Magistrates of the Sacred

Magistrates of the Sacred

Priests and Parishioners in Eighteenth-Century Mexico

William B. Taylor

STANFORD UNIVERSITY PRESS
Stanford, California

Stanford University Press, Stanford, California
© 1996 by the Board of Trustees of the
Leland Stanford Junior University

Published with the support of the
National Endowment for the Humanities,
an independent federal agency

Printed in the United States of America

CIP data appear at the end of the book

In memory of Charles Gibson and Fritz L. Hoffmann
Teachers and friends

Preface

Most of the work on this book was done alone, or so I thought. Looking back now, I see that a large circle of friends, colleagues, and institutions helped me at every step.

Thanks to the archivists and librarians who care for the materials cited in the notes, I never had a bad day of research. And thanks to grants from the John Simon Guggenheim Foundation, the University of Virginia, Southern Methodist University, the Social Science Research Council, the Albert J. Beveridge Fund of the American Historical Association, the Center for Latin American Studies of Tulane University, the Institute for Advanced Study in Princeton, N.J., and the National Humanities Center in Research Triangle Park, N.C., I could complete the research and writing.

Gary Allinson, Herbert Braun, David Carrasco, Inga Clendinnen, Brian Connaughton, Ramón Gutiérrez, and Nancy Mann read what I wrote, listened when I spoke, and sustained me with their advice and encouragement. I am grateful, too, to Eric Iversen for his advice on the conclusion, to Cecilia Brown for her careful attention to parts of Chapter Eleven, to David Szewczyk for lending an eighteenth-century manuscript from his collection, and to Walter Hauser for introducing me to his vibrant field of South Asian studies.

The following colleagues wished me well with helpful criticism and more: James Axtell, Edward Ayers, Peter Bakewell, Lewis Bateman, Woodrow Borah, Martinus Cawley, James Early, John Elliott, David Frye, Richard Graham, Richard Greenleaf, Charles Hale, Dwight Heath, Stephen Innes, James F. Jones, E. William Jowdy, Friedrich Katz, Melvyn Leffler, James Lockhart, Kenneth Mills, Mieko Nishida, David Parker, Ross Parmenter, Rebecca Scott, Felipe Teixidor, John TePaske, David Weber, John Womack, and Olivier Zunz.

Conversations with Michael MacDonald, Scarlett O'Phelan, Daphne Patai, Jeanne Stone, and Gerald Strauss at the National Humanities Center, and with Greg Dening, Gerald Fogarty, Rhys Isaac, Deborah Kanter, and Kimberley Raymond in Charlottesville led me to new possibilities in the subject.

In Mexico City, Guadalajara, and Zamora, Carlos Alba Vega, Carmen Castañeda, Agueda Jiménez Pelayo, Andrés Lira, Eucario López, and Salvador Victoria came to my aid repeatedly in personal and professional ways. In Seville, José Hernández Palomo welcomed me into his home and shared his enthusiasm for historical study and the Archivo General de Indias. For the photographs of Diego de Cervantes and the Sierra de Pinos parish church I am indebted to Bernardo del Hoyo.

At the Stanford University Press, the special efforts of Norris Pope, William Carver, and Barbara Mnookin got me through the uncertainties of how to finish.

But I owe most to Barbara, Karin, and Jill Taylor for their gifts of time and love.

A word on accents and locations. Modern pronunciation of many place-names derived from Nahuatl requires an accent (such as Cuautitlán, Tlaltizapán, and Tepatitlán); for many others it does not; and scholars familiar with this language in the colonial period have recently been inclined to drop accents (Tenochtitlán, for example, usually appears without an accent now). Rather than guess at how they were pronounced in the eighteenth century, I have left accents off all such names.

Communities mentioned in the text and notes generally are identified by their colonial district and modern state at first appearance in a chapter, or where references to them are separated by many pages. Occasionally, a place in the Diocese of Guadalajara is identified by diocese in order to distinguish it from others in a paragraph or series from the Archdiocese of Mexico.

W.B.T.

Contents

PART FOUR ≈ THE POLITICS OF PARISH LIFE

Figures, Maps, and Tables

TABLES

Magistrates of the Sacred

Introduction

Yes, I am a student of history, don't you remember? And
what we students of history always learn is that the human
being is a very complicated contraption and that they are
not good or bad but are good and bad.
—Jack Burden, in Robert Penn Warren's *All the King's Men*

On his trip to central Mexico in 1856, young Edward B. Tylor, future founder
of academic anthropology and the study of cultural evolution in England,
was impatient with the Catholic churches that interrupted his line of sight at
every turn:

Columns with shafts elaborately sculptured, and twisted marble pillars of the bed-post
pattern, are to be seen by hundreds, very expensive in material and workmanship, but unfortunately very ugly. . . . As to the interior decoration of the churches, the richer ones are
crowded with incongruous ornaments to a wonderful degree. Gold, silver, costly marbles,
jewels, stucco, paint, tinsel, and frippery are all mixed up together in the wildest manner.[1]

The seventeenth- and eighteenth-century walls, altars, and sculpture that dis-
concerted Tylor often fit Elizabeth Wilder Weismann's description of late colonial Mexican art as folk baroque—delighting in profuse ornamentation, movement, and intimacy; full of invention, borrowings, and irregularities. The makers
of these objects, and the generations of parishioners and priests who commissioned, arranged, and cared for them, had little academic training or concern for
stylistic purity. These old churches and meeting places were an unwelcome intrusion of European colonial history that had spread exuberantly over, through,
and beyond the pristine native ruins Tylor sought. They were altogether too
alive and luxuriant for his taste, too full of the idea of spiritual capital (in which
much of a society's wealth was invested in things to honor Christ the redeemer
and provider).

Even in the smallest former colonial settlements, parish churches and chapels
remain vital community places of devotion. At close range, these hundreds of

(a)

(b)

(c)

FIG. 1. *A parish church in the making: Sierra de Pinos, Zacatecas (Diocese of Guadalajara).* Construction of this church
apparently began in the late 1670's and continued to about
1700 with the encouragement of pastor Juan Enríquez
de Medrano and bequests by two local landowners. Two
naves remained unfinished in 1700, and the sacristy was
not added until after 1728. The first building phase is best
seen today in the church façade (a). Joseph Jacinto Llanos
y Valdés, another bricks-and-mortar pastor, who arrived in
1785, spent more than 15,000 pesos on various improvements before he was replaced in 1800, but money to cover
the naves ran out, and they were never completed. Some
of their spaces were later closed in for use on a smaller
scale (b). The atrium is now defined by a modern cement
block wall. The interior of the church also has a long history of addition and subtraction. A chapel to Our Lady of
Guadalupe was built with money from an hacendado who
died in 1710. When it was enlarged in the 1930's, one of
the retables was dismantled. Only a few of its solomonic
columns and ornaments were salvaged. A main altarpiece
and side altars made of wood were added after 1742. They
were removed in the early 1850's by a modernizing pastor
with a taste for neoclassical lines and a touch of Gothic.
The bare side walls and present altarpiece are his legacy
(c). The stone fountain in the sacristy is about all that
remains of the interior's 18th-century Baroque splendor.
Few of the silver ornaments mentioned in late colonial
inventories survive.

country churches present a jumble of three or four centuries of building. The atrium and present single-nave church may have been erected in the mid-seventeenth century; the roof, offices, choir, and bell towers repaired or rebuilt to suit later patrons; the original stone steps and floor worn into waves or replaced; the elaborate façade and original altarpiece preserved largely intact, perhaps restored recently by experts from Mexico City or some time ago by a priest or parishioners to their own tastes. There may be a side chapel and sacristy redone by an energetic parish priest in the 1750's; a rectory rebuilt most recently in the 1940's; colonial graves in the atrium; images of saints and small side altars to different advocations added and moved at various times; portable pews acquired in the twentieth century; and furniture, vestments, and other equipment for mass, some of it original, much of it worn out or replaced. The smell of incense and candle wax in the sanctuary is both fresh and old. And there are the places where other objects once stood, according to the parish inventories.

In some decisive respects, these eclectic, remodeled, well-worn buildings represent the subject of this book: the history of priests and parishioners together during the late colonial period. The churches were mediating points between the congregation and the divine, and gathering places for public expression and rites of passage. Within their walls, there was an intimacy between priests and parishioners and a converging experience of the sacred that were rarely achieved elsewhere. These buildings were also the seats of the parish priests' authority as magistrates of the sacred in the world, and they sometimes still bear the marks of that conflicted and celebrated authority in what has been added and subtracted— a confessional in dark wood with intricate carvings, a side altar to a favorite saint promoted by a former pastor, a battered portrait of him, or his silver-tipped cane propped in the corner of the sacristy. But the parish is to be found not so much in the church itself as in the succession of people who built, paid for, maintained, used, and rebuilt it; who prayed, rejoiced, wept, witnessed, confessed, learned, delivered sacraments, instructed, punished, and had words there. The parish is, above all, located in the relationships among these people over time, but it also involves people who were outside or only occasionally ventured into its visible boundaries.

I have used this study of priests and parishioners to offer several perspectives on how public life was organized in eighteenth-century Mexico and to gauge the scope and consequences of some Bourbon administrative reforms. The colonial relationships described here have especially to do with inescapable intimacies that Richard Bausch calls the obdurate forces of love—different experiences of the everyday exercise of love in circumstances of inequality, with their possibilities for conflict, fear, violence, and painful disappointment, as well as warmth, hope, trust, and communion. Parish priests, as agents of the state religion and as intermediaries both between parishioners and higher authorities and between the sacred and the profane, are a promising point of entry into this world of connections and perspective. Their history repeatedly opens out to local affairs and colonial relationships of authority and power. In pursuing these colonial relationships, I have concentrated on rural parishes in the Archdiocese of Mexico and the Diocese of Guadalajara. These parishes comprised mainly Indian communities in Mexico and a larger proportion of non-Indians in Guadalajara. While the following pages touch on various subjects, they do not pretend to be a comprehensive history of the two dioceses.

Some slow-moving, elusive changes are evident in the collective biography of parish priests, in the habits of speech and writing that organized and enlarged the experience of what was real for the speaker and writer, and in local political arrangements and religious practices. Sometimes demographic and economic changes—especially those worked by taxation and natural disasters—were so swift and acutely felt that they were widely remarked on at the time, but much of the "manifest history" in this study centers on the broader and more lasting changes brought about by the Bourbon reforms directed at the parish clergy from the 1740's, changes reserving to the royal governors authority that had previously been shared by pastors. How did these reforms affect the place of the church and religion in public life? the strength of the colonial state? the counterpoint of coercion and consent in public life? the crisis of authority after the Napoleonic invasion of Spain in 1808?

To catch elusive changes in society and thought, reflect on their relationship to these political questions, and move beyond the Spanish monarchy's well-known rationalizations of its power, I sought connections among an array of events, structures, places, times, and people. I liked J. H. Hexter's proposal to focus such a search for connections on paradoxes and pursued four of them in this study: (1) how this colonial system of great inequalities and little upward mobility continued for three centuries without a standing army or much use of force (that is, how the relative equilibrium of the colonial era was achieved and sustained, and how Indian subjects could be at once compliant and aggressively resistant); (2) how parish priests of late colonial Mexico were "separate but in the world," as they had been trained to think of themselves; (3) why, at the end of the colonial period, some of them led a double-barreled revolution for independence and social change that could threaten their own privileged position; and (4) how anticlericalism could develop in places where Catholicism apparently was not in decline. A study of priests in their parishes has a better chance of resolving the last three than the first, but it can, at least, enlarge the discussion of how colonial rule was maintained by taking into account the local practice of legitimacy and authority.

The main story in this study, then, turns on political culture in a time of rapid change, on the decline of what Richard Herr called "the state of mind necessary for the continuation of the old order."[2] But it does not argue for a cultural determinism. Common understandings and values constrained, enabled, and deflected; they did not determine. Political culture is never a monolithic variable independent of other circumstances; and in the eighteenth century, customs, values, and metaphors were increasingly contested, unsettling old meanings, accommodations, and habits of assent. This book is more about those conflicts than I imagined it would be, but it does not take them to be a direct, primary cause of the early independence movements. Conflicts of the kinds described here usually validated people's places in colonial society, even though they demonstrate new or growing rifts that were weakening the authority and power of the Bourbon monarchy.

Two views of religious change that remain controversial for sixteenth-century studies—difference-and-transformation (in which conversion necessarily meant displacement) and difference-and-resistance (in which natives and their descendants strategically accepted some surface features of Christianity but rejected the religion)—have less relevance for the eighteenth century and local religious practices. Theories focusing on syncretism, which is the most widely accepted way of representing religious change in highland Spanish America, stress adaptation, combination, and mutual influence, but theorists perceiving syncretism in Mesoamerica have tended to overemphasize a continuity of belief and the early completion of religious change. They have also implied more open, irreconcilable conflict between parishioners and priests over matters of faith than most late colonial evidence warrants.

The possibility of congruence and enlargement may be a better way to reckon with how colonial Indian parishioners combined and recombined practices and beliefs without subversive intentions. They may not have seen the similarities between particular Spanish and Indian forms and beliefs as proof that the new religion was really just the old one in new dress. Rather, the great continuity and consistency lay in habits of conception—in ways of representing and entering the sacred. While both native and Catholic religious traditions had imperial uses, at the local level they were not necessarily competing or mutually exclusive choices, unlike the decline of "magic" and miracles in competition with institutional religion, science, and faith in self-help that Keith Thomas describes for England in the seventeenth century. And there was enough distinction between particular priests and Catholicism to allow parishioners to feel anticlerical without rejecting the religion or the priesthood as such.

Parishioners, then, did not make local religion alone. Their practices existed with, more than against, the priest, and those practices took the sometimes surreptitious forms they did partly because the priest was an important resource for the community. In the late eighteenth century, the mounting friction between priest and Indian parishioner usually turned on political authority. When the opposition to him was expressed in religious terms, it was less often a matter of "pagan" versus Christian or of low religion versus high religion than of who deserved to be regarded as the superior Christian.

Religion and priests were integral to colonial political culture. They provided a focus for authority, a cosmic model for human order in a society where one's dying thoughts still turned to confession and salvation, and an institutional framework for expressing social relationships and mediating inequalities. But I have not treated religion as only a gloss on politics—as only a vehicle for government manipulation or a subject people's resistance. Church and state were combined throughout the colonial period and often mutually reinforcing, but they were not coextensive.

I view the state as the institutional expression of social relationships, as the formal aspects of power in public life organized through government, not just as an instrument of social control by rulers. Rulers and their offices are an obvious place to start, but no person or group was fully in charge; rulers in one setting could be ruled or checked in another, and the colonial state was not only the king and his Spanish agents, the viceroys, audiencias, district governors, tax collectors, and priests. The Bourbon government—rulers and their offices—was, I think, more active and more consequential than some fellow students of colonial Latin America consider it, but its officers certainly could not do or get just what they wanted in the late eighteenth century, nor was it as independent as its own policy makers imagined. Among other things, its power depended importantly on its right to rule, which had long rested on partnership with the church and on a religious ideology that had the potential to oppose, as well as support, that power. (*Power*, the ability to make and carry out decisions binding on others, is a larger category of relationships than *authority*, the right to make and carry out decisions, or the *state*, its formal, institutional expression. Power includes extralegal knowledge and force, as well as legal authority and institutions.) The exercise of political power in this history is filled with contingencies; it seems unlikely that "Indians" under Spanish rule in the heartland of New Spain forged their own communities in direct opposition to colonial masters or were forced into wholesale imitation of them. Their lives were deeply affected by powerful outsiders without being determined by them.

These questions and ways of asking have been influenced by social and political theories that explore reciprocities within inequalities. Antonio Gramsci and E. P. Thompson opened the way with their inquiries into subordination, which called attention to allegiance beyond coercion (without neglecting coercion)—to what rulers espouse and subjects also honor.[3] Thompson's insistence that categories like class, state, and culture emerge from ever-changing contested relationships rather than being things in themselves and that plebeian culture is neither fixedly deferential nor revolutionary is particularly germane. James Scott, too, regards most relationships of domination as reciprocal and incomplete, containing alternative meanings and values that could challenge rulers' versions of the social order, but he finds a larger role for subordinate groups in those relationships (at the expense of the role of leaders, a critic might say) and much evidence of "pragmatic submission" on their part.[4]

I have found Ashis Nandy's reflections on colonial and postcolonial political culture in India particularly rich in questions and leads that can help colonial Latin American historians move beyond the implicit metaphor of conquest.[5] Nandy treats colonialism as a "shared culture" in which the colonized accommodated and appropriated rather than simply submitted; relationships were transacted, contested, and reformulated, not stationary or crystallized; and frontal assaults by either side were rare. Fighting their own battles for survival, his Indians were participants in westernization more often than desperate opponents of it. His reflections invite a study that would look for points of union and conflict among colonial priests and parishioners—the accommodations and acceptances, the balkings and refusals on all sides, that made Catholicism into an American religion.

An array of mutual obligations, expectations, and changing associations made American Indian parishioners active participants in this history of consent and struggle. Points of friction were inevitable. Most parishioners lived directly from the land; the priests did not. Priests found their parishioners too concerned with propitiation, the profane, and miraculous images that spilled beyond clerical control, and too little interested in sin and contrition. As a rule, priests were educated outsiders who promoted their understanding of orthodoxy and were expected to maintain a distance from parishioners, a distance that could widen when they attempted intimacy or collected fees.

But local religious practices and beliefs were not particularly divisive matters in the late eighteenth century, even though the relationship between priest and parishioners became more complicated. Popular devotion and engagement with Christianity were plainly not declining (as they often were in Europe at the time), and there was no great conflict between priests and parishioners in matters of belief. Priests complained that Indian parishioners had too much religion and were too literal-minded in their practices or did not understand the articles of faith well, but they rarely said that Indians rejected the fundamentals of Christian doctrine or their own spiritual authority. For their part, the parishioners wanted access to Christian power, usually respected the priest's command of spiritual knowledge, and perhaps admired his charity, though they might regard the liturgy he provided as incomplete. By itself, it did not match their sense of well-being and popular participation in the sacred or their understanding of the pervasive presence of the divine. Not surprisingly, they often failed to follow the priest's distinction between internals and externals.

*   *   *

After a section of introductory chapters that surveys the politics of church and religion in the late colonial period (Chapter 1), similarities and differences between the Archdiocese of Mexico and the Diocese of Guadalajara that are important to the regional patterns of this study (Chapter 2), and issues of religious change (Chapter 3), the book is organized as three related studies. All three are concerned with the associations of priests, parishioners, and colonial government. The first is a social history of parish priests at work—their backgrounds, education, careers, roles, and conduct, and patterns in the sentiments they expressed about their professional lives during the second half of the eighteenth century. It explores common experiences and shared expectations, a range of differences among parish priests, and some memorable situations and individuals that help to place them in their parishes. The second study centers on the religious culture of lay people, without assuming that their practices, institutions, offices, and views of themselves as Christians were always markedly separate from priests, authorized beliefs, or formal organization. It attends to their participation with and without priests in the regular cycles of personal and collective obligations and celebrations; the expenses that went into maintaining and improving the church fabric and dignifying public devotions; the veneration of saints and images; and the activities of lay officers and organizations. The third study concerns local politics and institutionalized male authority, in which parish priests exercised influence along with village officials, royal governors, hereditary chiefs, popular spokesmen, specific community groups, and neighboring landlords. Their growing struggles over clerical fees, leadership in temporal affairs, and the rights and duties of fatherhood stand out here. The book concludes by moving a step beyond the conventional termination of colonial history in 1810 to consider the famed role of parish priests as fighters and leaders in the struggle for Mexican independence. An appended essay (Appendix C) provides one extended regional illustration for the districts of modern Morelos, where rural revolution without much reference to priests and Christianity would occur a century later.

This approach, and the wealth of written records in which parish priests appear, required a longer book than I intended to write. Since little of the basic information about the careers, thought, associations, and institutional history of late colonial parish priests was available in print, these essentials had to be dug out for my main enterprise—discerning the connections among rural parishioners, priests, and other royal officials—to make sense. Parish priests did have much in common, but that professional kinship must be substantiated from the array of information about them rather than inferred from common sense and the arresting, but contradictory, observations of a few contemporaries. Clearly, parish priests were significant figures to many people, endowed with social as well as spiritual power that was formalized in rituals of deference and obedience. As experts in sacred language, writing, and rites of passage, they were expected to mediate both between man and God and among members of a divided, multi-racial colonial society. They were bound to be influential, and sometimes they used force to get their way, but their control was not a reign of unrelieved terror any more than it was the "yoke of flowers" imagined by one late colonial pastor.

In writing about one well-documented case of conflict between priests and parishioners over clerical fees, I found that, as rich as it was in action and the particular, and as much as it seemed to suggest about colonial authority and the late eighteenth century, it could not stand for the hundreds of other cases I knew about. Some cases turn out to be more representative than others. For instance, more of the history of parish priests before and during the Independence War is revealed in the career of José María Morelos than in that of Miguel Hidalgo, but one cannot make this judgment without studying that larger history; moreover, the two careers together reveal more than either one can by itself. It takes a number of cases to illustrate the patterned tendencies and connections in the larger body of evidence. Most of the chapters offer a counterpoint of patterned tendencies and particular cases in order to describe the conventional and general without losing the individual and local—to reveal the open ends, blurred lines, peculiarities, and changes in colonial relationships involving parish priests. And most of the chapters turn to words spoken and heard, written and read, by the subjects themselves. My intention in doing this is to go beyond summarizing "their" views in my vocabulary, to come closer to the language of the time, with its strong feelings and its distinctive, sometimes surprising voices.

Contrary to the inviting simplicity that Catholicism is a religion of the image and Protestantism a religion of the word, colonial Catholicism was always as much about words, principles, ceremonies, and institutions as about images. It is in all of these facets together that the meetings and struggles taking place inside the parishes and those remodeled churches of eighteenth-century Mexico begin to reveal people's faith and the lived inequalities of the time.

PART ONE

Politics, Place, and Religion

CHAPTER ONE

Parish Priests in Bourbon Mexico

The King's jurisdiction extends not only to what is definitely within the purview of the Patronato, but also to
doubtful cases.
　　　　　　—Antonio Joachin Ribadeneyra y Barrientos,
　　　　　　later judge on the Audiencia of Mexico, 1755

Were parishes instituted for the benefit of the curas or for
the well-being of souls?　—Intendant of Durango, 1789

The role of the parish priest in Mexico's past is an incendiary topic. Like the
Spanish Conquest and the North American invasion of 1847, the history of
the church, especially of the priesthood, is passionately remembered in Mexico,
and foreign travelers and scholars like me have found it irresistible, at least in
passing. Although the wars of the nineteenth and early twentieth centuries separated church and state and greatly reduced the power, wealth, privileges, and
numbers of Catholic priests in Mexico, the history of the clergy is still controversial. About the only thing most commentators agree on is the great power
of priests in Mexican parishes, but even that is a largely unexamined claim and
inevitably needs qualification.[1] Beyond that supposition, parish priests usually
are depicted as either saintly or vicious. José Joaquín Fernández de Lizardi presented a classic disreputable priest in his picaresque novel *El periquillo sarniento*,
published in 1816. His young protagonist, nicknamed "the itching parrot," casts
about for a livelihood and decides for a time that parish service offers the ripest
opportunity for a comfortable, respectable, and carefree life with the least preparation. As one of the parrot's friends observes, the parish priest "never lacks for a
peso [even] if he has to get it for a mass badly said at top speed." In Fernández de
Lizardi's anticlerical view, ordination was a license to steal and otherwise abuse
privilege. His grasping, irresponsible priests "make a mockery of Christian conduct and the ideals of pastoral work."[2]

John Lloyd Stephens reached the opposite conclusion. During his search for
lost cities and the furtive statesmen of Yucatán and Central America in the late
1830's, Stephens came to regard country priests as his benefactors and comrades,

and accept them as benevolent community leaders who enjoyed unquestioned paternal authority. Remarking on his stay at Esquipulas (Guatemala) in 1839, he wrote:

In the course of the day I had an opportunity of seeing what I afterwards observed through all Central America: the life of labour and responsibility passed by the *cura* [pastor] in an Indian village. . . . Besides officiating in all the services of the church, visiting the sick, and burying the dead, my worthy host was looked up to by every Indian in the village as a counsellor, friend, and father. The door of the convent was always open, and Indians were constantly resorting to him: a man who had quarrelled with his neighbour; a wife who had been badly treated by her husband; a father whose son had been carried off as a soldier; a young girl deserted by her lover; all who were in trouble or affliction came to him for advice and consolation, and none went away without it. And besides this, he was principal director of all the public business of the town.[3]

These visions of parish priests as grasping, randy tyrants or selfless servants and trusted fathers find anecdotal support in the judicial and administrative record, but a head count of good and bad priests as they appeared in contemporary descriptions will not go far toward comprehending their place in the parish, the changes in their public lives and thought toward the end of the colonial period, or the enduring importance of popular devotion. The record has a history of its own, and each case has a context to consider. Parish priests' descriptions of themselves as isolated, lonely, defenseless servants of God, mitre, and crown, and their Indian opponents' descriptions of them to colonial judges as omnipotent tyrants are important social facts in themselves, but case records show that few late colonial pastors were poised to be martyrs or martinets. Furthermore, many priests served in minor country parishes and enjoyed less influence than most commentators have imagined. They spent a substantial part of their adult lives in spiritual exercises, visiting the sick, saying mass, and coordinating the observances of small numbers of the faithful in far-flung places, without exercising great influence in any of them; in looking after personal affairs; and in planning their departure for better assignments or retirement.

Still, from the beginning of Spanish colonization, parish priests were located at sensitive intersections between Indian subjects and higher authorities, and the state religion was an important source of public discipline and restraint. In the Spanish Hapsburg conception of the state during the sixteenth and seventeenth centuries, no sharp lines had divided secular and religious life. Until the mid-eighteenth century, an energetic cura might operate quite freely as keeper of public order and morals, punishing adulterers, gamblers, and drunkards, and reporting more serious offenses to royal judges. He and his assistants, the *vicarios*, had also been expected to report to the higher levels of royal government on agricultural conditions, natural disasters, and local disturbances and other political news; to record the population; to supervise the annual elections of village officers in communities within the parish; and to help maintain social control in other ways. He could be a patron in times of illness and want. As a moral and spiritual father and healer, and a literate local resident often able to speak the native language of his parishioners, the priest had been well placed to represent the state's requirements to rural people and interpret their obligations, as well as to intercede for them with higher authorities. They were sacred instruments, expected to mediate between Christians and God, as well as between members of a divided colonial society. But they were rarely the sole local leaders, and rarely unquestioned. And in the late colonial period, challenges to their influence gathered momentum.

Bourbon Reforms Affecting the Parish Clergy

Aiming to increase royal power and augment colonial revenues, the Spanish Bourbon monarchy (which for the Viceroyalty of New Spain, with its capital at Mexico City, held sway from 1700 to 1821) eventually introduced in America a new vision of royal absolutism. As Stanley and Barbara Stein have suggested, its manifestation was a "defensive modernization" that came late in the century largely in response to the fall of Havana (1762), the cession of Florida (1763), and other effects of foreign commercial intervention and the Seven Years' War.[4] But the vision itself was older, and pieces of it were in place in New Spain before the 1760's.[5]

From its beginnings, the Spanish Empire in America had been built on a conception of royal absolutism matched to elaborate hierarchies of status and authority, belief in divine sanction and judgment, organic metaphors of wholeness, a dual government of crown and church, and strategies of divide and rule. These principles and strategies continued in the eighteenth century, but in contrast to Hapsburg practice—which had left distinctions between the jurisdictions of royal governors and the clergy poorly defined, sought to deflect confrontations by intercession, and treated tradition almost as a sacrament—the Bourbon monarchy honored centralization under the authority of royal governors, standardization, systematic efficiency, precise measurement, and the rule of law. Hapsburg administration had treated justice as the highest attribute of sovereignty, balancing its laws with the discretion of appointed magistrates, the weight of custom, and overlapping lines of mediation to higher authorities. Quite tolerant of ambiguities that did not threaten its legitimacy, it relied on a balance of countervailing forces such as fear and love, law and custom, reason and emotion, and the "mutual suspicion" of *alcaldes mayores* (royal governor-judges at the district level) and parish priests as competing yet complementary magistrates and protectors of Indian subjects.[6] Late colonial Bourbon administrators invoked Hapsburg law to justify their reforms whenever possible, but they saw themselves as proselytizers for the new, the improved, and the progressive against the customary and traditional. They intended law to supersede custom, and they encouraged litigation as a way to enforce it. Their watchwords were "fixed rules" (*reglas fijas*) and obedience to the law "without interpretation."[7]

Bourbon absolutism encouraged new uniformities: every recognized town (*pueblo*) must have a community treasury (*caja de comunidad*); every parish should follow a standard schedule of fees; and all subjects of the Spanish crown should speak Spanish as their primary language. The parental metaphor of the "Two Majesties" (Dos Magestades)—with the crown as father and the church as mother of the Hispanic family, or the two together as the collective head of the social body—gave way to a fully masculine conception of politics, with only one head and one parent, the king.[8] Regalism—the subordination of church authority—became a hallmark of the Bourbon reforms.

By midcentury, especially during the ministry of the Marqués de Ensenada (1746–54), the Spanish Bourbons started to develop a far-reaching, if disjointed and only partly realized, program of reforms for the parish clergy. Like other reforms directed at the priesthood, especially those restricting immunity from royal prosecution, this program intended to treat religion and the institutional church as both more distinct from and more subordinated to the crown, not to separate church from state or crown from religion. It intended to redefine the clergy as a professional class of spiritual specialists with fewer judicial and administrative responsibilities and less independence than in Hapsburg times. In this, the Bourbons followed the lead of other European states in which religion was being "converted from the keystone which holds together the social edifice into one department within it."[9] Although this vision of change was not an open attack on religion, and although the Bourbons had ample precedent in both the Council of Trent decrees (which sought to reform the parochial clergy in the mid–sixteenth century) and Hapsburg law for their directives that parish priests concentrate on "the spiritual welfare of their parishioners," it had an anticlerical edge. Despite the labors of various regalist bishops, Bourbon administrators were inclined to regard priests as usurpers of royal authority and the church as an obstacle to material progress, a bastion of entailed, unproductive wealth, and the agent of revelation and tradition rather than reason and efficiency.

The priests' livelihood became a major issue when a concerted attempt was made by Bourbon reformers to fix a standard schedule of fees for their services, restrict the range of labor service they could command, and reduce the crown's cash contributions to their ministrations. The Bourbons' financial interests and zeal for efficiency combined to produce a minor moral crusade against lavish and disorderly holidays, Indian laziness and vagrancy, and any personal conduct that might impair a priest's capacity to increase the flow of revenue to Madrid, economic growth, and obedience to the crown. By these measures and others, including the secularization of parishes (the transfer of pastoral care in a parish from members of a religious order to the diocesan or secular clergy), the crown opened the way to unprecedented litigation against parish priests and a heightened anticlericalism. But except for the clerical-fees issue, which was a matter of hot dispute throughout the viceroyalty after 1767, there were significant regional differences in levels of conflict evoked by these administrative changes. In the Archdiocese of Mexico, for example, the secularization of parishes in the 1750's and 1760's was closely associated with legal battles and violent protests against priests in the districts of Xilotepec, Cuernavaca, Cuautla, and Chalco, but not in Texcoco or Coyoacan.

Scattered Bourbon initiatives in the first half of the eighteenth century aimed both to reduce the royal stipends for pastors and to expand the judicial and enforcement authority of royal governors and their supervision of parish affairs.[10] But in 1748–50—a decade before the coronation of Charles III, who usually is credited with initiating most of the important Bourbon reforms—there began a more concerted program of parish reform established by royal decree and implemented by the viceroys, *audiencias* (high courts), and district governors. Partly because various constituencies in the colonies could be enlisted for support, the new program was enforced with added determination. In August 1748 a royal *cédula* (royal decree) calling on district governors to control local drunkenness implicitly challenged the traditional role of the parish priest in policing public morality. And in 1749 came the first of a series of decrees calling for the secularization of parishes still administered by the Mendicant orders, a process that was largely carried through by the mid-1760's. That year there was also a royal order to remove from office any priests who did not know the native language of their parishioners. Then on January 31, 1750, viceregal edicts (*bandos*) redefined public and church property, enlarging royal supervision of community property at the expense of the parish priests. In October, another royal decree limited the traditional practice of using churches as asylums from arrest.[11] There followed a steady stream of decrees on parish administration in New Spain that quickened in the 1760's and again in the 1790's. Areas of shared jurisdiction were being redefined as essentially civil, and therefore subject to review only by royal courts. Increasingly, parish priests were expected not to enforce spiritual or moral obligations on their own authority, but rather to request "royal *auxilio*"—the assistance of royal governors.

The 1760's decrees were more administrative than fiscal, calling, for instance, on priests to refrain from criticizing the government, to promote the Spanish language and the primary schools, and to limit feast-day celebrations (*fiestas*). The crown also directed its officers to create new parishes, place a priest in residence at least every four leagues (about ten miles), see that priests did not leave their parishes without official permission, and restrict asylum privileges.[12] During the 1770's and 1780's, the crown required yet fuller information about the activities of pastors and parish finances; insisted on their residence in the parish and their prompt administration of the sacraments; sharply restricted their role in local elections, reducing them to honored spectators; limited their judicial authority over cases of drunkenness, adultery, "idolatry," and property disputes; moved to limit the jurisdiction of episcopal (referring to a bishop and the exercise of his office) courts over priests who were disrespectful toward royal governors; deprived the church of its exclusive supervision of marriages; and dramatically reduced the royal treasury's contributions to the livelihood of pastors (thus shifting the burden of their support to the portion of the tithe controlled by the bishops).[13]

The last major legislative initiative, accompanying the establishment of provincial governorships—intendancies—on the Spanish model after 1786, pushed for greater uniformity and the "recovery" of royal authority. The laws of this period were filled with calls for "fixed rules" and "avoiding unnecessary expenses to my Royal Treasury" (evitar gastos a mi Real Erario). Sometimes they were strongly anticlerical, as in the royal cedula of September 30, 1789, on *capellanías* (chaplaincies, a type of ecclesiastical endowment that required payment of a 5-percent annual stipend, usually in exchange for memorial masses), which chided priests for "the despotism with which the clergy tried to squash Royal Authority."[14] In these years, royal decrees enlarged on the earlier restrictions of the parish priests' judicial and fiscal roles, enlarged as well the jurisdiction of royal courts over priests, reiterated earlier decrees on financing parish activities, added regulations on transfers of pastors between parishes, emphasized royal prerogatives in elections and community property, and introduced new procedures to oversee church construction. After 1797, the only decrees of consequence ordered that construction be funded from church rents rather than the royal treasury (1799) and reiterated that parish priests could not act as judges in local criminal cases (1801).[15]

In the audiencias of Mexico and Guadalajara, there was a complementary shift in judicial opinion by the early 1770's. Before then, verdicts warned against "innovations."[16] Thereafter, the royal government more often made changes without apology. *Fiscales* of the audiencia (the chief legal advisers) might inquire into customary practices and cite law from the *Recopilación* (the great compilation of colonial law published in 1681) before rendering an opinion, but they were likely to ignore custom or disparage it, as the fiscal of the Audiencia of Guadalajara did when he opined in 1772 that much custom reflected the unwillingness of weak district governors in their capacity as judges to get involved in a dispute ("meterse en un pleyto").[17] By the 1770's, taking their cue from royal decrees, the courts and viceroys were increasingly involved in the details of parish administration, extending the boundaries of royal jurisdiction and urging district governors to implement royal orders and provide auxilio. The high courts might well support a parish priest against insolent parishioners or malicious charges,[18] but rarely would they side with the clergy against district governors and pueblo officials; in fact, their verdicts were usually critical of the parish priests. A priest's word still counted in court but with less force than before.

Colonial government in the Viceroyalty of New Spain had long included a network of district governor-judges—116 alcaldes mayores (and their analogues, the *subdelegados*, after 1786), plus their 250 or so lieutenants in the audiencia district of Mexico, and 33 more plus their lieutenants in the audiencia district of Nueva Galicia, where the Archdiocese of Mexico and the Diocese of Guadalajara, respectively, were located.[19] Although these district governors had seen their own power restricted when their monopoly trading privilege (the *repartimiento de mercancías*) was challenged by the ordinance establishing intendancies in New Spain in 1786, they stood to gain substantially from the post-1749 parish reforms that tipped the balance of authority away from the parish priests. More of the district governors than before had military experience, if not a commission, and most were faithful agents of Bourbon policies. Administrators more than magistrates, men of the regla fija, they were increasingly called on to supervise local politics and pueblo finances, which included properties previously treated as belonging to the church. Under the circumstances, further jurisdictional conflict with parish priests was virtually guaranteed. Moreover, the very intensity of the anticlerical rhetoric in royal law and judicial opinion in the 1790's implicitly encouraged district governors to greater provocations.

The bishops and archbishops of Guadalajara and Mexico responded somewhat equivocally to these initiatives. They supported most of the Bourbons' regalist programs with alacrity, promising "the most exact fulfillment" of royal instructions in jurisdictional disputes,[20] and warning their priests to stay out of secular affairs. These prelates were, after all, peninsular Spaniards hand-picked by the crown. Several of those who served in the 1760's and 1770's, including Archbishop Francisco de Lorenzana, were what William Callahan calls "perfect examples of what the absolutist state expected of its bishops."[21] They were learned, energetic men who cooperated with the crown's reforming policies on education, the promotion of agriculture and manufacturing, popular religion, and the personal conduct of priests. In the name of unity and loyalty to the crown, urging "the conformity of the members with the body" (conformidad de los miembros con el cuerpo), they acceded to the restrictions placed on the parish priests' judicial and administrative prerogatives.[22] Their own plans for the reform of clerical conduct—combating luxury and loose morals, emphasizing a good education and spiritual exercises, especially as preparation for the now paramount duty of teaching, and encouraging parish priests to regard charity as the essence of their public role—either accorded with the crown's redefinition of the parish clergy's subordinate role or did not directly interfere with it.

The high point of the bishops' regalism came with the Fourth Provincial Council in 1771, over which the 1767 expulsion of the Jesuits from Spain and its possessions had cast a long, if largely unacknowledged, shadow.[23] Under Archbishop Lorenzana's guidance, the bishops and other prelates at this conclave declared their intention to unify the two worlds of Spain and America and create "a single rule" (una misma regla) in the Bourbon spirit. They called upon parish priests to be loving fathers, "well loved and accepted," to withdraw from all disputes, to remember the "gentleness of Christ," and become "peaceable teachers" who would join with the king in a common front of "peace and cooperation" against atheism. But even in this most regalist of meetings, there was official ambiguity about the public role of parish priests. At one point, the council instructed priests to stay out of secular business "in order not to divide your heart between God and Mammon"; at another, it exhorted them to look out for the Indians' "spiritual and temporal well-being."[24] The prelates' resistance to paying stipends to parish priests from the tithe, and some of their standardizing practices (such as the 1767 *arancel*, or schedule of fees, and discrimination against priests who had qualified for ordination by studying native languages), in fact went against the interests of parish priests; but prelates, including Lorenzana, also defended the priests' custom of appointing lay assistants and resisted the crown's redefinition of sodality property as community property and its modifications of the right of asylum. Prelates also opposed the royal cedula of October 25, 1795, which reduced the immunity of priests from prosecution in royal courts to minor offenses and spiritual matters. This law caused a great stir among bishops and the cathedral clergy (the prebends and dignitaries of the cathedral chapters), who saw their powers being eroded,[25] but it caused only a ripple of dissent among rural pastors, since most of them had little to do with the bishop's court in the first place. The reforming side of episcopal regalism was muted after Lorenzana's departure in 1772. Later archbishops, and bishops of Guadalajara such as Juan Cruz Ruiz de Cabañas (1796–1824), promoted the spiritual mission, moral reform, charity, and new economic activity, but they knew their subjects better than Lorenzana and were less enthusiastic about institutional reordering.

Political Conflict and Religious Change

Juan de Ortega y Montañes, one of the archbishops to serve briefly as viceroy under the Hapsburgs, could write to his viceregal successor in 1696 that "the state of the parishes has been, and continues to be, tranquil and calm, without disputes. . . . Accordingly, there is nothing here worth bringing to Your Excellency's attention."[26] The same could not be said of the dioceses of New Spain in the late eighteenth century. Although the interests of parish priests, on the one hand, and of the bishops and the cathedral clergy, on the other, perhaps diverged more than at any time previously, conflict between them is less evident than the growing tensions between priests and parishioners in the archdiocese, and between priests and district governors in both dioceses. The potential for intraclerical conflict was usually overridden by the sentiments and interests the two parties shared: an interest in maintaining certain customary practices;[27] an opposition to some royal initiatives (usually mounted for different reasons); the fear that their hands were being tied by excessive royal absolutism; the advantages they gained at the expense of the religious orders (mainly the Franciscans, Dominicans, Augustinians, and Jesuits); and an antagonism toward the Napoleonic secular state.

The heaviest concentrations of conflict in the late 1760's to 1770's and from 1789 to 1796 correspond roughly to the sequence of administrative initiatives in which the colonial government sought to increase its role in the lives of ordinary people.[28] All kinds of conflict involving parish priests grew quite dramatically during the second half of the eighteenth century, although disputes over clerical fees and conflicts between head towns (*cabeceras*) and subordinate settlements (*sujetos*) had been common before 1750 as well, with some important spillover into the early 1760's. Conflict over the selection of a pastor's lay assistants was concentrated in the years 1763–74. The late 1760's and early 1770's were a peak period of community protests against parish priests in the archdiocese, of conflict over fiesta practices, and, in certain places, of personalist struggles for power. Fees disputes and other resistance to parish priests receded to a high plateau in the 1780's, only to rise to new heights in the late 1780's and early 1790's. Disputes and protests over elections, sodalities, community property issues, clerical fees, fiestas, and divisions within communities all were most numerous at that time. In the first decade of the nineteenth century, fiesta disputes, sharp political divisions within communities, and cabecera/sujeto disputes remained high, but conflicts over clerical fees and between pastors and district governors declined. The concentration of cases in the late 1760's and early 1790's is more than a reflection of efficient recordkeeping: the administrative initiatives issued at that time effectively invited the expression, in court, of certain kinds of conflict that could take on a dynamic of their own in local politics.

By the late eighteenth century, the often-voiced fear of an earlier day that evangelization was failing—that Indians either had returned to "idolatry" or had never given it up—had all but disappeared, judging by the corpus of writings by priests. Like their early-seventeenth-century predecessors, priests were still inclined to think in terms of a "pagan"/Christian duality, and a few waged energetic campaigns against suspected "idolatry," with unsettling results, but the standard view among bishops and parish priests now was that the Indians' many deviations in practice were merely the superstitions of ignorant children. Indian drunkenness remained a preoccupation of parish priests, but more as a social problem than as a gateway to "idolatry." Priests acknowledged that rural parishioners, including Indians, generally fulfilled their sacramental obligations, provided them with a livelihood (perhaps grudgingly), and rarely challenged their spiritual authority.

The late colonial cathedral clergy and royal councils encouraged change in religious sensibility that also bears on the politics of parish life. The bishops and cathedral chapters promoted a new theology that was consistent both with the redefinition of the parish priest's role in public life as the gentle teacher and with a more optimistic view of Indians as pupils who had enough willpower to become good Christians. Religious art, learned treatises in theology, and the bishops' pastoral letters were presenting God less as a stern judge than as a loving father, and the crucified Christ less as a wounded figure in agony than as a sublime human form that anticipated the resurrected Lord. The Ten Commandments and the epistles of Saint Paul came into new prominence as guides to human potential and standards of charity, love, and sociability. Fewer references were made to the Devil, to the Seven Deadly Sins, and to Saint Augustine's sour view of the human condition, all of which had been so prominent in the seventeenth century.

But how much this softened, more loving faith became part of local religion or was centered there in the first place is unclear. Given a more loving, accessible God who could be approached without intercession, there should have followed —as there did in Spain—a decline in the veneration of saints. But no such decline seems to have occurred in the dioceses of Mexico and Guadalajara. On the contrary, the growing veneration of Mary there in the eighteenth century suggests that her intercession was needed more than ever. Royal government began to rely less on tangible religious events like public spectacles on the feast of Corpus Christi to symbolize the wholeness of society under the crown and more on the potential for economic development and social integration in reforms in education, rational organization, and practical science. Indians became less the epitome of weakness, laziness, and sin, and more the objects of improvement, if not perfectibility, capable of full "conversion" into the new Hispanic order.[29]

Some colonial counterpoints and tensions between priests and parishioners expressed in local religious practices are discussed in Part III, especially in Chapter 11 on the contrasting local histories of Saint James and the Virgin Mary. In both cases, these powerful Catholic symbols had multiple meanings for veneration and social order. Saint James, or Santiago, introduced as Spain's crusading patron saint but also promising to defend all Christians, became an ambivalent figure in colonial terms, increasingly appropriated by parishioners as a local patron and protector. The Virgin Mary, even in the guise of the renowned painted image of Our Lady of Guadalupe, was always more than an Indian patroness. She was the greatest intercessor of them all, humanizing the colonial hierarchy and the route to salvation. But her protection also could be turned to other purposes, as it was in the early nineteenth century, for resistance by the chosen against their enemies, including the colonial government.

Socioeconomic and Intellectual Change

Eighteenth-century New Spain experienced important demographic and material changes—economic and population growth, migration within and across districts, alterations in land use and tenure, the reorganization of a declining textile industry, new tax demands by the crown, the expansion and diversification of urban markets, and an increase in wage labor and the use of cash. Much is still unclear about the scale and ramifications of these changes, and the evidence on them is not always conclusive, but recent scholarship no longer treats the late colonial period as a golden age of prosperity and development, despite impressive growth in silver mining, construction, and trade, and some important regional expansion of commercial agriculture. The growth, it appears, was more nominal than real, vitiated by inflation and stagnant per-capita productivity. The distribution of the new wealth was increasingly unequal; large private estates were the main beneficiaries of the modest overall increases in agricultural production; real wages and per-capita income actually declined; and silver production did not relieve the shortage of currency, capital, and credit.[30] In the late eighteenth century, even the nominal economic growth, especially in rural areas, seems to have lost momentum, leading John Coatsworth to speak of a "depression" in the 1780's and a "crisis" in agriculture.[31] Depression or not, the period of easy growth was largely over by the time Charles III came to power in 1759.[32]

Colonial taxpayers paid a dear price as the Bourbons' revenue-generating reforms, coupled with a stagnant or declining economy, led to proportionally larger exports of capital from New Spain. Spanish America between 1782 and 1797, writes John Lynch, was treated as "a pure colony, to be possessed, primed, and plundered."[33] Tax farming, a system in which the crown sold its right to collect taxes in a particular district, usually for several years at a time, largely disappeared in favor of direct collection; the *alcabala* (sales tax) was raised in 1744 and then extended to new items several times; tribute levies rose; there were new taxes on shopkeepers in the 1780's; and the royal monopoly on tobacco and taxes on liquor and playing cards drove up the price of these popular consumer goods. At the same time, the costs of empire were rising. Periodic wars with England or France, which were almost continuous after 1789, required additional American revenue for the defense of Spain's far-flung possessions and often interrupted the trade between Spain and the New World that was essential to it.

Most recent scholarship sees the nominal growth in production as driven more by population growth than by silver mining, leaving little room for upward social mobility for the native-born after 1750. From about 3,360,000 inhabitants in 1742, the Viceroyalty of New Spain grew to 6,122,000 in 1810. Central Mexico, where this study is centered, grew from 2,094,000 to 3,254,000 in the same interval. The number of people designated as Indians in central Mexico rose about 50 percent between 1720 and 1800 (about 0.5 percent a year), with spurts of growth between 1765 and 1775, and between 1790 and 1800. Though the non-Indian population grew faster, especially in regions north and west of the Valley of Mexico, it was still smaller than the Indian population of New Spain in 1793.[34] More people producing at about the same rate seem to account for many of the pockets of increasing agricultural production. As per-capita income dropped and land became unavailable to many in the villages, country people migrated to other rural areas, to mining centers and their hinterlands in the Bajío region north of Mexico City, or to the cities.[35] The rise in the prices of staples apparently resulted from the twin circumstances of substantial population growth and a stagnant agricultural economy in which maize production actually declined, rather than from higher wages and more money in circulation.[36]

These material changes made life more precarious for the rural parishioners of central and western Mexico. More and more villagers, increasingly hemmed in by expanding private estates and their own growing numbers, resorted to seasonal wage labor on the estates. Even so, they were still susceptible to the devastation of drought and epidemic, especially in 1785–86 and 1808–10. In a time of economic stagnation, their tax burden was growing without an increase in wages. At the same time, a greater stratification by wealth and power and a greater mixing of legally separate Indian and non-Indian populations were expanding villagers' political and cultural horizons. The result could be lawsuits or violence, increasingly with parish priests in the spotlight.[37]

But the connections between these material conditions (assuming that the new scholarship has not exaggerated the stagnation and depression story) and the relationships among priests, parishioners, and district governors, or between these conditions and the insurrections of the early independence period, are rarely clear and straightforward. The beginning of the independence struggle in September 1810 hard on the heels of severe grain shortages and high maize prices may be "concrete evidence of the fundamental role played by economic forces in the determination of political events," [38] but it is not so clear just what that fundamental role was or why there was no comparable social and political violence during the more profound famine and epidemic that brought a similar rise in prices in 1785–86. Despite the apparent objective conditions for decisive conflict between the metropolis and the colonies and within colonial society, recent inquiries into the origins of the popular movements of 1810 to 1815 have identified only loosely connected contingencies that do not satisfactorily explain the actions of particular people in particular places.[39]

A single factor like population increase is even less satisfactory as an explanation of political action. Mexico did participate in the worldwide surge in population beginning about 1750, a development that William H. McNeill regards as a prime reason for the Industrial Revolution in Europe, the French Revolution, and new levels of political violence in "ex-frontier lands" like Latin America.[40] And this jump in population clearly contributed to urbanization and other movements of people in central and western Mexico, to new pressure on agricultural capacity, to some "proto-industrialization," and to rural politicization. What is not so clear, however, is its direct relationship to the political and technological events that concern McNeill.

Yet population increase does help to explain some of the conflicts between priests and parishioners in late colonial central Mexico. The protracted conflict over the 1767 schedule of clerical fees was due in part to tensions between head towns and subordinate settlements that were fueled in the first instance by population growth and the adjustments required by the crown's demands for cash contributions and tax payments. Another demographic change, migration, also appears to bear a close relationship to these eruptions. Those very parts of modern Hidalgo in the north and Morelos and Guerrero in the south that were favorite destinations for Indian migrants, for example, were also centers of priest-parishioner conflict.[41] Still, there were some areas of high in-migration, like the Bajío and the hot, rugged lowlands of Michoacán and Guerrero, that did not show any notable increase in tensions between priests and parishioners, yet became focal points of insurgency after 1810, and others that went just the opposite way. The pueblos of the Morelos region that had especially bitter conflicts with priests showed less commitment to the insurgency, even when it finally burst onto the scene at the end of 1811. Migration did not by itself guarantee either local conflict or pro-insurgent sentiment, though it did at least expand the network of communications that insurgency could follow.

Antedating the recent findings in demographic and economic history, but enriched by them, is another theory commonly used to describe the conditions for, if not the causes of, the popular movements after 1810: that many classes of people in late colonial Mexico were (and understood themselves to be) deprived. In Masae Sugawara's view, for example, the economic changes and Bourbon reforms resulted in the "brutal exploitation" of the underclasses and rising class conflict with revolutionary possibilities.[42] But other economic forces besides pure material deprivation were at work, since the insurrections were centered in growth areas of the Bajío, Jalisco, Michoacán, and Guerrero. Recognizing the importance of perception in the experience of deprivation, John TePaske and John Lynch have argued that new taxes and other fiscal demands connected material conditions and political protest by giving a name and a face to latent material changes in the lives and livelihoods of protesters. Many historians believe that the manifest fiscal event that gave political focus to economic grievances in this case was the *consolidación de vales reales*—the crown's plan, announced in December 1804, to appropriate capital from the corporate reserves of the church and Indian pueblos in exchange for 5-percent annual interest payments.[43] In force for more than four years, the consolidación netted the Spanish government between 10,500,000 and 12,750,000 pesos, and the annual interest promised to former owners of this capital was rarely paid in full.[44]

The consolidación, however, does not fully explain political behavior in 1810. The 1804 order did elicit complaints, but according to Asunción Lavrin "the Church suffered only relatively small losses of property, and the majority of lay owners did not lose theirs either."[45] Brian Hamnett and others have argued that it was the parish priests who were most affected by the crown's delinquent interest payments and by the appropriation of capellanía endowments, but few parish priests in the Guadalajara and Mexico dioceses held capellanías at the time.[46] Most parish priests who joined the insurrections against colonial rule from late 1810 to 1815 had other grievances. According to Lavrin, "Indian communities were much harder hit [by the consolidación order] than [were] clerical groups," yet the communities most affected did not rise en masse after September 1810.[47] And the biggest losers in the consolidación, private owners of large rural estates with capellanía obligations, were in general not active opponents of the colonial government before the Hidalgo insurrection, though their resentment did weaken their support for the royalists after 1811.[48]

To demonstrate connections between economic forces and political action requires more than single cases or sweeping statements about "the masses" or whole communities acting in concert. Who actually joined insurrection forces in different places? When? Were they among the most deprived? Did they regard themselves as particularly deprived? If money was in very short supply, how did pueblos manage the house-to-house collections that covered their frequent litigations and extraordinary community expenses? And why did they often opt to pay their parish priests more for their services than they would have under customary arrangements? For now, Hamnett's vision of the Independence War as the violent expression of previous tensions and a mounting war of words after 1808 (rather than as a sharp departure from the past, or as simply the product of those tensions) seems most appropriate. The key connection between economic circumstances and political action after 1780 may be, as Pedro Pérez Herrero observes, the decline in royal revenues (coupled with growing expenses) and a growing dependence on the continued willingness of colonial elites to give resources to the crown in exchange for economic protection and loyalty to colonial structures: "the interests of elites, government, and the church had traditionally been intertwined during the whole colonial period—an equilibrium which the Bourbons broke, at their own peril." [49]

Habits of thought associated with the Enlightenment in Western Europe had obvious implications for parish priests, not to mention the place of kings and state churches in public life. Reason as an absolute standard of evaluation pointed toward religious skepticism and anticlericalism, a questioning of hereditary privilege and the divine right of kings, and a new valuation of individual liberty as an unqualified good in itself and increasingly associated with equality. By the end of the eighteenth century, betrothed couples had begun giving romantic love as their main reason for marriage, a fact that pointed to the growing importance of free will and personal happiness as social goals.[50] The Spanish crown and high clergy attempted with some success to promote a moderate, practical Enlightenment that would apply reason and the new science to the benefit of Bourbon absolutism.[51] During the years before 1810, French, British, and American political writings that might have challenged the old regime in Spain and Spanish America were read by some and circulated more widely in conversation, but they lacked the momentum of a political program or a cultural imperative.

What did have some momentum in New Spain, thanks partly to the endorsement of royal administrators, was a more secular, more questioning outlook, less confidence in the old absolutes, and an interest in the history of New Spain and its parts—all of which anticipated independent changes and "improvement" in the future. Regalist bishops in New Spain criticized Jesuit "probabilism" for having gone too far into empirical relativism, but Bourbon leaders themselves toppled old axioms and endorsed material measures of success and legitimacy that came close to affirming the pursuit of happiness as worthy in its own right. The growing anticlericalism in late-eighteenth-century New Spain came mainly not from the writings of Voltaire or Rousseau, but from this panoply of diffuse changes, from the constrained political and economic circumstances in which parish priests sought nonetheless to make a living from clerical fees, and from the moderately anticlerical policies of the imperial government, enforced by some of the more provocative district governors.

Parish Priests in the Middle

In the Bourbons' vision of a new order, the function of parish priests beyond the altar and the confessional was reduced and largely undefined. Their overlapping, sometimes contradictory roles as father, mother, brother, pastor, gardener, servant, judge, soldier, physician, and ambassador, among others, were being circumscribed all the while their role as teacher was being emphasized. Formally, they were no longer treated as so essential to social cohesion and political order, although they were still the literal and figurative interpreters of that imagined order. Where were the new boundaries between spiritual and temporal affairs? The influence of most parish priests had always been limited and had varied greatly from place to place and individual to individual, but the Bourbon reforms and other changes of the late eighteenth century altered the old, shifting limits, in ways that were encapsulated in the new rules governing access to each pueblo's community chest (*caja de comunidad*). Containing the cash, land titles, contracts, account books, and other legal records of the pueblo, the caja ordinarily required three keys before it could be opened (hence its other name, the *arca de tres llaves*). Traditionally, one key had been held by the district governor or his lieutenant, one by the parish priest, and one by an elected leader of the pueblo, usually the *gobernador* or *alcalde*.[52] Now the priest was expected to relinquish his key altogether.

Both parishes and parish priests in Mexico and Guadalajara increased in number in the late eighteenth century—by at least one-third between 1750 and 1810. By 1800, nearly all pastors and their assistants were diocesan, secular priests, displacing the members of the Mendicant orders (Franciscans, Dominicans, and Augustinians in the case of these two dioceses) who had predominated until the mid-eighteenth century. They moved more often than their Mendicant counterparts and depended more heavily on clerical fees and private commerce for their livelihood as royal stipends and the benefits of labor service were withdrawn. After 1767, when the arancel (or schedule of fees) was heavily promoted, clerical fees would become the greatest single source of conflict between priests and parishioners in the archdiocese (but not in the Diocese of Guadalajara).

Late colonial parish priests were accordingly on the defensive. No longer such privileged partners of the crown, they were now thrown back on appeals to custom and tradition against various initiatives taken by royal lawmakers, district governors, and parishioners. The growing notoriety of clerical misconduct reflected both administrative interest in supervision and a mounting anticlericalism that treated priests more as meddlers and obstacles to colonial integration than as intermediaries and agents of the state. By the 1770's, priests' confident claims to authority in disputes before the audiencias were turning into laments about the enmity of district governors and the unbridled license of Indians. Furthermore, in losing some of their partnership with the crown, priests also lost some of their capacity to serve parishioners in public life, and thus some of their standing with their flocks.

Nevertheless, the pastors in these two dioceses, even in many minor parishes, were not poor except by choice. Nor were they either functionaries "held firmly in the grasp of popular control," as contemporary Russian Orthodox priests seem to have been,[53] or mere creatures of the colonial state. They were still needed, still influential, not the "hired hands" they had evidently become in Yucatán.[54] For their part, curas had a vested interest in the traditional order and were appointed by a royal governor who exercised the king's power of appointment to church offices. Most curas received an acceptable evaluation from the king's district governors—the subdelegados—in 1793, and were attached by strands of colonial patronage and authority to the viceregal capital in Mexico City and their cathedral city. Most were also attached, by virtue of their cultural identity as *criollos* (American-born, of Spanish descent), to city life and the company of non-Indians. They expressed their feelings about change in a traditional, professional vocabulary. Their hearts, they said, throbbed with pain at the disobedience of parishioners and the godless arrogance of district governors. Fire in its positive usage could mean zeal, illumination, and purification, but these priests saw its energy turned toward destruction.[55]

When the regalist rhetoric of Christian love and charity did enter into priests' presentations to the bishops, audiencias, and viceroys in the late eighteenth century, it could imply a critique of misguided regalist reforms and callous district governors. The political implications of such criticism came to full bloom at the end of the independence struggle in 1821, when priests praised Agustín de Iturbide for his defense of "the endangered religion of Jesus Christ" against a Spain that had abandoned its Christian motives and works.[56]

The social and political order of New Spain and the role of the parish priest in that order were filled with tensions, intimacies, and ambiguities that tugged and pulled people in different directions. Many of the tensions were perennial, if not universal: custom and law, separation and union, misoneism and reform, reason and emotion, mind and body, church and state, sacred and profane, rights and duties, obedience and responsibility, liberty and mutual obligation, means and ends, standards and performance. As an intermediary in this society, and a royal appointee and an agent of higher authority, the parish priest faced them all. He was both a father and a stranger, traditionally required to stand apart and above, his conduct to be measured by a higher standard. Parishioners were drawn to the priest by his spiritual power, his ability to sanctify the local community, and his patronage in parlous times, but they found themselves distanced from him by his demands for money, labor, and obedience, by his institutional ties, and sometimes by the experience of confession.

By heightening these tensions, Bourbon initiatives complicated the lives of all but the most submissive parish priests. Lawsuits mounted over their relationships to lay officials of the church, as well as to district governors, pueblo governors, and parishioners at large or in groups. District governors and their superiors were inclined to blame parish priests for lavish and unruly feast-day celebrations, yet encouraged the use of fireworks. Parish priests were expected to concentrate on their pastoral duties, yet were rarely promoted or otherwise professionally rewarded for exemplary service alone. They were still educated to feel responsible for "reducing the Indians to rational life," yet were stripped of most of the old means for controlling their charges' behavior.

The disaffection felt by some parish priests, with its potential for political dissent, was only one of the unintended consequences of the late-eighteenth-century parish reforms. Bourbon administrators in Spain had removed the political resource—both for villagers and for themselves—of a countervailing power, replacing it with little more than the glorification of the king, a chimerical vision of efficiency and prosperity, and additional force. The mounting disputes that this change opened among priests, parishioners, and district governors could gather their own momentum, especially when the crown distanced itself from a legitimating religious ideology that still retained its power and could be put to other uses by laity and priests. Religious symbols like the Virgin of Guadalupe—multivalent and attached to American places—might authorize and mediate Spanish rule, but they also had the potential to replace it. Religion and custom could become the basis of a powerful critique of the late colonial state.

As incomplete as they were, the Bourbons' administrative reforms before Napoleon ousted them from power in 1808 had far deeper consequences than they could possibly have foreseen. New Spain was not ripe for a self-starting national revolution in 1808, but the Bourbon reforms joined with the gradual changes in New Spain's regional societies and economies since the seventeenth century and the growing importance of foreign intervention and commerce in the eighteenth century to hasten the political decline of Spain in America. In a fully formed hierarchy, weak lateral connections among components (say, in this case, pueblos, *altepetls*, or the local native states that remained important in the colonial period, and "Indians") make it easier to establish and sustain strong vertical connections. Bourbon reformers were fond of vertical classifications and graded inequalities, but their standardizing policies, such as promoting the Spanish language and non-Indian settlement in Indian pueblos, strengthened lateral connections and hastened the decline of some vertical ones, a decline that was well advanced for other reasons in the Bajío and the Diocese of Guadalajara, and was gaining ground in parts of the Archdiocese of Mexico.

* * *

Few of the parish priests in this study were much like Graham Greene's whiskey priest in *The Power and the Glory* except in their sense of duty to the sacraments. They expressed heartache and solitude but were not so solitary and marginalized, not so much driven by anguish in their public actions, and not placed in such mortal danger. Most were more like the "family doctors of the soul" J. F. Powers writes about in his stories of Minnesota priests. But to the extent that they lived in charged circumstances and expressed a growing sense of operating on the edge, they were at the same time much like the priests in Agustín Yáñez's *The Edge of the Storm*, which is set in a rural town of the Altos de Jalisco on the eve of the Mexican Revolution of 1910. Like the parish priest in that novel, some were mainly spectators—too weak, scrupulous, or self-absorbed to hold back the oncoming force of violent change with their spiritual and moral authority and unwilling to join or direct it. Others, however, would exercise a more active choice about making the world whole when their storm broke in September 1810.

CHAPTER TWO

The Archdiocese of Mexico
and the Diocese of Guadalajara

Mi vida! What delight your countrymen take in those hor-
rid mountains of ours! I wish we could export them in exchange for your beautiful farming-country in the North.
—Franciscan friar-pastor to an American traveler, 1875

Most of the documentation used in this study of priests in their parishes
comes from two of the ten late-eighteenth-century dioceses located within
modern Mexico's borders—the Archdiocese of Mexico and the Diocese of Guadalajara (see Map 1).[1] Both were large and comparatively prosperous, and both
experienced the population growth and accompanying increases in production
common throughout eighteenth-century Spanish America.

The Archdiocese of Mexico was the richest and most populous Catholic territory in America in the late eighteenth century, with about 1,100,000 people (perhaps a fifth of the Viceroyalty of New Spain's total) and annual tithe revenues of
about 712,880 pesos in 1793.[2] Its highlands and valleys embraced the capital city
of Mexico, important provincial cities and towns, and varied hinterlands with a
heavy concentration of Indians (the term applied especially to people descended
from the native population who were attached to nucleated communities designated in colonial law as *pueblos de indios*), migrants, silver mines, and private
estates. It encompassed the enduring heartland of the Viceroyalty of New Spain.

The Diocese of Guadalajara, with about half as many parish priests earning
on average about half as much from clerical fees as their counterparts in the archdiocese, was located to the northwest, beyond the Diocese of Michoacán, in a
more open, drier area, where large-scale ranching and long-distance travel were
common. Though it covered one and a half times as much land as the archdiocese, it had about half the population in 1793 (roughly 600,000) and less than
half as much income in tithe revenues (316,310 pesos).[3] It experienced rapid economic and social change in the late colonial period, but did not seriously rival
the power, wealth, and prestige of the city and archdiocese of Mexico. It was less
populous, less Indian, more provincial, and more homogeneous culturally.[4]

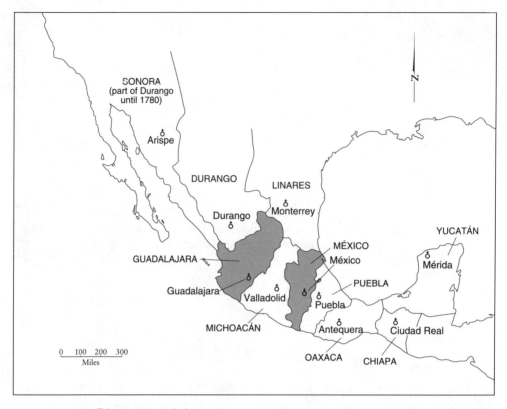

MAP I. Diocesan boundaries

Both dioceses lay south of the Chichimec Frontier, a floating zone defined mainly by rainfall patterns that separated the sparse, seminomadic groups of part-time farmers and hunter-gatherers who lived in desert or near-desert conditions in the north from the denser, sedentary indigenous farming communities to the south. Long-term changes in the spring and summer rainy season could shift this frontier north or south, affecting the ability of groups near the old margins to support permanent agricultural settlements and resist invasion.

This frontier was in fact a doubly porous one. "Chichimecs" (as they were known by their more sedentary enemies to the south) made forays across the frontier throughout the colonial period, affecting much of the northern and western parts of the Diocese of Guadalajara and, to a lesser extent, the northeastern part of the archdiocese (through Cadereyta, Querétaro, Xilotepec, and Metepec as far as Tula in Hidalgo state and Tenango del Valle in Mexico state, and from Meztitlan and Ixmiquilpan to Cempoala, Apam, and Tulancingo, all in Hidalgo state). But their "frontier" was in turn repeatedly breached, first by Spanish colonizers, sometimes accompanied by Tlaxcalan and Otomí Indian allies from central Mexico, in the sixteenth century; and then by an assortment of ranchers, prospectors, laborers, drifters, missionaries, soldiers, and traders in the seventeenth and eighteenth centuries, sometimes scattering on their own, sometimes arriving in larger groups and better order at the crown's behest, but always promoting ongoing contacts with the center in any case.

Like much of modern Mexico, the most populous parts of the Archdiocese of Mexico and the Diocese of Guadalajara were situated in a rugged, relatively high and dry landscape (more than half of Mexico is over 3,000 feet above sea level). About two-thirds of the land is too steep for good agriculture, and nearly four-fifths requires some irrigation for successful farming. While maize was cultivated and European domesticated animals were raised almost everywhere during the colonial period, thorny brush, cactus, maguey, and other xerophytic plants were part of the natural vegetation even in the greener valleys and slopes of the more temperate central plateau south of the Chichimec Frontier.

Human occupation wreaked havoc on this fragile landscape. Some effects of cultivation—a deforestation of the mountains and erosion on the slopes and depressions—were evident before the arrival of Europeans. But heavy colonial demands for timber and the overgrazing of plains and piedmont by sheep and other livestock degraded some farmlands and woods to the point that only cactus, maguey, short grasses, and Old World weeds thrived. Such changes were most dramatic in the Valle del Mezquital of modern Hidalgo and near the colonial cities and mines.[5]

The mountainous terrain, whose chief interest for the Spanish was its pockets of silver ore, is marked by great variations in altitude and temperature over short distances. The climate is mild to cool in many of the highland valleys and on the plateau between the ranges of the Sierra Madre Occidental and the Sierra Madre Oriental in central Mexico, but canyon floors, even in the central highlands, can be oppressively hot and humid. The mountains and steep canyons were obstacles to travel, long-distance trade, and state building throughout the precolonial and colonial periods.

The result of this broken terrain and its resource base for the human history of the dioceses of Mexico and Guadalajara before railroads, paved highways, and airplanes was the prevalence of many small, distinct settlements. Despite the pull of the mining economy and colonial urban centers, the relative isolation of these clusters of small settlements, the competition for scarce water sources and arable land, the dramatic decline in the size of the indigenous population in the sixteenth and early seventeenth centuries, and the divide-and-rule strategies of Spanish colonialism contributed to strong local attachments—the aggressively *patria chica* outlook that is so characteristic of the history of rural Mexico.

Before the arrival of Europeans there was a bewildering number of language groups, local identities, and largely independent political entities. The altepetl, which James Lockhart highlights as a remarkably stable indigenous territorial unit among the Nahuas of central Mexico before and after the Conquest, was usually not much larger than a municipality. There had been relatively large native states in central and southern Mexico, but most were short-lived, relied heavily on warfare to expand and stabilize their boundaries, and lacked elaborate organization. Beyond the central highlands, the strongest political units tended to be even less stable and about the size of the small altepetl. Spanish colonial politics, which promoted the first integrated state that reached (and exceeded) Mexico's national boundaries, legitimized the altepetl as a convenient unit of administration and, in time, worked to reduce Indian territorial loyalties still further by recognizing pueblos within the old native territories as the basic unit of civil society. Especially in the eighteenth century, colonial courts designated various formerly subordinate pueblos as political centers in their own right. Private estates of whatever size, from the largest hacienda or plantation to the tiniest rancho, added another kind of settlement to colonial society that created strong local attachments as well as connections to regional and viceregal markets.[6] (Unlike the hacienda and the plantation, which were usually owned by criollos, or American-born Spaniards, the rancho was almost always occupied by its owner: a *casta*, or person of mixed ancestry who was not officially classed as Spanish or Indian; a free black; or an Indian detached from a pueblo.)

In the colonial period, as in prehispanic times, earthquakes, high winds, floods, hailstorms, freezes, and droughts destroyed property, divided families and communities, and brought famines and early death, but the effect of these perennial disasters was magnified by the degradation of forests, farmland, and waterworks. The epidemics of measles, smallpox, and typhus that accompanied Spanish colonization joined with intestinal complaints and other endemic ills to decimate the native population. Within a century of Cortés's arrival in 1519, the Indians' numbers declined by at least 90 percent, to about one million. Despite this devastation, Indians continued to represent more than half the total population, even in the seventeenth century, as the Spanish population and distinct miscegenated groups began to grow significantly. In 1774, Pedro Alonso O'Crouley estimated that 54.5 percent of the population of the dioceses of Mexico, Puebla, Michoacán, Oaxaca, Guadalajara, and Durango were Indians, 36.4 percent castas, and 9.1 percent American-born Spaniards. But the devastation of the native population had been great. Whether the precolonial population south of the Chichimec Frontier was ten million, fifteen million, or more, those numbers would not be surpassed by the total population of Mexico until the twentieth century.

The Archdiocese of Mexico

Centered on the political and religious capital of Mexico City, the Archdiocese of Mexico traced a broad band from coast to coast, from Tampico in the northeast to Acapulco in the southwest. It embraced the northernmost part of the modern state of Veracruz; eastern San Luis Potosí; a corner of northeastern Guanajuato; the eastern and southwestern portions of Querétaro, all of Hidalgo, the Estado de México, the Federal District, and Morelos; and much of Guerrero.

Dwelling on the Archdiocese of Mexico's place as the richest colonial diocese in Spanish America obscures great internal differences.[7] The remote coastal areas and their adjacent uplands did not offer the natural resources, population, or climate to attract much attention from the great center at Mexico City. The *alcaldía mayor* districts of Pánuco and Valles on the Gulf coast plain were hot and often swampy (see Map 2). In the late colonial period, they supported only small, dispersed Indian settlements and private ranches on their grasslands. The neighboring districts rising into the Sierra Madre Oriental of San Luis Potosí, Guana-

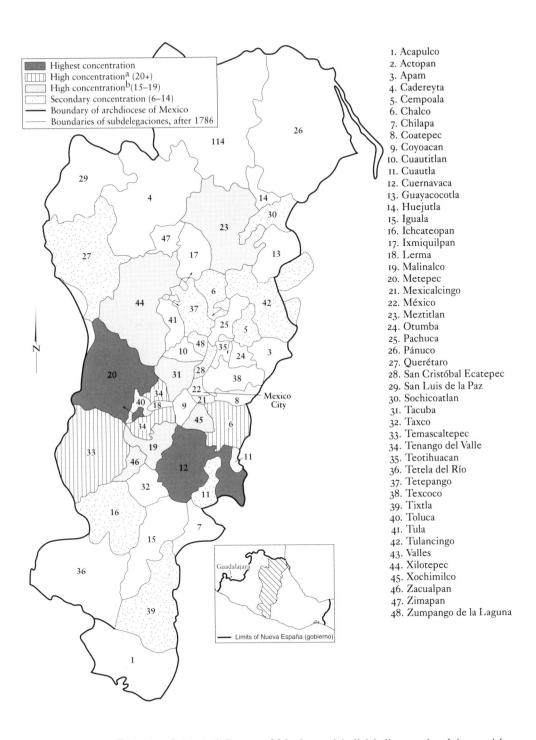

Legend:
- Highest concentration
- High concentration[a] (20+)
- High concentration[b] (15–19)
- Secondary concentration (6–14)
- Boundary of archdiocese of Mexico
- Boundaries of subdelegaciones, after 1786

1. Acapulco
2. Actopan
3. Apam
4. Cadereyta
5. Cempoala
6. Chalco
7. Chilapa
8. Coatepec
9. Coyoacan
10. Cuautitlan
11. Cuautla
12. Cuernavaca
13. Guayacocotla
14. Huejutla
15. Iguala
16. Ichcateopan
17. Ixmiquilpan
18. Lerma
19. Malinalco
20. Metepec
21. Mexicalcingo
22. México
23. Meztitlan
24. Otumba
25. Pachuca
26. Pánuco
27. Querétaro
28. San Cristóbal Ecatepec
29. San Luis de la Paz
30. Sochicoatlan
31. Tacuba
32. Taxco
33. Temascaltepec
34. Tenango del Valle
35. Teotihuacan
36. Tetela del Río
37. Tetepango
38. Texcoco
39. Tixtla
40. Toluca
41. Tula
42. Tulancingo
43. Valles
44. Xilotepec
45. Xochimilco
46. Zacualpan
47. Zimapan
48. Zumpango de la Laguna

Mexico City

Guadalajara

Limits of Nueva España (gobierno)

MAP 2. Districts of the Archdiocese of Mexico and judicial disputes involving parish priests, 1750–1810.

juato, Veracruz, and Hidalgo were not much more inviting. Their terrain is very rugged—creased by deep canyons that are too low (1,200–2,500 feet) to escape the heat and humidity—and offering no important mines or other very attractive resources. There was either too little rain and running water, as in Cadereyta and San Luis de la Paz, or too much, as in Sochicoatlan and Guayacocotla. All of this territory was exposed to Chichimec raids. Some of the poorest parishes in the archdiocese at the end of the colonial period were located here, or the Indian settlements were left to Franciscan missionaries—another sign of the area's marginal place in the affairs of the archdiocese.

Except for the natural harbor at Acapulco, which served as the American port for Spanish trade with Asia, the Pacific area of the archdiocese was also poor in resources. Rising quickly from the coast to the hot, mostly dry hills, mountains, and gorges of modern Guerrero, it was a frontier zone even in precolonial times, fought over by Tarascans and Aztecs in the early sixteenth century. Its chief settlements were garrison towns. Even in the Balsas River drainage districts of Tetela del Río, Guaymeo, Ichcateopan, and Iguala, where water for irrigation and domestic use was more plentiful and agriculture more successful, indigenous settlements were small, scattered, and often in conflict. Communications were poor throughout this rugged area of thorny underbrush. Roads were undeveloped except for the route from Acapulco to Mexico City, which passed through a natural corridor at Chilpancingo. In some places, as many as five languages were spoken in settlements located only a few miles apart.

Neither archdiocesan officials nor their parish priests could muster much enthusiasm for this Pacific territory, which, like the Gulf, was seen as poor, unhealthy, and particularly difficult to administer. A pastor might be called on to travel for three or four days over barely passable paths in wilting heat to hear a confession; parishioners in the area were noted for their tepid response to the initiatives of priests; and few communities sponsored decent churches. Some places never saw a priest. Ceutla, an interior site northwest of Acapulco on a fertile stretch of the Papagayo River, was more than 50 miles from the nearest parish seat. An inspector for the archbishop described it in 1780 as an isolated area of scattered huts and hamlets (*rancherías*) occupied by outcasts who raised illegal tobacco and "lived like beasts." They reportedly left their children unbaptized, and some were thought to be apostates.[8]

As these coastal regions give way to the highlands and Valley of Mexico, the topography, vegetation, and climate become more varied and inviting. Here, in the center of the archdiocese, where the Sierra Madre Occidental and the Sierra Madre Oriental join, mountains dominate the landscape, enclosing more temperate highland valleys. Lakes and fast-moving rivers were more plentiful (although hardly abundant) than in regions to the north, and afternoon rains during the late spring and summer promised good crops of maize, beans, and other vegetables in the valleys, and forage in the uplands. The ubiquitous maguey and other xerophytic vegetation bore witness to the basically semiarid climate even of central Mexico. An important part of the center of the archdiocese, especially to the north and northwest in Hidalgo and Querétaro, consists of stark, cold areas of eroded hills, the wild Sierra Gorda, and rather barren plains.

While many highland pueblos, haciendas, and ranchos mainly produced maize, *pulque* (fermented juice of the maguey plant), livestock, hides, and wool, the center's varied topography made possible different kinds of production and active market exchanges among nearby pueblos. The Meztitlan district, in a broken, mountainous part of Hidalgo, offered arid to rainy conditions, temperature extremes (although most of the district was hot or temperate), and some heavily forested uplands among cultivated valleys. Cereals, timber, a little sugarcane, and cattle (including an abundance of feral cattle) were produced there. Tanneries, cotton textile shops, and a few sugar mills employed the small nonagricultural population. To the southeast, the topography and climate are almost as varied, where elevations ranging from 650 feet to nearly 10,000 feet produce a zone that encompasses the hot, rainy country of Tututepec, cold little mountain valleys, and the relatively temperate situation of the town of Tulancingo, with a perennial river, before giving way to the dry plains of Apam in the south.

Highland districts closer to Mexico City on the north and east without these extremes of terrain and climate also had complex local economies and were actively involved in regional trade. Querétaro, well known for the cattle, horses, and sheep raised on its numerous haciendas and ranchos, had vineyards, lime deposits, woolen textile shops, and potteries. Ixmiquilpan, among other places in Hidalgo, sold rope, grains, the fruit of the prickly pear cactus, exotic birds, and hides. The plains of southern Hidalgo and the Valley of Mexico were especially well known for their pulque, while Tula (Hidalgo), with its mules, carts, and haulers, depended on transport. Districts in and near the Valley of Toluca in the Estado de México produced much maize and livestock, along with local specialties: Metepec traded in wheat, pigs, fruit, and pottery; Toluca traded in snow and ice gathered from the Nevado de Toluca; chickens were the commercial specialization of Ixtlahuaca; and Lerma had tanneries in addition to its grains and livestock. South of Toluca toward Malinalco, Temascaltepec, Zacualpan, and Sultepec, the cold mountain reaches, with their silver mines, quickly gave way to a more temperate zone, where a scattering of farming pueblos and private estates produced grains, fruit trees, rope, lime, baskets, shoes, wood articles, and even sugarcane.

The Valley of Mexico, with its dense population and varied ecosystem of mountains, hills, woodlands, plains, ravines, rivers, lakes, and bottom lands that could be swampy or dry depending on the location and season, was especially rich in natural resources and local products. Mexicalcingo specialized in fishing and quarrying volcanic rock. Xochimilco rented out its surplus farmland and produced maguey, firewood, straw mats, vegetables, and flowers for Mexico City. Cuautitlan offered maize, wheat, and pottery; Cempoala produced pulque from its abundant fields of maguey. In addition to farms and maguey fields, the Zumpango de la Laguna district harvested fish, ducks, and frogs for the market. Texcoco produced hats and wooden furniture, as well as crops (its production of textiles having declined in the face of competition from Querétaro). Chalco, in the southeast portion of the valley, was among the most important districts economically. Ranging in elevation from about 5,000 feet on the temperate plain to more than 16,000 feet at Mt. Popocatépetl, it produced large maize and wheat crops from irrigated fields and supplied much of the timber used in construction in Mexico City. Lakeshore pueblos there also manufactured canoes.

Hardly any two towns in this great valley enjoyed the same land and weather conditions. Texcoco occupied "an immense plain" with low hills—a more healthful site than Mexico City because it was higher and drier. Coyoacan had similar advantages at the other end of the valley, along with an abundance of river water and fresh air. Xochimilco, swampy and surrounded by water in the rainy season (as was Mexicalcingo), was regarded as an unhealthful place, its residents subject to intermittent fevers and other illnesses because of the dampness and a diet that was thought to be too rich in pork and cane alcohol concoctions.[9] San Cristóbal Ecatepec was regarded as more salubrious, being close to the mountains, but its lands were less fertile. Zumpango de la Laguna was located on a fertile plain but had little fresh water. Teotihuacan was colder and rather bleak, with less rain. Salt deposits were worked there, and much of Teotihuacan's land was controlled by private estates producing maguey and maize.

Even including the sparsely settled coastal areas, the population of the archdiocese in the eighteenth century was about three times as dense as that of the Diocese of Guadalajara. The rural population of the center, which consisted mainly of village Indians, was densest in the two largest and best-watered highland valley systems: the Valley of Mexico, with its network of lakes, rivers, and piedmont; and the Lerma River drainage in the Estado de México from Temascalcingo in the north through Atlacomulco, Ixtlahuaca, Toluca, Lerma, Metepec, Calimaya, and Tenango del Valle, and surrounding mountains and valleys. Nearly half (45.8 percent) of the 1,224 pueblos of the archdiocese and more than half of the total population were located in these two areas. The bulk of the other Indians lived on the semitropical river valleys and ridges of the Cuernavaca and Cuautla districts in modern Morelos (despite its reputation for a hot, unhealthful climate), on the broader but drier and increasingly eroded plains of Apam and adjacent valleys of modern Hidalgo from Meztitlan south, or in southwestern Querétaro, where the great plateau of the Bajío region, punctuated by mountains and mining towns, opened out to the northwest. This central portion of the archdiocese supported the important provincial towns of Cuernavaca, Querétaro, Toluca, Tulancingo, Chalco, Texcoco, and other district seats, as well as important silver mines at Pachuca/Real del Monte, Temascaltepec, Zacualpan, Cimapan, and Taxco, among others.

Indians attached to formally constituted, landholding pueblos were an especially numerous social category in the Archdiocese of Mexico, accounting for nearly two-thirds of the Intendancy of Mexico's population (with boundaries approximating those of the archdiocese) in 1810. Though the heartland of the archdiocese (and part of Michoacán) had larger native states than other parts of central Mexico did at the time of Spanish colonization, and Nahuatl was widely spoken there, the political situation was complicated and in flux. There were many small, semiautonomous states, especially in Guerrero and the Lerma River basin in the Estado de México. Nahuatl was the main native language of Morelos, but Morelos, too, had small states that stood in an uneasy relationship to the larger polities in and near the Valley of Mexico. And within small states there were distinct dependent communities (*sujetos*) and neighborhoods (*barrios*) that accentuated localized identities in the late colonial period. Though more numerous in Morelos and Mexico City than elsewhere in the archdiocese, *indios forasteros* (Indians who did not live in their pueblo of origin) were not nearly so common as in the Diocese of Guadalajara. Politically separate Indian pueblos were especially numerous in the greater Toluca Valley and the nearby mountain valleys of the Temascaltepec and Sultepec districts in the eighteenth century.

Indian languages, for all that they were changing under the influence of Spanish,[10] were more widely spoken in the archdiocese than in the Diocese of Guadalajara in the eighteenth century. Even in Morelos and the Chalco district near the Valley of Mexico, people from the pueblos were often described as "indios cerrados" (closed Indians), which meant mainly that they spoke a native tongue and manifested little interest in learning Spanish. But the pattern of few members of pueblos being fluent in Spanish, except where a large non-Indian population lived nearby or where there was considerable trade with other pueblos and a regional center, was apparently changing by the late 1770's. Spanish-language primary schools had become permanent fixtures in the Valley of Toluca by 1779, and the archbishop's pastoral visitor that year could detect a generation gap in the parish of Ichcateopan (Guerrero), where the young Indians spoke Spanish as well as they spoke their own language, whereas their parents still spoke little or no Spanish.[11]

In most of the archdiocese, non-Indians were concentrated in cities and larger towns, mining areas, and on haciendas, ranchos, and sugar plantations.[12] The *cabeceras* (head towns) of predominantly Indian districts were still mainly Indian in the late eighteenth century, except for those of Morelos where, by 1759, non-Indians had come to outnumber Indians.[13] Blacks—slave and free—as a category of non-Indians were found mainly in cities, on sugar plantations (one thinks of Morelos, but there were also 300 slaves on a sugar-producing Jesuit estate in the Malinalco district), on Jesuit properties near Mexico City, and scattered among private estates.

The Diocese of Guadalajara

Situated in the modern states of Jalisco, Zacatecas, Nayarit, Colima, and part of northwestern San Luis Potosí, the Diocese of Guadalajara had a resource base and colonial history more like those of central Mexico than like areas farther north. Some of its highland plains and valleys were more fertile than northern Mexico; its population, at about 550,000 in the late eighteenth century, was larger and more settled; its climate was more temperate; the spring and summer rains were more dependable; and Lake Chapala was an incomparable source of fresh surface water. The more than 250 farming and fishing Indian villages of the central and southern areas of this diocese contrasted with the wanderings and warfare of the sparser "Chichimecs" to the immediate north and west.

Like the heartland of the archdiocese, the central and southern parts of the Guadalajara diocese experienced Spanish expeditions of conquest in the 1520's, *encomienda* assignments (grants of Indians, mainly as tribute payers), new administrative and commercial towns, an urban capital with its own high court (*audiencia*) at Guadalajara, epidemics and Indian depopulation, draft labor systems, the formation of haciendas and ranchos, extensive wheat and maize cultivation, miscegenation, and—in the late eighteenth century—substantial growth in the economy, in cities and towns, and in the Indian population.

But a closer comparison of the diocese's principal regions—the largely arid north; the adjacent plateau of the Altos de Jalisco; the central area of the city of Guadalajara and its agricultural and ranching hinterland; southern Jalisco; and the coastal west and south of modern Nayarit, Jalisco, and Colima—reveals some striking contrasts to the archdiocese in terrain, natural resources, population, society, and colonial experience.

Guadalajara was more arid, hotter, lower, less varied, and more sparsely populated than Mexico. Even though within a short distance of its long Pacific coastline tropical vegetation gave way to the scrub cover of hot, dry plains interrupted by shallow arroyos, much of the diocese was a bumpy plateau occasionally cut here and there by deep canyons. The natural vegetation on the highlands of the two areas was of a kind, but not of the same size and spacing, being smaller and sparser in the Guadalajara diocese.

These conditions conduced to separate and scatter people, as well as plants, before and after Spanish colonization. While much of the land was flat enough to make travel by horse and mule easier than in the archdiocese (and it seemed as if everyone owned a horse or mule), most roads were described as wretched ("pésimos"). Communications improved some in the eighteenth century with a few good bridges and work on the roads from Guadalajara to the Bajío via San Juan de los Lagos and La Piedad, but settlements along other roads without adequate bridges were still cut off during the summer rainy season. Ranching, which amounted to a dispersed, extensive use of land, became a hallmark of the Diocese of Guadalajara, in contrast to the more intensive land use in much of the archdiocese. And about two-thirds of the population was classified as non-Indian (compared with about a third in the archdiocese). The nucleated Indian villages that had been formed under Franciscan administration in central Jalisco were usually surrounded by Spanish estates with substantial resident populations of their own.

The northeast half of the diocese, along the Chichimec Frontier in modern Zacatecas and Aguascalientes, included some of the driest land in Mexico. Here were barren high plains and valleys, mountains reaching elevations of 9,000 feet and freezing temperatures at night, hot, dry canyon floors, and salt flats. Except in the greener valleys of Juchipila and Tlaltenango, the native population was sparse and often hostile to Spanish colonization. (These and other civil districts in the diocese are shown in Map 3.)

Even though Indian pueblos and surface water were scarce, some of the most lucrative late colonial parishes were located in this part of the diocese—in the cities of Zacatecas and Aguascalientes, and in Fresnillo, Sierra de Pinos, Mazapil, Charcas, and Jerez—thanks to the rich silver mines worked in the mountains near Zacatecas and the minor strikes that quickened the pace of settlement near Pinos, Bolaños, western Aguascalientes, and several other sites. Surrounding areas, especially in modern Aguascalientes and Jalisco, benefited from the mines as suppliers of meat, hides, draft animals, lumber, grains, fruits, and vegetables. Forests that had once covered the mountainsides of Zacatecas near the mines were depleted during the sixteenth century, and those of the Bolaños dis-

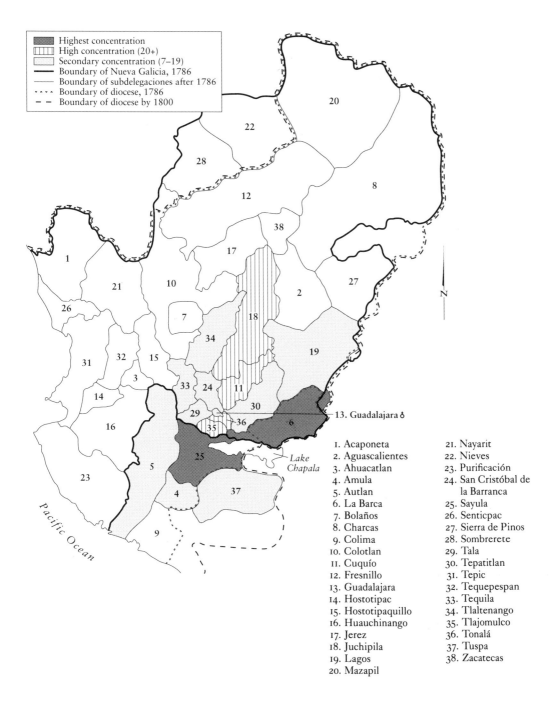

13. Guadalajara ♂

Lake Chapala

Pacific Ocean

N

1. Acaponeta
2. Aguascalientes
3. Ahuacatlan
4. Amula
5. Autlan
6. La Barca
7. Bolaños
8. Charcas
9. Colima
10. Colotlan
11. Cuquío
12. Fresnillo
13. Guadalajara
14. Hostotipac
15. Hostotipaquillo
16. Huauchinango
17. Jerez
18. Juchipila
19. Lagos
20. Mazapil

21. Nayarit
22. Nieves
23. Purificación
24. San Cristóbal de
    la Barranca
25. Sayula
26. Senticpac
27. Sierra de Pinos
28. Sombrerete
29. Tala
30. Tepatitlan
31. Tepic
32. Tequepespan
33. Tequila
34. Tlaltenango
35. Tlajomulco
36. Tonalá
37. Tuspa
38. Zacatecas

MAP 3. Districts of the Diocese of Guadalajara and judicial disputes involving parish priests, 1750–1810.

trict virtually disappeared in the eighteenth, thanks also to the requirements of mining operations. (Only in the southern part of diocese were there still forests at the end of the colonial period.)

Most of the countryside in this part of the diocese was lightly populated and dominated by great haciendas running thousands of head of cattle. The exceptions were the irrigated plains of Aguascalientes and, again, the valleys of Juchipila and Tlaltenango, where farming prospered. For the most part, employment was in ranching, mining, transport, and military service, with scattered tanning, soap, weaving, and pottery operations. Because of the mines and the Chichimec Frontier, the area had a more militarized history than the southern section. As a corridor to "tierra adentro" (the interior north) and a nexus of trade routes, it had, as well, a reputation for transiency, insubordination, and highway robbery that kept the royal constabulary (Acordada) occupied in the late eighteenth century.[14]

The western end of the Diocese of Guadalajara, sloping upward from the coastal areas of Jalisco and Colima into modern Nayarit, had been heavily settled by dispersed farming communities before the arrival of Europeans. They supported many small states, in which a variety of languages were spoken. But the Indian population declined precipitously in the sixteenth century, and there was little else to attract large settlements or a dense rural population in the late colonial period. The provincial towns of Tepic, San Blas, and Colima had a certain importance, as did the smaller district seats of Hostotipaquillo, Huauchinango, Santa María del Oro, Mascota, and Ahuacatlan, but in general the area contained some of the diocese's poorest and least desirable parishes. All the districts in this area (with the exception of Colima and Tequepespan) registered more mestizos and *mulatos* than Indians in the late colonial period; and in remote parts of Nayarit, the Indians could hardly be called Spanish subjects, so limited were their contacts with missionaries, royal administrators, and regional trade.

The coast and adjacent uplands were defined more by the ubiquitous dense, thorny scrub and deep canyons that discouraged travel, and the heat at lower elevations than by any symbiotic meshing of ecological zones. Without dams, the rivers of all but the coastal area of Colima were too deeply entrenched, fast flowing, and intermittent to be of much use; and the forested mountains of the rugged Hostotipaquillo, Huauchinango, and Ahuacatlan districts were too far from important mines and cities to be worth harvesting. Ranching on haciendas and the farming of maize, wheat, sugarcane, and a little cacao on many dispersed small holdings were the main activities in the valleys and upland meadows.

With this combination of resources and physical features, the area near the coast did not attract much of a colonial presence or regional market activity. Deposits of silver led to mining camps and occasional boomlets in the more mountainous parts of the Tequepespan, Hostotipaquillo, Ahuacatlan, Hostotipac, and Huauchinango districts, but most of the mines were small, scattered, and worked only intermittently. The narrow coastal plain of Acaponeta in the north had salt flats, mangrove lagoons, and marshes, but their perishable products were too far from prospective markets, and the salt could not be hauled to consumers at a competitive price. The rocky bluffs, small deltas, and sandy beaches of the Valle de Banderas and Purificación districts had little more to offer than their scenery, even though they, too, had been quite densely settled in precolonial times.

The Sierra Madre Occidental cuts through the lower third of the Diocese of Guadalajara south of Zacatecas, defining a region of high plains, hills, and scattered mountains that slope south to the gorges of the Río Santiago (the only great river of the diocese, flowing from Lake Chapala northwest to the sea above San Blas). Known as the Altos de Jalisco, this series of stepped plateaus at 5,000–7,000 feet was comparatively cool and dry, and still subject to "Chichimec" raids in the early colonial period.

Whereas Indian pueblos predominated as the centers of rural settlement in the archdiocese, especially in and near the Valley of Mexico, ranchos were more common in the Altos area by the late colonial period. For example, Tepatitlan, described as a poor district with soapmaking as its only industry, consisted of 1,528 ranchos, nine towns (including Indian pueblos), and three haciendas. There were more Indians in the Altos than in districts to the north, but they were in the minority.

Not all of the Altos area was poor. Two of the richest parishes in the diocese were located in the important commercial and agricultural center of Santa María de Lagos (Lagos de Moreno) and the market town and pilgrimage site of San Juan de los Lagos. Lagos was one of the four most densely settled districts of the diocese (the others were Guadalajara, La Barca, and Sayula in the center and south). Much traffic in farm and ranching produce passed through the area destined for Guadalajara, Mexico City, or the mines.

The central area and southern Jalisco are especially well represented in the parish documentation. Together, they accounted for much of the colonial Indian population and much of the best farmland and flattest terrain in the diocese. The central area alone, stretching from the eastern shore of Lake Chapala to Cocula on the west, and from near Tepatitlan on the north to Zacoalco on the south and containing the city of Guadalajara, had over 180,000 inhabitants in the 1790's—about a third of the diocese's population on less than a fifth of its territory.

The city of Guadalajara shaped the rural development of this semiarid central area, especially during the city's rapid growth as a commercial and manufacturing center, market, and administrative capital in the late eighteenth century. With the construction of new roads to the Bajío and Mexico City, new contacts with northern Mexico, an independent merchant guild (*consulado*) in 1795, a university in 1791, and the posting of a provincial intendant there, also in 1791, Guadalajara attracted much new activity and many new residents. Its population tripled between 1760 and 1803, to 34,697. The old elite families combined forces with prosperous merchants through intermarriage and credit relations to control the largest and richest of the haciendas of central Jalisco that produced for the urban market. As the century wore on and the Guadalajara market grew, these large estates turned increasingly from ranching to wheat farming. This shift in production was accomplished at the expense of small-scale market production by the pueblos and ranchos. With ever more land and water diverted to the large estates and ever more villages losing or renting out some of their croplands, the haciendas succeeded in cornering the market on cereals in the city. Haciendas, ranchos, pueblos, and the transient population alike were drawn in and changed by the region's growth.[15]

Much of southern Jalisco (and Colima), covering the plateau lands south of

Lake Chapala, was added to the Diocese of Guadalajara only in the 1790's (when diocesan boundaries were redrawn to conform more closely to civil jurisdictions). Nineteenth-century visitors to the area wrote of green oases in a wilderness of mesquite and cactus. The most arid, eroded part of this thirsty land, in the district of Amula around Tuscacuesco, became famous in Juan Rulfo's stories as "the burning plain." The more varied but still rather marginal late colonial districts of Amula and Autlan experienced the familiar pattern of a patchwork of populous, small precolonial states giving way to a smaller, dispersed population of creoles, mulatos, mestizos, and Indians by the eighteenth century. Once well known for their cochineal, these districts mainly produced cattle, timber, some sugar, and a little silver.

The heaviest concentrations of people and production in southern Jalisco were in the districts of Sayula and Tuspa, where an internal regional market in woven fabrics, clothing, ironwork, leather, and soap complemented ranching, maize, and wheat in the pueblos, and ranching, wheat, and sugar on the haciendas and ranchos.[16] The main urban markets and centers of manufacturing and commerce were Sayula and Zapotlan el Grande, where non-Indians predominated. The usual pattern of ethnicity recorded in late colonial population counts showed pueblos as about half Indian and half casta and creole. About half the 47,460 people of the Sayula district were classified as Indian, about a quarter as creoles, and a quarter as castas.

Overall, about half the rural population of central and southern Jalisco lived in settled communities of Indians that in precolonial times had belonged to a *señorío* or small state similar to the least elaborate altepetl of central Mexico. Though these states did not have a history of sustained conflict with "Chichimecs," they had been subject to efforts at incoporation by the Tarascans of Michoacán. During the late colonial period, the Indian pueblos of this area stood more open than many of their counterparts in the archdiocese to the larger colonial system, its social and cultural concepts, its administrators, and its economic activity. As early as the first decade of the seventeenth century, chroniclers remarked that Indians of the Diocese of Guadalajara imitated Spaniards in their dress, taste for meat, horses, habits of travel, and what they liked to grow and trade. The replacement of local Indian languages by Spanish was widespread in the pueblos, as were distilled alcohol and the laughter and music of taverns and neighborhood parties.

People from the pueblos of central and southern Jalisco were on the move for employment, to transport their products to distant markets on their own strings of mules, or to take up residence in an hacienda or another pueblo. In part, this mobility responded to a terrain and distant markets that invited travel, and to a ranching economy that required seasonal pastures and depended on distant markets. From early colonial times, this was a society on horseback, less wedded than central Mexico to maize agriculture. Another reason for movement was economic necessity. Most Indian pueblos had little farmland, usually much less than was needed for subsistence. Many villagers depended on crafts, petty trade, and work outside the community for their living. Some pueblos, like Tonalá (pottery), Tlajomulco (weaving), Zacoalco (shoes and soap), Atoyac (salt), and Mescala and several other towns on Lake Chapala (fishing), prospered from their specialized commerce and possessed adequate farmland and pastures. Others sold small surpluses of fruit, grain, swine, and leather in the city when they could. Many others were reduced to cutting firewood and lumber and preparing charcoal for sale, which put them in fierce competition with one another for the few remaining stands of pine trees on the denuded hills of the Tala and Zapopan districts. In other places close to the city, most Indian men worked all or part of the year on private estates, in mines, or as muleteers, depending on wage labor for their livelihood.

There was more confusion in the Diocese of Guadalajara than in the Archdiocese of Mexico about who was an Indian and who would be allowed to claim membership in a particular pueblo. Some designated Indians moved from one pueblo to another; communities descended from African slaves claimed Indian status; and pueblos frequently encouraged mestizos, mulatos, and even creole Spaniards to register as Indian tributaries and live within the townsite to share in the lands assigned to Indian families and the responsibilities for village expenses. Castas were also reported to be marrying Indians and taking up residence in their spouse's pueblo. Most pueblos—not only the administrative centers of a local district, as in the highlands of the archdiocese—had neighborhoods of recognized non-Indians, a pattern that grew stronger in the last years of the eighteenth century, when the long-standing segregation laws were changed.

The importance of outsiders and the colonial state in community affairs of pueblos de indios in the Diocese of Guadalajara can be detected also in the role of local Spaniards in district politics, litigation, and the state of pueblo finances. Spanish merchants and estate owners frequently served as district governors, using the position to consolidate their place in local merchandising, and they often found themselves accused in colonial courts of meddling in pueblo politics and demanding personal service.

The political institutions of pueblos in this diocese were in general weaker than in central Mexico. Few pueblos maintained the municipal coffers and collective property required by law to cover public expenses such as primary schools and road repairs. Compared with the central highlands of the archdiocese, factions in Guadalajara's pueblos were more likely to take their political disputes to colonial courts, and community lands were more often informally sold or rented out.

On the whole, late colonial Indian pueblos in the center and south of the Diocese of Guadalajara were less tightly knit and more exposed to an emerging society of cash and classes than their counterparts in the archdiocese. Their members were usually less rooted in the land and political territory of the pueblo, and there was an increasingly unequal distribution of wealth and political conflict inside pueblos. Most members owned some land but could not, or at least did not, make a living from it alone. They were of, but frequently not in, the pueblo. The remade appearance of public buildings in these pueblos reflected the colonial history of this area. Their unprepossessing early colonial churches and town offices were periodically replaced or renovated in ways that added new forms and fashions, especially in the late eighteenth century.

But this does not mean that the Indian villagers in the diocese had lost a sense of land-based community. Rural pueblos showed great variety in their adjustments to late colonial pressures, and pueblo identity in one form or another continued almost everywhere. The feast of the patron saint and the high holy days were popular community events each year, and some pueblos had their own "Indian" dances, which, if not precolonial in origin, gave a pueblo something that distinguished its members from their neighbors. There are many examples of local pride, especially of villagers boasting about their communities as places privileged by an illustrious past or a miraculous religious image. Virtually every little pueblo maintained its own church and wanted its own resident priest.

In tracing features common to most pueblos in a diocese or one of its regions, it is important to recognize that there could be great differences between nearby pueblos. For the central part of the Diocese of Guadalajara, two of the largest and most prosperous Indian pueblos, Tonalá and Tlajomulco, had few non-Indian residents, possessed comparatively large landholdings, and tended to be conservative and inward-looking. Indians of Zacoalco (the largest pueblo in the diocese, with about 2,400 Indians) owned the most land and prided themselves on their relative prosperity, hard work, and independent spirit, but they also shared their town with a Spanish and casta population of almost equal number. Surrounded by large haciendas, and engaged in all manner of work, from farming and ranching, to day and resident labor on estates, to cottage industries in soap, tanning, shoes, and saddles, Zacoalco's Indian population was exposed over many years to a wide range of commercial opportunities and colonial pressures from the creole centers of Guadalajara, Zapotlan el Grande, and Sayula. At the other end of the spectrum from Tonalá and Tlajomulco were submerged vestiges of Indian pueblos in communities like Atotonilco el Alto and Tequila that consisted mainly of forasteros and castas, already mixed into the larger town of non-Indians. They were faint remnants of earlier Indian settlements that survived until Mexico's national independence in 1821 largely because colonial law and local custom said they existed as corporate groups and because their legal status gave them a townsite and an elected council.

Some Regional Patterns Traced by This Study

There were differences between and within the two dioceses for the history of priests and parishioners that make this something of a comparative regional and intraregional study, as well as a presentation of common patterns and particular experiences. Rural communities of the Diocese of Guadalajara were more ardently Catholic in conventional ways. Guadalajara was particularly rich in reputedly miraculous sites and images, and most people routinely fulfilled their sacramental duties. Parish priests there generally enjoyed more dependable support from parishioners, or at least occupied a less controversial place in public life than in the archdiocese: here the two parties more often came into conflict not with each other but with their common adversary, the alcaldes mayores and other district governors (as in the archdiocese, the hostility toward district governors was most intense in places farthest from the audiencia seat at Guadalajara). The heated controversies there between priests and parishioners turned mostly on two matters: propertied sodalities or *cofradías*, which were a major source of parish revenue in the diocese (again in contrast to the archdiocese), and pueblo elections in the 1790's (over which parish priests of Guadalajara had traditionally had considerable influence, an influence the crown was moving decisively to check). In the archdiocese, there was more reliance by parish priests on the collection of fees for their living, and more disputes over clerical fees; more truancy on Sundays; more powerful district governors; and more *tumultos* (collective violence) directed against priests. On the whole, the conflicts over clerical rights and duties were somewhat sharper and of longer standing in the archdiocese.

Other differences between the dioceses are related to broad differences between their rural communities. In the Diocese of Guadalajara, there was less coordinated political action by single pueblos and less resistance in the form of flight by whole communities, but more instances of resistance to colonial authority that united people from different communities. Sharp conflict within a rural pueblo was more likely than conflict between pueblos. There was also relatively more evidence of personalist leaders and political factions within Indian pueblos of Guadalajara; nevertheless, parish priests there tended to praise the Christianity of the parish as a whole, not the piety of individuals, as their brothers in the archdiocese were wont to do. Personal struggles for power and the influence of private landowners could be found in varying degrees almost everywhere, but there were more conflicts between cabeceras and their dependencies in the archdiocese.

Some of the most outstanding differences occurred within dioceses. There were great variations in parish income and facilities, in the village resources that a parish priest could command, and in devotion to the liturgy and respect for him, especially within the archdiocese. By all accounts, the city of Querétaro was a center of fervent devotion, whereas the residents of the haciendas and *obrajes* (textile workshops) in the surrounding area reportedly lived "in a deplorable state of ignorance about Christian matters." [17] Most districts had reputedly miraculous images that expressed popular devotion, but some did not (such as Huejutla and Teotihuacan). In the Diocese of Guadalajara, the whole Altos region was said to be especially devout, whereas Zapopan, Santa Anita, San Juan de los Lagos, and towns near Lake Chapala were renowned for their miraculous images.

Each diocese had its hot spots of priest-parishioner conflict (see Maps 2 and 3). For the Diocese of Guadalajara, these were the districts of La Barca, Sayula, Tlajomulco, and Tonalá, near Lake Chapala and the cathedral city of Guadalajara, and Juchipila in modern Zacatecas, all with substantial Indian populations. For the archdiocese, the hot spots were the Toluca region (especially the districts of Temascaltepec, Zacualpan, Tenango del Valle, and Metepec) in the southwest portion of the modern Estado de México; the Cuernavaca and Cuautla districts of modern Morelos; parts of modern Hidalgo; and the vicinity of the Valley of Mexico, in the Chalco, Tacuba, and Xochimilco districts.

Differences among—and within [18]—the archdiocesan centers of conflict are evident, too. Hidalgo was well known for labor disputes involving parish priests; Hidalgo, the vicinity of the Valley of Mexico, and Temascaltepec-Metepec for cabecera-sujeto struggles; and Hidalgo and Morelos for personalist political conflict. Temascaltepec and Metepec figured less frequently than did other contentious places in conflicts between parish priests and district governors or disputes rooted in divisions within pueblos.

For the most part, the poorest, least desirable districts were not the hot spots of priest-parishioner conflict (the districts of Xilotepec and Yahualica in modern Hidalgo, and Ichcateopan and Tixtla in modern Guerrero were exceptions). Nor were the poorest parishes within a district certain to be the trouble spots, except perhaps in Chalco. The frequent or especially intractable disputes between priests and parishioners were more likely to appear in prosperous rural districts of the archdiocese and in some of the most lucrative first-class parishes within those districts. For Guadalajara, the richest as well as the poorest parishes were largely outside the primary zones of conflict between priests and parishioners.

The Toluca region and Morelos were notorious in the archdiocese for their disputes with priests and their resistance to paying clerical fees; rural parishioners in both areas actively participated in devotion to the saints and had cofradías and other pious works to support them; and, in both areas, pueblos de indios had a strong sense of local identity and continuity with the past and a reputation for defending community property. In their conflicts with parish priests, they were sometimes accused of wanting to be "the proprietors of the church." But these broad similarities mask important differences in local religious practices and in the relationships between priests and parishioners. There was more outright, persistent disobedience toward parish priests in Morelos and less compliance with official practices. Fees disputes had a longer history there, and there were more reports of churches in disrepair, cofradías in "a deplorable state," and parishioners uttering blasphemies and failing to meet their sacramental obligations. In more private behavior, such as sexual abstinence during Lent, they also may have been less compliant.[19]

In the Toluca region (including the districts of Toluca, Metepec, Tenango del Valle, and Lerma), the conflicts with priests were less obviously anticlerical. Parishioners were quick to lodge complaints and sometimes to run the priest out of town, but they were quicker to accept the mediating efforts of a pastoral visitor (the bishop or his delegate on a tour of inspection of the diocese) than their neighbors in Morelos. Like their counterparts in Morelos, leaders of pueblos de indios in the Toluca region were likely to invoke the 1767 arancel against their parish priests, but they were also more likely to meet its terms. When they called for a priest's removal, they usually were ready to accept a replacement. The Toluca area pueblos were more likely to appeal for parish standing in the late eighteenth century, or at least to want their own resident priest. Oddly (considering that the Indian population was absolutely and proportionately larger than in Morelos, and that native languages would have been more widely spoken), Indian pueblos of the Toluca region were less resistant to the campaign for Spanish-language schools headed by parish priests in the late eighteenth century and seemed to be accepting Spanish as a second language more readily.

Pueblos of Morelos stand apart, too, from other parts of the archdiocese in the way they responded to the archbishops' pastoral visits in the late colonial period. In contrast to Indian parishioners of Hidalgo and the Toluca region, who often approached the pastoral visitor with individual and collective petitions, Morelos villagers generally kept their distance, minimizing their dealings with the church hierarchy and the visitor's message of reconciliation. (For further discussion of the regional example of Morelos, see Appendix C.)

* * *

Counterpoints of center and periphery underlie some of these patterns of geography, settlement, and politico-religious history. While Mexico City was the great administrative city of the Viceroyalty of New Spain, Guadalajara was the other seat of a high court in the future Mexico, as well as a diocesan capital, and elites of both cities shaped much of the political, cultural, and economic life around them in the late eighteenth century. The cathedral city was a place of powerful attachments for parish priests who served under its bishop. Nearly all of the priests in the dioceses of Guadalajara and Mexico were trained in their cathedral city, many were natives of that city, and most returned to it frequently in their thoughts, correspondence, and travels. And the timing of petitions against parish priests suggests that many Indian pueblo leaders and lawyers took their cues from metropolitan edicts.

To judge by their political and ecclesiastical territories, the reach of these two cities was vast. But the strength of that reach and its influence on local affairs varied considerably. Distance from the center was an important variable. Both colonial cities had been established near the densest concentrations of native people in their jurisdictions, places that also had the prime agricultural lands and water resources, and a relatively temperate climate. Priests were concentrated in this area in and around the center, among many of the first-class parishes. They were less numerous among the third-class parishes toward the periphery, where in general people and natural resources were comparatively scarce, roads poor, and the climate often inhospitable. Conflicts between parish priests and district governors were especially intense in these remote places.

But the counterpoint of center and periphery alone does not account for many of the events, people, and patterns of religious practices presented in the following chapters. The presence of more priests in the heartland did not ensure greater piety and orthodoxy or less anticlericalism there. The many small, distinct communities with strong local attachments in both dioceses (but especially in the archdiocese) complicate, and sometimes confound, center and periphery patterns. There were poor parishes within nearly every alcaldía mayor, and in the Diocese of Guadalajara, some of the most important towns and richest, most desirable parishes were far from the cathedral city, in the Altos de Jalisco and the modern states of Zacatecas and Aguascalientes. The places of greatest priest-parishioner conflict did not correspond closely to distance from the center. Although easier access to the courts of the cathedral city made for some concentration of judicial complaints from districts close by, the most intractable disputes between parishioners and their priests in the archdiocese were concentrated in prosperous, densely populated rural districts, whatever their proximity to the city. In the Diocese of Guadalajara, the hottest spots were middling parishes—neither the richest nor the poorest—beyond the immediate vicinity of the city.

Moreover, the significance of center and periphery for colonial Indian affairs and the history of priests in their rural parishes was not exactly the same for these two dioceses. There was a clearer divide in the Archdiocese of Mexico between the populous, prosperous center, with its dense webs of local community, and the poorer, more remote areas with weaker attachments to the city and its immediate hinterland. The divide was less marked in the Diocese of Guadalajara, where the drier, flatter terrain was exploited in ways that separated and scattered much of the population onto ranchos and into wage labor; Indians were comparatively fewer and less distinguishable from other rural people; and more silver mining made for settlements and periodic explosions of resettlement that owed little to the spatial logic of administrative center and periphery. Still, the generalization can only be pushed so far. Even in the archdiocese, a town or city famous for its piety, like Querétaro, might be surrounded by settlements that were indifferent to the standard liturgy and sacramental obligations or openly anticlerical.

In the Diocese of Guadalajara, sacramental duties were fulfilled routinely, miracles were anticipated, and there was less conflict between parishioners and priests. The written record for the Archdiocese of Mexico suggests more anti-clericalism and conflict over priests and religion—conflicts that could turn on any number of things—though in general the archdiocese, too, remained an area strongly marked by Catholic devotions, desire for a resident priest, and care for community churches. Only in a few places did confrontation with priests signify a rejection of Catholicism and the social order it modeled, or indifference to its leaders and the promise of well-being.

CHAPTER THREE

Issues of Local Religion

They answered that we had hardly entered their country yet we were already ordering them to forsake their
teules [gods], which they could not do. But as for giving
obedience to this King we spoke of, this they would do.
—Bernal Díaz del Castillo (writing in
the mid-sixteenth century about his
experiences in the conquest of Mexico)

They easily confuse Our Holy Catholic Faith with their
own superstitions. . . . And there is nothing for which
someone does not pray.   —Fr. Antonio Arias, 1673

At first the noise during mass will bother you, but soon
you will become so accustomed to it that you will miss its
absence.   —Manual for assistant pastors
in Indian parishes, 1766

How Indian parishioners conceived of the sacred and otherwise made sense
of their place in the world bears on how they understood and responded
to Christian teaching, and on the difficulties of Catholic priests ministering to
them in a time of administrative reform and unsettling material changes. Their
lived allegiance to a cosmic order that transcended human power in colonial circumstances is a barely accessible subject—thinly documented, remote from the
experience of most colonial and twentieth-century observers, and complicated
by changes before as well as after the arrival of Europeans that are as yet poorly
understood.

The long descriptions of faith in practice—and there are comparatively few
of them—were written by parish priests in various times and places, or drawn up
for ecclesiastical court inquiries. They are texts that need to be situated in their
time, not impartial archives that are easily mined for representative ethnographic
nuggets. The more abundant but fragmentary documentation of local religious
practices also contains this problem of interpretation. Aside from the early colonial Nahuatl administrative records used by James Lockhart in his treatment of
Indian religion,[1] most of this documentation was generated by policing institutions, which were preoccupied with order and orthodoxy, and is skewed toward
the unusual. The administrators and their assistants often knew little about local
practices and rarely cared to solicit lengthy descriptions from those who knew

them well. The colonial record of Indian religious practices is most striking for its patchiness, for how much is missing compared with other aspects of social and political life. For the eighteenth century, there was no great compiler and interpreter of contemporary Indian religion like Bernardino de Sahagún for the sixteenth century, and regional variation was too great in any case for one place to represent many others. The written record, then, comes mostly in small pieces from particular times and places. Only with many such pieces, evaluated separately and together, can patterned tendencies be discerned with much confidence.

In discussing interpretations of parishioners' religious practices and connections to priests in this introductory chapter and Part III, I have tried not to separate localities from the wider society or to treat "popular" religion as neatly separable from state religion and largely resistant to incremental change. Here I follow William Christian's view that "local" religion provides "ways to deal with the local natural and social world, as well as the wider social, economic, and political network of which they are a part." As Christian says, the "practical impingement of the institutions of a central religion on the religious life of peasants" is as much a part of this history as the ways in which local practices may have departed from and challenged doctrine.[2]

Priests, Indian Religion, and the Local Practice of Catholicism

Most priests in Indian parishes during the late eighteenth century would have agreed with the canon who remarked to Henry G. Ward in the 1820's that lay people of his diocese were "very good Catholics but very poor Christians."[3] They were, in his estimation, wedded to the forms of Catholicism, to outward display, rather than to the inner spirit of piety or Christian principles.

The idea that Indians were good Catholics but poor Christians meshed with the view often expressed by late colonial bishops and dignitaries that there was much superstition but little idolatry in Indian religious practice. "Idolatry" and "superstition" expressed an official Christian view of what was false in religion. Idolatry was a serious deviation: rejection of the one, true God by the worship of alien gods, implicitly of Satan. Superstition was a lesser, venial sin, more the product of ignorance than a willful violation of what was correct or a rejection of God.[4]

This idea of good Catholics but poor Christians also reveals both the theological distance that many priests felt from their Indian parishioners and their own reliance on practical means of promoting the faith that glided over theological complications. The "externals" of the religion *were* very important, but a radical separation between lay practice and church doctrine, between externals and essentials, the natural and the supernatural (a distinction particularly foreign to the Indians), often existed mainly in a priest's mind. And from the beginning of colonization, priests had themselves introduced ritual expressions and objects of devotion. The veneration of saints, colorful images, elaborate displays of wealth and beauty in places of worship, the recitation in unison of prayers and doctrine, and feast-day celebrations all were promoted by priests in Spanish America after the Council of Trent prescribed the reform of Catholic practices in the 1560's. It is a standard criticism of "Baroque Catholicism," which grew out of the Council of Trent decrees and continued well into the eighteenth century, that it was pre-occupied with outward display and "stressed the pathos rather than the ethos of religion." [5]

What most disturbed clergymen in late colonial Mexico was how readily these attractive forms and rites could be taken from their control and put to local uses. Parish priests were expected to direct local religious practices into ortho-dox channels. Their success in this task varied greatly and was inherently lim-ited even in better times, but the task was made especially difficult in the late eighteenth century by the diminished formal role of priests in public affairs and by the regalist reforms intended to reduce religious spending, remove parish finances from local control, augment royal revenues, and make feast-day celebra-tions less extravagant.

The frustrations of pastoral service in late colonial parishes of Indians and rural non-Indians stemmed partly from differences between the formal church doctrine laid down to the priest, his personal experience of religion, and the prac-tices and beliefs he encountered in the field. These differences could be great, but they did not have to be exclusive or antithetical. Late colonial priests tended to focus on such Indian practices as idol worship and ancestor worship, blood sac-rifice, and the special importance of mountains, caves, and powerful creatures, rather than on their parishioners' broader habits of conceiving and participating in a universe that transcended human powers.

Because many local religious practices in Mexico corresponded to folk prac-tices in Spain, some have argued that they were essentially Spanish in origin.[6] Magical healing, divination, love magic, and fertility rites were indeed living fea-tures of local religion in Spain (not to mention other Christian agricultural soci-eties in the eighteenth century), but these were all well-established practices in Mexico long before the Conquest; in neither conception nor content were the New World forms simply European.

Precolonial religion, in fact, was not so much transformed by Spanish folk beliefs and practices as it was potentially congruent with them. Much of what Spaniards dismissed as superstition or worried about as animistic and idolatrous in colonial Indian practices had to do with a strong sense of the sacred penetrat-ing every aspect of the material world and daily life, overpowering people but possibly responsive to their entreaties and their efforts to harmonize with cosmic order. There was effectively no distinction between the sacred and the material. Stone, wood, clay, seeds, and maize pith were not simply inert materials to be shaped into images that symbolized or evoked divinity. Nor was the scented smoke from copal resin simply incense. These materials—and all others—were alive with the sacred, not just symbolic of it.[7]

Similarly, new religious ideas, such as Satan, hell, and a radical separation be-tween this world and the next, did not require a transformation in prior and persisting convictions about order in the sacred.[8] These ideas did not have to be rejected, accepted, or digested in ways that created or maintained a fixed, monolithic religious vision. The practices and beliefs discussed in Part Three suggest other possibilities as well: that two religions could be practiced together at different levels without explosive tension; that parishioners felt no particular need to make sharp distinctions between Christian and non-Christian aspects of their religion; and that mixtures of practices (as in contemporary rural Europe) were part of a continuing process of religious change, one in which parishioners might accept fundamentally new beliefs without understanding them or expressing them in practice just as their priest would have it. Christian monotheism, for example, could be understood in terms of an exceedingly remote, all-embracing God served by specialized tutelary spirits—the saints and miraculous images— with great powers in their own right; and colonial Indian conceptions of an underworld often remained out of step with the Christian idea of hell as a place of eternal damnation. (Late colonial priests repeatedly complained that they had difficulty instilling a fear of death and hell in their Indian communicants.)

Christian doctrine was quite dualistic—given to sharp dichotomies such as this world and the other world, body and spirit, heaven and hell, good and evil, man and animal, true God and false gods, and God and nature. Native ideas about duality were conceived in more monistic terms—that opposite tendencies like destruction and creation could be contained within a single deity or saint, and were mutually constituting. This native conception persisted even as beliefs and practices were modified and confused by Christian teachings.[9] Even where Indians accepted the concept of Satan, their local practices could continue to be deeply disturbing to a priest. Indians might agree in principle that witches got their powers from Satan, yet not regard all witchcraft as an abomination.[10] Such diabolical materials as hallucinogenic drugs had great, palpable powers and needed to be treated with the same care as was accorded the great powers of God. As L. Marie Musgrave-Portilla notes, "Indians appreciated the opposition between God and the devil, but . . . gave their allegiance to both." [11] To a priest who believed that religious purity and orthodoxy were the route to good order in this world and salvation in the next, this ambivalence about good and evil seemed agnostic, if not duplicitous and even "pagan."

Another religious difference that made Indians seem preoccupied with externals was their clear preference for supplication (humble entreaty) over contrition (remorse for having sinned). Propitiation and penance were common to both local practice and ideal Christianity, but, from the priests' point of view, Indians were entirely too focused on supplication for material ends and collective well-being in this world; they were more preoccupied with omens and prognosis than with spiritual diagnosis and remedial action.[12] Indians paid too little attention to the soul's eternal salvation and, therefore, to the scrutiny of personal sin, thought many of their Catholic priests. As a result, their infrequent confessions seemed disappointingly superficial and formulaic.

Ancestor worship and a cyclical conception of time were also areas of continuity, congruence, and missed understandings in this religious history. Ancestor worship could be channeled into the Catholic concept of purgatory and the remission of the sins of departed souls through penance by the living, but would not be confined there. Colonial Indian practices continued to center on the palpable presence of one's ancestral kin in particular places (recalling the blurred meaning of physical death and the idea of rebirth in Nahua religion), beliefs that their parish priests again would have regarded as superstitious and literal-minded.[13] Rather than conceiving of a linear human destiny culminating in a final act of judgment and salvation or damnation, the biological cycles of germination, fruition, reproduction, and death of all living things folded in upon each other in native thought, in ongoing cycles of cosmic creation and destruction.

Unfettered collective engagement versus individual introspection was a long-standing, universal tension between laity and priests, but "religion as performed" in public by colonial Indians in the Mexican heartland had features that Catholic priests found particularly troubling.[14] To the priests' ears and eyes, the Indians' ecstatic entry into the sacred through noisy action, vigorous scourging, drunkenness, and lavish decoration were childish and potentially threatening to good order. They were the opposite of the controlled, moderate religious fervor that was appropriate to all Christians except the privileged, official few who experienced God directly in mystical visions. But it was rarely within the priests' power (or in their financial interest) to dampen altogether such unseemly and possibly dangerous enthusiasm.

These differences and tensions between precolonial religions and Catholic Christianity can be easily overdrawn. Catholicism as it was presented and practiced in colonial Mexico was not as exclusive and individualist as some scholars suggest.[15] Catholicism, too, thrived on collective practices, including public feasts, processions, cofradías, and community responsibility for supporting public worship. And Indian villagers in the dioceses of Mexico and Guadalajara generally regarded themselves as Christians and practiced a core of Christianity.

The church always drew a certain line, to be sure. Late colonial priests, like their earlier brethren, had no intention of compromising on fundamental matters of doctrine such as monotheism and the Trinity, the temptations of Satan, and transubstantiation in the mass; but in other respects, they tolerated combination and "superstition." From the sixteenth century on, priests had encouraged (or at least tolerated) converging beliefs and forms—for example, by constructing churches and shrines on ancient sacred sites.[16] Certainly by the eighteenth century, the state was no longer bent on systematically eradicating the private and nonproselytizing worship of objects and images. As long as the basic rites of the church were performed, the sacraments were accepted, the catechism was more or less learned, the fees were paid, and the community was at peace, other local practices were secondary. Nor did a late colonial truce in the battle against what the clergy had once regarded as idolatry and continued to regard as superstition necessarily signal the priests' withdrawal from deep involvement in the religious life of their parishioners. Priests learned to live with the local sorcery and spirits.

Current Views on Religious Change

Most modern interpreters of Indian religion in Mesoamerica (from the Chichimec Frontier to the highlands of Central America) hypothesize one of three processes as central to the transition from precolonial to colonial life: Christian transformation, "pagan" resistance, or syncretism. All three approaches have focused attention on the sixteenth and early seventeenth centuries, as if the process both began and was largely completed in the first generations of colonization. The first two interpretations have been especially concerned with the issue of conversion, which centers attention on religion as belief and considers religious change in terms of one system competing with another, as a contest with one winner.[17] This emphasis can—and in fact does—lead to opposite conclusions.

Transformation and Resistance

Colonial historiography is rich in works that emphasize what Spanish friars did to and for despairing natives in the "Spiritual Conquest," the title of Robert Ricard's landmark study of the sixteenth-century evangelization. Deep in this vein of interpretation are George Kubler's and John MacAndrew's studies of early colonial architecture, which regard the replacement of native forms with Spanish forms in early churches as a metaphor for cultural transformation. For Kubler, religious beliefs and practices were the least likely to survive the imposition of colonial rule. Spaniards were the agents of this colonial history, thoroughly imposing their religion in those areas they settled. He concludes, "In the seventeenth century, so much had been forgotten, and the extirpation of native observances by the religious authorities was so vigorous, that the last gasps of the bearers of Indian rituals and manners expired unheard."[18] At this pole of the literature, Catholic priests were preeminent figures in their parishes, followed without much question by "the masses."

At the other pole, Indians are regarded as having maintained a triumphal, idols-behind-altars resistance, only pretending to "convert" to new beliefs, doing everything they could to avoid contact with the colonial government and its church, and succeeding where Spaniards were not able to impose their will by force. In this view, priests were insignificant players in local religious practice, hardly worth mentioning beyond their acts of oppression. This hypothesis was especially popular in the 1920's and 1930's, during the postrevolutionary waves of enthusiasm for *indigenismo* by Mexican politicians and artists (and foreign visitors),[19] and continued in the scholarship of Gonzalo Aguirre Beltrán and Fernando Benítez, among others. A stimulating refinement of it, grounded in formal Nahuatl texts and an emphasis on fragmentation and collapse as well as resistance, is being worked out by Jorge Klor de Alva, who speaks of a pervasive Indian resistance to conversion in central Mexico rather than a "true spiritual conquest," at least in the sixteenth and seventeenth centuries. He acknowledges the possibility of individual "conversion" and the inevitability of "mass subordination" under Spanish rule, but concurs with Miguel León Portilla that "the majority of urban and rural natives . . . simply borrowed from Christianity whatever elements were necessary to appear Christian . . . without changing their religious convictions."[20]

For both Klor de Alva and Aguirre Beltrán, the prime examples of this militant resistance are *naguales* (wizards believed capable of transforming themselves into powerful animals that worked their will in human affairs) like Martín Ocelotl, one of a line of Cuauhtémocs-in-the-wings, ready to oppose the new faith. Aguirre Beltrán's colonial naguales were underground descendants of pre-Christian wizards who emerged in the conflicts with Spanish rulers as cultural innovators guarding the purity of Indian culture and providing the social stability and continuity that helped to fortify their communities during the time of great troubles in the seventeenth century. He describes them as a virtual priesthood, fasting and practicing sexual abstinence.[21]

Syncretism

Standing somewhere between these poles are the scholars who emphasize mutual influences and adaptations among different religious traditions. "Syncretism" has been used in various ways to suggest either a fixed state or a process variously described as mixture, amalgamation, fusion, confusion, coalescence, or synthesis in the meeting of different religious traditions. Overarching much of this variety has been a general view that colonial Indian communities independently achieved a more or less full and, by the mid-seventeenth century, stable synthesis, a synthesis in which Christian traits had been absorbed incrementally into native religion. Approaches to syncretism have also emphasized the similarities of forms and sensibilities between religions in contact that made convergence and confusion possible. In their emphasis on the ability of native religions to add Christian traits without fundamental alterations, and their minimizing of the role of Catholic priests in local beliefs and practice (treating Catholicism as "high" religion), interpretations stressing syncretism have been closer to the resistance hypothesis than to the transformation hypothesis.

One standard way of describing religious syncretism in colonial Mexico has been to start with similarities between Christianity and precolonial native religions that contributed to a blurring of their distinctions. José Corona Núñez, for example, suggested the following points of theological and ritual convergence: both believed in divine intervention in human affairs independent of human will; both practiced a form of monotheism; and there were equivalences between Christ and Quetzalcóatl (both partaking of the two natures of man and god, both associated with the cross), between the Virgin Mary and Tonantzin (as mothers of divinity, both associated with the moon), between incense in the mass and the smoke of copal and tobacco as food of the gods, and between communion and human sacrifice. William Madsen and Wigberto Jiménez Moreno added the importance of ceremony in both, as well as similar practices of baptism, confession, penance, and communion; an association of darkness with mystery and danger; a stoic ideal and respect for celibate priests; parallels between the saints and the tutelary gods; and the importance of ritual calendars (with striking coincidences between the commemoration of Christ's sacrifice at Easter and the Mexica festival of Toxcatl, when an impersonator of Tezcatlipoca was sacrificed, and between All Soul's Day and the festival honoring the dead during the month of Tepeilhuitl, both of which included offerings of food to the dead).[22]

Some of these examples treat doctrine as if it were local practice; but the differences could be as great as the similarities. While there was room for convergence and confusion, the saints and the tutelary gods were quite different. In principle, the saints were perfect beings and mainly intercessors; the gods or spirits partook of the dual nature of divinity and were more malevolent and independent. The fact that ablution rituals were common to both obscures the profound importance of baptism in Christianity as a one-time initiation that was indispensable to salvation. Because simple substitution or equation was not likely, the cumulative effect of adopting similar elements like these would not have been immediately evident to the Catholic tutors or their pupils.

Whether or not such similarities were salient, late colonial Indian communities in these two dioceses did accept priests, the sacraments, and the saints. The desire for a resident priest, or at least the services of a priest, was strong, even when the church doors were locked against him, or when parishioners temporarily refused to call him for last rites. Attendance at mass and the fulfillment of the Easter duty of confession and communion were generally high. Even though the costs of public worship were considerable, they were usually met without much hesitation. Churches were constructed, furnished, and well cared for, and private endowments, community property, and special collections often covered the costs of the annual round of fiestas and special masses.

The desire for a priest, however, does not necessarily imply any great respect for the man himself. Though some priests were loved and followed for their exemplary Christian conduct, the core of this desire had to do with fulfilling ritual obligations that protected the individual and the community, and with achieving the political independence that came from being a parish seat or having a priest in residence. These motives could work for or against the priest's power in the parish. The piety of alms, sacramental fees, blessings, masses, and festivities in honor of the saints hid a fear that priests could play on—the fear that something terrible would happen if the contributions were not made, the rites not performed. On the other hand, faithful Indian parishioners could separate ritual from ethics, affirming their own standing as benefactors of the liturgy, yet judging their priest by the standards of the "other" Christianity of charity and self-abnegation, a Christianity that he might preach about more than he practiced.

Christianity in this colonial history was not just ideological domination. True, there were signs that colonial Indians accepted the idea of Christianity and Spanish rule as a step toward a more just world. In learning Catholic rules of propitiation, the Indians were also learning colonial lessons about intercession: both God and the king worked through mediated hierarchies—an old habit in central Mexico.[23] Yet, in accepting this subordination, they also had a claim on righteous indignation—on the radical demand that Christian masters reciprocate, that they live up to their values.

There were spontaneous reworkings of Christian forms and principles in local terms (as the history of Santiago, the Virgin Mary, found crosses, and feast-day celebrations discussed in Chapters 10 and 11 suggest), but local religion was not made by Indian laity alone, entirely separate from the guidance or knowledge of the priests and the doctrine of the universal religion.[24] The spreading veneration of Our Lady of Guadalupe in the seventeenth and eighteenth centuries was often guided by parish priests and missionary preachers. Yet the histories of both Santiago and Mary in rural parishes show that even a colonialist Christianity could contribute to firm resistance against new demands by the colonial government. Santiago was not only about homage to the victor or about humiliation and submission. He was also about power and resistance at the local level. The Virgin Mary offered more potential for large-scale political resistance, but not until about the mid-eighteenth century, when Our Lady of Guadalupe became patroness of the Viceroyalty of New Spain and popular devotion to her image began to spread widely among Indian communities of the center and west.

Anthropologists primarily concerned with ethnographic evidence like William Madsen have had the lead in studies of syncretism for Mesoamerica. Taking central Mexico as his area of concern and influenced by Wigberto Jiménez Moreno and his 1958 article on Indians and Christianity, Madsen sees syncretism as a fusion of religious forms and beliefs, a branch of acculturation in which traditions from different cultures "coalesced."[25] This syncretism can take two forms: one in which new gods and ways were added or assimilated into an existing religion without important change; the other in which beliefs were fused as well, bringing an emotional acceptance of the new religion without a simple imitation of it. For central Mexico (mainly the Valley of Mexico in Madsen's evidence), Madsen would have a weak version of this second form of syncretism working itself out spontaneously and independently in Indian communities in ways that resisted most of the values of Christianity and gave essentially "pagan" meanings to Christian elements. That is, Indians mainly adopted the externals, the forms of Christianity. Beliefs could change somewhat in this process of acculturation, but they were directed by lay people and retained an essentially "pagan" ethic.

Three ideas about the history of local Indian religion in central Mexico are pivotal to Madsen's discussion of syncretism as a fusion of beliefs and forms that remained fundamentally pre-Christian. First, fusion was carried out by Indians largely on their own terms, after a few generations of Spanish coercion and intentional confusion of practices, and Indian resistance and internal conflict over whether to accept Christianity. Relying on Jacinto de la Serna's and Hernando Ruiz de Alarcón's accounts of Indian "idolatry," Madsen suggests that by the seventeenth century, Indian syncretic Christianity was largely autonomous and stable. Second, "the most important stimulus for fusion" was news of the apparition of the Virgin Mary at Tepeyac in 1531, with her miraculous image as the Indian madonna, Nuestra Señora de Guadalupe.[26] Devotion to her entailed accepting a Christian idea of divine benevolence, an idea largely missing from precolonial beliefs; but Madsen argues that this acceptance was coupled with an Indian redefinition of the Christian God as a hostile, destructive deity that one dared not approach.[27] Third, Spanish Catholicism was introduced formally by a foreign priesthood in ways that could alter local beliefs and practices largely through force or through convenient similarities to Indian religions.

Although these ideas about the process and timing of religious changes provide a plausible substitute for the transformation and resistance hypotheses, and although they recognize local variations, they are not consistent with much of the late colonial evidence examined in Part III. Catholicism in the dioceses of Mexico and Guadalajara was not only a high religion, formal, institutional, and separated from the disparate versions that Indian communities worked out spontaneously and independently;[28] Catholicism even as it was introduced by the Spaniards had its own local and informal aspects, like Cortés presenting the Virgin Mary as rainmaker, or the twin messages of Santiago in the sixteenth century as the embodiment of the Spanish destiny to conquer and as the protector of all faithful Christians.

Madsen's emphasis on independence and completion leaves out parish priests as a factor in the history of local religion after the first generations; and in presenting local practice as an integrated fusion, he misses the loose ends, reworkings, conflicts, and contradictions, and, above all, the likelihood that change is ongoing and that great changes may come late.[29] What is known about the conception of God and the veneration of the Virgin of Guadalupe and Santiago in colonial Indian communities does not fit these ideas of early fusion and reconceptualization. God was introduced by Spaniards as remote, judgmental, and even vengeful; this was not simply an Indian invention. The syncretic possibilities of the cult of the Virgin of Guadalupe were realized incompletely and relatively late for most of Mexico; and the cult of Santiago was reworked to fit local meanings throughout the colonial period.

Madsen's main source, Jiménez Moreno, gives the colonial history of syncretism a somewhat different twist by tracing Spanish as well as Indian responses to conversion programs and emphasizing the changes in Christianity itself. He regards the incidents described by Serna and Ruiz de Alarcón as evidence of "new outbreaks of pagan practices," not syncretic completions, and sees the seventeenth century as a time of energetic Christianization leading toward a "long-term victory for Christianity." Less inclined than Madsen to attribute religious change to force in its early stages, Jiménez Moreno speaks of continuous resistance in some places, periodic resistance in others, and an enthusiastic acceptance of Christian doctrines and practices in many others.[30] But he provides the framework for Madsen's interpretation of "two worlds in conflict" and for Madsen's emphasis on a sixteenth-century fusion centering on the Indians' attachment to the Virgin of Guadalupe and reinterpretation of God as a menacing force.

As a way to highlight their meaning of syncretism, both Madsen and Jiménez Moreno contrast central Mexico with Mayan Yucatán, where "idolatry" and "pagan" rites were widespread even in the late colonial period.[31] Madsen recognizes changes in both areas but concludes that the Maya "retained paganism as the meaningful core of their religion,"[32] whereas the Indian communities of central Mexico worked many Christian elements into their belief system. Except for remote areas like the Petén, where the Spanish presence was always weak,[33] Madsen's contrast is too stark, but it highlights an important difference—the colonial Maya retained a clearer sense than the Indians of the center of what was pre-Christian in their religious practices.[34] The cross, which Madsen treats as the prime example of popular syncretism among the lowland Maya (in contrast to central Mexico, where it was less important before the Conquest), had a more powerful continuity with the pre-Christian past than the Virgin of Guadalupe or the Christian saints did in central Mexico. It was a point of union with Christianity, but its great appeal to colonial Maya stemmed mainly from its older associations with fertility, water, sacred space, and sacrifice. Madsen attributes the difference to the greater isolation of the Yucatán Peninsula from colonial rule, its more dispersed and more remote Indian communities, its later and less complete political conquest, and the Maya's hatred for Spaniards. In central Mexico, by contrast, early Spanish rule had destroyed "the focal values" of war and sacrifice, public worship of the gods, priesthood, and the authority of the local nobility.

The broad regional contrast Madsen underlines is, indeed, evident in descriptions of "pagan" practices in both areas. Few of the accounts for central and western Mexico note secret ceremonies comparable to those exposed by colonial authorities in Christianized settlements of Yucatán, Campeche, and Tabasco. The ceremonies in those parts honored particular "idols" with "dinners, banquets, and general drunkenness" and perhaps the sacrifice of a dog.[35] They included events on a community scale, with the *cacique* (the main, hereditary chief) and other leaders as prominent participants, alongside the private, mainly family rituals practiced with a shaman or healer/conjurer (*curandero*) that were common in central Mexico. They were large, often night-time gatherings, wholly separate from the supervision of parish priests but not overtly anticolonial. In the dioceses of Mexico and Guadalajara, what few large secret gatherings there were tended to be anticolonial cum religious actions; the two main examples occurred in the district of Yautepec, Morelos, in 1761 (see Appendix C) and the Sierra de Tututepec in the district of Tulancingo in 1769.[36]

Nancy Farriss's study of the colonial Yucatec Maya, which argues that religion was the main source of their community cohesion, points to both differences and similarities between Yucatán and the dioceses of Mexico and Guadalajara in the eighteenth century. Farriss implicitly mutes Madsen's contrast, joining the Mesoamericanists' vocabulary of syncretism—fusion, amalgamation, merging, and synthesis—with the idea of convergence to describe local religion. Her Yucatán seems rather like Madsen's central Mexico, effectively removing his essentially "pagan" type and narrowing the contrasts between south and center. The "creative synthesis" she describes for Yucatán amounts not to a clean shift from precolonial religions to Christianity, but to a layered convergence of religious practices and a merging of tutelary deities and saints that led the Maya to regard themselves as Christians without feeling a strong sense of conversion. "Idolatry" as Spanish Catholics thought of it was practiced, but not usually in ways that the Maya would have regarded as anti-Christian.

Christianity and Maya beliefs and practices operated at different levels—family, community, and state—that were not in direct conflict.[37] Maya communities had their local divinities that received most of the ritual attention. Christianity was represented by a more remote, all-encompassing divinity and distant priests who had little impact on local religion, except in community rituals centering on the veneration of saints. These practices are much like those proposed by Pedro Carrasco for central Mexico, with public ritual being largely Christian and private observances more pre-Christian.[38] In neither case was religion reduced to a personal relationship to God. The principal difference between the two regions, by Farriss's account, seems to be that Christian public worship in Yucatán was deeply mayanized through the cult of saints under the control of the local native nobility.

Farriss makes a strong case that a "synthesis" was achieved more or less independently by Maya communities, as classic syncretism would have it. But the main reasons she adduces—the independent power of the local Indian nobility from precolonial times throughout the colonial period, the autonomy of local cofradías, and the peripheral place of the peninsula in the colonial economy and polity—distinguish Yucatán from central and western Mexico. Although Farriss has little to say about parish priests, they apparently were in a weak position in Yucatán, able to exercise little influence over local religious practices and institutions.[39] They were comparatively few in number and usually resided in Mérida rather than in the parish seat, or were otherwise distant from the religious life of the parish. They appear in her account mainly as men who extracted a substantial income from the parish and were much involved in the manipulation of Indian labor. The eighteenth-century parish priests of Yucatán promoted church construction, and some supervised the financial affairs of cofradías, but they apparently practiced little charity and enjoyed little more support from the non-Indian laity than they did from the Maya.[40]

Curiously, despite (or maybe because of) the parish priest's weak position in Yucatán, anticlericalism seems to have been more widespread and enduring there than in all but a few districts of the Archdiocese of Mexico. By contrast, the *batabs* and *principales*—the local Indian nobility—enjoyed high status and wielded more local power than most of their counterparts in central Mexico both before and throughout Spanish colonization. They, rather than the *macehuales* (Indian commoners), were the active force in "creative adaptation" to colonial changes.[41] Unlike most of the parish priest's lay assistants in the dioceses of Mexico and Guadalajara, the *maestros cantores* of Yucatán were routinely drawn from the native elite and often constituted a virtual priesthood, controlling public worship in almost everything but the delivery of the sacraments.[42] The cofradías, sponsors of the community saint's day celebrations that Farriss regards as the core of the region's independent local religions, were created and controlled by the batabs, usually without license from the bishop.[43] They and the cajas de comunidad (community treasuries) appear in her account as autonomous Indian institutions (in contrast to most cofradías of Mexico and Guadalajara, even the wealthy and pivotal cofradías of rural Jalisco). Farriss relates this independence of local religion to the Maya themselves and their material circumstances. The peripheral situation of Yucatán—as "a periphery of a periphery of the world market"—meant a reduced Spanish presence, less of a spiritual conquest, weaker supervision, and more time to adapt to changing circumstances within Indian traditions before the late eighteenth century.[44] "Collective survival" was made possible by this cushion from the full impact of mining and export agriculture, as well as by the Maya's attachments to their decentralized local communities, the strength of the local elite, and the ability to slough off dissidents.[45]

Farriss vindicates for Yucatán the idea that syncretism was a more or less stable, harmonious, Indian-made synthesis. But colonial Yucatán seems almost as different from central and western Mexico as Madsen's "paganism" is from his syncretism. If Mayan Yucatán fits the classic syncretic model in an intricate way, local practices in Indian communities of the Diocese of Guadalajara were much more deeply influenced by the Christianity dispensed to them, even while they remained centered on the community and provoked the despair of priests who yearned for orthodoxy. Central Mexico presents a more complex and less settled situation, where the practice of religion was more a mixture than a stable, complete synthesis. In his travels to take the measure of Indians in central and southern Mexico, Frederick Starr observed in 1897 that Indian Mexico ranged from south of the Valley of Mexico to the border with Guatemala. To the north was mestizo Mexico, where although many Indians were to be found—even on the outskirts of Mexico City—the population was predominantly mixed in race and culture, and Spanish was widely spoken. Starr's boundary was crude and more evident in the 1890's than a century earlier, but it underlines an important distinction between Yucatán, where non-Indians were a relatively small minority who found it useful to learn Maya, and much of central Mexico, where Spanish was in wide use, non-Indians resided in Indian centers without needing to know the native language, mines and commercial farming were shaping forces in the economy, and the civil and religious institutions of Spanish colonization had a greater place in local affairs.

Beyond Syncretism

Except for Farriss, then, the syncretic school posits little religious change among the Indians of the colonial heartland. As Barbara Tedlock has observed of the theorists of syncretism for Mesoamerica generally, the proponents of this view have used incompatible sets of mechanical and organic metaphors—welding, blending, fusion, synthesis, amalgamation, and hybridization—and have focused on an end state of completion and wholeness. Process is invoked, but there has been little examination of what it entails beyond the addition or fusion of Catholic elements into a native worldview, producing a stable, "syncretic" religion.[46]

Students of syncretism in Europe have understood more clearly that a given combination of Christian and "pagan" elements was inherently transitional and incomplete, a mixture or combination more than a fusion.[47] It was not, in itself, a synthesis of religions or a selective assimilation of one religion by another, but part of an incomplete process that might be reversed or redirected and could not be measured by traits added or subtracted. Local religion in central and western Mexico during the eighteenth century was not unified, fixed, and uncontested from top to bottom, or simply set against the religion of Catholic priests. Any explanation of religious change there needs to account for the local conflicts over religious practices and the multiple meanings of religious symbols; for the understandings that were shared between rulers and ruled and the misunderstandings that could divide them; for the development of parallel and complementary practices, as well as mixed or fused ones; for ways in which religion could still be altered by groups and individuals in conflict; and for the late popularity of Our Lady of Guadalupe in pueblos de indios outside the Valley of Mexico.

A promising step beyond these limitations of syncretism as the key to religious change in colonial Mexico has been to examine sixteenth-century texts in native languages prepared by the friars in their evangelizing efforts. Louise Burkhart's study of sermons and a Franciscan moral "dialogue" prepared for this purpose reveals some of the inevitable missed understandings and incomplete conversion that followed from attempting to translate Christian concepts into Nahuatl. Though Burkhart describes the emergence of a "hybrid Nahua-Christian religion" without a synthesis, this formal, theological approach centering on questions of belief does not fully warrant her conclusion that "the belief system of the majority of Nahuas remained essentially untouched" and that, as Mendicants were replaced by diocesan priests (she assumes this secularization was largely completed in the sixteenth century), colonial Indians were on their own as practitioners of a faith that would not become more Christian.[48]

In an ingenious essay that posits ways of experiencing the sacred as the key to the Indians' ability to retain their local religions under colonial rule, Inga Clendinnen likewise avoids the confusing metaphors attached to syncretism in Mesoamerican studies. She finds colonial Indians of central Mexico shaping their local religion and "appropriating" the Virgin Mary and human representation in their sacred art while accepting Christian forms and the idea of being Christian.[49] Focusing on religion as practiced rather than religion as belief, and studying the Indians' "loosely scripted" public performances, she reaches a conclusion similar to Elizabeth Wilder Weismann's in her studies of colonial sculpture—that habits of conceiving the sacred continued while various practices and beliefs changed.[50] Indians in central Mexico adopted a whole series of Christian practices that were familiar or readily understandable to them, such as attendance at mass, penitence by flagellation, pilgrimage, liturgical theater, sacred dancing, and other forms of worshipful movement, but carried them far beyond what the priests regarded as decorous and reverent conduct. There were mass flagellations that spattered blood on bodies and walls; vigorous dancing and mock combat without obvious liturgical purpose or structure, but with much shouting, clanging, and drinking; noisy, apparently inattentive people at Sunday mass; and others slumped on the church floor, reeking of alcohol.[51]

This "undesired exuberance" was a route to the sacred that repeated and enlarged on the ecstatic piety of pre-Christian times. Harsh colonial sanctions against ritual warfare, human sacrifice, and the open use of hallucinogenic drugs increased the importance of alcohol as a means to approach the sacred through, as Clendinnen suggests, intense evocations of distinctive moods and experiences— in effect being possessed of the sacred.[52] Community leaders were feted with an abundance of alcoholic drinks—pulque, *mezcal* (distilled maguey juice), or *aguardiente de caña* (cane alcohol)—on many ceremonial occasions; and in the late colonial period, the major feast days came to involve large numbers of people, not only dignitaries, in collective drinking. The function of this drinking in the quest for heightened experience of the sacred becomes even clearer when it is recalled that a digitoxin, *cuapatle* (the bark of the *Acacia angustissima* tree), was much desired as an additive to pulque in the colonial period. It made the heart— that organ of the life force so fascinating to the pre-Christian societies of Meso-america—race and seem about to explode. If the Mexica are representative, the ideas behind such ecstatic practices (which included other kinds of dramatic action and emotion, such as blood sacrifices and the processions, mystery plays, and other ceremonial performances that early Catholic priests encouraged) centered on transformation and submission to the sacred—of consciously entering new phases, of the living human body as a stage in a vegetal cycle of transformation uniting the human and the sacred.[53]

Clendinnen's approach, like Farriss's, Burkhart's, and Weismann's, casts doubt on the use of "substituted" or coincidental traits (such as baptism) to measure religious change, and opens the possibility that Indians innovated in order to maintain the familiar.[54] Priests' worries about their parishioners' uncontrolled, anarchic, and possibly "idolatrous" mock battles, drunken and noisy dances and processions, and excessive reverence for Mary testify not only to the distance between them but also to a local construction of Christianity that reached for the sacred in much the same way as before. It is not surprising that late colonial Indians made Baroque art their own in some inventive ways. Baroque was a style without strict rules, a style of excess, of lavish decoration and dramatic light and shadow that attempted to create an experience of the sacred, not merely to symbolize it.

The local religious practices described in Part Three generally reflect the colonial Indians' identification as Christians, interpreting and adjusting to the expectations of priests and their superiors, without simply being directed by them. Priests in Indian parishes supplied the framework for Catholic practice, introducing if not controlling it. They were central to rites of the life cycle, weekly mass, annual confession and communion, the periodic feast days and blessings, and the administration of institutional affairs and public morals. They might also exercise considerable influence through their economic interests, literacy, knowledge of the colonial world, and spiritual authority; but, in general, they appear to have been a good deal less important to the religious aspects of everyday life, especially outside the parish seat. Weismann conveys a sense of the minglings, congruences, impositions, and appropriations of seemingly incompatible values, practices, and influences without simple displacement or full fusion when she writes that popular art in the heartland of Mexico toward the end of the eighteenth century was "not so much disrespectful of [official] tradition as untamed by it, surmounting it."[55]

As Henry Ward's canon implied, the forms of the colonial Indians' Christianity were more orthodox than the content. Like the hollow, papier maché-like images of Christ on the Cross known as *cristos de caña*—made from corn stalks and corn pith, orchid-bulb glue, carpenter's paste, and a fine clay stucco surface wrapped around a wooden frame—their Christianity appeared outwardly well formed to a European eye, but its texture and weight were different; and when the surface was broken even the appearance was foreign. These light crucifixes from the early colonial period, whose materials connected Christ's passage through birth, death, and resurrection to the regeneration of the sacred food plant, maize, sometimes contained writings that would have added to the figures' sacred energy, at least for the maker. In the case of the cristo de caña of Mexicaltzingo (Mexicalcingo, an Indian pueblo in the Valley of Mexico south of the city), the chest cavity, abdomen, and upper arms were formed around pages of sixteenth-century community tax records in native style and substantial fragments of Nahuatl texts in Roman script. The intention was not to insert secret idols behind a Christian altar (or to use meaningless scrap material), since the Nahuatl texts concerned the life of Christ written on Spanish paper, to which was added a stencil (perhaps an embroidery pattern) of Raphael's painting, "Il Pasmo de Sicilia," depicting Christ's fall on the road to Calvary.[56] In this way, the image of Christ was both associated with the community (through the tax records) and bonded to a powerful new means of communication with the sacred (through the Spanish inscriptions about him).[57]

The great persistences within great changes in colonial Indian religions, then, have more to do with habits of conception and ultimate concerns than specific practices and doctrine; that is, with faith more than belief.[58] Religious changes in this colonial history cannot be charted by adding up substituted traits, or by treating apparent substitutions as the digestion of forms and practices, one mouthful at a time, with no important changes in a fundamentally precolonial religion. Without much self-conscious theorizing (which is not to say that villagers did not have beliefs), local religious practices sought to explain and domesticate Spanish colonial rule. Indians sought access to the Spaniards' spiritual knowledge and power in order to fortify the connection between the sacred and the profane in ways that responded to the overshadowing importance of natural forces in their lives. Gaining access could well mean accepting fundamental aspects of Catholicism such as intercession, the doctrine of good works, the spiritual authority of priests, and the concepts of Satan, black magic, and Christian monotheism without necessarily transforming local religious life. The local explanations and domestications were facilitated by Catholicism's sense of hierarchy and its tolerance for categories of thought and practice that did not threaten the practices essential to reconciliation and salvation—this despite the Spaniard/Indian antithesis that Spaniards believed in and the formal exclusivities their religion called for. By viewing Indian parishioners as child-Catholics with an instrumentalist, literal-minded view of devotion, children who easily lost their way on a variety of doctrinal points, the parish priests both acknowledged and narrowed the gap between them.

Suspicions of "Idolatry"

Departures from Catholic dogma and liturgy were common in Indian districts of colonial Mexico, but it is often difficult to distinguish essentially precolonial practices from European introductions and colonial innovations. The precarious experience of peasant societies almost everywhere contributed to similar creation myths and to practices related to fertility and protection from harm, of the kind Mircea Eliade emphasizes in his comparative studies of religion. Divine participation in the landscape, analogies between the fertility of women and the land, and the counterpoint of local practices and an official religion directed by professional priests who infrequently came to stay are common features of peasant experience around the world that may overshadow local differences. But the experience of colonial Indian villagers in central Mexico as nominal Christians was not interchangeable with that of Iberian peasants. What Clendinnen calls the "appetite for a certain kind of [ritual] experience"—a "calculated assault on the senses"—made for differences that went beyond forms.[59] Tridentine Catholicism's sudden and relatively late entry into Mesoamerica as a colonial state religion that intended to supplant the elaborate, often institutionalized practices and beliefs of native religions also is an important source of difference.

Students of Latin American history have an understandable fascination with the nature of this encounter between two "worlds"—what continued after the Conquest, what was displaced in the process of colonization, what was driven into latency but eventually returned, and what changed in substance and form. Answers are incomplete and contested. The precolonial religious practices of the Indians are imperfectly known, especially outside the Nahua and Maya centers, and the study of colonial changes must consider local and regional differences that are even less well known. There is room for confusion, too, in the tendency to speak of two worlds repeating their first encounters centuries after Cortés met Moctezuma.

Throughout the colonial period, priests reported local practices that they regarded as idolatrous or superstitious survivals of precolonial religion. The fullest such accounts come from southern Mexico—from Oaxaca, Chiapas, and the Yucatán Peninsula—and from the northern reaches of the viceroyalty, where Spanish rule was weakest. In the dioceses of Mexico and Guadalajara, reports of "idolatry" and "pagan" magic were numerous but ambiguous, suggesting individual and small-group practices that were neither pristine survivals from precolonial times nor outright rejections of colonial Catholicism.

Even the most richly ethnographical of these Catholic sources on Indian "idolatry" are biased by their own historical context. What the church regarded as idolatry could change, and some peculiarities of its outlook—such as the association of idolatry with alcohol—led priests to read more diabolical meaning into Indian conduct than the practitioners likely understood. In the priests' manuals, idolatry was commonly understood as the "worship of false gods" that denied the existence of "the one and true God," as if the difference was between monotheism and polytheism.[60] But during much of the colonial period, clergymen did not treat idolatry as an all-or-nothing proposition. Some "idolatrous" practices, such as the propitiation of mountain and animal spirits, did not directly challenge the supremacy of one, true God. Other practices were regarded as merely "external" beliefs, the superstitions of ignorant people who did not intend to deny God or worship Satan.[61] One reason why there were comparatively few reports on Indian "idolatry" or trials of Indian "idolaters" is that Indians were considered ignorant people whose superstitions were "purely external" and "without formal error in the question of faith."[62] Indian exemption from the Inquisition's jurisdiction in the 1570's followed from this conviction, a happy circumstance for the Indians but not so for the historian, precluded in consequence from a potentially rich source of documentation on colonial Indian religion.[63]

Indian "idolatry" reported by non-Indian elites was much in the eye of the beholder. Particularly in the late-sixteenth and seventeenth centuries, even "external" beliefs were likely to be taken as signs of dangerous infidelity and a retreat from the promise of the initial conversion. Priests writing from the late sixteenth century to the end of the colonial period about the history of the church in Mexico looked back with nostalgia on the "heroic age" of the first Conquest years, when "so many souls were harvested," and heaps of images were destroyed.[64] For these authors, the subsequent history up to their own time was at best a holding operation, marked by signs of decay, weakness, and backsliding in this great unfinished enterprise. A yearning for purification and a "New

Conquest" of the spirit deeply affected their accounts. Mixture and ambivalence meant adulteration, and old practices meant infidelity. For these authors, the meaning and direction of history was the final triumph of Christianity. Their historical world was centered in Europe and the unfolding of God's design revealed in the life and teachings of his son, Jesus Christ. Whatever blocked this unfolding was the work of Satan. And they saw abundant signs that the kingdom of God was slipping away from human reach in the "invisible war" against Satan's influence.[65]

Was there a surge of Indian infidelity in the seventeenth century, as the clustering of famous ecclesiastical accounts implies? The evidence is not conclusive. For one thing, it is shaped partly by events in Europe. The Catholic Reformation, especially in the edicts of the Council of Trent confirmed by the pope in 1564, exalted the clergy and commanded decisive action to defend Christianity's True Church. Religious unity was collapsing, and the Protestant heresy seemed to be divine retribution for loose conduct and indifference to God's plan for the final victory of Christianity. Catholic jeremiads warned that it was necessary to reform the laity, rally the priesthood against the errors of rustics, and rein in popular attempts to gain direct and independent access to God. From the 1570's well into the seventeenth century, when the famous idolatry accounts for central Mexico appeared, the Inquisitions of Mediterranean Europe moved more decisively to suppress magical beliefs and practices as Satan's work. Magical healing, divination, love magic, and fertility rites, once considered ignorant but essentially harmless superstitions, now loomed as dangerous works of the omnipresent enemy.[66]

Thanks to these official preoccupations with moral reform and magic after the Council of Trent, as well as to the Indians' obviously incomplete conversion to Christian orthodoxy, we have some marvelous accounts of Indian "idolatry" from the hands of early-seventeenth-century priests. Not surprisingly, they dwelt on practices that deviated from Christian doctrine and generally neglected to describe those that conformed to it.[67] The best known of these accounts were composed by Jacinto de la Serna from his experience in the parish of Tenancingo and other communities in and near the Valley of Toluca (Zumpahuacan, Zacualpan, and Tenango del Valle); Pedro Ponce for the parish of Zumpahuacan, overlapping Serna's account; and Hernando Ruiz de Alarcón for the parish of Atenango in the modern states of Guerrero and Mexico.

Ruiz de Alarcón, in particular, located his descriptions of "pagan idolatry" in time and place. For example, he summarized a letter received from the Augustinian *doctrinero* (pastor) of Tlapa, Agustín Guerra. While on his way to celebrate mass in an outlying hamlet, Father Guerra said, he had seen an Indian climb to the top of a hill where ancient roads had come together, and suspecting that the Indian had gone there to practice some form of idolatry, he had followed. By the time he reached the top, the Indian had disappeared, but Father Guerra found his offering with the candles still lit in front of a stone idol.[68] Ruiz de Alarcón noted a special reverence among the Indians for fire, water, and the sun, within an encompassing animism. Even the clouds and winds were regarded as angels and gods, he reported, part of a pantheon that resided everywhere, but especially where man was dwarfed by nature—in hills, mountains, caves, precipices, rivers, and valleys.[69] To this priest, Indian shamans were agents of Satan, working their magic through stone "idols" as well as alcohol and psychotropic drugs. The Indians' secret rites were conclusive evidence of diabolical intentions:

Because in this manner the Indians of this land, like those of Peru, hide [these practices] sedulously, I believe [they are] advised by the devil in his interest. Here the priests advise that the heaps of stones that the Indians call *teolocholli* are suspect because in many of them I have found incense, candles, bunches of flowers and other things that they offer on particular days.[70]

In many instances, he wrote, Indians had even hidden idols in the bases of crosses; in one such case, God vouchsafed a sign of his wish that his people should repent and give up their idolatry:

Even God Our Lord pointed them out, as happened in the mountains of Meztitlan [Hidalgo] in the jurisdiction of the Augustinian friars, where lightning struck repeatedly at the base of a cross. Informed of this, the friars had it dismantled in their presence, and they found inside an idol. Since its removal, no lightning bolt has struck [the cross] in more than twelve years.[71]

Fathers Serna and Ponce also noted the influence of Indian curers and wizards, and described ceremonies and invocations for planting, rain, and the harvest, for restored health and safe travel, and for the dedication of a new house or sweat bath. Serna was particularly concerned where these "externals" were coordinated by what he called the "Old Master[s] of idolatrous ceremonies," since their place in the ritual life of the community could challenge the authority of the priest.[72]

For Ruiz de Alarcón, Serna, and Ponce, animistic "superstitions," ceremonies, and offerings, as well as ritual drinking, signaled the survival of ancient beliefs in other gods. In Ponce's account, Indians worshipped a god they believed to be the lord of the clouds and invoked Quetzalcoatl at planting time and on journeys. He found that Indians of all ages in his parish remembered the names of their gods, whether or not they worshipped them.[73] Serna too noted the multiplicity of Indian gods and saw his time as one of great idolatry. The epidemics and other disasters suffered by the Indians were, he believed, God's punishment for their persistent idolatry.[74] Like Ponce's, Serna's examples of suspicious practices and idol worship were instrumental—birth and curing ceremonies, rituals seeking to discover secrets, and rites aimed at placating the forces of nature that threatened and nurtured human life. In one example, he described how an Indian shaman vigorously poked at the sky with a stick wrapped with a live snake, and puffed, chanted, and moved his head to influence the movement of clouds and storms.[75] Serna was particularly impressed by the Indians' reverence for caves and mountains.[76]

The equating of heavy ritual drinking with "idolatry"—which had some basis in fact, since the Indians had long regarded drunkenness as a passageway to the sacred—was virtually automatic for priests throughout the colonial period, not just for these seventeenth-century writers.[77] Another seventeenth-century chronicler, Fr. Francisco Mariano de Torres, found an analogy in the fifth chapter of the Book of Daniel, which tells how "Belshazzar the king made a great feast to a thousand of his lords, and drank wine before the thousand. . . . They drank wine, and praised the gods of gold, and of silver, of brass, of iron, of wood, and

of stone."[78] In a late colonial echo of this view, Benito María de Moxó, a digni-
tary of the cathedral of Mexico, wrote in his 1805 advice on how to reduce Indian
"idolatry":

> Returning now to my Indians, I can do no less than repeat once and a thousand times that
> those who would cure them of their violent propensity to idolatry must, above all else,
> little by little get them to abandon their habit of drunkenness and teach them little by
> little to be sober and chaste.[79]

Unlike Ruiz de Alarcón, both Serna and Ponce occasionally remarked on an
interplay between native and Christian beliefs and practices. Serna was deeply
troubled by the Indians' practice of mixing their gods and "idolatrous" rites with
"good and saintly things," including the sacramental rites of Christianity.[80] He
noted, for example, that on the eve of festivities for a community's patron saint,
Indians offered food to the fire. The next day they would eat the same food,
which was also offered to the image of the saint in the church. They would spill
a little wine or pulque before the fire or the image just as they did before the
altars in their homes.[81] They were, to his mind, cynically mimicking Christian
rites in order to hide their infidelity, "fleeing from the light and clarity of truth"
and meeting secretly at night for their diabolical rites.[82] Ponce was more troubled
by what he regarded as the ignorant superstitions that continued to sway his
Indian parishioners than by the intertwining of beliefs, perhaps because the Son
of God had acquired a privileged place in Indian religious practice. He observed
that "among all these gods, they put Christ our Lord and Redeemer as the ultimate god."[83]

It would be a historical stretch to assume that the last 50 years of Spanish rule
saw exactly these same kinds of religious practices (which is the tacit assumption
of studies that generalize about the long-term process of religious change from
early colonial evidence), although various trial records, Moxó's description, and
some vivid traveler accounts from the early twentieth century tell similar tales.[84]
More than documenting specific continuities in belief and practice, Ruiz de Alarcón, Serna, and Ponce provide clues to a process of change and continuity—a
process that was not simply a matter of ignorance or a rejection of Christianity.
While the covert, apparently ancient practices these priest-authors described
may indicate that old religions survived behind a screen of Christian practice, or
that they and Christian religions were thoroughly blended, another possibility,
as Weismann and Clendinnen suggest, is that old habits of conception survived
in ways that could accommodate Christian devotions without great tension. The
Indian "superstitions" described by the three seventeenth-century authors focus
on health, safety, fertility, and prosperity in this life; they might have complemented otherworldly Christian practices intended to guarantee salvation and
eternal life for the soul freed from the flesh. Ruiz de Alarcón, for example, documents mainly curing rites, auguries, rituals to discover lost or stolen property,
and what he regarded as "pagan" invocations and offerings, especially in connection with the critical matters of subsistence: hunting, fishing, finding beehives
and firewood, firing lime ovens, planting, and bringing in a good crop.

By the late seventeenth century, the church's campaign against "idolatry" had
lost much of its momentum.[85] Practices that had been taken as manifestations of

idolatry—magical invocations to natural forces, auguries, love potions, medicinal magic, and devotion to animal figurines and other effigies—became relatively harmless superstitions. The records of late colonial pastoral visits in the archdiocese indicate that Indian parishioners were occasionally reprimanded for superstitious acts as evidence of Satan's influence, but rarely did the pastoral visitor act as if he suspected idolatry.[86] A priest's eyewitness report of suspicious rites in San Lorenzo Huicicilapan (Lerma parish, Edo. de México) in 1817 caused only a small ripple of concern in the archbishop's court (although the nearly two years that the accused were held in custody awaiting the court's investigation and findings served to warn others that even suspected idolatry could be costly). The assistant pastor reported on December 14 that he had surprised eighteen Indians worshipping "idols" in a house two blocks from the parish church. Among them were prominent men of the community—the fiscal, his assistant, a past gobernador, and the son-in-law of the current gobernador. He and the pastor found images of Jesus and Mary on a table in the center of the room, with various crosses and six candles alongside. In front of them were two tables covered with food, pulque, and a basket (*chiquihuite*) containing miniature representations of dogs and roosters resting on a bed of cotton, colored wool, and cigars. The fiscal had been playing a guitar while the men and women danced in groups of three, passing the basket and little flags from hand to hand, frequently bowing toward the altar and imploring the lord of the mountains (*llemixintle*) to keep them from harm and look upon them as his children. In a nod toward the Bourbon program of Hispanicization, the priest attributed this "great ignorance or liberty in idolatry and other excesses" to the remote, mountainous location of the pueblo and the absence of non-Indians (*gente de razón*) and schoolmasters in the district.

The bishop's chief legal adviser (*promotor fiscal*) responded to the assistant pastor's report by ordering the pastor of Lerma to investigate and execute whatever punishment the court might order. Twenty months later, the investigation was finished and the verdict rendered. The accused's sworn testimony and manifest repentance satisfied the promotor fiscal that no idolatry was intended and that these people had not performed the rites before. Blind Domingo Francisco was the only participant judged culpable, and the promotor concluded that he had acted spontaneously and out of ignorance rather than evil intent. His story was accepted more or less at face value: a resident of Mexico City to whom he delivered charcoal had suggested that, to effect a cure for his blindness, he do what his ancestors had done in times of trouble. On this man's advice, Domingo Francisco bought some little clay animals in the plaza plus cotton and cigars. A contrite Domingo Francisco testified that he and the others did not think they were engaging in an idolatrous sacrifice. He said he believed only in the one true God and proceeded to recite the catechism to prove his point. He and the others had invoked Macquetla Xhant, which he said meant Christ or his divine visage. It was true, he said, that people of San Lorenzo venerated an image of Christ's face at a shrine in the mountains, but that did not mean that they worshipped a god of the mountains. He repeated that he had never believed the figurines were gods. For his errancy, Domingo Francisco was ordered to do penance by attending mass for fifteen consecutive days and swearing at each session his faith before the pastor.[87]

More serious cases were occasionally reported in the archdiocese.[88] About 1750 in the parish of Xilotepec (Edo. de México), "idol worship" taken up in a wave of opposition to the pastor reached such a pitch that the bishop ordered six Indians into service in a textile workshop.[89] In Tepecoacuilco (Guerrero) in the late 1750's, the Indian pastor spoke of pursuing eleven prosyletizing shamans (magicians and healers) before the archbishop decided to transfer him to another parish for his own protection.[90] At Tlamatlan (Hidalgo) in 1777, the pastor complained of his parishioners' "lack of religion." The Indians did not know the catechism and engaged in "idolatries and enormous excesses": "some even adore a clay idol that they call *chicomexochitl* [seven flower, an ominous calendrical sign usually associated with bad luck and contagious disease among women] and attribute Divine Providence to the clouds."[91] Also in 1777, the pastor of Chipetlan (Tlapa district, Guerrero) wrote that he had discovered various Indians paying tribute to false gods on a hill that looked down on the parish seat. He described the "idols" as seven "most horrible and abominable" stone heads "of different human and animal forms." He was convinced that these were false gods "worshipped by their ancient ancestors," but he evidently did not feel threatened by the attention they received. As he said, the Indians "cannot completely forget about them, asking for relief from their illnesses and rain for their fields."[92] In the 1780's at Asunción Malacatepec, a "closed" (*cerrado*) community in the district of Metepec, a son of the gobernador reportedly "claimed to be 'the oracle and the god of the Indians,' burned crosses, and incited the Indians to sack the Spanish estates."[93] And in 1801 a parish priest in the district of Tehuacan (Puebla) lamented that the Indians of San Gabriel Chilac were "the most superstitious in all America," practicing witchcraft, performing animal sacrifices, staining holy garments with the blood, drinking without restraint, and disobeying him in many other ways.[94]

Apart from the uprisings in Yautepec in 1761 and the Sierra de Meztitlan in 1769, the major cases of large-scale, combative "idolatry" reported in Mexico after the 1570's occurred in the southern dioceses of Oaxaca, Chiapas, and Yucatán.[95] It was also in these southern regions that curas complained most often of the Indians' "irreconcilable hatred" for them.[96]

Memories of old manifestations of divinity and respect for ancient sacred places were alive in the late colonial period, but most of the evidence of "idolatry" that priests produced was considered too circumstantial for the ecclesiastical and criminal courts to pursue. Navarro de Vargas, for example, searched diligently for proof to verify his suspicions of idol worship in his parish of Churubusco (Valley of Mexico) in 1734. He knew that Indians continued to respect the old holy places such as the Hill of the Serpent; even if they did not worship idols at the hill, some refused to take rocks and clay for adobe bricks from it. He and his friends discovered several "idols" and implements of sacrifice buried in Christian places. One "idol," reported an agitated Indian *sacristán* (sexton), had been found in the wall of the church at Zumpango; another, a Huitzilopochtli (the Mexicas' patron god) was discovered buried in the cemetery of Santísima Trinidad Zapotlan; and sacrificial flint knives had been put into the base of an old cross at Sitlaltepec. But it was not clear to Father Navarro that his Indian parishioners knew of these hidden additions. The Huitzilopochtli was put on display before it was destroyed because so many parishioners were curious to see it. The flint knives, as sacred implements of human sacrifice, may have been a translation into local iconography of the sacrifice of Christ. Even if the 1734 parishioners knew about them, their "idolatrous" significance may have been as uncertain to the Indians as it was to the priest.[97]

The most common kind of "idolatry" identified in the late-eighteenth-century judicial records was associated with fertility rites. As Nicolás de Castilla recounted in his 1760 resumé, when he had been the designated ecclesiastical magistrate (*juez eclesiástico*) of Atitalaquia (Hidalgo) in 1737, two Indian women and one man were discovered worshipping "idols" associated with water and planted fields. To impress his parishioners with the gravity of the offense, Father Castilla staged a solemn little "auto de fe," as he called it (auto-da-fé in English; a public ceremony at which the Inquisition's sentences for crimes against the church were announced and the offenders were presented in procession), complete with pointed paper coronets of infamy and green candles of absolution for the "idolaters," a high mass and a sermon by the cura of Tetepango, and a procession to the cemetery, where the idols were destroyed and the pieces thrown into a hole in the presence of all the Indian officials and priests of the district.[98]

The frequent glancing references to such practices in the late colonial period document enduring beliefs in witchcraft and the propitiation of powerful natural spirits. The kind of witchcraft case that usually came to the priest's attention involved reputed black magic by a marginal member of the community. It was fairly safe, even commendable on all sides, for parishioners to bring the priest into such cases. In contrast to exorcism and other beneficent Christian magic, witchcraft distinctly qualified as part of the black magic the church condemned as Satan's work; and marginal individuals could be denounced with little political danger to the accuser.[99] It usually came out in testimony that the accused was a person of solitary habits, chronic drunkenness, melancholia, unpredictable or violent temper, recent good fortune, friendship with outsiders, or few kin. In any event, the accused witch stood out as different and untrustworthy.[100] Following are four short examples of black-magic accusations against adult men in which the victim or accusers sought the protection of the alcalde mayor or the spiritual and political power of the church against demonic powers and false accusations, to marginalize rivals and to punish enemies.[101]

In 1716, a principal of San Martín Quautlalpan in the district of Tlalmanalco (Edo. de México) complained to the alcalde mayor that the Indian alcalde had spread the rumor that he was a witch, thereby discrediting him in the community. He added that he was respected by the Spanish residents of Tlalmanalco and the resident priests.[102]

In 1746, Marcos Antonio of the San Gerónimo barrio of Tlayacapan, Morelos, went to the alcalde mayor for protection against various Indians he said had tried to kill him as a witch. They got him drunk and tried to make him say who had wished evil on Pedro Nolasco, son of Pascual Laureano. Marcos claimed that he had escaped alive only by pretending to cure Pedro.[103]

Francisco Xavier, an Indian of Colipa in the parish of Misantla (Veracruz), came to the priest's attention in 1784 when his wife ran to the pastor's residence for protection, with her machete-wielding husband in pursuit. Local people feared Francisco Xavier as a devotee of black magic whose pact with Satan enabled him to cause illness.[104]

At Atemajac near Guadalajara in 1795, an Indian principal was charged with witchcraft by a rival non-Indian registered there as a tribute-paying member of the community. The non-Indian claimed that he had become ill from an evil spell cast on him by the accused, and that a bird sang its ominous song in the tree outside his house every night. The Indian declared himself innocent, saying that his accuser, jealous because he had recently opened a profitable quarry, had threatened to kill him and was only pretending to be sick from an evil spell.[105]

If a village outcast suspected of witchcraft was a dependent of the parish priest, the villagers were unlikely to have much legal recourse. At Amalco in the jurisdiction of Metepec (Edo. de México) in 1792, a violent protest arose when the parish priest elected to have Isidro Hernández, a local Indian reputed to have caused the illness and death of many local people in recent years, assist him in taking a census. In response, an excited crowd of villagers (in a state of "alegría"—euphoria—reads the description) overran the church and parsonage but caused little damage. The violence ran its course only after the crowd captured and battered Isidro, causing him to bleed.[106]

Late colonial church officials often suspected that such charges were motivated by revenge on the part of the accusers rather than by pious horror at the evil deeds of lost souls in league with Satan. In circulars of June 15, 1754, and November 20, 1759, the archbishop warned that many cases of *maleficio* against Indians coming before his court resulted from rumor or out-and-out malice. In only one of the recent cases was detention by his attorney general warranted, the archbishop added.[107] Among the many accusations of witchcraft that were dismissed was the charge by an Indian of Tenango in 1780 that a fellow villager had cast a spell on his wife and caused "supernatural sores" to appear on her body. The accused denied that he had engaged in witchcraft, and the case was closed as "inconsequential."[108]

Perhaps the archbishop was too complacent, for not all reputed wizards and magical healers (curanderos) were outcasts or scapegoats. Some were feared and respected for their presumed ability to transform themselves into fierce animals or communicate with superior natural powers. Why were such people rarely denounced to the cura in the late colonial period? because Indian parishioners feared them? because they represented authentic dissent and experimentation on the part of the community? because the priest regarded them as inconsequential? because he did not know of them? because they cooperated with him and were regarded mainly as purveyors of harmless superstitions? If such shamans openly opposed the priest, they could be the kind of formidable threat to the cura's authority that Fathers Serna, Ponce, and Ruiz de Alarcón had worried about. That they often threatened what the priests regarded as their authority seems doubtful because so few cases were reported to higher-ups. Like the shamans of precolonial Tenochtitlan, they could be "providers of part of the local scaffolding for the larger system" more than competitors to the priests.[109] An exception was documented by Juan Silverio de Nava, the cura of Terrenate, Tlaxcala, who defended himself before the Inquisition in 1768 against false charges of solicitation in the confessional and other abuses of office. His parishioners had turned against him en masse, he claimed, because he had punished an old Indian with the portentous name of Juan Diego (the Indian to whom the Virgin of Guadalupe was believed to have appeared in 1531) for incest with his sister and procuring for his wife. Juan Diego was regarded as an especially powerful shaman in the community.[110]

Conjuring, divining the whereabouts of lost property, predicting future events, and other magical practices attracted the colonial administration's attention especially when they were associated with hallucinogenic drugs such as morning glory seeds (*ololiuhqui*) and *peyote* (a buttonlike cactus bud native to parts of northern Mexico). With some cause, colonial officials suspected that the use of hallucinogens in covert ceremonies raised petty "external" superstitions to a more dangerous level of magical power and the possibility of pacts with the Devil. For the users and their witnesses, drug-induced nausea, visions, and predictions attested to peyote's superhuman powers. The more accurate a witch's predictions and visions, the more a diabolical pact was indicated, especially to early-seventeenth-century colonial officials.[111] The Indians treated peyote with reverence, and their tendency to combine it with Christian imagery made it doubly suspect to church officials concerned about the purity of the faith. It was sometimes called the blessed herb (*hierba bendita*), administered ground up in holy water, and taken "with great faith, as if it were the Holy Sacrament."[112] The cross, and the infant Jesus, Mary, and other saints were sometimes included in peyote ceremonies. Christian prayers, especially the rosary, were sometimes recited.[113]

Details of a 1761 curing ceremony using Christian elements performed by an Indian of the Villa de San Felipe (district of San Miguel el Grande, Guanajuato) were reported by the patient's brother. Ground peyote in a cup of water was placed on an altar with lighted candles late at night. The saints on the altar were perfumed with incense while the sick man knelt before it. Those present then said the rosary and sang the *alabado* (a hymn or praise sung as the Host is placed in the tabernacle). The sick man drank part of the peyote brew, followed by the curer and others present in a kind of communion. Then the curer played the guitar, and the sick man danced with a bow and arrow in his hands. The patient's brother said that he next saw his brother dead, and cried out. The curer told him to kneel, pass the smoke of incense over the saints, and say the Apostles' Creed three times. When he turned around, he saw his brother sitting up. The witness passed out until morning, when he found his brother somewhat better though not cured.

It is difficult to chart changing patterns in the use of peyote and its association with religious acts during the colonial period. Too little is known about the drug's use in precolonial times to establish a baseline or even to determine the direction of change on the eve of Spanish colonization. Equally important, the colonial documentation is distorted by the intermittent activity of the Inquisition, which generated most of the documentation on peyote practices. Because the Inquisition effectively lost its jurisdiction over Indian religious practices by the 1570's, Indians enter its records obliquely, as sellers of the plant or specialists commissioned to use it for a non-Indian client. Community and Indian-to-Indian uses receive little attention. The records on peyote and witchcraft are concentrated (not coincidentally) in the 1620's and in the early eighteenth century, when the Inquisition engaged in campaigns against diabolical sorcery and divination, with which peyote was purportedly linked. Its use in witchcraft at other times largely escapes official documentation, as do its extensive medicinal uses.

Despite these serious problems with the evidence, three aspects of peyote's association with witchcraft in central Mexico are fairly clear and apparently continuous from the seventeenth century to the end of the eighteenth: (1) although peyote's natural growth area was to the north of the Archdiocese of Mexico and the densest settlements of the Diocese of Guadalajara, the plant was traded and used in both dioceses; (2) there, it apparently was used by Indian specialists (often women) for curing and divination, but rarely in community rituals [114] (largely, perhaps, because it was a scarce and expensive commodity); and (3) the trade in peyote and the magical practices associated with it brought Indian specialists and non-Indians into close contact. Non-Indians (but probably few upper-class Spaniards) sought out Indian practitioners and sometimes learned their art in order to discover its magical potential for themselves.

If the Inquisition records are a fair indication, the uses of peyote in Indian witchcraft south of its natural growth area were mainly individual, instrumental, and associated with Christian elements. Its most important uses may have been medicinal, but it was also widely used by diviners to find missing articles, to discover secrets, and to predict the future.[115] Though curanderos and diviners alike used the drug surreptitiously because of the church edicts against it, they aroused little suspicion as idolaters or diabolical agents building an alternative religion and threatening the authority of the parish priest.[116]

Even if "idolatry" seldom ignored or openly rivaled Christianity, local religious practices routinely went beyond the church's prescriptions and knowledge. These practices were more often understood to be compatible with or part of Christianity than an alternative to it, but they might become an alternative under the right conditions and leadership. Much of the documentation comes in the form of compendia of examples collected by treatise writers and treated as typical, like a collection of ancient stone masks removed from their contexts of time, place, and use. Father Pérez de Velasco, in his 1766 guide for parish assistants in the Diocese of Puebla, described some Indian beliefs that impeded a firm understanding of Christianity but did not constitute a rejection of it. His main examples were great fear of the owl and rituals that made the dead a living presence. The owl's hoot was thought to anticipate the death of someone nearby. If a relative died after the owl hooted, the family cursed the bird—a fact that Pérez de Velasco took as a welcome sign that Indians did not regard it as a god. Indians would leave the clothing of deceased relatives for a week at the place where death overtook them, and would bury them in sandals—in preparation, Pérez speculated, for the trek to heaven. On All Hallow's Eve, Indians awaited deceased parents and other relatives, paying their respects by sweeping the streets and patios and setting out fruit and bread.[117]

Another small compendium of Indian religious practices by a late colonial official is Antonio de Ribadeneyra's background report for the Fourth Provincial Council of bishops and other prelates (1771).[118] Although Ribadeneyra made no attempt to distinguish ancient aspects from colonial combinations, and occasionally remarked that a particular belief was common in Spain and among non-Indians in Mexico as well as among Indians,[119] his examples of beliefs and practices follow the general line of the priests' accounts. They center on the natural world—protection, health, fertility, propitiation, and predictions for the benefit of the living—and ancestor worship. Like Serna, he noted the important role that hilltops and clouds played in rain ceremonies. When the rains were late in coming, old Indian men would go to the nearest hilltop to summon them, taking food, money, incense, and candles as offerings. Supposedly the old men removed their pants and addressed the clouds with their penises displayed. These and other fertility rites were so common that some priests simply ignored them, he reported. According to this author, Indians of central Mexico believed that their deceased relatives became oxen or the first animal that ventured past the church door after the death occurred. Believing also that the deceased would have to work in the afterlife, relatives placed farm implements, money, and provisions for the journey in the burial; milk was placed there in gourds for infants who died unweaned, as were toys for older children. Ribadeneyra was charmed by "superstitions" and "abuses" that underlay Indian practices to ensure an individual's well-being, including feeding parrot soup to infants so they would speak; eating *epasote* (a native condiment known in English as Mexican tea or wormseed) for good memory, specifically red epasote for learning one's prayers; and sending Indian messengers out with a skunk's tail as a good luck charm to ward off fatigue, assault, and other mishaps of the road.[120] Indians also were said to believe that the sun was the face of God, to be greeted at sunrise and taken leave of reverently at sundown.

In describing quaint "abusos," Ribadeneyra, like many late colonial officials, was domesticating the strange—reducing local practices to minor departures from orthodoxy and representing Indians as ignorant, literal-minded children.[121] He glossed over much of the religious experience that underlay the "abusos," especially the ways in which the material world remained suffused with the sacred for late colonial Indians. As Father Arias had observed in Nayarit in the 1670's, "there is nothing for which someone does not pray."

While "pagan" practices were concentrated in private, household devotions intended to nourish and protect family members, they were not confined there. But even the cave ceremonies with stone effigies and invocations to spirits of the wind and rain, and other practices that priests considered superstitious or idolatrous, were rarely expressed in anti-Christian ways or as direct challenges to the parish priest's authority in the matters of spiritual well-being that concerned him most. As Omer Stewart suggests for Indian peyotism in North America since the late nineteenth century, people may operate comfortably in more than one religious tradition at a time, enlarging their cosmovision and repertoire of world renewing.[122] Colonial Indians could have resisted some of the priests' ways of being "truly Christian" and added others to fill out their understanding of the divine and sense of well-being without rejecting Christianity. "Idols" on altars when the priest was away or hidden in church walls and the bases of crosses could just as well attest to dual worship or native expressions of Christian faith as to an underground "idolatry" that repudiated Christianity or the utter failure of native and Spanish "worlds" to communicate.[123]

PART TWO

Priests

CHAPTER FOUR

Becoming a Parish Priest

> We no longer find ourselves at the beginning of the Conquest of these kingdoms, when to be a parish priest was to be a missionary—poor and exposed to great labors, even to martyrdom. —Archbishop Lorenzana, 1768

> Apparently insoluble questions, but actually quite soluble, once you accept the fact that in an archbishop there may be two archbishops—the administrator and the man of God. —Machado de Assis, *Epitaph of a Small Winner*

Parish priests were both spiritual specialists and men of the world. Inevitably they were administrators and members of a profession in regular contact with other priests and royal officials, family and friends, local notables, and other laymen who might be compatriots, rivals, or enemies depending on the circumstances. Familiar as their priestly failings and feelings may seem, they were not just interchangeable agents of a universal priesthood but individuals and men of their place and time. Their personal backgrounds, training, classifications, livelihoods, careers, and sense of responsibility as churchmen in colonial society, then, are important to a study of parish life. Their influence in the parish could depend as much on these individual and institutional constraints and experiences as on the spiritual authority of the office.

Just as speaking of "the church" gives a misleading impression of unity and uniformity, it is hazardous to generalize about the parish clergy. Nevertheless, as a first approximation, the next three chapters identify large patterns in the organization, training, careers, and livelihood of parish priests. Individuals appear here as examples of the patterns or exceptions to them. Most of the singular circumstances and personalities are left to subsequent chapters that draw closer to the priests' activities in the parish during this time of rapid change.

Numbers and Distinctions

Many clergymen in the eighteenth-century dioceses of Guadalajara and Mexico remain on the edges of this study because they were not full-time pastors. Some

diocesan priests lived among the educated elite of the cathedral city or a principal town and never sought a parish assignment.[1] If they were not independently
wealthy, they often served as rectors of seminaries, vicars general, and legal advisers to the bishop's court.[2] Some of these privileged men disdained parish service, but others avoided it because they were excessively scrupulous or timid.
For example, Lic. Joseph Reies Gómez de Aguilar, described by his bishop as
a learned man who had served ten years as a rector and promotor fiscal, had
"never . . . wished to try for a parish benefice for fear of the responsibility."[3]

But even outside the cathedral city and its immediate vicinity, there were at
least as many diocesan priests who were not dedicated to parish service as there
were diocesan priests and friars serving as pastors. In the Diocese of Guadalajara
outside the cathedral city in 1796, there were 234 diocesan curas (pastors, titular parish priests) and assistants and 242 additional diocesan priests in residence
in the 98 parishes reporting.[4] Eighty-five members of religious orders also lived
there, but the regulars no longer played much of a role in parish work; only fourteen of the 98 parishes were still assigned to the Franciscans and Dominicans—
an important change from the middle of the eighteenth century, when more
than a third of all parishes in both dioceses were administered by Mendicants.[5]
In the principal towns and cities, the proportion of parish priests to other diocesan priests plus men and women religious was much smaller. For Mexico City
in 1790, there were 16 pastors and 43 assistant pastors to 517 diocesan priests,
867 monks and friars, 923 nuns, and 26 members of the cathedral chapter—only
2.5 percent.[6] Of the 6,827 male diocesan and regular priests in the viceroyalty
in 1810, only about a third were in parish service, though for the diocesan clergy
alone the proportion rises to half.[7]

The "sin destino" priests celebrated mass, but most did not administer sacraments or sit for confession. Many were chantry or chaplaincy priests—paid a
fixed stipend from capellanías to celebrate anniversary masses and other special masses for the dead. At least 147 of the 242 diocesan priests who lived in
the Diocese of Guadalajara outside the cathedral city in 1796 and were not in
full-time parish service held such endowments.[8] The average capellanía of 4,900
pesos should have provided its holder with an annual stipend of 245 pesos.[9] Some
priests deriving most of their modest means from these stipends devoted their
lives to spiritual exercises ("sheltered in his home," as one cura said of such a
priest living in his parish);[10] a few others were mainly occupied with the operation of haciendas, mines, and other properties (at least 14 of the 242 diocesan
priests not in pastoral service in 1796). Some of these priests maintained their
licenses to confess, preach, and administer sacraments, and occasionally helped
the cura and his assistants, especially during Lent and in the cura's absence. Still
other diocesan priests, about whom very little is known, were virtual vagabonds,
outlaws, or too sick, old, or poor to do any regular work. The poorest of them
lived from alms or the charity of the local cura or a benevolent lay patron. Some
old pastors retired to a favorite parish, their childhood hometown, or an agreeable climate, where they lived modestly from their savings and stipends.

The number of parishes—and therefore of curas—grew steadily in the eighteenth century. The archdiocese had 189 parishes in 1746, 202 in 1767, 235 in
the mid-1780's, 243 in the early nineteenth century, and 245 in 1827. Guadala-

jara went from 76 parishes in 1708, to 90 in 1767, 96 in 1774, 122 in the early nineteenth century (a jump that owed in part to the transfer of the districts of Ocotlan, La Barca, Zapotlan el Grande, and Colima from the Diocese of Michoacán in 1795 and 1797), and 135 in 1827.[11] In 1767, there may have been 465 or so parish priests in Mexico and 234 in Guadalajara; by the early nineteenth century, the archdiocese would have had about 575–600, and the Diocese of Guadalajara about 300. The number of parish priests had grown by about 29 percent for the archdiocese between 1767 and the first years of the nineteenth century, and by about 28 percent for Guadalajara between 1767 and 1796.

The diocesan parish priests fall into various formal and informal categories. The main formal categories were *cura beneficiado*, *cura ad interim*, *vicario*, and *co-adjutor*. The curas beneficiados or *párrocos*, who accounted for more than a third of all pastors, held the parish as a benefice or quasi-feudal property under the title of *vicario in capite* (rector or head priest). The head priest's license of office was "absolute and without time limit."[12] As the titular priest, he was entitled to the parish income, labor, and provisions permitted by law or custom, and the post was his for life (or until promotion), provided that he fulfilled his duties and did not commit serious or repeated violations of royal and ecclesiastical law. Usually he was appointed to the separate position of ecclesiastical judge (*juez eclesiástico*) in the territory of his parish; often he was also the local agent (*comisario*) of the Inquisition.

It is the curas beneficiados (or curas) who are best known from written records. Many of them left detailed professional resumés; also, their duties led not only to administrative reports but often to civil lawsuits, of which there were many in the late colonial period. As later chapters will show, these men need to be considered in clusters and individually, not only as a professional class. Some were wealthy and influential and could hope to move on to more prestigious posts in the cathedral chapter. Roughly one in five held a *curato pingüe*, or "first-class" parish, that provided a comfortable living and was otherwise regarded as very desirable. Some curas were scholars and lawyers, holding licentiates and doctorates; most had at least a baccalaureate in arts, although a few had been ordained without it. Some were posted close to the cathedral city and participated actively in the political life of the diocese. Others lived in remote or poor parishes and had little in common with the privileged minority except for their title. Since it took some years beyond ordination for most pastors to secure a permanent post, and this was the highest position most of them attained, the average age of the curas at any time in the late eighteenth century was quite advanced, nearly fifty years.[13]

A cura ad interim had the same rights and responsibilities as a cura beneficiado except that his assignment was temporary. Though by law he was supposed to fill in for a dead or departed titular priest for only a few months pending the appointment of a permanent replacement, professional resumés and administrative records indicate that many curas ad interim lasted for a year or more, at least until the next competition to fill vacancies was held in the cathedral city, and sometimes longer.[14] Substitute posts in the less lucrative parishes were usually filled by young unbeneficed men eager to display their management skills. It was a distinction they highlighted in their quest for a permanent parish assignment, though not a certain stepping-stone into a benefice. Often, at the time of the appointment, they had been serving as temporary assistants in the same parish or one nearby. A well-educated, independently wealthy, young urban priest, whose career pointed toward the cathedral chapter, a part-time career in canon or civil law, and a professorship in one of the seminaries, the Royal and Pontifical University in Mexico City, or, after 1792, the Universidad de Guadalajara, might occasionally take up such an assignment to get a taste of pastoral work, but rarely was this the prelude to permanent parish work.[15]

Nearly two-thirds of the parish priests in the eighteenth century were vicarios and coadjutores. Also called *ayudantes* or *tenientes*, the vicarios were unbeneficed assistants to the curas. If there was more than one vicario, the principal one might be designated the *teniente de cura* (lieutenant cura).[16] The function of these priests, as set out in a 1766 manual for vicarios in the Diocese of Puebla, was to relieve the cura of part or all of his pastoral obligations, "to undertake and do everything that the curas are unable to do."[17] Often, they were the priests who communicated with Indian parishioners in their native languages. In parishes that were large and prosperous enough to support more than one vicario, the cura usually stayed in the parish seat and relied on his younger assistants to visit the remote dependencies for mass, special celebrations, baptisms, and last rites.[18]

The vicarios are the hardest category of parish priests to describe, being the most heterogeneous, transient, and poorly documented. For some, being a vicario was an interlude between ordination and a parish benefice, an interlude to be concluded as soon as possible. Of those who never gained a parish benefice, most lived out their service with only the barest written residue of their actions and thought. Their profile has to be built from trial records, parish archives, and fleeting references in administrative reports. The reports on the parish clergy that were submitted with some regularity by late colonial prelates and judges of the audiencias to the Council of the Indies are of little help. They rarely reached beyond the 30 or 40 priests whom the bishop or judge regarded as particularly distinguished and worthy of promotion in the near future. "Distinguished" generally meant men who were well educated, well bred, or particularly assiduous in fulfilling their duties as curas beneficiados. Most of these prominent curas were serving in the conspicuously desirable parishes.[19] To the bishops and judges of the audiencias of Mexico and Nueva Galicia, the rest were a faceless crowd except when they got into trouble. After naming 38 meritorious priests in his report on the Diocese of Guadalajara in March 1755, Oidor Jorge de Basarte said that the rest were "not known either for their academic prowess or their virtue. If they apply themselves to their pastoral work, perhaps they will be worthy of some notice in the future."[20] The bishop expressed himself in similar terms in a report to the king of October 8, 1758. He was singling out only a few distinguished priests from his cathedral chapter, the cabildo of the Franciscan Colegiata de Guadalupe in Zacatecas, and the leading parishes, he explained, for the diocese consisted in the main of distant, isolated parishes, sparsely inhabited by uncouth Indians and administered by curas educated in Indian languages, very few of whom had advanced degrees or distinguished professional records in the university and administration. "All the rest are unfit for promotion as prebends or in any other line of advancement."[21] There was another reason why the bishops knew little about the vicarios. Under the canons of the Council of Trent, a cura could choose and dismiss assistants on his own account.[22] In New Spain, curas sometimes asked the bishop to recommend a young assistant, and vicarios sometimes spoke of being "assigned" to a parish by the bishop,[23] but curas could take the initiative and often did. Only when they needed assistants and refused to name them was the bishop expected to step in.

Many vicarios were in their mid-twenties and fresh out of seminary. The mean age of 57 vicarios for the Diocese of Guadalajara in 1796 was thirty-five, close to fifteen years younger than the curas.[24] But, as the median age of thirty-three suggests, there was also a large minority of vicarios in their forties and fifties who would never obtain a parish benefice. By the mid-1760's, royal authorities were determined to appoint more vicarios, insisting that the growing population and vast territory of many parishes left them understaffed but able to underwrite a vicario's salary (as a Spanish Capuchin visitor remarked, "a parish in America is larger than a diocese in Spain").[25] They sometimes added that increasing numbers of idle but willing priests were in need of employment. The viceroys and audiencias were prepared for the news that babies went unbaptized for months and parishioners were dying without last rites because of a shortage of priests. Moving toward a general policy of appointing more vicarios, on September 9, 1762, the crown issued a royal cedula in response to "idolatry" in the district of Cuernavaca that was thought to result from too little administration. The cedula ordered the cura of Yautepec to hire assistants: "one, two or whatever the territory of the parish dictates."[26]

But how many assistants were enough? The crown answered by cedula on October 18, 1764, that there should be a pastor in residence wherever pueblos were over four leagues from the parish seat:

We are informed of the vastness of many parishes in that America. We understand that some have various pueblos ten, twelve, fourteen, and more leagues from the parish seat where the parish priest resides, and no lieutenants. The parishioners in these places lack all spiritual nourishment, are without mass most of the year, and are constantly exposed to the danger that the cura will not arrive in time [to administer the last rites] when they are gravely ill. . . . We order that secular or regular priests be provided without delay to pueblos that lack this essential care and are over four leagues from the parish seat.[27]

The four-league standard was repeated on various occasions thereafter and served as the justification for suits against curas who had not appointed additional vicarios and were suspected of failing to administer the sacraments promptly.[28] Some vicarios were added in both dioceses, but the new laws produced no great change in parish administration.[29]

The idea of adding vicarios had been debated in the Council of the Indies and the chambers of the bishops and audiencias for some years before 1762. The bishop of Guadalajara made a telling point in his 1758 report to the crown when he acknowledged the shortage of assistant pastors and the abundance of priests but noted that most curas could not afford to pay more assistants an adequate salary.[30] Furthermore, a distance standard for assigning new vicarios made little sense in parishes with large territories and small, dispersed populations. No one seems to have proposed a population threshold for assigning more assistants — a curious omission, since the size of the Indian population had been a primary consideration when parish boundaries were established in the sixteenth and seventeenth centuries. (Both the authoritative seventeenth-century legal commentator Solórzano y Pereira and the *Recopilación* regarded 400 tributaries as the proper size of an Indian parish.)[31] One way to bring population and parish territories into line would have been to redraw parish boundaries, but some clergy and parishioners angrily resisted the few attempts by prelates and state officials to do so in the eighteenth century.

The main effect of the campaign from above to assign more pastors to large parishes may have been to encourage subordinate towns to petition for parish status or, at least, their own resident pastor. Some parishes had had such *vicarios de pie fijo* for many years, but curas were almost certain to oppose this threat to their own authority and livelihood. Effectively an independent cura in his own right, the vicario de pie fijo might be entitled to the emoluments collected in his part of the parish, rather than being paid a lower fixed salary by the cura; he could be appointed by the bishop; and it was not clear whether he could be removed at the cura's discretion. The bishops did not favor creating new parishes by dividing old ones except when it facilitated the secularization of the Mendicants' *doctrinas* (the proto-parishes administered by friars were called doctrinas rather than *curatos* in order to emphasize the legal point that this was a temporary assignment—that Indians were to be assigned to diocesan pastors once their basic indoctrination was completed), but they were concerned about the number of unemployed priests.[32] So they were inclined to accept the establishment of new vicarías de pie fijo as a reform that met the crown's desire to increase the number of parish priests and gave the bishops more control over appointments.[33]

The coadjutor was another kind of assistant to the cura with more authority than the ordinary vicario. The term denoted a temporary appointment, and though it was sometimes used synonymously with vicario and lieutenant, a coadjutor generally enjoyed a degree of independence from the cura not open to the vicario. According to Solórzano, a coadjutor was required for each Indian language spoken in the parish, and could be appointed by a cura only with the bishop's approval.[34] Usually in eighteenth-century New Spain, however, coadjutors were appointed by the bishop. A royal cedula of January 21, 1718, noted that the Council of Trent had given bishops the right to name a coadjutor when the cura was absent or where distances in the parish territory were too great for him to administer all of it properly.[35] Coadjutors might also be imposed where curas were sick, too old to carry on alone, or incompetent. Some, like the vicarios de pie fijo, were given full authority over part of the parish. Perhaps most galling to curas who had coadjutors imposed on them was the disposition of the parish emoluments. Arrangements varied (they were left to the bishop's discretion by the Council of Trent), but coadjutors were often entitled to the fruits of the benefice while they served, and owed their curas only a monthly stipend. Not surprisingly, there were disputes between curas and coadjutors over what was owed and when it should be paid.[36]

In addition to these official offices, a cura might avail himself of a network of temporary, part-time, and informal helpers in outlying rural areas. Some of the holders of capellanías attached to haciendas lived on the estates and performed most of the sacramental duties of a parish priest there as well as celebrating the anniversary masses.[37] The population of most estates was too small to keep such a priest busy full time or provide an adequate living. Sometimes he was related to the estate owner or owned the estate himself and spent much of his time on the property. In either case, if his licenses to confess and preach were current, he and priests from the cities and monasteries sometimes helped the cura with confessions and sermons during and after Lent, especially the week before Easter Sunday, and in emergencies, usually in exchange for a small stipend.[38]

The Secularization of Parishes

Thanks to the secularization of most doctrinas still administered by the Franciscans, Dominicans, and Augustinians, the history of pastoral service in late colonial Indian communities of Mexico and Guadalajara centers on diocesan priests.[39] Why the crown undertook such a reform at this time is suggested by that most passionate of regalists Archbishop Francisco de Lorenzana, who assured the viceroy in 1768 that "above all, the diocesan priests are completely obedient to Your Excellency in everything, and quick to execute your orders and mine."[40] Secularization supported the Bourbon intention to centralize and standardize political authority and supervise the clergy more closely, especially the regular clergy,[41] a policy that had resulted in the expulsion of the Jesuits the year before Lorenzana wrote these words. The members of religious orders in pastoral service were far too independent for the regalists' taste, inclined to keep their Indian parishioners at arm's length from royal authorities and less amenable to accepting the reduced role of the clergy in public life than policy makers wanted.

As usual, the Bourbons did not have to invent new legal principles to put their policy into practice. In the early colonial period, the Mendicants had nearly monopolized pastoral work in the two dioceses, but their activities as pastors were subject to termination almost from the beginning. Their papal dispensation to administer sacraments was understood to be a special circumstance appropriate to the first stages of conversion and indoctrination, always considered temporary by the crown and the secular church. It was subject to review by the crown, especially when unemployed diocesan priests were available for assignment in New Spain by the late sixteenth century, and as seminaries and American ordinations increased dramatically in the eighteenth. Even though the crown repeatedly renewed the administration of doctrinas by members of religious orders, it was expressed in highly conditional terms:

We regard it as good, and we order *for now*, and until we order otherwise, that the Religious may continue in the Doctrinas . . . and that the assignment and removal of the Religious curas, whenever it is necessary, shall be done by our Viceroys of Peru and New Spain, Presidents, and Governors who exercise our Royal Patronato in our name. . . . The Religious do not pretend to acquire a perpetual right to the parishes (emphasis in the original).[42]

Even Solórzano, who did not conceal his preference for men of the orders over diocesan priests, affirmed the principle that assignments of Mendicants to pastoral service were temporary: "If secular priests are found in equal number, merit, and competence," they should be appointed.[43]

Despite a wave of secularizations in the late sixteenth century, the Mendicants managed to hold on to a third of the parish units in the two dioceses. But by the late seventeenth century, they were under full attack in Guadalajara. In 1678, the bishop of Guadalajara sequestered two Franciscan doctrinas that he claimed were poorly administered.[44] In 1708, his successor wrote a scathing report to the Council of the Indies calling for complete secularization. Citing as precedent the removal of some doctrinas in Oaxaca from Dominican control, he thought it ludicrous to have a large number of unplaced diocesan priests when 41 of his 76 parish units were still being run by the Franciscans.[45] At stages from then until the 1790's, even as the number of Guadalajara parishes increased to more than 100, the Franciscans were reduced to only two doctrinas.[46]

This dramatic change in administration did not sweeten relations between diocesan priests and friars (but neither did the installing of a fee-for-service regime, as one might have expected, lead to a significant rise in disputes between parishioners and their new religious mentors in Guadalajara). Still, it is important to note that, despite the cases of conflict between the two that could be cited, and of instances where diocesan priests eagerly joined royal officials in the assaults on Mendicant doctrinas, secularization laws were enacted long before they were implemented in full, and curas in practice often relied on the support of neighboring Mendicants, and especially on the missions of Franciscans they invited in for parish revivals.[47]

The stakes were higher in the archdiocese, where a drive toward complete secularization began with a royal cedula of October 4, 1749, recalling that parishes had been assigned to the religious orders only until a sufficient number of qualified diocesan priests should be available. That time had come, said the cedula, and the final removal should begin with the archdiocese, at the discretion of the viceroy and the archbishop.[48] In 1753, the crown extended the secularization to dioceses throughout the American empire. It softened the edges of this order with an amendment that allowed the orders to retain one or two parishes of their choice, called for the transfers to be accomplished "with as much gentleness as possible," and specified that replacements from among diocesan priests should be well educated and fluent in the native language of their parishioners.[49] Though some exceptions and 20-year delays were granted, and action was often postponed until the current cura doctrinero died or left,[50] by 1777 at least 73 archdiocesan parishes, or nearly 40 percent of the archdiocesan total, had been carved out of doctrinas. Things went fairly smoothly in the two districts that were most impacted—Cuernavaca (Morelos), with fourteen newly secularized parishes, and neighboring Chalco (mostly in the Edo. de México) with twelve, but many of the later fee disputes were centered in some of the new parishes: Capuluac and Calimaya in Tenango del Valle; Zinacantepec in Metepec; and Xilotepec and Huichapan (Hidalgo).[51] Of the 50 secularizations that are dated by year, 26 occurred between 1751 and 1756. Thirteen others cluster between 1772 and 1776. By 1805, only nine doctrinas were still under Mendicant supervision.[52]

To the Franciscans and Augustinians of Mexico and Guadalajara, the cedula of 1749 seemed like a sudden attack on their prestige and well-being, especially since they had depended on pastoral work to support many of their members in New Spain for more than 200 years. In their initial entreaties to the crown, they

lamented the lack of gratitude for centuries of faithful service and declared themselves "martyrs of envy."[53] Once the secularizations began, remaining Mendicant
doctrineros were targeted in the periodic pastoral visits of the archdiocese for
mortifying criticism as negligent and irresponsible pastors.[54] For the Franciscans,
a financial crisis and decline in membership were almost immediate. The province of the Santo Evangelio concentrated in central Mexico reported 787 members in 1764, 699 in 1769, and 577 in 1776; 422 of the 577 members in 1776 were
attached to sixteen monasteries that had no doctrinas to help support them.[55]

Even if Solórzano was right in claiming that Indians "love and revere the
regulars more,"[56] the secularization process was not a simple tale of grasping, immoral, aloof diocesan curas replacing beloved, saintly friars. The history of the
Franciscans, Dominicans, and Augustinians as curas doctrineros remains to be
written, but the doctrinas probably were more closely administered than the parishes were—at least in practice the Mendicants received more direct attention
from their provincial than diocesan curas did from their bishop, and a doctrina
was almost always administered by two or more men.[57] Nevertheless, the colonial
judicial record offers evidence of friction between Indian parishioners and friars
over alleged excessive charges and cruelty, of some lascivious and ignorant friars
in the field, and of friars who knew little of the native language of their parishioners, as well as of well-prepared, charitable, and dedicated diocesan curas.[58]

The friars resisted secularization as best they could in the courts, hoping to
delay, if not reverse the process. In the 1750's and 1760's, the Augustinians made
complicated legal claims about what property in their doctrinas belonged to the
order and was thus not subject to secularization.[59] For more than 20 years after
the royal cedula of 1749, the Franciscans of the Santo Evangelio province in
central Mexico waged a campaign of petitions and legal actions to suspend the
transfers and even restore lost doctrinas.[60] Their strategy centered on claims that
they were more dedicated and charitable pastors than their secular counterparts,
and that their replacements did not know the native languages of the parish.[61]
In this polemic they were promoting the image of a lost utopia of exemplary
spiritual care and of peaceful, pious, hard-working Indian pueblos under Franciscan aegis.[62]

Regular and secular prelates jockeyed for position, often acrimoniously. The
Franciscan provincial in Mexico City argued in 1768 for a delay in implementing
Archbishop Lorenzana's order for the secularization of San Sebastián Querétaro,
representing the archbishop as an overeager intruder on a matter that should be
resolved by the crown and the Mendicants.[63] Not surprisingly, Lorenzana responded that the authority was his in consultation with the viceroy, and that the
time to act had arrived.[64] The ensuing struggles could pit viceroys against bishops, as well as regular against secular prelates. Viceroy Revillagigedo (the elder),
who held office during the first years of the secularization program after 1749,
would have agreed with Lorenzana's contention that the initiative belonged to
the bishops. As long as their actions conformed to royal law in this matter, his
role was to lend support.[65] However, his successor intervened to protect several
doctrinas from secularization, stirring a jurisdictional struggle with the bishop of
Michoacán and leading to Lorenzana's firm defense of episcopal initiative.[66]

Although most parishes were transferred to diocesan administration without incident (friars rarely tried to subvert the formalities of dispossession, but cautious bishops usually called for a military guard to oversee the proceedings),[67] the act of secularization could occasion resistance, resentment, and stronger feelings among parishioners as well as Mendicant priests. Few friars intentionally stirred political protest among parishioners, but some effectively disrupted local politics for years and warned darkly of the social dislocations that would follow.[68] At Capuluac, a pueblo in the district of Tenango del Valle (Edo. de México) where a bitter fees dispute with the diocesan cura would surface in the 1790's, the transfer of the parish from the Augustinian prior and his two assistants in November 1750 occasioned weeping among Indian women in the large group of parishioners that assembled for mass that day, insolence from the non-Indians of Santiago Tianguistengo who came as armed auxiliaries of the judge, menacing gestures and angry words from the two assistants, and a refusal by the prior to give up the keys to the sacristy without a viceregal decree.[69] The first diocesan priest of Xichú (San Luis de la Paz district, Guanajuato) in 1751 found the Indian parishioners insolent and resistant to his guidance. For a time, they even refused to attend mass.[70] At Atlatlaucan, in the parish of Ozumba near the Valley of Mexico, Mendicants, rather than the diocesan cura, were still being called for the sacraments in the 1750's, years after secularization.[71]

Some Indian parishioners clearly loved their doctrinero, and responded to the possibility of his departure with moving petitions that affirmed the Mendicants' rhetoric of a receding golden age. A beautifully prepared appeal of this kind was made in 1765 by the fiscal of Santiago Ayapango, with the support of his pueblo and leaders from San Francisco Zeltalpan and San Cristóbal Paxtlam in the district of Tlalmanalco (Edo. de México).[72] Leaders of Cuanacalcingo, Morelos, in 1775 even petitioned to have the diocesan cura removed and the regulars restored. As they put it, they wanted priests who would work for "the complete well-being of our souls, as in the time of the friars."[73] Coming from a district where complaints against Mendicants had been common, this pious memory was selective—at least for rhetorical purposes, the period of Mendicant administration seemed more like a golden age once it had passed.[74]

Some contemporaries, including at least one former alcalde mayor, complained bitterly about the neglect into which the spiritual life of Indian parishes fell after these late colonial secularizations.[75] Important, unsettling changes *did* follow,[76] but they seem to have had less to do with neglect ("abandono") than with new complications and the redefining of the parish priest's role. Change from the predictable circumstances of Mendicant administration inevitably raised questions about the new order of things.

Social Origins and Official Expectations

The family background and social origins of the curas and their vicarios are difficult to trace in detail. In addition to being of legitimate birth and descended from Old Christians without taint of foreign religion, a parish priest was supposed to be well educated, literate in Latin, and virtuous in his personal habits. Men born and raised in the diocese in which they competed for office were to be preferred for parish benefices. Though these rules were not uniformly followed, they and local circumstances did give the parish clergy a definite regional and creole cast. The large majority of late colonial priests were, or passed as, Spaniards of American birth.[77] For both dioceses, about a third of the parish priests in the mid-eighteenth century were probably from the cathedral city: in the early 1760's, 34.4 percent of the aspirants to vacant parishes in the competitions (*oposiciones*) for benefices in the archdiocese were from Mexico City, and in 1757, 32.4 percent of the aspirants in the Guadalajara diocese were from that city.[78] Nearly all the rest were from other parts of the diocese and were already in parish administration there. For the archdiocese, only 4.7 percent of the aspirants were from other American dioceses, and 3.1 percent were peninsular Spaniards. There were no peninsular Spaniards among the Guadalajara aspirants, but 8.3 percent were from other dioceses. The proportion of metropolitan priests may have fallen off somewhat in the late eighteenth century. In the 1770 oposiciones for Guadalajara, 28.6 percent of the aspirants were from the cathedral city, a decline of almost 4 percent from 1757.[79]

There were few Indian curas in Guadalajara, but in the archdiocese perhaps 5 percent of the parish priests in the late colonial period were identified as Indians.[80] All had demonstrated to the satisfaction of the examiners that they were men of noble ancestry and legitimate birth, and most were from one of the Indian barrios of Mexico City or a pueblo in the Valley of Mexico.[81] There were a few peninsular Spaniards among the curas, and occasionally a vicario was identified as a mestizo or a mulato. Since the late sixteenth century, colonial law had allowed the ordination of mestizos who were able, well educated, and of good habits and legitimate birth.[82] But mixed ancestry was not a badge of honor that aspirants to the priesthood paraded in public. Even though the Fourth Provincial Council had recommended in 1771 that one-third of future seminary students should be Indians and mestizos, the bishops then and later spoke of such men's "inferior spirit" (bajeza de espíritu) and did not actively promote preparing them for parish service.[83] Few colonial pastors described themselves or were described by their superiors as mestizos or mulatos.

Any description of the social origins of late colonial parish priests based on the professional resumés (*relaciones de méritos y servicios*) of the priests who competed for positions in the cathedral chapters and the better parishes or were closely associated with diocesan politics would be misleading, for these men tended to come from the upper ranks of colonial society.[84] Many listed their fathers as merchants, colonial officials, hacendados, and provincial notables. On the rare occasions when a cura inherited a noble title, like the Conde de Santa Rosa in Guadalajara in the 1780's, he was apt to be on his way up to the cathedral chapter or out of active service.[85] Priests from the wealthiest and most renowned families rarely took up parish assignments at all and were choosy when they did so. They occasionally competed for vacancies but were inclined to wait for an opening in one of the first-class parishes.

Scattered information on more than 100 other curas and vicarios for Mexico and Guadalajara indicates that most were of relatively humble origins. Shopkeepers, small-town traders, painters, carpenters, military officers, and rancheros and other small landowners fathered curas, as did provincial men with more family prestige than wealth. Especially, those parish priests who were drawn from provincial towns and hamlets had been born into the narrow middle of late colonial society. They rarely brought any income or property to their profession, and often enough were burdened with the care of unmarried sisters and aged parents. An unknown but surely substantial number of the vicarios who never became curas were from yet humbler origins. For example, Agustín Joseph de Bedoya, a forty-one-year-old creole vicario of Texmelucan (Puebla) in 1726, was the son of a local shopkeeper who sold general supplies; José Antonio Baldovinos, a young creole vicario in the Villa de Colima in 1799, was the son of an uneducated carpenter and the nephew of a tailor; and Mariano Calzada, former vicario of Sierra de Pinos, described himself in 1790 as the son of a mestizo trader from Zacatecas and the grandson of an Indian painter.[86]

Priestly Education

At least as important as social origins to a priest's career were his education and scholarly accomplishments. Only a small proportion of the late colonial curas— roughly one in seven—held advanced degrees in theology and canon law. The figure was much the same in both dioceses in the early 1790's: eight doctors and eight licenciados among the 98 curas of Guadalajara outside the cathedral city (16 percent), fourteen doctors and ten licenciados in the 145 Mexico parishes reporting in 1793 (17 percent).[87] Though an advanced degree was not a guaranteed ticket into a choice parish—young, unpopular, indiscreet, unassuming, or mediocre doctors could be found in middling parishes—most of the doctors and licenciados in parish service occupied first-class parishes or at least parishes positioned near the diocesan capital. The choice Guadalajara parishes—Zacatecas, San Juan de los Lagos, Santa María de Lagos, Aguascalientes, and Sierra de Pinos—were usually held by priests with advanced degrees, as were about half the "first-class" parishes identified in Appendix A.[88]

At a minimum, parish priests had to be literate, to know some Latin, and to have passed public examinations in the field of moral theology. The surest and most acceptable route to this expertise was formal education, all but the first years of it in the colegios and seminaries of the cathedral cities and a few provincial towns. A bachelor's degree gained from studies in one of these institutions was nearly indispensable for priests who hoped to win a parish benefice in the periodic competitions to fill vacant posts.[89] Even better was advanced study in theology or law.

The reputation and friendships a future parish priest made in seminary must have been important later on. This was especially true in eighteenth-century Mexico, where most seminary students would have known one another and where few left their home diocese when they took up pastoral work. The colonial documentation I have studied sheds little light on this important subject of generations of students and their networks, but Celedonio Velásquez, cura of Capuluac (Edo. de México), described such a generation of Mexico City baccalaureate students in his 1757 relación de méritos y servicios. Velásquez had taught a group of 28 students who received their bachelor of philosophy de-

FIG. 2. A young Mexican seminarian, 1820's

grees in 1734. All graduated with honors, and most became ordained priests, he said. Four went on to obtain their doctorates. Seven of the 28 had become curas (two in Mexico City parishes); six had been professors in the Colegio Seminario or the University; and one was then the rector of the Colegio Seminario.[90] Perhaps more important than a society of former classmates was kinship. Brothers, uncles, cousins, and nephews who were in parish service sometimes gravitated to the same town or district.[91]

To be eligible for admission to one of the colegios or seminaries of Mexico City and Guadalajara, a boy had to be at least seven years old (most were at least eleven) and able to read and write.[92] In taking the oath of initiation, the new arrival embraced his fellow students as a token of the love he owed to his community of scholars.[93] In the colegios of Guadalajara at the end of the colonial period, students' religious duties included confession once a month, daily attendance at mass, periods of prayer twice a day, attendance at the cathedral on all feast days, and ten days of spiritual exercises during Lent.[94]

The normal course of study leading to a bachelor of arts or bachelor of philosophy degree was grammar, rhetoric, and philosophy. The grammar course consisted of reading, writing, and pronouncing Latin. It was often completed close to home under a tutor before the student entered a metropolitan colegio. Rhetoric combined Latin with Spanish, and included the study of syntax, translation in both directions of selected works of Cicero, Virgil, Horace, Ovid, and Julius Caesar, and the techniques of persuasion employed by these authors.[95] Depending on the student's age and aptitude, the grammar and rhetoric courses took about five years to complete. A three-year program in philosophy usually followed.[96] It consisted of studies in logic, metaphysics, physics, moral philosophy, arithmetic, geometry, and algebra.

Courses were generally taught in a dialectical manner: each class opened with the teacher's lesson—the dictation and explication of a text, followed by a "theoretical brief" or hypothesis on its meaning and application—and closed with a student debate in which one member of the class was chosen to defend the text or the professor's theoretical brief and the rest argued against him.[97] To earn the bachelor's degree after completing these studies, the student had to submit to an oral examination by three professors on questions of logic, metaphysics, physics, ethics, and philosophy. Until 1793, the examinations took place in, and the degrees were awarded by, the Universidad de México in Mexico City. Thereafter, candidates in the Diocese of Guadalajara could be examined and earn their degrees at the Universidad de Guadalajara.

To reach ordination as a *presbítero* who could celebrate mass, the seminary student had to go on to study theology. The program, generally completed in four years, was divided into two parts, dogmatic theology and moral theology. Moral theology, dealing with the application of dogmatic principles to everyday life, was regarded as the easier course. As "applied" theology, it was the primary concentration for future pastors who would not pursue advanced studies, known grandiloquently as a "carrera literaria." Dogmatic theology consisted mainly of a study of Saint Thomas Aquinas's *Summa Theologica* through commentaries and parts of the original work.[98] There might also be courses in canon law (especially conciliar decrees and church discipline), sacred scripture (direct study of sacred texts, especially the Old and New Testaments), church history, elocution ("elocuencia sagrada," the preaching techniques), and Indian languages. Students could enhance their reputations by founding informal "academies" outside the regular curriculum as a forum for discussing and debating theological issues. At the end of the course of study, leading students were given the opportunity to display their expertise in public lectures.

The reputation of scholarly distinction was reserved for seminary students who pursued advanced degrees in theology (a one-year course) or law (a two-year course) at a university or colegio mayor and did well in the public examinations. Students with these advanced degrees often began to give courses in the colegios, and some went on to complete a university licentiate in theology or canon law in about four years and a doctorate in another two to four years. In the process, they became veterans in the public display of their knowledge—in sermons, lectures, disputations, examinations of various kinds, and the publication of literary works.[99]

For aspiring diocesan priests in the archdiocese who were not enrolled in one of the *colegios mayores* or the university in Mexico City, there was the Real Colegio Seminario de Tepotzotlan, founded in 1777. There, for a minimum of six months, went men in the final stages of preparation for ordination and pastoral service. The seminary, its charter specified, was a place for "the instruction, inculcation, and perfection of the ecclesiastical state," a place of "prayer, purification, separation from worldly preoccupations, imitation of Christ, and practice of the other virtues."[100] It was a place to sharpen the pastor's instruments: to learn to compose sermons and to preach them effectively; to celebrate mass and administer sacraments correctly; to read the Divine Office devoutly; and to prepare to inspire others with one's own self-discipline and probity.

Thanks to the publishing of the school's *Constituciones* in 1777, we can track the daily life of its students from the moment they awakened. Enforced silence and periods for introspection punctuated days of formal study and communal living. Seminarians heard mass daily, confessed weekly, fasted on holy days, did ten days of special spiritual exercises annually, and carried out mortifications of the flesh and mind prescribed by their confessors in imitation of Christ. As was true for seminarians in other times and places, the mental discipline of "interior mortification" was meant to control the passions and all "useless," "vain," and "illicit" thoughts, and to promote the virtues of charity, humility, obedience, chastity, and patience. The inevitable question every evening was whether the seminarian's actions that day had been born of charity and directed to the glory of God.

The Tepotzotlan seminarians arose at five o'clock and assembled in the Novitiates' Chapel at five-thirty for half an hour of silent prayer.[101] At six, resident priests said mass and the others assisted or attended. After a light breakfast from six-thirty to seven, the seminarian returned to his room for three hours to read his office and study lessons assigned by the professors. The class in moral theology met from ten to eleven, followed by preparation for the afternoon lesson and fifteen minutes of silent prayer in the chapel. At noon, the community assembled in the refectory for the main meal. Members were seated by rank and class, but no distinctions were made in the food, utensils, or service. A lesson from the Old

Testament or a martyr's life was read during the meal. Students spent the afternoon in seclusion, reflecting on the spiritual lesson, praying, and studying. The class in ecclesiastical history met from five to six, followed by a rest period from six to seven. From seven to eight-thirty, students said the rosary in the chapel, heard a spiritual lesson or a talk on the obligations of the priesthood, and engaged in further secluded reflection or study. Supper brought a lesson from the New Testament. Before retiring at nine-thirty, students meditated on the next day and examined their consciences.

The Tepotzotlan seminary was staffed by a professor of moral theology, a professor of ecclesiastical history, a professor of Nahuatl, and a professor of Otomí. Moral theology was the centerpiece of the curriculum. Class meetings included the professor's explication of a paragraph from the approved catechism and a lesson from the *Suma* of Padre Ferrer. Every Saturday, a member of the class was chosen to argue against a proposition officially condemned by the church. Other seminarians would dispute his arguments and propose cases for the professor to explicate. On Thursday, the lesson would be from the *Rhetoric* of Fr. Luis de Granada, which was designed to educate the prospective priests in composing sermons. The principles were put into practice at mealtimes on Thursdays and on Sundays and other holy days, when seminarians were called on to sermonize on a detested vice or exhort the audience to virtue "so that they may begin to lose their stagefright and become accustomed to preaching." Toward the end of the term, they were expected to preach from the Gospels. The course in ecclesiastical history was taught from an approved text by Padre Graveson, supplemented by a short list of other works. The Thursday class consisted of a lesson on rites and ceremonies from a standard work by former Archbishop Galindo. Works by Bishop Palafox, among others, were recommended for the seminarians' spiritual exercises.

Students in the colegios, seminaries, and universities of Mexico and Guadalajara during the late eighteenth century would have been exposed to much the same intellectual ferment that John Tate Lanning describes for the University of San Carlos in Guatemala.[102] The study of philosophy in Spanish American universities had begun to bring scholasticism's traditional reliance on authority into tension with probabilism, which exalted reason over authority and eroded confidence in absolutes. Lanning describes the authors of the Guatemalan bachelor of philosophy theses as "thoroughgoing moderns," young men with a skeptical, experimental cast of mind who rejected the old formalism and systems in philosophy and theology.[103] But few of the future parish priests of Mexico and Guadalajara who attended school in the late eighteenth century would have been among Lanning's thoroughgoing moderns.[104] As Lanning notes, even at San Carlos, the theses sustained in theology, canon law, and metaphysics—where future priests predominated—were scholastic and tangential to the debate with reason. And judging by their coursework and professional histories, most of the future parish priests examined here were less exposed to the new European philosophies than men who did advanced studies in the universities and lay students who did not intend to become priests.[105] Most completed only a bachelor of arts or bachelor of philosophy degree and moved off quickly into moral theology and Indian languages before ordination.

Ordination and Licensing

Ordination and licensing to administer sacraments were separate from an upper-level academic program. They depended on a candidate's age and personal conduct, as well as his knowledge of doctrine and rite.[106] Under the canons of the Council of Trent, boys who could read and write, knew the rudiments of the faith, and had been confirmed were eligible for the first vows.[107] They could be promoted to minor orders upon the recommendation of their pastor and the master of their school, and proof that they understood Latin.[108] Normally, future priests would have begun the minor orders at age fourteen after completing the grammar course and demonstrating knowledge of Christian doctrine and the mysteries of the faith.[109] To be raised to any of the major orders of subdeacon, deacon, and presbyter (presbítero, priest), they had to submit to a lengthy investigation of their personal background and moral conduct by a deputy of the bishop at least one year after receiving the last of the minor orders.[110] Subdeacons and deacons were expected to go to their parish churches on feast days to help teach doctrine to the local children, and to attend all the religious festivities in their parish.[111] Subdeacons assisted in the mass, passing instruments of the sacrifice to the deacons. Deacons in New Spain, in addition to being more senior assistants in the mass, were often licensed to preach and were encouraged to practice during Sunday services wherever they could. The presbyter, or full priest, was permitted to say mass, but he could not hear confession, administer baptism and last rites, or perform marriages without a license. License to preach seems to have been automatic with ordination, but the license to confess and administer sacraments was more carefully controlled. A priest could be licensed in perpetuity to perform all of these functions, but many younger priests and some poorly educated vicarios received restricted licenses—often only temporary, for a year or two; sometimes limited to their home parish or to confessing only men or to administering the sacraments only in a particular Indian language.[112]

The Council of Trent stipulated minimum ages for the major orders: "the twenty-second year of his age" for subdeacons, the twenty-third for deacons, and the twenty-fifth for presbyters.[113] In fact, promotion within the major orders often proceeded faster than this, although not so fast as has sometimes been supposed. Usually the wait was six months to a year between subdeacon and deacon and another six months to a year between deacon and presbyter. The intervals could be longer (but rarely were) or shorter.[114] Older men seeking ordination often passed through the minor orders even more quickly.

Ordination to the priesthood generally would have occurred within a year or two after the candidate finished school, since most students completed their basic theology courses at twenty-three or twenty-four. The Trent decree did not specify whether the twenty-fifth year had to be completed or simply begun before one was eligible for ordination. According to the Fourth Provincial Council in 1771, the Third Council in 1585 had specified twenty-five years completed; likewise in 1771, Archbishop Lorenzana decried the practice of ordination in the twenty-fifth year and recommended a firm age of twenty-five.[115] Scattered evidence of age at ordination for the late colonial period suggests that in both dioceses many priests were ordained at twenty-four and some even earlier. In Guadalajara, in the 1757 concurso, half the priests had been ordained at twenty-four; in 1770, 40 percent; and from the 1770's to 1821, at least a third. A bishop could grant individual dispensations for early ordination, and there were occasional cases of twenty-two- and twenty-three-year-olds reaching the priesthood.[116] The mean age at ordination was twenty-five years and two months; but the median and the mode were both twenty-four.

Though most of the priests who would successfully compete for parochial benefices held at least a university bachelor's degree, it would be misleading to let the earlier description of formal studies in established schools stand for the average parish priest's education and intellectual life. Viceroy Revillagigedo (the elder) could speak warmly about the "many learned individuals among the clergy" of New Spain in the 1755 instruction to his successor,[117] but royal and ecclesiastical officials who worked with the parish clergy outside Mexico City knew better. In 1758, the Archbishop of Mexico defended the education of his curas but added that they lost most of their learning after a few years of parish service:

These same men undergo two examinations in order to become *curas*, one in matters of moral theology and the other in an Indian language. This happens every time they try for a new parish. But there is little civility in most parishes, because the local people are so unrefined. Accordingly, even if the priests are very capable at first examination, their competence declines considerably thereafter. I have verified this by testing the competence of the *curas* and *vicarios* during six long journeys on *visita*.[118]

Even late in the colonial period, curas with advanced degrees or other intellectual pretensions were unusual. As the subdelegado of Taxco reported for his district in 1793, only two of the eight curas had pursued advanced study or held a teaching post.[119] Even some curas whom the bishops commended as virtuous were called "unlettered" or "practically unlettered."[120]

It could be that those men had never earned a degree of any kind, for some parish priests were ordained during the first half of the eighteenth century without one. Carlos Buenaventura Ramires de Arellano, for example, was ordained in 1730 after studying grammar with one of his brothers, and arts and moral theology with a Jesuit in his hometown of Sultepec (Edo. de México). He spent 25 years as a vicario in some of the most difficult parishes in the archdiocese before being "rewarded" with the poor, hot-country parish of Tetela del Río (Guerrero).[121] Of those vicarios who never became curas, the best that could be said was that they had "the instruction necessary to administer the sacraments."[122] Most had some formal education or a bachelor's degree but had not distinguished themselves in their studies. Their resumés and the descriptions of their careers in lawsuits rarely contain more than vague references to accomplishments in school. One former vicario in the Diocese of Guadalajara, Mariano Calzada, was described in 1790 as a *bachiller*, but his perfunctory description of his studies mentioned only the following: grammar with the Franciscan Toribio Xaques in Zacatecas; philosophy with Fr. Joseph Naranjo in the Dominican colegio there; "one or another conclusion" in scholastic theology; and moral theology in Guadalajara with Vice Rector Joseph Francisco Gutiérrez.[123]

Many men of modest academic accomplishments entered the priesthood through the loophole of ordination *a título de idioma* ("by right of competence in an Indian language"). Traditionally, curas in Indian parishes were required to know the language of their parishioners; those who did not could be removed for incompetence or at least required to hire a coadjutor approved by the bishop for each Indian language spoken in their parish.[124] This was the law and usually the practice until 1770.[125] To promote a corps of vernacular pastors—priests skilled in the various Indian languages of Spanish America—the crown waived the Council of Trent's requirement that all candidates for ordination prove their financial independence. For impecunious youths who were fluent in an Indian language, ordination a título de idioma was a means to a livelihood as well as to ordination.

This channel dried up in Guadalajara in the late colonial period as communicants increasingly forsook their native languages and Nahuatl. Of 85 priests who were up for promotion in the diocese in 1757 and 1770, only eight reportedly knew Nahuatl, but it is not clear whether any of them had been ordained a título de idioma.[126] By contrast, over half of the 93 candidates for promotion in the archdiocese in the early 1760's included mastery of an Indian language among their accomplishments. Of the 54 who gave details on their ordination, only ten had been ordained *a título de capellanía* or *a título de suficiencia* (having demonstrated a chaplaincy endowment or sufficient personal wealth); all the others had been ordained a título de idioma. Some of these specialists in Indian languages, like Lucas Figueroa, the cura of Huehuetoca (Edo. de México), and Juan Francisco Caballero, were native speakers of Nahuatl. Most said they had taken this route to ordination because they were poor and did not have capellanías. Even though some had strong academic records—Manuel Cassela, cura of Atotonilco el Chico (Hidalgo) in 1762, for instance, had taken an advanced bachelor's degree in theology at the University of Mexico but lacking a capellanía, had gone to the district of Xichú (Guanajuato) to master the Otomí language and returned there as vicario after ordination[127]—cathedral priests and royal officials still saw the priest ordained by right of language as good at languages but otherwise ignorant and uninterested in learning. As the subdelegado of Malinalco (Edo. de México) said of the vicarios in his district, "since they are ordained *a título de idioma*, they devote little attention to their powers of study."[128]

Some priests on the fringes of the profession fitted this stereotype quite well. Francisco Antonio de Urueta, a creole from Ozumba (Edo. de México), was sent to study grammar in Mexico City at age twelve. At eighteen, he left the Colegio de Santiago for his hometown, apparently without a degree. Within a few months, he went to Tepotzotlan with the intention of studying moral theology and being ordained. Since he already knew Nahuatl, he received minor orders a título de idioma at nineteen. He lived in Ozumba, with periods of residence in Tepotzotlan, for the next five or six years, until he was ordained at age twenty-five in 1783. Over the following fourteen years, he served as a vicario in at least eight parishes, distinguishing himself mainly for his illicit relations with women of the parish.[129]

Since most Indian priests were ordained a título de idioma, this image of the fluent ignoramus stuck to them in particular. The subdelegado of Acapulco said in 1793 that the cura of Coyuca "seems to me to be of limited talent and no culture, considering that he is an Indian chief and gained the benefice *a título de lengua*."[130] In a letter of June 9, 1794, to the Inquisition about the Indian cura of

Ichcateopan (Guerrero), Dr. Athanasio Joseph de Urueña was even more blunt: "he is an Indian and for that reason I presume that, as regularly happens with Indians who are ordained, he must be excellent at languages and an extremely bad student." [131]

Archbishop Lorenzana discouraged ordination a título de idioma. In his first pastoral letter to the clergy, on October 5, 1766, he granted that knowledge of the Indian languages was important but warned that he would ordain only priests with independent means and proper learning because "we find that many of the clergymen ordained only *a título de idioma* go begging [for a living]." [132] On April 16, 1770, the crown weighed in with a royal cedula ordering that vacant parishes be filled with the most meritorious candidates, even if they did not know the native language of their parishioners. [133] The intent was to provide livings for more of the well-educated creole priests, give peninsular priests a better chance to compete for overseas benefices, and weed out curas "of low birth, worse customs, and less merit" who held parochial benefices because they knew Indian languages. According to this plan, the Indian-language priest would be treated as a specialized assistant: the new breed of cura was to maintain a vicario de idioma for the urgent sacramental needs of monolingual Indians.

The cedula of 1770 implicitly combined Archbishop Lorenzana's program with old plans, recently revived, to make Indians learn Spanish. In a paraphrase of Lorenzana's first pastoral letter, the Fourth Provincial Council called for limiting ordination by right of language to men "of such customs, independent means, and learning that they are assured of never lacking a station and means commensurate with their circumstances." [134] Later, the council spoke of the variety of Indian languages as a cause of disorder and misunderstandings of church doctrine. It urged the parish clergy to promote the Spanish language vigorously but also to keep vicarios who were certified in the native language of the parishioners. [135]

Calls for Spanish-language schools in Indian towns and against assigning parochial benefices to priests ordained a título de idioma were common in the last years of the colonial period, but priests continued to be ordained on the strength of their language skills and to serve in rural parishes. [136] And in remote and poor Indian parishes, they continued to win parochial benefices. An archiepiscopal visita to remote parishes of the Sierra Gorda area of Querétaro and Guanajuato in 1808–9 identified at least sixteen curas and vicarios who had been ordained as vernacular priests in 32 diocesan parishes and vicarías fijas. Of the other parishes, only six were administered by curas who definitely were not language priests. They were described as active promoters of Spanish-language schools. [137] In the richer and more desirable Indian parishes closer to Mexico City, the campaign against vernacular priests apparently had greater effect in the last three decades of the colonial period. Parish priests continued to be ordained *a título de idioma*, but few rose above vicario. As the subdelegado of Malinalco said of the coadjutor of Tenancingo in 1793 in a backhanded compliment, "even though he is ordained a título de idioma, he aspires to appointment in a parish of his own." [138]

* * *

The circumstances for entry into parish service were changing in the late colonial period. Secularization had removed nearly all of the remaining Mendicants from pastoral service in the Mexico and Guadalajara dioceses. The diocesan clergy was growing. More young men sought to become priests, and there were more places for them in the new provincial seminaries and universities, where the curriculum was leavened by various Enlightenment ideas and texts. Although the number of ordinations continued to outstrip the benefices available, there were more parishes and vicariatos de pie fijo to be filled, and more parishioners to serve. And the priesthood was more open to elite Indian and humble creole and mestizo aspirants. The institutional church, in its insistence on episcopal control, its reforms for more ecclesiastical discipline and better formal education of parish priests, and its de-emphasis on Indian language skills, was becoming more Tridentine than ever. All together, the late colonial church offered a more intellectual religion.

But much about the formation of parish priests remained the same. Despite individual differences, the parish clergy was not a microcosm of colonial society. By no means all parish priests came from privileged families, but very few were sons of the peasants and wage laborers who made up the large majority of the population. As before, parish priests tended to be creoles—few Indians were ordained, few peninsular diocesan priests served in rural parishes, and few American-born priests identified themselves as mestizos or other castas. And they tended to be urban by birth or at least by training. Fluency in Indian languages remained an indispensable skill in many parishes of the archdiocese. Parish priests were educated to the idea that the spiritual life was preferable to mundane affairs, and that their highest purpose was the search for purification and perfection. Yet they were always administrators, as well as men of God. The learning and experience that could hold these two roles in creative tension amounted to moral theology—the ethical application of basic theological principles to the lives of believers, both as individuals and as a society. It was concerned with proper conduct in imitation of Christ, with nurturing virtues and combating vices. Those virtues reached beyond obeying specific rules of conduct to the idea of charity: good works inspired by divine love.[139] When these were voluntary acts, they moved believers toward God and salvation.

The Careers of Parish Priests

> The quiet, devout and conscientious parson, doing his
> duty day by day among his people, is the last man who
> attains notoriety.   —Augustus Jessopp

> Was there a pastor worth his salt who didn't have improve-
> ments in mind, contractors and costs on the brain?
>   —Father Fabre in "A Losing Game" by J. F. Powers

The organization of the diocesan clergy in colonial Mexico roughly divided
men according to "merit": a partly inherited, partly acquired quality combining family background, independent means, education, academic and literary
honors, positions of responsibility held by appointment of the bishop and carried
out with distinction, good works befitting the vocation, seniority, and reputation
for personal as well as professional virtue. The meaning of merit could vary with
time and those who judged it. This was not a straightforward ladder system in
which everyone entered on the bottom rung, with the most deserving climbing
faster than others; personal contacts and family connections inevitably came into
play. Some curas did not enter at the bottom, others never advanced, and still
others moved to the top without occupying intermediate positions. Furthermore,
the hierarchy narrowed sharply near the top, so that not all who were meritorious
in the obvious ways could expect to be rewarded with a promotion.

Advancement was measured in income, administrative responsibilities, and
choice locations; assignment to a first-class parish meant the luxury of time for
study, charitable works, and activities beyond the parish. For a few prominent
curas, a cathedral chapter appointment was within reach. Even a minor episcopate was not out of the question. The striving to improve one's position gave the
professional lives of many parish priests a dynamic, restless quality, especially
during the first 20 years or so after ordination. As one young cura with a doctor
of theology degree said, he had entered the priesthood "desirous of rising in the
profession."[1] This chapter on career patterns attempts to identify which were
the better positions, who moved where and why, how long curas and vicarios
stayed in their parishes, and which parishes had many priests moving through. It

also begins to discuss the tensions and harmonies between spiritual vocation and professional advancement.

The Mechanisms of Mobility

The careers of eighteenth-century curas were decided largely in the oposiciones, or competitions for vacant parochial benefices.[2] Organized in *concursos*, or assemblies, these competitions were held every year or two, generally after four or more vacancies had accumulated in a diocese.[3] Vacancies arose on the death, resignation, removal, or promotion of a cura or on the creation of a new parish. Resignations and removals were exceedingly rare.[4] Deaths accounted for most of the openings; but also, over 100 new parishes were created in the Archdiocese of Mexico and the Diocese of Guadalajara in the eighteenth century. The secularization of parishes after 1749 triggered more turnover in personnel as individual curas and vicarios came and went. Some of the former Mendicant doctrinas that had preserved their ample sixteenth-century boundaries were divided into smaller parishes (especially where the population had grown), a process that placed more diocesan curas in the countryside and divided loyalties between old and new head towns (cabeceras).[5]

The competitions usually offered relatively few opportunities for vicarios to break into the group of benefice holders, but even a few openings could touch off a burst of transfers among the curas. In the 1806 concurso for the Diocese of Guadalajara, at least 28 of the 38 appointments were to curas moving into positions vacated by men who had themselves taken up a vacated parish.[6] In general, curas who had no stain on their reputations had the edge over vicarios because they had a record of parochial administration and because they were vacating a post that could be assigned to someone else.

The concursos were advertised far enough ahead of the examinations for candidates to submit the requisite resumé or certified account of their qualifications.[7] By a papal decree issued in 1742, written as well as oral examinations were required. For the written examination, all the candidates assembled in a guarded room in the cathedral city on the advertised day. They could not leave the room until the examination period was over, and the papers were turned in. All the competitors wrote on the same questions, the same cases, and the same text for a sermon, which were dictated to them as a group at the beginning of the day.[8] The oral examination was administered individually by a panel selected by the bishop. Apart from probing the concursant's knowledge, the examiners were charged with judging whether he had the prudence, moral rectitude, seriousness, and dedication required of a pastor.

The examiners proposed to the bishop a list of candidates judged fit for appointment and identified those who had received votes for first, second, and third place.[9] For each vacancy, the bishop presented three candidates in order of preference to the vice-patron, who made the appointment in the name of the king.[10] For Mexico, the vice-patron was the viceroy; for Guadalajara, it was the president of the Audiencia of Nueva Galicia. In principle, the vice-patron could choose any of the three nominees or call for the bishop to submit additional names.[11] In fact, the bishop's first candidate was almost always chosen.[12] As Viceroy Revilla-gigedo (the elder) advised his successor in 1755, though the vice-patron was free to choose, prudence recommended the first name on the list "because experience indicates that doing otherwise stirs up resentments by the prelates, public gossip, and other troubles that can disturb the peace and harmony that are so necessary in the weighty enterprise of secular and ecclesiastical affairs."[13]

Promotion was not always the issue in a change of parishes. Two curas might exchange places in what was called the *permuta*, a process that was more common in Mexico than in Guadalajara. Proposed exchanges usually were initiated by the curas themselves and required approval by the bishop and the viceroy.[14] Approval depended on an investigation to establish that both curas had good reasons to move, that the parishes were of roughly equal value, and that the crown's interests were not adversely affected. Health was the usual reason for requesting an exchange, though other common grounds were that both were having serious trouble with parishioners in their current parishes, or that both knew only the native language of the other's parishioners.[15]

A typical case was that of the curas José de Ignacio Vásquez of Ayotzingo (Edo. de México) and José Mariano Laso de la Vega of Cempoala (Hidalgo), who requested permission to exchange parishes in 1796.[16] Both submitted two certified medical opinions that the change would improve their health and ability to carry out the pastoral duties. Vásquez's doctors testified that his stomach ailments were aggravated by Ayotzingo's humidity and its location next to a lagoon. Laso de la Vega's medical experts noted his rheumatism, inflamed lungs, headaches, and apoplexy, and concluded that his health would improve if he could move from the cold and wind of Cempoala to a more temperate climate. Laso de la Vega added that his 23 years of faithful service in some of the most difficult parishes had broken his health and made his request especially deserving of consideration. Witnesses were called to satisfy the authorities that both men were dependable pastors who had no ulterior motives for seeking the exchange. The archbishop recommended the permuta on April 27, 1796, and the viceroy approved it two weeks later. These were not pro forma proceedings, but the viceroys seem to have approved such lateral moves routinely—partly because both curas had to pay the *mesada* tax on their new positions (8.33 percent of the value of the benefice).

Royal and ecclesiastical laws preferred the most "worthy," "virtuous," and "well-prepared" priests, those "outstanding in their life and example," for parish vacancies.[17] But these ideals could be blunted by the application of other laws and expediencies. Curas involved in local disputes might be reassigned to a new parish in the next concurso, whether or not they were particularly "worthy."[18] Other things being equal, creole Spaniards whose direct ancestors had served the crown (especially in the Conquest) were to be preferred, according to the *Recopilación*.[19] The provision that appointments in Indian parishes were to go to priests who knew the native language was also much flouted from the mid-eighteenth century on, with candidates "best qualified" in learning and virtue excused from knowing the Indian language of their parishioners.[20] In practice, appointments to parochial benefices probably had as much to do with personal contacts as with formal qualifications. Royal law forbade prelates from awarding parishes to relatives or dependents of prominent royal officials who interceded on their behalf, but prominent officials continued to receive such appeals for help in securing posts.[21] How often the bishops obliged, the written record does not disclose. Firmer evidence of favoritism is provided by charges that royal officials extorted payments from priests who were awarded benefices. One chief judge of the Audiencia of Mexico, Eusebio Sánchez Pareja, was accused in 1783 of demanding 500 pesos in gratuities from curas appointed in the latest oposiciones.[22]

Despite the warnings of the Fourth Provincial Council,[23] a more common and acceptable kind of personal influence was that exercised by the bishops on behalf of their own advisers and relatives. The effect was to move a few peninsular priests and a few creoles from other dioceses into some of the better parishes.[24] Juan Gómez de Parada (bishop of Guadalajara, 1736–51) appointed one member of his household as cura of the choice parish of Santa María de Lagos. Two other priests who accompanied Gómez de Parada to Guadalajara were appointed curas of Sayula and Zapotlan el Grande by his successor, Fr. Francisco de San Buenaventura Martínez de Tejada (1752–60). Martínez de Tejada also chose a member of his entourage as cura of Teocaltiche.[25] Bishop Cabañas (1796–1824) eventually made his personal chaplain the sacristán mayor of Zacatecas and cura of Nochistlan, and his secretary was awarded the Our Lady of Guadalupe parish in Guadalajara.[26] Archbishop Vizarrón (1731–47) left behind at least two of his attendants as curas: Dr. Juan Joseph de Henestrosa in Tenango del Valle and Br. Luis Román González Fuentes in San Andrés Xumiltepec.[27]

With these exceptions and an occasional peninsular Spaniard, parish priests in the Diocese of Guadalajara were Americans, and many gravitated to one part of the diocese for much of their careers.[28] The same pattern of locally born and locally trained curas holds for the archdiocese, although several priests from Puebla took advanced degrees from the university in Mexico City and subsequently received parishes there.

Thanks to the bishop's power of nomination and the virtual assurance that his first choice would be appointed, curas and aspirants were tied to him personally as much as they were institutionally.[29] But direct ties were difficult to maintain once curas were in the field, complicated by distance, regulations that restricted their travel, and the intercession of members of the cathedral chapter and the community on behalf of particular favorites. The personal connection between prelate and parish priest was usually intermittent. The bishop's territory encompassed hundreds of churches and priests and hundreds of thousands of laymen scattered over thousands of square miles. Rarely was his contact with curas renewed in two-way correspondence unless they were in trouble; and the pastoral visit (tour of inspection expected of a bishop) usually meant only one face-to-face meeting outside the cathedral city, if that. The main opportunity to establish and renew contact was during the concursos.

By rights, the prelates' long stays in office ought to have worked to seal this personal bond. For nearly all bishops in both dioceses during the eighteenth century, Mexico or Guadalajara was their final destination. In Mexico, all but one archbishop died in office. Only Lorenzana was able to use the archiepiscopacy as a stepping-stone to higher office. He served in Mexico from 1766 to 1772, then returned to Spain as archbishop of Toledo. The six archbishops between 1700

and 1811 averaged about sixteen years in office (thirteen of the 112 years were interim periods when the cathedral chapter served in the prelate's place, "en sede
vacante"). The pattern for Guadalajara was similar, with nine bishops serving
from 1696 to 1824 for an average of something over twelve years each (with fourteen years en sede vacante). All died in office there.

The longevity of most of these prelates helped to defuse charges of careerism
that might have weakened their personal influence and deepened the gulf between them and the less privileged parish clergy.[30] Nevertheless, the gulf must
have been wide. Most bishops at this time came directly from Spain, with no
previous experience in America. Surrounded by their court of followers and preoccupied with the affairs of the cathedral and church-state relations, they tended
to be well acquainted only with curas already in key posts, those who arrived in
their entourage or served in the cathedral city, and those with expectations of
promotion into the cathedral chapter or a first-class parish. Some long-lived bishops like Cabañas in Guadalajara followed parish activities quite closely, made
detailed inspections and required specific changes when they visited parishes,
and, at the behest of the crown, occasionally solicited reports from the curas.
Most, however, took part in parish affairs mainly through the formulation of general policies and the exercise of their judicial powers.

The Merits of Curas

The resumés of candidates for promotion reflect their own understanding of
"merit": what made them worthy of their vocation and of promotion. The credentials of the successful candidates are, of course, even more revealing. That
the aspirant was the legitimate son of illustrious creole Spanish parents and descended from long, legitimate lines of Old Christians was virtually a formula
in the resumés. Men who could be more specific were. It was especially desirable—legally as well as in practice—to be descended from the original sixteenth-
century conquerors or a distinguished viceroy, or to have an archbishop among
one's collateral ancestors.[31]

Still, on paper, academic achievement counted most. Not all the curas holding
the best parishes in the late eighteenth century were doctors and licenciados, but
nearly all had gone beyond the bachelor of arts or philosophy degree and basic
training in moral theology. Curas and other competitors who had held scholar-
ships, won prizes in public examinations, written a history or treatise, or taught a
few courses in the university were certain to describe these feats at length, sometimes barely mentioning parish service and other standard accomplishments.
Judging by who was promoted, the fast track into the best parishes and beyond
was for the most learned. This was increasingly the case by the 1760's and early
1770's, when the Fourth Provincial Council's interest in promoting Spanish in
Indian pueblos coincided with Archbishop Lorenzana's de-emphasis on ordination a título de idioma and his preference for scholars.[32] When the cura of the
choice Sierra de Pinos parish in Guadalajara was asked in 1796 to describe the
twelve assistants and nine other priests residing there, it seemed natural to him
to classify them by their education.[33] In 1762, when Juan Ignacio Bustamante

prepared his resumé for the next oposiciones, he elaborated on his academic distinctions—his early training, advanced study in law, awards in academic contests, and teaching posts. He had been the cura of Tezontepec (Hidalgo) for eight years but excused himself from describing "the progress" he had achieved there "so as not to tire the attention of my superiors."[34]

If the aspiring diocesan cura was not much of a scholar, it was important to find something else to boast about. One sure way to make his presence felt was to build and rebuild churches in the parish and furnish them with costly ornaments. By law, the cura and other local notables were expected to contribute what they could to the construction, reconstruction, and outfitting of the parish church,[35] and the crown expected any repairs to be covered by the 8.33 percent of the tithe designated for *fábrica* (construction). But the bishops traditionally had reserved this fund for maintaining the cathedral building, not for parish churches.[36] Late colonial builder-priests therefore won considerable favor with bishops and dignitaries of the cathedral. Every cura who could do so, consequently, presented himself as a builder, listing among his accomplishments new churches and chapels, major repairs of existing churches, new altars, confessionals, pulpits, images of saints (especially of new saints and advocations of Mary to which the priest was particularly devoted), vestments, silver chalices and monstrances, and other religious ornaments.

One such cura was Br. Pedro de Ubiarco of the Diocese of Guadalajara. In his 1808 resumé, Ubiarco began by declaring himself the legitimate son of colonial Spanish parents, born in Guadalajara.[37] He said nothing about his education, stating only that he had been ordained in March 1785. In the next breath, he mentioned his first appointment as assistant in the parish of Tlaltenango (Zacatecas), and described his building and maintenance projects there: adding a bell tower, whitewashing the interior of the church, repairing the floor, and acquiring apparel for the religious images. After four years and five months, he was sent by the bishop to the *sagrario* (the cathedral parish) in Guadalajara. Ten months later, he was named coadjutor with full responsibilities for the parish, at the modest salary of 20 pesos a month (by comparison, an agricultural laborer earned about 50 pesos a year, plus a weekly ration of maize). Here he sponsored a "beautiful and splendid throne of flowers" that was refreshed every Thursday for the renovation of the Holy Sacrament, various ornaments for the mass, and a baptismal font, all at his own expense. When the cura died two years later, Father Ubiarco stayed on briefly as interim cura and served for another year and a half as an assistant. He continued his special devotion to the Blessed Sacrament, collecting 200 pesos for the repair of the carriage in which the Host was transported to the sick and dying.

In 1793, he was chosen to replace the deceased cura of Xalostotitlan but was unable to assume the post. Instead, he accepted the parochial benefice of Tizapan el Alto. Again he described his services there principally in terms of ornaments added, altars constructed, repairs made to the sacristy and presbytery, new bells, and the exclusive use of wax candles from Spain, adding that he preached and taught doctrina on Sundays and worked to control public disorder. In 1795, he was awarded another poor parish, Iscuintla (Nayarit), where he was placed in 1797. Despite the heat, poverty, and dangers of the assignment, he persevered— teaching doctrina, adding religious celebrations, repairing the ruined church, and paying half his emoluments to an assistant. In the oposiciones of 1800, he was promoted to the new parish of Tototlan. On a renta of 1,300 pesos, he hired two vicarios, repaired the parish church inside and out, dressed the images, and added various ornaments. He was still in Tototlan at the time he composed his resumé for the competition to fill the cathedral vacancies in 1808. He added that he had a clean record of service, personal conduct, and cooperation with royal officials.

Judging by their resumés, some parish priests regarded these building projects as their only works of charity worth mentioning. A few also said that they regularly gave what they had to the poorest of their parishioners and had sponsored hospital beds, wells, roads, and the distribution of medicines and grain during epidemics and famines. The public work most frequently mentioned was the founding of local schools to teach basic literacy and church doctrine: evidence that the priest was both fulfilling his teaching role and serving the crown's campaign to teach the Indians Spanish and literacy. The cura was quick to mention when he could that he paid the schoolmaster's salary where the townspeople refused or were unable to do so.[38]

Another form of merit was the sponsorship of cofradías—sodalities or lay brotherhoods and sisterhoods established to promote a particular devotion, such as an advocation of Mary (especially Our Lady of the Rosary, Our Lady of Sorrows, and Our Lady of the Immaculate Conception), the sacrifice of Christ, or souls in Purgatory, or to meet certain regular expenses of the parish. Ideally, a cofradía had income-producing properties to underwrite its expenses. During the late eighteenth century, the curas of Guadalajara were more likely than those of Mexico to list in their resumés the founding, funding, or financial management of cofradías. Sponsorship of cofradías does appear in some of the aspirants' resumés from the early 1760's for the archdiocese, but curas there were more likely to promote schools, or at least to advertise such promotion in their service records.[39]

Priests with pastoral experience but few academic distinctions usually emphasized their dedication to pastoral affairs. Some said they had served the most difficult parishes for years in great want and without a stipend; had risked their lives many times to give spiritual aid to the dying in epidemics and to reach those in need late at night, traveling to the far corners of the parish over treacherous mountain paths and across fast-moving rivers; had succeeded in reducing drunkenness, adultery, and "idolatrous and superstitious practices" ("correcting vices and protecting against public sins" was how parish priests often summarized these activities); had introduced new devotions; and were active teachers of doctrine, diligent preachers, or "forever in the confessional." They could not very well celebrate their own exemplary judgment and personal conduct without seeming vain, but some could and did report that no formal complaint had ever been lodged against them. Parish priests who were well known for outstanding records of service, personal virtue, and charity but had limited education and no powerful patron might nevertheless be rewarded with promotions to more comfortable parishes; their chances depended on the bishop's ability to judge outstanding service. In the archdiocese, the prelates of the 1750's and 1790's to 1810 appear to have rewarded outstanding service more often than those of intervening years. Of the Guadalajara bishops, Antonio Alcalde (1771–92) and Cabañas are best known for attending to the parish priests' piety and personal virtue in their evaluations.

Personal Impediments to Promotion

A priest's career was shaped mainly by his merits—education, relationships to influential leaders, social background, and the excellence of his conduct in office—but it could also be stunted, though rarely stopped cold, by the circumstances of his birth or his personal indiscretions. Occasionally, an ambitious cura who was widely regarded as capable, learned, and virtuous was informally barred from higher office by illegitimate birth or Jewish ancestry. One or the other was apparently the case with Dr. Juan Basilio Ramos Ximénez, cura of Bolaños (Jalisco) in 1755, who had "not achieved acceptance because of a presumed infection at the root of his lineage, which, if it has not disqualified him, at least has impeded and complicated the course of his pretensions."[40]

Misconduct in office was a more ambiguous impediment to advancement. If it is correct to say that parish priests with only a bachelor of arts or philosophy degree, no independent means, and few contacts in high places needed to excel in piety and service to advance, then legal proceedings against them made promotions less likely. But the bishops' courts did not assume that priests charged with crimes were guilty, nor did the bishops necessarily withhold minor promotions even from those who had been found guilty of immoral conduct, failure to administer their parishes properly, or doctrinal misconceptions. José Angulo Bustamante, cura of Huazalingo (Hidalgo) in 1789, was the object of more than 30 charges of extortion, cruelty, and sexual offenses but was cleared on the grounds that he was an apparent victim of revenge.[41] Two years later, he moved to the more important parish of Temascaltepec (Edo. de México), where he soon faced new complaints that he charged excessive fees, mistreated his Indian parishioners, and was insubordinate to the subdelegado.[42] Mariano Muñiz, vicario de pie fijo of Tepetlixpa (Edo. de México), was charged in 1789 with various "excesos." A priest commissioned to investigate determined that some of the charges were true, especially his weakness for parties and dancing, but concluded that Muñiz was repentant and active in his professional duties, and that the charges had been brought by someone who was highly partial. Muñiz was let off with a warning to be more moderate, judicious, and modest in his conduct.[43]

The ecclesiastical courts were remarkably lenient in sentencing first offenders or those who could claim extenuating circumstances. A simple, repentant vicario who admitted to having baptized a silver peso with the name Gregorio in the hope that his money would multiply on demand was released from the ecclesiastical prison in 1726 with a stern warning against future sacrilege.[44] In 1725, a creole Spanish woman from Sultepec brought suit against the cura, Juan Antonio Xil de Andrade, for having her mulata slave severely beaten. Witnesses testified to the cura's cruelty to Indians and other parishioners, and Andrade did not persuasively contest the charge, but the *provisor* (chief judge) recommended only that he be reprimanded and ordered to treat all of his parishioners with paternal love.[45] In 1781, Miguel Amador, a vicario of Mascota in the Diocese of Guadalajara, was denounced for repeatedly soliciting a respectable nineteen-year-old woman in the confessional. The local comisario of the Inquisition confirmed the charges, but the *promotor fiscal* recommended that the case be suspended if it could not be shown that Amador had solicited any other women.[46]

Apparently for the same reason—that only one woman had been involved— Francisco Marroquín escaped severe punishment in 1780 for his repeated and blatant violation of the vow of celibacy. He had seduced doña María Trinidad de Vega in Mexico City nine years before and had taken her with him as a servant to his new post in Tulancingo, where she gave birth three times before returning to Mexico City. Marroquín reportedly continued to pester her in the capital after he moved to the parish of Singuilucan (Hidalgo), and was furious when she preferred a quiet life with her mother and sister to his persistent advances. The promotor of the archbishop's court ordered Marroquín to leave doña María alone, pay court costs, and spend six months in confinement and spiritual exercises at the Colegio de Tepotzotlan.[47]

In each case, the offender received a solemn warning that future transgressions would be dealt with much more severely. In fact, repeat offenders did receive harsher sentences. Their actions not only violated church law and endangered their parishioners' salvation but also flouted specific orders from their superiors. One example is the Augustinian Francisco Cayetano Téllez, coadjutor of Tlaola in the parish of Huauchinango (Veracruz). He was first charged with solicitation in the confessional in 1736. The case was reopened in 1746 with a new complaint that quickly multiplied. It came out in the testimony of various women he had propositioned and seduced, and finally in his own confession, that he had committed this sacrilege at least fourteen times in the various communities he had served. His sentence brought not only a severe reprimand, but permanent loss of his licenses to confess both men and women, exile for six years from Mexico City, Madrid, and all the communities in which his crimes had been committed, three years of service in the convent at Chalma, confession every 30 to 40 days (he was forbidden to celebrate mass unless he confessed on schedule), and deprivation of rights to participate in church government for eight years.[48]

In spite of the harsher sentences for repeat offenders, it is a comment on the leniency of the church toward wayward priests that eighteenth-century pastors were rarely defrocked except in cases of murder and were seldom permanently stripped of their benefices.

The Mobility of Curas

A new cura's career began with an act of possession: as he knelt before the bishop, a clerical cap was placed on his head as an emblem of his benefice, and he took an oath of office with his hand placed on the missal.[49] Most curas went through this ceremony four or five times during their careers.[50] Despite growing numbers of parishes and parishioners, two external forces worked to restrict the mobility of parish priests. One was formal regulation. In 1771, the Fourth Provincial Council attempted to prohibit curas who had not served at least three years in their benefice from competing in oposiciones.[51] Though the council's decrees did not become law, the proposal may well have reflected the bishops' practice at the time. A second, more important restriction on curas' mobility was the superabundance of qualified priests.[52] In 1753, the ecclesiastical governor of Guadalajara reported that, for lack of capellanías, more priests were ordained to pastoral service than there were livings available.[53] A warning from the crown, in its directive to the Fourth Provincial Council, about "an excessive abundance of priests" in New Spain seemingly had little effect when we recall the comment in the 1796 parish reports on resident priests for Guadalajara that many were qualified but *sin destino* (without a position).[54]

Some parishes had higher turnover rates than others. To trace precisely the pattern of turnover, one would have to study the books of baptisms, marriages, or burials the curas kept and signed. A fair idea of which parishes changed hands most often, however, can be gleaned from the curas' and vicarios' resumés, and the records of the *mesada eclesiástica* (the tax imposed when a parish benefice changed hands). Table 1 shows the parishes with the highest rates of turnover in the late colonial period. There are good reasons why curas might have been quick to vacate 38 of these parishes (italicized in the table). A few of the least desirable parishes are not captured in the mesada records and resumés consulted: Alahuistlan, Escanela, Huejuta, and Xaltocan in the archdiocese; Zapotiltic in Guadalajara. They were the hardship posts of the diocese, mostly classified as third-class, with some combination of foul climate, meager income, dispersed settlements, uncooperative or ignorant parishioners, bad roads, and great distance from Guadalajara or Mexico City—no place, certainly, for those on the fast track. Unless a cura was attracted to one of these parishes out of a sense of calling or because it was his hometown, he was likely to leave as soon as he could.

It is easy to detect a clear relationship between income and turnover in the Guadalajara cases. In twelve of the parishes with two or more changes in the mesada records, the cura earned less than 1,000 pesos. The outstanding exceptions are Santa María de Lagos and Zacatecas. Both were among the most lucrative and prestigious parishes in the diocese, with reported annual incomes of 3,228 pesos and 6,588 pesos, respectively. Other things being equal, priests who occupied either of these two benefices were prime candidates for appointment to the cathedral chapter. But they might also decide to settle in: one cura stayed thirteen years in Lagos; another stayed 28 years in Zacatecas. Similarly, except for Ameca and probably the Nuestra Señora de Guadalupe parish in Guadalajara, the parishes with a high rate of turnover yielded incomes of less than 1,100 pesos. Ameca was one of the most desirable parishes near Guadalajara and may have served as a stepping-stone to the cathedral chapter or a choice urban parish. The Guadalupe parish in Guadalajara also was a desirable position that could lead to promotion into the cathedral chapter.[55]

Map 4 locates the fifteen parishes in the Diocese of Guadalajara with high turnover and low incomes. Some are scattered through the central and southern sections, but there is a cluster in the west, within the modern state of Nayarit. Six of the parishes are located there: Guaynamota, Iscuintla, Real de San Sebastián, Senticpac, Tepic, and Valle de Banderas. Priests competing in the 1770 oposiciones wore their service in this area like Purple Hearts. Felipe de Liñán, a native of Tepic and its current cura, spoke feelingly of his service in Iscuintla

TABLE I

Mexico and Guadalajara Parishes with Highest Turnover
According to Mesada Tax Records and/or Curas' Resumés, Late Colonial Period

Parish	Years of service	Cura's income (pesos) 1774, Guadalajara; 1771–76, Mexico	Other year
Changes from mesada records			
Guadalajara (2 or more changes)			
Chapala	—, —	750	
Guaynamota[a]	—, 4, —[b]	262	
Huejuquilla	—, 3	583	
Magdalena	—, —	750	
Montegrande	3+, —	497	
Real de San Sebastián[a]	—, —, 9	954	
Salatitan	—, —[c]		224, 1790
Senticpac	7, 3	611	
Tepic	—, —	1,089	
Valle de Banderas	—, —, —	301	
Villa de Lagos	13, —	6,588	
Xalpa[a]	5, —, —	1,004	
Zacatecas	28	3,228	
Zapotitlan	—, —	750	
Mexico (2 or more changes)[d]			
Acatlan			700, 1775[e]
Amatepec y Tlatlaya		750	1,500, 1775[d]
Atotonilco el Chico[a]	4, 4+	200	1,000, 1775;[e] 950, 1793; 3,453, 1805
Huexotla			1,000, 1775[e]
Huizquilucan			2,000, 1775[e]
Jonacatepec			3,000, 1775[e]
Naucalpan		500	
Temascalcingo		1,750	800, 1775[e]
Temascaltepec		1,250	
Teotihuacan		600	1,980, 1775[e]
Tepehuacan			1,500, 1775[e]
Tetela del Volcán		500	
Xalpan			
Xichú		500	
Yahualica		400	1,300, 1775[e]
Changes from curas' resumés			
Guadalajara (3 or more changes)			
Ameca	—, —, 16		1,778, 1790
Guadalajara[f]	—, —, —		
Iscuintla	—, 3, 7, —, —	681	232, 1772; 311, 1790
Mecatabasco	6, —, 7	1,092	704, 1790
Zapotlanejo	—, —	917	
Mexico (2 or more changes)			
Chilpancingo	—, 7		
Coyuca	1+, 4	500	600, 1775[e]
Epasoyucan	—, —, 5+		500, 1775; 800, 1793; 1,355, 1805
Huehuetoca	—, —		620, 1775;[e] 600, 1793; 1,209, 1805
Lerma	—, 9	1,750	
Pánuco	6+, —	250	
Tarasquillo			2,100, 1793; 2,264, 1805
Tolcayucan	9, 2+		600, 1775;[e] 550, 1793, 1805

SOURCES: *Guadalajara.* Mesada records, 1763–64, 1769, 1772, 1774, in AGI Mex. 2726–27; length of service, changes of curas and income drawn from resumés in 1757, 1770, and 1770's–1821, and scattered financial records in

TABLE I
(*Continued*)

CAAG, unclassified. *Mexico.* Mesada records, 1771–72, 1782–83, in AGI Mex. 2726–27; length of service and changes of curas, early 1760's resumés, in JCB; income, 1771–76 in AGI Mex. 2726–27, 1775 in BN AF 107 exp. 1475, fol. 53, 1793 in Texas, García Coll., no. 261, and 1805 in Florescano & Gil, *Descripciones económicas generales.*

 N O T E : Unspecified lengths of service were generally less than 5 years. Italicized parishes were regarded as the hardship posts of the diocese.
 [a]Also at least two recorded changes of curas, 1757–1821.
 [b]Length of service "declined."
 [c]Second of the curas resigned.
 [d]All Mexico parishes ranked as 3d class in 1775 except Jonacatepec, 1st, and Huizquilucan, Lerma, Temascaltepec, and Teotihuacan, 2d (BN AF 107 exp. 1475, fol. 53).
 [e]1775 figures represent "value of the parish" and may be gross receipts rather than income, since they exceed the 1771–76 figure in four of the six cases where both figures are available.
 [f]Nuestra Señora de Guadalupe parish.

and Senticpac, where he had suffered "more and greater plagues than those of Egypt," and had served as a "faithful watchdog" defending the church against the proverbial packs of wolves. Antonio Manuel Velásquez, who had also served in Iscuintla, described the swarms of insects and other afflictions of the flesh, and "the barbarous and crude people given to all sorts of vices." For José Ramón de Herrera, his parish of Guaynamota was synonymous with suffocating heat, running sores, and intractable Indians.[56] From a cura's point of view, service in the tropics of Nayarit was no better in 1810, when Pedro de Ubiarco composed his resumé. Three of his years as a cura had been spent in Iscuintla, and he remembered vividly its "extremely hot climate, the abundance of poisonous animals, and the scarcity of healthy provisions."[57] The parish was divided by the Río de Santiago, very dangerous to cross because of its fast current during the rainy season and the alligators that lurked in its waters. Claiming that he was still suffering from the effects of those years, Ubiarco felt that his hardships had earned him a spot in some American cathedral chapter. The parish of Valle de Banderas (which included what is now the popular beach resort area of Bahía de Banderas), with its small income, isolated location, and suffocating climate, was like a revolving door. The bishop of Guadalajara wrote in 1770 that it was difficult to find suitable candidates for this benefice "because of the bad climate and rough roads";[58] and indeed, the parish was often staffed by young substitutes.

 The Archdiocese of Mexico provides a somewhat more complicated picture. The fit between turnover and small incomes is not as close. Less overlap between the mesada records and resumés probably results from having only one set of resumés to draw from (compared with two sets, as well as miscellaneous resumés, for Guadalajara); sketchy data in both sources; and the fact that the archdiocese had over twice as many parishes in the mid-eighteenth century. But the looser fit also suggests that high turnover was less clearly a function of the parish's poverty and undesirability. Table I nevertheless does identify a number of parishes where high turnover coincided with small incomes: Acatlan, Amatepec, Atotonilco el Chico, Coyuca, Epasoyucan, Huehuetoca, Huexotla, Naucalpan, Pánuco, Teotihuacan, Tetela del Volcán, Tolcayucan, Xichú, and Yahualica. Tolcayucan, Huehuetoca, Xaltocan, and Epasoyucan also saw vicarios come and go every year or two during the late eighteenth century.

 The best fit of all in this case is with the third-class parishes found in two lists,

Most desirable parishes

1. Agua de Venado (Venado y La Hedionda)
2. Aguascalientes
3. Ameca, Autlan
4. Fresnillo
5. Jalostotitlan (Villa de Lagos)
6. Nochistlan, Juchipila
7. Ojocaliente, Charcas
8. Real de Asientos, Aguascalientes
9. S. Juan de los Lagos, Villa de Lagos
10. Sta. María de los Lagos (villa), Villa de Lagos
11. Sayula
12. Sierra de Pinos
13. Teocaltiche, Villa de Lagos
14. Tepatitlan
15. Tlaltenango
16. Xerez
17. Zacatecas
18. Zacoalco, Sayula
19. Zapopan
20. Zapotlan el Grande, Tuspa

Least desirable parishes

21. Chapala, Sayula
22. Guaynamota, Nayarit
23. Huejuquilla, Colotlan
24. Iscuintla, Senticpac
25. La Magdalena, Autlan
26. Mecatabasco, Juchipila
27. Montegrande, Aguascalientes
28. Real de San Sebastián, Colotlan
29. Salatitan, Tonalá
30. Senticpac
31. Tepic
32. Valle de Banderas, Tepic
33. Xalpa, Juchipila
34. Zapotitlan, Amula
35. Zapotlanejo, Tepatitlan

Other parishes with very low annual rentas

36. Amatlan de las Cañas, Huauchinango
37. Chimaltitan, Bolaños
38. Cuyutlan, Acaponeta
39. Ejutla, Autlan
40. Hostotipac
41. Huaxicori, Acaponeta

42. Huejúcar, Colotlan
43. S. Pedro Analco, Tequila
44. Sta. María del Oro, Tequepespan
45. Techaluta, Sayula
46. Teul, Tlaltenango
47. Tonila, Tuspa
48. Xala, Ahuacatlan

MAP 4. Most and least desirable Guadalajara parishes, late 18th century. Districts are provided in parentheses where district and parish names differ. The characterizations are based on high (low) income, favorable (unfavorable) location, and low (high) turnover.

from 1746 and 1775.[59] Some of the parishes on both lists, like Escanela (Querétaro), were so unattractive to aspiring curas that the archbishop had trouble filling them, and they do not appear on the mesada lists. Others, especially mining camps that were nearly abandoned in the 1740's, recovered at least briefly later in the century and would have become more desirable appointments.[60] Though the third-class parishes and the high turnover–low income parishes in Table 1 were scattered through much of the territory of the archdiocese, there were two concentrations (see Map 5). One was in a large pocket of northern Guerrero and adjoining districts of Temascaltepec and Zacualpan (Edo. de México), encompassing both mountains and hot country. Except for periodic mining boomlets, this was a comparatively poor and remote part of the colony. It was also an area with an unusually large number of bitter disputes between priests and parishioners. The parishes of Acapetlahuaya, Alahuistlan, Amatepec, Atenango del Río, Cacalotenango, Ichcateopan, Iguala, Oapan, Pilcayan, Tasmalaca, Teloloapan, Temascaltepec, and Tepecoacuilco were located in this pocket. The other concentration, embracing the parishes of Atitalaquia, Atotonilco el Chico, Epasoyucan, Huehuetoca, Teotihuacan, Tolcayuca, and Xaltocan, was situated in a highland zone of poor Indian villages north of the Valley of Mexico in southern Hidalgo and eastern Estado de México. It included Otomí speakers, large haciendas and ranchos, and precarious mining settlements.

Some 10 to 20 percent of the parishes of both dioceses were regarded as choice appointments. The lists of first-class parishes in 1746 and 1775 can serve as a rough approximation of choice appointments for the archdiocese. Though some of these parishes declined later in the century, to be replaced by others that were growing and producing more income (including some of the parishes that were secularized after 1749), the bulk continued to be occupied in the late eighteenth century by curas whom the archbishops regarded as among their most distinguished and worthy of promotion.[61] Adding to these lists the three other parishes where curas were reported to have incomes over 2,000 pesos in the 1770's (Jonacatepec, Mazatepec, and Zinacantepec), Map 5 shows a marked concentration of choice parishes west of Mexico City in the populous Indian districts of Lerma, Metepec, southern Tacuba, Tenango del Valle, and southern Xilotepec. Half of the 28 choice parishes were located in this area: Almoloya, Atarasquillo, Atlacomulco, Atlapulco, Huizquilucan, Ixtlahuaca, Malacatepec, Ocoyoacac, Ozolotepec, San Felipe el Grande, Tenancingo, Tenango del Valle, Tescaliacac, and Zinacantepec.

There are no comparable lists of first-class parishes for Guadalajara, but the choice parishes can be identified by four measures: the estimated incomes they produced for their curas, the relatively long tenure of the curas, the number of vicarios employed, and the appearance of the curas in the bishops' reports to the crown on leading priests of the diocese. Eighteen parishes pass these four tests best and are identified on Map 4. They are not as concentrated as those in the archdiocese, but fourteen of them do fall into three clusters: (1) the commercial, farming, and ranching centers in or near the Altos de Jalisco (Aguascalientes, Nochistlan, San Juan de los Lagos, Santa María de Lagos, Teocaltiche, and Tepatitlan); (2) the important mining settlements and hinterlands in Zacatecas (Fresnillo, Ojocaliente, Sierra de Pinos, Xerez, and Zacatecas); and (3) the three

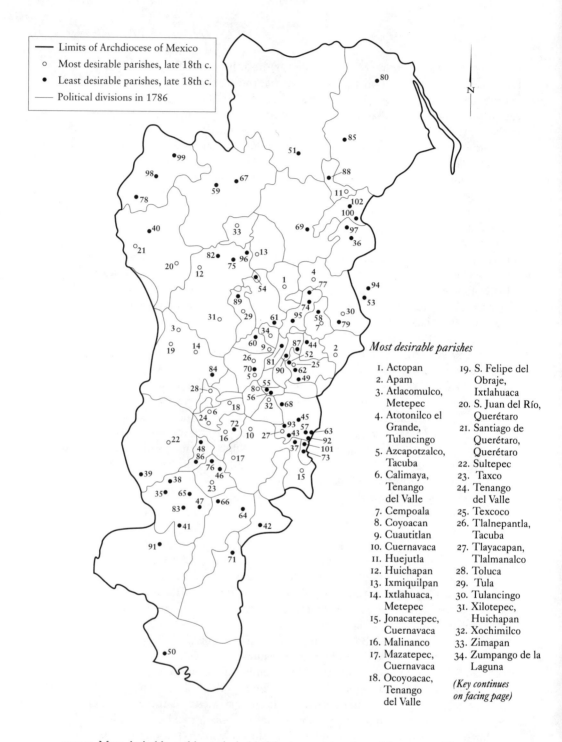

MAP 5. Most desirable and least desirable Mexico parishes, late 18th century. The "most desirable" parishes are those categorized as first-class in 1746 and 1775, with some additions and subtractions based on information about income and difficulty of administration. The "least desirable" are those rated as third-class with the highest turnover and lowest income. Districts are provided only where the district and parish names differ.

populous farming and ranching parishes with large numbers of Indians south of Lake Chapala (Sayula, Zacoalco, and Zapotlan el Grande).[62]

The mesada records for both dioceses in the late eighteenth century suggest how often curas left their parishes for new positions. For the archdiocese in 1771–72 and 1782–83, 117 promotions to parochial benefices were reported— 29 per concurso, or one turnover for every five parishes. For these four years, nearly two-thirds (64 percent) of the 143 parish benefices outside Mexico City changed hands at least once. Nineteen of these parishes (13 percent) turned over twice during the period; fourteen of them produced 1,000 pesos or less in annual income for their curas.[63] The figures are similar for Guadalajara promotions in 1763–65, 1768–72, 1774, and 1782: there were 10.6 promotions a year in a diocese with 96 parishes—one promotion for every nine parishes for each concurso. Three-fourths of the parishes turned over by promotion during these years, and those that turned over two or three times (excluding Zacatecas and Fresnillo) produced an average income to the cura of only 665 pesos a year (see Appendix A for lists of the parishes transferred in these mesada records). Since Mexico was a larger and richer diocese than Guadalajara, these differences in income and turnover rate by promotion are not surprising.

The career histories of concursants likewise indicate considerable mobility. It took most curas some years to win a parish benefice, and in the interim, they tended to put in short stints as vicarios in several parishes, applying for vacancies at each announced concurso. For Guadalajara, fourteen curas who provided

---

(Key continued from facing page)

Least desirable parishes

35. Acapetlahuaya, Zacualpan district
36. Acatlan, Tulancingo
37. Achichipico, Cuernavaca
38. Alahuistlan, Zacualpan
39. Amatepec y Tlatlaya, Sultepec
40. Amealco, Querétaro
41. Apaxtla, Zacualpan
42. Atenango del Río, Chilapa
43. Atlatlauca, Tlalmanalco
44. Axapusco, Otumba
45. Ayapango, Chalco
46. Cacalotenango, Taxco
47. Coatepec
48. Coatepec de los Costales, Zacualpan
49. Coatlinchan, Texcoco
50. Coyuca, Acapulco
51. Cozcatlan, Santiago de los Valles
52. Chiautla, Texcoco
53. Chiconcuautla, Huauchinango
54. Chilcuatla, Ixmiquilpan
55. Churubusco, Mexicalcingo
56. Culhuacan, Mexicalcingo

57. Ecacingo, Tlalmanalco
58. Epasoyucan, Cempoala
59. Escanela, Cadereyta
60. Huehuetoca, Cuautitlan
61. Hueypustla, Tetepango
62. Huexotla, Texcoco
63. Hueyapan, Cuautla
64. Huitzuco, Taxco
65. Ichcateopan, Zacualpan
66. Iguala, Taxco
67. Landa, Cadereyta
68. Mixquic, Tlalmanalco
69. Molango, Meztitlan
70. Naucalpan, Tacuba
71. Oapan, Tixtla
72. Ocuilan, Malinalco
73. Ocuituco, Cuautla
74. Omitlan, Pachuca
75. Peña de Francia, Xilotepec
76. Pilcayan, Taxco
77. Real de Atotonilco, Pachuca (pre-1805)
78. S. Jose Casas Viejas, S. Luis de la Paz
79. Singuilucan, Tulancingo
80. Tantima, Pánuco y Tampico
81. Tecama, S. Cristóbal Ecatepec

82. Tecozautla, Xilotepec
83. Teloloapan, Ichcateopan
84. Temoaya, Ixtlahuaca
85. Tempoal, Pánuco y Tampico
86. Tecicapan, Zacualpan
87. Teotihuacan
88. Tepehuacan, Huejutla
89. Tepetitlan, Tula
90. Tepexpan, Teotihuacan
91. Tetela del Río
92. Tetela del Volcán, Cuautla district
93. Tlalnepantla Cuautenca, Chalco
94. Tlaola, Huauchinango
95. Tolcayuca, Pachuca
96. Tozquillo, Huichapan
97. Tzontecomatlan, Chicontepec
98. Xichú, S. Luis de la Paz
99. Xichú, Real de, S. Luis de la Paz
100. Xochiatipan, Yahualica
101. Xumiltepec, Cuautla
102. Yahualica

dates of ordination and service in the resumés for the 1770 concurso waited an average of 8.7 years for their first parish.[64] For Mexico in the early 1760's, the wait was a year and a half less—7.1 years (in a sample of 30 curas). Once placed in a permanent post, the Mexico group averaged six to seven years there before moving on.[65] For the Guadalajara groups in 1757 and 1770, the average stay was also between six and seven years (6.8 years in 1757, 6.4 in 1770).[66] Between temporary assistantships and "permanent" parish benefices, most curas would have served in seven or eight parishes during their careers, but a few had served in as many as thirteen by the time they were sixty years old. As always, to speak of averages is to mask wide deviations from the general pattern. Ocotlan, for example, which became part of the Diocese of Guadalajara in 1795, had fifteen interim and beneficed curas between 1767 and 1821, for an average term of only 3.6 years.[67] At the other extreme, Huitzilopochco (Churubusco, D.F.) had only five curas in the 90 years from 1635 to 1725.[68]

One cura who moved a great deal was Joseph Manuel Sotomayor.[69] His career was distinguished more by long life and good fortune than by conventional accomplishments. A creole Spaniard born to a merchant family in Tulancingo (Hidalgo) about 1747, he moved with his parents to Acasuchitlan, where he learned to read and write from the local schoolmaster. At twelve, he was sent to Mexico City, where he studied grammar, rhetoric, three years of philosophy, three years of scholastic theology, and two years of moral theology.[70] Eventually he studied Nahuatl and was ordained a título de idioma in 1773, a year or two later than most of his contemporaries. A string of temporary assignments followed in the area of eastern Guerrero and Morelos. Sent first as vicario to Oapan (on the road to Acapulco), he soon fell ill and was reassigned to Tenepantla. After a short stay there, he went on to Guastepec for three years, Zacualpan de Amilpas for one year, and Jantetelco for one year. Only a few months into his next assignment, as vicario de pie fijo in Tlacagualoya, he was charged with violating his vow of celibacy and sent to Tepotzotlan for a period of confinement. At Tepotzotlan, he served as substitute professor of moral theology. Eventually he was given new assignments, serving first as vicario to Zacualtipan (Hidalgo), next as substitute cura in Escanela for three months, and then as coadjutor in Chilpancingo (Guerrero). After a stay of less than a year, he returned to Mexico City to compete for vacant parishes and renew his licenses to confess and preach. Next he was sent to Tamazunchale (San Luis Potosí) as coadjutor. Two years later, embroiled in a bitter dispute with the Indian parishioners, he was sent to Tochimilco (Puebla) as a vicario. He stayed there until the next concurso brought him back to Mexico City, and then went on to Tectipac (Guerrero) as coadjutor for two years before finally being awarded a benefice of his own—Oapan, where he had served his first vicariate nearly 20 years before. Only then were his licenses to confess and preach granted without term. In 1793, the subdelegado of Tixtla, reporting on priests in his district, said that Sotomayor was "of very limited learning and his parishioners consider him overly concerned with the collection of clerical fees, but nothing is known that would impugn his character, his outward conduct, and the fulfillment of his pastoral duties."[71] After six years in the third-class parish of Oapan, he gained the parish of Zacualpan, which he retained for five years before being awarded Jonacatepec in 1798 (both in Morelos).

By then, there was plenty to impugn his character and pastoral conduct. Since 1796 the Inquisition had been gathering a thick dossier on his irregular behavior. He was charged with twice breaking the seal of confession, committing many acts of incontinence and irreverence, engaging in illegal trade, failing to attend to his sacramental duties, making excessive demands on his parishioners, and more. Sotomayor readily admitted to violating the secrecy of the confessional and having at least two daughters and various liaisons with women, but only gradually acknowledged his other failings. Faced with a list of witnesses and 42 specific charges, he finally broke down, acknowledged his many errors, and pleaded for forgiveness. Yet even in his newfound remorse, he was quick to rationalize much of his outrageous behavior. (A particularly extravagant claim was that he smoked cigars while administering the last rites for health reasons, as if the smoke were a fumigant.) The Inquisition passed sentence on May 13, 1802: he was severely reprimanded, deprived of his licenses to confess and preach, exiled for ten years from Mexico City and the other locations of his crimes, and confined for two years in the Colegio Apostólico de Pachuca under a strict regimen of spiritual exercises, without permission to celebrate mass. In May 1804, he had completed the sentence, having shown himself to be of "good conduct, penitent, contrite, obedient, and a good example." Apparently he returned to his hometown of Acasuchitlan and assisted the cura in small ways. Early in 1808, he petitioned to retire to the Colegio de Tepotzotlan. Permission was granted as long as he maintained a strict retirement. But the irrepressible Sotomayor changed his mind about retirement and in November 1810 petitioned the archbishop from Acasuchitlan to have his sentence revoked so he could return to pastoral work. He was reappointed to the parish of Jonacatepec in 1812.

The careers of other marginal curas tended to be precarious and full of hardships, although few led lives as bold and off-color as Sotomayor's, and fewer still were as restless and durable.[72] Most of the better-educated and better-behaved curas who rose into middling or first-class parishes led safe, predictable, and outwardly dull lives. Pedro Ignacio del Castillo y Pesquera is a case in point. From his resumé of 1757 and supporting letters from his former teachers and colleagues, we know that he was born in Guadalajara about 1717, the legitimate son of creole Spanish parents. He took up studies for the priesthood "at a tender age," completing the grammar, rhetoric, and philosophy courses at the Jesuit college of San Juan Bautista. He claimed to have been an enthusiastic and successful student then and later, participating in academic competitions and giving public lectures; a letter from the Jesuit colegio supported the claim. He did four years of advanced study in scholastic and moral theology, presumably earning a second bachelor's degree. Then for four more years he led an academy of moral theology—a kind of study and discussion group—in his home and studied Nahuatl until reaching the age of ordination. He moved quickly into administration, first as assistant chaplain of the Convent of Santa Mónica in Guadalajara, then as coadjutor of the parish of Zapotlan.[73] He served there for nine and a half years, earning barely enough to support himself and the incapacitated cura. After the cura's death and a spell as interim cura, he was awarded the parochial benefice, which he held for six years before being awarded the more desirable parish of Ameca.

By Castillo y Pesquera's own account and those of his supporters, he continued his studious ways—his Jesuit and Mercedarian friends considered him one of the "most learned" priests in the diocese. But the accomplishments he stressed in his resumé were his building activities and his dedication to teaching and sacramental duties. He described rebuilding or restoring at considerable personal cost the churches and religious images he found in his parishes, and adding new ornaments of gold, silver, and diamonds to enhance the splendor of public worship. He declared himself equally proud of his dedication to teaching by formal instruction and the example of his well-ordered life and habits; his ability to win the love, respect, and obedience of his parishioners; and his success in reducing public drunkenness. Despite the settled appearance of his career and his long residence in Zapotlan, Castillo y Pesquera was a habitual participant in the competitions for vacant posts. As of 1757 he had participated in eleven concursos. Now, less than two years after moving to Ameca, he was applying for positions in the cathedral chapter.[74]

An example of the career advantages of academic success is Dr. José María Mansilla. Born in Zapotlan el Grande, he studied from the beginning in the seminario conciliar of Guadalajara—always, he said in his 1803 resumé,[75] in pursuit of an academic vocation (*carrera literaria*). He "interrupted" his formal schooling to serve as interim cura of Xala (Nayarit) for two years, then returned to study and teach in the seminary, compete for professorships in theology, and earn a doctorate in theology in 1794. He served as an examiner in various oposiciones to fill academic posts in Guadalajara and competed twice for vacant parishes. Both times he was rewarded with a parish benefice: first the *sacristía mayor* of Ayó el Chico, which he held for five years; then, in 1803, the desirable parish of San Juan de los Lagos.

Apparently, Mansilla's career was both helped and hindered by his academic pursuits. From 1803 on, he applied for vacancies in the cathedral chapter without success. Perhaps Bishop Cabañas, whose long episcopate coincided with Mansilla's career, blocked an appointment to the cathedral chapter because the studious doctor did not attend to his parish duties. He was said to indulge his passion for mathematics to the point of neglecting his responsibilities to confess, preach, baptize, marry, bury, and celebrate mass. An account (probably apocryphal in detail) of an exchange between Bishop Cabañas and Mansilla during a pastoral visit to San Juan de los Lagos has the bishop upbraiding the cura for neglecting his duties: "I do not want mathematical *curas*; I want *curas* who confess, *curas* who preach and who dedicate themselves to their pastoral duties." Observing Mansilla's ruddy complexion and light hair, the bishop supposedly observed, "Señor Doctor: Judas had your kind of hair." Mansilla replied, "Most Illustrious Sir: That is not what the Gospel says. It says that he was a bishop."[76] Whatever strains there were in the personal relationship between this cura and his bishop, Cabañas eventually approved his promotion in 1816 to Santa María de Lagos, one of the choicest of all the Guadalajara parishes, where he died in 1829.

The members of regular orders who served as pastors before the last round of secularizations in the eighteenth century also moved back and forth between doctrinas and provincial centers. They were not professional free agents to the same extent as their diocesan counterparts, but they usually were not kept in one doctrina indefinitely. The career of the Franciscan friar Joseph Yriarte illustrates their pattern of movement. Upon completing his formal education in Puebla in

1740, Yriarte received a general license to confess men and women and went to the Franciscan convent in Guadalajara for about eight months. From Guadalajara, he went to Juchipila for two years as a companion and assistant to the guardian-cura. After returning to Guadalajara for a year and a half to serve as *predicador sabatino* (responsible for the Saturday sermon), he went to the Franciscan Colegio de Nuestra Señora de Guadalupe in Zacatecas for fourteen months before returning to Guadalajara for another two years as a theology instructor. From there, he went to Santa María del Oro to assist the guardian, then replaced him for eight months. He moved on two years later to supervise activities of the Third Order at Tecolotlan (Nayarit), but became ill within a few months and returned to Guadalajara for close to five years, eventually taking up the duties of preacher again. He went to Yutla as guardian in 1759, only to be recalled to Guadalajara by the provincial on charges of incontinence.[77]

An important difference between the mobility of diocesan and Mendicant pastors was that friars could be shuffled around without the kind of disruption in administration that sometimes occurred when a parish priest was transferred. With three to five friars typically in residence in a doctrina, two or three men who knew the routine could carry on even when one or two left, and an assistant might well become the local guardian and cura. Or a guardian and one of his companions might change positions and still remain in the same doctrina.[78] The more prosperous parishes were in a position to weather a high turnover of diocesan curas, for one or more of the vicarios might be long-term residents. But such continuity was less predictable than that provided by the communal life of pastors and assistants of the regular orders, and was not possible in many of the smaller and poorer parishes where there were no vicarios or only one.

Still, many curas served fifteen, 20, or 25 years or more in the same parish. Curas in first-class parishes show up frequently among these examples of long-term service.[79] A good income and vicarios to aid in the pastoral work were powerful incentives to stay, not to mention that there were fewer promotions to compete for once a cura reached this level. But some parishes in the middle range of income and facilities also had their permanent tenants.[80] Even some modest parishes on the harsh outer edges of the archdiocese had curas who stayed more than fifteen years.[81] In some cases, this was a matter of a cura with an average record reaching his professional limit. In others, a particularly dedicated cura with promising credentials chose to stay because he found the climate agreeable and the company and his work there particularly fulfilling, or because it was close to home.[82] Joseph Anacleto Bernal, the cura of Purificación (Jalisco), simply did not harbor ambitions that would propel him beyond that parish. In a 1755 report from the Audiencia of Nueva Galicia, Bernal was described as the long-suffering cura in a harsh and poor place "with hardly enough income to maintain himself." He was "much admired by his parishioners," a "good pastor completely dedicated to the spiritual well-being of his sheep."[83] According to the report, he had made no move to leave. In still other cases, vice-patrons and bishops regarded a particular cura as indispensable to his parish. Even though he might be well qualified for promotion—in fact was especially deserving of it because of his exemplary parish service—they would not promote him unless he applied on his own.[84] The record of a pastoral visit into the Huasteca in the northeast fringes of the archdiocese in 1808–9 reported that the cura of Tancanhuitz (San Luis Potosí) had been there for 23 years, the cura of Huejutla (Hidalgo) for seventeen years, the cura of Huauchinango (Puebla) for eighteen years, and the cura of Zihuateutla (Puebla) for eighteen years. For the seventeen parishes included in this part of the visita, the average length of service was 8.3 years. But the median was only 2.5 years: the five parishes with curas who had served for seventeen years or more were offset by nine parishes in which the cura had served less than five years.[85]

The Vicarios

Priests without independent means or only enough to be ordained a título de idioma had little hope of moving into a parish benefice. If they did so, with few exceptions it was after many years of service and in one of the poorest or most isolated parishes. So long as they caused no scandal and attended to their pastoral duties satisfactorily, these men remained virtually unknown to their superiors. As the president of the Audiencia of Nueva Galicia put it in his report on the priesthood to the king in 1764:

Assuming they have undertaken studies, as soon as they conclude their philosophy and moral theology courses they leave for distant *pueblos* to help the *curas*, moving from one parish to another or operating rural estates. For this reason, it is not so easy to learn of their lives and habits, and for the same reason they have none of the merits and learning that would make them worthy of Your Highness's attention.[86]

This statement makes three observations about the careers of long-term vicarios: they were poorly educated; they moved a great deal; and they were not worthy of promotion unless they eventually exhibited some exceptional merit to overcome their meager learning. By implication, they also lacked influential friends who could bring their personal and professional merits to the attention of authorities in the cathedral city. The truth of the first and third observations is apparent from the evidence on curas and the emphasis on education for promotion that have already been discussed. Some longtime vicarios had even less education than the minimal bachelor's degree and were better versed in an Indian language than in the liturgy or the fundamentals of theology. We can add to our earlier examples two vicarios singled out by the subdelegado of Ixmiquilpan (Hidalgo), who in 1793 contemptuously dismissed both, Felipe Arévalo and José María Pérez, as "on the surface, God-fearing men; but only Your Majesty knows if they even understand what the missal says, because I know they did not even finish their grammar studies."[87]

The general transience of vicarios is clear from the records of service among competitors in the oposiciones. Most vicarios had had at least one assignment that lasted a year or less, and the overall average length of service in one parish was 2.3 years.[88] Some of the poor and generally undesirable parishes found it difficult to keep even one vicario for more than a year. In the archdiocese, for the early 1760's oposiciones, five different candidates had served in the parishes of Alahuistlan, Tizayuca, Tolcayuca, and Xaltocan. Sixteen of these 20 terminated assignments were for a year or less, three were for two years, and one was for three years. The other third-class parishes of Achichipico, Epasoyucan, Huehuetoca,

Ixtapalapa, Molango, and Tlahuac had each had three concursantes as vicario. Eight of these eighteen terminated assignments were for a year or less, three were for two years, two were for four years, and five were for unknown periods, probably less than a year. Some of the poorest Guadalajara parishes employing only one vicario also had large numbers of vicarios passing through for very short terms. Mecatabasco had thirteen former vicarios apply for the 1757 and 1770 concursos, Xalpa had nine, Tomatlan had eight, Mascota had seven, Zapotlan de los Tecuejes (Zapotlanejo) had six, and San Cristóbal de la Barranca had five. For various reasons—small salaries, a difficult cura, distance from the cathedral city, intolerable weather, and poisonous insects were mentioned—other parishes had difficulty finding anyone at all to serve.[89]

Though the vicarios as a group were more transient than curas, those on the move are overrepresented in the concurso records. An important minority were among the most settled of parish priests and did not elect to participate in the concursos. These two groups of settled and transient vicarios were roughly divided by age as well as education. The younger ones were likely to move every year or two for the first ten or fifteen years of service. Some who never secured a benefice continued to transfer to new situations, but the older the vicario, the more likely he was to remain in one place. A report on priests living in the district of Xilotepec (Hidalgo) in the early 1790's gives their hometowns and permits a glimpse of this pattern of rootedness for one type of vicario near the end of the colonial period.[90] Most of the eight curas in this district came from distant places—one from Spain, two from Mexico City, one from Saltillo, and one from Tulancingo. The other three were from the towns of Real del Monte, Tetepango, and Ixmiquilpan, ten to 20 miles from their parishes. In contrast, eleven of the fourteen vicarios had been raised in the district of Xilotepec or in towns within ten miles of their parishes (less than half a day's ride by mule in most cases). Only three were from more distant places—one from Mexico City, one from Toluca, and one from Otumba. Though this report does not give the ages of the vicarios, other examples indicate that older men were the ones most likely to find their way back to family and home district.[91]

Some vicarios were virtual vagabonds, moving from parish to parish every year or so for fifteen or 20 years or more. One of the more spectacular examples was Francisco Antonio de Urueta, a creole from Ozumba (Edo. de México). At thirty-nine years of age, he had served as vicario in ten parishes over the fourteen years since his ordination in 1785. He went first to the parish of Tlatlaya for a year. He then spent two months in Jantetelco, one year in Tochimilco, two months without employment, two years in Tenepantla Cuautenca, one month in Yecapixtla, six months again in Tenepantla, six months back in Mexico City to recover from an illness, a period coming and going between Yautepec and Mexico City, and a period of confinement and spiritual exercises in the Colegio at Tepotzotlan for acts of incontinence. From there, he went to Teoloyuca during Lent because he knew the Indian language. He stayed on in Teoloyuca for a while longer as vicario, then went back for two months to Yautepec, where he was arrested again for sexual misconduct.[92]

A similar pattern of restless movement for the Diocese of Guadalajara is exemplified by José Manuel Díaz Gallo. One witness to his activities described him as "usually in transit, without fixed residence." Licensed in Guadalajara in 1773 to confess and preach, Díaz Gallo served in at least twelve parishes before 1790. He went first to Cuyutlan for one year as vicario, then to Tomatlan as interim cura for three months, to Santa María del Oro as vicario for less than a year, back to Guadalajara without employment, and on to the Hacienda del Cabezón as chaplain for one year. From there, he went to the Dominican convent in Guadalajara for two months' confinement for incontinence, then resumed his bumpy career, going to Tapalpa as vicario for about two years, to Sayula for about one year, to Tizapan el Alto for about one year, to San Blas as substitute cura for a year in 1783, to Ameca as vicario for a year, to Jolapa for three months, to Xala for one year, and to Guaynamota as interim cura, where he was arrested again. He left behind a long trail of seductions, admitting to a total of seventeen—at least one in nearly every parish he had served.[93]

Less spectacular and more representative career histories of vicarios are those of Valentín Mariano Ximénez, Francisco Benites de Ariza, and Simón Thadeo de Castañeda Castro y Guzmán.[94] Ordained in 1775, Ximénez went to Xochitepec (Morelos) for six months as vicario and two months as interim cura, then spent two years (as vicario and interim cura) in Santiago Ayapango, where he was active in establishing schools. In 1778, he went to Totolapa as vicario, then as coadjutor when the cura was absent with the permission of the archbishop. Next came three months as interim cura in Coyuca, three years as vicario in Amecameca, and a reassignment to Totolapa as coadjutor, the post he held when he submitted his resumé in 1784. He had competed in three oposiciones and was judged qualified for pastoral work but received no appointment. Benites de Ariza described his career in handwritten resumés of 1760 and 1762, when he was the vicario of San Pedro Ecacingo. Born in Temascaltepec, he apparently had an extensive academic record in the Colegio de San Ildefonso and the University of Mexico, where he studied canon law, headed a student academy, and obtained first-class honors. After failing to secure an academic post, he lived among lowland Indians in order to learn their language, then was ordained in 1754. He had served as vicario in Alahuistlan, Acapetlahuaya, and Ichcateopan, where his uncle and brothers were the curas; returned to Mexico City to recover from an illness; and gone to Mixquic as vicario. He had been in his current post for two years now, he said in his 1762 resumé. No other priest, he claimed, "not even the friars," had lasted that long in Ecacingo.

Castañeda had also been ordained in 1754, after studying grammar and arts in the Colegio Máximo of San Pedro y San Pablo, and Nahuatl on his own. For the first two months after ordination, he served in Acolman as an unpaid assistant; he then stayed on for ten more months as a vicario. His next stop was Mixcoac, where he was responsible for mass in three tiny mountain villages of the parish; followed by assignments in Otumba, Tláhuac, Xumiltepec, and Alahuistlan; then a return to Tláhuac in 1762, where he composed his resumé. By then, he had competed in four oposiciones for vacant parishes. If his academic record and self-ascribed enthusiasm for parish service were true, eventually he should have gained a minor parish benefice. His chances of promotion would have been better after the tenure of Archbishop Lorenzana (1766–72).

Curas and the Cathedral Chapter

The culmination of an ambitious cura's career was, he hoped, to become a pre-bend, a salaried member of the cathedral chapter (*cabildo eclesiástico*). These offi-cers of the church assisted the bishop and met with him weekly as an administra-tive body with some legislative powers, exercised the bishop's authority during interim periods, and were responsible for protocol and the religious services of the cathedral church. Positions in the cathedral chapters were divided into four categories: at the top were the dignitaries (usually a dean, an archdeacon, a choir-master, a schoolmaster, and a treasurer), followed by the canons, the *racioneros*, and the half-racioneros.[95] The office of half-racionero was the usual entry-level position and the one most open to curas. There were six racionero and six half-racionero places in the cathedral chapter of Mexico in 1773, or nearly half of the 27 chapter posts at that time. The cathedral chapter of Guadalajara was modeled after that of Mexico, with five dignitaries, ten canons, six racioneros, and six half-racioneros, but many of the positions were left unfilled because the cathedral's portion of the tithe was too small to support them. In 1766, a royal cedula au-thorized filling eight empty positions (those of two dignitaries, two canons, and four half-racioneros),[96] but Guadalajara's chapter still had fewer than 20 members until 1807, when at least six new appointments raised the total to 24. Six of the 24 were racioneros and at least seven were half-racioneros.

The salaries of all but the half-racioneros were at least equivalent to the aver-age (but less dependable) rentas of a first-class parish. For the archdiocese in 1755, the dean received 6,018 pesos a year, the dignitaries 5,215 pesos, the canons 4,012 pesos, the racioneros 2,802 pesos, and the half-racioneros 1,404 pesos. By 1773, these salaries had increased slightly, to 6,525, 5,655, 4,350, 3,045, and 1,525 pesos, respectively. The prebends in the Diocese of Guadalajara earned much less than their Mexico counterparts in 1755, but their salaries had increased substantially by 1773, reflecting the growth in tithe revenues: the dean's rose from 800 pesos in 1755 to 4,437 in 1773, the dignitaries' from 700 pesos in 1755 to 3,846, the canons' from 600 pesos to 2,958, the racioneros' from 400 to 2,071, and the half-racioneros' from 200 pesos to 1,035.[97] Presumably these officials, especially the half-racioneros, earned additional income from fees, gratuities, and capellanías.

Unless new positions in the cathedral chapters were created, an aspiring priest had to wait for a vacancy on the death or promotion of the holder. It was likely to be a long wait, for there was little turnover. With very few opportunities for fur-ther advancement except to the next step in the cathedral chapter, appointees usually stayed where they were. As a result, aged and enfeebled prebends were common.[98] Vacancies in the cathedral chapters were filled by oposiciones similar to those for the parish benefices. An important difference was that the Council of the Indies, rather than the viceroy or the president of the audiencia, served as vice-patron.[99] At least in the late eighteenth century, the Council of the Indies seems to have reviewed the applications and taken its own vote on the candi-dates, rather than automatically accepting one of the bishop's nominees, as was the practice in selecting curas. Thanks to guidelines the crown had set out in the late sixteenth century and after, curas had some leverage in the competitions for vacancies. The first preference under royal law was given to learned men who had graduated from the universities of Lima or Mexico or from Castilian uni-versities.[100] The second was given to men who had already served in cathedral churches; and the third was to men who had served in parishes and been active in eliminating "idolatry."[101]

The applications and appointment records for the Guadalajara cathedral chap-ter from 1766 to 1819 reveal the basic pattern of promotion.[102] Nearly all the offices above half-racionero were filled by internal promotion—half-racioneros promoted to racioneros, racioneros promoted to canons, and canons promoted step by step, a few reaching the office of dean or treasurer. Since nearly all the canons and dignitaries were doctors or licenciados, a vacancy at that level would normally be filled from outside the cathedral chapter if none of the racioneros met the requisites of an advanced degree and a reputation for piety and good morals.[103] Most of the competitive appointments were made at the rank of half-racionero.

Before 1807, when at least six new positions were created, longtime curas with-out advanced degrees did not have good prospects for promotion to the Guada-lajara cathedral chapter. Except for an occasional sad case of an elderly cura who appealed for an appointment as a reward for decades of faithful service and hard-ships endured, few bothered to apply. The eighteenth-century bishops before Cabañas studiously ignored the crown's third order of preference, favoring only men with doctorates. As European Spaniards, some of them also favored their compatriots over creoles, though none ignored the custom of internal promotion. In 1758, one Hispanophile bishop, Francisco de San Buenaventura Martínez de Tejada, proposed to the crown a compromise in which half the chapter's posi-tions would be filled by peninsulares.[104] His reasons were that creoles over the age of forty were generally less healthy, that the three European Spaniards then serving were the best at their duties, and, more cryptically, that "the upbring-ing over there is different from what it is here." Although European Spaniards never predominated in the Guadalajara cathedral chapter during the late colonial period, they were more numerous before 1807. Of the nineteen appointees to half-raciones from 1766 to 1806 for whom biographical information is available,[105] four were European Spaniards. Of the remaining fifteen, eight were doctors or licenciados from distinguished families in Guadalajara; three were curas from first-class parishes in other dioceses; three were local curas from the leading par-ishes of Zacatecas, Zapotlan el Grande, and Ameca; and one was the cura of the less important parish of Tequila.

For the curas who were promoted to cathedral chapter posts, the most im-portant part of the formal record was their education and learning.[106] The case that José Joaquín de Unzueta, cura of Jonacatepec, built for himself as early as 1793 with friendly witnesses, records of achievement, and his own testimony was based on his wide learning and extensive library, rather than a record of unusu-ally effective parish service.[107] Though he was not promoted in the archdiocese, he did receive a half-ración appointment to Guadalajara before 1807 and rose to the rank of canon before his death in 1821. Like most prebends, he lived com-fortably in his own house in Guadalajara, surrounded by books, art works, and good furniture.[108]

With the advent of Bishop Cabañas in 1796 and particularly after the expan-sion of the half-ración level after 1807, the pattern of appointment shifted in favor of local men. Only one of the thirteen appointments between 1806 and 1817 went to a European Spaniard, and only one went to a man from another American diocese.[109] Six of the new members were local curas, four were doctors and licenciados from Guadalajara not serving as parish priests, and one was a local noble, the Conde de Santa Rosa. All six of the former curas moved from important parishes: Santa María de Lagos, the Guadalupe parish in the city of Guadalajara, Zapotlan el Grande, Fresnillo, Agua de Venado, and Real de Catorce. But for all the change in emphasis, two long-standing preferences remained the same: for sons of distinguished families from Guadalajara and for men with doctorates. Since Guadalajara was a smaller city and a smaller diocese with fewer doctors than Mexico, it probably provided a better opportunity for promotion to the cathedral chapter. But the difference is relative. Both dioceses had an abundance of candidates for parochial benefices and cathedral positions. In neither were many longtime curas able to enter the cathedral chapter. The few who did so were likely to be replaced by other well-connected priests with advanced degrees; such vacancies would hardly ever have been open to deserving curas stationed in second- and third-class parishes, let alone one of the perpetual vicarios.

The pattern of coming from and returning to the cathedral city that is evident in the careers of Urueta, Díaz Gallo, and Castañeda runs throughout the administrative and judicial records of both curas and vicarios. Mexico City and Guadalajara were the inevitable points of reference and standard of comparison for these priests. In their resumés, parish priests far from the capital expressed their feelings of longing and isolation in terms of distance in leagues from the capital city. Just as the Indian cura of Atenango del Río (Guerrero) in 1762, Br. Pasqual de Roxas Mendoza Austria y Moctezuma, deemed one of the great hardships of his parish being 40 leagues from Mexico City, so his counterpart in Guadalajara, Nicolás Ballejo, cura of Montegrande in 1770, remembered Totatiche, where he had served four years, mainly for its 50 leagues from the provincial capital.[110] Joseph Yriarte, a Franciscan doctrinero in the province of Xalisco, made so bold as to attribute his immoral behavior to being so far from Guadalajara for long stretches of time.[111]

The very act of participation in the oposiciones was evidence of the continuing attachment to the cathedral city. Of the scores of candidates for perhaps ten or fifteen vacancies, most competed not just on the slim chance that they might be favored over others with more impressive credentials and better connections, but because the competition meant a month or six weeks of leave from parish service and the opportunity to return to the place where most of them had been educated and where about a third of them had been born. It was like going to a professional convention in one's hometown—a chance to renew contacts, look after family business and commercial interests, renew one's sense of vocation, and hear the latest professional news.[112] The weaker candidates went to reconnect with family, colleagues, and what they regarded as civilization, as much as to compete for a better assignment. Bishops encouraged participation, both to personalize their relationship to parish priests and to reexamine the candidates' academic preparation for pastoral work.

This pulsating relationship between urban-minded pastors and the capital was reinforced by their habit of returning for medical treatment and convalescence, and by the standard license granted to faithful curas to leave the parish for two months a year (which they usually spent in the city).[113] Many well-educated priests were so reluctant to leave the city that they never took up pastoral work at all. Others chose to stay in lowly positions in middling parishes near the capital rather than compete for better posts at a greater distance.[114] Especially in the archdiocese, curas of the wealthier parishes were tempted to keep a home in Mexico City and spend as much time as they could there, relying on coadjutors and vicarios to do the routine work of the parish.[115]

* * *

Tracing the careers of late colonial parish priests reveals the priesthood as a profession. In their restless strivings, most priests recognized an elaborate ladder of advancement defined more or less by certain kinds of merit that rewarded some individuals and penalized others. Social background, education, intellectual achievement, and record of service were the objective ingredients of merit. Particularly recognized in the late colonial period were formal education and service beyond the routine pastoral duties: promoting primary schools, endowing cofradías, improving the physical plant, and the like. From the viewpoint of parishioners, most of their priests were not at home for long—young vicarios came and went, beneficed curas competed in concursos and were likely to move every seven years or so. Especially in third-class, contentious, and inaccessible parishes of oppressive heat or perennial cold, a minority of priests stayed to earn the full authority and confidence that could come with longevity.

Despite a great deal of small-scale movement, both to new assignments and from assigned posts to temporary resorts, older curas and vicarios knew the limits of mobility. Few curas moved outside the boundaries of the diocese in which they were born and trained, and many who gained second- or third-class benefices moved only within a circumscribed area of the diocese. Very few rose into the first-class parishes and the cathedral chapter. Once a parish priest was categorized by appointment as a vicario, coadjutor, vicario de pie fijo, or cura; by assignment to a first-, second-, or third-class parish; by ordination a título de suficiencia or capellanía or a título de idioma or ministerio; and by education, from the learned to the barely literate, it was not easy to climb out of his pigeon-hole. In the late eighteenth century, the distinctions sharpened especially between those who had been ordained as Indian-language priests and those who had not. The effect was to close more of the language priests out of parish benefices.

CHAPTER SIX

Making a Living

Since the income of these parishes generally depends on
obvenciones, it is greater or lesser according to the number
of parishioners, baptisms, marriages, funerals, *cofradías*'
feast-day celebrations underwritten with some livestock
and small estates in their possession, . . . and other kinds
of [irregular] earnings.
                          —Archbishop Rubio y Salinas, 1758

Five of the eight top revenue-producing dioceses of Spanish America at the
end of the eighteenth century were located within the borders of modern
Mexico. Together, the Archdiocese of Mexico (no. 1) and the dioceses of Michoacán (3), Puebla (4), Oaxaca (7), and Guadalajara (8) accounted for 39 percent
of the revenue reported for all 44 dioceses of Spanish America in 1796.[1] Mexico
and Guadalajara alone accounted for close to one-sixth (16.2 percent) of the total
revenue, yet church records of the late colonial period frequently lamented the
meager incomes of most parishes in New Spain. "Minerva's outstanding rewards
are exceedingly scarce. Only in the few richly endowed parishes can it be said
that scarcity does not reach extreme need," the dean of Michoacán's cathedral
declared in 1785.[2] In a more prosaic vein, the cura of Zimatlan, Oaxaca, noted in
1784 that "a boy would much rather be a businessman's cashier these days than
hold all our benefices."[3]

How priests in parish service made their living and how much they earned
cannot be settled with any confidence from such sweeping impressions or summary revenue figures. Some parishes yielded far larger incomes than others;
some were more costly to administer, and some curas spent much more on charitable works; and, despite established law on how parish priests would make their
living, there was no standard means of support in the colonies.

This chapter describes how parish priests made their living in the dioceses
of Mexico and Guadalajara during the eighteenth century, how much they may
have earned in different parishes, and how income and sources of income were
changing during the administrative reforms and material changes of the late
eighteenth century—all matters that bear on the tensions and affinities within
parishes.

Endowments and Royal Stipends

Ideally, all secular priests, including those in parish service, were to bring to their profession an estate or pension that would provide a "decent" livelihood.[4] Under the Council of Trent's decrees, ordination was not to be bestowed unless the candidate demonstrated that he had such a source of income.[5] This policy was reiterated from time to time by bishops in New Spain. Newly arrived in 1766, Archbishop Lorenzana made a point of it in his first pastoral letter: a candidate was to be ordained only if he could prove he had "ecclesiastical rents sufficient to provide for his proper maintenance," an income that "must be fixed, certain, and secured by property."[6] A "decent" livelihood for a cura supposedly consisted of enough income "to conduct himself honorably, dress and eat according to his station, maintain a pair of mules and servants to attend him, buy books, [and] reward his benefactors."[7]

In both the archdiocese and the diocese in the late colonial period, many secular priests held capellanías or other ecclesiastical endowments that provided them with a fixed income.[8] Often such endowments had been set up by the priest's parents or more remote ancestors for the express purpose of maintaining an heir in the clergy who would offer periodic masses for their souls, though some were attached to rural estates and did not require that the holder be a relative of the founder. Less often, capellanías were established by bishops to support outstanding or promising but needy candidates for the priesthood.

The holders of these endowments, however, were seldom in parish service.[9] Only 26 of Guadalajara's 234 parish priests in 1796 held capellanías, and 24 of the 26 served only on the haciendas to which their capellanías were attached. Moreover, these capellanías had an average principal of only 4,900 pesos. In the best of circumstances (it was common enough for interest payments to be in arrears or suspended altogether when they depended on marginal haciendas), such a capellanía would yield 245 pesos a year, which was not regarded as an adequate income for a cura. Further evidence that few parish priests had even this small fixed income from an ecclesiastical endowment comes from the data in a 1790 list of 297 priests who held capellanías in the diocese. Only eleven of them were listed among the parish priests in 1796: four curas and seven vicarios.[10] Most capellanía holders lived in the cathedral city and provincial towns or in parish seats. Few were engaged in pastoral duties, and many probably were not licensed to administer sacraments.

Ecclesiastical endowments and inherited wealth, then, did not provide a living for many parish priests. In light of the principle that independent means should be required for ordination, it was a sad irony that priests with substantial estates were among the least inclined to accept, let alone seek, parish office.[11] And capellanías did not narrow the margin. As Francisco de San Buenaventura y Texada, the prior of the Franciscan province of Xalisco and bishop-elect of Yucatán, said in 1753, "Because of the shortage of *capellanías*, . . . the loss of most of those that did exist, and the need for many priests in the administration of parishes, it has been necessary to ordain them *a título de ministerio*."[12]

Some parish priests did have private funds or owned haciendas and other income-producing property. For example, Francisco de Fuentes, the priest of

Yahualica (Hidalgo) in 1692, listed among his possessions a sundries shop and a half interest in a sugar estate inherited from his namesake uncle, who had also served as cura there.[13] Four pastors mentioned in the 1790's reports on priests in the Archdiocese of Mexico were identified as estate owners. Felipe Zeballos Franco, a vicario in the parish of Pachuca, owned a small hacienda in the district; Aniceto Orto de la Bastida, vicario in the parish of Ixtlahuaca, lived on his own hacienda; the cura of Tecozautla, Gracián de Agüero, owned two haciendas near San Antonio Capulalpan, which were run by his brother; and Marcel Perelleso, longtime vicario of Huichapan, owned a ranch and a string of mules.[14] A few land-owners also show up in the 1796 report on priests in the Diocese of Guadalajara. Laureano Alegría had been vicario of Chimaltitan, but withdrew from pastoral service to return to his hometown of Tlaltenango, where he owned a substantial hacienda; and Nicolás Antonio de Robles, serving in the parish of Mecatabasco, owned an hacienda he inherited from his father.

The ideal of an independent personal income for curas was rarely realized (except as a product of parish service), but there was another plan, formulated in the sixteenth century, to free pastors from material preoccupations and from dependence on their parishioners. As the patron of the church—with right to the tithe, power of appointment to ecclesiastical offices, and responsibility for propagating the faith—the Spanish crown and *encomenderos* (individuals who received a royal grant of Indians, mainly as tribute payers) were to provide parish priests with a "competent income," so they could live "with the appropriate decency."[15] Called the *sínodo*, this royal stipend or salary was fixed in law by 1570 at 50,000 *maravedíes*—184 pesos a year.[16] The stipend was to be paid from a two-ninths portion of the tithe designated by the crown for that purpose, or directly from the Indian tribute.[17] When a cura's sínodo came from Indian tribute, he was paid by the district governor (the alcalde mayor, corregidor, or subdelegado). Any shortfall from these sources was to be covered from another branch of the royal treasury.

Into the seventeenth century, sínodos were an important source of income for members of the religious orders. In the words of Juan de Palafox y Mendoza in his 1653 pastoral letter, "The King, our Lord, sustains the *minstros de doctrina* [and] provides wine and oil for the liturgy."[18] And to the end of the colonial period, the crown continued to sponsor with sínodos frontier missions and doctrinas manned by the regular clergy. Even though payment was often made years late, these royal salaries remained the principal income of regular clergy who served as doctrineros in more established areas of New Spain and Nueva Galicia.[19] Especially in the frontier missions, there was little other income to be had. In the richer doctrinas of the central area, the regulars had the reputation of living on their sínodos and allowing the diocese to recover at least some of the other income from fees.[20]

Few late colonial parish priests shared in this beneficence. Though some secular curas were still receiving a modest sínodo when the Bourbons came to power (most received between 100 and 300 pesos rather than the exact sum of 184 pesos), it could not be said to ensure the prescribed "decent" living. A parish clergy salaried from the tithe had not taken hold in either the Archdiocese of Mexico or the Diocese of Guadalajara. The bishops and cathedral chapters, who were supposed to pay the diocesan curas from the church's portion of the tithe, held back most of it for other purposes, as well as the 8.3 percent share that was earmarked for building grants. In the early eighteenth century, only nine parish priests in the Diocese of Guadalajara still received sínodos: those of Santa María de Lagos, Xerez, Aguascalientes, Sierra de Pinos, Saltillo, Purificación, Compostela, Monterrey, and Fresnillo—all Spanish *villas* and most of them already among the wealthiest parishes in the diocese.[21]

The crown continued to recognize responsibility for advancing the faith as the century wore on, but was increasingly inclined to leave the financial burden of parish support to others.[22] On January 21, 1718, a royal cedula was sent to the viceroy of New Spain ordering a cut-off of the sínodo to all curas with sufficient income from the tithe and other sources. The cedula observed that though royal stipends had been necessary at the beginning of colonization when parish priests had no other income, those conditions no longer obtained.[23] The viceroy was ordered to submit a report on which parish priests had an adequate income without the royal stipend and which did not. There followed various inquiries into the incomes of parish priests, first in 1724 and repeatedly after midcentury, that were intended to justify the suspension of stipends to most parishes.[24] By the 1760's, in some parishes the stipends were simply suspended or long delayed without judicial notice; in others, royal authorities withheld payments ostensibly for failure to comply precisely with bureaucratic regulations.[25]

From the 1760's, the crown sought to promote better pastoral care by ordering the appointment of assistants to reside in outlying areas of understaffed parishes, on the principle that a pastor should live no more than four leagues from the most distant parishioner. Though the first cedula to this effect (issued on October 18, 1764) provided that the royal treasury would pay a stipend to the new assistants if the parish priest or the income that accrued from vacant benefices could not pay them, it was clear in practice that royal funds would not be spent for this purpose.[26] When the bishop of Guadalajara and the cura of Tomatlan made an urgent request in August 1785 for support of a new teniente de cura, the audiencia demurred. The case seemed to fit the requirements of the 1764 cedula (and subsequent amplifications in cedulas of October 18, 1774, and June 1, 1775)—a poor parish in which many of the parishioners lived up to 40 leagues from the parish seat over the worst of roads—but when the audiencia finally responded eleven years later, it was to recommend that the parish priest pay the 300-peso stipend for the time being and try to find local contributors to relieve him of up to 100 pesos of this sum.[27] When resident lieutenants were established in Xalostotitlan and Juanacatlan in the late 1770's, they were paid from the income of vacant benefices and "the curas' ninths." [28]

That the crown was intent on eventually terminating the sínodos became increasingly clear during the second half of the century. Cedulas in 1749, 1772, and 1777 reiterated that the royal treasury and parish priests were being harmed by the failure of bishops to disburse the portion of the tithe that had originally been intended for sínodos.[29] Increasingly, royal policy made it clear that the bishops and parishioners were expected to fund the parish clergy properly. There was ample legal precedent for this policy, from the Council of Trent's decrees requiring that the needs of the curas in new or poor parishes be funded from the fruits of the mother church and exactions from the parishioners, to a law republished in the *Recopilación* that the prelates must give to the parish clergy whatever they needed.[30]

In practice, the Bourbons regarded the bishops' treasuries, especially the tithe, as the solution.[31] Bishops had stopped sending tithe monies to parish priests early in the colonial period because of the shortage of tithe-paying royal subjects and the small revenues generated for the prebends from this source. But conditions had changed, a spokesman for the parish priests of Puebla argued. The population had grown substantially in the eighteenth century, as had the tithe revenues. The prebends were already well paid and did not need this additional revenue as much as the parish clergy.[32]

Bishops of Guadalajara in the eighteenth century were slow to comply with the letter or spirit of the royal decrees on parish salaries. As early as 1710, the bishop had been ordered to draw up a plan to distribute the requisite portion of the tithe to his parish priests. He replied that the curas received 100 pesos a year, and the rest remained in the cathedral because of its many necessities.[33] "The" curas appears to have been a convenient locution, leaving vague the matter of how many curas received even this small stipend. In a January 1759 report to the king, also for the purpose of documenting the payment of sínodos, the bishop felt pressed to state more precisely how the tithe income was distributed. Of 150,025 pesos collected the previous year, 8,153 (5.4 percent) was paid to parish priests. Not only was this much less than the two-ninths (22.2 percent) standard; it was concentrated in the six rich Spanish parishes of Santa María de Lagos (1,852 pesos), Aguascalientes (1,534), Fresnillo (1,116), Xerez (758), Asientos (511), and Sierra de Pinos (431). Together, these six accounted for 76 percent of the tithe assignments to parishes. The remaining 24 percent (1,951 pesos) was divided among twelve parishes, leaving roughly 80 parishes with no allotment at all.[34] The value of the tithe increased by 71 percent in Mexico and by 36 percent in Guadalajara between the 1770's and the end of the 1780's; yet by 1796, only seven parishes had been added to the list, all with stipends of 150 to 300 pesos.[35] In 1811, Bishop Cabañas reportedly paid a total of 4,600 pesos in stipends from the tithe to eighteen poor curas (256 pesos average). This was nearly three times the sum paid out to needy curas in 1759, but it was barely equal to the salaries of two canons in the cathedral chapter.[36]

From the early 1770's, the crown pushed for an end to the sínodo. In 1771, the Fourth Provincial Council of the prelates of New Spain agreed to moderate or remove the sínodos, and the bishop of Guadalajara reported that none of his curas were receiving any of these funds.[37] By a cedula of March 13, 1777, the crown ordered the bishop to deposit up to two-ninths of the tithe as a fund to pay salaries to new tenientes de cura. The bishop and cathedral chapter of Guadalajara made some move to comply, claiming in 1795 to have supplemented from the cathedral treasury the incomes of poor curas up to the basic living standard. Most of these payments from the cathedral were said to have begun after 1765 (when the crown began to make regular demands for reports on the income of parish priests).[38] Still, the record is clear that the bishops resisted full disbursement of the two-ninths to pay needy curas and provide for the new assistants. Arguing that the cathedral would be in financial trouble and the canons would be forced to live in penury, the bishops moved slowly, making only small gestures to distribute these funds when the crown periodically ordered full reporting.[39] When forced to respond to the case put to them by royal officials in 1777 that, under law 1-16-23 of the *Recopilación*, two-ninths of the tithe must go to needy parish priests, the cathedral chapter argued that this law did not oblige it to distribute so much of the tithe to the curas. The bishops, it said, already permitted parish priests to collect the *primicias* (first fruits) for themselves, they had income from fees for services, and other laws of the *Recopilación* provided that the curas be paid their salary from the royal treasury.[40]

In fact, neither the tithe nor ecclesiastical endowments were a major source of income for more than a minority of parish priests in late colonial Mexico.[41] The crown's intention, clearly articulated by Solórzano in the mid-seventeenth century—to provide the priests with "good stipends" that would free them from the temptations of covetousness, profit, and unreasonable demands on their parishioners—was not realized in New Spain.[42] Particularly in the eighteenth century, they would have to live mainly from the fruits of their pastoral service or from their private ventures into production and commerce.

Direct Collections

Direct collections from parishioners took a variety of forms and varied considerably from place to place in the dioceses of Mexico and Guadalajara during the eighteenth century. One form was the *manípulo*, the periodic collection of a small sum of money from adult men and widows that would replace or supplement other contributions of money, goods, and services.[43] Hipólito Villarroel, a former alcalde mayor and polemicist against corruption in public life in the late eighteenth century, believed that a pro-rata collection like the manípulo in place of other kinds of collections would be a boon to Indian parishes.[44] But manípulos were not as widely used in Mexico and Guadalajara as in Oaxaca and Campeche.[45] And though a parish (or a community within a parish) occasionally struck an agreement with the cura to replace other fees with a weekly contribution of, say, one-half real per family, as did the Indians of Otlazpa (Tlaxpa) in the parish of Tepejí del Río (Hidalgo) in 1785,[46] in most places regular contributions of this kind supplemented rather than replaced other collections. In Yahualica (Hidalgo) in 1722, for example, the parishioners paid one real per married man and one-half real per widower for each of the six principal feast days of the year, plus the customary labor services, provisions, and fees for masses, baptisms, marriages, and funerals.[47]

Far more common was the practice of requiring Indian parishioners to pay a small sum on Sundays called the *dominica* to cover the expenses of the weekly mass (even though royal laws issued as early as 1578 forbade mandatory contributions by Indians attending mass), and to make other small contributions during the year for the celebration of special feast days.[48] Writing in 1809 in connection with a dispute over who should administer the funds collected, the Indian governor of Papalotla (Texcoco) described the collection of the dominica as follows:

It is customary that after the Holy Sacrifice of the Mass is concluded the governor and other members of the community gather to call roll and collect alms, which are given to the priest who celebrates the Mass, and the remainder is set aside for the building fund and whatever else is necessary for the reconstruction of the church [the collection yielded about seven pesos, of which two pesos went for the mass].[49]

The vicario claimed that the surplus funds had been kept in the *arca de tres llaves* (and therefore were jointly controlled by the gobernador, the cura, and the alcalde mayor's lieutenant), but he did not dispute the governor's description of how, when, and for what purpose they were collected. He added that the amount collected per person was one *tomín* (one real).[50]

Beyond this, parish priests could expect to collect certain other small, miscellaneous fees that varied from place to place according to local custom and their own initiative. These charges were called *manuales* because they involved the performance of minor services that required some degree of physical effort (as opposed to intelligence or knowledge).[51] These services included blessing religious images (usually two reales), blessing candles at Candlemas, Ash Wednesday, and Palm Sunday, special prayers and benedictions in marriage ceremonies or for rain or against plagues of locusts and disease, certifying local elections and the background and character of parishioners who moved away and needed formal identification (mainly for marriage), and investigating and mediating local disputes. In his role as ecclesiastical judge, the priest also collected small fines.[52] He collected commissions on the sale of indulgences, especially bulls of the Santa Cruzada, but could lose money on them: until 1775, he had to pay a deposit (*fianza*) and charges for the indulgences before selling them, and he often was pressured into this enterprise even when he knew his parishioners would resist buying them.[53] Some curas went beyond the bounds of what was legal or customary in these miscellaneous collections and faced judicial complaints as a result— for example, that they forced Indians to pay one real for confession during Lent (a practice regarded by bishops and the crown as particularly reprehensible), or that they appropriated wax and the alms collected for religious images venerated in the parish church.[54]

Although priests sometimes acquired grain and animals paid by Indian parishioners as tithe, they presumably did so by purchase or barter, since they had no right to collect the tithe directly, and few of them received a share of the tithe revenues dispersed by the cathedral. But some curas did collect primicias as a privilege of their benefice. This practice was more common in the archdiocese than in the Diocese of Guadalajara, but in neither case were first fruits a standard source of income for curas, despite attempts by the crown, bishops, and some priests to extend the practice in the eighteenth century. After village officials repeatedly appealed to custom and complained that the first fruits constituted a new tax, the viceroy declared in 1794 that Indian parishioners would not have to pay this tax unless it was the local custom.[55]

In parishes where the primicia was customary or where parishioners permitted it as a new collection in the eighteenth century, the manner of collection varied considerably. In some parishes, it was collected only on livestock; in others, only on grains; in still others, on both.[56] In some parishes, it was collected in kind, but not always as a fixed proportion of the early harvest. For example, whereas Indians of Chilapa (Guerrero) in the 1760's paid one *almud* (0.25 fanega; 1 fanega = ca. 1.5 bushels) of maize per married man or widower, those in Malacatepec, Metepec district (Edo. de México), were required to pay two almudes per person in 1774.[57] Or first fruits might be collected in cash as a proportion of the value of the crop or of the animals born that year (for example, in San Juan Alahuistlan,

Zacualpan district, half a real was collected for each calf born in 1786).[58] By law, the first fruits tax was not supposed to be collected on crops of less than six fanegas and was not to exceed half a fanega in any case, but there were complaints that priests collected a *carga* (a "load," generally of two fanegas) even on smaller crops. Where the tax was collected in Indian parishes, it could be expected to yield 200–300 pesos a year.[59]

Religious funds within parishes also contributed to the priests' income. For Mexico and Guadalajara, the main funds of this kind came from cofradías, endowed building funds, and small testamentary endowments for perpetual masses. Cofradías were important in both dioceses but tended to be older, more numerous, and richer in Guadalajara.[60] Although they sometimes collected alms or donations from members, those in rural Indian parishes usually derived their income from livestock, and those in urban and Spanish parishes, from houses, land, and interest-bearing liens on property. The funds were used to support religious feasts—usually one particular feast to the saint or image of the Virgin associated with the sodality, but sometimes Easter, Pentecost, and Christmas celebrations, too—to purchase sacred images, wax, oil, and wine for the liturgy, and sometimes to pay for a priest to come in routinely to say mass.[61] The feast days invariably involved a mass and other ceremonies for which the priests were paid.

The priests thus had a vested interest in the establishment of cofradías and the careful management of their properties and income. Parishioners, on the other hand, did not always want to donate animals and property for new sodalities or to use cofradía income according to the cura's plans. As a result, the operation of these sodalities became a sore point in the relations between priest and parish, especially when a cura was intent on managing the sodalities' finances himself or on injecting himself in other ways into their operations, compelling members to make a regular contribution of money or animals, for example, or initiating new religious feasts for their sponsorship.[62] Not a few curas, as we will see in Chapter 12, bought trouble for themselves by promoting new cofradías with funds and contributions that local people intended for the community treasury.

Endowed parish building funds, endowments for feasts,[63] and funds for perpetual masses from wills (called *legados* or *patronatos laicos*) varied greatly from place to place, but were rarely a major source of income for rural pastors. For Guadalajara, they were described in detail in the records of Bishop Cabañas's pastoral visit between 1797 and 1804.[64] They also varied greatly over time. In the case of the parishes of Tlajomulco, Tomatlan, and Purificación, all of the legados in existence in 1805 were founded after 1756.[65] Except for the poorest and wealthiest parishes, these funds ranged between 1,000 and 5,000 pesos, which would have produced 50 to 250 pesos annual income at best. The legados were often guaranteed with local houses that deteriorated over the years and came to be worth less than the original endowment.[66] As a result, the payments were frequently in arrears, if they were made at all, and in any case the recipient (the priest who celebrated the requisite masses) might not be one of the local pastors.

A less legitimate but important form of support was also open to the parish priests. By law, curas and vicarios were entitled to make use of Indian labor for the direct operations of the church.[67] It was in principle a circumscribed right. From the early seventeenth century, royal law stated clearly that parish priests were not to requisition Indian workers for any other purpose—including the curas' subsistence needs—without pay.[68] But this left considerable room for maneuver. Who in fact was to say exactly what constituted necessary service for the operation of the local church? There was general agreement that one or more *sacristanes* should be available to keep the church and grounds clean and orderly, that a *topil* (assistant) or two ("theopan topiles") act as watchmen and an experienced man as bell-ringer (*campanero*), that several boys be available for odd jobs, that local men carry official mail, that an acolyte assist the priest in his duties, and that the Indians provide the cura with a horse, a mule to carry his belongings, and lodging and meals when he went out on circuit.[69] These duties normally were performed in rotation, with a new group of servants arriving weekly.

The unpaid service rendered to parish priests usually exceeded these requirements. Often the additional service was by mutual consent, part of a longstanding, customary arrangement or in place of cash contributions paid to the priests of other parishes.[70] In other cases, the priest made new demands on his own authority, testing the limits of custom and necessary service. Sometimes the tasks were within the standard interpretation of church service, but the demands were excessive. For example, Indians of Acaponeta (Nayarit) in 1791 acknowledged their obligation to go to the parish seat with a horse for the priest and a mule to carry his bed, and to pay for his meals when they needed him in their pueblo, but they complained that he demanded horses and mules for his "housekeeper" and their children, and a cook to prepare fancy meals and hot chocolate for them all.[71] On the other hand, Indian parishioners might comply more with the letter of the service rule than its spirit. The cura of Zapopan, outside Guadalajara, complained in 1803 that the Indians of Santa Ana Tepetitlan sent him skinny and unserviceable horses.[72]

The additional service demanded was usually for household tasks. Many parish priests seemed to regard attendance to their daily personal needs as a right of office, and it may have been so by custom in many parishes. For the Franciscans of Calimaya (Edo. de México) in 1711, Indian boys served a week at a time guarding the friars' sheep, bringing firewood, charcoal, water, fodder, "and the rest that is usual."[73] The cura's self-defined or customary personal needs could be considerable indeed. According to the Indians of San Nicolás Acuitzio and Tiripitío (Michoacán), they supplied their cura weekly in 1770 with four bakers, four cooks, four grooms, four sweepers, two stableboys, two fodder gatherers, two water carriers, six wagon drivers, two shepherds, four carpenters, and eight boys who spent the day scaring birds from the cura's fields. Local Indians were also obliged to go into the hills to cut wood and to plant and tend his fields without pay.[74] In some parishes, the water was brought from two or three miles away.[75] Other common requirements were for widows to grind corn, make tortillas, wash dishes, and clean the kitchen; carpenters and masons to work shifts on the cura's dwelling and offices; labor drafts to clean the water conduits and irrigation canals; and young men to carry the cura's private mail to distant places and run other errands.[76] In some small communities, as many as sixteen *semaneros*—weekly servants—were expected to serve the cura.[77]

Some curas used Indians for commercial profit and appropriated the labor of schoolchildren. The cura of Lolotla (Hidalgo) in 1818 was charged with sending a group of laborers (a "flete de peones") to carry his maize from Ixtlaguautla to Lolotla and forcing some Indians to work in his sugar mill without pay.[78] Instead of teaching reading, writing, and dogma to the schoolchildren who came to him during the week, the cura of Guayacocotla y Chicontepec (Veracruz) in 1786 apparently used them as manual laborers. According to a local *vecino* (non-Indian resident), they worked in the church grounds during the mornings, and in the afternoons they gathered fodder for up to 30 horses and mules belonging to the cura and his visitors. Women who came to pray in the church during the week reportedly were put to work carrying jugs of water on their heads to irrigate the cura's large garden.[79]

By customary arrangement, priests might also have the use of land and other property owned by their parishioners.[80] Usually their quarters, the *casas curales*, were provided rent free.[81] Sometimes, they had the customary use of a piece of community farmland (and some curas were accused of forcing local Indians to work it without pay).[82] Occasionally, this was a substantial estate. For example, in 1693 the Indians and vecinos of Coatepec (Zacualpan district, Edo. de México) allotted two cultivated fields, half a flour mill, seed, and six yokes of oxen for a resident priest. Four years later, the cura of Tlachichico (Tulancingo district, Hidalgo) had the use of sugarcane fields and a mill about 30 miles away from the parish seat in exchange for forgoing sacramental fees.[83] Curas sometimes asked for and got the use of community land for stables and hayfields.[84] Several curas were even charged with seizing Indian fisheries and lands, and forcing Indians to rent community fields to them.[85] They might also collect food and other provisions from parishioners. For instance, the cura of San Juan Tetelsingo in the district of Tixtla (Guerrero) collected the following as part of the customary weekly charges against his parishioners in 1776: one fanega of maize, one almud of chile, one almud of beans, one real's worth each of salt, tomatoes, onions, garlic, and pitch pine, one-half real's worth each of *tequesquite* (salts used for making soap), lime, and *epazote* (a condiment herb), one dozen hens, 20 eggs, and two reales' worth of lard.[86] In other parishes, jugs, cookware, and other pottery were collected, and if parishioners were slow to pay their usual fees, the curas' topiles came to collect clothing, food, candles, reed mats, animals, or other possessions.[87] The cura of Capuluac (Edo. de México) in 1796 was entitled to the *miccatlaoli*, the "corn of the dead" paid on All Souls' Day (November 2) in the form of five almudes of maize or a cash contribution of two and one-half reales per household.[88]

Increasingly in the eighteenth century, the most important source of income to curas in these two dioceses was the *derechos parroquiales* or *obvenciones* and *emolumentos*—the direct collection of fees, both for ceremonies performed for individuals (baptisms, marriages, and funerals) and for community masses celebrated on Sundays in the parish seat and the visitas and on special feast days in the towns, neighborhoods, hamlets, estates, and cofradías of the parish.[89] While reiterating the principles that the crown provided the curas and vicarios with stipends sufficient for subsistence and a decent living, and that Indians were not to be charged for marriages, funerals, or other sacraments or priestly ministrations, royal law from the 1590's on opened the way for collections in all of these situations by ordering that they not exceed what might be established in the provincial councils, legitimate custom, and the *aranceles* (published schedules of fees).[90]

By the early seventeenth century, aranceles for clerical fees were published by the archbishops of Mexico and the bishops of Guadalajara as guidelines for parishes in which customary arrangements for the support of the priests were not in force. By the eighteenth century, church leaders in both dioceses regarded the clerical fees for the sacraments as the basis for the cura's "decent" living, assuming that the parish had at least the standard 400 tributaries.[91] As the secretary of the cathedral chapter of Guadalajara put it in 1795, the parish priests in his diocese "have an adequate income for their honorable and decent maintenance with the *obvenciones* they exact according to the *aranceles*."[92]

When a cura took up a new assignment in the second half of the eighteenth century, he usually began with an income of only the clerical fees or whatever arrangement of reduced fees, service, property, and manuales was customary in the parish.[93] The crown and prelates in both dioceses were by then promoting the idea of a standard schedule of clerical fees paid in cash to replace the welter of local arrangements for service, payments in kind, and cash contributions,[94] with Indian parishes free to choose whether they preferred the new standard fees or their customary contributions (the attempt to standardize clerical fees is discussed in Chapter Seventeen). One result of this program of standardization was to make the clerical fees even more important as the formal source of a cura's income. The prelates attending the Fourth Provincial Council in Mexico City in 1771 spoke as if the derechos parroquiales were the curas' only means of livelihood, and in some parishes, they apparently were the only lawful means.[95]

The most frequently cited and perhaps earliest arancel for derechos parroquiales in the archdiocese was published in 1637–38.[96] It distinguished four categories of parishioners: Spaniards; mestizos, negros and mulatos; Indian residents on private estates; and pueblo Indians. For each, it listed fees for funerals and marriages. For Spaniards, a first-class funeral (*de cruz alta*) was to cost 12.5 pesos, plus 0.5 peso for the Indian cantors (a gratuity also was expected for the gravedigger in all cases); an ordinary funeral (*de cruz baja*), six pesos plus 0.5 peso for the cantors. Various funeral masses and other ceremonies that could accompany or follow the funeral of Spaniards were listed with their fees. A Spanish marriage cost four pesos and the vigil the night before in the parish church with six candles cost eight. The fees listed for Indian marriages and funerals generally were smaller (and presumed less elaborate ceremonies): four pesos for a marriage and vigil combined; three pesos for the burial of an adult and two for a child. Masses for the Indian pueblos were assessed at four pesos each for high masses in the three *pascuas* (high holy days) of Christmas, Easter, and Pentecost; four pesos at Corpus Christi and for the *fiesta titular*, plus two pesos to the cantors; three pesos for sung votive masses to saints; and two pesos for any spoken mass in pueblos de visita. Voluntary offerings for baptisms were permitted for all classes, but there was no fixed charge except as established by custom in the parish.[97]

Of the three individual ceremonies, baptisms almost always produced the least revenue, especially in Indian parishes. In non-Indian parishes, funeral fees usually earned more for the cura than marriage fees because of the options for elaborate and costly funerals. In Indian parishes, it usually was the marriage fees that produced the most revenue, or marriages and funerals produced about the same and from one and one-half to four times the fees for baptisms. No matter how the relative proportion of these three ceremonial fees varied, together they represented an important part of the cura's income—generally about one-half and rarely less than one-quarter of the parish rentas.[98]

In 1767, Archbishop Lorenzana issued a new arancel for clerical fees that he intended for wide application, and that remained in effect until the end of the colonial period.[99] It divided the fee-payers into the same four categories and offered a somewhat more elaborate schedule for village Indians than had the 1637 arancel: for baptisms, no charge beyond the 0.5 peso offering paid by the godfather; for marriage, four pesos for the vigil, two pesos for the *información matrimonial* (premarital inquiry),[100] and 0.25 peso for the marriage banns; for funerals, three pesos for an adult and two for a child in the parish seat, plus 0.5 peso for the cantors; in pueblos de visita, an additional two pesos for the funeral and 0.5 peso more for the cantors. Elaborate Indian funerals ("de pompa") were to be charged at half the rate for Spaniards. Sung masses on the five principal feast days (Christmas, Easter, Pentecost, Corpus Christi, and the feast of the community's patron saint) cost four pesos, plus two pesos for the cantors. If a procession was included, the parish priest received an extra two pesos and other priests who participated received one peso. Sunday masses in the parish seat were to be celebrated without charge, but in the pueblos de visita, there would be a two-peso charge for a low mass, two and one-half pesos for a high mass. Other community masses were charged at the same rate for the pueblos de visita and at three pesos each in the parish seat.[101] (The arancel in effect for the Diocese of Guadalajara at the end of the colonial period specified the same charges.)[102] But even with the 1767 arancel, many parishes in the archdiocese operated on customary agreements or devised new agreements that modified the standard schedule of fees to provide for a mix of smaller cash payments, some labor service, and some provisions.[103]

The clerical fees for baptism, marriage, and funerals were thought, on average, to yield about 0.5 peso annually from a non-Indian parishioner and about 0.25 peso from an Indian in the Diocese of Guadalajara (assuming that an Indian lived about 40 years).[104] Espinosa y Dávalos estimated that a Spaniard there paid 20 pesos, three reales, in clerical fees over the course of a lifetime, compared with nine pesos, five reales, for an Indian.[105] An Indian parish with 2,000 people would theoretically produce about 500 pesos a year from these fees, a mainly Spanish parish perhaps 1,000 pesos. There was, again, great variation, and the yield could be considerably lower than projected. At the beginning of the nineteenth century, the mainly Indian parish of Pilcayan (Taxco district, Guerrero) produced about 310 pesos a year from 30 marriages, over 100 baptisms, and 25–30 funerals.[106]

The special community masses, even in a modest parish, yielded 100 pesos to the cura, and the income from masses and processions could rise to 1,000 pesos or more in prosperous and densely populated parishes.[107] In the parish seat of Temascaltepec (Edo. de México) in 1790, eight feast days required special masses: Christmas, Easter, and Pentecost at four pesos each; Corpus Christi and the feast of the patron saint at six pesos each, and three others at three pesos each, for a total of 33 pesos.[108] Pueblos de visita had additional requirements. For Tejupilco (district of Temascaltepec) in 1760, there were monthly masses at three pesos each and two local feasts to Our Lady of the Assumption and Our

Lady of Guadalupe that required mass and processions, at six pesos each.[109] A parish composed of a capital and two pueblos de visita with similar requirements would have produced 129 pesos a year in masses for the cura and his vicarios, and another 52 pesos or so if dominicas were customary. The parish of Zapotlanejo near Guadalajara in 1770 had five pueblos de visita (Santa Fe, Teocuitatlan, Ascatlan, Juanacatlan, and Matatlan), each of which paid for a monthly mass at 1.5 pesos, and three special feast-day masses costing fourteen pesos in all. This amounted to 32 pesos for each visita, or 160 pesos a year outside the parish seat for community masses and processions. If Zapotlenejo produced the same revenue from masses as the visitas, plus dominicas of one peso a week, the community masses would have approached 250 pesos a year in income for the cura and his vicario in this parish of 588 families (2,968 people) distributed among six towns and 41 haciendas and ranches.[110]

In the archdiocese, where there were fewer well-endowed cofradías supporting other money-making religious events than in Guadalajara, the fees from community masses, fiestas, and baptism, marriage, and funeral ceremonies were regarded as the main source of the parish priests' income.[111] Many special masses were added to the standard list. For example, in Achichipico (Cuernavaca district) in the mid-eighteenth century, there were locally sponsored masses every Friday at the Altar of the Holy Sepulchre, and on the nineteenth of every month to San José.[112] In 1807, the parish of Oztoticpac in the district of Otumba near Mexico City observed twelve feast days (beyond the standard five and those of the patron saints of barrios in the parish seat and the pueblos de visita): Saint Joseph; Monday, Tuesday, Wednesday, and Friday of Easter week; Ascension of Christ; Holy Trinity; Saint Peter and Saint Paul; Birth of the Virgin; All Souls; Saint Nicholas Bishop; and Christmas Eve.[113] For the parish of Ocoyoacac (Tenango del Valle district) in 1700, obvenciones and other emolumentos of the sort produced 1,719 pesos from the parish seat and four pueblos de visita.[114] Acapetlahuaya (Ichcateopan district, Guerrero) and its four visitas, with an unusually large population of 1,310 families, produced 2,588 pesos in emolumentos in 1788.[115] By comparison, the 270 families of Tetela del Río parish (also in Guerrero) in 1705 produced only 432 pesos (97 for baptisms, marriages, and funerals, and 335 for community masses and celebrations).[116]

Guadalajara on the whole had smaller and poorer parishes than Mexico. Intendant Jacobo Ugarte y Loyola, in a report of April 9, 1791, noted that the diocese's parishes "generally yield[ed] very small *obvenciones*" and depended heavily on the expenditures of the cofradías.[117] In the poorest parishes in the middle and late eighteenth century, such as Iscuintla or Purificación, a cura could expect only about 250 pesos a year from the derechos parroquiales.[118] A middle-rank parish like Tala produced 726 pesos of income from marriages, funerals, baptisms, and community masses in 1778.[119]

Even where an arancel was in force, especially in the archdiocese, fee disputes arose. Payment was often in arrears, or the cura had to settle for a few chickens or a reduced contribution if he was to collect anything at all.[120] Curas were sometimes accused of overcharging or of demanding fees even when they did not perform the services. Indians in the parish of Guipustla (Hueypustla? district of Tetepango, Hidalgo) accused their cura in 1768 of demanding fifteen or sixteen pesos for a marriage, ten to twelve pesos for an adult funeral, five or six pesos for a child's funeral, eighteen pesos for Friday and Saturday processions during the week of San Lázaro's day, five pesos for most special masses, and seven pesos for mass on the patron saint's day, as well as a twelve-peso fee for confession during Lent.[121] Fees collected for the cura in absentia were especially common for funerals in outlying areas where the local fiscal (the cura's principal lay assistant) or one of the cantors was the only church official in attendance.[122]

Annual Income

The curas' annual income from legal sources can be estimated from several tax lists for the mesada (8.33 percent of reported income on appointment) and *pensión conciliar* (depending on time and place, 2–3 percent of reported income for support of the diocesan seminary); summary lists of 1746 and 1775, and income reports commissioned by the crown to identify which parishes could manage without the sínodos. Reported income or "rentas" comprised fees collected for baptisms, marriages, funerals, and "other emolumentos" (that is, the various fees for masses and feast days, whether sponsored by the community or by cofradías and capellanías) and, presumably, the sínodos, if any.[123] It did not include the labor service many curas received or the fees and fines they collected as ecclesiastical judges. Whether the dominicas, provisions, and incidental fees were included is usually not clear.[124]

Late colonial parish rentas for four periods in the archdiocese and five periods in the Diocese of Guadalajara are given in Appendix A. Though there may be some question about the scale of change in rentas during the last two decades of the colonial period, the direction of that change is clear: in the archdiocese, rentas appear to have doubled for most parishes between 1793 and 1805, growing from an average of 1,653 pesos a year for 137 parishes in 1793 to 3,280 pesos a year for the same parishes (excluding Malinalco and Tepotzotlan, for which the published figures may be erroneous) in 1805. If the assembled figures can be trusted, the parish rentas in the Diocese of Guadalajara more often declined than rose between 1772 and 1790, falling on the average from 1,609 pesos a year in 1772 to 987 a year in 1790.[125]

In the early 1790's, the average parish in the archdiocese appears to have yielded half again as much income as its Guadalajara counterpart. Of the 145 parishes outside the five-league district of Mexico City reporting in 1793, 11 percent reported rentas of 3,000–4,800 pesos; 68 percent 1,000–3,000 pesos; and 21 percent under 1,000 pesos.[126] By contrast, fully 67 percent of Guadalajara's 92 parishes in 1790 yielded less than 1,000 pesos, and only 6 percent yielded 3,000–4,000.

As scattered records for particular parishes confirm, the figures in Appendix A give a fair representation of the relative incomes of different parishes even where the absolute figures are doubtful. Within each diocese, incomes ranged very widely between parishes. For Mexico in 1793, Escanela was low, with an estimated 400 pesos, and Actopan high, at 4,800. In 1805, the disparity was even greater, from Tetela del Volcán at 427 pesos to Tulancingo at 10,080.[127] Incomes bunched toward the bottom rather than the top, but there was a select group of about 10 percent of especially lucrative parishes. Some rose to the top and others fell, especially in mining areas, but the parishes that consistently produced the largest rentas for their curas in the archdiocese outside the immediate territory of Mexico City were Actopan, Amecameca, Apam, Atotonilco el Grande, Cadereyta, Calimaya, Cuautitlan, Cuernavaca, Huichapan, Jonacatepec, Mazatepec, Metepec, Meztitlan, San Felipe Ixtlahuaca (Villa de San Felipe), Temascaltepec and its mining community, Tlayacapan, Tulancingo, Xilotepec, and Zimapan. In Guadalajara, the richest parishes outside the city were Agua de Venado, Aguascalientes, Fresnillo, Jalostotitlan, Mazapil, Ojocaliente, Real de Asientos, Santa María de Lagos, Sierra de Pinos, Teocaltiche, Tlaltenango, and Xerez.[128]

What constituted a "rich" parish from the standpoint of the cura's rentas? It is risky to speak in absolute terms, since two parishes with the same rentas might vary widely in the expense and difficulty of administration, and contemporaries had varying ideas about how much income made for a rich parish. The dean of the cathedral of Valladolid in 1785 regarded any parish with an annual income of 6,000 pesos as a curato pingüe.[129] By that standard, no rural parish in either Mexico or Guadalajara would have qualified as rich in the early 1790's. But eighteen of the archdiocese's 205 parishes in 1808 would have qualified, as would three of the Guadalajara parishes reporting in 1772 and 1774.

A royal cedula of October 31, 1768, emphasized the irony of claims that the parish of Chacaltianguis in Oaxaca was of "little value" when it produced rentas estimated at 3,000 pesos a year; its author regarded this sum as far exceeding what was required for a modest, "decent" living.[130] A lengthy 1791 jeremiad against lax, materialistic curas written by a peninsular priest living in the Villa de Córdoba (Veracruz), Pedro Fernández Ybarraran, also scoffed at the persistent "sobs" and laments of curas about the small incomes their parishes produced. According to him, in three current cases of complaint, the cura had no less than 2,500 pesos income in rentas.[131] In the 1780's and 1790's, 2,000 to 3,000 pesos was considered a comfortable income, easily enough money to permit a cura to live "decently," perform his various duties fully and charitably, and even support aging parents and unmarried sisters, if necessary.[132] In 1793, nearly a third of the curas of the archdiocese had this much or more; by 1805, the proportion had jumped to two-thirds. But for Guadalajara, the proportion of curas in this comfortable position was less than one-third in 1772 and only about one-tenth in 1790.

An income of 1,000 to 2,000 pesos was generally treated in church records as providing a decent, but restricted living. Nearly half the curas in the archdiocese in 1793 had rentas in this range. Adding in those with larger incomes brings the figure to four-fifths in that year—and to nine-tenths in 1805. The 1,000-peso baseline, however, may be too low, since parishes like Jiquipilco, with about 1,000 pesos rentas, and Tecicapan, with 1,200 pesos in 1793, were described by civil judges as poor parishes producing small incomes.[133] In Guadalajara, the parishes of Huauchinango, with 1,200 pesos rentas in 1767, Hostotipaquillo, with 1,035 in 1770, and Tala, with 1,000 in 1772, had been described in a 1755 report as having very small rentas.[134]

If the 1,000-peso figure is somewhat arbitrary, there is little doubt that parish incomes under that amount were regarded by priests and royal officials as inadequate for a living suited to the profession. For the archdiocese in 1793, as noted, this would have been 21 percent of the parishes reported (30 of 145), for Guadalajara, 67 percent.[135] Where parishes listed in Appendix A as having rentas of less than 1,000 pesos are described in other records from this period, the words "poor" and "small income" are the usual adjectives.[136] These were the difficult, sometimes desperate situations that an occasional clergyman or observer represented for polemical purposes as typical cases.[137] In fact, however, most curas were neither poor nor exceptionally wealthy. Except for Guadalajara in the 1790's, most of their incomes fell in the middle, between 1,000 and 3,000 pesos.[138]

Most vicarios, coadjutors, and other assistants to curas lived on fixed incomes that were less than the rentas of all but the poorest curas. In the late eighteenth century, most were paid a salary of 200 to 300 pesos a year from the cura's rentas and collected some manuales. A few assistants received salaries of 600 pesos— even 900 where the parish was prosperous, and the cura generous.[139] The fortunate among them held capellanías that increased their incomes by a few hundred pesos.[140] When the livings of assistants are mentioned in the general reports on parish priests, they are described as enjoying little income and living a frugal life.[141] Viceroy Bucareli doubted that there would be any takers for the post of chaplain–assistant cura at San Blas (Nayarit) in 1775 without a stipend of at least 500 pesos because of the high cost of clothing there and the expenses of "maintaining their poor families."[142] The small salaries of assistants could be a sore point in cases where the cura left much of the hard work of the parish to them, took up residence in Mexico City or a provincial town, and demanded his full rentas. Since a cura who was absent without the bishop's permission was supposed to have his emoluments withheld, the bishops usually made sure that the coadjutor and others who were doing his work received a relatively large share of the parish income, and sometimes all of it except the sínodo, if there was one.[143]

Additional information on the income paid to curas by their parishioners, and on the curas' expenses, comes from miscellaneous administrative and judicial records. Periodically, curas reported on rentas that they received or that were due them in what were called *directorios* or *cuadrantes de obvenciones anuales*. Two of these reports from parishes in the archdiocese, for Jiquipilco in the mid-1780's and Capuluac in 1772, display the types of contributions made by rural parishioners for the support of their cura.[144]

The parish of Jiquipilco, in the district of Ixtlahuaca near Toluca, was regarded by the subdelegado in 1793 as a "parish of little income."[145] That year, its reported rentas were 1,000 pesos. A decade earlier, its gross renta receipts had been reported at 2,130 pesos. The text of the directorio describes the fixed income from community masses and feast days celebrated, and the "eventuales" or obvenciones from clerical fees, first fruits, and service. The cura, Luis Antonio de Veas, wrote in the margins his explanatory notes and comments on the difficulty of collecting his due. His initial comment was that, with few exceptions, the parishioners were cheats who defrauded him at every turn. Whenever possible, anyone assigned to this parish should collect the fiesta and marriage fees before the events took place, he advised.

The first category of receipts was for Sunday masses, which were celebrated in the parish seat and the pueblos de visita by turn every five weeks. These dominicas were valued at 992 pesos: 97 from the parish seat (counting one real from each resident laborer on two nearby haciendas), 117.5 from the towns of Santa Cruz and San Miguel and resident laborers of two other haciendas (also at one real per *gañán*); 40 from the town of San Felipe (at four pesos a visit); 77.5 from the town of San Bartolomé (40) and a neighboring hacienda (at one peso, six reales, for a visit); 20 from the barrio of Santa María; and 640 from five haciendas for masses every Sunday and principal feast day. The cura added in the margin that he collected dominicas from the devious pueblo Indians by garnisheeing their hacienda wages.

The second category of rentas was fiestas. During the year, Jiquipilco and the visitas customarily requested certain special masses, at charges of four pesos for a sung mass and two for a spoken one in the visitas, and three pesos for a sung mass in the parish seat. The Indians were responsible for feeding the priests when they went out to the visitas. The cura reported that in the past there had been 40 or 50 of these special masses, with a hypothetical value of 150 pesos, but that in his time, no more than 25 were requested annually. He complained that since 1781, the visita of San Miguel had asked only for a low mass in order to pay the smallest sum possible. He had eliminated the practice of each Indian giving the priest an egg at confession. During February, fiestas with a high mass and procession in two haciendas produced 34 pesos; Candlemas in Jiquipilco produced six pesos, and mass in an hacienda the next day another six. During Lent, the cura and his vicarios went to the visitas to hear confessions and sing a mass, for 73 pesos, six reales. On Friday before Palm Sunday, mass and a sermon produced thirteen pesos (including one peso to the cantors).

Easter week was the busiest and most lucrative. On Monday, mass and a sermon produced twelve pesos (of which 1.5 pesos went to the cantors). On Wednesday, mass and a sermon produced eleven pesos and a second sermon, at night, another eight (with one peso to the cantors if they sang then). On Thursday, mass and a sermon paid by the procession soldiers (with one peso to the cantors) and at night another mass and sermon paid by whoever was responsible that year produced 21. On Good Friday, the centurion paid eight pesos, the sermon in the afternoon produced ten pesos, and a second sermon at night produced eleven pesos. (From 1782 to 1784, the leaders of the processions collected 15.5 pesos for the sermon on the Crucifixion. Apparently this was not done before or after those years.) For Thursday, Friday, and Saturday, the Cofradía del Santísimo Sacramento paid ten pesos to the cura and one peso to the cantors; during the adoration of the Holy Cross, three or four pesos were usually collected, plus a little more in the offering plate at the foot of the cross. On Easter Sunday, the procession soldiers were supposed to pay three pesos for mass, and another six pesos was due for Easter services in the parish seat. In all, Easter week ought to produce about 103 pesos for the parish priests (not all of it free and clear, since the cura paid visiting priests to give some of the sermons). However, the cura noted that various fees dating back to 1780 were still pending, including Thursday of Easter week in 1781, when the captain, *alférez* (standard bearer), and centurion did not pay their contribution and held back a total of 24 pesos. The captain did not even bother to show up that day, and only after threats was he persuaded to pay six pesos of what was due.

In May, the village fiestas of San Felipe and Santa Cruz produced twelve pesos. In June, the feasts of Pentecost, Corpus Christi, and the Holy Cross in Jiquipilco produced eighteen pesos, and the Cofradía del Santísimo was supposed to pay ten pesos to the cura and one peso to the cantors for the fiestas del Santísimo (the cura noted that between 1778 and 1780 this cofradía accumulated debts to him of 141 pesos). During August, a high mass in San Felipe and the fiesta of San Bartolomé each produced six pesos; September brought eighteen pesos for the fiestas of the Barrio Santa María, the Barrio San Miguel, and the pueblo of Santa Cruz; five for a high mass to San Nicolás Tolentino; and six for the celebration of the "exaltación en el serro." In October, a local parishioner paid the cura three pesos for a sung mass for her great-grandmother. In November, he visited all the pueblos on All Souls' Day at four pesos each; responsories in the parish seat produced 40 pesos, responsories in the visitas produced 20 pesos (the cura noted that he had introduced the ceremony of the burial of the bones, for relief of the souls in Purgatory, for which he received about four pesos); and a feast for one of the archangels produced ten pesos (plus one peso for the cantors). In December, there was a mass for Our Lady of Guadalupe at twelve pesos; Christmas services in Jiquipilco at six pesos; two masses on the twenty-fifth and twenty-sixth, the consecration of the Host, and a procession in Santa Cruz for ten pesos; Christmas services in San Felipe for six pesos, and a low mass in San Bartolomé for two pesos. Ideally, the income in the fiestas category was about 865 pesos.

The third category was obvenciones. Here the cura listed labor service: a sacristán and a servant from the visita he was serving that week, plus one topil from Jiquipilco. If he wanted a woman to grind corn for him he had to pay her two reales a week. He also mentioned first fruits, noting that non-Indians in the parish paid about 60 pesos a year, while the Indians customarily paid nothing. The main revenues under obvenciones were the fees for baptisms, marriages, and funerals. Indians were assessed five reales for a baptism, non-Indians ten (of which 20 percent went to the sacristán). The other fees varied by place, according to whether villagers or estate residents were under custom or the arancel. The obvenciones produced about 273 pesos. In all, the dominicas could be expected to produce 47 percent, the fiestas 40 percent, and the obvenciones 13 percent of the yearly emoluments of Jiquipilco.

The second example, for Capuluac (Tenango del Valle district), is interesting as an illustration of a customary arrangement where the Indian parishioners paid the cura largely in services and kind. In 1772, the parish agreed to the following terms. Five times a year each family would pay the cura 0.5 real. They would pay four pesos and two birds (chickens?) for every marriage, plus 0.75 peso to the fiscal for publishing the marriage banns; 1.25 pesos for burials of adults and children; and 2.5 reales to the fiscal for baptisms. Married men were to pay the cura one almud of maize as first fruits, five almudes of maize at harvest, and four almudes of maize for miccatlaoli. He was also to get two loads of fodder a day from the *tepixque* (calpulli officers) from Ash Wednesday to the end of the year; two reales' worth of fish a day during Lent and four reales' worth a week during the rest of the year from the "raneros" (frog hunters, perhaps a neighborhood or lineage group); four pesos and five fowl from the gobernador for each of the three pascuas; 40 eggs and 80 tortillas a week for his semaneros from "los merinos" (merino sheep or sheepherders, perhaps another neighborhood or kin group?); 20 eggs a day during Lent and for vigils throughout the year (presumably from the community as a whole); four pesos and four chickens from the *regidores* (secondary officers of the cabildo) for the patron saints' festivities in their barrios and for the fiesta titular of the parish; and two pesos and four chickens from the regidores and fifteen pesos and five birds from the gobernador for the processions. A mule with saddle, harness, and attendant was to be supplied by the regidores whenever the cura wanted it.

By way of semaneros, the cura was to get a cook with her equipment, a labor boss, a charcoal supplier with a load of two fanegas, a *quilpixqui* ("so-called harvester"), a *clatlapo* (fieldhand?), a shepherd, a swineherd, a *cahuaio* (from "caballo," a groom), a *pixqui* (another harvester) with his tools, a *ateca* (porter), and a topil to serve in the church. The community at large was to farm two cornfields for him. He was also to have another porter on demand and could order farmworkers to carry loads wherever he wished, "whether to Malinalco, Lerma, Toluca, Mexico, or other places," for a fee of one real.

Expenses

Curas had a variety of expenses and deductions that reduced their income from rentas by a third or more. Those who spent more time away from their parishes than the church allowed were to have an amount proportional to their absence deducted from their income and placed in the parish fund for fábrica (for construction, repairs, altarpieces, images, and objects needed for the liturgy). In the first year after appointment to a parish, the cura paid about 12 percent of his reported income in direct taxes: 8.33 percent for the mesada eclesiástica, 1.5 percent (18 percent of the mesada) for collection and conveyance of the mesada and appointment papers to Spain, and 2 percent for the pensión conciliar.[146] He had to present collateral or a co-signer to guarantee that the mesada would be paid in full within four months of beginning his parish duties.[147] Thereafter, he paid the pensión conciliar every year, and frequently was expected to send money for Spain's wars in Europe and respond to other requests from the crown for extraordinary contributions. From 1802 to 1807, these extraordinary contributions were organized into a regular subsidy, a 3 percent levy on rentas.[148] By the end of the colonial period, in most parishes of Guadalajara and an increasing number in Mexico, the cura was paying for his food and necessary household services, as well as those of his vicarios.[149] In addition, though bishops were expected to visit the parishes of their diocese at their own expense, the parish priest was often responsible for feeding and lodging him and his party, if he could not pass on the expense to his parishioners.[150]

The largest category of fixed expenses for most curas was the salaries of assistants, and from midcentury on, the crown and some bishops were constantly pushing curas in populous and dispersed parishes to hire more of them. In practice, most curas had to support their assistants from their rentas, even though the law called for payments from the tithe and sínodos. Vicarios were typically paid

200 to 400 pesos a year, and some curas also gave them a share of their manuales and services. In 1732, Manuel García Berdugo of Tejupilco (Hidalgo) said he maintained a vicario at 600 pesos a year, supplied him with 25 fanegas of maize, and allowed him to collect the manuales.[151] In the prosperous mining district of Pachuca (Hidalgo) in the 1770's, vicarios made between 500 and 700 pesos from salary, masses, and manuales, although one received only seven pesos a week in fixed salary.[152] Closer to the norm were parishes like Cempoala near Mexico City, where the two vicarios earned 260 pesos a year each (five pesos a week), plus food and lodging, and Tamazula in Jalisco, where the vicario received 300 pesos, plus the occasional fee for a special mass.[153]

In addition to maintaining one or more vicarios or dividing the parish rentas with coadjutors and vicarios de pie fijo (or both), the cura often paid a sacristán, a campanero, acolytes, cantors, a notary, and perhaps an organist.[154] If the parish did not have an endowment or fund for construction and supplies, he also had to pay for the wax, wine, communion wafers, and lamp oil used in the services, and for the purchase, cleaning and repair of vestments and other "ornamentos." During Easter Week, most curas would hire licensed priests at 50 pesos or so to help with confession or give sermons. If these temporary assistants came for all of Lent, they might be paid 100 pesos.[155] After paying the priests and laymen who helped them with parish duties and paying for the supplies that "maintained the solemnity of the rites," most curas could expect to net about half the funds collected for masses and holiday celebrations.[156]

Curas who were faithful to the teachings of the church and their preparation for parish service, even curas situated in the most lucrative parishes, were expected to keep little of the income they received from fees and other emoluments for themselves. As Puebla's Bishop Juan de Palafox y Mendoza said in his *Manual de sacerdotes*, "I assign you to voluntary poverty. . . . Learn to be poor, to live without pretensions. . . . Be a canal, not a reservoir. . . . Strip yourself of all property and you will fly."[157] His message, like that of the eighteenth-century prelates of Mexico and Guadalajara in their pastoral letters to the clergy, was to "live humbly [and] decently," and attend to the needs of the poor.[158] In more practical terms, Quito's Bishop Alonso de la Peña Montenegro recommended in his *Itinerario* that a cura spend a quarter of his income from stipends and first fruits on charitable works.[159]

If the curas' own characterizations of their service in the poorer parishes of Mexico and Guadalajara can be trusted, some of them spent virtually all of their parish income on church construction, altarpieces and religious images, decent equipment for the mass, and charitable works.[160] It is certain, in any case, from less self-congratulatory sources, that some priests took Bishop Palafox's injunction seriously. In a report on the clergy in the Diocese of Guadalajara at the end of 1755, the president of the Audiencia of Nueva Galicia described Joseph Caro Galindo, the cura of Tepatitlan, as a man of limited education but great zeal, who spent all of his income above subsistence on the construction of the parish church.[161] In the same report, Anacleto Bernal, the cura of Purificación, was said to be a man "of few letters but solid virtue, exemplary in his personal conduct, and charitable." Of his small income, he "did not keep even enough for himself. It is all for the poor," added the judge. The cura of the wealthy parish of Zacatecas, Antonio Cabrera, was said by the same judge to spend half of the rentas on his church.[162] The alcalde mayor of Real del Monte (Hidalgo) in 1775 reported that the parish priest there regularly charged less for funerals than custom or the schedule of fees allowed, and often charged nothing at all. As a result, his rentas would have been substantially less than the figures reported for tax purposes.[163] The subdelegado of Huichapan (Hidalgo) in 1793 praised the cura of Aculco, Luis José Carrillo, as "so dedicated to the promotion of public worship that for some years he has only taken from his fees and other collections enough for his most basic needs. He has applied all the rest to the rebuilding of the parish church and the addition of side altars." [164] That same year, the subdelegado of Tacuba (D.F.) extolled the twelve vicarios of the parish of Tacuba as

distinguished by their probity, chaste conversation, superior conduct and disinterestedness. . . . You may be sure that among these twelve there is not one who has cast his lot with the perishable goods of this world or accumulated wealth by the handfuls and thereby earned renown as victims of that miserable idol of avarice.[165]

Exactly what curas typically made after expenses is difficult to say, for though the renta figures in Appendix A may have included deductions for the major expenses of administering the parishes (except for 1805 in the archdiocese and 1774 in the Diocese of Guadalajara), local records do not often put detailed figures for emoluments and expenses side by side. Three cases where net income from the emoluments can be figured are Sultepec (Edo. de México) in 1700, Hostotipaquillo (Jalisco) in 1787–97, and Yecapixtla (Morelos) in 1814.[166] Sultepec produced 1,645 pesos from emolumentos and obvenciones in 1700 and received a sínodo of 165 pesos for a total reported income of 1,810 pesos. The expenses listed were 548 pesos to four assistants and 40 pesos for the pensión conciliar. The net income, reported without subtracting charitable works and sacramental supplies, was 1,222 pesos.

Hostotipaquillo, a parish mainly of non-Indians, reported an annual average income to the cura of 1,360 pesos: 308 from baptisms, 226 from marriages, 550 from funerals, and 276 from masses and fiestas. From this, the cura paid an annual average of 68 pesos to the sacristán who assisted in the baptisms, marriages, and funerals, 46 to the bell ringer, 50 to priests who helped in the parish during Lent, 13 to priests who helped confess the sick in the parish, 5 to a Mercedarian who administered sacraments in an hacienda in the parish, 11 to priests who served whenever the coadjutor was ill; 4 for chrism, 8 for books and paper used for parish registers and other church business, 5 for rental of horses to go out to hear confessions, 42 for the pensión conciliar, 17 for a subsidio eclesiástico, 1 for a legal fee, and 150 for the support of his dependents, or 420 pesos of expenses in all. The average annual net income without reporting charitable works, miscellaneous supplies, or the coadjutor's salary was 940 pesos.[167]

The Yecapixtla records for 1814 break down the income and expenses by month. The income from baptism, marriage, and funeral fees, dominicas, and special masses and fiestas varied from a low of 158 pesos in June to a high of 220 pesos in May. For the year, the parish produced 91 pesos from baptisms (this was largely an Indian parish, so baptism fees would have been small), 267 pesos from marriages, 729 pesos from funerals, 444 pesos from dominicas, and 708 pesos from special masses, fiestas, and confessions. The gross income was 2,239 pesos. The expenses, totaling 1,164 pesos, were mainly the salary assigned to the priest who actually administered the parish for the cura (996 pesos), with the rest going to pay for paper and a scribe and for contributions to the royal troops stationed there. The cura's net income was 1,075 pesos.

Other Sources of Income

From the sixteenth century on, parish priests in Spanish America enlarged their incomes through retail and wholesale trade, mining ventures, moneylending, and landholding. From the beginning, these enterprises were regarded by the crown and bishops as violations of a priest's spiritual duties, dividing his life between the spirit and mundane preoccupations, diverting him from his principal duty to the parishioners, and leading to a life of cupidity and material cares.[168] Royal law reprinted in the *Recopilación* (1681) explicitly and repeatedly forbade parish priests to engage in trade and commerce ("tratos, negocios y grangerías") on their own account or for others, to serve as agents for encomenderos, and to own or operate mines.[169]

These royal injunctions were seconded by American prelates in their provincial councils, pastoral letters, and other writings.[170] The *Itinerario* instructed priests in Indian parishes not to engage in trade or make commercial contracts, not to raise animals for sale, not to run strings of mules, not to own mills or obrajes, not to operate mines, and not to work as tavernkeepers, bakers, butchers, and the like; these were mortal sins subject to excommunication.[171] Ecclesiastical laws for Mexican dioceses specifically prohibited priests from engaging in monopolistic economic activity, including tax farming, and from buying landed estates without the bishop's license.[172] The Fourth Provincial Council, meeting in 1771, repeated the restrictions on parish priests engaging in any mechanical art, retail trade, rental of rural property, operation of royal monopolies, or personal operation of mines, rural estates, or shops.[173] The provincial council went on at length to describe the kinds of trade in which parish priests could not engage (and in which some obviously did engage): buying for resale cochineal, honey, cotton, maize, blankets, woven goods, and other items that Indians paid in tribute.[174]

Bishops sometimes made their feelings about the priests' material pursuits edifyingly clear. Pérez de Velasco, in his guide for assistant pastors in the Diocese of Puebla in 1766, recounted how Dr. Manuel Fernández de Santa Cruz, bishop of Puebla during the last quarter of the seventeenth century, reacted in such a case. Receiving news of the death of a cura who had been universally admired and thinking his family might be in need, the bishop went to offer his help:

"How has he left you?" asked the bishop. "Not badly, Sir," the relatives answered, for he had left them an hacienda. "*The cura had an hacienda*!" responded the oracular bishop in a tone of great wonder and surprise. Turning his surprise into sorrow for the *cura*, this most discreet prelate continued, "So the *cura* had an hacienda! I am very sorry to hear it, because I believed him to be a good *cura*." And he said so because he knew very well (as he knew everything) that ministers of the church should not tend any other vineyard than the one they have been assigned, the one already planted and nourished with the Most Precious Blood of the Divine Tiller.[175]

Despite all of the injunctions and exhortations against profit-making activities and the accumulation of property, ecclesiastical law provided for exceptions. Colonial church law explicitly permitted the ownership of estates, the sale of produce, and other kinds of commerce under certain conditions. According to the *Itinerario*, curas were not to own ranches close enough to their parishes that they could employ their parishioners to work them. But they could own ranches and buy, raise, and sell young steers and mules that had been mistreated.[176] Similarly, to the rhetorical question whether parish priests could engage in trade and commerce, the *Itinerario* responded with a qualified yes: if the cura did not have sufficient income to meet his basic needs and live decently, he could farm and trade.[177] According to the ecclesiastical laws of the Diocese of Michoacán, curas could own haciendas "inherited, granted, or [acquired by] other just title" and could sell their produce, although they could buy a landed estate only with the bishop's license and only if it was not acquired from Indians in their jurisdiction.[178] The Fourth Provincial Council provided that parish priests could maintain personal property and sell the produce of their estates wholesale, but could not set up their own stores for that purpose or sell retail to the public.[179]

That eighteenth-century parish priests in Mexico and Guadalajara were actively involved in profit-making activities is certain. How many were involved and what proportion of their income they derived from these activities is less certain. Apparently, no general inspections of parish priests' estates and economic activities were made in the period.[180] The record of their economic pursuits is scattered through notarial, judicial, and administrative records. Here I can only summarize information gleaned from particular cases.

References to illicit commerce are common, but they do not usually go beyond phrases like "he has his private business affairs," "he mixes in the temporal business affairs of the laity," "he is inclined to personal interests and trade," he engages in "the forbidden commerce," or "he traffics in various goods."[181] Some curas had relatives or friends run retail stores in their parishes to maintain the fiction that they were not the real owners. The vicario of Tixtla (Guerrero) in 1793 reportedly kept a prostitute and had her tend the shop he established next to his house.[182] Manuel de Agüero, the cura of Yautepec (Morelos) in the 1790's, ran a candle and tobacco store out of his house, as well as a general postal service. Some priests monopolized the local sale of soap and other items they manufactured.[183] Curas were also charged with buying livestock and fattening them for resale, manufacturing cane alcohol for sale, and operating repartimientos in which Indians purchased mules and other goods from them.[184] Another kind of illicit trade had the cura operating as a wholesale merchant, engrossing local Indian produce for resale.[185]

Several curas and vicarios were also said to be active in mining. Rafael de Arce, a vicario of Mexcala and Sochipalan, in the Taxco area, was criticized by the subdelegado in 1793 for neglecting his parish duties to attend to mining ventures surreptitiously carried on under a brother's name.[186] Pedro Mauricio Lascano, a licensed pastor in the parish of Temascaltepec in 1715, was confronted with evidence that he was buying ore from local miners for resale. Unabashed, he reportedly replied that all the prominent and respected men of the community did the same. When the local vicario told him he should stop because the mineowners were complaining of Indian workers robbing their good ore and selling it to him, Lascano replied "Those are a nun's scruples. I buy the ore openly, in public."[187]

Perhaps most often, the cura acquired land in or near his parish to grow his own food and sell the surplus.[188] Some curas reported acquiring small farms to meet their personal needs, support their relatives, and provide for times of shortage. But despite disclaimers, others operated large farms exclusively for commercial purposes, planting them entirely in sugarcane or using them for ranching.[189] The cura of Huehuetoca (Edo. de México) rented and restored the Hacienda San Pedro beginning in 1753, then raised cattle on it to supply meat to Toluca.[190] These rural estates were sometimes part of a diversified personal enterprise. In addition to his store in Yautepec, cura Manuel de Agüero acquired the nearby Hacienda San Carlos Borromeo, which supplied his bacon contract on the outskirts of Mexico City. He also owned some houses in Mexico City.[191] Whether rented or bought, an hacienda was a distraction, likely to draw a priest like Agüero away from his parish for weeks at a time, and tempting him to requisition parishioners' labor for his personal use.[192] But the income from estates and trade could also contribute to harmony in the parish if it led the cura to forgive clerical fees and give up control over pueblo finances.

Though their property was more often inherited than acquired from the proceeds of office, some curas of Indian parishes became wealthy men by the standards of the time. At his death in 1754, Pedro de Zúñiga y Toledo, cura of San Bartolomé Ozolotepec (Hidalgo), left his heirs well over 1,000 pesos of plate, almost 100 books, clothes valued at nearly 500 pesos, a houseful of furniture and religious art, two carriages and trappings, the Hacienda de San Pablo, a shop in San Bartolomé, livestock, stores of grain, and various accounts receivable, including more than 1,600 pesos owed to him by nine individuals and two communities.[193] Every diocese had rich curas "with haciendas, houses, jewels, beautiful clothing and funds for perhaps less decent expenses,"[194] but the estates of most curas in rural Indian parishes were more modest. A priest was likely to need a little land if he stayed in the parish for a year or more. Almost inevitably he would acquire some livestock, then need a place to keep and graze the animals. That might be the extent of his interest in real estate.[195] A survey of priests living in the Diocese of Guadalajara in 1796 turned up a few who owned haciendas and ranchos, but none of them were curas or vicarios.[196] Some parish priests left little property behind. Mariano Calzada, former vicario of Sierra de Pinos, when arrested for solicitation in the confessional in 1792, owned only 45 books, two bundles of letters, some clothes (including two hats), a couple of trunks, a silver-tipped cane, his bed, sheets, a bookcase, two saddles, and spurs.[197]

* * *

In sum, parish priests were in principle to be supported financially by the crown and the bishop; but in practice, neither the crown nor the officers of the cathedrals made this possible in the dioceses of Mexico and Guadalajara. Without the tithe or other fixed income, most of a cura's livelihood from his profession came in the form of direct collections from his parishioners. These collections varied from year to year and depended on the parishioners' devotion and willingness to pay, as well as on the priest's exemplary conduct, public relations skills, and local power.[198] They took the form of cash payments, provisions, and labor service of various kinds, with cash payments becoming increasingly important after the 1760's.

Heavy dependence on direct collections could drive a wedge between the priest and his parish. Curas who depended heavily on these rentas for their living (and this was especially true of those who had not been in the parish long) struggled to collect as much as they could and were likely to violate customary arrangements, local expectations, and sometimes the law in doing so. Emoluments as the main source of income put charity in tension with the pastor's livelihood. He would think twice before burying a parishioner without charge, or agreeing to wait a few months for his fee, or allowing a young couple to marry outside the parish.

Parishioners naturally resented the face-to-face collection and strict accounting of these charges. The ceremonial fees were an especially tender matter because they were levied on individuals and families, not paid anonymously from a community fund. But even the community masses, processions, and other celebrations were frequently paid with collections of small sums from local families. This was especially true in the Archdiocese of Mexico. Forgetting the many indirect exactions made to the crown and its minions, the Indians of Malacatepec in 1774 could truly claim that "we pay much more in tribute to the *cura* than to our sovereign, the king."[199] Whether or not these payments were a great burden on their families and community finances, Indian parishioners were inclined to regard them as burdensome because "they do not believe that they have the obligation to personally bear the costs of public worship and the priests."[200] This feeling of resentment was magnified when priests threatened to withhold services if their fees were not paid promptly.[201]

Though the curas' incomes varied greatly, most collected enough to live "decently" and fulfill a pastor's basic obligations. Yet there was also a substantial minority who earned a more precarious living from their emoluments, and a class of unbeneficed parish priests—the rural vicarios and some coadjutors—who subsisted on their small salaries and miscellaneous fees.

Curas' incomes in the Archdiocese of Mexico differed rather sharply from those in the Diocese of Guadalajara in two respects. Rentas in the archdiocese were on the rise after 1770, whereas those for Guadalajara were in decline, at least into the 1790's. Also, while incomes were smaller in Guadalajara, they depended less on direct collections for services and more on cofradías. In Mexico, curas relied more on obvenciones and a variety of special masses in the parish seat and the visitas, and were edgy about the lack of income from fixed capital to support their services.[202] Greater conflict with villagers over parish revenues was built into the larger incomes of the Mexico curas.

In both dioceses, where the parish was poor or the parishioners resisted the idea of piecemeal payments for their services, most curas responded by exploiting extralegal sources of income or seeking another parish. Few followed Bishop Palafox's advice to "seek poverty so you can fly." Parish service for most diocesan pastors was their main source of income, and there was a tendency to equate the size of a cura's emoluments with his status and authority.[203] The pastorate was a living and a badge of dignity, as well as a calling.

CHAPTER SEVEN

Priests as Judges and Teachers

> My children, the office I hold—which is that of priest—
> has been given to me by God. Since I have not received it
> for my own good but for the good of your souls, I must do
> whatever I can for the good of your souls. So now I appeal
> to you that for the love of God you fulfill your duty as
> Christians and children of God, which is to fulfill the com-
> mandments of God and the Church. I also appeal to you
> to come to mass every Sunday and feast day, where we
> should give thanks to God for what he has given us, and
> where we should ask him for what we need. . . . You must
> be His true children, and this cannot be accomplished
> without knowing the doctrine. So that you may learn, I
> am going to teach you a little. Listen.
> —Opening words of a booklet of Chinantec and
> Spanish phrases useful to a priest in his pastoral
> work, composed shortly after Mexican Independence

In this way of presenting himself to his Indian parishioners, the pastor displayed his sense of the formal authority and responsibilities of his office. It
is a firm statement, without much qualification. In a society where expediency
and the pursuit of happiness in this life were shadowed at every turn by finalities
and divine judgment, where membership in the society required membership in
the church, the parish priest occupied a powerful place, or at least he expected
to.[1] Indeed, his open-ended sense of responsibility to do "whatever I can for
the good of your souls" was predicated on an equally open-ended authority. But
late colonial definitions of the priest's role varied widely and were changing significantly. It could be narrowly construed in terms of sacramental obligations or
broadly construed as involving responsibility for enforcing a wide range of personal and collective conduct that bore on the well-being of the soul.

   This chapter is the first of three in which I explore this ambiguity from the
priests' perspective, describing them at work in their rural Indian parishes and in
relationship to their parishioners in the late colonial context. I begin with a general discussion of the formal, normative aspects of the curas' professional lives,
the "poder del cura,"[2]—their responsibilities in the regulation of colonial Indian
life after the Council of Trent. The next chapter deals with the range of personalities, attitudes, and manifest behavior of colonial parish priests in the field.

Both of these chapters consider the figures of speech that the priests used to organize and enlarge their experience of what was real. Chapter Nine focuses specifically on the coercive aspects of their authority.

The Priest's Role

Priests were socialized, by seminaries, bishops, and professional manuals, to regard theirs as the most comprehensive of callings: "shepherd, priest, mediator, judge, celestial physician, teacher, treasurer, father, soldier, and light of the community," said Juan de Palafox y Mendoza, bishop of Puebla in the mid-seventeenth century; "priest, minister, deputy, ambassador, vice-God, and copy-likeness-image-representation of the Supreme King of Heaven and Earth," wrote Pérez de Velasco in his 1766 manual for assistant pastors.[3]

In more practical terms that regularly appear whenever parish priests described their duties in colonial records, as well as in the manuals they studied and the exhortations of their superiors, curas were expected to be, above all, vigilant spiritual guides, teachers, and examples of inspired conduct for their parishioners. Each of these three roles contained several attributes that connected and intertwined around the goal of the "spiritual health of the soul" and eventual salvation. The pastor's role of vigilant spiritual guidance was at once parental, fraternal, professional, and institutional.[4] He was the "spiritual father," "committed to the spiritual direction of his children."[5] He was to offer "fatherly consolation," nourishing his spiritual children "by the preaching of the Divine Word," and acting as a "brother, family member, and companion."[6] When necessary, however, he must also act the stern father and judge, playing out his role of soldier of Christ, fighting off Satan—the "common enemy"—with his sword of sacred scriptures and "winning souls for Heaven."[7]

In the most common image of all, the cura was a physician who must "cure the mortal ills of the soul" by "prescribing the proper medications according to the nature of the ailment."[8] His survival kit included prayers, blessings, exorcisms, the magical power of religious images, and the miracle of the mass, but his main medicines for the health of the soul and the Christian community were the sacraments of baptism, communion, penance, matrimony, and extreme unction and the popular practice of the precepts of the faith. Not only was he a dispenser of the sacraments that facilitated salvation, his office was, itself, a sacrament, lending a divine quality to the exercise of his duties.

The efficacy of the sacraments, however, depended on the recipient's understanding and believing in them, and therefore on the priest's teaching.[9] Formal teaching had two aspects: imparting the fundamentals of Christian doctrine in regular classes and preaching the divine word. The Council of Trent specified that classes in Christian doctrine were to be held "at least on all Sundays and solemn feast days, but during the season of fasts, of Lent, and of the Advent of the Lord, daily, or at least on three days of the week if [the priests] shall deem it necessary."[10] This schedule became the standard if not always the practice in colonial parishes.

The parish priest was the teacher, the guide, the physician, but what exactly was he to teach, and how? What map was he to follow? What medicines was he to administer? Such questions were answered in manuals and published guides that described the priest's duties in detail and gave advice about how to fulfill them. Priests—even those without scholarly pretensions—carried these hefty primers with them from parish to parish. In 1766, Dr. Andrés de Arze y Miranda, veteran cura of Indian parishes in the Diocese of Puebla, former canon of the cathedral chapter there, and bishop-elect of San Juan de Puerto Rico, recommended three areas of basic study for Mexican parish priests: the Indian language, the catechism, and moral theology. For the catechism or rudiments of the faith, he recommended the *Novíssimo cathecismo* of Ignacio de Paredes, *El camino del cielo*, by Fr. Martín de León, and a book of sermons by Juan de la Anunciación. For moral theology, Arze recommended, above all, "Montenegro."[11]

"Montenegro" was the *Itinerario para parochos de indios, en que se tratan las materias más particulares, tocantes a ellos, para su buena administración.* The nominal author, Alonso de la Peña Montenegro, bishop of Quito in the mid-seventeenth century, completed the text in 1663. It went through seven editions between 1668 and 1771 and circulated widely in Spanish America until the end of the colonial period.[12] It is the manual that eighteenth-century curas and vicarios in New Spain were most likely to take with them into the field, appearing frequently in the inventories of property owned by parish priests and in the footnotes of treatises they wrote (see Fig. 3).[13]

The *Itinerario* is a large work, running to over 700 pages of text in the quarto editions. In five "books" it covers (1) a definition of the cura and his many duties; (2) the nature and customs of the Indians, and what they must know to be saved; (3) the sacraments of baptism, penance, communion, extreme unction, ordination, and marriage, and how they should be administered to Indians; (4) the precepts of the church (the laws of the church governing the Christian conduct of Indians); and (5) a miscellany of matters, such as the privileges of prelates, regular clergy, and Indians, and pastoral visits. Concerned with rules having wide application, the *Itinerario* nevertheless wasted little space on platitudes. It was a practical guide to the basic and sometimes complicated issues that parish priests were likely to face in their work—explaining how to coax full confessions from reluctant Indians, what an appropriate penance would be, or how local marriage customs should be handled.

Above all, it provided detailed descriptions of the responsibilities of priests in Indian parishes and what they needed to know to meet these responsibilities. Because Indians were perpetual minors, the priests and royal governors were to be their special guardians, and the precepts of the church were not to be applied to them with the same rigor as to non-Indians. The priest was to lead by example, edifying his parishioners with good works and high standards of personal conduct,[14] but he must also govern their spiritual affairs and see that the Indians obeyed his teachings. Ideally, he would command their fear, respect, and love all at once.

The *Itinerario* placed the priest squarely into the public life of the parish as the keeper of community morality, glossing over the boundaries between spiritual and temporal affairs. Though the king was supreme, the parish priest was encouraged to mix in temporal affairs for spiritual ends, protecting the Indians

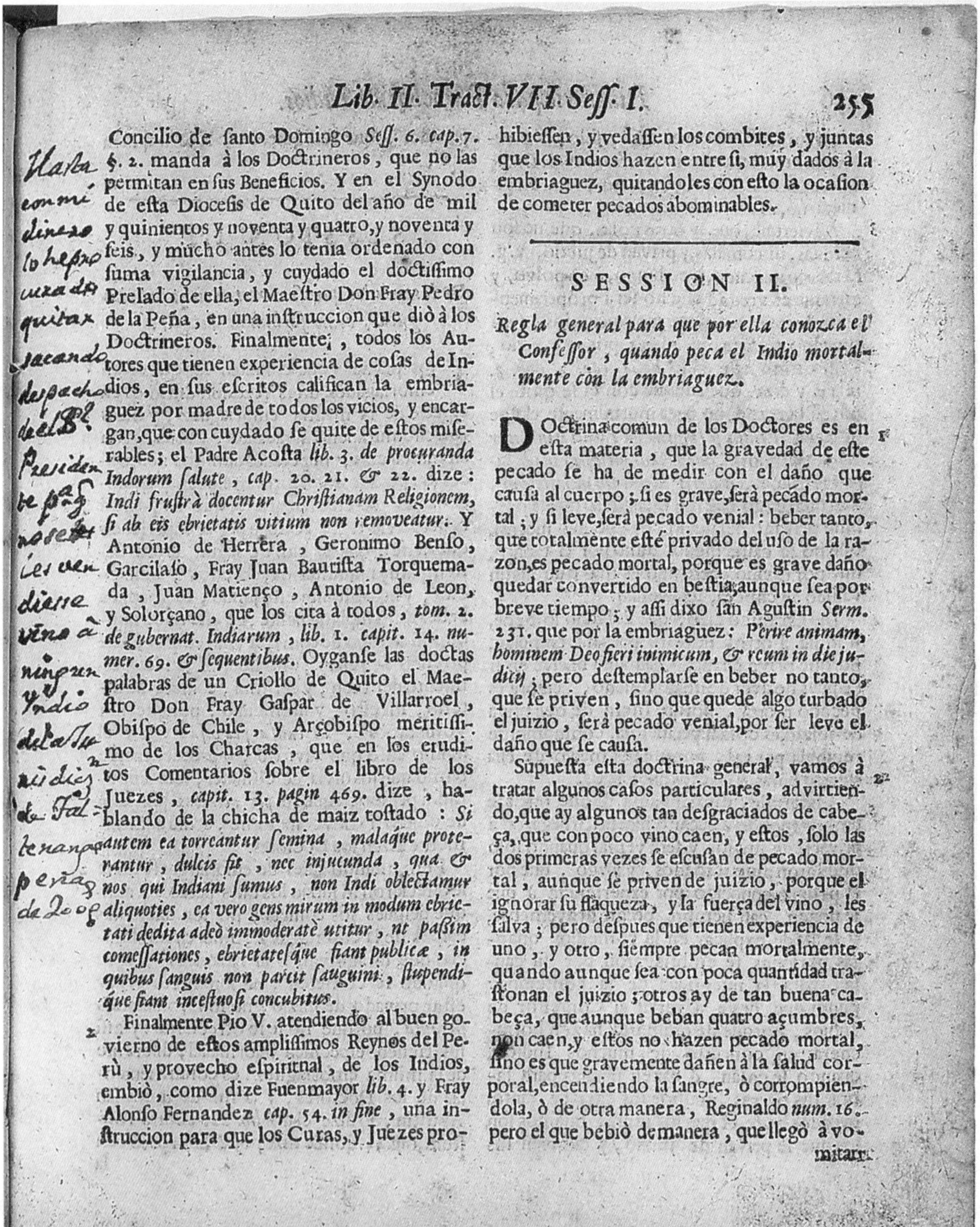

Concilio de santo Domingo *Sess. 6. cap. 7. §. 2.* manda à los Doctrineros, que no las permitan en sus Beneficios. Y en el Synodo de esta Diocesis de Quito del año de mil y quinientos y noventa y quatro, y noventa y seis, y mucho antes lo tenia ordenado con suma vigilancia, y cuydado el doctissimo Prelado de ella, el Maestro Don Fray Pedro de la Peña, en una instruccion que diò à los Doctrineros. Finalmente, todos los Autores que tienen experiencia de cosas de Indios, en sus escritos califican la embriaguez por madre de todos los vicios, y encargan, que con cuydado se quite de estos miserables; el Padre Acosta *lib. 3. de procuranda Indorum salute, cap. 20. 21. & 22.* dize : *Indi frustrà docentur Christianam Religionem, si ab eis ebrietatis vitium non removeatur.* Y Antonio de Herrera, Geronimo Benso, Garcilaso, Fray Juan Bautista Torquemada, Juan Matienço, Antonio de Leon, y Solorçano, que los cita à todos, *tom. 2. de gubernat. Indiarum, lib. 1. capit. 14. num. 69. & sequentibus.* Oyganse las doctas palabras de un Criollo de Quito el Maestro Don Fray Gaspar de Villarroel, Obispo de Chile, y Arçobispo meritissimo de los Charcas, que en los eruditos Comentarios sobre el libro de los Juezes, *capit. 13. pagin 469.* dize, hablando de la chicha de maiz tostado : *Si autem ea torreantur semina, malaque proterantur, dulcis sit, nec injucunda, qua & nos qui Indiani sumus, non Indi oblectamur aliquoties, ca vero gens mirum in modum ebrietati dedita adeò immoderatè utitur, ut passim comessationes, ebrietatesque fiant publicæ, in quibus sanguis non parcit sauguini, stupendique fiant incestuosi concubitus.*

Finalmente Pio V. atendiendo al buen govierno de estos amplissimos Reynos del Perù, y provecho espiritual, de los Indios, embiò, como dize Fuenmayor *lib. 4.* y Fray Alonso Fernandez *cap. 54. in fine,* una instruccion para que los Curas, y Juezes prohibiessen, y vedassen los combites, y juntas que los Indios hazen entre sì, muy dados à la embriaguez, quitandoles con esto la ocasion de cometer pecados abominables.

SESSION II.

Regla general para que por ella conozca el Confessor, quando peca el Indio mortalmente con la embriaguez.

D Octrina comun de los Doctores es en esta materia, que la gravedad de este pecado se ha de medir con el daño que causa al cuerpo ; si es grave, serà pecado mortal ; y si leve, serà pecado venial : beber tanto, que totalmente estè privado del uso de la razon, es pecado mortal, porque es grave daño quedar convertido en bestia, aunque sea por breve tiempo ; y assi dixo san Agustin *Serm.* 231. que por la embriaguez : *Perire animam, hominem Deo fieri inimicum, & reum in die judicij* ; pero destemplarse en beber no tanto, que se priven, sino que quede algo turbado el juizio, serà pecado venial, por ser leve el daño que se causa.

Supuesta esta doctrina general, vamos à tratar algunos casos particulares, advirtiendo, que ay algunos tan desgraciados de cabeça, que con poco vino caen, y estos, solo las dos primeras vezes se escusan de pecado mortal, aunque se priven de juizio, porque el ignorar su flaqueza, y la fuerça del vino, les salva ; pero despues que tienen experiencia de uno, y otro, siempre pecan mortalmente, quando aunque sea con poca quantidad trastonan el juizio ; otros ay de tan buena cabeça, que aunque beban quatro açumbres, non caen, y estos no hazen pecado mortal, sino es que gravemente dañen à la salud corporal, encendiendo la sangre, ò corrompiendola, ò de otra manera, Reginaldo *num.* 16. pero el que bebiò de manera, que llegò à vomitar.

[marginal handwritten notes, left side, partially legible:] Hasta comui dinero lo hepro uza des quitar jucando despachados del S. Presiden te paz nose es uen diesse uino à ningun Yndio de la su audiencia de Gual tenanga peñas de 2. de op

---

FIG. 3. Pages from a well-thumbed copy of the late colonial cura's field manual, the *Itinerario para parochos de indios* by Alonso de la Peña Montenegro. The owner of the Bancroft Library's copy, a parish priest of Tlaltenango, Zacatecas (Diocese of Guadalajara), in 1759, was given to adding marginal notes at points of particular interest. In the first example, from a chapter on the cura's obligation to combat Indian drunkeness, he wrote:

ral: por mas que Remeſal en el lugar citado lo contradiga, afirmando, que los Religioſos no tomaron el oficio de Curas con obligacion de Curas, ſino para adminiſtrar, *titulo Charitatis*; eſta razon ya novale, porque ya admiten eſte oficio de Curas, obligandoſe de juſticia à todo lo que pertenece por Derecho à los Curas, que con eſſa condicion les dàn las Doctrinas, como manda ſu Mageſtad por una Cedula Real dada en Madrid à diez y ſeis de Diziembre de mil y quinientos y ochenta y ſiete años, donde dize: *Y porque lo que ſanto importa, como es la Cura de las almas, y mas las de eſtos tan nuevos en la Fè, no conviene, que quede à voluntad de los Religioſos; los que eſtuvieren en las dichas Doctrinas, Curatos, y Beneficios, han de entender en el oficio de Curas, non ex voto Charitatis, como ellos dizen, ſino de juſticia, y obligacion, adminiſtrando los Sacramentos, no ſolamente à los Indios, ſino tambien à los Eſpañoles, que ſe hallaren vivir entre ellos. A los Indios por los indultos Apoſtolicos, y à los Eſpañoles por comiſſion nueſtra, para lo qual ſe la aveis de dar, dize à los Obiſpos.*

Aſſi lo Confeſsò Fray Juan Bautiſta en la 2. parte de ſus Advertencias, fol. 218. *Si Regularis acceptavit Eccleſiam Parochialem populorum Indorum, ut Curatus, abſque dubio tenetur in omnibus, ac per omnia, ad quæ Curatus ſæcularis tenetur, quia idem officium eſt, eningque.*

Y Supueſto que ſon propiamente Curas, y que de juſticia deven à los ſubditos lo que à eſſe oficio le toca, veamos aora la diferencia que ay de ſer Cura, à no ſerlo, para que cada uno conozca ſus obligaciones las quales pone Fray Juan Bautiſta en las advertencias que diò à los Confeſſores de Indios 2. part. fol. 212. y v. n. 32. y dize que en algunas coſas corren parejas los Curas con aquellos que no lo ſon; pongo por exemplo: Tanto paga el uno como el otro en adminiſtrar Sacramentos, eſtando en pecado mortal, y en darlos à los que conocidamente ſon indignos por no diſpueſtos, ſi falta en alguna coſa eſſencial de la

materia, ò forma, ò condicion neceſſaria en los Sacramentos que adminiſtra, pues por el miſmo caſo que ſe pone à exercitarlos, eſtà con obligacion de ſaber todo aquello que conviene à ſu oficio, que la razon natural lo eſtà dictando, como dize Santo Thomas *in 4. diſt. 17.*

6

Otras coſas ſon tales, que ſi las haze, ò dexa de hazer un Cura, ſeràn pecado, y aquel que ſolo acude de caridad, no lo ſeràn, pongo por exemplo: El no ſaber bien la lengua, el dexar de viſitar los enfermos, y no defender à los Indios de los agravios que les hazen; el no ſer muy puntual en la reſidencia en el Pueblo, que todos ſeràn pecados en el Cura, y no en aquel que ſolo acude de caridad; y para dezirlo todo de una vez, y dar una regla general, digo, que ay tres generos de deſcuydo culpable, que ſon, culpa lata, leve, y leviſſima; culpa lata es la que regular, y comunmente evitan todos, qual es la de aquel que dexò la joya que le avian pueſto en depoſito à la puerta fuera de la caſa, ò encima del eſcaño, eſto que ſe perdiò por ſu culpa lata, tendrà obligacion à reſtituirlo à ſu dueño, pena de pecado mortal en coſa grave; culpa leve es la que ſuelen evitar los hombres diligentes, qual es la de aquel que dexò el libro depoſitado en ſu apoſento, y deſcuydoſe de cerrar la puerta; la leviſſima es la que ſuelen evitar los hombres diligentiſſimos, como aquel que dexò el libro en ſu apoſento, y cerrò, mas no aſſentò el peſtillo, y por eſſo ſe quedò abierto. *Vide Leſſium fol. 77. diſp. 8.*

7

El Cura que tiene Doctrina, ora ſea Clerigo, ora Religioſo, ſiendo arititulado, ò Coadjutor pueſto por el Ordinario, ò por el proprio Cura, aviendoſe convenido con el, de que le ayudarà puntualmente en la adminiſtracion que ſe le encomendare de ſus Feligreſes, pecarà mortalmente en los deſcuydos graves por culpa lata, leve, y venialmente por la leviſſima; pero el Sacerdote que de una manera, ni de otra llega à adminiſtrar, ſino voluntariamente, no pecarà mortalmente, ſi el deſcuydo no fuere

"Even with my own money I have endeavored to eliminate it by obtaining an order from the president of the audiencia that wine not be sold to any Indian in the district of Taltenango [Tlaltenango] under penalty of 200 pesos." In the second, he strengthened de la Peña Montenegro's reminder that curas were responsible for defending the Indians with the comment, "To defend the Indians is the cura's obligation."

against abuse by employers and district governors,[15] but also protecting Indians against themselves, teaching them civility, cleanliness, and decency, and keeping them from drunkenness, adultery, and other vices that imperiled their souls. He was to share with the district governor responsibility for rooting out "idolatry" and keeping the Indians settled in towns and villages. Montenegro opposed the use of force in principle but held that the priest as judge could punish his parishioners in order to protect their souls and control sin.

The *Itinerario* is distinguished by its emphasis on the parish priest's role as a teacher, magistrate, and spiritual physician,[16] his duty to be a model of charity and good conduct, and the importance of confession. These were universal expectations for Catholic priests, but they gained a special priority in Spanish America, thanks to Montenegro's conception of Indians as particularly ignorant, morally weak, superstitious children. In this respect, even admirers criticized the *Itinerario* as partly a work of its place, shaped by the author's experience in Quito.[17] It is in any case clearly a work of its time. Its intermingling of spiritual and temporal affairs and its concern about Indian "idolatry," the punishment of spiritual offenders, the priests' need to know Indian languages, and sliding scales of responsibility for sin all fit the inclinations of mid-seventeenth-century church leaders far better than they do the policies and circumstances of the late eighteenth century. Yet there were no important changes in the later editions of this principal manual of applied theology.[18] All the editions placed the cura close to the center of public life, condoned corporal punishment, and emphasized the need to know Indian languages.

"A *cura* without books is like a soldier without arms," Bishop Palafox wrote in a pastoral letter of 1653.[19] He recommended a manual of sacraments, one of ceremonies, a Bible and concordance, one or two secondary works on biblical subjects, the decrees of the Council of Trent, a copy of the official Roman catechism, some books of saints, "two of the most practical and best" works on moral theology, a church history, and the *Summa Theologica* of Saint Thomas Aquinas.[20] Although few priests serving in rural Indian parishes of the dioceses of Mexico and Guadalajara in the late eighteenth century owned the writings of Aquinas, these men of words and the Word were reasonably well equipped. In addition to a copy of the *Itinerario*, they usually had the Bible, several books of sermons, a manual for administering the sacraments, and a separate manual for confessors in the Indian language of the parish if Spanish was not generally spoken. Many probably also had a copy of the decrees of the Council of Trent and a few other works of the kind Palafox recommended.[21] One of the books of sermons was likely to have been Ignacio de Paredes's *Promptuario manual mexicano*, published in Mexico City in 1759, with its lessons in Nahuatl for every week of the year, plus a sermon on Our Lady of Guadalupe for December 12. The manuals for sacraments were revised periodically, and parish priests were required to own and follow the latest version.[22]

Of the other practical guides to parish service, the one most frequently mentioned by parish priests and listed in their inventories was the *Farol indiano y guía de curas de indios*, written by an Augustinian, Fr. Manuel Pérez, and published in Mexico in 1713.[23] Pérez had served sixteen years in Indian doctrinas of the Diocese of Puebla and the Archdiocese of Mexico, mainly in Mexico City, it appears. His book focuses on the priest's sacramental role, and his aim was to anticipate problems the cura in New Spain was likely to encounter, especially ways in which Indians often misunderstood or misused the sacraments. Pérez's viewpoint is similar to the *Itinerario*'s. Indians are rustic but clever, like children. There is the same close attention to Indian practices that complicated Christian baptism and matrimony (but here with Mexican rather than South American evidence), and the same extra attention to the difficulties of getting Indians to make a proper confession. There is also the same leitmotif of drunkenness as the Indians' most intractable vice and the one that most challenged the validity of all the sacraments they received. The main difference between the two manuals is that Pérez was not an enthusiastic proponent of administering the sacraments in Indian languages. He argued that since Indian languages could not fully convey certain principles of Christianity, baptisms administered in the Indian language should be considered conditional.[24]

The expectations expressed in these manuals and other clerical utterances in many ways reflect the decrees of the Council of Trent, as did much of the colonial church's law and organization—not surprisingly, since a royal cedula of July 12, 1564, called for the canons of the Council of Trent to apply in Spanish America. Modern scholars properly warn against assuming an unqualified application of Tridentine doctrine overseas, but apparently most of the council's provisions were widely adopted in New Spain.[25] They were cited almost reflexively in royal cedulas, episcopal decrees, and manuals like the *Itinerario* through the end of the colonial period.[26] They influenced colonial practice—in the extensive authority of bishops, in sacramental practices, in the ways in which laity and clergy were separated, in injunctions on virtuous, exemplary behavior, and in the standard metaphors for the duties of parish priests.

We have already noted one important colonial departure from the canons of Trent: the waiving of the requirement that candidates for ordination have an ecclesiastical benefice or other independent means. Other, more elusive differences, implied in the *Itinerario*, pastoral letters, and royal law, concerned the public role of American priests. For instance, Tridentine decrees gave considerable attention to the mass, putting it solidly at the center of the parish priest's religious practice and balancing against it his other responsibilities as preacher, teacher, and exemplar. The colonial American guides accepted the central importance of the mass, but with little comment. Instead, they emphasized the pastor's responsibilities as teacher and enforcer of public morality—tasks that gained added importance in dioceses where Indian tributaries were numerous. The line between temporal and spiritual affairs had never been entirely clear, but in Indian parishes of the seventeenth and early eighteenth centuries, it was especially blurred. Bourbon administrators after the 1740's were determined to give it clearer definition.

Colonial politics had traditionally given priests an important public role. On the clerical side, the Third Provincial Council of New Spain's prelates (1585) declared that parish priests "should take away from the Indians those things that serve as an impediment to the health of their souls," including the dances, "idolatries," and dispersed settlements that kept them from a "civil and social life."[27] On the royal side, the legal commentator Solórzano endorsed the view set out by the First Provincial Council of Lima in 1583 that the cura's role included "overseeing [the Indians'] good customs in political matters"; and the *Recopilación* joined ordered town life and Christian instruction in ways that left open the public responsibilities of the parish priest.[28] Christian charity required that he do everything he could for his flock.[29] Well into the late eighteenth century, bishops exhorted their parish priests to attend to "the welfare of the republic," foster "a life of rationality among the Indians," and "maintain justice and peace in all [the king's] dominions."[30] The traditional expectation, then, was that the priest was to "govern his subjects not only in spiritual matters but also in the temporal, and everything that leads toward the welfare and benefits of their souls."[31]

But a decisive change in the parish priests' prescribed roles emerges from the eighteenth-century evidence. By the 1760's, the emphasis had shifted from the priest as judge toward the priest as teacher, a shift that fits both with some signs of change in religious sensibility and with the series of reforms that Bourbon lawmakers and administrators had in mind for parish priests.

After the Council of Trent, the formal conception of the priest's role reached for a balance between fear and love, punishment and charity, and judge and teacher. But this balance was not a fixed, fully accomplished synthesis. The role of judge received more emphasis in the Hapsburg period than it would later on. The *Itinerario*, for example, listed the principal roles of the parish priest as "juez, médico y maestro" in that order.[32] It could speak in the same breath of the priest as "serving as judge among his subjects" ("by the sacramental law of Penance he must judge them") and of his role as a "spiritual physician who prescribes the [proper] medicines."[33] There was always ambiguity in this balance and order, always a return to the single great purpose of redeeming souls.

A beneficed parish priest's standard title, "cura por su Magestad vicario in capite y juez eclesiástico,"[34] highlighted his traditional responsibility as judge in spiritual matters. His judicial function was most obvious in the confessional and the sacrament of penance; as the *Itinerario* put it, "in the confessional he is like a supreme judge, . . . pardoning sins and giving out sentences of life or death."[35] But he also had formal judicial authority in certain matters outside the purely sacramental domain, notably premarital investigations, the execution of wills, the handling of criminals who took asylum in the parish church, and the prosecution of Indian "idolatry," although his authority in all four areas was challenged in the late eighteenth century.[36] More broadly still, in the sixteenth and seventeenth centuries, many aspects of public life had been subject to moral law and clerical supervision. The blurred border between sacred and profane and a broad conception of what might endanger the soul left many early colonial curas with judicial authority over public morality, including drunkenness, gambling, and threats to the integrity of the nuclear family, especially sexual misconduct such as adultery, incest, and rape.[37] The clergy regarded marriage, sex, and the family as its special province; but troubles in the family inevitably covered more than sexual misconduct. Furthermore, in practice the parish priest was available to make quick work of minor conflicts that, in principle, should have gone to the alcalde mayor. This informal judicial authority could be a great source of local power, but its practice is rarely set down in writing because a written record was not required. Most of the evidence is incidental, appearing in disputes over re-

lated matters. In 1751, the cura of Chiapa de Mota (Puebla), Pedro Pablo de Ceballos, claimed that his notary was inclined to make many insignificant matters that
came to the cura into formal adjudications requiring fees. Ceballos meant especially the "many matters of little importance" that the Indians brought to him —
"an argument between a husband and wife . . . idle gossip . . . or other matters of
little substance with which *curas* are continually bothered." These were matters
for informal judgment ("juicios verbales"), in his view, and parishioners should
not have to pay for "the paternal consolation they seek."[38] Even when a cura did
not act as judge, he might influence legal affairs. For example, the cura of Tala
(Jalisco) in 1772 reported that he sometimes made investigations and recorded
local disputes at the request of the Indian officials.[39]

Some curas also acted as informal judges in local cases of assault and battery
that belonged in the royal criminal courts. For example, the cura of Zoquitlan
(Tehuacan district, Puebla) was said to have arrested an Indian in 1792 for stab-
bing a non-Indian resident and exacted a fine of twelve pesos (six for the medical
attention of the cura's scribe and six for the victim) before releasing him. Not surprisingly, it was the subdelegado who denounced the cura in this case — though
not at the time of this double violation of his judicial authority. He introduced
it in a subsequent complaint against the cura for manipulating local elections.[40]
Other curas overreached their judicial authority when they removed local officials on their own account.[41]

Eighteenth-century parish priests, especially before the 1790's, did not always
understand or were not always ready to accept the narrowing of their judicial authority. The cura of Actopan (Hidalgo) in 1763, Bernardino Alvarez Revolledo,
offered a ringing defense of his exercise of "the office of judge," with its responsibility "to warn, correct, [and] punish." He had in mind especially his responsibility for policing those who did not attend mass or observe the feast days, who
were irreverent in church or were known to live in sin, especially in concubinage
and adultery.[42] In a dispute over fees, the cura of San Simón Tototepec, in the
district of Zacualpan, in 1775 justified his jailing and punishment of disobedient
Indians on the grounds that it was "an ancient custom (as it still is) for ecclesiastical magistrates in such remote places to exercise their judicial prerogatives so
that crimes do not go unpunished." But he was drawn into this declaration by an
attorney who hammered away at his illegitimate claims to judicial powers — "he
wishes to play the role of judge" — and, consequently, his disobedience to the
audiencia.[43]

Part of the confusion over the public, largely judicial roles of the parish priests
resulted from the mixed signals of royal authorities, including the regalist bishops. Most of the decrees and audiencia verdicts restricted the priests' authority
in public affairs, but the *Itinerario*'s message of public responsibility was not revised in later editions, and before the 1770's, bishops were more apt to warn
against the abuse of judicial authority than against false pretensions to it.[44] Especially in emergencies, the curas were called back toward their traditional roles by
royal governors and prelates. At the beginning of the great famine and epidemic
in 1785, the viceroy exhorted "the *curas párrocos* and other ecclesiastics" to work
for the protection of Indians and against idleness by making their parishioners
understand that the crown would "punish severely vagrants, the disobedient, the

vicious, the incorrigible, and those who have given themselves over to idleness and drunkenness."[45] In the same year, the archbishop invoked "the spiritual and temporal harm that resulted from scarcity and hunger" to urge on his priests a campaign against monopolies and usury.[46]

As royal administrators moved more decisively in the late eighteenth century to narrow the judicial authority of curas and relieve them of jurisdiction over gambling, drinking, and sexual misconduct, teaching and preaching—persuasion rather than judgment—became their main function. Parish priests were still expected to work for the prevention of public sins such as idolatry, witchcraft, superstitious practices, concubinage, adultery, prostitution, gambling, and drunkenness, but they were now to assist the royal judges or make a secret report to the bishop.[47] Teaching was not a new responsibility, to be sure. Even leading propagandists against "idolatry" in the seventeenth century like Jacinto de la Serna spoke of "preaching and teaching the Gospel" as the principal tool against false gods.[48] But the decline of priestly judicial power gave it new importance.

The Council of Trent had underscored that every parish priest was responsible for teaching and explaining the essentials of the faith in the vernacular so that the faithful might approach the sacraments with greater devotion; and he was required to preach "at least on all Sundays and solemn festival days" and three days or more a week during Lent and Advent.[49] In the spirit of Trent, royal decrees of the late sixteenth and early seventeenth centuries collected in the *Recopilación* emphasized the teaching function of the parish priest ("enseñar y doctrinar").[50] The *Itinerario* and episcopal instructions also repeated and elaborated on his role as teacher, describing the essential beliefs required for salvation, and placing the burden squarely on the priest no matter how ignorant his Indian parishioners might be. Special attention was to be given to teaching doctrine in regular classes to children under the age of ten, with the cemetery as classroom in order to focus attention on mortality and the protection of the immortal soul.[51] But the priest was expected to continue with refresher instruction for adults, especially before the annual confessions during Lent, and to demonstrate how Christian teachings applied to new situations that arose in the parish.

Preaching was usually mentioned in the same breath with catechism classes as a principal means of fulfilling the priest's pedagogical duties. From its opening pages, the *Itinerario* underscored the doctrinero's obligation to preach to Indians "according to their limited abilities," warning that this required "ciencia," careful preparation; and the First Provincial Council in 1555 described sermons as "the clergy's weapons."[52] An occasional parish priest was famous for his stirring or numerous offerings, but most probably preached out of a standard book of sermons and homilies, and laid no claim to exceptional talent for the pulpit.[53] Those who spoke extemporaneously on Sundays about controversial local matters could find themselves in trouble with the episcopal court.[54] In the late eighteenth century, some conscientious curas made preaching a vital part of their pastoral work by bringing in someone from the outside or choosing a vicario with a gift for public speaking.[55] They might engage a troop of missionary preachers to revitalize popular faith and reform public morality. Up to twenty of the missionaries would visit the parish for two or three months, especially during Lent, preaching nearly every day and manning the confessionals from dawn to dusk.[56] For the

Diocese of Guadalajara, they were mainly Franciscans from Zapopan or the Colegio de Nuestra Señora de Guadalupe at Zacatecas. Many of the ones deployed in Mexico were also Franciscans, from the Colegio de San Fernando on the edge of Mexico City or the Colegio Apostólico in Pachuca.[57]

The new weight given to teaching is especially evident in the practical guides prepared for parish priests in the 1760's, during the terms of New Spain's most vigorous regalist bishops, Francisco Fabián y Fuero of Puebla (1765–73) and Francisco Antonio de Lorenzana in the Archdiocese of Mexico (1766–72).[58] Pérez de Velasco's *El ayudante de cura*, published in Puebla in 1766, opens with a ringing endorsement of the priest's role as teacher, warning that teaching doctrine to "coarse Indians and country people who are hardly less uncouth than the Indians" is a great challenge.[59] The instruments of fear, judgment, and punishment are conspicuously absent from this guide. If the priest would achieve his purpose of bringing Indians to peace with God ("reducirlos a la paz con Dios"), advised Pérez de Velasco, he would need to win them over with his benevolence, patience, and great charity even if his love was met with ingratitude. He offered a number of ways to improve instruction and the parishioners' command of essential doctrine. Since village men were in the fields from dawn to dusk, they did not "pray" the catechism at home, so the priest should have them recite the essential prayers, principles, and mysteries on Sundays. After celebrating mass and reading a passage from the Gospels in a visita on Sunday, the priest should take a seat and, for fifteen or thirty minutes, informally explain one of the mysteries of the faith or a commandment or a sacrament in the native language. During Lent, he should examine six or eight parishioners in the catechism every day.[60]

Far less well known but in the same spirit is a treatise composed by the cura of Tepecoacuilco (Guerrero), Ignacio José Hugo de Omerick, in 1769, "Conversaciones familiares de un cura a sus Feligreses Yndios." For Omerick, doctrine, if mastered, was the be-all and end-all. Simply teach the faithful "the fundamental maxims of divine and natural law," he wrote, and "idleness is done away with, neatness and cleanliness are achieved, ignorance and idolatry disappear, [and] a Christian inhabitant, father, and good republican useful to society is formed."[61] In an oblique attack on the *Itinerario*, with its endorsement of corporal punishment and emphasis on the priest as judge, Omerick argued that it was a priest's kindly approach and the example of his own efforts to be guided by virtue and good works that would teach the Indians about the fear of God. Omerick's grand plan was to educate "a new man" in the Indian parishes of Mexico, a "prudent, tidy, and polished" Indian.[62] In the process, he implicitly called for "a new man" among parish priests, too—a brother more than a father, a pastor interested in material works, charity, and his own education, as well as that of his parishioners.

The period from the arrival of Archbishop Lorenzana in 1766 through the meetings of the Fourth Provincial Council in 1771 marked a high point in the conceptualization of the priest as loving teacher. The decrees of the Fourth Provincial Council, which contained the regalist program of Lorenzana and Fabián y Fuero, were never officially approved, and Omerick's guide, which might have become a standard work had those decrees gained the force of law, languished in manuscript.[63] Lorenzana's successor, Alonso Núñez de Haro y Peralta (1772–1800), redressed the balance somewhat without raising the specter of the parish priest as judge. In his 1772 circular to priests, he pointedly urged love and moderation in punishment, and emphasized the priest's responsibility for educating children and establishing classes in Spanish. But he also reintroduced corporal punishment and if he did not return all the way back to an earlier day, his language indicates a more aggressive conception of the priest's public role than that expressed in the council's decrees. By profession, the assorted priests were at once "fathers, pastors, physicians, captains of the Christian Militia, and Sentinels of the house of the Lord."[64] Others also tried to wrap the older conception in the language of the new. In a treatise composed for the king in 1784, the cura of Zimatlan (Oaxaca) began by accepting that the cura was "neither judge nor prelate" and extolling the "rational milk of doctrine" before urging the crown to allow priests to flog their spiritual children.[65] But the image of the parish priest as affable teacher rather than judge was too deeply embedded in the late-eighteenth-century political reforms to be much changed. In their pastoral letters and instructions, late colonial bishops continued to underline the importance of teaching doctrine and rarely mentioned a judicial role.[66] And in their resumés and reports, late-eighteenth-century curas and district governors increasingly acknowledged that activity in founding schools and supporting instruction was a standard of achievement in parish service.[67]

"The Cure of Souls Is the Art of Arts"

Though teacher versus judge was at the heart of the debate over how exactly the parish priest ought to go about his practice of "the art of arts,"[68] his other roles in public life did not go unchallenged in the late eighteenth century. He was as indisputably above all a father as he had been in the Second Provincial Council's ordering of his roles in 1565:

> The *cura* is Father, and he ought to look out for his children; he is Pastor, and must take care that his flock does not scatter, become sick, or be destroyed; he is Judge, and must judge the Penitent with the most likely sentences; he is Physician, and must cure with the most proven remedies and medicines; he is Teacher, and must teach with the doctrines that are soundest and most in accord with reason.[69]

But the nature of that fatherhood was now less universally agreed on. To the subdelegados who described particular priests as "true fathers" in their 1793 reports on the parish clergy, fatherhood meant affability (toward the subdelegado as well as parishioners) and good works.[70] José Eugenio Bravo, in a 1796 report on priests living in his parish, characterized the teniente de cura of Zapotiltic as "the father of all through his piety and liberality."[71] In a jurisdictional dispute in 1763 between the cura of Actopan and the alcalde mayor, various witnesses said the cura behaved as a true father in "a multitude of ways." Their examples included his founding of schools, church construction, prompt pastoral care, instruction in doctrine, alms to the poor, and sale of foodstuffs to parishioners at low prices.[72]

For some priests, father-protector shaded into the activities of a semi-independent advocate and benefactor in mundane affairs. Occasionally, late colonial parish priests were known to distribute grain at cost, slaughter their cattle and distribute the meat during famines, lend money for tribute payments, petition the crown for land grants and loans to improve village farming, represent village parishioners in disputes over land and water and even pay for the litigation, negotiate rentals from neighboring landlords, and put into legal form the complaints of parishioners against abuse by district governors and landlords.[73] Some of these priests were licensed to practice law and litigated any cases involving their parishes or made the legal difficulties of their parishioners a particular charitable cause.[74] But most were drawn into legal affairs by their literacy, their city connections, and their standing as public men who in principle stood apart from partisanship.

These semi-secular benefactions were rooted in a traditional role assigned to the priesthood in Indian America since the sixteenth century and never fully revised: the protector of the Indians. Priests were not then or ever the only designated protectors of the Indians, and during the eighteenth century, the crown was inclined to shift the weight of the burden to royal judges. Even so, a July 12, 1739, royal cedula that pronounced the audiencia fiscales "the principal Protectors of the Indians" singled out bishops as guardians who should report any mistreatment of Indians directly to the viceroy and Council of the Indies.[75] The *Itinerario* is sprinkled with references to the responsibility of parish priests for the well-being of their Indian flock, for "defending these poor ones."[76] These were the passages that the anonymous pastor or assistant at Tlaltenango (Zacatecas) flagged in his copy of the manual in 1759. He was particularly concerned with a sentence in 1-1-14, referring to the cura's responsibility for "defending the Indians from harm that is done to them" (defender a los Indios de los agravios que les hazen), to which he added an emphatic marginal note: "to defend the Indians is the *cura*'s obligation" (defender a los yndios es obligazión deel cura). Many parish priests still reached deep into the analogy of the father and his children to include in their role supervision, consolation in everyday problems, and discipline.[77] As Miguel Antonio de Cuevas, cura of San Bartolomé Capuluac (Tenango del Valle district) put it in 1796, the doctrinero had "the economic authority that a father exercises over his children in order to correct their disobediences."[78] This was an unfashionable position for a cura to take in the late eighteenth century, especially since even the *Itinerario*, which sanctioned moderate discipline, emphasized the paternal role as one of love and mercy,[79] but it too was rooted in the traditional protective role.

The Second Provincial Council had placed the role of pastor second to that of father, highlighting the parish priest's duties as keeper and protector—keeping the flock together, drawing back wayward individuals with his metaphorical crook; sheltering them; and nourishing them on the "spiritual fodder" of doctrine and sacraments. This view was deeply embedded in Catholic practice and solidified by the Council of Trent. It was not eclipsed or replaced in the eighteenth century, but another old metaphor—that of the *hortelano* or gardener—gained new currency in the rhetoric about pastoral service. The result was a small shift in emphasis that fitted with other changes in the way parish priests and Indian parishioners were being conceived. Pastor and gardener were similar, if not entirely complementary roles (compare Jeremiah 12:10, for example, "pastors [are] destroying my vineyard"). Both looked after living things, nurturing their growth and multiplication, protecting them from harm in the expectation of a bountiful harvest. But the garden metaphor emphasized cultivation—the teaching role—more than protection, and implied a more sedentary, institutional setting. The church, as the *Itinerario* had it, was the gardener's *sementera* (tilled field), and the Indians were like "young plants" rooted in the soil of their community.[80] With the nourishment of doctrine, they would yield a "harvest" that could be turned into "the bread of Eternal Life" by the priest during Lent.[81] Even if the Indians were more like wild trees than tender shoots, Pérez de Velasco said in 1766, with cultivation they, too, could bear fruit.[82] There were sins to be uprooted from the hearts of the faithful like noxious weeds, but the wolf/devil did not lurk so conspicuously in the eighteenth-century garden as he did in the early colonial pasture.

"There Is No Religion Without Its Liturgy, and No Liturgy Without Its Priests"

The priest's first public duty was sacramental.[83] It was through him that the sacraments of the church were offered and the promise of salvation was kept alive. They were holy and perfect even if the priest was not. The simple act of administering them made him a semidivine intermediary working for "that priceless treasure," the immortal soul.[84] This intermediation came into play most obviously in the church's central liturgical form, the "holiest of holy things,"[85] the mass.

By the time the mass reached the New World, it had become a transcendental pageant of Christ's life, death, and resurrection, performed only by priests, with the greatest reverence and according to a detailed script.[86] It was a frequent event in parish life that both united and separated the priest and the community. He performed the ceremony at an elevated, railed altar in a whispered foreign language with his back turned. The congregation waited for the warning bell and the elevation of the consecrated wafer in a glittering monstrance, an act that completed the holy mystery and renewed the promise of salvation. The great miracle of sacrifice, the transformation in his hands of bread and wine into the body and blood of Christ, was something he did for the faithful, by the grace of God.[87]

Priests celebrated mass for the congregation weekly on Sunday mornings in the parish seat, and usually monthly or by rotation in the visita chapels on consecutive Sundays.[88] Each settlement also sponsored a special high mass on the day of the patron saint and on special holy days throughout the year. The rhythm of special masses quickened during Lent, culminating in the solemn and exuberant celebrations on the days before Easter Sunday, and at Pentecost and Christmas. And in nearly every parish, there were other masses during the week: those offered for the renovation of the Host on Thursdays, those said out of a particular devotion of the priest himself (e.g., for souls in Purgatory on Mondays or for the Holy Sepulchre on Fridays), and those sponsored by individual and corporate endowments for a departed soul or a particular saint or mystery.

Baptism, the most essential of the sacraments, was the least attached to ordained priests. A priest was expected to go to heroic extremes to perform infant baptisms, even to risk his life, but this sacrament of initiation was so essential, wrote Montenegro in the *Itinerario*, that "everyone, men and women, can be Ministers for baptism" in emergencies.[89] Midwives were the most likely to need to put this knowledge to use, but all adults were obliged to know how to do a proper baptism, and it was the priest's duty to teach them.[90] In practice, most baptisms were performed by a priest before mass on Sundays and registered by him in the parish *libro de bautismos.*[91]

Marriage was another sacrament over which priests did not, in principle, have exclusive authority. Like confirmation, it was the bishop's responsibility, but American curas received a dispensation to carry out all of its phases without his supervision,[92] from directing the prenuptial investigations and spiritual preparations of the participants to officially recording all the marriages celebrated in their parishes. The priest's role in marriage choices, however, declined after the Pragmatic Sanction of 1776 gave parents greater authority to cancel a child's marriage plans.[93]

For most parishioners, confession-penance-communion was the rite that best expressed the priest's paternal and sacral role. It was a requisite rite at least once a year, in the pre-Easter season. Lent became a two-month laboratory of instruction in the faith, culminating in a ritual cleansing of sin and reconciliation with the church.[94] Confession was the critical first stage of this communion, the cleansing that made the penitent worthy of "the bread of eternal life." The penitent knelt, head uncovered "like an accused criminal," and the priest was "seated and covered . . . because he represents the person of Christ as Judge."[95] The manual makers warned confessors not to rush through the encounter; especially with Indians, there was a fine art to teasing out an adequate self-examination and expression of contrition. It would be impossible to confess 60 or 70 penitents properly in a day, the *Itinerario* advised, but to confess only one in an afternoon was too few. Still, it was better to err on the low side—"It is better and more acceptable to God to confess two [well] than to confess twenty poorly and in haste."[96]

However carefully the priest went about the business, the *Itinerario* held out little hope for a proper result.[97] It was even prepared to excuse Indians from an adequate knowledge of the mysteries of the faith because of their "rudeza" (coarseness). Pérez de Velasco, writing a century later at the advent of the regalist-reformer bishops, also dwelled on the importance of confession, proper preparation by the penitent, and various tricks of the trade to elicit a satisfactory confession.[98] He was not over-optimistic about the potential of Indians to soar as Christians or thinkers, but he did have higher expectations than Montenegro had, because he assumed that Indians could at least learn basic doctrine fully and make a proper confession if the confessor had enough patience and ingenuity. Both authors glossed over one of the obvious reasons why confessions in Indian parishes might be inadequate: that the confessor did not know the native language well enough or used an interpreter, whose presence inhibited the penitents. For all this, heavy emphasis was always placed on confession as the cornerstone of the Easter communion. It was important to have 100 percent compliance. This sacrament was so important, so deserving of reverence, that no fee should be collected under any circumstances, and priests who violated the seal of secrecy or the decorum of the occasion could expect harsher punishment than for almost any kind of personal immorality.[99]

Traditionally, the mixed metaphor for the priest in the confessional was judge and physician. As the *Itinerario* put it:

If the Doctrinero exercises the office of judge among his subjects, and is to judge them for the sacrament of Penitence, he must clearly have knowledge and understanding of their sins; [and] being also their spiritual Physician, he must prescribe medicines according to the nature of their ailments.[100]

Increasingly, however, the favored image here, too, was the priest as gardener rather than judge, cultivating a sense of contrition and a full account of sin, and prescribing the proper remedies.[101]

Even in its formal aspects, the confessional had political uses. Bishop Cabañas advised the crown in 1816 that his priests were using their influence in the pulpit and confessional to dissuade parishioners from rebellion.[102] Confessors could and did withhold absolution until a penitent revealed details that the priest wanted to know or regarded as essential to a full confession. Absolution came into play as a way to gain compliance with ecclesiastical orders, as when the cura of Villa de Sinaloa in 1800 required every Indian parishioner guilty of tipping his hat to the subdelegado, who had been excommunicated on orders of the bishop of Sonora, to come to him for absolution.[103]

Besides his sacramental duties, the cura had other, related administrative and housekeeping chores to perform. He was responsible for the decency of the cult, which meant supervising the maintenance of buildings, altars, images, and grounds, keeping the vestments and implements of the mass clean and in good repair, maintaining an adequate supply of consecrated Hosts, wine, oil, and wax, and keeping the lamps for the Host always lit with olive oil and the fonts filled with fresh holy water.[104] He was responsible for parish recordkeeping—a vital task that required at the least maintaining registers for baptisms, marriages, and burials, an inventory of church properties, and a list of the people who confessed and took communion during Lent each year.[105] In some parishes, he customarily kept the records for cofradías and other properties that supported the cult.

On top of all this, the cura was charged with certifying the ancestry of parishioners who had moved away, conducting investigations into controversies involving priests and district governors in the vicinity, and carrying out audiencia commissions of various kinds.[106] He was often called on to give evidence in legal disputes and routinely served as a character witness for parishioners on trial or those standing for local office.[107] In these functions, his role as protector of community life was reaffirmed by the crown.[108]

Other customary activities, however, were challenged in the late eighteenth century (as discussed in Chapters 12–17). Parish priests had been accustomed to overseeing local elections, superintending community finances, and regulating religious processions of various kinds[109]—all tasks that now fell to the subdelegado. Church laws requiring that the faithful be baptized in their parish and that they confess and receive the obligatory Easter communion in their local church gave local priests some nominal control over the movement of parishioners, but late colonial priests found that the secular arm showed little interest in repatriating Indian parishioners.[110] And priests' official recordkeeping tasks sometimes extended by custom into serving as an informal community scribe, keeping the tribute, cofradía, and caja de comunidad accounts, making Indian wills, and supervising community lands and public works; but the audiencias were quick to reprimand parish priests for these extensions in the late eighteenth century.[111]

A less controversial change in administrative activity promoted by the crown and adopted enthusiastically by parish priests was an increase in both ecclesiastical and community construction projects. Late colonial curas sought to dignify public worship in their parishes with grander churches, repairs to existing structures, and interior decorations that would make the sanctuary more like a glimpse of heaven; and to carry out public works that contributed to the prosperity, peace, and stability of the community. Either kind of construction was regarded as an act of charity, an activity that "sacrificed self-interest for the spiritual welfare of souls," as Joseph Antonio Ximénez, cura of Jiquipilco, put it in the early 1760's.[112]

The late colonial record is filled with parish priests busy at constructing and refurbishing their churches, not least because, as one said, this activity displayed to their superiors their "devotion to the cult."[113] In principle, as we have seen, they had been doing so all along. Solórzano had long ago voiced the crown's expectation that curas and other local notables would contribute to the construction and maintenance of local churches according to their means, and some, if not most, probably subscribed to the rationale for the enterprise that his contemporary Bishop Palafox expressed when he noted that "in the Indies it is customary to say, and truly, that the Faith enters these poor natives through their eyes."[114] But the growing population and increasing parish revenues of the eighteenth century made building possible on a scale not seen in country parishes since the first decades of colonization.[115] Some pastors took a special interest in side altars, others in musical instruments, still others in pulpits, confessionals, statues, paintings, bells, silver implements, or vestments; at least one constructed a hospital, and another a boarding school for girls.[116] Looking back from the early 1760's on a lifetime of service in eight parishes, Antonio Flores Garcilaso de la Vega, the cura of Tantoyucan (northern Veracruz), was especially proud of his bricks-and-mortar legacy. Wherever he went, Flores said, he rebuilt or completed churches, bought precious implements for the mass, commissioned side altars and bells, and more.[117] The cura of Tlaltizapan (Morelos), Francisco Vásquez del Campo, claimed to have spent more in 1797 on repairs of the church and rectory, missals, silver furnishings, vestments, and gilding for an altar to Our Lady of Guadalupe than he collected in fees—2,560 pesos to 2,119 pesos.[118]

In the tradition of Fray Francisco de Tembleque, the sixteenth-century Franciscan doctrinero at Otumba (Valley of Mexico) who, in the protective company of a large brindle cat, devoted many years to the construction of an arched aqueduct that brought fresh water to his villagers from more than 30 miles away,[119] some late colonial curas undertook ambitious public works. Water projects were favored—Ignacio Munive, cura of Apango (Tixtla district, Guerrero) in 1793 led the construction of a stone-and-mortar aqueduct that drew water to a new public fountain from several miles away, as did Diego de Almonacid y Salasar for Huitzilac (Morelos) and Dr. Joseph Rodríguez Díaz for Real del Monte (Hidalgo) in the late 1750's, and Thadeo Castor de Aguayo for Villa Gutierre (Zacatecas) before 1754[120]—but pastors also built public washing facilities. One change from sixteenth-century public works was an emphasis on promoting new wealth and commerce. Royal law had long encouraged priests to see that their Indian parishioners tilled the fields, but the new projects were often infrastructural—roads and bridges built to tap markets for local produce as well as facilitate spiritual care, or the introduction of new crops and raw materials like cotton for cottage industries.[121]

The most admirable curas from the viewpoint of late colonial royal governors were the ones who did both kinds of building, making a double sacrifice of their time and wealth for tangible works of enduring value. In 1793, the subdelegado of Ixtlahuaca (Edo. de México) singled out the cura of Atlacomulco, Miguel Flores, for lavish praise because he had refurbished the church at his own expense, built a new rectory, and undertaken public works, including a new road in one direction out of town and a "very useful" bridge in another.[122] Antonio Manuel Velásquez's accomplishments in the impoverished Sierra de Nayarit (Diocese of Guadalajara) during the 1760's were less impressive, but his intentions were similar. The places he served were so poor, he said, he had to beg for his living, but he promoted better cultivation of the land and a successful search for mineral deposits that improved the local economy and allowed him to build up a cofradía ranch that supported the liturgy and improvements in the church buildings and furnishings.[123]

As a builder and teacher, José Joaquín de la Pedreguera, cura of Jalapa (Veracruz) in 1820, was an example of the "new pastor" who would make "a new man" of the Indian, as Omerick and Lorenzana had envisioned 50 years before. A veteran of 18 years' service in those parts and famous (in his own telling) for his sermons, Pedreguera had rebuilt parish churches wherever he had gone. But his crowning achievement had been in Coatepec, where he had drained the swamplands that had made the pueblo a place of pestilence, promoted coffee cultivation, and opened a new road to Jalapa, with seven bridges of mortar and stone, so that the locals could transport produce from the valley to promising markets.[124]

The Late Colonial Model of the Parish Priest

The late colonial written record is filled with images for model relationships between priests and parishioners, and with references to the mutual goal of "spiritual and temporal happiness."[125] On the Indian parishioners' side, the responsibilities were little changed from the sixteenth and seventeenth centuries: first, to fulfill the Easter duty, attend mass on Sundays and other holy days, and seal birth with baptism, family with marriage, and impending death with extreme unction; and second, to observe a "reverential fear" of the cura—to respect and fear him, and ideally to love him as their guide and guardian in spiritual affairs.[126] These two fundamentals—the sacraments and respectful obedience—entailed fulfilling an array of secondary obligations and displaying appropriate religious ardor.[127] To fulfill the sacramental duties, parishioners needed to know the doctrine of the church and follow its principles.[128] Respect and obedience meant deference to the priest but also implied a sweeping compliance with the political and social as well as the sacramental principles of church doctrine: Christians should not be idle, should practice cleanliness and good order in their personal and family affairs, should be useful to society, and should overcome ignorance and idolatry.[129] The obligation to be busy and useful translated into supporting the parish priests with fees, food, and household labor service, all of which became especially controversial matters in the late eighteenth century. In addition, from the clergy's point of view, respect meant docility.[130] If the priest was a pastor and father, his parishioners were sheep, followers, subjects, and children.[131]

In mentioning parishioners' obligations, priests were apt to speak first of their successes, as measured by people fulfilling the *precepto anual* (the Easter duty to confess and take communion). But for most, observance was of less concern than disobedience and disrespect.[132] Secular and ecclesiastical courts consistently backed up the worried curas, at least in a pro forma way, reminding villagers that they owed their priest "much respect and veneration."[133] The Audiencia of Mexico in 1782 pointedly reminded the Indians of Santo Domingo Hueyapan (Morelos) that they should "respect, revere, and obey their *cura*, and live in a Christian and politic manner."[134] Omerick, who looked on the bright side of Indian civility and spirituality, summarized ideal Indian parishioners in 1769 in a way that his less optimistic colleagues would have seconded: "well-instructed, docile, and dedicated to the divine cult and their work." Placing education first was a late-eighteenth-century ordering, but this combination invokes knowledge of the sacraments, respect, discipline, training, and work.

Colonial authorities were ready enough to instruct Indian parishioners in their duties, but the Indians had their own ideas on the subject. From a number of lawsuits between parishioners and curas, it is clear Indians believed their priests were bound by a reciprocal set of duties. Two cases are particularly noteworthy for setting out their view of the tit-for-tat nature of the relationship. In one, a 1785 dispute between the cura and Indians of San Luis de las Peras (Huichapan district, Hidalgo) over the removal of a vicario de pie fijo, the argument turned on the priest's liturgical duties: the cura complained that the Indians did not fulfill the Easter duty, attend mass regularly, or seek Christian burial or marriage; the Indians responded that he and the vicario did not "fulfill their obligation to provide spiritual nourishment."[135] More nebulous duties were invoked in the other case when the Indians of Teoloyucan, in a 1759 fees dispute, argued that they respected and feared their cura, and that in exchange he owed them "gentleness, kindness, and love" instead of the "violence and harshness" he meted out.[136]

Reciprocity between priests and Indian parishioners had always been the ideal. Archbishop Lorenzana offered an up-to-date statement of it in his advice for the good conduct of parish priests in 1769: the Indian parishioners were obliged to feel the holy fear of God, know the essential doctrine (especially in Spanish), educate their children well, respect their superiors, and obey the curas and judges. The cura was to "give his life for his sheep," attend to their spiritual needs promptly, suffer their impertinences patiently, and fulfill his duties as father, pastor, judge, physician, and teacher.[137]

Though Lorenzana did not make a point of it, he, like other prelates since midcentury, now saw the model priest as not only charitable, patient, obedient, and the rest, but also learned. To the bishop of Michoacán and his advisers in 1785, the "grave duty of instruction" fully justified giving priority for parish appointments to men of high education and "a brilliant academic record."[138] Archbishop Lizana y Beaumont, in even more exalted language, called learning the "science of the Saints" (ciencia de los Santos).[139]

Coupled with the emphasis on education were injunctions not to use rigor with the Indians and to "operate within the limits of your duties as *vicario*."[140] The archbishop's visitador in the Huasteca in 1806–8, for example, urged pastors on his itinerary to keep in mind that the Indians were in a state of spiritual illness and required ministration, not punishment.[141] Pérez de Velasco summed up the official position:

> Benevolence, affability, and sweetness are indispensable qualities in the Pastor, whose obligation is to win over the wills of men in order to bring them to peace with God. . . . We should not consider them [Indians] to be more brutish or fierce than tigers, for we can see how they become gentle, domesticated, and tractable (but by persuasion, not force). Cruel pastors will be feared by the Indians, no doubt, but those who are benign will be loved.[142]

Royal officials echoed the prelates' version of the model pastor in ways that emphasized the narrowing scope of his public duties and his love, gentleness, teaching, and obedience.[143] From the audiencia's point of view, the model cura — "the true father of his parishioners"—founded schools, promoted church construction, was prompt in his ministry, taught doctrine, often brought in revival missions, gave alms to the poor, and sold foodstuffs at low prices.[144] In a royal cedula issued in 1768, the year after the expulsion of the Jesuits, parish priests were ordered to set a good example of love and respect for their sovereign, to teach holy scripture to his subjects and inculcate its principles in the life of the people. Above all, they should abstain from "harangues" and "grumblings" against the government.[145]

The crown's image of the ideal cura's demeanor in his parish is abundantly evident in the 1793 district governors' reports on parish priests in their jurisdictions. The complimentary adjectives that appear repeatedly in these reports cluster around six qualities: gentleness (*blandura*), disinterestedness, exemplary personal conduct, love, charity, and zeal. The first—blandura—is the most common and richly elaborated characterization. Enthusiastic subdelegados amplified it or clarified its meaning with unusual expansiveness: the priest was "peaceful," "gentle," "humble," "modest," "upright," "benign," "mild," "God-fearing," "circumspect," "moderate," "peaceful and quiet," "very fond of peace," "prudent," and "given to the affability of a true father."[146] Picking out the traditional virtues of self-control, humility, and moderation, and embellishing them with adjectives that suggested subservience, the governors were constructing an updated ideal priest who understood and accepted his limited place in public life.

The other qualities that appear often in these reports recalled the traditional overlapping virtues underlined by the Council of Trent. But treated separately, they also emphasized the priest's more narrowly defined spiritual responsibilities. Disinterestedness (desinterés) here meant his separation from material preoccupations, especially his willingness to forgive sacramental fees and leave local financial matters to community officials (and thus to abandon any rivalry with the subdelegado over control of local wealth). Desinterés was closely connected with charity—the selfless, loving gift of himself and his possessions. The subdelegados, like everyone else, admired a cura who led an exemplary personal life (*arreglada*) and was "exact in fulfilling his duties," which is what "celo" meant to them. "Apostólico" was the subdelegados' highest word of praise. It summed up a combination of exemplary love, charity, and extraordinary parish service.[147]

The subdelegado of Ixtlahuaca was especially expansive in his evaluation of the cura there: Francisco Pico Palacio was a paragon of all the virtues district governors looked for in a cura, "a man whose discharge of the serious obligations of his high and delicate ministry [was] well known and attested to by all his parishioners":

He handles those obligations with complete order for we know him to be prompt and efficacious in everything. On holy days, he celebrates mass and explains the doctrine with brilliant clarity. Any day at any hour, he administers the holy sacrament of penance to whoever asks, even waiting long hours in the confessional in case he is needed. When there is a shortage of pastors he mounts up and leaves the parish seat for the hamlets and *haciendas* that are without mass and the sacraments. From his own purse, he has paid for rebuilding the choir and roof supports of the church. . . . He asks only for his just fees and those with great moderation, and often postponing collection from those who do not have money at the moment. He gives continual proof of discreet and politic behavior for, within the limits of his responsibilities, he keeps his parishioners at peace and in good order.[148]

Parishioners, though they had the most to gain or lose in a less-than-perfect priest, tended to have a small (but substantial) wish list. Well versed in the language of the ecclesiastical and royal authorities, attorneys for Indian complainants in the late colonial period reduced the ideal priest to a formula of gentleness and kindness. The attorney for Alahuistlan (Zacualpan district) in 1786, for example, wanted the cura to punish only "with the gentleness and kindness that their misery merits."[149] In virtually the same words, the attorney for Tlaltizapan (Morelos) petitioned that the cura "should treat his Indian parishioners with the kindness and gentleness that their misery demands and that is appropriate for a beneficed *cura*."[150]

In the mouths of Indian parishioners, moreover, the meaning of these words was likely to narrow in ways that reflected their direct encounters with their cura. Above all, they expected the cura to do what his title required—"to administer spiritual nourishment to them"[151]—but when they addressed the courts, desinterés, suavidad, and caridad were their watchwords. In 1757, an Indian official praised his cura for desinterés, by which he meant that even though many parishioners owed him fees, he continued to provide the sacraments and blessings without complaint. Desinterés also meant that the cura did not demand labor service not directly connected to maintaining the church buildings and the cult.[152] Suavidad and caridad were most likely to mean that he did not give heavy floggings for insignificant transgressions, that he applied only the "moderate punishment" of a loving father.[153] Caridad sometimes encompassed both desinterés and suavidad—meaning that the cura did not treat parishioners harshly, that he used little or no force and did many good works at his own expense.[154] Moderation and love (*moderación* and *amor*) together formed the general principle that was invoked by the Indians in this period, just as, in a more elaborate form, it had been invoked by bishops since the sixteenth century.[155] On occasion, parishioners looked beyond these concerns to express other aspirations for their ideal priest, as the Indians of Tuscacuesco (Jalisco) did in the 1820's when they observed that he should "protect the church as he would a pious mother."[156]

Finally, what of the curas themselves? Not surprisingly, in their formal en-counters with superiors, they inevitably reiterated what they had been taught and were expected to say. But some personal preoccupations nevertheless show through. They spoke of their charity and zeal, self-control and gentleness; of using "the most gentle and prudent means," of being impelled to "gentleness and suffering in order to root and nurture peace" (even as they were defending their judicial role).[157] Above all, they spoke eloquently and expansively of their faithful completion of their sacramental and teaching duties. As an investigating cura said of the cura of Zapotitlan (Jalisco), he "serves without taking note of the inconvenience of time, weather, or roads, negotiating even the most rugged ba-rrancas with unperturbed serenity as if he were crossing the smoothest plain."[158] Or as the cura of Huejutla (Hidalgo) said of his vicario in 1791:

He was such an effective pastor that he mounted his horse as soon as he was called to a confession no matter what the weather or whether he would have to travel across barran-cas, steep precipices, or deserted wastelands. . . . When he did not have the proper mount to cross a swollen river, he took off his clothes and swam across.[159]

But priests high and low also repeatedly expressed their sense of obligation to control immoral conduct among the Indians for the sake of their own salvation and the integrity of their families.[160] Most curas and late colonial bishops were deeply ambivalent about the rights and liberties of settled Indians. The word *libertad* carried mixed messages throughout the colonial period. On one side, it meant the opposite of servitude and captivity; on the other, it meant personal freedom unrestrained by social virtue or the sentiments that drew the individual toward God. The Fourth Provincial Council in 1771 repeatedly referred to Indi-ans as "free, not slaves," but the bishops had in mind freedom of trade and exemption from the kind of coercion over labor and property to which a slave was subject. In the same breath, they spoke of Indians being little children in need of the instruction and protection of "Our Catholic Kings." When the poli-tics of Indian freedom went beyond lawyers' briefs, episcopal pronouncements, and excessive restraint on economic choices, the sentiment usually was negative. For example, the cura of Tolpetlac (Edo. de México) in 1780 complained of his Indian parishioners' "criminal liberty," and Dr. José Manuel Ruiz y Cervantes, cura of Zimatlan (Oaxaca) in the 1770's and 1780's, argued that the Indians must be restrained because their "wicked manner of government," in which "every-one rules," was the source of continual disorder.[161] The Indians' "liberty"—their natural freedom[162]—must be kept in check so that it would not become *liberti-naje* (licentiousness). They were people of "the greatest liberty," who readily fell into sin—"dominated by an urge to gamble," as one cura put it, or to drink, liti-gate, steal, commit adultery and incest, mock their superiors, or be excessively slothful, lazy, wasteful, and greedy for meat.[163] "These Indians," said the cura of Tlacotalpan (Veracruz) in 1790, "are excessively libertine and insubordinate"; "given to the utmost high-handedness and libertinism," said the cura of Tlalti-zapan (Morelos) in 1781.[164]

J. H. Parry has pointed out that

the liberty of the Indians in the sense in which Spanish legislators used the word, meant . . . the kind of liberty which a legally free peasant enjoyed in Spain; liberty within the context of the whole society to which he belonged and subject to discharging the appropriate obligations towards that society as laid down by custom.[165]

Liberty in these terms had as much to do with dependence, protection, and obligation as with freedom.

Priests' Conflicting Views of the Indians

Priests' views of their Indian parishioners affected their expectations, were likely to increase the tension between old and new models of parish service, and sometimes lengthened the distance between them and their congregations. Though neither simple nor fixed, those views were thoroughly rooted in the experience of colonial rule and traditional conceptions of parish service, an influence of the past that was bound to complicate the priests' adjustments to declining judicial and administrative responsibilities in the daily affairs of the parish.

The vocabulary priests used to describe Indian character and behavior was quite elaborate and sometimes contradictory.[166] The number of terms increased over time, and their combinations and meaning could change, but many of the eighteenth-century characterizations still used the terms of the sixteenth-century encounters: ignorant, barbaric, savage, malicious, cunning, disorderly, uncontrolled, lazy, prone to drunkenness, lustful and gluttonous, meek, humble, obedient, long-suffering, docile, innocent, simple in spirit, patient, hardworking, modest, rational, and teachable.

As this list indicates, these terms cluster around two inconsistent notions: Indians as simple, timid, obedient, perhaps stupid, innocents; and Indians as deceitful, malicious, and cunningly disobedient subjects—children of the Seven Cardinal Sins. Sometimes a commentator seemed to hold both notions at once or was undecided about which was the real Indian. More often, the two views were held by different men, though the contradiction was rarely disputed openly and was subject to some change according to circumstances.

The most common negative adjective was "malicious." Malice essentially meant ill-will, but it could be used in various senses: to designate ill-will toward Spanish authorities or toward other Indians; to describe particular acts of ill-will or to draw a deeper conclusion about psychological motivation. The most positive comments, extolling settled Indians' "very superior talent" and holding up as examples the few Indians who had "prospered in letters, high office, and honorific positions," usually came from the pens of bishops and other dignitaries of the church. The common sixteenth-century view of Indians as innocents was heard less often in the eighteenth century, partly because the achievements of more than two centuries of proselytizing seemed so disappointing. Those late-eighteenth-century clerics who looked favorably on Indians were more likely to call them humble, guileless, or—sometimes—hardworking. But the idea that Indians were lazy was deeply ingrained and growing deeper in the late colonial period, when the Bourbons' emphasis on human industry and production encouraged images of Indian parishioners as potential "busy bees" and the lazy Indian as a "drone in the hive." [167]

Despite these mixed signals, there were common denominators in nearly all the clerical commentaries. In particular, Indians in general were regarded as vulnerable dependents with diminished capacity and understanding. The expressions that show up repeatedly in connection with this idea are *miserables, ignorantes, rudos, flexibles,* and *niños. Miserable* was the term most widely applied to Indians. Meaning helpless, unfortunate, and impoverished in possessions or spirit, *miserable* implied that Indians required protection and pity.[168] Occasionally, the implication of material poverty comes to the fore in a sharply pejorative way, as if Indians led a subhuman existence, but most often *miserable* appears in the same sentence with words for ignorant, unfortunate, and innocent.

Another word that was often paired with *miserable* in the ecclesiastical sources is *niño,* child. The *Itinerario* calls Indians "simple children." Cura Ruiz y Cervantes, in his learned treatise of 1784, called Indians "bearded children" and "children of punishment" (borrowing from the *Itinerario*). He described them epigrammatically as "people who eat without revulsion, live without shame, and die without fear."[169] In Ruiz y Cervantes's view, Indians' fear of hell was essential to the colonial enterprise and the good order of society, but it was not the kind of fear that came naturally to them. It had to be instilled, like honor and shame.[170] Other curas spoke of Indians as "by nature cowards," "timid and cowardly," and needing to be menaced or punished to be made to work.

Next to *miserable, ignorante* and *rudo* were the most common and enduring adjectives for Indians, and they frequently appeared together, one serving as an elaboration of the other. *Ignorante* meant destitute of knowledge, uninformed, and—like *rudo*—unsophisticated. It might imply innocence, especially to a charitable Spanish bishop who, from his lofty place, was ready to forgive what he regarded as quaint superstitions and incidental idolatry. But to most parish priests it suggested "misguided" at best. Mainly, *ignorante* and *rudo* implied little intelligence and limited rationality. The *Itinerario* urged priests to avoid abstractions in their teaching and use graphic examples whenever possible, for Indians were "more moved by examples than by reason."

A closely connected term was *flexibilidad*. It indicated that Indians were mercurial and undependable, like the child in the old Castilian saying, "amor de niño, agua en cesto"—a child's love is like water in a basket. Whether that flexibility was good or bad was a matter of opinion. Presented as a witness in a 1778 dispute between his parishioners and the alcalde mayor, the cura of Ocotlan, Jalisco, advised the court that Indians had "such flexible and waxlike hearts that they are easily stamped with iniquities." The more optimistic Omerick found virtue in Indians being "like paste or a lump of wax to be shaped as one wishes."

Commentators who were inclined to think of Indians as perverse rather than innocently ignorant saw a logical connection between flexibility and studied dishonesty. Ruiz y Cervantes thought he had found a key to this aspect of Indian character in their marketing habits: "In the baskets of *tortillas* that they sell in the *plazas* of our America, they usually put on top of their small yellow ones a great white *tortilla* for show. . . . And this is the way they act when they appear before ecclesiastical and civil judges."

In this lexicon, one term led to another, but not in endless variations or particularly complex ways. *Miserable* and its elaborations and extensions toward fear, shamelessness, ignorance, rusticity, laziness, and the rest led back to the idea that

Indians were incomplete humans, lacking in willpower and reason. This is what Omerick meant when he said they had "small hearts and lowly spirits." Sometimes in bitterness, sometimes with protective intentions, other parish priests said that Indians were "half alive," "like a leafless tree with barely some life in the root, which, if it is not watered soon, will be fit only for the fire." The manuals repeatedly noted that although Indians were rational and had some willpower, they had "weak use of reason."

Impaired or poorly developed rationality left Indians prey to their passions. Bishops, parish priests, and writers of manuals occasionally elaborated on this point, declaring that Indian rationality was overridden by "insatiable thirsts" for lawsuits, alcohol, and sex; or, as one parish priest said, that their will was itself colored by desire. Because rationality was the basis of civility, parish priests sometimes expressed fear that settled but barely rational Indians would be drawn back into infidelity and savagery. To a Franciscan doctrinero of Mexico City in 1719, Indians who lived outside their pueblos were "moors without a lord." Indian "reversion" to a solitary life was a serious threat to the colonial elite's self-image and values, and to actual colonial power. Settled Indian subjects made possible the colony as Spaniards intended it to be. They were vital as builders, farm laborers, market producers, taxpayers, responsible Christians, underlings, and buffers against hostile frontier tribes. Without their incorporation into colonial Christian society, the religious justification of Spanish rule in America dissolved.

But were Indians naturally inferior or were other circumstances largely responsible for their behavior? To cite only two of many examples, a Franciscan doctrinero from the district of Cuernavaca spoke of Indians in 1752 as having "a natural aversion to all that is good," and a natural propensity to lie and deceive. "Cowardly by nature," said Ruiz y Cervantes in 1772; "by nature unreflective," he added in 1784, "they do not seem to have free will." The mainstream view, however, expressed by bishops, published manuals, and other high colonial authorities was that Indians were neither noble innocents nor cunning brutes by nature, and that they had redeeming qualities that could make them faithful Christians and loyal, productive subjects of the crown. As Omerick put it, Indians were simple but rational and with a curiosity to learn.[171]

This tempered optimism went hand in hand with a renewed interest in a kind of social engineering through education: Indians were capable of improvement and should be improved; a "new conquest" was needed. By the 1750's, there was not so much a new as a more insistent emphasis on the education and improvement of ordinary Indians. Archbishop Manuel Rubio y Salinas claimed that 228 parish schools were founded in his jurisdiction during 1754. Many of the schools were short-lived, but new rounds of school foundings were attempted. The growing importance assigned to the enterprise is reflected in the parish priests' narrative of their services. Few of the Guadalajara priests seeking promotion in 1754 listed establishing or improving local primary schools among their accomplishments. But by 1770, most claimed to have supported schools, and some described their efforts at length. By the end of the century, this was a standard entry in a priest's resumé.

To the question of whether Indians' limited rationality and civility were inherent or conditioned, the answer for most parish priests and their superiors was "both." Indians were inferior by nature but still human, rational, and capable of improvement and salvation. "Miserable" and "niño" capture the essence of this intermediate category of teachable minors, neither savages nor fully rational and civil in their conduct. Anthony Padgen's account of a sixteenth-century deterministic theory of racial inferiority that regarded Indians as natural children—a theoretical position wedged in between theories of Indians as natural slaves and as noble innocents—fits well with much of the opinion expressed by New Spain's priests at all levels in the eighteenth century.

But this theory could contain a variety of antitheses contrasting Spaniards and Indians, and could be stretched under the changing conditions of the eighteenth century without collapsing in the face of environmental determinism or scientific relativism. The antitheses that are well documented in the eighteenth-century priests' comments about Spaniards and Indians include (besides the venerable one of civility/barbarism) Christian/pagan, reason/passion, moderation/excess, and love of virtue/fear of punishment. Given the fairly rich colonial lexicon for Indians and the acceptance of intermediate categories, it is a telling fact that the one term widely used to distinguish the rest of society from Indians at the end of the colonial period was "gente de razón," rational people. Perhaps the term was so common by then that people used it without considering its literal meaning, but it was at least a subliminal inversion that questioned the full rationality of people called Indians.[172] Labels like "miserable" and "niño" called for submission to paternal authority, and there was no doubt in this lexicon about who the children were.

The "paradigm of polarity" that Robert Berkhofer proposes as the lasting conception of Indians in British North America underlines a sweeping similarity across colonial American history. "Indian" was a generic term that summarized a whole continent of native people and distinguished them from the European colonists who adopted the term. But the Spanish colonial terminology for descendants of native Americans in the eighteenth century was not limited to inversions and polarities. The word for Indian in Spanish was a naked noun waiting to be dressed in adjectives that would answer the question, which Indian? It did not assume that all Indians were alike.[173] Here was an ample, convoluted vocabulary of distance, incorporation, and subjugation generated at close hand over many years. The polarities involving colonial Indians were tendencies, not static or absolute.

Protection and instruction, two distinct intentions embedded in the natural-child theory, were less closely linked than its sixteenth-century proponents would have liked. The key legal term, *miserable*, which corresponds most closely to the natural-child theory, had more to do with protection than instruction. Through most of the colonial period, the emphasis on control by means of protection, punishment, and segregation deflected attention away from how far Indian behavior could be positively changed. In the pale light of Spain's Enlightenment, especially from the 1770's on, the emphasis was reversed: Indians needed to be civilized and incorporated, their rationality nurtured. Protection, in the sense of segregating Indians in pueblos and assigning them the rights of minors, did not disappear from law, rhetoric, or practice, but it came into question and took second place to the idea of controlling Indians within colonial society as a whole.

The best of the eighteenth-century parish priests did not dwell on the Indianness of their parishioners. While few had broken free from the category of Indian or a European ideal of civilization to enter Tzvetan Todorov's dialogue of cultures "in which no one has the last word," some looked on their parishioners mainly as fellow Christians in need of a priest's services. They, like some of their superiors and precedecessors, understood that protection flowed in two directions. Even Ruiz y Cervantes realized that "the Indian's cloak covers us all."

Parish priests and other men of authority and privilege in this colonial society regarded non-noble Indians in many of the same terms they used for peasants and the lower classes generally. The connection was occasionally made explicit in eighteenth-century records, as when witnesses at the 1789 judicial inquiry into the conduct of the corregidor of Tequila spoke of "Indians and other poor people."[174] The tendency to conflate Indians and the *plebe* (the lower classes generally) would have gained strength in the late colonial period as miscegenation, newcomers moving into rural pueblos, and Indian villagers dressing in city clothes and speaking Spanish made it increasingly difficult to say who was an Indian. Even royal policy was shifting away from the idea of Indian pueblos as segregated reserves.

Still, in law and to a lesser extent in practice, settled Indians in Spanish America had a special claim upon the crown's protection, and most of them had a corporate legal identity as members of ancient landholding pueblos that distinguished them from other groups of the dependent, laboring, usually landless poor. Indian commoners as a group were inferior to Spanish masters, but not in a vertical line of status and wealth running from viceroys, bishops, landed nobles, mine owners, and merchants at the top to Indians and black slaves at the bottom. As wards of the crown, the objects of a large body of law concerning their rights and obligations, Indians evoked a continuing interest in their nature and origins that other groups did not. Settled Indians were sometimes considered meek and less covetous or envious than other groups—ideas rarely associated with the lower classes generally in New Spain. Indeed, blacks, mestizos, and other mixed groups were regarded as "infected races"—provocative, grasping classes of people who could easily contaminate weak, impressionable Indians.

* * *

Not all parish priests were wealthy and influential, but all occupied a position of official standing that drew them toward the colonial government and toward other educated and genteel classes of people. In principle, they stood between colonial rulers and Christian communities, as appointees of a Christian monarch and shepherds of a Christian flock. In practice, they might achieve a balance between these roles or be more one than the other. But rarely were they simply world renouncers, agents of colonial government, or embodiments of local autonomy.

The priest's distinguished place in the parish depended first on his priesthood. Ordained by the single official church, appointed by the crown as well as his prelate, educated into the mysteries of the faith, and adept at rites that summoned the divine to sanctify human life, he had a legitimacy unavailable to spiritual leaders who lacked such a great institutional base. Where a shaman whose auguries did not come to pass might pay dearly for his failure, the priest could deflect blame onto the deity or the congregation. Though his power, no less than the shaman's, rested on mediations that made the remote accessible—between what can be taken apart and explained empirically and what remains mysterious—it was buttressed by his influence in purely temporal affairs. Parishioners might look to him to intercede with higher authorities, settle a land suit, or resolve issues among disputing parties. How extensive this mediating role in public life was often depended on regional, local, and individual circumstances. Unquestioned paternal authority was not guaranteed by the pastor's priesthood or his role as a social integrator. It depended especially on his ability to fulfill the overlapping and sometimes contradictory and changing roles prescribed for him, and on the willingness of parishioners to follow his lead. It was a kind of mediating leadership open to the priesthood in this society, whether or not the priest enjoyed the formal authority of an adjudicator.[175]

"Separated but in the world," a favorite way for colonial prelates to describe the situation of parish priests,[176] was less a paradox than a vital tension to be held in balance. The rural pastor could not escape the world, for his subjects were there, but "the Lord's path always [ran] in the opposite direction to that of the world."[177] Maintaining the balance was a key to his successful exercise of the power of his office. Being in but not entirely of the parish and this world, both a stranger and a father, could make him an impartial intermediary between heaven and earth, and villagers and their superiors. The distance that in principle separated him from the parish also heightened his value to parishioners as a mediator.

But if the distance was too great or too small, the balance was upset, and the priest's moral authority was undermined. The distance often stretched into weakness if the cura was newly arrived, or took every occasion to be away from what he regarded as an unpleasant and temporary exile, or rarely visited outlying pueblos, or was of an especially cold and uncompromising bent, or was contemptuous of his Indian parishioners' abilities, or could not speak their primary language. The distance was also greatly lengthened if parishioners did not respect his spiritual authority fully—did not fulfill the precepto anual or regard themselves as Christians, were insolent or disobedient, or brought lawsuits against him out of vengeance. The distance could grow dangerously short if he failed to meet even the standards of personal conduct expected of his parishioners; or if he was too concerned about his livelihood and the affairs of the world, enmeshing himself too deeply in the local economy and politics; or if parishioners and district governors were intent on applying new laws or enforcing old ones that redefined his place in the public life of the parish.

The balance was therefore not entirely within the priest's control; and it was impossible to achieve once and for all. His power in the parish and the maintenance of the balance were complicated by the mixture and multiple meanings of the metaphors that traditionally described his role, and the changing emphasis given to some of them by the crown and regalist prelates in the late colonial period. Although loving father was the guiding idea behind descriptions of the Tridentine parish priest, he was also to be judge, teacher, physician, pastor, gardener, servant, brother, and more. How could a judge be a physician at the same time? a pastor and a gardener? a brother and a father? To succeed most of the time must have taken a synoptic vision that challenged his ingenuity and endurance. And if he did succeed in playing these many roles without much contradiction or controversy—in being both judge and physician in the confessional, both servant and father, both model of charity and man of means in the community—the late-eighteenth-century revisions that emphasized the gentle teacher, physician, gardener, and builder over the magistrate and pastor who judiciously mixed love with fear must have been even more distressing to him than to those priests who failed to balance so many roles. Traditionally, the priest's duties, which converged on his responsibilities as protector and spiritual father, had always shaded into public life, more or less, depending on the time and local circumstances. That public role could be modified but not easily transformed from the top of the political order without unexpected consequences.

CHAPTER EIGHT

Priests at Work

This solidarity among the Indians would not worry me if it furthered peace and tranquility, and were expressed with the appropriate recognition of and respect toward their superiors—me their parish priest and their own *gobernador*. . . . I expressed to them the pain in my heart and the torment it gave me as their pastor to see that the efforts I had made in earlier years to get them to fulfill their annual obligations to the church had been completely fruitless.
—Joaquín Trujillo, cura of
San Miguel Acambay (Hidalgo), 1761

Parish service required various talents and commitments beyond a spiritual vocation. It attracted men with some of the qualities of the ideal pastor and occasionally one with all of them. It also attracted men with little sense of calling or the strength to resist the opportunities for personal enrichment and power. The variation was almost endless. Some priests were humble, introspective, gentle men, praised for their "Christian simplicity" and quiet resignation. Some were an inspiration to their parishioners as exemplars of Christian conduct; others were so modest and otherworldly that they had little impact on them and were virtually forgotten by their superiors. Others were so hot-tempered and haughty that they alienated their subjects. Many suffered from physical ailments, and a few were considered demented. Some were delicate flowers, reclusive and studious, so timid and of such a refined conscience that they shrank from all but the sacramental responsibilities of a pastor; others were robust, outgoing, and determined to shape the public and private lives of those around them. Some were excessively tidy—punctilious, rigid, and didactic to a fault. Others responded more to the spirit of charity than to the letter of the law. Some were unabashedly "interesados," exacting as much money as they could for masses and fees, putting parishioners to work for personal gain, or moving off into trade and the management of rural estates. Some were professionally ambitious men, intent on the next promotion; others seemingly had no higher ambition than to serve their parish and dignify the liturgy, or to lead an ordinary, if socially elevated, life in their hometown in the company of relatives. Some were energetic and prepared to spend their health and wealth in parish service; others were phlegmatic and self-indulgent. Some vicarios were hardly distinguishable from rustic parishioners in their learning and manners. A few were mildly sacrilegious in their habits.[1] Some priests were rooted in one place; others were frequently on the move. There were picaresque characters right out of Fernández de Lizardi's *El periquillo sarniento*—rogue priests who gambled, seduced women, brandished knives and pistols, and dressed like rancheros.

Whether such personal qualities were admirable, regrettable, or inconsequential depended on how they came together and where and when the priest served. Selfless dedication to an older conception of parish service could result in angry confrontations with parishioners and district judges; great energy could be put to very different uses; introspection did not save some priests from self-importance and a selfish notion of charity; and punctiliousness could be regarded by parishioners, as well as superiors, as a virtue. It was not unusual for parish priests who were judged to be scoundrels and cynics in their personal conduct to be attentive to their sacramental duties and efficacious in the pulpit and the confessional ("exact in fulfilling their obligations" was the usual way of saying this). These were extreme cases, but most priests must have experienced this tension of a life split between the ideal of the soaring eagle and their earthbound weaknesses and mistakes, a tension inherent in Christianity's emphasis on mankind's fall from grace and the stain of original sin. It could be eased, even resolved temporarily, for priests as well as laymen, by good works, penance, and absolution, although priests were expected to answer to a more demanding conscience.

This chapter examines the individual actions and sentiments of these men, identifying patterns in how they regarded their duties, how they interpreted change in their own situations, and how they experienced divided lives and loyalties. Sentiments and imagination sometimes are more clearly expressed in what people did in specific circumstances than in what they said later or in the abstract. But mental life does not divide neatly into what is implicit in the actions of the many and what is explicit in the ideas of the elite. Even grand ideas about social order and human destiny could express deeply felt passions, longings, and frustrations that brought rulers and subjects together on the same stage and close the distance between intellectual and social history.

There are broad patterns, but they must be inferred and situated from an incomplete record. The record of sexual misconduct by priests, for example, is deceptively abundant, and the general comments about it in colonial sources can be misleading.[2] It is more difficult, probably impossible, to gauge the incidence of sexual misconduct for parish priests as a group than to describe individual cases and to infer, from their comments, how priests, parishioners, and royal governors regarded sexual transgressions. Certain ideas and ways of thinking run with great force through the priests' actions (or at least through the accounts of them). Four that are especially prominent here and throughout the book are the tendencies to use organic metaphors, honor custom, value charity, and expect reciprocal obligations.

The main division in this chapter between conduct (which the judicial and administrative record was likely to treat as misconduct or exemplary conduct) and sentiments is artificial, since sentiments pervade the accounts from which the discussion of conduct is drawn. Still, the division has its logic—the second part deals mainly with how priests felt about their profession, whereas the part on conduct is more concerned with how individual acts and reputations drew priests close to or away from their parishioners.

Misconduct

There is considerable evidence for central and western Mexico in the late colonial period of parish priests who were perceived to act in unpriestly ways, but most of the detailed cases come from the Inquisition—that trap for the offbeat. Relying heavily on such records gives a strange and distorted view of priests in their parishes. This section combines them with other kinds of evidence of forbidden conduct and conduct unbecoming a priest (acceptable behavior carried to unacceptable extremes) that were more common and more revealing of the place of the priest in the parish, and sets them off against evidence of exemplary conduct to suggest how the definitions of unpriestly conduct were shifting in the late eighteenth century.

Writing about eighteenth-century Spain, Antonio Domínguez Ortiz suggests that diocesan priests lived like laymen.[3] For colonial Mexican pastors, there is a kernel of truth to this claim, but much of the support for it comes from a small number of extreme cases, and it is not often possible to establish which habits were widespread or universal. Cases of avarice and obsessive preoccupation with personal wealth were well known in the eighteenth century, if not typical. The seventeenth-century legal commentator Solórzano Pereira thought that material greed was a common vice among priests and the root of evil, and that the complaints of curas' "black greed," "insatiable avarice," and "excessive attachment to possessions," their reluctance to hire vicarios to meet the spiritual needs of the parish, bitter disputes over clerical fees, property interests, and interference in parish finances, indicated an overactive involvement in worldly affairs that left them open to criticism.[4]

Cases of improper dress point to another recurrent problem that usually took a less extravagant form: diminishing the office by failing to exhibit exemplary personal habits. The purpose of proper dress was described by the Council of Trent: "That by the propriety of their outward apparel they may show forth the inward uprightness of their morals."[5] More specifically, it meant dress that was chaste ("honesto") in its color, cut, and fabric—long and black, with a clerical collar, and no colored gloves or other fancy accessories. The black garments symbolized the priest's perpetual mourning, "carrying in his mind the memory of the crown and sacrifice, and in all his actions mortification and humility."[6] Hair was to be short and unstyled. Stockings had to be black or a drab gray, brown, or purple. And the only suitable footwear was sandals, also symbolic: "the foot was exposed above and covered below where it touched the ground to signify that the Gospel is not to be hidden, nor is its preaching to be based on interests and worldly comforts."[7] The priest had to appear for mass in the proper surplice and cap.[8] Priests were supposed to dress in clerical garb when they appeared in public, but if they went out gambling or to a dance in it, they compounded their sin by besmirching the office.[9]

The few scandalously dressed parish priests who appear in ecclesiastical court records were out of uniform altogether or in torn and dirty attire. For example, José María Texeda, a young priest sent to the parish of Salinas in 1819, reappeared in the city of Zacatecas without license and in the company of disreputable friends wearing a torn priest's cloak and no cassock.[10] José Antonio Baldovinos, an amorous vicario of Colima, was in the habit of dressing in a ranchero's outfit with chaps and boots.[11] Cura Joseph Manuel Sotomayor of Zacualpan, careless in so many ways, reportedly could be recognized as a priest only by his skull cap.[12]

The more routine excesses in clerical dress that rarely led to individual description were the subject of several of Archbishop Lizana y Beaumont's pastoral letters. These were unseemly decoration and finery ("adorno y luxo")—luxury fabrics such as silk, velvet, or damask, colored accents, fancy stitching, and the like. Just what constituted excessive display is not clear, since Lizana found a moderate elegance ("moderada gala") acceptable, and other episcopal instructions made silk, although a luxury fabric, appropriate for clerical garb in hot weather. It was, in Lizana's terms, the perception of excess that counted most: "provocative" finery was inappropriate.[13]

The extravagant dressers, especially those who appeared in public out of uniform, were usually among the most scandalous in other respects as well. Baldovinos was fond of dances, gambling, and young women.[14] José Pablo Torreblanca, the cura of Chacalinitla in the district of Tixtla in 1793, lived very much like a layman. He shed his clerical collar for a green-coated military outfit and arms when he went out at night, and spent much of his time in Tixtla rather than the parish.[15] Miguel José Losada, the cura of Xichú (Guanajuato) in the late 1790's, reportedly dressed more like a criminal than a priest ("un hombre facineroso que sacerdote de Jesucristo"), operated an illegal cane alcohol still, carried firearms, and went off to Mexico City with three women, giving fandangos along the way.[16]

Another common complaint was drunkenness. A few late colonial curas and vicarios were plainly alcoholics. Like Graham Greene's whiskey priest in *The Power and the Glory*, and unlike those who dressed improperly, they were not necessarily given to an array of disreputable conduct except for sometimes failing to fulfill sacramental duties. José Roberto Gonzales, vicario of Tescatepec (Guayacocotla district), was charged in 1805 with sometimes being violently drunk and unable to administer the sacraments.[17] Mariano Calzada, as vicario of Sierra de Pinos (Zacatecas) in the 1780's, reportedly drank to the point of passing out.[18]

Even though more priests were in parish service in the late eighteenth century, complaints of absenteeism and inadequate spiritual care were common. The lapse was understandable in parishes with large territories, steep mountain paths and rushing streams, and small, widely scattered populations. It was impossible for a cura, even with assistants, to be everywhere he was needed, and special trips to remote corners of the parish were exhausting, dangerous, and often unrewarding, either spiritually or financially.[19] But absenteeism and incomplete spiritual care were common problems for other reasons as well, especially in the Archdiocese of Mexico. Most diocesan priests were city men by education. The core of their professional community and often their families and business contacts were located in the cathedral city.[20] Repeatedly, parish priests of the archdiocese were reported to maintain residences in Mexico City or spend months at a time there. Some, like Ygnacio Espinabarros of Ixtapalapa, who held parishes in or very near the Valley of Mexico, were commuters, traveling to the parish for Sunday services, special events, and emergencies but living in the city.[21] Others, especially the better educated curas assigned to more distant places, resided in the city and virtually farmed out their benefices.[22] Responding to the vicar general's order to return to his parish of Calimaya in the Valley of Toluca in 1792 after an absence of nearly nine months, Dr. Miguel de Araujo offered this delphic explanation: he needed to be in Mexico City on "very grave and important business concerning my church, in which I am not only an interested party but the legal advocate of their [my parishioners'] clear rights." There was, he said, no place for him to live in the parish seat, and he feared the disobedient parishioners who failed to do their Easter duty and peppered the courts with eight lawsuits against him.[23] Parish priests were entitled to an annual leave, which many spent in the capital; but others had a habit of taking additional, unauthorized leaves there. Mariano Matamoros, the national hero who served as cura of Jantetelco (Morelos) at the start of the Independence War, had earlier held the backwater parish of Escanela. During that time, he was reprimanded for virtually abandoning the parish for Mexico City. Others facing complaints of inadequate pastoral care spent months at a time in the city or a provincial town.[24] Some were simply too old, sick, drunk, lax, or distracted to do better.[25]

Residence in the parish became a visible if secondary issue in the regalist reform program of the late eighteenth century. The traditional standard of "personal, formal, active, efficacious, and conscientious residence" was reiterated and publicized by prelates and royal governors. The archbishop of Mexico issued a circular on February 2, 1762, that hit hard on parish residence, criticizing curas who left their parishes for no better reason than to "find amusement," as if "there were no objection to leaving whenever they wish," and warned of stiff penalties for absenting themselves without license. With license and faithful service, they would be granted the two months' leave prescribed by the Council of Trent.[26] A royal cedula of August 25, 1768, ordered bishops to notify the vice-patron when licenses were granted for longer absences than that.[27] The bishops were also to inform the vice-patron of appointments of coadjutores and vicarios. The aim was both to police the appointment of assistants and to move against curas who violated the rules of residence. The crown was still wrestling with the problem 20 years later. A cedula of August 4, 1791, concerning a 1784 order to place coadjutors in parishes where the cura was incapacitated, noted that there were also circumstances where a coadjutor ought to be imposed at a salary that approached the cura's revenues from the parish: some curas had been using this income to take up residence in the cities and devote themselves to private business and a disorderly life.[28] Agustín Durán, the cura of San Sebastián Querétaro, was forced into this arrangement. In 1805, the archiepiscopal court ordered him to accept a paid coadjutor, since he declined to reside in the parish. Durán objected that he had to remain in the capital for health reasons, and that his vicarios were more than capable of meeting the spiritual needs of the parish. But the order stood, and a coadjutor was appointed at a salary of 80 pesos a month even though Durán promised to move to San Sebastián.[29]

Most absentee curas were less brazen than Father Durán, living or traveling outside the parish without license but returning when warned to do so.[30] Some resided not in provincial towns or capital cities but on their own estates, or were away for weeks at a time on personal business.[31] Others remained in the parish but abandoned some of their duties for other pursuits. The 1793 subdelegados' reports occasionally identify priests of this kind. Their reasons ranged from the pursuit of excitement—which usually meant card games and cockfights—to commercial activities, a love interest in a distant place, indolence, and selective engagement in the calling. One was faithful in attending to the sick throughout the parish but remiss in preaching and teaching doctrine; another exempted himself from administering the sacraments altogether in favor of his studies and preaching; another had spells of introversion when he lived in virtual seclusion; another was an avid miner.[32] The subdelegado of Taxco singled out his rival, the cura of Acamistla, Manuel de Burgos, for comment as an able man diverted from his pastoral duties by worldly concerns:

He has had a brilliant literary career, is talented, well educated, and one of the best theologians in the archdiocese. His conduct has caused the greatest harm to many residents of this mining settlement, where he has resided most of the time since he became the *cura* of Acamistla. During his residence here he has spent his time fomenting disputes and discord among the residents, insinuating and drawing up petitions to start these, and sometimes producing petitions against the same residents he had once defended.... And all of this harm comes from sponsoring unjust business. Even when there is some justice in it, he handles it so badly that he seems to confuse matters on purpose.... He has worked mines, unfairly wanting to get in on the Poder de Dios mine, which resulted in a noisy dispute.... Devoting himself entirely to secular business that is alien to his station, he has abandoned the care of his parish and his parishioners.[33]

But absenteeism was not the only or even the most important cause for complaint by ill-served parishioners. More often it was a case of a cura confining his operations to the parish seat. Some curas failed to provide the periodic masses in visita churches more than twice a year, and many were slow to provide confession on demand outside the cabecera.[34]

Despite the clerical vow of celibacy and exhortations to misogyny,[35] heterosexual relations were common among parish priests, especially monogamous unions involving longtime vicarios and curas in remote second- and third-class parishes. The most striking aspect of the documentation on clerical incontinence is how little concerned parishioners and the ecclesiastical courts were with discreet violations of celibacy. Heterosexual activity and fathering children were not, in themselves, regarded as particularly scandalous or worth prosecuting, and a priest known to have broken his vow of celibacy did not necessarily weaken his position as spiritual leader in the eyes of his parishioners. What counted more was his public conduct as a priest and his social morality. The Indian gobernador of Huitzuco (Guerrero), for example, rose to the defense of the village priest, Manuel Urizar, when he was investigated in 1805 for illicit relations with a local woman. Passing over the moral lapse, the gobernador made an earnest plea for the priest's restoration to the parish, describing his "steadfast, most honorable conduct [and] great many acts of charity," his generosity in forgiving clerical fees, and his punctiliousness in attending to confession whenever called and offering the sacraments in remote parts of the parish even when he was plagued with painful carbuncles. In short, "we have never seen a priest with such zeal for his parishioners, as is well known throughout the Tierra Caliente."[36]

Since simple fornication in a monogamous relationship was rarely the basis for lawsuits against parish priests, the evidence that it was a common occurrence comes up incidentally in other ways. Several of the district governors who submitted reports in 1793 mentioned that a pastor was living in sin. But hardly any made a point of it; usually the remark was made in passing or as part of a wider criticism of his hypocrisy or entanglement in worldly affairs.[37] The cura of Chucándiro (Michoacán), for example, was described by the intendant of Valladolid as "learned and devoted to his duties, but somewhat unchaste." The subdelegado of Tixtla (Guerrero), on the other hand, singled out a local vicario, José Miranda, for sharper criticism because he maintained the lie that he was supporting a cousin, "until her mother and sisters made public that she was a prostitute without the slightest kinship to him."[38] Even though royal policy and regalist prelates in the late eighteenth century highlighted the requirement of clerical celibacy and devised ways to ensure compliance, incontinence was rarely the primary basis for parishioners' complaints against a priest or an episcopal investigation.[39]

Heterosexual misconduct did strike a nerve in two kinds of circumstances. The first was a promiscuous, aggressive, and repeated pursuit of maidens and married women. Priests who invited the anger of aggrieved husbands and parents in turn attracted the attention of the ecclesiastical courts. For example, in 1806 a vecino of Tianguistengo (Hidalgo) discovered that his daughter, doña María Veitia, estranged from her husband and living with her parents, had not returned home from a dance at the district governor's house the night before. He discovered her in bed with the vicario, Juan Andónegui, with the full knowledge of the servants and sacristans. Outraged by the shame of it, the father began to drag the naked doña María from the room by her hair. When the priest, his brother, and a sacristán barred the way, the father ordered her to meet him at the church. But she disappeared, probably hidden by Andónegui, leaving her father to appeal to the archbishop. The case attracted the attention of the archiepiscopal court as well because Andónegui had resigned a pie fijo post in 1802 and been sentenced to two weeks of spiritual exercises at Tepotzotlan in 1804 for unspecified offenses.[40]

Usually, it took an utterly indiscreet repeat offender to activate ecclesiastical justice over incontinence. One such case came to light when, in 1780, doña María Trinidad de Vega denounced Francisco Marroquín. After he seduced her in Mexico City nine years before, she had gone as his servant to his next post in Tulancingo (Hidalgo), where she gave birth three times. She decided to return to Mexico City with her one living child in order to lead a quiet, respectable life with her mother and sister. Now assigned to Singuilucan (near Tulancingo), but making frequent visits to Mexico City, Marroquín would not leave her alone. The sentence of the court may have satisfied doña María Trinidad but was hardly a harsh penalty; he got off with court costs of 48 pesos, unspecified penance, six months' confinement in the seminary at Tepotzotlan, and a restraining order against future contact with her.[41]

The occasional suits against parish priests for incontinence usually involved dozens of offenses over a period of years. The accused generally were vicarios

who had escaped the social and political consequences of their aggressive pro-
miscuity by moving from place to place every year or two, or curas in large parishes who manipulated women in the visitas. The Yriarte brothers, Gregorio and
Joseph, Franciscan doctrineros in the province of Xalisco, were particularly indiscreet in their lechery before being brought to court in 1758. In the past ten
years or so, Gregorio, who was 38 years old at the time he was roped in, had made
lewd propositions to at least nineteen women, mostly Indians at Ajijic, Poncitlan,
and Atotonilco el Alto, during Lent and often in the confessional. Most of the
offended penitents had fled and refused to confess to him again. One woman testified that he fondled her breasts in the confessional; another said he insisted that
she chew his tongue so he could know her sins.[42] The younger brother, Joseph,
had a similar history of obsessive lust while serving as guardian of Santa María
del Oro and in the communities of Tecolotlan, Ayutla, Tepic, Huaxicori, and
Juchipila in the 1750's. He reportedly pursued all younger women who confessed
to him, "even the Indians," urging them to give him a finger to bite, calling them
to his rooms, and exposing himself.[43] Both Yriartes were relieved of their duties
and placed in seclusion.[44]

The other kind of sexual misconduct the church actively prosecuted was
solicitation in the confessional. The court's interest here was less in the vow of
celibacy and the honor of the woman than in the sanctity of the act of confession.[45] A single, well-supported instance of a priest propositioning a woman in the
confessional or making sexual contact there could lead to an inquisitorial investigation. But for the same reasons that incontinence was greatly underreported,
a priest was rarely charged at the first attempt, and cases of solicitation often
brought to light a long history of sexual encounters in and out of the confessional.[46] The confessional was a priest's main opportunity for private communication with women, especially young unmarried women, and the temptation to
use that privacy to express amorous desires was more than some could resist.
Some priests charged with solicitation said they made their advances before the
confession commenced or declined to confess the penitent altogether, believing
that this did not violate the sanctity of the confessional. Others confessed and
absolved the penitent, then invited her to their rooms on the pretext of further
spiritual instruction. Some priests were so far gone that they offered blandish-
ments, launched into passionate talk about copulation, and fondled women on
the spot.[47]

Parish priests could find other ways to violate their *hijas de confesión*. Joseph
Díaz Conti, while cura of Xochicoatlan in the district of Molango (Hidalgo) in
1795, persuaded the parents of some of his young penitents that they were in
need of intensive spiritual exercises, instruction that he could provide if they
boarded with him in the rectory. At least five women stayed with him on this
pretext before he accepted a lesser post as vicario in Atotonilco el Grande, eventually ending as an assistant to the sacristan of the Colegio de San Ignacio in
Puebla. According to one of his young penitents, Antonia Valentín, an illiterate
creole from the town of Molango, he had asked her in the confessional to come
to his house as his maid. When she declined, he persisted in urging that, for
the good of her soul, she should come to stay in his house, and he would care
for her. Her parents objected, but he eventually persuaded the mother by let-

ter that certain spiritual exercises under his supervision were needed. No sooner had Antonia returned to Xochicoatlan than Conti seduced her. Two days after she left home, her father sent a message that she should return, since there were priests in Molango to confess her. A week later, he removed her from the rectory over the cura's objection that this would be damaging to her soul. As Antonia's mother later put it, "No confessor, no matter how saintly, can have women penitents in his house."[48] Such cases were unusual, but they became part of the folklore about priests and inspired satirists like Fernández de Lizardi.

Beyond the general acceptance of discreet heterosexuality by parish priests, there are two strong reasons why the documentation on heterosexual misconduct is not more abundant and why a priest could safely risk a few indiscretions. One is that prosecutions depended on denunciations by the women involved. Married women, especially, feared the consequences. Some undoubtedly lived with the private shame and guilt of a solicitation or seduction rather than risk public ridicule and possible reprisals from a dishonored husband or the harm to him if he attempted revenge.[49] Village women, in particular, might be unaware that an attempted seduction by a priest, especially in the confessional, was a serious offense, or they might know well enough that it would be filed away by the ecclesiastical courts unless a larger case was building against the man. An Indian widow of Sahuayo (Michoacán), brought before the Inquisition in 1744 to testify that the Franciscan doctrinero there had caressed her and solicited sex in the confessional, said that she had not come forward for two years because she did not know she was obligated to do so (and apparently had not mentioned the incident in her annual confession the year before).[50] Those married women who did denounce parish priests for propositioning them often did so years after the fact and under great pressure from their current confessor.[51] To a penitent in anguish for her soul, the confessor held a powerful spiritual weapon that could move her to risk the shame and uncertainty of a denunciation: he denied her absolution until she revealed the dark secret to the Inquisition.[52]

Second, the ecclesiastical courts were inclined to protect their own. They rarely prosecuted for the first or second offense in these circumstances,[53] and did so thereafter only if a formal charge was lodged independently, usually at the insistence of another priest. Even when the transgressions were many, and the evidence overwhelming, the verdict in an ecclesiastical court was not certain to be guilty or the sentence severe. In the case of Juan Antonio Xil de Andrade, the cura of Cempoala (Hidalgo) in 1777, the Inquisition narrowed the scope of the investigation to whether he had told one of the women he seduced that it was no sin to submit to his desire. In doing so, it glossed over the various seductions and pregnancies themselves.[54] Vicario Juan Centeno's aggressive and repeated seduction of women in the parish of Sierra de Pinos was well documented in 1798, and the Inquisition judged him "a very lascivious, ignorant, and imprudent man," but it suspended the case in 1799 without reaching a verdict.[55]

In their sentencing, the Inquisition and episcopal courts effectively condoned heterosexual misconduct. The harshest punishment for even repeated solicitations in the confessional and dozens of seductions was ten years' exile (at least 20 leagues away from the sites of the misdeeds), a loss of the license to confess, and a period of confinement with rigorous spiritual exercises for up to three years. The convicted cura or vicario was removed from service, but there were no excommunications, no sentences at hard labor, and no confiscations of property. Those who completed the sentence without incident stood a good chance of having their licenses restored. Since the curas rarely lost their rights as propietarios, they could petition for reinstatement or assignment to a parish of comparable value with some hope of success if they had been exemplary penitents.[56]

Sexual relations between parish priests of Mexico and Guadalajara and other men (or animals) rarely appear in the records of the Inquisition or other ecclesiastical courts. These were especially grave offenses—the term most widely used for sodomy in the colonial period, *el pecado nefando*, meant sacrilegious sin, and Castilian law made it as great a crime as heresy or treason. In the seventeenth century, a priest convicted of sodomy would have been regarded as a heretic, and subject to execution. Though offenders were probably dealt with less harshly in the next century,[57] late colonial priests were nevertheless under considerable pressure to suppress or hide such relations, and the pecado nefando may have been so threatening to the church that the Inquisition suppressed most rumors and poorly established accusations of it against priests.[58]

Unpriestly behavior of these kinds is less abundantly documented in the judicial and administrative record than cases of what amounted to a priestly abuse of office. Their prominence in the written record probably reflects their relative frequency, as well as the viceregal and ecclesiastical courts' concern for anything that disturbed the political order and the readiness of laymen to pick up cues from policy makers. In any event, they occupied the shifting ground between proper and improper conduct into which colonial justice was so often drawn.

The most common complaint was excessive anger and combativeness. As in so many of the acts identified as misbehavior on the priest's part, the feature highlighted was excess. Excessive passion destroyed the loving detachment that allowed the priest, as pastor, father, magistrate, and physician, to judge and punish with moderation. It broke the balance between fear and love and led to rash decisions, vengeful acts, and unchristian violence. By no means unique to the late colonial period, this accusation was, nevertheless, particularly characteristic of the time. District governors used it as evidence of the priest's failure to cooperate with them and as evidence of their own judiciousness, and parishioners used it as evidence that the priest had broken the family compact, had not behaved as a father should. Excessive anger was an offense that parish priests rarely admitted to, or that they justified as a reply in kind to outrageous behavior by royal officials and parishioners who did not behave as good spiritual children.[59] They would have had occasion to be provoked into it often in the late colonial period.

The documentation on overwrought priests is eye-catching but backed up mainly by district governors and other witnesses who had an interest in presenting the priest in a bad light. The most damaging aspect of their testimony was that it usually claimed to represent the priest's character, not only his behavior on a particular occasion. "Genio," meaning temper or character, was often invoked in the descriptions of his angry acts: "de genio inquieto y contencioso"; "genio áspero"; "genio intrépido y precipitado"; "genio violento"; "genio ardiente"; "genio soberbio"; "pasión orgullosa, poco amor"; "demasiada pasión";

"genio colérico"; "genio violento, es iracundo"; "temperamento cálido y seco"; "genio intrépido y altivo"; "genio arrebatado, violento, turbulento." [60]

The towering anger of José María Piña, vicario of San Andrés Jimilpan in the district of Xilotepec (Hidalgo), in an encounter with an old adversary in 1789 is well documented in a series of reports and depositions submitted to the archiepiscopal court. They began with a formal complaint Piña fired off after fleeing to a nearby rancho for refuge. He claimed that a tumulto had been mounted against him by Francisco Ordóñez, a local creole who had married into the Indian community; that about a hundred Indians had followed Ordóñez to the rectory and threatened the building and its occupants. The clearest description of the meeting between Ordóñez and Piña comes from a notary of the Juzgado de Indios who went to take his leave of the priest that evening and, at Ordóñez's request, tried to resolve the strained relations with the priest. How the Indians waiting outside behaved is hard to establish—the testimony of eyewitnesses in these emotionally charged and confusing circumstances is contradictory—but the receptor's description of the actions of Piña and Ordóñez was not challenged:

After I put before Br. Piña Ordóñez's proposal, and the former having consented to the reconciliation and meeting that the latter proposed, . . . Ordóñez knelt, kissed the priest's hands and, intending to satisfy him, said that there was no good reason for the quarrels because what the Father had heard second-hand about his statements was untrue, and that it was the Indian *alcalde*, Antonio de Santiago, who was spreading the rumors. . . . And he begged his pardon if he had offended him in some way. . . .

At this, Br. Piña (perhaps because of his violent and intrepid nature) answered with haughty words and in a bad manner, telling him: that he [Ordóñez] had said the priest went around as if he were God, that he had testified to his conduct and would have him removed from the *pueblo*. To all of this, Ordóñez replied by saying that it was untrue, but the priest insisted that Ordóñez had said he would have him removed from the *pueblo* and the parish. Thus harassed, Ordóñez realized that no words of his would satisfy the priest and said: "I did not say it, but if I had, I would have followed through." These words so aroused the priest's anger that he shouted and pounded on the table, saying "I'd like to see you try to get rid of me. I'll take care of you," and uttering many other statements that obviously sprang from his anger. Ordóñez's repeated attempts to calm him by kneeling, embracing him, and kissing his hands failed, as did my efforts to do so.

While this was happening I noticed that Br. José María Peña [Piña's assistant] went out in the corridor and returned suddenly, grabbing a cane or club, saying that some Indians had come in irreverently as far as the corridor, chewing tobacco. I restrained Br. José María and the priest, who, becoming even more angry over this than he had been, wanted to go out and club them.[61]

Another kind of pastoral conduct that seems to have drawn more attention as excessive in the late colonial period was undue zeal and inflexibility in defending old privileges against the pretensions of other authorities, and an authoritarian law-and-order approach to treating with parishioners.[62] Rightly or not, legalistic, "hard-hearted" priests were blamed for causing disputes with villagers or district governors.[63] According to Indians of Camotipan, their cura, Nicolás Mariano Ladrón de Guevara of Guayacocotla y Chicontepec (Veracruz), demanded labor service without regard to their safety and their need to make milpa and imprisoned those who did not serve. On one occasion in 1786, he forced many Indian men and women to marry against their will, gathering them in a room and arbitrarily pairing them off.[64]

Provoked or not, some curas and vicarios hurt themselves in court with their punctiliousness and legalistic maneuverings. José Ysidro de Santa María, cura of Tepetitlan, near Tula, gained the reputation of being severe ("áspero") and fiery ("ardiente") by forcing Indians in the visitas to sign a pledge to pay for wax; requiring that they come to him for the annual confession and communion; and refusing to sign a document ordering him to follow the arancel on the grounds that it was directed to his predecessor and that the subdelegado must request the signature in person rather than delegating the responsibility.[65] Others could damage their credibility and local trust and be marked as of "impulsive and reckless character" (genio intrépido y precipitado) by overusing their conditional authority to excommunicate and treating jurisdictional disputes as if they were purely local issues unconnected to royal policy.[66]

An occasional priest was reported to be very lazy and careless in handling the sacraments and attending to the spiritual needs of parishioners, but, if the surviving record is representative, intentionally sacrilegious behavior by priests unconnected to their sexual appetites was rare.[67] Pastors knew that failure to celebrate mass properly or administer the sacraments in a timely way was the least pardonable violation of professional conduct, and that faithful ministration could gain exoneration from ecclesiastical courts for a variety of other kinds of misbehavior.[68]

In the last decades of colonial rule, a few loose-tongued, freethinking priests were denounced to the Inquisition for heretical propositions that priests should be permitted to marry, that simple fornication was not a sin, that Christ shed his blood for some but not all, that the apparition of the Virgin Mary at Tepeyac was a pious invention, that one could be saved in any religion, and that good works had little to do with salvation.[69] The Inquisition's increasing focus on political sedition as heresy brought into its field of vision others who condoned regicide or were intrigued by the French Revolution and its emphasis on liberty and equality.[70] But superstitious sacrileges by priests were rare.[71]

Exemplary Conduct

For every notoriously unpriestly cura or vicario, four or five apparently satisfied their parishioners and superiors. One measure of their relative importance is the confidential surveys of parish priests generated by royal decree after the 1750's. One, the 1793 set of subdelegado reports, was composed by royal governors; the others were prepared by or for the bishops. The bishops' reports tend to identify a handful of men with good prospects for promotion and dismiss the rest with a wave of the pen.[72] An exception is a report for Guadalajara dated January 3, 1764, in which the bishop commented on all of his curas.

The surveys are naturally more superficial than the individual investigations of misconduct, especially surveys that were composed by officials new to the district, or not good at evaluating the work of others, or uncritically pious, but this sketchier evidence of solid performance is consistent with satisfactory service done without fanfare and self-promotion. It met expectations and so attracted little attention. The judgment made by the governor of the State of Mexico in his biennial report for 1826–27 could well have been made by the viceroy in 1800, in spite of the intervening years of insurrection: there were some claims in court, but "the pious zeal of many *párrocos*" was evident.

These surveys identify dozens of priests who went about their duties without much notoriety or worked with a dedication that earned official praise. The Guadalajara bishop's report of 1764 specifically noted the very good to exemplary conduct of 45 curas, accounting for well over half the 65 parishes staffed by diocesan priests at the time.[73] There were old curas who had served well in obscurity, like "the virtuous" seventy-year-old cura of Nochistlan, José de Cara, and the eighty-year-old Joseph Tello de Orosco, "formerly a very good *cura*," who still held the benefice of Ojocaliente; young men on the rise, like Dr. Asencio Palomera, "a man of advantageous, resplendent learning and virtue," who at thirty had already spent three years as cura of Huauchinango, "where he fulfills his duties precisely"; men in the major parishes who did their duties with care; and various older men in lesser parishes who laid no claims to intellectual distinction but were busy at their work (like Francisco de Dios Sobrados, forty-five years old, in Sayula for seven years, who "does not have much learning but does have great virtue and zeal"; Joseph Caro Galindo, over fifty years old, with six years in Tepatitlan, who "does not have much learning but is virtuous and fulfills his responsibilities"; Agustín de Acosta, sixty years old, with four years in Saltillo, who "has little learning but much virtue"; and Anacleto Bernal, forty years old, with six years in Purificación, with "little learning but solid in virtue, exemplary, and charitable. . . . He does not take even enough for his needs; it is all for the poor"). The 1808–9 pastoral visit to the Huasteca by the archbishop's delegate, which commented on the comportment of priests in the parishes visited, generally found them to lead an "orderly life, fulfilling their duties without complaint."[74]

Even the 1793 subdelegado reports for districts in the archdiocese, which were likely to be more critical of clerical conduct, had no quarrel with most parish priests. Some were singled out as exemplary pastors (which could mean that they bowed to the subdelegado's wishes); but a large majority come across as men who fulfilled their duties—whether in virtual obscurity or in the limelight—even when they were not outstanding in all ways.[75]

Here is a sample of exemplary curas in the two dioceses described by the subdelegados. They include an old man of great energy; a well-seasoned Augustinian friar; two curas from the Burgo de San Cosmé, Zacatecas (from which Dr. José María Cos, one of the famous parish priests in the Independence War, would come in 1810); a coadjutor who lived only for his parish duties; and an urbanized doctor of theology who took his pastoral duties to heart:[76]

> *Lic. Juan de Dios Castro Tobio, cura of Tulancingo, Hidalgo*: "Truth obliges me to say that even in advanced age he excels in exemplary virtue, renowned learning, notorious zeal, selflessness and charity, and the fullest performance of his pastoral duties."

> *Cura of Meztitlan, Hidalgo*: "This parish has belonged to the Augustinian, Fr. José Gamboa, for the past thirty years, and the exacting performance of

FIG. 4. Lic. Diego de Cervantes, longtime cura of the first-class parish of the present Lagos de Moreno, Jalisco (Diocese of Guadalajara). According to a 1755 audiencia report, Father Cervantes was a model parish priest: "the most estimable cura in the diocese," a pastor of "singular application and zeal in the spiritual service of his flock," and a man of "profound humility" who sponsored the Capuchin convent of Lagos with his own funds and lived in poverty. The author of the report urged that Cervantes not be promoted to the cathedral chapter because he was indispensable to the parish—an unusual compliment (AGI Mex. 2549). Nine years later, Cervantes, by now 60 years old, with more than 20 years' service at Lagos, was again praised in glowing terms, as a pastor who was "always most diligent," "very charitable," in fact, "a perfect exemplar of a cura" (AGI Guad. 566, 1764). This portrait of him, from the Lagos parish church, makes him exceptional in another way: pictures of parish priests for colonial Mexico and Guadalajara are rare and usually of men on the way to higher office.

this *párroco* is evident to me. His zeal for the welfare of souls is extraordinary. He is renowned for good personal conduct and selflessness, and he is indefatigable in spiritual care, even in looking after the pastors in mountain dependencies attached to this parish."

Former and current curas of Burgo de San Cosmé: "[The former cura Br. José Valerio Aldrete] is a talented person, very virtuous and indefatigable in fulfilling his duties—so much so that in the calamitous years of 1785 and 1786 his charity and efficacy for confessions carried him sixteen, eighteen, even 25 leagues away, without rest. He was promoted to Mazapil, where he is still. He was succeeded by Lic. d. Salvador María de Ayala, a talented person adorned with sufficient learning, notable virtue, and constant attention to the confessional, pulpit, and other obligations of his office."

Unnamed coadjutor of Epasoyucan, Cempoala district: "[He] is so strict in fulfilling his duties that he never leaves his parish unless compelled by the requirements of his office, maintaining this spiritual absorption as an example to his parishioners and to be sure that none of them is deprived of his spiritual assistance when they ask for it. This evinces his zeal, his virtue, his upright conduct, and how far he is from wasting time on amusements. He excuses himself from them all in order to be ready to fulfill his obligations."

Cura of Coyoacan, Valley of Mexico: "Dr. d. José Angel Gasano, cura of this *villa*, is exact in fulfilling the duties of his ministry; a man of consummate prudence and irreproachable conduct who is an example to his parishioners. He possesses sublime talents, profound learning, integrity, and selflessness; treating his parishioners with characteristic modesty, paying the schoolmasters of the district from his own purse."

Exemplary priests were sometimes remembered long after their departure. Fr. Martín de Valencia in Amecameca and Tlalmanalco is perhaps the most famous, but eighteenth-century Indians of Matlalcingo in the Valley of Toluca reportedly remembered their sixteenth-century Franciscan doctrinero, Fr. Andrés de Castro, with great affection, "revering him as an apostolic superman full of heroic virtues."[77] Over a shorter span of years, the creole and mestizo rancheros of Mesticacan (Jalisco) in 1755 admired their former diocesan cura Dr. Antonio Mercado y Zúñiga in similar terms for his charity and pastoral care.[78]

The obscure but dedicated priests who caused no trouble are less richly described in the subdelegado reports, but here are four who can stand for the best of them:

Cura of Huizquilucan, Tacuba district: "[José Mariano Guerra] plainly has not inherited a mind that is much talked about, and he moves [too] quickly; but he is certainly scrupulous and most exact in his duties. Although he does not deserve to be called a soaring eagle, he is blessed with more than what is needed to carry out his job."

Cura of Tepeapulco, Apam district: "In [this] *pueblo*, . . . the cura is Br. d. Josef Marcos Vélez de el Burgo, with whom the author of this report has communicated only once. By reputation, he fulfills the duties of his office and is a person of judicious conduct, distinguished ability, learning, and selflessness."

Vicario of Acambay, Huichapan district: "[Mariano Ruiz Miranda] fulfills the obligations of his office with exactitude, is well versed in everything, very diligent in the confessional and pulpit. He maintains himself with restrained dignity, and only has his salary and miscellaneous fees."

Cura of Huehuetoca, Cuautitlan district: "The *cura* is Br. d. José Onofre Zamorano, who, I am told, is an orderly man who fulfills the duties of his office scrupulously. He has no *vicario* because the resources of the parish are very limited."[79]

As far as parishioners were concerned, what counted as good conduct at least as much as dutiful service was charity. It was a virtue that prelates since the Council of Trent had highlighted, and it received clear and repeated attention in the *Itinerario*.[80] Charity as good works received increasing attention in the formal communications of church leaders in the late colonial period, especially in pointed references to the epistles of the Apostle Paul. In his introduction to Pérez de Velasco's 1766 guide for vicarios, Andrés de Arze y Miranda quoted 2 Corinthians 12:15, "And I will very gladly spend and be spent by you; though the more abundantly I love you, the less I be loved," and added, "If necessary I will gladly give my life for the well-being of your souls." In his pastoral letter of September 24, 1807, Archbishop Lizana y Beaumont devoted chapter 27 to the good example priests must set as a manifestation of their Christian charity. Referring pointedly to Paul's exhortations to the Romans to "provide things honest in the sight of all men," "overcome evil with good," and "bear the infirmities of the weak, and not . . . please ourselves," he added his own gloss: "Let every one of us please *his* neighbor for *his* good to edification."[81]

Charity was a quality that the subdelegados too were likely to mention in their 1793 reports. The key word in many of these descriptions is desinteresado—"disinterested," unselfish.[82] But the characterizations often are more elaborate and specific, identifying priests who practiced charity on an unusual scale. For example, Miguel Flores, cura of Atlacomulco, whom the subdelegado of Ixtlahuaca regarded as the model of curas ("pauta de los curas"), practiced "so much charity and unselfishness that his income from the parish falls short of his alms to parishioners and his expenditures on public worship and the decoration of his church." Equally praiseworthy was the cura of Apango (Tixtla district, Guerrero), Ignacio Munive, whose "unselfishness and charity are so singular that he gives up everything he has when he sees his parishioners in need." Of José Ignacio Azcárate, cura of Alahuistlan, the subdelegado of Zacualpan noted, "One doesn't find any attachment to possessions; on the contrary, he is too generous in distributing what he acquires."[83]

In practice, charity meant different things to different priests. From their own descriptions in their resumés, a few saw charity mainly in terms of contributing to the gravity and brilliance of public worship, especially in building or repairing the church edifice and adding altars, vestments, and silver instruments of the mass.[84] But most recognized wider obligations that approximated the pauline exhortations to good works, mercy, and self-sacrifice generally. For some, charity meant giving alms to the poor, forgoing sacramental fees when the parishioner could not pay, and providing for their own extended family of parents, siblings, and cousins. For others, it meant especially providing grain and medicine in famines and epidemics or fearlessly responding to the endless call for confession in epidemics. Pedro Gómez García wrote that, as vicario at Colotlan (Jalisco) during two years of epidemic in the 1760's, he spent many days and nights without sleep or food caring for the sick in distant places. One day, he administered last rites to 40 parishioners. Some days he was so sore and tired that he could not even mount a horse by himself, and eventually he himself fell ill.[85] For still others, charity meant sponsoring local primary schools or promoting public works.[86] Dr. Joseph Verdugo, who became one of the first prebends of the Colegiata of Our Lady of Guadalupe at Tepeyac in the 1750's, was regarded as a shining example of charity. He spent 20 years in parish service, leaving it "without a feather" because "he gave away all of his income in alms, and his health was badly damaged from the work of the ministry."[87]

Hardships

Verdugo's exemplary devotion suggests some of the purifying hardships of the work—what curas called "the grievous ministry of the cure of souls," "the imponderable tribulations of the cure of souls," and "the grave weight."[88] A conscientious parish priest who had ridden circuit among the scattered settlements of a mountain or lowland parish and frequently encountered death could speak without hyperbole of his professional resumé as an account of merits and perspiration ("relación de méritos y sudores").[89] Juan Diego de Cuevas, vicario in the district of Tepatitlan in the early 1760's, summed up the priest's hardships from experience as "inclement weather, the [beating] sun, winds, gloomy nights, rough roads, swollen rivers, broken health."[90] He was not the first pastor to have his idealism blunted by the physical hardships. That there were real hardships is indisputable; but we know them mainly through the priests' words. Perhaps not so many souls passed away in the dead of night; nor was there always bad weather to brave. The burden of the work was partly in the eye of the beholder and varied according to individual circumstances and conscience.

For curas who took their pastoral responsibilities seriously and did not rely on assistants to do much of it, the schedule could be brutal. The work of confessor alone could seem endless.[91] For those in large parishes with scattered populations, it was, especially in times of epidemic. Hugo de Omerick warned that a parish priest should not try to find more than two hours a day for study. On top of all the other work that had to be done, it would quickly break a priest's health. He wrote of returning to the parish seat of Tepecoacuilco from a circuit ride to find a smallpox epidemic. Attending to sick parishioners, he had no time to read his office, much less to study or write. Then the annual confessions commenced, lasting from Ash Wednesday to Corpus Christi.[92]

When parish priests described their work, they usually mentioned travel,

often involving great distances, foul weather, terrible roads, and physical depriva-
tions.[93] Antonio Flores Garcilaso de la Vega wrote in 1762 of the "almost unimag-
inable work he [had] endured in the forty-one years and some months that he
has served the sacred mitre," of "traveling in the dark in mortal danger from the
poor roads," and of "spending nights on the ground with no more cover than his
cape, eating the most vile meals, if that."[94] Simply celebrating mass outside the
parish seat kept the more fortunate pastors on muleback for four hours or more
two days a week.[95] Others had to travel ten, fifteen, and twenty-five leagues to
outlying pueblos and ranchos, sometimes through dense woods that tore at their
clothing and flesh. A witness for the Indians of Atlacaoloaya, who were seeking
a vicario de pie fijo within the parish of Xochitepec in 1791, testified that one vicario making the journey had left "various pieces of his cassock . . . behind in the
trees."[96] A conscientious pastor was even more often on the road to administer
last rites, which might take him anywhere in the parish anytime. Some described
themselves as being on the road morning and night under the full force of the
sun and gloom of night. Sisto Luna of Ixtlahuacan del Río (Jalisco) wrote that
he commonly left his home at two or three in the morning, returning at three or
four in the afternoon.[97] The violent jolting of travel by horse or mule caused skin
rashes, hemorrhoids, and swollen joints, and rubbed sores that might never have
time to heal.[98]

The hot lowlands, far from the centers of population and teeming with insects
and reptiles, were especially dreaded, but the mountains presented their own
rigors. Tiburcio de Salazar, cura of that most undesirable parish of Escanela in
the Sierra Gorda of Querétaro, wrote in 1762 of the "excessive work and scarce
emoluments" in this parish "destitute of everything," of "the inclemency of that
country," and of the "many downpours and storms, [which were so] continuous
in that mountain range" that travelers might at times be literally left "clinging to
a tree."[99] Bernardino de Sahagún, the famous sixteenth-century Franciscan missionary and Nahuatl scholar, left a haunting description of the dangers of highland travel and the psychological effect of the wild mountains of central Mexico
on the minds of urban Nahuas and Catholic pastors that applies to the late colonial period as well:

The mountains are as follows: they have much very green moss; they are windy and
damp, and it freezes there. They are sad, solitary places, places to make one weep. They
are cavernous and steep places, rocky and muddy, of soft dirt and yellow dirt, and places
with great peaks and great, steep hills full of moss and trees. There are plateaus in the
mountains, and many woods and dry trees; there are somber places in the mountains and
flat lands where neither grass nor moss grows. There are rocky places and depressions
like valleys. The mountains are also terrifying places where ferocious beasts dwell, where
there is no rest for men, only dry stones and crags and caves where tigers and bears and
lynx dwell; and where maguey grows wild and very thorny, and brambles and thorns and
wild *tuna* cactus, and very rough pines. [It is] a place where beasts eat men and where
men kill treacherously.[100]

An added burden for many priests was their own poor health. Some were not
very fit to begin with, perhaps having chosen their profession (or having had it
chosen for them) because of physical weakness and studious inclinations. Others

had good reason to believe that they had been ground down by the physical labor of parish service and the insalubrious places in which they had served. Br. Salvador Ordóñez, cura of Malacatepec (Edo. de México) in 1762, wrote of how his health had been broken by the "soakings, evening dew, snows, late nights, beating sun, freezes, drafts, and long fasts" he had endured in Xocotitlan 40 years earlier.[101] And for Antonio Arias de Puga, seeking a new place in 1770, his service in Iscuintla (Nayarit) over the past three years had been a veritable trial of Job. Apart from the "insufferable weather" and the dangers of insects, reptiles, and wild mammals, he was covered with sores, had lost a leg to infection, and had been gravely ill three times.[102]

The work itself could be dangerous. Priests worn out from the extra effort of caring for the sick and ministering to the spiritual needs of the dying in an epidemic were themselves prey to the contagious disease. Some were thrown from their horses or slipped on errands of mercy in bad weather, with crippling or fatal consequences.[103]

Whatever the cause, the surveys of rural priests in Mexico in 1793 and Guadalajara in 1796 describe many parish priests as "habitually ill," "in broken health," "disabled by illness," "suffering continual fevers," or laid low by sores and poisonous bites.[104] Some had to resign their posts or take extended leaves of absence.[105] The bishop of Guadalajara in 1758 made use of the popular impression that American priests over forty were chronically ill to promote the appointment of more peninsulares to his cathedral chapter, "because they enjoy more robust health." [106]

Joseph Diego Gómez offered a personal panorama of the hardships of his few years of service in third-class parishes of the Diocese of Guadalajara in his resumé of 1802. He had begun his career as substitute vicario for San Cristóbal de la Barranca during a smallpox epidemic. In serving the distant corners of the parish for three years, he had twice nearly lost his life on the steep mountain roads and swollen rivers during the rainy season. Suffering from a persistent fever, he returned to Guadalajara to recover, paying a priest double his fees to care for the parish. While there he competed in the oposiciones for vacant parishes and was awarded Techaluta, but its old cura decided to stay, and he was named instead to San Sebastián Huaxicori. Without income, he waited four months for his appointment, then on the trip to the parish, his luggage and that of his sister were stolen. He had not left the parish during his two years there, and the life was proving difficult. The alms to the church and fees on which he had to live were meager because his only parishioners were Indians who lived in small dispersed communities in the mountains, people who were not just poor but also inclined to rebellion. Even so, with the help of the lieutenant of Acaponeta, he had established a cofradía ranch for the support of the Eucharist and made some small additions to the church interior. Despite this small success, the cabecera had few residents, and he felt utterly isolated, "without any human consolation." He returned to Guadalajara for the 1802 oposiciones and requested of the bishop that if he left him in Huaxicori, a stipend from the tithe be added in order that he might carry on decently.[107]

In these accounts of parish service and the summary reports, there are glimpses of unusual courage and self-sacrifice—of a vicario burdened with the cure of 25,000 souls who spent virtually all of his time in the countryside confessing the sick; of robust, indefatigable curas in the worst of parishes feeding the needy and supporting widowed mothers and unmarried sisters on top of everything else; of impoverished priests facing down local rebellions to protect privileged non-Indians; and of priests working alone in epidemics for years at a time without taking annual leave, watching their own estates dwindle away.[108] But most of the heroism was on the smaller scale of carrying on, doing a job, keeping the flame alive.

Familiar Sentiments

Though colonial parish priests rarely wrote memoirs or kept diaries, the kinds of sentiments one might find there creep into their public writings. These sources have their limitiations, to be sure. Few priests would have found it appropriate to express the affection some undoubtedly had for birds, plants, games, food, sunsets, and antiquities in a professional resumé and other formal utterances, let alone speak of their dreams, even though theirs was a mental world replete with symbolic nuances. On the other hand, the profession did effectively encourage a keen sense of pain, anguish, sorrow, and shame, sentiments that were expressed readily and taken as a badge of honor. Harriet Doerr catches the tension, intensified by this cultivation of sentiment between the priests' lives of mundane pursuits and their spiritual responsibilities, in her story, "Picnic at Amapolas":

At the same time Padre Miguel, on his knees at the altar, prayed to be assigned to another parish, a larger place, where he could be in the company of people who talked well, had talents, examined ideas. Then, for having asked this, he prayed to be forgiven.[109]

Aside from overheated indignation at having been thwarted, questioned, or accused by parishioners, perhaps the strongest sentiment that comes through in unguarded moments is loneliness. Joseph de Piña y Banda, vicario of Huizquilucan, said that "he suffered the dead calm of solitude and bad roads."[110] Some curas simply meant that they longed for the civility and good company of the city, and felt alienated from Indian parishioners.[111] Joseph Yriarte went so far as to excuse his excesses on the ground that Amacueca (Jalisco) was a "desert . . . with nothing but Indians and very solitary."[112] Even Omerick, for all his upbeat reflections on parish service, spoke of himself and his parishioners together as "withdrawn into solitude."[113]

Most curas identified with the refinements and domestic comforts of the city. Many stayed close to the parish and administrative seats, where non-Indians, news, and traffic from colonial centers were concentrated. They also tended to seek out the society of other gente de razón. They usually had dependents with them—a mistress and children or a widowed mother and unmarried siblings, and perhaps more distant relatives if they were posted to the parish of their birth; a scribe or notary; and assistants. Some paid out half of a meager income as much for the sake of an assistant's companionship as anything else.[114] Many eagerly looked forward to the long Lent season and the temporary camaraderie of the urban priests who poured into the countryside to assist with masses, confessions, and Holy Week celebrations. Special revivals and retreats led by missionary priests sponsored by the cura provided another source of fellowship for pastors and their assistants.[115] Assisting a neighboring cura in an emergency was a chance to seal a friendship as well as help a comrade and have a change of scenery.[116] More often it was the cathedral city that beckoned as the destination.[117] And in between travels, most parish priests kept up an active correspondence.[118]

The preference for living and working among non-Indians was not universal; some late colonial curas in Indian parishes viewed gente de razón as a threat to local peace.[119] Pérez de Velasco confided to his readership of novice vicarios that parishes of "pure Indians" were preferable because the Indians "provide more benefit than irritation, while parishes of *gente de razón* are very bothersome, they grumble not a little and serve very little." If Indians were corrupted, he added, it was due to the bad influence of gente de razón.[120] But Pérez de Velasco's little primer was out of phase with royal and regalist church policies on education and segregation almost as soon as it was published. The many late colonial curas and vicarios who had faced their Indian parishioners in court, or witnessed a village tumulto, or been rescued from attack by non-Indian friends, or been insulted in public, would at least have understood the vicario José Antonio Hurtado de Mendoza's petition not to be reassigned from Sierra de Pinos to Pueblo Nuevo in 1815:

[My reason] is that since this parish is composed mostly of Indians who made trouble in a thousand ways for the deceased cura Cervantes, making charges against his conduct before yourself and the superior government, I fear that my luck will be the same. There is good reason to think so because I am tenacious about making people in my charge fulfill their obligations in every detail, and I lack the tact and good judgment necessary to treat with these people, who require great knowledge of their character and customs.[121]

The segregation issue tended to draw out extreme opinions of this kind. Still, such social isolation was not simply a consequence of racism. As we will see in Part Four, conflict and support did not simply follow ethnic lines—a rural pastor in these dioceses rarely had all of his Indians or non-Indians against him.[122]

For most priests, admitting loneliness was more than an expression of weakness, self-indulgence, melancholy, or alienation.[123] It was also an expression of penitential self-abnegation and suffering, of the burden of being in-between, of being called upon to forgo the material pleasures of this life. The priest was taught to see a rather isolated individualism and stoic mental discipline as a source of his power—he was to command respect by being aloof, dignified, reserved, and impartial.[124] Daniel Berrigan describes such a priest: "I told of the austere elderly Jesuit once held up to us for emulation. It seemed he was approached by someone who dared say, 'I met a friend of yours the other day,' or some such passing remark, only to be brought up short by this soul of iron, 'I have many acquaintances, but only one Friend.'"[125] None of the Mexican priests described here claimed such strength, and few voluntarily sought grace in this extreme. But the resumé of José Antonio Barragán for the oposiciones of Guadalajara in 1770 suggests both the pain of loneliness priests experienced and their view of its value as penitential suffering. Barragán emphasized his service between 1762 and 1768 as a vicario of Tlaltenango, where during two years of epidemic he alone had often served this parish of 6,000 people, including Indians dispersed in trackless canyons. The illness was terrible, and sometimes there was nothing to eat except his own livestock, which he slaughtered to feed Indian parishioners. But the worst of these years of "unspeakable sadness," he said, was isolation from the company of other priests: "There is no priest nearby [to turn to] when I need to make sense of my situation or to help me in illness. The fear of this [dying without last rites] has mortified me greatly." [126]

Priests were educated to the view that this life would be a vale of tears. Archbishop Lizana y Beaumont gave this expectation the classic construction in his pastoral letter of March 25, 1803: "It is right that we also live between sighs and tears, for we were conceived in sin and we break divine law many times." Expect no thanks in this world, Arze y Miranda warned in 1766: "This world is a thankless land; the only place of gratitude is Heaven. God sees my work and is grateful for it." [127] But most parish priests would have been torn between these theological truths and their desire for accomplishment, meaning, and reward in this life. When a priest in a ruined little mountain parish of central Mexico or the scorched hills and barrancas of Guerrero said, "there I sacrificed my youth and now my health," it was a poignant lament at least as much as a gift serenely given.[128] When priests like Juan Joseph de Monroy, interim cura of Xocotitlan in 1762, wrote in their resumés of "untiring efforts, . . . always with the hope that eventually one will be granted rest," [129] they were thinking of promotion to a parish with more assistants or a cathedral chapter post, more than the eternal rest of a good Christian.

Whatever their formal training, priests were encouraged to think of their calling as "a grievous burden that even angels would fear to shoulder." [130] Though some shouldered rather little of the weight of their spiritual duties and the struggle for perfection, others were so tormented by the relentless introspection that they failed to take final orders, resigned, or gave up the calling altogether. A letter written to the archbishop in February 1823 by Antonio González Calderón, a deacon in Mexico City, expressed an anguish that other aspirants may have felt as they prepared for ordination. He spoke of his nine years of "bitterness and affliction" seeking spiritual happiness, "and with it, my eternal salvation." Having begun his studies believing that he had a pious and compassionate heart and hoping that a brilliant record as a student would assure him of "an honorable and decorous living," he had taken the subdeaconate in 1813 and the deaconate in 1814, but his "spirit was afflicted" with many doubts. He had continued his studies of theology in the Colegio Mayor of Santa María and the University of Mexico, completed an advanced degree, and thought about becoming a Jesuit. Now he believed that his spiritual struggle threatened his health and his soul. While he added that he might be deceiving himself through "self-love, prejudice, and a thousand other causes," he asked to be released from his vows.[131]

Manuel Cobarruvias, another early-nineteenth-century cleric, completed his ordination and was appointed to the parish of Salatitan near Guadalajara but was soon overwhelmed by a sense of inadequacy and felt compelled to resign. The act of resigning a parish benefice was itself a painful humiliation. It had to be done in a formal audience with the bishop, with notice to the viceroy, the president of the audiencia, or the governor.[132] Cobarruvias's troubled letter to the bishop on June 7, 1816, reads:

When I expressed my desire to have the parish of Salatitan, which Your Most Illustrious Highness generously gave me, I presumed a greater capacity on my part than was warranted. I had little understanding of the thorns and dangers to which the least of these posts is exposed. Experience very quickly made me realize this, as well as my own inadequacy. From that moment, I should have, and would have, resigned the post, except for the prideful fear of seeming to be fickle and worth little, and the conceit that I could make myself worthy of the responsibilities. Or if my conscience's remorse had abated, I would not have delayed as I have. I am now utterly convinced by the very testimony of my conscience that my salvation is imperiled by continuing in this state. I assure your Most Illustrious Highness that this is not a matter of frivolity or a paroxysm of passion, but the result of serious reflection, supported by sound advice from knowing and mature persons. So I have resolved to send you my humble request that with the same kindness given to my petition for this benefice, I may be allowed to resign it.[133]

Some royal officials would have liked to see pastors in their district follow Cobarruvias's example. The subdelegado of Tehuacan (Puebla) in 1792 complained that Gaspar Antonio de Rivera, cura of Zoquitlan, "does not have the aptitude of a *cura*." [134] Evidently few of the priests who remained in parish service agonized over their vocation as the scrupulous Cobarruvias did.

Loneliness and the sense of burden were often accompanied by fear. The judicial record for Mexico and Guadalajara is replete with curas' nervous accounts of threats on their lives and narrow escapes from lethal attack (though, to my knowledge, few were ever injured, much less maimed or martyred like some frontier missionaries). The cura of Malacatepec in the district of Metepec in 1774, describing the Indian parishioners' threatening behavior over a fee dispute, wrote "I fear death"; and the new cura of Amecameca, embroiled in a bitter dispute over fees with parishioners in 1796, reported that an angry crowd of parishioners came into his rooms with mutiny on their minds and would have attacked and maybe killed him if another priest and two non-Indians had not come to his rescue.[135] The cura of Apaxtla (Guerrero) in 1809 understood that the Indians of Tanicpatlan "have promised to kill my *vicario* and me," and indeed they gathered outside his residence, shouting "Death to the *cura*" and grew more angry when the priests tried to calm them with words.[136] In some cases, including those of Domingo Joseph de la Mota in parishes in and near Morelos in the 1740's and 1750's (discussed in Appendix C), Francisco Franco, an impetuous cura of Apaxtla in the 1780's, and the teniente de cura of Pozontepec (Sultepec district) in 1758, controversy over a priest's rash behavior or determined campaigns against local vices did lead to attacks on his residence or, in Franco's case, a nighttime escape.[137]

The priests' account of these narrow escapes and mortal threats do express genuine fear, but few were unguarded intimacies spilling out into the official record. Rather, they were presented as further evidence of sacerdotal self-sacrifice and especially as damning evidence of the terminal extremes of which the unrestrained plebe were capable. Cloaking themselves in public authority, priests were touchy about the respect and obedience due them as God's agents, and threats to their persons were the ultimate in disrespect.

There is no way to know for certain whether disrespect really increased in the late eighteenth century. Parishioners had made insolent fun of their curas for centuries, whether in idle gossip, individual defiance, or periodic rituals of reversal,[138] and priests had always been sensitive and usually inclined to consider piety and respect in their time to be on the wane. But circumstantial evidence presented throughout this book suggests that parish priests were now more sensitive to disrespect, or at least had occasion to express this sensitivity more often than before.

Laments over lack of respect were probably the most common incidental response parish priests made in the growing litigation against them in the late colonial period, and a common justification for their occasional use of the whip and imprisonment.[139] Open disrespect had shock value, because it was still considered unusual. As an Inquisition official observed in 1795, the public at large was afraid to "say anything against a priest." [140] Disrespect was a broad category that could embrace face-to-face insolence, men addressing the priest with their hats on or approaching the confessional in spurs and reeking of cheese,[141] denunciations to higher magistrates of church and crown, and imagined slights and insults. Whatever its manifestations, disrespect implied to the priest a deeper disobedience that threatened authority and order in society, especially his own ample conception of spiritual authority. As the cura of Zacualpan put it in 1775 in his dispute with Indian parishioners of San Simón Tototepec over fees and with the alcalde mayor over judicial rights, he was "obligated to give spiritual direction to his children, to tame the disobedient . . . and insolent [of their] unruly audacity." [142]

There was an unwritten contract implicit in this conception of respect. If a priest acted honorably and "decently"—dressed, ate, and otherwise behaved according to his station—he deserved a commensurate respect and obedience from his parishioners.[143] But it was not always an equal contract, for many priests saw failure to show respect, even if the priest had not fully met his side of the bargain, as more than a violation of their professional honor. It was an affront to their personal honor as well, reason enough in the minds of some for righteous indignation. That may even have come first for the cura of Capuluac, judging from his statement in a 1796 fee dispute that his purpose in responding to the exaggerated charges of his parishioners was to vindicate "my personal and professional honor." [144] This dual honor could be of incomparable importance to the cura. In a long and bitter litigation with non-Indian parishioners during the late 1790's, Manuel de Agüero of Yautepec declared that their charges "wound my honor, a jewel more precious than life itself." [145] Some curas expected extravagant public expressions of respect as a validation of their authority and became irate if parishioners "did not show every kind of submission" when they met them on the street.[146]

In correspondence and litigation related to their parish service, late colonial curas expressed strong feelings about unity, order, the endless struggle against "indecencies," and pernicious liberty in society, fear of disrespect, feelings of loneliness, gnawing scruples, and sometimes even their boredom with a career of ordinary service.[147] The sense that pervades these personal statements is one of being trapped in a paternal dilemma. Priests were schooled to think of themselves as dignified superiors, as fathers and leaders with a special responsibility for protecting and disciplining their flock, which they sometimes expressed in the homely metaphor of the human body, with themselves as the head and their parishioners as the feet. But they were, they thought, heads and fathers with dwindling parental authority; the feet were trying to take over the work of the head, and the crown at best stood by with its arms folded.[148] Parish priests were concerned about their responsibility for the plebe's souls, worried particularly about their failure to fulfill the annual obligation of confession and communion. The plebe, especially Indians, were said to be governed by uncontrolled passions and could not be trusted to act as Christians without close direction; yet the priest was increasingly left without the power to control them except by Christian love and compassion, humility and prudence.[149] The result, said one Oaxaca cura, was "total spiritual ruin."[150]

Apocalyptic hyperbole was not new, but there was a growing sense among parish priests that they were being constrained by limitations on their power to punish in a fatherly way and by the litigation against them that Indian parishioners were being permitted, even encouraged, to pursue. Even for men who believed that God would punish failures to follow his law in the next world,[151] it was painful to watch that law ignored and flouted without retribution in this one. Since God's law was superior to human law, there was a poignant disjunction between priests' sense of their superior responsibility and their feelings of powerlessness. Though God may have been, as the Franciscan doctrinero Fr. Martín Calderón put it in 1734, "the universal king for whom the earthly king governs his vassals by His laws," the cura had only a wooden staff. It was the royal governors, with their staffs of iron, who must enable God's law to reign.[152] Yet far from lending support to the clergy, the royal courts seemed to be letting loose the forces of disorder and disobedience. Craving "the proper respect and obedience" from his Indian parishioners, the cura of Tepetlaostoc (Texcoco district, Valley of Mexico), in a response to their 1759 lawsuit against him, linked litigation to disrespect and political impotence:

They have treated him disrespectfully. . . . They have totally denied him their submission and obedience. . . . He has suffered the insolences of the Indians, who think that they have license to act that way just because they initiated a lawsuit against him, believing that it cancels his ability to discipline them.[153]

Despair, frustration, and sometimes rage over the naked passions of their parishioners and the failure of gentle Christian instruction to restrain them run through late colonial priests' representations of themselves in public conflicts.[154] One was willing to "sacrifice myself entirely for the spiritual and temporal welfare of my parishioners," but found that he could do little more than sacrifice himself.[155] The cura of Totomaloyan in the district of Sultepec in 1798 wanted to put a stop to the drunken Indian fiesta held annually on December 12 for the election of caretakers of the saints, but discretion forced him behind the doors of his rooms with the bolts securely fastened. "All [of my efforts] have been useless," he wrote.[156] In the 1760's, the cura of Actopan (Hidalgo) explained that as judge, he was bound to be hated by many, even though he proceeded with the "greatest gentleness":

These [Indian parishioners], like crazed invalids, have turned against their pastor and spiritual physician, abusing the protection they have had from me, treating me with disrespect. They have set about discrediting my conduct and impugning my honor with the repeated complaints they have made against me.[157]

It was the lack of restraint in the behavior of Indian parishioners (and occasionally a district governor) that upset the priests—their perverse, disobedient ways, their unbounded appetites, their detestable pride and pernicious liberty.[158] The cura of Tenango del Valle in 1796 reduced his feelings on the subject to a sentence: "They don't wish to understand reason and I see that they are blind with passion; [they are] ingrates . . . who promise one thing but don't do it; they follow custom only when it suits them." [159] The cura of Tlapanaloya (Hidalgo) in 1765 said of his parishioners, who followed an influential local family into litigation against him over clerical fees, "they live so arrogantly . . . denying me the proper obedience. They do not want to appear before this court even for the smallest matter." [160]

By the 1770's, some parish priests were beginning to argue more explicitly that by taking moral authority away from them and ignoring custom, royal officials were responsible for this growing predicament. In 1775, Juan Nicolás Cortés, cura of Alvarado on the steamy delta of the Papaloapan River in central Veracruz, was accused by the district governor of terrifying his parishioners by sermonizing on the first Sunday of Advent that universal judgment was imminent owing to the growing presence of anti-Christs who persecuted the church and its priests. Cortés escaped conviction and punishment by the Inquisition because eyewitnesses said he offered this as one of several opinions to illustrate the difference between universal and individual judgment, without advocating one or another. They added that he did denounce various vices of the time, including magistrates who acted unjustly, but that he did not mention anyone in particular.[161]

Others were less circumspect. In a 1790–91 suit with his Indian parishioners over an array of property issues, the cura of Temascaltepec complained openly that "the royal decisions tie my hands to proceed against even the most ordinary offenses." [162] Less directly, the cura of Mazatepec in the district of Cuernavaca expressed the same sentiment in 1800 when he wrote that his "peaceful character and good disposition" did not work in the present situation, in which "one sees in this country, sir, only drunkenness, concubinage, adultery, rape, parents offended by the robbery of their daughters, woundings, deaths, and other wrongs without any way to remedy them." [163]

It would be a mistake to regard this expression of frustration as a meaningless or timeless stage performance, the standard lament of priests since Saint Augustine. It was different from the Conquest and Catholic reformation rhetoric of the sixteenth century. Even in the late-sixteenth and seventeenth centuries, with their strong sense of a fall from the golden age of evangelization and of neophytes slipping back into "paganism," the problem was still perceived as laying mostly within the clergy and within the plebe's propensity for evil.[164] It was the priests' mission to rouse themselves and root out that evil. They understood themselves to have an active, central role to play from within the colonial government. The dilemma for late-eighteenth-century parish priests was that they were being kept by the crown from controlling the dangerous license of the plebe.

*   *   *

It is in the nature of the administrative and judicial record to expose the exceptional, the dramatic, and the exemplary extremes in the conduct and thinking of parish priests—the notoriously bad and the famously good, according to the standards of the time.[165] Most priests were neither. Like José Ignacio Azcárate, cura of Alahuistlan in 1793, they combined strengths and weaknesses. Azcárate was described as a man of talent and learning, temperamental but of generous intentions ("su genio violento pero de penzamientos muy humanos").[166] Others were charitable with parishioners but weak as teachers and preachers; or fond of gambling and distracted by their own estates.[167] Still others were scrupulous in their pastoral duties but grasping in money matters, rigid in their demands on parishioners' resources and personal behavior, or fun-loving or vicious in their personal conduct.[168] All but the most wanton of them at least had the scruples of Graham Greene's whiskey priest, marveling at the miracle of the mass and divine forgiveness, of which they were the instruments despite their personal failings. Few neglected their sacramental duties.

But curas and vicarios who were among the most dedicated to their pastoral duties were not necessarily successful or warmly appreciated. Pedro José Moreno, cura of Santa María Tututepec (Tulancingo district, Hidalgo) in the early 1790's, knew the Indian language of his parishioners well and was committed to the arduous work in his mountain parish, where anticlericalism and millenarian aspirations had been manifest only a generation before, but he was so thorough in pursuing his lofty spiritual expectations and so firm in demanding his fees that the Indian parishioners apparently would have no more of him.[169]

Regalist treatises about the need for moral reform, notorious cases of misconduct in the ecclesiastical court records, and the growing number of diocesan priests in parish service, together with the reputation of the regular orders for better moral discipline and fewer material concerns, have led some writers to suggest that there was a decline in the morality and dedication of parish priests in the late colonial period. But abuses and unpriestly behavior were always part of this colonial history. Reports of misconduct by parish priests in all its forms did reach new levels in the eighteenth century, but that is not certain evidence of a more corrupt parish clergy. It seems more a case of increased conflict over their authority.

The traces of parish priests' sentiments and public behavior reveal some deep tensions that were both inherent in the pastoral duties and more acutely and widely felt at the end of the colonial period. For most curas and vicarios most of the time, theirs was a career of ordinary service. They were torn between "the counsels of perfection and doing the job."[170] They were trained to contemplate and forgive weakness in others, yet they themselves were called to a higher standard of conduct. Such tensions were not necessarily disruptive, but these parish priests were called to act as parents to a very large family, and their paternal authority in the struggle against evil was, they felt, being greatly diminished. The anger that sometimes rises from the manuscript page came both from their sense of being thwarted in the work of salvation and from their sense of dishonor to the office and their person. These men were not inclined to temporize about disobedience and disrespect. They understood themselves to be concerned with order and precedence in this world, as well as in the kingdom of God.

CHAPTER NINE

Sanctions and Deference

> Father Gregorio came up suddenly on horseback and [I] heard him say "Hail Most Holy Mary," to which the *gobernador* replied "who was conceived in grace," taking off his hat. —Testimony of Indian parishioner of San Miguel Almoloya, 1762

To the extent that parish priests were accepted as leaders and obeyed by their village parishioners, how was this obedience evoked? How were the model role of the cura, the view of Indians as natural children, and the ideal relationships to Indian parishioners put into practice? The divided images of the parish priest embedded in the Council of Trent decrees and the *Recopilación*—the gentle shepherd who leads by example and exhortation, and the father who judges and disciplines—sanctioned both loving persuasion and force. For some curas, obedience was a yoke of flowers that rested lightly and sweetly on the Indians' shoulders, a gift offered and accepted, not forced on them; for other curas and other situations, good order and salvation required stronger direction—a heavier, rigid yoke.[1] In either case, laymen were under the yoke, and priests were among the drivers.

These divided images of shepherd/father and yoke of flowers/yoke of iron implied a deep ambivalence about the cura's authority to enforce obedience, an ambivalence that came into the open in the late eighteenth century.[2] For sixteenth- and seventeenth-century lawmakers, these divisions were reconciled by moderation and balance: the rod should be used gently and only when necessary, and should be balanced by love. Some boundaries of moderation became clearly marked in colonial law and custom, but others were local and informal, established at the discretion of individual bishops, pastors, and magistrates, and by what parishioners would tolerate. There was always some uncertainty about when and how the priest could resort to force.

The cura's use of force, his position of authority, and the social customs of deference toward him were among the main instruments of his political power in the parish. But they were not the only ones, especially for parish priests who were well rooted in the community. A cura might be able to control local elections and see that his favorites were placed in the strategic offices of gobernador, alcalde, and fiscal; he might spread gossip as a way to weaken the influence of a local family; his literacy, judicial role, and contacts outside the parish could make him an important legal adviser; he might have influential friends in Mexico City or Guadalajara who would work on his behalf (or so parishioners were led to believe) if formal complaints were lodged against him; he might enjoy the special favor of the district magistrate; and he might be able to bribe local people and officials.[3] Furthermore, as a landowner, shopkeeper, or trader, the cura might wield economic influence with political ramifications. These and more formal aspects of the priest's power are addressed here and in the chapters of Part Four, especially in terms of how some of the instruments of obedience were changing in the eighteenth century as the image of the gentle shepherd officially overtook that of the stern disciplinarian.

Imprisonment

In the cause of salvation and the protection of the family, parish priests could use fear and force, even though colonial directives discouraged these methods from the beginning. In the eighteenth century, the forms of corporal punishment still used by parish priests and backed by the weight of custom and the ambiguity of law were incarceration and whipping. Excerpting royal cedulas of 1560, 1613, and 1619, the *Recopilación* made it clear that ecclesiastical judges could not sentence Indians to cash fines or forced labor service,[4] but colonial law was less clear about whether parish priests could order imprisonments and operate jails. Early bishops discouraged but did not forbid confinement and corporal punishment. A meeting of New Spain's bishops in 1539 concluded that Indians should not be put in jail or stocks or whipped for not knowing the catechism. Rather than prison or lashes, the bishops thought, the appropriate punishment was to forbid an Indian offender to enter the church for a period of time.[5]

In principle and practice, early colonial authorities were more concerned with controlling the use of prisons and corporal punishment by priests than with prohibition. The questions were, what was the purpose of imprisonment, and who had the right to order and execute it? Following a 1613 cedula, the *Recopilación* treated imprisonment as a punishment: Indian alcaldes could administer a day of prison or six to eight lashes for drunkenness, absence from mass, or "committing a similar transgression."[6] But as late as 1815 an audiencia fiscal maintained that "imprisonment is not a punishment but a form of custody."[7] Episcopal decrees in the sixteenth and seventeenth centuries also called for Indian officials to punish local parishioners for failing to attend Sunday mass or learn doctrina, but they forbade the priests to do the incarcerating or whipping.[8] By implication, it was the priest who ordered the Indian official to arrest and punish in these situations. Still, the laws were clouded by exceptions: priests were not supposed to arrest Indians or order corporal punishment except in cases that fell within their jurisdiction; they were not supposed to incarcerate or use other physical restraints except with formal permission from their bishops.[9]

These uncertainties were exacerbated by practical difficulties. Every settlement in the New World was to have a public jail, according to a 1578 cedula, but it had to be built and maintained without cost to the royal treasury.[10] Understandably, in many places the response was to put up a flimsy adobe building that could accommodate few prisoners, was not secure, and soon needed repairs. In these rural communities, rooms in the stone church compound were the most secure quarters for temporary incarceration. The use of church property for this purpose came increasingly into question in the eighteenth century, however, as colonial officials energetically pursued the idea of a unitary, absolutist state in which the monarchy was the arm of the law in all mundane affairs. Beginning in 1716, the crown promoted construction of new and more secure jails in the district seats.[11] Viceroy Revillagigedo (the elder) advised his successor in 1755 that parish priests should not operate jails, period.[12] Eusebio Ventura Beleña's compendium of laws and court decrees for the Audiencia of Mexico in 1787 excerpted a May 4, 1656, cedula that ordered alcaldes mayores not to allow parish priests to imprison Indians. Ventura Beleña underscored this rediscovered law with a 1786 audiencia decree that ecclesiastical judges could not order imprisonments without the permission of the corregidor.[13]

Regalist bishops of the late colonial period added their voices to the new rhetoric of the unitary state and the docile cura as spiritual specialist: at the Fourth Provincial Council (1771), the bishops agreed that parish priests should not use fetters or jails, that these forms of coercion contradicted the model of the priest as the "pacific teacher."[14] There had always been a tension between instruction by love and instruction by punishment—even so strong an advocate of corporal punishment as the anti-idolatry campaigner of the seventeenth century, Jacinto de la Serna, spoke of "repression with rigor and love"[15]—but late-eighteenth-century bishops were more inclined to see the two as antagonistic opposites than as a complementary pair. Archbishop Rubio y Salinas, in his pastoral letter of February 1, 1762, urged his parish priests to lead with tenderness ("suavidad") and love. He did not absolutely forbid corporal punishment, but he made it clear that lashes should be used infrequently, and that Indians should be corrected "with charity and not with rigor." In practice, the bishops discouraged but sometimes condoned the use of parish jails. In disputes that came before the episcopal courts at the end of the colonial period, the provisor objected less to the use of prisons by parish priests than to their abuse, to "violent imprisonments."[16]

Even when imprisonment was accepted as a holding device, there was the question of the reach of ecclesiastical jurisdiction. What a parishioner could be held for or punished for on a priest's orders was subject to change, especially in the eighteenth century. Typically, incarceration by priests had been tolerated for Indian parishioners who had failed to fulfill their religious obligations (had not attended Sunday mass, had not learned the catechism, or had not confessed or taken communion at Easter); had not paid fees owed to the priest for baptism, marriage, burial, or other services; had committed fornication or adultery; had appeared drunk in public; or had committed some other deliberate but minor offense against public decency. Priests had also been allowed to arrest people suspected of witchcraft, but the suspicion had to rest on more than a simple refusal to make voluntary contributions.[17] By the late eighteenth century, the policing powers of the parish priest were increasingly confined in principle

FIG. 5. One kind of parish jail. Most were makeshift and crude at best or assigned to some part of the church complex. A granary much like this was used for that purpose at San Luis de las Peras (Huichapan, Hidalgo, Archdiocese of Mexico) as late as 1785.

to religious practice—attendance at mass, mastery of doctrina, observation of the sacraments, and annual confession and communion. Only the crown's district governors were to police public morality. Even the power to jail parishioners who had not paid their sacramental fees was withdrawn in the archbishop's pastoral letter of February 2, 1762, as violating the spirit of charity in which priests were expected to live.

The issue of incarceration by priests was taken up rather obliquely by royal authorities in the late eighteenth century as part of the requirement of royal *auxilio* (royal approval and assistance) for any quasi-judicial punishments priests considered necessary. It was a long-standing legal principle that ecclesiastical judges should rely on civil authorities to enforce the law. From the sixteenth century, the crown had forbidden parish priests to arrest or punish laymen without the auxilio of a royal magistrate, and stipulated that royal officials were to aid them in fulfilling their spiritual duties.[18] Royal auxilio was required for crimes that fell entirely within the priest's jurisdiction (such as absence at mass and ignorance of the catechism), as well as for those in the gray area of jurisdiction shared by civil and religious authorities (such as drunkenness and illicit sex). In a 1536 cedula that instructed both royal judges and prelates to see that Indian adulterers were not branded or fined, the crown gave precedence and a slightly greater emphasis to the royal judge's responsibility: "We order [*ordenamos*] our magistrates and we commission [*encargamos*] our ecclesiastical prelates."[19]

After the 1740's, the right of royal auxilio was claimed by the audiencias and district governors with growing frequency. Had the cura requested royal auxilio? Had it been granted? Sometimes the answer was yes to both questions. Whether from a sly cynicism or from excessive allegiance to the rules, the cura of Cuautitlan in the late 1780's was so assiduous about soliciting the royal auxilio that the alcalde mayor's lieutenant became fed up: the cura was forever sending him Indians who were charged with "insignificant debts and other trivial matters."[20]

In cases where the auxilio had not been requested or received, the audiencias were increasingly firm that it should have been. This was not so much a new policy as a sharper definition and more active enforcement of an old one. The change is evident in two orders, one from the Audiencia of Mexico in 1740, the other from the viceroy in 1789. The 1740 audiencia order required lieutenants of the alcaldes mayores to help the curas ensure that all parishioners fulfilled the annual duty of confession and communion. At the same time, the curas were ordered to seek the lieutenants' aid rather than arresting parishioners on their own.[21] It was as if the lieutenants had to be urged in 1740 to take a more active role. The 1789 order from the viceroy, directed to the intendant of Valladolid,

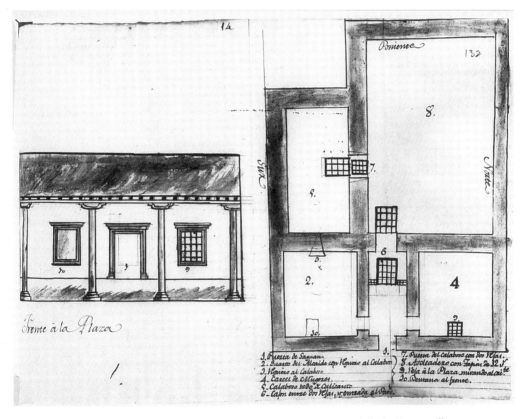

FIG. 6. Plan for a royal jail in Ario, Michoacán, 1804. Sturdy new jails built according to similar designs in many Indian pueblos during the late colonial period served as local monuments to the district governor's growing authority, as instruments of royal auxilio, and as replacements for the priests' impromptu parish jails.

instructed subdelegados and lesser judges *not* to accede to the curas' appeals for arrest without reviewing the charges and evidence. If the crime was secular in nature, the judge should be careful not to permit the priest to exercise jurisdiction.[22] Here the district judges were assumed to be actively intervening—now involving themselves not in response to the priest's initiative, but under their own authority as independent agents empowered to scrutinize the priest's actions and protect and extend the royal jurisdiction. District judges in growing numbers complained of priests not securing their permission to arrest and punish.[23] Even at that, the issue of auxilio was often overshadowed by more pressing disputes involving the same officials and communities.

While priests sometimes were called onto the carpet for making arrests without royal auxilio before the 1770's, they could justify their actions either as a necessity in remote places or as a matter of long-standing tradition. When the alcalde mayor of Actopan complained in 1763 that the cura was arresting women without his auxilio, the cura replied that he was just trying to do his duty and, besides, royal auxilio customarily was not required for the imprisonment of women in the archdiocese. The audiencia fiscal agreed with the cura but added that he should not be allowed to exceed the church's authority: "he is not free and independent to exercise it against all reason, because the secular judge is superior to the ecclesiastical judge, and his jurisdiction must be recognized and acknowledged."[24] In a similar case in 1760, the priest received a laconic order from the audiencia not to imprison Indians "without authority."[25]

By the early 1770's, the climate of administrative opinion that had accepted parish jails and corporal punishment was noticeably chillier. A priest might appeal to custom and necessity, but the courts were almost certain to disregard those arguments in favor of the principle of royal auxilio.[26] Indians and their attorneys who understood the shift began to lodge their own complaints against curas who acted without state approval, as the gobernador of Tlalmanalco (Edo. de México) did in 1772.[27] Priests in the last decades of the colonial period were not always apologetic about failing to secure royal auxilio, but they were careful to document their efforts to comply before acting on their own.[28]

Even with mounting royal opposition, the record is full of cases of priests maintaining parish jails and ordering imprisonment in the period 1710–1809.[29] The largest share of the archdiocese examples, 34 of 44, date from 1760 and after.[30] Nearly all are documented in an incidental way: a dispute over clerical fees, involuntary service, or general cruelty and misconduct was taken to court, and the fact that the priest operated a jail or ordered arrests came up in testimony as further evidence of his misconduct. Although parish jails were illegal, the courts usually did not seize on them as the main issue or follow through with a full investigation and resounding verdict.[31] These late colonial examples did not cluster in the most remote parishes or on the fringes of the archdiocese far from Mexico City and the district seats of the alcaldes mayores and subdelegados. They were located in districts throughout the area—in places near Mexico City, such as Coyoacan, Xochimilco, Zumpango de la Laguna, and Otumba; in important provincial centers such as the Valley of Toluca and the district of Cuernavaca; and in more remote parishes like Cadereyta and Zacualpan.

In most cases, witnesses or an inspector said only that the priest had arrested local Indians on his own authority, but the testimony is detailed enough to establish that three of these curas controlled the town jail, and that 20 others operated their own facilities.[32] A parish jail might be a detached building near the priest's quarters, such as a chapel, oratory, or granary. Indians of San Luis de las Peras in the jurisdiction of Huichapan (Hidalgo) in 1785 said they were held by the priest in a wooden granary near his residence, "which serves as a jail and which has no light or air except for a cat hole through which a cup of food barely passes. . . . It is worse than the cruelest dungeon" (see Fig. 5).[33] Occasionally, the church itself or the sacristy was used.[34] If the prisoner was female and the term of confinement long, the priest might order her kept "en depósito" in a private house in the parish seat, supervised by a respectable older woman.[35] Usually, however, the parish jail was a locked room attached to the cura's living quarters and guarded by his servants.[36]

Who was arrested and why suggests the range of the priest's power of imprisonment and the results he expected to achieve by it. Most of the jailings conformed to the traditional and legal conceptions of the pastor's duty. As the priest of Tepetlaostoc put it in 1758, he used the jail only for deliberate but minor spiritual transgressions, which he called moral matters ("casos morales"): "that is, the Indian who does not know *doctrina*, who balks at sending his children to school, or who does not attend the weekly mass, roll call, or catechism class after he has been warned."[37] The traditional conception of a priest's moral purview remained strong, too. Some parish priests at the end of the eighteenth century were quick to defend their use of imprisonment as necessary to control "public sins, drunkenness, and libertine conduct."[38] Where an old-fashioned parish priest operated a jail, parishioners who were drunk in public, committed adultery, had not brought infants in for baptism, or had not learned the teachings of the church could expect arrest and sometimes a beating.

Priests also arrested Indians who had not paid burial or baptism charges in full, owed money to a cofradía, or had not performed customary personal service for them. Incarceration in many of these cases was imposed largely as a form of leverage.[39] The priest might make it clear to his prisoner that he would not be released until the fee was paid or a cosigner came forward.[40] After a few days in jail, men usually paid what the priest claimed they owed, or promised to pay or to perform labor service. In a similar way, some innocent relative might be held hostage. Near Mexico City, the cura of Tecospa imprisoned one Indian woman for more than fifteen days because her husband refused to give up land he had seized from a neighbor.[41] Another Indian wife was held by the cura to force her husband out of hiding.[42]

Although far fewer women than men were taken into custody by curas in the eighteenth century, they could be arrested for most of the same "moral matters," including failure to recite doctrina or attend mass, drunkenness, and illicit sex (especially a wife's adultery).[43] Perhaps there were fewer women arrested because Indian women did not hold office, rarely appeared drunk in public, and were more likely to act respectfully in the priest's presence, to know church teachings, and to attend mass. It may also be that since women were regarded as the weaker, less responsible sex, secular and religious officials were more reluctant to incarcerate them and inclined to leave their discipline to husbands and fathers. An unusual but notorious use of confinement on orders of the cura was in cases of pregnancy from incestuous unions. The cura of Temascaltepec in 1796 made this one of his pet projects, ostensibly to spare such young women the public shame of their pregnancies. When one of his pregnant girls escaped with the aid of her mother, he promptly had the mother arrested.[44]

A striking pattern in the arrests is that pueblo officials were so frequently the victims. The cura's lay assistants, the fiscal and the sacristán, were sometimes arrested for failing to collect fees and fulfill other duties,[45] but most of those arrested were gobernadores, alcaldes, and elders who had a less direct relationship to parish administration. Sometimes, pueblo officials and other notables were incarcerated for moral and spiritual offenses or for acting in other ways that the priest found provocative. A gobernador who failed to attend mass, did not know the catechism, or was disrespectful to priests in public was particularly offensive, since the cura's standing in the community depended on official respect for and obedience to authority.[46]

More often, these officials were held hostage in order to force the community to fulfill its obligations to the cura or bend to his will in other ways.[47] A pueblo gobernador and his constable (topil) might be arrested when the cura's servants for the week did not appear, as happened at Tlaltizapan in 1781.[48] Or the cura might pull in an alcalde or a former alcalde when labor service that he regarded as his legal right (but the community regarded as voluntary) was not provided.[49] Arrests on these grounds were especially common after 1767, when many pueblos opted for the new schedule of clerical fees that freed them from all labor service to the priest. The priest's strategy was to hold the local notables until a settlement was reached or until they agreed to enforce his rules.

Imprisonment could be used like a fine-tipped brush or a heavy stamp to mark parishioners' habits and obligations. For the minor offenses that came before a parish priest acting as juez eclesiástico, the offender was kept in jail for two or three days; but if the issue was money, the stay could be indefinite, depending more on the offender's willingness to settle and bow to the cura's will than on any standard of how much time served was enough. The Indian fiscal of San Cristóbal in the parish of Zinacantepec (Metepec district) had languished for two months in the cura's jail for failing to pay the fees he was charged with collecting by the time his complaint reached the audiencia in 1791.[50] Where one priest might arrest one or two drunkards or officials in order to make his point, "as an example and warning to the rest,"[51] another might hope to punish every case of deliberate transgression he could find. But few curas had the time, the desire, or the power to identify and arrest all transgressors. Practical considerations, plus the model of moderation and paternal conduct, made exemplary punishment the norm.

Finally, some curas used imprisonment for patently self-interested and immoral purposes. The cura of Tianguistengo in 1815 imprisoned Indians who refused to work on his estates; and the cura of Zacualpan in 1796 reportedly arrested the Indian husband of Joana de Lía of Songosotla for drunkenness, then approached her for sexual favors in exchange for her husband's freedom.[52] A more common misuse of imprisonment was to punish behavior that was lawful but threatening to the cura. Indian officials who supported lawsuits against priests were arrested by the curas of San Gerónimo in the district of Cholula

(Puebla) in 1729, San Bartolomé Capuluac (Tenango del Valle district) in 1796, and Santiago Amatepec (Temascaltepec district) in 1806.[53] Priests accused of incarcerating their political enemies usually claimed that there were other reasons for the arrests, but they also justified their actions as essential to good order in the parish. They knew that vengeful and hostage-taking arrests were risky acts that could set off angry protests from royal officers, as well as villagers.[54]

Corporal Punishment

Whippings by parish priests were both more common and more controversial than detention and parish jails. Colonial magistrates accepted the whip as a standard instrument of control. As the alcalde mayor's lieutenant for Choapan in the Villa Alta district of Oaxaca put it in 1789, "the whip does wonders."[55] Some owners of private estates used corporal punishment freely, and little heed was paid to it.[56] But whether the priest and the whip should go together was hotly disputed at the end of the colonial period: whippings were an unambiguous intervention by the cura in public affairs, and Bourbon colonial policy was especially clear about their prohibition in the late eighteenth century; yet many parish priests regarded the whip as an efficacious instrument of order and salvation for Indian parishioners, made more acceptable by long use and good results.

The seventeenth-century publications of law and legal opinion that restricted the use of parish jails also referred to corporal punishment. Solórzano's *Política indiana*, like the *Recopilación*, enjoined parish priests from whipping parishioners without the permission of their bishops, but was far from set against the idea in principle, declaring that experts considered most Indians so careless and possessed of so little shame that if they were not whipped they would not learn the doctrina or fulfill their sacramental duties. For them (but not for the nobility and other superior Indians who led orderly lives and understood shame), the whip was a necessary instrument of civility and salvation.[57]

Perhaps because it was more widely used than the parish jail, the priest's whip became the object of a more emphatic campaign of reform and eradication in the late eighteenth century. Apparently in the early 1780's, the crown decreed that parish priests could no longer administer whippings at all (at least priests who wrote urgent letters to the Council of the Indies in 1784 assumed that such an order had been made).[58] And the *Recopilación*'s law granting them conditional rights to do so attracted new attention. Viceroy Marqués de Branciforte, in his 1794 plan for the good order of missions in New Spain, criticized priests for grossly exceeding their authority to administer whippings under this law (1-13-6). Besides, to the viceroy's way of thinking, law 1-13-6 had now been effectively superseded. He denounced the practice of missionaries ordering whippings "as a thing so opposed to the laws and latest disposition of the matter in which priests are absolutely forbidden to take cognizance of and punish the offenses of laymen with temporal penalties."[59] Six years later, the audiencia fiscal actually construed 1-13-6 to forbid whippings "unless [the priest had] the *auxilio* of the secular arm."[60]

Church policy followed a similar course of development. In most of the provincial council decrees, manuals, and pastoral letters of the sixteenth and seventeenth centuries, the moderate use of corporal punishment was accepted. Bishops and other clerical writers regarded preaching and exhortation as the most desirable instruments of the priest's influence, but they also recognized a need for corporal punishment and a place for the priest in administering it.[61] The *Itinerario*, that most popular of manuals for priests in Indian parishes in the eighteenth century, reiterated the principle of moderation and the restriction to parish priests who had been appointed ecclesiastical judges or had a special commission from the bishop, but it registered a series of legitimate uses for the whip. Preoccupied with Indians' moral weakness and conceiving of them as "children of punishment," the *Itinerario* regarded the whip as key to Indian devotion, decency, and good order.[62]

In the late eighteenth century, clerical opinion on the use of force was divided and in flux. Church leaders, now gripped by the idea of the parish priest as the gentle teacher, instructed their priests not to resort to corporal punishment. Archbishop Rubio y Salinas, in his pastoral letter of Feburary 2, 1762, urged priests in Indian parishes to correct with charity, not rigor.[63] His successor, the energetic regalist Lorenzana, skirted all mention of corporal punishment in his pastoral letters (an omission that, as one might expect, was repeated in the decrees of the Fourth Provincial Council he convened in 1771). His model parish priest was a man of exemplary personal conduct and refined education, a teacher of Christian doctrine and moral virtues who would win his parishioners over with good works and love.[64] Inspired by Lorenzana's pastoral letters, Omerick's unpublished 1769 guide for parish priests drew out the implication for corporal punishment of this vision of the good pastor. Omitting any reference to the *Itinerario*, he said that disciplining the Indians should not consist of the whip and the frown. Like Lorenzana, Omerick exhorted parish priests to govern with love and affection, to be familiar, humane teachers and edifying examples. The eventual result of the crown's campaign for royal auxilio, episcopal acquiescence, and the developing image of the loving pastor was a firm prohibition of whippings by curas in the archdiocese on March 4, 1814.[65]

But the men on the spot were more inclined to the old ways of their training manuals. Most of the parish priests who expressed an opinion in writing argued strongly for corporal punishment. The virtually unrevised eighteenth-century editions of the *Itinerario* remained their guide to office, and the new manuals published in Mexico by the experienced curas Manuel Pérez and Pérez de Velasco echoed its view that the whip was an essential instrument of the faith in Indian parishes.[66] "What rational father would not punish his child when he needed it?" asked Pérez de Velasco in 1766. The priest of Zimatlan (Oaxaca) in 1784 reworked a verse from the Book of Ecclesiastes to the same purpose in his defense of corporal punishment: "a father who does not punish [his child] with lashes does not love him." Both he and his contemporary in the parish of Tlalixtac, Miguel Francisco de Ferra, followed the *Itinerario* closely in their spirited arguments in favor of corporal punishment. For both, fear of the lash was an appropriate method to bring naturally pusillanimous people under control. Ferra claimed that for many years he had tried to administer his parish without corporal punishment, but experience had led him to the conclusion that it was impossible to "establish order" without it.[67] Indians had to be compelled to farm, to live civilized and Christian lives. Without an occasional flogging, they could not be "maintained" (*conservado*).[68] By the last years of colonial rule, some parish priests were talking as if these gloomy predictions had come true. The Franciscan doctrinero of Cocula (Jalisco) in 1802 contended that when the whippings stopped, so had his Indians' obedience: "since the end of the punishment they received with the whip," they no longer performed customary service for the church, resisted paying clerical fees, and acted like infidels.[69]

The whipping issue was one of the most convenient ways for alcaldes mayores and subdelegados to invoke the principle of royal auxilio and strengthen their position at the expense of the parish priest. Once it became clear in the 1770's and 1780's that the audiencias and viceroys were siding with the Indians in such cases, the number of lawsuits they entered over clerical whippings increased dramatically.[70] Indian officials who had other reasons for opposing the cura were not above fabricating stories of illegal whippings and other abuse, knowing that the crown was receptive to such complaints.[71] In any event, there was a tendency on both sides to exaggerate. It is hard to know the right of it, when the same vicario depicted by the Indians of Mochitlan in 1800 as unfair and generally abusive was defended by the coadjutor as a mild, peace-loving man who would not "harm a fly." The coadjutor claimed that during his two and one-half years in the parish, the vicario had whipped only two drunken cantors who failed to perform their Sunday duties, the assistant fiscal for being drunk and missing mass, the fiscal for failing to see that local children attended school, and one prospective groom who did not know the catechism.[72]

Indians apparently did not object to clerical whipping in principle. Implicitly, they accepted moderate whippings that related directly to spiritual obligations—for failing to attend mass, memorize the catechism, confess, and take communion. What they did object to was excessive cruelty, unwarranted punishment, or humiliation. The first two abuses, especially, had been a source of Indian complaints since the sixteenth century. Cruelty had to do with the number of lashes, the force applied, and the wounds inflicted. The sense of what was an appropriate number of lashes changed dramatically with time. Where in the sixteenth and early seventeenth centuries, curas normally ordered 50 lashes (and occasionally threatened to castrate offenders),[73] such severity seemed excessive to curas, as well as Indians, in the eighteenth century, and more brutal forms of torture by curas rarely came to the attention of the courts.[74] The cura of Tlalixtac (Oaxaca) in 1784, determined to show that he did not use excessive force, said that he ordered six to twelve lashes for minor offenses and fifteen to 25 for serious offenses: abusive behavior toward magistrates, fathers, wives, and children; scandalous behavior or drunkenness in church; and lack of respect to the cura or the temple of God.[75]

The standard of six to twelve and fifteen to 25 lashes is fairly consistent with scattered examples in the trial records, where priests said they ordered three or four lashes for Indian men and two or three for women who did not attend mass, recite the doctrina, or confess and take communion.[76] Repeated failures to fulfill spiritual duties constituted more serious offenses from the cura's point of view. By repetition, they became deliberate sins, mortal rather than venial in the eyes of church fathers, as did insolence to the cura, adultery, and other threats to the sanctity of the family. Several late colonial curas reported giving fifteen to 20 lashes to a few local Indians for gross insolence.[77] Curas also regarded town officials who were derelict in their duties as guilty of a serious offense. As leaders, they were held to a higher standard of conduct than the average parishioner. The cura of Tulyahualco in 1817 ordered 25 lashes for an Indian alcalde who was drunk while collecting clerical fees.[78] In this and other cases from the same decade, 25 lashes for such offenses was considered excessive both by the Indians who complained and by the civil courts that passed judgment.[79] Twenty-five lashes—an "arroba de azotes"—was deemed a harsh but deserved punishment for serious transgressions.[80] Any more than 25 constituted cruel punishment.[81] Cruelty could also be gauged by whippings that drew blood. An Indian man of San Nicolás Coatepec in the district of Malinalco received a favorable hearing from the Audiencia of Mexico when he reported that the cura had struck him so hard his flesh split open.[82]

So far as the Indians were concerned, punishment of any kind was cruel if it was perceived as unwarranted or out of proportion to the offense.[83] Complaints often concerned whippings for failure to pay clerical fees or perform labor services, either because these obligations were in legitimate dispute or because the parishioners had been advised that debts and service were not among the offenses that justified corporal punishment by the priest.[84] But it was the first category—whippings on any pretext—that was regarded as particularly offensive by Indian petitioners and their attorneys. They complained that the cura had whipped cantors, alcaldes, and others "without cause," "on frivolous and specious pretexts," "even for the most trivial reasons," or because he did not like a particular official.[85] Among the victims were young men who refused to marry as the cura ordered them to do and men intimidated into serving on his estate.[86] For the presiding magistrate, attorneys highlighted two distressing ramifications of such whippings: that the offending priest was capricious, perhaps sadistic or lascivious; or that he was terrorizing his parishioners in order to make them elect his favorites as village officers and cofradía administrators or serve his personal interests in other ways.[87]

Complaints of this kind measured the cura's conduct against the model of charitable teacher and loving father. As teacher and father, he might justifiably use punishment when it was directed toward correction and commensurate with the offense. Otherwise, the whippings violated not only specific rules of conduct but also the reciprocal obligations between just leaders and loyal subjects. By going to court over abuse and baseless cruelty, the petitioners were affirming these rules of reciprocal obligation. In the title of his memorable book about the struggle over land in Morelos, Arturo Warman quoted villagers who appealed to state officials to protect their rights: "We come to object." But in these eighteenth-century cases, the posture of petitioners more often was respectful and conciliatory: "We come to ask" (Venimos a pedir).[88] These Indians were responding to cues from the colonial courts that particular complaints would be welcomed; and as long as the courts took these complaints seriously, such conflict was not likely to turn into regional violence.

Late colonial complaints against clerical whippings were brought by Indian officials (either on their own behalf or in the name of the community or individual macehuales), and they were particularly sensitive to humiliating violations of rank and privacy. Their complaints affirmed the most basic colonial values of order and respect, and were expressed in terms that would have appealed to audiencia judges even without the royal campaign against parish jails and clerical whippings: here was a parish priest, a royal appointee, whose actions disregarded royal supremacy, fatherly conduct, rank, the honor of women, and personal dignity.

Village leaders' complaints about whippings frequently centered on social rank and sex. Indian leaders of Guayacocotla in 1731 said the priest did not "distinguish between married women [and unmarried women or men], between men of noble ancestry and plebeians."[89] The leaders of San Luis de las Peras, Huichapan district, made the same complaint about their cura in 1785: "he orders lashes without distinction as to standing or sex."[90] It was one thing to whip a macehual for missing mass but quite another to whip a gobernador or other elected official or elder, especially in public.[91] To do so led, in the view of the Indian leaders of Churubusco in 1739, to macehual disrespect toward their principales and *oficiales de república*.[92] Repeatedly, Indian petitioners to the audiencia complained that the cura "strikes even the most important people," including gobernadores, fiscales, alcaldes, principales, and caciques.[93] There was an unresolved tension here that was bound to create trouble: officials were leaders and examples for ordinary parishioners, so their transgressions were more serious threats to public order and merited more severe punishment; yet their honor and privilege customarily exempted them from the humiliation of the whip.

The idea that the young of both sexes might occasionally need a corrective whipping was widely accepted.[94] A whipping was more humiliating for an adult, especially a married woman. When such a whipping was called for, another woman was supposed to administer it out of public view. For adult women, rank and privacy were powerfully intertwined. The most vehement complaints against priests whipping adult women, whether single or married, occurred when the whipping was performed in public and with the woman's buttocks or breasts exposed to view. Inquisition and criminal court records for the eighteenth century contain some grim examples of humiliating, sadistic, or lascivious whippings of Indian and non-Indian women by priests in rural parishes. The priest of Guayacocotla in 1731 reportedly forced a young creole woman to strip off her clothes to receive a public beating on the shoulders for leaving church before mass ended, stripping her modesty (*pudor*) in the process, according to the complaint.[95] In some cases, the priest did the whipping in the privacy of his bedroom as a prelude to sexual assault.[96] Priests who defended the whipping of women were careful to establish that it was done for acceptable reasons, in a private place such as the baptistry, and in the priest's absence.[97]

For many village officials, the most galling thing of all was to be chastised in public. A gobernador might conceivably have held his tongue if he had not been kicked and insulted by the priest in front of the church door after mass, or dragged out of his house for a ceremonious whipping in the plaza, or hit by the priest in a chance encounter.[98] The ultimate humiliation for a local notable was to be forced to drop his pants before being whipped. Ordered to do so by the cura of Tampomolon (eastern San Luis Potosí), the alcalde of Tancanhuitz vehemently refused and menaced the priest with a knife. After two of the alcalde's companions refused to restrain him at the cura's order, he was arrested by other officials and whipped only with great difficulty.[99] The depth of feeling about humiliating disregard for rank and honor is clear in the spontaneous anger and violence villagers sometimes showed when the priest acted this way. Throughout the eighteenth century, whippings of these kinds set off village resistance in which the cura said he had to hide or flee for his life.[100]

It might be argued that to go to court over such humiliations was to admit weakness and inability to defend one's own honor. But these were not matters of personal honor between men of roughly equal standing; they were cases of damage to official standing, as well as personal reputation. They were cases of honor across classes of royal officials—where the honor of a lower official was impugned by a higher official or by an outsider of higher rank. The crown had long been the arbiter in such cases; it was most securely in the royal courts that a village official might have his personal and official reputation vindicated without risking fatal consequences or punishment even for an assault on a royal official.[101] And despite sometimes interminable delays, the late colonial audiencias were more inclined than ever to look favorably on complaints of this kind.

The audiencias tolerated whippings by priests or on their orders mainly by omission—most cases probably escaped their attention. The high courts depended on district magistrates and local Indians to bring the violations to their attention. In about one out of five cases, the cura had clearly violated the laws against administering whippings himself. Indians sometimes testified that the offending priest asserted that he was the master and could do what he wanted,[102] but priests did not claim in court that they had the right to whip and beat. When cases of priests doing the whipping or beating came up, the courts rarely bothered to question the priest's justification: that he struck out in a moment of passion, responding instantly to an act that violated his honor or the good order of the parish. But whether or not he wielded the whip himself, they were not likely to favor the cura in these cases.

Why Indians and curas said parishioners were whipped follows roughly the patterns for imprisonment, with which such complaints were sometimes linked. In court, the curas outlined reasons for whippings that fell safely within acceptable limits, where their parishioners sometimes saw only arbitrary acts or ulterior motives. Still, there was a rough consensus when the issue was penance for mortal sins confessed or for failure to fulfill religious duties. For parishioners, these duties centered on attendance at mass, knowledge of doctrina, support of catechism classes for children, annual confession and communion, timely reports to the priest of communicants who were gravely ill, and the presentation of dead infants for Christian burial.[103] But for the many priests who still saw themselves as the protectors of the family and the keepers of public morality or who were especially sensitive about their honor, any act of defiance toward them was also a violation of religious duty. For these curas, the whip was the appropriate remedy for disobedience of all kinds, especially public drunkenness, gambling, billiard-playing, illicit sex and lewd behavior, marital disputes, disrespect to the cura, and ignoring his advice (especially his warnings to cease disputes and litigation).[104]

The priests of Zimatlan and Tlalixtac outlined the purposes of whipping in equally broad, traditional terms in their 1784 appeals to the crown. For the Zimatlan priest, Dr. Ruiz y Cervantes, these purposes were religious duty and public order: "to punish the parishioners' abuses and make them hear mass, learn *doctrina*, and fulfill their obligations to the church"; and "[to see that] they live pacifically, that they become tame, domesticated, and obedient not only to their *curas* and *vicarios* but also to the secular judges."[105] In arguing for the whip, he was quick to separate it from the parish jail. The whip was a positive force, indispensable to salvation and public order; the jail was counterproductive because it instilled too much fear and caused too much unhappiness. Indians, he said, looked on imprisonment as a fate worse than death. Cura Ferra of Tlalixtac also divided his reasons for using the whip into two categories, but he focused more directly on what he regarded as the root cause of Indian crimes and sins. His second category was Ruiz y Cervantes's first: compelling parishioners to fulfill their Christian obligations. His first category was the control of drunkenness, which he regarded as the source of, or pretext for, many other evils that the priest had an obligation to control, including rape, incest, adultery, concubinage, theft, mistreatment of family members, and disrespect to God and his temple and priests.[106] But few royal officials in the late eighteenth century would have agreed with Ferra's and Ruiz y Cervantes's appeal to traditional prerogatives, even if the priest's whip promoted social order and respect for secular judges.

Order was a watchword for the curas who were called to justify their use of the whip in Indian parishes at the end of the colonial period: Indians were disorderly; they needed restraint and punishment for their "detestable abominations."[107] These justifications echo the conception of Indians as natural children. Schoolchildren required the threat of the whip to learn their letters, and the same rule applied to adult Indians. Pedro Ugaris, the cura of Tlalmanalco in 1766, made the analogy explicit and added a bitter postscript when he explained why he had whipped a disrespectful Indian: "It is the custom to do so, as if he were a child beginning to learn his first letters, even though this individual is well versed in every bad habit and entirely too diligent in his drunkenness, for he uses it to loosen his tongue and speak without restraint."[108]

Sacerdotal Powers

The lofty position of the priest, his separation from parishioners as a person with special spiritual and judicial powers, was represented in the ceremonies he conducted and the array of fine vestments he wore for special masses throughout the year. He oversaw the community's rites of passage and passed judgment on its moral well-being. As the expert in Latin, the esoteric language of God, he had access to privileged information. His actions were invested with mystery. The magical power of religious images was in his hands.[109] His blessing of a new home, his prayers for rain, his propitiation of unseen powers and colonial superiors were valued remedies. Sometimes, it was enough for him to elevate the Host or display the cross or the image of a revered saint to calm a public disturbance.

The parish priest's symbolic and substantive authority at once separated him from parishioners, acknowledged other divisions in nature and society, and served as a powerful point of union. It was the priest who performed the mass, with parishioners as onlookers and respondents. He was the master of the sacred texts, the teacher of timeless knowledge. The idea that the majesty of the divine diminished the human project was powerfully evoked by Christianity as well as by precolumbian religions; but the church and its priests represented a way for believers to transcend their own mortality and participate in that divine majesty. By withholding the sacraments or extinguishing the lamp, the priest could jeopardize their salvation. By preaching and teaching, he strengthened his spiritual leadership across a wide range of social life.

The most powerful of the priest's sacerdotal weapons was "the sword of excommunication," "the terrible arms of the church." [110] Since expulsion from the church effectively meant expulsion from society altogether, it was a powerful tool of social control if used sparingly. Excommunication was, therefore, not taken lightly; but it was rarely irreversible. A parish priest's order was provisional; it depended on review by the bishop's court, where the victim was encouraged to repent. Parish priests very occasionally excommunicated an Indian official for disobeying or attacking them or a royal magistrate of the district, violating the church as a sanctuary from arrest, impeding the priest's spiritual activities, or repeated blasphemy.[111] But in each case, the excommunicated person was reconciled and restored to membership in the church, if not to his place of authority in the community.[112] One priest, Dr. Agustín Río de la Loza of San Sebastián Querétaro, resorted to a mass excommunication of parishioners who did not fulfill the annual obligation of confession and communion in 1777. In this case, so many parishioners had not taken communion—more than a thousand—that the excommunications and the priest's use of the prison for a few recalcitrants look more like futile gestures than acts of great coercive power.[113]

Words were the cura's main instrument for obtaining obedience: sermons, admonitions at baptism and marriage, interrogations in the confessional, informal exhortations and warnings,[114] and the continuous instruction of parishioners in basic doctrine. As the bishops of the First Provincial Council put it in 1555, "Declamations are the priest's weapons." [115] Or, as the Council of Trent more gently emphasized, the priest should use exhortation and persuasion rather than force.[116] It was an approach that Domingo de la Peña, the interim cura of Almoloya in 1805, employed so well that his Indian parishioners petitioned the archbishop's court to appoint him as titular priest:

He has preached the Gospel to us morning and afternoon on holy days, fitting his style to his audience in order to nurture in all of us the fruit of the divine word. . . . In the confessional, in the pulpit, and even in our own homes he exhorts us and persuades us to follow him with his gentle teaching and with his example. . . . He leads by dint of the power of his explanations, not by force.[117]

After independence, the pulpit was often used to spread political rumors and warnings.[118] It is not clear how common this practice was in the late colonial period, but once the Independence War broke out in September 1810, curas used the Sunday sermon to proclaim their political sympathies.[119] A few sermons by parish priests from this period were published for wider distribution. One was the "advice" of the cura of Apam (Hidalgo), Pedro José Ignacio Calderón, to his parishioners on December 12, 1810.[120] It is a good example of exhortation by flattery. Father Calderón began by expressing his gratitude for their response to news of the insurrection: "I shall never forget, my beloved parishioners, the religiosity and patriotism you showed on November 4 when some seductive tongues spread among you the sad news that American insurgents had seized the capital." He praised their solidarity with Spaniards and the Spanish government ("Driven by the wish to defend religion and the state, you sought out the peninsular Spaniards with well-equipped horses in order to hide them in the woods"), outlined their special rights as Indians and the legitimacy of the colonial system, and ended with an exhortation against revolution on the grounds that America already belonged to Americans: "We already possess these dominions and do not need to acquire them anew for, with Ferdinand VII at our head, we Americans are the owners of America."

Words could also be used to intimidate, whether they came from the pulpit, in public or private speech, or in writing to a local official. Indians of Santa María Atengo and San Francisco Zayula in the parish of Tepetitlan (near Tula), who moved a suit against their cura over clerical fees and services in 1790, complained to the ecclesiastical court that he threatened them with damnation if they insisted on the new schedule of fees.[121] Indians of Tultitlan in 1809 complained that the cura used the pulpit to make cruel fun of parishioners he disliked, and to damn their souls.[122] In 1796, an array of witnesses, including a young priest, testified that Joseph Manuel Sotomayor used classes in doctrine to satirize his enemies.[123] In these cases, the witnesses' word for what the cura said is all we have. But in a letter to the gobernador of Atlapulco, José Bargayanta, the priest of Ocoyoacac (Tenango del Valle district), spoke for himself:

My son: All of you with your continual bouts of drinking want to obey neither God nor your superiors in this world. . . . I paternally order you to come for the benediction mass that is soon to take place, and to the regular mass on Sundays. If you do not, I shall go to the superior authorities, and they will oblige you to be obedient and not to live drunk. In the name of God in his Holy Grace. Ocoyoacac, June 9, 1767.

Your Cura who in God loves you.[124]

In fact, Bargayanta was attempting to intimidate his parishioners, who were involved in a legal dispute with him over clerical fees. His strategy in this letter was to dispense with the initial pleasantries of formal correspondence and begin with banners of authority flying in all directions. Here on paper was what Graham Greene called "the old parish intonation"—the "manner of authority and impatience."[125] The cura's tone and message were quite different in his formal responses to the audiencia during the same litigation. There he took the tack of meekly pledging to obey the old arancel while doing his best to delay compliance, first by requesting further clarification from the high court and then by arguing that, since a new arancel was being prepared, he should strike an interim agreement with the pueblo.

The confessional could be an especially powerful instrument of spiritual and social control, involving both the hortatory and the intimidating uses of words. More than just a formal accounting of sins, a mere prelude to the sacraments of penance and communion, confession was supposed to be an "act of contrition" in which a "holy fear" of damnation and feelings of shame would move the sinner to repentance and virtue. On the priest's part, it was an act of instruction, persuasion, judgment, and reconciliation. Confession was an arena in which licensed priests sat as judge and tutor over the personal conduct and intentions of every communicant. As a confessor, the priest occupied a position of unquestioned authority as "supreme judge," able to interrogate, exhort, or reprimand the humble penitent.[126] He was seated and covered, "for there he is representing the person of Christ as Judge." The penitent was on his knees with head bare, "like an accused criminal."[127]

Because of the seal of secrecy, we cannot know how effective the confessional was as an instrument of spiritual and temporal direction and how invasive its messages about conscience and personal guilt were.[128] Scattered comments by bishops and rural parishioners, lengthier discussion in the confessional manuals, and a few Inquisition trial records offer some evidence of how priests tried to use the confessional for social control, but indicate more strongly that confession had a limited impact on the behavior of peasant parishioners.

Bishops occasionally reported that they had instructed their parish priests to use the confessional to make a political point or exhort their parishioners about a particular issue. Bishop Cabañas assured the crown on March 15, 1816, that his parish priests were using the pulpit and the confessional to sway parishioners against the independence movement.[129] The confessor could also withhold absolution from a penitent who had not made a full confession or followed his instructions. As we saw earlier, priests who solicited sexual favors from women in the confessional occasionally threatened not to confess or absolve them until the women consented. Others threatened to withhold absolution until a pregnant, unmarried penitent confessed the name of the child's father.[130] More frequently (and justifiably from the ecclesiastical courts' standpoint), confessors withheld absolution from women who confessed to having been propositioned or seduced by a former confessor until the women denounced the offender to the Inquisition.[131]

Printed confessional manuals document the ideal: what the confessor should ask, what sins he might expect to find, and what kind of admissions he should elicit, in an unhurried confession by a penitent who was responsive to the wide-ranging probings of a persistent examiner, who fully understood the meaning of sin, and who had reflected deeply on his behavior since he last knelt beside the priest.[132] But these ideal conditions rarely obtained in rural parishes of the eighteenth century. Even with the help of visiting assistants, the cura and vicarios of an Indian parish would not have been able to spend more than a few minutes with most of the thousand or so penitents who pressed in to confess each spring. The task was enormous. Juan Miguel Tinoco wrote in the early 1760's that he assisted the cura of Zinacantepec in the confessional from sunrise to sunset from the second week of Lent to Pentecost. During that time, he confessed over 1,300 Indians plus the non-Indians of the parish.[133] There was little time even to ask many of the questions in the manuals, let alone to probe the answers or explore the penitent's thoughts and actions during the preceding twelve months. The lack of privacy during the Easter rush also inhibited full confessions. If confessions were whispered so that others in line would not overhear them, the priest might also have trouble hearing what was said. He could ask the penitent to speak louder, or he could gloss over a soft-spoken declaration. Some parishes had no confessional furniture, or not enough for all the priests at work during Lent.[134]

But the problems undoubtedly ran deeper than lack of time and equipment. A hundred years earlier, the *Itinerario* had been resigned to Indian parishioners making inadequate confessions even under intense scrutiny. The *Farol* (1713) observed that since Indians were so given to vices, a confession every twelve months could barely begin to plumb the depths of their sins. Indians, Manuel Pérez averred, acted as if they thought they were responsible only for sins committed during Lent; or they would abstain from adultery, drunkenness, and other willful sins for a few days before confession in order to prove their repentance; or they did not regard themselves as having sinned if they were given the meat that they ate on Friday or got drunk at someone else's expense. Other commentaries on Indian confessions add to the examples of misconstrued sins and omissions. Antonio de Ribadeneyra, the oidor with a special interest in church-state relations, said Indians ate game on Friday, thinking it was like fish. Or they would confess early in Lent and eat meat on Fridays thereafter, as if their lenten duties ended with confession and absolution.[135]

Confessors would have to accommodate themselves to the Indians' opacity: even after more than a century of Christianity, lamented the *Itinerario*, they often withheld their serious sins and did not seem to be contrite.[136] The challenge was to instill enough repentance to justify absolution; a full accounting of sins was too much to hope for.[137] And if all the willful, mortal sins could not be teased out, absolution could still be granted if the omissions were judged to be the result of ignorance rather than malice.[138]

El ayudante de cura (1766) repeated these laments. Its author, Pérez de Velasco, a veteran of 40 years' parish service, thought that Indians confessed in empty formulas when they did not lie or conceal their more serious sins.[139] The typical Indian penitent would, he said, mention five or six venial sins. When the confessor asked how many times he or she had committed each of them, the answer would be the same: if he said three for the first, he would say three for the rest. Asked to continue, he would say that he had nothing more to confess. "If you continue examining him about matters he has not identified you will find that he has sinned in many of them, sometimes seriously"; but in many cases, even an exhaustive interrogation would not produce a satisfactory confession. For the confessor of Indians, he concluded, book learning was less important than long experience in their customs, and much charity and patience.[140]

Occasionally, a parish priest commented on Indian confessions in his petitions or reports. In a long letter to the viceroy in 1790 about the need for Indian schools, the parish priest of Tlaola (Huauchinango district, Veracruz) used confession as an example of Indian ignorance, insolence, and lack of good Christian habits. He found it especially hard to get his Indian parishioners to "feel the anguish of their sins." When he warned them that

God will punish you with eternal afflictions, they answer, "let God do as he pleases"; and I have to remind them that God does not wish to condemn anyone, that he only wants the sinner to change his ways and truly live. To this they respond that they have only a few sins and therefore little need to repent. . . . This is how many of them make their confession.[141]

Even when they did feel contrite, he suspected that they withheld many sins out of fear. He acknowledged that he was usually called to administer the last rites but thought that his parishioners did so with "mundane ends in mind," fearing that if they did not notify him, he would whip the fiscal or one of the bystanders who ought to have summoned him. He arrived "eager for their salvation," but the sick confessees would make only a "very superficial and perfunctory" confession.

Under the circumstances, curas probably regarded confession more as an annual rite of reconciliation with God and community, and an opportunity to insist that parishioners know the rudiments of doctrina, than as a time to probe deeply into the penitent's conscience.[142] The most consequential confession, where a more thorough probing by the priest was sometimes possible and a more willing penitent likely, was the deathbed encounter. For believers who remained lucid, this may have been a moment of earnest desire for final reconciliation. But since the penitent usually died within hours or days, its usefulness as a means of social control lay mostly in anticipation and in the sense of remorse it may have induced in observers. If the Tlaola case is representative, even the final confession was a disappointment to the cura. It also must have been an inhibiting disappointment to the penitent if the confessor was chewing on a cigar or would not draw near enough to hear a weak voice.[143]

The quality of the confessions also had to do with the confessor's preparation, his character, and how long he had served in the parish. An effective confessor in a rural parish needed to know the parishioners and gain their trust. A new pastor, or one who regarded time in the confessional as a numbing routine or had violated the seal of secrecy, would have had great difficulty drawing out an extensive confession under the best of conditions. A new cura or vicario did not have the advantage of knowing his parishioners' habits or having heard their confessions before. But experience was not enough. To get results, the confessor also had to be dignified and patient. Indians testifying for the gobernador of Huazalingo (Hidalgo) in 1789 complained that their cura rushed them through confession: "Because he does not want them to linger, they go to the confessional like someone going to kiss an image." And the gobernador claimed that local people did not confess serious sins because they did not trust the cura to hold his tongue.[144]

Trust and extensive confessions also depended on the confessor's knowledge of the parishioners' native language. Especially in the archdiocese, Indian parishioners had confessed in their first language since the sixteenth century, and though by the end of the colonial period, many spoke Spanish too, they did not want to confess in Spanish. Ribadeneyra recounted a story from the confessional of Dr. Josef del Pinal, a canon of the Collegiate Church of Our Lady of Guadalupe at Tepeyac, that illustrates this continuing preference and the communication gap. An Indian came to the canon for confession and began to speak in Nahuatl. "Not understanding the Mexican language, [the canon] urged [the Indian] to confess in Castilian, finding him to be very fluent in that language. But the Indian stopped him short with his reply, 'And you, Father, will you confess in Latin?' "[145] Confession through interpreters was even less satisfactory, since penitents would have been inhibited by the presence of a neighbor or stranger in this private and potentially embarassing encounter.[146]

The priests' concern for teaching Indians to feel contrition was part of a more general preoccupation with their lack of shame. The senses of shame and honor (*pundonor*) were signs of adulthood, maturity.[147] Indians were regarded as having too little of both, and serious curas groped for ways to cultivate those feelings in their charges. The chosen means was sometimes a crude public spectacle. In 1761, the cura of San Miguel Acambay (Hidalgo) had grown impatient with the failure of Indian adults to learn the catechism properly. Following a familiar strategy, he arrested several men and ordered them whipped for not knowing doctrina and not confessing. But this time he went further:

> The next day I held the catechism exercise that I had established in the *cabecera* every Saturday for children five to ten years old. And I made the Indian prisoners attend, arraying the children before them and making them pray the *doctrina*, telling the men they should be ashamed to see that the little ones knew it, and that they, adults, married, and with children of their own, did not. Having returned them to the parish jail and seen that they were fed, I learned the next day that they had escaped, breaking out through a window.[148]

There were limits to how much edifying humiliation even respectful villagers would take from their priest. Here the cura had gone too far. The men had endured a whipping and a night in jail, but after being ridiculed in front of the children, they would not endure another affront. If a late colonial priest whipped Indian officials in public, his victims were more likely to start a lawsuit than to flee. And a cura could even set off a village uprising with too much humiliation if he had only his personal authority to rely on. How much was too much he would have to learn by experience and a knowledge of his parishioners.

Gestures of Deference

Imprisonment, whippings, excommunication, and denial of absolution were not everyday events. Routine obedience involved not just brute force and verbal intimidation, but bonds of respect, prestige, mutual advantage, and predictable conduct. These bonds of respect and rules of conduct expressed the asymmetrical relationship between the priest and his parishioners. The priest was to be a father, the parishioners his children. The priest's main obligation was to direct the moral and spiritual life of the parish with compassion and justice; the parishioners' main obligation was to follow his direction. This relationship was confirmed daily in words, gestures, and silences, and in special rites throughout the year.

Which of these acts of deference were performed fervently or routinely and which grudgingly or from fear—or whether such distinctions would have made sense to people then—can be determined only from an accumulation of acts of obedience and defiance anchored in time and place.[149] This chapter draws mainly on examples of compliance, and there *was* a general willingness to defer to authority; but acceptance of many aspects of the colonial order was compatible with conflict and open resistance, as the chapters of Parts Three and Four suggest.

Indian parishioners were expected to use physical gestures of appreciation and devotion in the presence of the priest that implied supplication, gestures that recalled the priest's deferential genuflections during the mass, the posture of many images of saints at prayer (such as Saint Dominic before the Cross or the penitent Saint Peter), and the devotion demanded of all believers when the consecrated Host appeared in public. In the case of the consecrated Host, deference was more than a norm. It was a rule that carried legal sanctions. *Recopilación* 1-1-26 provided that all believers were to kneel when the Host passed and follow the procession to its destination.[150] Since all Indians were presumptively believers, any Indian over fourteen years old who did not comply was to be brought before the local magistrate. And since the Host was carried by the cura or a vicario, the gesture of devotion was expressed toward the priest, as well as the sacrament. When the parish priest of Temascaltepec complained in 1805 that the subdelegado had not knelt to honor the sacrament, he emphasized that it was he, the cura, who had passed the subdelegado bearing the Host.[151]

From the beginning of the colonial period, Indian parishioners would have associated kneeling, bowing, and kissing with respect and entreaties to their priest as spiritual father. The first bishops of New Spain, meeting on April 27, 1539, designated appropriate gestures of respect as a way to control excessive deference. Indians were to be advised to show esteem according to rank,

without kneeling, crossing themselves, or wounding themselves in the chest, nor any other act that appears to be adoration. They should kneel only when receiving the bishop's blessing. When seeking pardon from a regular priest or any priest who is not a prelate, it is enough to kiss his hand or the regular's habit.[152]

Of course, kissing the habit or hand also required at least a bow.

Despite the bishops' efforts, some parish priests expected and received extravagant gestures of deference, instituted out of a desire to impress parishioners with their "stately superiority" (predominio magestuoso).[153] The Franciscans of Texcoco in 1722 complained of the "imperious conduct" of the secular vicario foráneo, Pedro Güemes, who staged solemn entrances into Texcoco and the parish's villages. The Indian fiscal would precede Güemes in his carriage, raising high the staff of office. The Franciscans complained that Güemes encouraged the Indians to address him by the exalted title of Señoría, as if he were lord of the territory. The Indians received him with flowered arches and tolling bells, and great numbers of them clustered around him and followed his orders—thanks, thought the Franciscans, to "the extraordinary estimation they have of him from the imperious way he acts and treats them."[154]

If the Franciscans can be believed, Güemes was unusually successful in his manipulation of ceremony, but they, like other priests, well appreciated what it accomplished: pomp and gestures of respect heightened the priest's standing and acknowledged his leadership; they located him above the rest for all to see.[155] All parish priests expected to be received ceremoniously when they entered a village, with some combination of flowers, arches, bells, music, and a little procession of the local notables. It is not always clear whether this was done willingly, even eagerly, or as a routine emptied of special reverence, or under duress. Fear was definitely involved in some cases, and in any event, a fine distinction between fear and consent (even willing consent) would be misleading in situations where people complied because they had no choice. Since fear—"holy fear"— was regarded as a positive instrument of the faith, one of the two wings of flight toward God,[156] and Indians were sometimes referred to as "children of fear," it would be surprising if fear were not intended and felt, at least subconsciously.

A priest could sometimes evoke fear without force or overt threats—by withholding services, by showing great anger, or with changes of expression like furrowing his brow, puffing out his cheeks, flashing his eyes, and opening them wide.[157] But fear as a means of bringing parishioners to heel was not enthusiastically supported by official policy. The curas who are documented in judicial records near the end of the colonial period as ruling by fear were charged with abusing their authority. In a complaint against the cura of San Juan Atlistaca (Tlapa district, Guerrero) in 1795 for spiritual neglect, village officials said he instilled "fear and horror" by his conduct.[158] Even the *Itinerario*, which approved of moderate corporal punishment and spoke optimistically of "fears that serve as spurs to virtue," referred repeatedly to abuses of the Indians' "reverential fear" of the cura.[159] This fearful respect was not to be used to extract donations, force Indians to marry, or make them agree to contracts or unnecessary service. If an Indian had good reason to fear the cura, he was not required to attend mass.[160]

An Indian parishioner who understood the cura's appetite for deference might save himself some grief and atone for provocative conduct with an extravagant display of humility. An Indian alcalde of Poncitlan (Jalisco) in 1727 angered the cura by appearing in the priests' residence with his staff of office. When the alcalde declared that he "had to enter with it," the cura grabbed him by the hair, knocked him down, kicked him, and wanted to have him whipped. By kissing the cura's feet (at the urging of the Inquisition commissioner, who witnessed the exchange), the alcalde escaped the whipping.[161] The gesture here was one of both intimacy and distance. The priest, like the image of Christ at the altar, was above the Indian parishioner. He could be approached, even touched reverentially, but with some fear. He stood above the parishioner in two senses— guarding and looking down upon him.

In this case, as in many others, the kneeling and kissing were more than gestures of respect. They were supplications for indulgence, which the priest as father and confessor had a moral obligation to grant. Indians of San Simón Tototepec in the parish of Acapetlahuaya (Zacualpan district) and their cura-coadjutor, Gregorio Agustín de Villavicencio, were in a heated dispute in 1775 over whether Indians had to pay first fruits. Lately, the cura had sent out his lay assistants to make house-by-house collections. They tried to tie up and arrest María Francisca, whose husband had not paid, but she resisted and could not be captured. When he heard of this, the cura told his assistants, "We are going to find that woman and make her pay the first fruits." They found María Francisca in the company of two other women. All three said that their families had already paid. The cura noticed some pieces of wood in María Francisca's patio that were the right size for clubs and asked what they were for. "Do you want to fight with me?" he asked. No, replied the women, those sticks were for torches. The cura again insisted on payment, and the women replied: "It would be better for you to leave here and see that the people confess and fulfill their spiritual duties to the church. That deserves your attention, not trying to collect *primicias*." Furious, the cura kicked one woman, hit another with a stick, and had all of them tied up, whipped, and imprisoned for several days. According to the women, after they had provoked the cura with their remark, they got down on their knees and pleaded with him not to have them whipped on the buttocks, but he refused. After the whipping, they knelt again and asked for his pardon, pleading with him not to punish them further, but he had them locked up anyway.[162] Beyond the question of the first fruits, the women's complaint against the cura was that he had not heeded their abject pleas. Their very indignation affirmed the rules of hierarchy: submission merited pardon and forgiveness.[163]

The habit of seeking pardon from the priest carried over to other colonial officials who were regarded as fathers and patrons. Indian petitions to the district magistrate or his lieutenant were often made in figurative genuflections. The Indians of Santa Ana Tetlama, writing through their escribano to the alcalde mayor of Tancítaro (Michoacán) about abuses by their cura in 1699, began their appeal with the words, "Prostrate and kneeling at your feet, we come to ask, . . ." and closed with "We kiss the feet of Your Excellency."[164] The petition of Indians from Oztoticpac and Cuautlancingo (Valley of Mexico) to the Audiencia of Mexico in 1807 to enforce the customary arrangement for clerical fees emphasized their helplessness and the patronage of the crown: "We are sad, confused, and upset. . . . We have always been willingly and affectionately under the favor and protection of our sovereign [the king of Spain]."[165] District magistrates and provincial governors undoubtedly encouraged or even demanded this kind of submission. As the governor of Puebla stated in response to a complaint against his harshness in 1772, it seemed to him that people obeyed royal officials more from habit than obligation, and that without fear their authority would be endangered.[166]

The carefully deferential tone Indians took in their supplications does not prove that they believed wholeheartedly in the hierarchy to which they paid respect, but it would be a mistake to assume that the pleas were all sly obfuscations, empty gestures, or artifacts of fear. The bishop of Oaxaca's observation in 1777 that Indians generally hated Spaniards but loved and even worshipped the king should not be discounted.[167] Petitions addressed by Mexican villages to the king of Spain many years after Spanish rule ended and "the miracle of monarchism" that Alfonso Reyes observed in the popular culture of modern Mexico are vestiges of that colonial loyalty. Where Indian villagers did accept the paternal metaphor and the colonial order, they were capable of acting out of faith more than fear. Their appeals to "royal piety and protection" were rewarded often enough to preserve the appearance of reciprocity.[168] Members of stable, prosperous communities that had been favorably treated by the colonial courts undoubtedly had the best reasons to believe in gestures of respect.

Perhaps the most common gesture of deference and respect between men in the colonial period, including the parish priests, was tipping or removing one's hat.[169] The two *politesses* were not equivalent. Tipping was mostly used as a gesture of courtesy and respect between equals—two Indians or two Spaniards tipping their hats to each other on the street—or as a gesture of deference when

FIG. 7. A customary show of deference. An English visitor to central and northwestern Mexico in the 1820's found the male gesture of removing one's hat in greeting such a distinctive and widespread habit that he included in his account a drawing of bedraggled country men (with long hair similar to Indian *balcarrotas*) in the act.

a villager passed a cura, magistrate, or other official but did not stop for a more formal greeting.[170] Removing the hat was typically a prelude to further face-to-face communication. But when the cura or magistrate was being addressed in this way, he did not have to remove his own hat unless he was dealing with someone who was his social equal or from whom he was about to ask a favor.[171] The cura of Cuautitlan, even while bursting with anger over the local magistrate's repeated failures to provide the judicial assistance he needed, went to the man's offices and removed his hat, offered a civil greeting, and asked after the health of the alcalde mayor. The civilities ended when the magistrate again refused assistance, and the cura hit him with his cane. Once the magistrate had refused to help, the cura felt that deference was no longer required because the man had not reciprocated, had demeaned him by not acting as a magistrate should. The cura's *bastón*, the symbol of his office and judicial authority, became the avenging instrument of a higher duty to order and honor. But since the cura was supposed to be a model of moderation and gentility, it would not do for him to brain a magistrate, even when provoked. He was not supposed to act out of anger or to administer punishment. The conclusion to this particular impasse must have pleased the royal officials in Mexico City. The magistrate and the priest had a public reconciliation, thanks to the efforts of the archbishop during his pastoral visit of 1788.[172]

A parishioner who failed to uncover before the priest invited trouble. In 1815, Tomás Miramontes, the Indian escribano and cantor of Tepechitlan (Zacatecas), was imprisoned by the magistrate for his many vices and disruptive acts. When called to bear witness against the Indian's conduct, the interim cura, José María García Diego, recalled Miramontes' habit of speaking to him in an imperious way and with his hat on. During the tense transfer of parish authority in Capuluac from the Augustinians to a secular priest in 1750, the new coadjutor, Anastasio de Santa María, kicked an Indian for not uncovering in his presence.[173]

In effect, removing one's hat before the cura, the magistrate, or a local Spaniard was a rite of access that at once recognized inferiority and requested indulgence. Just as the main altar of the parish church where the priest celebrated mass was a visible but remote stage—elevated and often protected by a railing—and just as relics and images of saints in the smaller and more proximate side altars were often encased, elevated, or otherwise separated from the touch of worshippers, the priest and other authorities were set apart in these gestures of deference. Even in moments of spontaneous anger and violence against acts of the cura or his allies, the priest was rarely harmed—much less often than were district magistrates, tax collectors, and village officials.

Bastones and Balcarrotas

The mixture of love and fear, natural authority and punishment, and persuasion and coercion in parochial practice was symbolized by the priest's cane, often called the bastón.[174] Usually a long, stout staff, it served as both a walking stick and a weapon. Above all, like the Indian alcalde's or the alcalde mayor's staff of office (*vara de justicia*), it represented his authority and justice, although unlike the district magistrate's staff of office, it was not an indispensable emblem. A priest would be recognized without his staff, whereas a local or district magistrate might not be.[175] Still, a priest who held the title of juez eclesiástico was not likely to leave home without it.[176] It was as much a part of his regular apparel as his cassock and hat. One of the few extravagances in which a lowly vicario might indulge was a fancy, silver-tipped bastón.[177] Occasionally, a cura wrote metaphorically about his authority in terms of his staff, comparing it with the stronger, rigid one of the district judge. In 1734, the Franciscan cura of Toluca, lamenting the bad habits of Indians in his parish, said that the priest had only a fig limb for a staff (*vara de higuera*) while the ministers of the king's justice had an iron staff (*vara de hierro*) with which to reduce them to the yoke of Christian law.[178]

Bastones appeared in the judicial records mainly when used as weapons or instruments of punishment.[179] These records suggest that the cura used his ubiquitous bastón to assert precedence and power, not only to symbolize it. This menacing, sometimes wounding use of the bastón was usually directed at Indian parishioners or at the district magistrate's lieutenant. In 1758, Indians of the village of Aquiapa in the parish of Pozontepec (Sultepec district) contested certain fees that the cura claimed were owed to him. When he went to Aquiapa for the feast of the patron saint, some parishioners shouted that "the *padre* couldn't order them around like those of Pozontepec." The cura became angry and struck a woman with his bastón.[180]

According to Indian witnesses in other cases, the priest used his bastón to instill fear and effect submission. During a 1760 dispute over whether Indian parishioners had to pay first fruits, villagers in the parish of Tejupilco (Edo. de México) claimed that the cura had ordered his vicarios to hit them with their bastones and cut their hair.[181] In 1783, Indians from San Lorenzo Huichilapan in the district of Tenango del Valle complained of cruelty by their vicario de pie fijo, Joseph María Rodríguez. They expected to be punished for not knowing doctrina, but lately, as a suit over clerical fees progressed, they said he was acting with excessive cruelty. Now when he summoned an Indian, right away he hit him with his bastón and knocked him to the floor; and he used the bastón in the same way on the street if the Indian parishioners did not treat him "with every type of submission."[182] The Indian alcalde of Ocotlan (Guadalajara), who had been beaten in anger by the cura, also expressed fear of his cura's arbitrary ways ("el mucho mando del cura").[183]

Curas also struck or menaced lieutenants of the district magistrate with their bastones as an act of precedence and disapproval. In 1790, relations between the coadjutor of Ajuchitlan and the subdelegado of Tetela del Río (Guerrero) were strained over fees and cofradías. One day, the subdelegado's lieutenant went to the cura's residence with a message from his superior and was told by a servant that the cura was indisposed, that he was taking a bath. According to the lieutenant, he waited outside for an hour before he lost patience and burst into the cura's room to find him lying on his cot. The lieutenant withdrew to the corridor, whereupon the cura came out and shook his bastón at him.[184] Curas were likely to defend these uses of the bastón as an application of their authority as teachers. As the cura of Cuautitlan put it in 1788, he hit the lieutenant "not to wound but to correct."[185]

Curas shared the symbols of authority with the saints' images, and expected to share the same relations of deference. The parish priest of San Pedro de la Cañada (Querétaro) in 1795 was particularly outraged by a story his predecessor recounted of how an Indian, needing a staff with which to dance in a local fiesta, "dared to ascend the altar and despoil the archangel Michael of his *bastón*." To the cura's mind, this was a fitting example of "the little veneration and respect with which such people can treat the images and sacred articles."[186]

Indians' hair was another important article of the cura's figurative and literal claims on Indian obedience. Hairstyles varied somewhat by region and rank, but in general Indians wore their hair long, often divided on each side of the head (see Fig. 7). These gatherings of long hair, or *balcarrotas*, as they were called in the late colonial period, were an important symbol for Indians and non-Indians alike. To the Indians, they were a proud reminder of old ways and local identity. How one looked, moved, and spoke was part of what it was to belong to a family, a lineage, and a residential group. To their non-Indian contemporaries, the balcarrotas distinguished Indians as a social category, another in the series of gratifyingly visible markers between two increasingly porous social classifications. As the cura of Ocuilan reported when he confidently identified the rebels in a 1772 tumulto, "most were Indians with their *balcarrotas*."[187] The hairstyle was so closely associated with Indianness that, as the cura of Santo Domingo Hueyapan reported in 1782, some castas took to going about in Indian dress and balcarrotas, trying to pass as Indians in order to escape their tax obligations and gain access to Indian lands.[188] The cura of Ixtapan (Zacualpan district) in 1773 documented the opposite behavior: some Indians were cutting off their *balcarrotas* in order to pass as non-Indians and avoid paying tribute.[189]

Partly because dress and appearance were convenient distinctions between Indians and Spaniards, colonial lawmakers supported Indians in their preference for long hair. But there was more to the meaning of long hair than a class distinction or a quaint sumptuary rule. To have one's hair cut or pulled out was a deep humiliation, as Ylario Antonio Cabrera, former Indian gobernador of Tecomic (Xochimilco district), testified in 1796: "Indians regard the loss of their balcarrotas, even if they are scissored off for an offense or injury, as an extremely grave offense by whoever ordered or did it."[190] To Cabrera, it was not a question of social standing; any Indian would have been deeply offended and threatened.[191] Ribadeneyra recognized that hair was intimately connected to a sense of wellbeing. He wrote in his commentary on issues raised in the Fourth Provincial Council that "Indian children have their hair trimmed so that it forms a serpent adorning their entire head, believing this ensures the child's health. And if it is shorn, they believe that he is sure to die."[192] *Recopilación* 1-1-18 quoted royal cedulas of 1581 and 1587 recognizing that Indians in some parts of America regarded long hair as an "ancient and venerable ornament." Since they took any cutting of their hair as a humiliating affront and punishment, priests should not cut it even for baptism: "they are to be left to wear it as they please."[193] This must have been a sore point for Spaniards who regarded long hair as a link to the Indians' "pagan" past, but the law stood and was repeated as authoritative.[194]

Opinion was divided on whether cutting Indian hair was to be forbidden altogether or, since it was a great humiliation, restricted to especially serious offenses. The *Itinerario* opposed haircuts for baptism but, mirroring the rigor of its time, asserted that Indians who gave false witness should be whipped in public and have their hair cut "so that they may be defamed."[195] Late-eighteenth-century sources returned to a general rule against cutting Indians' hair. In his prologue to the *Ayudante de cura* (1766), Arze cited *Recopilación* 1-13-6—which ordered magistrates to see that church officials did not jail or whip Indians or cut their hair—as a definitive prohibition on haircuts as punishment.[196]

Curas did not abandon their shears altogether as the teachings of the *Recopilación* spread in the eighteenth century, although haircutting was now more likely to result in criminal charges. The cura of Cuanacalcingo (Cuernavaca district) allegedly had the widower cacique there arrested in 1781 for carrying on with a woman, and made him pay for his lewd behavior with the loss of his balcarrotas, 25 strokes of the lash, and a forced union with his mistress (with the payment of the appropriate marriage fee).[197] The cura of San Felipe del Obraje, in the district of Metepec, admitted in a bitter 1771 dispute over the arancel that he had shorn several Indians. The Spaniard sent to investigate the charges of cruelty added a revealing detail: the Indian he had sent with a message to the alcalde of San Lucas had been whipped and shorn ("tuzado") on the cura's orders, and his locks had been hung from the church entrance as a warning to anyone who would support the arancel. Apparently another local man who subsequently declared himself a supporter of the arancel also lost his hair.[198]

A less provocative way for the priest to express his displeasure and his eminence was to grab a parishioner by the hair. This was an act that Spaniards and Indians alike understood to be degrading. Precolumbian codices sometimes represented conquest by one warrior grabbing another by the hair, and sixteenth-century pictorial manuscripts often show Spaniards grabbing Indians by the hair. The Franciscan cura of Poncitlan (Guadalajara) in 1727 beat one Indian for grabbing the cura's nephew by the hair, and himself grabbed another Indian by the hair for disobedience.[199] Indian officials of Ozoloapan in 1769 dragged an Indian man out of church by his hair and whipped him at the church door.[200]

When priests grabbed an Indian by the hair, it was usually a spontaneous response to disobedience. But the act was likely to be more violent than simply tugging at the victim's locks. When the cura demanded that the gobernador and other officials of Alahuistlan in the district of Zacualpan identify persons who had not attended mass on November 1, 1786, the gobernador and the alcalde replied "the whole town" (el pueblo). According to the alcalde, the cura became furious and chased after him with his paper shears, finally throwing them at him, then grabbing his balcarrotas and trying to force him to the ground.[201] The cura of Tescaliacac, Tenango del Valle district, charged in 1801 with the physical abuse of Indian leaders, was also said to "have given hard yanks at the hair" of a principal's wife.[202] The cura of Tancanhuitz in 1749 said that he had grabbed an insolent Indian by the hair in order to humble him, to force him down to the ground.[203] In other cases, the complaint was that the cura had grabbed the victim by the hair and dragged him or her off to the church compound.[204]

*   *   *

Though it is misleading to regard Indian parishioners only as "the survivors of three centuries of violence and intimidation," violence, fear, and intimidation were indeed part of the relationship between priest and rural parishioners in eighteenth-century New Spain. "Respect and fear" were understood by church and state officials to be partners in the good order of Christian society and the journey toward salvation generally.[205] It was their view that Indians, especially, had to be made to feel the anguish of sin and the meaning of shame, and had to be taught submission to the priest's authority. Similar gestures of respect were demanded also by royal officials and other Spaniards, lending an aura of legitimacy to privilege in this stratified social order. Of course, there is much more to the history of priests in their parishes than their own representations and authoritarian impositions, and there is the persistent complication of variation by place and time. But compared with Imperial Russia as Gregory Freeze describes it, rural Mexico gave considerable scope to fear and the cura's claims on power. In eighteenth-century Russia, parish priests "were held firmly in the grasp of popular control," hesitant to expose immorality, persecute deviants, or demand deference and obedience.[206] Priests in villages of central and western Mexico expected to exercise great influence over their parishioners' lives, and many had the potential to do so, because they had not only more formal authority to instruct, intimidate, and lead than their Russian counterparts, but also the weight of habitual deference behind them. Even in pueblos where the priest's intervention in public life was openly challenged and successfully resisted, whippings were still accepted for spiritual misconduct, and the person of the priest was almost always respected even when opposition to his authority turned violent.

Yet while some priests may have ruled mainly by force—at least one had his own constabulary [207]—most cannot be said to have ruled at all, much less by force. Their influence was drawn from a more varied and contingent kit. The formal rules of conduct and the priests' institutional activities provided ample room to influence by persuasion, legitimacy, fear, and limited coercion. The rules of conduct and order represented by the bastón, the balcarrotas, the confessional, and gestures of deference required reciprocity and adherence to the complex, contradictory ideal image of the parish priest. When the priest did not reciprocate a plea for pardon or indulgence, or when he acted with excessive anger or force, the bonds of mutual obligation were strained and righteous indignation and disobedience could result.[208] Furthermore, even the role of loving and just father depended on the threat of punishment, so that as the crown moved to replace the pastor's whip and jail with more imposing town jails and an enforcement of royal auxilio, some parish priests found it more difficult to elicit obedience.

PART THREE

Parishioners

CHAPTER TEN

Christian Duties
and Local Celebrations

"The Indians have too much religion," a padre once said
to me; "and they want more than is good for them."
                                        —Carl Lumholtz, 1902

Although rural curas sometimes complained of their Indian parishioners'
tepid faith or even atheism,[1] the late colonial documentation shows much
less indifference than passionate engagement with Christianity and its priests—
whether that passion was wholehearted, theologically informed, fearful, submissive, irreverent, combative, or devious. How villagers viewed and practiced
their Christianity was partly determined by what church officials expected them
to learn. From the beginning, pastors were given printed catechisms of Christian doctrine that were to be taught to American neophytes for their salvation. They were brief but highly concentrated little manuals of belief that prescribed the Persignum Crucis (signing the cross and the accompanying prayer),
the Apostles' Creed, the Lord's Prayer, the Salve Regina, the fourteen Articles
of Faith, God's Ten Commandments, the Church's Five Commandments, the
Seven Sacraments, the Seven Virtues, the Seven Mortal Sins and their opposites, the nine ways to expunge venial sins, the four steps to expunge mortal
sins, the eight beatitudes, the three powers of the soul, the three enemies of the
soul, and the five physical senses.[2] Indians were to be instructed in the fourteen
Christian acts of mercy (such as feeding the hungry, clothing the poor, caring for
the sick, forgiving trespasses, and praying for sinners), and they were to pray to
God for the seven attributes of the Holy Spirit, and for grace and thanksgiving
at meals. The general confession they were to learn emphasized the role of the
priest and the saints (especially the Blessed Virgin) in mediating sin and expressing the sinner's plea for mercy and forgiveness.

The catechism taught rules of conduct and belief that emphasized monotheism, the individual soul, a deep division between the sacred and the profane,

the love of God and man, the Trinity, the sinfulness of the physical world and the weakness of mankind, Satan as the source of evil in this world, the idea of a physical and spiritual struggle against sin, the need for intercession with God, and the special role of Mary as intercessor. It also taught the need for sacraments and ritual redemption, the attributes and exalted potential of the soul, and the virtues of mercy, forgiveness, charity, poverty, meekness, peacemaking, temperance, and good works. All of these rules brought parishioners and priests together in an ongoing conversation about self-control, salvation, and leadership. The more social rules—the need for intercession, ritual redemption, and good works—took hold most readily.

Although villagers were sometimes declared to be ignorant of the mysteries of the faith,[3] curas in both dioceses usually reported that their parishioners had memorized the basic doctrine of the catechism. This knowledge was the essence of their formal education—in the primary school classes for children, in the weekly recitations of doctrine by adults led by the fiscal or the priest after mass every Sunday,[4] during Lent for everyone over fourteen in preparation for confession, for couples preparing to marry, for parents and godparents before a baptism, and in exemplary situations, as when a man suspected of "idolatry" was obliged to recite the Apostles' Creed in public. What was directly understood from these lessons in doctrine or which items contributed most to religious change is rarely certain. Most of what can be learned about the penetration of Christian beliefs comes from evidence of local practice.

There was great variation in how faithfully and meaningfully the obligations of the church were practiced. Priests wondered whether parishioners had done much more than commit the prayers and doctrine to memory.[5] Some laymen, especially in the pueblos de visita, were in the habit of fulfilling only the Easter duty and not attending Sunday mass regularly. Confession there was more likely to be rushed or poorly attended because the priests tried to pack a year's worth of confessions into a brief Lenten visit.

Emphasis on the Easter duty was part of a general pattern of seasonal intensity. The long Lent and Easter season was the high point of the religious calendar for Catholics generally, and especially so for Indian villagers.[6] It was during Lent that villagers were most likely to extend themselves to attend mass and obey the moral injunctions of the catechism. Even then, curas encountered irritating deviations that marred the spirit of the season. Instead of fasting on all the Fridays of Lent, some Indians ate meat as soon as they had taken communion.[7]

In the late colonial period, villagers sometimes resisted attending Sunday mass when curas attempted to celebrate it more often than customary in pueblos de visita. In a few parishes, especially in modern Morelos and districts in and near the Valley of Toluca, there were occasions when fewer than half the parishioners reportedly fulfilled the Easter duty and attended weekly mass. This was more likely to become a long-term pattern in urban parishes or parishes with large transient populations. It was difficult to remain a member of the community without participating in rural parishes, especially in the cabeceras, where an accurate census was kept, roll was called after mass on Sundays, and receipts were signed and distributed by the cura to those who had taken communion. But it was also true that most lay people were less preoccupied with conscience and sin than the clergy and were more concerned with the supplicatory and propitiatory aspects of the faith. Frequently, whole communities (especially pueblos de visita) would skip mass or another of the mandatory rites in protest of high clerical fees or some other source of conflict with the cura.[8] At Mochitlan (Tixtla district, Guerrero), during a suit against the cura over fees and mistreatment in 1800, the parishioners, both children and adults, remained silent when the priest called on them to recite the catechism after Sunday mass.[9]

The principles of the faith were commemorated in ritual occasions and obligations prescribed by canon law. Indian parishioners were obliged to attend mass every Sunday and on the feast days of Christ's circumcision (New Year's Day), Epiphany, Candlemas, the Annunciation, Saints Peter and Paul, Mary's birth, Corpus Christi, the Ascension of Christ, the Assumption of the Virgin, Christmas, Easter, and the Day of the Holy Spirit. They were to fast on the seven Fridays of Lent, Christmas Eve, and the eve of Easter Sunday.[10]

The Precepto Anual

The crowning rite for the laity was the *precepto anual*—the Easter duty or annual obligation to confess and take communion during the season of Christ's sacrifice, between Ash Wednesday and Corpus Christi. It was through this annual rite that one remained in good standing with God, the community, and colonial society. But the crush of communicants during the week before Easter Sunday or during a priest's brief journey to a pueblo de visita and the perfunctory confessions likely under those conditions made some curas doubt the validity of this reconciliation with the church.[11] And at least in some pueblos of Tenango del Valle, Indian parishioners distanced themselves from confession and communion by not practicing these rites until they married.[12]

All parishioners fourteen and over were expected to prepare themselves for communion by renewing their knowledge of church doctrine, confessing, and doing the penance prescribed by the priest (typically a modest devotional act, such as reciting a series of Hail Marys).[13] For confession/penance and communion, unlike the other sacraments, no fees were to be charged. Though confession was a private communication between the priest and the penitent, separated by a screen for anonymity, it was to be done in a public part of the church in order to discourage improprieties and gossip: the confessional was to be placed where there was good light, not in a remote corner or dark place; and women were to be confessed before vespers (that is, before dark).[14]

To complete the precepto anual was normal in both dioceses, but many exceptions are recorded for the late colonial period.[15] A few suggest outright rebellion against the church and clashes between Catholic and unorthodox practices. During a pastoral visit to 45 parishes and missions in northern Hidalgo and San Luis Potosí in 1808–9, the archbishop's delegate reported that in the Huehuetlan mission and in three of the eleven pueblos in the parish of Tepehuacan, the Indians simply refused to practice the faith. They did not attend mass, or complete the precepto anual, or call the priest for the last rites.[16] Four visitas in the parish of Huizquilucan near the Valley of Mexico in 1769 reportedly had a long history of refusing to confess and of practicing their own secret rites in caves.[17] Seven years earlier, the cura there, Joseph de Zelada, observed that the Indians' periodic suits against his predecessors were timed to enable them to evade the precepto anual. As a result, one elderly ex-gobernador had only taken communion twice in his life.[18]

Some failures to confess were sly individual evasions of institutional religion rooted in anticlericalism or personal dislike of the priest. Mexico City provides clear examples for the late colonial period. One early-eighteenth-century manual writer alerted readers to a common trick that Indians with more than one residence used to avoid confession: whenever either priest came looking for them, they would just say: "Father, even though I have a house here, I live in such-and-such place." Other evasions were commercially motivated. In 1788, some Indians in the city were reported to take communion two or more times in order to sell their extra cedulas (certificates of confession) to people who did not want to confess.[19]

Most of the instances of wholesale evasion of the precepto anual had religious roots of one kind or another, but in a few cases, local politics figured in heavily. In the parish of Mazatepec (district of Cuernavaca) in 1800, the cura lamented his failure to gain universal compliance. Although he had sponsored a preaching mission by members of the Colegio Apostólico de Pachuca and had made up to nine priests available for confessions during Lent, the number of evaders had continued to grow during his five years there, reaching 2,000 by his count.[20] Breaking this round figure down by community reveals that most of the evaders were residents of a few haciendas (79 percent) rather than pueblos. On top of the typical isolation of haciendas from parish life in Indian districts was the opposition between the hacendado and the priest in this case. As another parish priest in this district observed in 1816, the hacendados made it clear that "they give the orders in the churches [the hacienda chapels]."[21]

Parishioners were most apt to evade confession in large numbers during a heated dispute with the cura. One dramatic boycott occurred in the parish of Calimaya near Toluca in 1792. The cura, Dr. Miguel de Araujo, submitted a 72-page list of nearly 5,000 parishioners who had not confessed or taken communion that year. Roughly three-quarters of them were Indians. That some lay people in this parish failed to fulfill the precepto anual was not new, but these numbers were unprecedented. They apparently originated in the change of curas nine months before and the eight ensuing lawsuits against the newcomer over fees, services, and abuses. The audiencia concluded that there had been some neglect on the cura's part because he was not well versed in Nahuatl, but this alone did not account for 5,000 apostates. It ordered that the district governors aid the cura in enforcing the precepto anual and recommended a preaching mission by Franciscans of the Colegio de San Fernando to revive the parishioners' enthusiasm.[22]

Less volatile or less political circumstances also contributed to recurrent abstentions from the precepto anual. Three of these were a priest's using the confessional to proposition his women parishioners or extract information unrelated to personal sin; his violation of the secrecy of the confessional; and his inability to hear confessions in the parishioners' native language.[23] For example, Indian representatives of San Juan de Imala, Santiago de Navito, and San Pedro Cuilan in the district of Culiacán (Sinaloa) in 1726 said that many of them had stopped going to confession in the last two years because the cura interrogated them about their lawsuit against him:

We can't confess with this *cura* because it is said that various people have placed themselves at his feet, only to find that instead of confession, he submits them to another kind of examination—about our complaints against him. The result is that they left without having confessed (which they should have done), which humiliated them and made them more hesitant about their religious obligations than before.[24]

The secrecy of the confessional was broken in several ways. Occasionally, the priest himself divulged confidential information. More often, an interpreter was present[25] or the priest made penitents speak so loudly that their sins were overheard. In one case from Oaxaca, a cura who was always in a hurry when he visited the outlying visitas insisted on confessing the faithful two by two.[26]

Language was most often mentioned as a barrier to confession in the archdiocese, where many parishioners could not speak Spanish or did so haltingly. There was undoubtedly some truth to the claim by Indians of Almoloya in the Tenango del Valle district in 1792 that they did not go to church often or confess regularly because they did not understand the priest's words.[27]

Some late colonial priests—especially those attuned to the reforming rhetoric of the crown and regalist bishops—questioned whether the confessions of their village parishioners were sincere or their sense of guilt deeply felt. A year was too long between confessions, Joseph Tirso Díaz, a priest from Mexico City contended in 1770, especially since many people confessed only out of fear and showed few signs of genuine contrition.[28] A pessimistic peninsular Spanish priest in Córdoba in 1791, Pedro Fernández Ybarraran, believed Indians dissembled in the confessional because of their lukewarm religious convictions and their deep distrust of gente de razón.[29] And Manuel Morales, cura of Tlaola (Veracruz) in 1790, reported that not only did Indians withhold many sins in their confessions in preparation for the last rites, but also, if they recovered, they assumed that they would never have to confess again. He concluded that his parishioners were too literal-minded to be deeply devout unless their devotion was motivated by fear. Had the cura seen God? Had he seen Hell? they asked. No? Then they doubted these existed. When he responded that God would punish them eternally, they responded, "Let God do as he pleases."[30] Language barriers, especially, left room for obscure or mendacious confessions of serious transgressions. Ribadeneyra gave the example of a Nahuatl-speaking Indian who confessed, "My Father, I have sinned by returning to myself" (Totacine onimo cuepac). Only after careful probing in Nahuatl did the confessor discover that the penitent had had intercourse with his mother.[31]

With confession, as with the other rites of the church that called for lay people's participation, few parish priests in the archdiocese would have said that their Indian parishioners were ardent Catholics.[32] In some pueblos de indios, curas reported that only women came to mass regularly, which was a familiar pattern in non-Indian parishes.[33] Especially in the visitas, villagers were content to bury their dead and have midwives do conditional baptisms if necessary, and, in a rebellious mood, to suspend obligatory practices and hold religious fiestas on their own without mass.[34] And where Christian duty involved paying a fee, there was likely to be resistance unless the priest would accept partial or late payment.[35] Still, most parishioners evidently fulfilled their basic obligations, knew the rudiments of the catechism, and supported the works of the church and the priest with their labor, cash, and sodalities.

Indian Christianity and Parish Priests

With regard to doctrine, the meaning of the mass as a reenactment of Christ's sacrifice, and of communion as food of the spirit, seems to have been widely understood, if not always granted the awe that was expected.[36] But it was the lessons of the catechism about the Blessed Virgin that lay people in rural communities most readily accepted. The *santocal* (little altar or display of religious images) that was common in the houses of villagers and rancheros, whether Indians or gente de razón, was almost certain to display an image of the Virgin (see Fig. 8).[37] But devotions to these images and prayers at home were less regular than some priests would have liked. As Pérez de Velasco observed, the men were in the fields during the daylight hours and went to sleep almost as soon as they returned home; women were busy all day with food preparation, spinning, weaving, and child care.[38]

Of the "compulsory" aspects of Catholic religious practice, the clergy succeeded best in establishing the importance of baptism and extreme unction.[39] With many exceptions, attendance at weekly mass and the fulfillment of the Easter duty were widely accomplished, too.[40] Formal marriages may have been the norm, but parish priests often reported that a substantial minority of couples were living in carnal sin.[41] Many were galled more by the evasion of the sacrament than the loss of the sacramental fee. Frustrated by the number of unmarried adults in his parish, the cura of Guayacocotla in the late 1780's resorted to confining over 200 single men and women in one room one Saturday and forcing them to choose a marriage partner. At mass the next day, he read the marriage banns. Those who refused to get married were whipped and imprisoned.[42] Lay people may have regarded formal marriage as less important than baptism or last rites because it was less immediately linked with eternal salvation. But the main reason may have been that young village couples and their families could not afford to pay the substantial clerical fees for the ceremony, amounting to a laborer's wages for six weeks or more.[43] The cura of Tepoztlan in 1778 decried his parishioners' common-law unions but added that the couples often came to him for formal marriage after three or four years.[44]

Priests in the Diocese of Guadalajara were more likely than their Mexico counterparts to write enthusiastically about Christian fervor in their Indian pueblos. Mariano de Torres claimed in the late sixteenth century that Indians of Nueva Galicia showed "incredible devotion," with whole neighborhoods marching in file to mass on Sunday behind their banner and singing a Te Deum in Nahuatl. Antonio Tello wrote in the early seventeenth century of Indian hospital officials rising at midnight and dawn to sign the cross and pray in Spanish and their native language. Alonso de la Mota y Escobar, another early-seventeenth-

FIG. 8. A home altar. An English couple espied this "fine collection of religious plates" displayed against a *petate* (woven reed mat) in one of the four "wretched hovels" they found at El Bozal, on an arid plain near Real de Catorce (Diocese of Guadalajara), in 1827.

century source for Nueva Galicia, considered Indians there to be good Christians who participated actively in the religion and kept their churches well stocked with ornaments that enhanced the dignity of public worship.[45]

The archdiocese's priests were apt to dwell instead on the piety of individual parishioners. Even some of the treatises that were preoccupied with Indian "superstitions" recognized exemplary Indian Christians. Joseph Navarro de Vargas, writing in 1734, paid a backhanded compliment to Indian women of Churubusco when he noted that the impressive construction program under his predecessor had been accomplished "with daughters of the *pueblo* who were truly Venerable Matrons, helping him manfully."[46] The Franciscan doctrinero at Papalotla in the district of Texcoco in 1809 wrote that the pueblo was "vast, pious, and Catholic," although the churches were in poor repair despite the generous donations of parishioners. He singled out three wealthy Indian nobles as particularly devout, reserving special praise for Gregorio Alonso as "perhaps the most rational and virtuous Indian in all of New Spain."[47] Also in the Valley of Mexico, the cura of Tepetlaostoc's account of exemplary piety was less happy. Serving the people of Santo Tomás Apipilhuasco had been an impossible challenge, he said in 1758, until Nicolás López became the alcalde and his brother became the fiscal. But despite the brothers' devotion to the faith and generosity in covering essential church costs when the community would not, they were opposed by "the vicious ones" and effected little change.[48]

Leaving aside the edifying exceptions, priests regarded their village parish-

TABLE 2
Devotional Expenses from Community Income, Tequila (Jalisco), 1787

Item	Amount
30 jars of coconut oil for the lamp*a*	50p
Flour for the sacramental wafers, incense from Castile, and soap	13p, 4rr
Blessing and distribution of candles	5p
Castilian wax, music, and rockets for Pentecost	31p, 6rr
Semana Santa functions of the cura	10p
Refurbishing of the monstrance	6p
One arroba and 20 pounds of Castilian wax	67p, 4rr
Meals for those who played the apostles	3p
Feast of the Ascension	31p, 6rr
Feast of Corpus Christi	37p, 6rr
Feast of the patron saint, Santiago, (including sermon, rockets, wax, etc.)	56p
24 pounds of wax used in the procession of the Eucharist	36p
Paperwork for the tithe	9p, 3rr
Violin for the church choir	6p

SOURCE: AGI Guad. 352 exp. Tequila, Dec. 22, 1787.
*a*Ordinarily more expensive olive oil from Spain was required for the lamp.

ioners' devotion as literal-minded, especially likely to become attached to images of saints and other sacred objects. The sympathetic bishop of Oaxaca in 1778 recalled

an incident that happened to me this March when I was making my pastoral visit to the parish of Ixtepeji. Those poor Indians asked me to consecrate or bless a bell because almost every year their cacti [for raising the dye-rich cochineal insect] were devastated by storms and frosts. I agreed to do it, and the word quickly spread throughout the district. Forty-eight hours later the town was filled with bells. More than sixteen [bells] came in from various *pueblos*, some from eight and ten leagues away. During that time, these *miserables* had taken the bells down from their towers and carried them on their shoulders (and some of them were very heavy).[49]

Many village Catholics may have known deeply only the rudiments of the faith, but within those limits, their devotions were enthusiastic. Pueblos underwrote a wide range of supplies for the liturgy, services, and celebrations every year. The head town of Tequila (Jalisco) paid almost 364 pesos from its community income in 1787 for the items shown in Table 2. But its total devotional expenditures, including individual sacramental fees, would have been much larger, since the list omits payments in kind or cash for Sunday masses, other fiestas, special masses, the tithe, first fruits, extraordinary collections, sacramental wine, the support of the priests, the upkeep of the church buildings, and the purchase of church ornaments.[50]

At the same time, pueblos expected a return on their money. Complaints were loud and frequent when the cura and vicarios did not provide all of the necessary services or did them too quickly and halfheartedly. Charges by Indian parishioners against priests in the late colonial period were often made with the vehemence of righteous indignation. The common terms of opprobrium were cheerless and blunt: "avarice," "servitude," and "tyranny." To the petitioners of San Pedro Cacaguatepec in the district of Acapulco in 1782, their priest was a law unto himself, and that law was boundless avarice. He "converts our misfortune to a perpetual slavery."[51] Leaders of Chapula, Tianguistengo district, also regarded their cura's greedy quest for fees as an "unjust servitude."[52] Straining for eloquence, the 1774 spokesmen for Malacatepec in the district of Metepec described (in words perhaps fashioned by their attorney) a virtual martyrdom for the cura's sake:

My people pay much more tribute to the *cura* than to Our Majesty, . . . with the result that the small advances they might achieve by the drops of sweat spilled in their labors benefit only the *cura*, and they are left eating a piece of stale *tortilla*. . . . This schedule of fees was established with the sainted purpose of permitting the Indians to experience the greatest relief possible, not to swell the *cura*'s purse.[53]

The wolf was a popular metaphor that parishioners used for parish priests who abused their office and failed to do their pastoral duties. In 1789, for example, the Indians of Ocuilan in the district of Malinalco charged their cura, who had the unfortunate name of Antonio Joseph Lobo, with beating them and exacting exorbitant fees. All in all, they said, this was a priest who, "like his surname, lunges to destroy them entirely."[54] The wolf metaphor, like the frequent charge of avarice, had Old Testament roots and was used by colonial priests and high civil officials in a variety of situations. In the mid-seventeenth century, Jacinto de la Serna wrote of Indian "idolaters" as "wolves in sheep's clothing"; in a pastoral letter of 1803, Archbishop Lizana y Beaumont described priests who were not pure in their mundane and spiritual lives as "mercenaries or wolves rather than pastors"; and in 1800, the fiscal of the Audiencia of Nueva Galicia spoke of Juan José Lombide, a parish priest who joined the Hidalgo revolt, as "a wolf who devours his sheep."[55] The Ocuilan Indians' critique of their priest's conduct used Christian terms to express a self-consciously Christian anticlericalism.

The many bitter disputes between curas and village parishioners over clerical fees went deep into Christian identity and practice. If the priest violated the laws of the church and seemed to be selling the sacraments, his own Christianity was in doubt; parishioners could present themselves self-righteously as the meek and humble who, living closer to Christ's example, wanted only the "solace of Christian rites" from the priest.[56] Protesting the removal of their vicario de pie fijo in 1781, the Indians of San Luis de las Peras in the parish of Villa de la Peña de Francia (Villa del Carbón, Edo. de México) charged that the cura had eliminated their resident priest simply out of selfish financial interest. Now many were dying without last rites, and they missed their weekly mass at home and could not reach the distant cabecera on Sundays.[57]

A case from Ixmiquilpan (Hidalgo) in 1807 highlights another dimension of the potentially disruptive contradiction between church doctrine and the priest's behavior—Indian petitioners presenting themselves as good Christians who were denied the benefits of the faith. The pueblo leaders fashioned a damning complaint to the archbishop against their cura, an aged and infirm man who, they claimed, reserved most of his meager energy for card games and cockfights. He did not confess, preach, or celebrate mass for the parish: "In a word, he does nothing. . . . His only activity as *cura* is to tyrannize." They concluded with a loaded question: "Is it possible, Most Illustrious Sir, that your pious and charitable zeal would allow our *cura* to nurture us—both adults and children of tender age—on this harsh and unjust milk?"[58]

Association with a local miraculous image could extend this feeling to a prideful claim of being something more than just good Christians. According to the Amecameca priest in 1806, his Indian parishioners considered themselves superior Christians because of the old tradition that their image of Christ had spoken to the saintly Franciscan Martín de Valencia at the beginning of the evangelization of Mexico.[59] A more common form for the idea that the local spiritual landscape was separate from, prior to, and in a sense superior to the cura was the assertion that the church building belonged to the community. When the cura of Actopan (Hidalgo) asked for a fee for burials in the churchyard in 1748, the reply by the pueblo officials was that the church was theirs, so no fees should be required.[60]

But if the priest was not wholly inflexible, an identification as Christians could draw parishioners away from self-righteousness and toward forgiveness and obedience. That, at least, is what Indian parishioners of Tlamatlan (Meztitlan district, Hidalgo) expressed during the Easter season of 1777 after a year of bitter conflict with their cura: "a bad settlement is better than a good lawsuit, and we are Christians and in the midst of a holy season."[61]

Pueblos in both dioceses almost always made a point of their desire for the sacraments and for a resident priest in their appeals to higher authority. During a dispute with the cura over clerical fees in 1807, the leaders of Ostoticpac and Cuautlancingo in the Otumba district near Mexico City expressed dismay that church services had been withheld: "We are all sad, confused, and upset at the very thought that such sacred remedies are kept from us, and our consternation rises much higher at the thought that no guardian can be found to protect us."[62] In the Indian parish of Tzontecomatlan (Veracruz) in 1808, pueblo officials wrote to their district lieutenant complaining that five villagers had recently died without confession. The lieutenant, in turn, wrote to the subdelegado that he feared an uprising of the district's five pueblos if they were not served with regular spiritual care soon.[63]

Villagers occasionally made excessively abject vows of loyalty to the cura while flouting his authority or, at least, failing to follow his direction with equal alacrity. What curas read in the contradiction was insincerity. At Santa María Apaxtla in the district of Zacualpan, the cura lodged a complaint against the Indian gobernador, Marcos Juan, for turning the town against him over fees and encouraging the inhabitants to stay away from Sunday mass and other feast-day rites. Marcos Juan replied that he and his people respected the priest and loved him "like Jesus himself," but he demanded exorbitant fees that they could not pay.[64] Father Ruiz y Cervantes of Zimatlan (Oaxaca) sarcastically quoted his typical Indian: " 'I don't have' (this is their way of presenting themselves to us), 'I don't have any other father or mother than you'; and even when they don't feel this, all those living within the pale of the Catholic Church assert it as a certainty."[65] The authority of parish priests was put to the test spontaneously in times of community violence. Sometimes, approaching the crowd with a cross or a revered image lifted high was enough to quell the violence; sometimes, it was not.[66]

Despite the great many suits against individual priests by their communities and the inflated condemnations of some and the false flattery of others, reverence for the parish priest and the wish to have a priest in residence were widespread in both dioceses (especially, again, in the Guadalajara diocese). Much of the abject respect that Ruiz y Cervantes found disingenuous would have been sincere in pueblos where the priest's authority was not challenged, where he was accepted as a holy man who guided people in times of grief, illness, and important decisions.[67] When a move was made to replace a beloved cura of San Agustín de las Cuevas in the Valley of Mexico in 1728, Indian parishioners asked the viceroy to exercise his power as vice-patron and restore their priest (which he did).[68] In 1803, Indians and gente de razón of Miacatlan in the district of Cuernavaca pleaded for the return of their "beloved pastor so that we might enjoy the spiritual nourishment that he gave us superabundantly and without delay."[69] Two years later, the Indian and Spanish parishioners of Almoloya in the district of Metepec asked the archiepiscopal court to grant their interim cura the parish as his benefice. They praised in lavish terms his spiritual zeal, his tireless pastoral work, his persuasiveness in the pulpit, and his charity.[70] In 1824, the subdelegado of Tonalá, frustrated by the local sway of the cura of Salatitan, Ignacio Negrete, left a memorable comment: "these rustic *alcaldes* believe that the aforementioned *cura* is infallible in his words and is incapable of deceiving or being deceived." When Negrete was suspended from office over his jurisdictional dispute with the subdelegado, the town council urgently requested his restitution: "We miss the spiritual care of Our Beloved Párroco. . . . He has looked out for our spiritual and temporal welfare in every way, with his words and advice, as well as by his example."[71]

But this kind of loyalty could carry a divisive edge. One part of the community might admire the priest fervently, while another thoroughly detested him.[72] Or the replacement for a popular priest might get a hostile welcome. In 1801, the Indians of Amanalco in the jurisdiction of Metepec expressed great affection for their interim cura, but they so bitterly opposed his permanent replacement that he stayed in Mexico City out of fear for his life.[73] The former priest of Tlatlauquitepec (Puebla), who rose to bishop-elect of Manila in 1765, recalled how the cura from 30 years before his time, Lorenzo de Orta, was still so fondly remembered by parishioners that they always sang a response for him on the Day of the Dead. But they also remembered those who had been disliked for various reasons.[74]

However strongly parishioners professed their loyalty, few late colonial priests seem to have enjoyed the kind of unqualified obedience and deference that they were schooled to expect. Indians involved in disputes against their priests expressed a clear sense of boundaries that the priest should not cross. This sense of limits was not new, but it probably took on a new intensity and bite as the royal government bent its efforts ever more strongly to confining the priests' activities and regulating their income from direct collections. Pedro Alcántara, Indian of San Francisco Tecospa in the parish of Milpa Alta, complained to the Audiencia of Mexico in 1792 that the cura's intervention in a local land transaction was "very alien to his pastoral work."[75] When the cura of Zacualpan confronted a group of Indian women at San Simón Tototepec in the course of a bitter fee dispute in 1775, one of them (who addressed him as "father of my soul" to emphasize that his hold was in spiritual matters only) declared that "it would be better if you got the people to confess and meet their spiritual obligations, that that deserved attention, not the collection of first fruits."[76] When a new cura arrived in Techaluta (Jalisco) in 1824, the village elders responded without enthusiasm. As one of them said, it was all the same to him who served as cura as long as he "has not intervened nor tries to intervene in anything."[77] Carrying to a sometimes rigid extreme the crown's own principle in the late colonial reforms, villagers such as these were arguing that the priest should stick to strictly spiritual affairs.

These sentiments were partly a product of the crown's encouragement and of the tension built into the relationship between local interests and an authority that usually looked beyond the parish. But they were nourished by a sense of locality and continuity. Priests "came and went," as the town officers of San Juan de Alaya put it during their suit over clerical fees in 1793.[78] So did gobernadores, at least as gobernadores. It was the community and its members that continued, and time was on their side. Current gobernadores did not feel much responsibility for the uncollected fees of their predecessors. If fees were not paid on time, eventually they were no longer owed. As the gobernador of Santo Domingo Hueyapan said in 1770 when he declined to recognize old debts, "Time has passed, and various *gobernadores* have succeeded each other, and they advised him not to pay."[79] Determined local leaders understood that though they could not have much influence over the appointment of their priest, they might have something to do with his tenure. A complaint founded on written law or custom or touching sensitive jurisdictional interests of the crown could remove the priest from the community pending investigation and judgment. And it was likely to hasten his departure even if the case was decided in his favor. Bishops had permutas at their disposal to cool down disputes of this kind.

Fiestas and Fandangos

Public celebration was at the heart of religious devotion in eighteenth-century central and western Mexico. The sacred and the profane intermingled in penitential pilgrimages to popular shrines, processions bearing local images through their hometowns and into the countryside in times of trouble and thanksgiving, processions accompanying the Host to the door of a dying parishioner, funerals, gatherings to mark the arrival of the bishop on visita or the parish priest in an outlying hamlet, and the annual religious feasts that culminated in the emotional public events of anguish, hope, and reconciliation during Easter week.[80] These solemn and spirited collective expressions of faith were the least managed of public Catholic practices in rural Mexico.[81]

Local fiestas or feast-day celebrations were particularly important community activities. Linked to the high holy days and special saints' days, they were often expensive, noisy, colorful displays of devotion and consumption that freed participants from the routine of hard labor from planting to harvest. In the sixteenth century, between Sunday devotions and annual feasts, there were 95 obligatory holy days a year (or over a quarter of the days of the year).[82] By the late eighteenth century, the number had been reduced to 71 for non-Indians (19.6 percent) and

TABLE 3

Expenses for a Village Fiesta, District of Tepospisaloya (Jalisco), 1788

Item	Amount	Item	Amount
Saffron, pepper, cloves	4rr	Butter	5rr
Anise, cumin, rice	2rr	A large slice of lard	4rr
Cinnamon, almonds, candies	3rr	Sausage, blood pudding	2rr
Sugar	2rr	Two bottles mezcal	1p
Chile, onions	3rr	Chocolate	4rr
Garlic, garbanzos, oil	3rr	Cook's wages	1p
Flour, wine, sacramental wafers	3rr	Candles, soap	1r
Bread	4rr	Priest's travel charges	1p
A quarter steer	4rr	Half fanega maize	2p, 4rr
Two lambs	2p	Three almudes beans	3rr
Half a pig	1p	Offering of lamb, maize, chickens	1p, 4rr
Eight chickens	1p	Two masses and wax	13p, 3rr
		TOTAL	30p, 2rr

SOURCE: AGI Guad. 352, cuad. 1, fol. 86v.

64 for Indians (17.5 percent), but these figures do not include the feast of the patron saint, other special devotions of the community, and the extended Christmas and Easter seasons, which would bring the total back close to the sixteenth-century level.[83] Some pueblos, like San Miguel Totomaloyan (mentioned below), observed a feast day for virtually every saint represented in the local church. In rural parishes, the great feasts generally were for the patron saint, for other special local devotions like Saint Francis and various advocations of Mary, and for Christmas, Epiphany, Candlemas, Easter, Pentecost, Corpus Christi, All Souls, and the feast of the Immaculate Conception.

Each parish had its own practices, devotions, and means of support, but lavish expenditures for religious fiestas were the rule. Yahualica (Hidalgo) in 1739 supported fiestas for Corpus Christi, San Juan, San Nicolás, and All Saints, and the Christmas and Easter devotions, from contributions of one real by married men and one-half real by widowers. Cofradías to Our Lady of the Rosary, the Holy Sacrament, Souls in Purgatory, the Holy Sepulchre, Our Lady of Sorrows, the Holy Trinity, and San José supported their own annual fiestas for the parish, as well as weekly masses. A Congregation of Our Lady of Guadalupe also funded a weekly mass and an annual fiesta. In addition, each of the parish's ten pueblos observed the day of its patron saint, which would have been attended by at least some other parishioners.[84]

Annual expenses for fiestas in a modest Indian parish generally ranged from 300 pesos to more than 1,000.[85] Some parishes spent much more. According to the fiscal of the Audiencia of Nueva Galicia in 1791, the people of Sayula district were so attached to "an infinity" of fiestas that they spent more than 13,000 pesos annually, "and this doesn't even begin to include the fiestas that are permitted."[86] Even in a small visita, the basic cost of food, candles, and the services of a priest for a fiesta could cost over 65 pesos, as Table 3, showing the estimated figures for pueblos in the district of Tepospisaloya (Jalisco) in 1788, indicates.[87]

In this case, the items indicate that a lavish feast was laid on. Although such spreads were sometimes mounted for the whole community, more commonly it was the *república*—the current officeholders and elders—who enjoyed these protein-rich, spicy meals. Arrangements for the feast were generally made by the saint's mayordomo for the year as his culminating duty. At San Miguel Almoloya in the parish of Tescaliacac (Tenango del Valle district), a breakfast feast for the república on the Day of the Holy Cross in 1760 was interrupted by the vicario. He understood from his fiscal that the feastgoers had been clandestinely practicing their own religious rites to the cross with chains of roses.[88] Such celebrations staged by lay people aroused the clergy's suspicions of ignorant error, if not heresy and rebellion. To some extent they *were* violations of good order and hierarchy, but as long as they did not spill over into everyday life and politics, most were tolerated, even encouraged.

The popular wisdom among colonial administrators of the late eighteenth century was that Indians were devoted to fiestas and commonly spent more on them than they had, going into debt for the sake of unrestrained celebration and devotion.[89] But it would be a mistake to think here of selfless officials holding pueblos back from a life on fiesta. Colonial Spaniards were quick to regard excess and disorder as typically Indian, whether that was their experience or not. Some pueblos celebrated few fiestas, and few late colonial pueblos wanted more. It was often the parish priests, dependent on clerical fees and festival masses for their income, especially in newly secularized parishes, who were most eager to promote new fiestas. Indians of five pueblos in the Sultepec district in 1756 complained that the new vicarios in that recently secularized parish were introducing unwanted fiestas.[90] Playing their legal angles, the spokesmen for the Indians of San Miguel Almoloya in 1760 argued that priests were making them contribute for fiestas that were not obligatory.[91] The response in some communities was simply to stop celebrating most religious feasts and refuse to pay the fees. In 1796, in a dispute over clerical fees, leaders of Santa María Tututepec in the district of Tulancingo promised their constituents (or so the cura said) that there would no longer be expenses and celebrations for Easter week, All Soul's Day, Corpus Christi, and other familiar fiestas, only the fees for Sunday mass, baptisms, marriages, and burials.[92] In the same year the Indian fiscal of Zinacantepec in the district of Metepec reported that, in protest against what the parishioners regarded as excessive charges, no fiestas were being celebrated there except Easter Sunday.[93]

In the end, the law-and-order issue outweighed the rural priests' drive for more fiesta fees. In the name of good Christian habits, firmer control over colonial subjects, and the economic welfare of Indian communities, late colonial governors and prelates were bent on reducing the number and extravagance of fiestas, especially where they smacked of religious deviation. The campaign against fiestas began in earnest at the religious level, with a spate of edicts from New Spain's prelates, led by Archbishop Lorenzana during 1769–71. On February 7, 1769, the archbishop prohibited various Indian performances that he regarded as superstitious and possibly idolatrous. Two years later, the Fourth Provincial Council called for no new fiestas and forbade banquets and other mundane celebrations during the Easter and Christmas seasons.[94] The royal government launched its own campaign later, with a cedula of May 2, 1789, that went beyond the council's call for no new fiestas, to order a reduction in the existing ones. That cedula was barely published in a viceregal bando in November when it was followed by another on March 23 (supplemented by one of April 16, 1790), reiterating the order and directing attention especially to the Holy Week celebrations in Mexico City. Audiencia judges, intendants, subdelegados, and bishops leapt to echo the calls.[95] All 28 late colonial cases of adjudication over fiesta practices located for this study took place after 1755. The bulk were concentrated in three periods following the arrival of Lorenzana and the royal government's joining of the battle: 1769–73 (five cases), 1791–96 (nine cases), and 1800–1807 (six cases).

The response to these two campaigns largely dictates the timing of the written evidence and makes it difficult to document other changes in fiesta practice in late colonial years. The judges and priests commissioned to report on public celebrations rarely went beyond brief descriptions and rarely recorded the views of lay participants. Nevertheless, those descriptions, fleshed out with a scattering of administrative reports, financial records, and other materials from earlier and intervening years, point to some broad patterns of fiesta behavior, as well as the tension of the late eighteenth century over proper religious conduct.

Fiestas meant exuberance. Inside the church, the effect of a solemn sung mass with choir and organ was enhanced by as much candlelight and as many flowers and paper decorations as possible. Outside, there were profane resonances in which parishioners led rather than followed—more music and singing, food (a meal heavy with meat rather than sacramental bread), drink (pulque, cane alcohol, mezcal, and mixed punches in place of the priest's sacramental wine), and the light and noise of fireworks, plus dancing. From the beginning of Spanish colonization, clergymen were worried by these profane versions of communion—the vigorous dancing, singing, eating, and drinking of Indian neophytes, and the gathering together of many people from neighboring pueblos.[96] A 1539 meeting of prelates called for an end to these extravagant practices in religious fiestas because "the entire cost falls to the *macehuales*," and the result was often deaths, sacrifices, and other "things that are far from exemplary."[97] More than two centuries later, village fiestas still seemed to prelates, royal governors, and many parish priests to be excessive, beyond official control, and tinged with "paganism."

The comandante gobernador of Guadalajara remarked in 1778 that Indians liked dancing and heavy drinking in their fiestas, whereas non-Indians had a weakness for gambling and bullfights in theirs.[98] This was an old chestnut that had had more truth to it in the sixteenth century than in the eighteenth. In many late colonial pueblos with substantial non-Indian populations, it is not easy to say who the celebrants were, and pueblos de indios in parts of both dioceses (especially in the Guadalajara territory and the future state of Morelos) had a soft spot for bullfights.[99] But even in the more open, mixed pueblos of the Guadalajara diocese, Indians kept their own fiesta practices with unusual dances, heavy drinking, and comparatively little gambling. Priests commented extensively on Indian drunkenness and associated it with a lack of self-control, a lack of moral scruples, social disorder, and idolatry.[100] Pérez de Velasco, off his long experience in Indian parishes of Puebla, advised confessors to question their Indian penitents especially about those occasions when they drank to the point of passing out, which came mainly during fiestas.[101]

Although the dances are rarely described in detail in the colonial judicial records, some bear exotic names that seem to echo an Indian past or barely

Christian reworkings of colonial experience, like Malinchis, Tlaxilacalis, Hue-huentris o Tlaxcaltecos, Nescuitiles, Tastuanes, Palo de Volador, and Danza de los Negros. Others suggest Moorish-Christian encounters—*moros y cristianos* and *matachines* (the second derives from Arabic and refers to elaborately costumed, masked dancers who fought with wooden swords). Still others were clearly Christian in form but went beyond the conventional representations that the official church found acceptable, such as live representations of the passion of Christ.[102]

Most of these performances were noisy mock battles with masks, costumes, and much vigorous movement and drinking.[103] Spanish Christians knew about mock battles, costumes, and masks, but if Sahagún's descriptions of Mexica ceremonies are indicative of practices elsewhere in Mesoamerica, the fiesta dances of the period retained the heart of late precolonial performances: the ceremonial sacrifice of the *ixiptla*, the masked god-impersonator decked out in fine regalia who was the leading figure in the Mexicas' festivals. It may have been the tradition of this culminating event that charged many masked processions and battles with the special feeling of excitement and anticipation that officials sensed but apparently did not fathom.[104] What was new in the colonial performances, in addition to the forms, was the amount of drinking by participants and spectators.[105] At fiesta time, it could be dangerous for outsiders to enter a pueblo where heavy drinking was taking place, but the descriptions—even by colonial officials who had fled for their lives—indicate that the drinking was usually convivial, and that members of the community drank together, sometimes from a common pot.[106] Here the general use of alcohol validated an old attachment to community in a new way. That Indian elites did not control public festivities now as closely as their forebears did before the Conquest (or so Indian nobles claimed), a local identity attached to the past—at least a long colonial past mixed with the sense of a still longer native past—was being confirmed.

One kind of performance that came under scrutiny in the late colonial flurries of administrative interest was Easter week celebrations in which male parishioners dressed as "centurions" or soldiers. They were supposed to guard the tabernacle for the Host that was consecrated on Maundy Thursday and saved for Good Friday devotions, and participate in the processions and other Holy Week devotions. In February 1771, the parish priest of Xaltocan (Valley of Mexico) petitioned for an end to this practice because the Indians who dressed up as soldiers got drunk and acted indecently, and because of the costs entailed in providing clothing, gunpowder, food, and drink to the captains and soldiers. The Juzgado de Indios concurred, noting that the practice had been introduced long before to encourage Indian devotion, but that it had degenerated into "atrocious disorder ending in drunkenness that profanes this Holy time." The court ordered that Indians of Xaltocan might attend processions during Holy Week with candles but not dressed as centurions.[107] In 1796, the cura of Capuluac complained that the Indian centurions in his parish committed "sacrilegious and irreverent abuses" by virtually taking over the parish church—not allowing the building to be closed on the nights of Thursday and Friday of Holy Week and permitting people to profane the sanctuary with drinking and other dissolute acts.[108]

Several curas in the Mexico and Guadalajara dioceses made dramatic reports on fiesta practices that got out of bounds, in which their only role was helpless onlooker. The cura of Alahuistlan in the district of Sultepec reported in 1798 that Indians of San Miguel Totomaloyan celebrated saints' days with meals that led to general drunkenness. On these occasions, with most of the pueblo "publicly losing its grip on reason," he locked himself in his rooms for safety's sake. He said he had been unable to stop these practices and appealed to the audiencia to forbid the excesses of the meals and drinking.[109]

The Dominican doctrinero of Azcapotzalco near Mexico City in 1799 apparently exercised more authority than his counterpart in Alahuistlan, but he, too, was worried about local fiestas spinning out of control. He had heard a rumor that for the inauguration of a grand side chapel, the gobernadores of the Tepanec and Mexican sections of the community were planning a "scandalous fiesta" like the one he had forbidden them to celebrate for Corpus Christi. Because the Indians now dared to defy him over that ban, thanks to the protection of an unnamed person the cura was bound to respect (perhaps the subdelegado), he took his case to the audiencia. He had banned the celebration, he explained, because the high mass and procession of the consecrated Host had typically been followed by the "most ridiculous dances and superstitious, even brutish acts." The dancing before the Host had been led by "several large figures disguised in masks and very ridiculous costumes." The cura added that Indians spent lavishly on these fiestas, and people came from all around, contributing to the disorder. The gobernadores agreed to no more "ridiculous and perhaps indecent masks" for Corpus Christi (even though masks were used in many pueblos near Mexico City). They also promised to control the drinking but assured the audiencia that it was the castas and creoles of the vicinity, not Indians, who acted impiously in these fiestas.[110] Clearly, they wanted the procession to continue at all costs; it was, they said, an essential part of their Christianity.

Community fiestas, especially in the Diocese of Guadalajara, could be dangerously unpredictable occasions. The danger was sometimes part of the fun, but the consequences could be deadly, as Diego de Alcalá, a young married Indian of Atemajac near Guadalajara, learned on the night of the All Souls celebration in 1820. In high spirits, Alcalá and four friends set out for his brother's house with "some small sacks or chairs belonging to the officials of the Señor de Esquipulas." In the dark, they encountered three other young men from their town, who attacked them with the leather whips that everyone carried that night for protection. This was a traditional All Souls sport played in Atemajac. As the victim's brother explained, "It was a sort of established game on that night in the *pueblo*, tracking down people carrying offerings in order to take them away." Alcalá's group shouted, "Are you playing at lashings?" The other group shouted something in reply, and the fight was on. But this time, more than whips and fists flew. There had been heavy drinking already, and one of the offenders claimed that Alcalá struck him with a machete as fighting began. In the struggle, Alcalá was cut to death.[111]

Intercommunity hatreds also could rise to the surface in community fiestas and lead to violent death.[112] José Gregorio, an Indian from Tesistan outside Guadalajara, had gone to the fiesta of Santiago at Nestipac on July 25, 1810. On his way home at 5:00 P.M., three men from Nestipac attacked him with long knives and a staff of office at the Bajío de Santa Lucía, wounding him mortally.

José Gregorio said that he knew none of his attackers but that one shouted to him, "Now you'll see, *grandísimo carajo* [you damn prick]." The three attackers continued on toward Nestipac, attacking various people and seriously wounding two other men from Tesistan. According to witnesses from that community, the attacks were planned because Tesistán rather than Nestipac had won the patronage of a powerful local don, Alfonso Leñero. Vicente Cobarrubias, one of the victims, claimed that his attacker, Rafael Guzmán, an Indian of Nestipac residing in Guadalajara, had called him a *peladillo* (an unmanly man) and said, "You're the one who crawls over to your master, don Alfonso Leñero."[113]

The victims of a fiesta fury could easily be third parties. At the Feast of the Assumption in Atemajac in August 1819, a celebration that drew men and women from Guadalajara and the surrounding towns, José Rulfo Meza, a prominent Indian from Ixcatan and mayordomo of the hospital there, tried to intervene in a drunken argument over a stolen hat between a friend of his and José Antonio Méndez, a twenty-two-year-old creole supernumerary frontier soldier (*corredor supernumerario*) from Durango. Méndez turned on Meza and wounded him severely with his saber. The Indian officials of Atemajac tried to arrest Méndez, but he resisted and later fled. When the authorities caught up with him, he claimed that Meza had intervened for no reason, that Meza had insulted him, saying, "Here come these hungry ones," and had attacked first, and that he had resisted arrest because he did not realize that the Indian officials had the authority to arrest him. The audiencia fiscal concluded that Méndez's story was a string of lies and ordered him held in custody and tried.[114]

Fireworks were essential to virtually any important religious fiesta. Rockets —especially rockets—plus "bulls" studded with firecrackers, reed frames of churches and castles ready to explode into light, "feet-seekers," "flyers," and "chambers" were listed among the expenses for religious fiestas and mentioned in official complaints throughout the two dioceses.[115] Stanley Brandes suggests a promising explanation for the importance of fireworks among modern Tarascans of Michoacán in terms of historical continuities and syncretic combinations of light and percussion. In the precolonial Tarascan tradition, light and fire were ever present, associated with "the sacred male principle" and the sun; and rites of transition may have been associated with percussion. Roman Catholicism's use of candles, the lighted lamp, and fireworks on important religious occasions was sufficiently similar to be readily adopted. Fireworks, in Brandes's view, validated traditional masculinity. Men built and set off the fireworks, and the rockets reiterated male assertiveness and the male sexual role of penetration and explosion.[116]

Other specific associations could be advanced—for example, the airborne flash of light and bang of rockets with lightning and thunder were rich in possible connections to fertility, the god Tláloc, and Saint James (Santiago)—but a more general and, I believe, more immediate reason for the appeal of fireworks to Christian Indians was their resonance with the vigorous movement, sound, and light in precolonial ceremonial life. Fireworks brought dramatic sounds, surges of movement, and flashes of illumination—precisely the qualities that sixteenth-century friars associated with Indian religious practices, and that they hoped to moderate without extinguishing.[117] Fireworks introduced by Spaniards heightened these expressions of the divine within a conventional form—rockets soaring and exploding, castillos lighting the ground, with pinwheels whooshing and spinning and hundreds of lights sizzling and bursting, sending off sparks. Fireworks meant excitement and festivity to virtually everyone, not just Indians; and they were readily connected to Christian faith, announcing the joy of religious celebration and simulating the soul's elevation to heaven and the dramatic illumination of faith (like the rays of light that surround so many representations of Mary of the Immaculate Conception and the Annunciation, or the haloes that illuminate the saints). These were associations that the parish priests would have encouraged.

There was also a strictly mundane but no less important reason for the popularity of fireworks in the colonial period: their value to the crown as a source of revenue. Whether administered directly or rented out, monopoly rights on the sale of gunpowder were held by the king. Even after the campaign against extravagant religious fiestas began in 1769, fireworks were promoted by official order. On June 28, 1780, the viceroy published a decree in accord with the crown's wishes to encourage fireworks as an important branch of the gunpowder monopoly and an important source of employment for "Indians and poor people." The viceroy's subordinates were ordered "to see that the use of fireworks continues in the functions that are celebrated." [118]

Despite the murder and mayhem that these revelries could produce, colonial authorities were not of a mind to try to stamp them out altogether, still less the Indians' community celebrations. When Indians resisted the fiesta reforms of the 1770's and 1790's, the plan of provincial governors and audiencia judges seems to have been to push where they could but fall back on the old principle of moderation when challenged. In 1778, the commander-governor of Guadalajara put it this way:

> It is not useful to suddenly abolish at one strike the ideas, amusements, and ridiculous *fiestas* to which the Indians are prone; nor, for the same reason, to forbid those to which Spaniards and other people profess a passion. . . . To forbid either is to keep everyone's spirits inflamed; but to permit everything without restrictions and moderation is repugnant to good order, and incites vice and the ruin of families and wealth.[119]

His sentiments were echoed by the fiscal of the Audiencia of Mexico in 1799 in response to the cura of Alahuistlan's troubling report of wild breakfast parties on feast days in the parish. While favorably disposed to the cura's request for a ban on these disorderly events, he cautiously recommended that the subdelegado make a thorough investigation "because, in matters of customs in the *pueblos*, one should not move to remove them without perfect knowledge of the cause." [120]

Such caution was justified by the complex conflicts that could arise over changes in fiestas. An example from the last years of Spanish rule comes from Amecameca, with its famous Christ in the cave that the venerable Martín de Valencia had used as a hermitage in the 1540's. In January 1806, the cura of Amecameca complained of the "disorders and abuses" committed by Indians during the feasting and revelry just before Lent. During the four-day celebrations when the image was brought down to the parish church, there was much drunkenness, lewd behavior, and gambling. He blamed the subdelegado for failing to help control the disorders. The audiencia fiscal responded in a sweeping gesture, recommending to the court that local processions with this image be banned; such processions were by then widely thought by crown reformers to be at the root of disorders and profanation of the faith throughout the Catholic world. The cura of Amecameca was far from satisfied with this solution. Because local Indians fervently believed that this Christ had spoken to Fray Martín, the ban on all processions and short pilgrimages to Amecameca was certain to meet with righteous, potentially explosive opposition.

Writing again in February 1807, the cura claimed that the disorders had indeed been even worse in 1806 (when the processions were forbidden), and that the subdelegado had made no effort to control the gambling. Now the audiencia retreated to a ban on gambling and on the sale of food and drink after 6:00 P.M. But this angered the *asentista de gallos* (the local cockfight monopolist), whose lucrative concession was suddenly worthless. Merchants warned darkly of an Indian tumulto, pointing out that Indians from the outlying pueblos worked during the day and expected to do their festival drinking in Amecameca at night. Nevertheless, sensing the direction of the political wind, the subdelegado now supported the audiencia's modest reform (but not soon enough to avoid a fine of 500 pesos for negligence). He judged the 1807 celebrations to be less disorderly than before, and no worse than was to be expected when so many Indians congregated in one place. In his opinion, the great source of the problem had been the drinking, which was the "chief source of merriment" among Indians. Unfortunately, he added, they were strangers to moderation, a fact that inevitably led to crimes, prostitution, and other indecorous conduct. In this case, both the cura and the fiscal moved zeal to caution, while the initially permissive subdelegado was drawn into a more active part than he apparently would have wished. Only the asentista's interests were neglected (and those perhaps only temporarily).[121]

Organized religion was the great source of public festivity, but not all festivities were primarily religious or supervised by the parish clergy. There were periodic feasts to renew the rental of a community rancho, semireligious gatherings with music and dancing like those commemorating the death of a child, and *gallos* or serenades in the streets at night sponsored by a private party.[122] In the early 1790's, the Indians of Juchipila (Zacatecas), with the subdelegado's support, even turned the coronation of Charles IV into an annual celebration of thanksgiving.[123] By the end of the colonial period, *fandangos* had emerged as popular occasions for diversion in both dioceses, but especially in Guadalajara.[124] These were nighttime parties to celebrate a wedding, a person's saint's day, the return of a relative, or some other special occasion. The essential ingredients were music, dancing, and drinking.

Whether in a home or a tavern, fandangos were noisy, high-spirited occasions that spilled out into the streets and often grew spontaneously by attracting neighbors and strangers, blurring the line between private and public without becoming community events. Invariably, there was the music of guitars, violins, and sometimes a harp; and dancing, shouting, and heavy drinking, especially by the men. These were occasions when people stepped out of their ordinary lives but not into supervised religious devotion, and without the masks and costumes of the fiesta. In fandangos, village men were more likely to express their feelings, act extravagantly, and pick a fight. The combination of excitement, escape from routine affairs, drinking, and a general belief that drink gave one courage could lead to tests of manhood, arguments, and bloodshed. Personal grudges and less personal feelings of anger might come to the surface and be released as a gratuitous insult or shove that led to fistfights and drawn knives. Attacks on individuals at fandangos were more than incidental. In central Jalisco in the late colonial period, more homicides in rural districts occurred at fandangos (16 percent) than in any other setting. People went to fandangos knowing they were dangerous places. There was the expectation that crowds of people drinking and dancing could mean violence as well as high spirits (*alegría*). This is how the audiencia's fiscal explained a wedding fandango in Amatitan in 1813 that turned into a bloody melée: "A great mob of strangers were drawn together. . . . Excesses, wantonness, music, and drunkenness put all those present in the mood for offending someone and defending themselves."[125]

Village life was never really private, and the music of a fandango readily drew a crowd, as in the case of Doroteo Salazar. Identified as an Indian of Zoquipa (Zapopan district, near Guadalajara) in the trial record, twenty years old, he returned to town from his duties as a shepherd and charcoal maker on December 17, 1809. On the spur of the moment, two friends invited him to go to a house in the pueblo where harp and violin music was playing. Salazar said he refused several drinks that were offered to him there and was shoved and abused verbally for doing so. But he must have been drinking heavily, because he pawned his hat for liquor, and several witnesses said he was drunk and abusive before he left the fandango. The unfortunate victim of Salazar's drunken rage was another Indian of Zoquipa, Secundino de la Cruz, who was walking home from his nephew's house when Salazar appeared on the street swinging his sword. Salazar demanded to know where Cruz was coming from and, without delay, ran him through three times. The bewildered victim testified that there was no motive, that they had been friends until then.[126]

As often as not, the fatal violence at fandangos was indiscriminate, spontaneous, or misdirected. At a rowdy party in the house of Juan Felipe at the cofradía rancho of San Gaspar Escacalco (Tlaltenango district) on the eve of the Day of the Three Kings, January 5, 1820, a local Indian was killed, and no one seemed to know why. The fandango ended at 10:00 P.M., but a number of local Indian men remained, "speaking in a disoriented way like drunks," according to witnesses. None of those present could or would say what happened next, but about midnight, Juan Doroteo de la Cruz argued with Juan Felipe and killed him with an *estoque* (a long narrow sword), which, according to Cruz's wife, he had taken to the fandango "to fight bulls if there were any, as happens in these functions." Cruz claimed to have been so drunk he did not remember what happened and did not know if he had injured Juan Felipe. He did say that he had been drinking distilled vino mezcal that night instead of the usual maize beer, *tesgüino*.[127]

In another fandango, at the ranch house of the mayordomo of the Cofradía del Señor San Antonio of Totatiche (on the Jalisco-Zacatecas border near Tlaltenango) in June 1818, an Indian constable was killed while trying to intervene in a fight between two creoles, Sinforoso Gallegos and Domingo Guisar. Earlier in the year, Gallegos had been arrested by the constables during a dispute at the cofradía ranch's roundup. Now Gallegos came up to one of them, Dionisio Valenzuela, and asked if he still bore a grudge over that incident. Valenzuela said no, and Gallegos replied that he must drink with him—"that he had to drink the wine I gave him." Valenzuela answered that he would drink what he could. The dancing and drinking carried on all night. As Valenzuela put it before he died, the fandango was filled with "a multitude of provocative drunks." During the night, Gallegos and Guisar fought over a card game, and Guisar left. At sunrise, he reappeared waving a spear, calling for Gallegos to come out, calling him an "hijo de una tal" (son of a bitch), and shouting "a thousand insolences." Guisar and Gallegos began to fight again in the house. Guisar was wounded and demanded that Valenzuela arrest Gallegos. When Valenzuela tried to make the arrest, Gallegos knifed him through.[128]

The Case of Zapotlan el Grande

As parish priests feared, community fiestas could become occasions for scandalous, barely Christian devotions. The town of Zapotlan el Grande (modern Ciudad Guzmán) in the Diocese of Guadalajara was well known at the end of the colonial period for its large and unruly fiestas. This seat of an alcaldía mayor south of Guadalajara had become a substantial trading and agricultural center inhabited by Indians and non-Indians (largely separated by neighborhood). Most of the creole families, of which there were about 200 in the town, were farm owners, producing maize and sugarcane. Cattle ranching was important, but there were comparatively few ranchos (roughly three for every hacienda). Indian villagers in the district grew maize and produced mezcal; those who lived in the town were artisans, servants, and day laborers. If the town followed the pattern in the district, about 40 percent of the residents would have been classified as Indians, 40 percent as mulatos and other castas, and 20 percent as creoles.[129] Though Indians and non-Indians maintained their own fiestas and public spectacles, they were similar in their taste for processions and their distaste for colonial authorities. Judicial records for Indian fiestas there in the early 1780's and a non-Indian disturbance in late December 1793 permit a brief description and comparison.

In early April 1782, the cura of Zapotlan, Bernardino Antonio de Lepe y Rivera, wrote to the viceroy seeking his aid in controlling the elaborate celebrations and unruly conduct of his Indian parishioners, especially during Easter week. Events that week had left Lepe shaken and afraid for his life, but not surprised. He remembered that in 1774 Indian parishioners had raised a frightening commotion when the Maundy Thursday processions were ordered curtailed. A crowd of Indians had gathered at the parish church, demanding the keys and threatening to kill the priests if they did not accede. The priests hid for safety as Indians stormed the building and remained there for the night prowling around in noisy disarray (Lepe spoke of them "formando algazara"—shouting and murmuring like a force of Moors happening on the enemy). The militia was unable to contain the Indians' insolence, and the aggressors went unpunished except for some acts of public penance.

The result of the 1774 disturbance, said Lepe, was that the Indians continued their old fiesta ways and were emboldened in their insolence to him. He felt powerless to contain any of their scandalous fiesta customs and public drunkenness, knowing that a similar scene was sure to follow. One custom he considered especially pernicious because of its extravagance and great expense was the flowered arches the Indians insisted on constructing for the church, the hospital, and other chapels on fiesta days. Many of the 30 or so arches were huge, requiring fifteen to 20 Indians to move one. Great bunches of marigolds, speedwell, roses, and other flowers that were not grown locally had to be brought from distant pueblos, sometimes at a cost of 50 pesos an arch. The arches were constructed the night before in great unruly parties of men and women drinking all night as they worked, accompanied by profane music. The cost was considerable, said Lepe, in both money and human dignity—over 1,000 pesos a year and many arguments, injuries, and acts of rape, incest, and adultery. Accordingly, the year before, he had banned the arches and ordered the Indian alcalde to punish violators. Subsequently, a crowd of Indians ("over a thousand," claimed Lepe) gathered at the alcalde mayor's office armed with knives and clubs, demanding that he prevent the cura from whipping two men. Fearing for his life, the alcalde mayor, Vicente de Leis y Oca (a peninsular infantry second lieutenant), ordered Lepe to release the Indians. The Indian community was in turmoil, Leis y Oca said, with some selling their house lots and leaving town, and others who stayed simply refusing to pay their royal tribute and clerical fees.

The disturbance of April 6, 1782, that Lepe now complained of was the fourth that had erupted over his attempt to control dangerous and unchristian rites at fiestas. Lepe touched off one disturbance by interrupting a Candlemas "mogiganga," in which men dressed up as bulls, wearing wooden frames covered with a skin of palm matting with bull's horns attached to the head. According to Lepe, vengeful Indians disguised this way used the merrymaking as an occasion to gore their enemies, with many resulting wounds and some deaths. Then he tried to prevent the risky celebrations and costly banners that were customary on Whitsunday (Pentecost) in the public plaza and during wedding celebrations. They began decorously, he said, but often ended in fights with rocks and clubs. The Indians formed units with banners, and went about singing and drinking all night.[130] This year's Maundy Thursday disturbance against the cura followed his order that they not flagellate themselves so violently in their drunkenness and his reminder that one man had died of self-inflicted wounds in 1779. Alcalde Mayor Leis y Oca had denied the request to allow some of the Indians to continue the practice of bloody flagellations in the procession, but they had gone ahead—"with notable indecency," said the alcalde mayor—drinking and drawing blood as they marched.[131]

The militant separation of Indians' religious identity at Zapotlan was played out in court again in 1797, when Indian leaders of Santa María de la Asunción complained to the audiencia that the cura of Zapotlan, Felipe Figueroa, would not allow the bells in the newly finished church to be rung for their events and buried only gente de razón in the courtyard. "We are on our ground; the *pueblo* is ours," they said. Although the subdelegado, Tadeo de Therán, was mentioned in the Indians' complaint, he was fearful of further Indian violence and helped the audiencia frame a response that would mollify the Indians without making an example of the cura. In his letter to the court, Therán noted that the Indian population was large—1,259 tributaries in this place alone—and easily provoked. These Indians were, he said "little educated and lacking the necessary enlightenment." Taking away their customary privileges could well lead to protests he would not be able to contain. Once, he added, when the cura refused to allow an Easter Week procession to pass along its usual route, they rioted, and the gente de razón had to hide for safety. The audiencia issued an order to the cura along the lines suggested by the subdelegado: he was to avoid innovations and their potentially unfortunate consequences.[132]

As the subdelegado had already learned, he could not count on even the most privileged non-Indian citizens of Zapotlan to support a campaign against festive excesses. The freewheeling processions on the night of December 28, 1793, were neither Indian nor part of an organized religious event, but they were just as disruptive as any Indian fiesta. They amounted to a high-spirited private celebration that turned public and ugly. The more the subdelegado tried to intervene, the more he turned the matter into a defiance of civil and ecclesiastical authority.

Therán had the first words in the judicial inquiry into the disturbance, which he called a gallo.[133] By his account, a disorderly, drunken party of many men and women had wound its way in and out of the plaza for much of the evening, ignoring the curfew that the subdelegado had ordered the previous August on public displays of this kind. Attempting to break things up by taking the musicians in hand, he learned that they had been hired by José Manuel de Orbe, the administrator of the tobacco monopoly. Sensing that this circumstance, combined with the reputation of Zapotlan for insolence and licentiousness, might be truly dangerous to public order, he thought better of it, and took no other action that night.

The depositions Therán later took from leading participants give a clearer idea of what a gallo of this magnitude involved. It had grown spontaneously from what had begun much like the posadas at Christmastime, with families making stops at different houses. In the course of their trips, they had called in at the shop of José Antonio López for some rum. López and his family joined the crowd, as did many other *gente plebeya* as well as *gente decente* "excited by the merriment and vigor of the gallo" and by the effects of the rum.

The evidence pointed toward Simón de Figueroa, the head of the local militia, as the evil genius of the disorder, but it was not pursued. Instead, attention focused on a common soldier, Miguel López, and his wife, mostly because they had the effrontery to balk at the subdelegado's investigation. Therán reported on January 18 that the wife would not give her deposition unless he went to her house, as if she and her sister were "some high and mighty women," rather than "mere orphans." Ever protective of his official dignity, Therán refused, but the damage was done:

By this example, Sir, a variety of women in this *pueblo* refuse to come to the government offices to face the *subdelegado* so that even the tamale vendors refuse, saying that they are ladies, all of them believing that they would lose respect unless the Judge is made to act as everyone's servant when in fact his office makes him the most distinguished of all.

Only a notary could go to their houses to take such a deposition, Therán added, and there was no notary in town. Now he wanted these insults punished. The audiencia was more circumspect. On July 4, it judged López and his wife to be the root of the problem and exonerated all the others involved. Nearly a year later, the fiscal of the audiencia added a note that López had lodged a complaint against the subdelegado but had not pursued it. Since all parties had long since been absolved of blame, he ordered the case "archivado"—placed in the inactive files.

That people of the district of Zapotlan, whether Indian or not, had a reputation for flouting authority and for customs bordering on blasphemy is further evident in a denunciation to the Inquisition in 1793 from the cura of Zapotiltic. He said that some non-Indian men there had tattoos of half-naked women on their arms and legs and the Blessed Virgin on their backs, and he had heard of a man in Tamazula who was fond of saying that "God is very good, but the Devil isn't so bad since he helps men." The Indians of Zapotlan, he said, had superstitious practices for the funerals of dead children in which they seemed to worship death and personify it. They were also famous for keeping a great many images of Christ, most of them exceedingly ugly, which they took out on procession during Easter Week and which contributed more to rivalries and verbal abuse than to devotion and respect.[134]

But there was more to conflicts over religious practice in Zapotlan than tensions between local ways of celebrating and colonial authority. By the 1780's, open conflict within the colonial elite—between priests and district governors, and creoles and district governors, over property and political duties—contributed to the climate of provocation and disobedience in religious life. In 1786, the viceroy received a bitter (and ultimately unsuccessful) petition calling for the removal of Alcalde Mayor Leis y Oca "in the name of Christ's blood."[135] The main charges against him were substantiated by creole and peninsular witnesses, even by his predecessor, the popular Guillermo Aguirre, who defended Leis's character and the recent improvements in his personal conduct but could not defend his public life. One of the charges was that he was ineffective, commanding little respect even among his lieutenants. His chronic drunkenness and failure to set an example of public piety were said to be important reasons for his poor reputation as a governor. But it could also have been a legacy of his weak response to the Indian tumulto in 1782. The result, the cura's notary later claimed, was that "the people here live like Moors without a Lord." The other main charges were that he levied excessive fees on estates before their distribution to heirs and failed to put into operation the municipal granary that had recently been built (with a capacity of 5,000 fanegas). Finally, in late 1787, Leis y Oca was denounced to the Inquisition by a visiting Franciscan for sexual advances. Asked by the court where the alcalde mayor could be found, the cura he had much maligned, Bernardino Lepe y Rivera, replied (no doubt with some satisfaction) that he had gone to Guadalajara, and it was not known if he would return.[136]

*   *   *

The enduring, often lavishly expressed Christian identity in predominantly Indian parishes of Mexico and Guadalajara during the late colonial period contained tensions between priests and parishioners over correct practice, financial support, and limits to the priest's authority that could erupt in protest. The late-eighteenth-century evidence of public celebrations expresses these tensions between local lay people and their priests, and adds to them the mounting intervention in local religion of royal policy and district governors. It documents colonial officials' efforts to restrict local practices that confused the sacred and the profane, to gain control over the public life of the plebe, and to restore some of the decorum and sobriety of everyday life to feast-day events and non-religious celebrations. The administrative message was clear: public processions and other festivities should be edifying spectacles. It was an old message, but the royal government's insistent interest and overshadowing activity in pursuit of it were new. But even more salient than the tension between colonial policy and local practice was the tension between parish priests and royal governors.

Ironically—at least to curas who were quick to criticize their parishioners for unseemly religious exuberance—it was priests who the intendants and subdelegados were inclined to blame for the excessive number of fiestas and the disorderly behavior in them.[137] The blame was sometimes well-placed, since parish priests had a financial interest in introducing new celebrations. Most district governors increasingly took it upon themselves to supervise religious fiestas ("in order to contain the Indians in good order," as the subdelegado of Xochimilco put it in 1793 when he visited the feast of the patron saint in Milpa Alta), regulate the priests' funeral processions, and promote secular celebrations for events like Charles IV's coronation that reduced the priest to an honored spectator.[138]

CHAPTER ELEVEN

Saints and Images

Look at an Indian man or woman kneeling on the step of
some altar where a Crucifix is placed, and you will notice
that, with hands pressed together, sighing and bathed in
tears, he repeats his prayers. Then he rises, goes up to
the altar, and draws near the image. He reaches his hand
out to touch [the image], then withdraws it in a timorous
gesture; he kisses it, signs the cross with it, and leaves.
What will this Indian think—after so many genuflections,
such expressive demonstrations of his devotion, approaching the image with such fear, and barely daring to draw
his hand close because it seems overly bold to touch the
image of Jesus Christ—if he sees the priest elevate and
lower the consecrated Host quickly, without special feeling or reverence? What will he think if he sees the priest
bless it and sign the chalice with it in a disorderly way,
with extravagant flutterings as if he were dancing with
it? Regarding the Pastor as his Teacher and Director, will
he learn from this Mass the respect and reverence that is
owed to Christ Our Lord in the Eucharist?
—Pérez de Velasco's manual for novice pastors, 1766

Pérez de Velasco's account of Indian devotion, written as a warning to young
priests, points to the important place of sculpted and painted images of
Christ and the saints in local religion, and links official intentions and the religious practices of lay people. The Indian's actions were a model of the respect
and devotion that the church encouraged. The Christian Indian Pérez de Velasco
portrayed came to his devotions feeling the full weight of the divine presence in
the church. In this sense, he was a better Christian than the priest who swooped
through the mass. But he came to the figure on the cross more as a supplicant
seeking intercession than as a contrite sinner,[1] and that figure was barely approachable. Intimate intercessors—"advocates"—were needed to carry the supplicant's message to God and his godly Son.

Miracles and Frauds

The veneration of saints and Christian images in eighteenth-century pueblos
has an obvious beginning and a more transparent history than precolonial prac-

tices and conceptions that continued yet changed in ways that are largely hidden from the written record or are otherwise difficult to describe and date. In discussing the importance of saints and images in rural parishes, priests and foreign visitors before and after Mexican independence were inclined to stress the Indians' mistaken identifications and their supposedly superficial understanding of the faith. But the tension between priests' theology and local practices went far beyond Indians—to the very nature of Catholic devotion. Especially after the mid-sixteenth-century Council of Trent, Catholicism focused attention on the display of sacred *things*—relics of saints and other holy objects; beautiful (and therefore divinely inspired) paintings and statues of the heroes of Catholic history; medals, crucifixes, rosary beads, pilgrimage mementoes, cheap prints of saints, and printed bulls of the Crusade; chestfuls of fine vestments and costly (therefore more precious) implements of the liturgy; and altars, furniture, and other adornments for the House of God.[2] These "things" made parish churches not only places of worship but also models of the kingdom of heaven.[3] Like much of Hispanic Baroque art, they were intended less to engage the intellect with theological propositions than to provide an experience of divine order and grandeur.[4] They helped to build "a bridge that reached from the mundane world to the threshold of the divine spirit."[5] The elaborate altars, the paintings and sculpted figures, the play of light on polished silver and three-dimensional forms coated with gold leaf created precious surfaces pulsating with life. Especially in the seventeenth and eighteenth centuries, to be inside a well-furnished colonial church or chapel was to approach the heavenly realm, to be transported toward the divine in an atmosphere of worship that engaged all the senses—the smell of incense, candle wax, and damp earth; the feel of holy water, a saint's robes, the points of the cross signed on one's forehead, shoulders, and chest, and the hard ground or tiles under one's knees; the sound of organ music, the cantors' voices, the priest's mysterious speech and the echoes of his footsteps at the altar, the bell that signaled the presence of Christ, and the murmurings of prayers and confessions; and the sight of precious objects, colors, movement, and shafts of light that drew the eyes up and out.

If such churches modeled the kingdom of heaven and were charged with the divine presence, then divinely charged images could show signs of life—blinking, bleeding, twitching, shedding tears or perspiration—and could serve as the agents of other marvels. A will to believe in such incarnations bridged ethnic groups, regions, and classes. To village believers, the possibility was realized in different ways many times over in colonial Mexico. For example, in the mid-seventeenth century, Fr. Francisco Tello recounted the Passover legend that circulated among the Indians of Tuspa in southern Jalisco, in which they claimed that by painting crosses on their houses, they had been spared from the fearsome epidemic of 1577.[6] Antonio de Alcedo, in his *Diccionario geográfico de las Indias Occidentales o América* (published between 1786 and 1789), described the trembling Christ of Santa Ana Amatlan in the district of Tancítaro (Michoacán) and its trinitarian symbolism:

[The town of Amatlan] has a monastery of Franciscan friars in whose church an image of the crucixion called the Christ of the Miracle is venerated with magnificent elegance. It carries this title because at three o'clock on the third day of Easter in 1739, in the house of

V.R. de la Hermosissima Imagen de N.S. Crucificado milagrosamente Reno-
bada que se venera en el Convento Antiguo de Señoras Carmelitas
Descalzas de Mexico.
El Eminentisimo S.D. Luis Antonio Arzobispo de Toledo, Concede, 100, dias de Indulgencia
à todas las personas q. delante de esta estampa rezàre un Credo, Padre Nro. ò hizieren alguno de los
Actos de Fee, rogando à Dios por la paz &'.

FIG. 9. A "living" image. Print of a decrepit crucifix from near Ixmiquilpan, Hidalgo, that
reportedly sweated, groaned, and restored itself to fine condition in 1621. The archbishop
ordered the crucifix brought to Mexico City, where it was placed in the convent church of
the Carmelite nuns.

some Indians of the *pueblo* of Xalapa where it was placed, the image began to tremble as if it wanted to break loose from the cross. Astonished, those present brought their neighbors together and they witnessed the movement until six o'clock, when the *cura* arrived. This prodigious event being evident to them all, they formed a procession and took the image to the church and placed it on the high altar, where it repeated its movement three times.[7]

Images like the Christ of Amatlan that had given a visible sign of their spiritual power and approachability were especially favored intercessors between ordinary Christians and God.[8] In this case, the priest of Amatlan succeeded in appropriating the trembling Christ from Xalapa for his parish church. But often priests were less than happy about religious images and places that enraptured their parishioners and complicated the cross's official meaning of submission and humility. Images of Christ discovered in the neighboring woods, fields, and waters or associated with caves and hills were particularly appealing to native believers in colonial Mexico. There, as in the sixteenth-century Spanish areas studied by William Christian, discovered images usually appeared in the countryside, away from the parish center and the priest. Such images, found by tillers or gatherers or shepherds or fishermen in the villagers' own domain, signaled a direct association between lay people and the divine, even if the image was moved to the parish church or to a sanctuary closely supervised by the clergy.[9] The Christ of Chalma near Malinalco and the painting of Christ in Fr. Martín de Valencia's cave on the Sacromonte of Amecameca, both in the Estado de México, and especially Our Lady of Guadalupe at Tepeyac in the Valley of Mexico, gained large followings beyond the local area, but there were many others.[10] Whether associated with miracles or not, Christian images placed far from the parish church were problematic. At Amanalco (Metepec district, Edo. de México), where Indians and their curas were often in conflict, the pastoral visitor in 1792 was determined to persuade parishioners to bring into the parish church for "proper devotion" the crosses they kept in the mountains and other remote places.[11]

An area particularly given to this kind of devotion was the vicinity of Lake Chapala in modern Jalisco and Michoacán. Most of the eleven renowned images that Fr. Matías de Escobar reported for the Diocese of Michoacán in 1729 were located near this lake, close to Guadalajara.[12] Escobar gives pride of place in his account to an image known as Our Lady of the Root kept in the parish church of Xacona. Consisting of two intertwined roots—one a "perfect image of most saintly Mary," the other "a most perfect Child nestled in his mother's bosom"—the image was found floating in the shallows of Lake Chapala by an Indian fisherman from Paxacoran, who took the piece of root home and dried it. Later, as he made to burn it, his friend Juan of Xacona happened by, and noticing some features of an image on the root, retrieved it from the flames. Escobar emphasized the providential signs associated with the discovery: it was found along a reeded shoreline like Moses among the bullrushes; it survived the fire like Shadrach, Meshach, and Abednego; and it paralleled the apparition of the Virgin of Guadalupe to an Indian named Juan on the shore of another great lake. In fact, to this pious promoter of his diocese, the Virgin of Xacona was Michoacán's Guadalupe.

The other ten images in Escobar's account are crucifixes, bringing the Christian cross into close association with trees and the sacred energy they contained (especially in precolonial conceptions of a layered universe joined at the cor-

ners by cosmic trees)—at La Piedad and San Pedro Piedra Gorda in the parish
of Tlazacalco, Santiago Ocotlan, San Miguel de Atotonilco, Jocotepec, Villa de
León, Tupátaro (near Pátzcuaro), Tamazula, Valladolid, and Ziragüén in the
parish of Guiramángaro.[13] The cases that he describes in some detail follow the
same pattern: a humble campesino, gathering wood in the countryside, discovers
the image when he tries to burn it.

The Jocotepec image had already turned up in a case that reached the ecclesiastical and civil courts earlier in the 1720's. The record in the episcopal court
begins with a petition of August 22, 1720, to the bishop of Guadalajara by Francisco de la Cruz Godoy, an indio principal of Jocotepec.[14] De la Cruz stated that
three months earlier, he had ordered a large mesquite tree cut down for a calvary
cross. His carpenter reported that the six-foot cross he had cut from the tree was
better suited for a crucifix because it already showed the form of Christ on it.
Calling it "Our Master and Lord," Cruz wanted the bishop's permission to build
a chapel for his Christ on the hill used for the Calvary, where, conveniently, de
la Cruz had a small farm.

Miguel Aznar, the guardian of the Franciscan monastery at Ajijic and assistant
pastor for Jocotepec, contributed a more complicated version of the story. The
Jocotepec church, he reported, already had a miraculous crucifix, known as the
Santo Cristo de la Expiración, with its own cofradía, an endowment of land from
d. José de Cara, and the bishop's license to collect alms for the image.[15] Indeed,
the mayordomo of this crucifix, Matheo Lucas, had been taking it to neighboring pueblos to collect alms. (This was the image, cut from a guaje tree, to which
Escobar referred in 1729.) In 1718, de la Cruz Godoy had persuaded the elders of
the pueblo in one of their drunken meetings to name him mayordomo in Lucas's
place. But Lucas refused to give up the image and gathered another group of
elders ("viejos principales"), who voided de la Cruz Godoy's appointment. An
angry de la Cruz then went out looking for a tree with a cross shape that was large
enough for another crucifix like Matheo Lucas's. Having found the big mesquite
and brought the trunk to his house, de la Cruz first contacted a mestizo amateur
sculptor ("medio escultor") of Ajijic to carve a Christ on the trunk, then settled
on an Indian from Istahuacan, who produced the poorly sculpted figure that now
appeared there.

That accomplished, Fray Aznar said, de la Cruz had proceeded to build a
chapel for his "Miraculous Christ of the Calvary" with the poisonous intention
of obtaining a license to collect alms and grow rich from the proceeds. The completion of the chapel was celebrated with so great a hubbub of music, dancing,
and beating of drums that the entire town went there to give alms, forgetting all
about the cross in the parish church. On the wall of the new chapel, a forged episcopal decree was posted, granting indulgences to those who prayed there.[16] Word
spread of the miraculous cross, and Indians throughout the area (*comarca*) flocked
to the place. The friar ordered the alcaldes of Jocotepec to whip de la Cruz and
bring him the cross, which he covered with a sheet and locked in the baptistry.

In short, Aznar reported that de la Cruz's cross was a dangerous fraud and
should not be licensed or otherwise recognized by the bishop. But the friar had
few kind words for Matheo Lucas and his cross, either. Matheo Lucas, he said,
lived a respectable family life, but he had been exiled from the community two

years before with five or six followers and lived about a league from town (on the cofradía lands?), where he had built a small "chapel." He had been selling live-stock from the cofradía herd without permission and had not accounted for the "plentiful" alms collected in the name of the cross. How, wondered the priest, had the once poor Matheo Lucas acquired houses and a substantial estate? The parish church was falling apart, and only the chapel with its cross was being maintained. He lamented the gullibility of common people "who are deceived in these supposed and false miracles by superstitious and deceitful Indians." "I confess," concluded the priest, "I am not comfortable with these Christs that ap-pear to Indians. Based on my understanding and experience in the past year with the Indians of this *pueblo*, if my inadequacy would allow me and if I were asked for my judgment, I would suggest in conscience that you order the burial of these images."

Despite Aznar's earnest recommendation, Matheo Lucas's cross, with its promise of providential rewards and political mischief, remained an important factor in the public life of Jocotepec. In 1748, a barrio of Jocotepec residents moved out of town to the land where the image of Christ had appeared. They petitioned for town status, only to be told that the land belonged to d. Sebastián de Caros. In 1773, the separatists, now calling themselves the people of San Martín Texiutlan [Teccistlan], again petitioned for town status. They said they had moved to vacant royal land ("baldías y realengas"); their population had grown from 50 family heads, including widowers, in 1748 to 72, not counting widowers; they had established a school and hired a schoolmaster to teach the catechism, Spanish, and reading, writing, and counting; they had elected their own cabildo in 1772, with the approval of the cura of Ajijic and royal authority; and, thanks to an order from the alcalde mayor, the miraculous Christ now was housed in a sanctuary in their community. In the alcalde mayor's investigation that year, the Indians of Jocotepec opposed the petition as a thinly veiled ma-neuver by the people of San Martín to escape paying their share of the town's expenses. But the alcalde mayor apparently sided again with the people of San Martín, because pueblo status was approved by the end of the year. Since the recent secularization of the parish, the alcalde mayor had emerged as the deci-sive figure in the old factional dispute dating from Matheo Lucas's time and the struggle for control of the Santo Cristo de la Expiración. The image and its sepa-ratist faithful had found their place.[17]

Saints and Intercessors

Unlike the troubling discovered images that offered lay people direct commu-nication with the divine, the saints were a conventional, ubiquitous part of the local practice of religion and the design of the colonial world. In principle, social and religious unity was achieved through hierarchy. At the pinnacle of all order, God sat in judgment, remote from the everyday affairs of lay people. He had to be approached through those who themselves had a measure of divinity or spe-cial access to the divine. Priests were intercessors, to be sure, but few claimed to speak directly to God. The principal intercessors were the many saints of the church—some mainly two-way translators of messages, others advocates engaged in protecting the interests of believers.

Individual Christians had a special relationship with the saints after whom they had been baptized; and even if not named after the saint on whose day they had been born or baptized, they often had a special regard for that saint too. In addition to the family altars and images of saints that were served in Indian homes as if the saint actually resided there,[18] every colonial town and most neighborhoods had a patron saint. As in sixteenth-century Spain, villagers assumed "a series of obligations, many of them explicit and contractual, not unlike their obligations to secular lords,"[19] and involving labor service, offerings of money, flowers, clothing, artwork, candles, and incense, and other signs of devotion. There was always an annual fiesta in the patron saint's honor, renewing the bonds of obligation and loyalty. Also, thanks to the initiatives of local laymen or parish priests who arrived with their own favorites, the parish and visita churches inevitably acquired images of other saints and a special devotion to many of them.[20] Sculpted figures, paintings, and side altars dedicated to particular saints were supported from cofradía property, individual sponsorship, and collections. The appeal of particular saints was often perpetuated in the parish by private endowments. As the subdelegado for Tenayuca (Valley of Mexico) reported in 1818, "There is this custom among the Indians who have the use of a plot of community land to will it to the saints upon their death."[21] The cura of Huitzilac (Morelos) in the early 1760's, Diego de Almonacid y Salasar, reported that an Indian had willed money for the construction of an altar to San Bartolomé about 20 years before, and that he, the cura, had recently completed the work.[22]

The annual round of religious feasts for universally popular saints like Mary, Peter, and Paul, visits to festivals for saints of neighboring towns, and longer pilgrimages to special shrines further enlarged the inventory of personal and collective spiritual intercessors. Some of the more portable and less fragile images, like the Virgin of Zapopan and the Chapalan Christs, were taken out on pilgrimage to expand and renew the devotion among residents of outlying settlements.

Approaching the saint through an image raised the troubling old problem in Christianity of what was being venerated. Was it the figure of wood, paint, and stone or the symbolic association? The sixteenth-century Franciscans in particular struggled against the lay fascination with images, but there was a persistent tension between object and symbol throughout the colonial period. In practice, the line between them was not sharp, for it was through the image that the saint was most accessible. With the discovered images that worried Fray Aznar, there was little of this tension: it was the image that counted most.

The devotion to saints and images in late colonial central and western Mexico was neither a simple imposition nor a collection of local practices independent of the episcopal and universal churches. Lay people in rural Mexican parishes took the saints given to them, discovered others, and made many of them their own in ways that combined instruction, invention, and prior experience of the divine. A saint like San Isidro Labrador, with his oxen and plow, appealed to farmers and was especially revered in central and southern Mexico. San José (Joseph) was promoted by the early bishops of New Spain as the special patron of the new church in America,[23] but, overshadowed by his wife and not readily distinguished from other male saints, he did not gain the hoped-for universal popular devotion. With Franciscan missionaries among the first in the field, their founder gained exceptional Indian devotion early on (or so Motolinía said),[24] but Saint Francis lost ground in rural parishes during the late colonial period.

Each parish has its particular history of saints that, separately and together, would reveal much about the practice of local religion and a triangle of political power connecting priests, royal governors, and community officials. The rather distant evidence of the directorios (detailed reports on parish income) and other account records for the devotion to saints can be supplemented by colonial disputes that reached ecclesiastical courts. In 1775, Indians from the Simapantongo rancho in the district of Xilotepec complained of their cura's misbehavior. He wanted them to be treated as a pueblo, with mandatory masses and other obligations. To punish their resistance to the new obligations (apparently they had signed an agreement with him), he had confiscated the images of saints scattered about in their oratories and their "Most Holy Virgin in the captain's house." They appealed to the Inquisition to order the return of their saints "for our consolation."[25]

Without a bank of parish and saints studies to turn to, the remainder of this chapter focuses on Spain's two special patrons—Santiago (Christ's apostle, Saint James the Greater) and the Virgin Mary—two widely popular saints with substantially different histories that expose some of the complexities of change in local religious practices and how their meanings were reworked in colonial Indian pueblos.

Santiago and His Horse

Of all the saints, Santiago stood most clearly for the violence done to native Americans by Spaniards in the Conquest period; yet he continued to hold their attention long after the imposition of Spanish rule. In Spain, Santiago was the symbol of the Reconquista—Christianity on the march, the holy war against Islam in Iberia.[26] In the sixteenth century, he crossed the Atlantic as a central image also in the Spanish expeditions into mainland America, invoked by the invading troops for his aid and protection against the Indians, and claimed by the Franciscans as patron for their evangelical province of Xalisco and by the Dominicans for their province of Mexico.[27] To Spaniards, he came to symbolize their destiny to rule and the Indians' destiny to submit. He was eagerly promoted by Spanish evangelizers as a personification of Christian conquest, and widely accepted by Indians as a force to be propitiated.

The Humilladero (Chapel of Submission) in Pátzcuaro, Michoacán, was known as one of the colonial monuments to this meaning of the saint and to the memory of the Conquest. According to the Spanish Capuchin Francisco de Ajofrín, who traveled in New Spain during the early 1760's, it was built on the site where Santiago had appeared to the Spanish forces two hours before dawn on the day of a pivotal battle. The Spaniards awoke "invigorated and full of courage," while the Indians awoke "confused and scared. Then without raising their weapons, they gave up, humble and submissive."[28]

Images of Santiago and human impersonators of the saint were important props in the dramas of mock combat that Spaniards staged for themselves and promoted among Indian neophytes during the sixteenth and seventeenth centuries. In one of the standard forms for these ritual military engagements, the moros y cristianos dances, Indians reenacted the Reconquista, with Santiago leading the Christians into glorious victory over the infidel.[29] The parallel with the Spanish conquest of native America would not have been lost on the spectators and participants. As Richard Trexler has suggested, these early spectacles were more than exercises in piety. They were intended as instruments of Spanish political control, "conquest through behavioral control," as he puts it, that "conjured a world safe for Hispanicism."[30] Through Santiago as bellicose patron of the Spaniards, the memory of violent conquest remained alive, and villagers might welcome the sting of his sword at fiesta time as penance for their sins.[31] But Indian understandings were not carbon copies of Spanish intentions.

Even the intention was not so simple. In a late-sixteenth-century account of missionary activity in the Franciscan province of Xalisco, Fr. Francisco Mariano de Torres associated Santiago and Indian submission, but with the added implication that Indians might also share in the saint's protection. He reported that the Indians of the province, especially at Tonalá, where they had made him their patron saint, were well disposed to the friars because the Apostle Santiago had fought there for the Spaniards,

showing himself to be a true son of thunder by conquering and frightening the Indians . . . and brandishing lightning to illuminate them. As soon as the venerable Padre Segovia [the evangelizing Franciscan] arrived, they recounted the events for him with astonishment. And taking advantage of this, this holy man began to preach to them of Christ's fidelity to Christians.[32]

As Padre Segovia understood, while Santiago was a powerful symbol of the destiny of Christian Spaniards to rule over Indians, the saint's patronage also conveyed the idea that Christian Indians might share in his formidable power.[33]

Containing this dual message, Santiago grew into an important, if ambiguous, symbol in colonial times. He was the patron saint of at least 81 colonial settlements in Mexico.[34] In the sixteenth century, many prominent Indian men (like the cacique of Tonalá) were baptized Santiago or took Santiago as their surname.[35] Especially during the seventeenth and eighteenth centuries, his representations in sculpture and painting—dressed in armor and mounted on a white horse with his sword raised to strike the Muslims arrayed at the horse's feet— were acquired and carefully preserved by villagers throughout the central areas of Spanish America.[36]

From the beginning of the introduction of Christianity, the ambiguities that made devotion to the images of Santiago more than cults of Indian humiliation went beyond this mixed Spanish message, to the gulf between official explanations and local understandings. Before the 1560's, there were few friars and secular priests in the Mexican heartland. No matter how energetic their efforts, they were hampered by their small numbers, faulty understanding of native beliefs, and limited ability to communicate the subtleties of Catholic dogma in the local languages. Not surprisingly, native converts elaborated in their own terms on the outlines of new beliefs.[37]

Santiago's attraction to Indian neophytes consisted partly in his horse. Judging

by the monumental representations of fanged serpents and the intimate association between eagles or jaguars and the most esteemed warriors, the precolonial
societies of central Mexico prized the large, fierce animals around them as important agents of divine power and authority. According to Inga Clendinnen, Mexica
warriors regarded the Spaniards' horses not as obedient brutes or emblems of
the owner's social standing, but as courageous and powerful animal warriors that
may have acted in unison with their riders, but were independent of them.[38] In
the *Relación de Michoacán*, a 1541 account of native history and ceremony for western Mexico, Aztec emissaries and their Tarascan rivals shared this conception of
horses as powerful, independent agents during the Conquest. They thought of
the horses as armored deer with manes and long tails, possibly even as gods in
their own right. The horses were said to talk to their Spanish riders and wield
deadly firearms. They were worthy of the same tribute in food as the Spaniards.[39]

Indians had no large domesticated animals and thus, in the beginning, might
well have perceived trained responses as expressions of the animal's will. Even
at a distance, the sights and sounds of a cavalry charge left lasting impressions
of strength and ferocity—the ground rumbling under the horses' hooves, metal
shoes flashing and kicking up dust and bits of earth, eyes rolling, nostrils dilated,
big teeth showing behind foaming lips, and unearthly whinnying and panting—
that were epitomized in Santiago's mount.[40] Writing after 1620, Chimalpahin, the
Indian chronicler from Amecameca (near the Valley of Mexico), reportedly recorded a local tradition about the Conquest in which Santiago's horse killed and
wounded as many of the enemy with his mouth as the saint did with his sword.[41]

Spaniards and Indians both associated the horse with power, albeit perhaps
different kinds of power: social and military for Spaniards; mystical as well as
social and military for Indians. The rider's position sitting above earth-bound
onlookers, coupled with his trappings, his horsemanship, and the quality of
his mount, suggested superiority, virility, and wealth, not to mention mobility.
Horses were luxury transport, faster but not as durable on the rough and mountainous roads as mules and donkeys, and rarely used as draft animals.

Indians and horses, pageantry, and the Conquest come together in Joel R.
Poinsett's observation from his travels in central Mexico in 1822 that "the Indians
are particularly fond of appearing in processions, clothed in the armour and other
habiliments of the followers of Cortes. This dress is associated, in their minds,
with majesty and power, and they delight to ride on a war horse, armed from head
to heel with helmet and mail."[42] Poinsett leaves the reader to wonder whether the
Indian conquistadors he saw were saluting the Spaniards' power in this exchange
of roles or felt they had become, at least for the moment, Santiago's lieutenants.

Another native belief widespread in central Mexico that would have been
folded into early colonial understandings of Santiago was that animals were
agents of greater forces working on human destiny. An animal could be the manifestation of a deity; it could be infused with the migratory spirit of a *nagual* or
wizard; or it could be the protective yet vulnerable counterpart that every human
being had.[43] Animals as a manifestation of the divine, especially when infused
with a wizard's spirit, could directly injure and destroy, as well as protect. They
could also signal an impending disaster, as in the belief that when an owl's hoot
was heard or a large fly called the Miccarayoli was seen circling a house, someone inside would soon die.[44]

Precisely how beliefs in animal associations with the spiritual welfare of humans affected Indian attraction to and understandings of Santiago remains deeply uncertain. Was the saint regarded as a Christian wizard exercising great power through the horse? Could he, like a prehispanic god, transform himself into the horse? Did the horse's whiteness suggest the color's ominous associations with death and uncertainty in Nahuatl thought, and thereby reinforce the message of defeat and humiliation? Or could the horse, as a powerful domesticated animal that protected Christians, be separated from the saint and appropriated by Indians? Perhaps the answer varies for different places. As the seventeenth- and eighteenth-century examples that follow suggest, over time there would certainly be local departures from the Spaniards' use of Santiago to symbolize Indian defeat and humiliation.

The moros y cristianos dances introduced by Spaniards in the first colonial generation could be reworked by parishioners and priests.[45] By the late sixteenth century, Santiago's providential aid to Christians in battle was being transferred to mock engagements between mounted Indian townsmen and impersonators of wild, heathen "Chichimecs." Well before the Europeans' arrival, sedentary communities and states indiscriminately lumped the semisedentary people to their north as "Chichimecs," or barbarous invaders and looters.[46] By the late sixteenth century, the moros y cristianos theme was sometimes re-scripted, to make Chichimec interlopers the targets of the local heroes' efforts. For instance, in 1590 the Franciscan Alonso Ponce was welcomed into the village of Patamba, Michoacán, by about 20 Indian guards on horseback (one on a white horse, like Santiago), dressed as Spaniards and armed with wooden swords and pikes, who beat the roadside trees and brush shouting "Santiago, Santiago," and skirmished with ten or twelve "Chichimecs" who came out of the woods on foot.[47] In another spectacle enacted in Michoacán on the Day of the Holy Cross in 1643, the engagement of Christian Indians and Chichimecs followed the moros y cristianos scenario more closely. The Christian Indians assaulted a "castle" defended by "Chichimecs." The spectacle culminated in the arrival of Santiago, who vanquished the enemy and recovered the cross.[48] Like the moros y cristianos pageants, these new spectacles represented the triumph of Christianity over "paganism" in America and warned settled Indians about barbarism and backsliding. But they could carry another, more indigenist message that was less apparent in the mock battles between Moors and Christians: Santiago protects local places against their enemies. This message would have been especially appealing in Michoacán, which provides the two examples. As in the territory of modern Jalisco, Querétaro, and Hidalgo, there were parts of Michoacán where Chichimec incursions were remembered in the sixteenth century as more than distant legends.[49]

By the middle of the colonial period, Santiago ceased to be mainly a symbol of the Conquest; or, at least, not mainly a terrifying or paralyzing signal to submit to the force of Spanish authority. As the moros y cristianos dances came to be overwhelmingly Indian events,[50] Santiago took on the role of local patron or foil to a sense of community autonomy. Even where he was not the patron saint, his power was being harnessed to local purposes—to heal, protect, and fertilize. In 1624, at Ixmiquilpan in central Hidalgo, where nomadic "Chichimecs" still threatened colonial peace, an Indian named María reportedly claimed that her renowned curing powers resulted from having had intercourse with an invisible

Spaniard who came, like Santiago, on a white horse. In María's vision, the power of this man was transferred to her directly, without mediation or supplication.[51] Here the Spanish Conquest was turned on its side: by union with the phantom Spaniard, she was magically empowered. Her vision contained a radical independence that is a short step from the idea that Santiago's power could be acquired and turned against one's enemies, individual or collective.

But more often, once the Chichimec threat began receding, Santiago was invoked to prosaic purposes. In particular, he was often called up for help with the weather, recalling his association with thunder and lightning. According to Jacinto de la Serna, who had served in the Tenango del Valle district early in the seventeenth century, an Indian shaman there tried to alter the direction of clouds and storms as the corn harvest approached by appealing to Christ, the Blessed Virgin, and Santiago. His supplication to Santiago referred to the saint's virility, courage, and military might: "Santiago, young man, help me, virtuous man, strong conqueror, and courageous man, make me powerful and help me so that the works and deeds of God Almighty are not lost."[52]

In the eighteenth century, while the old images of Santiago in the parish church were approached by Indian villagers for the same favors, attention increasingly was drawn to the horse, as if the animal had become the saint. According to the crown's counsel Antonio de Ribadeneyra, if a pregnant Indian was unable to give birth, an offering of corn would be made to Santiago's horse.[53] In 1769, Indians of Tescala in the district of Huizquilucan near the Valley of Mexico were reported to have danced the forbidden dance of the Santiaguitos, in which a pony was adorned, incensed, and venerated. The saint, again, had left the spotlight.[54]

As with Tescala's pony, late colonial examples generally express a shift away from the saint himself and suggest community more than individual practices. Community fiestas centering on Santiago appear quite often in the records of the 1760's, perhaps largely because colonial authorities at that time intended to eliminate what they regarded as uncontrolled village celebrations generally, and the dance of the Santiaguitos in particular.[55] It is also possible that the dance became more popular in the preceding years, although that is purely speculative. In any case, prelates attending the Fourth Provincial Council were worried about the "pagan" and anticolonial implications of the dance as they understood it, especially the song that accompanied the dancing.[56] The Franciscan provincial said he had heard from reliable witnesses that the song was a lament by the Indians over their conquest by the Spaniards. According to Ribadeneyra's account, "The *cura* of Otumba added that he had not been able to comprehend the language [of the song]. When he asked the Indians what the words meant, they replied that they meant the same as arrogant or haughty, which referred to the sainted Apostle."[57]

The dance of the Santiaguitos may not have been as threatening as the church leaders imagined in 1771, but in an 1815 celebration at San Andrés in the district of San Pedro Tlaquepaque (outside Guadalajara), Santiago was the symbolic focal point for both submission and resistance to colonial authority. In August of that year, the Indian officials of San Andrés unsuccessfully petitioned the audiencia for permission to hold their traditional dance of the Tastuanes on the Day of San Pedro (September 8). According to the subdelegado, a man dressed as Santiago would ride through the plaza hitting masked Indians with the flat of his sword.

Explaining that the dance ended with the people surging forward to manhandle the "saint," he concluded that "the worst of the matter" was "the many obscenities that they mutter both in Spanish and Nahuatl, and also their indecent actions once they turn to 'stripping the skin' from the one who acts as Santiago." [58] The ending should have been doubly disturbing to a district governor (1) as an inversion of the moros y cristianos scenario in which Santiago appears at the decisive moment to rout the Moors; and (2) as a strange echo of the precolonial festival of Toxcatl in Tenochtitlan, which ended with the deity impersonator (ixiptla) of Tezcatlipoca being assaulted and stripped of his mask and regalia, then sacrificed. [59]

What had begun in sixteenth-century Jalisco as a commemoration of Santiago's timely aid to Spaniards, and had grown by the early seventeenth century into an annual reenactment of the miracle in Indian pueblos of Nueva Galicia,[60] became strangely twisted in this late colonial performance from the same region. In sum, there were multiple meanings and a growing ambivalence in Santiago's significance to late colonial Indians of central and western Mexico. His various meanings were rooted not only in the official Spanish messages about conquest and conversion, but also in native understandings of animals and the sacred, and in adjustments to colonial rule at the local level. Even in the sixteenth century, when the performances were more likely to be directed by colonial officials, Santiago's official significance was mixed. The early message of Indian submission and Spanish power included the problematical (to colonial governors, at least) idea that Indian converts could also be protected by the Spaniards' patron saint of war. He remained an armed avenger, but his enemies were the enemies of Christ, not Indians in particular.[61]

The notion of protection would become more complicated and localized as it grew in importance toward the end of the colonial period. The saint could be propitiated and invoked for his protection;[62] crop failures and other misfortunes could be explained as his punishment for individual and collective sins; and he could be attacked and insulted in spectacles of inversion that also separated him from his horse. In some cases, the saint had virtually disappeared or become the horse, a force of nature and potential protector physically more powerful than man but possibly harnessed to his uses. The common threads in these variations from the original messages seem to be that in spite of continuing interest in Santiago, the way was prepared for his demotion unless he was the patron saint of the community, or for his transformation into an animal benefactor with mainly local meaning.[63]

In all of these cases, whether regarded as a source of special favor or as an object of ridicule, Santiago (like most other saints) was a focal point of local expression, attached to pueblos and individual believers. Father Serna's shaman apparently was little concerned, if it occurred to him at all, that his appeal to Santiago to move the rainclouds might deprive another community of life-giving moisture.

The Virgin Mary and the Image of Guadalupe

Important as Santiago was, he was never the central figure that the Virgin Mary became in local religion. Early Spanish colonists devoted to Mary invited Indians to regard her as their special intercessor, too,[64] and she came to occupy an unrivaled place in the history of Christian saints in Latin America. Unlike other saints, she was represented in many different forms, including Our Lady of Mercy, Our Lady of the Rosary, Our Lady of the Remedies, the crowned Madonna, and the Madonna and child, and especially in forms recalling the joyful and sorrowful events that connected her life to Christ: Our Lady of the Annunciation, Our Lady of the Immaculate Conception, Our Lady of the Purification, Our Lady of the Sorrows, and Our Lady of the Assumption. Of all these representations, the Immaculate Conception was the most widely venerated in New Spain.[65] Hundreds of distinctive individual images of Mary became identified with particular places and people, and were believed to contain the power to protect and favor them. Some of these painted and sculpted images gained a wide following, and their sanctuaries became important centers of pilgrimage and popular devotion.

Among the many colonial representations of the Immaculate Conception, one has been particularly popular and ideologically important, especially from a nineteenth- or twentieth-century perspective: Our Lady of Guadalupe. By the time of independence in 1821, the Guadalupe image had become the most powerful symbol of an elusive national identity. Along with the national flag, it was the symbol most universally recognized as Mexican. But its popularity in the colonial period had more to do with its miraculous properties (defined in the sixteenth and seventeenth centuries) than with a precocious providential nationalism. Like the discovered images of Michoacán and Jalisco—divinely created objects of devotion found by humble Indians or mestizos away from their towns, without the aid or intervention of authorities—it promised direct access to the divine. Furthermore, the Guadalupe image was associated with an apparition of the Virgin, one of the few apparition stories to gain official recognition in the colonial period. The Virgin was said to have appeared three times to a humble Indian, Juan Diego, at Tepeyac, the sacred place of a precolonial mother goddess in the Valley of Mexico, finally leaving her beautiful image on the Indian's cloak as a sign of her presence for a doubting bishop. That the image was believed to represent Mary as an Indian Madonna and to have appeared on the cloak of a humble Indian gave it a nativist appeal for creole nationalists and self-conscious Indians and mestizos at the end of the colonial period.[66] Firm evidence of the tradition in the sixteenth century is scarce and inconclusive, however, and there is debate over whether the image of the Virgin of Guadalupe venerated at Tepeyac then was the famous American portrait on cloth or a replica of the Spanish image—a sculpted Madonna and child—or both.[67]

The emphasis on the Virgin of Guadalupe, especially the treatment of her as a "syncretic, Christo-pagan" goddess with a vast Indian following since the sixteenth century and as the "spiritual aspect of protest against the colonial regime,"[68] overlays a more ambiguous history of the Virgin Mary in local religion. Like Santiago, Mary was introduced by Spanish masters as their own patroness, in hundreds of different images; and she came to stand for several meanings that were subject to change, and that may or may not have moved people to political action. How she came to be so widely popular in Indian villages during the colonial period is known better at the beginning from the Spanish side. Despite the convenience and popularity of the blending of Indian and Christian female representations of the divine (triggered by the spiritual orphanhood of colonial Indians, Octavio Paz would say), research has yet to show the place of native religions and colonial circumstances in the widespread devotion to Mary during the seventeenth and eighteenth centuries. There were female deities in the pre-colonial religions of Mesoamerica, and Tepeyac itself was the sacred place of one of them—Tonantzin, by whose name the Virgin of Guadalupe was sometimes known to Indians in and near the Valley of Mexico during the colonial period— but they were less conspicuous than the Blessed Virgin would become, and often had a cold edge of intimidation and violence and an association with disorder that also separate them from Mary.[69]

The following pages describe how devotion to Mary began in New Spain and how it may have grown, especially through images of the Immaculate Conception, including the American Guadalupe. For the eighteenth and early nineteenth centuries, given names and political symbolism reveal some of the history of Marian devotion in rural parishes and the interplay of local and translocal practices and beliefs, especially the role of priests in promoting devotion to Mary.[70]

Spaniards, the Virgin Mary, and the American Guadalupe

In the Conquest period, the Virgin Mary was represented especially as La Conquistadora, a heavenly protectress of the Spaniards and—like Santiago—a symbol of Spanish power. For example, Cortés's campaign banner displayed a picture of Mary, along with Constantine's motto "Brothers and comrades, let us follow the cross, and under this sign we shall conquer"; and the province of Tabasco was given the name Holy Mary of Victory. She and the crucified Christ are the two religious images that the *Lienzo de Tlaxcala*, a native pictorial of the Conquest, adds to its representations of meetings between Spanish and Indian leaders. Although Spanish accounts do not present her as engaging in combat— except at one point to throw dust in the Indians' eyes—Bernal Díaz says that the Spaniards commended themselves (not just their souls) to "Christ and his Blessed Mother."[71] Robert Padden has suggested that Indians, as well as Spaniards, in those earliest years understood the Virgin Mary to be the embodiment of Spanish sovereignty in a confrontation of cosmic forces, with the Spaniards intent on dethroning the old gods and replacing them with Mary in the native temples and sacred places.[72] Certainly, religion and sovereignty were inseparable to those early Spaniards, and Cortés brought a generous supply of pictures and statues of the Virgin, which he gave to the Indians as symbols of divine mission and Spanish rule or placed on the altars of the "idols" wherever he could.

After the military conquest, what may appear to be purely indigenous folk beliefs about the Virgin Mary and a peculiarly strong reverence for Mary among colonial Indians look on closer inspection much like the popular beliefs of contemporary Spaniards. It is true that in the formal religion of the Catholic church, the Virgin Mary carried a variety of symbolic connotations—as queen, virgin, bride, the new Eve, innocence, mother, and intercessor; whereas in rural Latin America she was revered mainly in the last two roles. It would be a mistake, however, to equate the religion of Spanish colonists simply with the formal and doctrinaire. What Indians understood about the Virgin from the first Spaniards was also determined by the common sense of the time. As William Christian describes it, at about the time of the military conquest of Mexico, a truly extraordinary reverence for Mary blossomed in Castile, where she eclipsed all other saints and heroes of the church.[73] Over two-thirds of the curing shrines there in the early sixteenth century were dedicated to Mary, and she accounted for most of the wave of apparitions from 1400 to 1525—apparitions that were, as Christian says, "eminently social visions, validated by widespread public devotion."[74]

In Spanish popular belief, God and Christ were more feared than loved. God was a remote and brooding eminence, and Christ was represented either as a child or as sacrificed on the cross—images that Christian says were references to plague and judgment.[75] Mary, on the other hand, was the beloved intercessor who worked to deflect or soften the harsh judgments of a stern God.[76] The Virgin Mary in Spain also was closely associated with the land and fertility, an association that Cortés conveyed in an informal way when he encouraged Indians at Tenochtitlan to pray to the Virgin Mary for rain.[77] The point here is not that the meaning of the Virgin Mary to Indians in colonial Mexico was simply borrowed from Spanish folk beliefs. It is that Spanish conceptions of the Virgin were not purely abstract and formal, and Indian conceptions purely informal and unconscious. There were no neatly separable great and little traditions in this respect.

The formal counted, to be sure. Devotion to Mary was actively promoted by the church hierarchy from the beginning. Four of the twelve high holy days that the First Provincial Council (1555) required Indians to observe were associated with her birth, the annunciation, the purification, and the assumption.[78] Two centuries later, in 1760, Clement XIII declared the Virgin of the Immaculate Conception the patroness of Spain and the Indies (hastening to add that this would not prejudice the standing of Santiago as patron of Spain).[79] Many of the colonial bishops were special devotees of a particular advocation of the Virgin.

One of the most eloquent of the Virgin's episcopal devotees was Juan de Palafox y Mendoza, the bishop of Puebla. In his 1649 pastoral letter, Palafox appealed directly to lay people to give Mary their special devotion as "the Queen of the Angels," the great source of communication with her son: "Propitiate and call out to the Virgin, for this devotion will bring excellent results, especially if the whole family prays to her together at night."[80] Four years later, in an especially long pastoral letter, he instructed his priests to give special attention to the Rosary: "After the sacraments, I take it as one of the greatest consolations and remedies for the faithful. The Virgin's favor is our entire remedy. Through the Mother, one reaches the Son."[81] In a little book of epigraphic notes from his seminary lectures published in Mexico City in 1664, he advised future priests to

crown these recommendations with devotion to the Queen of the Angels, MARY, whom you should keep at the center of your heart: as a preacher, preach her; as a priest, serve her in your works, your conversations, and your prayers, with spiritual exercises during the day and contemplation at night, always yearning to merit her grace and favor.[82]

Official promotion and concern for the proper veneration of Mary continued to the end of the colonial period. The Pope's elevation of Mary Immaculate as patroness of Spain and the Indies was a benchmark. At the meetings of the

Fourth Provincial Council in 1771, both the prelates and the royal representative expressed concern about improper representations of her—especially dressing her immodestly in styles of the day or skimpy costumes, or in excessively fine clothing and jewels.[83] And when the reforming Viceroy Conde de Revillagigedo (the younger) issued a bando in 1789 to restrict the number of religious holidays, he specifically exempted special advocations of Mary, notably Our Lady of Carmen, Our Lady of the Angels, and Our Lady of the Pillar.[84]

Mary came to mind at critical moments in the lives of colonial Catholics. Priests and parishioners often invoked her as a special advocate in their final testaments and set aside a portion of their estates for masses in her honor. Petitioners to the colonial courts, whether ecclesiastical, civil, or criminal, frequently pleaded for justice and mercy in her name, as did Manuel Salbador, gobernador of Atlistaca (Tlapa district), who wrote that "Most Holy Mary is my only guardian; that is, my Lady of the Sorrows."[85] And it was often an image of Mary that was brought out for display when priests tried to subdue an unruly crowd or an irate district governor.[86]

In central and western Mexico, devotion to Mary Immaculate (of which Guadalupe was one of many representations) was especially strong in the territories that had been assigned to the Franciscans and Augustinians in the sixteenth and seventeenth centuries. The Franciscans, in particular, managed to associate "the good little grandmother" in the New World, as in Spain, with healing, mercy, and charity, making her the centerpiece of the hospitals they founded.[87] Working first in the parish seats, the order extended its efforts to smaller subject villages during the critical years of the early seventeenth century, when the Indian population was reduced to perhaps 10 percent of its precolonial number.[88] Usually supported by a cofradía, each hospital invariably included a chapel with an image of the Virgin Mary of the Immaculate Conception.

Even when Indian hospitals closed or reduced their services in the late eighteenth century from the decline of their cofradías and the last great wave of secularization of parishes, the chapels to Mary Immaculate remained at the center of local religion in many pueblos.[89] She was like a second patron saint and a locus of village religion, a source of health and recovery. Secular priests complained that the Indians maintained their hospital chapel but let the parish church fall to ruin without a second thought and refused to do voluntary labor on it.[90] In one case, the collapse of a parish church's roof while the sturdy little chapel to the Virgin survived an earthquake intact seemed like a providential vindication of the villagers' faith in her patronage.[91] According to late colonial parish priests of central Jalisco, the hospital chapels also were being used as meeting places for village deliberations and drinking parties, which many supposed to be occasions for secret plottings against them.[92] As late as 1804, the cura of Ocotlan on the shore of Lake Chapala refused to celebrate mass in the hospital chapel and tried to prevent praying there at night, to discourage both nocturnal gatherings and this locus of devotion.[93]

These local examples, all with their own images of Mary and associated with the protection and destiny of particular villages, occurred at a time when the population of Indian pueblos stabilized, and distinctive forms and institutions emerged to reinforce local community attachments. Inventories of parish ornaments for the eighteenth century suggest that virtually every parish and visita church displayed an image of Mary, if not an altar to her. Several had gained a reputation for miraculous cures or mysterious associations. The image of Our Lady of the Immaculate Conception in the Chapel of the Third Order at Cuernavaca (Morelos), for example, came to be associated in the eighteenth century with a mysterious visit by two handsome travelers to the home of a virtuous woman named Agustina at a nearby sugar mill "in the time of Hernán Cortés." They left a locked box in her care, which she dared not open, expecting them to return. Eventually, after sweet music began to come from the box, she informed the cura and alcalde. They opened it in the presence of many neighbors and found this image of the Virgin in the dress of a pilgrim.[94]

By the mid-seventeenth century, several images of Mary had gained a wider reputation for favoring the faithful and had become important centers of penitential pilgrimage:[95] the Virgin of Candelaria at San Juan de los Lagos, the Virgin of Zapopan outside Guadalajara, Our Lady of Guanajuato, Our Lady of the Refuge at Zacatecas and Puebla, Our Lady of La Bufa at Zacatecas, Our Lady of the Pueblito at Querétaro, Our Lady of the Angels of Tecaxique near Toluca, the Virgin of Los Remedios and Our Lady of Tulantongo near Mexico City, the Virgin of Ocotlan outside the city of Tlaxcala, Our Lady of the Sorrows at Oaxaca, the Virgin of Itzamal in Yucatán, and especially the Virgin of Guadalupe at Tepeyac. Pilgrims also journeyed to various secondary shrines in other cities, especially to the north of Mexico City, at Querétaro, Guadalajara, Zacatecas, San Luis Potosí, and Santa Fe (New Mexico).[96]

The providential story of Guadalupe's apparition apparently was more popular among creole clergymen of the mid-seventeenth century than among Indian villagers, although these priests clearly attempted to use her as a pious sign to bring Indians into the church. Miguel Sánchez's 1648 book, which first proclaimed the miraculous apparition story in print, was both the culmination of growing interest and the catalyst for a wave of new activity intended to spread the word and reap the rewards of the tradition in other parts of the archdiocese.[97] On Christmas day of that year, the mayordomo and administrator of the sanctuary at Tepeyac petitioned the archbishop for permission to collect alms throughout the archdiocese on the grounds that important works were under way for the "greater devotion and brilliance of this divine cult," and that to make a large enough collection they would have to canvass the whole territory.[98]

Still, in the sixteenth- and seventeenth-century evidence of where Guadalupe was venerated and by whom, the viceregal capital of Mexico City stands out. As early as 1556, the Franciscan Francisco de Bustamante criticized the devotion of "the people of this city" to the image of Guadalupe at Tepeyac as a bad example for the Indians.[99] Those "people" presumably included Archbishop Montúfar, whose see was in Mexico City. By 1557, he was as strong a patron as any of the devotion to Our Lady of Guadalupe. Seventeenth- and eighteenth-century successors followed his lead, sponsoring ever more elaborate events and church buildings at Tepeyac.[100] Montúfar's efforts also stirred the interest of the viceroys, who soon began habitually visiting the shrine, sometimes as often as once a week. In the late seventeenth century, even before construction was started on the great church that stands next to the new concrete basilica at Tepeyac today, the viceroys solidified the connection between capital and shrine by building a grand highway from the main square in Mexico City, with its viceregal offices, to the sanctuary of Guadalupe about three miles away.

In the late sixteenth century, Miles Phillips (an English sailor stranded in Mexico from 1568 to 1582) underscored the appeal of Our Lady of Guadalupe to Spaniards traveling to and from the city. Phillips observed that any Spaniard passing the shrine "will alight and come into the church and kneel before the image and pray to our Lady to defend them from all evil." [101] Even earlier, in the 1550's, Archbishop Montúfar had observed its attraction to Spanish women from the city, "who walk there barefoot with their pilgrim's staffs to visit and praise our Lady." [102] Located on the principal road into Mexico City, which led to the port of Veracruz and on to Europe, the shrine of Guadalupe came to define the edge of the city's territory. By the 1560's, dignitaries from Spain were met there by the viceroys and archbishops, and colonial records generally describe the location of the shrine as "extramuros" (outside or adjoining), "contramuros de esta capital" (at the border of this capital), or at the city's "salida principal" (principal exit) "through which the necessities of that city enter." [103] At Tepeyac, the principal highways east to Veracruz and north to the silver mines and *tierra adentro* ("the interior") branched off.

Most of Guadalupe's early recorded miracles also are connected to Mexico City. She was reported to have stemmed the great flood of 1629.[104] She was also credited with ending the *matlazahuatl* epidemic of 1737–39, during which the archbishop formally proclaimed her patroness and protectress of "this Imperial City [and] its territory," and made December 12 an obligatory day of devotion.[105] The 1737 epidemic was pivotal in confirming the link between the city and the image of Guadalupe, and then in expanding its importance to the whole viceroyalty. According to the *Gazeta de México* for December 1737, various miraculous images had been enlisted before the archbishop acted to recognize the image of the Virgin of Guadalupe as the city's patroness. Only then did the epidemic start to subside.[106]

Despite the growing interest in the sanctuary at Tepeyac, especially after 1737, and despite the promotion of the miracle by bishops in other dioceses, there was still a strong tendency to associate Our Lady of Guadalupe with the capital city. Writing from Guadalajara in 1742, Matías de la Mota Padilla judged that "the whole world may envy Mexico City its good fortune in having the appearance of a sign as great as Holy Mary, who protects it." [107] José Joaquín Fernández de Lizardi, writing in 1811, recounted that when a large meteor shower was sighted in 1789, most people of Mexico City believed it was fire from heaven. In panicky disarray, they fled to the shrine of Guadalupe, shouting "To the sanctuary, to Our Lady of Guadalupe." [108] When blanket statements about widespread devotion appear in the record, the chroniclers' specific examples are for Mexico City (and to a lesser extent for San Luis Potosí, Valladolid, Puebla, Guadalajara, Zacatecas, and other large towns, but self-conscious appeals to her by these other cities are recorded mostly for the 1730's).

Several formal changes between 1733 and 1756 encouraged a widening circle of devotion to the Virgin of Guadalupe. In 1733, the viceroy elevated Tepeyac to the status of villa (the rank just below ciudad) and separated the Indians who

FIG. 10. An 18th-century Guadalupe image. As devotion to Our Lady of Guadalupe increased in the late colonial period, paintings, prints, and medals of her image that were said to be "exact replicas" proliferated. This 1743 engraving depicts her coming to the aid of the faithful in Mexico City during the epidemic of 1737.

resided there from the immediate jurisdiction of Santiago Tlatelolco, one of the principal Indian districts of Mexico City. In 1746, the bishops and cathedral chapters of New Spain united to proclaim the Virgin of Guadalupe the patroness of the viceroyalty. In 1749, the establishment of the Villa de Guadalupe was completed and the shrine became an endowed *colegiata* or college of canons (as papal bulls had authorized in 1725, 1729, and 1746). In 1751, the officers of the colegiata took possession of their posts, and on December 12, a formal coronation ceremony for the Virgin of Guadalupe at Tepeyac celebrated her as the "Universal Patroness of this Kingdom of New Spain." Then, in 1756, Mexico City and other principal towns held fiestas to commemorate the Pope's formal confirmation in 1754 of Our Lady of Guadalupe as patroness of the "entire kingdom," completing the official elevation of her image and her town.[109]

The celebrations of 1756 appear to have been pivotal in the promotion of the image by church leaders in New Spain. Certainly this promotion increased in the late 1750's and 1760's. The *Promptuario manual mexicano*, the book of sermons and lectures that the Jesuit Ignacio de Paredes published in 1759 for the use of curas in their teaching duties, includes a sermon on Our Lady of Guadalupe and a short history of the apparition suitable for presentation to Indian neophytes, "so that this [history] may be known to all the Indians, who are especially favored by the same lady"—as if the story of the apparition was not yet so well known among Indians.[110] Archbishop Lorenzana actively sponsored the veneration of the Mexican Guadalupe in the late 1760's, especially in his "Oración a Nuestra Señora de Guadalupe: Non Fecit Taliter Omni Nationi," in which he recounted the apparition tale, described the painting, and urged that the message of this "divine favor . . . to Americans" be taken to Indians: "May all the Indians come, may all the Indian women come to pay their respects to this Lady, may the children come from afar, and may the Indian women believe."[111] Lorenzana's successor, Alonso Núñez de Haro y Peralta, issued a circular on August 12, 1776, declaring his obligation to promote the devotion ("solicitar el mayor culto") of the Virgin Mary and her "marvelous apparition in the image of Guadalupe" as the patroness of "this entire kingdom." And Archbishop Lizana y Beaumont lent his full support in a pastoral letter of March 25, 1803:

Shortly after the conquest of this Imperial and Most Noble City, you were sent from Heaven the Sovereign Queen of the Angels as a sign of how much she loves you, and as a certain omen of the treasures the God of mercy would provide from the hands of your sweet Mother.[112]

Also from the late 1750's on, the judicial record shows concerted efforts by curas in rural parishes of central Mexico to establish or increase popular veneration of the Mexican Guadalupe. In 1760, for example, the Indians of Tejupilco in the district of Temascaltepec (Edo. de México) lodged a complaint against their cura for forcing them to hold an annual celebration commemorating the apparition. The cura responded that the Indians had celebrated the apparition in 1758, and he was working to institutionalize the event. Manuel Cassela, cura of Atotonilco el Chico (Hidalgo), noted in his resumé that he had actively promoted devotion to the image after he arrived in 1758, when the residents had decided to declare the Virgin of Guadalupe their patroness. Nicolás Ximénez, cura of

Epasoyucan (Hidalgo), founded a cofradía to the Virgin of Guadalupe sometime between 1751 and 1760 and had an altar to her constructed in the parish church. And Mariano Joseph Loretoyturría Mora, coadjutor in the parish of Tezontepec in 1762, had arranged for Our Lady of Guadalupe to be made patroness of the school of the Hospital Real in Mexico City when he had taught there in 1761.[113]

The clustering of cases like these in the late 1750's and early 1760's appears to be linked to a marked attachment to the Virgin of Guadalupe by curas trained in Mexico City at that time: the curas mentioned as particular promoters were trained there; the published panegyrical sermons to the Virgin of Guadalupe collected in the Biblioteca Nacional increase in number from 1757 on; and the professional resumés of aspirants to parishes in the early 1760's begin to list sermons the priests gave at Tepeyac and their participation in competitions for posts in the colegiata in previous years.[114] The deep reverence of one Indian cura from Mexico City in the late 1750's is recounted in the resumé of Juan Faustino Xuárez de Escovedo, the son of Indian nobles of the Barrio de la Candelaria. Shortly after his appointment as cura coadjutor of San Juan Cozcatlan in the Huasteca, he was called out of town to hear a confession: "While he was crossing the Axtla River, the waters suddenly rose and swept him downstream; inside he cried out to the Most Holy Virgin of Guadalupe, and the Indians pulled him out, almost dead."[115] This concentration of clerical activity in the 1750's is also illustrated by the complaints it elicited from Indian parishioners. The residents of Tejupilco were not alone in their protests. Their counterparts in the Zacualpan jurisdiction (also Edo. de México) suspected in 1757 that their priests were introducing feast days in honor of Guadalupe as a way to increase their incomes.[116] Complaints about added fees of this kind appear occasionally in later ecclesiastical court cases, as when the Audiencia of New Spain ordered the cura of Acatlan (Hidalgo) in 1817 not to collect from local Indians for religious celebrations in honor of Our Lady of Guadalupe and San Miguel.[117]

How extensive and self-starting this midcentury movement was in the pueblos of Mexico and Guadalajara is difficult to determine. Ajofrín made the connection to the Indians explicit, observing that the image looked like an Indian noblewoman, and that almost every day many Indians visited the sanctuary with votive offerings. He was especially taken by the simplicity and great love with which these "dear little Indians," "these poor little people," venerated "their beloved Mother and Lady of Guadalupe."[118] But he was a peninsular with only a superficial knowledge of the Indians, who viewed the sanctuary from his residence in Mexico City, did not inquire into where the Indian pilgrims had come from, and did not mention the Guadalupe image in his section on Indian religious practices.[119] Late colonial church administrative records suggest that pueblos outside the Valley of Mexico were slower to show their enthusiasm for Guadalupe than their priests and some hacendados and rancheros were. In the directorio for Jiquipilco in the district of Metepec from 1773 to the early 1790's (a region where devotion to the Virgin of Guadalupe was unusually vigorous), masses in honor of this image of Mary on December 12 were sponsored only by two haciendas. The parish had formerly supported a mass and celebration costing twelve pesos from a stand of magueyes, but in 1780, after several years in which the plot had not produced any income, the celebration had been suspended. The Hacienda

Boximo had thereupon assumed responsibility for the twelve pesos needed to support the devotion. The Hacienda Sila was the sponsor of the only other mass for Guadalupe within the parish.[120] In the records of an 1808–9 pastoral visit in part of the archdiocese in northern Hidalgo and the fringe of San Luis Potosí, seven pueblos were reported to have established pious works in her name, but none had yet grown into a cofradía, suggesting that they had been founded recently or for some other reason were not strongly supported; three of the seven were mission communities, where veneration of Guadalupe was likely to have been promoted by missionary priests.[121] In southeastern Hidalgo in 1790, cofradías to Guadalupe were reported in the pueblos of Zempoala, Singuilucan, and Zihuateutla, but two of the three were about to be reduced to an obra pía or combined with another cofradía because of long-standing neglect.[122]

Most of the early copies of the Guadalupe image were probably produced in Mexico City, just as the altars, saints, and ornaments of village churches usually came on order from the city's workshops. In any event, painted copies of the image found their way into other parts of Mexico before the 1650's: first, apparently, to the city of San Luis Potosí early in the century, then to Querétaro, Antequera, Zacatecas, and Saltillo.[123] By the early eighteenth century, Tepeyac was the major pilgrimage site in New Spain. By the 1770's, there were reports of apparitions of the Virgin of Guadalupe in western Mexico, and chapels were dedicated to her in district seats as far north as New Mexico and Texas.[124] Clearly, by then there was a substantial and widely dispersed network of devotees to the American Guadalupe.

The evidence suggests four patterns in the expansion of Guadalupe's popularity. First, its greatest pull concentrated in Mexico City, the Valley of Mexico, and places within a few days' travel of the sanctuary. Second, it grew especially through an urban network. For example, Andrés Cavo's account of what he called "unprecedented celebrations" in honor of the Virgin of Guadalupe in 1756 says that they took place in Mexico City and "all the cities of New Spain."[125] Third, when the devotion spread outside the Valley of Mexico, it grew first and most broadly to the north (the least Indian part of the viceroyalty). By the end of the colonial period, a resident of rural San Luis Potosí could report that "if you travel through the *ranchos* of this entire kingdom you will find that two things rarely are lacking: an image of Our Lady of Guadalupe and a poor schoolmaster who teaches reading and Christian doctrine."[126] And fourth, to the extent that there was a popular Indian devotion to Guadalupe as Tonantzin before the eighteenth century, it may have been centered in the Mexico City wards of San Juan and Tlatelolco, among Indians who lived or settled near the sanctuary, and in the district of Cuautitlan, where testimonials to the apparition were taken from local Indians in 1666 as part of an official church authentication.[127] In any case, the few clear examples we have suggest that the Day of the Virgin of Guadalupe was not much celebrated in outlying Indian villages of central and western Mexico before the 1750's, and that it was less a spontaneous devotion than one fostered by parish priests, few of whom were Indians, and nearly all of whom had been educated in cathedral cities.[128] Perhaps this is a case of the great preindustrial city as style center, as Paul Wheatley calls it,[129] the place from which values are disseminated and specialized expertise provided.

María and Guadalupe as Names of the Newborn

Establishing who believed in Mary and how people expressed their devotion is not easily done. Occasionally, suggestive evidence of devotion appears in judicial records—in appeals to colonial judges in her name, and in dated references to pilgrimages to the shrine of Guadalupe and village celebrations of the apparition—but these are scarce fragments. It would be especially helpful to have serial evidence of a homogeneous kind that spans several centuries. Serial evidence of pilgrimages would be best. At some European shrines, "books of miracles" and "books of benefactors" were kept, recording the miracles attributed to a sacred image and registering the groups of pilgrims that went there bearing gifts. So far as I know, no scholar has yet reported such registers for the Guadalupe sanctuary during the colonial period.

Although it may never be possible to establish who made pilgrimages to the shrine at Tepeyac, something of a spiritual geography of the devotion can be recovered from baptismal and property records that indicate where and when parents named their children for her and where there were estates and settlements called Guadalupe. One could, for example, map place-names (including barrios, ranches, and haciendas, as well as towns, rivers, and other physical features).[130] By the early eighteenth century, scores of haciendas, ranchos, sugar mills, and mines were named Guadalupe, especially in central and northern Mexico. Both Indian and non-Indian pueblos, barrios, and cofradías were sometimes named for her, but they appear in the record less often than Spanish haciendas and ranchos, and mainly in the late colonial period.[131] Though names do not tell a full story of faith, the patterns of naming by place and time give a first approximation of long-term shifts in devotion that can be compared with other, more scattered evidence. A sample of baptismal records from several parishes in the dioceses of Mexico, Guadalajara, and Oaxaca suggests that the name Guadalupe gained popularity in provincial cities, district head towns, and creole ranching areas in the second half of the eighteenth century, but was not well favored in Indian districts and rural villages outside the vicinity of Mexico City until after the Independence War.

The sample consists of 18,771 baptisms from the late eighteenth and early nineteenth centuries distributed among eight parishes. Of the eight parishes, six were in the Diocese of Guadalajara (Guadalajara city, Tlajomulco, Tonalá, Zacoalco, Arandas, and Acatlan de Juárez—all in modern Jalisco), one in the archdiocese (Tenango del Valle, Edo. de México), and one in the Valley of Oaxaca (Mitla). The six Jalisco parishes offer a range of communities and ethnic composition: an urban parish (the sagrario metropolitano of Guadalajara); a largely non-Indian parish of ranches and small hamlets (Arandas); a parish near Guadalajara in transition from Indian to mestizo and mulato, where many of the residents were landless laborers (Acatlan); a large parish with roughly equal numbers of Indians and non-Indians (Zacoalco); and two parishes near Guadalajara with a majority of Indians (Tonalá and Tlajomulco). The two parishes from central and southern Mexico—Tenango del Valle and Mitla—both had large Indian populations and were selected to allow a comparison with the naming patterns in Jalisco. Better than half of the newborns—10,658—were classified as Indians; the other 8,113 were classified as Spaniards, mestizos, and mulatos. For each parish and time period, the total number of baptisms and the number of infants who bore the name María (or other direct references to the Virgin), or Guadalupe have been tabulated by sex and racial designation. For the Guadalupes, the month and day of baptism were also recorded.[132]

Irrespective of race, women named María and Guadalupe outnumbered men —by about ten to one for Marías (9.4 : 1 for non-Indians and 9.8 : 1 for Indians) but by less than three to one for Guadalupes (2.45 : 1 for non-Indians and 2.25 : 1 for Indians). More non-Indian women than Indian women were Marías, by 87.5 percent to 73.9 percent, but the percentages are high in both cases, suggesting a powerful devotion to Mary generally. And the importance of the name María was growing during the years represented in the sample, roughly 1740 to 1840. There was an increase in the percentage of women named María, whether Indian or not, for nearly every parish, decade by decade from the 1740's to 1820. Somewhat more non-Indian men than Indian men carried the name María (usually as José María) or Mariano (9.3 percent to 7.6 percent), but the absolute difference between them is not as great as for the women, and the pattern for men does not show the increase that is so clear for the women. If anything, men were less likely to be given the name María as time went on.

Guadalupe appears much less often than María in these baptismal records, but, again, non-Indians were three times more likely than Indians to be given that name (3.2 : 1 for men and 3.4 : 1 for women). Of the Indians, 0.62 percent of the men and 1.4 percent of the women were Guadalupes, for a total of 0.99 percent of Indian baptisms. The figures for non-Indians are 1.97 percent of the men, 4.78 percent of the women, and a total of 3.35 percent of all non-Indian baptisms. The given name Guadalupe seems to have gained initial popularity in the second half of the eighteenth century. For the parish in Guadalajara, there was more than a twofold increase in the frequency of Guadalupes between 1745 and 1781 (from 0.84 percent to 2.2 percent). In the rural parishes of Jalisco, there were often no Guadalupes at all in a year, or at most one or two before the 1750's.

The distribution of Guadalupes over the course of the year for all parishes except Arandas also indicates a more widespread veneration for Guadalupe among non-Indians than among Indians in the 1750's. As Guadalupe became a more common name in the late eighteenth century, Indian Guadalupes generally were born and baptized in December—Guadalupe's month—and most of these were born near her day, December 12, or were baptized within a week thereafter. This suggests that the pattern of Guadalupe namings for Indians followed the usual pattern of naming in Spanish America in the eighteenth century—an infant received the name of the saint or saints on whose day or in whose month he or she was born or baptized. Naming, then, had more to do with date of birth or baptism than with the personal preference of the parents or godparents, or of the priest who baptized the infant and registered the birth.[133] The monthly distributions for the two groups were different enough to suggest that Guadalupe was becoming a popular choice for non-Indians irrespective of the season: 70 percent of their Guadalupe baptisms occurred from January to November (compared with the Indians' 32.9 percent). Only 18.3 percent of non-Indian Guadalupes were born or baptized within a week of December 12, compared with 45.6 percent of the Indian Guadalupes. Overall, 42.7 percent of all Guadalupes were born in

December, and 27.2 percent of these namings were made close to December 12. Arandas is the one exception to this seasonal pattern and to the contrast between Indian and non-Indian Guadalupes. For all Arandas groups, Guadalupes were quite evenly distributed over the twelve months, with only 11.8 percent of the Indians and 12.6 percent of the non-Indians baptized in December.

Though the name Guadalupe became more popular in the late eighteenth century, the pattern of increase is not so clear and consistent as for the Marías. A plateau of popularity seems to have been reached in the 1780's, holding good through at least the 1830's. In Tenango del Valle and Tlajomulco—two parishes where there were Indian pueblos with a substantial non-Indian population, near large estates—Guadalupe namings increased during the War of Independence (from 1.06 percent in 1786–1804 at Tenango del Valle to 3.06 percent there in 1809–17, and from 0.19 percent during 1800–1806 at Tlajomulco to 0.92 percent in 1810–11). A comparison of the Guadalupe namings across the sample exposes Mitla and Arandas as the extreme examples of the differences between Indians and non-Indians. The least Indian parishes of Arandas, the Guadalajara sagrario, and Acatlan had the highest percentages of Guadalupes; the most Indian parishes of Mitla, Tonalá, and Tlajomulco the lowest. For non-Indians, it seemed to make little difference whether they lived in a city, on ranchos, or among Indians. Perhaps to distinguish themselves from Indians, non-Indians were somewhat more likely to be named Guadalupe if they lived in parishes with a majority of Indians. Guadalupes were less frequent among non-Indians in Guadalajara than they were in the Tonalá and Tlajomulco parishes.

Mitla stands apart from the other parishes in this sample for its well-landed Indian pueblos and few Spaniards. Its place in the pattern of Guadalupe namings is equally distinctive. Even as late as the nineteenth century, very few Guadalupes appear among the names in the baptismal registers of Mitla—only three of 1,476 baptisms over the years 1808–43, or 0.20 percent, by far the lowest frequency in the sample. And all three of these infants were born or baptized on December 12. By contrast, Arandas had 22 times Mitla's frequency of Guadalupes (112 of 2,257), and two to six times more than in other parishes. Arandas also experienced a larger increase in Guadalupes between the 1770's and 1820 than the others did: from 2.4 percent in 1771–76 to 4.6 percent in 1790–1819. One obvious reason for the popularity of Guadalupe as a personal name in Arandas is that Mary in this guise was the patroness of the parish. But other parishes dedicated to Guadalupe do not seem to have had such a clear pattern of naming so early. Another possible explanation is that many of the local rancheros, traders, and laborers of Arandas had traveled beyond the confines of their parish and felt a stronger regional identity than the people of other rural parishes in the sample. Also, children in non-Indian parishes (and in Arandas in particular) in the eighteenth century were usually christened with two to three names, increasing the likelihood that one of the names would be María or Guadalupe.

From this sample, it appears that naming followed the saints associated with the date of birth or baptism, but there were no absolute rules and no simple differences based on place, race, or gender. Still, two large patterns are evident. First, the special attachment to Mary and the new frequency with which children were named Guadalupe in the late eighteenth century suggest that the popularity of Guadalupe followed and depended on a deeply rooted devotion to Mary. The name Guadalupe was far from ubiquitous in the late colonial period, but given the custom of naming for the saints associated with the date of birth or baptism and the frequency of Guadalupes from the 1740's to the last decade of the eighteenth century, the 3.35 percent of non-Indians named Guadalupe is substantial. Second, the non-Indians' greater use of the name Guadalupe and almost random choice of it during the year suggests an earlier and stronger self-generating attachment to this Mexican image of the Virgin. Indians did not approach the same pattern until after 1840.

Symbol, Ideology, and Insurgency

Whether one considers Guadalupe separately or as only one of many venerated images of the Virgin in New Spain, the messages of Mary in general bear on how Spaniards ruled in America and how their rule ended. In colonial Mexico, especially outside large cities, she was venerated time and again as mother and intercessor. For farming villagers, an important layer of meaning came from her position as a unique mother of miraculous, spontaneous fertility. Motherhood in this marvelous form was naturally connected by village farmers to the fertility of the land they worked. Mircea Eliade speaks in universal terms of the earth being "endowed with manifold religious significance," with significance especially as "Mother Earth," woman and soil, and, by extension, of women as "centres of sacred power." [134] The case of Mexico before and after the initial encounters of native Americans and Spaniards is no exception. Ancient beliefs in the efficacy of propitiatory agrarian rites did not lose their strength, and the Virgin Mary had become a main point of contact. Mary, especially Guadalupe, came to be associated in central Mexico with pulque, the milky fermented juice of the maguey plant. In some colonial Indian villages, there were fields of maguey named for her, and in the late eighteenth century, the Virgin of Guadalupe was sometimes called the Mother of Maguey. As a symbol of health and hospitals, the Virgin Mary of the Immaculate Conception also had great appeal as a guardian against epidemics and other illnesses.

But it is especially as intercessor that Mary Immaculate contains one of the master principles of religious life and political relationships within the colonial system. The mediation of her womb between the spiritual and the physical, as the means of the Incarnation, was only one aspect of her mediation between heaven and earth. Mary retained her special hold on popular piety partly because God had not been softened in Spanish America, just as the great gulfs in the social and political hierarchy had not been spanned. There was need of her intercession with her son and his father, not only to create a bridge into heaven for the believer, but to bring healing and consolation to the living. Although her place in the journey to personal salvation was very important, for rural people in the future Mexico, she was less a broker in the journey after death than a protectress in this life. Part of her appeal was that she did not seem to play favorites. She was mother and mediator for all, while other saints appeared more as special advocates for particular people and special purposes.

The images of the Immaculate Conception assume the posture of prayer.

Prayer was the instrument both of Mary's intercession with God and of the believer's appeal to her. The art historian Elizabeth Wilder Weismann noticed that this appeal was associated with distinctive images of the Virgin Mary that were believed to contain her power. Unlike the representations of Mary as a young, idealized beauty that were popular in the academic art of Europe in the seventeenth and eighteenth centuries, the favorite representations from rural Mexico were friendly, approachable, even homely little women.[135] As Marina Warner says about Mary as intercessor, "she is approached as a human mother who brims with a mother's love." [136]

This central meaning of the Virgin Mary in Indian Mexico as mother and intercessor carries paradoxical messages for colonial political life. Modern scholars who have considered the Virgin's political significance see revolutionary and messianic messages, the Virgin as a symbol of counterculture inviting her believers to escape the restraints of established order in the hope of communion.[137] She was the only mortal to have escaped the stain of the sins of Adam and Eve. Her purity carried the promise of redemption; her child was the source of a new beginning. Colonial Indians could have understood this new beginning as liberation in the widest sense—spiritual salvation, escape from taxes and oppressive labor service, and protest against alien power. As a symbol of liberation and the embodiment of Indian interests, Mary was proof that her faithful were a chosen people. In effect, devotion to the Virgin was a critique of the existing social order, a rejection of Spanish values and a guide to action—as if she represented a "confrontation of Spanish and Indian worlds." Because the political history of the Virgin Mary has been considered largely in association with uprisings, especially with the Independence War and the Revolution of 1910, the impression lingers that this message of protest was the only one, that Guadalupe was *communitas* for Indians from the 1530's on, the opposite of structure and of everything hierarchical, paternalistic, and Hispanic.[138]

But there is another political message embedded in faith in the Virgin Mary that on the surface contradicts the symbolism of liberation: as mediator, she was a model of acceptance and legitimation of colonial authority. The success of Spanish rule in Mexico for nearly three centuries without a standing army depended on a system of administration and justice that worked through intermediaries and specialists, defusing or postponing independent action by offended subjects. It succeeded largely because the elaborate hierarchy of colonial judges was, in the end, believed to be just or at least was widely accepted as a way to resolve disputes. Village Indians in colonial Mexico were inclined to take their grievances over land and taxes to the courts, to work through legal intermediaries, and to appeal to a higher authority within the colonial structure, if the verdict went against them. Mary, too, was an intermediary who would intercede with higher authorities on behalf of the believer. Believing in her was like having a friend in high places. She gave country people a stake in the colonial system. Ritually, the Virgin was approached as the colonial governors were—humbly, hat in hand. One had to trust in the Virgin and give her time, just as one had to accept that justice worked slowly in the colonial courts. Here was a statement about self-control and hierarchical social relationships that joined religion and the politics of deference discussed in Chapter Nine. The Virgin Mary personified the church (colonial records often refer to the church as "the pious mother"), and, like the church, she was the intercessor between Christians and God. But she had also become the mediator between the king of Spain and "the Americans," as the sermonizer and chronicler Itá y Parra put it in *El círculo de amor* (1747).[139] In this way, she sanctified both an American identity and the authority of the colonial system, affirmed the unity of that society, and carried a message not to take matters into your own hands, not to right your own wrongs. Turn them over to Mother Mary.

This political message of accommodation worked especially well so long as curas had the king's support in exercising moral and political, as well as spiritual leadership, in their parishes. Where the Virgin Mary had not been appropriated by the local community or used against the authority of the priest, she was part of the priest's domain, and many times curas displayed her image as a way to stop local uprisings against Spanish tax collectors and governors. Where curas lost much of their moral authority in the late eighteenth century during the Bourbon reforms, or where they chose to identify more closely with their parishioners than with the cathedral chapter or the king, or where they disdained their posts for the city, the Virgin's message of reconciliation and stability was jeopardized.[140]

The Virgin's messages of accommodation and liberation were not perceived as contradictory or as simple alternatives. The importance of each message waxed and waned, but neither disappeared. Mary's message of liberation dominated the last years of colonial rule, during the struggle over independence after 1810. As in the Spanish Conquest, she had become a patroness of partisans in an armed struggle. But the tables were turned; she now surfaced as the patroness of Mexicans against Spaniards ("Mexicans" meaning here people who consciously thought of themselves as Mexicans). Now Mary represented division more than unity, for she was invoked just as fervently by loyalists. The image of the Virgin of Guadalupe, in particular, was sometimes taken up as a spiritual ally of common people in revolt after the war broke out, partly because of a change that had been in the making for many years. The Virgin Mary had gradually come to be a general protectress, not only a specialist in supplications to a distant God, a guardian against floods and plagues, and a source of fertility. Increasingly, she was approached for aid against hated new taxes, and in other ways that had political meaning for an ideology of community autonomy and protection of the poor. For example, Toribio Ruiz, *mulato* scribe (escribano) of the Indians of Zacoalco (Jalisco), proclaimed in 1783 that "Most Holy Mary is praying for us" in a protracted land dispute. When a Spanish resident joked that since the high court in Guadalajara had issued a definitive judgment against the Indians in the suit, the Mother of God must no longer be pleading his case, Ruiz replied ominously, "Consider the temporal and eternal judgments."[141] And in the complaint the Indians of Chacaltianguis (Cosamaloapan district of Veracruz) lodged against their cura in 1768 for collecting excessive fees, they appealed to the Viceroy's "royal piety" and to the "protection of the Virgin Mary to free us from these many oppressions."[142]

The Virgin Mary also found her way into popular conceptions of the Trinity. The cura of Otumba, on the northeast edge of the Valley of Mexico, in 1795 doubted the story of the apparition of the Virgin of Guadalupe but kept a print that depicted the Trinity with three figures: God the father on the right, Christ on the left, and the Virgin Mary in the center, with the Holy Spirit springing from her body.[143] Twenty years before, the alcalde mayor of Colima reported having seen a painting and drawings on rocks at a spot near the foot of the Volcán de Colima where local mulatos were believed to worship the Devil.[144] One painted image, according to his drawing of it, placed a crowned Virgin Mary—the largest of the figures—in a vertical line between a small figure of Christ and God in heaven, with a dove representing the Holy Spirit at the very top. These misconceptions of the Virgin Mary as part of the Trinity or as the source of the Holy Spirit were not new or uniquely American, but they may have been more common in the late eighteenth century. Omerick, in his 1769 treatise on teaching in Indian parishes, inveighed against the conception of the Trinity that had the Holy Spirit emanating from the Virgin Mary, as if such a conception were common in Mexico.[145]

At first in isolated instances and then throughout central and western Mexico, the Virgin of Guadalupe became attached to an idea of millennial reconquest during the last decades of colonial rule. In a regional Indian uprising in the jurisdiction of Tulancingo during 1769, the leaders called for the death of Spanish officials and the creation of an Indian priesthood. They dreamed of the day when bishops and alcaldes mayores would kneel and kiss the rings of Indian priests. The leader of their theocratic utopia called himself the New Savior, and his consort was known as the Virgin of Guadalupe.[146] And during the chaotic first months of the independence struggle, the Virgin of Guadalupe was used not only by Miguel Hidalgo, the parish priest who adopted this image as the symbol of his movement shortly after he began his march on Mexico City in September 1810, but also by other curas seeking protection against the *gachupines* (peninsular Spaniards).[147] Small bands of rebels even looked to her to justify their acts of destruction. In December 1810, Father Hidalgo ordered the Indians of Juchipila (directly north of Guadalajara in the state of Zacatecas) not to sack the estates of the local Spanish tax administrator. The Indians refused to obey, even after a direct order from their parish priest. They did it, they said, with the permission of the Virgin of Guadalupe.[148] What had been forbidden only months before could now be accomplished under the higher authority of their protectress.

The connection between the Virgin of Guadalupe and Indian rebellion in the late colonial period, however, was far from unambiguous. In 1800, Indians in Tlaxcala and Nayarit were rumored to have plotted with a creole aristocrat in Mexico City to start a rebellion against the crown on December 12, the Day of the Virgin of Guadalupe. The details of this aborted rebellion are sketchy, but the men and women from Nayarit who were called to testify in early 1801 said that it was to begin by setting fire to the church at Tepeyac—they made no mention of rescuing the sacred painting—and at the same time setting off explosions at the viceregal palace in Mexico City.[149] Victor Turner's bold and penetrating essay "Hidalgo: History as Social Drama" makes the image of Guadalupe the inevitable symbol of national protest and mass revolt in 1810.[150] In Turner's words, Guadalupe was by then "the supreme mobilizing symbol of nationalism" and "national community," a "populist symbol that activated the masses." Eric R. Wolf said much the same thing about the Virgin of Guadalupe as an image with mass appeal to Indians and mestizos in colonial Mexico, carrying a message of power to the people, when he spoke of the War of Independence as "the final realization of the apocalyptic promise of Guadalupe," the return of Tonantzin, which had "guaranteed a rightful place to the Indians in the new social system of New Spain."[151] But the Hidalgo movement was concentrated in the Bajío region north of Mexico City—the most prosperous and populous area of the viceroyalty, and one of the least Indian in the conventional pueblo sense at that time (although one in which Indian class identity was comparatively strong). It was second only to the Valley of Mexico in its devotion to Guadalupe. Many of its residents had migrated from areas closer to Mexico City or had visited the shrine of Guadalupe. Given these ties and even stronger devotion to Guadalupe in the Valley than in the Bajío, if the sacred image had been sufficient to "activate the masses," Indian villagers there should have flocked to Hidalgo's cause as he approached from the north, and Indians of Morelos, Puebla, and Oaxaca should have joined José María Morelos in large numbers. They did not.

It is difficult to say why something did not happen. For many communities, local attachments apparently overrode any automatic interest in a mass movement claiming the image of Guadalupe as its patron. Two other considerations further complicate the history of this image in the late colonial period and the first months of the war: first, that devotion to Guadalupe was not mainly Indian or necessarily political, and second, that not all her politically partisan devotees were attached to the cause of independence.[152] Even at the end of the colonial period, the prophetic appeal to an Indian past through the image of Guadalupe was promoted mainly by creole intellectuals. Fr. Joseph Joaquín Sardo, an Augustinian writing of the Christ of Chalma in 1810,[153] celebrated it and the Virgin of Guadalupe as connected signs that Mexico was a chosen realm, both images appearing to humble Indians at places sacred to precolonial mother and father deities, with the Christ at Chalma making his seasonable appearance several years after his mother Mary at Tepeyac (1531 and 1539). In September or October of 1811, Fernández de Lizardi composed a poem, "La muralla de México en la protección de María Santísima Nuestra Señora," in which he ascribed the failure of Hidalgo's insurgents to occupy Mexico City the year before to the Virgin Mary. She was the city's "fortress, the surest wall, defense, and castle"; and the shrines dedicated to her that ringed the city were the capital's "valiant squadron." But the two images he singled out as the bastions of "this happy and fortunate" city were those of Guadalupe and Los Remedios.[154] Clearly, some Indians who were devoted to the image of Guadalupe were as stoutly opposed as he to the Hidalgo movement. For example, when the Indians of Zacapoaxtla (Puebla) requested permission in 1813 to build a temple to the Virgin of Guadalupe, they explained that it was to honor her for her protection in 1810–11. When they heard that Father Hidalgo was using the name of the Virgin of Guadalupe, they declared her their patroness against the insurgents and attributed to her their repeated victories over Hidalgo's forces.[155]

By concentrating on the Virgin of Guadalupe, as well as by assuming mass Indian support, we lose some of the complex and contingent meaning of religious symbols at the time of the independence struggle. For instance, Hidalgo's popular movement was probably connected both to the Virgin of San Juan de los Lagos and to widespread devotion to Mary Immaculate in general. Hidalgo planned his uprising to coincide with the fair of this widely venerated image at San Juan de los Lagos on December 8, which is also the date of the universal feast of the Immaculate Conception and close to Guadalupe's feast day. Many of the areas of central and western Mexico where Indians did join the Hidalgo forces by the hundreds or thousands had been evangelized by the Franciscans and maintained strong local attachments to an image of Our Lady of the Immaculate Conception. Guadalupe, as a representation of the Immaculate Conception with a large following among creole priests, townspeople, rancheros, and some villagers in many places north of Mexico City, could have served as the bridge between them and villagers who were devoted to their local images of Mary Immaculate. If this was so, Guadalupe as a symbol of nationhood and liberty for Indians and common people would have been more a product of the war than a universal, dominant symbol ready to "activate the masses."

The attachment of this image to Indian justice and nationalism seems to have grown during and after the war in relationship to three public men in particular. First, in the course of the fighting, there were dislocations and migrations of villagers in central and north-central Mexico who came into sustained contact with devotees of the Virgin of Guadalupe. This would have been especially true during the height of José María Morelos's movement from 1811 to 1814, since Morelos, even more than Hidalgo, invoked the name of the Virgin of Guadalupe as the rallying cry of the revolution. His flag was blue and white, the colors of the Virgin's dress; "Virgin of Guadalupe" was used as a countersign by his troops; and he publicly attributed his victories to her.[156] Second, there was the association between the Virgin of Guadalupe and Hidalgo, the martyr to independence, regarded as the "Father of Mexico," an association that became automatic after 1828, when the name of the community at Tepeyac was changed from the Villa de Guadalupe to Guadalupe Hidalgo, with the rank of city.[157] Third, there was the reputation of a great military hero from Durango and Mexico City who changed his name during the Independence War from Manuel Félix Fernández to Guadalupe Victoria and went on to become Mexico's first constitutional president in 1824. He also presided over the ceremony at the sanctuary in 1828 in which the name of the community was changed.

Unlike the small host of images of the Virgin with local or regional appeal, the image of Our Lady of Guadalupe contributed to a loose and incomplete but still important network of connections among formally separated groups and places, especially among those groups and places that took part in the independence struggle during the early years: some urban creoles, especially in the Bajío; pueblos de indios where a strong Indian identity could bridge mutual suspicion; and deracinated mestizos and Indians in the Bajío and some parts of central and western Mexico. The image of Guadalupe had a special appeal in places where people thought of themselves as Mexicans, or as members of a social category without privileges, or as members of a group whose privileges had been lost—notably creoles, the lower clergy, and landless farmworkers, including Indians who thought of themselves as Indians. But the Virgin of Guadalupe also represented the nation by the location of her sanctuary in the Valley of Mexico and her long-standing association with the unrivaled political and cultural capital, Mexico City—the place of intercession.

* * *

Alexander von Humboldt's statement that Mexican Indians "know nothing of religion but the exterior forms of worship" is, itself, an excessively exterior view.[158] It mirrors his Enlightenment vision of the Indians he saw in passing during 1803–4 as broken remnants of a great ancient civilization dwarfed by a monumental landscape, a people too debased and sad to contemplate much further. Yet, through his European lenses, Humboldt was right to emphasize the concrete and to suspect a kind of "idolatry," even if he was wrong to argue that Indian religious understandings stopped there. Matter and spirit were inseparable. Colonial images and places *were* alive with the sacred and filled with literal meaning.

Saints and their images—so important to the practice of Catholicism generally—straddled a border between order and chaos in colonial life. They expressed the proper, hierarchical organization of religion and society, God's great power, and the need for official intercessors. Through them, Indian parishioners found their places in Christianity and colonial society. But the relationship between priests and parishioners over these objects and divine intercessors was problematic. Alternative understandings were possible, some of them created locally by Indian parishioners drawing on their knowledge and experience to make sense of subordination in the colonial order, others mainly learned from more official colonial sources, especially the parish priests.[159] The images of saints beckoned to ordinary people and could put the priest's conditional authority in jeopardy. He could not be everywhere the sacred dwelled or erupted; nor could he control its uses, even with his own considerable powers to transform. It was in his interest to bring wayward images and their followers into the central place of his authority, the parish church,[160] but even there his influence was incomplete.

In several ways, the Virgin Mary and Santiago traced a common course through the colonial history of local religion. Both were central figures in the conquest and early colonization of the Mexican heartland; both were presented by the Spaniards as partisans in the military enterprise; both were primary symbols of Spanish destiny to rule and stood for hierarchy in colonial society; devotion to both grew from promotion by the Catholic priesthood, as well as through native acceptance and appropriation; both gained new local meanings in the late-sixteenth and seventeenth centuries; and, by the eighteenth century, local attachments stand out for both. But there are striking differences within these broad similarities. Though both contained multiple meanings that changed over time, the meanings were not identical, and the changes differed sharply toward the end. In particular, Santiago's importance seems to have declined in the eighteenth century as Mary's became ever greater.

Despite Santiago's prominence in the Conquest period and his conspicuous part in the popular moros y cristianos pageants, he was one among many saints, not heavily promoted by the clergy after the sixteenth century. He was the patron saint of some communities and individuals, his day (July 25) was a popular if optional feast day, and he was treated as a forceful demigod, who could bring down rain and the arresting spectacle of thunder and lightning. But few priests in the middle and late colonial period adopted him for their special devotion, and most of the village performances in which he appeared were staged by the laity, not priests. He might protect, but he was treated more as a messenger and an independent power to be propitiated than as an advocate for lay people in their appeals to God. Still, if Elizabeth Wilder Weismann is correct that most of the images of Santiago found in rural Mexican churches were made and acquired in the seventeenth century, their popularity did not decline as obviously as the official promotion did.

From a primary symbol of the Spaniards' destiny to rule a Christian empire and deliver God's protection to converts, Santiago became a saint attached to local meanings (including the old ones intended by the colonial authorities) and a patron who defended the local community's sense of its independence. That sense of independence could find expression in appeals to the saint and his horse for protection against enemies. But by the late colonial period, it also took the form of disrespect to the saint—ridiculing him, defeating him in mock combat, and promoting his horse as the object of devotion and source of power. These reversals of the initial meaning of Santiago as Spaniards represented it suggest that the message of Indian humiliation was subject to change but had not been forgotten by late colonial Indian villagers.

In their late colonial performances involving Santiago, Indian lay people presented themselves as good, even superior Christians, not as agents of a prehispanic revival or enemies of the colonial state and its religion. True, where Indians who believed that they were chosen Christians went on to distinguish between Christianity and the church or Christian conduct and the conduct of privileged colonists, there were revolutionary possibilities. But such possibilities of a new order were rarely acted on; rarely, at least beyond the local level, where they had helped to define a colonial identity. As royal authorities suspected, there were potentially subversive if not "pagan" implications in departures from Cortés's original message, but only in the seventeenth-century vision of María, the healer from Ixmiquilpan, was Santiago's sword poised to challenge the colonial order. When a widespread struggle for political and social liberation came to Mexico in 1810, his sword was sheathed. Santiago was not the symbol to activate that national cause any more than he could hearten early-nineteenth-century royalists in their defense of New Spain. The veneration of Santiago, then, had become more than a form of homage to the Spanish victor and less than the kind of militant inversion of the Conquest that put villagers on the offensive, connected them in a classlike cause, and threatened colonial rule.

Mary was altogether more important, and devotion to her continued to grow without apparent interruption. As with Santiago, local images and local associations developed. The hospital images of Mary Immaculate were adapted to local uses and interpreted, as were those of Santiago, reinforcing self-conscious local identities. But Mary carried few of the complicating associations with humiliation, armed conquest, animal power, and Spanish rage that could make Santiago the object of ridicule. Penance was a route to Mary, but there were no humilladero chapels to her, no Marian memorials to Indians' paralyzing fear.

On the contrary, Mary helped to shape a wider political identity as Santiago never did. As a particularly famous pilgrimage shrine, the sanctuary of Guadalupe contributed to that development, but this image's place in the political culture of village Mexico is complicated. During the colonial period, the Guadalupe image was at least as much an official, urban, creole, and ranchero symbol of chosenness as an appropriation by Indian villagers. If it is accurate to say that "the Indians clamored for their right to partnership in erecting a supreme divine symbol, one which embodied an aspect of their past, of their values and aspirations,"[161] then that divine symbol in the colonial period was more likely to be a local image of the Blessed Virgin or the patron saint than the image of Guadalupe, and the process of enlargement was likely to be gradual and local more than sudden and uniform.

The relationship between devotion to Mary Immaculate and Indians in the colonial polity of New Spain seems to fall into three phases that were shaped by situations of conflict and disruption. In the generations after the first conquest, ideas of redemption and justice through mediation, prayer, and deference occupied an important place in the formation of a way of thinking and living that made Christianity and colonial rule generally acceptable to many established Indian communities. In the seventeenth and early eighteenth centuries, the rise of the Virgin Mary of the Immaculate Conception as a corporate protectress and intercessor for Indian pueblos may have been connected to a gradual reconstitution of Indian peasants in more ideologically "closed, corporate communities" (in many cases colonial settlements with precolonial roots, which were in fact neither closed nor simply corporate). In the late eighteenth century and during the Independence War, a time of increasing interest in the image of Guadalupe, the Virgin's protection more often implied a challenge to the political and social order directed from capital cities, and armed action against privileged people.

If devotion to Mary did not experience a gradual decline during the seventeenth and eighteenth centuries, this would distinguish Mesoamerica from early modern Spain as William Christian describes it. Spain experienced a decline in Marian devotion from 65 percent of all images especially revered to 55 percent between roughly 1580 and 1780. Christian's explanation for this apparent decline bears consideration for Mexico. He posits a growing devotion to Christ and his Passion, and a change in the representation of God toward a more positive, benevolent, helping deity in the eighteenth century. Disasters then were less likely to be viewed as punishment by an angry God than as the misfortunes of individuals, a change that Christian takes as signs of corporate religion giving way to individual faith, the erosion of local autonomy, fewer and less devastating epidemics, and generally improved material conditions of life beginning in the eighteenth century. A more benevolent God also fits with the regalist tendencies of eighteenth-century church-state relations and the shrinking of the church's (especially the parish clergy's) judicial role in matters of public morals and political loyalty. For Mary, it meant that her intercession was less required.

In Mexico, the devotion to Mary was, if anything, more intense than ever by 1800, and religious practices in pueblos de indios do not reflect much change in the conception of God. But this does not mean that the ideological changes Christian adduces were not present and being promoted from the top. Perhaps because a sense of local autonomy was challenged but not yet deeply eroded, physical hardships were not much ameliorated, and the acceptance of hierarchy remained about as strong as ever, her association with local places was undiminished, and her intercession was needed as much as ever.

The continuing appeal of Mary in eighteenth-century Mexico suggests that she was more than an intercessor. Her own volition was increasingly evident. She could act independently, and her actions were becoming more political. She guarded and protected; she healed. As patroness she might sanction rebellious acts that validated her believers' superior Christianity. And even a decline in local autonomy and corporate religion in the late eighteenth century could reinforce her importance, albeit in altered form, as devotion was transferred to the regional pilgrimage images that drew people out of their communities into wider political associations. Regional devotions were growing in central and western Mexico during the eighteenth century, although, as the pattern of namings suggests, the base of this change was not simply in Indian pueblos; nor was it simply a spontaneous, self-generating development there, little affected by pastoral initiatives.

A widespread devotion to Guadalupe among villagers in the dioceses of Mexico and Guadalajara came late in the colonial period. Even then it was less complete than the popular tradition supposes. She was not yet a "dominant symbol" with a "highly constant and consistent meaning" of liberation and protest against colonial rule. Before the 1730's, village devotion was concentrated in and near the Valley of Mexico, with pockets of devotees in more distant places that likely were connected to old pilgrimage routes to Tepeyac or to the popular devotion that was being promoted by the clergy. The more dynamic, popular devotion to Guadalupe seems to have emanated especially from Mexico City in official and unofficial ways, from other cities of the viceroyalty (especially San Luis Potosí, Zacatecas, Querétaro, Guadalajara, and smaller towns populated mainly by non-Indians), from the priesthood, and from the non-Indian population of the countryside in central and northern Mexico.

CHAPTER TWELVE

Cofradías

The *cura* has stuck his scythe into the ripe grain of others.
—Pedro Alcántara, Indian of
San Francisco Tecospa, 1792

The cofradías organized to promote particular devotions were especially controversial in the late eighteenth century. The capital of many of these important sources of parish revenue was being depleted at that point, pitting priests and parishioners against each other over control of what remained of this collective wealth and expression of faith.[1] The controversy also depended on Bourbon state making. Most cofradías had been governed more by local custom and informal agreements than by formal law until the Spanish reformers set out to expand royal authority at the expense of the clergy, control colonial wealth more fully, and stimulate revenue-producing enterprises.

Royal law governing cofradías in Indian and non-Indian communities collected in the *Recopilación* of 1681 was sketchy and reflected the ambiguities of an earlier colonial state conceived as a marriage of church and crown. By law, the nominally self-governing cofradías were under dual supervision. They were to be directed by members elected to office under by-laws approved by royal officials and church leaders, with active supervision by both majesties in all formal proceedings. The principal law regarding cofradías, cited repeatedly in late colonial litigation—a 1600 royal cedula abstracted in *Recopilación* 1-4-25—declared that cofradías required a license from the king, review and approval of their by-laws by the Council of the Indies, and authorization by the bishop. Meetings of cofradía members were to take place only in the presence of a royal representative and the local priest ("the prelate of the house where they meet"). Other laws of the *Recopilación*, decrees of the Third Provincial Council of bishops and provincials in New Spain (1585), and legal commentaries of the seventeenth century elaborated on the dual jurisdiction or emphasized the particular responsibilities of priests and royal governors for the proper conduct of cofradía business.

Generally, the initiative in cofradía affairs during the Hapsburg period remained with the clergy. *Recopilación* 1-2-22 called for bishops to visit Indian churches and hospitals (which were supported principally by cofradías) and inspect their accounts "in the presence of a representative of the Royal Patron," who, in the ambiguous wording of this law, might "take part and attend" (*intervenir y asistir*). The Third Provincial Council decreed that all expenditures from the property of the church required a special episcopal license, and that the bishops were to promote and increase the property of pious funds (such as cofradías).[2] And Solórzano, the great seventeenth-century legal commentator, described an active role for priests in the selection and tenure of cofradías officers when he declared that "as for *mayordomos*, they should be to the *cura*'s satisfaction."[3] But the *Recopilación* also outlined the responsibilities of royal officials to promote Indian and Spanish hospitals, keep accounts of Indian contributions to hospitals, determine that Christian services were readily available, and ensure that Indian pueblos had *bienes de comunidad* (secular community property).[4]

Here was a small body of law and legal opinion that seemed to favor the clergy's supervision of locally governed cofradías but left room for royal initiatives, rather like the overlapping authority of viceroys and audiencias. Late colonial records provide ample evidence that, in practice, many parish priests dominated the selection of cofradía officials and kept the financial records of cofradía properties, income, and expenditures; and that some priests effectively managed the cofradía properties as if they were their own.[5] These practices were apparently more common in the Diocese of Guadalajara than the Archdiocese of Mexico, where, as in most other facets of the political and social history discussed in this book, the patterns varied more from place to place, and the conflicts over parish priests' rights were somewhat sharper and of longer standing. Although total ecclesiastical rents were much higher in the archdiocese, cofradías were a more important source of parish income in Guadalajara.[6]

The operation of formally constituted cofradías depended on one or more officers elected at the end of each year, when the accounts of property, income, and expenditures kept by the outgoing officers were reviewed. The principal officer for the year was the mayordomo (sometimes called *prioste*, a term that could also refer to lower cofradía officers), who managed the property and paid the customary devotional expenses from its income and from contributions by the *cofrades* (cofradía members) and parishioners at large.[7] In some communities, the mayordomo shared responsibilities with other officers, as at Temascaltepec (Edo. de México) in 1790, where the Cofradía del Divinísimo's mayordomo was assisted by a rector and nine diputados.[8]

If a pueblo had only one cofradía, it was likely to be dedicated to the Divinísimo or Santísimo Señor Sacramentado (the Holy Sacrament, literally "The Most Holy Lord in the Eucharist"), also known as Nuestro Amo (Our Master). Where there was more than one cofradía in the community, that of the Divinísimo would usually be designated the archicofradía and serve as an umbrella sodality for the whole pueblo or parish.[9] It was the first cofradía established in most pueblos that had none before the eighteenth century; and usually it was the last to be dissolved. For instance, when several cofradías of Tlajomulco (Jalisco) were in decline during the 1770's, the bishop decided to combine them into the one for the Señor Sacramentado.[10]

Reinforcing the Council of Trent's emphasis on the doctrine of transubstantiation, a cofradía to the Divinísimo had general responsibilities for supporting the mass. It covered the costs of the weekly Misa de Renovación (the Thursday mass to renew the Host), the supply of wafers, oil for the lamp, sacramental wine, flowers, and other supplies that made for a dignified mass. A cofradía del Divinísimo would also pay for the parish's Corpus Christi celebrations in June.[11] Its activities might be expanded beyond the ceremony of the Eucharist to cover the costs of other principal feasts, such as Easter week and the day of the parish's patron saint.[12] Its membership was equally broad, typically comprising all adults in the community. The breadth of its membership and responsibilities is recorded in a brief 1793 description of the cofradías of Huiciltepec, district of Tecali (Puebla). After mentioning various cofradías in the parish, it states that "there is one general [cofradía] dedicated to the Santísimo, in which all the *barrios* participate."[13]

Communities with several cofradías often had one dedicated to the Virgin Mary of the Immaculate Conception and another dedicated to the Souls in Purgatory.[14] These, again, were cofradías that enrolled all or most members of the community and sponsored weekly masses and special feast days—in these cases, the Day of the Immaculate Conception (ordinarily December 8) and All Souls' Day (November 2). Thanks to the Franciscans' hospital-building efforts of the sixteenth and early seventeenth centuries, cofradías to the Virgin Mary of the Immaculate Conception were especially common in these two dioceses. Ordinarily, each of these institutions had a cofradía that supported both the hospital proper and its attached chapel to Mary.[15] Jalisco had the greatest proportion of cofradías dedicated to this advocation. Other popular advocations for cofradías with a general membership were the Holy Sepulchre, Our Lady of the Rosary, and the Holy Trinity.

Ideally, but not often in fact, there would be a cofradía or *hermandad* ("brotherhood"; formally, a less important lay organization) for every special advocation, fiesta, or major image in the parish and visita churches. These more specialized sodalities might be made up of people from a particular barrio who were especially devoted to one saint or religious image or a nucleus of families that donated the property and labor to promote a particular devotion. The Santo Cristo de la Expiración of Jocotepec, for example, had its own cofradía in the eighteenth century, which looked after the image and sponsored celebrations in its honor.[16] Short of establishing a formal cofradía to each saint, some pueblos like Totomaloyan in the district of Sultepec in 1798 elected a "mayordomo" for each saint venerated during the course of the year. This officer's responsibilities were to furnish candles daily for the saint's image in the parish church and a feast rich in meat and tepache for the community officers and principales on the saint's day.[17]

In both dioceses, cofradías were established mainly from the late sixteenth century to the 1770's. At the end of the seventeenth century, the Franciscan chronicler Agustín de Vetancurt reported cofradias in most pueblos of the Archdiocese of Mexico, although fewer there than in Guadalajara were attached to the chapels of Indian hospitals.[18] By then, Guadalajara pueblos were virtually certain to have two or three cofradías, and many had five or more. But in the archdiocese, though most larger communities had at least one cofradía or hermandad, curas often complained that none existed in the visitas, or that they had ceased operation or were in a "deplorable state," and that non-Indians were more inclined to favor them.[19] Cofradías were especially numerous in the area of modern Hidalgo—for example, in 1767, Soquisquiapan had eleven in the cabecera, Molango ten, Xochicoatlan six, and Tianguistengo four—but even here most were losing capital and income by the 1790's.[20]

Property and Activities

As Vetancurt found for the archdiocese's cofradías generally, and Emma Pérez Rocha found for the district of Tacuba (Valley of Mexico) specifically,[21] most late colonial cofradías supported their activities from community-owned livestock and lands. Typically, the lands and animals were either rented out for cash or worked by hired laborers or the cofrades themselves.[22] In the early colonial period, before endowments of livestock and land had accumulated, the expenses of cofradías in rural parishes were likely to be covered by general contributions (*derramas*) of cash and labor, combined with some individual sponsorship.[23]

Especially in the Diocese of Guadalajara between 1660 and 1770, sheep and goats virtually disappeared from the cofradía herds in favor of cows, oxen, horses, and mules. The Tala Immaculate Conception cofradía, for example, increased its livestock holdings from 495 cows, steers, and oxen in 1708 to over 600 head in 1764.[24] In the mid-eighteenth century, most hospital cofradías in Indian pueblos of central Jalisco had 150 to 500 head of cattle and horses, plus grazing lands and 100 to 500 pesos in cash.[25] In contrast, non-Indian cofradías in mixed Indian and Spanish towns like Zacoalco, Tecolotlan, Ocotlan, and Atotonilco el Alto rarely owned livestock. Instead, their main assets were liens on rural estates at 5 percent annual interest. Some of the liens were voluntary encumbrances by estate owners to provide a small annuity to pay for special masses; others represented cash loans to the estates. Typically, non-Indian cofradías in rural Jalisco had cash on hand of 500 to 1,000 pesos, and mortgages totaling 500 to 10,000 pesos.[26] In Tepatitlan, for example, the non-Indian cofradías of the Santísimo, Souls in Purgatory, and Our Lady of Sorrows held 37 mortgages and loans totaling 9,724 pesos in 1798, whereas the Indian cofradía of Acatic in the same parish had 173 cows, steers, and oxen, 167 horses and mules, and 1,072 pesos in cash.[27]

In the late colonial period, some Indian cofradías diversifed their economic activities. In 1798, the hospital cofradía of Tequila owned three houses, 143 furrows of sugarcane plantings, and lands with 6,703 mezcal plants, all of which were rented out for a cash income of 1,000 pesos a year.[28] In 1803, Salatitan, near Tonalá, planted mezcales on its cofradía land which was also used to graze cattle. Other cofradías raised chickens, produced cheese, and stored grain harvested from small fields donated to the Virgin.[29] Especially in the archdiocese, many cofradías supported themselves on a comparatively modest scale from a mix of liens, livestock, magueyes, small plots of arable land, and the labor of the membership. Where expenses exceeded the income from these sources, members were called on to make up the difference. For example, the difference between the 100 pesos in expenses of the Cofradía del Santísimo of Ozoloapan (Edo. de México) and the 20–30-peso income from a small lien and labor service by members in 1792 was prorated among twelve diputados.[30]

Though popular devotion was a fundamental factor in the long history of cofradías and the veneration of saints in rural Mexico, late colonial cofradías and their properties rarely began simply as a spontaneous expression of collective piety. Many were founded or actively promoted by interested parish priests, who regarded them, in the words of one, as a principal means "to promote the liturgy and maintain its pastors."[31] They were a way to increase public religious devotions, maintain the physical plant, and make more secure the priest's income from masses and fiestas. When the cura of Tepejí del Río (Hidalgo) in 1785 discovered that the Indians of Tlaxpa had no cofradías to cover the costs of public worship, like many late colonial curas, he attempted to organize one in which all parishioners would participate. His plan was for all adults to contribute one-half real a week—a kind of institutionalized derrama—to support the activities of a general cofradía. Not surprisingly, his parishioners resisted this proposal for yet another general tax.[32] The cura of Huaxicori in the Guadalajara diocese, facing the same absence of cofradías in 1802, chose a less provocative course. He and the district lieutenant went outside the parish to the district capital of Acaponeta to solicit donations of cattle for a cofradía ranch in his parish dedicated to the Divinísimo. There they succeeded in securing 70 cows for the project.[33] In some cases, new devotions were underwritten from the increase of livestock belonging to established sodalities, as at San Simón Tototepec in the district of Zacualpan, where growing numbers of cattle from the Cofradía of the Immaculate Conception—the original herd having been acquired by the farm labor of local men and blankets woven by their wives—were transferred to ranches that supported eight new cofradías by 1803.[34]

A cofradía often began when a group of parishioners agreed to donate a few steers and cows to cover the basic costs of public worship or a particular advocation. Occasionally, the donor was a pious alcalde mayor, the parish priest, or a resident merchant; but usually it was local parishioners, whether Indian or gente de razón. For example, at Tizapanito near Guadalajara, a cofradía was founded by five men and a woman, each giving a few head of cattle and a little land to be held in common, then naming a mayordomo and caretakers.[35] At Zacoalco, Jalisco, a cofradía was created in the 1730's with 154 *ganado mayor* (cattle and horses) donated by 137 non-Indian parishioners, including the cura.[36] At Huetamo (Michoacán) in 1714, a cofradía was established by several Indian and non-Indian residents with livestock and grazing lands, then maintained by the Indian community.[37] Even in the last years of the colonial period, when the future of endowed cofradías was uncertain, a few communities in the Diocese of Guadalajara continued to donate livestock and make community lands available for the creation of new sodalities.[38]

Above all, a village cofradía supported the annual fiesta for the community's patron saint or advocation. Rarely, however, was this the only activity it supported. Cofrades also looked after the altar or image of their advocation in the parish or visita church, supplied the candle wax and incense for the standard devotions, and paid the district judge and the priest for presiding over cofradía meetings, overseeing the annual election of officers, and certifying the accounts.[39] Most cofradías sponsored an annual requiem mass in honor of deceased members. Weekly or monthly masses were another common expense that kept priests busy at the altar and added to their incomes—on Mondays for the souls in Purgatory, on Thursdays for the Blessed Sacrament, on Fridays to commemorate the life of Christ, and on Saturdays for the Blessed Virgin. The cofradías of the Santísimo Sacramento and the Immaculate Conception of Atoyac in the jurisdiction of Sayula, Jalisco, in 1787 provide a minimal example. Together, they paid for high masses on the four feast days of the Virgin, Maundy Thursday, and Corpus Christi; two requiem masses for deceased cofrades; and low mass every Saturday and the second and third Sundays of each month.[40]

Propertied cofradías not closely supervised by the cura were likely to stretch the expenses for religious festivities beyond what he regarded as dignified devotion and the proper use of limited resources. The cura of Alahuistlan in 1804 complained of Indian cofrades spending large sums for "superfluous meals," "continual drunkenness," and unnecessary assistants (*conmilotones*).[41] Likewise, the cura of Santa Fe, near Guadalajara, in 1765 objected to the town cofradía providing the ingredients for homemade liquor and quantities of meat that encouraged townspeople to drink heavily and break their obligation to fast on certain Fridays.[42] The cura of Achichipico (Diocese of Guadalajara) in 1795 wanted cofrades to spend much less on candle wax so that the sodality could pay the standard fee for the masses it sponsored.[43] Often most troubling of all to curas were expenditures that were unrelated to the support of the church and of no direct benefit to them. Indians of Huiciltepec (Tecali district, Puebla) in the 1790's used cofradía funds to pay for public works and—particularly galling to the cura—a lawsuit against him over sacramental fees; various pueblos in the Diocese of Guadalajara paid for land measurements and title verifications from the cofradía treasuries; some covered part of their royal tribute from cofradía funds; and many dipped into the cofradía treasury in times of famine and epidemic.[44]

Still, most of the cofradía expenses that went beyond the feasts and masses of the advocation benefited the parish priest, as well as the cult and the community, and were sometimes actively encouraged by him. The cura of Zumpahuacan in the district of Malinalco in 1765 demanded a cofradía calf every two weeks for his table.[45] Cofradías in other parishes were obliged to provide horses and mules for the priest's use when he went on circuit or was called out to administer the last rites.[46] The list of materials and services that Indians of Mascota, Jalisco, provided to the cura from their Immaculate Conception cofradía in 1786 consisted of barriers for bullfights on feast days, repairs and additions to his residence, repairs and improvements to the church and sacristy, two mounts for his travels to hear confessions, cedar wood for a new altar, the construction of a cemetery and bell tower, the maintenance of the hospital, and silver for new ornaments in the church.[47] Like Mascota, many pueblos in both dioceses resorted to the cofradía treasuries to pay for a new side altar, repair damage to the church, or buy a new monstrance or other ornament for the church.[48] Such uses of cofradía funds technically required the bishop's license, and episcopal court records for the late colonial period contain many petitions of this kind. Curas could have mixed feelings about these petitions and sometimes opposed them out of concern that cofradía funds for the support of masses and other regular observances might be depleted.[49] But normally, they were waved through, if not actively promoted by bishops and curas.[50]

Church Property or Community Property?

The various uses made of cofradía funds in rural pueblos—especially for tribute, land litigation, emergency relief, and other secular purposes—expose a long-standing tension between curas and parishioners that was rooted in different conceptions of pious funds and the old ambiguity of church and crown jurisdictions. Curas were inclined to view land and livestock used by parishioners to support public worship as "bienes de la iglesia," "bienes eclesiásticos," or "bienes espirituales"—church property that was independent of other community holdings. Cofradías and hermandades were the classic forms of collective support for religious activities, and curas were inclined to speak of properties so used as belonging to cofradías, whether or not there was a formally constituted sodality. Villagers might bend to the priest's desire to institutionalize and manage these properties, yet continue to think of the lands and livestock as bienes de comunidad, inseparable from other community properties that were not used to support public worship. Royal officials attempting to build up the anemic community treasuries (cajas de comunidad) in the 1780's and 1790's gave such villagers added encouragement.[51] Indian petitioners from Ixcatepec (Guerrero) elaborated on this conflation of bienes de la iglesia and bienes de comunidad in 1802 during litigation with the cura over who should administer the property of six community ranchos:

From the beginning of our settlement, individual members voluntarily established six *ranchos* . . . for the purpose of assuring the *pueblo* a subsistence sufficient to meet the basic expenses of the church, the cost of its religious ornaments, [and] the alms for masses to different advocations [but] also to pay for various public necessities, which formerly were satisfied by the sweat of community members.[52]

Because the ranchos mainly supported religious activities, the Ixcatepec petitioners said, their parish priests had long been determined "to reduce them to ecclesiastical control." The cura responded that since the pueblo elected mayordomos every year, they *were* cofradías, which elicited a final retort from the Indians through their attorney: "Under the cover of such claims, the curas applied the bad name of *cofradías* to the aforesaid *ranchos*." The audiencia decided for the Indians, ordering that control over the ranchos be returned to them.

The clear line that late colonial priests often said existed between bienes de la iglesia and bienes de comunidad was not so clear either in principle or in practice. Many pious funds in rural Mexico that seemed to operate as cofradías attached to a particular advocation and administered by an elected mayordomo originated without the formalities of a license or written by-laws; and Indian parishioners were inclined to mix community land and livestock with livestock marked for the church.[53] People who were assigned what amounted to inalienable plots of community land (part of the pueblo endowment or *fundo legal,* as it began to be called in the 1790's) for their personal use sometimes willed them to the church for the support of a particular saint.[54] Were these bienes de la iglesia or bienes de comunidad?

Before the 1790's, the question was rarely raised. The nine cattle ranches that the pueblo of San Simón Tototepec owned in 1803 were used to support both religious and community activities. Eight had been acquired as the first rancho's herd increased—a rancho that belonged to the Cofradía of the Immaculate Conception.[55] So, many of the ranchos' animals descended from what was clearly cofradía property at the start. But they were raised on land that was mainly community property, not specifically deeded to the church. The issue, then, was whether the herds were bienes de la iglesia or not. Legal precedent provided no clear answer. In 1734, for example, Indians of Huetamo had struggled with their cura over rights to control the livestock and other property of their informal pious funds, and over his attempts to coerce them into creating new cofradías. They claimed that the animals were bienes de la comunidad grazing on pueblo lands and therefore should not be treated as bienes espirituales. The audiencia supported the Indians' position that they should not be forced to establish new cofradías or celebrate more than the mandatory feast days but left open the issue of whether cofradía properties were bienes de la iglesia.[56]

Without a formal constitution, it was not clear whether a pious fund in the parish was the equivalent of a cofradía. Even if there was a written constitution, Indian parishioners usually preferred customary practices. And colonial law had never defined clearly the boundary between community and religious property. As Intendant Ugarte y Loyola documented in his reports on bienes de comunidad for Nueva Galicia after 1787, rather than separating their religious and secular affairs, Indian pueblos often regarded the treasuries of cofradías and the comunidad as one. This was a useful ambiguity that Indians could manipulate for their own purposes. In 1732, the cura and district governor for Temascaltepec complained that when they tried to settle accounts with the Indians of San Pedro Tejupilco from the reserves of a community ranch, the Indians would tell the alcalde mayor that he could not take any of the animals because they belonged to the church, then tell the cura that he could not intervene because they were bienes de la comunidad.[57]

The Bourbons' venture into the law of cofradías and ecclesiastical jurisdiction over them in New Spain began rather tentatively with a viceregal bando on January 31, 1750.[58] This bando reiterated law 1-4-25 of the *Recopilación* and the principle of dual responsibility, but in describing the procedure for establishing cofradías and convening their meetings, it stressed the crown's responsibilities. The crown took the initiative to order reports from all parish priests on the number of cofradías, their income, and whether their constitutions had been formalized according to the law.[59] At the time, little apparently came of this general bando and the implication that the crown might assert its primacy over cofradías in order to promote community treasuries at the expense of pious funds. A viceregal bando in 1776 went a step further by coupling a repeat of the order for curas to report on the number of cofradías and their properties with a reminder that the conta-

dor general de propios y arbitrios, in his legal opinion of June 6, 1775, had concluded that the many pious funds in pueblos de indios had contributed greatly
to the poverty of community treasuries, which had been mandated by law since
the sixteenth century.[60] Again, the new decree did not lead directly to dramatic
royal initiatives, but it added to the growing resentment of clerical control over
the substantial properties of cofradías that expressed itself in vehemently anticlerical treatises like Hipólito Villarroel's *Enfermedades políticas*, which circulated
in the capital after 1785. Influenced by his own experience as an alcalde mayor,
Villarroel argued against any involvement by priests in the operation of cofradías
because their ranches were not ecclesiastical properties and because cofradías
prejudiced the economic well-being of pueblos by encroaching on limited farmlands for pasture. By the early 1780's, viceroys of New Spain were moving in particular cases to enlarge the pueblo bienes de comunidad by reducing payments
for church activities and making alcaldes mayores their financial supervisors.[61]

The 1786 Ordenanza de Intendentes for New Spain (in effect by 1789) proved
to be a catalyst for a more active engagement of the cofradía issue by crown authorities. Article 13 called for Spanish judges to preside over elections in Indian
pueblos, and article 31 called for all communities to report in detail to the intendants on their community properties. The accuracy of the reports was to
be verified by the subordinate judges, presumably the subdelegados.[62] Priests
were conspicuously absent from these assignments of responsibility. The question soon arose whether community properties included those of cofradías. The
subdelegado of Santa María del Oro in the Diocese of Guadalajara judged that
they did, and ordered the curas in his district to turn over to him all their cofradía records. The bishop questioned the subdelegado's authority to inspect the
cofradías, which he regarded as "the patrimony of that church." He appealed to
the crown to excuse any defects of the foundation records of cofradías in his diocese and to confirm ecclesiastical jurisdiction over them. The incomplete result
of this dispute was a royal cedula of July 20, 1789, requesting the viceroy's advice
and ordering that no innovations be made in the interim. "The interim" apparently outlasted Spanish rule in New Spain, but this cedula and the Ordenanza
de Intendentes led to a series of inspections and audiencia rulings that extended
secular control over cofradías and supported village initiatives against curas. For
the province of Nueva Galicia (including the Diocese of Guadalajara), Intendant
Ugarte y Loyola compiled an extensive dossier on bienes de comunidad between
1786 and 1791, from which he concluded that nearly every pueblo had cofradías,
but very few had the requisite community treasury.[63] In the report that he presented to the audiencia on April 9, 1791, Ugarte took a conciliatory position. He
was not, he said, opposed to cofradías as a rule, only to their abuses. He wanted
the legitimate cofradías to be identified and their fiestas made less lavish in order
not to deplete community resources. But the die was cast. When the fiscal of
the audiencia expressed his concern about the misuse of pueblo lands three days
later, cofradías were on his mind. He said that in various pueblos, community
lands had been divided up unequally for private use, and that the Indians of the
Cuquío jurisdiction were founding new cofradías from their bienes de comunidad, even taking lands of the fundo legal for this purpose.[64]

The fiscal of the Audiencia of Mexico in 1791 took the earlier cedulas and

bandos to their logical conclusion. In a cofradía dispute involving Temascaltepec, he recommended that any sodality that did not have its constitution in order
should be dissolved.[65] Audiencia fiscales debated the issue of dissolution through
the 1790's but consistently expressed their concern over the decline of Indian
community lands, disorder in the pueblo treasuries, the extravagance and excessive number of religious celebrations, and the need to protect lands of the fundo
legal.[66] In 1799, and again in 1800, during the bitter dispute over cofradía properties in the district of Tecali (Puebla), the civil fiscal of the Audiencia of Mexico
urged that the cofradías of Huiciltepec be dissolved because they were not properly established and the properties were being mismanaged. He went on to make
a sweeping recommendation that all cofradías without formal constitutions ("las
solemnidades necesarias") be abolished, and that the subdelegados preside over
commissions to dispose of the property.[67] But the fiscal was out of touch with
a decided shift in administrative policy. By 1796, the viceroy and audiencia had
concluded that, although proper constitutions were necessary, cofradías were
very important to the Indians' Christian devotion and should not be dissolved on
the pretext of faulty titles.[68] The following year, the crown gave the cofrades of
Totolapa (Tlalmanalco district, near the Valley of Mexico) two years to get their
constitutions up to legal standard.[69] In the Tecali case, the *asesor general* (general
counsel) on June 3, 1800, deflected the fiscal's recommendation, saying that this
was no time for a definitive judgment. For two more years, the fiscal de lo civil,
backed by the fiscal protector de indios, promoted his recommendation to dissolve the four cofradías of Huiciltepec, but on July 25, 1802, he recommended
that the Indians decide for themselves. The next year, the audiencia ordered the
cofrades to draw up proper constitutions.

Although the weight of audiencia opinion in Mexico and Guadalajara shifted
against ecclesiastical rights over cofradías, the question of whether cofradía properties were bienes de comunidad had been left dangling by the cedula of July 20,
1789. Increasingly, cofradía property was judged to be secular by the courts, but
audiencia officials were hardly of one mind on the thrust of that decree. In March
1798, one fiscal in Guadalajara cited the 1789 cedula to support his judgment that
cofradía lands were royal property, even though it had only broached the question, not given a clear answer. Two years later, another fiscal in the same audiencia invoked it to a different end—to forbid all innovations in cofradías, whether
or not their constitutions were well formed, thereby attempting to convert the
cedula's temporary injunction against alterations into a general principle governing cofradías as institutions.[70]

Though the audiencias backed away from radical proposals to dissolve propertied cofradías altogether, they moved to tighten their control over them. A
viceregal bando of August 17, 1791, reinterpreted *Recopilación* 1-4-25 to give the
state sole authority in the supervision of elections and other meetings of the
sodalities: now only the royal representative (*ministro real* or *justicia real*—usually
the district governor or his lieutenant) could preside over meetings of cofradía
members.[71] Audiencia rulings in cofradía disputes after that date put the policy
into practice. The first test came in 1794. In a case involving Real de Huautla
(Morelos), the Audiencia of Mexico decreed that the priest could attend cofradía
meetings only in the passive role of "rector de la casa."[72] A decision in a dispute

at Aculco in the district of Xilotepec (Edo. de México) two years later pretended to protect the pueblo cofrades' right to manage their own affairs but decreed that the justicia real who presided over their meetings should have the decisive vote in the selection of the mayordomo.[73] By the first years of the nineteenth century, judges ruling in such cases consistently applied the principle of royal supervision and expanded on it. Responding to the question of whether community ranches used to support the public worship at Alahuistlan between 1802 and 1805 belonged to the church and could be managed by the cura, the audiencia concluded on August 22, 1805, that they were bienes de comunidad and outside his jurisdiction. It ordered the subdelegado to take special care to safeguard the property of these cofradías, and to ensure above all that the Indians not waste the resources of their sodalities on lavish meals and drunkenness at fiesta time but invest them strictly in "pious objects and purposes."[74]

By 1805, few sodalities had been dissolved for lack of proper titles, but in both policy and practice, especially in the Audiencia of Mexico, their properties did not belong to the church and were subject only to the management and supervision of the cofrades and the royal representative.[75] Royal officials used their expanding authority in cofradía affairs to control spending and disorderly conduct, and to require accurate accounts.[76] During the last years of colonial rule, formal constitutions and written accounts proliferated to check clerical initiatives and unauthorized cofradía expenditures.[77]

Especially in the Archdiocese of Mexico, custom favored the independent local election of cofradía mayordomos in some parishes, but before the late 1780's, the cura often had an important, sometimes decisive influence over who was selected.[78] He had the home field advantage. The elections had been sanctified events, ordinarily held inside the church and under his supervision. "Supervision" could effectively mean that he proposed candidates for election, which made opposition to his choice awkward. After the crown's campaign to reduce the curas' role in cofradía affairs, villagers generally named their own mayordomos, under supervision by the district governor or his lieutenant, or petitioned to do so.[79]

More Conflict, Less Property

In rural pueblos of both dioceses, the crown's shift in policy led to increased disputes between curas and parishioners and curas and district governors over the control of cofradías, and brought growing pressures to spend and break up their corporate wealth. Or what corporate wealth they still had. For population growth and natural disasters had already contrived to reduce the livestock of many cofradías. In the Diocese of Guadalajara, the herds of cofradía cattle and a growing human population began to threaten local self-sufficiency in basic foodstuffs as early as the late seventeenth century: cofradía pastures were crowding out corn fields.[80] Despite more rapid population growth during the eighteenth century, cofradía herds in most Indian villages of central Jalisco held their own or continued to grow into the third quarter of the eighteenth century. However, after the 1770's, most Indian cofradía herds there as elsewhere became notably smaller.[81] In the case of Tala, there were only 104 cows, steers, and oxen, and 23 horses in the Immaculate Conception cofradía's herd in 1802, compared with over 400 ganado mayor in 1770.[82] For seven cofradías in the parish of Tlajomulco on which livestock figures are available over the period 1767–1821, the herds decreased by 67 percent from 1767 to 1801 (from 1,128 animals to 373) and by another 45 percent from 1801 to 1821 (from 373 to 204).[83]

Reports by parish priests suggest that the famine and epidemic of 1785–86 accelerated the decline. Villages with little food available from their own lands began to sell the cofradía animals in large numbers or to slaughter them for food. But there were other causes. In his pastoral visit to parishes in central Jalisco during 1801–3, Bishop Cabañas attributed the substantial decreases in the preceding years to Indian mismanagement. He and others reported that some corrupt Indian officials with newfound authority over cofradía property had taken animals and land for themselves, and cofradía animals had been sold or slaughtered without authorization to pay for community feasts and extraordinary community expenses.[84] Whether much cofradía livestock was sold following the royal cedulas of 1805–7 that authorized the *consolidación de vales* (consolidation of government treasury bills through the expropriation of mortgages) and sale of obra pía properties is not yet clear.[85] The decline in cofradía livestock in Mexico and Guadalajara between 1801 and 1821 was probably due in large part to the confusion and insecurity of the Independence War in this part of Mexico. Animals were requisitioned by combatants and taken by bandits. A rebel or royalist encampment could deplete a cofradía's herds of cattle and horses in a few weeks. The insecurity of the time and the breakdown in the administration of cofradías also led some communities to try to sell their cofradía lands (because renters could not be found) and convert the cash into interest-bearing loans.[86] But even before the war, cofradía reserves in Guadalajara had been further depleted after Cabañas's visita. In Ixtlahuacan, near Chapala, the Immaculate Conception cofradía herd dropped from 129 cattle and horses in 1802 to 61 in 1807. Most of this decline apparently resulted from poor care—animals wandering off, stolen, or neglected.[87]

Priests consistently claimed that Indian officials were depleting the herds to pay for tribute and litigation, or distributing the animals as private property to members of the community. Intendant Ugarte corroborated the decline in cofradía livestock in the Diocese of Guadalajara—which he termed "drastic"—in the survey of cajas de comunidad and cofradías he completed in April 1791. However, he attributed it not to Indian mismanagement (Indian management was only beginning to expand then) but to recent years of famine and disease, and to some curas' stealing from the cofradía treasuries.[88]

In sum, the late eighteenth and early nineteenth centuries brought the secularization of parishes, royal initiatives to remove the capital of obras pías from the curas' control, increasingly independent administration of cofradías by Indian mayordomos and town councils, the epidemic and famine of 1785–86, and the depletion of cofradía herds. The result was a surge of open confrontations between parish priests and village officials and between parish priests and district governors. Some priests, not easily reconciled to their loss of influence over parish finances and local politics, carried disputes from the porticoes of the parish church to the episcopal and audiencia courts. Twenty-five of the 33 cofradía disputes between curas and rural parishioners examined in this study—nearly two-thirds—date from 1790 to 1805. Only six occurred before 1773. Eight of the ten formal disputes over cofradías between curas and district governors that reached the high courts of Mexico and Guadalajara also occurred between 1790 and 1805. In some parishes, there had long been disputes between curas and cofrades over the election of mayordomos, over how cofradía revenues should be spent and who should decide, and over curas treating the cofradías' wealth as their personal property or selling or renting cofradía lands and animals to non-Indians as an inducement to settle there and support the priest. The novelty now was in the number of such disputes.[89]

The open conflicts between priests and district governors over cofradías were more obviously a product of the shift in royal policy. At Aculco in 1796, for example, the cura objected strenuously to what he called the "intervention" of the subdelegado's lieutenant in cofradía affairs. Citing decrees of the Council of Trent and the Third Provincial Council, he argued that only the cura should supervise the cofradías, hold the mayordomos accountable for the properties, and preside at elections. The lieutenant replied that the cura had usurped royal authority by continuing to control the 40,000 pesos' worth of property in three cofradías. He called on the audiencia to confirm his right to administer the properties and cast the deciding vote in cofradía elections. The verdict of the audiencia in this case was a qualified endorsement of the lieutenant's position and a complete rejection of the cura's. Only royal judges were to preside over cofradía meetings. The cofrades were to manage the properties themselves, but the lieutenant was to control the election of mayordomos, exercising a vote equal to that of the cofrades.[90] The audiencia had ignored an early warning of conflict between the cura and the lieutenant over cofradías at Aculco in the form of an anonymous letter in December 1792. Evidently inspired by the cura, the letter accused the lieutenant of adultery with his sister-in-law, arresting local people on long-forgotten charges as a pretext to collect fines, and squandering great sums of money as the administrator of the parish's pious funds.[91]

Embattled as the curas were, some still found room to maneuver; a few even managed to control cofradía properties unopposed. At the end of the colonial period, there were curas who kept the accounts for illiterate cofrades, selected and removed mayordomos, imposed non-Indian mayordomos on Indian cofradías, treated corporate properties as their personal possessions, and otherwise acted as if there had been no change in policy.[92] At Mochitlan (Tixtla district, Guerrero) in 1800, the subdelegado complained that the cura persisted in overstepping his authority by managing the property of an hermandad "with complete independence" and not convening the cofrades to elect a new mayordomo in three years. In defense of the cura, the coadjutor denied none of these charges. Instead he said that the cura had acted in the best interest of the brotherhood and had donated some of his own money to the cofradías for church expenses and construction. Even his failure to convene an election was said to be "clear proof of his zeal and disinterest."[93]

But after independence, especially in the Diocese of Guadalajara, where substantial cofradía properties remained, even the priests understood that the corporate properties of cofradías would inevitably disappear along with the curas' oversight of cofradía affairs. The litigation of the 1820's increasingly found curas charged with taking cofradía livestock for themselves or petitioning the bishop to permit the sale of cofradía lands and animals.[94] In a report to the bishop of Guadalajara in 1829, the cura of Cuquío wrote of the urgency of a deteriorating situation, various reasons for the decline of cofradía properties, and the need for quick action to salvage what little remained:

The Indians have divided the capital among themselves to the point that not only the pastures where the cattle of the Immaculate Conception *cofradía* graze are gone but also the corrals and round-up plaza. As a result I am forced to rent another pasture or sell the few animals that remain, both because of what might happen in moving them and the petty thieves who would finish them off little by little. I am even more pained by the contempt with which the said natives behave, seduced as they are by some knuckleheads ["calaveras"] who need not be named. They have even gone to the extreme of selling a hospital.[95]

In some communities, the struggle over cofradía properties continued in the 1820's and 1830's, though the church and its priests were no longer parties to it. At Tizapanito (Villa Corona, Jalisco) in 1828, groups of eight to eleven natives vied with the municipal council over ownership of what cattle remained to the Holy Sepulchre, Santa María Magdalena, and Our Lady of Sorrows cofradías. The groups claimed that they, the legitimate heirs of the cofradía founders and the rightful owners of the livestock, were being despoiled of their property by the council because it had few other funds. The council replied that since cofradía properties were "common to the *pueblo*," they were subject to use for the common good of the community, which included the schoolmaster's salary and rations for prisoners in the municipal jail. Just now the funds were needed for a land suit against two neighboring haciendas, but the council promised that the cofradías' obligations to the church would be fulfilled, even though the plaintiffs wanted the animals for their personal use. The heirs of the cofradía founders responded that the reason why the council members wanted to control the cofradía herd was to keep the cattle for themselves.[96]

Some cofrades had managed their own affairs and property as long as anyone could remember. For example, the Cofradía del Santísimo of Tequisquiac (Valley of Mexico) was said in 1795 to have always controlled its affairs without reference to the cura, submitting its annual accounts to the pueblo council, deputies, and other Indians who constituted a board of overseers.[97] In another case from the turn of the nineteenth century, San Simón Tototepec (Zacualpan district, Edo. de México) in 1803, the cura reported that cofradía accounts had not been submitted to his predecessors in decades.[98] But by the late 1770's, the claim to this privilege was asserted with new audacity and frequency. At Tuspa (Jalisco) in 1776, Indian cofrades made the ringing claim that they had "absolute power" over the government of their cofradía.[99] Indians of Ixcatepec in 1802 also made a strong declaration of their rights over cofradía management that echoed recent audiencia verdicts when they petitioned the crown to "restore" their rights "because they [the cofradía properties] are profane and alien to ecclesiastical control."[100] In a show of defiance that elicited an exasperated complaint from the cura, Indian officials from Mecatabasco (Zacatecas) in 1792 ceremoniously carried the treasury chest of their cofradía from the church to the town offices. Although the cura protested, they kept him away from the chest and proceeded to divide up the money among members of the community.[101] More commonly, cofrades stopped submitting their accounts to the cura and resisted—sometimes by force, but usually by petition to secular authorities—his efforts to impose mayordomos in the annual elections. And (as we shall see later) some pueblos allied themselves with subdelegados who were anxious to extend royal authority over cofradías and thwart traditional prerogatives of the curas.

The declining corporate property of cofradías in Indian pueblos before 1810 required some response if community fiestas were to be celebrated in the customary fashion. Villages might have reduced their expenses by holding fewer fiestas or consuming less food, drink, and fireworks—this is what the crown repeatedly proposed to its district governors—but little evidence has come to light that such reductions were common. Another adjustment in the late eighteenth century to the decline of corporate property was more sponsorship by individuals. When the corporate income of the cofradía no longer met expenses, the mayordomo would naturally have been expected to bridge the gap with collections from the cofrades and the community or from his own funds.[102]

Informal, individual sponsorship of the cult is documented before the 1785–86 disasters and the crown's move to reform cofradía practices—but more of the evidence dates from the 1790's and 1800's, and suggests a response to the decline of income-producing corporate property.[103] But even then the shift from community to individual responsibility was not abrupt or as yet widespread. At Temascaltepec in 1790, the Indians' attorney claimed that mayordomos there covered expenses of their sodality that were not met by the cofrades or by produce from a field of wheat and maize. Individual sponsorship of this kind was simply expected, he said, so the mayordomos were chosen from "among those Indians who are comparatively wealthy." [104] They were not ruined by the expenses and cheerfully accepted their posts, he added. But individual sponsorship was not always as desirable to Indian parishioners as this attorney made it seem. In Tepatitlan and Atotonilco el Alto, Jalisco communities that by the late eighteenth century had non-Indian majorities, Indian cofrades had started requiring non-Indians to sponsor fiestas in exchange for matriculation (which offered newcomers exemption from the alcabala tax and a share of the corporate Indian lands).[105] Private, especially individual, sponsorship was not a new solution to shortfalls in corporate support, whether for secular or religious activities, and would have been a natural solution to the decline of cofradía wealth for devout parishioners; but there is also some evidence that parish priests and bishops pushed for private sponsorship at this time.[106] Joseph Manuel Sotomayor admitted that while serving as cura of Zacualpan in the mid-1790's, he urged a private sponsorship plan on non-Indian cofradía members there.[107] The cura of San Miguel Almoloya in 1790 reportedly demanded private contributions for religious festivities that lacked a sponsoring cofradía.[108]

While individual sponsorship was not yet the rule in the dioceses of Mexico and Guadalajara at the end of the colonial period, it was well established by the eighteenth century in Oaxaca, where formal cofradías had been founded relatively late and were less often well endowed even before the decline of cofradía income from endowments. The immediate reasons for individual sponsorship there seem to have been pressure from secular priests for better support of the public worship and administrative policies that forbade universal contributions, more than home-grown ideas of elite recruitment or redistribution of wealth within the pueblo.[109]

Judging by the limited evidence adduced here for the dioceses of Guadalajara and Mexico, the need to move toward sponsoring village fiestas from private sources would have increased greatly in the first 40 years of Mexico's national history, from 1821 to 1860. The cofradía properties that remained to pueblos in 1821 were much diminished by 1840 and no longer covered even the basic costs of maintaining the faith.[110]

The Case of Alahuistlan

Indian resistance to the curas' involvement in cofradía affairs during the late colonial period reached full intensity in the central Mexican parish of San Juan Bautista Alahuistlan, located along watercourses that thread through the hot, barren hills and barrancas of north-central Guerrero. The great majority of residents of the parish seat and the visitas of San Miguel Totominaloyan, San Pedro, San Francisco Metlatepeque, San Sebastián Axuchitlancillo, and Rancho San Antonio were Nahuatl-speaking Indians. In 1789, the parish priest, Germán José Sánchez, counted 760 Indian families and 26 non-Indian families ("Spanish families whose racial background is not known for certain because they are outsiders recently settled in this jurisdiction").[111] The few non-Indians were concentrated in the rancho and the parish seat, and, like the Indians of San Miguel and some from Alahuistlan, they spoke both Spanish and Nahuatl.

The local economy centered on the production of salt and cotton cloth for the mining center of Sultepec and the production of maize, fruit, and cattle for local consumption. In the late 1780's, Indians in the parish were under pressure to produce more mineral salts for the processing of silver ore at Zacualpan, as well as Sultepec, in exchange for mules and other goods controlled by the active *repartimiento de mercancías* trade—the forced sales monopolized by the alcalde mayor at Zacualpan. Lieutenants of the alcaldes mayores were apparently forcing them to sell their salt in Zacualpan, and they complained to the audiencia through their attorney that they were losing control over their market—when to produce, where to sell, and at what price.[112] Since the salt pits were more than a league from Alahuistlan, the added demand and indebtedness kept the men away from their homes for long periods.

Alahuistlan was located in one of the two large pockets of parishes in the archdiocese where priests reported especially low incomes and left as soon as they could. Classified as a third-class parish by Villaseñor y Sánchez in 1746, Alahuistlan yielded an annual income of only 750 pesos in the early 1770's. Like many late colonial parishes of modern Guerrero, it was regarded as difficult to administer, with a small population dispersed over a large area, poor roads, and a harsh climate—but without the reputation for Indian indifference or hostility to priests of neighboring parishes in Morelos.[113] With the expanding market for salt and cotton cloth, the priest's income reportedly rose to 950 pesos in 1793 and 2,616 pesos in 1805. Qualifying by then as a second-class parish, Alahuistlan was no longer one of the poorest; still, thanks to its heat, remote location, and increasingly contentious Indians, late colonial priests with any prospects were no more inclined to stay long than earlier ones. The ambitious construction project Father Sánchez launched to replace the "indecent and inappropriately small" parish church would not be completed during his tenure.

The priests and parishioners of Alahuistlan carried on particularly vigorous, prolonged, and inconclusive disputes before the Audiencia of Mexico over a span of 20 years. The action began in April 1786, with six past and present Indian officeholders engaging an attorney in Mexico City to represent them in all of their future litigation.[114] In November, he entered a sweeping complaint on behalf of the pueblo against the cura, José Antonio de Zúñiga. Father Zúñiga was accused of demanding unpaid service in the fields and salt pits for his personal benefit, allowing his livestock to destroy Indian plantings, demanding first fruits, exceeding the published schedule for sacramental fees, and ordering cruel whippings of some parishioners and humiliating others. Cofradías were a secondary issue in this initial complaint: the cura allegedly demanded that parishioners take care of the cofradía cattle without compensation.

On the audiencia's order, the alcalde mayor of Zacualpan fixed a copy of the schedule of fees to the church door and took depositions. Witnesses included the schoolmaster, Carlos Rodrigo de Castro, and two castizos and an español from Sultepec who had resided in Alahuistlan for three, twelve, and 30 years, respectively. Castro swore that the cura's demands for fees and service conformed to the customary practice of the parish: true, Indians had farmed an additional plot under the fiscal's supervision on land made available by the town council (instead of supplying fodder for the cura's horses), but they had done so without complaint; and true, Indians had been whipped, but the punishment had not been excessive or without cause.[115] Concerning the complaint over cofradía service, he said that the gobernadores named the mayordomos and cowboys at the end of the year, and that it was customary for these men to serve without provisions or wages.

The lengthy testimony of the other witnesses supported Castro: Zúñiga, like curas before him, had nothing to do with the operation of the cofradía except during the annual accounting of livestock, when he was paid four pesos for his attendance (and presumably his certification of the count). He evidently was pushing to increase parish income—sometimes using the customary service in new ways and proposing to charge the tithe on grains—and was liberal with the whip, but they regarded him as moderate in his demands and operating within traditional limits. From the parish archive, Zúñiga produced a convenio of 1775 in which the Indians agreed to the customary fees and duties rather than the published schedule of fees and were exempted from paying first fruits. The alcalde mayor concluded his investigation in February 1787 with a report that the labor service required of the Indians conformed to the convenio, that the complaint against the cura about cofradía service was without merit, and that the whippings were not especially frequent or cruel. Father Zúñiga had in fact sought to add the tithe on grain and had sometimes ordered whippings when none were called for, he noted, but the other charges were false or inconsequential.

The alcalde mayor also reported that there had been trouble that year on the Day of the Three Kings when the cura arrested Pascual Hipólito, the *alcalde de segundo voto*, for his frequent absences at mass. That event, as it can be reconstructed from the records of the alcalde mayor's investigation, reveals the rising tension over the priest's authority in the parish. The gobernador and other alcaldes released Pascual Hipólito without Father Zúñiga's permission. The cura wrote to the alcalde mayor describing their disobedience and appealing for the crown's intervention. Later, he confronted the officials for an explanation. The gobernador replied that Pascual Hipólito had been released by "the *pueblo*." When the cura demanded to know "Who is 'the *pueblo*'?" one of the alcaldes, Agustín de Santiago, raised his voice ("insolently," said the cura) to repeat "THE PUEBLO," and threatened the cura with his staff of office. The cura broke away and rode to Zacualpan (a hard two-day trip from Alahuistlan) to request the alcalde mayor's intervention. The gobernador, Agustín Pedro, later testified that after Santiago spoke and gestured, the cura threw his scissors at Santiago, wounding him in the head, before the witness intervened to calm the cura. The Indian officials retired, and Santiago later left for Mexico City.

Schoolmaster Castro had witnessed the events and testified at length that after the cura wounded Santiago with the scissors, the two grappled, and the cura hit the Indian and grabbed his hair. The alcalde broke loose and grabbed for the cura, scratching his hands. The gobernador and another alcalde pleaded with the cura to calm himself. At that point, the cura called for help, and Castro and three other non-Indians came forward to restrain Santiago, only to retreat when he menaced the one holding the shackles. The cura continued to call for help—"Is there no one who will help Our Holy Mother Church?"—but the assembled Indians held back. The cura then grabbed the fiscal and ordered him to call the pueblo together and find out who had released the prisoner. When an angry crowd assembled, the schoolmaster pleaded with the cura to release the alcalde in order to avoid a rebellion. The cura agreed to turn Santiago over to the gobernador for incarceration (another witness added that the cura warned the gobernador not to speak to Santiago because he was now excommunicated), then left for San Miguel on his mule. The Indians remained in large groups the rest of the day, but nothing more happened except the alcalde's departure for Mexico City the next day.

In his defense, the fifty-year-old Agustín de Santiago described the cura's actions more than his own. He declared that in confronting the cura over the release of Pascual Hipólito, he had simply repeated what the gobernador had said—that the whole pueblo had done it. The cura had wounded him with the scissors, hit him with his fists, grabbed him by the hair, and tried to throw him to the ground. Naturally he resisted, he said, then resisted again when the cura ordered another Spaniard to put him in shackles, because he had committed no crime. The next day, he had gone to Mexico City to present his complaint against the cura to the archbishop.

At the start, the case seemed sure to go in the cura's favor. The alcalde mayor wrote to the audiencia on February 24, 1787, that the Indian alcalde was at fault—his intemperate reply had led to the cura's violence—and the injury was not serious. Now it was obvious, he added, why the cura had for some time requested a resident lieutenant to police the vices of these Indians and keep order and respect for "the many Spaniards who enter [Alahuistlan] in the salt trade and *repartimiento de efectos*." The alcalde mayor's main concern was to relieve what he called the "grave shortages" of salt for the mines in his jurisdiction, and Alahuistlan was a principal supplier. A permanent lieutenant would suit his purpose very well, as well as the cura's.

But for all the alcalde mayor's enthusiastic support, the case tailed off later that year with no stunning vindication of the cura and two partial defeats. The Indians secured an order on October 25, 1787, for the cura to follow the arancel, which ended their obligation to perform extraordinary labor service and apparently avoided the placement of a hated resident lieutenant in their midst. The cura took steps to continue the litigation in February and April of 1788, but the record is silent on what, if anything, resulted. Perhaps he was replaced by Father Sánchez shortly thereafter.

Disputes over parish administration in Alahuistlan were muted for a few years under Sánchez's successor, José Ignacio Azcárate, but the events of 1786 and 1787 were not forgotten, and the royal policies on cofradías after 1789 invited further litigation over that issue. Father Azcárate was known during his tenure there in the 1790's for his professional zeal and for sponsoring the construction of a "magnificent" parish church.[116] Still, he managed to create a new explosive issue by taking on what seemed to him an excessively prominent and expensive part of Alahuistlan's parish life. In 1798, Azcárate appealed to the audiencia to reform the practice in San Miguel Totomaloyan of having a mayordomo for each of the various saints venerated in the community. He argued that the money wasted on this practice could be put to better devotional use, and the annual banquets occasioned much public drunkenness and disrespect. Having failed in his efforts to bring change through persuasion, exhortation, punishment, and an order from the subdelegado, he appealed to the audiencia to prohibit these mayordomos de santos, leaving the care of the images to the sacristán and the fiscal; to order that no one be required to supply candles or wax to be burned before the images; and to prohibit vigils and banquets for the saints without the cura's permission.[117] The fiscal de lo civil was receptive to the cura's appeal, but he hesitated to act against local religious customs without a full investigation. In 1799, the audiencia acceded to the cura's requests, although it warned that "in matters of customs in the *pueblos*, they should not be removed without a perfect understanding of the reason."

Again, the record does not disclose how the cofrades reacted. But three years later, the cofradía conflicts set in motion by the shift in royal policy reached Alahuistlan with full force, thanks to aggressive Indian leaders who knew their rights and an uncommonly single-minded cura who came to stay. The cura, Mariano Dionicio Alarcón, offered his version of the conflicts in a letter to the vicar general of the archdiocese in December 1802.[118] He had arrived in the parish to find that the six cofradías and hermandades that should have provided most of the support for masses and feast-day celebrations were squandering their wealth on extravagant expenditures and payments to royal governors. Such payments violated the terms of their early-eighteenth-century constitutions requiring that they spend their funds only on prescribed religious activities: masses, various feast-day costs, fees to cantors, wax from Castile, ornaments and missals for the local church, and building repairs. He said he had brought these violations to the Indians' attention and warned them not to kill or sell livestock from the cofradía ranches without his permission. For five months now, the Indians had retaliated with "a thousand absurdities and insults" and had obtained a judicial order from the viceroy that they be left to manage the cofradías as they wished. The cura regarded this order as contrary to canon law and concluded that it must have been issued because the Indians presented false and misleading evidence.

From his letter, it would seem that Father Alarcón did not realize that the royal government in Mexico City not only accepted the substance of its order as a general principle but had toyed with the idea of dissolving corporate cofradía properties altogether. In an attempt to reestablish the church's control over the cofradías of Alahuistlan as bienes espirituales, the archbishop's promotor fiscal sent a report to the viceroy summarizing Alarcón's account. The audiencia's fiscal de lo civil responded on December 31, 1803, that the matter would be reviewed by the fiscal protector de indios. The file offers no further evidence of review or a verdict, but given the audiencia's position in other such cases after 1800, the cura had little reason to hope for a vindication of his claims in the royal courts.

The apparent lack of a definitive verdict in 1803 played into the cura's hand, for when the unresolved dispute reached the audiencia again in August 1804, Father Alarcón was claiming that he had always been in charge of

the economic supervision of the *cofradías*' products, the investment of them, the branding and counting of the cattle, and their care; so that nothing concerning [the cofradías] can be done without my intervention, and no change or alteration in their constitutions can be made without the intervention of the bishop's court, which is corroborated by a succession of orders from the pastoral visits for this parish from Archbishop Aguiar y Seixas to Haro y Peralta.

After his judicial complaint to the vicar general and the viceroy, Father Alarcón must have proceeded to take over the operation of the cofradías and declare to his parishioners that their management was his by canonical right. His ignorance of royal policy seems to have been disingenuous. A marginal note written on his high-flown letter of August 1804 by "Saviñon" (the juez real de propiedades?) and dated August 12, 1804, said that the cura's claim that these cofradías were bienes espirituales was false. It cited an order of November 25, 1802—just before Alarcón made his initial appeal to the vicar general—to the subdelegado of Zacualpan to inform the cura that "those *ranchos* are secular property [*profanos*]" and should be administered by the town government and the mayordomo named by it, under the supervision of the juez real de la Contaduría General de Propiedades.[119]

Father Alarcón followed this exchange with another letter to the archbishop on October 12, 1804—composed "with deep pain in my heart"—in which he repeated his complaints that the church was being left with nothing and declared his commitment to "the defense of my jurisdiction." The Indians, he said, considered it enough to pay the cofradía masses; they no longer permitted him to review the annual accounts. Speaking like an exalted son of the *Itinerario*, he observed that the dissipation of cofradía wealth by the Indians violated the orders of the pastoral visits (as if those orders overruled the recent direction of royal decrees and audiencia judgments).

In February 1805, Father Alarcón was finally drawn into direct correspondence with the audiencia. Stressing his "incontrovertible rights," he appealed on February 14 for an end to the unauthorized sale of cofradía cattle and excessive expenses on banquets, drinking celebrations, and "gifts to Mexico City." Rich Indians, he said, squandered the wealth of the cofradía treasuries, practiced no charity, and bribed officials to expunge from the record their many misdeeds. He claimed not to have received until May 18, 1804, an audiencia order sought by the gobernador of Alahuistlan and sent to the subdelegado of Zacualpan on November 6, 1802. A second order from the audiencia concerning ecclesiastical property was sent to the subdelegado on September 8, 1804, but he seems to have withheld it from the cura. If so, this was more than a broad hint that the subdelegado had been bribed to turn against him.[120] Reaching for whatever he could salvage from a bad situation, Father Alarcón proposed to the audiencia that double-locked strong boxes be purchased to hold the accounts and cash reserves of each cofradía and ensure that the use of corporate wealth conform to their written constitutions. Two keys would be needed to open the box, one for the cofrades and one for him.

But the string finally ran out on the cura's bluff. On June 5, 1805, a new subdelegado, Mariano del Pozo, promised the viceroy that he would soon report on the cura's petition that the natives not be allowed to admininister the cofradía ranchos on their own:

For the present, I can advise Your Excellency that said properties are known by the natives themselves as *cofradías*, but they are neither church property nor religious property. It is common knowledge that they are purely *bienes profanos*, and none of the other *curas* [in the district] have pretensions of this sort, for they are aware of the true principle involved.[121]

On August 17, the audiencia's fiscal protector de indios endorsed the subdelegado's preliminary evaluation: cofradías were "purely *bienes profanos*; that was the legal practice." He advised the audiencia to rule that mayordomos and pueblo officials alone could administer these properties; that priests should not have a key to the cofradía treasury boxes because they contained no ecclesiastical property; and that subdelegados should be instructed to give close attention to maintaining and increasing the cofradías' wealth. The audiencia concurred on August 22. Apparently, this verdict was unequivocal enough to silence even the persistent Father Alarcón, for no other appeals or complaints appear in the record.

* * *

From this brief survey, it is clear that the activities of cofradías in the dioceses of Mexico and Guadalajara were infrequently the elaborately staffed, individually sponsored affairs familiar to twentieth-century ethnographers. The late colonial evidence of limited individual sponsorship, few offices, and promotion by priests does not readily fit the modern pattern of an elaborate civil-religious hierarchy where community life and service were concentrated.[122] Colonial cofradías generally lacked a large or elaborate ladder of offices that all men of the community would have mounted, and most cofradía expenses were covered by corporate property more than individual prestige-spending. Cofradías were not the only way that local devotion was organized; nor (as we will shortly see) were cofradía officeholders the only important lay religious figures.

As an essential source of income for the parish clergy and funding for public worship, cofradías from the beginning attracted the participation of priests. Priests fostered cofradía development in Indian pueblos during the late sixteenth and seventeenth centuries; and as the corporate property of cofradías declined in the late eighteenth century, priests pressured parishioners to create new ones and make private contributions to the established ones, intervened to conserve their properties, and sometimes endowed them from their own savings. Given the opportunity, curas treated the cofradía mayordomos as their agents, responsible for promoting public worship in ways the cura thought best.

What the role of curas should be in the administration of cofradía affairs, and what distinguished bienes de la comunidad from bienes de la iglesia, remained largely unsettled in law until the late eighteenth century. Under the Hapsburgs, parish priests had the initiative, although their influence was mainly over the financial and political affairs of the sodalities—overseeing the election of officers, conserving the corporate property and putting it to income-generating use, and making sure that the masses and supplies were paid for before other expenditures were considered. They had less power, and perhaps less desire, to control the festivities and rituals sponsored by cofradías, which thus became a locus of more or less independent religious expression.[123] Under the later Bourbons, the government took the initiative in cofradía affairs away from the parish priests in order to promote the cajas de comunidad and otherwise strengthen royal authority and access to community wealth. Sacred and profane properties were now in competition rather than being partners or in a blurred relationship that allowed cofradía cattle to graze on municipal lands. District governors, backed by royal policy and the audiencias, were inclined to move the curas out of cofradía affairs.

Even though the influence of priests and district governors over the cofradías loomed larger in these two dioceses in the late colonial period than it did in some others, such as Yucatán,[124] the history of cofradías there is not mainly the history of priests and district governors. In many respects, the cofradías and less formal pious works were local institutions maintained by local people. The creation of new cofradías even in the late eighteenth century, the longtime accumulation of endowments, the growth of individual sponsorship, and the unbroken line of mayordomo service in many pueblos ultimately depended on popular devotion and willingness to serve, feelings that a priest might tap but could not expect to create and control.[125] These reserves of active piety gave substantial leeway to the cofrades to do as they wished. Where parish priests depended on the financial support of the cofradías, they were less likely to interfere in the group's devotional life. The mayordomos were, as a rule, less controlled by curas than the fiscales, even before the royal initiative to reform elections and administration after 1789. Mayordomías (individual sponsorship of local devotions) requiring attentive and costly veneration of local images of saints without a corporate organization were particularly independent of the cura and brought him little income. And the contests between curas and district governors over the supervision of cofradías diverted attention from their daily affairs and gave the cofrades and town councils even more room to maneuver.

The surge of cofradía lawsuits and pressure for individual sponsorship of devotional practices after the late 1780's was more than coincidental with the shift in royal policy and general assault on the authority of priests in public affairs. But the origins of these local changes and conflicts were not simply external. Crown policy and the actions of subdelegados encouraged local initiatives that were already familiar, and built on accumulating pressures: population growth, competition with private estates and neighboring communities for cropland, the increasingly unequal distribution of community lands, rising liturgical costs, more royal taxes, and a general climate of change.

The case of Alahuistlan from 1786 to 1805—during the 20 years when clashes over cofradía administration were at their peak in New Spain—exposes some of the economic, as well as political, circumstances for conflict. Alahuistlan had enjoyed considerable independence in its local religious institutions before 1786—with a network of unregulated mayordomías, and with cofrades managing cofradía properties under little supervision. Popular discontent with the curas there focused on cofradías precisely because local Indians had exercised authority over them. The people of Alahuistlan did not want to lose that authority, not only because cofradías were a source of wealth and religious autonomy, but also because at just this time they were losing control over the core of the local economy, with the salt market and their labor increasingly controlled by the alcaldes mayores and subdelegados. The crown's campaign against the priests' administration of cofradías gave Alahuistlan the legal means to claim control over this part of community life and keep the cura at a distance. His effort to control the cofradía cattle and accounts was too much like the subdelegado's intrusion into the salt trade; and the idea of a resident lieutenant was transparently advantageous only to the subdelegado and the cura. But this resistance to in-roads on established practice was not an anti-Catholic move or even deeply anticlerical. The Alahuistleños objected to the cura's interference, but they faithfully paid him the fees for masses that the cofradías customarily sponsored.

CHAPTER THIRTEEN

The Curas' Lay Network

What the *cura* says is not true; rather, the poor natives are angry because their children are not being taught well. The cura has told the *maestros* not to teach them to read or write in the Castilian language, but only [to teach them] the standard prayers because if they should learn these other things well, individually all will then know how to fend for themselves.

—Juan Miguel, *gobernador* of Huazalingo (Hidalgo), 1789

In modern villages of central and southern Mexico, cofradía mayordomos and the ladder of fiesta sponsors are the conspicuous lay officials of Catholicism. In the late eighteenth century, however, there were other offices that curas regarded with great interest, if somewhat less controversy. Fiscales, sacristanes, and cantores variously assisted the parish priests in their sacramental duties, in maintaining the church buildings and ornaments, and in policing the faith, and maestros de escuela were largely responsible for teaching children the catechism and Christian discipline. Part of the priest's administrative power in the parish depended on this network of officials doing much of the routine work that supported him and the property of the parish. They extended the priest's reach but were not simply subject to his authority.

Fiscales

The most prominent lay assistant to the parish priest in Indian pueblos was the fiscal mayor. He and his assistants were responsible for "promoting the divine cult" within their community, which meant, above all, seeing that local people fulfilled their religious obligations, behaved morally, and paid the clerical fees.[1] Especially in remote pueblos de visita, church officials expected the fiscal to be the cura's eyes and ears, advising him of suspicious behavior.[2] The promotor fiscal of the archdiocese described these local fiscales in 1763 as the cura's tireless constables, charged with inquiring into who does not attend mass; who does not observe the feast days; who is irreverent in church; who lives in public sin; whether the taverns or public houses are open and doing business during mass where public attendance is required; and whether proper modesty is observed in processions. It is also by their hand that the corrections and punishments are to be meted out to Indians. They also read the Indians' marriage banns in their language; teach the catechism in church; place the fiancées in confinement [en depósito] until married; collect the clerical fees; inform [the cura] about known cases of concubinage; and in unavoidable cases, conduct burial services.[3]

The charge was broad and the methods of choosing fiscales varied, so that local custom and circumstances largely determined what these officials did and how far the cura could expect them to conform to his wishes. The fiscal could be an influential leader, but in the late colonial period, his post was often regarded as a minor office controlled by the priest. Candidates then were likely to shun what more often meant onerous responsibilities and costs than income, prestige, or power.[4]

In late colonial times, most small hamlets with a church had a fiscal, and most large pueblos had two (the fiscales mayor and menor), as provided by law.[5] Apart from the fact that the fiscal mayor and the fiscal menor both resided in the parish seat, they were very different positions. The fiscal mayor was likely to exercise some authority over fiscales in the visitas, as well as over the fiscal menor.[6] He was the principal lay official in the parish. His fiscal menor (also called the *fiscalito, teniente de fiscal, teopa alguacil,* or *alguacil de la iglesia*) was junior even to such other officials as the sacristanes and cantores. Like fiscales in the visita, he was sometimes referred to as a *topil* (deputy) or *teopanpile* (topil of the church), indicating a position roughly on a par with that low and often despised community office. In the written record for the larger Indian towns, he is often indistinguishable from other assistants and petty deputies of the fiscal known as *mayores,* who were also called *topil del fiscal* or *topil de la iglesia.*[7] He did many of the menial duties assigned to the fiscal, carried messages, assisted in arrests and the delivery of orders, and rang the church bells.[8]

The fiscal mayor was supposed to be a reputable elder of the community, fifty to sixty years old.[9] Royal and ecclesiastical ideals for the post near the end of the colonial period varied mainly in emphasis. A viceregal bando of December 11, 1770, stressed that the fiscal must know the Spanish language; an instruction for vicarios in the Diocese of Puebla in 1766 stressed that the fiscal should be "of advantageous age, married, pacific, moderate in his drinking habits, reliable, dedicated to the church, and with a perfect knowledge of the catechism."[10] With the rural population growing in the late eighteenth century and approaching a standard age pyramid, local custom could more easily conform to the age requirement (a trend interrupted by the dearth and epidemic of 1785–86). The fiscal mayor, at least, was usually over forty years old and sometimes described himself as a *cacique y principal* who had served the community as gobernador or alcalde.[11]

The fiscal mayor's activities varied by place more than time, depending on the cura's influence and expectations, on local definitions of the responsibilities of the office, and on how the man was selected. The fiscal's duties could range from such important tasks as witnessing deathbed testaments and managing the communal plot that supported the maestro de escuela, to polishing church ornaments and carrying messages; but what the cura mainly wanted was an informant, policeman, and tax collector.[12] Sometimes his expectations were satisfied, sometimes not. Some conscientious fiscales were willing to gather intelligence on suspicious movements, drunkenness, lewd behavior, improper marriage practices (such as lengthy matrilocal residence), deaths without final rites, "idolatry," and escapes from jail.[13] Others were reluctant to reveal all they knew about local habits and scandals, a silence that could cost them dearly. A fiscal in the jurisdiction of Tenango del Valle (Edo. de México) in 1780 was whipped at the cura's orders because he would not divulge who was behind a pending lawsuit against the cura.[14]

As religious policemen, the fiscales and their assistants were called on to arrest parishioners on the priest's orders, to communicate his orders for parishioners to come for confession, to place betrothed women under bond (en depósito) until their marriage, to take roll at Sunday mass and pass out the receipts for attendance, and to act as truant officer for the catechism classes. If there was an ecclesiastical jail in the community, the fiscales were likely to be in charge of it. They were responsible for the transfer of prisoners to a superior court and accompanied the priest when he went out to break up a late-night party or look into a suspicious gathering.[15]

The fiscal's most provocative activity as law enforcer was to administer corporal punishment for the cura, something that had been debarred to the priests themselves since the time of the Third Provincial Council in 1585.[16] The problem was, as noted in Chapter 9, that more than the prescribed light whipping sometimes occurred—and for matters that had little to do with religious practice. One of the most common causes of legal action by Indian parishioners was against fiscales who were too free with the whip. Clearly, more than a few fiscales were violent and irresponsible in carrying out their duties, especially when they had been drinking. For example, Diego Juan of Tlalmilalpa (Metepec district) died at the hands of a drunken fiscal in March 1724 when he and other parishioners were whipped after mass for failing to pay their clerical fees.[17] In February 1775, the fiscal of Xilotepec (Edo. de México), on orders from the cura, went to the Rancho de Simapantongo to arrest two men who were involved in a jurisdictional dispute with the head town. He pushed and slapped their wives and threatened to whip them when they objected to the arrest. The next day, he and the Indian gobernador threw the two men to the ground and gave them a brutal lashing that left them half dead (or so the wives said).[18]

The fiscal's most onerous administrative duty, and one that implicated him in the most common source of conflict between the priest and parishioners, was the collection of parish taxes. It was the fiscal who usually collected the dominica or Sunday contribution for mass, if this collection was customary in the parish. He was also sent out to collect sacramental fees that were in arrears and to oversee the weekly labor force that was owed to many parish churches and priests.[19] Some curas pressed their fiscales to collect all the other clerical fees, including special fees for fiestas.[20] This task was both an unpleasant chore and an opportunity for personal gain. Villagers who were upset by a cura's persistent and heavy-handed attempts to collect old and new fees sometimes confused the collector with the collection and accused the fiscal of capricious innovations, excessive force, and unjust demands.[21] More directly costly to the fiscal was the cura's common demand that he pay the difference between what the community owed for mass and other services and what he had been able to collect.[22] In both of these circumstances, fiscales may well have overcollected and held back money for themselves, as their opponents charged.

The fiscal's variable roles of instructing in doctrina and assisting with the sacraments led to some confusion and could add to his spiritual power. Under the *Recopilación*, his primary responsibility was to bring the Indians together for instruction in the faith,[23] and the records show that fiscales regularly convoked the catechism classes for children and adults. Some fiscales were called on to teach the elements of the faith, as well.[24] This practice did not become a major issue in the bishops' courts in the eighteenth century, but when it did come up in guides and treatises, clerical opinion was divided. Pérez de Velasco (1766) accepted the idea that the fiscal was responsible for ("regentear") the teaching of doctrina; Tirso Díaz (1771), taught like other priests that fiscales were supposed only to convoke the catechism classes, made a scathing comment about how little these men understood of the religion and therefore how little of it they could communicate to other Indians.[25] Whether the cura voluntarily delegated this responsibility or the fiscales assumed it on their own, perhaps because the cura and a maestro de escuela were not in residence, teaching the catechism helped to establish some fiscales as spiritual masters. (On the other hand, teaching poorly could also diminish their local authority and prestige.)

The fiscales' participation in administering the sacraments carried the same possibilities for both a greater spiritual role and conflict with parishioners. Some fiscales were sent out to hear confessions; others served as interpreters for priests who could not take confessions in the Indians' language.[26] More commonly, they assisted at baptisms, marriages, and funerals, receiving a small sum for their services.[27] Also, fiscales might be sent out by curas to oversee burials and say the appropriate prayers.[28]

The fiscal's relationship to the cura—how closely he followed the priest's orders, fulfilled his many responsibilities, and identified himself with the priest and the church—varied considerably among communities and individuals. A critical ingredient was the method of his selection. Before the 1760's, there was no firm rule. Some communities elected the fiscal in January, along with the officers of the Indian cabildo.[29] In many others, the cura appointed the fiscal on his own.[30] Early colonial law had specified that curas were not to appoint ("poner") fiscales,[31] but this meant that appointments were, in the end, the responsibility of the bishops, not that local curas could not take the initiative.

In a royal cedula of September 19, 1763, the weight of the law came down decisively on the side of pueblos selecting their own fiscales during the annual elections.[32] Where local groups then moved quickly to replace the cura's fiscales with their own selections, priests were bound to object;[33] and in fact the objections were so loud and long that in 1772 the crown backed down. Archbishop Lorenzana led the campaign against the 1763 policy. In a July 18, 1772, cedula that acknowledged Lorenzana's letters of March 23 and April 25, 1771, the crown sought the middle ground. Customary practice at the time of the 1763 cedula was affirmed: where curas had chosen the fiscales before that date, they could do so again; where the pueblos had chosen the fiscales before 1763, they could continue to choose them.[34] By viceregal bando of January 31, 1774, the Indian pueblos of New Spain were notified of this return to pre-1763 practice[35]—as if all parishes had had clear, uncontested selection procedures before 1763.

The lingering effect of this attempt at legal reform, followed by a retreat toward the variety of custom, was to make the selection of fiscales a more widely contested issue, an opportunity for enterprising village politicians and curas long after the 1774 bando. For example, in 1787 Indians of San Pedro de la Cañada (Querétaro) charged the cura with violating their custom of electing the fiscal, sacristán, and maestro de escuela. After reviewing the cedulas of 1763 and 1772, and hearing testimony that fiscales had been elected by the pueblo before 1763, the viceroy issued a cedula on June 23, 1791, recognizing these Indians' right to elect the fiscal and stating as a general principle that the authority to choose fiscales rested with the elected officials of the town council.[36] In San Pedro de la Cañada, the issue was still not settled, for the alcaldes of the pueblo were back in court in 1809 against another cura who claimed the right to choose the fiscales.[37] Although lawsuits over the election of fiscales were not numerous in the late eighteenth century by comparison to those over clerical fees or cofradías, they were growing in number. Most often, the pueblos involved were testing the will of newly appointed curas by claiming that their fiscales had always been elected.

Even in a pueblo where the cura did not choose the fiscales, he retained a voice, if not a veto. It was the parish priest's job to ensure that men put forward for the bishop's selection conformed to the general requirements for the position. If the priest certified that a nominee was not qualified, he would ordinarily not be confirmed unless further investigation showed that the priest had misrepresented the man's personal qualities and qualifications for the job.[38]

The priests' proprietary feelings and established role in the selection of the fiscal followed naturally from the idea that he was a crucial assistant, that without his cooperation a parish's religious mission and finances were endangered.[39] Some priests demanded full obedience of the fiscales, as if it was theirs by right and the fiscales were responsible to no one else. A few went so far as to appoint non-Indians without any ties to the parish, hoping to create unrestrained partisans for themselves.[40] As the bishop of Oaxaca put it in 1777, the fiscal was someone the Indians "have been accustomed to *give* [my emphasis] to the parish priests since the beginning of the just acquisition of the Indies."[41] One particularly authoritarian cura demanded the release of an abusive fiscal on the grounds that the man was empowered by him and subject only to his discipline. "My *fiscales* represent my very person," he declared.[42]

It is not surprising, then, that some priests treated their fiscales like personal servants and ordered them about in endless petty matters, in spite of a provision of the *Recopilación* that they not be used for purposes outside their office without their consent and payment for their services.[43] Because curas depended heavily on the fiscales as exemplary Christian tributaries who managed essential activities in the parish and because they were likely to regard them as personal dependents, some curas were particularly uncharitable when a fiscal failed them. One

had his fiscal arrested and beaten for losing a letter belonging to him; another had
the man flogged for disobedience and for failure to correct others; a third grabbed
the fiscal by the hair and dragged him to the parish offices; a fourth had the fiscal
whipped about the feet for not obliging the children to attend catechism classes.[44]

In some of these cases, the cura may have correctly detected sabotage, passive
resistance, or indifference.[45] Ecclesiastical and criminal court cases show that fiscales could act independently of the cura and become adversaries and sometimes
rivals for spiritual leadership. In late colonial cases accusing priests of excessive
fees and labor demands or other abuses, fiscales occasionally appear as principal
plaintiffs.[46] The fiscal of Terrenate (Tlaxcala) was among those who brought false
charges against the cura in 1764; and the fiscal of San Luis Xocotla (Chilapa district, Guerrero) was one of the officials who lodged complaints against the cura
on behalf of the community in 1781 (the cura responded that the fiscal was taking
revenge after being punished for letting a woman die without confession).[47]

Some fiscales went further in their opposition to the cura. A 1772 tumulto in
Zimatlan (Oaxaca) was reportedly led by four men: two fiscales, the cacique, and
a principal.[48] The fiscal of the Barrio San Diego in Tlayacapan (Morelos) participated in a boycott against the cura in 1769, in which the parishioners refused
to pay for Easter services, blocked entry to those who tried to attend, and took
away the palm fronds on Palm Sunday as part of a protest against excessive fees.[49]
In San Felipe del Obraje (Edo. de México) in 1771, the cura reported that a dispute over fees had led to disobedience and virtual withdrawal by the fiscales of
the parish (he claimed to have seen the fiscales of only two pueblos in the parish
during the past two years). He added that the Indians of this parish elected their
own fiscales, and one of his enemies had persuaded or forced the Indians to elect
him to the office that year.[50] Finally, in the Huizquilucan district near Mexico
City in 1769, fiscales were reported to dispense justice from caves where "idolatry" was practiced. The evidence here is sketchy, but it suggests both that covert
shamans might be chosen by parishioners as fiscales because of their spiritual
powers and that fiscales could become spiritual leaders through their position as
representatives of the priest.[51]

In most of these cases of an outright stand against the cura, the fiscal had been
elected rather than appointed;[52] but the means of selection was only one of the
possible sources of opposition. Fiscales occupied a particularly sensitive spot in
community life. They were of the pueblo—often they were elders who had held
or would hold a major office—but their positions made them directly responsible
to the cura, whose requirements might be opposed by pueblo leaders and followers. Many found themselves caught between their responsibilities to the cura
and their standing in the community. They were supposed to inform the cura
when they heard that the rules of the faith were being violated, and some were
asked to interpret in the confessional, but if they did so, they might be regarded
as *soplones*, irresponsible windbags who told the cura every bit of unsubstanti-
ated gossip and knew entirely too much about villagers' private affairs.[53] In any
event, it would have been difficult to carry out all the cura's orders without anger-
ing members of the community. In 1775, the alguacil de la iglesia of San Simón
Tototepec (Zacualpan district, Edo. de México) chose to face a whipping from

the cura rather than arrest and restrain a local woman who had refused to pay the first fruits levy. As he explained, "I can't tie up [such a woman] because she has a husband, and I don't want to become ensnared in misunderstandings."[54]

Fiscales were especially likely to be caught between conflicting interests when they collected clerical fees. The fiscal of Tultitlan (Tacuba district, Valley of Mexico) in 1809 chose to join a complaint against the cura for demanding excessive fees rather than be brought to court as a party to them.[55] Yet a fiscal was certain to be disciplined by the priest if he did not follow orders to collect the fees. If a cura demanded that the fiscal collect a standard lump sum for a religious feast day in a year when some men of the community had gone to work elsewhere or had died in a recent epidemic, he either had to get each family to pay more than usual or make up the difference himself, an unenviable choice for a community member of modest means.

Occupying this difficult but strategic middle ground, some fiscales brought trouble on themselves by misusing their authority. There was a temptation to bring down local rivals and enemies by charging them on the flimsiest of evidence with violations of the faith.[56] The animosities provoked by such charges are well documented, although the ulterior motives are not so clearly fixed on one side only. For example, the allegations of a fiscal in the district of Tescaliacac in 1760 that a local man, Juan Mestitlan, practiced witchcraft apparently had no foundation. The pueblo officials in this case were outraged, the gobernador calling the fiscal two-faced and a soplón. But by the cura's lights, the leaders of the pueblo were not model Christians either. Their anger in court stemmed partly from the fact that the fiscal had told him about a secret religious rite in which some of those very leaders were involved.[57] The fiscal's explanation for his unhappy relations with the pueblo officials was that he had been appointed by the cura, rather than elected. It was for this reason, he said, that his efforts to collect the fees, take attendance at mass, and see that the children attended catechism class always met with resistance.

For whatever reason—fear, religious conviction, personal ambition, sense of duty, respect for the cura, dependence on the cura's favor, the gratification of power—some fiscales cooperated wholeheartedly with the cura, identifying with him, enforcing his orders, and informing on their fellow villagers. The evidence for these relationships is generally routine and is scattered incidentally through the formal disputes between curas and villagers in the late eighteenth century.[58] Occasionally, the fiscal was so intimately involved with unpopular demands made by the cura that his life was endangered by the association. The cura of Guayacocotla (Veracruz) apparently demanded mass labor drafts during the second year of the great famine and epidemic of 1785–86 for a church he was building at Camotipan, forced Indians to marry against their will and buy various goods from him, and made other extraordinary demands. The fiscal acted as his faithful enforcer, sending Indians on errands without pay and managing the forced sales. A faction that opposed the cura kidnapped the fiscal and an alcalde, put them in stocks at a neighboring hacienda, and threatened to force scalding eggs into their mouths and hang them.[59]

In the dioceses of Mexico and Guadalajara, few if any fiscales were killed for political reasons, but those in other areas who were closely identified with the cura were not always so fortunate. A bloody Indian revolt at San Francisco de Caxonos in the Villa Alta district of Oaxaca on September 14, 1700, began after the two fiscales (one the cacique, the other a principal of the community) warned the cura that acts of idolatry were being planned. After the effigies were confiscated, Indians from Caxonos and neighboring pueblos laid siege to the Dominican convent, where the cura and the fiscales had taken refuge. The besiegers wanted the fiscales, not the effigies. They broke through the convent doors, seized the fiscales, tied and whipped them, and then killed them.[60]

Fairly or not, it was often assumed that the fiscales were the cura's allies. In court cases, doubt was cast on the credibility of the cura's presentation if his main witnesses and supporters were his fiscales. In the 1771 dispute over clerical fees between the cura of San Felipe del Obraje and various pueblos, the investigating judge was unimpressed by the cura's side of the case because his "bando" (side, faction) consisted mainly of his "employees," the fiscales and oficiales de república.[61] In a lawsuit involving charges of misconduct by the cura of Xichú (Guanajuato) in 1796, the Indians tried to discredit the cura's defense by pointing out that fully five of his ten witnesses were fiscales.[62]

An account by the cura of Huitzilopochco (Churubusco, Valley of Mexico) in 1728 of his quest for a suitable fiscal elaborates for one place and time several facets of this ambiguous relationship and offers one variant of the tensions inherent in it:

> My predecessor's *fiscal* had the nerve to issue marriage certificates, and even though he was punished, it was not as he deserved. Then I came along asking that these unfortunate circumstances be remedied, and since I did not know the local people, and the *fiscal* I found in place was very old (although a good son) and no longer able to exercise his office, I had to tell the Indians to choose another who would do things well and help me in teaching the Christian doctrine. In their depraved malice, they brought me the man my predecessor had reproved and punished for his lies and excesses. And I, not knowing this, admitted him and kept him on for several months until I could take him no longer.
>
> I determined to choose a young man, having decided that even if he was contaminated by drunkenness and other bad habits, he would be easier to correct. Asking God's help, I ordered brought to me a young man I knew only by sight. He was not found in his *pueblo* because he was working in another, but finally he came, fearful because he thought he was being sought for something else. He was not so young, being over twenty-six years old, married, and with children.
>
> The Indian *gobernador* objected to my choice. Shouting and insulting me, he opposed my selection of such a *fiscal*, saying that an elder should be chosen instead, that what would other *pueblos* say of them when they heard that Huitzilopochco was governed by a child. I gave him many reasons, even telling him that a priest need only be twenty-four years old to attain such an exalted office, and that to teach doctrine, even a young man would do. All this was done to provoke me, to create a disturbance with his allies, and treat me with disrespect. But I knew his depraved intent, and since my only desire is to bring him and all of them to the observance of God's law, I endured this and sent them on their way, and I continue with my *fiscal*. He is wronged and scorned by them, and in the beginning this unfortunate fellow fell in with them and joined in their drunkenness because he favored them, but, thanks to God, he no longer pays attention to them, and he is helping well and suffering through [the way they treat him].[63]

As this account suggests, even before 1763, the tensions between the cura's pastoral concerns and local Indian interests could change the relationships between curas and fiscales, at least in a cyclical fashion. Both curas and village leaders tried to squeeze and stretch the local custom of appointment and service to their own ends.

In this case, if the cura's account is credible, it was the Indians who gave in. By the 1770's, a dispute of this kind would have led to litigation, and the cura may well have been forced to withdraw his appointment of so young a man. In the earlier part of the century, as long as the fiscales were expected to do little more than the routine tasks of seeing that parishioners attended their lessons, requested the sacraments, confessed and took communion, and paid their customary fees, mutually acceptable fiscales could usually be found. The exceptions were numerous, but they were concentrated in pueblos that were deeply divided or that elected their own fiscales, and they lacked the momentum of the wave of disputes over clerical fees that was building after 1768. Even then, the conflict between pastoral and village interests was tempered by a common concern for salvation, the availability of a priest on important ritual occasions, and the preservation of the parish.

Sacristanes and Cantores

Since the *Recopilación* called for every pueblo to have a sacristán and two or three cantores, these officials would have been more numerous than the fiscales.[64] But they appear much less often as controversial figures in the written record. At least in their formal duties, they were in a less sensitive position and exercised less power than the fiscales.[65] In law, the sacristán was the caretaker of the church buildings, responsible for the security and good order of both the structures and their contents.[66] The main requirement for eligibility at the end of the colonial period was the ability to post a bond against a failure to account for the property under his care at the end his term.[67] He was also obliged to post censures on the church door and read in church the edicts sent to the parish by the bishop and the crown.[68] His emblems of office were the keys he held—to the church, to the sacristy, and to the cabinets where the linen, chalices, and other equipment for the mass were kept.[69]

Additional responsibilities beyond those spelled out in law varied from place to place. The sacristán often assisted at marriages for a small fee, and helped the priest celebrate mass; occasionally he was put in charge of funerals and burials.[70] Whether the sacristán would also be the local schoolmaster for the Spanish language (maestro de la lengua castellana), "as in the rural settlements of the kingdoms of Castile," was contested in the late colonial period—attempted by priests in some parishes but apparently not a widely accepted practice.[71]

There was considerable variation in the selection and tenure of sacristanes, but filling these slots apparently provoked relatively few disputes. Colonial law did not specify how old a sacristán had to be or how long he might serve, and the crown made little attempt to standardize the selection of sacristanes by election, as it had with the fiscales. Some sacristanes were elected, as at La Cañada

(Querétaro) in 1795 (over the cura's objection), but it was more common for the cura to appoint the sacristán.[72] The Indians of Tejupilco complained in 1760 of the cura appointing a creole sacristán, but an investigation revealed that long-term appointments to the post were customary in this parish, and that the creole in question had served for all but eight years since 1732 (and during those eight years, one Indian had held the post). Another creole had been the sacristán there for 20 years between 1685 and 1705.[73] The sacristán of a parish seat frequently managed a group of assistants, also called sacristanes, who served on a rotating basis.[74] Parish priests seem to have treated these short-term assistants and the sacristanes in outlying villages as janitors, table servants, and errand boys.[75] Whether they were dealing with the principal sacristanes or their assistants, the curas and fiscales had to exercise some restraint in their demands on them and in how they punished unsatisfactory work or, as in Churubusco in 1739, no one would agree to serve.[76] One reasonably sure way for a cura to guarantee their support was to give them some kind of supplementary income. The cura of San Cristóbal Ecatepec (Valley of Mexico), for example, provided his sacristanes with the use of some church lands during their period of service.[77]

Controversy broke out over the sacristán and his assistants mainly when the cura increased the scope of the job or made excessive demands, or when the incumbent abused his trust. Curas occasionally raised complaints over sacristanes who buried parishioners without notifying the cura first, lost valuable ornaments, sold oil for the lamp to parishioners for magical purposes, or were otherwise disobedient and dishonest.[78] When sacristanes were used by the curas to arrest parishioners, inflict whippings, and escort prisoners to the alcalde mayor, they were open to the complaints made by parishioners against fiscales, with the additional irritation that these were almost certainly not their customary duties.[79] Parishioners conscripted as assistant sacristanes without pay began to complain in the late 1760's, when it was no longer so certain that a cura could demand unpaid service, even in parishes where this had been the custom in earlier years.[80] Likewise, in the eighteenth century, sacristanes who were enlisted to refurbish the cura's living quarters rather than look after the church and its possessions began to lodge complaints.[81]

Among the lay assistants to the cura, the cantores had the most specialized and often the most permanent position. Mainly they assisted the priest in celebrating mass and led the choir in the sung masses.[82] Since it took months to train a cantor in the liturgy and music of the sung mass, a cura was likely to stick with the ones he had for many years, though in principle he could replace them every year.[83] Cantores were to be chosen from among the most able parishioners,[84] and enjoyed a certain independence because of their specialized skills. In prosperous parishes, theirs was a desirable job; it usually paid four reales for the sung masses, generally exempted them from other community service, and rarely required the kind of administrative work and fee collection duties that could prove costly to a fiscal's savings and reputation. Furthermore, their participation in the mass and occasional performance of burials and baptisms in outlying villages gave the cantores' office a spiritual dimension that heightened their status.[85]

As with the fiscales, the greater the cantor's spiritual prowess and the longer he stayed in office, the more likely he was to be a political force in the parish.[86]

However, his influence, like that of a sacristán, seems to have derived less from the office than from his connections and standing in the community. For example, the longtime Indian cantor of Tlaltenango (Zacatecas) was uncooperative with the new cura in 1815 and was reportedly prone to gambling, drunkenness, and insolence to authorities. But he had also served several times as the local scribe and keeper of the community land and cofradía records, duties that he performed in exchange for the use of a piece of the fundo legal. As scribe, he was chosen by the cabildo and given extensive responsibility for protecting the community's interests: "the conservation of our rights, peace, and tranquility without putting us in conflict with the sovereign's intentions, . . . with the privilege of substitute power where he sees fit, especially in pursuing the pending petition concerning the hardships of forced labor." [87] No sacristán or cantor would have received such wide authority simply because of his office. Here the cantor's literacy and long service placed him in a position of trust that permitted him to lead a legal offensive against the lieutenant for trying to force the community to build a barricade around the town. Younger, inexperienced cantores could be punished and bullied into serving the cura outside the church.[88] A lot depended, again, on whether the cantor had been appointed and trained by the current cura. Since curas moved every seven years on average (and many vicarios moved much more often than that), the chances of a cantor being the veteran official and the priest the newcomer were greater than in the case of the fiscal.

The Schoolmasters

On the whole, the relationships between rural priests and schoolmasters were reasonably amicable, unmarred by the conflicting loyalties and interests that often pitted fiscales against their curas. The "notorious struggle between priest and teacher" that Eugen Weber detected in France during the nineteenth century is only occasionally evident in eighteenth-century Mexico.[89] In France, parish priests and schoolmasters had roughly the same social background and level of education, and struggled over local authority on more or less equal terms. Rural French schoolmasters often regarded themselves as independent messengers of the Enlightenment who were unfairly treated as underlings by hidebound *curés*. In Mexico, the rural schoolmasters were not so well established or self-important. As the creole schoolmaster of San Juan del Río said to the district lieutenant in 1700 when the cura approached them to start an argument, "with such men being priests, the best defense is to flee." [90] More often than not, in fact, the schoolmaster was a dependent of the priest, operating under his supervision and patronage.[91] Even after civil authorities became more involved in village schools in the 1750's, and more rural pueblos of central and western Mexico engaged schoolmasters, priests and schoolmasters tended to work together to carry out the crown's new priority on Spanish-language instruction as a way "to improve the Indians and make them more useful to the State." [92]

The maestros' personal histories also suggest why few of them were serious rivals to the curas. The ideal was avowed to be a literate, virtuous, Spanish man examined in doctrina to instruct the boys, and a woman with similar qualifications for the girls.[93] Reality rarely matched the ideal, although d. José Antonio Flores, the maestro de primeras letras for Tenayuca (Valley of Mexico) during the Independence War period, fitted the model quite well. His large family and twelve years of service in this pueblo suggest a settled and professional life. The parish priest, a newcomer by comparison, spoke of Flores as an "hombre de bien."[94] In most cases, it proved difficult to maintain schools at all, much less to provide for more than one qualified teacher. Writing from his experience as alcalde mayor for Cuautla Amilpas (Morelos) and Tlapa (Guerrero) in the 1760's and 1770's, Villarroel grumbled that the maestros were rustics of unenviable habits who did more harm than good, especially when they taught the catechism.[95] In the late eighteenth century, maestros would have known how to read and write, but very few had the bachelor's degree of most parish priests.

Many of the colonial teachers who escaped the administrative record would have been local Indians. A viceregal decree of September 30, 1716, to promote Indian schools expressed a preference for local men who were competent in Spanish. The reasoning was that the more alike teacher and students were, the greater the understanding and affection between them, and the more the children would learn as a result.[96] In some pueblos, the maestro was the community escribano, a local Indian who sometimes had served the parish before as sacristán or cantor.[97] Outsiders who became maestros in pueblos and rancherías near the end of the colonial period generally were unmarried men in their twenties or thirties. About half identified themselves as españoles and used the honorific don before their Christian name (which was automatic for the priests). The others were mulatos or mestizos or were not identified by race.[98] Most had worked in their current teaching post for only a short time before they appeared in the record. Their situation bears some comparison to that of vicarios in the sense that both lacked the security of a tenured appointment and were paid small salaries. But the vicario could count on a more secure position, one established by long tradition or solidified by the request by parishioners for additional assistant pastors. In most pueblos, the schoolmaster's post was likely to be new or recently reestablished. Village schools seem to have closed about as often as they opened, and the initiative for new schools typically came from the top, from royal cedulas, viceroys, intendants, bishops, and parish priests. Rarely did a pueblo actively campaign for a school and master.[99]

One extravagant example of a powerless maestro is documented in the 1777 Inquisition trial of Juan Joseph Aguirre, a creole from Guanajuato, twenty-seven years old and crippled in one leg.[100] Aguirre barely clung to the margins of polite society. Having learned to read and write in a Jesuit school, he left Guanajuato when his mother died in 1770, going to Mexico City and Puebla, where he begged and taught fitfully in order to survive. In 1774, he went north to San Juan de los Lagos, then west toward Guadalajara, teaching in rancherías. At Loma Larga in 1775, he was employed to teach reading and the catechism to the children of a ranchero. Aguirre fell in love with the ranchero's thirteen-year-old daughter. Desperate to win her favor, he wrote out a pact with the Devil in his own blood, promising to sell his soul for ten years in exchange for money and favors that would make him a prosperous and respected man. The girl took the letter from Aguirre and gave it to her father, who informed the cura of Ocotlan. Aguirre was arrested, but during the long delay before the Inquisition took up the case, he moved again, to the hamlet of San Juanico in the nearby district of La Barca, where he was teaching school when his case was opened in February 1777. In the proceedings, he was condemned by his own literacy: the pact was there for all to see. Despite Aguirre's pleas that he had never made such a pact before or since, had wanted to destroy the letter before anyone saw it, and had been blinded by love and the despair of his poverty, the court levied a heavy sentence of public humiliation, 200 lashes, ten years' exile, eight years' hospital service, monthly confession, and reciting the rosary every week.

Though several of the royal cedulas, viceregal decrees, and bishops' instructions that touched off waves of school foundings called for the maestro to be "assigned an appropriate salary from the *arcas de comunidades* [the pueblo treasuries]," or "a sufficient and secure salary to be paid monthly,"[101] a schoolmaster's living was rarely so dependable. There was little agreement on what constituted an "appropriate" and "sufficient" salary, and some consideration was to be given to the community's ability to pay.[102] In any case, the pay was modest. In seven examples from the second half of the eighteenth century, the maestros were paid 100 to 120 pesos a year, or about 50 pesos a year plus a ration of maize.[103] By comparison, a rural cura was considered to live "decently" only if he earned more than 1,000 pesos. His vicarios were rarely paid less than 200–300 pesos a year, and they were said to live very frugally. Enterprising maestros supplemented their salaries by acting as interpreters, conducting a small business like the local monopoly on the sale of tobacco, or assisting the cura in the sacristy.[104]

The source of the teacher's salary was less settled than the law made it seem. Many pueblos had no community chest or had too little money in it to pay the full salary.[105] In these cases, the law and episcopal instructions called for villagers to work a milpa large enough to cover the difference.[106] But the intendant of Guadalajara reported in the early 1790's that few pueblos planted a communal crop for this purpose.[107] Failing the community chest and the communal crop, each villager was expected to contribute an animal or a small cash sum.[108] Apparently there was widespread resistance to such levies on all families. Two modifications sometimes worked. One was to assess the levy only on families with children in school.[109] The other was to organize the collection by turns. When the Indians of Zitácuaro (Michoacán) resisted the levy in the 1770's, the alcalde mayor organized the households into teams of 20, each with a captain who was to collect one real from each member of his team when it was their turn to pay the weekly salary of 20 reales.[110]

Whatever the reasons—minimal financial support from the crown; local resistance to new taxes; or the priest's desire to solidify his traditional association with village schoolmasters, promote the Spanish language, and fulfill the orders of the prelates and royal authorities—the salary of the maestros sometimes came directly from parish sources. In Tepetlaoztoc (Texcoco district, Valley of Mexico) and Zoyatlan (Tlapa district, Guerrero), a dominica or Sunday collection paid for both mass and the maestro de escuela.[111] In Villa Alta (Oaxaca), the mayordomo of a local chapel paid for the school with income from an endowment of land.[112] More often, the cura paid the maestro from his own purse and represented this action as prime evidence of his Christian charity.[113]

Though some curas would have opposed new Spanish schools with maestros appointed by the district governors, the practice of paying the maestro's salary fit the long-term pattern of church patronage and direction of the schools and teachers. Curas had long been held responsible by the crown for seeing that doctrina was taught to Indians in Spanish,[114] and before the 1790's, they were credited with founding most of the schools. It was to the curas that maestros turned when the villagers resisted payment or did not send their children to class.[115] It was the curas who complained to the audiencia when the schools were not operating properly.[116] It was the curas who were charged with making official weekly visits to the school on Saturday; and it was they who still, in the 1790's were responsible for certifying the competence of maestros in Catholic doctrine once a year.[117]

The resumés of concurso candidates clearly reflect the crown's new interest in establishing and maintaining primary schools. An accomplishment that had rarely been mentioned before the 1750's was now more and more often highlighted by aspiring candidates in both dioceses. For example, Br. Manuel Cassela, cura of Atotonilco el Chico (Hidalgo), an applicant in the 1763 concurso for the archdiocese, presented himself as the enthusiastic patron of village schools. He had taught Indians in the district of Xichú even before ordination and founded schools in all the pueblos there for "reading, writing, and all the prayers and other appropriate recitations" when he took up his first assignment as vicario in 1752. Moving to Tlalnepantla (Valley of Mexico) for less than a year in December 1754, he founded a school in each of the six pueblos of the parish. When he finally obtained the parish of Atotonilco in 1758, Cassela continued to give schools his highest priority.[118] As we saw earlier, where few concurso candidates in the Diocese of Guadalajara had thought to mention establishing or improving local primary schools in 1754, this was a standard entry in their resumés by the end of the century.[119]

For many maestros, especially for those brought from outside the community, the practical consequence of the cura's patronage (and of the natural affinity among men of words, who were in, more than of, the community) was that they were his dependents and allies. In passing, late colonial judicial records make this close association clear. In the record of a 1758 tumulto at Pozontepec (Sultepec district, Edo. de México) in which the vicario's house was set afire, it is evident that the maestro lived with him.[120] In a 1772 uprising at Ocuilan (Malinalco district, Edo. de México), the maestro was the one who was stoned and lost an eye, although Indian witnesses said the violence really was directed against the cura's imposition of whippings and a head tax.[121] In a 1775 petition against the cura, Indian women of Tototepec mentioned that two schoolteachers carrying firearms went out with the cura to collect fees.[122] In 1789, the Indian gobernador of Huazalingo (Sochicoatlan district, Hidalgo) complained that whenever one of the pueblos celebrated a fiesta, the cura would summon all the maestros in the parish. Every time this happened, the schools were closed for a week, and the unlucky fiesta pueblo was burdened with lodging and feeding all the maestros.[123]

In some communities, the cost of moves to replace priests with district governors as the main promoters of Spanish-language schools was no school at all. The cura of Tlacotalpan (Veracruz) reported in 1790 that a school had not operated there in twelve years. He had pressed the matter with the Indians and the district governor without success during his two years in the parish.[124] At Tlaquiltenango (Morelos) in 1803, the new cura and the lieutenant clashed over local education, the cura claiming that the lieutenant had failed to sponsor the required schools. The cura had started a school in January, but in May the lieutenant had removed the maestro as useless and disrespectful. For the sake of peace, the cura said, he acquiesced, but the lieutenant had not helped to arrange for a replacement. Mexico and Guadalajara were apparently less affected by such rivalries than Oaxaca, where, according to a 1777 cedula, the founding of Spanish schools had not been widely achieved because the curas and alcaldes mayores could not agree on who would appoint the maestro and how he would be paid.[125] Fifteen years later, Oaxaca's governors and curas continued to argue over who could appoint and remove the maestros.[126]

The district governors' new role in education should have made maestros more independent of the curas, if not allies of the governors, but little evidence of such a shift has come to light. Miguel Barrera, dismissed by the cura of Tlaltizapan (Morelos) before 1775 as the maestro de escuela for Cuanacalcingo, was accused of stirring up the pueblo against the next cura.[127] The district governor is not mentioned in this case, and it reads like the kind of tension between an independent-minded maestro and an assertive cura that is occasionally documented in earlier years. In a civil case resulting from a bitter public argument between the cura and the lieutenant of San Juan del Río (Querétaro) in 1700, the key witness was the maestro de escuela, Ysidro de Torreblanca. Judging by his account, he and the lieutenant were close friends. At the time of the unhappy encounter ("pesadumbre"), Torreblanca was helping the lieutenant execute an impoundment order. Torreblanca acknowledged that the lieutenant had unsheathed his sword and threatened the cura, but he added that the cura had provoked the argument. He did not speculate on the cura's motive for the argument or the complaint to the archbishop's court.[128]

The Cuanacalcingo and San Juan del Río cases show that the maestros were not always the curas' faithful constituents; but as unusual examples 75 years apart, they also suggest that uncooperative maestros (at least as a proportion of all schoolmasters) were not much more common in the late colonial period than they had been earlier. Except in parts of Oaxaca, the emergence of maestros who operated as free agents or allies of the district governors against the cura seems to have lacked the momentum of a great change.[129]

More serious obstacles to formal schools and the priests' influence over teachers in the late colonial period came from within the Indian pueblos.[130] Archbishops' reports, letters from maestros, and lawsuits initiated by parish priests show that Indian pueblos often resisted the schools, and that the harder the crown and the bishops pushed for them in the last third of the eighteenth century, the more resistance they were likely to meet. After 1770, curas who complained at length against their Indian parishioners for being insolent and ungovernable generally included in their bill of particulars failure to support the school.[131] Villagers not only opposed the establishment of schools but also let those that were established close after a few years.[132] Funding the schools had always been a problem; failure to pay the maestro's salary was the most common reason why schools closed, and the most common reason why priests brought suit against pueblos over education. The cura of Tescalapan and Aquiapa (Temas-caltepec district, Edo. de México) in 1799 reported that his parish was without schools because

there is no way to pay the *maestro* either a *congrua* [a rent, normally ecclesiastical] suf-ficient to support him or what the Indians contracted to pay him. They either withhold the salary altogether on some feeble pretext or delay payment so long that, without the means to survive, the *maestros* are compelled to leave their posts.[133]

Some villages complained through their leaders that they were too poor to fund a school.[134] Others resisted what amounted to a school tax, just as they resisted any contributions that were not understood to be customary and "just."[135]

Even when the maestro was paid, Indian villagers were known to keep their children away. A pastoral visitor to the highland parishes of Hidalgo in 1808 dwelled on the difficulty of maintaining schools there and repeatedly noted that where they existed, Indian parents resisted enrolling their children.[136] Similar reports came in from Iguala (Guerrero) in 1771, Tlaola (Huauchinango district, Veracruz) in 1790, and Cozcatlan (Villa de Valles district, San Luis Potosí) in 1791.[137] The standard reason given was that the children were needed for work in the fields and at home.[138] According to the intendant of Guadalajara in 1791, "during the growing season, the Indians take their children out of school for the entire rainy season until the crop is harvested." Intendant Ugarte probably hit the mark when he added that Indian villagers saw school as an unnecessary lux-ury, especially when they were suffering through illness or food shortages.[139]

Abuses by the curas and maestros fortified villagers' opposition to the schools. The pueblos of Guayacocotla and Chicontepec (Veracruz) in 1786 and Tultitlan (Valley of Mexico) in 1809 claimed that the curas put schoolchildren to work rather than providing instruction. The leaders of Huazalingo (Sochicoatlan dis-trict, Hidalgo) in 1789 accused the cura and the maestro of demanding fodder and chickens from the schoolchildren, as well as sending them to work in the fields.[140]

The school issue could drive a wedge between parish priests and maestros. Obviously, if villagers refused to pay the maestro or send their children to class, in the long run there would be no school and no maestro. Without allies among the leaders of the community or the means to coerce payment, the curas and district governors could not hope to sustain schools for more than a few months unless they were willing to pay the maestro themselves and could find an inde-fatigable truant officer. In general, curas would have had less influence over local Indians who served as maestros than over outsiders whom they hired. As with the fiscales, the curas' influence would have depended in large part on how the local maestros were selected and paid. If appointed or elected by the república and paid from the bienes de comunidad, they would probably have been less inclined toward the cura's interests and less under his control. Two cases suggest that priests had to contend with this possibility. In 1744, the cura of Mechoacanejo (Jalisco) complained that the Indians there had named the maestro without his permission.[141] In 1790, the cura of Tlaola accused the Indians of appointing a vice-ridden maestro who was willing to hide their bad behavior from him.[142]

In this colonial order, making Indians literate in Spanish was a more difficult enterprise than the reformers had anticipated. Maestros recruited into rural villages rarely knew the local language well enough to succeed in teaching villagers with little or no Spanish, as an Indian priest, Julián Cirilo de Castilla, observed in the early 1750's.[143] Added to this communication barrier was the lack of school-books in Indian languages.[144] Social and cultural values within communities also impeded instruction. Beyond the financial burden and doubts that school was more important than planting and reaping, villagers had reason to be ambivalent about the education of their children in the Spanish language. Parents suspected that children were being educated to forget their native language, a process that would separate them from their elders. According to one Oaxaca cura in the 1770's, Indians of Zimatlan menaced the maestro when he tried to keep the children from speaking their native language.[145] Formal education and a good command of Spanish could isolate an Indian villager from his community as well as provide him with an instrument of respect and mediation. Father Ignacio José Hugo de Omerick, the cura of Tepecoacuilco (Guerrero) in the late 1760's, observed that Indians might admire their schoolchildren but, once educated, they were ridiculed as "ladinos," "bachelor-degree holders," and "garrulous," untrustworthy individualists who were faithless to their own people and should be made to serve in the lowest and least prestigious offices of the community.[146]

To be sure, not all pueblos and their leaders resisted paying for schools or kept their children away. Perhaps the most resourceful Indian patron of a primary school was Juan de San Pedro Andrade y Bejarano, the Opata cacique of San Juan Tecomatan (Sonora?). In 1799, he sailed to Spain to lay his petition for an "escuela general pública de enseñanza religiosa y civil" before the Council of the Indies. Predictably, the council ordered him to return home and make his request to the viceroy. To soften its rebuff, the council affirmed that Juan de San Pedro was himself well qualified to be a maestro de primeras letras and should be provided with what he needed for his own support. But the cacique was not so easily removed. For nearly two years he remained in Sevilla and continued to petition for his school. By August 1800, he secured a small stipend from the council for his studies, and an order that a school be established in his pueblo "if possible." [147]

Of course, evidence that a primary school existed in a pueblo in the late eighteenth century does not mean that it was permanent. Many of the hundreds of schools founded at the insistence of bishops, royal governors, and parish priests were abandoned in a few years: a dedicated parish priest or alcalde mayor departed; parishioners were indifferent or actively resisted because they were burdened with the costs or did not want their children to learn Spanish or attend classes taught by outsiders. But a discontinuous history did not mean that many schools were not refounded and maintained, or that nothing was learned. The schools apparently took hold best in the parish seats, but in some districts, they also were well established in subordinate pueblos.[148] In the same sentence that the archdiocese's visitador mentioned Spanish-language schools in pueblos of Ichcateopan parish (Guerrero) in 1780, he observed that the pueblos' young people ("jóvenes") in particular were quite well versed in Spanish.[149] Did the pastoral visitor overstate a generational difference in 1780? If not, how was the difference related to the success of schools there? It may be impossible to answer these questions with much confidence, but the visitador's observation is an intriguing hint of a watershed in accumulating cultural changes that had reached some colonial Indian communities of central Mexico earlier, and would reach others later or hardly at all.

* * *

In the case of fiscales and maestros de escuela, as in the case of the cofradía mayordomos, centralizing, standardizing Bourbon reforms sought to remove the selection and control of local officials from the curas. These reforms generated some bitter struggles between curas and district governors, but such conflicts were often muted by the parties' common interest in promoting the use of Spanish and by a measure of royal flexibility (encouraged by widespread complaint and expense to the royal treasury). However, this royal initiative opened a less easily muted conflict between priests and village parishioners.

Since the positions of fiscal and maestro de escuela were not so closely connected to community finances, they attracted less royal attention and generated fewer lawsuits than the cofradía offices did. The fiscales were a potential locus of tension between cura and parish long before the Bourbons moved to detach them from his control, and they appear more often than other lay religious officers in the late colonial lawsuits against parish priests. Still, many remained under the cura's influence—with less independence, spiritual authority, and prestige than the cofradía mayordomos, with their saints and sacred images.

There was great local variation, especially in central Mexico, where some fiscales were major officeholders or had a claim on spiritual leadership as shamans, but in the dioceses studied here, few fiscales, sacristanes, and cantores enjoyed the spiritual authority and political power of their counterparts in Chiapas and Yucatán. The Tzeltal Rebellion of highland Chiapas in 1712 revealed Indian fiscales who regarded themselves as a virtual Catholic priesthood under the providential patronage of the Virgin Mary.[150] For Indian parishes of Yucatán, the *maestros cantores*—who in many respects played the twin role of the fiscales and the maestros de escuela in central Mexico—also enjoyed more independence as a rule, and have been described as virtual priests.[151]

In Mexico and Guadalajara, the maestros de escuela were more likely than the fiscales to be dependents of the cura. As the pressure to recruit literate, Spanish-speaking teachers mounted in the late eighteenth century with the opening of new schools, more maestros entered the pueblos de indios from larger towns and cities. They were outsiders, often hired and paid by the cura to teach doctrina primarily, despite plans for community sponsorship and selection and royal supervision. Unlike the local men who served as fiscales, these maestros were socially isolated from the community, often staying only a few months or years and sometimes living in the cura's quarters. Few of the maestros would have been formidable rivals to the parish priests unless they were elected, local men of influence or enjoyed the patronage of the district governor and his lieutenant.

Although more was at stake in the struggle over the control of the cofradías and their officers, and more open conflict resulted from it, the crown's initiatives on schools and the independent election of fiscales also elicited strident expressions of local autonomy. Innovations of this kind were riskier than colonial governors understood, but for the time being, this minuet of words pleased the royal officials who had composed and conducted it. When the elders of Huazalingo wrote in 1789 of wanting schools that would teach them more than prayers, schools that would make them independent of priests and other mediators, their plea for the new education decreed by the crown was directed to the magistrates they understood to be their most receptive audience—the oidores of the royal audiencia.

PART FOUR

The Politics of Parish Life

CHAPTER FOURTEEN

Officials, Popular Action,
and Disputes with Parish Priests

In former times they delighted in the voice of their pastors, and they followed their whistles like gentle lambs;
but now they flee their caresses as they would the ferocity
of the wolf.   —Dr. Joseph de Zelada, cura
of San Felipe del Obraje, 1771

After finishing his confession and receiving absolution,
[an Indian of the parish of Huiciltepec] asked me if it was
a sin to get drunk and to fornicate and to steal, . . . because he had heard his cura . . . preach in the pulpit that
[these were not sins], and that it was only a sin to engage
in lawsuits.   —Francisco Antonio de Abila,
vicario of the parish of Santo Tomás
in the city of Puebla, 1800

This part examines in close detail the local political relationships and struggles for power that took place in the two dioceses among and between the
three components of the "triangle of authority": priests, parishioners, and district governors.[1] Much of the material comes from litigation and pastoral visit
records, which reveal Indian parishioners as players more than counterplayers or
nonplayers in the colonial order, even in their resistance to colonial officials and
new laws. Sections of chapters report on the concentrations of cases by time and
place. Some sections overlap; they are not additive categories. They represent
different ways of looking at a body of evidence on local politics that is not as
neatly divisible as the classifications on the title pages of judicial cases suggest.

This chapter and Chapter 15 concern colonial Indian communities and their
secular leaders; Chapter 16 discusses the royal district governors and their associations with the priests and Indian communities. These three chapters touch on
various issues that were legislated into the relationships by Bourbon reformers.
Chapter 17 examines the most contentious issue of all—clerical fees—over which
there was an explosion of disputes in the second half of the eighteenth century.
But numbers alone are not what command attention. Rather, it is the fact that in
many cases, the fees were as much a pretext as the cause for dispute, an opening
advertised by the colonial administration that engaged deeper tensions over control among competing interests and order within the community or local territory.

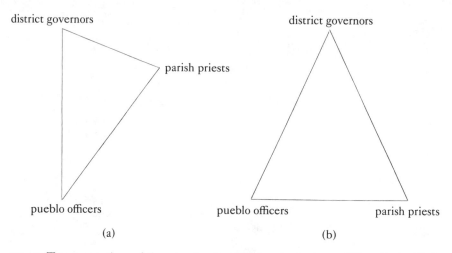

FIG. 11. Two conceptions of the triangle of political authority in rural New Spain. Early colonial policy makers thought in terms of authority shared more or less equally by district governors and parish priests (a). In principle, the late Bourbon reformers shifted much of the authority to the district governors (b).

I have tried to expose the local interests, personal and political ambitions, and rivalries involved in these disputes, and to follow their sources and outcomes. Despite appearances, the disputes almost always amounted to more or less than a pueblo versus a priest, and few resulted in a serious political breakdown. The familiar early modern triangle of authority, with priests, secular colonial powers (district governors, estate owners, and merchants), and pueblo leaders at its corners, was never quite equilateral. Bourbon policy makers had more clearly in mind than their Hapsburg predecessors an elongated shape tipped on one corner, with royal governors above and priests and pueblo officials below, rather than an inverted shape with the district governor and the priest sharing the top (Fig. 11). It makes sense to combine pueblo officials with resistance because elected officials usually were in the forefront of community resistance, and it is often through evidence of conflict and resistance that the counterpoint of obedience and challenges to the cura's authority can be identified and evaluated at the Indian point of the triangle. We begin, in this chapter, with the curas' side of things, specifically (1) their attempts to control personal and collective behavior (moral and religious) and their individual and community resources (land, labor, livestock, and money); and (2) the priest as a challenger to local autonomy and customary practices. Chapter 15 comes at the issue of control by examining how internal contests for community authority and power in the late colonial period affected parish priests.

Pueblo Officials

The formal political life of colonial pueblos centered on their elected officials, who served for one year at a time and were subject to removal by the district governor and sometimes the parish priest. The offices varied, but every cabecera or head town of a local district had a gobernador and a cabildo of alcaldes, regidores, and an escribano, among others. The sujetos, or dependent pueblos, usually had at least one alcalde of their own. These elected officers were ministros de vara—holders of the staff of office, "those who command."[2] Generally, the senior offices of gobernador and alcalde were held by men over forty years old.[3] The power of the offices varied greatly, not least with the qualities and ambitions of the holder, but both indigenous and European traditions held them in esteem.[4] A detailed description of native herbal medicine from the Valley of Mexico in 1552 reserved a special category for "trees and flowers for the fatigue of those administering the government and holding public office."[5]

The body of pueblo electors and advisers (the "república" or "comunidad política") also varied considerably from place to place, and there were growing pressures in the late eighteenth century to broaden the electorate, but colonial law and local practice still favored a select group of principales composed of former officeholders, elderly men, and members of the traditional elite.[6] Even if their authority had diminished since preconquest times, late colonial principales regarded themselves as superior to ordinary tributaries. As the gobernador of Malinalco put it in 1796, the many were his "subalternos."[7] Principales, especially the leading officeholders, regarded themselves, and were often regarded, as political fathers. The gobernador of Zacoalco (Jalisco) in 1769, for example, brushed aside a complaint by three principales against the new district lieutenant because he alone, as "padre de Nuestra República y tributario de Su Magestad," spoke for the community. Indians of Tlajomulco in 1808 complained that their alcalde had acted "not as a benevolent father, but as a devouring lion." And the subdelegado of Tonalá in 1791 criticized the Indian alcalde of San Martín for designating new principales who, "even though they are elderly, lack the service, training, and merits that would make them *padres de república*."[8] (But in their dealings with the colonial state, rural Indians of all categories inevitably were treated as "hijos del pueblo.")

Under colonial law, senior officials were expected to represent the community and comply with the requirements of colonial authorities. These open-ended expectations might mean testifying to the age, occupation, and reputation of local people called to court; organizing the community's response to emergencies; assembling residents for meetings in the casa de comunidad; soliciting contributions to support litigation in defense of pueblo interests; and doing administrative jobs such as supervising collective labor and managing community property, or even naming cofradía mayordomos and caretakers.[9] Archbishop Lorenzana wanted gobernadores to be responsible for seeing that all Indian men over twenty-five years old worked as farmers or wage earners in another occupation, and that they married and built solid houses "suitable for rational people, not beasts" (como para racionales, y no para bestias).[10]

Petitioners from Atotonilco el Alto (Jalisco) in 1715 summarized their understanding of the main duties assigned to their oficiales mayores by colonial law: "to administer Royal Justice, collect the royal tributes, and attend to the urgent needs of our *pueblo*."[11] All three duties connected the officials to interests within their communities, superior officers of the state, and Indian and non-Indian neighbors. In all three, they were expected to act for the community. To advance local interests while meeting colonial obligations was a delicate task for which some were better qualified than others. In any case, the expectations were high, and elected officials were often neutralized by the contradictory interests and obligations they faced. Except in especially harmonious communities, powerful officials needed more resources than the office. Their authority to speak for the community was not automatic or unqualified.

The second duty—tax collection—was foremost for their royal and ecclesiastical superiors. It inevitably led to other demands for collection, by parish priests as well as district governors. In the early nineteenth century, gobernadores were called on to collect contributions for Spain's European wars, and in some parishes, curas succeeded in making gobernadores, alcaldes, and regidores responsible for collecting clerical fees, first fruits, and fiesta costs.[12] (One gobernador spoke for many when he responded that these collections should be made by fiscales and cofradía mayordomos.)[13]

But it was as judges (*justiciales*) that the gobernadores and alcaldes exercised much of their authority, and their staffs of office were, above all, a sign of their power "to render justice" ("justificar").[14] Their role as criminal judges was outlined in *Recopilación* 6-3-16 and 17 in the qualified Hapsburg way that invited uncertainty and customary arrangements. Indian alcaldes had only the authority to "investigate, apprehend, and bring delinquents" (i.e., Indians) to jail in the district's *pueblo de españoles*. Yet they could impose punishments of a day in jail and six to eight lashes on Indians who were absent from mass on Sunday, were drunk, or were guilty of "similar misconduct" (otra falta semejante); could mete out stronger sentences in cases of group drunkenness; and could even act outside their jurisdiction to the extent of holding unruly negros or mestizos until the alcalde mayor or his lieutenant arrived. But few gobernadores and alcaldes adhered to the narrowest construction of the law. For example, the gobernador of Tenango del Valle (Edo. de México) in 1753, backed by a large number of local Indians, claimed that he had as much right to try a local assault case as the alcalde mayor's lieutenant.[15] Only an ample interpretation of "otra falta semejante" would allow him that right, but local custom must have kept many such cases from the attention of alcaldes mayores and curas, and in others, the gobernador had their tacit consent or encouragement. An alcalde of Mechoacanejo (Jalisco), who had served several terms despite complaints by members of the community, said in 1790 that the cura and lieutenants found him indispensable because he was the only one who could control his townsmen's "excesses."[16] Gobernadores and alcaldes tried and punished villagers on their own account for adultery, disrespect to officials, and the mistreatment of children; and there were cases of local arrests for sorcery and witchcraft.[17] Some Indian gobernadores and alcaldes operated jails and stocks without interference by royal officials. When the Indian gobernador of Malinalco (Edo. de México) complained to the viceroy in 1796 that he was not being allowed to operate the jail and stocks he required to punish Indians for drunkenness and "otros excesos," the viceroy ordered that he not be impeded, that he could have a jail "like the *parcialidades* de San Juan and Santiago of this capital do and like those of other *pueblos*."[18]

No matter how limited their legal authority, judging by the many complaints, from community members as well as parish priests, gobernadores and alcaldes wielded substantial power. It appears that their most sensitive duties, and those affording the widest room for abuse, were the collection of tribute and the administration of punishment. Throughout the seventeenth and eighteenth centuries, gobernadores and alcaldes were accused of skimming off a portion of the tribute (and occasionally other taxes) by collecting the full amount but underreporting the number of tributaries, or collecting more from their macehuales than was required.[19] They were also charged with favoring their associates in the distribution of community lands, diverting communal labor to their own uses, accepting bribes, and extorting contributions.[20]

The opportunity for the abuse of judicial authority was especially great. Common complaints alleged the use of excessive force in making arrests, severe and repeated beatings for minor transgressions (especially for questioning an official's judgment), and arresting people and imposing fines without cause.[21] Ironically—since these officials derived their colonial judicial authority partly from their duty to control drunkenness—their acts of violence in an official capacity were often committed while they were drunk.[22] Manuel de Aguilar, the gobernador of Tetela del Río (Guerrero) in 1748, was described as particularly abusive and chronically drunk, terrorizing Indians with cruel whippings, selling minor offenders into service in textile sweatshops, keeping money from the tribute for himself, and selling community lands.[23] Other officials and their relatives took their authority as license to rape local women and indulge in adultery.[24]

On the other hand, there were hardships, dangers, and constraints that could make officeholding a risky and thankless business. If there was money to be made by manipulating tribute accounts, there was also money to be lost. Vicente Isidro of Azcapotzalco (D.F.) claimed that serving as supervisor of the communal planting in 1779 cost him some of his meager savings. Now, in 1782, as regidor mayor he estimated the cost of the office at 150 pesos and asked that other, "wealthier people" be required to serve.[25] The escribano of Capuluac (Edo. de México) in 1795 testified that officeholding was a sacrifice because it left him no time to earn his living.[26] But at least he did not pay out of pocket for the privilege of serving, as many gobernadores, alcaldes, and other tribute collectors had to do. These officials were entitled to 1 percent of the collection as a "reward" but were not allowed to dip into the caja de comunidad to cover defaults. If they were unable to collect the full tribute levy (some members of the community were inevitably absent, which was a good reason for local officials to underestimate the number of tributaries), they were expected to make up the shortfall themselves. If they failed to do so, their property could be confiscated, and they and their relatives could be arrested. Either way, they could be beggared by the job.[27] The Audiencia of Guadalajara commented in 1791 that officers "ought to suffer for their offices."[28]

There were physical risks as well. Trying to collect taxes from recalcitrant members of the community could lead to a beating. In 1804, when the gobernador of Acatitlan (Sultepec district, Edo. de México) tried to collect 25 pesos from his predecessor for the use of bulls belonging to the community, the man had him whipped.[29] Enforcing the law could also earn enemies and a beating.

When the alcalde of Jocotlan (Tala district, Jalisco), José Doroteo, tried to enforce an eleven o'clock curfew on the night of Mardi Gras in 1807, five revelers in a local tavern became abusive, resisted arrest, assaulted him, and threw him in jail at the instigator's command—"So what if he's the *alcalde*? I'm in charge here, so put the *alcalde* in the stocks."[30] José Doroteo at least escaped with his life, if not his dignity. The alcalde of Tuluapan in the district of Colima was not so fortunate when he intervened in a fight between two local men in 1809.[31] Some communities habitually made officeholders objects of ridicule. At Nestipac (Tala district) in December 1814, the Indian alcalde stepped in to stop an apparently unprovoked drunken assault by Damasio Cárdenas on his wife at a fiesta at the Rancho de Nuestra Señora de los Dolores. Cárdenas and his brothers had a reputation for provoking and assaulting local judges and carrying firearms. Three years before, he and his brothers had set up a commotion in the cemetery and knocked down a Franciscan who went out to calm them. This time, with his wife seriously wounded, Cárdenas insulted the alcalde ("no *carajo* was going to interfere with him. That was his wife and he would do whatever he wanted with her"), attacked him, and paid with his life.[32]

As the representatives of the community, elected officials could be held responsible for the faults of the pueblo. Some gobernadores and alcaldes were incarcerated for no other reason than to bring their insubordinate fellows to heel. At Tepetlaostoc (Valley of Mexico) in 1758, the vicario reported that Indians of Santo Tomás Apipilhuasco had begun to perform the required labor service now that the gobernador had been arrested.[33] Such a strategy was acceptable to the Audiencia of Mexico, as a 1781 case from Huispaleca and Cuanacalcingo (Tlaltizapan district, Morelos) indicates. It decided that if no instigators could be identified for the insolence and refusal of local people to serve the parish church, the gobernador and alcaldes of the two pueblos could be arrested until the villagers complied, and could be removed from office.[34] Removing pueblo officials for community, as well as individual, misconduct was well within the power of the district judges and higher courts, and was done often enough in the late colonial period to restrict a village gobernador's or alcalde's authority.[35]

The gobernadores and alcaldes were certain to come into close contact with the curas. Traditionally, the cura was expected to train local leaders and hold them to a high standard of personal conduct. *Itinerario* 1-4-10 called on parish priests to train Indian leaders ("caziques y mayorales") to be exemplary in "propriety, cleanliness, modesty, and good manners." At least before the 1780's, the cura's traditional power to veto candidates for office whose personal conduct and religious practices were not exemplary made him something of a benefactor to those who gained office.[36] The gobernadores' and alcaldes' specific charge to control drunkenness, which was a basis for their wider customary judicial authority, was also a primary responsibility of parish priests, one that concerned them greatly for religious and political reasons. Indian officials who did not satisfy the priest in policing drunkenness and adultery, especially those who themselves appeared drunk in public or seemed to promote drunkenness and disrespect for higher authorities, could face charges by the priest in the district court and a loss of office.[37]

But the gobernador or alcalde who won the cura's approval as a faithful ally against local vice could lose far more than he gained from such patronage if he was perceived as cozying up to the priest at the expense of others. Miguel Santana Silva, for example, paid heavily for his close collaboration with the cura and subdelegado in prosecuting drunkenness and other crimes while he was alcalde of San Pedro Tlaquepaque (Jalisco) in 1814. According to his testimony, after his term expired, most of the Indians of the pueblo became his enemies, "to the point of chiding me at every turn, looking upon me with disgust, and shunning me in every kind of *pueblo* activity." Then, on April 28, 1815, the current alcaldes took their revenge. They called him to the pueblo offices, where five alguaciles tied him up and whipped him. He demanded that the subdelegado or at least a meeting of principales be consulted, but they laughed and said, "Didn't you think you would have to pay?" Several of the alguaciles involved testified that they had whipped Miguel Santana Silva on the alcaldes' orders, and that the alcaldes said to Santana at the time, "You, when you had your year as *alcalde*, punished all the *principales*; so now we are punishing you." Another added that Santana was hated "because he corrected everyone and because he is more inclined to the maxims of the *gente de razón* than to those of the *pueblo*." The alcaldes admitted that the testimony of the alguaciles was true but defended their punishment of Santana because he had insulted them as judges and "mistreated the entire *pueblo*." [38] At Tixmadeje in the district of Huichapan (Hidalgo) in 1789, when the gobernador whipped many Indians who were charged by the cura with ignoring their Christian duties and confiscated their property, he found himself the object of a mass uprising. Surrounded by over 600 angry Indian men and women of all ages armed with slings, goads, and sticks, he was taunted and accused of being the cura's creature and spy. He was badly beaten, then imprisoned for several days without food. His life was spared only, he claimed, because his captors said that killing him would end their fun.[39]

Escribanos de la república occupied a unique position that made them more important than other holders of "oficios menores," which, according to a principal of the district of Tacuba in 1818, included topiles, alguaciles, merinos, regidores, and fiscales, as well as escribanos.[40] Especially in communities where the gobernador and alcaldes did not read or write and knew little Spanish, pueblo secretaries could be pivotal political figures, mediating and representing community interests to higher authorities. They wrote out, signed, and sometimes composed the official communications of the community, counted the votes and certified the election results for the district judge, kept the records of council meetings and collections of various kinds, and often appeared in court for the community with the gobernador or alcaldes.[41] Their literacy and knowledge of Spanish also made them likely candidates for maestro of the community primary school in the late eighteenth century.[42]

Though theirs was an elective office and purportedly a minor one, escribanos could accumulate considerable power through continuous service. Even in the eighteenth century, some served indefinitely because no one else was sufficiently literate or trained in recordkeeping. Others were chosen because they were close relatives of the gobernador or an alcalde.[43] Since the office was nearly indispensable to fulfilling colonial obligations and transacting business in the colonial courts, a lack of a suitable candidate allowed some non-Indians to thrust themselves into the position and exert substantial influence on political decisions, especially the pursuit of litigation.[44]

The escribano had more responsibility and potentially more independence than all but the most senior elected officials of the pueblo. As the formal charge to the new Indian escribano at Tlaltenango (Zacatecas) in 1815 stated, he was responsible for

preserving our rights, peace, and tranquility without troubling or abusing us, or disturbing our sovereign will, . . . with the authority of substitute power as he sees fit and especially to press the pending petition concerning the trouble over our personal labor service.[45]

An aggressive escribano could promote land litigation; and, if unsuccessful, he might lead an illegal occupation.[46] In the disputes over land, elections, and clerical fees, escribanos sometimes pretended to be the sole (or at least most important) spokesmen of the community, cloaking themselves in the will of the república. In 1801, both the alcalde and the escribano spoke up for San Agustín (district of Tlajomulco, Jalisco) against a land possession, declaring, "we don't obey, we don't consent, we don't agree." But the escribano then lapsed into the singular, declaring that "this is what my *república* says."[47] Similarly, during a political protest in Ocoyoacac (Edo. de México) in August 1810, it was the escribano who supposedly claimed that "he has at his disposal 500 Indians to fight against the Spaniards; that this conquest won't be like that of Hernán Cortés."[48] The cura of Mechoacanejo (Jalisco) in 1744 blamed three principales, including the escribano, whom he called "the boldest and most depraved of them," for instigating a dispute over elections.[49] With the current and past alcaldes in the background, the escribano of San Luis Xocotla (Chilapa district, Guerrero) spearheaded a lawsuit against the cura in 1781, apparently because he alone was literate.[50]

The escribano's special knowledge of legal forms and responsibility for official recordkeeping provided opportunities to enrich himself outside the law. There were cases of escribanos falsifying official documents and the signatures of district judges and curas, drawing up bogus episcopal decrees, composing petitions in the name of the community without the consent or knowledge of the cabildo, and tampering with testaments and local land records to benefit themselves and their sponsors.[51]

Open Resistance

Conflict between priests and Indian parishioners appears to have reached a peak in the 1760's and 1770's following the Seven Years' War, which was an especially active period of Bourbon administrative and fiscal reform, and to have remained relatively high through the end of the colonial period. Of the 82 cases of open resistance in the court records for 1720 to 1809, 35 (43 percent) occurred in the 1760's (18) and 1770's (17).[52] This is not firm evidence of the incidence of dramatic conflict—the sample could be enlarged with more research, especially for

1720 to 1770, and the evidence reflects the administrative concerns and activity of the Bourbons at the time—but it is probably still a fair approximation of the growing importance of such conflicts, the changing place of priests in many parishes, and the tender spots in their relationship with parishioners.

The vast majority of these cases (71 of the 77 that could be placed geographically) occurred in the Archdiocese of Mexico, and all but a few were regionally concentrated in five areas: the immediate vicinity of the Valley of Mexico (fifteen cases), adjacent districts of Metepec, Temascaltepec, and Zacualpan in the Estado de México (eighteen), districts of modern Hidalgo (fourteen cases), the districts of Cuernavaca and Cuautla in modern Morelos (eight cases), and parts of modern Guerrero near Morelos and the Estado de México (eight cases). A similar pattern—highlighting the southwestern Estado de México and modern Hidalgo—appears in the 38 complaints by pueblo officials registered in pastoral visit records for the archdiocese beyond Mexico City from 1765 to 1792: seventeen cases for Metepec, Temascaltepec, Malinalco, Tenango del Valle, and Lerma; nine cases for Hidalgo and districts of northern Veracruz; five cases for the Valley of Mexico; four cases for Cuernavaca and Cuautla; two cases for neighboring districts in Guerrero; and one case for Querétaro.

Though the records focus on these areas as the chief centers of trouble between priests and parishioners, other places were not conflict-free, as incidental testimony and administrative reports sometimes reveal. Still, the spotty geographical and temporal distribution and the nature of the cases themselves also suggest that even where disputes were most evident, priests tended to be respected and obeyed in public. Pueblos and their members usually paid their clerical fees and other taxes, responded to calls for contributions toward the defense of the empire, maintained their churches, attended mass, took communion, summoned the priest for last rites, and consented to the docility and obedience prescribed for them by the colonial government.[53] Even the people of Amanalco (Metepec district), who were notorious in the 1780's and early 1790's for running their priest out of town, leaving the parish church in poor repair, resisting clerical fees, and dotting the landscape with shrines of their own, cheerfully accepted the coadjutor introduced by the pastoral visitor in late 1792 and pledged to obey him, repair their church, buy new ornaments, and more, "in order to avoid the bad reputation they have in other places."[54] The many long-running lawsuits document the habit of compliance to higher authority at the same time that they express conflict.

Issues of Political Authority

The issues raised by parishioners in their complaints to pastoral visitors, episcopal courts, and royal judges, and in their violent protests had little to do with the kind of loose moral behavior by priests that seems to have so exercised rural Frenchmen in the early eighteenth century.[55] Political authority and, especially, clerical fees and other economic demands were at the heart of most disputes.[56]

Elections

Elections were only a matter of occasional dispute before the intendancy reforms of the 1780's. Most of the cases requiring adjudication turned on the *Recopilación*'s ambiguity on the point. By specifically charging curas to be present
in one law and failing to mention them in another, it left the parish priest's super-
visory role in doubt.[57]

What is most revealing in this handful of challenges is that, with some striking exceptions, priests exercised considerable influence in local politics. This
was especially true in the Diocese of Guadalajara, where election issues involving parish priests were more numerous and contentious than in the archdiocese.
The cura of Mechoacanejo in 1744, for example, faced fourteen principales of the
parish seat in litigation over his manipulation of the election of the alcalde. The
cura had vetoed the choice of the majority of electors and imposed another candidate because, he testified, he did not know the man and heard that he was
licentious. The cura made no apologies for holding the elections in his rooms and
believing that these Indians could not be trusted in their choice of officials (nor
was an apology or explanation demanded).[58] The cura of Xala (Ahuacatlan district, Jalisco) summed up a common view of the local election practice in 1749:
"the sons of the *pueblo* are to propose, the *cura* to elect, and the *alcaldes mayores*
to appoint."[59]

In some parishes—for instance La Barca in 1708, Atotonilco el Alto in 1715,
and Tetapan in 1767 (all in the Diocese of Guadalajara)—district governors had
supervised the elections uncontested, especially when they had the informal
support of the parish priest.[60] But the cura's role remained strong even when
contested, thanks to disputes within pueblos. At Hueyapan (Morelos) in 1768,
a group of former officials obtained an audiencia order for the cura or vicario to
certify to the suitability of candidates for office because the alcalde mayor had
capriciously admitted to office disreputable men promoted by a small group who
controlled the elections.[61]

The viceregal government began to put its new interest in pueblo elections
into legislative action in 1763. That year, the viceroy implemented a royal decree
for fiscales to be elected in the annual elections like other village officials. In
1770, he ordered that all elected officials must be Indians who knew the Spanish
language. Three years later, he went further, ordering that all these candidates
must have resided for at least three years in the community. By 1777, it must
have been a tacit assumption that royal judges certified elections, since the viceroy declared that alcaldes mayores and their deputies were not to charge a fee
for doing so.[62]

But the flash point for this kind of dispute between priests and parishioners
came after the Ordenanza de Intendentes was put into place in 1789. Articles
13 and 14 made it unequivocally clear that only the royal judge was to preside
over the annual elections of pueblo officers; neither article mentioned a role for
parish priests. In August 1789, the corregidor of Mexico City, Bernardo de Bonavía, attempted to reconcile the new law with the *Recopilación*'s provision that the
cura was to be present at the elections. Because the cura was present there, declared Bonavía, did not mean that electors were obliged to select officers of his

choosing.[63] In 1787 and 1788, after the ordenanza was published but before it was implemented, the Audiencia of Guadalajara's fiscal protector and fiscal de lo civil formulated the following instructions for Indian elections: they should be held during December (because it was a month of little agricultural work) in the community where the officers would serve; the alcalde mayor or his deputy (another "persona española decente") was to preside but must not charge any fees for his services; the alcalde mayor or his deputy was to approve the election in writing, and give the certification to the Indian officials for safekeeping in a locked box; and the cura should attend, if possible, "contributing greatly to the splendor and solemnity of the occasion with his presence but having no jurisdiction whatsoever over it."[64]

With the weight of law now clearly against the parish priests, the many suits brought against them over local elections in the 1790's removed them further from the supervision of local politics.[65] Whereas in earlier cases curas had advanced confident claims about what was rightfully their duty, as the cura of Xala did in 1749, now curas were more likely to complain that the royal governor or his lieutenant was abusing his powers or, where the cura was on good terms with the man, to respond as the cura of Capuluac did in 1796, when pueblo officials accused him of blocking the election of a local favorite—that while he did not favor their candidate, he had merely postponed the election because "both judges" must be present for a valid election.[66]

The audiencias moved decisively at this time to make the fiscal and the sacristán elected community officers, as the 1763 viceregal decree and a supplementary 1774 circular provided. A long-standing complaint by the pueblo officials of San Pedro de la Cañada (Querétaro) about the cura's interference in their way of selecting the community's fiscal, sacristán, and maestro led to a royal decree on June 23, 1791, that these officials should be freely elected by the community.[67] In 1795, the cura returned to court to protest the election of a sacristán who was an unbonded and untrustworthy drunkard. The sacristán was confirmed after the audiencia's legal counsel urged a ringing endorsement for "the right of the *república* to elect its *fiscal* and *sacristán*" as long as the Indians posted a bond for him with the court.[68] The audiencias received repeated petitions as well for the election of cofradía mayordomos without the cura's interference—as at Ajuchitlan (Tetela del Río district) in 1790, where Indians told the interim cura that "they, not the *cura*, have the right to name the *mayordomo* of the *cofradías*"; and at San Simón Tototepec (Zacualpan district) in 1803, where the gobernador asserted that "the *mayordomos* have always been named by the *república*."[69]

Because of the curas' long-standing political influence in the Diocese of Guadalajara, implementing the new policy frequently required judicial action. The parish of Juchipila (Zacatecas) in 1791 is a well-documented example. Called to explain himself to the audiencia, the cura rather meekly requested that the judges clarify his role, expressing his "intense desire to please my superiors." Was he still to certify to the fitness and Christian aptitude of the elected? he asked.[70] But the subdelegado would have no part of this performance, retorting that the cura was interfering outright in the elections and should be restricted to ascertaining whether the officers knew the catechism; that only the royal judge should decide whether or not they were Indians and of good character. The audiencia issued a laconic order for the cura to desist from his interference. Simultaneously, Indians of Moyahua in Juchipila parish protested the cura's rejection of their elected alcalde on "frivolous pretexts."[71]

Whether judicial action was necessary depended partly on whether the cura had been in place for many years and was accustomed to supervising elections. The cura of Zoquitlan (Tehuacan district, Puebla) expressed his angry bewilderment to the audiencia in 1792, after the subdelegado announced that his attendance and approval were no longer needed. Was he not supposed to certify elections "in order to prevent dissensions in the *pueblo* when individuals are elected from infected *castas* who despicably disturb the peace?" In his twenty years as cura there, he added, he had always certified elections, "even in the time of the intendancies." The audiencia was moved more by the subdelegado's argument that because of the cura's intrigues, a suitably free election could not be held.[72] Here, as in most parts of New Spain, the cura was being reduced to lending gravity to the occasion and advising the district governor whether candidates knew the basics of Christian doctrine, and, if the governor wished, confirming their race and residence qualifications.[73] That left the cura with little more than the negative power to exclude some potential candidates for office.[74]

Another sign of the parish priests' declining role in elections is that more complaints began to be lodged against subdelegados and their lieutenants for abuses of the election laws. At San Pedro and San Martín (Tonalá district, Jalisco) in 1789 and 1791, the subdelegado was charged with delaying his confirmation of some new officials and capriciously overturning the election of others.[75] In 1794, the attorney for Mecatabasco in the district of Juchipila requested that the Indians be allowed to elect the next group of alcaldes because the current officials chosen by the lieutenant were doing great harm to the community.[76] And the subdelegado of Tlaltenango in 1805 found himself in the same predicament as the curas 30 years before when he nullified the election of an alcalde as unfit for office and appointed an interim alcalde, only to have residents of the barrio from which the rejected candidate came take him to court for inserting himself unfairly in the electoral process.[77]

The surge in proceedings against curas in the 1790's was great and obviously related to the legislative opening, but beneath the much longer run of election disputes during the eighteenth century, there were often internal disputes over the franchise and vote fraud.[78] With great local variation, the trend was away from a voting group restricted to the fifteen or 20 principales who enjoyed hereditary privileges or were former officeholders, and toward adult male suffrage.[79] The more politically divided and contentious the community, the more likely someone was to appeal for a wider electorate. Rival groups in Atotonilco el Alto (Jalisco), which was famous for its political divisions in the eighteenth century, enlisted more than 100 voters—far more than the score of principales who had monopolized office—in their quest for local power in 1715.[80] At Tlajomulco (Jalisco) in 1808, one group of principales allowed certain macehuales to vote in order to tip the electoral balance in their favor.[81] Sometimes it was the cura who moved a community toward general male suffrage, as the cura of Guipustla did in Joloapan (Tetepango district, Hidalgo) in 1768 in an effort to break the influence of the traditional electors, who were divided among themselves and more or less united against him.[82]

The Community Treasury

Just as the tension between curas and villagers over the control of cofradía wealth dated back to the sixteenth and seventeenth centuries, so the caja de comunidad (community treasury) issue was not new. But this was not a major point of conflict before the late eighteenth century because the crown was flexible about the use of these funds; because cajas hardly existed in many of the pueblos of these two dioceses; and because it was well established in law that parish priests should not take anything from the caja de comunidad on their own account.[83]

New attention was drawn to the cajas after the 1770's, when administrative responsibilities shifted from the audiencias and viceroy to royal treasury officers as part of a plan to increase fiscal efficiency and accountability. In 1776, a report by the contador general de proprios y arbitrios concluded that the many cofradías in Indian pueblos of New Spain were the principal reason why the bienes de comunidad in these pueblos were lacking or inadequate. His office began to organize investigations into community treasuries and cofradías, and to undertake inspections for the audiencia.[84] In 1783, the contador moved to increase the funds of the cajas de comunidad by calling for an annual contribution of one and a half reales per tributary or the produce from ten varas of community land (as royal law had prescribed in 1582).[85] This marked the beginning of a concerted administrative effort to create and enlarge community treasuries. With the support of the district magistrates and intendants, cajas became a regular feature of pueblos in central and western Mexico during the 1780's and 1790's.[86] As is indicated by the crown's resort to the pueblo cajas for loans to the Banco Nacional de San Carlos and the Real Caja de Filipinas, as well as "patriotic loans" for Spain's European wars, the reform had less to do with principles of community property than with access to the royal patrimony broadly defined.[87]

Litigation and administrative activity over the cajas peaked between 1786 and 1810 and centered on whether bienes de comunidad could be used for religious purposes. It had long been necessary to secure a license to do so from the audiencia or viceroy, but the license was usually granted.[88] Though the answer now was rarely a definite no, the message conveyed in the audiencias' judgments was that royal judges would scrutinize such requests closely, and that the answer might well be no, depending on the circumstances. In 1786, when Indian officials of San Juan Xicotlan in the district of Chiautla de la Sal (Puebla) petitioned the audiencia, over the alcalde mayor's objections, for permission to cover Easter week expenses from the caja, the court ordered an inspection and report but granted the license, ostensibly because the sum involved was small (68 pesos).[89] In later cases, before deciding, the court considered closely the proposed uses (usually for construction or to pay ceremonial expenses), the funds available, and the amount requested.[90] In the case of Popolotla's request to build a new chapel next to the parish church in 1805 (Tacuba district, Valley of Mexico), the answer was no, as it was in 1791, when the former cura of Texupa (Oaxaca) asked to be pensioned from the community's caja in compensation for fees still owed to him.[91] The requests of Santiago Tlatlaya, Santa María Cuatepec, and Aquiapa (Sultepec district, Edo. de México) in 1788 to use caja funds for church repairs were granted only in part: they could use interest on the capital toward covering the expenses but not the capital itself.[92] Detailed accounts of pueblo cajas from the 1790's in central Mexico, surviving as artifacts of this administrative interest, indicate that over half their funds were still being expended on clerical fees and religious functions.[93]

Labor Service

Judicial complaints against curas by Indian officials in the name of their pueblo over involuntary service were especially common in the late eighteenth century (and connected to the arancel cases discussed in Chapter 17). As with the larger pattern of conflict between pueblos and priests in the late eighteenth and early nineteenth centuries, the labor disputes were concentrated in the districts of Metepec and Temascaltepec-Zacualpan in the modern Estado de México, in modern Morelos, and near the Valley of Mexico in the districts of Xochimilco, Tacuba, Huizquilucan, Milpa Alta, and Otumba. The one striking departure from the resistance pattern is the heavy concentration in the area of modern Hidalgo (eighteen of 61 disputes between 1720 and 1820, with nine of these in the districts of Meztitlan and Yahualica), perhaps because more labor service had been demanded by priests there earlier in the colonial period, and because Meztitlan was a district of marked political conflict in the second half of the eighteenth century.[94] Typically, outlying villages were the most inclined to resist labor service for the church and the cura, adding as it did the burden of traveling to the cabecera, a place they may not have regarded as their own.

Like other conflicts, the protests over labor service were concentrated in the period 1760 to 1810 and peaked in the 1790's, but they followed an unusual trajectory that reflects a different history from that of other sources of dispute. Labor disputes were comparatively numerous throughout the eighteenth century. Within the 1760–1810 bulge, almost as many disputes dated from before 1780 as after (24 vs. 28). The main reason for this more even distribution is probably that, though new attention was drawn to labor service in the late eighteenth century, it had been a sensitive issue since the early colonial period. The law was well established before the publication of the *Recopilación* and changed very little thereafter.

The basic law was set out in books 1 and 6 of the *Recopilación*. In one of the earliest pronouncements, Philip II in 1594 specified that the regular clergy could not require service from Indians "except in essential cases and things, and then paying them what they deserve and what the Government has decided for their wages . . . since the Religious are to be concerned only with the teaching and relief of the natives." [95] Responding to specific abuses, other laws at the turn of the seventeenth century confirmed that no parish priest, regular or otherwise, should demand personal service from his parishioners, and that if they did serve him, it was to be at the going wage.[96] This body of law was summarized in 1610 in response to labor drafts: "*Curas* in Indian parishes may have been assigned Indian men and women to cook for them, make *tortillas*, and fish for them on meatless days. Because this is very harmful and prejudicial, we order that such drafts not be allowed for these purposes or any other, and that what [we have decreed] for personal services be followed."[97] The two initiatives that drew added attention to the issue in the late eighteenth century were the new schedules of fees for the archdiocese in 1767, which gave Indian pueblos the option of additional payments in cash in place of labor service; and a viceregal circular of October 20, 1793, advertising the fact that parish priests were forbidden to demand personal services from their parishioners.[98]

The issues and interested parties in these labor suits were the same whether the dispute happened in the 1720's or the 1790's. The plaintiffs appealed to earlier laws against forced labor; the amount of service expected was said to be excessive; the cura did not pay, or paid too little, for personal service; Indians of visitas were the usual protagonists; and the arancel was invoked.[99] For instance, in 1721 Indian representatives of Huazalingo in the parish of Yahualica (Hidalgo) complained of being burdened not only with "a thousand impositions of errands to Mexico City and many other places without the one-half *real* benefit" (mil pensiones de enviado a México y otras muchas partes sin el interés de medio real), but with the cura's demand for the weekly service of one assistant, one hay gatherer, one grinder, and one tortilla maker. They requested the arancel.[100] In 1775, at Cuanacalcingo in the district of Cuernavaca, the complaint and the legal grounding were much the same: the parishioners claimed the cura forced them to run long-distance errands without "the required wage" and to provide weekly servants to fetch his water, collect fodder and charcoal, cook his meals, bathe his horses, and tend to the oxen without pay. The cura argued that these services were ancient, and he resisted any change, even if the Indians wanted the arancel.[101]

Even with this long history of disputes and delinquency, before the 1767 arancel, many curas felt entitled to certain personal services. Above all, they expected kitchen help and care for their animals. In the parish of Cempoala (Hidalgo) in 1755, the pueblo of Santo Tomás was expected to supply a dining-room servant, a sacristán, and a cook every week, the pueblo of San Gabriel a sacristán, a pastor, and a cook, and the pueblo of San Mateo a janitor and a groom (*cagnayopisqui*).[102] At Yahualica (Hidalgo) in 1739, the cura demanded the weekly services of three sacristanes, two church assistants (*theopan topiles*), four children (*piltopiles*), two hay gatherers, two grinders, and a tortilla maker.[103] At another site in Hidalgo, Tasquillo, as late as 1796, Indians were still required to provide two unmarried men as general servants, a bellringer, a groom for the cura's horses, a water carrier from each barrio, a grinder, and enough men to work a corn field and a wheat field. At Chilapa (Guerrero) in 1774, the cura claimed that two villages had provided his predecessors with twelve "Indians to farm, enough for his domestic needs, and a messenger whenever there was mail to carry."[104] At Malacatepec (Metepec district, Edo. de México) in 1755, the cura demanded by right of custom and over the parishioners' objections the use of six grinders and eight young men every week.[105]

The arancel of 1767 brought a new flurry of complaints over personal services. Within a year, the Indians of Joloapan (Hidalgo) had sought an order requiring the cura to conform to the new fee schedule. The plaintiffs said that they had willingly rebuilt the parish church but objected to the cura compelling four sacristanes to serve two weeks a month without pay, largely on personal errands.[106] Over the cura's objections, parishioners of San Felipe and Santiago in the parish of Malacatepec (Metepec district) went to the audiencia in 1774 to claim the arancel and avoid further servicios involuntarios. The cura, in his turn, pleaded that "he ought to be privileged when it comes to service," and that each pueblo had to supply only a few Indians for household service six weeks a year (the Indians responded that seven was more than a few). What he regarded as a standard feature of the office was now involuntary, unpaid labor. Predictably, the verdict went against the cura.[107] Priests who defended old labor service arrangements now actively opposed by the crown and bishops found themselves in the uncomfortable position of defending custom against law. They had little choice but to accept the arancel, if that was the wish of their parishioners.

The secularization of parishes between 1749 and 1780 may have been as important as the new arancel in generating complaints over labor service. According to the diocesan cura of Chilapa (Guerrero) in 1774, the Indians of San Luis Xocutla and Santa María Nazintlan had provided twelve servants a week until the parish was secularized in 1771. Now, he said, they refused to serve, and when he required them to do so, they sued him.[108] Whether inspired by the arancel, secularization, or local hardships such as illness or famine, late-eighteenth-century Indians wanted to serve less, even if they recognized some continuing obligation. As the attorney for an Indian from Milpa Alta (Xochimilco district, Valley of Mexico) put it in 1797, the sixteen servants that the pueblo had customarily supplied every week since the sixteenth century were too many.[109]

The main differences between earlier suits over labor service and the many new ones after 1760 were that (1) Indian plaintiffs increasingly demanded pay for their labor and seem to have been more keenly aware that unpaid labor for the parish priest could be regarded as intolerable servitude; and (2) royal courts were inclined to narrow the scope of what constituted appropriate church service.

Indians and their attorneys were more confident and more vehement in the late-eighteenth-century complaints over servicios involuntarios to the curas. In the Tasquillo case of 1796, for example, Indian petitioners spoke bitterly of "offering their sweat for free" and of the cura's treating them like "common slaves, imposing on them as he pleases." Often enough, it was an entrepreneurial attorney speaking for the pueblo who turned up the rhetorical heat of these petitions and encouraged a more adversarial stance toward the cura.

Unpaid labor of some kind would continue with the crown's blessing, despite the hopes raised by some local leaders that the arancel and royal policy exempted them from service of any kind. But what was still owed by communities that chose the arancel? What were the limits of essential church service? Service that enabled the priest to fulfill his pastoral duties—providing a horse or mule for confessions outside the cabecera,[110] maintaining the church building, and performing the duties of the fiscal—was endorsed. For Tlaltizapan (Morelos) in 1781, essential service meant keeping the church grounds clean and supporting the mass and other fundamental rites—servants to ring the church bells, keep the lamp lit, police the parish, and assist at mass and funerals. The audiencia judged this to mean a weekly crew of seven, in addition to cantors: two sacristanes, two acolytes, one bellringer, one topil, and one fiscal.[111]

In the case of construction, the *Itinerario* had charged parishioners with the tasks of building and repairing both the church and the priest's residence, and even approved working on Sunday after mass if the situation was urgent.[112] But by the eighteenth century, anything beyond the upkeep of the church was likely to be challenged. Despite some early successes, as when the audiencia decreed in 1756 that the Indians of San Luis de las Peras (Tula district, Hidalgo) could not be forced to make adobes for the priest's residence without pay,[113] the courts initially tried the tack of accommodation. For example, San Lucas in the parish of Tecualoyan (Malinalco district, Edo. de México), which was willing in 1768 to help maintain the parish church but refused to work on the residence without pay, was eventually brought to agree to work there, too, as long as the whole parish did.[114] Similarly, in a 1779 case, the audiencia fiscal recommended that the Indians of San Juan Tetelzingo in the parish of Oapan (Guerrero) help repair the residence because the building had collapsed and the work was not onerous if all the pueblos in the parish helped.[115] In the 1790's, however, as the Indian complaints about labor demands for church and rectory construction mounted, royal judges were increasingly inclined to give them a sympathetic hearing.[116]

In some cases, parishioners accepted terms for service that were broader than the royal policy. Even then, they could do so with reservations. In 1788, Indians of Cempoala were willing to concede to the cura the service and food he needed "to live," in addition to his income from ritual services, but they were not prepared to support him in grand style ("with the magnificence and comforts that the *cura* wants").[117] One thing that the courts clearly would no longer permit in parishes governed by the arancel was agricultural and ranching services. For example, in 1789 the fiscal of the Royal Treasury ordered the cura of Tlaquiltenango (Morelos) to pay parishioners for the services he demanded for his maize and hay fields, orchard, and flocks "according to the custom of the land and the wage they could earn in other occupations."[118]

The demands that curas pay for any personal services became ever more frequent, especially in the archdiocese, once the arancel of 1767 gave pueblos the option of paying clerical fees in cash. It was an option that many were eager to pursue but few could manage without new sources of income. Indian leaders were quick to grasp the potential of requiring payment for household work and other forms of personal service. It is hardly surprising, in the circumstances, that many of the late colonial suits turned not on serving the cura, but on doing so without fair wages.[119]

The disputes over labor service tapered off after the 1790's, but they did not end. Uncertainties and defiant violations continued. In pueblos that did not choose the arancel option, unpaid service that substituted for higher fees was still lawful. And in some parishes where the arancel applied, curas were understandably reluctant to give up the convenience of at least a few rotating household servants. For example, when the cura of Temascaltepec (Edo. de México) was called to account for involuntary labor in 1790, he admitted requiring a kitchen servant, a grinder, a firewood gatherer, an acolyte, and a gravedigger.[120] But it was a sign of the times that by the 1760's, more curas answered their parishioners' complaints with evidence that they did, in fact, pay for household labor.[121]

Miscellaneous Causes of Action

In addition to the disputes focused specifically on personal services, elections, community treasuries, cofradías, and schedules of fees, Indians brought suits against their parish priests for a variety of overlapping reasons. There were sweeping, often rather vague, formulaic complaints that expressed conflict but were tailored to the legal setting in ways that could mask precise motives.[122] The old charge of curas physically abusing their parishioners did not die out. Neither did the allegations of excessive rigidity and "tyrannical" rule.

Especially interesting were the suits brought against curas for "innovations." Bourbon administrators were themselves innovators, but allegations of *novedad* or *inovación* among colonial subjects appealed to their sense of privilege and responsibility. The meaning of the word novedad at the time invited this kind of appeal: "change in things that usually have a fixed condition or that one believes ought to have a fixed condition."[123] Indian litigants invoked custom to argue against the priest's "innovations" in fees, in the number of masses, in local religious practice—removing an image from the local church, refurbishing an image without local approval, refusing to bless images, forbidding a traditional procession, adding fiestas, or placing or removing a resident priest in an outlying visita.[124] "Innovation" suggested that the priest acted on his own, "at his pleasure," contrary to the organic metaphor in which the body acted on the instructions of the head and heart. Most of the salvos against innovation imply an irresponsibility on the part of the priests more than blind adherence to custom on the part of their parishioners.[125] As defendant priests sometimes observed, their Indian parishioners loved custom as long as it suited their interests. In a 1785 fees dispute with Huispaleca and Cuanacalcingo, the cura of Tlaltizapan remarked that his parishioners "embrace custom with the utmost tenacity whenever it favors them and they follow the *arancel* in the parts they find useful."[126]

These various complaints against parish priests expressed two more or less separate kinds of tension. One was tension over moral and spiritual behavior, arising when parishioners objected to the priest's excessive zeal in attempting to reform them. Issues ranged from attendance at mass and the fulfillment of feast-day obligations to drunkenness and cohabitation without marriage. The second was tension over pueblo resources, which produced claims that the cura was controlling villagers' lands and community finances, and making unreasonable demands (requiring them, for example, to supply horses for his travel as needed). All of the complaints asserted a strong community identity. Invoking the "liberty" of their communities, Indian leaders criticized their curas for interfering too much or betraying the ideals of their office.[127] In either case, they represented themselves as truer Christians.[128]

Litigation, Flight, and Other Means of Resistance

Learning to lay claims to legislated rights and express complaints against priests through legal channels was an important part of Indian participation in the colonial polity. The habit of litigation had been well established in Indian pueblos during the sixteenth century, but the number of suits initiated, especially against parish priests in the Archdiocese of Mexico, increased dramatically in the second half of the eighteenth century.[129] In part intentionally, the crown encouraged this activity by enlarging and advertising the class of circumstances under which it was not likely to take the priest's side. And Indian litigants and their attorneys borrowed the language of Bourbon administration to make their claims more appealing. The Indians of Coatepec in the parish of Malinaltenango (Zacualpan district), for example, emphasized the key word "fijo"—fixed, standard—in their 1784 complaint that the cura was not obeying the 1767 schedule of fees.[130]

Indian lawsuits could be a form of harassment and delay. They were costly and time-consuming, and even if the priest won the case, his career could be damaged or he could spend years waiting for his parish revenues. The cura of Tejupilco in 1732 added another dimension to Indian reasons for lawsuits over clerical fees: he claimed that such suits were started and prolonged in the hope that accumulated fees from before the suit would be forgotten (especially when a new cura arrived) or forgiven.[131]

Despite the growing penchant of late-eighteenth-century Indian parishioners for litigation, and the prospect of some success, there were constraints that no doubt made some reconsider. District governors began to warn their subjects against pressing their cases so hard. For example, during the long-running suit over clerical fees by Indians of Huiciltepec (Puebla) between 1793 and 1803, the lieutenant advised the Indians to stay home with their families and be at peace, "without wasting on lawsuits (as they are doing at present) what they have acquired with so much effort and ought to use to support themselves, roaming about and leaving their fields untended."[132] Nor was the appetite for litigation so unlimited as it seemed to some defendants. As one observer of a lengthy suit noted, "The expenses have turned the complainants into cowards."[133]

As an adversarial encounter, litigation invited exaggeration that the judge was challenged to take into account.[134] Since litigation was expensive (although not to the individual Indian officials, since the costs were covered from community property or special household collections), it tended to respond to signals from the crown about what kinds of complaints had a chance of "victory" (as the litigants put it). But the parish reforms of the late eighteenth century also brought riskier suits that were calculated to discredit or remove a parish priest. Occasionally, the charges were pure fabrications. A particularly well-documented example involved Juan Silverio de Nava, cura of Terrenate (Veracruz) in 1768. Nava was brought before the Inquisition as a perpetrator of an array of abuses, including repeated solicitations in the confessional. At least three Indian women residing on haciendas in the parish claimed that he had propositioned them in the confessional (one claimed he had done so for nine straight years during Lent). It took two years to unravel the evidence and clear Nava of the most serious charges. Behind the false charges was a long-standing rivalry with an influential elder of the community bearing the portentous name of Juan Diego, whom Nava accused of being a soothsayer and personal enemy, and whom he had punished for sexual misconduct.[135]

Sometimes the path of resistance was the path of least resistance. Archbishop Lorenzana, in his pastoral letter of October 5, 1766, cautioned his parish priests that if they stretched things too far with their Indian parishioners, they would "flee to other *pueblos* or to the hills and the settlement [would be] ruined." Four years later, Tirso Díaz, the Mexico City priest who had been an interim cura in the district of Córdoba (Puebla), had second thoughts about the Indians' vaunted attachment to their place of birth: "Although Indians are believed to be lovers of their land and attached to it, the truth is that they know very well how to leave it for long periods when it is in their interest to do so. No, they are certainly not as simple as many believe."[136] These were more than the self-revealing comments of two European Spaniards. The late colonial record is filled with incidental evidence of flight as an oblique form of resistance.

In central and western Mexico, the temporary migration of a whole pueblo or a large number of its residents had long been a common stratagem for security and survival. Mota y Escobar at the beginning of the seventeenth century found it difficult to estimate the number of Indians in Nueva Galicia because so many were not to be found in their pueblos; they were off working in the mines, ranches, and farms, or as muleteers.[137] In central and southern Mexico in the early seventeenth century, there were reports of congregaciones abandoned and exoduses from provinces.[138] The eighteenth century brought reports from throughout central and western Mexico of Indian vagrancy, and of Indians absent for long periods as traders or residing much of the year on private, non-Indian estates as agricultural workers and ranch hands, working salt mines and fields several hours' walk from the pueblo and returning there only on the weekend.[139] In Metepec district of the Valley of Toluca, with its densely settled pueblos, Indians were so "in the habit of moving" that it was difficult to collect the tribute.[140] As the subdelegado of Santa María del Oro (Tequepespan district, Jalisco) put it in 1798, they were "readily inclined to leave their belongings and flee to the mountains."[141] Shorter term departures by large numbers of villagers were reported in times of dearth and disease.[142]

So, departures from pueblos, even on a large scale, for reasons of occupation, adventure, or personal health and safety were ordinary enough that they could inspire a political strategy. But flight for political reasons was not limited to areas like the Diocese of Guadalajara, the Bajío, or the tierra caliente of Michoacán and Guerrero, where other kinds of departures were especially common; and, as one might expect, it was a choice many made in areas where direct confrontations (in the form of lawsuits or tumultos) were concentrated, including the central Mexican areas of modern Hidalgo and the district of Temascaltepec. It was, in part, an additional strategy in the negotiation of disagreements with colonial officials: sometimes a strategy of passive resistance and sometimes mainly a product of fear.

Flight as a negotiating tool is evident in the occasional threats to abandon pueblos. As the Indian leaders of San Gregorio, Saigupa, Santa Catharina, and los Remedios in the district of Xerez, put it in 1713, in requesting the Audiencia of Nueva Galicia to remove the local lieutenant because of his abuses, "all of us from the *pueblos* are of a mind to pick up our families, abandon the *pueblos*, and come to live in Galicia for some peace and quiet if the said Chaide continues with the *vara de justicia*."[143] Three-quarters of a century later, the Indians of Ocuilan (Malinalco district, Edo. de México), engaged in a dispute with their cura over fees and labor service, also threatened to "abandon the land." (The threat must have been taken seriously, for the cura left soon afterward.)[144]

Since colonial order as the Spanish conceived it depended on Indians residing in a settled community under the supervision of royal magistrates and taking the sacraments in their home parish, the many actual desertions gave bite to such threats and could serve as a strategy for subsequent negotiation, as well as a gesture of protest and an escape from punishment or further abuse. Coordinated flight as protest was less common in the more densely settled parts of the Diocese of Guadalajara than in the Archdiocese of Mexico.[145] The most frequent reason participants gave for their action was to escape the priest's cruelty, but since flight was usually a prelude to further litigation, it was also a way for them to dramatize their case to the colonial courts.[146] In some cases, 20 or 30 households left, suggesting decisions by extended family clusters.[147] In other cases, where the entire pueblo was abandoned or all of the men left, a more concerted, community action was apparent. According to the cura of Malacatepec in the district of Metepec in 1803, Indians had retreated to the mountains under the evil influence of a local hacendado in order to dramatize their demand for the arancel and avoid their duties to the church.[148] Disappearing on Sundays was a way to avoid the fee for mass and express an ongoing disagreement with the cura over other matters.[149]

Sometimes the flight of whole communities or large groups, as well as individuals, was mainly avoidance rather than public gesture—avoiding the charges an alcalde mayor might make on his tour of inspection or the services a cura might require; avoiding the abusive labor practices of crown officials, neighboring hacendados, or a pueblo notable; avoiding the anger and punishment of a cura; or avoiding the recriminations that were sure to follow a tumulto or defiance of orders from the cabecera.[150] In most of these cases, it is difficult to tell whether the departures were permanent. The more they resulted from individual choices and economic hardship, the more likely it was that the emigrants would not return, especially in areas where migration was common in the eighteenth century, such as Morelos, Guerrero, Jalisco, and the Bajío.

Political flight had a special twist for members of pueblos in or near the Valley of Mexico. Their escapes were less to the mountains than to Mexico City, where they could hide themselves in urban anonymity and had some hope of a hearing from an attorney and one of the high courts.[151] Flights to the city were acts of access and direct judicial action more often than of retreat. Macehuales, as well as Indian officeholders, within the five-league radius of the audiencia's original jurisdiction were quickest to go there over even minor disputes with their curas. Indians living beyond the valley, in modern Morelos, Estado de México, and Hidalgo, were also frequent visitors to the city when they had grievances against their curas. The Indians of Tlaltizapan, Huispaleca, and Cuanacalcingo in modern Morelos were reported to have virtually abandoned their pueblos in

1781 to appeal directly to the audiencia against the parish priest over labor service.[152] Indians of the Toluca Valley and the district of Temascaltepec made similar moves throughout the eighteenth century.[153] And in separate incidents, in 1756 and 1789, Indian alcaldes from two communities in the district of Xilotepec (Hidalgo) fled to Mexico to take refuge from the wrath of the district magistrate.[154] If it was a community matter, representatives of more distant pueblos were likely to hire an attorney in the city or the district seat to press their complaints for them.[155] Even so, the increasing migration of litigious villagers to Mexico City and provincial capitals in the late 1790's strained urban supplies and rural agriculture enough that the viceroy ordered pueblos to send no more than two representatives at a time.[156]

Another common form of aggressive but nonviolent collective protest was a boycott of sacramental obligations: failing to attend mass on Sunday or locking the church doors so the priest could not enter; not appearing for instruction in doctrina; not making confession during Lent or declining to confess serious sins; and not calling the priest for last rites, baptisms, and burials.[157] Occasionally such boycotts amounted to open anticlericalism (see Appendix C), if not anti-Catholicism or anticolonialism. But generally, even a mass failure to fulfill the annual obligation was not a sign of widespread irreligion, only a protest against scheduled fees or services, changes in parish boundaries, or mistreatment.[158] It was a dramatic act that was certain to worry both the church hierarchy and royal officials rather than a permanent rejection of the religion. Rural parishioners also resisted by refusing to appoint a fiscal or accept the cura's choice for fiscal. Lay officials sometimes refused to do their duties.[159]

An especially irritating kind of passive resistance for curas must have been villagers' humbly agreeing to a settlement over fees and services, then refusing to follow it, or hiding an earlier written agreement from a new cura. At Nochtepec in the mountains above the parish seat of Pilcayan, near Taxco (Guerrero) in 1809, the pueblo agreed to the customary arrangement for clerical fees but would not adhere to it. Then, the villagers demanded the arancel and failed to follow that arrangement as well. The cura declared them to be "inflexible" in their demands and petitioned for an audiencia order "that they be obedient to their *cura* in everything," a blanket request that the court declined to grant.[160] This kind of complaint by curas was especially common in fees disputes after the 1767 arancel was available to Indian parishioners.

Occasionally, Indian parishioners insulted the priest to his face—calling him a robber, making fun of him in public—or openly defied him.[161] Usually, some specific grievance was involved, and the parishioners cloaked themselves in community rights or customary privileges (this pattern changed somewhat in the last decades of the colonial period, as the next section of this chapter suggests). Villagers of Mochitlan (Tixtla district, Guerrero), embroiled in a fees dispute with the cura in 1800, dutifully assembled for a recitation of the catechism after mass on Sunday, only to "act as if they [were] dumb and refuse to respond, even the children." [162] Indians of San Luis Xocotla and Santa María Nazintlan in the district of Chilapa (Guerrero) also turned a cold shoulder to their priest during litigation over services and mistreatment in the 1780's: "They treat me as if I were a nonentity, and do not speak to me. In short, they act as if I had inflicted the cruelest affronts."[163]

Although it was rare for a parish priest to be physically attacked, late colonial protests against his conduct sometimes turned violent. When they did, it was almost always in response to a provocative act by the priest. Moving or destroying objects belonging to the local church was especially likely to arouse general anger and violence. For example, friction in Tanicpatlan (Ichcateopan district, Guerrero) in 1809 originated in the cura's campaign against drunkenness and a poorly maintained church, but violence broke out only when he removed a worn altar cover and ceremoniously took it to the cemetery to burn.[164] Priests also touched off collective violence by selling building materials set aside for the church, humiliating or arresting local officials, imposing a resident vicario, demanding fees, or exchanging angry words with Indian leaders.[165]

Except for some concentration in the late 1760's, the 23 examples of tumultos against priests examined for this study were scattered through the period 1743–1809. The regional distribution, however, is striking. Some hot spots of resistance in general—especially the districts of Metepec, Cuernavaca, and Cuautla—are not so prominent among the tumultos. But the district of Zacualpan had five tumultos (Zacualpan 1747, Pozontepec 1758, Tototepec 1775, Apaxtla 1793, and Tanicpatlan 1809), and the vicinity of the Valley of Mexico had six (Xaltocan 1747, Tlalmanalco 1773, Churubusco 1785, Cuautitlan 1785, Amecameca 1796, and Atlautla 1799).[166] In three of the five cases for districts in modern Hidalgo, the priests were attacked and injured.[167]

Some Indians considered burning down the priest's residence. In a 1771 dispute with the cura over providing for his household needs, Indians of Iguala (Guerrero) inquired of a neighboring vicario whether "burning the priest with his house and all would get them into trouble."[168] During their tumulto against the cura of Ocuilan in 1772, Indians of Azingo (Malinalco district) reportedly threatened to burn down his residence.[169] In at least two instances, priests' houses were actually burned—at Tepecoacuilco (Guerrero) in 1743, and Pozontepec (near Sultepec, Edo. de México) in 1758[170]—but both were secretive acts, and it is not clear whether their inspiration was collective or individual.

Violence directed against parish priests in these two dioceses rarely approached a declaration of war against the church as an institution, but it did occasionally express a militant distance from the cura and a localism that bordered on a rejection of the church's version of Christianity as mediated by ordained priests. Huizquilucan near the Valley of Mexico, discussed in Part Three, is one case. Santa María Tututepec in the turbulent district of Meztitlan, where a millenarian movement against colonial authority had been quelled in 1769, is another. Twenty years later, the priest at Tututepec faced a bitter dispute over fees, services, and the parishioners' failure to maintain him. He told the audiencia that the parishioners had a tradition of tumultos and disrespect for the parish priest; that they worshipped idols in caves; and that two of his predecessors had been attacked and one injured. A former gobernador testified to the pueblo's frequent drinking bouts and affirmed that "this entire people has always been very restive and opposed to the *curas*."[171]

A "Spirit of Independence" and a Sense of Liberty

The late colonial judicial record repeatedly testifies to a spirit of independence, even lawlessness in colonial terms, in pueblos of the archdiocese. Some of the most eloquent testimonials come from parish priests—not surprisingly, since they were men of words and the defendants in many of the lawsuits. In 1758, at the beginning of a long-running dispute over fee payments at Tepetlaostoc and Apipilhuasco, the Dominican doctrinero observed that his Indians "have been studying ways to return to their old style of life. . . . Since they always keep control of the government, the *cura* and *alcalde mayor* will never know what is going on there. Rather, they will always keep local business to themselves." Three years later, the doctrinero added that these Indians lived like "so many heathens or brutes without the slightest recognition or obedience to any ecclesiastical or secular superior." Fifteen years later, his diocesan successor said of the people of Apipilhuasco:

Their character has always been audacious, full of wickedness, arrogance, and a continual unruliness not only toward their *cura*, but also toward the secular magistrates who could hold them in check if they wanted to because they can punish them with greater freedom and rigor; [these Indians] only recognize their *tlatoques* as their superiors.[172]

In a bitter dispute over fees that culminated in 1771, the cura of San Felipe del Obraje (Edo. de México) criticized the Indians' "idiocy" and "desire for freedom of conscience. . . . They live without law and like barbarians." The principal instigator of the pressure for the arancel, he said, had passed out slips of paper (*cedulillas*) with the word "aranzelado" written on them, "and with these as the authentic instrument of his liberty, the Indian believes he can govern himself independent of any superior authority."[173] Recall also the response of the alcalde of Alahuistlan in 1786 when the cura demanded to know who had released a local man he had jailed: not once, but twice, and with repeated heat, he shouted that it was "the *pueblo*, everyone big and small."[174]

Even where the elaboration is exquisite, these propositions about particular pueblos are subject to some doubt because they express the priest's self-justification.[175] But the geographical and temporal distribution of twenty cases in which priests' descriptions of "pernicious Indian liberty" are corroborated by testimony of witnesses in the same records suggests that they are distorted truths more than simply the interested claims of dishonored or frustrated pastors. Rather than appearing all over the map, these characterizations by priests are concentrated in and near the district of Zacualpan in the modern State of Mexico, adjoining districts of Metepec and modern Morelos, and Hidalgo. And they are scattered in time from 1758 to 1809, representing the claims of many priests, not just one or two.[176]

Several cases from these places contain other testimony to habitual resistance. The judge in a prolonged land suit involving Coatepec (Malinalco district, Edo. de México) concluded in 1798 that the Indians there "live at liberty, employed in their vices, especially drunkenness and robbery."[177] After a tumulto involving two small pueblos in the district of Meztitlan (Hidalgo) in 1777, several non-Indian witnesses testified that no royal judge had dared to venture into the area in more than six years.[178] The schoolmaster of Pozontepec in the district of Temascaltepec testified in 1758 that local Indians resisted having a resident priest because they wanted to "live free to indulge in their chronic drunkenness."[179] Intendant Ugarte of Guadalajara believed that Indian pueblos even very close to Mexico City resisted learning Spanish and clung to their own languages because they wanted to hide their thoughts from Spaniards.[180]

Colonial law had long encouraged Indians in pueblos to express their rights in terms of *libertad*, although it had in mind mainly their exemption from slavery and a rather nebulous community privilege, always tempered by obligations and restrictions.[181] Indian petitioners were likely to acknowledge these limits. As Santiago Tecali's representatives said in 1735, "we are using our legal resources in order to free ourselves from so many exactions, [but] we know very well that we have a king, an *alcalde mayor*, and a magistrate to obey (except in the matter of *repartimientos* because royal law says we are exempt)."[182] Still, their sense of liberty gave rise to some grand, metaphorical claims about slavery and freedom, and to a tetchiness about their rights.[183] In the 1781 Tlaltizapan case, in which the cura wrote that "they live in total independence and complete libertinism, and I cannot find any way to subjugate them," the Indian villagers of Huispaleca and Cuanacalcingo shot back that he treated them as if they were "perpetual slaves, without rations or pay from the *cura*."[184] Sixteen years later, the people of Tlaltizapan renewed their complaints against the cura's demands for money and service and his role in local elections. Their claim then was for the "full liberty they ought to enjoy in their elections."[185] The parameters of this pueblo "liberty" became less clear after 1808, with the suspension of the Bourbon monarchy in Spain.

*   *   *

Although the kinds of resistance to parish priests described here might have prepared individuals and communities for the idea of political combat in the future, they did not become instruments of more than very limited social and political change at the time. Nearly all had a collective dimension that reaffirmed community membership and intended to restore a right relationship with colonial authorities in colonial terms. They expressed membership in that larger society and acceptance of its hierarchy even as they intended to express local autonomy. But collective or representative action was not always a timeless affirmation of tradition. Especially in the archdiocese, many Indian parishioners in the late eighteenth century took their cues from Bourbon policies and questioned the place of the priests in the public life of the parish and their influence over local leadership.

There was more of an anticlerical edge to these actions now, especially in the greater Toluca Valley (from Zacualpan and Temascaltepec to Xilotepec) and Morelos, but it was not deeply anti-Catholic. Local religion itself was not sharply anticlerical, and priests remained the object of reverence and a vital resource in local society even as the political confrontations increased. On the curas' side, these changes again put them in the position of defending custom—here against local leaders who were turning to their own advantage the Bourbon revival of formal law and standardized regulations.

CHAPTER FIFTEEN

Leadership and Dissension in Pueblo Politics

Harassed for ages and compelled to a blind obedience, he [the Indian] wishes to tyrannize in his turn. The Indian villages are governed by magistrates of the copper-coloured race; and an Indian *alcalde* exercises his power with so much the greater severity because he is sure of being supported by the priest or the Spanish *subdelegado*. Oppression produces everywhere the same effects, it everywhere corrupts the morals.
—Alexander von Humboldt, 1805

These unfortunates are very inclined to lie about their *curas*. . . . If their leaders did not find it so easy to make believers of the Indians, they would not have the parishes in such an uproar. —Dr. Joseph de Zelada,
cura of San Felipe del Obraje,
district of Metepec, 1771

The attention of modern scholars to collective expressions of religion and politics in colonial communities has helped to correct an earlier historiographical tendency to reduce Mexico's rural history, at least before the Revolution of 1910, to a tale of unrelieved victimization, starting with the armed conquest of the sixteenth century.[1] Exposing a more complex past than this, one that is not simply littered with deracinated descendants of the precolonial population, has been important. But it is easy to overemphasize the solidarity of colonial Indian communities. Whether described as approximations of the earlier altepetl, districts of cabeceras and sujetos, pueblos, or combinations of extended families, neighborhoods, and moieties (halves; the typical dual organization of Indian settlements), these communities were not anthills in which the individual's actions were unconditionally determined by his or her position in a fixed social order. Many of the great number of lawsuits brought to colonial courts in the name of Indian pueblos were fashioned by a few people claiming to represent the community. Sometimes they did represent the community, but it was not always clear who could speak for the whole. Most communities did not speak with one voice, and some were more prone than others to internal conflict, factionalism, and caciquismo.[2] This chapter completes the colonial Indian corner of the triangle of local authority by considering it from within and among communities rather than out from solidary cabeceras. It focuses less on the authority of Catholic priests in their parishes than on fights for authority within districts, parishes, and pueblos.

Tensions Between Cabecera and Sujeto

As Charles Gibson recognized, colonial Indian governments changed especially in the promotion of sujetos to cabecera status: "The conflicts of status between cabeceras and sujetos repeatedly took the form of disputes over political organization," with sujetos sometimes separating off to form their own cabildos.[3] This kind of political dissent was especially evident during the eighteenth century, as the population grew, economic pursuits shifted, and the numbers of non-Indians residing in rural districts increased,[4] affecting the distribution of wealth and interests within old territories.

There were far more cabecera-sujeto disputes in the second half of the century than in the first half, with concentrations during 1755–69 and 1785–94. Of 35 cases documented between 1710 and 1819, only six occurred before 1754, compared with eight between 1755 and 1769 and nine between 1785 and 1794.[5] All but one were located in the Archdiocese of Mexico. Given the social and economic organization of parishes and districts in the Diocese of Guadalajara, this imbalance is not surprising. They were larger; their populations were more dispersed; and they were less rooted in the boundaries of former native states (which, in any event, were being stretched by late colonial demographic, economic, and political changes). More people were drawn out of the Guadalajara pueblos onto haciendas and ranchos, and into long-distance trade that kept them away from the pueblo for months or years at a time.[6] And fewer sujetos grew sufficiently to rival the cabecera as a center of population, production, and trade.[7]

Within the archdiocese, these struggles were concentrated in the modern state of Hidalgo and the southwestern part of the Estado de México, plus the vicinity of the Valley of Mexico. The district of Temascaltepec led with eight cases (which fits with an 1801 report that cabeceras were exceptionally numerous in this district).[8] The neighboring Toluca valley had five cases, and the Valley of Mexico area six, so that a relatively small part of central Mexico accounts for over half the cabecera-sujeto disputes. The districts of Xilotepec, with five cases, and Meztitlan and Guayacocotla, with six, give Hidalgo most of the remaining cases. Modern Morelos accounts for three, and the district of Tixtla (Guerrero) two.

The Hidalgo and central Mexico cases can serve to describe some larger patterns in the sample, although in the Meztitlan and Guayacocotla cases, which date from 1786 to 1818, the sujetos were not appealing for political separation or a separate parish. In effect, they already enjoyed a de facto separation from their cabeceras, or at least enough independence to cause their curas and gobernadores to enter legal complaints against them for lack of obedience and service to their superiors.[9]

In the district of Xilotepec, four of the five cases of resistance by sujetos (dating from 1761 to 1790) were closely associated with administrative changes.[10]

San Luis de las Peras's 1785 complaint of a lack of spiritual care followed the parish priest's removal of its vicario de pie fijo, a position created after Lorenzana's pastoral visit in 1769. In Santa María Atengo and San Francisco Zayula, the secularization of the parish led to confusion over what was owed, new demands by cabecera leaders for cash payments and labor, and resistance by sujeto Indians to paying and serving the cura in Tepetitlan.

In the other two cases, sujetos reacted against the division of their parishes. In the new parish of Acambay, throughout the 1760's, the pueblo of San Pedro and three rancherías that had recently been separated from their political cabecera of Xilotepec resisted paying for more frequent local masses and were undecided about whether they would provide the customary labor service in Acambay or opt for the arancel. In the other case, the cabecera of Chapatongo had trouble establishing administrative authority over communities added to the parish in 1755, especially the rancho Simapantongo.

Simapantongo had originated as an estate of the Cofradía del Santísimo Sacramento of Xilotepec in the early 1600's, and the people there still regarded the mayordomo of the cofradía as their governor. As part of the parish of Xilotepec, they had received visits by the cura or vicario every three weeks for mass, and for two special fiestas, annual confession, baptisms, and last rites. After the division of Xilotepec, the cura required the rancho residents to come to Chapatongo for weekly mass, baptisms, marriages, and burials. (Simapantongans had given up having Sunday masses in their community in exchange for the cura's forgiving their 177-peso debt, a decision they later regretted.) They wanted to go on having their relatives buried in Simapantongo, and the trips to Chapatongo for Sunday mass were a special hardship because many of the local people were potters who needed to travel to Sunday markets in other towns. The cura's position was that they should have mass in Simapantongo only if it were treated as a formal sujeto, which meant paying for a weekly mass at the prescribed fee (the 1767 arancel called for a higher fee in sujetos and provided for it to be levied three times as often as Simapantongo had been used to). The cura blamed the cofradía mayordomo for interfering and acting as if he were the judge and governor of the settlement. He also objected to the local practices of ringing the bells when the mayordomo arrived and using the community's chapel at night for "músicas y bailes indecentes" without his permission.

A written agreement between the cura and leaders of Simapantongo was signed at the beginning of 1775, but the tension continued for at least another four years, with the cura withholding the bells and images of saints he had taken from the local chapels and the capitán's house. A "final" judgment was issued in April 1779, specifying that the images and bells were to be returned, and that the priest would come for mass every three weeks, and would come for burials in the chapel, annual confessions, and the two special feast days. Except for the potters, local residents were to go to Chapatongo for Sunday mass two weeks out of three and equip their chapel properly for services; and the cofradía officials from Xilotepec were to limit themselves to the operation of their estate. Celebrations for a saint were to be held only with the cura's license and instruction, and both the cura and the parishioners were to perform their mutual duties.

The Temascaltepec cases, combined with those from the adjacent Toluca

Valley and districts in and near the Valley of Mexico, reveal more initiative by the sujetos themselves and a deeply adversarial relationship with their cabeceras (and, consequently, often with the cura). The disputes here seem to have been more intricate than those in Hidalgo, but sujetos in both areas moved at about the same time toward administrative independence and enthusiastic petitions for the arancel of 1767 as a way to escape service to the cabecera. By 1760, pueblos in the Temascaltepec parish of Tejupilco had already prepared for separation by building and maintaining fine churches. Their complaints were directed more against the cura than against the gobernador of the cabecera, whom they supported in his appeal for the arancel and against the new cura's objections to local fiesta customs and the use of a native oil for the lamp.[11] The pueblo of San Simón Tototepec (Zacualpan district, Edo. de México), with the support of Santiago Ixcatepec and San Agustín Almoloya, petitioned for a separate parish in 1788 because the cura had effectively denied their coequal standing with Acapetlahuaya. Though they had succeeded in getting a vicario de pie fijo some years before, the three pueblos kept pressing to be formed into a parish because their residents still had to serve in Acapetlahuaya and go there for marriages and confession.[12]

The Toluca Valley cases spread across the eighteenth century but otherwise followed the pattern of initiatives for separate parishes.[13] At least half the cases in and near the Valley of Mexico fell in the 1740's and 1750's, and most combined moves toward a resident vicario de pie fijo or an independent parish with objections to serving the cura in the cabecera.[14] One striking exception was an uprising against the cura by the Indians of Xaltocan (Zumpango district, north rim of the valley) in 1747, when he tried to move their holy images to the new parish seat of Santa Ana Xaltengo. What with the transfer of the church ornaments (especially a revered image of Christ), the demotion of the Xaltocan church to visita status, and the priest building himself a sumptuous home in Xaltengo, a serious conflict had been growing for more than a year.[15]

Divisions Within Pueblos

Resolute as some pueblos were in the struggle for authority, more fought that battle out internally. In 58 instances between 1685 and 1819, these contests for pueblo leadership were serious enough to reach the courts. Both the timing and the geography of these cases are interesting. The clearest temporal concentration was between 1790 and 1810, suggesting that such struggles were not immediately triggered by the reforms of the 1750's and 1760's. The regional pattern has several unusual features. The districts of Temascaltepec and Metepec, which are heavily represented in other kinds of conflict, appear less often in these cases (nine cases between them), suggesting that political conflict there was directed more against colonial officials than against rivals within the community. Hidalgo had eight cases, about the same share as for other kinds of conflict documented there. The more "open" or "centrifugal" settlements of the Diocese of Guadalajara are conspicuous in this kind of conflict, with sixteen cases,[16] as are communities in and near the Valley of Mexico (eleven cases) and modern Morelos (five cases).

What was in play in these internal struggles? Were they factional disputes that threatened parish priests as well as the community? Some striking differences both between individual pueblos and across regions are evident, but the limited vocabulary of the documentation tends to obscure the particulars in most of these cases. Only a few Spanish terms were used to characterize rival groups within a community. The most common were *parcialidad* and *bando*. Parcialidad could denote a large section of a town, but both terms also meant "faction" in the loaded sense of "an oligarchical clique . . . with selfish or mischievous ends or turbulent or unscrupulous methods," as well as dissension and sedition.[17] The terms themselves reveal more about colonial preoccupations with order and wholeness than about actual divisions within communities and their implications for power relationships. Often enough, the divisions involved rivalries that could turn violent; and the willingness to take such disagreements to court indicates some reluctance or inability to resolve them without mediation. But, as Duane Champagne warns, an indiscriminate use of the term "faction" to characterize the actions of groups within a community assumes crisis and the onset of a permanent separation, where only routine conflict and contained competition may be involved.[18]

What parish priests, district judges, and Indian witnesses said about the circumstances of particular events, apart from these headline words, suggests three main generators of internal political conflict: local elections, clerical fees, and personal struggles for power. Priests and district governors were involved, but judging by the kinds of struggles that entered into nearly every case, they were incidental to many of them.

A particularly common locus of internal disputes in the Diocese of Guadalajara was the election of community officers. At La Barca (Jalisco) in January 1708, for example, eleven petitioners, including the newly elected alcaldes, complained to the alcalde mayor and the audiencia that the previous year's officials and their allies had left the election meeting without voting and were trying to keep their own people in office by contesting the results before the audiencia.[19] At Tututepec (Hidalgo) in 1796, two groups struggling to capture the oficios mayores accused each other of cultivating alliances with, respectively, the cura and the lieutenant. One group of past officials and their allies claimed that the current gobernador and his supporters were able to manipulate the elections with the lieutenant's help; he, in turn, accused the accusers of supporting the cura's abusive collection practices and demands for service, and claimed that the cura had had people arrested so his supporters would be in the majority on election day. This was not the kind of dispute that would be resolved with a bland order from the audiencia for all parties to obey the law and the lieutenant to supervise elections.[20]

These disputes over elections generally pitted groups of principales against each other, especially in situations where one group was gaining advantage, where the cura or a district judge had become an influential partisan, or where the community was divided over some particular issue. At San Martín (Tonalá district, Jalisco) in 1791, for example, a group of twelve principales denounced the subdelegado for encouraging the candidacy of young men with no experience, whom they called a *pandilla* or gang. The subdelegado admitted that there were bitter arguments among the voters and that he had removed the escribano for just cause, but he claimed that he had simply confirmed the election results submitted to him, without favoring any candidate. The trouble, he said, stemmed from the carelessness and contempt of the current alcalde and regidor; they ignored the traditional principales and were appointing new ones without consultation or a formal vote.[21] At San Gerónimo Xomulco (Ahuacatlan district, Jalisco) in 1749, a divided electorate apparently had led to a rift between the Franciscan doctrinero and the alcalde mayor. The doctrinero complained that the alcalde mayor had chosen the new alcalde; the alcalde mayor responded that he had merely broken an impasse when the two parcialidades of electors had been unable to decide on a candidate.[22] And at Tlajomulco (Jalisco) in 1817, a newly inflamed division between two rival groups of Indian electors reportedly resulted from disagreement over whether the current officials had done well in allowing non-Indians to move into the community and share in its lands.[23]

Especially after 1767, some pueblos in central Mexico divided over whether to petition for the arancel or continue with customary arrangements for the support of the parish priests. At the cabecera of San Simón Tototepec in 1775, Indian officials and the cura blamed eleven Indians and a mulato of Tehuistla for persuading nearly half of their pueblo to oppose the arancel.[24] And at Capuluac (Tenango del Valle district) in 1796, an anxious cura explained the persistent complaints against him over clerical fees as the result of a lack of consensus about whether the community should choose the arancel or custom: "I notice that the Indians are divided, some favoring custom and others the *arancel*. To resolve this predicament will require all of Your Excellency's authority."[25] More was involved in the internal divisions of the late 1740's in the district of Actopan (Hidalgo) over whether to seek the arancel. In 1746, most non-Indians in the area, especially the owners of haciendas, wanted the cura tied to the arancel. The principales and some local Spaniards favored custom, but most macehuales of the cabecera apparently preferred not to perform the customary labor service. Thirty-one of them joined the non-Indian vecinos in a successful petition for the arancel. But the matter did not end there. By mid-1748, the Indians of Actopan were, according to the alcalde mayor, deeply divided over the new regime. The cura had mobilized a large number of them to request a return to custom, while another influential priest, a local hacendado who served as the juez eclesiástico of the parish, firmly supported the arancel. The non-Indians also were more divided than before.[26]

These internal disputes often coalesced around kin and residential units, especially moieties and barrios. In the Diocese of Guadalajara, for example, the prolonged disputes over elections in Tlaltenango (Zacatecas) at the end of the eighteenth century (described later in this chapter) involved rivals from the barrio de arriba and the barrio de abajo (upper and lower barrios).[27] Barrios also initiated action at Xalpan (in the district of Juchipila, near Tlaltenango) in 1797 and 1818, and Teocaltiche (Jalisco) in June 1810.[28] In central Mexico, where dual divisions of this kind are better known, some of the political friction also involved ethnic groups or formerly separated communities that were resettled as barrios of a larger community.[29] At Azcapotzalco in the Valley of Mexico, for example, a land dispute between the Mexicanos and Tepanecos parcialidades (large ethnic sections of the town) was resolved in 1753 by assigning each of them one half of the *tierras de comunidad*.[30] The cura of Cempoala, just north of the Valley of

Mexico, responded to a 1788 suit over fees and forced labor by claiming that the community did not speak with one voice on the matter: one of the two barrios served without complaint and preferred the customary arrangement. As it happened, the barrio that supported him was a former pueblo called Zacuala, which by the late seventeenth century had moved to the eastern edge of Cempoala to form the barrio San Lorenzo.[31]

In some cases, disputes cut across residential and kinship groups—for instance, in election disputes where macehuales pressed for voting rights against the principales of the community. The area in and near the district of Metepec (Edo. de México), already shaken by the issue in 1641–42 and 1685 (at Ixtlahuaca and Atlacomulco, respectively), witnessed additional pressures by macehuales for voting and officeholding privileges at Ixtlahuaca and Temascaltepec in 1768.[32] Violent action on New Year's Day of 1799 at Tlaylotlatlan, a barrio of Amecameca (Chalco district, southeast of the Valley of Mexico), also pitted macehuales against privileged Indians of the community, but the issue here was land, not elections. A servant of the Riberas, hereditary nobles whose leading member was described as a mine operator at Real del Monte (Hidalgo), was attacked by a crowd demanding that the Riberas not be put in possession of lands awarded to them by the audiencia. In the alcalde mayor's judgment, the gobernador was to blame, stirring up the Indians of Tlaylotlatlan as a "caudillo y cabeza de bando."[33] If the curas can be believed, many of the suits and disturbances against them were really the work of a few "bandos" (factions) of ambitious or vengeful men who seized the initiative in the name of the community and occasionally gained wide support. (Sometimes the curas were right.)

Divisions crosscutting kin and residential groups also occurred when outsiders insinuated themselves into local politics, as they reportedly had at Hueyapan (Morelos) in the 1780's—becoming electors, winning office, and redistributing land in favor of their partisans in ways that brought rivalries and violence to the surface[34]—but these situations seem to have developed mostly where there were problems with the cura. Again, curas claimed that these movements were the machinations of small minorities, as at Zinacantepec (Metepec district), where in 1796 a past alcalde and five active allies were able to magnify their personal resentments against the cura into a fairly widespread defiance of his authority and judicial complaints against him in the name of the community. Indian witnesses later testified that they were basically content with the cura and would not have joined the opposition to him without the prodding of these "cabecillas" (rebel leaders).[35] At Ajuchitlan (Tetela del Río district, Guerrero) in 1790, the cura reportedly stirred rancorous divisions in the community by creating what amounted to a personal police force and winning over some Indians of the cabecera with promises of revenge against their enemies.[36]

Legal Entrepreneurship

The Fourth Provincial Council (1771) identified a particularly troublesome kind of leader in late colonial pueblos de indios: an aspirant to political power, though not usually an elected officer, who depended on the power of litigation and his knowledge of legal forms, royal decrees, lawyers, and court procedures:

Experience teaches that Indians often present briefs with charges against priests in the name of the *gobernadores*, *alcaldes*, magistrate, and community, without a signature. And it turns out that the brief is the work of one devious person, [usually] a non-Indian. To stop this kind of activity, this Council orders that the bishops determine if the complaints of the natives are true, if they are induced [by someone else], if they are the product of malice, if the *gobernadores* and magistrates are involved, and if the signatures are authentic.[37]

These legal entrepreneurs might, as prelates and curas imagined, be a devious outsider leading gullible Indians into malicious complaints; he might be a self-important man with private ambitions that would one day propel him into personalist power far beyond these beginnings; but he might also have gained broad support by asserting rights in the name of the pueblo, expanding its political freedom, and overcoming local political divisions.

In any case, late colonial legal entrepreneurs perched on the edge of legitimacy. In the name of the law, they circumvented constituted authority. They took the name of the community without holding the offices that would have allowed them to do so; or, if they did hold office, they exceeded their authority in the eyes of their colonial superiors. They went outside traditional authority to mediate a colonial relationship, taking a risk that might disgrace them or add greatly to their local influence. Their staying power depended largely on whether they were able to displace the usual authorities or fill a vacuum by coercion and intimidation, and on whether they won at court. And their chances of winning were, at this period, much improved if the object of their briefs was a parish priest.

The mixture of coercion and consensus building used by such leaders is reflected in how they financed their activities. Rather than demanding funds from the community chest or seizing lands, at least at the beginning they drew upon a customary colonial device with precolonial antecedents: the derrama or collection of a small sum from every household. Colonial derramas had been sanctioned in the backhanded Hapsburg way and used by Indian officials and parish priests from the sixteenth century. Late-sixteenth- and early-seventeenth-century laws of the *Recopilación* specified that parish priests were not to "echar derramas" among their Indian parishioners on their own no matter what the circumstances. If they considered such collections essential, they must go to the viceroy or president of the audiencia for a determination.[38] From the sixteenth century, Indian gobernadores had exacted derramas to cover the tribute of absent community members and pay for religious fiestas (with the attendant complaints that they were keeping for themselves some of the money collected).[39]

Parish priests requested and sometimes received permission to collect derramas throughout the colonial period, both to cover extraordinary expenses and to institutionalize responsibility for recurrent ones. But generally these initiatives were grounded—or at least said to be grounded—in traditional practices. When the cura of Tejupilco (Temascaltepec district, Edo. de México) proposed in 1732—over the Indians' objections—that the people of San Lucas pay off their 170-peso debt to him by derrama, he cited the long-standing custom there of Indian burials being covered with a donation of one-half real from every family, and major feast days being supported with a collection of four reales per macehual.[40] At Xochiatipan (Sochicoatlan district, Hidalgo), until the early 1790's,

Indian parishioners customarily paid what was called the *mextomín*—two reales per family for each new moon.[41] The manípulos discussed in Chapter 6 were a form of derrama based on local agreements between the priest and pueblo officials; and late colonial curas were quick to use them as a precedent for additional collections or new agreements to avoid the arancel.[42] To ease their dependence on the community's obligatory payments, secular curas urged the use of derramas as a convenient way to create new cofradías and pay for essential supplies like chrism and oil for the lamp.[43]

Some priests understood themselves to be in competition with other officials for collections. The cura of Sultepec (Edo. de México) complained in 1750 that his Indian parishioners were not paying their obvenciones on time because others went to them for "extraordinary donations." Indian villagers, then, knew and generally accepted derramas as a form of taxation in the community interest. Indeed, given the option of working on a communal farm or contributing half a fanega of grain or a small cash sum for the pueblo treasury, late colonial Indian families of central Mexico typically chose the family payment plan.

Community lawsuits were often financed through derramas. The possibility of coercion was real enough, but curas and district governors recognized that villagers often willingly supported derramas for litigation. In Omerick's words, Indians of central Mexico had "an insatiable thirst for land suits" and complaints against their curas.[44] The Franciscan doctrinero of Xiuctepec (Morelos), writing about Texalpa in 1752, was convinced that if the Indians did not have litigation pending, it was only because they could not get enough money to fight:

Their way of getting it is to collect *derramas* of a *peso* or four *reales* per person to begin, proceed with, and finish the lawsuit. The *cabecillas* [leaders] do not hesitate to ask for [additional contributions], nor do the rest hesitate to contribute with great pleasure as often as they are asked, even if the dispute goes on for a long time.[45]

Derramas for this purpose were granted or not according to the district governors' sizing up of the situation. They were understandably inclined to back an enterprise in which they stood to profit from the need for notarized documents and judicial proceedings. For example, when the community leaders of Santa Ana Tepetitlan near Guadalajara petitioned for permission to "echar derramas" to cover the costs of pending land suits and boundary measurements in 1808, the subdelegado (who was going to benefit from the resulting legal work) warmly recommended the license, arguing that "almost all the Indians are quick to contribute *derrama*."[46] The trick was to take the measure of the promoters of the derramas and their motives. As the curas of Cuanacalcingo and Tepoztlan (Morelos) complained in the late eighteenth century, local men were undertaking derramas not only to make trouble for them in court but to make a comfortable living for themselves.[47]

But, then, legal entrepreneurs like these were hardly working under license. In 1690, the gobernador of Tlapanaloya (Atitalaquia district, Hidalgo) collected money from villagers to bring suit against the alcalde mayor for extortion.[48] The Zinacantepec pueblo of San Antonio (Metepec district) habitually paid derramas to support litigation in the name of the community by a local specialist—a seventy-year-old elder who had been collecting two reales a week from each family for community land suits between 1785 and 1797. He reportedly took clothing or chickens from those who did not pay in cash and was accountable to no one. The villagers never objected, but the parish priest did.[49]

Indeed, it was usually parish priests and district judges rather than villagers who complained of collections for community litigation. Nevertheless, communities were divided in ways that could give a coercive edge to the derramas. In a 1795 case from Capuluac (Tenango del Valle district), for example, the community scribe and his wife had been beaten when they refused to contribute one and a half reales to four men who were collecting for a suit against the cura over fees and services.[50] According to the subdelegado, the informal cabecilla of the pueblo, Yldefonso Reyes, had long been an enemy of the curas and collected two reales per household when he wanted to make trouble for them in court. Giving flesh to this indictment, the scribe portrayed Reyes as a man who acted as if he feared no judge, intimidating past officials to sign his petitions and repeatedly telling the cura that the Indians would pay him nothing "because they have a good lawyer." One of Reyes's accomplices testified that they had gone out collecting for an injunction against the cura (for half a real, not one and a half), and that they did it "on their own authority," without seeking the gobernador's or the cabildo's permission. Reyes, a thirty-five-year-old tributary, testified that he had promoted the suit over manípulos but denied injuring the scribe and his wife. The cura and scribe wanted Reyes depicted as a lone seducer of ignorant Indians, but the record shows that the original suit against the cura was brought by the gobernador and other Indian officials, not just Reyes, and that it was the scribe who was the villain in the eyes of the community: when Reyes was arrested, a crowd of more than 40 people had taken the scribe to the subdelegado for punishment and demanded the release of Reyes and two others.

Legal entrepreneurship directed against the cura was not a new development in the late colonial period. One early-eighteenth-century case that is well documented from more than one viewpoint occurred in the district of Metepec in 1711. In that year, the gobernador of Calimaya complained to the audiencia that San Mateo Mexicalcingo, San Miguel Chapultepec, Nativitas, and a fourth pueblo de visita were demanding a resident priest for their part of the parish. Seeking to protect his own community's territorial influence and the financial base of the parish church, the gobernador argued that the visitas' petitions did not really represent the will of the pueblos but had been confected by Lorenzo de Santa María and an assistant, who had "undertaken to manage and promote the natives' lawsuits and extract from them large sums of cash." These two men were continually creating new lawsuits as a way to increase their influence and enrich themselves. Now that the visitas had secured resident Franciscans, they were acting as if they were a separate parish, refusing to provide laborers to rebuild the parish church in Calimaya.

Although the interests involved were murky, there apparently was a large core of truth to the gobernador's claims. The judicial inquiry, which relied heavily on the testimony of elderly creole landowners in the vicinity who had known Santa María for many years, established that he was a native of Tepemaxalco who had married into the pueblo of Asunción and resided there until he was expelled after an unspecified dispute. He had gone to live in San Mateo Mexicalcingo and had eventually become the gobernador there for at least one term after the pueblo gained its own government. He maintained his home in San Mateo but reportedly was a frequent visitor to pueblos in this and other districts, promoting lawsuits against neighboring communities, local officials, and parish priests. He had succeeded in obtaining a resident Franciscan for Mexicalcingo after taking chickens, money, and other gifts to Mexico City, and now had persuaded Mexicalcingo and Chapultepec to stop performing service in Calimaya.[51] Baltasar Atencio, a seventy-year-old creole native and lifelong resident of Calimaya, testified that Santa María bore the nickname Trampa ("trap" or "trickster") and was "exceedingly untrustworthy and rebellious." Atencio claimed that he had been a corporal in a militia troop that had arrested Santa María in 1692 and found him in possession of forged land records relating to haciendas of the Conde de Sano. Another witness implied that Santa María represented a faction of San Mateo, not the whole community. The witnesses unanimously believed that Santa María was behind many of the disputes within and between pueblos in the district, and that he lived comfortably from the derramas.

The visitas involved clearly did not speak with one voice. Representatives of Nativitas testified that leaders of San Mateo (Santa María's base) had gotten them into this suit against their better judgment, and that they had always regarded Calimaya as their parish seat and preferred to serve it rather than San Mateo. But even as the audiencia wrestled with this case, San Mateo and Chapultepec were continuing to press the case against serving in Calimaya since they now had their own resident priests. Meanwhile, Santa María had been arrested by the gobernador of Calimaya, and on October 8, 1712, representatives of San Mateo appealed for his release on the grounds that he had simply been defending the interests of his pueblo. Santa María himself admitted that he had collected 25 pesos one week but said it was all for litigation in defense of community lands.[52]

While legal entrepreneurship as a basis for political power was not new, it did increase in the late eighteenth century in response to new opportunities opened by changing royal policy,[53] especially in the 1760's and between 1790 and 1810. Of 42 cases that I could document between 1708 and 1818, fully 38 occurred in the 1750's or after. In the 1760's (nine cases), the main issues were new policies on clerical fees, labor service, corporal punishment, and the judicial role of parish priests. The 1790's and 1800's cases (sixteen) were associated with the intendancy reforms and a second phase of concerted parish reforms.

The regional distribution of the 40 cases that could be located by place only partly follows the pattern for resistance to parish priests in general. Temascaltepec-Zacualpan and districts in the modern state of Hidalgo lead the way with eight and seven cases, respectively, concentrated in the years after 1765; and Morelos is well represented with six cases, all in the second half of the century. In all three places, the proportions are close to those for divisions within pueblos and all categories of resistance combined. But the area in and near the Valley of Mexico offers only two cases of legal entrepreneurship (Apipilhuasco in the district of Tepetlaostoc in 1758 and Milpa Alta in the district of Xochimilco in 1790), compared with eleven cases of local divisions (in the seventeenth and eighteenth centuries) and general resistance to curas. The district of Metepec is represented equally in cases expressing local division and legal entrepreneurship, but was much more likely to experience cabecera-sujeto conflict and general resistance to curas. Pueblos of the audiencia district of Nueva Galicia (including the Diocese of Guadalajara) predictably are better represented in cases of local divisions (sixteen) than of effective legal entrepreneurship directed against parish priests (two—La Barca in 1708 and Zapotitlan in 1805–6).

Sometimes it was the gobernador, alcaldes, and a few other officials out in front acting on their own. Although the gobernador's credibility ultimately depended on performance,[54] he had a legitimate claim to speak for the community. But these lawsuits were a way to expand his power beyond the office, to establish a claim to a more durable personal leadership. In 1752, the cura of Juchipila (Zacatecas), Antonio Ruiz Olachea, attempted to rein in one such elected leader when he accused Francisco Bentura, the alcalde of Guanusco, of disobedience. He and his witnesses claimed that Bentura encouraged local people to disobey the lieutenant and the cura, did not attend mass, interfered with prosecutions of illicit sex, incited the community to violence against Indians of Mecatabasco, and made virtually all decisions in dealings with outsiders.[55]

Gobernadores generally consented to pueblo litigation, if they did not lead it,[56] but since they were not likely to serve successive terms, their opportunities for wealth and power through litigation were unpredictable. In many communities, a gobernador's pursuit of litigation required a local consensus (at least among the principales) and was usually understood to be in the defense of community interests. The gobernador of Temascaltepec promoted a suit against the recently arrived cura over fees, services, and the management of cofradía property in 1790 after the cura moved to rent cofradía lands to non-Indians.[57] In doing so, the gobernador responded to his constituency's fears that the cura was proceeding "to destroy the *pueblo* and make it into a community of Spaniards" (destruir el pueblo y hacerlo de españoles).[58] Still, the gobernador of Tejupilco in the same district 30 years before had managed to elevate his fortunes and power substantially through litigation and reelection. According to the cura, the gobernador was "accustomed to go about soliciting the Indians' power of attorney in this and other districts," bribe judges, and promote disputes against curas with derramas that made him rich in the process. His reelection, said the cura, was made possible by the collusion of the alcalde mayor (a partnership that he disdained as a disreputable mixture of "the characteristic malignity of the *alcalde mayor* and the seditious ambition of the *gobernador*"). It was a story of rags-to-riches corruption in the cura's telling: from "a poor Indian reduced to his cotton cloak enduring the distresses that are common among his kind, [the gobernador] is now very well dressed, carries arms, raises livestock, and owns a *rancho* and a mill."[59]

Although any elected community officer could pose as the voice of the community,[60] litigious Indian alcaldes and minor cabildo officials were in a weaker position than the gobernador to turn litigation to personal advantage. They had neither his high authority (and could more easily be dismissed by the courts as cranks) nor the freedom of action of a non-officeholder. Without strong local support, their role as spokesmen could deteriorate quickly. At Alahuistlan (Ichcateopan district, Guerrero) in 1795, a petition to expel the local tobacco monopolist was discredited because it was brought by an alcalde whom the defendant labeled an inveterate litigator ("pleitista").[61] At Huiciltepec, Puebla, legal complaints against the cura from 1793 to 1803 over fees and cofradías were ultimately disregarded because the driving force behind them was an alcalde who persisted in going to court even after promising to desist. The intendant finally ordered the subdelegado to replace him with someone more "tranquil and discreet."[62]

Among other officeholders, escribanos were particularly well placed to promote lawsuits in the name of the community and increase their personal prestige and local influence, especially if they had a good command of Spanish. They were most likely to know something about colonial law and have contacts in the administrative capital. Gerónimo Gutiérrez, for example, the Indian escribano of La Barca (Jalisco), was quick to advise a disgruntled faction of leading men who had lost the pueblo election of 1708 to appeal the results to the audiencia and even offered them lodging in a friend's house near the court in Guadalajara.[63] At San Simón Tototepec (Zacualpan district, Edo. de México) in 1803, the lieutenant understood the escribano to be the moving force behind the suit against him over the control of community lands. Even though the pueblo's case was well received by the audiencia, the escribano was reprimanded as "the seducer of the Indians of his *pueblo*, getting them agitated and stirring up this matter."[64]

Past gobernadores usually enjoyed particularly high standing and occasionally led formal complaints against curas over fees and service.[65] In a more unlikely case, an ex-alcalde of Zinacantepec (Metepec district) was arrested in 1796 by the subdelegado's lieutenant for fomenting a suit against the cura over fees and for not fulfilling his sacramental obligations. The ex-alcalde then sued the lieutenant for false arrest. The fiscal protector accepted the subdelegado's view that this was a situation in which a few local men had "usurped the voice of the community," exacted derramas with the approval of the gobernador, and used the money to make malicious charges against the cura. He recommended a whipping for the ex-alcalde and a warning to stop bringing these minor conflicts with the cura to court.[66]

Legal entrepreneurship depended less on the person's age or service than on his expertise—bilingual skills, literacy, some knowledge of the law, and contacts in the audiencia seat. It attracted some young men impatient for power or the opportunity to serve the community. It also attracted some non-Indians, as the prelates had surmised in 1771. For example, a complaint against the cura over fees and services by Cuanacalcingo (Morelos) in 1780 revealed the influence of the pueblo's former schoolmaster, Miguel Barrera, a mulato who had married a local india. The cura blamed Barrera for the insolence and litigiousness of the pueblo since 1775, an allegation whose truth was experienced by the magistrate of the Juzgado de Bienes de Difuntos in April 1781, when Barrera, wishing to protest a property settlement, marched into his chambers with nearly the entire pueblo plus Indians of Tlaltizapan and Huispaleca.[67] Sometimes non-Indians or outsiders induced Indian protests but did not lead them. According to the cura of Coxcatlan in the district of Villa de Valles (San Luis Potosí) in 1791, three Spaniards in the district urged his Indian parishioners to bring false charges against him over fees and other matters.[68]

Whatever their age, race, or office, the personal interests of those who claimed to represent the community cannot be easily detached from their standing in it and their sense of responsibility to it. As the veteran cura Omerick observed, no one attracted a pueblo's attention like a *capitulero*—"a promoter of lawsuits who promised independence and material advantage to the community" and who was typically addressed respectfully as "yxtlamatqui," meaning "prudente" (prudent one) or "sabio" (wise man).[69]

It is often difficult to tell from the record whether one or a few people were responsible for the litigation, but the apparently willing payment of derramas suggests that more was usually involved than a single leader manipulating ignorant masses. The core organization, where one can be identified, is reminiscent of Paul Friedrich's Naranja (Zacapu district, Michoacán) in the 1920's,[70] where a principal figure depended on an inner circle of close relatives that was buttressed by outer circles of less firm support. At Tlapanaloya (Tetepango district, Hidalgo) in 1765, the cura blamed the gobernador, Francisco Ramírez, and his Ramírez relatives for fostering the vehement claims against him over fees and persuading other Indians not to contribute to the feast of the Assumption. According to the cura, the Ramírezes had held various community offices, collected derramas for their lawsuits, and controlled the cofradía properties, thereby "depriving the saints of their proper devotion and me of my meager emoluments."[71] A 1796 suit launched by the gobernador of Tututepec (Hidalgo), Juan Tolentino, against the cura over involuntary services exposed a bitter, complex dispute over local political power that involved rival groups in the pueblo, as well as the cura and alcalde mayor. According to several former officials, the gobernador and his son the escribano had terrorized villagers into supporting the suit and contributing three reales each to cover costs. The father and son had joined other relatives in alliance with the lieutenant to mortify the cura, reduce clerical fees, secure themselves in office, and reap the attendant rewards. The past officials, who evidently belonged to a group that was losing power in the pueblo, had supporting testimony from the cura of Achiotepec. He cast doubt on the Tolentinos' motives in his description of an expanding, branch-office legal entrepreneurship. According to this cura, Juan's son, Nicolás, had moved into Achiotepec and persuaded local Indians to put him in charge of a petition against the cura. Nicolás collected over 300 pesos by derrama and started the lawsuit, but it ended with his expulsion from the community when a preliminary investigation determined that the charges were false.[72]

Legal entrepreneurs in these situations were rivals to the cura, and their actions could arouse defiance, some of it openly anticlerical, especially if the men had been disqualified from office by the cura or he had punished them for disobedience, sexual misconduct, or failing to fulfill the precepto anual. In addition to examples already cited, three can be mentioned from Guerrero, Morelos, and Veracruz:

1. The longtime cura of Iguala responded to a judicial complaint against him in 1771 for overcharging fees with the claim that the petition had been entered in the name of the community by one man who held no office and was acting out of personal revenge.[73]

2. The cura of Tlaltizapan (Morelos) claimed in 1797 that he was being sued nominally over fees but really because of his opposition to Bernavé Antonio for gobernador for the past four years. Since the complaint had been initiated by a former gobernador and the current gobernador and escribano, the cura's attorney

was exaggerating somewhat when he asserted that the suit was the work of a few Indians who aspired to political office; but Bernavé Antonio certainly was a principal figure in the litigation.[74]

3. A flurry of lawsuits against the cura of Tzontecomatlan in the jurisdiction of Guayacocotla (northern Veracruz) led to his suspension, then restoration in 1808, when the charges proved exaggerated. The subdelegado declared that the town was plagued with "cabecillas seductores" who habitually launched overblown legal claims of various kinds. At the time he wrote, a former gobernador, Juan Baptista, was the cura's leading opponent, having been deprived of his political rights by the cura on the rumor that he had organized a secret junta. There was more than one side to this story, however, and the archbishop's provisor advised the cura to calm down and expect less from his campaign against drunkenness and fireworks, especially since the Tzontecomatleños agreed to obey him.[75]

The Pressures of Caciquismo

Rural Mexico in the nineteenth and twentieth centuries has been known for a kind of local personal rule called *caciquismo*. Originally a Caribbean term, "cacique" was adopted by colonial Spaniards in the sixteenth century and applied to hereditary Indian chiefs throughout their American empire. In the late eighteenth century, it still referred to Indians but was used more broadly to mean "lord of vassals or superior in a province or a *pueblo de indios*."[76] The emphasis was now more on superior position and the exercise of authority than on hereditary rights. Many principales in the late eighteenth century claimed to be caciques by ancestry, but few exercised the old authority. By the mid-nineteenth century, the term had become a synonym for local ruler without term and with arbitrary personal power (in Spain as well as Mexico).

However used, "cacique" implied willful personal power exercised over a rural territory and not requiring election. Where personal power was decisive in late colonial pueblos, the precolonial bases for it were overlaid with what Humboldt regarded as the collusion of local Indian officials in colonial oppression (see the chapter epigraph). But the material basis for that partnership, if it can be called that, changed enough to alter how such power could be acquired and held.

Fernando Díaz Díaz, studying the first decades of Mexico's national history, emphasizes military power and personal qualities as the essence of caciquismo. Alan Knight draws a close connection between caciquismo by the 1850's and the control of land and labor.[77] For the eighteenth century, however, Luisa Paré's description of caciquismo in the twentieth works better:

the informal and personal exercise of power at the local or regional level in rural areas, characterized by its mediating activities between the *pueblo* and the governmental apparatus—activities made possible by controlling and manipulating the channels of communication, especially of the system of authority.[78]

Paré's cacique exercised personal power in the name of the community, claiming to protect his people. Then, as now, his power depended partly on fulfilling this function, and therefore on his access to resources, including control over vital relations outside the locality and at least the threat of force.[79] During the eighteenth century, laws and courts were among the important political resources tapped by local leaders.[80] But force or the threat of force was always involved.

Caciquismo "flourish[ed] with the crisis of legitimacy that followed the breakdown of colonial power."[81] The prolonged Independence War undoubtedly enfeebled the old legitimacy and made armed force a more important political resource, but local militarization and intimidation began earlier and increased in the late eighteenth century. The growth of bandit gangs invited vigilantes, local strongmen, and more police action by a state that had already moved to establish the Acordada.[82] The promotion of a standing army and the arming of civilians in coastal settlements, haciendas, and villages to combat brigandage, foreign incursions, and political disorder fostered a growing resort to force at the local level, as did the weakness of provincial and national governments thereafter.[83] For example, in 1805, Indians of Meztitlan complained to the viceroy that soldiers stationed in their community frightened off the men and beat the women or carried them off to the woods on their horses.[84] In 1809, Indians of San Andrés Huisculco (Cuquío district, Jalisco) complained that vagrant men were moving into town, stealing from local people, and threatening to kill the Indian alcalde when he tried to control their criminal acts.[85] During the war, there was evidence that royalist as well as insurgent troops exercised arbitrary power in their localities— "despotismo" as one cura called it—presenting themselves as caudillos who had the authority to order decapitations, or muscling the cura aside with a display of force.[86]

There are many examples of abusive Indian leaders in pueblos during the eighteenth century, but these are not clear evidence of caciquismo unless caciquismo includes the acts of a whole class of elders (who were often divided against each other) rather those of single leaders. At this time, power and authority were usually relatively diffuse, belonging more to groups than to individuals. Most of the documented cases of abuse and coercion reveal less than complete personal power. They involved officials who wanted to dominate and moved to do so, but were checked in one way or another, including through the judicial system. For example, Pedro Felipe, a principal of Xamay on Lake Chapala (Jalisco), was the object of repeated complaints by other principales, who tried over and over to exclude him from officeholding and voting rights because of his authoritarian behavior ("he tries to control all events of the *pueblo* and subordinate all the members of the *república*"). They managed to get him stripped of his political rights in 1807, only to see him regain them in 1809. It was not long before a group of principales went back to court seeking to ban him from office because of his record of tampering with the vote count, upsetting elections, selling cofradía livestock below market value, and being continually drunk. The persistent Pedro Felipe was denied political rights again in November 1809 and September 1810.[87]

Many of the complaints of authoritarian abuses were lodged by other Indians rather than the parish priests or district judges. Some centered on cruel punishments, which the official usually justified as his duty; others turned on the arbitrary distribution of community lands, unjust demands for labor service, and similar acts of self-aggrandizement in office.[88] Documented cases represent only a small fraction of arbitrary abuses by local officials, because it was risky to lodge complaints. In a 1756 case against the alcalde of San Luis de las Peras (Hidalgo) for the infliction of cruel punishments and other abuses of his authority (which came into the open because an important segment of the community denounced him), some community members declined to testify or withheld information, apparently fearing reprisals from a man they still regarded as very powerful and connected to influential outsiders, including the cura.[89]

When the cura stepped in to make such a complaint, it was often because the man clearly did exercise enough power to challenge his place in the parish. At Acapetlahuaya (Ichcateopan district, Guerrero) in 1790, the cura complained that the former gobernador/cacique was intimidating local men and bribing officials to harass them. According to the cura, this man boasted that he could do anything he wanted, and that he had blackmailed various local men by having his daughter-in-law seduce them and then telling them, "you can deny me nothing because I know the whole story. Don't be afraid. With my pesos I can arrange everything." What seemed to concern the cura most was the unusual respect paid to this man. Getting drunk instead of attending mass on Sundays, he would appear in public afterwards in the pueblo offices, attending the council meetings. "There and in his house the men of the *república* attend to him and take care of his needs for all to see, as if he were a great personage and their oracle."[90] It was also the cura who denounced a young Indian "cacique" of Huatzalco (Yahualica district, Hidalgo) in 1749 for beating the alcalde of Santo Tomás and an Indian of San Francisco. According to him, the "cacique," himself an ordained priest and the son of the current gobernador, used his family's wealth and position to force local Indians into labor service, exercised a "tyrannical dominion" and "exceedingly great oppression" over them, and forced them to oppose the cura. As a result, the cura claimed, many people were leaving the community.[91]

Terror in the service of personal power could be deeply rooted in divisions within the community and could in turn deepen those divisions. At Chiapa de Mota (Hidalgo) in 1727, Indians from the cabecera and sujetos complained that the gobernador had been elected five consecutive times with the support of his core of "partisans" and "friends" and by intimidating others. By now, they claimed, he treated the position as personal property, using it to extort money and service.[92]

Newcomers and non-Indian residents of the pueblo were likely to be involved in these bando-based moves toward caciquismo. The cura of Huipuztla argued in 1768 that an extended family of non-Indians had taken over the government of Axoloapan (Hidalgo) and created a deep internal division:

There are certain families, the Hernándezes, who (not being tributaries or useful for anything at all) seek with increasing determination to become *gobernadores* in order to have the poor natives under their control and make use of them. The result is that that unfortunate *pueblo* is frequently divided into two *bandos*.[93]

At Santa María Atipac (Coatepec district, Valley of Mexico), a "coyote o morisco" married to a local india became the focal point for political divisions in the community. According to his opponents among the Indian principales, Joseph Antonio "managed to take control of the *pueblo*" (se dió maña de apoderarse del pueblo) once he became the alguacil mayor. Since he enjoyed the alcalde mayor's confidence, the many people who objected to him could do nothing. In 1773, an Indian was elected alcalde on the first two ballots, but a third round of voting was made and Joseph Antonio was elected because, his opponents said, he was nominated by a principal whom the others did not want to cross and who was also the alcalde mayor's ally. Now, as alcalde, he was

disrespectful to the officers and to everyone, beating them as if they were his servants. He has taken lands from the *pueblo*, giving them to other people. Even worse, he has whipped even widows with his own hands. If he catches their sons, he jails them and takes their money in fines. In the face of these abuses, many have been obliged to abandon the *pueblo* because they cannot go to the *alcalde mayor* for protection.

Though it was evident that Joseph Antonio had supporters as well as detractors in his quest for authority and personal power, the viceroy—determined to "cut [the problem] at its root"—made him ineligible for office by ordering that only Indians of three years' residence could stand for office.[94]

The Indian pueblo of the district seat of Tlaltenango (Zacatecas) provides a particularly interesting case of attempted caciquismo because it involved at least in part the question of who was an Indian (a common source of conflict in this part of the viceroyalty). In 1795, d. Blas de Santiago, a former regidor and alcalde, was charged by a group of principales with usurping power by terror, defrauding the treasury of 300 pesos, promoting drunkenness, using force to impose his will, and taking revenge on principales who opposed him. He replied that the three principales who had brought the complaint did not represent the pueblo's opinion, and furthermore, that even though they were officeholders, they were not Indians at all, but mulato troublemakers who wanted him out of office so that they could monopolize positions of influence. The audiencia's response at this point was to warn Blas de Santiago of harsh punishment for future abuses and declare him and his ally, Francisco Rebeles, ineligible for office for three years. In 1798, the two asked for a certification from the audiencia that they were again eligible for office. This time, their opponents objected on the grounds that they would take revenge once they were back in office and demand that the pueblo pay them 400 pesos for the court costs in 1795. In response, Blas de Santiago and Rebeles again raised the non-Indian issue, arguing that it was mulatos who were objecting and using their authority as elected officials to steal from the cofradía and the treasury. But Blas de Santiago had no better success with the argument now than he had in 1795. He was denied his political privileges in 1798, and again in 1800. Despite the claims of both sides to represent the real interests of the community, this was a deeply divided pueblo. Blas de Santiago had won election in 1792 with only a plurality of votes—ten to eight to five.[95]

In 1805, the political divisions and power moves in the Indian pueblo of Tlaltenango again reached the courts. On May 5, the alcalde del barrio de abajo, six or seven elders, and a large number of young Indians went to the lieutenant's office urging that Miguel de Lucas be appointed interim alcalde of the pueblo, since the current alcalde, from the barrio de arriba, was ill. But the lieutenant demurred because Lucas had been arrested and punished for assaulting an earlier lieutenant; instead, the lieutenant's choice was Rebeles, now evidently restored to the franchise. Lucas and two of his followers refused to accept the interim appointment of Rebeles and struck him in the chest during the installation ceremony at the rectory. The lieutenant failed to calm the gathering and had to call for the aid of soldiers. The leaders fled, pushing the lieutenant to the ground on their way out. With four local Spaniards and the troops, the lieutenant went out to arrest the cabecillas and disperse the crowd that had gathered. Only two men were captured. One of them, Doroteo Alverto, a thirty-year-old indio farmer, said that his barrio regidor had told him to go to the rectory with the others. He had grabbed the lieutenant's wrist, he said, only so that the lieutenant would not strike his father. In his court appearance, Lucas insisted that he, not Rebeles, was the proper alcalde of Tlaltenango.[96] Clearly, the struggle there had not been resolved, and the state's intervention served at best to restore an uneasy balance and to raise a few assertive men to the spotlight.

As the examples of legal entrepreneurs suggest, personal power in rural communities could come from contacts with higher authorities and the manipulation of the law; personal power was less often extralegal in the colonial period than later. Omerick, for example, was convinced that the "jefes" (bosses) of Indian pueblos he had encountered in Tepecoacuilco (Guerrero) in the 1760's were the same insulting men who had gained the support of villagers in malicious lawsuits.[97]

In 1790, a legal entrepreneur on the way to becoming a cacique in Milpa Alta (Xochimilco district, Valley of Mexico) was charged before the audiencia with being a "lazy vagrant, rebellious, and an agitator of Indians" (vago osioso, revoltoso, e inquietador de los yndios). The gobernador of Milpa Alta claimed that Ysidro Giménez "assembles the Indians, induces them to bring suit, exacts large contributions from them, and frequently is away in Mexico City pursuing his legal affairs." The gobernador described Giménez as an outsider—a mestizo whose parents were from the neighboring community of Tuyahualco—who openly disobeyed him and protected Indians he had ordered arrested. An Indian alcalde added that Giménez's only occupation seemed to be "composing documents in the name of Indians for this court [and] also making himself their agent and going in their name to stir up their petitions. . . . He has the *pueblo* in an uproar."[98]

The subdelegado regarded Giménez as a menace who had been arrested many times and had led the Indians to insubordinate conduct, including a noisy movement against the Franciscan doctrinero, for which he was deprived of his political privileges in the community. But he did not dismiss Giménez's influence or say that it was based simply on threats and force. Giménez had won the support of villagers, he said, by promising that they would not have to pay taxes to any collector, and local Indians willingly brought him food and money when he went to Mexico City. He always represented himself as an Indian of the community and was treated as such by many of them. The cura was particularly critical of Giménez, but he too recognized his power. Giménez might be often absent from the pueblo and a heavy drinker who did not fulfill the Easter duty or obey his superiors, but he had "won over this *pueblo* and his faction" and was "their agent in all of their legal affairs."

In his defense, Giménez identified himself as an Indian son of a Tuyahualco father and a Milpa Alta mother who grew maize for a living. If he was acting as a legal agent for the community, it was because the role had been pressed on him: Indians came to him "for his direction, which he provide[d], giving them instructions for the attorney." He claimed to have a license from the viceroy as "legal agent of the Indians" (apoderado de los indios), but when asked to show it, he replied that it was at home in Milpa Alta. In response to the cura's charges, he said that he did intend to fulfill the Easter duty but was waiting for the feast of the Holy Ghost to do so, and that he drank pulque because water was scarce. That Giménez was more than just one man tyrannizing a community is suggested by the witnesses he produced: four ex-gobernadores, one ex-alcalde, and an ex-escribano, who referred to him as an indio cacique and swore that they had authorized him to serve as the pueblo's legal agent since 1783. The Juzgado de Indios recognized ambiguities in the case that may well have reflected deep pueblo divisions (it is suggestive that past gobernadores were opposing the current gobernador), but it was concerned about Giménez's growing influence and his overactive promotion of litigation. It ordered Giménez released from prison without additional penalty except a severe warning not to involve himself further in Indian legal affairs.

The temporal distribution of late colonial caciquismo suggests that personal power of the complex and contingent kinds described above and in earlier chapters was an old pattern. Twelve of the 62 cases located for the 1720–1820 period occurred before 1760. As with much of the evidence of resistance to parish priests, there was a concentration in the 1760's and 1770's (eleven and ten cases, respectively, or 34 percent), a drop in the 1780's (four), and another concentration in the 1790's and 1800's (thirteen and eight cases, or 34 percent). The regional distribution of would-be political caciques highlights districts in Hidalgo (thirteen cases) and Morelos (ten). The Diocese of Guadalajara is also well represented with eleven cases. Temascaltepec-Zacualpan and the vicinity of the Valley of Mexico had fewer cases of caciquismo than one might expect from their prominence in the larger body of evidence of political conflict (five and seven, respectively).[99]

In a 1796 dispute with the cura of Tututepec (Hidalgo) over fees and services, the bishop of Puebla's investigation revealed that the gobernador was a very powerful figure and the principal promoter of this and other lawsuits in the name of a pueblo where the Indians were "notorious" litigators, "the most perverse of all those who live in these mountains." His power evidently stemmed more from the office than from his personality or intimidation: local people enthusiastically subscribed to the idea that a gobernador, not the cura, "is the principal head and father of the *pueblo*, and the one who is always ready to defend them. As a result, what a *gobernador* wants is done; and even though many are disgusted by him, they keep quiet and obey."[100]

A lesser official might command similar support. In the late 1720's, the Franciscan guardian of the convent and doctrina of Poncitlan (Jalisco) faced frightening opposition to his actions as judge and father. Indians were releasing people he had arrested and had menaced him when he ordered a man whipped for not fulfilling the precepto anual. His familiar complaint that the Indians "live very much on their guard and quite at liberty" (viven mui sobre sí y con bastante libertad) carried a sharp edge in this case because the alcalde of the cabecera had organized elected officials throughout the district to join the people in their defiance. He convened many of them in the cabecera for a march on the doctrinero's cell to "show me their disrespect," then organized a march to the cathedral in Guadalajara to appeal to the bishop for the arancel.[101]

Plainly, the power of some local officials (and the frustration of their parish priests) increased substantially as the priests' role in elections and other aspects of local affairs shrank in caciquismo cases. At Hueyapan (Morelos) in 1767 when a suit was launched against him over fees and accounts, the cura blamed four Indians for trying to "gain control over the *república de naturales*." He appealed to the audiencia to order the alcalde mayor not to certify elections without the advice of the cura "about the suitability and circumstances of the candidate." In the background to this dispute was Indian resistance to various fiestas and conflict with the priest over an orchard his predecessors had been allowed to use.[102] According to the cura of Tultitlan (Tacuba district, Valley of Mexico), the gobernador there in 1777, the forty-eight-year-old Marcos Antonio, had been given dictatorial powers by the Indians, who repeatedly reelected him despite the cura's warnings that this was illegal. The cura claimed that Marcos Antonio was constantly drunk and allowed public drunkenness even in church. His non-Indian witnesses added that Marcos Antonio raped local women and sold their husbands to haciendas, but he denied it all and the audiencia dismissed the charges.[103]

Of course, not all gobernadores who were reelected (and presumably, therefore, could exercise substantial influence in the community) were political caciques or proto-caciques. They might be men who were trusted by all, who shrank from the exercise of power and posed a threat to no one, who spoke no Spanish, or who were constrained by the countervailing powers of rival leaders and their groups, priests, merchants, hacendados, and district magistrates. In one unusual case, the gobernador of Tenancingo in the district of Malinalco went to court in 1787 to protect himself from future service. He was, he said, loyal and dedicated to his pueblo, and would accept the fourth nonconsecutive term to which he had recently been elected. But the service was impoverishing him, and he wanted others to have the "distinction of the *gobernador*'s *vara*." His request for exemption from future nomination was granted by the audiencia.[104]

Much of the written record on caciquismo is no more than tantalizing, especially when it rests on the testimony of a parish priest or district judge. Some of the examples of personalist rule are couched in terms remarkably familiar to students of nineteenth- and twentieth-century caciquismo. But these terms probably expressed colonial rulers' fears and frustrations over disobedience and the possibility of disorder as much as they described actual patterns of local leadership. It is sometimes evident that local leaders did not exercise the kind of unconditional power the cura or alcalde mayor imagined. For example, the subdelegado of Tonalá (Jalisco) in 1818 charged the Indian alcalde, Toribio Covarrubias, with thwarting him, releasing some Indians he had imprisoned, pushing a lieutenant when he tried to arrest another Indian, falsifying the subdelegado's signature on fraudulent documents to keep local men out of the royalist army, and leading a tumulto when the subdelegado and a lieutenant "tried to disperse a bunch of drunkards." Covarrubias had clearly defied the subdelegado, but it

is less than certain that he was the political boss of the pueblo. The subdelegado noted that he was illiterate and depended on his literate adviser ("asesor"),
Ignacio Delgadillo, who was an even greater menace. Covarrubias's authority apparently depended mainly on his staff of office. The cura praised him as a good
Christian, and his own testimony indicated that he had been imprisoned several
times at the behest of other prominent officials who were his rivals. Speaking ad-
miringly of the alcalde's exemplary Christian conduct, the cura seemed to agree
that he represented much of the community in his call for the subdelegado's residencia and in his defense of community rights; and that as a leading citizen, he
worked for public tranquility, primary education, and loyalty to the crown.[105]

In another example, the cura of Apaxtla (Ichcateopan district, Guerrero) in
1809 reported that the Indians of Tanicpatlan had threatened to kill him and his
vicario and were now complaining that the vicario would not go there to confess
them. In his opinion, there were eight main leaders who terrorized the populace
with threats of imprisonment and floggings—"like despotic lords"—and made
travel to the pueblo dangerous. But he singled out one man, Josef de la Cruz,
"alias Bonaparte," as the main problem. Cruz supposedly presented himself as
"the king of the *pueblo*, who has the *subdelegado*, the *cura*, and the rest of the colonial authorities under his feet":

> This man's domination has reached the point that whenever he went to the *casa de comu-
> nidad*, he ordered the *alguaciles* to ring the bells. He would summon the entire commu-
> nity and have the ringing continue until he returned home. . . . He and the other *regidor*
> named Domingo went from house to house persuading all the Indians to rise up against
> my *vicario*, d. Bernardo Martínez y Sandoval, because he had placed in confinement at
> the request of her mother an *india* who had been in an adulterous relationship with a mar-
> ried man.[106]

The details about the bells and the house-by-house canvassing confirm that the
cura had powerful local opponents who were prepared to defy his authority. But
was Josef de la Cruz a petty tyrant imposing a reign of terror on a cowed populace? It is difficult to tell from the priest's account. The fact that there were at
least seven other "cabecillas principales" in the pueblo, and the fact that Cruz
had to make a personal, house-to-house appeal to mobilize villagers against the
vicario suggest that he was not yet the new Bonaparte of his little world. What
does seem clear is that his apparently considerable personal power depended on
representing himself as the defender of local autonomy, and that he enjoyed a
kind of public recognition (exemplified in the bell ringing) that was supposed to
be reserved for higher colonial dignitaries.[107]

The cura of Soyatlan (Tlapa district, Guerrero), in his 1806–8 suit with the
pueblo of Xalpatlahuaca, identified a legal entrepreneur who, at least in the cura's
mind, was considerably more. The suit centered on the thorny legal issue of
ecclesiastical versus community property that the crown had highlighted in the
1790's. The cura was charged with withholding 1,600 pesos from the pueblo treasury. He responded that the treasury chest was a "sacred repository" (sagrado
depósito) because it contained money for rebuilding the church, and that a sacrilegious person had broken the lock and taken money for other purposes. By the
cura's account, that person was Christóval Zevallos, the pueblo's legal agent who,

having persuaded the pueblo officials to use some of the treasury to press land disputes against Zacatipan, had then seen fit to help himself. When the cura had thwarted Zevallos's plan, he countered with the suit against him. Zevallos, said the cura, "keeps [the community] in a continual uproar [and is] the main axis around which the entire *pueblo* revolves": he had imposed derramas, influenced local people to disobey him and his vicarios, and closed the school. He was also the legal agent of Jonacatlan and had spent nearly 2,000 pesos from collections on lawsuits. The subdelegado ordered that essential church repairs be made from the pueblo treasury but left unaddressed the larger issue of Zevallos and control over the treasury.[108]

The kind of violent, unchecked personalist power that was familiar after the Independence Wars was more likely in places that were not primarily Indian and to reach beyond a single pueblo. One example comes from the parish of Chicontepec (northern Veracruz) in the late 1780's. The cura claimed in 1787 that residents of the settlements of Camotipan, Francia, Aragón, and Xicalango had been "induced by some evil individuals" to balk at their Christian duties. The Indian gobernador and ex-fiscal of Chicontepec judged that the Indians of these four rancherías were being manipulated by three Indians, known for criminal activity in the past, who had been in hiding or living on neighboring haciendas for many years "and who now [had] taken control" (y ahora se han apoderado del mando y gobierno) of the rancherías, intimidating other local people with threats of violence and keeping them from doing their religious duties. Their motive, the gobernador testified, was to "place themselves outside the law by arousing the rest of the natives against their *cura* and the *gobernador* and *república*," and to collect derramas, ostensibly for lawsuits and petitions, so that they could bribe officials and enrich themselves. One Indian of Camotipan testified that he had not been allowed to go to the cura and request last rites for his wife.

The cura saw a moving force behind these "evil individuals." He had no doubt that the powers behind this defiance of authority were a cavalry captain and local hacendado, d. Manuel Valdés, and his estate administrator, d. Pedro Retureta, supported by their dependents and servants. According to the cura, they encouraged Indian rebellion against the priest and protected those who engaged in it, exercising "an absolute despotism." He judged that Valdés was the principal

caudillo . . . in these lands because of his wealth, farflung activities, favoritism, and consummate cunning. . . . He exercises a decisive influence over everything important that happens in these parts, having completely dominated the magistrate. . . . He wields an unlimited despotism not only with his dependents and soldiers but with all kinds of people. . . . Those who could testify to these and other matters tremble at the thought.[109]

Valdés had, the cura said, a supply of false witnesses waiting in the wings to testify against him. He thought the Indian principales were men of good conduct for the most part but were intimidated into supporting Valdés. Alcaldes mayores from Pánuco, Huejutla, and Chicontepec provided some support for the cura in the subsequent investigation, explaining that this had been an "extremely turbulent" area before he arrived, and saying that he held parishioners to high standards of religious conduct.

A case from Tlalmanalco near the Valley of Mexico exposes the internal struggles and divided loyalties—to curas, district judges, neighboring landlords, and cabeceras—that often escape the written record of late colonial pueblos.[110] It provides glimpses of sharp divisions within a pueblo, exacerbated by an alcalde's favoritism with the community's most vital resource; the shadowy rule of neighboring estate owners, who formed personal bonds that gave them access to community lands and added to internal divisions; at least one local Indian who enjoyed some of the power of a political cacique; and differing views of local power on the part of the cura and the lieutenant.

The case involved the division of community lands among Indians of the pueblo of Ayotzingo in 1766, and began when a former regidor mayor and a current regidor menor came forward in the name of the community to criticize the cura's and lieutenant's interference, and to petition for the restoration of redistributed lands to their former holders. The root of the problem, as the cura explained it, was that much of the best land of the pueblo was in the hands of neighboring non-Indian landowners, who rented it extrajudicially from Indian holders. The Indians, he said, were divided into various factions (parcialidades), each organized around one of these renters, "who is their Adalid or Patrono," and

> to whom the Indians defer and obey in all matters for no better reason than the mistaken idea that they were gaining some benefit. [But] when there were lawsuits over land, they were made in the name of the Indians and at their expense. . . . The costs accrue to the landowner and the benefits accrue to the renter with his *parcialidad*. No wonder there have been endless lawsuits over land in this *pueblo* for thirty years.[111]

The cura added in his defense that during recent litigation, three different groups of men had represented themselves as spokesmen for the pueblo when, in fact, each represented only a political faction. Four years earlier, the audiencia had decided against the renters and ordered a new distribution aimed at inducing the Indians to cultivate their best lands for themselves. Under its terms, after the best lands had been distributed among the tributaries, the remaining 36.5 *fanegas de sembradura* (area planted with this many fanegas of seed) were auctioned to Juan Francisco Guerrero, a Spanish resident of Ayotzingo. The proceeds of 328.5 pesos per year were to go to the pueblo treasury. But the Indian alcalde acted improperly, the cura claimed, playing favorites in the distribution and failing to maintain the dikes that kept a nearby river from ruining arable lands assigned to some families. And Indians had continued to rent out their assigned plots, despite the audiencia order. So he had called on the lieutenant to remedy the situation with another, more equitable distribution to Indians who would actually work the land.

The plaintiffs, he said, were aroused because they had lost the unusually privileged place they had held in earlier distributions and their ability to rent choice lands to their patronos. Antonio de la Rosa lost his plot because it was not all his; during his father's term as alcalde, he had seized enough choice land to support four families. One of those he had victimized was d. Simón de Castilla, "the best Indian and most meritorious person in this *pueblo*, who served for seven straight years as *alcalde* without a hint of misconduct in all that time, and who was largely responsible for terminating the extrajudicial rentals." (Clearly the cura had his own notion about who was worthy of favor.) But de la Rosa had resumed the practice, despite orders not to do so. Moreover, he had received payment in advance, so he had an obvious reason to object to the latest distribution. It was for these reasons, the cura said, that this—the most "disobedient, impudent, and audacious" Indian in the pueblo—had lost his former plot in the new distribution. Though he had been assigned land in another location, he was not satisfied and had promised "to do whatever he could against the *cura* and the lieutenant." The cura also made a detailed reply to the complaint of Juan Hilario, who had apparently been especially favored by de la Rosa's father.

Perhaps because the lieutenant enjoyed friendlier relations with the neighboring non-Indian landowners and knew less about the internal politics of Ayotzingo, he was more convinced than the cura that the problem was de la Rosa's unchecked personal power, as distinct from the practice of land rental. He was the most feared man in town, the lieutenant thought. Some years before, he wrote, when an Indian alcalde had tried to arrest de la Rosa for his long-standing adultery with a married woman of the pueblo, de la Rosa had hit the alcalde over the head with a rock, and no one dared to protest. De la Rosa's wife had complained many times of being beaten by him, but the local and district judges had not risked arresting him for fear of the uproar it would cause. He was so feared in the pueblo, the lieutenant said, that no one dared to denounce his criminal acts to the secular or ecclesiastical magistrates. As a result, he lived "insolently, . . . laughing at the system of justice."[112]

* * *

Derramas, litigation, and cabecera-sujeto struggles were potent expressions of the paradox of freedom in community in late colonial pueblos de indios. But whose freedom was being expressed? The república's?—yes, but often in ways that fostered conflict within this group and threatened the place of current members. The macehuales'?—less so, and mainly in a collective sense, with others acting for them or making demands on them. It was especially the legal entrepreneurs, officeholders, and would-be caciques, with their circles of supporters, who benefited from the defense of the community's freedom. Their kind of patronage could create a situation in which "the idea of freedom is the mask of a tyrant," as Octavio Paz has put it.[113]

Clearly, there were powerful individuals in the rural parishes. This chapter focuses on the pueblo members among them. Some were from old families with hereditary privileges, wealth, and education since the sixteenth century, if not before; others were ambitious macehuales, secondary principales, or newcomers and castas who used the law, allies in and beyond the community, and intimidation to gain prominence. As Humboldt maintained, some powerful men drew strength from an alliance with the cura or district governor. The colonial record, however, suggests that more of them were rivals of the curas—men who were thwarted by the cura in pueblo elections, who took revenge for a flogging, or who greeted a new or controversial priest with lawsuits.

Individual power in these communities could feed on a mystique of invincibility, even a defiance of higher law. But as Humboldt also suggested, personal power gravitated toward officeholding. It was likelier to depend on communication and mediation between colonial authorities and the locality than to operate in open defiance of them. As the Chicontepec and Tlalmanalco examples suggest, owners and overseers of private estates, among other influential outsiders, also could exercise the kind of arbitrary personal power associated with caciquismo. Parish priests and district governors might enjoy virtually unchecked power in a locality, but their institutional ties made them less likely candidates for this kind of power.

In most cases, the judicial and administrative record reveals a far more complex and contingent kind of individual power than Humboldt's petty Indian tyrants exercising arbitrary power as alcaldes. Aspirants to the personal power of caciques usually were hemmed in by personal and sectional rivalries within the community, by officeholders and other members of the república who were jealous of their own standing and suspicious of individual ambition, and by priests or district governors. While there were veritable local rulers in some places, and men who seemed on the way to becoming that powerful, there was no simple type, no single origin of nineteenth-century caciquismo in colonial politics and culture. The political and economic culture stressed hierarchy, mediation, and personal power backed up by the authority of office, but an individual with some personal power was not necessarily on the way to becoming a local ruler, and resorting to colonial law and personal alliances could as easily subvert an individual's power as promote it.

CHAPTER SIXTEEN

District Governors
and Parish Priests

Indians shall be favored and protected by the ecclesiastical
and secular courts. . . . It is our will to entrust the viceroys,
presidents, and *audiencias* with looking after them, so that
they may be protected, favored, and treated leniently. . . .
And we request and entrust the ecclesiastical prelates . . .
that they all guard the Indians' privileges and prerogatives,
and keep them under their care.
—*Recopilación*, 1681 (1580)

Even though the Royal Authority is so powerful and worthy
of respect, priests are not for that reason contemptible.
—Cura of Tehuacan, 1792

The third corner of the triangle of formal authority in local and district politics
—the alcaldes mayores or corregidores (replaced in the late 1780's by subdelegados) and their lieutenants—faced unsettling challenges themselves, in the
Bourbon parish reforms, especially to their role in local commerce.[1] But on balance the king's district governors (a term I use here to embrace the lieutenants as
well as their superiors) benefited from the changes. Though this is not the place
for a full study of the public lives of these officials, one must understand their responsibilities and sources of income to grasp the principles and practices of their
associations with parish priests, their conflicts with parish priests in the late eighteenth century, and the clergy's views of the changing relationship. Despite an
increasingly abrasive confusion of authority in district politics at the end of the
eighteenth century, only a minority of governors came into open conflict with
the priests, and the disputes between them rarely led to irreconcilable ruptures.

As administrators of territories that often incorporated as many as five or six
parishes, alcaldes mayores and subdelegados tended to be more removed from
the majority of their subjects than were the parish priests. Their lieutenants
were less removed, but even they were likely to supervise more than one parish.
Most alcaldes mayores and subdelegados saw themselves, and were seen by their
subjects, as temporary. Their tenure in one district in the late eighteenth century was usually limited to a five-year term.[2] Curas stayed several years longer
on average, and since the parish was a benefice, there was no fixed term or great
concentration of transfers around the average. Unlike many of their lieutenants,

few alcaldes mayores and subdelegados were from the area or spoke the indigenous language, and few lived outside the cabecera or the viceregal capital. Their contact with subjects was largely restricted to men; except as judges, they dealt mainly with their own dependents and lieutenants, village officials, trading partners, resident non-Indians, and the priests.

The governors' substantial influence, then, stemmed less from regular contact than from their judicial and administrative authority and traditional commercial activities. Apart from their specific title—alcalde mayor, subdelegado, lieutenant—they were most often addressed individually as *el justicia*—"the court" (more often than as juez or judge, which was the way priests as judges usually were identified). This term cloaked their judicial role in a somewhat distant and institutional yet paternal authority.[3] Their judicial powers and sometimes arbitrary use of force earned many of them, especially in the Audiencia of Mexico territory (the high court district of central Mexico), a fearful, distancing respect as men who could bend the law to their own ends.[4] Except for petitions from individual curas and occasional complaints by whole pueblos, serious allegations against the district justicias, unlike those against the priests, were usually anonymous.[5] As the lawyer for Indians of Tecamachalco (Tacuba district) observed in their 1787 dispute with the alcalde mayor over the scrawny mules he forced them to buy at 30 pesos each, "Since he is the judge . . . these unfortunates fear that he will arrest and ruin them."[6] To cross a justicia without the active support of the community and its officers or some sign of a favorable reception by higher authorities in Guadalajara or Mexico City clearly involved greater risks than challenging the parish priest.[7]

Still, there were spontaneous local protests and vehement individual and collective displays of disrespect toward these district governors, and a popular lore about their personal corruption. Such disrespect, especially toward lieutenants, was particularly evident in the Diocese of Guadalajara, at least in comparison to the defiance of parish priests there.

Much of this chapter is devoted to disputes involving district governors brought by or against parish priests that reached the audiencias of Mexico and Guadalajara. Such disputes were not new, nor were they based on much new law. Since the early colonial period, there had been tensions between curas and governors over individual misconduct and their jealously guarded and poorly defined roles as judges. But the new balance of judicial authority mandated by the crown in the late eighteenth century contributed to greater conflict. The judicial responsibilities of district governors increased, and the high courts usually failed to support the claims of parish priests against them. Open disputes between the two increased in number and were more often expressed in a categorical rhetoric that policy makers invited in some of their decrees and in their emphasis on law and obedience without interpretation. Rural parish priests, nearly all of whom were American-born, chafed at the redefinition of their place in public affairs, and many were quick to respond to imagined slights by district governors who stood for the changes. For their part, the alcaldes mayores and subdelegados of the late colonial period were likely to be peninsular-born and anticlerical (if not antireligious). Many were military men with little legal training.[8] They knew their authority was increasing; some provoked parish priests by stretching

TABLE 4

Priest-Governor and Priest-Parishioner Lawsuits by Decade, 1700–1819

Decade	With district governors		With parishioners	
	Number	Percent	Number	Percent
1700–1709	2	2.2%	2	0.6%
1710–1719	0	—	2	0.6
1720–1729	0	—	11	3.5
1730–1739	3	3.3	13	4.2
1740–1749	3	3.3	14	4.5
1750–1759	3	3.3	22	7.1
1760–1769	10	10.8	38	12.3
1770–1779	16	17.4	38	12.3
1780–1789	19	20.6	41	13.2
1790–1799	18	19.5	65	20.1
1800–1809	15	16.3	46	14.8
1810–1819	3	3.3	18	5.8
TOTAL	92[a]	100.0%	310[b]	100.0%

[a] 63 from Mexico, 29 from Guadalajara.
[b] 259 from Mexico, 51 from Guadalajara.

the limits of royal jurisdiction and humiliating them in public. It was the district governors more than parishioners or the high clergy who charged priests with sexual misconduct.[9] In their turn, parish priests were quick to raise their voices early and late in the eighteenth century against district governors' repartimientos (monopoly trading ventures) when royal decrees invited such complaints.[10] Coupled with additional Indian taxes and the secularization of many parishes after 1749, this shift in authority generated what John Lynch has called a new level of "competition between exploiters," [11] as the court cases over bienes de comunidad, cofradías, elections, and clerical fees suggest.

But a temporal distribution of the 115 judicial cases pitting parish priests against district governors examined in this study traces neither a high plateau from the 1750's nor a smooth ascent to the eve of independence.[12] As Table 4 indicates, the cases rose to a new level in the 1760's, then jumped in the 1770's, to reach a peak in the 1780's and 1790's. The greatest concentration of cases (39, or 33.9 percent of the total) occurred between 1785 and 1796. Nearly a quarter (28 cases) date from 1789 to 1796. Evidently the initial rise in the 1760's and 1770's was associated with the acceleration of administrative and fiscal reform measures under Charles III, including José de Gálvez's visita (especially between 1765 and 1771, when he exercised his fullest authority), the expulsion of the Jesuits, the continuing secularization of parishes, and the regalist programs of prelates like Archbishop Lorenzana. The rise continued during Gálvez's tenure as Minister of the Indies until his death in 1787. It was recharged, even boosted temporarily, during the first years of the intendancy reforms.

The regional distribution of these cases exposes four distinctive patterns (Table 5). First, the Metepec-Tenango del Valle-Malinalco-Temascaltepec-Zacualpan jurisdictions of the modern Estado de México, which are so heavily represented in the overall record of conflicts involving parish priests, are less conspicuous in these priest/district governor cases (the conflicts there were mainly between priests and Indian parishioners). Second, the modern state of Hidalgo—

TABLE 5
Priest-Governor and Priest-Parishioner Lawsuits by Region

Region	With district governors		With parishioners	
	Number	Percent	Number	Percent
Hidalgo-Querétaro-San Luis Potosí-Veracruz	22	24.0%	57	18.4%
Guerrero-Morelos	15	16.3	74	23.9
Valley of Mexico area	12	13.0	41	13.2
Metepec-Tenango del Valle-Malinalco-Temascaltepec-Zacualpan	14	15.2	87	28.1
Diocese of Guadalajara	29	31.5	51	16.4
TOTAL	92	100.0%	310	100.0%

particularly the jurisdictions of Meztitlan and Xilotepec—is especially prominent (23 cases in all). Third, districts in modern Guerrero also stand out in comparison to the whole body of judicial conflicts involving parish priests there (16 cases). And fourth, priests in the Diocese of Guadalajara were much more likely to be embroiled in lawsuits with district governors than with parishioners, reflecting their comparatively strong position as public figures.

But these regional and temporal data reveal little about the depth of the disputes. The most bitter ones seem to have occurred far from the centers of the two audiencia districts: for Guadalajara, in the remote districts of Acaponeta (Nayarit) and Chametla (Sinaloa); for Mexico, to the northeast in the district of Cadereyta, as well as Meztitlan and Xilotepec; and outside the Archdiocese of Mexico in modern Puebla and Oaxaca. Remote places that were "first-class" alcaldías mayores and subdelegaciones (first-class because of the income that local commerce promised for the district governor) were especially likely to have bitter disputes between district governors and priests: for example, Tlapa (Guerrero) in the 1770's, Villa Alta (Oaxaca) in the 1790's, Tecali (Puebla) in the 1730's, and Zacatlan (Puebla) in the 1780's. And though the disputes that reached the high courts in the 1770's were not the most numerous, they were among the most fiercely contested.

The Role of District Governors

"Swear to God . . . that you will fulfill your duties well and faithfully, . . . that you will attentively serve God and Your Majesty," the *Recopilación* instructed in 1681. "If you do so, may God help you, and if not, may He hold you accountable."[13] Invoking God so emphatically in this oath of office for alcaldes mayores suggests how deeply intertwined royal and ecclesiastical administration were in the Hapsburg conception of the state—intertwined, but not equal, unchanging, or indistinguishable. The alcalde mayor was father. Royal instructions encouraged an affectionate possessiveness on his part. The Indians in his territory were his people, for whom he was responsible. He was to be their protector, director, inspector, and judge; he was to supervise their attendance at mass and catechism classes, and see that they did nothing contrary to "Our Sacred Religion"; but, above all, he was to look after their material well-being and productivity.[14] More than the parish priests, he was to enforce the rules of productive labor, land use, residency, and good order in their communities.[15]

Good order during the eighteenth century increasingly required the district governor to intervene as a criminal judge and police commissioner, political and financial administrator, royal investigator, and economic promoter. The construction of new, more secure jails in some cabeceras in response to royal directives as early as 1714 symbolized his expanding responsibilities to control public drunkenness, contraband liquor, gambling, fiesta behavior, adultery, and other "public and scandalous sins." As a royal administrator, he was also responsible for promoting and protecting the bienes de comunidad; reporting on local conditions, such as natural resources, population, and resident priests; certifying elections; and removing Indian officials who disobeyed orders from above.

As guardians of the colonial economy, these officials had always supervised tribute collection, the periodic markets, and local weights and measures. Their work as judges reinforced this economic role. Property relations—especially land transactions—were their special responsibility. Their permission was required for the rental and sale of local Indian lands and the periodic distributions of pueblo lands for private use, and they had the authority to sequester personal property.[16] If the inventory of more than 200 cases processed by the court of the subdelegados of Tonalá, Jalisco, between 1788 and 1802 is a fair indication, over half the disputes they adjudicated concerned land, buildings, and cash debts. Domestic disputes, especially estrangements that the judge presumed to reconcile, account for about 10 percent of the cases, followed by robberies, assaults, and a scattering of other offenses.[17]

How the alcaldes mayores and subdelegados behaved as judges and administrators, and how they were regarded, depended partly on their social backgrounds and career patterns. Intended to promote impartial administration and loyalty to superiors, the short terms of office and restrictions on property ownership and marriage in the district worked to limit their local associations. But isolation and transience were not automatic. Those who did reside in their districts formed working relationships and personal ties with Indian officials and non-Indians, to their mutual advantage; their family circle was likely to include brothers, cousins, and other dependents who served as business partners and informal assistants; and occasionally extended families broadened the network of close relationships and influence. For example, the corregidor of Tlajomulco (Jalisco) in 1728 noted that his father had served in the same office for three terms, as well as in Senticpac, and that his mother's brothers were also district governors in Nueva Galicia.[18]

Close studies of the backgrounds and careers of district governors have not yet been done, but two late-eighteenth-century changes appear to have affected how they performed their duties and how they were regarded: more were former military men or held military titles;[19] and more were peninsulares. In keeping with the growing importance of military affairs following the Seven Years' War (1756–63) and later, with the Acordada's all-out campaign against highwaymen, various alcaldes mayores carried the title of *capitán a guerra* (war captain). Both Mexico and Guadalajara had a full measure of them in the late 1760's, in Cadereyta, Colima, Chilapa, Pánuco, Tampico, Villa de Valles, Huichapa, Meztitlan,

Sayula, and Lerma.[20] Francisco Javier de Arriola, alcalde mayor of Santa María de Lagos (Jalisco) in 1771 and subsequently of Teocaltiche, had had a military career in Cuba before taking up administration in New Spain; and the justicia of Zacatecas in 1783 was a cavalry lieutenant.[21] It is not certain that fewer alcaldes mayores had legal training, but military experience and the emphasis on administrative duties do seem to have inclined them toward summary justice and quicker recourse to force.[22] Whether or not the appointment of peninsulares increased the distance between governors and subjects or contributed to the efficiency of a centralizing administration, this change added to the antipeninsular sentiments that were openly expressed during the second half of the eighteenth century.[23]

The lieutenants—the administrative and judicial officers with whom parish priests residing outside a district capital would have had the most contact—were appointed by the alcalde mayor or subdelegado.[24] Most of them were probably faithful subordinates. As the fiscal of the Audiencia of Nueva Galicia observed in 1795, the lieutenants "depend on the *subdelegados* who name them."[25] But lieutenants were not simply subordinates. Although their terms of service coincided with those of the alcalde mayor or subdelegado, many were reappointed, especially if the office was sold. Some served for more than fifteen years. And unlike the alcaldes mayores and subdelegados, most lieutenants were longtime local residents and had their own personal networks. Some of the local landowners, merchants, or retired military officers who served for many years acted largely on their own authority, especially if they had purchased the office or been foisted upon the subdelegado by a merchant who had cosigned his bond of office.[26] A lieutenant might operate at cross purposes from his superior not because he was naturally independent-minded, but because he was controlled by powerful local merchants or landowners. For instance, according to the cura of Mazatepec (Morelos) in 1802, local peninsular merchants threatened to have the lieutenant removed from office and bribed him to proceed with litigation against the cura.[27]

Reports for various districts north and east of Guadalajara in the late 1780's offer some information on the circumstances of lieutenants there. Several alcaldes mayores reported that their districts would not support lieutenants at all (e.g., Real de San Pedro Analco, Real de Comanja) or that the lieutenants earned insufficient incomes (Cuquío, Yahualica, Mesticacan, and Tequila). Nearly all complained that the income was too small to appoint any but local men, and that they could not find well-qualified local men to serve. Most of the lieutenants in the Altos de Jalisco were reported to be landowners native to the district, and those from Tepatitlan and La Barca were beholden to local notables for posting their bonds of office. In Hostotipaquillo, the lieutenants were modest creole and mestizo ranchers, farmers, and miners, one of whom had served many years. In Ahuacatlan and Santa María del Oro, they were local men of some means who did not depend on the income of the office for their living. The lieutenant for Teuchitlan was an Indian cacique who had asked the alcalde mayor several times for permission to resign. In some poor districts, the lieutenants were "reputedly [creole] Spaniards" without judicial authority because their superiors were uncertain whether they could be trusted. The unusually prosperous district of Fresnillo had all peninsular lieutenants. According to the alcalde mayor, all of them were men of high quality, although some had only modest means of their own.[28]

Means importantly affected the district governors' relationship to subjects and parish priests. The crown's assumption had been that a salary, judicial fees, and concessions for the sale of stamped paper and bulls of the crusade would provide them with a comfortable income. But royal officials discovered in 1766 that few alcaldes mayores in the heartland of the viceroyalty had received salaries since 1717.[29] Despite a royal cedula on September 9, 1771, ordering that all alcaldes mayores receive their salaries, a survey made the following year revealed that many were still going unpaid, and, with a few exceptions, the ones who did receive salaries were not even close to getting a sufficient income.[30] In only four of 149 districts did the salary amount to more than 500 pesos annually: Veracruz, 5,000 pesos; Puebla, 4,000; Oaxaca, 665; and Michoacán, 525. Forty districts listed no salary at all, and the other 105 averaged 304 pesos, with a median of only 150 pesos. The administrative costs of taking office alone amounted to 425 pesos for Huejotzingo (Puebla) in 1768.[31] By law, alcaldes mayores were also required to post a bond before taking office.[32] The intendancy reforms called for higher salaries, which were to be the subdelegados' main income, but royal officials acknowledged during the 1790's that a salary of 5 percent of the local tribute, plus the judicial fees and other collections regulated by arancel, was still not an adequate income for most of them.[33] Yet most alcaldías mayores and subdelegaciones were prized appointments, so they obviously did offer advantages, including a lucrative living. According to one interested source—the peninsular priest Tirso Díaz—an alcalde mayor in the 1770's should have been able to accumulate between 20,000 pesos and 50,000 pesos during a five-year term.[34]

One way district governors could augment their income was to milk the judicial and administrative fees by generating business for themselves, misrepresenting taxes owed, levying excessive fines, and overcharging for services. In criminal courts, this bureaucratic entrepreneurship included frivolous arrests, extra maintenance charges for incarceration, and fines instead of corporal punishment.[35] Or the justicia made little effort to prevent drunkenness or illicit sex in order to increase the number of arrests and his income from fines.[36] In any case, reliance on judicial fees for income encouraged both bribery and an over-energetic enforcement of criminal laws at the district level. As a style of justice and source of income, incarceration was habitual in the late colonial period.

Taxes and fees were manipulated in other ways as well. Tax reporting could be turned to profit by undercounting the number of tributaries, and exorbitant or unauthorized fees could be demanded for land measurements, certifying wills, doling out vending privileges, inventories of estates, periodic visitas to dependent settlements, confirming elections, and supervising cofradía meetings.[37] The subdelegado of Tonalá in 1817 allegedly required a fee for virtually every public act he performed.[38] Some district governors demanded produce and money for their own use from all households.[39] Others forced cofradías to sell them livestock below market value.[40]

Requisitioning Indian labor was another source of income for some district governors, despite early colonial laws that forbade them to "make use of [Indians'] services" without pay.[41] In the late colonial period, labor was usually acquired obliquely, by forcing prisoners to work off their fines and prison costs.[42] But some district governors were apparently brazen enough to require communities in their jurisdictions to provide labor gangs for their agricultural estates.[43]

In principle, such abuses of office should have come to light and the perpe-trators been held accountable in the residencia—the judicial inquiry into the performance of district governors at the end of their term. But, as the archbishop noted in 1762, residencias were often not carried out with "disinterest and recti-tude."[44] The cura of Ixtapan in 1773 put the matter less delicately: "When the cash is at hand, giants become pygmies, which you can verify by asking your-self whether any *alcalde mayor* has done badly in his *residencia*."[45] Ten years later, the regent of the Audiencia of Nueva Galicia in Guadalajara was accused of de-flecting serious charges against his compadre, the corregidor of Tepatitlan, and naming his own nephew to preside over the residencias of the alcaldes mayores of Hostotipaquillo, Huauchinango, and Tala.[46]

The district governor's commercial activities, which usually were his most important source of income, had an ambiguous legal history. Under *Recopilación* 5-2-47 and 2-16-54 and a 1719 cedula, alcaldes mayores and their lieutenants could not have commercial relations with Indians.[47] Yet the repartimiento (their mo-nopoly on the sale of certain goods in the district, usually including mules) was a common practice during the seventeenth and eighteenth centuries,[48] one that they defended as indispensable to good government, Indian productivity, and royal revenue. In 1751, another cedula acknowledged the repartimiento as a nec-essary evil—damaging to the interests of local Indians, but essential to making them produce above subsistence and attracting qualified candidates to the office of alcalde mayor. The solution, this cedula concluded, was closer regulation—an arancel to fix the prices of repartimiento goods.[49] In the name of free trade and honest government, the intendancy ordinance applied to New Spain in 1789 called for an end to the repartimientos. It is not yet clear where and when the prohibition was enforced.[50] Writing as if the law was in fact widely applied, Vice-roy Revillagigedo (the younger) observed in 1789 that the best-qualified candi-dates were not applying for the subdelegaciones, and that those in office now had to resort to illegal means to make their living. In his opinion only an adequate salary for the subdelegado could replace the legal repartimientos and resolve this administrative problem.[51]

With their administrative authority and repartimiento sales as a wedge into the market, eighteenth-century alcaldes mayores traded in whatever was produced locally, sometimes with the financial backing of merchant houses in Mexico City and Veracruz if export goods like cochineal were involved.[52] A general report from the 1770's on district governments in the viceroyalty, with brief entries for each alcaldía mayor, indicated a broad range of commercial activities, including trade in wheat, maize, rice, chickpeas, sugar, honey, pulque, fodder, livestock, lumber, charcoal, salt, cotton textiles, and cochineal.[53]

Higher officials assumed these commercial interests to be the reason why a large number of alcaldes mayores were often absent from their posts. Noting in February 1785 that as many alcaldes mayores resided in Mexico City as outside its busy borders, the crown ordered all corregidores and alcaldes mayores, "with-out exception or admitting excuses of any kind," to return immediately to their districts.[54]

The financial circumstances of many lieutenants in rural districts mirrored those of their patrons: they were likely to enter office with administrative debts and no salary.[55] The sale or "rent" of the office—another source of income for alcaldes mayores—was apparently a common practice in New Spain when it was ordered abolished in 1784.[56] A lieutenant might pay as much as 800 pesos a year for the office.[57] Why would anyone pay such a price for an unsalaried post, aside from the prestige and local authority of a judgeship and the slim possibility of promotion? The reason is much the same as for the alcaldes mayores. Although lieutenants usually did not operate their own repartimientos, it would have been hard for subjects not to patronize those who traded in the local market, as many did.[58] And they tapped the same array of miscellaneous fees for judicial and administrative services, and the same possibilities for extralegal income. Lieutenants were famous for the money they made from direct collections—informally allowing gambling, bootleg liquor enterprises, and illicit liaisons in exchange for a *propina* (gratuity); levying heavy fines; arbitrarily arresting local people, then extorting payments for their release; charging excessive jail costs; and using their judicial powers to mobilize unpaid labor for themselves and others.[59] The cura of Meztitlan de la Sierra (Hidalgo) in 1774 was convinced that bribery was a way of life for the district lieutenant ("everything is settled with money," he charged).[60]

The district governors' largely unsupervised institutional power, their sources of income, and their distance from most people of the district offered many opportunities for abuses. The surviving record of late colonial complaints against them for bribery, physical mistreatment, graft, extortion, contraband, coerced labor, gambling, and sexual misconduct is no more than suggestive. It is probably biased against them because priests and parishioners became more sensitive to abuses as the powers of the governors grew; but it is also biased in the other direction because the governors' power to intimidate would have deterred many complaints. Taken together with the evidence of other kinds of resistance against them, the record suggests that the personal bonds between district governors and their rural Indian subjects were weak even during the period of parish reforms. Without their coercive powers, few could command automatic obedience.

Aside from passive resistance and minor provocations like failing to tip one's hat, the acts of resistance against district governors typically took the form of community tumultos in the core area of the archdiocese and more dangerous individual or small-group defiance in Nueva Galicia. The tumultos, in which governors were sometimes threatened with knives or rocks but were rarely injured, were touched off by intervention in a community land dispute, the incarceration of a pueblo official, the collection of what were considered excessive or arbitrary taxes, the repartimiento, forced labor, demands for local produce, or harsh corporal punishment. Occasionally, a tumulto expressed a deeper resistance to an alcalde mayor's political authority, as the shout of "We have no other judge than our *gobernador*" in the pueblos of San Nicolás and San Simón (Mexicalcingo district, Valley of Mexico) in 1701 documents.[61]

In the Diocese of Guadalajara, some of the defiance was political, even though the district governor called it personal disrespect. When the lieutenant of Etzatlan, Jalisco, decried the "insolence" of local Indians in 1786, he meant that they had invaded the realm of royal justice by "assuming jurisdiction over all sorts of Indian cases, civil as well as criminal, making wills, hearing petitions, and passing judgment on them." [62] Merely trying to implement a royal decree could evoke angry protest. At Zacoalco in 1756, the lieutenant's attempt to take a new census

met with menacing gestures and shouts of "We're not sheep" and "teniente de
mierda."[63]

But in most cases there was little doubt that personal insult or harm was intended. Twice, in 1805 and 1807, the lieutenant of Cañadas in the Altos de Jalisco
was attacked at night and wounded by unknown assailants.[64] Spontaneous out-
bursts against a district governor when he attempted to make an arrest or interfere in a private dispute were more common. A case from Mesticacan in the Altos
in 1803 can illustrate this kind of personal resistance in the Diocese of Guadalajara. In the lieutenant's account, after curfew on September 24, he heard a crowd
of people gathered in a corner of the town plaza. He went out to find three *obra-
jeros* (weavers in textile workshops) still there. One of them, an Indian in his
mid-twenties named Ubaldo Matías, pretended to be drunk. When he resisted
his companions' efforts to take him home, the lieutenant warned Matías that he
could go to jail if he did not return home quietly. About two blocks from the
plaza, Matías again resisted and began to shout. At that, his companions released
him, and the lieutenant approached.

He found Matías flat on his back, motionless "as if he were dead." Hearing
the lieutenant order the other two men to carry him to jail, Matías sat up and declared angrily, "What jail, and what damn coward [*pendejo*] says so? Since when
do you think you can take me to jail, don Juan? What shit [*carajo*]. You'll have
to tear me apart before I go to jail. I ought to destroy you as one of those who
uses the staff of office to offend men." The lieutenant said that he endured these
insults and more for about fifteen minutes, all the while trying to calm Matías,
reminding him that "I am *your* judge. Remember that you must treat me with
respect, that I can punish you."

"I don't have to go to jail," the defiant Matías replied, "and you aren't man
enough to take me. Now we'll see," and he picked up some rocks. At that, the
lieutenant drew his sword, hitting him five or six times with the flat side. They
wrestled; then the lieutenant withdrew, with Matías in pursuit, armed with rocks.
With the help of seven leading citizens, the lieutenant disarmed Matías and
placed him in stocks, "the only prison we have here." Four days later, his brother,
José de la Cruz, showing a cobbler's knife, helped Matías escape, warning the
lieutenant, "Now the dispute is with me, not my brother. If anyone approaches,
I'll kill him." In July 1810, the two men surrendered to a new lieutenant. Matías
admitted that he had been arrested four times before in the pueblo, twice for
drunkenness and twice for failing to pay the royal tribute. He claimed to have no
memory of insulting the lieutenant or fighting with him—"he insists that since
he was drunk, he remembers nothing." A year later, he and his brother again disappeared, perhaps to join an insurgent band or one of the gangs of highwaymen
then active in the Altos.[65]

District Governors and Parish Priests

The essence of the relationship between district governors and parish priests,
as early colonial law and eighteenth-century audiencia judges described it, was
countervailing power—"to maintain a harmonious relationship" (*guardar armonía*) and check arbitrary acts by either authority.[66] Deep conflict between them

was obviously undesirable from the colonial government's point of view, but so was collusion (*estrechez*). A balanced polite but cautious cooperation would ensure that serious disputes at the district level reached higher courts, thereby preserving a semblance of justice and reducing the possibility of anticolonial wars by Indian subjects.[67] And the subjects also benefited from separation and respectful competition in the relationship between district officials and parish priests — what John Phelan described as institutionalized mutual suspicion.[68] If the priests and magistrates were not in league, Indians might have a natural ally in one or the other when disputes arose.

"Guardar armonía de ambas magestades" continued to be invoked in the late eighteenth century as the watchword of proper relations between district governors and parish priests. In their disputes, a district governor or a parish priest (or both) would claim that he had been particularly forbearing in the relationship, that he had always maintained "la buena armonía" even when his counterpart had not reciprocated.[69] Audiencia judgments routinely warned either or both to follow this principle, as did the ecclesiastical courts and the Fourth Provincial Council of prelates.[70] And when contending priests and governors were reconciled without a judicial decree, they formally promised to "guardar armonía." [71]

A preponderance of responsibility in spiritual matters fell to the clergy and in temporal matters to the justicias, but sixteenth- and seventeenth-century colonial law and practice did not distinguish clearly between the spiritual and the temporal.[72] Shared responsibilities included policing public morals (especially sexual misconduct, drunkenness, and gambling), supervising pueblo elections, uprooting Indian "idolatry," and promoting schools for instruction in church doctrine.[73]

Colonial law also called for mutual assistance and mutual supervision. *Recopilación* 3-1-3 (1563) called on "prelates and other ecclesiastical judges to give secular judges the necessary help and favor." The justicias were, above all, responsible for lending royal auxilio to the doctrineros "whenever necessary" in order to make certain that Indians attended mass, studied doctrine regularly, and fulfilled the Easter duty.[74] Royal auxilio was both assistance and supervision, as *Recopilación* 1-10-12 (1530) made clear: no parish priests could make arrests or administer punishment without it.[75]

For the priests' part, early colonial orders required that they report to the crown when Indians were not treated well, and early-eighteenth-century instructions required that they report on the conduct of justicias.[76] For alcaldes mayores and audiencias, the instructions were more numerous and detailed. Sixteenth-century laws published in the *Recopilación* called on justicias to see that curas did not abuse Indians. Priests enjoyed a substantial measure of immunity from prosecution by state courts, but the audiencia fiscal was to urge prelates to take appropriate action against incorrigible doctrineros and in extreme cases to advise the prelate to remit the case to the secular authorities for prosecution.[77] Late-eighteenth-century district governors were called on to testify to the merits of individual parish priests, to select witnesses and submit reports on the conduct of priests in their districts, to report on the income of parish priests, and to investigate charges against them.

How these complex hypothetical relationships operated in practice has been little studied. Assessments made in passing usually treat curas and district governors as natural allies who joined forces for personal profit.[78] The judicial and administrative record of the eighteenth century suggests a less predictable relationship, one in which conflict, more than collusion or the ideal balance, was increasingly evident.

Though the familiar language of balance and harmony continued into the late eighteenth century, legal practices and administrative policies changed in ways that revised the terms of countervailing power. The requirement of royal auxilio, for example, was now invoked more often as a means of supervision and a way to display delegated royal authority than as a means of assistance. Indeed, the crown intended to make such assistance less automatic, as when the viceroy specified in 1789 that no auxilio should be extended to curas who wanted to incarcerate Indians unless a written justification had been presented and reviewed by the justicia ("sin examen de autos").[79] The application of royal auxilio became a perennial issue before the audiencias. In a few cases, it was raised by a district governor: parish priests were flooding their offices with requests for help over every petty incident of misconduct, or a certain priest was ignoring the requirement of royal auxilio by arresting and punishing offenders on his own.[80] But most of the complaints were brought by priests: the justicia had been too slow or indecisive in giving assistance; he had released prisoners the priest had arrested without determining the reason for the arrest; or he had failed altogether to provide auxilio when parishioners were insolent, behaved immorally, did not pay their clerical fees, or were absent from Sunday mass or the Easter duty.[81] Once a priest appealed to higher authorities over royal auxilio, the working relationship with the district governor deteriorated, as it did at Misquiahuala (Tetepango district, Hidalgo) in 1793 and Mazatepec (Morelos) in 1800–1802.[82]

Jurisdiction over Indian "idolatry" underwent another kind of shift in the overlapping responsibilities of curas and justicias. Judging by a handbook of legal procedures prepared for the cura of Huamantla (Puebla) in 1746, the practice of "mixed jurisdiction" in such cases before the 1780's assigned the alcalde mayor or his lieutenant an auxiliary role: the secular governor should respond to the juez eclesiástico's requests for arrests, the sequestering of personal property, the joint inspection of the physical evidence, and the execution of the ecclesiastical court's sentence.[83] In a 1783 "idolatry" case, the Council of the Indies called for a substantially different arrangement. It judged that secular magistrates had jurisdiction "over all civil matters, including Indian idolatry." Ecclesiastical judges might adjudicate "idolatry" cases, but only if a formal delegation of authority was made by the secular magistrate. This judgment was published in a royal cedula on December 21, 1787.[84]

As earlier chapters indicate, parish priests were also losing their traditional influence over the administration of pueblo finances and ecclesiastical property. From 1789 (when the intendancy reforms for New Spain were being put in place), a new vehemence, sometimes even an anticlerical edge, to royal decrees on property rights and taxes invited aggressive moves against priests by district governors and audiencias. A royal cedula of March 22, 1789 (published in a viceregal bando on September 30), which emphatically assigned jurisdiction over the properties of capellanías to royal courts, contained a sweeping indictment of clerical influence. Responding to abuses by priests in collecting the interest on their capellanía endowments, the bando denounced "the despotism with which the Ecclesiastical Jurisdiction has tried to squash Royal Authority" and demanded clerical subordination:

The Kingdom of Jesus Christ was and is spiritual. It has not given its ministers any rights at all over temporal goods. Nor has it altered the order of civil society, by whose power the Church possesses its properties and the clergy their privileges. [This is] to declare not only that all judicial notice of matters that are not spiritual belongs to the Royal Jurisdiction, but also that laws should be issued to suppress the acquisitions and usurpations of [past] ecclesiastical invasions.[85]

Also in 1789, the Audiencia of Mexico warned the cura of Tlaquiltenango (Cuernavaca district, Morelos) in a fee dispute with his parishioners that the royal tribunals have "indisputable authority to make him observe everything that is just." He was, the court added, not to repeat his "outrages and abuses against Royal Justice."[86] The balance had clearly tipped against ecclesiastical justice in the daily life of rural parishes. More frequently now, parish priests lamented the disobedience of Indian parishioners and complained either that they needed a resident lieutenant and more royal auxilio or that the parishioners obeyed the district governor more than their cura.[87]

If Tirso Díaz can be believed, already by 1770 curas were afraid to challenge abusive district justicias and denounce their lax control over local sexual misconduct, drunkenness, gambling, and contraband:

The *cura* and other ecclesiastical ministers now are careful about speaking and intervening to remedy such scandals because a few days later [the district governor] or others will lodge an elaborate complaint, replete with witnesses, that will send [the cura] off to seclusion [by the bishop], and result in the loss of the merit he acquired in the exercise of his office and his reputation and good name with the prelate (and consequently with everyone).[88]

There was at least a kernel of truth to Díaz's claim—priests were feeling more embattled, and district governors could act with a freer hand. But, as the chapters in Part II indicate, few parish priests were as bereft of allies and other resources as he implied.[89]

In any event, it is clear that most district governors and parish priests continued to work together routinely without great conflict. In 1793, only one subdelegado in four mentioned any real problems in his report on the priests in his district, and some subdelegados, as we saw earlier, were positively enthusiastic about certain priests, praising them for their political conduct and contributions to the "peace and tranquility" of the district.[90] Many district governors continued to act on curas' requests for auxilio, some even deposing pueblo officials the cura found unsatisfactory; and some governors and priests supported each other in more than routine ways, including enthusiastic testimonials in court.[91] This is not persuasive evidence that the ideal balance was achieved. Judging by the 1793 reports, where subdelegados mainly praised priests who accepted the narrowed conception of their public role ("que no sale de cassa si no es a sumpto de la administración") or did not cause trouble on their own, routine order would be largely on the governor's terms or reflect his distance from the curas' affairs. But the judicial record does suggest that neither had much appetite for a humiliating confrontation, and that mutual deference and the prompt application of royal *auxilio* at the cura's request went far to maintain a balance that both could accept.

A case from Coatepec (Malinalco district) provides a fine example of a delicately worked out relationship between the two sides. In early March 1798, a local Indian had come to the cura with a complaint against his neighbor over the ownership of construction materials. The cura refused to hear the complaint, advising both parties that it was for the lieutenant (who did not reside in Coatepec) to decide. But when that did not settle the matter, he had some of those involved punished without the lieutenant's *auxilio*. Sensitive to the niceties of the situation, he then sent the lieutenant a letter of explanation that appealed to their common sense of justice and respect for authority, and bowed to the lieutenant's right to enforce the law:

Very Dear Sir:

Yesterday morning, Santiago appeared, asking me to call Pedro Juan and his wife who [Santiago claimed] were carrying off some building stones, wanting me to order them to stop and return what they took. I, as a great foe of Indian gossip, persuaded them to take the matter to you. At that point, Juan's wife came up, followed by Juan and others, menacing Santiago. All were drunk and failed to pay me proper respect, making as many insulting remarks as they wished. Juan's wife even had the nerve to put her hands in my face with great insolence. So I struck them a few times. Please summon them and punish their drunkenness and insolence.

The fact is that during this season of confessions, *tepache* is consumed endlessly. . . . Even though the others who have approached me in such a drunken state, like the *escribano* and Salvador el Temachti,[92] have not been insolent, it would be a very good thing if you warned them. That way they might control themselves for, I tell you, this and worse behavior should not be tolerated during Holy Lent.

May God keep you many years, your most devoted chaplain who kisses your hands,

Cornelio López[93]

This lieutenant not only had given Father López his timely *auxilio* in the past; he chose not to make an issue of the priest's punishment on the spot in this case. Such cooperation did not require personal loyalty or a sense of institutional solidarity.[94] In one case where an alcalde mayor acceded to the cura's request—that the Indian who had received the most votes for alcalde of Joloapan (Hidalgo) in 1768 not be installed—he emphasized that he had done so because he accepted the cura's judgment that the man and his family were a pernicious force in the community: "as a priest and *cura*, I assumed he would not deceive me." But several months later, when the cura wanted the new official removed as well, the alcalde mayor demurred, concluding that the cura's judgment about local officeholders could not be trusted.[95]

But the Coatepec example is more typical. Because of their standing as colonial officials and their shared view of Indian subjects, many district governors and curas managed to cooperate despite the unsettling changes of the late eighteenth century. Though the pattern was far from uniform, many curas, like most district governors, identified with the polite society of Spanish descent more than with their Indian subjects.[96] In his frustration at litigation against him by Indian parishioners, the cura of Tlaltizapan (Morelos) urged the audiencia to ask "all the *hacienda* administrators and *vecinos de razón* . . . whether I oppressed my parishioners or treated them with great love." [97] Other curas admitted that they wanted to recruit more gente de razón into their head town and urged such people to participate in parish affairs.[98] As the cura of Ocoyoacac (Edo. de México) put it when he decried the Indians' hatred of gente de razón residing among them, "all the *gente de razón* are devout and God-fearing." [99] When both the cura and the district governor were the objects of Indian disrespect, tumultos, or litigation, each one's sense of solidarity with the other and with gente de razón increased.[100] That solidarity was grounded in a common fear that Indians were disorderly and unpredictable—people of "excessive liberty and no fear." [101] The local justicia put it this way in a case brought against the cura of Huiciltepec (Guerrero) in 1800 for failing to fulfill his parish duties:

[I can testify to] the meager truthfulness of these people, the hypocrisy with which they cover their malice, especially when they harbor some particular grudge in their heart— as they undoubtedly do against their *cura* over the litigation they have undertaken against him for the last six years now over *aranceles*, clerical fees, *cofradías*, and lands.[102]

Judging by occasional Indian petitions to the audiencia and the fiscales' opinions, cooperation could well become collusion, with a justicia or priest allowing the other to do as he wished. A justicia might, for example, fail to process Indian complaints against the cura, or intervene aggressively to break the staffs of Indian officials who protested the cura's demands, or fine an Indian heavily for disrespect to the cura.[103] Indian plaintiffs complained bitterly of the unchecked abuses and miscarriages of justice when district governors and priests were allies. As three Indian officials of San Pedro Cacaguatepec, near Acapulco, put it in 1782:

If we take these [complaints] to the priests, besides ignoring them and abusing us, they do worse. If we take our complaints to the secular judges, the same thing happens because they temporize with the priests. It is precisely for these reasons that in our bad luck we are reduced to a perpetual slavery.[104]

The fiscal of the Audiencia of Guadalajara noticed the problem in a 1789 dispute in Atotonilco el Alto, when he, too, spoke of the "tight unity" (estrecha unidad) between parish priests and district governors as a source of mistreatment of Indians.[105]

Conflict and Criticism

Public estrangement between priests and district governors was neither new nor pervasive, but there was a growing sense on the part of a growing number of priests that the relationship had deteriorated, that conflicts had become more intense. As we have seen, various issues set late colonial district governors and priests against each other: pueblo elections, primary schools, cajas de comunidad, cofradías, clerical fees, royal auxilio, churches as asylums, public morality, the priests' personal conduct, and the governors' repartimientos. The underlying sore spot in these and other conflicts was jurisdiction—identifying and respecting the boundaries between secular and ecclesiastical affairs. Those boundaries had always occasioned conflicts, but by the late 1760's, they were sharper, were drawn along different lines, and were interpreted in different ways. Previously, when a parish priest was accused of usurping the king's jurisdiction, it was likely to be a literal claim. At Zacoalco (Jalisco) in 1753, for example, the cura reportedly tried civil and criminal cases himself and advised the lieutenant that "Your Royal Jurisdiction is nil and despised in this *pueblo*." [106] But as royal jurisdiction expanded into new areas, isolated or minor violations acquired a more figurative meaning—as at Joloapan (Hidalgo), in 1768, where the lieutenant saw the priest's punishment of a messenger for losing an important letter as an infringement on royal authority; or at Patatlan (Michoacán), in 1799, where the cura's release of a man from the public jail was read as emblematic of "the excesses that *curas* and other priests commit in order to impose fitting punishment on the guilty." [107]

Jurisdictional disputes sometimes brought into play the priest's most fearsome and humiliating weapon—excommunication—a weapon brought out often enough apparently that the Audiencia of Mexico felt the need to warn ecclesiastical judges in 1786 not to use it in such cases.[108] A particularly fierce battle that ended in excommunication took place in the parish of Autlan (Jalisco) between 1784 and 1787. A string of small disputes between the priest and district governors over the sale of meat on Sunday mornings and local people carrying arms came to a head over a case of rape. The learned, punctilious cura, Dr. Salvador Brambila, claimed that the case belonged in his court because rape, as much as incontinence, endangered the soul. When the alcalde mayor refused to cede jurisdiction, Brambila excommunicated him and his associates. While the jurisdictional issue was debated at higher levels, Brambila and the lieutenant of Autlan kept the community in an uproar. Brambila reportedly held parishioners in fear while he fattened the audiencia's dossier with his long disquisitions. He accused the lieutenant and alcalde mayor of concubinage, gambling, haughtiness, and caprice, and, at first, would not lift the ban even when ordered to do so by the audiencia. An audiencia decree issued on September 11, 1786, deplored Brambila's disrespect to "ministers of the Royal Jurisdiction," and concluded that the cura had invaded their territory and made excessive use of his authority to excommunicate. The cura was ordered to lift the ban or face a fine of 200,000 *maravedíes* (about 735 pesos). Four months later, Brambila was engaged in another jurisdictional dispute, in which he expelled the lieutenant from Autlan. Brambila granted a general absolution on September 18, 1787, but he had already gone too far. The bishop of Guadalajara would soon comply with another audiencia order calling for his transfer from Autlan.[109]

The Archdiocese of Mexico saw a few notorious confrontations in which curas defended their customary authority and refined sense of personal honor by defying district governors, but most of the extravagant clashes and acts of open disrespect by parish priests come from the Diocese of Guadalajara, especially from curas with fifteen or twenty years of service in the parish.[110] The most extravagant example of all may have been Salvador Parra. As a cura's assistant in San Pedro Analco, Parra was charged with "violating the Royal Jurisdiction" in September 1796 by insulting and striking the lieutenant of Tequila, who had come to his house to arrest a fugitive from the district jail and a woman who had committed incest.[111] Six years later, now as interim cura of Zapotlanejo, Parra was charged with insulting the lieutenant and driving him out of town. The lieutenant claimed that Parra had become powerful there by protecting criminals who, in turn, protected him.[112] Then, in 1806, as the cura of Valle de Topia (Diocese of Durango), Parra was charged by the district governor and the cura of Escanela with new offenses, including concubinage and the sacrilegious use of his vestments by his young mistress. The most serious charge was that he had attempted to kill the local comisario (sheriff), who had come to his house to arrest a man and a woman one night. As the couple resisted, Parra came forward in his underwear, brandishing two pistols, which he tried unsuccessfully to fire. When the comisario presented his warrant, Parra responded that the couple were soon to be married, and he would not allow the arrests until after the wedding mass. The comisario objected that they were not even engaged. Parra countered by telling the couple to hold hands and saying, "I marry you now." The comisario replied that there was a legal impediment to their marriage and proceeded to arrest them over the cura's objections. Parra was arrested for attempted murder but escaped from jail in July 1808.[113] He resurfaced in the judicial record on June 22, 1810, accused of seditious remarks in a Durango store about abusive peninsulares, cowardly members of the Junta Central of Sevilla, and his willingness to take up arms with other creoles against a French invasion from the United States. His last petition to the audiencia—requesting release after more than two years in irons—is dated January 18, 1813.[114]

Parish priests and district governors occasionally clashed over ceremonies and rites of deference and precedence. At Tlaquiltenango (Morelos) in 1803, the pretext for the lieutenant's sweeping claim that the cura was "diametrically opposed to everything that relates to the Royal Jurisdiction" was his supposed failure to celebrate a requiem mass in honor of the Prince of Asturias's marriage. The cura's delayed response reveals deeper sources of conflict, including his own exasperation. The reports by the lieutenant were, he said, demeaning and false, acts of revenge, the work of "an arrogant, imprudent, lying, reckless, and audacious man." He himself was true to his "character and religion," which called him "to humility and suffering in order to root and cultivate peace." Furthermore, the "real reasons" for the slander, which made the truth of everything he claimed "as certain as the noonday sun," were the tensions between a schoolteacher he had hired and the lieutenant, his own participation in a suit brought against the subdelegado by the Indians of Tlaquiltenango, and the lieutenant's irritation at the many appeals he had made to him on behalf of the Indians. The cura also seized the opportunity to make countercharges that the lieutenant arrested people without cause in order to collect fines.[115]

At Tlalmanalco (Edo. de México) in 1817, a bitter dispute broke out during Easter week when the lieutenant accused the cura of "harming Royal Justice" by not serving him first at the communion rail on Maundy Thursday and not presenting him that day with the key to the tabernacle for safekeeping until Saturday. In a testy reply, the cura wrote that it was the lieutenant's arrogance, rather than his zeal for the faith and royal justice, that occasioned these charges "designed to slander me." He had served the lieutenant as soon as he came to the rail, he said, and had placed the key around his neck as soon as the church was closed—a contravention of canon law that he allowed because it was the custom in those parts. The cura received a double dose of criticism in this case. The archbishop's counsel reprimanded him for giving out the key to the tabernacle, and the fiscal of the audiencia wanted the archbishop to warn him to "guardar armonía" and show secular officials proper respect.[116]

The lieutenant of Ajuchitlan (district of Tetela del Río, Guerrero), Joseph Victor de Sámano, and the vicario de pie fijo Juan Baptista Lecca (a veteran of 20 years there who had called for the removal of the two previous lieutenants) stood even more firmly on their separate rights as they assailed each other in 1790–91 with charges of disturbing the peace, invading the other's jurisdiction, and "mortal hatred." When the lieutenant brought an audiencia order to Lecca's house commanding him to stay out of the affairs of the lay brotherhoods, Lecca menaced him with his bastón and shouted that the intendant had been deceived by the subdelegado and the lieutenant. Later, Lecca agreed to sign a receipt but argued with the lieutenant over who should sign first.[117]

Judging by the testimony of local witnesses, some of these disputes shaded into open anticlericalism on the district governor's part. In a 1771 complaint against the alcalde mayor of Taxco (Guerrero) by a longtime vicario, witnesses stressed the alcalde mayor's hatred of priests. Evidently, there was animus on both sides (as well as unfortunate timing for the vicario during the regalist Archbishop Lorenzana's administration), because the provisor eventually reprimanded the vicario for "insults to royal ministers" and "lack of moderation, humility, and gentleness."[118] At Chametla (in southern Sinaloa) in 1805, various witnesses testified that the lieutenant hated the cura—insulting him in public, threatening him with a knife, and encouraging his parishioners to continue in their grossly immoral ways.[119]

Parish priests in these suits often spoke of the district governor as "my pertinacious enemy," "my greatest enemy," "the capital enemy of priests," and "the self-proclaimed enemy of the *curas* and other ecclesiastics," sometimes with good reason.[120] But an accusation of anticlericalism could have little basis other than the priest's need to defend himself in court. That seems to have been the case when the cura of Meztitlan claimed in 1785 that the alcalde mayor was "ill-disposed toward the clergy" and violated "ecclesiastical authority." He was facing the well-documented charge that he had demanded 500 pesos for burying the Indian gobernador, and resisted when the alcalde mayor tried to negotiate a discount to 200 pesos.[121]

Some priests and parishioners accused particular district governors not only of anticlericalism but also of irreverence toward the church and its teachings. Curas and witnesses from Cuquío (Jalisco) in 1786, Zapotiltic (Jalisco) in 1795, and Tututepec (Hidalgo) in 1796 testified that the district governor did not fulfill the Easter duty. According to a Spanish witness in the last case, the lieutenant had not confessed or taken communion during his 21 years of service.[122] The military subdelegado of Tlajomulco in 1815 not only did not attend church; he reportedly made fun of the cura and destroyed a cemetery cross where many parishioners recently had gathered for a blessing. His explanation was that the cross had become a secret meeting place for insurgents.[123] According to the bishop of Puebla in 1772, the provincial governor's behavior in church was so inappropriate that his absence would have been preferable:

No one could miss the lack of reverence he displays on those occasions he does attend—with his legs indecently wide open (please pardon [this vulgarity]), craning his neck to look around as if he were out in the street, failing to kneel when all of the faithful did so in veneration of the temple or when the representation of one of the mysteries demanded it.[124]

Witnesses also reported mildly sacrilegious remarks by district governors—as in 1792, when Alejandra Francisca Gonsales of Nochistlan (Jalisco) reported that the lieutenant tried to get her drunk on maize beer, proclaiming that "in this town only the Holy Sepulchre doesn't know how to drink it"; or in 1785, when parishioners of Meztitlan (Hidalgo) displayed an engraving of Nuestra Señora de los Dolores and pleaded with the alcalde mayor in her name not to whip a local man, but the official declared that he would rescind the order only if the Virgin spoke to him.[125] In an earlier, more serious case, the alcalde mayor of Autlan (Jalisco) was charged in 1705 with declaring in public that he did not believe the cura was the agent of transubstantiation, and that for him "there was no God other than money." He was also charged with smashing the collection box for Santa Efigenia.[126]

But the most common evidence of irreverence on the part of governors adduced by the priests was their failure to help ensure parishioners' compliance with the Easter duty, regular attendance at mass, and decorum during services; or their active encouragement of immoral behavior. For example, in 1793 the corregidor of Coyoacan (D.F.) was accused of abetting a scandal in the Carmelite church at San Angel, in which drunken people vomited and fought on Christmas Eve. The corregidor supposedly did not even attend church that night, instead lingering outside with a widow and her daughters, "giving a not very good example of himself."[127]

Clashes were bound to occur when a justicia with an exalted sense of his authority ran into an equally officious parish priest. The lieutenant of Ocotlan (Jalisco) in 1778, frustrated by the cura's insistence on his traditional prerogatives in public affairs and threats of excommunication, stretched his criticism of the priest nearly to a charge of sedition: the cura acted as if he were the "absolute owner of the royal jurisdiction that I administer."[128] Responding in 1805 to a complaint by the cura of Chametla (Sinaloa) that he had released a woman from his custody, the lieutenant of Rosario explained that she was about to give birth and deserved the medical care she would receive outside of confinement. In a revealing letter to the cura, advising him of his intention, the lieutenant indicated that he was coming there (like some Lone Ranger) to *do justice*:

In short, I shall be in that *pueblo* as soon as possible, either in person or represented by a commissioner, to purify the matter; for, to administer justice, nothing can stand in my way (except the duties of service to the sovereign). I have never, nor will I ever, judge in anger . . . because my job is to hear and to administer justice to all; and lastly, you know that in this and all else, [I] may order whatever [I] please.[129]

District governors were quicker than parishioners or the ecclesiastical courts to label particular parish priests sexually incontinent, as well as quick-tempered, high-handed, selfish, and immoderate in other ways,[130] and it must have been galling for them to find that the ecclesiastical courts were lenient toward these and other kinds of misconduct. Priests seemed to them altogether too far above the law. In 1790, Bernardo de Bonavía, the subdelegado of Villa Alta (Oaxaca)—a district notorious for conflict between priests and district governors—wrote of his dissatisfaction that the intendant had turned his reports of various curas' abuses of Indians over to the bishop for prosecution. The most the bishop had done, said Bonavía, was to send out an investigator who was a close friend of one of the accused curas. In any case, he found no justice in these matters when the ecclesiastical courts were in charge.[131]

A particularly full exposition of a peninsular district governor's view of parish priests is Hipólito Villarroel's *Enfermedades políticas*, the work of a man dispatched to the third-class alcaldía mayor of Cuautla (Morelos) in 1761 and, after a return visit to Spain, to the first-class district of Tlapa (Guerrero) in 1774.[132]

Exactly what befell Villarroel in his first post is unknown. He may have been removed but more likely served out his term and was not reappointed. At any rate, he could not have had an easy time of it, arriving in a period when the secularization of parishes was still fresh; when troubling revelations of "idolatries" and religious protest nearby at Yautepec (see Appendix C) and in the district of Chalco resulted in a report by the archbishop that placed much of the blame on avaricious district governors;[133] and when charges of misconduct had been leveled against him personally.

Tlapa was hardly an improvement. Villarroel no sooner got there than he became embroiled in an ongoing dispute with the cura of Chipetlan and Indian pueblos over the alcalde mayor's control of textile production by the forced distribution of cotton to Indians and the repartimiento de efectos. Shortly before Villarroel's arrival, the then alcalde mayor had impugned the cura's initial complaint about the repartimiento as an act of revenge for "the light punishment I administered to his *mulato* godson in the line of duty." The cura responded self-righteously that his actions were altogether consistent with "the zeal and care with which I am obliged to attend my poor parishioners in temporal as well as spiritual matters."

Villarroel's scathing report from Tlapa on July 10, 1774, shortly after his arrival, suggests that his presentation of himself in the *Enfermedades políticas* as a militant defender of royal justice with an almost apocalyptic vision of disorder in the colony was deeply colored by his experiences there and probably even more so, at Cuautla. It was a sweeping indictment of parish priests as power-crazed, disobedient enemies of district governors, and of Indian parishioners as their willing dupes. The district governors, as he saw it, were innocent victims of the priests, whose machinations threatened the good order and prosperity of the area. The report reads in part:

If complaints have been leveled against my predecessor, they are certainly unfounded, since during the two months that I have exercised the office, I have not heard the slightest complaint against his conduct; nor to my knowledge has he engaged in extortions of any kind.

I am convinced that it is all a slander, and that it must have been brought to the high court through the influence of some *cura* or other, the source from which discord usually flows, as experience in this unfortunate kingdom reveals to us. There is no *cura* who does not directly or indirectly use his influence against an *alcalde mayor* in order to strength his position through the destruction of his adversary. By this misguided means, he seeks to exercise his authority as he sees fit, which he judges is his to insert in every case and matter foreign to his ministry.

The style and fundamental propositions that such *curas* regularly teach the Indians is: whenever they receive an order or decision from the *alcalde mayor*, they should bring it to the *cura* and follow the course of action he advises; he tells the Indians whether or not they should obey the *alcalde mayor*. If the *alcalde mayor* opposes this corrupt practice (as is just), gossip, protests, and complaints to higher authorities immediately follow, and the result is trouble for the *alcalde mayor*, the disruption of proper relationships [*buena armonía*], the desolation of the district, a lack of respect by the Indians for judicial authority, and *curas* gripped by the conceit that they are authorized to destroy one and all who subsequently take up the office [of *alcalde mayor*].[134]

Villarroel apparently composed the *Enfermedades políticas* in 1785, more than five years after his term at Tlapa ended, with litigation against him from that time still pending. This treatise was in the tradition of seventeenth-century Spanish *arbitristas*—framed as an exposé of political and social ills, accompanied by the author's prescriptions. His interpretation had become more elaborate and apocalyptic, but it was much the same as in 1774. He warned darkly about "chaos," "disorder," and "the total dissolution of justice not only in the capital but throughout [the viceroyalty]."[135] Secular parish priests were rich, avaricious men, the "dedicated enemies of *alcaldes mayores*," who encouraged Indians to lodge "ruinous complaints" against the state's agents and were thereby leading the pueblos down the road to extermination. Above all, they must be separated from the temporal affairs of their parishioners. Echoing the cedulas of the 1760's and 1770's, Villarroel emphasized financial affairs, especially the administration of cofradía properties. To demonstrate that he was not an enemy of religion or the Catholic church, he praised the Mendicant priests who had preceded the diocesan clergy in parish service. Indians, he concluded with an Augustinian twist, were nearly ungovernable. "Given over to superstition, idolatry, and other detestable vices," they "[fled] from all correction, control, and instruction [and exercised] complete freedom by suppressing the *alcaldes mayores* and their lieutenants."[136] His solution was to restrain the parish priests and to appoint "capable judges" who would exercise wider judicial powers, be allowed to serve longer than the standard five-year term if their record warranted it, and be assured of their repartimiento de efectos privileges.[137]

Two Cases from the Periphery

Clashes between district governors and curas on the northern fringes of the two dioceses, in the Sierra Gorda of Querétaro in 1777 and Acaponeta, Nayarit, in 1791, concentrate the main features of estrangement and conflict that were played out in the high courts for other places. (These cases may have reached such extremes because awkward, self-important men were likely to win appointments to parishes and alcaldías mayores in marginal places, which for all their undesirable features did afford them greater freedom from supervision by higher authorities.)

The Sierra Gorda case opened with a report to the viceroy from the alcalde mayor of Cadereyta, Lázaro Joseph Figueroa Yáñez, in which he complained of liberties taken by the interim cura of Xalpan, Manuel de Villalpando. Father Villalpando had taken control of the town plaza that had been marked out in 1770 when the Franciscan doctrina was replaced by a diocesan parish, refusing to allow secular activities in the space and claiming that it contained Christian graves and was therefore under the church's jurisdiction. From his seat in Cadereyta, Figueroa Yáñez had objected that Villalpando was invading the crown's jurisdiction. He claimed that his defense of the crown's rights had aroused the cura's "rancor and ill-will" and led him to plot vengeance with some Indians and soldiers from two frontier posts.

In a note to the archbishop, the viceroy summarized the alcalde mayor's version of events and asked the prelate to warn Villalpando to maintain good relations with the justicia and not stir up local people. The provisor of the archbishop's court acknowledged that the cura had twice sent troops to arrest the alcalde mayor—both times the confrontation was settled without arrests, thanks to the cura of Escanela—but thought that because he was now in Mexico City, sick and contrite, a year's confinement at Tepotzotlan, plus court costs after he recovered, would be the right punishment.

Appealing to the viceroy for relief from this judgment, the cura recounted his version of events. A commander of the Saucillo frontier post had asked for his help when the alcalde mayor passed through there on inspection and charged the soldiers a fee. Villalpando said he had advised the soldiers to take their complaint to the capitanía general, where they secured an order warning the alcalde mayor not to charge for his visit and promising a 1,000-peso fine if he did so in the future. Similarly, when the alcalde mayor aroused three Indian pueblos by demanding visita fees and they came to the cura for relief, he again offered legal advice that resulted in a royal provisión ordering the alcalde mayor not to make such demands. According to the cura, the alcalde mayor ignored the royal provisión and "looked for a way to mortify me because I took up the law to protect the residents."[138]

Both parties then became bolder. Villalpando had judged it "convenient" not to allow the alcalde mayor to construct a bull ring next to the cemetery (presumably in the new town plaza) and had told him to return the money he had taken from the caja de comunidad of Concá as a "reward" for an inspection. Yáñez appeared with 100 armed men to release a parishioner whom the cura had imprisoned for sacrilegious acts. (The cura glossed over his own violation of the requirement of royal auxilio by saying that he had appealed to the commander of Saucillo for *his* royal auxilio.) In the cura's account, the alcalde mayor had withdrawn when faced by the Saucillo troops, promising to take revenge and reduce the pueblo to rubble.

The cura wrote that he had merely been defending the church under the terms of the Council of Trent—that *ministros inferiores* who did not respect the rights of the church should be severely punished. Since the parish was more than 100 leagues from Mexico City and prompt action was required, he had resolved to have the alcalde mayor arrested and sent to the capital. Meanwhile, the alcalde mayor had made a formal complaint to the archbishop, who had summoned the cura to Mexico City, where he fell ill. Now, Villalpando sought a pardon from the viceroy, "since everything I decided and undertook was done in the belief that I was serving God, Religion, Our Catholic Sovereign, the sacred mitre, and the Republic."[139]

The record ends with a ruling from the fiscal of the Audiencia of Mexico: the cura's case against the alcalde mayor was flawed by his enmity and without legal foundation; the charges were accordingly not a matter for the courts but should be taken up in the alcalde mayor's residencia; and the cura ought not to be pardoned. Given the likely outcome of charges in a late-eighteenth-century residencia, it must have been evident to interested observers that district governors would escape serious punishment from higher civil authorities if they seemed to be protecting the royal jurisdiction against incursions from priests.[140]

Acaponeta was still a Franciscan doctrina when conflict between the doctrineros and the district governor reached the Audiencia of Guadalajara in 1791.[141] The incident that exposed the array of provocations and resentments between them was a fireworks display during Pentecost. The new subdelegado complained to the audiencia that the senior doctrinero had allowed unauthorized fireworks on two consecutive days and had even touched off a few rockets himself when he knew the subdelegado was watching. When the subdelegado, removing his hat, approached the doctrinero about not using fireworks without his permission because of the danger of fire, the Franciscan supposedly responded that "he would do as he pleased" and called the subdelegado a frivolous drone ("sángano patarrato").

The subdelegado used the occasion to make a great many accusations against the doctrinero, including incontinence, drunkenness, gambling, an attack on an earlier alcalde mayor when he failed to pay a gambling debt immediately, performing a marriage ceremony even though he knew the groom was already married, and failing to carry out the traditional ceremony of presenting the subdelegado with holy water from the hyssop. According to the subdelegado, the Franciscan had also confiscated his horses when his servant brought them to the corner of the convent to drink; burdened visita residents with feeding and housing his common-law family to his demanding specifications; and showed little respect for the poor (for example, farting loudly and shouting "Adiós, pendejo" when a poor but respectable man passed by).

The heart of the subdelegado's complaint was that his own authority counted for little. The doctrinero, who had been in Acaponeta for more than ten years, was, he said, in league with the richest and most powerful man in the community, the *gachupín* Pedro Quinteros. Together, they and their minions ruled Acaponeta, "flouting the Royal Jurisdiction." Thanks to Quinteros's influential friends in Guadalajara, they escaped punishment for these serious abuses.

The audiencia directed the Franciscan provincial to punish the doctrinero under *Recopilación* 1-14-73 and 1-6-38, to order him to avoid such confrontations with royal authorities, and to consider removing him from the district.[142] The provincial did issue a "severe warning" to maintain good relations with the justicias reales but refused to admit that the Franciscans had been at fault (and apparently did not consult the three priests who, according to the subdelegado, could testify to the doctrinero's misdeeds). Perhaps smarting from the crown's long assault on the Franciscans' standing as doctrineros, he replied to the audiencia that the personal honor of his friar and the corporate honor of the order had been stained; that the subdelegado bore personal resentments that distorted the charges; and that the only public issue in this case was the fireworks. Whether or not the provincial knew of the crown's new interest in regulating fiestas and their expenses, he claimed that the subdelegado's order for licensing fireworks displays was no more than a thinly disguised device to make money from new fees. On this perhaps unintentionally provocative note, the case apparently ended.[143]

As heated as the conflicts between priests and district governors became in the late eighteenth century, few had consequences so grave that they seemed to be leading to revolution. Conflicts in particular places were subject to change, and their legacy was diffuse. Particular political resentments tended to dissipate with time. Decisions in some court cases were postponed until one or both parties ceased litigation, left the district, or died in office, when they were "archivados"—filed away without a verdict. Some priests resigned or were transferred to another parish by their bishop; some lieutenants were removed from office by their superiors; some district governors and priests heeded the audiencia's warning to cooperate or were formally reconciled, usually by the prelate during a pastoral visit or by the cura of a neighboring parish. And the political tension in a parish might change from one year to another. In Ocotlan (Jalisco) in 1778, the lieutenant and cura were openly hostile to each other, the lieutenant complaining bitterly of false charges made against him by the parish priest. Five years later, local vecinos complained that the lieutenant and cura were compadres who cooperated all too closely.[144]

But of the disputes that went to a verdict by the audiencia, few provided much comfort to the parish priest. The result of a dispute between the alcalde mayor and the cura of Sierra de Pinos (Zacatecas) over funeral processions in 1772 can stand for many others. In January, the alcalde mayor was irritated by a lavish funeral put on by the cura for "a resident of low standing and middling means," and particularly by a procession with stations or stopping places (*posas*) in the street and plaza, and "similar ostentation." Since "the street belong[ed] to the king," he demanded that the cura obtain his written permission to conduct funeral processions with stations outside the church grounds.[145] The cura balked at this demand, insulted the bearer of the order, and enlisted the support of the archbishop's promotor fiscal. Each party suggested that the other was threatening the harmony they were expected to maintain.

The promotor submitted a brief to the audiencia arguing that the alcalde mayor was introducing a "remarkable innovation" (novedad notable), which violated a revered custom going back to the sixteenth century. The processions were, he wrote, for salvation, not for profit, and he feared that alcaldes mayores would use the power to license processions as an instrument of revenge against parishioners and curas they did not like. Would licenses then be required for all religious processions through public streets, including Corpus Christi, Rosary and penitential processions, Holy Week, and carrying the Blessed Sacrament to the sick for last rites, he asked? The audiencia was not impressed by the reports of fourteen justicias and two former curas of Sierra de Pinos that licenses for funeral processions with stations were not customary in their districts or the promotor's observation that no such licenses had been required in the capital of Guadalajara. On the fiscal's advice, it decided that such licenses from the alcalde mayor should be required in order "to protect the Royal Jurisdiction" (as the alcalde mayor had put it). The fiscal observed that the processions with stations "should be considered ostentation and grandeur of the living more than aid or relief to the souls of the deceased." Since the act was not purely religious, he reasoned, it was the duty of secular authorities to judge what was deserving of splendor in order "to protect proper class distinctions and give preference to the worthy and distinguished" (guardar en la república la debida distinción de clases y preferir a los beneméritos y distinguidos).[146]

The Clergy's View of a Changing Relationship

Faced with royal initiatives to alter their place in public life and these mounting tensions with district governors, prelates and members of cathedral chapters wavered among the old language of balance, regalist sentiments that endorsed the crown's supremacy, and a fear of new disorders coupled with a decline in popular devotion. In his 1768 pastoral letter, Bishop Diego Rodríguez Rivas of Guadalajara worried about the loss of the secular clergy's "credit and honor" with the expulsion of the Jesuits, but the following year, he affirmed the regalist position that the alcaldes mayores and other justicias were the "padres de familia" who would enforce the law of God.[147] Lic. José María Oñate, priest and attorney to the Audiencia of Mexico, responding in 1801 to a royal decree denying clergymen the privilege of serving as attorneys in the civil and criminal courts of Spanish America, bemoaned the loss of the king's protection and his apparent indifference to creole interests: "Ha, Sir! What anguish the American clergy feels to see their King and Protector so far removed, their Monarch the Sun of Spain in whose light the fortunate European Spaniards bask."[148]

The high clergy had especially strong feelings about preserving ecclesiastical immunity and stood fast against any infringements of the jurisdiction of the ecclesiastical courts.[149] A dispute in 1798 over who would prosecute a priest's sedition stirred the bishop and cathedral chapter of Michoacán to wonder how the crown's claim to jurisdiction could be consistent with the principle of secular and ecclesiastical union, and to invoke France as an example of the consequences of such claims, warning that to weaken the church was to undermine political and social order: "priests are the only members of the state in these countries who can appeal to the heart of the people; they are also the ones who have worked most to keep them docile and obedient to the Government and the laws."[150] As the case continued into 1799 and 1800, the bishop added some explosive polarities to his spirited defense of customary privilege:

If centuries of ignorance produced confusion and abuses in the exercise of ecclesiastical jurisdiction and immunities, the so-called enlightened century—which disputes even the most holy matters and, like a rushing torrent, mixes up truth with error, piety with fanaticism, and authority with superstition—has completely destroyed these sacred rights or has reduced them to a shadow of what they ought to be.[151]

The high clergy had less to say about changes in parish administration, but when they did venture an opinion in litigation involving parish priests, it was to extol custom as the "wise interpreter of the law" and warn that "great disorders are born of small beginnings."[152] The gobernador de la mitra for Mexico, responding to trouble between the cura and parishioners of Tanicpatlan (parish of Apaxtla, Ichcateopan district, Guerrero) in 1809, advised the high court that those "great disorders" might lead to the collapse of colonial rule:

In various *pueblos* of the parish of Tepehuacan, there are Indians who do not hear mass, do not fulfill the precepts of Our Holy Mother Church, do not summon a priest for confession of the sick, do not want schools, and have completely given up obedience to the priests—which is the obvious beginning of complete disobedience to the secular powers as well. As history affirms, the Catholic Religion has always been the most solid support of monarchies.[153]

Peninsular priests in Mexico who were not bound by pastoral duties, writing in the arbitrista tradition of their homeland, were more pointed in their comments about district governors. Writing from Mexico City in 1770, Tirso Díaz acknowledged that Indians sometimes staged violent protests against alcaldes mayores but added that a wise governor did not dwell on these incidents, since the Indians would have been drunk at the time and were repentant when they sobered up. What needed attention, he said, was the drunkenness itself and other Indian vices, for which both alcaldes mayores and parish priests were largely responsible through their negligence. But Díaz reserved his sharpest criticism for the greed of the alcaldes mayores. Here his indignation soared as high as Villarroel's did in the opposite direction: the alcaldes mayores "fail to act as true fathers, tutors, and guardians of the Indians. . . . Their refined greed [drives them to] innumerable acts of usury and injustice." He concluded that the district governors' repartimientos must end if these officials were ever to live up to their responsibilities.[154]

Pedro Fernández Ybarraran, a fellow peninsular priest residing in the Villa de Córdoba (Veracruz) in 1791, had few compliments for the American clergy, but he, too, reserved his harshest criticism for the district governors. If religious devotion and obedience to the king were crumbling, he wrote, it was especially the fault of the justicias: "It is undeniable that many subaltern governors have abused their authority by encouraging [their subjects'] passions. This has caused injury to the church, detriment to justice, and the dismantling of the state and the *pueblos*."[155]

Parish priests involved in lawsuits with district governors and parishioners had more intimate experience of the political changes at the local level. Most would have shared in their prelates' deep misgivings about the political reforms, but usually without the regalist ambivalence. Like the peninsular priests who wrote treatises on the ills of the colony, these curas were critical of the district governors, even if their criticism was muted by the recognition that they would nevertheless have to deal with the governors, and that audiencia judges were not sympathetic to strong criticism of them. Even so regalist-minded a priest as Omerick could not resist a cutting remark about greedy corregidores who kept down promising Indian individuals. Perhaps he was influenced by his own brush with an alcalde mayor over the limits of a priest's sacramental jurisdiction in a 1765 abduction case.[156]

Curas who voiced opinions in these lawsuits clearly felt embattled. From the early 1750's on, they complained that Indian parishioners were becoming more unruly and insolent—litigating every little thing and treating them with contempt, in imitation of the district governor.[157] The cura of Mazatepec (Morelos) wrote in 1800 of a complete moral collapse in the parish and sensed a conspiracy against him by the lieutenant and various hacendados.[158] Some curas expressed a nearly apocalyptic vision of order and religion collapsing around them, and of district governors transformed "from judges into tyrants."[159] In an appeal to the viceroy, the cura of Villa Alta (Oaxaca) claimed in 1793 that the alcalde mayor was

influencing and persuading the natives not to obey, respect, or revere us; favoring as many deals as the natives want to undertake against us; and giving them to understand that we are subject to their jurisdiction without exception. This most perverse principle has yielded just the fruit in the heart of these neophytes that their wicked heart desires, for now we, their *párrocos* and other ecclesiastical ministers, are treated as worthless individuals; they show us neither obedience nor respect. But even worse—and this we draw to your attention with the deepest sorrow—is that the devotion and fervor that these natives were achieving in things sacred are growing cold.[160]

Less stridently, others lamented their powerlessness, implicitly criticizing the reforms that were taking away their judicial and administrative authority. The cura of Tepetlaostoc in 1758 and the cura of Temascaltepec in 1790 used the same words to lament their inability to control the degenerating moral conduct of their parishioners: "my hands are tied."[161] The ever-active Omerick proposed "a new conquest" to counter what he regarded as the growing disobedience to curas and justicias and the loss of religion among Indian parishioners; but for most curas who spoke of a solution, it was to honor custom and roll back mistaken reforms.[162]

* * *

Society in this political culture was described as the nuclear family writ large or as a living body: hierarchical, in large part corporate, and headed by the father. Parenthood was a particularly exalted source of authority. The family and organic metaphors had always been tangled—both cura and alcalde mayor could be described as father or head; either could also be described as both father and mother or both head and arm—but now the metaphors were changing as well as confused. There were too many fathers.

Later Bourbon decrees muted the parental union of the crown as father and the church as mother. The crown was now the parent usually mentioned; and the crown delegated its fatherhood to the district governor. While parish priests were supposed to use only the "wing of love" to promote their parishioners' salvation, the district governors remained fathers in the fuller sense: "amoroso y severo," loving and severe. District governors were often seen as capricious and remote, and they were gaining a reputation for irreverence, if not for sacrilegious opinions. Yet they were increasingly the designated and self-identified fathers. Antonio de Udias, subdelegado of Tzontecomatlan (Veracruz) in 1808, claimed to be the Indians' "true father." Calling the cura's complaints against Indian parishioners "gossip" that "seems to come from a vengeful spirit," he warned the cura that he would not punish innocents. Indian subjects and the cura in this case validated their respective roles as children and lesser parent. Leaders of Tzontecomatlan addressed Udias in a March 21 letter as Most Beloved Little Father ("Amantíssimo Padrecito"), and three months later, the cura sighed over his parishioners' disobedience in the subdelegado's absence: "even the young Indians I have raised and now see unfortunately corrupted make fun of me to my face."[163] The alcalde mayor of Actopan (Hidalgo), responding to the cura's complaint against him and Indian parishioners for disrespect in 1763, dismissed the cura as "the stepfather, not the father, of that community" who "unjustly usurps the secular jurisdiction."[164]

Whether because it seemed politic to do so or because the habit of speech had taken hold, late colonial Indian petitioners increasingly couched their appeals to the district governor in these terms. For example, in 1783 a regidor and four principales of Tepetitlan, on the outskirts of Guadalajara, complained to their corregidor against another four principales, appealing to him "so that as father you may tell us the route to travel."[165] When the vicario of Sayula (Jalisco) charged the alcalde mayor with failing to provide royal auxilio in 1776, the accused produced letters from parishioners appealing for his help against false arrests by the cura. One of them read: "After God, there is no one for me to approach because you are our father."[166]

Late Bourbon decrees called for the parish priest to stand aside in nearly all judicial matters; but could he afford to do so? Would he not be accountable to a higher authority for the protection of his Indian parishioners? In practice, a parish priest had to weigh the merits of each particular case that would involve him with district governors. For most of those who were in trouble with the district governors at the end of the colonial period, their traditional fatherhood in parish life was decisive. Some continued to believe that they were entitled to the same authority that "a *padre de familia* exercises over his children."[167] In 1775, the cura of Zacualpan defended his conduct against complaints by Indians of San Simón Tototepec in similar terms. The Indians were, he said, "my true children, as you can see by the punishment they receive, which is more like that of parents to their children than like judges to criminals."[168]

The Bourbon political reforms may have strengthened the crown's hand in America and conceived the state in more modern, categorical terms, but by legislating the withdrawal of curas from public affairs without the power or will to enforce the new regime systematically, they blurred responsibilities and sharpened disputes between parish priests and district governors. As parish priests lost leverage in the colonial bureaucracy and district governors gained power, Indian villagers lost one kind of local political resource, experienced new difficulty in negotiating the extractions of the market and greater estrangement from the colonial state at the district level, and made more demands on the audiencias and viceroys.

CHAPTER SEVENTEEN

Arancel Disputes

This [arancel] was enacted with the saintly purpose of
giving the Indians some comfort, not to make the *curas'*
fortunes greater.   —Indians' attorney, 1774

Tell the sons and daughters of the *pueblo* that the clerical
fees are required by natural law, divine law, ecclesiastical
law, and royal law, that they are not voluntary offerings, as
all of you seem to think. Just as I am obliged to give you
spiritual nourishment, you are obliged to give me corporal
nourishment, as Saint Paul says.
                      —Cura of Huichapan (Hidalgo)
          to gobernador of San Luis de las Peras, 1786

The most common and persistent source of friction between parish priests
and Indian parishioners in the late colonial period was the fees for spiritual
services that curas treated as an indispensable part of their living. The parochial
economy and direct collections from laymen had long been sensitive issues in
the history of Christianity, placing priests in the awkward position of seeming to
have put the sacraments on sale, and extracting wealth directly from those who
were asked to respect them. Indian parishioners reputedly escaped such fees
whenever they could. As the cura of Jiquipilco wrote in the preamble to his detailed 1773 guide to annual charges for his parish:

In order not to lose most of the parochial dues, one must realize that, with very few exceptions, [the Indians] are swindlers and will go to great lengths to achieve their purpose,
even if it means defaming the *cura*. Whenever possible, the fees should be collected before the *fiesta* commences, before the fiancé is married, etc.[1]

An Overview of Arancel Disputes
in the Late Colonial Period

As the fiscal of the Audiencia of Mexico noted of an arancel dispute in 1757,
"This is an exceedingly frequent kind of controversy between *curas* and their
Indian parishioners, and it has been so for a long time."[2] But the disagreements
over clerical fees in the two dioceses have a history; they were not unchanging and timeless. An examination of 162 adjudication and administrative reports
from 1670 to 1820 invoking the arancel suggests that fee disputes were common

from at least the 1720's, with the most decisive increases coming after about 1755. (Since fee disputes were perennial and bishops had begun issuing aranceles in the early 1600's, a look farther back in the records might well show a frequency of conflicts at about the same level as in the 1720's and 1730's, perhaps with bursts of activity in the years following the enactment of each arancel.) Table 6, which breaks down the 1700–1820 disputes by decades, shows two peaks, in the 1760's–1770's and the 1790's. The first was especially related to the secularization of parishes in the archdiocese beginning in 1749 and the archbishop's declaration of a new arancel in 1767 (more than half of the 1760's cases occurred between 1767 and 1769). By the 1790's, few curas could claim that they had never faced their parishioners in a dispute over fees or received an order to conform to the arancel.[3] As the pastoral visitor to the remote Huasteca region of Guanajuato and San Luis Potosí put it in 1808, "There is no Indian today who does not want to be released from what he used to pay his *cura*."[4] The impetus for the second peak was clearly the intendancy reforms of the 1780's and the further erosion of the parish priests' authority in public life.

All but four of these cases come from the archdiocese. However, a fuller representation of Guadalajara would probably not change the picture much. Though the court records of the cathedral archive at Guadalajara are less complete than the court records of the archdiocese, and were less well organized and accessible when I consulted them in 1980, I found only one arancel dispute in six boxes of late colonial records for parish affairs, in Tlajomulco in 1817. My survey of the more extensive Audiencia de la Nueva Galicia civil and criminal records, where much of the documentation on arancel disputes should appear, produced just three more cases (Poncitlan, 1727; Achichipico, 1795; and Zapotlan, 1805); and the unusually rich four-volume digest of cases and issues before the audiencia in Guadalajara at the end of the colonial period compiled by the court fiscal, Juan José Ruiz Moscoso, yielded no additional evidence of protracted fee disputes linked to the aranceles.[5] It may seem surprising to find so few cases, and the number undoubtedly would be enlarged with further research, but this pattern fits with others described in this study: Guadalajara priests generally occupied a less controversial place in local political affairs than their counterparts in the archdiocese; were subjected less often to the kind of anticlericalism that accumulated near the end of the eighteenth century in some parts of central Mexico; and were more dependent on cofradías for the support of spiritual activities, so that their money conflicts with parishioners tended to be centered there.

Within the archdiocese, the greatest concentration of arancel disputes was in the adjacent alcaldías mayores or subdelegaciones of Metepec, Tenango del Valle, Malinalco, Temascaltepec, and Zacualpan in the southwestern part of the modern Estado de México. Together, they account for 60 (37 percent) of the cases by place. Metepec alone had 22 cases, concentrated in the localities of Zinacantepec (1749, 1792, 1796, 1804), Almoloya (1775, 1792, 1795), and Malacatepec (1755, 1774, 1803).[6]

There were four other regional concentrations. One was the 32 cases in districts of the modern state of Hidalgo, with clusters in the districts of Xilotepec and Huichapan (1721, 1761, 1768–90, 1775, 1785, 1789, 1796, 1806), Meztitlan (1777, 1780, 1785, 1799), Tulancingo (1769, 1796, 1799, 1817), and Yahualica

TABLE 6
Arancel Disputes by Decade, 1700–1820

Decade	Number	Percent	Decade	Number	Percent
1700–1709	1	0.6%	1770–1779	20	12.6%
1710–1719	0	—	1780–1789	17	10.7
1720–1729	9	5.7	1790–1799	33	20.8
1730–1739	10	6.3	1800–1809	12	7.5
1740–1749	8	5.0	1810–1820	7	4.4
1750–1759	17	10.7	No date[a]	3	1.9
1760–1769	22	13.8	TOTAL	159	100.0%

[a]All are inferentially 1750 or later.

(1721, 1739, 1794). A second was the 33 cases in or very near the modern state of Morelos; a third, 18 cases in the Valley of Mexico; and the fourth, 11 cases in the modern state of Guerrero that were located on or adjacent to the corridor between Acapulco and Mexico City, especially in the district of Tixtla (1726, 1740, 1776, 1779, 1793, and 1794).

Within these regional concentrations, there were two departures from the temporal pattern. The Morelos cases were especially numerous in the 1780's and 1790's, but were also conspicuous among the few late-seventeenth- and early-eighteenth-century cases; apparently this was an area where fees collection and a standard schedule had become an issue well before the late-eighteenth-century administrative initiatives. This early history of arancel disputes in Morelos fits with other evidence of a precocious anticlericalism there (Appendix C). In the Valley of Mexico, where ready access to the audiencia and news of changing royal policies might predict a more continuous history of arancel disputes, the cases cluster between the decisive royal cedula on the secularization of parishes in 1749 and the intendancy reform in 1789. This was certainly a period of policy changes, but the legal cues of the intendancy reforms and seventeenth-century changes in fee schedules apparently did not prompt the kind of continuous history of fees litigation that might be expected.

The secularization of parishes was an important ingredient in the fee disputes of the 1750's and early 1760's. For example, Simón Thadeo de Castañeda Castro y Guzmán wrote of the troubles he had in the parish of Mixcoac (Valley of Mexico) in the early 1760's, when three mountain visitas resisted their parish duties, believing that secularization had freed them from obedience to the cura.[7] The new secular curas sometimes brought different ideas about how they should be supported by the parish and how they should enforce those expectations (more often by incarceration and withholding services). Dependent as most were on the collection of clerical fees, they seem on the whole to have been more determined than their regular counterparts to maximize their returns by seeking out unmarried couples; promoting new or higher fees; collecting for special projects; and encouraging additional masses, fiestas, and veneration of saints.[8] If the Mendicant doctrineros did not leave behind instructions, enterprising Indian parishioners could take advantage of the confusion to redefine their financial obligations. At Zacualpan de las Amilpas (Morelos) in 1763, the Augustinians had left the new diocesan cura, Juan de Ayuso Peña, with no guidance about the fees normally charged for spiritual services. Eventually, he determined that Indians from the visitas of Temoac, Guazulco, Tlacotepec, and Popotlan had been defrauding him with what they called the "ancient *obvenciones*." He discovered in the parish archive that in November 1757 parishioners and the Augustinians had signed an agreement to abide by an arancel published in the 1720's. De Ayuso Peña had done some tinkering of his own that added to the local tension. Twice he had refused a license for Temoac to hold its customary dances—which he regarded as idolatrous—and pressed for removal to the cabecera of its periodic market.[9]

Another example of the unsettling effects of secularization expressed in a fee dispute comes from the parish of Acambay (Hidalgo). In 1758, shortly after the removal of the Franciscans, the parish boundaries were redrawn, and a section of Xilotepec was absorbed by Acambay. In 1761, four Indian rancherías in this section refused to pay the half real per family the cura of Acambay expected when he traveled to the visitas to say mass, and refused to fulfill the Easter duty or attend catechism classes. When the cura went to the district judge for help in getting them to pay for his services, the Indians, led by the "captain" of San Pedro, said they wanted to pay only the fees required by the current arancel. Then they decided they wanted a *convenio* (extrajudicial agreement) instead of the arancel. They settled on the convenio the cura demanded in the first place—one-half real per family per month—but there were other disagreements rooted in the new boundaries. The cura blamed the gobernador of Xilotepec for encouraging the Indians' resistance, and the Indians made it clear that they did not want to obey or serve the gobernador of Acambay, whose pueblo was now the parish seat. Finally, in 1768, Archbishop Lorenzana thought he had the solution. The convenio, he observed, obviously had not resolved the dispute. It was time to apply his new arancel.[10]

The Arancel of 1767

Archbishop Lorenzana's arancel for the archdiocese of July 7, 1767, had unusual importance. Though at the time, the fees for spiritual services in most parishes were determined by custom and convenio, schedules of fees intended for wide use dated back more than a hundred years. The Council of Trent prepared the way for them in the mid-sixteenth century by permitting direct collections from parishioners for the support of the cura and the parish.[11] As early as 1538, the crown called on provincial councils of prelates in the Indies to draw up aranceles for masses, funerals, and other spiritual services in collaboration with the highest colonial governors.[12] From 1560 to the 1640's, royal cedulas and legal commentaries reiterated that parish priests were to follow aranceles for "funerals, marriages, baptisms, and all the rest."[13] In 1585, the Third Provincial Council for New Spain assumed that an arancel would be available to govern clerical fees, and it ordered the curas to keep detailed records of their collections.[14] Divided into descending charges for (1) españoles, (2) negros, mulatos, and mestizos, (3) *indios de cuadrilla* (Indian laborers residing on private estates), and (4) indios de pueblo, aranceles were published by the dioceses of New Spain on various occasions in the early seventeenth century, modified slightly from time to time, and eventually superseded in the late eighteenth century.[15]

The publication of an arancel did not mean that its charges would be followed in any particular parish or by all pueblos in a parish. Although early aranceles contained orders for parish priests to follow their terms, the operating principle seems to have been that the schedule would apply if a parish or pueblo requested it and the priest consented (as Lorenzana provided in 1767).[16] In fact the clergy in most Indian parishes in the mid-eighteenth century worked under hundreds of local fee arrangements that mixed cash payments with goods and labor service. Some places paid manípulos and/or primicias as well.[17]

One instance of the resulting confusion is documented in a 1760 case brought by Indians of the parish seat of Tejupilco and the visitas of Ixtapan and Acatitlan in the district of Temascaltepec.[18] The parishioners documented that they had "aranceled their cura" ("arancelaron a su cura") in 1733. They had not demanded it of the cura then in office because he did not charge at all for burials, but they had had two of his successors (who asked for more than it allowed) served with the arancel. One was Carlos Antonio López de la Torre, who no sooner arrived in 1755, according to them, than he began to "innovate," charging off-scale fees for burials, promoting an annual celebration for the Virgin of Guadalupe, and demanding first fruits. They had provided him with a local oil for the lamp and chrism, but he refused to use it, saying that only olive oil from Castile was acceptable. The Indians had him served with the arancel, but they complained again in 1759 that he was making extra demands for fees and prepayment and jailing and whipping the tardy. They also complained that he imposed a non-Indian as sacristán and mistreated their officials:

He treats them with abusive words, whether to the *gobernador*, the *alcaldes*, the *regidores*, or other elders who have served in such offices of the *república*. Often he has even ordered them to be whipped for exceedingly petty reasons at the church door on Sundays for all to see. His mistreatment of them has reached the point of ordering his *vicarios* to do the same without exception, even to cut off their *balcarrotas* with their own hands and to beat them with their staffs. I [the Indians' attorney] have been told that the *cura* wants to whip the interim *gobernador* and the *alcaldes* and three elders of the *cabecera* and the *pueblo* of San Simón. Fearing he will act on his threats, the men have fled and, consequently, are not attending mass.[19]

To show that their absence from mass was not an act of bad faith, they said they supported the liturgy enthusiastically, kept their churches in good repair, and only wanted the cura to follow the arancel and treat them as he should. Instead of denying most of the Indians' charges, the cura put them in a different light. He had ordered whippings, he said, but only within the limits of his office. There was, indeed, a Spanish sacristán who also served as maestro de escuela, but he had been appointed in 1732, long before López de la Torre became cura; and the preceding eight-year period in which Indians had held the post had proved to be a disaster for the parish buildings. If the parishioners meant to follow the arancel, why, he asked, had they kept their royal provisión secret for nearly eighteen years? They wanted it now, he judged, because they were no longer able to avoid clerical fees altogether. He said his income of about 2,500 pesos a year barely covered operating expenses, including salaries and provisions for three vicarios. The burial fees, in particular, were needed to purchase the proper European holy oil. It was not that his parishioners were too poor to pay their share, he said; they were simply lazy and disobedient. He blamed the gobernador—who, he noted, had been illegally reelected—for stirring up the litigation in order to make himself rich.[20]

The arancel that Lorenzana replaced dated back to January 18, 1638 (later citations to it usually mention August 3, 1637, the date of the royal provisión calling upon the archbishop to issue a standard schedule of fees).[21] Although much amended and elaborated (in 1670, 1683, 1691, 1720, and 1757, among other years), this fee schedule was effectively in force until 1767.[22] Most of the early-eighteenth-century rural fee disputes that invoked any arancel at all referred to the 1638 document, as did most of the lawsuits in the 1750's and early 1760's that petitioned for an end to customary practices.[23] For pueblo Indians, the 1638 arancel called for the following funeral payments: three pesos for a mass for an adult; two pesos for a mass for a child; and three pesos for a high mass with vigil, plus four reales for the Indian cantores. In addition, an offering "according to the *calidad* [standing] of the deceased" was expected.[24] For marriages and nuptial masses (*velaciones*) the charge was four pesos. For baptism, the arancel called for a voluntary offering. Masses for Easter, Christmas, and Pentecost, the feast of the Holy Ghost, and the feast of the community's patron saint were valued at four pesos, plus an offering. For sung votive masses for the saints, the charge was three pesos, and for unscheduled low masses outside the cabecera, two pesos.

The Lorenzana arancel of 1767 eliminated the vague provisions for "offerings" in the old schedule except in the one case of baptisms, which in principle were still free of charge but in fact now required four reales "por razón de ofrenda." Otherwise, it mostly tinkered at the edges, raising a few fees and adding a couple of others. It raised the fee for a funeral mass with vigil to four pesos, plus seven reales for the Indian cantores; fixed cantores' fees at four reales for funeral processions and two pesos for special holiday masses; and added two pesos for the premarital report (*información matrimonial*), two reales for each bann that preceded a marriage, and two pesos for the cura and one peso for every other priest who participated in processions for one of the special holiday masses. The change that proved the most controversial distinguished between cabeceras and visitas for funerals and regular masses: funerals outside the cabecera were charged an additional two pesos; Sunday mass in the cabecera was free, but the visitas were to pay two pesos for low mass and two pesos, four reales, for high mass.

With what amounted to fairly modest changes, why did the Lorenzana arancel immediately spark so many heated disputes? Local circumstances work against a simple, universal answer, but in every case, new imperial plans and pressures were involved in one way or another, providing a focus for the unsettling effects of new material conditions and magnifying tensions between the actions of curas and the perceived interests of local Indians.

For the crown and regalist bishops, the new arancel was part of a move toward standardization and centralization following the Seven Years' War. The new watchword of colonial administration was the *regla fija* (fixed rule). Lorenzana spoke of a regla fija in his preamble to the 1767 arancel, which, he said, was "for all the *curas* of the archdiocese"; audiencia fiscales and judges used the term or a synonym in their explanations of verdicts thereafter; and an occasional cura picked it up in his arguments with parishioners who seemed to be remaking custom before his eyes (as did at least one Indian representative).[25] Universally applied, an arancel was supposed to eliminate the confusion of customs, which one audiencia fiscal called a "seminary of complaints, commotions, and lawsuits."[26] It would go far, in Lorenzana's vision of 1767 and that of a 1785 royal provisión, "to cut off the disputes at their roots."[27] There had never been such an active promoter of an arancel for parish fees as Lorenzana, convinced as he was that it would bring order and harmony to parochial administration. He judged that the 1638 arancel could not serve as that desired regla fija because its ambiguities and the qualifications and clarifications added to it over the years caused more confusion than order:[28] what was required was a new one that incorporated the old. Bishops of other dioceses in New Spain eventually acted on Lorenzana's desire for a single arancel to apply across diocesan boundaries; Bishop Cabañas of Guadalajara applied the 1767 arancel to his diocese in 1808.[29]

The royal government had pressed for a new arancel in the archdiocese since 1746—"in order to bring this long-running controversy to an end"[30]—and would promote Lorenzana's and other episcopal schedules long after the high-flying archbishop's departure in 1772. On September 13, 1775, a royal cedula ordered the audiencias to examine the aranceles then in force and report on abuses that required attention.[31] On March 22, 1785, the viceroy issued a bando for curas to collect only their legitimate fees, to do so without coercion, and "to pardon from payment the poor and unfortunate."[32] What those legitimate fees should be was clear from the audiencias' laconic judgments in post-1767 disputes in which Indians petitioned for the arancel: all parties were to obey the arancel without interpretation or deviation.[33] The audiencia fiscales and judges placed great faith in the efficacy of the arancel as a regla fija. Going beyond Lorenzana's plan that the arancel should be adopted by mutual consent of the cura and his flock, the audiencias effectively made it applicable on demand by Indian parishioners.[34] This was a clear invitation to litigation. Even a wholehearted testimonial from the alcalde mayor of Zacualpan could not rescue the cura there from an exaggerated complaint brought in 1769 by Indians of Ixtapa who requested the arancel. The audiencia's verdict, then as later, was a short, flat order to the cura to conform to the arancel.[35]

Many Indian pueblos took up the invitation with alacrity. Their petitions rejected "the *cura*'s custom" and invoked the arancel as if it were sacred writ, claiming that "the *cura* abhors the *arancel*," or that "he neither observes nor keeps any *arancel* except for that which his greed dictates."[36] It was understood to be *theirs*, a regulation that would lighten their tax burden and strike a more favorable balance in their formal relationship with the parish priests. They would use it to protect themselves against certain old and new demands for material support. Litigation over the arancel sharpened local sensitivity about parishioners' contributions to the priest's living, and about any alterations he might make. Taking a cue from royal policy statements and the advice of their attorneys, Indian plaintiffs increasingly depicted the priest as arbitrary and uncharitable. They criticized priests for operating "at their pleasure," either to impose old customs or to flout both custom and the new rule.[37] And the arancel became a political weapon with which to criticize the priests on various fronts and advance personal and collective interests. Especially if the cura pressed for a weekly contribution, whether it was customary or not, pueblo representatives responded with an invidious comparison to the amount of royal tribute they paid.

An unstated purpose of the 1767 arancel that became evident in pueblo petitions and the courts' judgments was to eliminate personal services. Aranceles had occasionally been used for this purpose long before 1767. Traditional arrangements almost always included some personal service, but colonial law condensed in the *Recopilación* clearly opposed involuntary personal service in general and provided a foundation for associating the arancel with the abandonment of unpaid personal service. In August 1720, Indians of Tecomatlan in the district of Malinalco (Edo. de México) complained that the cura demanded involuntary services and exorbitant fees. The audiencia immediately confirmed their right to the arancel and exemption from personal services, as it did in their subsequent petitions of 1722 and 1723.[38] Indians of the district of Poncitlan (Jalisco) presented their cura with a published arancel in 1727 "in order to deny him our service." When the alcalde mayor in this case offered the opinion that the Indians would be wise to follow "the customary fees and services," he assumed that their choices were the arancel without service or customary arrangements with it.[39] Indians of San Lucas, a visita of Tejupilco parish, in 1732 asked that their cura "conform to the *arancel* and not demand involuntary services."[40] The same pattern appears in some cases closer to 1767. The 1762 complaint from San Juan and San Francisco in the parish of Huizquilucan (near the Valley of Mexico) began by quoting laws of the *Recopilación* against personal service, a tactic that gained the immediate and emphatic approval of the audiencia, which "ordered that an affidavit be drawn up to serve as a royal *provisión* according to their request, with a penalty of 200 pesos for noncompliance." The cura replied that the farm and household labor he commanded was "an age-old custom," but the verdict stood.[41]

After 1767, the audiencia received more strongly worded petitions for the arancel that intended to eliminate unpaid, involuntary labor service. Representatives of visitas usually led the way in these petitions, reflecting the growing tensions between cabeceras and sujetos. The arancel enabled visitas to reduce, if not eliminate, labor service that benefited only the cabecera and put them under the direction of the gobernador.[42] The cura, with his headquarters in the cabecera, was likely to resist such initiatives. The cura of Malacatepec in the district of Metepec in 1774 opposed the Indians' request for the arancel because the Indians "had agreed of their own free will" in 1767 to a customary arrangement that included service, which he regarded as essential to his livelihood. It amounted, he said, to only two Indian men and one woman to grind corn. The Indians' attorney retorted that this was a form of slavery. The audiencia agreed with the cura that his parishioners were rebellious but still ordered that the arancel be applied.[43]

A late arancel dispute from Zacualtipan (from the modern state of Hidalgo, where the labor issue was particularly sensitive) is notable as an example of both vehement Indian complaints and the colonial government's determination to stand by the 1767 schedule. In 1799, a former gobernador and four former alcaldes hired a Mexico City attorney to present their claim that the cura of Zacualtipan collected twice the fees provided in the arancel and used semaneros for his own benefit. Rather than following the arancel, the cura was, they said, acting according to his "whim and caprice" and his "boundless greed." They also complained that the subdelegado was in league with the cura to subvert the arancel, so they requested a reissue and posting "in a public place." The subdelegado claimed that he had never received a royal provisión for the arancel, but the audiencia made it clear that one had been sent, and ordered him in January 1800 to pay for replacing it. The cura complained in writing to the subdelegado that the Indians were insubordinate and not paying him enough, but in 1801 the audiencia again ordered the arancel.[44]

An audiencia order by itself was not likely to resolve a local dispute, even if the bruises of litigation healed quickly. At Malacatepec, Indian parishioners refused to adhere to the terms of the arancel, and more than two years later, the cura was still petitioning the court to make them pay.[45] In other cases, parishioners thought that being "arancelados" meant the cura could not command service of any kind. More adjudication was needed to clarify that only personal service, not parish service, was being eliminated.[46]

In some cases, the cura continued to demand personal service or extraordinary service in the name of the parish.[47] In others, the Indians were willing to perform personal service if it was voluntary and they were properly paid. "Proper payment" could then become the issue. But the line between parish service and personal service was not always clear, and that could be a source of especially bitter litigation. When a topil was sent on an errand, was it parish business or the cura's personal affair? Was repairing the cura's house personal or parochial service? The courts decided such issues in an ad hoc way. In 1779, at Tetelcingo in the parish of Tixtla (Guerrero), the villagers declared that they had been arancelados since the 1767 schedule was published and should not have to work on the cura's residence. The fiscal of the audiencia concluded that since it was a small job, they should do it as long as the entire parish participated, and it was understood that this was not a precedent for the cura to demand personal service.[48]

From the 1750's to 1810—what with secularizations, divisions of parishes, the high turnover of diocesan curas, and the crown's invitation to Indian parishioners to litigate over clerical fees—newly arrived curas were frequently greeted with a lawsuit demanding the arancel or complaining of excessive charges for their spiritual services.[49] Some asked for trouble by insisting on full payment and looking for legal, but innovative, sources of income. Most defended their clerical fees energetically as a right of office, as the essence of their benefice and authority. And each cura brought his own temperament and priorities to the issue. A priest who undertook a concerted campaign against public drunkenness or for a village school might be regarded by parishioners as an intolerable meddler but see himself as simply fulfilling the traditional duties of a cura or the direct orders of his superiors. Whether or not a particular accusation was well founded, the idea that parish priests were irresponsible innovators had become a common feature of the arancel cases by the 1760's, partly because it was plausible.[50] The attorney for Santa María Atengo and San Francisco Zayula associated this idea with secularization in his complaint against the cura of Tepetitlan (Tetepango district, Hidalgo) in 1790:

Since the parish was secularized (and the friars, whom they regarded with the greatest piety, were replaced), they have had to exercise their patience and suffer a great deal in the exaction of the parish fees and innovations that each *cura* has introduced at his whim.[51]

In most of the 27 late colonial cases in which new curas faced fees disputes or were served with the arancel, the legal action was a kind of initiation—a pretext to restrict the priest's position in the community or a solid wedge behind which to enter a more sweeping complaint.[52] Many of the judicial complaints were made within a few weeks of the cura's arrival, before he had time to do much more than state his intentions. As the attorney for Carlos Antonio López de la Torre put it in his fee dispute with the Indians of Tejupilco in 1760, "Since they are in the habit of seeking an order for the *arancel* whenever a new *cura* is sent there, they also sought it for my client as soon as he arrived, before they had any idea of his conduct."[53] Testifying in an arancel suit at Capuluac in 1796, the subdelegado also blamed the Indian parishioners and exonerated the cura:

[I have] been in frequent contact with this *cura* and can assure [the court] that few surpass him in personal conduct, zeal, and activity in carrying out his ministry. He treats his Indian parishioners with the love and fairness that his honorable and orderly Christian ways demand. . . . Some unruly spirits, like those heard in the preceding document, wallow for the most part in misrepresentations. They resent the corrective measures the *cura* seeks in order to cut out the deeply rooted vice of drunkenness that possesses them.

To the best of my knowledge, the entire basis for their noisy petition is that the *cura* posted the *arancel* for them to obey in their payment of parochial fees, since they do not want to meet those that are designated by custom.[54]

Before the 1790's, the arancel disputes followed a common pattern. Nearly all began as complaints by pueblo spokesmen against their parish priests for "excessive charges" and other kinds of professional misconduct. Often, the Indians also complained of collusion between the curas and district judges to impose arbitrary charges. Aside from the increasing number of cases, the main differences between the early-eighteenth-century cases and those from the 1750's to the 1780's were that (1) pueblo plaintiffs complained more often of curas' "innovations"; (2) as more pueblos adopted the arancel, more charged that the cura was not following its provisions ("no se arregle al arancel"); (3) after 1767, personal service to the priest became a more prominent issue; and (4) the bishops were more eager to defend diocesan curas against what they took to be false charges by Indian parishioners of fee-gouging and innovation.[55] Innovation and "novedad" were loaded terms, political epithets that both parties to these disputes used against each other. In this patrimonial society rich in organic and familial metaphors, novedad suggested an irresponsible, even "criminal" liberty that disturbed the social order.[56]

An accumulation of *despachos*—a satisfyingly thick bundle of official papers covered with the printed arancel—was taken by eighteenth-century petitioners to confer a kind of collective license, much as colonial land titles, with their legal formulas, seals, signatures, and boundary maps had stood since the sixteenth century for community property, well-being, and independence.[57] Official emphasis on paperwork encouraged a more militant legalism on the parishioners' part, reaching the point at Ixtapan (Edo. de México) in 1773 where the cura claimed that they refused to obey his directions about spiritual duties "unless it is by written order of [my] superiors."[58]

Curas and third parties described parishioners acting as if the official papers were a kind of writ of independence from wider obligations.[59] Joseph de Zelada, the cura of San Felipe del Obraje (Edo. de México) in 1771, complained that an influential group of six or seven Indians from the visitas of San Lucas and San Juan who had pressed for the arancel had now persuaded parishioners that

> the *arancel* orders an end to fees, so that they think anything asked of them must be a violation of the *arancel*. . . . They imagine that Indians under the *arancel* cannot be obliged by the *cura* to fulfill God's law. As a result, they do not allow *doctrina* classes in their *pueblos*; nor do their children come to the *cabecera* for instruction on Saturdays.

He claimed that the leader of this movement, Bernardo González, presented himself as the heaven-sent emissary of the Eternal Father, "assuring [the Indians] that the *arancel* was made to let them live as they wished." González reportedly did a brisk business in certificates entitled "aranzelado," which he sold to the Indians as "an authentic instrument of your liberty . . . for your protection." [60]

In spite of the crown's stated intention to reduce lawsuits by standardization, royal authorities welcomed litigation over parish fees. It gave them a way to manage conflict that might otherwise erupt into the kind of popular violence discussed in Chapter Fourteen, and to strengthen their authority at the expense of the curas. But it had a perhaps less welcome side for them, giving parishioners a legal footing to air other grievances that might not receive a hearing on their own. Many of the arancel cases turned into long, looping complaints against a priest's "excesses," "mistreatment," and "offenses"—especially his cruelty, interference in community affairs, deficiencies in administering the sacraments, lack of charity, and excessive demands for labor, goods, and money. An arancel dispute at Yahualica (Hidalgo) in 1739, for example, grew to include charges against the cura for operating a jail, cruelly whipping Indians and cutting off their hair, naming fiscales on his own, and engaging in illegal commerce. At Temascaltepec in 1790, Indian parishioners turned their complaint against the cura over excessive fees and services into charges that he was appropriating community lands and cofradía property, and trying to turn the pueblo over to non-Indians. [61]

Many pueblos vacillated about what they wanted, suggesting that Indian parishioners were often seizing a political opportunity rather than reacting against abusive innovations by the cura. In some parishes, local opinion was divided from the start. A single leader or group or pueblo might take the initiative and obtain the arancel, perhaps for personal reasons; once it went into effect, others might object and want the customary arrangement restored. Often it was only visitas (less often just the cabecera) that pushed through petitions for the arancel. [62] Some villagers were especially eager to escape labor service in the cabecera but, on discovering that the arancel required higher cash payments, had second thoughts. In other situations, the original petitioners became divided over whether to continue with it, request a return to the previous arrangement, or seek a revision of the arancel that would suit them better. In any case, audiencia judges were inclined to regard such confusion as further evidence of congenital Indian inconstancy and annoying departures from the principle of the regla fija. [63] Curas who asked the court to require that the Indians decide on one plan or another got a sympathetic hearing. [64] But even at the end of the colonial period, when the arancel was widely applied, it was common for various pueblos within a parish to adhere to different arrangements for meeting their financial obligations to the cura, especially for visitas to have opted for the arancel.

By the 1790's, at least parts of most parishes of the archdiocese had come under the arancel.[65] Pedro Antonio de San Juan y Barroeta, the subdelegado of Yahualica (Hidalgo) in 1794, could report that the goal of the framers to "eliminate discord" and "cut the disputes at their roots" was working now that most curas acquiesced in this standardized method of support.[66] Yet there were even more—and often more heated—arancel disputes in the archdiocese during the two decades before the Independence War began. Why? Had Barroeta indulged in wishful thinking? Was his district unusual?

The explanation lies partly in the momentum and accumulation of experience since the 1750's. Pueblo representatives knew how to litigate this issue, had reasons to pursue it whether or not the cura violated the arancel's terms,[67] and were confident of victory. In more remote parts of central and western New Spain, Indian pueblos were just then demanding the arancel. The report of a pastoral visit into the Huasteca region and beyond in 1808–9 noticed a series of new petitions for the arancel. At Tampamolon (San Luis Potosí), the Indians were so eager to be arancelados in order to avoid personal service to the cura that they asked the visitador to witness a public ceremony in which they and the cura agreed to follow its provisions.[68] The viceregal government continued to advertise the prospect of a favorable verdict with a notice for general circulation of October 20, 1793, that forbade personal service to the parish priests and ordered them to abide by the arancel.[69] New curas continued to arrive—some of them with their own ideas about payment and service and prepared to test whether the arancel really applied; and nearly all of them in a debate with the parish over their duties and authority. More established curas increasingly complained that Indian parishioners did not obey the arancel, which suggests both that the arancel had become the norm, and that it could occasion other demands for change in the relationship between priest and parish.

The Intendancy Reform

The intendancy reform of the late 1780's was a new ingredient that helps to explain the surge in arancel disputes. Article 224 of the Ordenanza de Intendentes provided that curas must not demand "excessive" fees from their Indian parishioners, that "equitable aranceles" must be drawn up in keeping with the level of poverty, and that secular magistrates must make certain that the aranceles were obeyed.[70] With the promotion and implementation of the arancel now the particular responsibility of the subdelegados and lieutenants—and an instrument with which to assert their authority over the curas—the complaining party in the arancel disputes of the 1790's and 1800's was as likely to be a district governor as a group of parishioners; and Indian representatives were less likely to complain of the collusion of curas and district judges in the matter of clerical fees.[71]

These new conflicts between priests and district governors over the arancel took at least four forms. In one, the cura's resistance led to official criticism by the subdelegado (as when the subdelegado of Malinalco reported in 1793 that the cura of Tenancingo followed his own "arbitrary *directorio*" rather than the arancel).[72] In the second, the district governor challenged the cura by encouraging local protests and petitions for the arancel. In the third, the governor's act of serving notice on the cura that the arancel now applied led to an angry scene and litigation over disrespect for authority. And in the fourth, the cura complained that the subdelegado did not energetically enforce parishioners' obligations under the arancel.

Three examples will serve to illustrate both the depth of feeling between curas and district governors over this issue at the end of the colonial period and how it placed the curas on the defensive. At Tlaquiltenango (Morelos), the pueblo leaders complained in 1786 that "they have much to be angry about with their *cura*" over his failure to follow either custom or the arancel. The result was a royal provisión from the audiencia that the cura be bound by the arancel. Then, in 1789, a new cura was installed, and the Indian parishioners wanted an order for him to obey the arancel, too. The order was drawn up and delivered to the district lieutenant, who presented it to the cura on July 22, 1789. The cura's reaction led to further judicial action: "the said parish priest became furious and let loose a barrage of intemperate and undignified words that are ill-suited to his station and calling." Another order to obey the arancel came down from the Juzgado de Indios in Mexico, along with a cold warning not to repeat "your outrages and abuses against Royal Justice."[73]

In 1794, the cura of Chilpancingo (Guerrero), Pablo Aycarde, made a blistering complaint against the subdelegado for interfering with his pastoral duties and stirring dissension between his vicarios and parishioners. In particular, the cura claimed that the governor encouraged parishioners to resist paying their clerical fees in full. A secret report to the viceroy by his investigator, Pedro Ossorio y Motezuma, on April 18 was mildly critical of the cura: he was often absent from the parish, and there was nothing to suggest that the subdelegado interfered with the collection of clerical fees. Ossorio was apparently not aware that the year before, the subdelegado had written a sharp rebuke of Aycarde in his report on priests in his district for "his unbridled materialism and, since his entry into this *pueblo*, his failure to follow the *arancel*, collecting clerical fees according to the arbitrary quota he imposes."[74] A second secret report, written a few days after Ossorio's by Ramón Flores, brought into the open a dispute between the subdelegado and the cura over charges of more than 500 pesos for a marriage. The viceroy swept aside Aycarde's complaint, judging that the exorbitant marriage charge was behind the dispute with the subdelegado. The real problem, he concluded, was the cura's blatant violation of the arancel, which must be stopped.[75]

At Asuchitlan (Guerrero) in 1790, the longtime coadjutor, Juan Baptista Lecca, found himself involved in a bitter struggle over the control of cofradía finances and officers, and the object of a request to the archbishop by the intendant of Mexico that he be reassigned. Glossing over the legal question of jurisdiction in cofradía affairs, the archbishop wondered in reply whether the subdelegado and the lieutenant wanted to keep the cura out of cofradía affairs because they had misappropriated cofradía property. Clearly, the cura and the lieutenant were taunting each other with charges and countercharges of the abuse of office. In May 1791, a fees complaint against the cura and an order for him to follow the arancel were added to the controversy. On May 26, the subdelegado spoke to the cura's friend d. Isidro Gonzales Taboada, who offered this account of their conversation:

As soon as I greeted him, the *subdelegado* said, "How is the *cura* doing? He must be very angry about the *pueblo* of San Miguel's *arancel*. But do me a favor and tell the *cura* that neither I nor my lieutenant had anything to do with it. D. José de Navas drafted the letter that the said Indians presented to the *audiencia*, which led to the *arancel* being issued."

I answered that the *cura* was not angry about the *arancel*, only about the way your lieutenant presented it. The *cura* was bathing and, instead of letting him finish, the lieutenant burst into the room, telling his followers, "Go right in, sirs"; this and more.[76]

Most cases of conflict in the 1790's and 1800's are not so easy to classify. Responsibility for the 1795 conflict between the cura of Tututepec (Hidalgo) and the lieutenant is particularly difficult to establish from the written record, partly because witnesses from the pueblo were divided in their loyalties. The witnesses for the cura—three past officials and a resident mestizo—claimed that the lieutenant was able to control the current officeholders because he was responsible for their election, and that he persuaded them to petition for the arancel as a way to lower their fees, escape labor service, and weaken the cura's campaign against drunkenness. They swore that the cura was blameless in this dispute, was "always very correct in his conduct," was scrupulous not to use the semaneros for his personal benefit, and had suffered greatly from the "scorn he has tolerated" from the lieutenant. The lieutenant's animosity, they thought, dated from the cura's attempts to get him to fulfill the Easter duty. The subdelegado countered on behalf of his lieutenant that the Indians had agreed to follow the arancel, and that it was the cura who made trouble by "interpreting it to his own advantage." The cura's harassment of the Indians, the subdelegado warned, could lead to more hostilities of the kind for which Indians in this district were well known.[77]

The late colonial arancel disputes placed most parish priests in the awkward position of defending customary practices when colonial policy had shifted decisively to law and standardization (in this they remained faithful to the spirit of the *Itinerario* and what they understood to be their religious mission, as well as their material interests).[78] Though a few curas favored the arancel from the outset, most responded to attorneys' aggressive demands for it with arguments that customary practice was in their parishioners' interest and worthy of respect.[79] In the Diocese of Oaxaca, where similar tensions surrounded a new arancel in 1805, curas argued that a standardized schedule of fees cut into income needed to pay for the additional vicarios now required by the crown.[80] In 1808, their bishop criticized the arancel for terminating the "agreements and compromises" that suited local circumstances. So far as he was concerned, these arrangements had been "the keystone" of the colonial order.[81] Many of the curas who expressed themselves openly in the arancel suits were torn between feelings of despair over Indian disobedience and outrage over being treated as thieves.[82]

In the course of litigation, parishioners and third parties often testified that curas pressed for obedience to custom, removing the posted arancel or keeping it from being displayed in the first place, and openly disregarding its terms.[83] The cura of Tepetitlan (near Tula, Hidalgo) in 1790 reportedly told his parishioners that "with the *arancel* you won't reach heaven."[84] But though some curas plainly continued to be rigid and arbitrary, insisting on immediate and full payment for their services—whether under the terms of the arancel, custom, or their personal sense of what should be owed[85]—others succeeded in avoiding arancel suits by being unusually flexible about fees. The interim cura of Almoloya, district of Metepec, was praised in 1805 for contenting himself with the fees his parishioners decided they could pay and covering some of the operating costs of the parish from his savings.[86] Still, occasional generosity could backfire.[87]

The best solution, according to Antonio Bonavita, cura of Yecapixtla (Morelos) in 1795, was to do away with clerical fees entirely and have the government pay parish priests a reasonable salary. Bonavita mixed this idea with an admiration for the French Revolution that brought him before the Inquisition, but his solution to the fee disputes was one that some more conventional clergymen also favored, and was raised again during the Independence War by José María Morelos.[88]

Three Instructive Cases

Three protracted fee disputes that spanned the years before and after Lorenzana's schedule illustrate some of the complex local issues, the weak position of parish priests in these disputes, and the counterpoint of pueblo resistance and accommodation to colonial pressures that characterize the arancel cases. The first, between the priests and Indian parishioners of Ozoloapan, was understood by all of its participants to involve the cura's authority to direct the public life of the parish. The two priests who served at Ozoloapan over the dispute's nine-year course (1767–76) repeatedly complained of the Indians' refusal to pay the proper fees and perform the customary services, and of their disrespect for clerical authority. The Indians, for their part, complained that the priests oppressed them — imposing excessive fees and employing unwarranted violence. Both parties appealed to colonial superiors, especially to the audiencia, to define the limits of colonial authority and local autonomy within the parish.

Located on the temperate to hot western edge of the mining alcaldía mayor of Temascaltepec and Sultepec in southwestern Estado de México, Ozoloapan parish stretched over a wide area, with the farthest of its three subordinate pueblos (San Juan Atexcapan, San Juan Sacasonapa, and Santo Tomás el Cristo), six haciendas, and numerous small ranchos some eleven leagues away from the parish seat. Most Indians of the parish reportedly spoke Spanish as well as Nahuatl in the late eighteenth century. The population of this large territory numbered only 4,000 in 1792; it was the one part of the alcaldía mayor with fewer people near the end of the century than at the beginning, having been severely hit by the epidemic of 1737.[89] Atexcapan seems to have recovered faster than the head town of Ozoloapan, and began to press claims for special recognition. This was a third-class parish in 1775, with a reported income to the priest of 800 pesos — too little to support a vicario as well as the cura.[90]

The record begins in 1767 (shortly before the publication of Lorenzana's arancel) with a complaint by the cura, Manuel Ruis Coronel, against the Indians of San Juan Atexcapan. Father Ruis reported that within a few weeks of his appointment to the parish, in December 1766, the Indians of this visita had secured an order from the archbishop for the new priest to follow an old arancel.[91] The Indians had presented the arancel to him in a haughty manner, saying that they had secured it only for their pueblo, not for the parish as a whole. Now, "under cover of this order" and on the "frivolous pretext of the litigation" and their alleged poverty, they were "behaving in such an insolent and disorderly way that they are paying none of the parish duties" and refusing to perform all of the customary services agreed to in writing in 1758. The cura felt personally injured by the Indians' "malice": they intended "to do damage to my personal reputation and station," even though he had always acted "in a benign, loving, and impartial way."

In response to the priest's complaint, the audiencia ordered the lieutenant in Ozoloapan to see that the Indians paid their fees according to the arancel. Father Ruis replied with thanks but lamented that because of "the isolation of this place, the broken terrain, the insolence of the Indians, and difficult access to the markets," there was no one he could count on to help him hold the Indians to their obligations.

By 1768, the Atexcapan arancel dispute had bubbled over into the other Indian settlements, including the one in the head town, and the four pueblos together secured a court order that required the cura to follow the new arancel. On December 8, 1768, as Father Ruis was preparing to leave for Atexcapan to celebrate the feast of the Immaculate Conception, an Indian of the head town died. The priest sent the Indian fiscal to the mourners with a message that the burial fee would be four pesos. Before leaving town, he authorized his notary to permit the burial once the fee was paid. According to Father Ruis, the next day the entire village council, including the fiscal, buried the body in the church with full honors and the cross raised on high—ignoring the notary, who had confronted the mourners at the church door to indicate that they must first pay the fee. On December 13, Ruis wrote a complaint to the audiencia and added that the Indians of the parish were not showing him or the Holy Church proper respect; for example, Indian officials had pulled a parishioner out of church by the hair during mass on the eve of the Immaculate Conception feast and whipped him on the doorstep. Ruis repeated that he could do nothing because there was no one to help. He asked for a judicial order that the Indians of all four pueblos must obey the first audiencia order for the Indians of Atexcapan to pay their fees according to the arancel. The Indian officials of the head town replied that they had waited for the cura's return to start the burial, and that after they paid three pesos, he had authorized them to proceed.

In early 1769, Indians of one of the pueblos complained to the alcalde mayor and the audiencia that the lieutenant for Ozoloapan had arrested two of their officials at the cura's request for not paying the customary fees. The audiencia responded that the Indians were to be released if the arancel dispute was the only reason for the arrests. It added that the cura was to obey the arancel. Apparently, the claims in court were suspended at this point, although the dispute itself had not been resolved. Ruis left Ozoloapan in 1770, having won a more desirable parish.

The judicial record picks up again in August 1771, when the Indian alcalde of Atexcapan accused the new cura, Simón de Castañeda, of using "loathsome force" in violation of royal laws and in disregard of the arancel; of whipping Indians, including the fiscal in public with his pants down; and of not permitting confession at Easter until the fees for mass in the outlying pueblos were paid. The alcalde went on to complain of the villagers' "life of oppression" under this cura, who, he said, claimed to be the king of the parish. The audiencia responded with the standard, terse order for all parties to follow the arancel.

Indian parishioners in this dispute were remarkably reluctant to compromise with the cura and settle with him extrajudicially (where the cura was intransigent, compromise would have been all but impossible in any case). In this case, as in some others, they were determined to go directly to higher authorities in Mexico City, bypassing the cura's traditional authority as mediator and judge. The growing inclination of villagers to avail themselves of the high courts in disputes with their parish priests strengthened the mediating role of not only the audiencias, but also the Indians' attorneys in Mexico City and Guadalajara, who were often retained permanently to look after whatever legal actions a community might have pending.

In August 1772, Father Castañeda wrote a strongly worded reply to the Indians' complaint, emphasizing what he called their "perverse nature." He knew that trouble awaited him when he first arrived because, although it was "customary for the entire village council to meet me and accompany me to the head town, none of the officials except the *fiscal* did so." The Indians of the outlying pueblos, he added, resisted the new arancel's fees for masses in visitas, and the Indian alcalde ignored his call for the establishment of a school. During the ceremony in which he had formally invested the village officials with their staffs of office, he had exhorted the alcalde to fulfill his obligations, only to have the man retort:

The cura should stick to mass and confession, and only when he is called. Otherwise, he should stay in his house because [I] alone suffice to govern the *pueblo* because of my office of *alcalde*, which is a very great office.

Turning to the *fiscal* [the cura continued], he added that the *fiscales* run to the *cura* with gossip in order to inconvenience and bother the Indians, so he had ordered the *fiscal* of his *pueblo* to stop doing so; and if the *fiscal* did not stop, he would make him do so.

Since then, Castañeda said, he had repeatedly called on the alcalde to open a school in his pueblo, "but he has never replied, disobeying my orders completely; all of which I have suffered and endured, acting with the greatest discretion." [92]

Father Castañeda went on to recount how the same alcalde came to the parish seat escorted by his village councillors during Easter week in 1772. The cura rebuked him for his disobedience in not attending church in the head town and not making other Indians from his pueblo do so. According to Castañeda, the alcalde's reply was so heated and offensive that he had to order up twelve lashes. At this point, one of the councillors rose to the alcalde's defense, shouting to the other Indians to help him, and "they threw themselves upon me, shoving their staffs of office in my face and saying they would defend themselves with the staffs, for the king had given these to them for that purpose."

Now, in August, the alcalde had gone to Mexico City, promising to obtain another cura for the parish. In the meantime, the Indians were not fulfilling their Christian duties. They went elsewhere for baptism and did not call him to administer the last rites, so that, "thanks to their depraved character and addiction to a brutal licentiousness, they have gone to eternity without the slightest spiritual aid." The alcalde, he had heard, had been collecting small contributions of a real or two from all households to continue the lawsuit against the cura. Castañeda blamed the "malevolence" of the Indian alcalde and the creole administrator of a nearby hacienda, Francisco Maroto. Indians in general were easily taken in by outside agitators, he said, and some of the recalcitrants were Maroto's sharecroppers, and thus under his control. The cura continued his litany of complaints against Maroto, especially that he buried Indians in the hacienda chapel without the priest's permission, saying he was the lord of the chapel as well as of the hacienda, and "in both, he alone gives the orders."[93] Castañeda also blamed the Indians' attorney in Mexico City, an "unprincipled defense counsel and source of discord between *curas* and their parishioners." Castañeda said he had complained to the deputy district governor but received no help. Later in 1772, the audiencia issued yet another short decree for the parish of Ozoloapan: the cura was to follow the arancel, and the Indians were to do their Christian duties.

The record ends on October 6, 1776, with the attorney for the Indians of Atexcapan petitioning for better spiritual care, claiming that Father Castañeda had been cruel to his clients, was levying excessive charges, and was not obeying the arancel, despite two audiencia verdicts to this effect. Castañeda, it was claimed, had imprisoned the alcalde when payments were not to his satisfaction, had failed to confess anyone at Easter, did not celebrate mass in Atexcapan, and rarely came to confess the dying. When asked to do so, he had allegedly replied, "Let the devil take them." No reply from the audiencia or further action by the priest or parishioners is recorded in these files, but Castañeda's death on the road to Mexico City in 1778 or early 1779 gave him a small measure of revenge. He had taken with him, without authorization, 425 pesos belonging to the cofradía of Nuestra Señora de los Dolores. As of May 1779, the cofrades had not been able to recover the money.

Shortly after Castañeda's death, the parishioners of Ozoloapan were described by a visitador pastoral as "quiet and obeying the *arancel*," but the peace was temporary. During the next pastoral visit in 1792, all four pueblos complained that the cura was mistreating them and overcharging for his services. The visitador determined that while the cura charged more than the arancel allowed for some services, he charged less for funerals, so that the differences canceled out. On the other hand, he concluded that the priest had good reason for a countercomplaint, "because the Indians act as if they own the church and bells, and want to do things just as they wish."[94]

After failing to win a clear victory at court, the Ozoloapan curas, previously so energetic in defense of their local interests, withdrew from the fray. Father Ruis Coronel found another post; Father Castañeda spent less and less time in the outlying pueblos. Both were familiar career patterns. But for these two curas, the prolonged arancel disputes also lengthened the emotional distance between pastor and parish. The formal disputes hardened their feelings of isolation, fear, and helplessness, as well as their worst judgments of Indians as cunning imbeciles who were adept at using their protected legal position to win unjust orders from the audiencia. The Ozoloapan priests' failure to gain more than minimal support from the lieutenant when local defiance peaked in 1767 and 1772, and the disappointing verdicts from the audiencia, added to their frustration over the challenges to their traditional duties as father, judge, and enforcer in the moral life of the parish.

The Ozoloapan case also highlights three kinds of brokers and men of influence in late colonial villages who contributed to the suits against parish priests. One was the hacienda administrator, who used his association with Indian sharecroppers to feed the conflict. Another was the attorney in Mexico City, who pressed the case and gave it an anticlerical tone. The third was the local Indian who took up a collection from fellow villagers to launch lawsuits in the name of the community. In the Atexcapan example, he was a village official, but, as Chapter Fifteen suggests, that role could as easily have been filled by a self-appointed legal agent with connections to a lawyer in Mexico City—a political entrepreneur who had not yet ascended the ladder of community offices. If he succeeded in court at the priest's expense, his reputation soared, and the path was cleared for his election to a leading community office and further enrichment.

The second case reveals some unanticipated local repercussions of the 1767 arancel, as well as the general tensions between priest and parish and cabecera and sujeto. Unlike Ozoloapan, Tepetlaostoc in the Valley of Mexico was a second-class Dominican doctrina with the same priest in residence during both phases of the formal dispute, in 1758 and 1776. In 1758, representatives of the visita of Santo Tomás Apipilhuasco protested the weekly contribution of one real per family that Fr. Salvador de Villafaña demanded from them for mass and the pueblo school, and his effective control over the community treasury (he and the pueblo alcalde held the two keys needed to open it). One real a week was an unusually heavy burden, amounting to about three times the annual tribute payment of an adult male head of family. The protest over the treasury implied that the cura took from it when family contributions were not paid in full.

Villafaña answered the complaint by juxtaposing the "disobedience," "lack of respect," and "malicious behavior" of the people of Santo Tomás against his duties "to lead all the Indians to that Christian and orderly life; to make sure that they have a school, that they attend mass, roll call, and instruction in doctrine, [and] that they avoid their continuous adultery, drunkenness, and other sins."[95]

Schooling, as we have seen, was a growing concern of late colonial parish priests, especially in the 1750's, when Archbishop Rubio y Salinas made it his pet program.[96] The problem was how to pay for it and guarantee attendance. The archbishop's solution to the financing was a weekly contribution, which Villafaña had implemented. Villafaña claimed that the Indians of Santo Tomás had always been unruly, that they had rebelled against the friars he had sent there as his assistants and now were not fulfilling the Easter duty regularly. He brushed aside the complaint about the weekly fee as an issue trumped up by a few Indians who resented the punishments they had received from him for their vices, and who wanted to shut down the school and free themselves of any government control.

Clearly, this heavy new collection had touched off the complaint, but Villafaña's observation that people in Santo Tomás were acting out their desire for political independence had a large kernel of truth to it. Santo Tomás was the most remote visita in the parish and apparently the largest.[97] Its residents refused to pay the contribution in Tepetlaostoc or have anything to do with the gobernador there. They would recognize only the local authority of their own alcalde, they said. Cabecera-sujeto friction, then, was a powerful ingredient in this dispute. Nevertheless, the issue was resolved in 1758 by mutual agreement, with the Indians paying a reduced contribution of one-half real every two weeks (and probably being allowed to pay it in their own pueblo).

The agreement appears to have held until 1776, when the Indians of Santo Tomás, now joined by those in the visitas of San Andrés and San Pedro, again stopped making regular contributions for school and mass, and declined to send their children to school. They complained that the aging Friar Villafaña was charging them for first fruits, overcharging them for his spiritual services when he came to the visita, and operating an illegal jail. Now they wanted the arancel, and they wanted it affixed in a conspicuous place for all to see. The archbishop responded on June 20 that they could have the arancel but emphasized that they must follow it in every detail. Villafaña answered on July 4 that the Indians' charges against him were false, and that the people of Santo Tomás were acting as if they could speak for the entire parish. To document their disobedience and malice, he produced a letter from his assistant there, Vicente Verdura, written a few days before the archbishop's response:

Very Most Esteemed Compatriot and Very Dear Sir—
The Indians of this *pueblo* have turned insolent to the point that even the Sunday roll call is mocked (for there is no way to make them attend); and the few who do attend cannot be made to pay the biweekly one-half *real*. When I press them, they turn and run. And [though] now with the imprisonment of the *gobernador* (which caused some respect), [the Indians of the parish] have suspended their insolence in the *barrios* as well as the *cabecera* . . . what is collected does not even pay for mass. It is the same with the school. They will not send their children no matter how often the *fiscal* and his *topiles* call them. As a result, the school is almost deserted at present.[98]

As in 1758, the Indians, Villafaña believed, were looking for an excuse to stop paying the biweekly contribution and to shut down the school; and they were using the litigation to resist his authority and keep him from judging and punishing them. The arancel was only a pretext; Villafaña blamed the intervention of several colonial officials, especially the escribano of Texcoco, who had encouraged the Indian leaders of Santo Tomás to bring suit.

Villafaña provided enough commentary to suggest that his version of Indian motives was very selective. Fees and the language issue were still sore spots and a legitimate source of complaint for the people of Santo Tomás. Villafaña admitted that in addition to the two pesos for mass in the visita listed in the arancel, he charged four pesos for travel and meals. He also admitted that in order to improve the Indians' command of Spanish, he confessed only pregnant women near term, the old, and the sick in Nahuatl.

But the priest, too, had cause for indignation. Villafaña had served 25 years as the doctrinero of Tepetlaostoc, and the last seventeen without a judicial complaint against him. Why, he wondered, had the representatives of Santo Tomás renewed their complaints when he had followed the convenio of 1758 and done no more than fulfill his spiritual duties and promote the schools and language program as ordered? He thought they had ulterior personal and anticlerical motives. If there had been excessive fee collections, he surmised, the mayordomos must have kept the difference for themselves. Evidently, he did not regard the maintenance charge as either illegal or excessive.

The friction between Villafaña and the people of Santo Tomás depended only partly on the cura's actions. The most important underlying issue was local autonomy from the parish and district seat of Tepetlaostoc, but the issue of segregation was also involved. Villafaña knew that fees disputes were inevitable in Santo Tomás if he demanded full payment under the arancel because the population was composed of many castas as well as Indians. When it suited them, mestizos claimed to be Indians, and creoles claimed to be mestizos. Yet Villafaña himself had stirred the ashes of the dispute by complaining of disrespect by the people of Santo Tomás in the report to the crown he was commissioned to write for the parish in 1776.

Although the audiencia skirted the most difficult issues in 1776 by simply ordering the Indians of Santo Tomás to pay the first fruits they had agreed to and validating the arancel, time soon took care of the rest. Villafaña apparently died in 1777, for the parish was secularized on August 19 of that year, and Santo Tomás soon gained cabecera status. No further fees disputes from this parish seem to have reached the high court before independence.

One of the salient aspects of the third case, from the district of Metepec between 1749 and 1774, was the struggle to reduce the labor service the cura could command.[99] Labor was an especially important issue in this district, as it was in the other region where these arancel disputes were most common, the modern state of Hidalgo. The case opened with an attorney's petition on behalf of the Indians of San Gaspar, a visita in the second-class parish of Metepec, which denounced the Franciscan cura doctrinero, Manuel Antonio Martínez, and his assistants, for forcing them to perform personal services, especially as burden bearers, in the name of "just perquisites and fees." The petition, which called on the audiencia and viceroy to order the priests to follow the arancel and refrain from demanding personal service, was prompted by the Franciscans' incarceration of five pueblo officials over this dispute. On May 7, 1749, the audiencia ordered the release of the officials, compliance with the arancel, and personal service only with the Indians' consent and at the customary wage. Soon thereafter, the Indians of San Gaspar entered another complaint against Martínez, this time over fees. They claimed that he had made each of the ten "barrios" of the doctrina sponsor a separate Corpus Christi fiesta, when the custom had been for each to contribute four pesos to a single fiesta in the cabecera. They complained also of charges of twelve reales for a baptism instead of the normal four. Again, on June 6, the audiencia ordered Martínez to obey the arancel, and the alcalde mayor to enforce the order.

Other complaints from San Gaspar were made to the audiencia against Martínez's successors, in September 1752 and July 1756. The target of the 1756 complaint was the first diocesan cura of the parish, Dr. Cayetano de Sotomayor. Sixteen years later, yet another complaint was registered against Sotomayor, this time by Metepec and its barrios, as well as the pueblo of San Gaspar, for various abuses, including grossly exceeding the terms of the Lorenzana arancel. He reportedly had charged 52 pesos for a simple Indian funeral and burial, asked 100 pesos for the funeral of the widow of a former gobernador, demanded personal services, and "ignominiously" cut off Indians' hair. The petitioners claimed that for five years, crews of fifteen to 20 local Indians had worked at demolishing the old Franciscan convent and building the cura's new house without pay. Those who did not serve were whipped or fined one and a half reales per day. He also was said to demand three reales a year as a school tax from each Indian man, even though classes often were not held. The petitioners called for the arancel to be applied.

These were serious charges, and the cura's attorney requested that the audiencia examine the petitioners. His contention was that the arancel complaint was a contrivance of the alcalde mayor, who wanted to weaken the cura's power and reduce his income. The audiencia ordered seventeen witnesses to appear: the gobernador, the alcalde ordinario, two alcaldes, eight past gobernadores, and the escribano of Metepec, and the gobernador, two alcaldes, and escribano of San Gaspar. The examination of witnesses was made in Mexico City on October 6 by the oidor Antonio de Ribadeneyra (who had been a key figure in the Fourth Provincial Council). Nine of the witnesses called did not appear, including the two current gobernadores.

Ribadeneyra was unusually careful in his procedures. He called the witnesses to him one by one, keeping the others isolated so that they could not talk to one another or listen to the interrogation. The first witness, Phelipe Antonio, alcalde ordinario of Metepec, offered somewhat contradictory testimony—first that he had not been a party to the complaint, and that it was promoted by the alcalde mayor's lieutenant; then that he had consented to it voluntarily because the cura had treated the officials with disrespect during the Sunday roll calls "merely because they did not have their cloaks tied properly." The second witness, a past gobernador, Antonio Andrés, was a close associate of the cura, having served as the fiscal mayor for many years. He said that his name had been used in the original complaint without permission, and that the charges were false. It was the alcalde mayor who wanted the arancel, not the Indians, he said, adding that though the cura did punish parishioners, it was only with four to six lashes for absence from catechism class and mass and their failure to meet "other obligations." He admitted to a strained relationship with the alcalde mayor, who recently had denied him the position of interim gobernador and "wanted to put him in stocks and beat his feet." Ribadeneyra found the remaining witnesses no more reliable or forthcoming (he said they did not "speak honestly," and considered the one witness who spoke reasonably good Spanish to be "sly as a result"), but they did present the gobernador of Metepec as a leading figure in the complaint and seemed to clear the alcalde mayor. Notwithstanding the problems in the testimony, Ribadeneyra concluded that "the *arancel* prepared for the *curas* should be generally obeyed," because custom involved personal services and "some improper contributions." The result was a brief order of November 2, 1772, for the cura to obey the arancel.

Sotomayor replied on December 17 that the alcalde mayor had interfered and convinced the Indians that they did not have to pay their duties. He sought and received an interim order, announced by the lieutenant on January 4, 1773, that the customary fees should be paid. Through their Mexico City attorney, the Indians responded with a sharp attack on the cura, who had "never . . . followed any rule in his collection of parish fees." They wanted to be governed by the arancel because they had been providing the cura with one campanero, two sacristanes, and over ten fiscales weekly to carry out personal as well as parish work without pay or food. The weekly roll call was a tense time, they added, because it was used not to mark attendance at mass but to requisition labor. On October 14, the audiencia fiscal responded favorably to the Indians' request for the arancel as "the only effective way to avoid the stream of petitioners and complaints that almost daily weary Your Excellency's attention." He used the occasion to promote Lorenzana's vision of his 1767 arancel as a regla fija: "I advise you to order that the *aranceles* be obeyed generally and universally in all the parishes of the kingdom." He said he realized that the customary arrangements could be less burdensome in some parishes but still opposed "this freedom to vary," leading as it did to "continual movements and disruptions because of the ease with which the Indians change their minds at every turn." In March 1774, the audiencia again simply ordered the cura to follow the arancel.

* * *

More than any other late colonial issue, the arancel of 1767 spotlighted parish priests in a negative way and promoted the idea of the greedy cura. In practice, it tended to turn the relationship between curas and Indian communicants into a financial transaction. The increase in the fee for mass in the visitas was a particularly sore point, so much so that a cura or his vicarios could find the church doors locked against them when they traveled outside the cabecera for the service of the Eucharist.

In a moral economy that was particularly sensitive to "excessive" charges, the arancel had the advantage of reducing labor service and overall payments, but it increased cash payments, which were especially resented. Coming at a time when the tax burden on rural pueblos was increasing, it convinced many Indian parishioners that the cura mainly wanted their money.[100] And with the collection of clerical fees often now in the hands of elected fiscales (who were less beholden to the cura), demands by the curas for prepayment also increased. In these circumstances, the arancel of 1767 contributed to more—and more vehement—suits and overt anticlericalism in various parts of the archdiocese.

Indian parishioners in these fees disputes were reluctant to settle with the cura extrajudicially. This litigiousness strengthened the authority of the audiencias and the mediating role of the Indians' attorneys in Mexico City and Guadalajara. It also both expressed and reinforced parishioners' greater freedom from the parish priest's moral and political influence.

In the Atexcapan dispute, the Indian officials' staffs of office were featured in dramatic confrontations involving both threats and the kind of violence that left broken bones and aching hearts. Defiant Indians brandished their varas; priests responded by striking out with their own silver-tipped canes and angrily seizing the officials' staffs. One priest who was particularly fond of minatory gestures even confiscated and "imprisoned" the Indian council's staffs. Staff against cane highlights the revision of the judicial role of parish priests that was part of the Spanish Bourbons' reformulation of church-state relations in the late eighteenth century, redefining the priests as spiritual specialists in narrowed terms.

With pueblos demanding, and colonial courts encouraging, the arancel, some curas chose to stand on the uncertain ground of their "incontrovertible rights,"[101] but most appealed to precedent and the sanctity of custom in defense of their traditional sources of income. But standing behind custom and traditional values so decisively in the fee disputes left parish priests open to accusations that they were materialistic, that they were resisting royal laws and the interpretations of royal judges, or that they resembled slave masters or feudal lords.[102]

Ironically, priests who balked at the arancel also faced accusations of "innovation." Even the most conservative late colonial curas were thrust into novel situations that made them look like innovators to parishioners and royal judges—replacing friars in the secularized parishes, pushing ahead with the schools and language reforms required by their superiors, and working within traditional categories to increase their incomes. Curas were quick to deny this charge and retaliated with claims that parishioners were the ones who disturbed a stable, equitable relationship and failed to fulfill their duties as Christians, not to mention the terms of the arancel.[103]

Despite the Atexcapan Indians' hostility toward their curas in the 1760's and 1770's, they were not leading a "pagan" revival or a separatist movement. They accepted the dogma of the church as it was taught to them; they wanted a priest and the sacraments; they were concerned with salvation in Christian terms (with the "welfare of our souls," as their representatives put it); and they claimed to fear and respect their cura. Even when Indian parishioners' feelings toward him ran more to fear and anger than to love and respect, the late colonial cura was an important spiritual figure, not often an object of indifference or simply an adversary or an agent for hire. In the pastoral visit records and some of the suits over aranceles, visitas hoped for a cura or vicario de pie fijo of their own. And although these petitions and lawsuits were always presented in the name of the community, they did not simply express Indian solidarity against intrusive outsiders. As Chapter Fifteen suggests, they could also express personal ambitions, divisions within communities, and other kinds of local dissension.

Arancel suits sought local rule and protection against increasing demands from Spanish authority, but they did not directly challenge that authority or contribute much to an Indian class identity. The parishioners' bundle of litigation papers—like Santiago's horse, a found cross, or the titular saint—stood for a localized Christian identity that interpreted and adjusted to the received beliefs and expectations of priests and other colonial officials more than it rejected their authority. Litigious pueblos, like Indian officials shaking their royal staffs of office at the cura, were resisting the acts of one kind of colonial official while validating colonial authority at a higher level. Disputes over clerical fees, like those over election procedures and bienes de comunidad, took their cue from royal and archiepiscopal decrees. These late colonial lawsuits and protests may have expressed a determined opposition to labor service, externally imposed alterations of clerical fees, and other perceived injustices, but they were framed as supplications for the king's favor. The typical opening was a humble "Venimos a pedir" (We come to request), not a militant "venimos a contradecir" (We come to object). And the audiencia's mechanical rulings that all parties must follow the arancel seem to have been a sufficient victory for most Indian litigants.

Parish Priests and Insurrection, 1810–1815

I give shade and shelter, as God commands me.
—Manuel Villalpando, interim cura of
Xalpan, district of Cadereyta, 1779

To follow the late colonial history of priests in their parishes is also to wonder about their prominent place in Mexico's War of Independence. The conclusion moves between these subjects in an effort to understand both better—using the history of local religion and politics to illuminate the choices priests made between 1810 and 1815, and using their actions during that struggle to offer some final reflections on the changing circumstances of parish priests before 1810.

Separate But in the World

The main story of late colonial priests in their parishes is of men whose sense of their duties and interests was changing more slowly than their circumstances. In addition to foreign threats and powerful pressures on the rural communities they served—from population growth, migration, land shortages, growing social differences within communities, increasing labor demands from commercial agriculture, mining, and manufacturing, higher taxes, and other initiatives to incorporate Americans more fully as colonial subjects—those changing circumstances included Bourbon reforms pointed at the parish clergy and new ways of thinking about the relations between church and state.

Among the Bourbons' church reforms, the revision of ecclesiastical immunity from royal courts was uppermost in the minds of the cathedral clergy (and historians who have relied on the record they produced).[1] But this was only one of many initiatives designed to increase the power of the monarchy in church affairs and restrict the place of the priesthood and religion in public life. To be sure, Bourbon administrators were unable to implement all of their reforms for the parish clergy, or even all of any particular facet for that matter, but what they did accomplish contributed directly to changes in who the parish priests were, how they thought about their service, how they made a living, and how they dealt with parishioners and district governors.

The importance of Bourbon reforms to priests' changing circumstances and their subsequent actions comes not only from how far Bourbon designs for the parish clergy were implemented. In proposing to reconstitute the clergy as a professional service group and presenting a more absolutist, modernizing conception of government that emphasized law over custom, standardization, royal absolutism, and the enlargement of the royal patrimony, the reforms invited local conflicts that increasingly centered on the authority of parish priests in public affairs. That the reforms were inspired by centralizing initiatives in Spain, rather than petitions from Americans, and were designed to serve peninsular interests best virtually guaranteed resistance and some expressions of patriotic outrage in America. Parish priests were pulled in several directions by these royal initiatives. They were agents of the Spanish crown, but also called to a higher law; and they were overwhelmingly American-born and -educated.

For parish priests who succeeded in performing their many traditional public roles without much contradiction or controversy, the late-eighteenth-century reforms that sought to curtail their roles as judge and pastor were more distressing than the challenge of pastoral service itself to the priest who was perennially unable to succeed as both judge and physician in the confessional, or both servant and father in the community. Traditionally, the pastor's duties, which originated in his responsibilities as protector and spiritual father, had always shaded into public life, more or less so, depending on the individual and local circumstances. That public role in colonial society could be modified but not easily transformed from the top without consequences for the political order.

Bourbon policies had recast the old parental metaphor in ways that weakened both the political authority of the church and the legitimacy of royal authority, and with them, the ability of some priests to command their parishioners' allegiances. Many late colonial curas who became embroiled in lawsuits got a lesson in royal supremacy, as well as a disappointing verdict. The royal tribunals, one was advised, had "the indisputable authority . . . to make [priests] act in accord with all that is just."[2] As if the judges of royal tribunals alone knew what was just, more than a few cura defendants must have thought.

The attempt to strengthen the state could alter the relationships between priests and the moral-political order of society at the local level, but not simply by removing parish priests from public life. The central areas of Spanish America were not Europe, where a similar expansion of secularizing governments in the eighteenth century came closer to the intended results. Parish priests in Spanish America were more important to the legitimacy and bureaucratic operations of the monarchy, and their place in local affairs had not eroded gradually, as it had in much of Europe. Nor does a loss of religious fervor seem to have occurred before the Bourbon reforms in the dioceses of Mexico and Guadalajara. Religious observances overseen by parish priests were as popular as ever, and local cults of the Virgin Mary and the saints were growing.

Saying that the parish reforms, however incomplete, were extensive and consequential is not to suggest that most curas became insurgents because of them or that these reforms go far to explain the nature of the Independence War. External events and local and regional circumstances have too much to do with the complex, turbulent history of that period to allow sweeping, categorical explanations. Priests were not automatically leaders of the early struggles, even if they aspired to lead; only a few seem to have been indispensable; and most curas and vicarios did not join an insurgent movement before 1821. But their actions were still important to the course of the war in less obvious ways. Although there is little evidence that they could simply "call out the masses" in many places—little evidence even in the Bajío of whole pueblos or parishes marching off behind their parish priest, as some have suggested—it would be easy to overestimate Indian resistance to parish priests and miss the points of union between them. The church in its full sense of the body of communicants—priests and laity—remained an especially powerful set of relationships in the late colonial period.

Many influential parish priests chose a deliberate neutrality that was most damaging to the royalists. Curas in the heartland of New Spain were after all part of the colonial elite in terms of status, education, and wealth. In fact they were, on average, the wealthiest parish priests in the Spanish empire and still powerfully attached to strands of colonial patronage and authority. But, on the defensive, divided in their loyalties, and feeling thwarted in what they saw as their indispensable duties, they were less likely than their predecessors to regard themselves as full partners in the colonial enterprise. As agents of the colonial state, they were considerably less royalist after 1810 than their lay counterparts, the subdelegados and lieutenants.[3]

The shifts in outlook parish priests experienced did not center on Enlightenment political thought that emphasized individual rights and a subversive union of liberty and equality. Some parish priests did embrace the terms of French and British Enlightenment political philosophy. Liberty was coming to have a more positive meaning, but few parish priests who spoke of it had abandoned their ideas about hierarchy, custom, submission, and mediation in favor of unfettered personal freedom and private virtue.

Enlightenment ideas with a more important, if diffuse, impact on the outlook of parish priests included several that Bourbon policy makers and regalist bishops themselves found congenial, especially the idea of improvement through human agency. For Bourbon absolutists, this idea carried with it greater optimism about human nature in general (and the capacity for goodness and productivity of hispanized Indians in particular), the efficacy of formal education in unifying the state and promoting the material well-being of rulers and subjects, and a new interest in history as a guide to future progress.[4] For curas, it was the idea of change—of living with the prospect of change and disorder, and seeing themselves in history, with a mission, whether or not they were optimistic about their ability to influence its future course—that affected them most.

Some religious concepts and sensibilities were also changing in ways that suited Enlightened absolutism, if their depiction in painting, sculpture, and pastoral letters is any indication. Doctrine took on a new sweetness as it moved away from the old balance of opposing forces that mirrored the decline of the two-majesties principle and the clergy's judicial role, and emphasized official optimism about human nature and the future. The focus of church teaching shifted from fear and love as the two wings of flight toward heaven to love alone as the guiding principle of Christian order and the means of salvation; from God as remote father-judge to God as a more accessible, loving father; from images of Christ on the cross that emphasized his suffering to a more serene, idealized representation of his body that anticipated the resurrection.

A new emphasis by church leaders on the Ten Commandments at the expense of the Seven Capital Sins also fitted the official optimism of the time. Both were prescriptions for Christian conduct, but the seven sins, which had been at the heart of doctrine in the seventeenth century, directed the believer inward to personal imperfections and the dark corners of human nature. Pride, covetousness, lust, anger, gluttony, envy, and sloth were willful excesses of passion, violations of divine law that had to be curbed. The Ten Commandments, especially as priests were being taught to present them in late colonial Mexico, were more affirmative and sociable. The commandments stressed the individual's relationship to God, family, and fellow humans, and the messages they were meant to convey included respect for authority, "reform of customs," "social well-being," and love as the means of achieving grace.[5] Taught this way, the commandments could support the Bourbon's selective combination of Enlightenment thought and centralized, regalist authority, a combination that rationalized change in terms of old laws and Christian principles whenever possible. But the Ten Commandments were also associated with older ideas about moral conduct centering on charity, personal sacrifice, hierarchy, and mutual obligation that could serve to critique, more than justify, Bourbon reforms.

Insurgents and Royalists

When large-scale movements against Spanish privilege and the threat of French rule began in September 1810, parish priests were prominent enough for Henry G. Ward, Britain's chief emissary to Mexico in the 1820's, to call the early years of Mexico's War of Independence "the insurrection of the clergy," and for Lucas Alamán to claim that "almost alone they [the curas] sustained it."[6] More than a dozen parish priests appear as pivotal leaders or conspicuous insurgent fighters and administrators in the standard histories of Mexico's beginnings as a nation, whether by the conservative Alamán or the insurgent and moderate liberal Carlos María Bustamante. Because of this handful of leaders, the history of the Independence War as reduced to a few lines or a mural painting has highlighted the role of parish priests. But when one asks how many insurgent parish priests were involved and why, the sharp lines of the picture dissolve into very different opinions. Pablo Richard claims that thousands of clergymen "supported the revolution"—about three-fourths of all priests, in his estimation.[7] Jesús Bravo Ugarte's statistical study led him to the opposite conclusion. As basically firm regalists who remained loyal to Spanish authority, most clergy actively opposed the popular insurrections between 1810 and 1819.[8] Bravo Ugarte's conclusion is in the spirit of Manuel Abad y Queipo's claim in his pastoral letter of September 26, 1812,

TABLE 7
Insurgent Parish Priests, 1810–1819

Position	Confirmed supporter	Alleged supporter	Total	
			Number	Percent
Curas	72	25	97	66.9%
Vicarios	25	10	35	24.1
Coadjutors and interim curas	6	2	8	5.5
Hacienda chaplains	3	2	5	3.5
TOTAL	106	39	145	100.0%

SOURCES: See Appendix B.

NOTE: The table excludes 3 men who were apparently not in service and 3 who may not have been priests. I have chosen also to exclude the 25 men identified in 1813 by district governors in the Archdiocese of Mexico, which would have badly skewed the data, especially in respect to the geography of the participation.

that few curas were involved as insurgents. Abad y Queipo acknowledged that some insurgent curas came from his diocese of Michoacán ("even among Jesus's disciples, there was a Judas"), but that for each of them "there have been . . . twenty-eight or thirty Peters and Pauls."[9] All of these views assume that curas, whether insurgents or royalists, were natural leaders of masses waiting to be led—an assumption that is not fully supported in this study.

In fact, parish priests participated in the insurgency in smaller numbers than Richard and Ward imagined, but in larger ones than Bravo Ugarte and Abad y Queipo thought. Although Alamán's opinion was colored by his vision of "the common people" as a disorderly rabble and of priests and religion as the linch-pins of social and political order, his assertion that "warrior clergy [were] every-where" is a revealing exaggeration.[10] Enough priests participated for one or two to appear in nearly every major engagement and congress, and many minor ones. And parish priests were favorite targets of kidnappings on both sides, either to recruit these men of influence or neutralize them as opponents.[11]

As shown in Appendix B, at least 145 of the parish priests within the borders of modern Mexico either supported or were alleged to have supported the insur-rections between 1810 and 1815, including as many as 97 of the country's 1,027 curas. The proportion of curas, 9 percent, though substantial, is far from the massive participation that Alamán claimed (see Table 7 for a breakdown by posi-tion). Additional research undoubtedly will show that some of the unconfirmed partisans listed in the appendix should not be included, and that others should be added, especially from the dioceses of Michoacán and Puebla. Even if these figures were increased by half with additional evidence, only about one cura in seven and one vicario in 40 joined an insurgent movement by 1815.[12] In short, perhaps one priest in twelve participated in an independence movement before 1820, and two-thirds of these participants were not in parish service at the time.[13]

The insurgent parish priests were concentrated in two areas: the Bajío and adjacent highlands of modern Jalisco and Michoacán; and the tierra caliente of Michoacán, Guerrero, and Puebla, and adjacent highlands of the Estado de México. These two areas account for about 60 percent of the 108 parish priests identified by region in Table 8.[14] Of the 111 insurgent priests whose diocesan af-filiation is known, 34 (30.6%) were from Michoacán, 24 from México (21.6%),

TABLE 8
Insurgent Priests by Region and Modern State
(N = 108)

Area/modern state	Number	Percent
Bajío and adjacent areas (in dioceses of Guadalajara, Michoacán, and Mexico)	34	31.5%
Jalisco	12	
Guanajuato	10	
Michoacán	8	
Zacatecas	3	
Querétaro	1	
Tierra caliente of the west and south (in dioceses of Michoacán, Puebla, Mexico, and Guadalajara)	31	28.7%
Guerrero	16	
Michoacán	9	
Puebla	4	
Colima	2	
Central highlands (in dioceses of Mexico and Puebla)	22	20.4%
Mexico	12	
Hidalgo	4	
Morelos	3	
Puebla	3	
Gulf: Veracruz (in dioceses of Mexico and Puebla)	8	7.4%
South: Oaxaca (in Diocese of Antequera)	8	7.4%
Northwest (in dioceses of Arispe and Durango)	5	4.1%
Sinaloa	3	
Sonora	1	
Durango	1	

NOTE: The table does not include the 25 insurgent parish priests reported in AGN OG 5 because these reports cover only districts in the Archdiocese of Mexico. This additional group of 25 has the following temporal and geographical concentrations: in the modern state of Hidalgo in 1811; and in southwestern Estado de México both in 1810–11 and in the months before the reports were composed at the end of 1813 (when some priests were drawn to Morelos's movement, which was then centered in adjoining districts of modern Guerrero and Michoacán). The Sultepec area in the Estado de México was home to more than a third of these additional insurgent priests.

22 from Guadalajara (19.8%), 20 from Puebla (18.0%), 9 from Antequera (8.1%), 1 from Durango (0.9%), and 1 from Arispe (0.9%).

Curas and vicarios fought on both sides, but the patriotic interest in insurgent priests has neglected their royalist counterparts. Royalist pastors attracted little attention from colonial recordkeepers unless they were exemplary fighters and propagandists or, like José Francisco Alvarez ("el padre chicharronero"—"the chitlin priest," who was said to have burned insurgents alive), gained notoriety for their atrocities. Judging by the sample in Appendix B, more pastors in the Archdiocese of Mexico (82 of 105 in the 1813 district reports and 37 of the 66 who could be identified by place in other sources) were active royalists than insurgents.[15]

Being classified as an insurgent or collaborator did not always mean early and unwavering support. Even some of the most important cura-insurgents, such as Mariano Matamoros and Lic. José Manuel Herrera, were reluctant to join. As insurgents approached Matamoros's parish of Jantetelco (Morelos) in late 1811, he petitioned the archbishop for permission to take refuge in Mexico City. He joined José María Morelos, he said at his trial in 1814, after the district tax collector falsely accused him of being a collaborator and the accusation stuck.[16] Herrera, who joined Morelos in 1811, was supposedly discovered by insurgents hiding in the cobwebs behind a side altar of his parish church in Huamuxtitlan (Guerrero). Some parish priests were active in the insurgency or lent aid and comfort for only a brief time. Dr. Antonio Labarrieta of Guanajuato and Dr. Francisco Severo Maldonado of Mascota (Jalisco), for example, became outspoken royalists after raising their voices for Hidalgo in late 1810. Other priests who were identified in one way or another with insurgents quickly faded from political view with a pardon and stern warning.[17] Most pastors stayed in their parishes.

The numbers are small enough, the pool of parish priests diverse enough, and the decision to join contingent enough that it would have been difficult to predict in September 1810 who among them would have become insurgents. Insurgent pastors were not mainly young radicals who acted as if they were oppressed by the upper clergy or swayed by French and Anglo-American liberal ideas. More, in fact, were men of modest learning in mid-career who had not been conspicuous in the politics of self-promotion or protest before 1810 and seem to have been dedicated pastors. The bishops and doctors and licenciados of the cathedral chapters were more likely than parish priests to be versed in the new politics of freedom, and the most "Enlightened" of these high clergymen remained royalists in the early years of the war. There were reasons for conflict between the upper and lower clergy, but insurgent curas rarely targeted the church hierarchy as the object of their wrath or an obstacle to a new order independent of Spain and peninsulares, despite the anathemas heaped on them from cathedrals once the insurrections began.

Some doctors and licenciados in parish service imbued with the spirit of progress did join the insurgency. Most did not. Dr. José Ignacio Couto of Texmelucan (Puebla), an especially prominent cura-insurgent when Morelos's forces spread into his diocese in 1812, was reminiscent of Father Hidalgo. Well-educated and placed in a secondary parish, he had directed much of his restless energy as a pastor toward the application of eighteenth-century ideas about material progress through road-building and initiatives in commercial agriculture. But Lic. José de la Pedreguera, the cura of Jalapa (Veracruz), who was active in similar programs of road- and bridge-building, industry, and commerce, became an ardent royalist, earning the title "benemérito de la patria" for his part in the reconquest of Coatepec.[18]

Apart from the fact that many insurgent parish priests were curas, came from second- and third-class parishes in the modern states of Guerrero, Michoacán, Guanajuato, México, Hidalgo, and Jalisco, and had connections with Morelos's movement between 1811 and 1815, there is little else that obviously united them. Arancel suits and conflicts with subdelegados and lieutenants may have fueled the anti-peninsular feelings of some.[19] Kinship and close associations with creole hacendados probably had the same effect on others.[20] The sensitivity to social injustices and determination to act on charitable intentions that brought some curas into disagreement with royal authorities, especially after the 1785–86 famine and epidemic, would have played a part, too.[21] And a fierce, almost apocalyptic resolve to combat spiritual decay—a resolve sometimes nurtured by years of arduous service and near isolation in remote parishes—may have prompted others to join.[22]

Alamán offered another hypothesis about priests as insurgents that does not

stand up well to the available evidence: that it was the most dissolute priests—
"the most corrupt ones of every place"—who took part.[23] Priests with dubious
nicknames like Father Rotgut and Father Chocolate were, he wrote, among the
"most atrocious and bloodthirsty" men of the insurgency.[24] But on the rare occasion that a parish priest who made his way into the colonial record because of
his misconduct turns up in the standard sources on the Independence War, it
is usually as a royalist. For example, Francisco Garrido left the parish of Tochimilco (Puebla) in the archdiocese early in the 1790's under a cloud of complaints
over concubinage, drunkenness, and failure to perform his sacramental duties.
He received a negative report from the subdelegado in 1793 in his next parish of
Zinacantepec, and another series of complaints by parishioners forced him out
of there, too. But in 1811, he reappeared as the cura of Sultepec, declaring his
loyalty to the crown, denouncing the insurgent sentiments of various priests and
townspeople who were kinsmen of Miguel Hidalgo, and expressing his disincli-
nation to be among people who were so prejudiced against peninsulares.[25] José
María Torres, the Indian vicario of Tepehuacan, was judged in 1808 to be a priest
of less than good conduct, "inclined to drink in a disorderly way." He openly affirmed his loyalty to his bishop and the crown in 1811.[26] And then there is one of
the prime examples we met earlier, Joseph Manuel Sotomayor, who had been removed from his parish of Zacualpan and suspended from service in the late 1790's
for outrageous conduct, but resurfaced as an ardent royalist in the war and was
restored to his parish.[27] If breaking the vow of chastity or engaging in commercial
activity was the standard of disreputable conduct, many—perhaps most—parish
priests on all sides of the independence question would have qualified. Such misconduct was not a clear expression of rebellion against the colonial order.

   Alamán's fixed vision of clergymen in the war is of an immoral, often ignorant
cura leading "an unruly multitude" of "poorly armed people from their *pueblos*"
into a district capital. He cites as examples the forces of Mariano de las Fuentes
Alarcón (cura of Maltrata) and Juan Moctezuma Cortés (cura of Zongolica) converging on the administrative and commercial center of Orizaba in March 1812.[28]
This, for Alamán, was the bad cura corrupting the clergy's great influence, leading the ignorant, fanatical masses into anarchy and the devastation of property
and civilization.[29] Both Alamán and Bustamante, in their histories of the war,
lingered on the case of Moctezuma, a prominent insurgent in the Diocese of
Puebla until his death in 1816. Alamán wrote of Moctezuma's unbridled taste for
gambling and dissipation as a sign of how unsuited he was to lead a moral cause.
Bustamante described him first with some admiration as "the living image of
the emperor of this name. . . . He was not born to be a general but to intone a
good sermon: he had a beautiful way of speaking and knew how to arouse the
troops with the double prestige of a priest and a descendent of the emperor of
the Aztecs."[30] But Bustamante found him vain and irresponsible. "Poor Oaxaca,
in the hands of the *cura* of Zongolica," he said of Moctezuma's brief tenure as
interim governor there in 1813.[31] Irritated that he was not named a voting member of congress at Tehuacán in November 1815, Moctezuma, according to Bustamante, ascended the church pulpit for a sermon "filled with outrageous remarks
[dos mil disparates] made in a self-satisfied tone."[32] For Alamán, he was the

epitome of the insurgent priest; for Bustamante, he was an absurd figure whose flawed humanity lent a little bizarre humor to the upheaval.[33]

The Moctezumas of the insurgency were more than matched by the Joaquín de la Plaza y Castañedas. This longtime cura of Otumba, denounced by the subdelegado as an insurgent in 1811, was the familiar type of pastor devoted to his parish duties and discreet in his personal affairs who occasionally fell into dispute with parishioners over clerical fees and with royal governors over jurisdiction. He was praised in 1793 by an earlier subdelegado for exemplary conduct—"exact in fulfilling his duties and of sufficient talent and learning." He had refurbished the church largely at his own expense and acted "with restraint" in collecting clerical fees.[34] But in 1807, two pueblos in the parish brought suit against him for charging the fees of the arancel rather than the lower customary schedule established in the 1760's and withholding services until payment was received.[35] Then, in the early months of the Independence War, Plaza, caught up in a jurisdictional dispute with the subdelegado in an adultery case, was rewarded with a charge of sedition.[36]

The Neutral Majority

José Antonio de Zúñiga, cura of Temascaltepec at the time the Hidalgo insurgency swept through the Valley of Toluca, can illustrate some of the contingencies and counterpoints at work when parish priests met insurrection and made choices. Fifty-five years old in 1810, Zúñiga had been a cura since 1783 in the second- and third-class parishes of Alacotlan, Alahuistlan, Hueypustla, and finally Temascaltepec, all in the vicinity of Zacualpan on the margins of modern Guerrero and southwestern Mexico state. Although Indians of Alahuistlan brought suit against him in 1786 for demanding excessive fees, tithe, and first fruits, and meting out cruel floggings, he was largely inconspicuous.[37] The subdelegado of his district of Tetepango in 1793 described him as an acceptable pastor, not particularly talented or learned.[38] But he was willing and able to exercise some political influence in the parish of Temascaltepec on the eve of the insurrection. In particular, he cooperated with a neighboring hacendado to propose that several dispersed rancherías of Indians be resettled into the pueblo of Acatitlan in exchange for land, water, new houses, and 200 pesos for church furnishings. When some of the people targeted for resettlement objected, he attempted to "persuade them with Christian arguments" (persuasiones cristianas).[39]

In March 1811, at the urging of the district administrador de rentas, the Inquisition charged Zúñiga with treason for not urging his parishioners to oppose the insurgents or teaching them that the insurgency was against their religion and the king. According to the administrador, Zúñiga had failed to help mobilize 100 local men for the royalist ranks. The cura responded that the charges of sedition were false, that in fact he had made a 3,000-peso donation in support of the royalist cause and could give other evidence of his loyalty. But local witnesses presented a more complicated history. An Indian shopkeeper testified that the cura's behavior before September 1810 had been "good," and that he had initially preached against the "revolution." But he caught the new spirit and began to urge his parishioners "to join the insurgents, reject those who took away their liberty, . . . for they, not the King of Spain, were the legitimate owners [dueños] of America." He organized a cannon foundry and reportedly proclaimed to some of his parishioners:

> Boys, now we have cannons to kill all the *gachupines* who have usurped our America for so long. Now that Spain is finished, we won't have brandy, Brittany cloth, and other things, and we won't be kicked around, but we'll still have our *charape* [mixed drink from fermented maguey juice], homespun, and other cloth we make for ourselves. Long live Our Lady of Guadalupe and death to the *gachupines* and their lackey friends![40]

The shopkeeper added that Zúñiga accepted the title of commander at arms of this pueblo, and his house served as a meeting place for insurgents. Another witness testified that Zúñiga had greeted the insurgents in full regalia, with the image of Our Lady of Guadalupe, the cross elevated, and the church bells tolling, and that before any insurgents entered the parish, he stirred up public sentiment by spreading seditious gossip against the gachupines.

Zúñiga's response again was to deny all charges of sedition: he accepted the title of captain from the insurgents, but only so that the Indians would obey him as cura; the church bells had indeed tolled when the insurgents entered, but the Indians had rung them on their own; and he had met the insurgents with the image of Our Lady of Guadalupe because that was what the insurgents told him to do.[41]

Most parish priests were more cautious than Father Zúñiga in their uncertain commitment to one side or the other. They wanted first to ensure the safety of their parishioners and themselves, and did what they could not to antagonize armed partisans—tentatively and discreetly supporting one group or another.[42] Curas also looked for ways to strengthen their position of local influence while avoiding risky political choices, especially when they could play their customary role as mediators and messengers of mercy. Sometimes they negotiated surrenders by insurgents or royalists in their midst, or interceded for the safety of their parishioners and other priests. The cura of Apam (Hidalgo), Pedro José Ignacio Calderón, reported on August 27, 1811, that he and the other priests resident there had successfully pleaded against executions when insurgents entered the cabecera several days before. Calderón then hurried to Almoloya to plead for the life of the royalist captain of Molango, who had been captured there.[43] José María Alvarez, cura of Ocoyucan (Puebla), negotiated the surrender of Huamantla in 1812 and arranged for the release of captured royalists, while the cura of Olinalá (Guerrero) led his parishioners in appealing for the pardon of their insurgent leader, Miguel Bravo, when he was captured in April 1814.[44] In several famous cases, the lives of insurgent curas were spared because of the entreaties of other curas who were respected for their impartiality and piety: Dr. Valentín, the cura of Córdoba (Veracruz), on behalf of Dr. José Ignacio Couto, and "the venerable" Nicolás Santiago Herrera, cura of Uruapan (Michoacán), who persuaded disaffected insurgents to spare the life of Dr. Cos.[45]

Most parish priests remained above the struggle in ways that particularly distressed royalist leaders. Bishop Cabañas of Guadalajara lamented in a pastoral letter of April 4, 1812, that few of his priests were even sending news of local unrest that could help royalist soldiers locate the insurgents; and in May 1813, Manuel Toral, cura of Aculco, blasted the priests of Querétaro for their "criminal indifference" in not doing more to suppress the insurgency.[46] The next year, even as the insurgency was losing momentum, Félix María Calleja, the royalist military commander, complained that priests assuring their parishioners of the justice of the insurgency in the privacy of the confessional were subverting popular support for the royalist forces.[47]

Not a few curas took their political cue more from where insurgent forces happened to be than from a considered choice. As with the decision to flee or to decline reassignment to a pueblo notorious for its support of insurgents, a purely practical concern for personal safety was what motivated some to cooperate with the group then in power locally (as Labarrieta and many others did), to ring the church bells on the approach of insurgent forces and offer them holy water at the door, to straddle the fence by sending occasional reports to the bishop but eschewing a more partisan role, or even to publicly support one side while helping the other.[48]

The timid, weak, and demoralized among them were not likely to make a daring move in any case; and many comfortably situated curas could be expected to protect their local privileged positions by not making permanent enemies. Parish priests who accepted the regalist definition of their office could regard neutrality as the proper way to remain true to their calling, even when their superiors chided them for inactivity. For those whose public authority in the parish had been much diminished by the lawsuits against them that Bourbon policies on floggings, ecclesiastical jails and courts, the administration of community property, and local officeholding encouraged, the risk of joining the insurgency still was great. Even if they sympathized with the independence side of the struggle, they, like the priests of Ozoloapan in the 1760's and 1770's, had reason to question the blessings of popular sovereignty and an armed plebe. Even if some parishioners joined the insurgency for reasons of religion (the reasons were rarely so clear, as Eric Van Young has pointed out), curas and vicarios in central Mexico could not count on a firm base of personal support.

Latent nationalism was also involved in the determined neutrality of parish priests. Most curas represented themselves as creoles, celebrated the signs of Mary's and Christ's special favors, and probably shared the popular prejudice against European Spaniards.[49] Accused of aiding insurgents in the first months of the war, Dr. José Antonio Muñoz had given a sermon in 1809 in which he referred to European Spaniards as "Jews."[50] Other curas expressed their anti-gachupín sentiments at the beginning of the war by calling them "heretics" and "despots."

But the dissatisfaction among curas that could lead to neutrality or insurgency depended more on a sense of a traditional and proper role in public life being wrenched from them, a sense that order and the conditions for salvation were disappearing. It was not usually because "their own sense of vocation had grown dim."[51] Most curas in the late colonial period were involved in bitter conflicts with parishioners and royal officials that they interpreted as evidence of mounting anticlericalism and the disintegration of society and Christian principles. For these students of moral theology, it would have been hard to miss the implication that misguided royal policies and godless philosophies threatened the providential order of an America that the Blessed Mary had chosen as her own. Few of the American priests encountered in this study were expressing high hopes about the changes they experienced or anticipated.[52] Country priests facing the political changes in public confrontations often stood on their personal and professional honor and appealed to tradition. By the 1770's, their confident claims to authority in disputes before the audiencias were becoming laments about district governors as enemies and the unbridled license of Indian liberty. By the 1790's, some anticipated a thunderous collapse of the political and social order. Their vocabulary had little in common with the "new man" that regalist bishops of the 1760's had in mind. Rather, it was rich in old metaphors from their training in moral theology and allusions to sentiment, a professional habit of men who were educated to take emotions seriously.

Some old ambiguities and tensions in parish service were becoming troubling contradictions for them. Parish priests were expected to concentrate on their pastoral, teaching duties, yet there were few professional rewards for exemplary service, especially in the 1760's, 1770's, and 1780's. They were still educated to feel responsible for "reducing the Indians to rational life," which meant nurturing the Indians' willpower so they would drink the "rational milk of doctrine" and subject themselves "to peace with God."[53] This responsibility also meant combating the vices that interfered with salvation, especially drunkenness, which was regarded as the root of other evils among Indians. Given this conception of their role, it is not surprising to find the cura of Chipetlan (Guerrero), José Mariano Hurtado de Mendoza, still claiming in 1772 that his obligation was "to attend to my poor Indian parishioners, not only in spiritual matters but also in temporal affairs."[54] Curas like Hurtado de Mendoza would be slow to accept the narrowing of their judicial role. The more optimistic vision of the Indian's capacity for moral and economic improvement that prelates and Bourbon administrators promoted was likely to increase the frustration of priests who faced mounting lawsuits from parishioners and found that pious acts did not go far to elicit support in the parish. When the regalist emphasis on Christian love, charity, and material improvement entered into late-eighteenth-century parish priests' communications with the bishops, audiencias, and viceroys, it could contain an implicit critique of misguided reforms, callous district governors, and selfish merchants. The political direction of this implicit criticism of Bourbon clerical reforms blossomed most fully in the safety of Spanish defeat in 1821, when one Mexican priest publicly praised Agustín de Iturbide for his defense of "the endangered religion of Jesus Christ" against a Spain that had abandoned its Christian motives and works.[55]

Whatever its origins, the neutrality of most curas in the war was more damaging to the royalist cause than it was to the insurgents, since parish priests had been fixtures of the royal administration for three centuries and received their appointments from the crown. Most had benefited in status and wealth from this close association of church and state. Under the circumstances, neutrality was, as Calleja and the bishops recognized, a form of defection.

Priests and Parishioners

Insurgent leaders and followers often designated religion as part of their motivation or call for action. Priest leaders mixed ideas of freedom and divine protection in addressing their audiences. Hidalgo had emphasized the defense of Catholicism from the start, speaking of "maintaining our religion, our law, our country and the purity of our ways."[56] Matamoros, Morelos's leading military commander, declared in his letter of thanks to the people of Oaxaca on August 10, 1813:

Yes, Oaxacans, you are very precious objects of Eternity's eyes. . . . Even though unfortunate Mexico is afflicted with tyranny, . . . you enjoy the protection and vigilance of heaven. . . . We are doing no more than leaving the bedroom of this beautiful home in order to locate ourselves in its doors and entrances. . . . You are, without contradiction, free, happy, and independent.[57]

From the first weeks of insurrection, popular voices echoed the insurgent curas' righteous talk about a holy war against gachupín anti-Christs. For example, an anonymous threat to the cabildo of Querétaro fixed to a regidor's door on September 18, 1810, declared, "If Christianity is lacking in some, it is among the peninsular Spaniards, for it is clear that you have no other purpose than avarice. And this is the cause of our movement, . . . for we are defending our Homeland and Religion."[58]

Respect for the authority of the church, even in districts where late colonial conflicts with parishioners were fierce and protracted, could move villagers to follow the cura's lead or at least to seek his support when political crises came to town. Dr. Eusebio Sánchez Pareja, cura of Alfajayucan (Hidalgo), reported to the archbishop that on November 4, 1810, the district governor, the Indian gobernador, and other residents burst in on his prayers to report that insurgents were entering the pueblo. They asked for his guidance, and he told them that it was their duty to defend the royal government against the rebels. They answered that they did not have the people or weapons to do so. They wanted to receive the insurgents in peace and asked him to accompany them in order to prevent a mishap. He refused, and also denied their request to ring the church bells as the insurgents entered. According to Sánchez Pareja, the next day three young men from the pueblo came to him in tears, begging him to leave because the insurgents planned to kill him. He heeded their warnings and fled, and later learned that the insurgents executed the district governor and his brother that same day.[59] Other curas of parishes in modern Hidalgo reported in those early days of insurrection that parishioners had joined the insurgents over their entreaties to defend the crown or at least remain neutral.[60] In the Sierra de Meztitlan and some of the Huaxteca region to the east and northeast, where at least several thousand villagers had ignored such appeals by royalist curas in 1810–11, parish priests appear to have persuaded many to accept pardons in 1813.[61] Apparently as a result of the pardons, Indians of Tututepec—where parishioners in the late colonial period were locked in unusually bitter struggles with curas, and where some had mounted a millenarian rebellion in 1769—became ardent royalists, attacking an insurgent band with bows and arrows in early 1816.[62]

As Parts Three and Four suggest, anticlericalism was more evident in local politics than in local religious expectations and practices during the late colonial period. The Marian devotion that was so important to the sense of mission among insurgents could cut in several directions. An ardent veneration of the Virgin Mary served to justify both preserving the political and social status quo and mounting protests against it. And the religious vision of rural insurgents did not require priests as their leaders. The practices of local religion described in earlier chapters sometimes point to mounting tensions between parish priests and Indian parishioners over who was the better Christian. These tensions usually expressed a spirit of local independence from outside authority that is now a familiar part of the history of highland Indians under Spanish rule. The cura of Zacoalco (Jalisco) encountered this independence in 1783, when his Indian parishioners were assured by a community leader that "no Christian can be condemned to hell."[63] The villagers' moral economy of just demands and mutual obligations among unequals was expressed during the late colonial and independence periods in terms of Christian charity and love battling the capital sins of gachupines, but it was also expressed in localistic, even millenarian terms, which saw the arancel and other checks on the authority of parish priests as "heaven sent."[64] (This moral economy was expressed in still another way, in the new language of free trade, of "libertad de comercio," with villagers demanding to sell where and when they wanted, which usually meant in the local markets where they were used to selling;[65] intended to promote the improved and unified against the customary and separate, the Bourbon reform program here served to reinforce the old ideology of autonomy in pueblos de indios.)

Not all Indian parishioners of central and western Mexico were impassioned millenarians or apathetic bystanders as insurrection spread from the Bajío. Like their parish priests, they could be resolutely neutral, committed mainly to their own survival, as Br. José Antonio Díaz, an insurgent chaplain in western Mexico, testified in his 1814 confession. When pressed for information about the strength of the insurgents in the tierra caliente, he answered that the crown could recover the region because wealthy families there were royalists at heart and could use their influence with "los humildes" (the masses): "No force can stop the royalist troops, since those natives would rather give the rebels their money and horses than their lives."[66]

Even as insurgent leaders, parish priests could differ philosophically from their followers. In those parts of central and western Mexico where curas led Indian villagers into an anti-gachupín insurgency, their shared Christian critique of selfish elites might contain an important difference. Where the parish priests—identifying themselves as creole Spaniards—clearly directed their attacks at Europeans in America when they spoke disparagingly of gachupines, village followers may well have meant all privileged Spaniards, both American and European, priests included.[67]

Still, priests, the sacraments, and other objects of devotion were generally respected and desired by insurgents, who condemned royalists for their lack of Christian piety. In an 1813 letter to the commander of royalist operations in Oaxaca, the insurgent chief Juan Pablo de Anaya defended the insurgency as a holy way and dwelled on the sacrilegious and uncharitable conduct of the royalists.[68] There were differences in how royalists and insurgents treated priests. Neutral or partisan curas who were captured could generally expect more generous treatment at the hands of insurgent forces than they could from the royalists. Royalist forces showed little respect or patience for uncommitted curas and were relatively quick to execute those who were implicated in the insurgency.[69] Alamán described occasional disrespect by insurgents for curas who did not join them, and the murder of the aged cura of Santa Ana Chautempan, Tlaxcala,[70] but the treatment received by Felipe Benicio Benítez, cura of Cempoala (Hidalgo), apparently was more common. Benítez reported to the cathedral chapter that insurgents had threatened the local gachupines and royal officials but were respectful to him when they occupied the parish seat on May 9, 1811. Only at his urging did they promise to spare the district judge's life.[71]

Instances of anticlericalism seem to have been especially common among royalists.[72] In Morelos's movement, priests kidnapped by insurgent forces were more likely to become committed supporters, even though he evidently did not insist that curas in his domain become active insurgents as long as they fulfilled their pastoral duties and were not partisan royalists.[73] Conversely, royalists were notorious for sacrilegious behavior. Alamán and Bustamante both reported cases of royalist forces defacing religious images, especially those of the Virgin of Guadalupe, after they captured an insurgent town.[74] According to Bustamante, royalists, unlike insurgents, denied last rites to prisoners they executed. He described the "americanos" as by and large pious and more concerned to provide spiritual care for the population during the war.[75] The fervent tributes to Our Lady of Guadalupe and her patronage suggest the importance of religious symbols, especially the Virgin Mary, to insurgents.[76]

José María Morelos: Moral Theology and Insurrection

Nearly two of every five parish priests identified with the insurgency in Appendix B were associated with José María Morelos—a cura from the Diocese of Michoacán between Mexico City and Guadalajara—and the political programs of the congresses of Chilpancingo and Apatzingán between late 1810 and early 1815. According to Bustamante, over one-third of the delegates to the congress at Chilpancingo in September 1813 were parish priests.[77] This concentration suggests that Morelos and his ideas influenced dozens of little-known curas and vicarios to commit to the insurrection. He is a fascinating enigma, whose career discourages simple answers about what parish priests believed and did in the Independence War. Frances Calderón de la Barca could speak of him with reason as "the mildest and most merciful of these soldier-priests," yet Alamán could produce chilling examples to support his view of a man so fiercely cruel that he was unworthy of the priesthood.[78] The apparent confusions and contradictions in Morelos's thought and political action have puzzled both his detractors and his admirers.

By origin and background, Morelos was little different from the hundreds of inconspicuous parish priests who faced the choices of the independence struggle. He was not from the educated elite; he was not a doctor of theology or canon law who was moved by new political ideas before the war; and he was not torn between faith and reason the way doctors and licenciados of the church were more likely to be.[79] Like most of the less prominent insurgent priests and many of those who remained on the sidelines or became royalists, he never served in a choice parish (he described his parish in June 1810 as "poor"[80]) and had few prospects for professional advancement. Nevertheless, despite more than a decade of service and travel in the wilting heat of the Carácuaro-Nocupétaro parish of southeastern Michoacán, his great energy remained constant.

Morelos came to the priesthood comparatively late. Born in the provincial capital of Valladolid, he was ordained at thirty-two in December 1797, after a youth of labor on an hacienda in the district of Apatzingán, located west of his eventual parish in the Michoacán lowlands.[81] He impressed his seminary superiors as a capable, eager, and diligent student—"aplicado" is the adjective that appears in his academic record—and earned a first place in philosophy during his Bachelor of Arts studies. But as an older, less-polished seminarian, Morelos took a short program of formal study for ordination to parish service. Moral theology—the application of dogmatic principles to everyday life—was the focus. He suffered from a limited knowledge of scholastic logic and formal theology, as his "barely passing" mark for promotion to deacon in 1796 and his request for permission to return to Valladolid for further study in 1800 suggest.[82]

There is little reason to think that he was particularly disenchanted with his professional situation in 1810 or ambitious for greater recognition and power. He was a steady, attentive pastor, who avoided controversy and enjoyed good relations with his superiors. He had been favored with an interim appointment at Churumuco and La Huacana in the tierra caliente on ordination, for which he expressed "incredible joy." He wrote of the humbleness he felt that the bishop would "choose the small for great undertakings" and of his intent to lay down his life in order to obey the bishop and "cultivate the Lord's Vineyard."[83] But his next assignment, as interim cura at Carácuaro in 1799, was disheartening at first. As in many late-eighteenth-century appointments, within a few months of the new pastor's arrival, parishioners lodged a humiliating complaint against him over clerical fees and mistreatment. Morelos, in return, complained of their insolence, vicious habits, and laziness, noting that he had exercised restraint in not making a prior complaint against those who refused to pay their fees and serve the parish, even though they had the means to do so. He also suspected that the subdelegado had put them up to it.[84] The bishop's verdict reduced the fees but vindicated Morelos by reprimanding his parishioners for exaggerated claims.

In 1800, a discouraged Morelos reported that about 20 percent of his parishioners still did not fulfill their Easter duty, and he sought permission to return to Valladolid. But his fortunes were beginning to turn. From December 1800 onward, he could report 100 percent compliance with the Easter duty, and in 1801 or 1802, the bishop made him the beneficed cura of Carácuaro. He was now well settled. He would father at least two children by Brígida Almonte of Carácuaro, and his financial circumstances improved.[85] He took up residence at Nocupétaro, acquired a ranch on the edge of the parish, and a house for his sister in Valladolid, part of which was rented out for a shop, and organized trade between the city and his parish in grains, livestock, and rum. He could begin to act on his charitable intentions and became especially active in construction, completing the church at

Nocupétaro at his own expense. As late as 1808, he was among the parish priests who answered the bishop's appeal for contributions to the king's war chest.[86]

When the independence struggle began in September 1810, Morelos did not show immediate interest. It was only in mid-October, after he was ordered by the bishop-elect of Michoacán to make known in his parish the excommunication of Miguel Hidalgo and his followers, that he resolved to consult Hidalgo, his old seminary rector, about the justice of his cause.[87] Reduced to the sentiments expressed on Hidalgo's campaign banner, that cause would have appealed deeply to Morelos: "Viva la religión, Viva Nuestra Madre Santísima de Guadalupe, Viva Fernando VII, Viva la América, y Muera el mal gobierno" (Up with religion, Our Lady of Guadalupe, king, and America; down with the bad government [of selfish European Spaniards and Frenchmen]).[88] Even when he was convinced of the need for an insurrection against the French and the corruption of Spanish rule, Morelos's first act was to request a leave of absence with partial pay; he still looked to his superiors for approval and support, regarding the insurrection as a defense of religion and virtue. He was not disappointed by their initial response. The Conde de Sierra Gorda, acting as gobernador de la mitra in the absence of Bishop-elect Abad y Queipo, appointed a substitute cura for Carácuraro and instructed him to forward one-third of the parish rents to Morelos. On October 16, this same executive also lifted Hidalgo's excommunication, an act he would soon regret.[89] Without his acquaintance with Miguel Hidalgo, Morelos might well have stayed home in October 1810, and his name would likely be lost in the sparse shade of local memory as a busy, charitable pastor, rancher, and trader, a doer with his hands as well as words, a member of the community who trained his energies on local matters. He was not the kind of parish priest to start a revolution, either a political or a social one. But extraordinary leaders do not always start out as visionaries.

Between his commission by Hidalgo to organize forces in the southern lowlands in October 1810 and his capture and execution in late 1815, Morelos came to lead the most effective insurgent force of the independence period. His force operated freely for four years in the lowlands of modern Michoacán and Guerrero, in parts of Puebla, Veracruz, and México for three, and more fleetingly in Oaxaca and Morelos. Beginning with 25 men of his parish in October 1810, he recruited an armed following of about 3,000 from the pueblos and rancherías of the hot lowlands of Michoacán and Guerrero in less than two months.[90] His forces remained at about that strength until his death, a sign of the comparative discipline of his troops and Morelos's ability to manage the tensions involved in mixing the liberal political ideas of his ranchero and urban allies with a popular movement bearing strong religious overtones. Even the conservative Alamán, who felt betrayed by what he regarded as caudillo priests who mesmerized the ignorant masses, paid Morelos grudging respect as "the man who played the principal role in the history of the revolution of New Spain," "the most extraordinary man that the revolution of New Spain produced," and "an original character who [gave] evidence of a great store of good reason in the midst of a confusion of ideas."[91]

Morelos revealed himself more in short bursts of words that responded to concrete problems than in sustained reflection. Still, his evolving understanding of the struggle as one year of leadership became five can be gleaned from his occasional writings, as well as actions he did not personally record. Ernesto Lemoine Villicaña and Agustín Churruca Peláez, the leading students of Morelos's thought, have discerned multiple origins but emphasize that his originality came especially from his personal response to the movement—particularly from what Luis Villoro calls "the intoxication of liberty"—and his immersion in a collective creole consciousness that was nationalistic and sensitive to social injustices. Lemoine and Churruca suggest that by 1812, he had increasingly come under the influence of the liberal ideas of an intellectual following that centered his attention on popular sovereignty, liberty, and equality.[92] Liberty for Morelos was becoming less a negative concept—freedom from oppression—and more a positive force paired with equality.[93]

What did not change through all this was his strong sense of American identity coupled with a hostility to European Spaniards that would make him a firm advocate of political separation from Spain and reinforced his social contract with the poor. He detested the hypocrisy of European Spaniards in America, seeing them as cruel despots and "enemies of mankind," who were blinded by the sins of pride and greed and bound up in "Machiavellian schemes," taking more and more in taxes and profits from the labor of others and giving little in return.[94] This moral indignation over their social hypocrisy and his identification with native Americans of all classes account for his uncharitable treatment of royalist European Spaniards who fell into his hands, actions that Alamán took as hypocrisy of an even less pardonable kind.[95] In his unbending refusal to pardon peninsular prisoners and his determination to expel the rest, he was, indeed, a fierce avenger.[96] But he was equally unyielding toward his own followers who were insubordinate, cowardly, treacherous, or guilty of "any disturbance which is opposed to the law of God, the peace of the kingdom, and the progress of our arms."[97]

Morelos's unrelenting criticism of European Spaniards expressed in a negative way his American identity and social conscience. He grew increasingly opposed to serving Spain's interests and hereditary distinctions, especially slavery and other social classifications that divided Americans against one another and impeded the pursuit of individual and collective virtue. Consistent with his feelings as a colonial official in the fees dispute against him in 1799, Morelos valued hard work in others, but he also favored the rights of workers to enjoy more of the fruits of their labor, and of pueblos to own and control their own lands and rents.[98]

Despite Morelos's sometimes seemingly contradictory stands, his political philosophy was not incoherent. His simultaneous attachment to monarchism and democracy until late 1812, his shift toward the views of the jurists of Apatzingán, and his growing belief in liberty and elements of equality despite a preference for hierarchy, precedence, status, and religious exclusivism all hark back to a common source. The moral theology he had studied and taken to heart as a parish priest was the wellspring of his emerging political and social thought and many of his actions in the war, notwithstanding the ambiguities and blank spots.

Throughout his years as an insurgent leader, Morelos wrote of his cause in terms of "the true religion and the *patria*," and he filled his political propaganda with the idea of a religious destiny.[99] He warned the royalist commander Calleja on April 4, 1812, that "God will punish you and yours at the appointed time." Later in 1812, in an appeal to the people of Tehuantepec, he urged them to "trust in the Power of God (more than in your own powers) and the intercession of his Most Holy Mother, who in her marvelous image of Guadalupe visibly protects us." On February 17, 1813, from Yanhuitlan (Oaxaca), he explained to Intendant Ignacio Ayala why he would not break his word to the pueblos of the region in such terms: "I do not want to leave them exposed, much less sacrifice them. I am a Christian, I have a soul to save, and I have sworn to sacrifice myself for my Motherland and my Religion rather than renege on a single point of my oath."[100] The next month, he presented the people of Ajuchitan with a vision of a society ruled by the commandments of God and the church.[101] And he set great store in providing spiritual care for people within his territory and in making the last rites available to royalist prisoners.

To the end, Morelos represented himself as an orthodox believer and loyal priest, not a renegade. Granted, he had left his parish in October 1810, but his appeal to the bishop's office for license to serve as a chaplain with Hidalgo's forces had been approved, and he had provided for the spiritual care of his parishioners.[102] He knew of his excommunication but said he considered it invalid since the godless Napoleon commanded the Inquisition and the bishops at the time.[103] Moreover, while he was a sinner, fathering children and failing to pray his office daily during the war, as Matamoros found time to do, he argued that he fulfilled his sacramental duties as a Catholic, and that his actions in the war were consistent with the defense of his religion. Finally, the extraordinary circumstances of the war, he claimed, produced pressing spiritual needs that justified his making unauthorized parish appointments and allowing some marriages without priests.[104]

Morelos firmly denied the charge of heresy made against him by the Inquisition after his capture in 1815. However, the record of his interrogation shows that he was troubled by the inquisitors' insistence that signing the Apatzingán constitution and swearing to uphold it proved he was a reader and follower of heretics like Rousseau, Helvétius, and Voltaire. Perhaps regretting having signed the constitution, Morelos claimed that he had had no real hand in it: he had merely been present for its promulgation and had had only one hurried day to consider it. He offered the enigmatic judgment that the constitution was "mal por impracticable" (bad because it was impracticable).[105]

The effect of American and French revolutionary thought on Morelos is unclear. While he undoubtedly learned more of both during the war, no evidence has come to light that he read the *philosophes* or Thomas Paine, or understood himself to have been directly influenced by their ideas. The few writings he told the Inquisition he remembered reading, and the books in his possession at the time of his capture in 1815, related mainly to his pastoral service. One of the titles he recalled having read—the *Itinerario para parochos de indios*—appears often in these pages as the rural parish priest's primary guide to moral theology in eighteenth-century Mexico.[106] What might Morelos have found in the *Itinerario* that kept it close to his thoughts at the end, and was his mention of it intended as a rebuke to interrogators who judged him a heretic?

The *Itinerario* is not a text that Morelos would have swallowed whole. It was grounded more in the author's experience in Ecuador than in the circumstances of more sedentary colonial Indians and castas encountered by parish priests in the heartland of New Spain. Some of its seventeenth-century social outlook would have seemed repugnant or anachronistic to Morelos. The emphasis on rooting out "idolatry" was dated, as were the focus on the Seven Capital Sins and the view of the Indian faithful as "hijos del castigo" who would require repeated floggings to practice a moral life. As Enrique Dussel observes, it is an elitist ("class-ridden") text that assumed the justice of Spanish rule and the inferiority of Indians.[107]

But there was more that Morelos could accept, even thrill to, in the pages of this book. It is filled with the language of balance, the moderation of opposite tendencies, and the grave responsibilities of priests. The fear of anarchy manifested in the discipline he imposed on his followers, and the rewards, sacramental attention, and harsh punishment he used to that end, recall this balance of fear and love, the value of exemplary punishment, and the simultaneous role of judge and teacher for which parish priests were educated.[108] It conveyed a heroic image of the parish priest as father engaged in the endless, exhausting struggle to save his flock. The priest's sacramental mission to the laity is his most sacred. According to the *Itinerario*'s logic, his additional roles as judge, teacher, pastor-protector, and spiritual physician were necessarily temporal, as well as spiritual.[109] Above all, the compelling importance of charity appears in expressions that could have sharpened Morelos's sense of justice and equality. The *Itinerario* repeatedly returns to the obligation of both material and spiritual charity, since Indians were materially as well as spiritually *miserables*. Certainly priests, but also the rich, must help those in great need.[110] The tension between hierarchy and equality in both the *Itinerario* and Morelos's thought—between the dignity and equality of all souls and the value of calidad (a social hierarchy based on race, occupation, wealth, prestige, and personal virtue)—was resolved by the practice of charity.[111]

The insurgent title Morelos took for himself, Siervo de la Nación, had strong religious overtones. As Carlos Herrejón recognized, it alludes to the biblical verse, "and whosoever of you will be the chiefest, shall be the servant of all."[112] "Siervo" had been used for centuries in the hagiographical literature of New Spain to praise worthy bishops and parish priests—the "buen Siervo," "the Siervo del Señor."[113] But Morelos expanded the term's meaning to present himself as the servant of the patria as well as of God. He was on a double mission of collective salvation—spiritual and political—that church leaders in New Spain had urged on their priests in the struggle against Napoleon before Hidalgo's Grito.[114] The leader as servant expressed the ideas of Christian charity and hierarchy as Morelos knew them from his education in moral theology. In this sense, the leader would give rather than receive, serve rather than be served, be an aqueduct rather than a reservoir: "And I will very gladly spend and be spent for you; though the more abundantly I loved you, the less I be loved" (2 Corinthians 12:15). The related passage in the *Itinerario* is, "Since Christ gave his life for us, we should risk ours for the sake of our neighbor who is in extreme need."[115] These passages at once capture Morelos's sense of sacrifice and charity and attest to the growing popularity of Paul's epistles in the late eighteenth century.

The Virgin of Guadalupe was an especially powerful link for Morelos between religion and patria. Not only was the image an increasingly important symbol for Americans, but it represented the Immaculate Conception, a mystery of the faith that Morelos held especially dear, and that he urged the town fathers of Oaxaca in 1813 to defend.[116] The pious tradition of this particular image of the Immaculate Conception, which had been recognized by the papacy as well as in local practice, held it to be a sign of Mary's special favor for Mexico and her power to intercede with God. Politically and personally, Mary and this image were at the center of Morelos's patriotism.[117]

During the independence struggle, Morelos took considerable interest in securing an appropriate income for parish priests. Though he opposed taxes generally (finally settling on only the alcabala and tobacco monopoly as sources of government revenues), Morelos consistently called for the public support of parish priests through the tithe and first fruits (and even favored, for a time, the controversial clerical fees).[118] Emphasizing the tithe was both an appeal to tradition and a criticism of the privileged cathedral clergy for keeping most of the revenue that by early royal law was supposed to go to the parishes. Morelos opposed Indian tribute and the pueblo treasuries (cajas de comunidad) that were reorganized in the late eighteenth century to funnel local wealth to royal administrators, but his silence on cofradías suggests that he favored them. As a parish priest fighting in the name of religion, Morelos had good reason to discriminate between cajas and cofradías. Cofradía properties and income were being transferred to the cajas and royal administration during his years of service, and he had complained in 1808 of the "grave matter" of declining cofradías and parish income that had arisen since the curas were ordered to stop administering those funds in 1802.[119]

The example of Morelos demonstrates how the late-eighteenth-century emphasis of regalist prelates on Christian charity could lead to insurrection. Such a focus on charity could rouse the social conscience of a priest against the colonial order in the long political crisis for Spain that followed the Napoleonic invasion. Morelos explained himself in just these terms to a royalist adversary in April 1813:

I am a pitiful man [a sinner], more so than others, and my nature is to serve honest people, to lift the fallen, to pay for him who has no means, and to share what I can from my possessions with those who need them, whoever they may be.[120]

The simple desire to practice Christian charity—combined with the priest's responsibility to protect the weak and defenseless—could be as revolutionary an idea as any.[121] While Morelos accepted the idea of inequalities in private wealth, the conduct of European Spaniards in New Spain epitomized for him their lack of Christian virtue and charity; and their suspicious francophilia and sacrilegious plunder and destruction of church property subverted Catholicism and Christian morality, if it did not indicate outright heresy.[122] Perhaps he remembered the *Itinerario*'s maxim that "an Indian who stole a sheep because of extreme need neither sinned nor is obliged to replace the animal. In extreme need the rich man has the obligation to give to the poor man who suffers."[123] If he did remember it, Morelos ignored the manual's warning that this was a lesson Indians should not be taught because they might use it as an excuse to violate the property rights of others. On the contrary, Morelos was optimistic that charity and justice of this kind would reduce the threat to property, since the poor were motivated by need, not greed.[124] With this reasoning, Morelos closed the gap between principle and practice contained in the *Itinerario*'s warning, a gap that had blocked the realization of Catholic values of charity and love that regalist bishops were forever recommending to their priests at the time. Unlike the Spanish missionary preachers who, after the French Revolution began, muted their criticism of the proud and powerful as they rose to defend king, church, and unity, Morelos thought to defend the church and king in 1810 by attacking the proud and powerful with the sword of the same Christian charity that his manuals and bishops invoked.[125] While he did not abandon the ideal of status, balance, and moderation as the source of order, he would not use it as an excuse to do nothing.

Morelos did not see any great violation of his Christianity in his actions, any contradiction between his independence movement and being a Catholic and a priest. It was not, he declared to the royalist commander at Acapulco in 1813, a revolution, as the commander had called it, but an exercise in virtue:

It is for me, and it will be in the eyes of God, the angels, and mankind, an exercise in virtue . . . in which each will receive what is his and the people will be held in check so that no blood will be shed, even the blood of the guilty.[126]

Like many of his fellow priests in parish service, he believed implicitly in the old parental metaphor for the political order in which the king was the father, and the church and Mary were the mother. When the father was absent and the family—the patria—was threatened from outside, the mother should take up the defense with the aid of her children, first in the father's name, later in the family's. Morelos would not have warmed to the reworkings of the biblical metaphor of filial piety—Honor thy father and thy mother—proposed by regalist priests like Joseph Mariano Beristáin de Sousa (canon of the cathedral of Mexico), who in his call for the defense of the mother in the absence of the father in 1809 urged fellow colonials to consider Spain their mother and patria.[127]

Though Morelos had little to do with the framing of the Apatzingán Constitution, he made his fullest political statement, the "Sentimientos de la nación," at the opening session of the Chilpancingo congress on September 14, 1813.[128] Morelos's familiar reference to the patronage of the Virgin of Guadalupe (art. 19) and his pointed anti-peninsular convictions (arts. 9 and 11) are there, but the three pages of his text contain much more. Usually regarded as a homegrown "liberal" document enshrining popular sovereignty, liberty, and equality,[129] the "Sentimientos" take on a somewhat different meaning if Morelos's pastoral service and training in moral theology are remembered. He did not lightly refer to this proposal as "*sentiments* of the nation." For Morelos, ideas expressed passions, longings, and frustrations, not just principles and rationalizations.[130] Religious sentiments and the social values behind them pervade the document, giving it a homiletic quality and a connection to the past, while critiquing the present and breaking with colonial rule and its hereditary inequalities.

Morelos's thinking in the text can seem contradictory. The "Sentimientos" open with a clear call for national independence from any sovereign power, but the second, third, and fourth of the original 22 articles turn immediately to religion in ways that seem to confuse the liberal cast of the document: article 2 declares Catholicism to be "the only religion, without tolerance of any other";

article 3 provides for the financial support of the priesthood; and article 4 affirms the responsibility of the church hierarchy to keep Catholic dogma pure.

Yet to simultaneously affirm hierarchy, religious intolerance, popular sovereignty, and equality before the law would not seem contradictory to Morelos the parish priest. A unifying idea behind these seeming ambivalences was the old regard for moderation and balance. Morelos could speak of liberty and equality among Americans without accepting these principles as absolutes or abandoning his conviction that hierarchy was essential to social order, that the poor and humble—like Indians in the colonial conception—required parental care, and that salvation was the highest purpose of human activity. Liberty for Morelos still centered on the freedom to fulfill a Catholic Christian destiny. It still centered on freedom from unjust restraint, rather than freedom as an absolute good in its own right. It was not freedom to practice false religion. Nor was it, in J. H. Parry's words, "freedom to be idle, to be left to one's own devices, to refrain from making any contribution to the well-being of society."[131]

Articles 12 and 13 of the "Sentimientos" sought to ameliorate social inequalities, not abolish them—"to *moderate* opulence and indigence, so that the wages of the poor worker will *increase*, that his customs will *improve*" [emphasis added]. It meant "separating [him] from ignorance, [and the need for] plundering and theft." The laws would apply to all, including corporate groups (art. 13)—*except* for matters applying to the exercise of the professional duties of corporate members (such as priests or soldiers). Slavery and other hereditary distinctions would end—"with all to be equal"—but there would still be a hierarchy of the wise and virtuous ("sólo distinguirá a un americano de otro el vicio y la virtud"), and elections would be indirect. A family was entitled to the fruits of its labor, as Morelos had declared from the beginning, but property rights—the basis of much inequality—would be protected (art. 17). The articles abandoned monarchy, but the vision of balanced political powers derived as much from the past of countervailing and complementary qualities as from the future of individual rights and liberties and unrestrained interests. Morelos as well rejected the old unitary, hierarchical model of authority, was confident of the benefits of national independence, held a relatively optimistic view of the goodness of the plebe, and accepted a diminished political role for religion. But he did not abandon the metaphor of balance or dismiss the importance of virtue, religion, and government in favor of the newer eighteenth-century metaphor of a web of interdependent self-interests with its optimism about the social and political efficacy of unbridled individual freedom.[132]

The "Sentimientos" and other evidence of Morelos's actions and sense of purpose reveal the "man of praxis" he is famous for being. He was, as Churruca Peláez says, a leader who thought for himself—learning from various sources, especially from the experience of leadership and struggle in the insurgency, but captive to none. But too many signs of Christian moral theology underlie Morelos's utterances to suggest that the man of praxis grew out of an alternative logic gleaned only, or even mainly, from the experience of his political struggle.[133] Morelos, in Michael Weinstein's terminology, was a "finalist" from the beginning. He rejected the "instrumentalism" of Bourbon policy makers and Europeans in America who viewed people as resources to be put to use for maximum advantage with minimum effort from themselves, and who measured honor in the currency of status more than virtue. His was an ethic of charity and virtue in which minimal personal advantage accrued from maximum effort.[134]

Parish priests' vision of self-rule, especially as we can know it through Morelos and anticipate it in the actions of curas before 1810, centered on the virtues taught by their moral theology: charity, personal sacrifice, hierarchy, and mutual obligation. For some resolute priests in 1810, these virtues in turn exerted their own pressures toward social justice.[135] It was a short step from Christian charity as the *Itinerario* or Grosin taught it to Morelos's political program, in which Indian personal and property rights under law were to be protected, no one should go hungry, the rich should be less rich and the poor less poor, and social distinctions depended on the exercise of virtue. Taking this short step animated the popular insurrections of the early nineteenth century during the political crisis in Spain more than proto-liberal aspirations. Insurgent priests like Morelos were not consciously questioning Catholic doctrine. They wanted it to be practiced more fully as a social ethic and in a way that reaffirmed the clergy's familiar place in public life.[136] The ancient quest to ensure "the harmonious coexistence of the Profane with the Sacred, . . . to restore the pristine calling of Christianity from its adulteration, or simply its domination, by secular aims,"[137] had become a political cause.

*   *   *

Spain's political crisis in 1808 turned sentiment against the political and social institutions of its American empire (monarchy, hereditary nobility, corporate fueros, tribute, slavery, and a familial partnership of church and state), but the credibility of those institutions was already in doubt. Unwittingly, the Bourbons would contribute to the national revolutions of the early nineteenth century by effectively cutting themselves loose from divine right. Their path to modernity was to clear away thickets of custom and tradition in order to maximize efficiency and promote the public good. In the process, political power was becoming desacralized (although not so much from Enlightenment skepticism) and increasingly separated from familiar patterns of attachment, convenience, and consent long before Liberal politicians came to power in the 1850's. Religion had expressed the ideology of the colonial order, and it was priests who had taught the message of unity in hierarchy and had been among its chief mediators. But with a diminished partnership of the "two majesties," moral theology could become the common language of righteous opposition to colonial rule, especially as American priests came to see in the Napoleonic invasion of Spain and the effects of Bourbon reforms a dreaded breakdown of order.

The Bourbons' claim on Enlightened absolutism, in which the crown acted within a framework of older laws and customs, was increasingly seen as a despotism of arbitrary and capricious demands without the ideal of a protector's principled generosity. Especially in the colonial setting, the Bourbon state did not appear as the benign arbiter of traditionally useful bodies and active promoter of new interests, as some Enlightenment absolutist states in Europe could present themselves. Honor as virtue (in the old sense of virtue as disinterested conduct that serves the common good) seemed to Morelos and others to have given way in America to honor as status in the galling form of private peninsular privilege.

Even though a substantial reserve of loyalty to the king and royal institutions persisted, colonial administrators, merchants, and miners were increasingly regarded as the embodiment of selfish foreign and personal interests.

Perhaps there was little the Bourbons could do to guard against the collapse of their American empire, but their path to modernity contributed to that collapse after the Napoleonic invasion of Spain. The "destruction of the state of mind necessary for the continuation of the old order" did not consist simply of colonial Americans of various classes venturing beyond the Enlightened absolutism of the Bourbons in pursuit of happiness, equality, and unfettered liberty. Nor did the Bourbons simply destroy a stable balance or accomplish a new political synthesis in New Spain that was shattered in 1808. Hopes were raised and a sense of change was felt, but the critique of Bourbon initiatives and colonial inequalities that served to justify independence from Spain came more from within the ideology of the old order than from beyond it.

Appendixes

APPENDIX A

Reported Parish Income
in the Late Colonial Period

Figures in the following three tables contain information on many parishes at different points in the late 18th century, which makes possible comparisons within and between the two dioceses over time. But there are problems that diminish their utility:

1. Round numbers for incomes based on many small collections obviously are approximations rather than exact figures.

2. Most of the figures for rentas were extrapolated after the fact by the colonial compilers or had to be converted from tax records for this appendix. (A contemporary critique of the 1774 renta figures extrapolated from the pención conciliar tax claimed that they underestimated the actual rentas. It recommended figures based on the mesada tax, which presumably were based on the average of the preceding five years' rentas. Curiously, a full comparison of the parish rentas extrapolated from the pención conciliar and the mesada for the 54 parishes where figures for both are included indicates that the estimated rentas from the pención are higher by an average of 182p per parish.)

3. The tax records were supposed to be based on the average of the previous five years' rentas but do not make clear who reported the renta figures and how they were computed. If the curas reported their own rentas, there may have been a tendency to underreport. How great the underreporting was is not clear. At the end of the colonial period, curas were required to report their rentas in the form of detailed directorios in which they listed one by one the masses and other emoluments to which they were entitled. This should have worked against serious misrepresentations of income. When the cura of Teoloyucan in 1759 mentioned his rentas in the course of a dispute with parishioners over fees, he said they amounted to about 1,100p a year (a figure that is in line with the reported rentas in 1793 and 1805). The Indians replied that it was closer to 3,000p. AGN CRS 68 exp. 1, fols. 1-18. The discrepancy here is great, and I cannot determine how much each party exaggerated or whether the Indians had in mind total income and the cura only the masses and obvenciones minus his expenses.

4. The fact that the same renta figures for a parish appear over several years in some cases suggests that the figures were not regularly revised.

5. In the occasional cases where parishes were divided in two in the late 18th century, the apparent decline of rentas is misleading.

6. Finally, the increase in rentas for the archdiocese from 1793 to 1805 looks suspiciously large. Some of the figures for 1805 may have been recorded incorrectly—the increases in Malinalco, Mazatepec, and Atitalaquia are out of proportion to the rest, and there is no clear reason why incomes in these parishes would have grown so much—but these cases do not discredit the 1805 list as a whole. Three complementary considerations may account for the apparent increases in the 1805 figures. First, there were real increases. That a general increase accompanied population growth and more assiduous tax enforcement seems certain, although the increase in curas' incomes (not adjusted for inflation) is larger than other material changes in the 1790's and early 1800's. Second, the distortion may come more from underestimates in 1793 than from overestimates in 1805. (3,000p for the Zacualpan parish in 1800 is consistent with the 1805 figure of 2,816p for this parish. AGN Inq. 1304 exp. 3, fols. 28–32. The tendency in these figures was not always to underestimate rentas. Reported rentas presumably were for fees to which the cura was entitled. Since the cura rarely could collect everything due him, the reported rentas would be inflated by the amount he did not collect, assuming he tried to collect only what was reported.)

The 1793 figures are in round numbers and may be five or ten years out of date. For example, the Yautepec rentas for 1793 were reported as 2,100p, yet in 1796 another source estimated them at over 5,000p. AGN CRS 140 exp. 4, fols. 132ff. The 1790 renta figures for Guadalajara also may be low. Estimates in round figures from another source, José Menéndez Valdés's detailed report on districts in the Intendancy of Guadalajara in 1791–92, are consistently higher for the parishes he mentions. (Cuquío, 2,500p reported in Menéndez Valdés v. 1,171p for the rentas listed in AGI Guad. 544; Encarnación, 2,500p v. 1.172p; Jalostotitlan, 5,000p v. 1,711p; San Juan Lagos, 3,000p v. 1,412p; Lagos, 6,000+p v. 3,342p; Linares, 1,000p v. 587p; Tapalpa, 1,200p v. 800p; Teocaltiche, 4,000p v. 1,432p; Tepatitlan, 5,000p v. 2,158p; Tequila, 2,000+p v. 748p; Tonalá, 1,000p v. 689p; Yahualica, 1,000p v. 436p; and Zapopan, 2,000p v. 370p.)

Another consideration that would help to explain the low figures for 1790 and 1793 is that the 1805 figures may be for gross income from emoluments while the 1793 figures included various deductions and expenses incurred in administering the parish. This apparently was the case in the 1790 figures for Guadalajara. In Hostotipaquillo, a parish in the Diocese of Guadalajara for which I have income and expenses accounts from 1787 to 1797, as well as the reported renta for 1790, certain expenses were deducted from gross emolument income to reach the renta figure. The accounts list 13,615p income from burials, marriages, baptisms, and masses for the period September 1787 to April 1797 (treated in the accounts as a ten-year period). The accounts also list various expenses to the cura during this period, most of them related to the cost of administering the parish. These deductions amounted to 4,191p. The net income calculated for the decade by subtracting 4,191 from 13,615 amounted to 9,424p, or 942p a year. In the 1790 renta list for Guadalajara, Hostotipaquillo was reported to yield 941p a year. AGI Guad. 544.

The sources for all three tables appear at the end of the appendix.

TABLE A.I
Parish Income, Archdiocese of Mexico, 1771–1805
(in pesos)

Parish	Class of parish	Parish income			
		1771–76	1777–83	1793	1805
Acambay		1,000		1,200	2,165
Acamistla	2		1,000		
Acapetlahuaya	3		600		
Acapulco	1				
Acatlan		400	750	700	1,109
Achichipico				850	1,023
Acolman	1[a]		1,500		
Actopan	1[a]			4,800	9,606
Aculco		1,000		1,450	3,880
Alacotlan			750		
Alahuistlan	3	750		950	2,616
Alapusco		200			
Alfajayucan				2,150	4,507
Almoloya	1[b]			2,200	4,349
Amanalco				1,500	2,990
Amatepec y Tlatlaya		750		1,200	
Amecameca	1[a]			2,800	6,425
Amitepec	3				
Apam		400		3,100	6,695
Apaxtla	2				
Aplanta		400			
Atenango del Río	3	500	500		
Atitalaquia	3		800	1,000	(?)7,778
Atlacomulco	1[b]			1,500	1,853
Atlapulco	1[b]				
Atlatlaucan		750		1,300	2,733
Atotonilco el Chico	3	200	200	950	3,453
Atotonilco el Grande	1[a]		3,400	5,362	
Ayacaputlan			1,250		
Ayapango				1,500	2,447
Ayotzingo		1,250		1,400	1,616
Azcapotzalco	1[a]				
Cacalotenango	3				
Cadereyta				2,400	6,719
Calimaya				3,000	5,743
Calnali				1,500	1,416
Capuluac				1,600	2,015
Cempoala	3			2,800	3,399
Chalco				1,800	2,532
Chapatongo				950	910
Chiautla			500		
Chiapa de Mota	1[b]			1,900	3,530
Chiconcuauhtla				970	1,797
Chilcuatla				1,000	2,539
Chimalhuacan				1,800	5,198
Churubusco	3				
Coatepec Chalco				900	906
Coatinchan		250			
Coyoacan	1[a]				
Coyuca		500			
Cozcatlan	3				
Cuautitlan		1,500		2,800	5,770
Cuautla Amilpas	1[a]			1,800	5,974
Cuautzingo				1,100	1,758
Cuernavaca			2,000	3,600	7,486

TABLE A.I
(*Continued*)

Parish	Class of parish	Parish income			
		1771–76	1777–83	1793	1805
El Doctor		1,000		1,200	3,896
Ecacingo				600	658
Epasoyucan				800	1,355
Escanela			300	400	2,917
Escaneco	3				
Galileo (El Pueblito)		500			
Guacazaloya		750		1,600	3,616
Guayacocotla	2		1,250	1,000	1,460
Huacotla		500			
Huauchinango				1,800	4,147
Huazalingo		1,000			
Huehuetoca	3			600	1,209
Huejutla	1[a]	500			
Huepuxtla	3			1,100	1,945
Hueyapan				700	1,459
Huichapan				3,600	5,291
Huizquilucan	1[b]	2,250	2,250		
Ichcateopan	3				
Iguala	3				
Ixmiquilpan	1[a]			2,600	3,640
Ixtacalco		400			
Ixtapalapa	3	500			
Ixtapalucan				1,600	4,066
Ixtapan	2			1,600	1,694
Ixtlahuaca	1[b]			2,400	4,086
Ixtlahuaca, S. Felipe	1[b]		3,800	6,557	
Jacala				750	706
Jalapa		1,000			
Jalatlaco	2			1,600	2,222
Jamiltepec			750		
Jantetelco		750	750	1,500	2,180
Jiquipilco	3			1,000	1,492
Jocotitlan	2			1,600	2,317
Jonacatepec	1[a]	2,000	2,000	3,300	4,814
Landa		200		500	1,274
Lerma		1,750		2,100	2,264
Lolotla		1,250			
Malacatepec, Asun.	1	1,500		1,500	1,919
Malinalco	1[a]			2,100	(?)12,028
Malinaltenango	2	1,000		2,100	2,732
Mazatepec		2,000		3,000	11,111
Metepec				2,200	4,767
Mexicalcingo		250			
Meztitlan	1[a]			2,600	4,433
Milpa Alta		1,500			
Misquiahuala	2		1,000	1,100	1,943
Mixquic				700	1,366
Molango				1,100	2,407
Naucalpan		500	500		
Oapan	3	750	750		
Oaxtepec	1[a]			1,950	4,270
Ocuilan		750		750	(?)4,105
Ocuituco		500		950	1,524
Ocoyoacac	1[a]	1,500		1,800	2,228
Omitlan	3			750	602

TABLE A.I
(*Continued*)

Parish	Class of parish	1771-76	1777-83	1793	1805
			Parish income		
Otumba		300			
Ozoloapan	2			1,600	1,238
Ozolotepec				1,500	3,806
Ozumba				1,400	2,323
Pachuca	3			2,000	2,733
Pacula			500		
Pánuco	3	250			
Pasayucan		500			
Peña de Francia				1,400	4,195
Pilcayan	3	500			
Real del Cardonal				1,900	3,995
Real del Monte	1 [b]	1,750		1,800	3,025
Sagrario (Mex. City)	1 [a]	2,000	2,000		
Salto del Agua (Mex. City)		500			
S. Agustín de las Cuevas		1,000			
S. Antonio de las Huertas		650			
S. José (Mex. City)		1,500			
S. Juan del Río	1 [b]				
S. Miguel (Mex. City)	1				
S. Sebastián Querétaro		1,240			
Sta. Catharina (Mex. City)	3				
Sta. María la Redonda (Mex. City)		500			
Sta. Veracruz (Mex. City)		1,250			
Santiago, à Sta. Ana (Mexico City)		1,750			
Sto. Tomás (Mex. City)		400			
Santuario de Nra. Sra.de Guadalupe	2				
Santuario de los Remedios	2				
Singuilucan			750	950	2,066
Sultepec	1 [b]			1,150	9,202
Tacuba		1,000			
Tampamolon					
Tantima			600		
Tarasquillo	1 [b]				
Tasquillo				750	2,356
Taxco	1 [b]	1,000			
Taxmalac	3				
Tecama		500			
Tecicapan	3			650	1,200
Tecozautla				1,800	2,999
Tecualoyan				1,450	2,507
Tejupilco				2,100	5,515
Teloloapan	3	500			
Temamatla		700		1,400	3,784
Temascaltepec	2	1,250	1,250	2,000	4,709
Temascaltepec, Real de	2			3,600	5,540
Temascalcingo	1 [b]	1,750	1,750	1,100	3,463
Temoaya	3			800	2,633
Tempoal		500			
Tenancingo	1 [b]			2,400	4,721
Tenango del Valle	1 [b]			2,100	4,867
Tenango Tepopula		1,000		2,100	3,169
Teoloyuca	1 [b]			1,600	2,134
Teotihuacan		600	600		
Tepeapulco		400		2,000	4,953
Tepecoacuilco	3				

TABLE A.1
(*Continued*)

Parish	Class of parish	Parish income			
		1771–76	1777–83	1793	1805
Tepehuacan		1,000			
Tepetitlan				1,100	1,217
Tepejí del Río				2,700	2,472
Tepexpan			500		
Tepotzotlan	2	1,250		1,200	5,770
Tepoztlan			1,250	1,500	2,407
Tequisquiac	2			1,000	2,702
Tequisquiapan	2	750			
Tescaliacac	1[b]			900	2,768
Tetela del Río	3	400			
Tetela del Volcán		500	500	550	427
Tetepango				950	3,370
Tetipac		1,250			
Texmelucan	3				
Tezontepec				1,300	2,217
Thematla		700			
Tianguistengo				1,800	2,095
Tizayucan				2,300	4,550
Tlachichico	3	1,250		800	833
Tláhuac			1,250	1,800	2,295
Tlalmanalco			800	2,200	1,970
Tlalnepantla Cuatenca			1,000	953	
Tlaltizapan			1,250	2,100	3,487
Tlanichol				1,000	2,418
Tlaola		550		1,000	1,383
Tlaquiltenango	1[a]	1,500		1,700	3,786
Tlayacapan	1[a]			3,000	4,886
Tochimilco				1,600	3,988
Tolcayuca	3			550	550
Toliman		1,000			
Toluca				4,000	
Totolapa				1,800	1,954
Tula				3,600	6,881
Tulancingo				4,200	10,080
Tultitlan			600	2,000	2,974
Tzontecomatlan	3			1,200	
Xalpan		250	250	700	1,701
Xaltocan	3	750	1,900	2,717	
Xichú		500	450		
Xilotepec		1,250		3,100	7,821
Xiuctepec				2,000	5,575
Xochiatipan		400			
Xochicoatlan	1[a]			1,600	2,332
Xochitepec				1,200	5,097
Xuchitepec		1,000		1,000	1,137
Xumiltepec		750		420	932
Yahualica	1[b]	400	600		
Yautepec	1[a]	1,500		2,100	
Yecapixtla	1[a]			1,900	3,220
Zacualpan de Amilpas		2,425	2,816		
Zacualpan, Real de	1[b]			1,900	3,040
Zacualtipan				1,600	2,666
(Zacuculpan ?)		1,250			
Zimapan				3,200	7,737
Zinacantepec		3,750		1,900	
Zihuateutla			350	600	

TABLE A.1
(*Continued*)

Parish	Class of parish	Parish income			
		1771–76	1777–83	1793	1805
Zumpahuacan	2			1,000	1,896
Zumpango de la Laguna	1 [b]				
Zumpango del Río	2				

NOTE: All parish classifications are from Villaseñor y Sanchez (1746) except as noted. I have included some parishes on which no data are available whose classification may provide at least a hint of their income.

[a] Classification from an updated, apparently early-19th-century manuscript in the volume entitled "Aranzeles" in the Bancroft Library.

[b] Villaseñor y Sanchez classification confirmed by the Bancroft manuscript.

TABLE A.2
Parish Income, Diocese of Guadalajara, 1696–1790

Parish	1696	1763–70	1771	1774		1790
				Mesada records	Pensión conciliar records	
Acaponeta				2,000		471
Agua de Venado		2,449	2,450	2,450		2,265
Aguacatlan					3,000	
Agualulco				1,500		380
Aguascalientes	8,333	4,993	4,993	4,993	9,000	3,194
Amatlan de las Cañas			450	450	750	386
Ameca	2,000		2,000			1,778
Atotonilco el Alto		1,521				
Atoyac				1,000	560	
Autlan				2,000	263	
Axixic		600		1,000		
Ayó el Chico		1,514				
Boca de Leones				750		
Bolaños			2,130	2,129	3,000	1,067
Burgo de San Cosmé						1,576
Cadereyta				1,500		
Cerralvo				500		
(Cocastlan?)	333					
Cocula				2,500		1,341
Colima				1,500		
Colotlan		1,572	1,573	1,573		873
Compostela	1,000		1,353	1,353		703
Cuquío			2,000	2,000	1,500	1,171
Cuyutlan		500	500	750		397
Chacala				750		
Chapala		500		750		112
Charcas						1,410
Chimaltitan	833					445
Ejutla				300		
Encarnación						1,172
Fresnillo	2,333		6,535	6,535	3,500	3,502
Guadalajara	1,667		4,176	4,176	2,500	2,604
Guainamota		242	463	262	500	440
Guauchinango	1,000	1,200	902	902	500	532
Guaxicori		283	283	400		
Guaximic						503
Gutierre de Aguila		1,862				

TABLE A.2
(*Continued*)

Parish	1696	1763–70	1771	1774 Mesada records	1774 Pensión conciliar records	1790
Hostotipac	500	239	239	239		
Hostotipaquillo	833	1,035	1,036	1,036		941
Huejúcar			630	631		329
Huejuquilla		409	583	583	750	305
Jalostotitlan	2,000	4,508	4,508	5,656[b]	3,000	1,711[c]
Jocotepec						682
Juanacatlan	833					
Juchipila		1,488	1,488	1,488	2,000	1,010
La Barca		605				
Labradores				500		
Lagos, San Juan		1,149	1,149			1,412
Lagos, Sta. María	6,667		10,886	6,588	10,000	3,342
Linares				2,000		
La Magdalena		400		750		750
Mascota			1,046	1,749	1,000	2,051
Mazapil	2,333	2,897	2,897	2,897	3,500	1,099
Mecatabasco			1,092	1,092	1,250	704
Mesquital			411	411	500	518
Mesquitic		833	833	833	500	608
Mexicalcingo						457
Mojarras				1,026	1,250	
Monclova	500					
Monte Escovedo			400	693	1,000	676
Monte Grande	833	300	497	497	750	455
Monterrey	3,333	2,259		5,000[d]		
Nochistlan	2,667		2,000	2,172	4,000	763
Ocotlan		844				
Ojo Caliente	833	2,414	3,014	3,014	1,250	2,583
Pánuco	833		800	1,054	1,250	2,430
Pilón				1,500		
Poncitlan		359	838	838	1,250	633
Punta de Lampasos		718				
Purificación	833	618	(?703 or 609)		1,250	730
Ramos	833					
Real de Asientos		3,154	3,154	3,153	3,500	1,656
Real de Catorce						3,873
Riemanica (?)						396
Salatitan		88	85		224	
Saltillo		2,000		3,000		
S. Blas						853
S. Cristóbal de la Barranca			368	368	600	
S. José Analco				2,500		717
S. José de Gracia		800	800			480
S. Pedro Analco			131			349
S. Sebastián	500	954	954	954	750	478
Sta. María del Oro				300		382
Sayula				2,250		1,953
Senticpac		710	611	611	2,000	103
Sierra de Pinos	2,667	6,629	6,629	6,630	4,000	1,659
Tala			1,000	1,000		653
Tamazula				500		
Tapalpa				1,000		800
Techaluta				350		582
Tecolotlan				1,500		

TABLE A.2
(*Continued*)

Parish	1696	1763–70	1771	1774 Mesada records	Pensión conciliar records	1790
Tenamastlan				1,250		
Teocaltiche	3,000		3,000	3,000	4,500	1,432
Teocuitatlan		320		600		381
Tepatitlan	1,000		1,200	1,200	1,500	2,158
Tepic		560	1,089	1,089	1,500	1,343
Tequepexpan			500			
Tequila	4,667		1,200	1,200		748
Teul				500		136
Tizapan el Alto		250		600		404
Tlacotlan	1,000					
Tlajomulco				1,250		613
Tlaltenango	3,333		3,000	3,000	3,000	1,662
Tomatlan			619	703	750	476
Tonalá						689
Tonila				300		
Totatiche			1,030	1,030	1,500	690
El Tuito	500					
Tuscacuesco			697	1,250		826
Tuxpan		320		2,000		
Valle de Banderas	667	300	(?253 or 301)	301	1,000	625
Valle de Salinas		1,171				
Valparaíso						1,209
Villa Gutierre			1,862			
Villa Nueva				1,862	750	709
Xala		861	862	862	2,000	409
Xalisco		262	262	263	500	784
Xalpa	1,333	900	1,005	1,005	1,000	1,121
Xerez	2,333		2,424	2,424	3,500	703
Yahualica						436
Yscuintla		681	232	681	500	311
Zacatecas		3,175	3,228	3,228	4,500	4,782
Zacoalco				1,500		448
Zapopan	1,333		2,000	2,000	2,000	370
Zapotiltic				500		
Zapotitlan			535	750		278
Zapotlan (del Rey?)		916	917	917	1,000	

[a] 2,500 per Menéndez Valdés (1791–92).
[b] Includes San Juan.
[c] 5,000 per Menéndez Valdés (1791–92).
[d] Includes Salinas, Guajuco, and Lampasos.

Archdiocese of Mexico Parishes by Jurisdiction, Income, and Class, 1744 and 1775

Jurisdiction and parish	1744		1775	
	Income	Class	Income	Class
Alcaldía Mayor of Tacuba				
Azcapotzalco	1,515	1	2,200	1
Huizquilucan	2,300	1	2,000	2
Naucalpan	—	3	1,536	3
Tacuba	2,049	2	1,830	2
Tlalnepantla	3,968	1	8,369	1
Corregimiento of Coyoacan				
Coyoacan	1,207	1	3,000	1
Mixcoac	1,068	2	1,600	2
S. Agustín de las Cuevas	1,290	2	2,500	2
S. Angel	1,345	2	1,808	2
Tacubaya	1,131	2	2,000	2
Corregimiento of Mexicalcingo				
Churubusco	301	3	452	3
Culhuacan	656	3	1,000	3
Ixtapalapa	1,300	2	2,886	3
Mexicalcingo	—	2	—	2
Corregimiento of S. Cristóbal Ecatepec				
Ecatepec	1,476	3	2,700	2
Tecama	957	3	1,300	3
Tultitlan	971	3	2,000	2
Alcaldía Mayor of Zumpango de la Laguna				
Huepuxtla	659	3	800	3
Tequisquiac	879	2	1,020	3
Xaltocan	998	3	1,700	2
Zumpango	1,896	2	3,000	1
Alcaldía Mayor of Tetepango				
Atitalaquia	1,678	3	878	3
Misquiahuala	583	2	1,500	2
Tetepango	1,662	2	1,000	2
Alcaldía Mayor of Cuautitlan				
Cuautitlan	1,972	2	3,500	1
Huehuetoca	3—	2	620	3
Teoloyucan	478	2	2,000	2
Tepotzotlan	1,261	2	1,660	2
Alcaldía Mayor of Pachuca				
Epasoyuca	983	3	600	3
Omitlan	801	3	800	3
Pachuca	1,959	1	2,402	2
Real de Atotonilco	503	3	1,000	3
Real del Monte	1,227	2	2,150	2
Tezontepec	450	3	1,800	2
Tizayuca	1,486	2	2,400	2
Alcaldía Mayor of Otumba				
Axapusco	—	3	1,155	3
Otumba	?3,153	3	1,600	2
Alcaldía Mayor of Cempoala: Cempoala	1,228	3	3,500	1
Alcaldía Mayor of Apam				
Apam	3,762	3	3,800	1
Tepeapulco	1,882	3	2,800	2
Alcaldía Mayor of Tulancingo				
Acatlan	1,192	3	700	3
Atotonilco el Grande	2,677	1	4,000	1
Huatzatzaloyam	1,303	1	1,600	2
Singuilucan	984	3	1,000	3
Tulancingo	4,792	1	4,500	1

TABLE A.3
(*Continued*)

Jurisdiction and parish	1744		1775	
	Income	Class	Income	Class
Alcaldía Mayor of Huauchinango				
Chiautla	—	3	1,154	3
Chiconcuautla	—	3	800	3
Huauchinango	?5,391	2	2,200	2
Tlaola	—	3	1,300	3
Alcaldía Mayor of Texcoco				
Acolman	1,250	3	2,255	2
Coatinchan	515	3	800	3
Huexotla	552	3	1,000	3
S. Andrés Chiautla	525	3	800	3
Tepetlaostoc	1,254	3	2,101	2
Texcoco	3,887	1	6,000	1
Alcaldía Mayor of Ixtlahuaca				
Atlacomulco	3,039	2	1,400	2
Ixtlahuaca	2,173	2	3,000	1
Jiquipilco	1,075	3	1,450	3
Temascalcingo	1,596	2	800	3
Temoaya	990	3	925	3
Villa de S. Felipe	3,097	2	3,250	1
Xocotitlan	2,685	2	2,000	2
Alcaldía Mayor of Chalco				
Amecameca	3,743	1	2,000	2
Ayapango	—	3	800	3
Chalco	1,747	2	1,300	2
Cuautzingo	—	3	1,480	2
Tlahuac	1,703	2	2,000	2
Xuchitepec	942	2	1,200	2
Alcaldía Mayor of Xochimilco				
Milpa Alta	1,487	1	2,600	2
Xochimilco	4,907	1	5,600	1
Alcaldía Mayor of Tochimilco: Tochimilco	2,500	2	800	3
Alcaldía Mayor of Tlalmanalco				
Atlatlaucan	616	3	1,400	3
Ayotzingo	869	2	1,500	2
Chimalhuacan	2,614	2	3,040	1
Ecacingo	500	3	700	3
Ixtapalucan	1,332	2	1,000	3
Mixquic	774	3	750	3
Ozumba	828	3	1,000	3
Temamatla	1,601	3	1,950	2
Tenango Tepopula	2,838	2	1,500	2
Tlalmanalco	?3,453	3	1,800	2
Tlalnepantla Cuatenca	591	3	900	3
Tlayacapan	2,201	1	3,500	1
Totolapa	9—	3	2,000	2
Alcaldía Mayor of Cuautla				
Cuautla	2,025	1	1,800	2
Hueyapan	235	3	515	3
Ocuituco	383	3	990	3
Tetela del Volcán	282	3	500	3
Zacualpa Amilpas	1,716	1	2,500	2
Xumiltepec	283	3	541	3
Alcaldía Mayor of Xiliapa (Puebla Diocese):				
Tenango del Río	800	3	600	3
Alcaldía Mayor of Tlixtlan (Puebla Diocese)				
Oapan	1,041	3	750	3
Zumpango del Río	666	2	1,100	3

TABLE A.3
(*Continued*)

Jurisdiction and parish	1744		1775	
	Income	Class	Income	Class
Alcaldía Mayor of Acapulco				
Acapulco	1,396	2	3,000	2
Coyuca	500	3	600	3
Alcaldía Mayor of Meztitlan				
Jacala	1,000	2	875	3
Lolotla	1,110	2	1,000	3
Meztitlan	?6,348	3	2,280	2
Molango	2,349	3	1,390	3
Tepehuacan	—	2	1,500	3
Tianguistengo	2,210	1	1,784	2
Tlanchinol	4,076	2	1,140	3
Zacualpan	2,344	2	1,450	2
Alcaldía Mayor of Chicontepec (Puebla Diocese)				
Guayacocotla	1,058	2	1,000	3
Tlachichico	1,978	2	1,009	3
Tzontecomatlan	1,200	3	1,000	3
Alcaldía Mayor of Yahualica				
Calnali	—	2	1,664	3
Huazalingo	1,019	2	1,400	3
Xochiatipan	—	3	1,200	3
Xochicoatlan	2,669	2	1,130	3
Yahualica	1,817	3	1,300	3
Alcaldía Mayor of Sultepec/Temascaltepec				
Amatepec y Tlatlaya	1,361	3	1,500	3
Ozoloapan	660	2	800	3
Sultepec	2,258	1	3,200	1
Tejupilco	1,415	2	2,000	2
Temascaltepec	1,595	2	2,130	2
Temascaltepec del Valle	1,639	2	2,230	2
Alcaldía Mayor of Metepec				
Almoloya	1,111	2	2,200	2
Amanalco	—	1	1,800	2
Asunción Malacatepec	1,071	2	1,600	2
Metepec	1,689	2	2,700	2
S. José	—	2	2,000	2
Zinacantepec	1,647	1	1,400	2
Corregimiento of Toluca: Toluca	6,924	1	3,950	1
Corregimiento of Santiago de los Valles				
Cozcatlan	1,913	3	1,500	3
Tamazunchale	1,809	2	1,300	3
Tampamolon	2,905	2	1,700	3
Tancanhuitz	—	2	1,700	3
Alcaldía Mayor of Pánuco and Tampico				
Pánuco	761	3	550	3
Tantima	—	3	600	3
Tantoyuca	2,275	2	1,000	3
Tempoal	1,100	3	1,000	3
Corregimiento of Lerma: Lerma	3,376	2	2,800	2
Alcaldía Mayor of Huejutla: Huejutla	?761	1	3,450	1
Alcaldía Mayor of Coatepec				
Chimalhuacan Atenco	1,390	3	1,720	2
Coatepec	1,232	3	500	3
Alcaldía Mayor of Teotihuacan: Teotihuacan	663	3	1,900	2
Alcaldía Mayor of Tula				
Tepejí del Río	1,735	3	2,200	2
Tepetitlan	931	3	1,200	3
Tula	1,157	2	3,201	1

TABLE A.3
(*Continued*)

Jurisdiction and parish	1744		1775	
	Income	Class	Income	Class
Alcaldía Mayor of S. Luis de la Paz				
Real de Xichú	685	3	776	3
S. José Casas Viejas	—	3	1,020	3
Xichú	1,125	3	1,155	3
Alcaldía Mayor of Huichapan				
Acambay	883	2	1,200	3
Aculco	424	2	1,500	2
Alfajayucan	2,132	3	2,140	2
Chiapa de Mota	1,558	2	1,800	2
Huichapan	3,278	2	3,600	1
Peña de Francia	—	3	1,100	3
Tecozautla	1,120	3	1,920	3
Tozquillo	—	3	800	3
Xilotepec	895	3	4,000	1
Alcaldía Mayor of Zimapan				
Escanela	300	3	300	3
Zimapan	4,092	2	3,500	1
Alcaldía Mayor of Cadereyta				
Cadereyta	1,339	3	2,380	2
Real del Doctor	—	2	2,000	3
Alcaldía Mayor of Tetela del Río:				
Tetela del Río	703	3	800	3
Corregimiento of Querétaro				
Amealco	—	3	1,400	3
El Pueblito	451	3	1,500	2
S. Juan del Río	2,834	1	6,000	1
S. Pedro de la Cañada	641	3	1,800	2
S. Sebastián	—	2	2,550	2
Santiago	8,412	1	5,503	1
Tequisquiapan	859	2	1,500	2
Toliman	1,072	3	1,400	2
Tolimanejo	—	3	1,250	2
Alcaldía Mayor of Cuernavaca				
Achichipico	—	3	825	3
Cuernavaca	4,349	1	4,000	1
Jantetelco	862	3	1,700	3
Jonacatepec	2,101	1	3,000	1
Mazatepec	—	1	3,000	1
Oaxtepec	1,319	2	2,000	2
Tepoztlan	1,600	2	2,000	2
Tlaltizapan	2,100	2	2,000	2
Tlaquiltenango	1,500	2	2,200	2
Xiuctepec	1,948	2	2,700	2
Xochitepec	—	2	2,000	2
Yautepec	1,664	2	2,200	2
Yecapixtla	1,344	2	2,000	2
Alcaldía Mayor of Taxco				
Acamistla	1,070	2	1,100	3
Cacalotenango	1,046	3	900	3
Huitzuco	986	3	1,200	3
Iguala	1,601	3	1,500	3
Pilcayan	709	3	1,100	3
Taxco	1,888	1	3,100	1
Tepecoacuilco	1,033	3	3,400	2
Tetipac	936	2	1,000	3
Alcaldía Mayor of Tenango del Valle				
Calimaya	2,098	2	3,500	1

TABLE A.3
(*Continued*)

Jurisdiction and parish	1744		1775	
	Income	Class	Income	Class
Capuluac	1,276	2	1,500	2
Jalatlaco	1,250	1	2,100	2
Ocoyoacac	1,900	2	3,000	1
S. Bartolomé Ozolotepec	2,136	2	2,000	2
Tenango del Valle	1,486	1	2,200	2
Tescaliacac	1,110	2	1,100	3
Alcaldía Mayor of Malinalco				
Malinalco	1,775	1	2,100	1
Ocuila	1,030	3	1,100	3
Tecualoya	1,366	2	2,450	2
Tenancingo	1,995	2	2,500	2
Zumpahuacan	1,167	2	1,320	3
Alcaldía Mayor of Zacualpan				
Acapetlahuaya	1,003	3	950	3
Alahuistlan	847	3	900	3
Apaxtla	—	3	600	3
Coatepec de los Costales	1,500	3	700	3
Ichcateopan	1,158	3	900	3
Ixtapa	1,617	2	2,000	2
Malinaltenango	1,383	2	2,400	2
Teloloapan	754	3	1,100	3
Texicapan	713	3	600	3
Zacualpan	1,800	1	2,200	2
Alcaldía Mayor of Ixmiquilpan				
Chilcuatla	1,222	3	1,270	3
Ixmiquilpan	3,318	1	2,673	1
Real del Cardonal	1,201	2	2,163	2

NOTE: Question marks identify figures that seem significantly out of line with the parishes' class rankings and might be clerical errors.

Table Sources

Table A.1: *1771–76 and 1777–83* derived from mesada tax records in AGI Mex. 2726–27; *1793*, Texas, García Coll., no. 261, Miguel Valero Olea, "Descripción de el estado eclesiástico secular y regular del arzobispado de México . . ."; *1805*, Florescano & Gil, *Descripciones económicas generales*, pp. 185–92.

Table A.2: *1696*, derived from pensión conciliar payments in Castañeda, p. 133; *1763–70*, derived from mesada payments in AGI Mex. 2726–27; *1772*, AGI Guad. 348; *1774 mesada*, AGN Hist. 318 exp. 3 (extrapolations of compilers from mesada payments said to be based on preceding 5 years' rentas); *1774 pensión conciliar*, AGN Hist. 318 exp. 2 (extrapolations of compilers from pensión conciliar tax); *1790*, AGI Guad. 544.

Table A.3: *1744*, Villaseñor y Sánchez; *1775*, "Plan exacto y puntual de todos los curatos y misiones que hay en este arzobispado de México," BN Archivo Franciscano caja 107 exp. 1475, fol. 53.

APPENDIX B

Parish Priests in the
Independence War, 1810–1819

The list of insurgents does not include parish priests who criticized the colonial system or took part in conspiracies before 1810 unless they were active after the Grito de Dolores. The dates are based on document references and do not necessarily reflect the entire period of activity or stated choice (cura Cano, no. 18, for instance, was with Morelos in 1812 but cannot be traced beyond that year).

Asterisks are used to denote the 14 parish priests who played major roles in the early years of insurgency; they appear repeatedly in the standard narratives of Bustamante and Alamán. A dagger identifies a priest who was rumored to be an insurgent sympathizer but for whom the evidence is inconclusive (some were cleared of the charges; a few became outspokenly royalist and are included on both lists). This group of rumored insurgent sympathizers includes most of the secular priests Farriss identifies as collaborators or subversives in the appendix to *Crown and Clergy*. Dioceses are given in parentheses.

For archival references, I have used essentially the same abbreviations I used in the notes. The two departures are that I routinely drop AGN on the sections from that archive, and use AJANG without further identification to refer to the documents in Criminal, the only section cited here. The following abbreviations are used for the printed sources (for complete authors' names, titles and publication data, see the Bibliography).

Alam	Alamán, *Historia de México*
Amad	Amador, "El clero mexicano"
BU	Bravo Ugarte, "El clero y Independencia"
Bus	Bustamante, *Cuadro histórico*
Farr	Farriss, *Crown and Clergy*
G&P	García and Pereyra, eds., *Documentos inéditos*
HyD	Hernández y Dávalos, *Colección de documentos*
López	Juan López, ed., *Insurgencia de la Nueva Galicia*

MiV   Miguel i Verges, *Diccionario de insurgentes*
M&H   Montiel and Huesca, eds., *Documentos de la guerra*
Mor   *Morelos: Documentos inéditos y poco conocidos*
MyC   María y Campos, *Matamoros*
PI   *Proceso instruído en contra . . . Matamoros*
RP   Riva Palacio, *México*, 3: 775–77

Reputed Insurgents

1. †Aguilar, Mariano, vicario of Nopala, Hdgo (Mex); suspected subversive, 1810 [Farr; MiV]

2. Aguilar, Pablo, vicario fijo of Totomaloyan, Sultepec dist (Mex), and cura of Alahuistlan, Gro (Mex), 1812–13 [Farr; OG]

3. †Aguirre, José María, vicario foráneo of Villa San Sebastián, near Mazatlán, Sin (Guad); charged with greeting insurgents under Hermosillo with a peal of the church bells, released on bond July 1813 [AJANG caja 4 leg. 3 exp. 1]

4. Alvarez, Francisco, cura comandante (of Nochistlan?), Jal (Guad), 1812; per woman arrested in May 1812, her husband, José Ignacio Camarena, had joined Alvarez and lost his life [AJANG caja 3 leg. 1 exp. 12]

5. Ames y Argüelles, Antonio, cura of Coscomatepec, VC (Pue), 1813; pardoned 1817 [BU; Farr]

6. Angeles, vicario of Temascalcingo, Mex (Mex), 1813 [OG 5]

7. Arévalo, Dr. Ignacio Vicente, cura of Asunción Malacatepec, Mex (Mex), 1811 [Amad; OG]

8. Argandar, Dr. José Francisco, cura of Baniqueo(?) (Mich), 1814; at Chilpancingo Congress and signing of the Apatzingán Constitution [Farr; MiV]

9. Arroyo, Fr. Miguel, cura on coast of Oax (Anteq) [M&H, p. 166]

10. Ayala, José Antonio, vicario de pie fijo, Tetela del Río, Gro (Mex), 1817 [Farr]

11. Ayala, Rafael, cura of Ajuchitlan, Gro (Mich), 1817 [Farr]

12. Balleza, Mariano, vicario of Dolores, Gto (Mich); executed 1812 [BU]

13. Baños, Victoriano, cura of Talixtacan, Hdgo? (Mex), 1817? [Bus, 2:498]

14. Barreda, Jose Antonio, vicario of Zapotlan, Jal (Guad), 1811; pardoned after expressing repentance [BU]

15. Bravo, Eugenio, cura of Tamazula, Jal (Guad); pardoned March 1811 [BU]

16. Bustamante, Juan María, cura of Tianguistengo, Hdgo (Mex); said to be capellán to insurgents in 1810–11; pardoned and still serving as cura in 1815 [G&P, 5:206; Bienes 663 exp. 25; OG]

17. Calvillo, José María (Pablo?), vicario of Colotlan, Jal (Guad), former cura of Huejúcar, Ags (Guad); led Indians from his district at Battle of Calderón 1811; last mentioned in attack on Aguascalientes Aug. 1812 [BU; MiV; Farr]

18. Cano, Juan Miguel, cura of Pichátaro, Mich (Mich), 1812; with Morelos [Farr; MiV]

19. Cardozo, Mateo Mariano, cura of El Colector, Hdgo (Mex), 1813 [OG]

20. Castañeda, Francisco, cura of Valle de Santiago, Gto (Mich), 1816 [BU; Farr]

21. *Castellanos, Marcos, vicario of La Palma, Ocotlan, Jal (Guad), 1816; surrendered [BU]

22. Clavijo, Manuel, cura of Taxco, Gro (Mex), 1813 [OG]

23. Collado, vicario of Tlalchiapa, Gro (Mex), 1813 [OG]

24. *Correa, José Manuel, cura of Nopala, Hdgo (Mex) [BU; Bus, 1:415–23]

25. *Cos, Dr. José María, cura of Burgo de S. Cosmé, Zs (Guad), 1811; pardoned, d. 1819 [BU]

26. *Couto, Dr. José Ignacio, cura of S. Martín Texmelucan, Pue (Pue), 1812; captured

and escaped in 1817; applied for cathedral chapter post in 1821, admitting only that he took refuge among dissidents in the war [BU; AGI Mex 2550]

27. Crespo, Manuel Sabino, cura of Río Hondo, Oax (Anteq), 1812; political leader with Morelos, executed 1814 [Farr; MiV; Bus, 1:449]

28. Delgado, Fr. Pablo, OFM, cura of Urecho, Mich (Mich), 1808; conspirator of Valladolid; with Verduzco in 1813; killed in 1814 [BU; MiV; Bus 1:58]

29. Díaz, Guadalupe, vicario of Sierra de Pinos, Zs (Guad), 1811; operated in Bajío [BU]

30. Díaz, Joaquín, Tlayacapan, Mor (Mex), 1812; not clearly parish priest [*Mor* 1:219–20]

31. Díaz, José Antonio, former lt. cura of S. Francisco Almoloya, Colima (Guad), without a ministry in 1810; 1810–14 associated with Hidalgo and Morelos; appointed priest and military gov. of Jilotlan, Jal, 1812; tried for infidencia and sent to Manila, 1814–15 [AJANG caja 3 leg. 1 exp. 6; RG]

32. †Díaz Conti, Lic. Joseph, former coadjutor in Molango dist, Hdgo (Mex); capellán of Regimento de Tlaxcala (Pue) 1808; denounced for defending Hidalgo's movement in conversation, Mex City, Jan. 1811 [Inq. 462 exp. 5]

33. Domínguez, Fr. Joseph, OFM, missionary in Acaponeta dist, Sin (Guad), 1811; found with band of insurgents; still in jail in June 1813 [AJANG caja 4 leg 3 exp. 11]

34. †Estrada, Isidro, cura of Tenango del Río, VC (Pue), 1812; "subversive" [Farr]

35. Fernández del Campo, José María, cura of Huatusco, VC (Pue), 1813; at Chilpancingo Congress; pardoned 1817 [Farr; MiV]

36. †Florez, Fernando, cura of Acámbaro (or Acambay?), Mich (Mich), 1812; "subversive" [Farr; MiV]

37. Francio, Manuel, vicario of Atargea, Gto (Mich), 1811 [G&P, 5:119ff]

38. Fuentes Alarcón, Mariano de la, cura of Maltrata, Pue, near Tehuacán (Pue), 1812; arrested 1814; pardoned [BU; Alam, 3:225; MiV; Bus, 1:435]

39. García, José, vicario of Tepetitlan, Hdgo (Mex), 1813; loyal to Morelos but had not taken up arms [OG]

40. García, Manuel, cura of Tetela del Volcán, Mor (Mex), 1813 [OG]

41. †Garfías, Domingo, cura of Tehuantepec, Oax (Anteq), 1814; "spy" [Farr]

42. †Garibay, José Jesús, vicario of Ario, Mich (Mich), 1815; "collaborator" [Farr]

43. Garnelo, Manuel, cura of Tlapa, Gro (Pue), 1813; at Chilpancingo Congress [Farr; Bus, 1:618]

44. Gil, cura, Querétaro dist (Mex) [RP]

45. Gomes, Francisco Javier, cura (of Guastepec, Mor?) (Mex); aide to Guadalupe Victoria with rank of general [MiV]

46. Gomes, Pedro, vicario of Guitepec, Mor (Mex), 1813 [OG]

47. Gómez, Felipe, vicario of Almoloya, Mex (Mex), 1813; pardoned [OG]

48. †Gómez, Francisco, cura of Toluca, Mex (Mex), 1816; "subversive" [García Ugarte, "Andares políticos"]

49. Gómez, Miguel, cura of Petatlan, Gro (Mich), 1813; Morelos's confessor, executed [BU]

50. González, José Antonio Teodoro, cura of Huichapan, Hdgo (Mex), 1813 [OG]

51. Gudiño, Pedro, former interim cura of Santa María del Oro, Jal (Guad), 1812; convicted of infidencia Sept. 1812, completed sentence of two years' seclusion 1814 [AJANG caja 4 leg. 3 exp. 15]

52. Gutiérrez, Joaquín, cura of Guayacocotla, VC (Pue); with Morelos [BU; *Mor*, 2: 362–63]

53. Gutiérrez, José Antonio, cura of Ahuistlan, Mex (Mex), 1813 [OG]

54. Gutiérrez, José Mariano, cura of Huamelula, Oax (Anteq), 1814 [Farr; MiV]

55. Gutiérrez de Terán, cura of parish "in the south of Mexico," 1812; diputado suplente to congress at Tehuacán; [RP]

56. *Herrera, Lic. José Manuel, cura of Huamuxtitlan, Gro (Pue); with Morelos; pardoned 1816; joined Trigarantines 1821 [BU]

57. Herrera, José María, cura of Coatepec de los Costales, Gro (Mex), 1813 [OG]

58. †Herrera, Nicolás Santiago, cura of Uruapan, Mich (Mich); saved Cos (q.v.) from death penalty [Farr]

59. Herrero, district of Cuernavaca, Mor (Mex), 1812; not clearly parish priest [Farr; MiV]

60. *Hidalgo y Costilla, Miguel, cura of Dolores, Gto (Mich), 1810-11; executed

61. Jiménez, Ignacio, vicario of Huango, Mich (Mich) [Farr]

62. †Labarrieta, Antonio, cura of Guanajuato, Gto (Mich), 1810; per Bustamante, gave sermon against the tyranny of the Spanish government when Hidalgo entered Guanajuato in 1810, but Alamán seems to disagree; in any case, requested pardon Dec. 1810 and became active royalist [Farr; Bus, 1:95; Alam, 2:67-68; HyD, 2:371-72]

63. Ledesma, José Mariano, vicario of Tulancingo, Hdgo (Mex); pardoned by 1813 [OG]

64. Lezama, Mariano, cura of Huichapan, Hdgo (Mex), 1813 [OG]

65. Llave, Lic. José María, cura of Puebla diocese, 1813; at Chilpancingo Congress [RP; Alam 2:567; Bus, 1:455]

66. †Lombide, Juan José, cura of Guad diocese; jailed on district governor's assertion that he had a suspicious relationship with Xayme (q.v.); admitted answering a letter from Xayme but denied publishing his manifesto or joining the insurgency; also acknowledged that insurgents who came to his parish seat had killed peninsulares [AJANG leg. 1 for 1800; doc. is post-1811]

67. †Lopez, Jose Vicente, vicario of Ayó el Chico, Jal (Guad), 1812; sentenced July 1812 for allegedly trying to get soldiers to rebel, telling them they were "más napoleonistas que realistas"; admitted joining insurgents at the beginning in order to seize some peninsular Spaniards in la Barranca, but claimed to have repented on realizing the injustice of the insurgency; still in prison 1815 [AJANG caja 5 leg. 1 exp. 14]

68. López Cárdenas, José, interim cura of Tlatlaya, Mex (Mex), 1813 [OG]

69. Macías, Antonio, cura of La Piedad, Mich (Mich), 1811-14 [BU]

70. Maldonado, Dr. Francisco Severo, cura of Mascota, Jal (Guad); pardoned March 1811; became royalist spokesman [RP; Alam, 4:209]

71. Martínez, Ignacio, vicario of Tlatlaya, Mex (Mex), 1813 [OG]

72. Martínez, José, cura of Chilapilla, Gro? (Pue) [BU]

73. †Martínez de Segura, José Antonio, cura of Tetela de Xonotla, Pue (Pue), 1815; sheltered Carlos Ma. Bustamante from royalists (then over 80 years old, Martínez was a firm financial supporter of the insurgency, per Bustamante) [Farr; Bus, 2:196; Alam, 4:255]

74. *Matamoros, Mariano, cura of Jantetelco, Mor (Mex), Dec. 1811; executed 1814

75. Medalla, Joseph, cura of Huitzuco, Gro (Mex), 1813 [OG]

76. †Medina, Rafael, cura of Xilotlan, Col (Guad); accused of infidencia June 1813, which he denied [AJANG caja 4 leg. 3]

77. Melgarejo, Francisco, cura of Tetepango, Hdgo (Mex), 1813 [OG]

78. Mendoza, Pedro, vicario of Chilapa, Gro (Pue) [BU]

79. *Mercado, José María, cura of Ahualulco, Jal (Guad), d. Jan. 1811 [BU]

80. Miranda, Tomás, cura of Malacatepec, Mex (Mex), 1813 [RP; Farr; OG]

81. *Moctezuma Cortés, Juan, cura of Zongolica, VC (Pue,); with Morelos; d. 1816 [BU; Alam 2:228, 4:722; Bus 1:434, 2:16, 232-34]

82. †Montes, Hermenegildo, vicario of Dolores, Gto (Mich), 1811; "subversive" [Farr]

83. †Montes de Oca, José Antonio, cura of Tiripitío, Mich (Mich), 1813; "conspirator" [Farr]

84. Morales, encargado of Tizacapan, Mex (Mex), 1813 [OG]

85. Morales, Manuel, cura of Zacualpan, Mex (Mex), 1813 [OG]

86. *Morelos y Pavón, José María, cura of Carácuaro and Nocupétaro, Mich (Mich), Oct. 1810–15; executed 1815

87. Ocampo, Pedro Joseph de, cura of Acamistla, Gro (Mex), 1813 [OG]

88. Ortega Muro, J. Mariano, cura of Hueytlalpan, Pue (Pue), 1812–13 [BU; Bus, 1:546]

89. †Ortiz Navarro, José María, interim cura of Ozoloapan, Mex (Mex), 1818; as vicario de pie fijo of Acatitlan, Tejupilco (Mex), in 1817, accompanied the insurgent leader Vargas, but said he went unwillingly and was threatened with death if he refused [Acervo 49 caja 45]

90. †Palafox, Antonio, cura, courier for Ignacio López Rayón, 1811 [Bus, 1:462]

91. †Palancares, Domingo, cura of Tuxtepec, Oax (Anteq); "collaborator" [Farr; Bus, 2: 22–23]

92. †Parra, Salvador, cura of Valle de Topia, Sin (Guad), from 1796; though in trouble with the audiencia for loose talk in early 1810 criticizing gachupines and declaring creoles' right to rebel, apparently not involved in the subsequent insurgencies [AJANG caja 9 leg. 3 exp. 68]

93. Patiño, Mariano, cura (diocese unknown), 1813; at Apatzingán Congress; arrested 1817 [Bus, 1:617; MiV]

94. Pedraza, Germán, cura of Nopala, Hdgo (Mex), 1813 [OG]

95. Pedro, cura of Tepecoacuilco, Gro (Mex), 1812; with Morelos [*Mor*, 1:326]

96. Pérez, José, cura of Zapotlanejo, Jal (Guad); executed as presbítero faccioso y revolucionario [BU]

97. Pérez, Salvador Antonio, cura of Chimaltitan, Jal (Guad), 1811; imprisoned in Zacatecas for infidencia; sought pardon 1817; still in prison 1820 [AJANG 1820 leg. 5 (27)]

98. †Plaza y Castañeda, Joaquín de la, cura of Otumba, Mex (Mex), from mid-1790's; accused of treason by subdelegado during their dispute in 1810 [Tulane VEMC 51 exp. 6]

99. †Ponz, Fr. Tomás, OP, cura of Cutzmala, Gro (Mich); preached in favor of insurgency and welcomed Morelos in early 1815 [Alam, 4:282]

100. Ramos, José María, cura who operated in Zacatecas and Aguascalientes [Amad; also referred to in AJANG caja 13 leg. 2 exps. 10, 12, April 1812 arrest record of eight robbers suspected of belonging to "the band of cura Ramos"]

101. Ravadan, cura (diocese unknown), 1812; attacked Taxco [BU]

102. Rodríguez, José Antonio, vicario of Tacotan, Jal (Guad), 1811; charged with being capellán of the insurgent Miguel Gómez Portugal; claimed to have twice refused to join and been taken by force [AJANG caja 9 leg. 3 exp. 72]

103. Rodríguez, Marcelino, cura of Tlaltizapan, Mor (Mex), 1813 [OG]

104. Romero, Juan Antonio, vicario of Tlalpujahua, Mich (Mich), 1818; executed [BU; Bus, 2:153]

105. Romero Soravilla, Juan de Dios, former vicario of Irimbo, Mich (Mich); executed [BU]

106. Rosado, Mariano, cura of Misantla, VC (Pue), 1812–17 [Farr]

107. Rosas, cura [Amad]

108. Ruiz, Mariano, cura of Santiaguito, Hdgo (Mex), 1813 [OG]

109. Ruiz Calado, Joseph, cura of Yautepec, Mor (Mex), 1813 [OG]

110. †Ruiz de Chávez, Manuel, cura of Huango, Mich (Mich), 1809; conspirator at Valladolid 1809, but apparently not an active insurgent and pardoned 1813 [RP]

111. Sabino Crespo, Lic. Manuel, cura in Oax dist (Anteq), Dec. 1812 [M&H, p. 53]

112. Sáenz, cura of Nombre de Dios, Dur (Dur), 1810 [BU]

113. Sáenz, Vicente Rafael, OFM, cura of Temapache, VC (Mex), 1811 [G&P, 5:119ff]

114. Salgado, Mariano, cura of Cuahuayutla, near Petatlan, Gro (Mich), 1812–17; at Chilpancingo Congress; "collaborator" [Farr; Bus, 1:617]

115. *Salto, José Guadalupe, vicario of Teremendo, Mich (Mich), 1811–12; tried and pardoned July 1811; took up arms again; d. May 1812 [BU; Alam, 3:210–11; Bus, 1:447]

116. Sánchez, José Francisco, cura of Molango, Hdgo (Mex), 1813; pardoned [OG]

117. †Sánchez, Juan José Crisanto, capellán of Hacienda del Astillero, Villa Nueva dist, Zs (Guad), 1811; pardoned for publishing Hidalgo's proclamations, which he said he did under duress [AJANG caja 9 leg. 3 exp. 18]

118. Sánchez, Vicente, former vicario of Yautepec, Mor (Mex), 1813 [OG]

119. Sánchez de la Vega, José María, vicario of Tlacotepec, Pue (Pue), 1812–21; with Morelos and later Trigarantine [BU; Alam, 2:563, 3:223]

120. †Soria, Francisco, cura of Jiquipilco, Mex (Mex), 1811; "collaborator" [Farr]

121. Soria, José, interim cura of Petatlan, Gro (Mich), 1811; sent to ecclesiastical prison 1798; transferred to hospital in Valladolid 1803; disappeared and reportedly insurgent colonel 1811; d. 1811 of fever at Hacienda Pedernales, Turicato dist [Civil 1603 exp. 5]

122. †Subiano, Manuel, vicario of Ajuchitlan, Gro (Mich), 1817; "subversive" [Farr]

123. *Tapia, Mariano, vicario of Tlapa, Gro (Pue); with Morelos, d. Oct 1812 [BU]

124. Terán, cura of Teypan, Gro (Mich), 1812; with Morelos [*Mor*, 2:62–63]

125. Tirado, José Luis, vicario of Tenango (Tenango del Valle, Mex?) (Mex), 1812; executed when royalists took town [RP; Farr]

126. Tonalá, cura in Anteq diocese, 1814 [M&H, p. 168]

127. Torreblanca, José Pablo, cura of Acatlán(?), 1818; Miquel speculates that this is José Antonio Talavera, vicario of Ajuchitlan and Pungarabato, Mich (Mich), an ally of Morelos, active 1811–18 [Farr; MiV]

128. *Torres, José Antonio, vicario of Cuitzeo, Gto (Mich), 1810–19; "el azote del Bajío"; killed [BU]

129. Torres, José María, cura of Olintla, Pue (Pue), 1812 [BU; Bus, 1:315]

130. Uraga, Francisco, cura of San Miguel (Mich), 1810; adviser to Junta de Policía of Aldama [M&H]

131. †Urquijo, Joaquín de, cura of Acayucan, VC (Anteq), 1812; "subversive" (palabras sospechosas) [Farr]

132. Valdivieso, José Antonio, cura of Ocuituco, Mor (Mex), 1812–14; executed at Tlapa [RP; Farr; Bus, 1:389]

133. Vásquez, Pedro, cura of Ajuchitlan, Gro (Pue); captured 1817 [RP]

134. †Vega, José María de la, cura of Sola, Oax (Anteq); "collaborator"; declared innocent [Farr; M&H]

135. Velasco, José Mariano, cura of Tescaliacac, Mex (Mex), 1810–13 [Farr; OG]

136. †Vera, Fulano, vicario of Santo Domingo, Izúcar, Pue (Pue), 1812; spied for Matamoros [*PI*]

137. *Verduzco, Dr. José Sixto, cura of Tusantla, Mich (Mich); with Morelos; active to 1818 [BU]

138. †Victoria, Pablo, "cura" of Hacienda de la Pala, near Sahuayo, Mich (Mich), 1813; arrested for advising insurgents and publishing their proclamations; denied charges, produced 33 witnesses, and was pardoned [AJANG, bundle labeled "1813 leg. 3 (42)"]

139. Vilchis, José Agustín, encargado of Pilcaya, Gro (Mex), 1813 [OG]

140. †Villanueva, Agustín Mateo de, cura of Ixtlahuaca, Mex (Mex), 1810; "collaborator" [Farr]

141. Xayme, Santiago Mariano, capellán of Hacienda de San Nicolás de Pánuco, Son (Arispe), 1812; imprisoned Tepic for wearing an insurgent uniform, serving as lt. col., and

preaching on behalf of Hermosillo; repented and pardoned Oct. 1812 [AJANG, bundle labeled "1719–1787, leg. 1"]

142. Yllanes, coadjutor of Tejupilco, Mex (Mex), 1813 [OG]

143. Zavala, Eduardo, of Tlayacapan, Mor (Mex), 1812; not clearly parish priest [*Mor*, 1:219–20]

144. Zavala, Matías, vicario of Tlayacac, Mor (Mex), 1812; Matamoros's lt. cura [MyC, p. 32]

145. Zimarripa, Fernando, vicario of S. Luis, Dolores, and S. Miguel el Grande, Gto (Mich), captured April 1812 [BU]

146. †Zúñiga, Francisco, capellán de la Valenciana, Gto (Mich), 1810; preached for insurgency; Trigarantine by 1821 [BU; MiV]

147. Zúñiga, José Antonio, cura of Temascaltepec, Mex (Mex), from 1796; charged with infidencia 1811 for not preaching against the insurgency; strongly anti-gachupín and apparently urged parishioners to fight for "liberty" as the best form of government because Americans were the "rightful owners" of America; reportedly met with insurgent leaders, organized a cannon foundry, and received title of capt., all of which he denied; no verdict as of 1811 [Inq 462 exp. 34]

148. †Zúñiga, Nicolás, cura of Sultepec, Mex (Mex), 1813; "collaborator" [Farr; OG]

Reputed Royalists

149. Aguado, Ignacio, cura of Tepehuacan, Hdgo (Mex), 1811 [G&P, 5:144ff, 185ff]

150. Agüero, Dr. Gracián, cura of Tecozautla, Hdgo (Mex), 1813 [OG]

151. Aguirre, Gregorio, cura of Acatlan, Hdgo (Mex), 1813 [OG]

152. Alana, Liberato, vicario of Atotonilco el Grande, Hdgo (Mex), 1813 [OG]

153. Albarran, Manuel, vicario of Ocoyoacac, Mex (Mex), 1813 [OG]

154. Alcántara Villaverde, Fr. Pedro de, OSA, cura of Meztitlan, Hdgo (Mex) [Alam, 4:411]

155. Alonso, Juan, cura of Capuluac, Mex (Mex), 1813 [OG]

156. Alvarado, Miguel, vicario of Cuernavaca, Mor (Mex), 1813 [OG]

157. Alvarez, José Francisco, cura of Matehuala, SLP (Guad); sent by Gen. Callexa against insurgents at Colotlán in June 1811 and elsewhere; committed numerous atrocities, as noted by Alamán and Bustamante (who calls him a monster), earning him the nickname "el cura chicharronero" [BU; Bus, 1:216; Alam, 2:253–54]

158. Aragón, Francisco, vicario of San Bartolomé Ozolotepec, Mex (Mex), 1813 [OG]

159. Arévalo, cura of Tlalpujahua, Mich (Mich); as companion of "Torre" in 1811, tricked insurgent Indians into letting him pass by handing out prints of Virgin of Guadalupe [Bus, 1:171–72]

160. Avila, Manuel, cura of Tulancingo, Hdgo (Mex), 1813 [OG]

161. Ayala, Miguel José, vicario of San Cristóbal Ecatepec, Mex (Mex), 1813 [OG]

162. Azcárate, José Ignacio, cura of Huascaloya, Hdgo (Mex), 1813 [OG]

163. Barco, Joaquín Mariano Soto Posada del, cura of Tepatitlan, Hdgo (Mex), 1811 [G&P, 5:135ff]

164. Barreiro, Joseph, vicario of Tepecoacuilco, Gro (Mex), 1813 [OG]

165. Bear, Diego, cura of Armadillo(?) (Guad?); protected Zacatecas in 1812 [BU; Alam, 2:283]

166. Benítez, Felipe Benicio, 1811 [G&P, 5:135ff]

167. Benosa, Manuel, cura of Xilotepec, Hdgo (Mex), 1813 [OG]

168. Benzanilla, Lic. José M., cura of Silao, Gto (Mich), 1811 [G&P, 5:91]

169. Bravo, Eugenio, cura of Zapotlan, Jal (Guad), 1812 [HyD, 4:411–12]

170. Caamaña, Dr. Tiburcio, cura of León, Gto (Mich) [Amad]

171. Cabeza, 1810–11 [HyD, 2:907]
172. Cacela, Mariano, cura of Tejupilco, Mex (Mex), 1813 [OG]
173. Calderón, Pedro Ignacio, cura of Apam, Hdgo (Mex), 1813 [OG]
174. Calera, Dr. Rafael José de, cura of Temascaltepec, Mex (Mex), 1811 [G&P, 5:156]
175. Carrasco, 1810–11 [HyD, 2:907]
176. Chávez, 1810–11 [HyD, 2:907]
177. Clavijo, Felipe, cura of Huejuco(?) [*Mor*, 2:235]
178. Cortásar, Juan, interim cura of Yautepec, Mor (Mex), 1813 [OG]
179. Cortés, 1810–11 [HyD, 2:907]
180. Dávila, Patricio, cura of Tlalnepantla, Mor (Mex), 1813 [OG]
181. Díaz, José Hipólito, cura of Huazalingo, Hdgo (Mex), 1813 [OG]
182. Domínguez, Juan José, cura of Ocuilan, Mex (Mex), 1817 [Alam, 4:646]
183. Escarcega, Alonso, vicario of Tulancingo, Hdgo (Mex), 1813 [OG]
184. Esquivel, 1810–11 [HyD, 2:907]
185. Estrada, Joseph, cura of Tlaquiltenango, Mor (Mex), 1813 [OG]
186. Fernández de la Somera, Juan, cura of Teotihuacan, Mex (Mex) and his two vicarios, 1813 [OG]
187. Flores, 1810–11 [HyD, 2:907]
188. Flores, Miguel, cura of Atlacomulco, Mex (Mex), 1813 [OG]
189. Frera, Lic. José Antonio, cura of Calimaya, Mex (Mex), 1813 [OG]
190. Fuentes, Victorino de la, cura of Irapuato, Gto (Mich); capt. of local royalists [BU]
191. Gallardo, vicario de pie fijo of Santiago Tianguistengo, Hdgo (Mex), 1813 [OG]
192. García, Pablo, cura of Aculco, Mex (Mex), 1811 [G&P, 5:211ff]
193. García, Lic. Timoteo, cura of San Gregorio Cuaxingo, Mex (Mex), 1813 [OG]
194. García Jove y Seijas, Dr. Cayetano, cura of Chiautla, Mex (Mex), 1820; had urged loyalty to the crown while interim cura of Chimalhuacan, Chalco, and Ixtapalapa [AGI Mex 2550, 1820 relación de méritos]
195. Garrido, Francisco, cura of Sultepec, Mex (Mex), 1811 [G&P, 5:229; OG]
196. Garza, cura of Aguayo(?); self-proclaimed royalist though pursued for insurgent sympathies [Bus, 1:259]
197. Gavito, Vicente, interim cura of Tizayuca, Hdgo (Mex), 1813 [OG]
198. Gil, José Mariano, interim cura of Ocoyoacac, Mex (Mex), 1813 [OG]
199. Gil de León, 1810–11 [HyD, 2:907]
200. Gomes de Selis, Francisco, interim cura of Chalco, Mex (Mex), 1813 [OG]
201. Gómez, Francisco, cura of Alfajayucan, Hdgo (Mex), 1813 [OG]
202. Gonzales, José Julián Teodoro, cura of Atitalaquia, Hdgo (Mex), 1811 [G&P, 5:130ff]
203. González, Pantaleón, vicario of Huascasaloya, Hdgo (Mex), 1813 [OG]
204. Gorostiza, 1810–11 [HyD, 2:907]
205. Guevara, Juan Bautista, cura of Guastepec, Mor (Mex), 1813 [OG]
206. Gutiérrez, Mariano, former vicario of Ixtlahuaca, Mex (Mex), 1813 [OG]
207. Hermosa, cura of Exutla, Oax (Anteq) [*Mor*, 2:70–71]
208. Hernández, Manuel, vicario of Atlacomulco, Mex (Mex), 1813 [OG]
209. Herrera, José, cura of Jamiltepec, costa chica of Oax (Anteq), 1814 [BU; Alam, 4:77]
210. Herrera, Manuel, vicario of Tulancingo, Hdgo (Mex), 1813 [OG]
211. Hiaorta, José Cristóbal, cura of Huitzuco, Gro (Mex), 1810- 11 [G&P, 5:109ff]
212. Huamantla, cura in Tlax dist (Pue), 1816 [Alam, 4:407]
213. Huitzilac, vicario in Cuernavaca dist, Mor (Mex), 1816 [Alam, 4:421]
214. Inurriaga, Félix, cura of Zitácuaro, Mich (Mich), 1811–12 [HyD, 4:452]
215. Irigollen, cura of Xuquila de la Costa, Oax (Anteq) [*Mor*, 2:70–71]

216. Iturbe, cura of Tenancingo, Mex (Mex), 1813; peninsular [OG]
217. Iturribarría, Mariano, cura of Tejupan, Oax (Anteq), 1812 [M&H, p. 40]
218. Jaso, 1810-11 [HyD, 2:907]
219. Jaso y Osorio, Alejandro, cura of Temoaya, Mex (Mex), 1813 [OG]
220. Jocotitlan, cura of Ixtlahuaca, Mex (Mex), 1811 [Alam, 2:355]
221. Labarrieta, Antonio, cura of Guanajuato; *see entry 62 under insurgents* [Alam, 2:67–68]
222. Landa, cura in Queretaro dist (Mex) [BU]
223. Lara, José María, interim cura of Xuchitepec, Mex (Mex), 1813 [OG]
224. Larrainzar, Manuel, cura of Tempoal, VC (Mex), 1813 [OG]
225. Laso de la Vega, Felipe, interim cura of Amecameca, Mex (Mex), 1813 (OG)
226. León, José, cura of Acasuchitlan, Hdgo (Mex), 1813 [OG]
227. Lloreda, Manuel, interim cura of Sta Clara, Mich (Mich), 1811-12 [HyD, 4:452]
228. López, José Antonio, cura of Tinhuindín, Mich (Mich) [Bus, 2:151]
229. López Aguado, José Ignacio, cura of Tampamolon, SLP (Mex), 1813 [OG]
230. López Cárdenas, 1810-11 [HyD, 2:907]
231. López Escudero, Manuel, cura of Temamatla, Mex (Mex), 1813 [OG]
232. Lozano, J. Ignacio, cura of Mesquitic, Jal (Guad) [BU]
233. Maldonado, Dr. Francisco Severo, cura of Mascota; *see entry 70 under insurgents* [RP; Alam, 4:209]
234. Marques, Carlos, cura of Ayutla, Gro? (Mex) [*Mor*, 2:235]
235. Martín, Bernardo, vicario de pie fijo of Tepepa, Valley of Mex, 1813 [OG]
236. Martínez, Diego, interim cura of Ixtapaluca, Valley of Mex, 1813 [OG]
237. Martínez, José María, vicario of Real del Cardonal, Hdgo (Mex), 1811 [G&P, 5:128ff]
238. Maruri, Antonio, cura of Chapala, Jal (Guad), 1814 [AJANG caja 1, leg. 5, exp. 18]
239. Maturana, 1810-11 [HyD, 2:907]
240. Mayol, cura of Tixtla, Gro (Pue) [Bus, 1:344]
241. Meana, Dr. Mariano, interim cura of Huejutla, Hdgo (Mex), 1813 [OG]
242. Meras, 1810-11 [HyD, 2:907]
243. Mesa, Mariano de, vicario of Huejutla, Hdgo (Mex), 1813 [OG]
244. Monasterio, Domingo, cura of Milpa Alta, Valley of Mex, 1813 [OG]
245. Mondragón, 1810-11 [HyD, 2:907]
246. Mondragón, Joseph, vicario of Tepoztlan, Mor (Mex), 1813 [OG]
247. Monrroy, Rafael, interim cura of Ixtlahuaca, Mex (Mex), 1813 [OG]
248. Moreno, Ignacio, vicario of Xocotitlan, Mex (Mex), 1813 [OG]
249. Moreno, José María, coadjutor of San José Malacatepec, Mex (Mex), 1813 [OG]
250. Muñiz, 1810-11 [HyD, 2:907]
251. Nava, José Manuel, vicario of Malinaltenango, Mex (Mex), 1813 [OG]
252. Niño de Rivera, Manuel, cura of Chicontepec, VC (Mex), 1813, [OG]
253. Olloqui, 1810-11 [HyD, 2:907]
254. Osores Sotomayor, Félix, cura of Santa Ana, city of Querétaro (Mex), 1810-20 [García Ugarte, "Andares politicos"]
255. Oyarzábal, 1810-11 [HyD, 2:907]
256. Parodi, Diego, cura of Amanalco, Mex (Mex), 1811 [Alam, 2:349; HyD, 2:907]
257. Patiño, Francisco, cura of Acapulco, Gro (Mex), 1814 [Alam, 4:67]
258. Paz, Mariano José de, cura of Huejutla, Hdgo (Mex), 1811 [OG]
259. Pedreguera, Lic. José de la, cura of Jalapa, VC (Pue); claimed he fought in the "reconquest" of Coatepec and was named Benemérito de la Patria [AGI Mex 2550, 1820 relación de méritos]
260. Peláez, Manuel, cura of Tototepec, Gro(?) (Mex), 1816; royalist spy [Alam, 4:,492]

261. Pérez, 1810–11 [HyD, 2:907]
262. Pérez, Francisco Ignacio, cura of Ixhuatlan, VC (Mex), 1813 [OG]
263. Pérez, José Miguel, cura of San Bartolomé Ozolotepec, Mex (Mex), 1813 [OG]
264. Quesada, Severino, vicario of Xochitepec, Mor (Mex), 1813 [OG]
265. Ramos, José, interim cura of Tlayacapan, Mor (Mex), 1813 [OG]
266. Raya, Juan José, cura of Tequila, Jal (Guad); fled when insurgents came to town Oct. 1811 intending to kill him; learned they decapitated a mayorodomo [CAAG July 21, 1812, report]
267. Rincón, Joseph, cura of Guitepec (Guastepec?), Mor (Mex), 1813 [OG]
268. Ríos, Pablo de los, vicario of Lerma, Mex (Mex), 1813; peninsular [OG]
269. Rodríguez Bello, Francisco, cura of Chilapa, Gro (Pue), and his vicario [BU; Alam, 3:248; Bus, 1:344]
270. Romero, 1810–11 [HyD, 2:907]
271. Rosas, Antonio, cura of Acasingo, Mex (Mex), 1813 [OG]
272. Rubén de Celis, Manuel, cura of San Cristóbal Ecatepec, Mex (Mex), 1813 [OG]
273. Ruiz Calado, José Mariano, cura of Yautepec, Mor (Mex) [*Mor*, 1:376]
274. Salazar, José Felipe, cura of Yecapixtla, Mor (Mex), 1817 [BU]
275. Salgado, Celedonio, cura of Jacala, near Zimapan, Hdgo (Mex), 1813 [BU; OG]
276. Sánchez, José Francisco, 1811? [G&P, 5:206ff]
277. Sánchez, Juan Nepomuceno, cura of Tepeapulco, Hdgo (Mex), 1813 [OG]
278. Sánchez, Pedro, cura of Cozcatlan, SLP (Mex), 1813 [OG]
279. Sánchez de Aparicio, Dr. Jacinto, cura of Actopan, Hdgo (Mex), 1811 [G&P, 5:246]
280. Sánchez Espinosa, J. Rafael, cura of Tlanichol, Hdgo (Mex) [BU]
281. Sánchez Pareja, Dr. Eusebio, cura of Alfajayucan, Hdgo (Mex), 1811 [G&P, 5:78; HyD, 2:907]
282. Sandoval, Santiago, cura of Xochiatipan, Hdgo (Mex), 1813 [OG]
283. Sansipuian, José, cura of Totolapa, Mor (Mex), 1813 [OG]
284. Semper, José María, cura of Real de Catorce, SLP (Guad), 1811 [BU; Bus, 1:223; Alam, 2:283]
285. Senil y Alderete, Vicente, cura of Zimapan, Hdgo (Mex), 1810–11 [HyD, 2:907; G&P, 5:207ff]
286. Servantes, Pedro, vicario of San Cristóbal Ecatepec, Mex (Mex), 1813 [OG]
287. Simbrón, Rafael, vicario of Tulancingo, Hdgo (Mex), 1813 [OG]
288. Soria Bustamante, Domingo, cura of Landa, Qro (Mex), 1811 [G&P, 5:119ff]
289. Sotomayor, Joseph Manuel, as informal assistant of Acasuchitlan, Hdgo (Mex), and cura of Jonacatepec, Mor (Mex) [Inq. 1334 exp. 3; Acervo 49 caja 146]
290. Telles, Agustín, cura of Oapan, Gro (Mex), 1811, 1813 [G&P, 5:201ff; OG]
291. Terán, Fr. José, cura of Petatlan, Gro (Mich) [*Mor*, 2:235]
292. Terrón, Ignacio, vicario of Tenango del Valle and Calimaya, Mex (Mex), 1813 [OG]
293. Tlalmanalco, Mex, cura of (Mex), Dec. 1813 [OG]
294. Toral, Manuel, cura of Aculco, Hdgo (Mex), 1810–13 [HyD, 2:907, 5:353–54; OG]
295. Torres, José María, 1811? [G&P, 5:243ff]
296. Travanca, Miguel, Zacapoaxtla, Pue (Pue), 1812; not clearly parish priest [Alam, 2:567]
297. Truxillo, Rafael, vicario of Xochimilco, Valley of Mex, 1813 [OG]
298. Ugalde, Joaquín de, cura of Zacualtipan, Hdgo (Mex), 1811 [G&P, 5:153; OG]
299. Ugalde, Pedro, cura of Lolotla, Hdgo (Mex) [BU]
300. Valle, José Ignacio del, Zacapoaxtla, Pue (Pue), 1812; not clearly parish priest [Alam, 2:567]

301. Varrientes, cura of Tlahuac, Valley of Mex, 1813 [OG]
302. Vázquez, Manuel, cura religioso of Meztitlan, Hdgo (Mex), 1811 [BU]
303. Vega, 1810-11 [HyD, 2:907]
304. Verdin, José Nicolás Santos, cura of San Blas, Nay (Guad), 1811 [BU; López, 1: 172-73]
305. Verdugo, Dr., cura of Cuernavaca, Mor (Mex), 1816 [Alam, 4:421]
306. Verdugo, Joseph Tivurcio, cura of Tepoztlan, Mor (Mex), 1813 [OG]
307. Viana, cura of Lerma, Mex (Mex) [Bus, 1:67; HyD, 2:907]
308. Vieyra, José María, interim cura of Tepetlaostoc, Mex (Mex), 1813 [OG]
309. Villar, Mariano del, cura of Amealco, Hdgo (Mex), 1811 [G&P, 5:161ff]
310. Violet y Ugalde, Luis, cura of Pachuca, Hdgo (Mex), 1813 [OG]
311. Vivanco, 1810-11 [HyD, 2:907]
312. Yañes, vicario of Xuquila de la Costa, Oax (Anteq) [*Mor*, 2:70-71]
313. Zamarripa, cura of Ixtapan, Mex (Mex), 1813 [OG]
314. Zimbrón, José Mariano, cura of Singuilucan, Hdgo (Mex), 1811 [G&P, 5:142ff]
315. Zúñiga y Ontiveros, Felipe, cura of Mixquic, Mex (Mex), 1813 [OG]

Morelos: A Regional Illustration of Priests, Parishioners, and Insurrection

One of the inevitable complications in the study of priests and parishioners in 18th-century Mexico is provincial, regional, local, and individual variation. As distinctive as the Diocese of Guadalajara and the Archdiocese of Mexico were, the sharpest contrasts in religious practices and parish histories occurred within them, especially within the archdiocese. Regional and local patterns appear throughout this book but usually in short bursts for different subjects. Another book or series of books about priests, and local religion might well be organized around more systematic regional descriptions and comparisons. These final pages of text offer one example of the fruits of a more sustained regional and local history that again looks toward the independence struggle and the arrival of José María Morelos.

Late colonial relations between rural priests and parishioners in the districts of Cuautla and Cuernavaca (roughly the modern state of Morelos) anticipate the defiant spirit for which country people there became well known during the 19th century and the Revolution of 1910.[1] This area was one of the hottest spots in central and western Mexico for political and economic conflicts involving parish priests, and the place where anticlericalism and poor church attendance were most evident. In this sense, colonial Morelos is an extreme regional case, not a particularly representative one. No place was simply representative of larger colonial processes; or, if any one was, we cannot know it without first building a composite of all places. But a regional case may be no less revealing of the larger history because it was unusual.

The districts of Cuernavaca and Cuautla covered a comparatively warm, wet basin in the heart of the central highlands, connecting haciendas and towns of the semitropical lowlands with cooler upland settlements. They were linked to the Valley of Mexico, the tierra caliente in Puebla and Guerrero, and the mining districts of Sultepec and Temascaltepec in the Edo. de Mexico and Taxco in Guerrero. These two districts were reputed to be among the most rapidly changing and politically turbulent places in the archdiocese.

There were important Indian pueblos, many with at least a substantial minority of recent arrivals from other parts of central Mexico, as well as Spaniards, castas, shopkeepers, and artisans.[2] Head towns of lowland Morelos were more evenly divided racially than in other areas of central Mexico with a large Indian population: one Indian to one or two gente de razón in Morelos, compared with about two Indians to one gente de razón in the Toluca region.[3] Late colonial judges found the racial composition of lowland pueblos complex and rather confusing. In litigation records they sometimes reported that individual "Indians" were actually mulatos or lobos. Some pueblos were tenacious in keeping district judges and priests at arm's length; many others were divided within by their ties to these and other authorities and men of property, and by competition for scarce resources. There were large estates, some of them veritable towns, that produced and processed sugarcane, grains, and livestock for Mexico City and other markets. There were also smaller sugar estates, dispersed hamlets or rancherías, and family ranches; prosperous peninsular and creole merchants in the pueblos, haciendas, head towns, and regional center of Cuernavaca; and a comparatively large slave, free black, and afromestizo population living on the sugar estates and rancherías, as well as in pueblos. The largest towns—Cuernavaca, Cuautla, Yautepec, and Mazatepec—were seats of some of the most lucrative parishes in the archdiocese.[4]

By the 1760's, the growing sugar economy had worked important changes in land tenure, labor requirements, and the size and distribution of the region's population. The pueblos, ranches, and haciendas had changed in ways that added to their complexity and intensified the contacts beyond their borders. Although there was a strong sense of local identity and continuity with the past in pueblos de indios, these were comparatively open settlements resembling the centrifugal pueblos and estates of central Jalisco and the Bajío.[5] As Antonio de Alcedo reported in the late 1780's, the area had become one of the most populous in New Spain.[6]

The persistent troubles involving parish priests were concentrated in the densely occupied, sugar-producing western districts of Cuernavaca, Mazatepec, Tlaltizapan, and Tlaquiltenango, and in the east from lowland Yautepec and Jonacatepec, up to Tepoztlan, Tlayacapan, Atlatlaucan, Zacualpan, and Ocuituco, and into adjacent upland parishes of Ecacingo, Atlautla, and Ozumba on the way to Mexico City. Draft labor was an especially volatile issue between priests and village parishioners, partly because of economic changes that increasingly drew villagers into wage labor, but also because onerous draft labor for the mining district of Taxco had been a source of local conflict for most of the colonial period.[7]

Recent Views

Morelos is fairly well known from primary and secondary sources. But its special attraction as a regional case for local religion and politics in the 18th century is its subsequent fame during two of Mexico's great national upheavals: the early years of the War of Independence, from 1810 to 1815 (especially in early 1812, when the state's eponym, José María Morelos, faced the royalist forces at Cuautla), and the Mexican Revolution of 1910, in which the villages of Morelos came to epitomize the agrarian cause and produced the nation's most famous campesino leader, Emiliano Zapata. As a dynamic, complex area and the stage for these principled heroes of the nation, the state of Morelos has an unusually important place in Mexico's usable past. The latest wave of historical and anthropological scholarship on the area is marked by increased attention to the 18th century, usually with Zapata and the Revolution of 1910 in mind. This recent literature is almost as intriguing and as much in flux as the region itself was when Miguel Hidalgo raised his voice at Dolores in September 1810. Two of Mexico's eminent social scientists, Arturo Warman and Guillermo de la Peña, opened the way in 1976 and 1980 with broad historical and structural interpretations grounded in studies of eastern Morelos—mainly the lowlands for Warman; mainly the uplands for de la Peña.[8] Both emphasized great transformations in the late 18th century that were driven by commercial agriculture.

Warman's rural Morelos was awash in agrarian capitalism by the end of the colonial period. In his view, the area witnessed extraordinary land pressures from the expansion of the sugar economy and population growth. These factors jointly reduced villagers to the marginal lands of their town sites and completed the conversion of land and water into commodities monopolized by private estates. Furthermore, the sugar estate owners were as much concerned with controlling the now "free" labor force as they were with acquiring agricultural lands. A corollary to this "definitive expansion" of sugar haciendas was the decline of communal institutions in the pueblos. Warman's Morelos in 1810 seems already ripe for *zapatismo* or some other kind of class war, not to mention the Decalogical egalitarianism of José María Morelos's movement.

De la Peña also emphasizes the expansion of sugar estates at the expense of villages in the late 18th century, and the growth among highland villagers of a free labor market and a free market in Indian produce. He treats villagers' access to land as the crucial variable in the agrarian violence of 1812, as well as 1910, and speaks of "strong support . . . among villagers and laborers of the Cuautla-Yautepec region" for the early insurgents.[9] De la Peña differs from Warman in positing that the colonial state occupied a controlling position—promoting the economic transformation, seeking to ameliorate sharp divisions between estate owners and villagers, and manipulating community loyalties through the fiesta system and symbols of spiritual unity. For de la Peña, the Bourbons brought on the First War of Independence by their aggrandizing ways and a rigid reassertion of colonial domination that left planters freer to attack village lands. Deep cleavages developed that left many local people, especially mestizos, creoles, villagers, and the lower clergy, without "a proper place in the colonial structure."[10] In places where villagers and ambitious creoles and castas did not organize to subvert the royal government after 1810, he believes, the concerted efforts of churchmen and colonial governors maintained an uneasy symbiosis between villages and the lowland sugar estates. In his view, it was especially the power of the church that held back a more torrential agrarian movement during the Independence War.

John Tutino, in his wide-ranging study of rural insurrection and revolution in Mexico from the mid-18th century into the 20th century, also highlights growing tensions over land in Morelos at the end of the colonial period, but he emphasizes a more durable, symbiotic relationship between private estates and villages.[11] It was the containment of conflict through social and economic symbiosis that accounted for what he regards as the weak support José María Morelos found in the area. In contrast to de la Peña, Tutino does not believe that symbiosis depended on judges, district governors, militias, and priests; and he points to the weakness rather than the potential strength of agrarian unrest in Morelos by 1810. For Tutino, it was only in the 1840's that the agrarian conflict gathered much momentum.

Cheryl Martin's study of land tenure and population in rural Morelos, Gisela von Wobeser's study of sugar estates, and Brígida von Mentz's study of rural communities in western Morelos provide essential details on the expansion of commercial agriculture and its ripple effects in the region from the 1760's.[12] Martin, in particular, demonstrates that this expansion was accompanied by a rapid growth in the non-Indian and migrant Indian populations (correcting Warman's impression that the labor force was drawn almost exclusively from local residents), new pressure on the lands of pueblos and small estates, and deep factional disputes within pueblos that could weaken the symbiosis with haciendas. She speaks of a "volatile political situation" that centered on struggles over land and water and was further destabilized by the Bourbons' secularization of parishes in the area after 1750, which "generated confusion and conflict over disposition of property once designated for ecclesiastical purposes."[13] Agreeing more with de la Peña than with Tutino, Martin concludes that José María Morelos's revolutionary message "held great appeal for the so-called lower classes of the region."[14] She speaks of Morelos's arrival as a convenient pretext for villagers and migrant workers to attack the haciendas. However, citing disputes over land, water, and political authority in the increasingly non-Indian town of Yautepec, Martin also suggests how conflict within communities could have moved some members to join the insurgents and others to support the royalists.

Von Mentz charts the structural changes Martin describes for villages in a part of Morelos where sugarcane production and processing were developing. The population of pueblos there continued to grow, merchants and other non-Indians were moving in, and villagers were turning to trade and working for wages outside the community more than farming their own lands. Internal divisions and land disputes were becoming more apparent in the pueblos, and their institutional authority was "dissolving."

The most recent contributions to the English literature on late colonial Morelos and its reputation for exalted protest are Serge Gruzinski's *Man-Gods in the Mexican Highlands* and Robert Haskett's *Indigenous Rulers: An Ethnohistory of Town Government in Colonial Cuernavaca*. Much of *Man-Gods* is devoted to a charismatic religious movement that developed in the district of Yautepec in the late 1750's under an Indian shepherd, Antonio Pérez, whose conception of leadership drew on the native man-god principle of the ixiptla, as well as Christ and the saints. Gruzinski treats Pérez largely in pathological terms, but his explanation of Pérez's radical rejection of Spanish domination on behalf of the dispossessed recalls de la Peña's view of the region's late colonial history. It was inflexible diocesan priests, determined to impose their regalist version of a purified faith, who excluded Pérez from even his marginal place in the colonial order. Gruzinski ends his book with a bold leap forward to Emiliano Zapata as the last incarnation of the man-god in Morelos, a kind of socially integrated successor to Antonio Pérez in the collective subconscious.

In his study of the inner workings of Indian town government, Haskett describes a local Indian society that seems worlds away from the Morelos of Gruzinski, de la Peña, and von Mentz. Using Nahuatl cabildo records, he is struck by the durability of a traditional ruling elite, their successful resistance to change, and the local society they "carefully crafted and maintained,"[15] without missing the many divisions and conflicts among them, with other Indian communities, and with Indian commoners over labor and taxes. He supplies a crucial missing piece of the historical puzzle for Morelos, but by concentrating on continuities, the agency of local Indian officeholders, and the "drive" to maintain traditional arrangements,[16] his study contributes less than it might to the history of power during the colonial period. It effectively leaves out other powerful individuals and groups living among or near colonial Indians of the Cuernavaca district, and most of the ways in which the communities represented by the officeholders were part of a larger political economy, constrained by demographic changes and colonial demands. Colonial government beyond the Indian cabildo enters the story mainly to show "the basic inability or unwillingness of the colonial authorities to intervene." And the documentation for *Indigenous Rulers* is richest for the 17th and early 18th centuries, before the economic and social changes described by Martin, von Mentz, and von Wobeser took hold.

This celebrated regional history becomes yet more complicated and a little clearer if more attention is given to priests and to local religion, as well to the intersection of regional and national history in 1812. Perhaps most importantly, such an examination discovers a long-standing anticlericalism that increased with the ecclesiastical reforms of the Bourbons after 1749 and the divisive effects of economic and social change noticed by

Martin and von Mentz shortly thereafter. With some striking exceptions,[17] the church in Morelos was not Gruzinski's and de la Peña's domineering institution unwittingly creating anticlerical sentiment by marginalizing many of the faithful. It was, I think, the curas more than eccentric believers who were being marginalized as spiritual and political figures in this region.

The Secularization of Parishes

One chain of events that immediately preceded the growth of disorders and lawsuits in the region was the secularization of doctrinas still controlled by the Mendicants. A disproportionate number of the mid-18th-century secularizations occurred in Morelos. Of the 70 parishes of the archdiocese known to have been secularized in 22 alcaldía mayor districts between 1750 and 1777, at least 16 (23%) were located in the districts of Cuernavaca and Cuautla. Twelve others (17%) were in or near modern Morelos in the district of Chalco. Franciscans, Dominicans, and Augustinians all had served in doctrinas in the area, and all three orders were affected.[18]

The precise effects of secularization in Morelos are difficult to determine. The argument against secularization made by Juan Bautista de Bolde, the Franciscan guardián at Ozumba, when the Augustinians were removed from parish administration there in the early 1750's, seems less convincing for the Morelos area than it might have been for other parts of central and southern Mexico: that the diocesan curas were unable to speak Indian languages and therefore could not perform their duties as well as the Mendicant doctrineros.[19] The large number of priests ordained a título de idioma before the 1780's ensured that most parishes had at least a vicario who could communicate in the native language; moreover, Indians in some of the larger lowland pueblos and villas of Morelos reportedly spoke Spanish fluently.[20] Bolde and others campaigning against secularization in the 1750's drew their examples from the part of Morelos (spilling over into the Chalco district) that suited their purposes best—the upland parishes of Atlatlaucan, Totolapa, Tlalnepantla, Ocuituco, and Tetela.[21]

On the whole, diocesan priests were no less dedicated to their sacramental duties than the friars. The claim that Indian villagers in this area felt betrayed by the removal of their benevolent friars does contain a kernel of truth—at least in the way some parishioners after the 1760's spoke about the past, and the way some Franciscans and Augustinians mounted their case against secularization in the 1750's—but these are only two sides of a many-sided question of authority and property in the late 18th century. Of course, today's popular contrast of "good Franciscans" with self-interested diocesan priests can be validated with colonial examples. Indians of Cuanacalcingo (or Pueblo Nuevo, near Tlaltizapan, Cuernavaca jurisdiction) in 1775 petitioned to have their cura, José Eusebio de Ortega, removed and three friars put in his place because, they said, they wanted priests who would "work wholeheartedly for the good of our souls, as in the time of the friars."[22] Indian parishioners in prosperous parishes of Morelos may have regarded the better-educated secular replacements as more remote, even unapproachable. In the secularized pueblo of Tlacochahuaya (Cuernavaca), Indian petitioners spoke of their priests in 1780 as "estos señores licenciados" (these gentlemen licentiates) in contrast to their former Franciscan "fathers."[23] And militia forces sometimes had to be sent out to ensure a peaceful transfer of authority to the diocesan cura.[24] But it is also clear that friars in parish service faced and perhaps invited the same kinds of disrespect and bitter opposition as some of their diocesan successors. In 1672, Indian leaders of Tetlama, Mazatepec, Coatlan, and five other Indian pueblos of southwestern Morelos entered charges against two of their Franciscan doctrineros from Cuernavaca for cruel whippings and excessive demands for money, goods, and labor. A Franciscan appointed to investigate the charges concluded that they were malicious exaggerations stemming from a recent incident in which one of the Franciscans had upbraided an Indian of Coatlan for leaving his church filthy and in disrepair. According to the ecclesiastical investigator, the Indian had reacted impertinently, nearly gouging out the friar's eyes and declaring that he had an order from Mexico City allowing him to disobey the Franciscans. The investigator agreed that the friar had been right to prescribe a moderate whipping, and judged that the new charges were motivated mainly by revenge.[25]

With a reputation for poor church attendance, the Morelos area was precocious in disputes between pueblos and doctrineros over clerical fees and demands for the arancel. Fees were in the background of the 1672 case against the Franciscans. Mazatepec and 12 other Cuernavaca pueblos had successfully petitioned for the 1637 arancel to replace what they claimed were excessive demands for labor, food, and cash payments made by their Franciscan doctrineros.[26] When pueblo leaders complained that the doctrineros had agreed to comply but had in fact disregarded the arancel, the Franciscans replied that the entire dispute over fees had been concocted by the alcalde mayor, "the capital enemy of said religion," in order to win the support of village officials for his own exactions. The Franciscans were, they said, complying with the arancel while the alcalde mayor was now moving the village leaders to make false claims to the contrary. When the coadjutor went to two of the pueblos to celebrate mass, only a few non-Indians came, and the Indians had hidden the chalice and other implements needed for the rite.

In another early arancel dispute, Indians from Tetecala complained that their Franciscan doctrinero, Pedro Araña, had refused to accept the terms of the arancel and had jailed their gobernador for resisting his wishes. The Indians went on to charge the Franciscans with forced labor, operating a private jail, and unnecessarily delaying the administration of justice. In 1730 and again in 1732, the Franciscans were ordered to follow the arancel and to treat their charges with the love best suited to the cure of souls.[27] At about the same time, the Augustinians at Jonacatepec were also enmeshed in an arancel dispute with local Indians who, the doctrinero said, paid less than the prescribed fees, refused to perform customary labor service, were often absent from church, and exhibited a general "malignity."[28]

Then, in 1748, Indians of San Pedro Istoluca, San Felipe y Santiago, and San Marcos Huispaleca in the Dominican doctrina of Tlaltizapan sought the arancel, believing it would reduce their payments and labor services to the friars under the customary unwritten arrangement. They were right about some of the service but wrong about the payments in cash, and when the district lieutenant went there to present the audiencia's decree for the arancel, he was stoned and nearly killed by Indian parishioners, who reportedly shouted in Nahuatl, "Kill, kill, because the audiencia deceived us with the *aranceles.* Now we are charged more than the friars used to."[29] The cura reported that when he asked for the fees prescribed in the arancel, the Indian officials refused to pay more than was customary and were otherwise "disobedient, audacious, and insubordinate." Fearing that this misbehavior would spread to other pueblos, he sought an order from the audiencia that the Indians pay the arancel rates and provide the labor service essential to support the church and its services, under penalty of four years at hard labor in an obraje. The case ended with a firm order from the audiencia to this effect. A similar dispute over labor service and fees at Santiago Xiuctepec (located between Yautepec and Cuernavaca) in 1752 stirred the Franciscan doctrinero, Antonio Arpide, to lament the decline of Indians' respect for their pastors since the golden age of evangelization in the sixteenth century and to denounce his charges as "lazy, uncouth, indecent, [and] rude" people who needed to be forced to work.[30]

As Arpide's complaints indicate, the tension between priests and parishioners in this region predated secularization. But it is also clear that the changes of the mid-18th century exacerbated things. Even before Archbishop Lorenzana issued the new arancel in 1767, some leaders of pueblos in recently secularized parishes of Morelos balked at meeting their financial obligations to the diocesan priests. Among other things, the departure of the friars left confusion about what was owed and stirred up old grievances among parishioners against serving and provisioning the curas. Indians of Tlacochahuaya in 1780, for example, claimed that their formal agreement with the Franciscans for service and fees was now disregarded because, they told the curas, the Franciscans were no longer in charge.[31]

Fees disputes continued to animate the conflicts between curas and parishes through the end of the 18th century, especially in the southwestern parishes around Tlaquiltenango and Tlaltizapan. In some cases, the fees do seem to have been the main source of dispute; in others, they were largely a smokescreen for political ambitions and a deeper opposition to the cura. Usually the disputes involved resistance to labor service, which is not surprising in a region where the labor demands of private estates were great and growing.[32] In the case of Tlaquiltenango, Indian officials of Jojutla lodged two separate suits against the cura (against Francisco de Aguilar in 1786 and Miguel Ruperto Gómez Negrete in 1789) over first fruits, unpaid service, and sacramental fees.[33] Although the pueblo officials' complaints may have been exaggerated and complicated by other motives, they seem to have had a strong case. Both curas failed to enter a full defense against the charges, and Aguilar provoked the parishioners' anger by demanding the full prescribed fees (if not more) during the hard times of dearth and disease in 1786. In 1789, the audiencia resolved both suits with emphatic orders that the cura should follow the arancel, pay for labor service beyond the immediate requirements of the church according to the prevailing daily wage for manual labor in the district, and not repeat his outrageous disrespect to the king's representative. The last, an allusion to the furious insults that Gómez Negrete had hurled at the lieutenant when he was notified of the order to obey the arancel, indicates that the audiencia was particularly out of sympathy with the priest.

The Tlaltizapan case was less obviously one-sided. Brought to court in 1797 on a charge of excessive fees, the cura, Francisco Vásquez del Campo, presented strong evidence that the suit against him had little substance and was the work of six local men who were using it to lever themselves into community offices and frustrate his influence over the selection of the gobernador. Vásquez del Campo had been the cura of Tlaltizapan since 1782. According to his testimony, shortly after he took over the pastoral duties, there was a dispute over clerical fees in which the parishioners were given two choices: the arancel or the customary fees and services. They chose custom.[34] The 1797 suit contains no claim that Father Vásquez did not follow this agreement to the letter, at least for the first 11 years of his service. He claimed that over his 15 years in Tlaltizapan he had spent 2,560p on parish improvements and taken in only 2,119p in parish fees, a claim that went unchallenged by the Indian leaders. The complaint by the current gobernador and his predecessor was that the cura not only had begun to vary the fees during the past four years but, more important, had blocked the election of their candidate for gobernador, Bernavé Antonio. The cura replied that he had indeed spoken against Bernavé Antonio for community office, because he was "a chronic drunkard of perverse character," but that he had not intervened further in the choice of officers. His last, perhaps telling point (the record is without a judgment from the high court in response to the Indians' complaint) was that the six plaintiffs were Bernavé Antonio's main partisans in the pueblo.

Unlike the Mendicants, the new curas did not belong to a special fraternity of priests that protected its members against the personal insecurities of earning a living; nor had they taken an explicit vow of poverty. These differences did not keep friars from abusing parishioners and demanding their fees, but the diocesan priests had reason to accumulate private property and use it for personal gain. Depending largely on their own resources and ingenuity, they were more likely to be either transient and distant from community life, or, in a few cases, entrenched and powerful. Those who were in their thirties and forties when the new parish benefices in Morelos became available and who stayed for many years were likely to become landowners and develop other local business interests. These were the sorts of distractions from the spiritual duties that the Council of Trent had tried to guard against, but they did not have to set the priest against most of his parishioners or make him a less effective pastor than his unencumbered colleagues. It was possible for a dedicated pastor who made a comfortable living from his private interests to enhance his spiritual standing with parishioners. Unlike younger and poorer curas recently appointed to modest parishes and dependent on fees for their livelihood, he had the means to forgive sacramental fees and support expensive charitable works. But in late colonial Morelos, few curas seem to have forgiven fees or used their personal incomes in this way; or, at least, they rarely enhanced their spiritual standing by doing so.[35]

One case, from Zacualpan de las Amilpas in 1763, illustrates as well as any, how Indian parishioners used secularization and some legislated changes in the authority of the cura to reassert their independent religious practices and distance the priests and colonial judges from local affairs. Complaining that "the only custom they adhere to is their own caprice,"[36] the cura of this erstwhile Augustinian doctrina singled out the Indians of Temoac for their "contemptuous and captious" refusal to pay him the just fees and first fruits, for celebrating holy occasions on their own, and for drawing Guazulco, Tlacotepec, and Popotlan into their disobedience. Using as an excuse the new royal cedula that forbade the cura to choose fiscales on his own account, they had made their own selections and demanded the cura's confirmation (rather than submitting three names from which the cura would choose one). Many of them failed to fulfill their obligations to attend mass and take communion before Easter. Creole and mestizo witnesses said that the Indian leaders of Temoac were disobedient to both the civil and the ecclesiastical judges, and that two of them had been sent to jail for inciting a riot against the constable of the jurisdiction. There had been rumors that the cura would be murdered, and one witness claimed that "the Indian women were worse than the men" in their resistance. The cura had also tried without success to prohibit the Indians' Santiago dances, which he regarded as "crazy, excessive, and idolatrous." After he twice denied Temoac's petition to perform its dances, the parishioners refused to pay for any church functions on holy days and proceeded to hold two days of bullfights, dances, and fireworks in the cemetery.[37]

Temoac and other Morelos pueblos de indios belied the distinction made by colonial authorities between an "Indian" preference for dances and drinking and a "Spanish" preference for gambling and bullfights in public celebrations.[38] At Tlayacapan, bullfighting was so much a part of the Candlemas fiesta that when the cura forbade a *corrida de toros* in 1756 as an unseemly event for a Sunday afternoon, villagers burned his house down and sent him and the alcalde mayor running for their lives. The alcalde mayor said that though he had known there would be trouble and had warned the cura that the Indians had always marked the occasion with bullfights, he had enforced the ban anyway in order to avoid excommunication and an open disagreement with the priest. Apparently it took 30 soldiers over three weeks and several skirmishes and killings to restore order.[39]

A militant sense of local autonomy and factional anticlericalism was understood on both sides in the recurring disputes between curas and pueblos de indios. As at Temoac, the complaint by the curas and district governors was often that Indian villagers in the region resisted all higher authority, but especially that of the priest.[40] Vásquez del Campo's predecessor at Tlaltizapan, José Eusebio de Ortega, had had his own troubles in 1781. The Indians of Huispaleca, Cuanacalcingo, and the cabecera had resisted paying sacramental fees and carrying out labor service for more than a year, even after an audiencia order was obtained, and the alcalde mayor and the alguacil mayor of Cuernavaca came to compel obedience. On November 13, the alcalde mayor ordered the Indian gobernador of Tlaltizapan and the alcalde of Huispaleca to assemble the village councils and other natives at Ortega's residence the next day to swear their obedience to the audiencia decree. They did so, and agreed to send the first crew of servants that afternoon, but the leaders of Huispaleca failed to return with their crew or a list of men eligible for service. When the alcalde mayor and his constable went to Huispaleca to enforce the order, they found only women and children there, who swore they had not seen the men in two days. A cat-and-mouse game ensued: when reports that the men had gone to Mexico City were investigated, the news was that they had returned to Huispaleca, and vice versa. The alguacil mayor considered the resistance a matter of bad character and anticlericalism: the Indians of Tlaltizapan and Huispaleca "manifest little or no respect for or attention to the said *párroco* and superior authorities," and "some of them are people of restless and rowdy spirit." The cura added in December that he could do nothing in the face of the Indians' "consummate arrogance and libertinism."[41]

Father Ortega's successor, Vásquez del Campo, as we have seen, enjoyed nearly 15 years of comparative peace. But his time came in 1797, when the new issue of the day—elections free from the cura's influence—was taken up by his opponents. The Indians' attorney argued for the "complete liberty" to which they were now entitled in their elections[42]—an appealing idea in this local context but a dangerous one in the larger tradition of colonial rule, in which "liberty" was understood to shade off quickly into "libertinism."

Alcohol: The Mal Inevitable

Morelos would have been a very difficult place to enforce the new regalist austerity of the late 18th century even if most curas there had been determined to do so. Part of the recipe for chronic conflict between priest and parishioners in Morelos was what colonial officials at all levels called the *mal inevitable*—alcohol. From the beginning of Spanish rule in Mexico, liquor had been considered by colonial officials to be the gateway to vice, disobedience, and idolatry. The Morelos area, like Jalisco, was already well known in the 17th century for its raucous fandangos and holy day celebrations and illegal production of potent distilled beverages.

Changes beginning in the 1690's brought liquor closer to the center of attention. Under the protection of royal authorities eager to tax colonial commerce, Indians of the Chalco, Cuernavaca, and Cuautla districts in the 17th century had cultivated maguey and produced pulque for sale as well as local consumption.[43] But sales fell off badly after 1692, when riots in Mexico City were blamed on excessive pulque drinking, and they continued to slide as private estates closer to the major markets (Mexico City and the mines) became the suppliers of choice.[44] By 1782, the administrator of the pulque tax for the district of Cuernavaca reported that it was hardly worth collecting any more: most of the 60 towns now grew only a few magueyes to satisfy their own needs.[45]

The growth of the sugar economy after the 1750's doomed most of the small commercial producers who survived.[46] The prohibitions against American distilled drinks, especially mezcal (made from maguey hearts) and chinguirito (made from sugarcane juice) were loosened and then lifted by the crown in the late 18th century for tax purposes.[47] Cane alcohol now became the drink of choice for non-Indians, was consumed along with pulque by local Indians, and was sometimes even used as payment for corvée labor.[48]

Capitalizing on a growing interest in the production of distilled drinks in America, Viceroy Marqués de Croix assembled a large file of reports and opinions of leading citizens in 1767 to make the case for legalization. The argument came down to three points: illegal production had proved impossible to control; it was a potentially rich source of tax revenue; and distilled beverages were more healthful (because purer) and less disruptive of social peace than pulque.[49] In January 1797, the last administrative decree legalizing cane alcohol in New Spain was put in place.[50] Now the colonial administration set about encouraging the commercial production of cane alcohol and destroying the illegal stills producing mezcal in the Cuernavaca district. Most of the cane alcohol was produced by non-Indians living on the larger estates or by petty entrepreneurs.[51]

Priests in this area were particularly frustrated by their inability to control their parishioners' drunken revelries and production of illegal beverages. In Morelos, it was natural for thwarted late colonial curas to consider drunkenness a major source of their parishioners' violence, insolence, and weak devotion to the church, especially because of what they regarded as the volatile mixing of Indians and castas in the pueblos.[52] But priests and royal judges who campaigned against drinking in the Morelos pueblos were likely to anger both the Indian and casta consumers and the hacendado suppliers of cane alcohol. When the alguacil mayor went to Tetelcingo in 1778 to end the local sale of mezcal and chinguirito by the creole schoolteacher, Josef Viscarra, about 500 Indians reportedly threatened him with clubs and rocks, shouting, "We're going to kill you and drink your blood."[53] Father Ortega's troubles in Cuanacalcingo after 1775 resulted in part from his attempts to punish Indian parishioners for "drunkenness and disorders."[54] Curas in the late colonial period were caught between their duty to check drunkenness on religious and moral grounds and the crown's promotion of alcohol production and consumption for revenue purposes.

Contentious Parishioners, Intemperate Priests

The Morelos area had its share of found crosses and popular devotion to the saints and parts of the liturgy, but even these Christian practices expressed contentious local identities that complicated relations with parish priests and made them antagonists or followers more than leaders in public life. Fittingly, the Christ of Tula, discovered by a muleteer gathering firewood in the parish of Tlaquiltenango in 1722, would insist on a home in one of the visitas. The pious tradition surrounding this image at its beginning is rich in meaning for a parishioners' view of the abrasive practice of religion and politics in the area—the militant identity of pueblos and clusters of small settlements, moves by an hacendado and priests in the cabecera to keep them down or appropriate their good things, and priests eventually bowing to "divine will."

According to the notarized accounts of the two Dominican doctrineros of Tlaquiltenango in 1723, the muleteer discovered the cross in a remote corner of the Hacienda San Gabriel in September 1722, when he chopped into an overgrown shade tree and found his axe splashed with blood. From his home in the Ranchería de Tula, the authorities took the image to the hacienda chapel. Four times in the next few months, it disappeared from the chapel, returning each time to the tree near Tula. Finally, the hacendado asked the Dominicans to take it to the parish seat because, with so many curious visitors to Tula, he feared the ranchería would soon become an independent pueblo. After its removal to the parish seat on January 1, 1723, the image again moved mysteriously, always to the altar of the church of Our Lady of Guadalupe in the visita of Jojutla. In the end, the Dominicans gave in. On September 14, the image was moved from Tlaquiltenango to Jojutla, accompanied by rejoicing Indians from Jojutla, Tetecalita, Nexpan, Theocalzingo, and other little settlements close by.[55]

Some Indian parishioners in the Morelos area expressed their independence by seeking the sacred on mountains and in caves and ritual books of their own, dressing images as they wished, taking them out of the church on unauthorized tours of the parish, and resisting accountability for the properties of their barrio chapels.[56] They might occasionally look to their priest for political support or move to a new location in order to enjoy the spiritual comforts he provided,[57] but in general the lukewarm enthusiasm for priests and sacramental obligations was expressed in the frequent complaints by curas that their parishioners were "rebellious sinners" who did not attend mass regularly or meet the annual obligation to confess and take communion, and that they paid the priest no heed or insulted him.[58] Parishioners were impertinent to their curas elsewhere, but rarely in other places did an Indian official behave as the gobernador of Cuanacalcingo did toward Father Ortega in 1780. According to Ortega, the man came up to him in a drunken state with his hat firmly planted on his head and said "that he was the new *gobernador* and that the *cura* would be leaving one of these days, while he would stay forever to pursue this litigation [over labor service for the church]." [59] The next year, the gobernador's successor and the pueblo's council members avowed that the Indians would serve the church only if paid, just as the cura did.[60] In despair, Ortega wrote that the local Indians "no longer pay attention to the parish, the needs of public worship, or the *cura*," and that such anticlerical insolence was spreading to other places.[61] By 1782, he reported that two of the three pueblos were finally beginning to do the labor service for the church that the audiencia had repeatedly ordered since 1780, but that the Indians of Cuanacalcingo no longer recognized him as their parish priest and ecclesiastical judge, and the last four times his assistants had gone there for mass, they had been locked out.

The tumultos and protests that occasionally flared in Indian pueblos against the parish priest exposed more of their objections and resistance to his spiritual guidance. In the investigation that followed a general protest against Manuel Gamboa, the cura of Tepoztlan in October 1778, Gamboa focused on the Indians' insolence and resistance to their Christian obligations. Few parishioners, he said, attended Sunday mass; many couples lived together without the sacrament of marriage; others buried their dead without informing the cura; the children did not attend school; and there was much drunkenness on mezcal and chinguirito that the villagers secretly produced in the mountains. Now they no longer confessed or provided the customary labor service for the church. On the Indians' side, the priest was accused of rough treatment, especially of humiliating whippings of naked women. Their recent violence resulted, they said, from the cura selling lime they had stored away for whitewashing their church. When they had stopped the mule train loaded with lime and the cura reacted by hitting an Indian with his bastón, some women led by Big María Juana ("la larga") laid hands on the priest. They testified that the real protest occurred that night when the lieutenant of Yautepec came to arrest the women.[62] In the confusion, the priest's bastón was taken from him and broken. Neither side demonstrated that the other's complaints were without merit, and the audiencia tried to resolve the conflict simply by admonishing the villagers to act as good Christians and singling out one presumed leader for exemplary punishment. With the archbishop's intervention, the leaders of Tepoztlan finally agreed to a reconciliation with their parish priest in 1779.[63]

The curas' relatively weak political, moral, and spiritual position in many parishes of Morelos was magnified by their conflicts with non-Indians. As in other regions, some Morelos curas identified and allied themselves with local gente de razón,[64] but the independence of haciendas and rancherías and the divisions within the non-Indian population virtually guaranteed that the priest would accumulate enemies as well as allies in every social group. Curas of late colonial Morelos repeatedly complained that estate owners and their administrators failed to attend mass or take communion, and kept their residents away from the parish church. At best, they hired an itinerant priest to say mass and hear confessions in the hacienda chapel, responding to the cura's objections with declarations like "I alone give the orders in this church." [65]

Bitter disputes between curas and local merchants, hacendados, and district governors were further evidence of a divided gente de razón in this region. In 1802, seven merchants and hacendados of Tetecala brought apparently false charges of concubinage and failure to perform his duties as a priest against Manuel Morales, cura of Mazatepec, in an effort to have him removed from the parish. The case took a strange twist when two disgruntled brothers of Morales were bribed to testify against him, then recanted their testimony; and the district lieutenant was said to have been threatened with the loss of his job if he did not support the peninsular merchants in this case. Threats aside, Lt. Felipe Matute had his reasons to oppose the cura. Two years before, Morales had complained to the audiencia of his failure to help round up the many parishioners who did not do their Easter duty. (Interestingly, Morales here unwittingly echoed a 1671 complaint by the Franciscan doctrinero against the alcalde mayor of the same jurisdiction when he accused Matute of having "no passion for justice" and being "in league with various *hacendados* to fight against me.")[66]

Besides Matute, the leader of the movement against the cura in 1801 was, according to one of Morales's brothers, an hacienda administrator who was said to hate priests and spread malicious rumors about their conduct. Another of the cura's enemies, d. José Salazar, boasted of having won lawsuits against the archbishop and shouted down Viceroy Gálvez. He reportedly had not confessed or taken communion in many years.[67] Although this priest's problems with the lieutenant, the hacendados, and the merchants seem to have resulted from his single-minded passion for saving souls,[68] these disputes often exposed divisive economic interests. Priests who competed for the control of land and water, who operated stores and tobacco concessions, or who blocked the profitable enterprises and independence of other local gente de razón could expect trouble.[69]

In 1794, parishioners and the cura of the mestizo mining settlement of Huautla came into conflict over another late colonial sore spot—cofradías and their properties. Presiding over a meeting of the Blessed Sacrament cofradía to receive the annual report of the outgoing mayordomo, Father Santiago Antonio Balderas noted that the cofradía owed him 2,891p. Father Balderas asked who would be the next mayordomo and take responsibility for the debt. The cofrades replied that no one would. The cura repeated his question twice more to the same response. In that case, he declared, he would be obliged to consume the supply of Hosts, leaving the parish without this essential material of the mass and communion. The next Sunday, he made good on the promise, letting the lamp burn out and swallowing the store of consecrated wafers. At that point, some of the brothers menaced him with a beating if he did not relight the lamp and renew the supply of consecrated wafers.

The lieutenant rushed the matter to the viceroy, describing "the [miners'] laments and tears" over the cura's shocking ingestion of the consecrated wafers, and using the occasion to complain that Balderas had illegally presided over a cofradía meeting and otherwise interfered in its affairs. In his defense, the cura underlined his loyalty to king and God, and the cofrades' betrayal of the fundamental order of Christian society: "If no example had been made with these people in such a case, higher authorities would have been left with their lives compromised, left to acquiesce in their evil maxims; the place and people would have been bereft of souls." On the order of the viceroy, the cura celebrated the renovation mass and restored the consecrated wafers, and the lieutenant convened a meeting of cofrades and neighboring hacendados to find a way to support the expenses of the Eucharist.[70]

The tension between curas and non-Indians in Morelos was heightened also by the entanglement of Indian and non-Indian political and economic interests. As in parts of Jalisco, considerable pueblo land was rented out to neighboring estates in long-term arrangements. Such rentals could draw together the parties involved or nurture resentment in the villages. Indian officials in Morelos were often joined by a faction of gente de razón in support of or opposition to the cura. In the 1802 suit against Manuel Morales, the Indian council of Miacatlan was joined by some local gente de razón in defending their cura as a vigilant, dedicated priest—"our beloved pastor." Together, they asked for his return to the parish.[71] In 1780, the cura of Tlaquiltenango charged that the former schoolmaster, a mulato named Miguel Barrera whom he had fired, was behind the labor suit lodged against him by the Indians of Cuanacalcingo.[72]

The district of Mazatepec, with 10 pueblos and 12 haciendas and sugar mills, was the site of many costly disputes in which these tangled social and political interests swirled around the parish priest. The 1671 suit the Franciscan doctrineros had brought against the alcalde mayor for allying with local hacendados against them was followed by decades of Indian resistance to clerical fees and labor service for the church at San Francisco Tetecala, beginning in 1730.[73] Even an upbeat pastor presenting his service there in the best light could not resist mentioning the political hardships. The vicario of Mazatepec, Joseph Lucas de Santibáñez, in his brief for a promotion in 1760, stressed his active pastoral service and establishment of Indian schools. He was particularly proud of having persuaded "by great effort" the difficult Indians of Tetecala to work two pieces of church land for the support of the priests, but admitted to little success with the "rebellious and quarrelsome" Indians of San Miguel Huajintlan.[74]

Conflict between hacendados at the Mazatepec town of Tetecala and the state administrators surfaced in a 1793 complaint against the alcalde mayor's lieutenant, Joaquín de Montenegro, for his promotion of gambling and the alcalde mayor's illegal repartimientos of bulls and mules. The hacendados also charged the lieutenant with scheming to collect more fees from the Indian pueblos of the district by undertaking unauthorized land measurements that led to new disputes between pueblos and haciendas. In this case the cura, Mariano Berdugo, who was commissioned to investigate the charges, supported the lieutenant and his superior, the alcalde mayor.[75] But several years later, his successor, Manuel Morales, complained that the lieutenant was not helping him to enforce the Easter duty. Since his arrival in 1795, Morales reported in 1800, some 2,000 parishioners had failed to confess and take communion, despite several missions to the parish by preachers and confessors from the Apostolic College of Pachuca during 1797–99. The rebels were concentrated on haciendas—565 of the 720 families that had not confessed were hacienda residents, 250 of them from the Hacienda de Miacatlan. The lieutenant agreed that the people of the Mazatepec district were "dispersed in *pueblos*, large farms, and *ranchos*, composed of Indians, Ethiopians, and the rest; a rustic and uncouth people," but said that their "vast [uncontrolled] nature" required "pastoral and doctrinal cultivation and an apostolic voice," which, he said, the cura had not provided.[76] But in the political countercurrents of these districts, enemies in one quarter produced friends in another. When the lieutenant struck back at the cura in 1802 with the aid of merchants and hacendados of Tetecala, some non-Indians, as well as the Indians of Miacatlan, rose to the cura's defense as character witnesses.

Into this region of potentially lucrative parishes, a relatively dense and varied population, and growing indifference if not hostility to the established church and its priests stepped some unusually temperamental and dissolute curas who sharpened the conflicts and confirmed anticlerical prejudices.[77] Francisco Antonio de Urueta, a vicario of Yautepec at the end of the 1790's, cut a particularly strange figure for a family doctor of souls. During ten years of service as an assistant pastor in three parishes, he left behind a long trail of solicitations in the confessional, seductions, and concubinage—serenely having his pleasure with more than a dozen maidens and married women. One conquest was the niece of his cura. Apparently ignorant of this betrayal, the senior priest wrote a glowing recommendation for Urueta's transfer to a more desirable parish. Twice Urueta had been confined to the seminary at Tepotzotlan as punishment, once escaping to a mistress's house in Mexico City. When the constables of the Inquisition caught up with him in 1799, he was hiding in a tree in his nieces' garden, dressed only in his undershirt and trousers.

Urueta was in much more serious trouble this time than before because the Inquisition now suspected that his long-standing intimacy with people "of all classes and stations" and his repeated offenses against the sacraments of confession and communion were evidence of heresy. At his trial, Urueta expressed remorse and denied any heresy. Forbidden by the Inquisition to hear confessions and therefore unable to obtain another parish assignment, he resurfaced in 1802 in Atlautla and Ecacingo as a producer of bootleg cane alcohol, living openly with a woman, enjoying the favor of local Indians and other common folk, well armed when he appeared in public, and rumored to have violated his sentence by confessing an Indian. He died of natural causes in February 1805 on the road to Amecameca. Hurrying to the spot, the district judge removed a key from the dead man's pocket and rode off to his rancho, where he unlocked a strong box containing jewelry and the substantial sum of 1,500p.[78]

An even more scandalous example of pastoral misconduct was Joseph Manuel Sotomayor (whom we met several times in the text), who took over the benefice of Jonacatepec in about 1798 after 25 years of service in 16 parishes, all of them in or near Morelos. The charges against him included dozens of carnal acts, solicitations in the confessional, personal business dealings, and great carelessness in his pastoral work. Deprived of his parish and his licenses to confess and preach, and sentenced in May 1802 to ten years of internal exile and two years of seclusion and rigorous spiritual exercises, Sotomayor found his chance for professional redemption in the Hidalgo and Morelos insurrections. In November 1810, he petitioned the Inquisition to restore his licenses to confess and preach so he could return to active ministry. The Inquisition initially refused, but the royalists desperately needed all the clerical support they could get. His petition was reviewed and granted in March 1811. At Acasuchitlan in February 1812, he fought bravely against bandits and insurgents, earning a glowing report from the subdelegado and reappointment to his old parish of Jonacatepec shortly after José María Morelos's occupation of Cuautla ended.[79]

A routine case of misconduct that was perhaps more damaging to clerical authority involved two parish priests of Tlaquiltenango in December 1804. Late that month, the cura, Miguel José Losada, reported to the archbishop a mildly scandalous sermon by Luis Venegas, his vicario de pie fixo of Tetelpa. According to the cura, Father Venegas had proposed in his sermon on the day of the Immaculate Conception that the Blessed Virgin be named the captain of armies, dances, bullfights, and plays. Almost playfully contemptuous of his old seminary classmate, whom he labeled "a [gullible] innocent," Father Losada judged that Venegas had made the suggestion without heretical intent in order to encourage the Indians' devotion. Unless Father Losada intended a cruel joke or wanted to discredit the vicario and ease him out of the parish, it is hard to imagine why he made a case of it to the archbishop. Whatever the reason, Venegas was mortified when the archbishop ordered him to forward a copy of the sermon, and took the opportunity to complain of Father Losada's antipathy. Losada responded on January 27, 1805, that Venegas had insulted him in public. Venegas countered that it was only when the cura had ridiculed him in front of others that he had lost his temper. Having helped the cura in his pastoral duties far beyond what was customary or required, he felt betrayed. Three months later, Losada wrote the archbishop again, urging him to remove Venegas, who no longer followed instructions and was too feebleminded ("escaso de luces") to continue. Apparently, Venegas was not removed, because the record ends with the court's investigator reporting that personal enmity was at the root of the dispute, and that Losada should thank Venegas rather than complaining that he had performed last rites in the Tlaquiltenango jurisdiction, since he had done so without compensation.[80]

This dispute with a tenured assistant seems especially self-destructive in light of Losada's public conflict with the local district lieutenant the year before (touched on in Chap. 16). On June 28, 1803, the lieutenant accused Losada, whom he called "an opponent of all that pertains to the royal jurisdiction," of failing to celebrate mass in honor of the Prince of Asturias's wedding, as ordered by viceregal bando. Losada held back his reply for five months "because my character and religion call me to gentleness and suffering so that peace may take root and flourish." In December 1803, however, he wrote a long defense that was anything but gentle: the lieutenant's informes were the "false and denigrative reports" of an "arrogant, rash, untruthful, daring, and outrageous man." Losada claimed he had given this thanksgiving mass, but only eight gente de razón, 20 Indians, and some women and children had attended—a sign, he said, of how the lieutenant's defaming complaints had influenced the parishioners. In his opinion, the root of the conflict was the lieutenant's determined opposition to his effort to found primary schools out of fear that his power over the Indians would be diminished. Both the priest and the lieutenant read sinister motives in the other's actions. Losada presented himself as the Indians' great protector against the lieutenant's tyranny and mistreatment; the lieutenant presented himself as the defender of royal authority against a haughty and disobedient subject whose actions threatened public order. Since Losada had performed the thanksgiving mass, after all, the case was dismissed, but the cost to reputations and cooperation between the cura and the district judge could not be so easily erased.[81]

Clearly, late colonial Morelos was marked by (1) a lukewarm enthusiasm for much of the Catholic liturgy and the priest's spiritual leadership and authority in public affairs; (2) an increasingly secular outlook on life; (3) local religious practices expressed in Christian terms that often crossed communities and ethnic groups with little reference to or supervision by the parish priest;[82] (4) Indian resistance to labor service for the church, the payment of clerical fees, and the regulation of drinking habits; and (5) bitter rivalries among non-Indians that were sometimes marked by extravagant anticlericalism.

Conflict at Yautepec

Next to Mazatepec and Tlaltizapan, Yautepec was the Morelos parish best known to late colonial authorities for bitter political disputes involving parish priests.[83] Consisting in the mid-1790's of a cabecera with 1,570 gente de razón and Indians, two pueblos, five sugar estates with village-sized populations in their own right, and various rancherías, Yautepec had the reputation of a contentious parish of questionable devotion to the church decades before its cura of unmatched longevity, Lic. Manuel de Agüero, found himself at the center of controversy in 1796.

Writing in 1769, the cura of Tepecoacuilco (Guerrero) referred to Yautepec as "a ridge of shadows, . . . a dikeful of notorious idolaters."[84] Perhaps he knew the reputation of Yautepec from his predecessor, Domingo Joseph de la Mota, the Indian priest who had been cura of Yautepec when "idol worship" was discovered there. In his relación de méritos y servicios for 1762, Father de la Mota recounted his eventful time in Yautepec. Upon arriving in 1759, he had waged a determined campaign against the manufacture of illegal alcohol, scandalous fandangos, and concubinage. (He neglected to mention the fees and forced labor complaint entered against him that first year.) On September 1, 1761, he and the lieutenant happened on a healing ceremony, in which about 200 Indians and some gente de razón were kneeling before a reputedly miraculous statue of the Virgin Mary, in the house of Pascual de Santa María. When Santa María was arrested, the faithful rose up with machetes, pikes, digging sticks, iron bars, rocks, or whatever else was at hand, and chased after the cura. Two days later, troops led by the alcalde mayor found a large group of the worshipers in a cave near the top of snow-capped Popocatépetl in the parish of Ecacingo.[85] Sixty-nine people were arrested; all were soon released except for 19 presumed leaders, who were still in jail in May 1765.[86] To Father de la Mota's mind, Yautepec was "the most tenuously [Christian parish], and its natives the most rebellious, ungovernable, and litigious people in the whole archdiocese. They have no order whatsoever, nor do they pay the sacramental fees according to the *arancel* or custom." It seems likely that Father de la Mota himself was a catalyst of the Yautepec violence, for he had touched off similar public disturbances before. By his own proud admission, he had been a tenacious persecutor of 11 shamans of Tepecoacuilco in the early 1740's, with the result that his house was set on fire and he himself nearly drowned in the Balsas River before he was transferred; and his campaign against adultery as cura of Zacualpan in 1747 had led to a local uprising, death threats, and another transfer.

Animating the events described by Father de la Mota was the spiritual leadership of Antonio Pérez, an Indian shepherd who had lived at Chimalhuacan and in several ranchos near the upland communities of Ecacingo and Atlatlaucan, east of Yautepec near Mt. Popocatépetl. Pérez apparently gained his reputation for spiritual power in the 1750's as a rather conventional healer using Catholic images and prayers as well as special concoctions. But he was hounded as a superstitious idolater by curas of the recently secularized parishes of Totolapan/Atlatlaucan and Yautepec, and ended up as something of a throwback to the man-gods of precolonial times—offering a radical critique of the Catholic church, its priests, and colonial rule, and representing himself as a superior Christian who had become both God and God's representative. The political and social message he was promoting at the time of his capture in 1761 resembled that of José María Morelos's "Sentimientos de la nación" of September 1813, but with a sharper line dividing Indian and Spaniard: "Everything should be for the *naturales* [the Indians]. . . . They alone should remain, while the Spanish and the *gente de razón* should be burned. . . . The world is a cake that must be shared among all."[87] By 1761, Pérez may have had about 500 followers in 12 pueblos, and practiced cave rites with 50 or more of the faithful at a time near Ecacingo.[88] Some were from Yautepec itself, but most lived in upland communities to the east, near Mt. Popocatépetl.

The importance of secularization and other religious reforms in the story of Pérez, noticed by Gruzinski, takes us still further back into the history of Yautepec. In August 1753, 13 Indian officials of Atlatlaucan (near Antonio Pérez's probable residence at the time) complained that their new secular priest, Joseph Manuel de la Peña,[89] had raised the sacramental fees, demanded contributions for a new side altar and threatened to whip those who refused, seized control of money and property that supported the veneration of San Mateo, and taken away many of the silver ornaments of their church. They also alleged that he rarely came to Atlatlaucan from his residence at Totolapa, gambled at home while infants died without baptism abroad, did not know Nahuatl, and used interpreters for confession. Clearly feeling abandoned and morally outraged, the Indian officials praised their former Augustinian doctrineros of Totolapa, "who regarded us as if we were their children" and were "very vigilant and God-fearing." But their strongest sentiments were reserved for the archbishop's court. Noting that their appeals to the provisor, like those of Ocuituco and Hueyapan, had gone unattended for seven months, the regidor mayor commented that "we have not been given justice, nor even attended; [the case] has been left to sleep. . . . Money talks." Now the officials of Atlatlaucan were appealing for justice from the audiencia, "where we would be treated as tributary vassals of His Majesty." Apparently this appeal, too, went unheeded.[90]

The collective action of 1761, then, exposed popular (but not necessarily anti-Christian) religious and social practices that priests wanted to control, connected with a long-standing alienation from authority in general, and, if de la Mota was right, not confined to Indians. It did not spread down the Río Yautepec valley to the parishes of Tlaltizapan or Tlaquiltenango, where the archbishop detected "superstitious" rites and a neglect of churches in his 1759–60 pastoral visit; but it did find adherents in Yautepec and Cuautla, and the upland parish of Yecapixtla, where de la Mota had also interfered.[91]

The crown used the Yautepec idolatry case to promote its agenda for change. A cedula of May 13, 1765, blamed the 1761 disturbances on inadequate spiritual attention from the parish priests, the avarice of the royal justices in the jurisdiction, and the Indians' excessive consumption of alcohol. The crown's idea for a solution to the problems of idolatry, disorderly conduct, and migration was to promote more schools to teach Christian doctrine in Spanish, assign more vicarios to large parishes, and control Indian drinking and adultery by forbidding district governors to sell alcohol to Indians or tax its sale.[92] The Yautepec case was the catalyst for royal decrees directed to all of Spanish America that vicarios be appointed for pueblos more than four leagues from the parish seat, in order to ensure adequate spiritual supervision.[93] The 1765 cedula also criticized the justices' pecuniary interest in Indian adultery, their use of the *reparto de mulas* (the monopoly on sale of mules in the district; part of the repartimiento de mercancías) to control Indian allegiance through debts and gain access to community lands, and the hatred they engendered by overcharging tribute. In this cedula and others like it from the reign of Charles III, the stage was being set for the intendancy reforms and the abolition of the repartimiento de mercancías.

Manuel de Agüero had held the Yautepec benefice for 24 years when his most notorious troubles began in 1796, during which time he had acquired the San Carlos Borromeo hacienda; the local tobacco, gunpowder, and playing-card concessions; a store, a chandlery, and a postal service in Yautepec; houses in Mexico City; and the bacon contract at the Puente del Carmen. Agüero did not enjoy a reputation for charity. Instead of raising his standing as a spiritual leader, his pursuit of wealth and economic power earned him some bitter enemies.[94]

Long before 1796, Father Agüero had been locked in disputes with the district governor, his parishioners, and a former estate owner that generated hundreds of pages of heated claims and counterclaims. In 1772, Indian parishioners of Yautepec complained of Agüero demanding unpaid servants. They requested that the arancel be applied. Lt. Rafael Blanco Casal became a principal in the dispute when he presented Agüero with the audiencia's order to obey the arancel. According to Blanco, Agüero refused to obey, and in a fit of "anger and great arrogance" called the royal governors "despicable thieves," threatening to have the lieutenant dismissed. Whether or not Agüero treated the lieutenant in quite this way, he began to display a notable zest for provocation and tenacious defense of his dignity and financial interests. Facing a second order on September 4, 1773, to obey the arancel, refrain from demanding labor service, and maintain "harmony and good relations" with the royal governors, Agüero fired back a long declaration in his own awkward handwriting. It was the kind of salvo that would become very familiar to audiencia notaries and judges who handled his subsequent cases. In it he declared that Lt. Blanco was behind the Indians' complaints, motivated by "venomous ill-will." Two more audiencia orders for Agüero to obey the arancel followed, in November 1773 and March 1774.[95]

In 1773, Lt. Blanco also charged Agüero with disobedience and defamation of character over a land possession: d. Francisco de Urueta of Yautepec had purchased the Hacienda Quatetelco from the Juzgado de Capellanías. Agüero, as the local juez eclesiástico, was supposed to have carried out the transfer, but he questioned the legality of the sale and refused to entitle Urueta when Blanco brought the matter to him. The upshot was a new exchange of insults and judicial complaints.[96] Then, in 1788, Agüero faced a long, bitter suit entered by Leonardo Calo, the Mexico City merchant who sold him the Hacienda San Carlos Borromeo. Calo charged that the priest still owed him thousands of pesos from that transaction.[97]

What triggered his troubles in 1796 was an anonymous letter to the vicar general accusing Agüero of a string of offenses: he stayed in Mexico City for long periods and had hired only one assistant to help in this large parish of dispersed settlements; breezed through ("se sopla") seven masses on holy days; extorted fees and allowed many parishioners to die without confession; left the Indian sacristans to oversee burials; neglected to repair the church; and controlled the properties of the cofradías and hermandades. No doubt Father Agüero left himself open to these and other charges against his service. As he said, by then the vicar general had come to regard him as a troublemaker (Agüero recounted a conversation in 1796 in which the vicar general said to him, "Fellow, you are very wicked").[98] But the unstated reason for the anonymous complaint, as he would later observe, was his struggle for irrigation water against other hacendados and residents of Yautepec, especially against Manuel del Cerro, who had served as lieutenant there from 1782 to 1792.[99]

Under house arrest in Mexico City, Father Agüero was not without allies as a secret investigation began. The first eight witnesses the hearing officer, the cura of Oaxtepec, called on November 17, 1796—the Indian gobernador of Yautepec, six Spaniards from Yautepec, Ayotepec, and the Hacienda Atlihuayan, and a mulato cantor—defended Agüero's pastoral service and testified that he did not charge more than custom allowed for the sacraments and forgave those who could not pay for burials. The last twelve witnesses criticized him in rather general terms, although nearly all noted his control of the cofradía properties.[100] Del Cerro and Miguel Cabrera, a 68-year-old Spaniard from Yautepec, excused themselves as witnesses because both had had public disagreements with the cura.

Nine days later, the vicar general received a secret letter signed by 21 non-Indians of Yautepec complaining that the cura of Oaxtepec's investigation had been biased in Agüero's favor—that he had called the witnesses favorable to Agüero first and had prompted them. Father Agüero also complained of this first investigation, saying that most of the witnesses were followers and dependents of the man who was surely his anonymous accuser, Manuel del Cerro.

In January 1797, a new investigation was undertaken by the archiepiscopal notary, Francisco Romero Blanco. The Indian gobernador of Yautepec was called again, this time with his council. They affirmed his earlier praise of the cura's conduct, though they did note that some parishioners had died without confession. The rest of the new investigation did not go so well for Father Agüero. Indian witnesses from Oacalco, Zamatitlan, and the barrio of Santiago said that he was often absent, mistreated them when he did appear, rarely came to administer last rites or explain church dogma, withheld mass and other services until the fees were paid, and left the vicario to do most of the work. The vicario, José Rodríguez, testifying only about the fees, said that he followed a schedule written for him by the cura. In his report, Romero Blanco noted that the parish registers were faulty, that the vicario had not allowed him to finish examining the archive as the vecinos requested, and that indigo was being processed on the consecrated ground of the cemetery.

Sensing that the case had turned against him, Agüero, himself a licensed attorney, dug deep into his kit of lawyer's tools, criticizing incorrect procedures and bias in the Romero Blanco investigation, then arguing that the entire case should be dismissed because it stemmed from an inadmissible anonymous letter. In April 1797, the case passed to the archbishop's Tribunal de Justicia de Indios, where it languished for nearly eight years while Agüero remained under house arrest in Mexico City and his nephew and other relatives represented his interests in Yautepec. Why the case was delayed so long is not clear. Apparently, Agüero was unwilling to push for a speedy resolution at the cost of a compromise or admission of guilt on his part. During this period, there were glancing encounters at court: in May 1799, del Cerro petitioned to have his marriage entered in the parish register, noting that it, "like many others," had been omitted by Agüero; the next month, Agüero petitioned for the case to be dismissed because del Cerro was his "capital enemy"; in 1801, del Cerro complained of the cura's "atrocious outrages."

By November 1802, the vecinos had had enough. Their lawyer indicated they were willing to withdraw the charges and live "in tranquility" with Agüero as their cura. Citing this statement, in January 1805 Agüero requested his release and agreed to make a confession. But his "confession" was hardly that of a penitent. He admitted long absences in Mexico City and failure to employ more than one vicario but claimed that illness and pressing litigation had drawn him to the capital, and that he could not find assistants to go to the tierra caliente. He insisted that he had gone out to parishioners whenever they called him: "neither sun, nor rain and flood, nor bad roads, nor any other thing has kept him from his parishioners' call, even when summoned in the least convenient hours of the night."[101] Still blaming del Cerro, he added a new countercharge—that the former lieutenant had been the enemy of earlier curas, too, and had spread rumors that all were atheists. Still insisting that he was "a person of docile temperament," Agüero conveniently neglected to mention his own troubles with another lieutenant, as well as parishioners. The archbishop's chief counsel concluded that the charges against Agüero were not untrue but had been exaggerated by the vecinos. With the eight years of house arrest, he had paid for his misdeeds and should be allowed to return to Yautepec as long as he employed two vicarios. The vicar general agreed, noting the cura's confession and the request by the non-Indian members of the community (*vecindario*).

The Agüero case and its background echo most of the persistent troubles between rural Morelos priests and their parishioners at the end of the colonial period. Several of the initial witnesses, as well as Father Agüero, noted the Yautepec parishioners' indifference to regular Christian devotions (their "poca asistencia"), their resistance to his directions about drunkenness, and the anticlerical remarks of some of the vecinos who had brought charges against him—all attitudes and actions that were common in the region. But like the parishioners of Mazatepec, the Yautepec parishioners were more anticlerical than irreligious. Their attitude that "the church is ours" fits with the "idolatry" events of 1761 and the troubles of Father Agüero and his immediate successors to indicate a long, though uneven, decline in the pastors' moral and spiritual influence.[102]

The cura of Yautepec, like many of his fellows, was a rather distant figure, a licenciado who may have fulfilled his basic duties but was often absent from the parish on private business, did little work outside the parish seat, and was not a dynamic or much loved spiritual leader. Although the archiepiscopal court in 1805 judged that the charges of private commerce had not been proved, it seems unlikely that Agüero's nephew was an independent agent in the enterprises he managed out of the rectory, and there was no doubt that Agüero operated the Hacienda San Carlos. And his persistent conflicts with the lieutenants, like those between other Morelos curas and district governors, tended to undermine his authority.

The complex allegiances of Morelos villagers also are evident in the Yautepec case. The slate of witnesses on both sides included Spaniards and Indians. A group of influential creole and peninsular vecinos of Yautepec, including the former district lieutenant, led the movement against the cura, but other vecinos of the cabecera testified for him. Indian leaders from the cabecera supported him, too, but those representing the Santiago barrio and the two pueblos opposed him, perhaps because he rarely visited them except to collect fees. But these divisions were not absolute or unchanging; after 1802, some of his influential enemies requested that he be restored to the parish. And at Yautepec, as elsewhere in Morelos, leaders from neighboring pueblos within and sometimes beyond the parish occasionally made common cause against the cura and other district officials.[103]

The Region and Its Eponym, 1812

Yautepec was a strong local eddy in the crosscurrents at play when José María Morelos briefly made his namesake region the center of insurgency. It would be wrong to suggest that Morelos found few recruits in the region, but it would be equally wrong to say that he found widespread local support based on sharp cleavages between, say, Indian villagers and Spanish or creole hacendados.[104] Morelos arrived in December 1811 with about 5,000 followers,[105] many of them from haciendas and ranchos in lowland Guerrero and Michoacán to the south and west. He occupied Cuautla at the beginning of February 1812, waiting there for the royalist troops that were closing in. In the only major engagement, the insurgents in Cuautla beat back three assaults by the royalists under Félix María Calleja on February 19. A siege of more than two months followed. Taking heavy losses, Morelos broke through the royalist lines on May 2 and retired with his remaining forces through the low country of Puebla toward Tehuacan.[106]

According to Morelos's testimony, 1,000 Indians near Cuautla and 250 men from Yautepec joined the defense of Cuautla. So Yautepec, famous as a center of unrest since the 1760's, did provide some support for José María Morelos.[107] But this support was neither particularly rooted in a local millenarian tradition nor particularly Indian; and it was far from unanimous. Unlike the name of Jacinto Canek in Yucatán, that of Antonio Pérez does not seem to have been a rallying point around Yautepec; and most of the Yautepec insurgents were estate residents or townspeople rather than village Indians spread across the district. (The supporters from Cuautla also included hacienda residents and at least one hacendado.) Finally, though the gobernador of Yautepec joined Morelos, the cura and one of Yautepec's Indian barrios, Santiago (which had opposed Father Agüero in the 1790's), backed the royalists in 1812; and at least 160 royalist cavalrymen drawn from ranchos in the region and commanded by a local hacendado largely offset the estate residents who joined the insurgency. Even though the western half of the district of Cuernavaca had been the site of much of the political agitation involving parish priests, hacendados, district governors, and Indians in the late 18th century, the residents do not seem to have thrown in their lot with either side.

The fact that Morelos was a priest apparently did not bring him much aid. Morelos himself did not attribute what support he got to his profession or his conspicuous display of the Virgin of Guadalupe and her colors, although altars to Our Lady of Guadalupe had become popular in the region during the 18th century.[108] Disgruntled curas—and there must have been plenty of them—certainly did not flock to him. Of more than 50 parish priests in the districts of Cuernavaca and Cuautla, only three are known for sure to have joined the Morelos forces (two other priests on his side may or may not have been parish priests).[109] The most notable defector to the insurgency was Mariano Matamoros, cura of Jantetelco in the southeastern lowlands, an intellectually inquisitive priest and restless, public man devoted to Our Lady of Guadalupe, who had been reprimanded in his previous assignments in the backwater parishes of Escanela and Misión de Bucareli (Querétaro) for long absences in Mexico City, where he fathered a son. Matamoros had made an early overture to Hidalgo in 1810 but failed to act on it, apparently because of religious scruples. Wavering again in late 1811, he finally joined the insurgents sent to arrest him at Jantetelco on the day of Our Lady of Guadalupe and went on to become Morelos's most trusted military commander.[110] He brought with him at least 47 supporters, including his vicario and the local schoolmaster.[111]

Parish priests rarely entered the independence struggle in Morelos on either side. Certainly, given the area's history of anticlericalism, they were unlikely to bring many of their parishioners with them. Matamoros was an exception, perhaps because Jantetelco was one of the few parishes more or less united behind its cura, a parish in which no bitter disputes over the cura's personal conduct or role in public life had reached the courts since long before Matamoros's tenure. Most Morelos parishes were not so peaceful. But a history of resistance to the cura did not predispose villagers to armed revolution against the colonial state. In testimony shortly before his execution in 1814, Matamoros suggested that rural support for the insurgency in central Mexico was very weak compared with that in the cities of Mexico and Puebla. In the countryside, he said, the people of most pueblos thought first of their own survival and tried to remain on friendly terms with insurgents and royalists alike.[112]

Late colonial Morelos was a place of deep conflicts and "consummate resistance," as one despairing cura put it in 1763. Collective actions there could be widespread and vehement, in contrast to collective violence in much of central Mexico and Oaxaca, which was largely confined to single villages and small territorial units. Yet in 1812 there was only limited support in the region for José María Morelos and his stirring message of political revolution, religious unity, and greater social equality.

Why wasn't the Morelos area ready for a broad-based political insurrection in 1810? The repressive power of the colonial state, emphasized by de la Peña and Gruzinski, is a reason; so is Tutino's economic symbiosis between haciendas and pueblos. But these explanations slide over the combination of sharp divisions within communities, local attachments, and anticlericalism that shows up throughout the area.

The colonial state did have the staying power of a traditional hegemony, but it also had weaknesses, especially the declining political, moral, and spiritual influence of priests in this region even before 1750, and sharp divisions between curas and district governors. There were indeed some intransigent curas who asserted themselves in political and spiritual affairs—Ayuso Peña of Zacualpan de las Amilpas in 1763, Balderas of Huautla in 1794, and Francisco Vásquez del Campo of Tlaltizapan in 1800. Domingo José de la Mota, the priest who persecuted Antonio Pérez, would seem to be the perfect example of a regalist agent determined to impose a more austere practice. But he is too perfect. I know of no other late colonial cura in this part of the viceroyalty who was repeatedly transferred to another parish after his zeal evoked threats to his life. The transfers also make him an odd choice to represent the rigidity of the colonial state (as Gruzinski does), since the archbishop and viceroy did not choose to resolve de la Mota's conflicts by backing him up with force. Emphasis on the power and rigidity of the colonial state also misses how intraethnic conflicts and cross-class alliances could both fuel political conflict and retard mass insurrection.[113]

Economic symbioses between pueblos de indios and haciendas did divide communities and work against a mass insurrection in 1812. But the Morelos region was almost as precociously proto-Mexican as the Bajío, where the insurgency began and continued. Both areas were rapidly expanding centers of commercial agriculture with many recent Indian and non-Indian migrants; both experienced powerful new pressures on land, water, and labor; both exhibited dense webs of political, economic, and social relationships with long strands that crossed many places and ranks at a time; and both prompted colonial officials to write gloomy reports about political unrest and general unruliness in the years before 1810.

If this study has a bearing on why the insurrection took hold in the Bajío more than in Morelos, two differences between them may have been especially important. First, even with the great economic and social changes of the 18th century, rural people of the Cuernavaca and Cuautla districts remained more rooted in pueblos and haciendas and more attached to local interests and their factional struggles, as Mariano Matamoros observed for central Mexico as a whole. Much of the Bajío's dense population was less rooted in this way by 1810, more dispersed among ranchos and rancherías, more transient, and somewhat less tied into the colonial system of administration and justice. As the subdelegado of Dolores, Guanajuato (Miguel Hidalgo's home district), observed in 1805:

> In this vast district, there is no judge but the *subdelegado* for the large number of inhabitants to obey. This lack of subordination gives rise to some disorders, particularly in the weddings and other events that are celebrated among the people of these *ranchos*. There one encounters brawls, drunkenness, illegal gambling, and other offenses . . . that cannot be prevented [by the subdelegado alone]. I fear that in the near future this unruliness will grow with robberies and murders, as is already becoming evident since the resignation of Provincial Lt. Manuel Vizente de Salas of the Acordada, whose presence controlled to a considerable extent the robbers in these parts.[114]

Second, in the Bajío, clerical leadership and popular piety promoted social alliances—from mestizo and mulato sharecroppers, mineworkers, and artisans, to village Indians and Indian migrants, to creole ranchers, hacienda administrators, and militiamen. In Morelos, the authority of the curas meant less to the webs of association and trust. Though campesinos, estate owners, and townspeople in Morelos still regarded themselves as Christians, they were unlikely to look to a priest for political and moral leadership, especially if he was implicated in local competition for land, water, labor, and money. A priest of shaky credentials who tried to assume leadership would probably have found as many parishioners opposing him as following him. Matamoros brought parishioners with him in 1812, but neither he nor Morelos could recruit the kind of following in this region that Morelos commanded in Michoacán and Guerrero, and Hidalgo mobilized in the Bajío and Jalisco.

The Morelos area stands near one pole of priest-parishioner experience in 18th-century New Spain. Most parish priests who had served there would have agreed with Antonio Arpide, the Franciscan doctrinero of Xiuctepec in 1753, that his flock resisted and discredited him at every turn. Those who did not have a lawsuit pending against him "either do not have lands to mortgage . . . or are too few in number to collect enough money to fight."[115] Such anticlericalism did not mean anti-Catholic; nor did it mean that priests were no longer needed. Curas and vicarios in the Cuernavaca and Cuautla districts were still provided a good living (albeit often grudgingly and late), and hundreds or thousands of people still flocked to the archbishop for confirmation at the stops he made on his pastoral visits to the area. In this sense, parishioners of rural Morelos were more like the 19th-century European Catholics described by Hugh McLeod: "many Catholics who were violently anti-clerical and never went to mass continued to turn to the saints in times of need, to ascribe supernatural potency to the church's sacraments, holy days, buildings—and indeed priests."[116]

But Catholicism had become a less powerfully unifying idea in Morelos than in other parts of central and western Mexico in the 18th century. Parish priests in Morelos were, as elsewhere, in the middle, but not so much in their accustomed role of a mediator who integrated worlds, struck the balance, and reconciled differences in spiritual and temporal affairs. Most found themselves lodged between contentious, secretive, or indifferent parishioners and regalist officials, without the option of simply joining one or the other. Little wonder that few of them warmed to the later Bourbons' Enlightenment vision of Indian goodness, of a loving Christianity stripped of fear and discipline, and of parish priests as spiritual specialists and public-works benefactors.

Glossary

Glossary

Foreign words that are used only once and defined in place do not appear here. Likewise, many foreign words that have passed into English (e.g., aguardiente) are not listed. A few English terms are included because of their special importance or special usage in this study. Terms that are listed separately (save for ones used over and over, such as curas and Indians) are given in small capital letters.

a título . . ., see under Título

Acordada. The court and royal constabulary established in 18th-century Mexico to combat highwaymen

afromestizo. Person of mixed African, Indian, and European ancestry (not a term used in the colonial period)

alabado. Hymn sung in praise of the consecrated Host when it is placed in the MONUMENTO

alcabala. Sales tax

alcalde. One of the OFICIOS MAYORES in a PUEBLO, *villa*, or *ciudad*; usually the chief office in a SUJETO or the subordinate office(s) in a CABECERA

alcalde mayor or *corregidor*. Royal district governor

alcaldía mayor. Territory of an ALCALDE MAYOR

alegría. High spirits, merriment, euphoria

alguacil. Town constable

alguacil mayor. ALCALDE MAYOR's constable

almud. Unit of dry measure, one-twelfth of a FANEGA

altepetl. Local native state that retained an important territorial identity during the colonial period

arancel. Published fee schedule; here for the services of a parish priest

arancelado. Person or community agreeing to accept an ARANCEL for clerical fees in lieu of customary clerical fees

arbitrista. So-called reformer and self-promoter who presented proposals to the crown for the renewal of Spanish greatness, especially in the 17th and 18th centuries

arca de tres llaves. Locked community chest requiring three keys to open. In Indian communities the keys were usually held by the parish priest, the district lieutenant, and the GOBERNADOR or ALCALDE of the community.

arroba. Measure of weight equal to 25 pounds; 25 of anything, here especially of lashes

audiencia. High court

auto de fe. Public ceremony at which sentences of the Inquisition were announced (in English-language works, usually the Portuguese *auto-da-fé*)

auxilio. Aid, assistance; here royal auxilio, or enforcement by crown officers of parishioners' obligations to the church. Invoked in the late 18th century to challenge *curas'* powers to arrest and punish, it amounted to supervision as well as assistance.

bachiller. Holder of a bachelor's degree. The academic distinction of most parish priests.

balcarrotas. Indians' long hair, often gathered in two bunches at the back

bando. (1) Printed proclamation, especially of a viceroy; (2) faction or party

barrio. Neighborhood of a PUEBLO

bastón. Walking stick or staff; an emblem of the pastor's office

batab. Native noble of Yucatán

benefice. Tenured ecclesiastical office with an income attached

bienes de comunidad. Community property subject to royal oversight; especially in the 18th century, distinguished from *bienes de la iglesia*, or church property

cabecilla. Leader of rebels; one who incites

cabecera. Head town of a municipality or parish (often of a former ALTEPETL)

cabildo. Annually elected council of a CABECERA and/or a SUJETO (sometimes elected only from the REPÚBLICA)

cabildo eclesiástico. The cathedral chapter or council. Its offices were benefices, and appointments were made by OPOSICIÓN.

cacique. Hereditary Indian chieftain; by the late 18th century, more broadly, any local powerholder in a rural area (*Diccionario de la lengua castellana* [1822 ed.]: "leader in a province or a *pueblo de indios*")

caciquismo. Personalist power over a locality

caja de comunidad. Community treasury; also the chest in which the treasury funds and records were kept

calidad. Individual's social standing based on religion, race, ethnicity, legitimacy, personal virtue, occupation, wealth, and relationship to others (e.g., as father or mother)

campanero. Bellringer

campesino. Lit., "person from the fields"; especially a village farmer

cantor. Leader of the church choir; also any choir member. The choir leader was a lay assistant to the priest and was often the local man most steeped in the liturgy.

capellanía. Type of ecclesiastical endowment; chaplaincy; an income-producing foundation that supported a cleric in return for the celebration of a specified number of masses

capitulero. Promoter of lawsuits

carga. Unit of dry measure, generally two FANEGAS

casas curales. Rectory or residence of parish priests

casta. Person of non-European ancestry; especially person of mixed Indian, African, and European ancestry

castizo. Light-skinned MESTIZO; in theory, person of three-fourths European and one-fourth Indian blood

caudillo. Chief; one who commands others, especially in war

cédula. Written authorization; here usually short for *real cédula*, a royal decree. (In English, it is used without an accent.)

Chichimec frontier. The area of north-central Mexico that divided sparse, seminomadic indigenous groups living in desert or near-desert conditions to the north from denser, sedentary agricultural communities to the south; roughly from Tampico on the Gulf coast to San Blas on the Pacific

ciudad, see under PUEBLO

clerical fees, *see under* DERECHOS PARROQUIALES

coadjutor. Coadjutor, assistant; here sometimes a synonym for *vicario* or *teniente de cura*, but usually a priest with a temporary, unbeneficed appointment who was responsible directly to the bishop. A coadjutor was generally sent out to fill in for a sick, absent, or incompetent *cura*; he might be assigned only part of a parish.

cofradía. Religious sodality or confraternity established to promote a particular devotion. A member was a *cofrade*.

colación. Conferral of an ecclesiastical office

colegiata. College of canons; here especially the institution established at the Basílica de Guadalupe in 1751

colegio mayor. Residential college in which various academic disciplines were taught

comisario. Commissary; someone charged with carrying out an assignment; a local agent, especially of the Inquisition

comisario general. Franciscan official subordinate to the superior general of the order, with authority over the provincials

concurso. The combined assembly of aspirants (*concursantes)* and officials in an OPOSICIÓN

congrua. A rent or source of income, normally ecclesiastical

consecration. Here the solemn blessing or dedication of a church

Consolidación (or Consolidación de vales reales). The consolidation of government treasury debts through the expropriation of mortgages; applied to New Spain after 1804

consulta. Here a written opinion

contador de propios y arbitrios. Chief royal treasury official for municipal lands and taxes

convenio. Extrajudicial agreement; here especially between pastors and parishioners over clerical fees

corregidor or *alcalde mayor*. Royal district governor

Council of the Indies. The royal tribunal that governed Spanish American affairs from Seville

creole (*criollo*). American-born person, especially one taken to be of Spanish descent

cuapatle. Bark of the *Acacia angustissima* tree; a digitoxin and common additive to PULQUE

cura. Pastor; the titular or beneficed priest of a parish (not "curate"). Also (though rarely used here), *cura beneficiado*, *cura párroco*, and *párroco*.

cura ad interim. Temporary appointment to the position of *cura*; substitute *cura*

curandero. Healer, conjurer; often a SHAMAN

curato pingüe. Especially lucrative parish

depósito. Custody, safekeeping; here the confinement of women, especially before their marriage

derecho. Law, right

derechos parroquiales. Parish fees, both for ceremonies performed for individuals (baptisms, marriages, funerals, blessings, etc.) and for community masses; also called *emolumentos, proventos,* or *eventuales*

derrama. A general collection of cash and/or labor services, usually assessed on households or adult men

diocesan priests, *see* SECULAR CLERGY

directorio. Formal list of the activities that generated income for the parish priests

district. Used here to designate the territory of an ALCALDE MAYOR or SUBDELEGADO. It usually contained three to six parishes.

district governor. Used here both specifically for an *alcalde mayor*, *corregidor*, or *subdelegado* and generally (in Chap. 16) for the crown's representatives as a class (i.e., for those officials and their lieutenants)

Divinísimo. The consecrated Host

doctrina. (1) Dogma of the faith taught to laity; (2) a proto-parish administered by the regular clergy for people who were in principle still neophytes but beyond the initial stage of conversion

doctrinero. Priest serving in a DOCTRINA; here especially members of the REGULAR CLERGY in pastoral service (head priests in *doctrinas* were often called *curas* or *curas doctrineros*)

dominica. Small sum collected on Sundays, usually from all household heads, to pay for the weekly mass

don (also d.), *doña* (also da.), pl. *dones*. Title of respect affixed to a person's Christian name; widely used in the late 18th century by ESPAÑOLES, Indian nobles, and all priests

Dos Magestades. The "two majesties" of crown and church

Easter duty. The annual confession and communion required of Catholics; usually fulfilled during Lent

ecclesiastical immunity. The areas of exclusive jurisdiction that put priests beyond the reach of the royal courts

emolumentos, see DERECHOS PARROQUIALES

encomienda. Grant of Indians, mainly as tribute payers; held by an *encomendero*

entierro de cruz alta, entierro de cruz baja. First-class funeral, ordinary funeral

epasote. Native condiment known in English as Mexican tea or wormseed

escribano. Scribe; PUEBLO office of secretary

español. Spaniard, whether born in Spain or America; "all white people" (Ajofrín, I: 66 [1763])

fábrica. Lit., "fabric"; fund for the repair and upkeep of parish churches

fandango. Party with music, dancing, and drinking, usually to celebrate a wedding, a person's saint's day, the return of a relative, or some other family occasion

fanega. Unit of dry measure, about 1.5 bushels

fianza. Deposit or bond in surety

fiesta. Community feast-day celebration

fiesta titular. Feast of a community's patron saint

fiscal. Assistant, adviser; here (1) a community's lay assistant(s) to the parish priest; (2) the chief legal counsel to an AUDIENCIA. An audiencia might have specialized chief counsels, such as the *fiscal de lo civil* (for civil suits), *fiscal de lo criminal* (for criminal suits), and *fiscal protector* (for Indian affairs)

fiscal mayor. The chief lay assistant to a *cura*

flexibilidad. Undependable, mercurial; sometimes applied wholesale to Indians

forastero. Indian who did not live in his or her PUEBLO of origin

friar. Member of one of the Mendicant orders in the Roman Catholic church; here especially a Franciscan, Dominican, or Augustinian

fuero eclesiástico. Corporate legal rights and privileges of the priesthood, especially immunity from prosecution in royal courts

fundo legal. PUEBLO patrimony or endowment in land (term used mainly after the 1780's); also called *tierras de comunidad*

gachupín. Popular term for peninsular Spaniard, often derogatory

gallo. Privately sponsored music and singing in a public place; generally regarded as an urban, non-Indian practice *gañán*. HACIENDA laborer; generally used for an unskilled laborer paid a daily wage

gente decente. People of good repute, especially ESPAÑOLES

gente de razón. People of reason, rational people; non-Indians, especially ESPAÑOLES

gente plebeya, see PLEBE

gobernador. Governor; here specifically an Indian governor in a CABECERA

guardián. The guardian (director) of a Franciscan house or monastery and its members, territory, and property; subordinate to a PROVINCIAL

hacendado. Owner of an HACIENDA

hacienda. Large landed estate engaged in farming and ranching. (I. Aguirre, p. 195 [a 1778 definition]: "Haciendas in these American kingdoms are rural estates with permanent buildings that belong to people of more than average wealth. The estates include grazing lands, breeding places, and farmlands. On these lands the art of agriculture is practiced to produce grains, and livestock large and small are raised.")

hermandad. Religious brotherhood/sisterhood; less important than a COFRADÍA

humilladero. Lit., "chapel of submission"; roadside chapel or shrine near the entrance of a town

Indian. *Indio, natural*; descendant of the indigenous population living under Spanish rule; a major social and ethnic category in colonial law. Distinguished from GENTE DE RAZÓN, Indians were tribute payers, legal minors, and usually associated with a corporate community known as a *pueblo de indios*. *Indio* or *natural* was not necessarily the primary identity of people so designated. "Indian" here is distinguished from "native" and "indigenous," which refer to people and practices antedating Spanish colonization.

información matrimonial. Premarital report; the record of a marriage application and investigation

intendancy. The province of an INTENDANT

intendant. Provincial governor; new territorial office instituted in New Spain after 1786

ixiptla. Masked deity-impersonator

juez eclesiástico. The ecclesiastical magistrate designated for a particular parish; usually the *cura*

juicio verbal. Informal judicial decision, without written charges or trial record

el justicia (or *justicia real*). The embodiment of justice; an official to whom royal judicial authority is delegated; especially the district governor (ALCALDE MAYOR, CORREGIDOR, or SUBDELEGADO), but sometimes also his lieutenants

legado (or *patronato laico*). Provision for perpetual masses in testaments

libertad. Liberty in the sense of freedom from servitude or captivity; often appears in colonial documentation in the negative sense of licentiousness

lieutenant. Used here only to designate the lieutenant or deputy of an ALCALDE MAYOR, CORREGIDOR, or SUBDELEGADO (as opposed to the cura's lieutenant, rendered in the Spanish TENIENTE DE CURA); usually served in a particular part of the district that was about the size of a parish or two

macehual. Indian commoner (from the perspective of a late colonial *hacendado*: "Indians who are not attached servants; rather, free people belonging to *pueblos*." AGN Acervo 49 caja 68)

maestrescuelas. Member of the CABILDO ECLESIÁSTICO in charge of the cathedral school

maestro cantor. Master cantor; principal lay assistant of parish priests in Yucatán, often regarded by Maya parishioners as a virtual priest in his own right

maestro de escuela (also *maestro de primeras letras*). Village schoolmaster

maguey. Native agave plant; the source of PULQUE

maleficio. Harm believed to be caused by witchcraft

malos tratos. Abuse (often a synonym in colonial documentation for *molestias* and *vejaciones*)

manípulos. Periodic collections by *curas* of small sums from adult men and widows in place of or as supplements for the OBVENCIONES

manuales. Clerical fees for the performance of services perceived as requiring more manual exertion than intelligence or knowledge

maravedí. Monetary unit; one–thirty-fourth of a REAL

matachines. Elaborately costumed and masked dancers who usually fight with wooden swords; mostly in only Indian performances in the late colonial period

matlazáhuatl. Typhus

mayordomo. Majordomo, chief steward; here especially (1) the principal COFRADÍA officer, elected annually; (2) the individual sponsor of a community devotion

mayores. Assistants, petty deputies, especially of a FISCAL

Mendicant. Member of one of the regular orders in the Catholic church committed to living without possessions through work and alms alone; here especially a Franciscan, Dominican, or Augustinian in pastoral service

merino. Shepherd

mesada. An 8.33% tax a priest paid on assuming a parish benefice

Mesoamerica. The area of dense, largely sedentary agricultural communities and states before the arrival of Europeans; from the Chichimec frontier to the highlands of Central America

mestizo. Usually a person of mixed Spanish and Indian ancestry

miccatlaoli. The "corn of the dead"; an offering in kind made to the priest on All Souls' Day

miserable. Helpless, unfortunate, and impoverished in possessions or spirit; often applied to Indians to suggest that they required protection and pity

monumento. Tabernacle or catafalque placed on the main altar to house the consecrated Host during Easter Week

moral theology. The application of dogmatic religious principles to everyday life

moros y cristianos. Pageants reenacting the victory of Christians over Muslims (or usually here the Moors) in the Spanish RECONQUISTA

mulato. Here person of mixed African and European ancestry or less often of mixed African and Indian ancestry; a free population but, like Indians, subject to the tribute tax

nagual. Wizard, SHAMAN; especially one whose spirit could inhabit an animal counterpart

nahualli. The spirit residing in the liver that a NAGUAL could release into a powerful animal counterpart

native. Reserved here for people and practices antedating Spanish colonization

New Spain. The Spanish viceroyalty that included the territory of modern Mexico; also the smaller area of central and southern Mexico over which the viceroy ruled in his capacity as *gobernador*

nopal. Prickly pear cactus

novedad. (1) "The state of things recently devised or revised"; (2) "change in things that usually have a fixed state or which one believes should have such a state" (*Diccionario de la lengua castellana*, 1822 ed.)

obra pía. Pious fund for the sponsorship of particular devotions; less important than an HERMANDAD or COFRADÍA

obrajero. Usually a worker in an *obraje*, a textile workshop

obvenciones. Periodic fees and collections to which parish priests were entitled.

oficios mayores. Major offices; here in local Indian government; collectively held by the *oficiales mayores*

oficios menores. Minor offices; here in local Indian government. The TOPIL, ALGUACIL, REGIDOR, FISCAL, and ESCRIBANO were usually classed as *oficiales menores.*

oidor. Audiencia judge

oposición. Periodic competition that priests entered for appointment to vacant offices such as parish benefices

oratorio. Private chapel; also home altar

ordinario. Ordinary; ecclesiastical official who exercises authority in a given jurisdiction in his own name, not that of another. The opposite of VICARIO.

orthodoxy. Conforming to established beliefs; here those beliefs stipulated by the Catholic church

orthopraxy. Conforming to established practices; here those practices stipulated by the Catholic church

parcialidad. (1) Division, large section of a town; (2) faction

párroco, see cura

parroquia. Parish

pascuas. The high holy days of Christmas, Pentecost, and Easter

Pase Regio. Royal permission for the publication of papal documents in Spanish dominions

pastor, *see cura*

pastoral visit. A bishop's tour of inspection to communities in his diocese; a requirement of the office of bishop at least once in his tenure

pastoral visitor. The bishop or his deputy engaged in the tour of inspection

patrimonialism. Sovereignty as the personal possession of the head of state; a conception of the state as the family writ large

Patronato Real. Rights and privileges of the Spanish crown in church affairs; especially the king's power of appointment to ecclesiastical benefices

pensión conciliar. Tax of 2% or 3% that priests paid on parish income (*rentas*) for the support of the diocesan seminary

permuta. Exchange of parishes by two or more *curas*

peso. Monetary unit; here the standard silver peso of eight *reales*, weighing about one ounce

peyote. An hallucenogenic cactus bud native to parts of northern Mexico

plebe. The common people, here with the connotation of rabble. (Lizardi, *Don Catrín*, p. 78: "'You are a plebeian,' I told him, 'a base, despicable, ordinary person. My genealogical trees, the coats of arms in my house, my pedigrees, and the merits of my ancestors which you see in the papers before you are worth more than you and all the nuns' houses.'")

de pompa. Term applied to a stately (and costly) funeral

prebend. Member of the cathedral chapter, paid from the income of the cathedral

precepto anual. Easter duty to confess and take communion

prelate. Usually here a bishop or archbishop. An ecclesiastical officeholder, secular or regular, who exercises "ordinary" power; *ordinario*

presbítero. Ordained priest

primicias. First fruits church tax

principal. Member of the local hereditary Indian elite, especially of the RÉPUBLICA DE INDIOS; more broadly, an elder, a person of standing in an Indian community

prioste. COFRADÍA officer, usually lower in rank than the MAYORDOMO, although the term was sometimes used for him, too

promotor fiscal. Chief adviser on canon law and on lawsuits before the bishop's court

propietario. Owner; here the lifetime holder of a parish benefice

propina. Gratuity

provisión. Written order; here always "royal *provisión*," an order issued in the name of the king by a royal tribunal, typically in this case the Council of the Indies or an AUDIENCIA

provincial. Head of a regular order's province of DOCTRINAS, houses, and members

provisor. Chief ecclesiastical judge of a diocese, sometimes also the vicar general

pueblo. Town; corporate residential community inferior to *villa* (a more distinguished town) and *ciudad* (a city); a legal term usually applied to recognized Indian towns

pueblo de visita, see VISITA

pulque. Fermented juice of the maguey plant; the most popular alcoholic beverage in central Mexico

ranchería. A small settlement not formally constituted as a PUEBLO

rancho. Small family estate often on marginal lands used mainly for ranching and owned by a *ranchero*

real. One-eighth of a silver PESO

real subsidio. Royal subsidy; a modest sum of money paid annually to missionaries and, occasionally, to parish priests

Reconquista. The long struggle of Christian kingdoms against Islam in Iberia, 711–1492

Recopilación. The great compilation of colonial law published in 1681

regalist. Here a priest or royal official who supported greater royal authority over the church; defender of the PATRONATO

regidor. Councilman; secondary officer of the CABILDO or town council

regla fija. Lit., "fixed rule"; principle of government frequently invoked by Bourbon administrators to emphasize strict enforcement of the written law

regular clergy. Members of religious orders (such as the Jesuits or Mercedarians) who lived according to the rules of their community; here especially members of the Franciscan, Dominican, and Augustinian orders who worked as DOCTRINEROS of the 18th century (cf. SECULAR CLERGY)

relación de méritos y servicios. Professional resumé or certified account of qualifications submitted by candidates in OPOSICIONES

relator. Clerk responsible for drawing up accounts of cases for judicial review by the AUDIENCIA

renta. Income pertaining to an office (here of *curas*)

repartimiento de mercancías. Monopoly trading privilege of a district governor within his territory

repartimiento de mulas. Monopoly on the sale of mules by a district governor within his territory

república de indios. Lit., "Indian republic"; voting body of an Indian political community; usually the current officeholders, former officeholders, and male elders

residencia. Trial held at the end of a term in office

royalist. Partisan of the Spanish crown during the Independence War

rudeza. Coarseness; term especially applied to Indians

sacristán. Sexton or sacristan in charge of church property, especially the ornaments and the priest's vestments

sagrario. Lit., the part of a church where the Host is kept; here the *sagrario metropolitano* — cathedral parish and church of Mexico City or Guadalajara

Santísimo. The consecrated Host

santocal. Home altar

secular clergy. Diocesan priests directly under the bishop's authority (cf. REGULAR CLERGY)

secularization. Conversion of DOCTRINAS administered by the REGULAR CLERGY into PARROQUIAS administered by the SECULAR CLERGY

Semana Santa. Easter Week

semaneros. Men and women of a district who work in weekly rotations; here Indian workers in the service of parish priests

servicios involuntarios. Mandatory labor service

shaman. Magician and healer whose power depends on achieving mystical communion
with the spirit world

sínodo. Royal stipend or salary (Solórzano 3-26-11 [1647]: "salary or stipend judged sufficient for *curas*")

sodality, *see* COFRADÍA

subdelegado. Royal district governor after the intendancy reforms of the late 1780's and
early 1790's; replacement for the offices of ALCALDE MAYOR and *corregidor*

subdelegación. Territory of a SUBDELEGADO

sujeto. Subject; here a PUEBLO subordinate to the authority of a CABECERA

teniente de cura. Assistant or "lieutenant" to a *cura*; sometimes specifically the chief VICARIO
of a parish; used here in Spanish or in full English to distinguish the position from
that of the district governor's LIEUTENANT

tequitlato. Community tax collector

tianguis. Indian market

a título de capellanía. Ordained with chaplaincies sufficient to meet the priest's basic needs

a título de idioma. Ordained "by right of competence in an Indian language," without proof
of self-sufficiency

a título de ministerio. Ordained to pastoral service without proof of self-sufficiency

a título de suficiencia. Ordained with proof of sufficient personal wealth to meet basic needs

tona. An individual's animal counterpart or associate

topil. Assistant; especially the office of lowest assistant in an Indian CABILDO

tributary. Payer of the tribute tax; sometimes treated in colonial documentation as a
synonym for Indian, although MULATOS also owed tribute

tridentine. Coming after the Council of Trent (1545–63) and influenced by its reforms for
the institutions and practices of Catholicism

tumulto. Uprising, commotion

vara de justicia. Staff of office, especially of an Indian gobernador or a district governor

vecino. Resident member of a town; here reserved for non-Indians

vicario. One who exercises power in the name of another; here an unbeneficed assistant
to the titular parish priest (not "vicar")

vicario de pie fijo. Priest who administered a portion of a parish territory from a fixed
residence outside the parish seat. He was salaried by the *cura* but enjoyed greater
independence than his other assistants did. Occasionally a *vicario de pie fijo* was
called a COADJUTOR

vicario en capite y juez eclesiástico. Rector or head priest and ecclesiastical judge; often
the *cura*, although the post required a separate appointment and could be held by
someone else

villa, *see under* PUEBLO

visita. (1) Community within a parish visited at intervals by the nonresident pastor or his
assistants; (2) tour of inspection by a bishop or his delegate (pastoral visit); (3) tour
of inspection commissioned by the crown

visitador. The inspector in a VISITA, especially a pastoral visit

Notes

Notes

For full authors's names, titles, and publication data on works cited in short form, see the Bibliography, pp. 811-47. When citations to the same section of an archive appear in the same note, the archive abbreviation is not repeated (e.g., AGN CRS 39 exp. 4; CRS 41 exp. 5). Circumstances have prevented my retracing a few incomplete citations. For this, my apologies to the reader. The following abbreviations are used in the Notes:

AF	Archivo Franciscano, in BN
AFRANG	Archivo Fiscal de la Real Audiencia de Nueva Galicia, in BEJ
AGI	Archivo General de Indias, Sevilla (cited by section, legajo, document, folio)
AGN	Archivo General de la Nación, Mexico City (cited by ramo, tomo, expediente, and folio)
AHJ	Archivo Histórico de Jalisco, Guadalajara
AHM	Archivo Histórico de la Mitra, Mexico City (cited by section, volume, and folio)
AJANG Civil	Archivo Judicial de la Audiencia de Nueva Galicia, sección Civil, in BEJ (cited by box and document, except for uncatalogued documents, which are cited by bundle label)
AJANG Criminal	Archivo Judicial de la Audiencia de Nueva Galicia, sección Criminal, in BEJ (cited by box and document, except for uncatalogued documents, which are cited by bundle label)
AMAJ	Archivo Municipal de Acatlán de Juárez, in AHJ
BEJ	Biblioteca del Estado de Jalisco, Guadalajara
Bienes	Bienes Nacionales ramo, in AGN
BMM	Mexican Manuscripts, Bancroft Library, University of California, Berkeley
BN	Biblioteca Nacional, Mexico City

CA	Cofradías y Archicofradías ramo, in AGN
CAAG	Cathedral Archive of the Arzobispado de Guadalajara
CDCh	Colección de Documentación del Castillo de Chapultepec, Oaxaca series, Instituto Nacional de Antropología e Historia library, Museo de Antropología, Mexico City
CPM	*Concilio provincial mexicano IV*
Crim.	Criminal ramo, in AGN
CRS	Clero Regular y Secular ramo, in AGN
DP	Derechos Parroquiales ramo, in AGN
Guad.	Audiencia de Guadalajara sección, in AGI
Hist.	Historia ramo, in AGN
Inq.	Inquisición ramo, in AGN
Itin.	Alonso de la Peña Montenegro, *Itinerario para Parochos de Indios* (cited by libro, tratado, and sección)
JCB	File B760 A973i, in John Carter Brown Library, Providence, R.I.
Mex.	Audiencia de México sección, in AGI
OG	Operaciones de Guerra 5, in AGN
RCO	Reales Cédulas Originales ramo, in AGN
Recop.	*Recopilación de leyes de los reynos de las Indias* (cited by libro, título, and ley)
resumé	relación de méritos y servicios
Templos	Templos y Conventos ramo, in AGN
Texas	Latin American Collection, Benson Library, University of Texas, Austin
Trent	Canons and decrees of the Council of Trent (cited by session, heading, and chapter)
Tulane	Latin American Library, Tulane University, New Orleans
VEMC	Viceregal and Ecclesiastical Mexican Collection, in Tulane

Introduction

1. Tylor, p. 47.
2. Herr, p. 444.
3. Gramsci, *Prison Notebooks*; Thompson, "Patrician Society."
4. Scott, *Domination and the Arts of Resistance* and *Weapons of the Weak*.
5. Nandy, *Intimate Enemy*.

Chapter One

EPIGRAPHS: Ribadeneyra, ch. 8, para. 1 ("No solo toca a el Rey el conocimiento de lo que ciertamente es de Patronato, sino aun en caso dudoso"); AGI Guad. 545 ("¿Se instituyeron los curatos a beneficio de los curas o a favor de las almas?"). The term Patronato embraces the rights and privileges of the Spanish crown in ecclesiastical affairs; especially the king's power of appointment to church offices.

1. Although Gibson, *Spain in America*, p. 149, sees the Spanish state as exercising "a controlling influence" over colonial Indians, he offered a dissenting view on powerful parish priests in his earlier *Aztecs Under Spanish Rule*, pp. 117, 118, 125, where he emphasizes the estrangement of Indians and the clergy, and the need for compulsion in priest-Indian relations. Hunefeldt offers a similar interpretation for late colonial Peru, suggesting that pastors seem to have exercised no effective influence in their parishes beyond their coercive business activities. Like several other recent works that stress the political weakness

of parish priests in the face of community solidarity, Hunefeldt starts from the position that the colonial state in general was weak. Porras Muñoz, *Iglesia*, pp. 508–30, also sees the church as comparatively weak in 18th-century Nueva Vizcaya, but here it was because of the special strength of the crown on this military frontier.

An emphasis on social history over the past 30 years has led some historians to dismiss the study of the state (usually taken to mean government institutions) as anachronistic (in the sense of imposing modern experience on colonial history) or practically irrelevant to the lines of consequential change and continuity in colonial history. In these terms, the priesthood, as an element of the colonial state, can safely be ignored or treated as a foil to local political autonomy or the tidal force of independent economic and demographical variables. A stimulating approach to the history of power and preindustrial states that considers organized religion as a source of discipline and legitimacy and is generally more akin to my study is Mann, *Sources of Social Power*. Mann, however, deals less with reciprocities, is inclined to speak of inert "masses" and regard popular revolt as absent or unproblematic in his theorizing, and tends, in his few comments on colonial Spanish America (e.g., 1: 123, 173, 531), to overemphasize Spanish military power and native powerlessness.

The more common emphasis on the great power of the church and curas in the colonial period appears in Farriss, *Crown and Clergy*, pp. 1–4, 238–39; D. A. Brading, "Tridentine Catholicism," p. 22; Van Oss, *Catholic Colonialism*; and Cahill, "Curas and Social Conflict."

The liberation theology literature—with its criticism of the institutional church in Latin American history—has turned in both directions. Berryman, *Liberation Theology*, celebrates autonomous Christian communities in general and sees Catholicism developing in rural Latin America during the colonial period practically without priests. Pablo Richard, pp. 27, 31, 48–52, looks for early churchmen who made the choice for liberation and were followed by the laity toward the creation of the true church.

2. Fernández de Lizardi, *Itching Parrot*, pp. 2, 37. Fernández de Lizardi milks the tale of a parish priest from Tixtla (Guerrero) who refused to order a burial for the husband of a poor, starving widow with a baby at her breast until she paid the prescribed burial fee in full. The author also presents the reader with a visiting parish priest, aptly named don Benigno, who secretly gives the woman the money from his own purse, but he leaves no doubt that the charitable priest is exceptional, *El periquillo sarniento*, pp. 52–57, 209–14.

3. Stephens, *Incidents of Travel in Central America*, p. 104.

4. Stein & Stein, pp. 88, 106, 113. John Elliott, in his forthcoming comparative study of British and Spanish colonization in America, highlights a Spanish American crisis of the 1760's and 1770's that resulted more from the reforms that followed the Seven Years' War than from foreign threats.

5. John Lynch has developed the idea, that Bourbonism aimed at a virtual second conquest, in several publications. See especially, "La segunda conquista." But the view that Bourbon initiatives constituted a second conquest rather than reform is not universally accepted. Gutiérrez de Arroyo, in her recent article on the intendancy reforms, speaks of "el nuevo espíritu reformista" as "la noble aspiración de procurar el mejoramiento moral y material de los súbditos" (p. 89). From the ministry of the Marqués de Ensenada (1746–54) forward, the goals of material progress and royal power were often reflected in public policies. The shifting administrative history of Spain in the 18th century is greatly clarified by Lynch in *Bourbon Spain*.

6. Phelan, *Kingdom of Quito*, p. 73, calls the association of church and state under the Hapsburgs "institutionalized mutual suspicion." On patrimonialism, legalism, and limited flexibility of Hapsburg administration, see Phelan, "Authority and Flexibility"; Crahan, "Spanish and American Counterpoint"; and MacLachlan, *Spain's Empire*. Changes within a Hapsburg political tradition and the dangers of over-essentializing that tradition are discussed by Hoberman, "Hispanic American Political Theory." For an illuminating

case study of Hapsburg politics, in which "royal authority learned to demand only what it could get, thereby saving face and preserving the façade of unchallenged supremacy," see Boyer, "Absolutism Versus Corporatism."

7. For example, the fiscal of the Audiencia of Mexico in 1771 spoke of "la variación que se advierte en muchas doctrinas sobre guardar la costumbre o los últimos Reales aranzeles para la exacción de derechos parroquiales" as "un seminario de quexas, disturbios y pleitos." He urged a "regla fija" to ensure "asertado govierno y la universal quietud de los yndios." AGN CRS 68 exp. 3, fol. 210v. A late colonial guide for assistant pastors informed them that the district governors were required to buy a set of the *Nueva recopilación* (of Spanish law) from the royal treasury before taking office, and that even their lieutenants usually had a copy of the *Recopilación de leyes de los reynos de las Indias*, "which is like the Bible to them." Arze, n.p.

The achievements, the methods, and even the intentions of Spanish Bourbon absolutism at home and abroad are still debated by historians, although almost everyone accepts a gap between intentions and results. Domínguez Ortiz identifies three fields of Bourbon reforms — (1) the reorganization of the government from the top, (2) state intervention in the economy, and (3) regalism toward the church (he also speaks of social reforms, offering little evidence of a coherent program beyond social control) — but observes that even with the regalism of Charles III (r. 1759–88), only some secondary aspects were modified in the direction of greater absolutism. *Sociedad y estado*, chs. 17, 18, 20. Considering government of the American colonies before 1760, Muro Romero, "Instituciones de gobierno," concurs. He finds that problems were identified but few solutions attempted before 1750; and that there was, in fact, a deterioration of imperial control at the time.

Lately, the view elaborated by John Lynch, David Brading, and J. H. Shennan, among others, that the later Bourbons carried through a "revolution in government" and the enforcement of old and new centralizing rules has been challenged from several directions. For Cuba and Chile, Allan J. Kuethe, G. Douglas Inglis, and Jacques Barbier suggest that Bourbon policy makers and high administators were eclectic pragmatists who could be adept at consultation and compromise (Kuethe & Inglis, "Absolutism"; Kuethe, "Desregulación comercial"; Barbier, "Tradition and Reform"). Bernard E. Bobb's portrayal of Viceroy Antonio María Bucareli as a cautious, efficient, tactful gradualist who was especially concerned with preserving harmony and unity encapsulates this interpretation for New Spain, although Bobb conveys the misleading impression that there were no important problems in church-state relations during Bucareli's term.

Pietschmann, "Consideraciones," offers a different interpretation, which is bound to continue the debate and deserves close scrutiny — that especially in the intendancy reforms, the later Bourbons did begin a "profound and invisible revolution," but it amounted to "liberalizing intentions," promoting decentralization and a more open society, not centralization and special privilege. While his interpretation demonstrates that doctrinaire centralization is not an adequate representation of Bourbon administrative policies, regalism and royal revenue — more than protoliberalism — seem to have animated the ecclesiastical reforms of this period, and Pietschmann misses the physiocratic quality of Bourbon economic policies: authoritarian, centralizing government to guarantee the market and individual freedom. Bourbon initiatives in the late 18th century clearly built on a long history of attempts to concentrate power in the monarchy.

8. Not surprisingly, it was under Charles III that Spanish and colonial coinage began to display the king's portrait as the emblem of monarchy. On European conceptions of order and the holiness of royalty and royal mediation by analogy to the human body — inspired by the idea of the church as the mystical body of Christ — see R. Gutiérrez, pp. 95–98 and the accompanying notes. Crahan, "Spanish and American Counterpoint," and

MacLachlan, *Spain's Empire*, consider the disturbance of mutual interests of the crown, peninsular elites, and creoles by Bourbon initiatives.

9. R. H. Tawney, quoted in Shils, *Center and Periphery*, p. xx. Brading, *First America*, ch. 22, provides a good introduction to Bourbon regalism in the colonial context, especially in terms of the thought of two influential Spanish ministers, Campomanes and Jovellanos. Also especially valuable on the secular state in the 18th century (as well as on the profound economic and social changes of the time) is R. Gutiérrez, ch. 10.

As Crahan, "Civil-Ecclesiastical Relations," notes, the "dual nature of government action" (in which the Hapsburgs intended harmonious relations with church authorities, and bishops accepted a principle of royal intervention) had already been challenged in the late 17th century by royal officials in America, who acted on their own in church-state relations and urged the crown to exercise more direct control over the church. The later Bourbons, then, represented a culmination of changing church-state relations that had been building for more than a century. Bourbon attacks on the clergy's traditional public role is a theme of Martínez Albiach, especially ch. 3.

10. AGN RCO 43 exp. 23, May 6, 1709, decree that vacant parishes should be filled quickly; RCO 37 exp. 85, Feb. 20, 1716 (in accord with cedulas of July 30, 1714 and Aug. 19, 1714), decree calling for the construction of new royal jails in the district seats; RCO 39 exp. 32, Jan. 21, 1718, decree allowing the viceroy to reduce the number of stipends paid to parish priests, and commanding priests not to demand fees higher than the published schedule allowed; RCO 46 exp. 11, 1727, decree urging bishops to punish parish priests for concubinage; RCO 132 exp. 154, 1737, decree reasserting the crown's right to the tithe; RCO 69 exp. 67, July 12, 1739, cedula stressing the royal authorities' role as protectors of the Indians, implicitly reducing the role of the clergy.

11. The 1748 decree was reiterated in AGN Bandos 4 exp. 9, June 20, 1749. The 1749 law on secularization is taken up in Ch. 10; on the other 1749 decrees, see Bandos 4 exp. 9; and AGN RCO 69 exp. 5. For the Jan. 31, 1750, bandos on sodalities and the supervision of community property, see Bandos 4 exps. 15, 16, and 17. A copy of the decree on asylum is in RCO 70 exp. 29.

The publication of Ribadeneyra y Barrientos's *Manual compendio* in 1755 was another event in the legal history of regalism and the redefinition of the place of priests in their parishes before the reign of Charles III. This treatise on the royal Patronato in the Indies by the fiscal del crimen of the Audiencia of Mexico went beyond amplifying the crown's power of appointment to ecclesiastical benefices. Giving special attention to parish priests, it asserted wider royal authority (albeit through bishops) to supervise the conduct of pastors and the education of Indians. See Ribadeneyra, ch. 11, paras. 27–30; ch. 12, para. 14; and ch. 13, paras. 1–11, 30. Ribadeneyra's regalist vision of church-state relations is discussed in de la Hera, *Regalismo borbónico*, pp. 165–67, and García Gutiérrez, *Apuntes*, pp. 185–90.

12. 1764: AGN Bandos 5 exp. 101; BEJ Papeles de Derecho, 3: 66–78; AGN RCO 85 exp. 99. 1765: Papeles de Derecho, 1: 389v–401r; AGI Guad. 345. 1766: Bandos 7 exp. 20; Matraya y Ricci, pp. 334–35. 1767: Bandos 7 exp. 8. 1768: RCO 92 exp. 102; RCO 93 exp. 47; Bandos 7 exp. 28; Matraya y Ricci, pp. 335–36. 1769: Bandos 7 exps. 47, 91; RCO 96 exp. 102.

13. 1771: AGN RCO 101 exp. 20; Matraya y Ricci, p. 343. 1772: BEJ Papeles de Derecho, 3: 66–78, plan de curatos (the resulting reports are found in AGI Guad. 348). 1773: AGN Bandos 8 exps. 28, 33. 1774: Bandos 5 exp. 68. 1775: Papeles de Derecho, 3: 500–504. 1777: Bandos 10 exp. 1. 1782: RCO 123 exp. 164. 1783: AGI Mex. 2582. 1786: RCO 134 exp. 27; RCO 136 exp. 135; Papeles de Derecho, 2: 178–79; RCO 138 exp. 238; R. Gutiérrez, pp. 315–18; Seed, pp. 200–215. A chronological review of royal cedulas con-

cerning the church in New Spain during the reign of Charles III in Floris Margadant, pp. 17–53, likewise gives the impression of more regulation and supervision of the church as auxiliary to the royal government. Floris Margadant distinguishes two phases of church reform under Charles III: 1759–71, period of "reformist euphoria," and 1771–88, onset of a more cautious reforming spirit.

14. AGN Bandos 15 exp. 27 ("el despotismo con que la Jurisdicción Eclesiástica procuraba deprimir la Autoridad Real").

15. 1789: AGN Bandos 15 exps. 2, 27; AGI Guad. 352, 545 (intendants' plans for parish reforms); AGN RCO 143 exp. 200; AGN Templos 24; Matraya y Ricci, p. 404. 1791: BEJ Papeles de Derecho, 3: 98v–99v. 1795: RCO 161 exp. 196 1796: RCO 163 exp. 79; Papeles de Derecho, 2: 263v–264v. 1797: Bandos 19 exp. 101; Papeles de Derecho, 3: 86–94; RCO 167 exps. 288, 291. 1799: RCO 174 exp. 199. 1801: RCO 182 exp. 95. 1803: RCO 190 exp. 33. In 1799 Manuel Abad y Queipo, then dean of the cathedral chapter at Valladolid, warned the crown that the royal cedula of Oct. 25, 1795, and related decrees restricting ecclesiastical immunity from prosecution in the royal courts were an attack on the very existence of the clergy, Hernández y Dávalos, 2: 823–52.

The *consolidación de vales* decree of 1804 was not directed at parish priests in particular. It affected those who owned rural properties encumbered with capellanías that were being called in, but few parish priests seem to have held capellanías, and those who had them lost income when the amortizations took place. (This royal cedula and instruction appear in Pérez Lugo, pp. 55–68.) But the crown was interested in tapping church wealth for revenue to finance international wars, especially between 1780 and 1808, as Marichal demonstrates. On Bourbon interest in church wealth as a source of royal revenue, see K. W. Brown, ch. 6.

16. AGN CRS 23 exp. 4; CRS 67 exp. 7. The stricture against departures from precedent was made as early as 1704, when the Council of the Indies recommended against "innovations" in the secularization of parishes "that might disturb peace among the natives" (que pueda perturbar la paz de los naturales). AGI Mex. 717.

17. AJANG Civil, box 80, doc. 2. Customary practices of pueblos in their own affairs were less often challenged. For example, the fiscal of the Audiencia of Mexico warned against violating custom when the pastor wanted to eliminate local Indian sponsors of the saints in Totomaloyan (Sultepec district, Edo. de México) in 1798: "no deve procederse para removerlas [pueblo customs] sin perfecto conocimiento de la causa." AGN CRS 206 exp. 3, fol. 202r.

18. For example, AGN Templos 25 exp. 8; AJANG Criminal, box 20, doc. 2.

19. See Gerhard, *Guide* and *North Frontier*.

20. AGN Hist. 319 exp. 21, 1772. De la Hera observes that 18th-century regalism was less a matter of new laws and institutions than the gradual extension of "a new juridical philosophy" based on the idea of a state church, in which royal authority replaced papal authority over ecclesiastical matters, and a clearer line was drawn separating spiritual and temporal affairs. "Notas," p. 410; *Regalismo borbónico*, pp. 18–21, 122. See also De la Hera, "Reforma de la inmunidad personal"; Lopétegui & Zubillaga, *Historia de la iglesia*, ch. 30; and Giménez Fernández. On the roots of regalism in the 16th-century Catholic reformation, see Parker; and Poole, *Pedro Moya de Contreras*.

21. Callahan, *Church*, p. 11; see also p. 68. Leading regalist bishops like Lorenzana, Fabián y Fuero, and Núñez de Haro y Peralta regarded royal absolutism as generally benign and in line with their own plans for ecclesiastical reform. They believed they could moderate excesses from within the legal church-state relationship. Morales, pp. 18–50; Malagón Barceló, "Obra escrita de Lorenzana."

In the Diocese of Michoacán, Bishop Pedro Anselmo Sánchez de Tagle, Lorenzana's older contemporary, made a firmer defense of ecclesiastical privileges and immunities against regalist initiatives, but without directly challenging royal authority. Mazín Gómez provides a penetrating study of Sánchez de Tagle's predicament in *Entre dos majestades*.

22. Lorenzana, *Historia de Nueva España*, Preface.

23. The legacy of the Fourth Provincial Council was not as great as it might have been, since its decrees were not formally approved by the papacy and crown and so did not have the force of law. But many of its novelties expressed the intentions of various bishops in their own dioceses at the time or were instituted piecemeal with royal support.

24. CPM, pp. 170–72, 189.

25. For the reaction of the bishop of Michoacán in 1798–99, BN Manuscripts, no. 1314 exp. 5; and AGN Civil 1603 exp. 5.

26. *Instrucción reservada*, p. 92.

27. For example, in a complaint to the Council of the Indies on Dec. 26, 1795, about the crown's directives on the tithe, the bishop of Puebla endorsed custom in the most glowing terms. AGI Indiferente General 2975.

28. Lynch, who does not discuss parish reforms, considers 1765–75 a "pause" in the Bourbon reform program. *Bourbon Spain*, p. 340.

29. The use of Corpus Christi rites to symbolize both social wholeness and social differentiation in late medieval England is explored in James, pp. 16–47. For a treatment of the beginnings of a more optimistic view of Indians and the idea at court of a social "conversion," see Tiryakian.

30. The crown actively encouraged silver mining by twice reducing the price of mercury by 25% in the 1760's-70's period and offering some special tax relief for new mining ventures. But despite an impressive nominal growth in production over the course of the 18th century (from 5,000,000p in 1702, to 18,000,000p in the 1770's, to a peak of 27,000,000p in 1804; Lynch, *Bourbon Spain*, p. 355) and a faster rate of growth than agriculture (averaging about 1.4% a year; Garner, "Prices and Wages," pp. 77, 92), the first quarter was evidently the only period of sustained growth in silver production (Van Young, "A modo de conclusión," p. 209).

The extent to which mining was the lead sector of the colonial economy remains an open question. Some recent works question the thesis that mining drove the rest of the domestic economy; among others, see Salvucci & Salvucci; Van Young, "Age of Paradox"; and Ouweneel, "Raíces del 'chiaroscuro.' " According to Garner, "Exportaciones"; and "Prices and Wages," p. 77, much of the silver produced in Mexico in the late 18th century was appropriated by the crown and shipped to Spain, and the mining industry had a limited multiplier effect on domestic production and consumption. Furthermore, Coatsworth's analysis of silver production in Mexico suggests that the real value of mining stagnated and then declined from the 1770's. "Mexican Mining Industry," pp. 26–45.

31. Coatsworth, "Historiografía," and "Economic History." (Garner, the Salvuccis, TePaske, and Van Young have joined Coatsworth in leading the way in this recent revision of Mexico's late colonial economic history; see their entries in the Bibliography). Reher's recent estimates of per-capita agricultural production lead him to agree that the last decades of the colonial period witnessed a declining standard of living (especially in the Bajío) and "a moment of severe economic depression." For a dissenting view, see D. A. Brading, "Facts and Figments."

32. Another author who warns against the idea of the 18th century as a golden age of prosperity is Pérez Herrero. Whatever increase in productivity there was, he argues, occurred before the reforms of Charles III were in place. In respect to silver specifically, he concludes that even the notable increase in production in the late years actually amounted to a decline in the real value of the output. "Los beneficiarios," pp. 240–41. See also his *Plata y libranzas*.

33. Lynch, *Bourbon Spain*, p. 21. (See also p. 371 for his estimate that the royal share

of American profits increased 20-fold in the 18th century, much faster than the nominal growth of the economy or the population). Coatsworth, "Mexican Mining Industry," pp. 28–30 disputes Lynch's dating. He contends that the real value of revenue collection grew fastest from the 1740's to 1775. TePaske, "General Tendencies," agrees, finding that the real value of revenue collection "stagnated or declined from the 1770's to 1810."

34. Indians still accounted for about 61% of New Spain's population in 1793. Lockhart & Schwartz, p. 338.

35. Ouweneel, "Growth, Stagnation, and Migration." Despite the overall increase in population, some regions lost out or grew slowly in the late 18th century, notably Puebla and the Guadalajara region. Van Young, "Age of Paradox," links abundant cheap labor to the expansion of commercial agriculture.

36. Garner, "Prices and Wages," p. 73; Garner, "Price Trends"; Coatsworth, "Economic History"; Coatsworth, "Historiografía"; Florescano, *Precios del maíz.*

37. On these changes for pueblos de indios, see especially Tutino, *From Insurrection to Revolution*; and Tutino, "From Colonial Reconstruction to Symbiotic Exploitation: Agrarian Structure in the Valley of Mexico, 1600–1800," in *Historia General del Estado de México*, vol. 3, forthcoming. For an example of the little-studied encouragement of Indians to move onto haciendas, see AGN Tierras 2772 exp. 17. On non-Indian residents in Indian pueblos in the late 18th century, see Mörner, pts. 4, 6; and Taylor, "Indian Pueblos."

38. Johnson & Tandeter, *Essays on Price History*, p. 2.

39. For one attempt to identify the roots of popular protest, see Halperín Donghi, pp. 36–93.

40. McNeill, chs. 1–2.

41. Ouweneel, "Growth, Stagnation, and Migration." In Hidalgo, the in-migration districts of Xilotepec, Actopan, Tulancingo, Ixmiquilpan, Yahualica, and Tetepango were among the areas of persistent conflict; while Apam and Guayacocotla in Hidalgo and the out-migration districts of Chalco, Teotihuacan, and the Valley of Puebla were comparatively quiescent.

42. Sugawara, "Reformas borbónicas." For Brian Hamnett, *Roots of Insurgency*, pp. 26–34, 71–73, lower-class resentment over "the social problems of incorporation into a market economy," the penetration of mercantile capital into the countryside, and rapacious white capitalist agriculture was given direction by a disgruntled bourgeoisie of creoles like Miguel Hidalgo. More tentatively, Garner, "Prices and Wages," pp. 71, 93, observes that an "inflationary spiral may provide a broader context in which to deal with the recurrent agricultural crises and the controversial political issues of the half-century before the 1810 uprisings." Van Young, "Age of Paradox," pp. 82–83, writes that the deteriorating material conditions—"secular changes in agrarian structure"—in the late 18th century helped create "pre-conditions for the rural rebellion." Garner and Van Young, like Hamnett, pull back from simply ascribing the early insurrections to long-term agrarian conditions, and Van Young notes that "agrarian issues . . . played very little explicit role in the ideological and programmatic expressions of the rebels."

43. Florescano & Gil Sánchez, "Epoca," pp. 204–5, describe the consolidación as "the most serious blow affecting the Church," provoking "the most violent and general reactions against the metropolis." (Their description seems to be based on Flores Caballero, ch. 2; and Sugawara, *Deuda pública*.) Similar views are expressed in Villoro, "Revolución," p. 311; Halperín Donghi, pp. 91–93; Lynch, *Bourbon Spain*, p. 373; Brian Hamnett, "Appropriation"; and Silva Riquer.

44. Brian Hamnett, "Appropriation," p. 85.

45. Lavrin, "Execution," p. 30.

46. This view is best expressed by Brian Hamnett, "Appropriation," p. 101: "The parish priests, who contributed many leaders and propagandists to the revolutionary forces

of Hidalgo and Morelos, depended on their income from chantries [capellanías] to supplement their meagre salaries."

47. Lavrin, "Execution," pp. 41–44.

48. Ibid., pp. 46–47; Brian Hamnett, "Appropriation," p. 102.

49. Pérez Herrero, "Beneficiarios," pp. 240–41.

50. R. Gutiérrez, p. 328. Palmer, *Sculpture*, p. 143, sees this outlook at work in the 18th-century sculpture of Quito, Ecuador. Private patronage and the novelty of small, fluid, free-standing figures—sometimes with secular subjects—suggest to her a "metaphorical step toward freedom" for the individual and the colony.

51. Callahan, passim; Nöel, "Clerical Confrontation"; Nöel, "Missionary Preachers"; Nöel, "Opposition"; and Connaughton, passim. Unlike Nöel and Connaughton, Sarrailh draws a sharp line between Catholic conservatism and the influence of Enlightenment thought on government leaders and others in Spain (*España*, pt. 2, and pp. 698 and 710), though he does note that the old spirituality was not overwhelmed by the new faith among the Spanish populace, that atheism gained little ground, and that even the Inquisition could show some flexibility. The Sarrailh interpretation of Enlightenment momentum and the forces of reaction arrayed against it is applied to New Spain's administrative history in Rees Jones's flattering presentation of colonial intendants, *El despotismo ilustrado*. The Enlightenment in America, its Spanish secular origins, and its importance to the coming of national independence in Latin America are celebrated in Córdova-Bello, *Reformas del despotismo*. Circulation of Enlightenment ideas among the high clergy and in seminaries is discussed in Cardozo Galué, *Michoacán*; and Lanning, "Enlightenment in Relation to the Church."

The more pervasive, less overtly political and libertarian ideas of the Enlightenment in which priests at all levels participated, at least in their formal education, were the vogue of rationality, optimism about the possibilities of applied science, and a more historical outlook that contained the idea of progress, a spirit of innovation, and the seeds of political action for change, even if in the name of traditional principles. Moreno de los Arcos, "Humanismo." Malagón-Barceló, "Obra escrita," gives close attention to Archbishop Lorenzana's active participation in the "historicist spirit of the age."

In any case, as Gibson, *Spain in America*, p. 23, suggests, Spanish American responses to Enlightenment thought "involved a gradual intellectual reorientation rather than a sudden inclination toward subversion and liberty." The lack of a powerful tradition of opposition thought in Spanish America helps to explain why the critique of colonialism after 1810 would be expressed as much in terms of the violation of traditional obligations as in terms of proto-liberalism. Aldridge, p. 57.

52. G. V. Vásquez, p. 339 ("reglamento para el pueblo de San Francisco Apasco," 1783). The three keys in this instance were to be held by the alcalde mayor, the gobernador, and the escribano de república.

53. Freeze, *Russian Levites*, p. 21.

54. Farriss, *Maya Society*, p. 343. In her earlier work, *Crown and Clergy*. pp. 1–3, 238–40, Farriss stressed the great power of parish priests. For late colonial Peru, the research of O'Phelan Godoy points toward an interpretation of anticlericalism, the influence of parish priests, and Catholicism in political conflict similar to mine. See, especially, the first three of her works in the Bibliography.

55. Late colonial bishops, even those who were reformers in other respects, continued to encourage these two metaphorical uses of fire. For example, in his Sept. 30, 1810, pastoral letter, bishop-elect Manuel Abad y Queipo of Michoacán exhorted his priests to "Desahogad el celo de vuestra ardiente caridad, inspirándola en sus corazones, para que se amen, se unan y tranquilicen" (Console with the zeal of your burning charity, inspiring in their hearts love, unity, and tranquility). Orozco Farías, p. 184.

56. Sermon delivered by Dr. José Julio García de Torres in the presence of Agustín de Iturbide at the Basílica de Guadalupe on Oct. 12, 1821 (printed in Mexico in 1821).

Chapter Two

EPIGRAPH: Oswald, *Summerland Sketches*, p. 179.

1. The other eight dioceses were Michoacán (located between Mexico and Guadalajara); Puebla, Antequera, Chiapas, and Yucatán to the south; and Sonora, Durango, and Linares to the north.

2. Florescano & Gil Sánchez, "Epoca," pp. 234–35, 286. The population of the archdiocese in 1793 would have been roughly that of the Intendancy of Mexico, which was listed as 1,162,856. At that time the archdiocese included some districts that were not in the intendancy (Valles, Pánuco, and Cuautla, and parts of Guayacocotla and San Luis de la Paz), but excluded others under its purview (Tlapa, Igualapa, Zacatula, and parts of Chilapa, Acapulco, and Tetela del Río).

3. Ibid. The archdiocese's population grew much faster than Guadalajara's in the two decades before the Independence War—by 37% versus 9%.

4. This is not to say that a colonial Indian population was unimportant in the Diocese of Guadalajara. See Taylor, "Indian Pueblos."

5. For an especially rewarding study of the environmental degradation of the Valle de Mezquital (encompassing much of Hidalgo) by sheep ranching in the 16th century, see Melville.

6. In popular usage, haciendas were distinguished from ranchos as landed estates mostly by their size and wealth. According to Patiño, pp. 195, 198 (he was the pastor of Tlajomulco, Jalisco, in 1778), an hacienda was "the country house and other buildings belonging to persons of more than average means, with their pastures and farmlands, on which grains and livestock are raised." Ranchos were "the modest country house and other buildings occupied by middling and poor people who cultivate the few fields they own or rent, and raise their [own] domestic and field animals." Beyond size and wealth, Patiño was indicating that hacendados might well not reside on their estate, whereas rancheros were residents by definition.

7. An especially rich source of information about population and economic activity in the Archdiocese of Mexico in the mid-18th century is the two-volume, *Relaciones geográficas del Arzobispado de México. 1743*, edited by Francisco de Solano. This section also draws on Gerhard, *Guide*; and several late colonial reports published in one or another of the three *Descripciones* compiled by Florescano & Gil Sánchez (see Bibliography).

8. AHM L10A/21, 1779–80, fol. 271v.

9. Florescano & Gil Sánchez, *Descripciones económicas generales*, 102–13.

10. Lockhart, *Nahuas After the Conquest*, ch. 7.

11. AHM L10B/21, 1779–80, fols. 7–105, 274–75.

12. Patterns described in this paragraph are gleaned from figures in the pastoral visit records of the archdiocese from 1752 to 1809 in AHM.

13. AHM L10A/8, 1759–60, records the following population figures for Indians and gente de razón in the head towns of modern Morelos (figures for both groups are not available for Cuernavaca and Yautepec): Jantetelco, 255 and 300, respectively; Jonacatepec, 337 and 410; Cuautla, 307 and 732; Tlaltizapan, 97 and 213; Tlaquiltenango, 106 and 168; and Xaltenco, 255 and 300.

14. Florescano & Gil Sánchez, *Descripciones económicas generales*, p. 37 ("inclinados por lo común al ocio y al latrocinio").

15. For details, see Van Young, *Hacienda and Market*.

16. Peña, "Evolución."

17. Loose leaf dated June 23, 1803, in AHM L10B/32.

18. The conflicts in Morelos, for example, were concentrated in the densely settled, sugar-producing west and in the center-east of lowland Yautepec, Jonacatepec, and adjacent upland parishes. In the Toluca region, with its great diversity of local settlement patterns and Spanish/Indian mixes, there were important differences even within parishes.

19. Pescador Cantón has discovered a striking pattern of resistance to sexual abstinence during Lent in Morelos. Estimating dates of conception from parish baptismal records, he finds a significant decrease in conceptions during Lent throughout the colonial period in Tianguistengo (Hidalgo), but no such decline in Yautepec (Morelos) in the 18th-century evidence. (By 1819–20, Tianguistengo, too, apparently had moved away from the habit of sexual abstinence before Easter.) *De bautizados*, pp. 67–77.

Chapter Three

EPIGRAPHS: Díaz del Castillo, p. 191; "Franciscan Report on the Indians of Nayarit," p. 217; Pérez de Velasco, p. 72 ("Algo perturbará a Vmd. el ruido en la misa, pero a pocas veces se habituará de modo que lo estrañe si falta").

1. Lockhart, *Nahuas After the Conquest*, especially ch. 6. Lockhart, too, looks beyond a conversion-or-resistance interpretation of colonial Indian religion in his study of the intermingling of religious life and altepetl politics. His interpretation and early colonial Nahuatl documentation, in which indigenous and Spanish patterns often reinforced each other, fits quite well with my emphasis on congruence in religious change, and they inform my discussion of other recent scholarship on colonial religion later in this chapter. We differ mainly in his emphasis on religion as belief, on officeholding elites, and on some unbroken continuities; and in the absence of Catholic priests from his understanding of local practice. His Nahuatl documentation—which tails off in the late 18th century where my study is centered—lends itself to these emphases. He acknowledges (p. 450) that the diminution of Nahuatl records at that time may represent a watershed in the history of cultural interaction; but I would add that it could also (1) be part of social and cultural changes that are not much evident in earlier Nahuatl records, and (2) reveal more about colonial administrative practices than signal a cultural watershed.

2. Christian, "Folk Religion." Luria, pp. 8–9, criticizes Christian for drawing too sharp a distinction between local religion and universal religion as opposed cultures, and muting the common beliefs and symbols among Catholics. But as Christian's words here indicate, such a sharp distinction along the lines of high religion and low religion is not his intention, or mine. On the contrary, speaking of "local" religion rather than "popular" religion means to question such a sharp distinction and opposition. But I depart from Christian in his passing thought that "the government was all-pervasive" in colonial Mexico (p. 373).

3. Ward, 1: 250. The passage in which this phrase appears reads: "One of the most distinguished members of a Cathedral Chapter, while lamenting, in a conversation with me, the debased state of the people of his diocese, used this remarkable phrase: 'Son muy buenos Católicos, pero muy malos Christianos'; . . . meaning (as he afterwards stated) that it had been but too much the interest of the lower orders of the clergy, to direct the attention of their flocks, rather to a scrupulous observance of the *forms* of the Catholic Church, than to its moral or spirit." Farther south, the bishops of Oaxaca would have been less likely to say that their Indian parishioners were good Catholics. The bishop there in 1726 wrote that they "have only the slightest exterior Christianity." AGI Mex. 877, letter of April 26.

4. Tulane VEMC 24 exp. 2 fol. 10v.

5. Phelan, *Kingdon of Quito*, p. 179.

6. Ricard, pp. 277–78.

7. Ruiz de Alarcón, especially p. 36; Nicholson, "Religion"; Nicholson, *Art*, especially pp. 17–27; López Austin, *Human Body*, 1: 282, 342; Markman & Markman, pp. xix–xxi, 8, 66. Synesthesia—the idea that one type of stimulation evokes the sensation of another and symbolizes the unity of the senses—may be a particularly good way to imagine the permeable boundaries in precolonial and colonial Indian religious ideas, the ways in which humans are *of* nature, and the idea that all nature is animated by spiritual power. For two suggestive introductions to synesthesia, see Eck; and Sullivan, "Sound and Senses." Striking examples of the idea of humans being of the earth are the myths and testimony in ethnographic accounts of the earth eating people. See Bierhorst, pp. 74–77 ("Why the Earth Eats the Dead"); and Segre, p. 30, where he quotes Indians of San Miguel Tzinacapan in the Sierra Norte of Puebla: "Somos frutos de la tierra. Es ella la que nos da la vida, la que nos da de comer. Ella nos mantiene y después nos come, después que regresamos a ella."

This sense of the sacred and the cosmos as indistinguishable from nature and daily life contrasts with the more dichotomized Christian conception of nature and the divine, heaven and earth. Compare, for example, this passage from *The Confessions* of St. Augustine, pp. 177–78: "I asked the earth, and it answered me, 'I am not He'; and whatsoever are in it confessed the same. I asked the sea and the deeps, and the living creeping things, and they answered, 'We are not thy God, seek above us.' . . . And I replied unto all the things which encompass the door of my flesh: 'Ye have told me of my God, that ye are not He; tell me something of Him.' And they cried out with a loud voice, 'He made us.' "

8. Monotheism was not a radically new idea to Mesoamerica, although it had a more prominent place in Christian orthodoxy.

9. The distinction between monistic and dualistic religions is made in other terms by Eisenstadt, "Religious Diversity." He contrasts "axial" religions like Christianity that maintain a sharp separation between "the mundane and the trans-mundane worlds" with "pagan" religions that do not. Burkhart, pp. 185–86, makes the same distinction for 16th-century Mexico, speaking in Robert Bellah's terms, of "archaic" and "historic" religions. That notion is also developed for New Mexico pueblos before and after Spanish colonization in R. Gutiérrez, chs. 1–2.

10. Madsen, *Christo-Paganism*, pp. 161, 163.

11. Musgrave-Portilla, p. 29. See also Aguirre Beltrán, *Medicina y magia*, pp. 110–11.

12. Nutini, *Todos Santos*, discusses propitiation as the dominant feature of syncretic Indian religions in Mexico; see especially p. 8. Aguirre Beltrán notices the contrast between diagnosis and prognosis in *Medicina y magia*, chs. 2 and 10. In a suggestive discussion of change within this continuity, Miller writes of how mountain Zapotecs safeguarded their ancient calendars in the colonial period by means of ritual booklets written in Latin script, and how unplanned changes in the form and function of the calendars and the concepts of space and time followed from this transliteration of knowledge.

13. Clendinnen, *Aztecs*, especially ch. 7 and the plate from Codex Vaticanus A described as "The bountiful 'Milk Tree'." The dead were a part of the living in precolonial Mesoamerica, as they were in Europe before the Reformation, but reverence for and propitiation of the dead seem to have had a greater place in rural Mesoamerican communities after the Conquest as well. Veneration of ancestors in Catholic Europe, in conjunction with the fear of hell and the doctrine of good works, made the dead primarily dependents—with the living working through divine intercessors to rescue their souls from purgatory. Chance, p. 162, calls attention to the importance of ancestor "worship" in the colonial period; and Nutini, *Todos Santos*, ch. 2, comments on the subject before and after Spanish colonization.

14. See Clendinnen, "Ways to the Sacred," on the Indians' public worship in the 16th century.

15. Jiménez Moreno, "Indians," is among those who draw the individual/collectivity contrast. Where Catholicism stressed the salvation of the individual soul, native religions put almost no value on the individual as such, emphasizing instead the preservation of the cosmic order and the well-being of the collectivity. Corona Núñez, "Religiones indígenas," speaks of seven points of theological and ritual convergence that contributed to mixture and confusion, but holds that native religions and Catholicism were ultimately in conflict because of Catholicism's exclusivity and Indian religions' elasticity.

16. For an illustration of the teocalli and church juxtaposed, see the map accompanying the relación geográfica of 1576 for Texupa (Tejupan), Oaxaca, in *Papeles de Nueva España*, vol. 4. Two famous examples of superimposition are the parish church of Mitla, Oaxaca, and the church of Our Lady of the Remedies at Cholula, Puebla.

17. If belief is emphasized and conversion is the phenomenon to be explained, Eric Van Young offers helpful categories and commentary in "Conclusions," p. 97.

18. Kubler, "On Colonial Extinction," p. 14. See also his *Mexican Architecture*. For other major art historical works that take the same approach, see MacAndrew; and Fraser. Foster, *Culture and Conquest*, is a historical work by an anthropologist that also emphasizes the importance of what came to Mexico from Spain.

The French scholar Serge Gruzinski offers a complex and richly documented vision of cultural (including religious) change in late colonial Mexico that is consonant with the transformation literature but does not require an early or stable completion. Gruzinski has considered several kinds of Indian resistance and appropriation, but his emphasis is on victimization—on the overwhelming power of the colonial state, on the Spaniards' thoroughgoing project of domination (including a relentless anti-idolatry campaign), and on "dominated cultures [being] swamped," so that colonial Indians were victims even in their resistance. See especially his "Segunda aculturación," p. 199; "Guerra de las imágenes"; "Red agujerada"; and *Colonisation de l'imaginaire*. In his discussion of several rebellious "man-gods" in colonial Mexico, Gruzinski concludes that they were "an exceptional formulation, at the opposite extreme from apathy, withdrawal, and deep deculturation—the fate of those marginal souls who still make up the bulk of the Mexican population." *Man-Gods*, p. 180. As in the transformation and resistance literature generally, Gruzinski's emphasis is on religion as belief and the poles of conquest and resistance by direct opposition. An exception is his 1990 article, "Indian Confraternities," where he explores the Indians' "wonderful capacity for adaptation to colonial society" and resistance of a different and more successful kind.

19. An enthusiastic North American study of this kind, which became a best-seller in the early 1930's is Stuart Chase's *Mexico: A Study of Two Americas*. It is illustrated with drawings by Diego Rivera, whose murals are famous examples of the indigenismo of the 1920's and 1930's. Sergei Eisenstein's unfinished film, "Que Viva México," is another example.

20. Klor de Alva, "Spiritual Conflict," p. 353. For Klor de Alva's views on "mass subordination" and a ubiquitous Spanish colonial regulation of Indians through the confessional, see his essay, "Colonizing Souls." His interpretation in "Spiritual Conflict" is similar to that of Aguirre Beltrán in *Medicina y magia* (especially ch. 5 and pp. 263–73). Aguirre Beltrán posits sweeping continuities in Indian religion in the colonial period and a radical separation between Spanish and Indian social spheres, and between the rational, high religion of Christianity and the magical, low religion of Indian pueblos (which, as he notes, were far more complex and coherent than "superstitious" suggests). He recognizes syncretism in the local Indian practice of religion, but regards it as a forced acculturation that was concentrated in the period 1614–30, when the Spanish campaign against "idolatry" was at its peak. Indians resorted to Catholic forms then in order to hide the old gods and resist Spanish attempts "to impose an alien culture on the great conquered masses" (p. 102).

21. The activities of colonial curanderos, naguales, and diviners in Indian pueblos de-

serve special attention in future research. If they were, in fact, virtual priests and adversaries of parish priests, it is curious that they appear so infrequently in colonial judicial records. If Aguirre Beltrán is correct that Indians regarded illness as divine punishment for the violation of taboos, religious duties, and rules of abstinence (*Medicina y magia*, p. 43), how could the naguales have enjoyed unbroken sacerdotal powers in the face of their impotence to control the devastating epidemics of the colonial period? He relies almost exclusively on Inquisition records, which rarely document directly the religious activities of colonial Indians; and parish priests and Catholicism are written out of his discussions of the late-17th and 18th centuries. The problem, as I see it, is that Aguirre Beltrán's colonial pueblos de indios are culturally stable (if not static) and aggressively resistant to colonial pressures. Their medicinal magic served, he says, to hold back economic changes introduced by European colonization, especially inequalities in personal wealth. I am suggesting more flexibility, more adaptation, less separation from colonial life, less radical resistance, and less fixed, indivisible, conflict-free communities. Aguirre Beltrán's portrayal would seem to work best for areas that he has elsewhere called "regions of refuge," on the peripheries of the viceroyalty.

22. Madsen, *Christo-Paganism*, pp. 126–32; Jiménez Moreno, "Indians," pp. 417–24.

23. López Austin, *Human Body*, 1: 282: "The concept of an invariable order in the universe was one of the bases for social relationships. A taxpayer could rebel against the despotism of the governing class, but not against the government itself. He was not an individual deprived of rights fighting for the downfall of an unjust regime. He did not think of it that way. He demanded equilibrium and moderation on the part of the rulers, respect for ancient laws, the legitimacy of his lords; but the breaking up of such an asymmetrical relationship was inconceivable to him."

24. Most anthropologists, including Nutini, have regarded local religion as spontaneous rather than guided. An exception is Brandes, who gives parish priests a prominent place in local religion in his book *Power and Persuasion*. See also the essays in Badone, *Religious Orthodoxy*, including Brandes's Conclusion.

25. Madsen, "Religious Syncretism," p. 369.

26. Ibid., p. 377: "The real turning point in the conversion came with the miraculous appearance of the Indian Virgin of Guadalupe in 1531." Similar views have been expressed by Jacques Lafaye and Octavio Paz, among others. See the notes and bibliography to Taylor, "Virgin of Guadalupe."

27. Madsen, *Christo-Paganism*, p. 152: "God became a destroyer as well as a creator." See also p. 175.

28. Hugo Nutini's richly detailed books and articles on modern ritual practices in the state of Tlaxcala (especially "Pre-Hispanic Component," and *Todos Santos*, pp. 8–14, 30–36), with their emphasis on propitiation, offer a historical interpretation of the colonial period that is not far from Madsen's. Both emphasize what Nutini calls a stable "spontaneous (as opposed to guided)" synthesis of belief by colonial Indians—"a single, undifferentiated system," "a single belief system"—that was more or less fixed during the 17th century. Both point to the separation of Christian forms from the ethical underpinnings of Christianity. Both are at their best in describing and interpreting what they have witnessed, and both are inclined to move across great stretches of time with plausible, thinly documented periodizations that, like earlier attempts at the periodization of acculturation for Mesoamerica by Oliver LaFarge and Charles Wisdom (summarized by Tedlock), seem more episodic than processual.

Pedro Carrasco, with whom Nutini studied, has given attention to cultural changes in Indian communities of central and western Mexico during the colonial period. In his article "La transformación de la cultura indígena," in particular, we find an interpretation similar to Madsen's in an emphasis on a syncretic state, and on Indians taking control of local religion in ways that separated their religion from "the church" after the initial adjustments of the 16th century ("Sin romper con la iglesia, los indios se apoderaron del culto local y de su organización y se estableció una marcada diferencia entre la iglesia y las formas locales de culto y de creencias"; p. 202). Relying again on Serna, Ruiz de Alarcón, and Ponce as archives rather than texts, he comes to an idols-behind-altars conclusion that "demuestran la continuidad de la religión aborigen que se escondió en la clandestinidad, mientras que al mismo tiempo se aceptaba exteriormente la nueva religión de los misioneros" (p. 199). For the Indians, he suggests, the fusing of their own gods with the saints was both a natural analogy and an act of defiance that consciously continued idol worship. Carrasco goes on to make a valuable distinction between private, usually family, religious practices that were continuous across the Conquest and public rituals that were Catholic in form, which he regards as separate, parallel "systems" (which Nutini adds to his unitary presentation; *Todos Santos*, p. 35). Public "pagan" rites for the benefit of the whole community continued only in very remote places. Carrasco regards the public, Catholic aspects as "politically convenient" more than complementary to private devotions directed toward immediate necessities; and he heightens the distance between official religion and local practice by assuming that the parish priest was a distant figure and "never was an Indian" (pp. 198–203).

29. Huber well illustrates ongoing, cumulative change and great changes coming late in his study of 20th-century fiestas in the Sierra Norte de Puebla. While tending to emphasize continuities, Lockhart's studies on the colonial Nahuas make a major contribution to this line of interpretation. See, for example, "Some Nahua Concepts."

30. Jiménez Moreno, "Indians," p. 410. Of 16th-century resistance, Jiménez Moreno says, "Many other Indians had very soon accepted with complete spontaneity the religion which the friars were preaching and . . . were convinced of its doctrines." Here he follows Ricard.

31. Ibid., pp. 412–13, 429; Madsen, "Religious Syncretism."

32. Madsen, "Religious Syncretism," p. 370.

33. The east and south of the peninsula were precariously incorporated into colonial society. The Lacandones' uprising of 1775, which overran the Presidio del Petén (AGN Crim. 306 exp. 2), seems more like the Indian uprisings in northern New Spain—such as the Pueblo Revolt of 1680–82—than like the political conflicts between Indian communities and the state in central and western Mexico. See Taylor, *Drinking*; and Taylor, "Conflict."

34. According to Madsen, "Religious Syncretism," p. 386, the Maya were inclined to compartmentalize pagan and Christian cults, doubt Christian doctrine, and feel no great need for a new religion; whereas Indian communities in central Mexico were relatively quick to make Catholicism their own. He cites an example of Maya doubting that Christ was "our Lord."

35. See, for example, AGN Inq. 789 exp. 31, 1721, Campeche; and Inq. 467, fols. 436ff, 1607, Yucatán.

36. In Tututepec, an old Indian claiming to be the True Savior assumed the authority of a Catholic priest, administering the sacrament of baptism, hearing confessions, and prescribing penance. AGN Crim. 308, unnumbered 8-folio expediente.

37. For an application of Farriss's model to the Sierra Zapoteca of Oaxaca that traces a different chronology of syncretic developments, see Chance, ch. 6.

38. But, as Wood, "Adopted Saints," shows, it would be a mistake to imagine that private practices were purely non-Christian. Wood emphasizes the "new—or syncretic—expressions of Christian spirituality at the very base of Indian society" (pp. 292–93).

39. On the secular parish clergy of Yucatán, see Fallon; and Harrington.

40. Farriss's parish priests bear little resemblance to the "petty barons" of the Guate-

mala highlands depicted in van Oss, *Catholic Colonialism*. The difference may be real, but the authors' particular research interests lead them to see more autonomy for priests or parishioners than a study of both together might suggest. Van Oss is concerned mainly with the clergy and parish economies. He gives little attention to local religion. Farriss is mainly concerned with the Maya and does not have much to say about priests.

41. Farriss, *Maya Society*, p. 351.

42. Ibid., p. 335. Farriss, p. 318, notes a virtual priesthood in Chiapas. Although she puts less emphasis on open confrontation and resistance to Christianity, the maestros cantores of Yucatán seem comparable to Aguirre Beltrán's sacerdotes naguales. Lockhart's findings, *Nahuas After the Conquest*, pp. 210–15, indicate that some fiscales in central Mexico exercised similar power.

43. Farriss, *Maya Society*, pp. 266–68, 325–26, 338, 350.

44. For evidence of precolonial rites and Indian names continuing, see ibid., ch. 11.

45. Farriss, *Maya Society*, provides a subtle study of continuity within change (finding little evidence of transforming change before the "modernization" of the late-18th and 19th centuries, she still conceives of this history as far from static before or after the arrival of Europeans) and a complex interpretation of local religion that rejects not only the antitheses of high and low religion and Christian monotheism and "paganism," but also the idea of a monolithic "syncretism." Two aspects of her analysis that would benefit from additional research are the emphasis on Maya communities as harmonious and integrated, and the treatment of religion solely as a force for social integration. Farriss's focus on how Mayas created, expressed, and sustained bonds of community (p. 263) leads to a somewhat one-sided emphasis on harmony and synthesis. See, for example, the analogy to Michael Zuckerman's much-criticized representation of New England villages as "peaceable kingdoms" (p. 198).

46. Tedlock, "Phenomenological Approach." Some of the recent literature on Mesoamerica by anthropologists speaks of syncretism in ways that are closer to my understanding of religious changes and local histories in rural central Mexico. Watanabe, "From Saints to Shibboleths," takes syncretism to mean recombinations of conventional forms that express local identity, rather than a completed fusion. He warns against measuring religious change or evaluating its significance by charting elements that have been transferred from one tradition to another. (For a similar approach, with evidence from western Nigeria, see Peel.) Merrill, "Conversion and Colonialism"; and Chance, *Conquest of the Sierra*, ch. 6, also have influenced my thinking about religious change in colonial Mexico.

47. See Colpe. W. Powers, p. 98, takes syncretism to mean the substitution of Christian for native beliefs and practices, and regards it as "a concept so abstract that it is almost useless as an analytical distinction." I agree that its limited value is descriptive, but no Mesoamericanist who has used the term in print would be satisfied with the definition of syncretism as substitution.

48. Burkhart, especially ch. 1 and the conclusion.

49. Clendinnen, "Ways to the Sacred," identifies appropriation (by both Indians and Spaniards) as the process of religious change that explains great continuities. Perhaps this gives too much weight to choice. On the Spanish side, she identifies dressing the religious images as a popular habit that followed Indian practice (although, according to Nolan & Nolan, p. 213, dressing images in elaborate costumes was popular in medieval Spain). Aguirre Beltrán, *Medicina y magia*, p. 266, adds the example of peyote and other hallucinogenic drugs that were well known to Indians as a means of divination and adopted by non-Indians for the same purpose in the colonial period. He sees this appropriation of Indian medicinal practices into the dominant culture as an ironic twist to the Conquest.

50. See Clendinnen, "Franciscan Missionaries," p. 241 (the notion of religion as lived here draws on Christian, *Local Religion*; and, among Weismann's works, *Mexico in Sculp-*

ture). For a more recent art historical study that pursues this idea of Mesoamerican concepts expressed in Christian terms, see Callaway.

51. Pérez de Velasco, p. 72.

52. Clendinnen, "Ways to the Sacred," pp. 124–25.

53. For a new introduction to the culture of the Mexica's capital of Tenochtitlan at the time of the Spanish Conquest, see Clendinnen, *Aztecs*.

54. The formulation "logical transformations based on earlier cultural content" (W. Powers, p. 124) describes much the same process. Clendinnen, "Ways to the Sacred," treats the 16th- and early 17th-century descriptions of Indian religious practices by priests as texts as well as archives. Her comments about the authors as "trans-local" men attached to horticultural metaphors and about a "trade store model" of religious change, in which religions are displaced and replaced, should give pause to anyone inclined to extract nuggets of ethnographic information from these sources for a description of religious practices without considering what is missing from them. Aguirre Beltrán, *Medicina y magia*, pp. 263–64, 271, contributes to a critical evaluation of clerical texts on Indian "idolatry" by identifying the period 1614–30 as the peak of Inquisition repression rather than the peak of "idolatry."

55. Weismann & Sandoval, p. 198.

56. Carrillo y Gariel, *El cristo*. The chest cavity of two other broken cristos de caña he examined were also formed around sheafs of paper. Ibid., pp. 79–83.

57. In the spirit of this metaphor, see Platt for a well-developed study of "an original Andean configuration of Christianity," in which colonial Indians incorporated Christian principles without abandoning older conceptions of divinity.

58. This distinction between faith (as a community's ultimate concerns, "one's primary apprehension of the sacred") and belief (as the smaller category of formulated understandings, "one's secondary articulation" of the sacred) is made by Boys. I am indebted to Kimberley Raymond for this reference.

59. Clendinnen, *Aztecs*, pp. 255, 258. Markman & Markman, p. 178, posit still greater continuity in Indian religion in the face of European colonization by suggesting that the ongoing tradition of masked rituals "carried within their symbolic features the same meanings they had embodied in pre-Columbian society, [allowing] the mask to retain its centrality as a metaphor for the most fundamental relationship between humanity and the world of the spirit that created and sustains human life."

60. *Itin.* 2-4-3.

61. *Itin.* 2-4-4. O'Neil, "*Saceredotes ovvero strione*," observes that superstition is an inevitably pejorative term "defined in opposition to a given culture's concept of true religion." Measured against the "militant monotheism" of Christianity, superstitions are by definition the products of false, excessive, and inappropriate religious attitudes.

62. AGN RCO 126 exp. 137, 1777, Oaxaca.

63. Greenleaf, "Inquisition and the Indians." There is some incidental documentation on Indian religious practices in AGN Inq., mainly short reports by people who were not aware that the Inquisition could not prosecute such cases. The episcopal and secular courts retained jurisdiction over Indian "idolatry" but apparently did not exercise it often in these two dioceses during the late colonial period.

64. Torres, p. 39 ("pescando tantas almas"). See also AGN CRS 68 exp. 3, cura's letter, Nov. 2, 1771; and BMM 135 exp. 18, 1719.

65. AGI Mex. 2588, Jan. 26, 1784, report.

66. O'Neil, "*Sacerdote ovvero strione*," pp. 53–83. See also O'Neil, "Superstition," which places the height of the Roman Catholic campaign against popular magic in Europe during the early 17th century.

67. One exception was the priest Joseph Navarro de Vargas, who reported similar evi-

dence of Indian "idolatry" but also spoke of Christian piety in his relatively optimistic account of 1734.

68. Ruiz de Alarcón, p. 42.

69. Indians were said to see shapes of gods in the clouds, especially serpents during the rainy season. "Franciscan Report," p. 212. The parish of Huizquilucan, in the mountains just north of the Valley of Mexico, was especially renowned for "idolatries" in the 18th and 19th centuries. In 1762, the parish priest, Dr. Joseph de Zelada, reported that he was trying to rid the community of "idolatries in the mountains," where many local charcoal makers lived and worked for extended periods. Tulane VEMC 39 exp. 15. Elaborate cave ceremonies, involving alcoholic beverages and stone idols, were reported there in 1769. AGN Crim. 120 exp. 25. As late as 1908, a visitor wrote that among these people— "one of the most conservative and reserved of Mexican Indian populations"—a great boulder known as the moon stone was the object of prayers and offerings. Starr, *In Indian Mexico*, pp. 56–67.

70. Ruiz de Alarcón, p. 29.
71. Ibid., p. 47.

72. Ponce, pp. 373, 379; Serna, p. 77.
73. Ponce, pp. 371, 375, 378.

74. Serna, pp. 17, 31.
75. Ibid., p. 37.

76. See Grigsby for the lore of caves as at once places of origin—the womb of the earth, associated with both rain (water rising through caves on prominent mountains to make rain clouds) and sustenance (as storehouses filled with valuables)—and places of death. Grigsby regards caves as preeminent ritual sites for communication with spirits of the underworld and rain. See also Heyden, "Caves."

77. The equating of heavy ritual drinking with "idolatry," is discussed in Taylor, *Drinking*, ch. 2. The same point is made by Navarro de Vargas in his description of Churubusco in 1734. For a troubled priest's letter about Indian drunkenness, irreverence, and "idolatry," see AGN Crim. 111 exp. 3, 1777, San Lorenzo Tultitlan, district of Tacuba.

78. Torres, p. 39.

79. Moxó, p. 243.

80. Serna, pp. 17, 19. Although Ruiz de Alarcón did not specifically get into the matter of the Indians' Christian practices, he did not, as Lockhart, *After the Conquest*, p. 258, points out, ever "suggest that he uncovered any disbelief in Christianity."

81. Serna, p. 69.

82. Ibid., p. 19.

83. Ponce, p. 372.

84. Examples such as Huizquilucan's Easter cave ceremonies in 1769 are mentioned in Taylor, *Drinking*, ch. 4. Moxó, pp. 203–4, 206, 218, dwells on the Indians' furtive "idolatry" in caves, especially at Easter and Christmas, when the general rejoicing of the season left them relatively free to act unobserved. After visiting the shrine of Chalma or Guadalupe, he says, they customarily went to their local caves and paid homage to their "idols" with the flowers, candles, and incense they brought back from their pilgrimage. Otherwise, they made offerings out of fear when struck by a crisis such as a crop failure or a sickness in the family.

85. Delumeau, p. 174. Delumeau's explanation, which seems to draw heavily on Keith Thomas's interpretation in *Religion and the Decline of Magic*, emphasizes the emergence of a new mentality. As "the critical spirit developed in the educated classes" and "the masses no doubt felt more reassured than before," fear of Satan diminished, and "in the combat between priest and magician, the former carried the day." Colonial Mexico is unrecognizable in this line of interpretation, which treats religion and magic as redundant, and the clergy and shamans as deadly enemies.

86. These late colonial pastoral visits included a *plática* (an inspirational talk and initial observations to parishioners by the visitador) or a generic auto general on the good

order of parish affairs that was read at every major stop in order to warn parishioners and pastors against various vices and superstitions. AHM L10A/4–8, L10B/9–32. Occasionally there was a more pointed warning against local superstitions, as at Tampomolon, Yecapixtla, and Cuajimalpa in 1767. AHM L10B/10, entries 15, 49, and 51. Only at Cuautla in the wake of the movement led by Antonio Pérez (AHM L10B/10, entry 50; see also App. C) and at Amanalco in 1792 (AHM 10B/28, fol. 107) did the visitador intimate that local practices might be more serious than superstitions. At Amanalco, he warned parishioners to avoid "supersticiones, abusos y vanas observancias y quizá cosas peores."

87. AGN Bienes 663 exp. 19. For a mid-18th-century sermon from the Diocese of Puebla to the effect that for the Indians, the Eucharist validated the Aztecs' "false belief" that by eating their sacrificed god, Huitzilopochtli, they would survive, see Andrés de Arce y Miranda, "En la mayor mentira, la mejor verdad. El verdadero Teoqualco, o Dios que se come, discurrido en el diabólico de los antiguos mexicanos," in Rivera, 2: 278–83.

88. The district of Ixmiquilpan was well known in the early 17th century for Indian "idolatry." For example, in 1624 an Augustinian pastor there claimed that local Otomí Indians were still barbarous and idolatrous. He was told by visiting Indians from Meztitlan that a local witch (hechicero) had turned into a tiger and approached them while they slept. They ran after him with sticks and rocks, but he got away and they were left faint and blinded. The pastor described other cases of Indians claiming that they had been bewitched, and that healers and witches sometimes transformed themselves into animals and killed defenseless people. AGN Inq. 303, fols. 69–71.

89. AGN Tierras 2179 exp. 3, fols. 34–36, testimony of Pablo de Cabañas. This cura called the Indians of his parish "gente perdida."

90. JCB, Domingo Joseph de la Mota resumé.

91. AGN Crim. 79 exp. 8, fol. 204.   92. Galarza, p. 247.

93. AGN Inq. 1331 exp. 4, fols. 107ff.   94. AGN Hist. 413, fols. 236–37.

95. AGN Inq. 467, fols. 436–42, 1607, Yucatán; Inq. 437, fols. 65–99, 1653, Sola de Vega; Inq. 456 exps. 16 and 18, 1654, Sola de Vega (Oaxaca); Inq. 457 fols. 64–76, Sola de Vega; Inq. Lote Riva Palacio 42 exp. 11, Sola de Vega; Inq. 734, fols. 323ff, 1706, Teposcolula (Oaxaca); Inq. 789 exp. 31, 1721, Sacala (Yucatán); Inq. 960 fols. 263ff, 1754, Oxitlan, Teutila district (Oaxaca); AGN RCO 138 exp. 229, 1787, Cotzocan, Villa Alta district (Oaxaca). The notorious case of Antonio Pérez and his followers in the highlands north of Yautepec (Morelos) is discussed in Appendix C and at length in Gruzinski, *Man-Gods*.

96. For example, AGN Acervo 49 caja 146, 1772 letter of cura of Xalapa, Teutila district (Oaxaca).

97. Navarro de Vargas, pp. 560, 562–63.

98. JCB.

99. On the dichotomy of black and white magic as a colonial conception of witchcraft, see Musgrave-Portilla.

100. In 1772 Melchor de Morales and his niece, of Tamazulapa in the Diocese of Oaxaca, were denounced for performing a ceremony with a lighted brazier, incense, and a jar of pulque designed to cause the death of the local alcalde or his removal from office. Morales denied the charge, saying that all the people of his pueblo were against him. According to those who testified, Morales was unemployed and a drunkard, facts that were taken as reason enough to treat him with suspicion. CDCh, roll 15, exp. 368.

101. Accusations of witchcraft were also made against women. One case in which the accused asked an ecclesiastical judge to intervene is recorded in the pastoral visit record of the archdiocese in 1791–92, AHM L10B/27, fol. 106: Micaela María Olguin approached the visitador to complain of Fermín Antonio, Indian of Xihuico (Hidalgo) who had spread the rumor that she was a witch and said he could prove it. She asked for an investigation of the charges and the punishment of Fermín Antonio if they were not proved. The visita-

dor determined from the parish priest that the charge of witchcraft was not fully justified ("no se justificaba lo suficiente"), and he ordered Fermín Antonio to desist from defaming Micaela María Olguín.

102. AGN Crim. 1 exp. 7.

103. AGN Crim. 145, fols. 493ff.

104. AGN Inq. 1255, fols. 9–10. Other examples of Indians accusing Indians of witchcraft are AGN Crim. 208, fols. 135ff, 1783, Santa Ana Gilozingo, and Crim. 208, fols. 226ff, 1782, San Bartolomé Ozolotepec.

105. AJANG Criminal, bundle labeled "1799, leg. 1 (65)," Esteban Aguilar.

106. AGN Crim. 243 exp. 1. Isidro Hernández was comparatively lucky. One Indian thought to have brought illness to the pueblos of San Felipe and Santiago Xalapa (Oaxaca) was dragged from his bed and killed in a noisy attack signaled by a trumpet blast. AGN Acervo 49 caja 146, 1772 letter of cura of Xalapa.

107. Tulane VEMC 62 exp. 1; VEMC 24 exp. 4.

108. AGN Crim. 148, fols. 94–105.

109. Clendinnen, *Aztecs*, pp. 55–56.

110. AGN Inq. 1074. Although it is not clear whether he was a shaman, Miguel de Santiago of Tzontecomatlan (in the mountains of Veracruz, not far from Meztitlan, Hidalgo) was an open opponent of the parish priest and his teachings. On Santiago's death in 1792, the priest had buried him in the mountains rather than the churchyard because he and Juan Julián Serna had promoted doctrinal errors among the Indians, telling them not to believe what the cura taught, including the Trinity and the providence of God. Santiago had refused to repent his errors even in his last hours. AHM L10/27, fol. 198.

111. AGN Inq. 510 exp. 112, 1625, Tlaltenango.

112. AGN Inq. 339 exp. 34; Inq. 373 exp. 4.

113. AGN Inq. 826 exp. 8, fols. 199–212, 1729, San Pedro Piedra Gorda, Zacatecas.

114. Peyote use was apparently not a part of community rituals in central Mexico before Spanish colonization either. Clendinnen, *Aztecs*, p. 339, cites Muñoz Camargo to the effect that its use was restricted to the lords.

115. AGN Inq. 1100, Chihuahua; Inq. 342 exp. 10, Cuautla; Inq. 1327 exp. 2, Guadalajara; Inq. 335 exp. 59, Inq. 342 exp. 15, Inq. 373 exp. 4, Inq. 308, all Mexico City; Inq. 377 exps. 146, 284, Inq. 377 exps. 155, all Puebla; Inq. 377 exp. 341, Querétaro; Inq. 1051 exp. 143, San Luis Potosí; Inq. 304 exp. 16, Mapimí; Inq. 356 segunda parte exp. 108, Inq. 872 exp. 4, both Tepeaca; Inq. 5 exp. 14, Inq. 826 exp 8, both Zacatecas; Inq. 332 exp. 2, Acahuato, Michoacán; Inq. 377 exp. 155, Huejotzingo; Inq. 510 exp. 112, Tlaltenango; Inq. 799 exp. 613, Nombre de Dios, Durango; Inq. 1328 exp. 357, Tehuacan; and Inq. 360, Tlalmanalco.

For specific mentions of the medicinal use of peyote, see: Inq. 486, fols. 229–36, 1621, Jalatlaco; Inq. 486, fol. 417, 1621, Cuitzeo; Inq. 339 exp. 34, 1621, Zacualpan; Inq. 356 2a pte, fol. 83r, 1626, Tepeaca; Inq. 304 exp. 26, 1632, Mapimí; Inq. 1328, fols. 357–64, 1713, Tehuacan; Inq. 826 exp. 8, fols. 199–212, 1729, San Pedro Piedra Gorda, Zacatecas; and Inq. 1327 exp. 2, 1799, Guadalajara. More references are likely to appear in the judicial records of alcaldes mayores, as in CDCh, roll 16, exps. 553–54, where a wealthy india of Tecomatlan reportedly sold peyote for leg pains in 1693.

116. Aguirre Beltrán's review of Inquisition evidence leads him to a different conclusion about "paganism" and peyote. He suggests in *Medicina y magia*, p. 147 that peyote was still a god to the natives, and that the Christian aspects of peyote rituals and the apparent "syncretism" between "pagan" and Christian beliefs was only a cover to avoid persecution by the Catholic Church (p. 147). He also suggests that Indians used peyote collectively to go into battle and not be afraid, and that they did not use peyote to predict the future. The differences in interpretation are more apparent than real, since Aguirre Beltrán describes

Indian uses in the area of natural growth north of the dioceses considered here, and urban, non-Indian uses in the center and south. Some of the Inquisition peyote cases he does not cite for central Mexico require that divination and "Indian shaman specialists" be introduced into the picture there. His idols-behind-altars interpretation of Christian elements in peyote practices is also a more likely possibility for places north of Guadalajara, where collective peyote rituals were practiced and the plant was harvested by its users. If peyote became more widely available to Indian shamans in central and western Mexico during the colonial period, its association with Christian elements could have been less compulsive and less a cover for a thoroughgoing "paganism" than Aguirre Beltrán suggests.

117. Pérez de Velasco, pp. 52–53, 84–86. Indian children were said to be especially fearful of the spirits of the dead. AGN Acervo 49 caja 49, 1739 criminal complaint against Francisco de Vergara by the Indians of San Mateo Churubusco. Attitudes toward burial varied substantially, from the preoccupations of Indians in Coatepec, Zacualpan district, with a proper Christian burial (AGN Templos 25 exp. 4, 1784), to the practices in Actopan (1763) and San Gabriel Chilac (1801), where the Indians, acting on the advice of their gobernador, threw their dead down the barranca and let the animals eat the bodies. AGN CRS 179 exp. 13, fols. 398–428; AGN Hist. 413.

118. John Carter Brown Lib., Spanish Codex Coll., no. 52, fols. 11–59. At the time, Ribadeneyra was an audiencia judge, legal scholar, and the crown's representative to this provincial council.

119. According to Ribadeneyra, one practice common to all of these groups was rubbing oil from the church lamp on a person suspected of stealing. If the spot rubbed with oil turned to sores, that was proof of the person's guilt. The same belief was described by a priest living in Temascaltepec in 1715. He regarded it as a "superstition of women." AGN Inq. 760 exp. 40.

120. Ribadeneyra mentioned the skunk's tail in terms of guarding against fatigue, but Ajofrín, 2: 151–52, emphasized the animal's ability to escape from predators.

121. The kind of paternalistic optimism that marks Ribadeneyra's view of Indians emerged in the late 18th century (as discussed in chs. 4–5), to replace the generally dark views of the Indians found in earlier proclamations and treatises of high royal and ecclesiastical officials. Only a half-century or so before, for example, the archbishop had issued a decree on the subject of "Indian idolatry, superstitions, and vestiges of heathenism" in which he lamented the Indians' inclination toward a nature that "produces only drunkenness, superstitions, idolatry, and obscenities." Tulane VEMC 62 exp. 1, June 5, 1714. Still, not all royal officials were so complacent about Indian religious practices as Ribadeneyra. Hipólito Villarroel, the former alcalde mayor of Tlapa, Guerrero, sounded an alarm against Indian "idolatry" in his treatise of the mid-1780's. He gave it an anticlerical twist, asserting that parish priests and bishops were at fault for "neglecting such an important matter." *Enfermedades políticas*, p. 56.

122. Stewart, *Peyote Religion*. In an extended discussion of dual religious participation among North American Indians, William Powers focuses on the Oglala Sioux people of South Dakota. His explanation is that the two religions serve different functions. Together, they are regarded by the Oglala people as the best guarantee for the survival of their community and its underlying values. Powers regards dual participation as a "transformation," an innovative rearrangement that conforms to a new way of life without changing basic values. From Gadow, pp. 235–37, we have a vivid description of the kind of simultaneous worship he encountered in his travels in Oaxaca and Guerrero in the early 20th century:

> The church, even in an out-of-the-way place, looks and is well kept; there are beadles and churchwardens and a choir, and when the bells are run for the "oración,"

vesper or curfew, the people take off their hats and cross themselves; some go to Mass, and they besprinkle themselves with the holy water, and they do all that and more. It is well to be on the safe side; and one can never tell what it may be good for. But go inside, on a day in mid-week. On the altar stand the customary images, etc.; the Madonna in front of the cross, before her a gaudy vase with withered flowers. On either side she is supported by the clay figures of native gods, also supplied with flowers, but these are fresh, and are put into the crown of the idol, which in reality is often shared so as to serve as a flower vase. These "idols" disappear toward the end of the week, when the padre is expected; they are put underneath the altar, or behind it, into a niche, and if the ecclesiastic is a zealous fool he finds them and makes a fuss, and then he cannot even get a "niece" to cook his supper.

In Totolapan, Oaxaca, Gadow was told by a man who presented him with a ceramic idol shaped into a vase that it was particularly efficacious because of its age. It was more experienced than the new statuette of the Virgin that the priest had recently given to the church. The images here were clearly more than symbols.

123. Stephen Greenblatt, in the last paragraph of his celebrated book, *Marvelous Possessions* (pp. 150–51), juxtaposes two images in a niche of the colonial parish church of Tlacochahuaya, Oaxaca, to call up just such a vision of utter incomprehensibility between native and Spanish "worlds."

Chapter Four

EPIGRAPHS: Tulane VEMC 57 exp. 17 ("Ya no nos hallamos en el principio de la Conquista de estos Reinos, en que el ser Párroco era ser misionero, pobre, y expuesto a trabajos, y aun a el martirio"); Machado de Assis, *Epitaph of a Small Winner*, tr. William L. Grossman (New York), 1952, p. 218.

1. In 1758, by the archbishop of Mexico's estimate, there were about 1,000 secular priests in Mexico City and close to another 1,000 in the rest of the archdiocese who had been ordained a título de capellanía. Those who were not in parish service or serving as chaplains on haciendas—and that would have been most of the priests who held these chaplaincies—lived from the interest on their endowments and personal wealth or depended on donations for masses they celebrated. AGI Mex. 2549, Oct. 8, 1758 report. The bishops at the Fourth Provincial Council in 1771 complained of "the large number of clergymen and the few useful pastors" because so many were ordained a título de capellanía. They proposed that all future capellanías were to specify the number of masses required and be attached to the benefice of a particular church. CPM, p. 17.

2. Of the "patricios" of Mexico City—people who by birth, wealth, or virtue stood above the rest—the archbishop said in 1758, "they abhor commerce, the only employment of their fathers; they dedicate themselves only to study and the ecclesiastical state, reduced to no small penury." AGI Mex. 2549, Oct. 8, 1758 report.

3. CAAG, responses to Oct. 31, 1796 circular requesting information on secular clergy residing in all parishes.

4. Ibid.

5. For the archdiocese in the 1740's, Villaseñor y Sánchez, 1: 29–31, lists 101 doctrinas administered by the religious orders (regulars) and 88 secular parishes. In the early 1800's, according to Navarro y Noriega, there were only eight doctrinas under the regulars: Azcapotzalco, Cuautla, Malinalco, Meztitlan de la Sierra, Texcoco, Toluca, Tula, and Tulancingo. The 1805 report in Florescano & Gil Sánchez, *Documentos económicos generales*, lists nine doctrinas. AGI Guad. 204, bishop's report, shows 43 Franciscan doctrinas, 33 secular parishes, and two Augustinian doctrinas for the Diocese of Guadalajara in 1708. By 1772, only 24 doctrinas (of 94 parishes and doctrinas) were left. Guad. 348. In 1796, the

number had fallen, but there were still 12 Franciscan doctrinas and two Dominican doctrinas (Amatlan, San Juan del Teul, Tlajomulco, Amacueca, Atoyac, Tuspa-Tonila-Pihuamo, Cocula, Tecolotlan, Acaponeta, Ahualulco, Etzatlan, and Ahuacatlan for the Franciscans, and Analco and Charcas for the Dominicans). CAAG, responses to Oct. 31, 1796 circular.

6. Humboldt, 2: 82–84. According to his calculation, these 2,392 priests and nuns represented 1.5% of the Mexico City population (compared with 2% priests and nuns for the Spanish city of Madrid).

7. Cuevas, 5: 46. The two-thirds of priests who were not in parish service includes secular priests and male members of the regular orders. The proportion of priests who were not in parish service would have been smaller in the Diocese of Guadalajara than in the viceroyalty as a whole. In 1796 there were 561 secular and regular clergy. Of these, somewhat fewer than 293 would have been in parish service—one for every 0.9 priest not in parish service. Fewer members of religious orders in the Guadalajara diocese account for most of this difference.

8. CAAG, responses to Oct. 31, 1796 circular. As these figures suggest, there were too few capellanías to support most ordained priests. The gobernador de la Mitra of the diocese reported on Feb. 3, 1753, that because of the shortage of capellanías, many priests without their own resources had been ordained for parish service (a título de ministerio). While awaiting a parish assignment, they reportedly lived in penury. AGI Guad. 210.

9. Only 15 of the capellanías in the 1796 report cited in the preceding note are listed with their income or endowment; the figures bunch together at 200p and 4,000p, respectively. Both the median and the mode for the endowments in this sample were 4,000p.

10. CAAG, Benito Antonio Vélez 1796 report on Tepic.

11. *Archdiocese*, 1746, Villaseñor y Sánchez, *Theatro americano*, 1: bk. 1, ch. 4. *Guadalajara*, 1708, AGI Guad. 204, bishop's report of March 20, 1708; 1774, AGN Hist. 318 exp. 2. *Both dioceses*, 1767, Cuevas, 4: 83–84; mid-1780's, Alcedo, 2: 435; early 19th-century, Navarro y Noriega, pp. 13–18, 33–36 (a summary table on p. 44 mentions 244 parishes in the archdiocese and 120 parishes in the Diocese of Guadalajara); 1827, Ward, *Mexico*, 1: 264. Since there were 125 parishes in Guadalajara in 1802, and Bishop Cabañas was reported to have recently established three new ones, the Navarro y Noriega figure of 122 should date from about 1800. See AGI Guad. 543, March 20, 1807, response to petition of Bishop Cabañas. Navarro y Noriega identifies a total of 1,069 parishes and doctrinas in the viceroyalty, only 60 of which were still administered by regulars.

Vera, *Erecciones parroquiales*, identifies the following parishes of the modern Estado de México as established in the 18th and early 19th centuries, but does not give precise dates in every case: Achichipico (1767), Aculco, Amacuzac (1785?), Amatepec (1739), San Miguel Atlacahualoya (1807), Atlacahualoya (1810?), Ayapango (1769), Ayapisco [Yecapixtla] (1767), Ixtacalco (1771), Malacatepec (1754), the Mexico City parishes of San José, Santa Cruz Acatlan, Salto del Agua, Santo Tomás la Palma, and San Cosmé (1772), Naucalpan (1775?), Nextlalpan, Ozoloapan, Ozumba (1785), Tasquillo (1775), Tecozautla (1756), Tecualoya, Temamatla (1759), Temascaltepec, Tepalcingo (1806), San Martín Tepanango (1790's), Tepexpan, and Villa del Carbón.

For 1767, Cuevas 4: 83–84, lists 853 parishes for the viceroyalty. Broken down by diocese, there were 202 in Mexico, 150 in Puebla, 120 in Michoacán, 110 in Oaxaca, 90 in Guadalajara, 76 in Yucatán, 60 in Durango, and 45 in Chiapas. According to Cuevas, 5: 46, the number had grown to 951 by 1810.

Though the total number of priests in pastoral service in the two dioceses is not available, detailed parish records for the early 1790's in CAAG (uncatalogued parish files) and AGN Hist. 578A show 234 secular pastors and assistants in 98 parishes for Guadalajara (2.39 per parish), and 472 pastors and assistants in 195 parishes for Mexico (2.42

per parish). A breakdown by parish in connection with Bishop Alcalde's visita of 1775–76 (AGI Guad. 341) and scattered records on various parishes suggest that the ratio was somewhat higher than this in Guadalajara in the mid-18th century—about 2.6 (2.8 in the report of the 1776 visita)—and somewhat lower in the archdiocese—about 2.3.

12. The meaning of benefice as a term for spiritual office is summarized in Oakley, p. 30: "Just as churches had come to be conceived of as pieces of real property, to be bought, sold, inherited, or granted out as a sort of fief, so too their incumbents had come to be regarded as quasi-feudal dependents and their offices as *beneficia* or rewards." In this spirit, Ribadeneyra, *Manual compendio*, ch. 9, paras. 15, 18, defined ecclesiastical benefice in 1755 as "a distinguished place granted by the king, endowed with an income for the fulfillment of the Divine service." On parishes becoming benefices after 1574, see Schwaller, "Ordenanza del Patronazgo"; and Padden, "Ordenanza del Patronazgo." Solórzano 4-15-87, spoke of Indian parishes as "beneficios curados"—parochial benefices. The "absolute and without time limit" license of the cura is mentioned in a royal cedula of July 23, 1718. AGN RCO 39 exp. 92.

13. The mean age for eight curas in the 1796 report for Guadalajara was 48.3 years, with a mode of 45 and 52. Scattered cases for the 1750's and 1760's also averaged about 50 years.

14. According to *Recop.* 1-13-16 (1553, 1591), an interim cura was to be replaced within four months. If there was a royal salary for the parish, he was to be paid on a pro-rated basis.

15. Two examples of priests who served as parish substitutes before going on to bigger and better things are Dr. José Julio Torres and Lic. Manuel Antonio Vidal, listed in Osores, 2: 253–54, 302. Another kind of temporary appointment was that of cura en encomienda. According to Solórzano 4-15-6, this priest was temporarily in charge of the parish "for a certain time and to serve the church's evident utility or need." He could enjoy the fruits of the parish "as if he were the true holder of the benefice." Unlike the interim appointments, an encomienda appointment could be expected to last for years, sometimes many years. Ribadeneyra, ch. 2, para. 73, specified that the term referred to a temporary assignment where there was no established parish or benefice, especially in haciendas, obrajes, and mills. The bishop of Guadalajara in 1757 reported that it meant an interim cura whose appointment was not submitted to the vice-patron for approval, and that in his diocese it was used for assistants placed in private haciendas by the cura. AGI Guad. 196. By the late 18th century, cura en encomienda applied mainly to members of regular orders who directed doctrinas. See the patronato de oficio records for 1725–30 in Tulane Mexican Administrative Records, vol. 38, where doctrinas were assigned to Franciscan priests as temporary possessions, "not in perpetual title." As the regulars' doctrinas were secularized, the crown continued to specify that their few remaining parochial benefices were granted "precariamente"—temporarily. AGN RCO 167 exp. 235, July 15, 1797.

16. For example, Manuel de Larrainzar Patricio is referred to as the teniente de cura of Ixmiquilpan in AGN Hist. 578A, Sept. 26, 1793 report by Ignacio Guerra de Manzanares.

17. Pérez de Velasco, p. 5.

18. On the duties of vicarios and other assistants to the cura, see ibid., passim.

19. Most of the "distinguished" priests did not hold parish appointments, and most of those who did were on their way to higher office. Very few of the parish priests in this study were among Félix Osores's "distinguished alumni" of the Colegio de San Ildefonso in Mexico City.

20. AGI Mex. 2549, March 21, 1755 report. Basarte's report of Dec. 30, 1755 (also in AGI Mex. 2549) was even terser: the rest of the clergy "were said not to be known for their letters or their virtue."

21. Ibid. Ribadeneyra, ch. 13, para. 22, was regretfully philosophical over the stunted careers of deserving but poorly connected priests—"los que van en tropa"—who were

passed over for benefices in favor of friends and relatives of the evaluators. These practices were wrong, he said, but they happened: "ésta es la frágil condición de nuestra humana naturaleza."

22. AGN RCO 39 exp. 92 cites the Council of Trent (21st Session, Reform, ch. 4) to this effect. In an 1800 suit labeled "Sobre que el cura del pueblo de Mochitlan, Br. d. Juan Valerio Barrientos, maltrata y exige derechos indebidos a sus feligreses" (AGN Hist. 437), the Audiencia of Mexico's fiscal de lo criminal acknowledged a cura's authority to remove a vicario, but added that in the case at hand the cura should be compelled to remove the vicario or see that he reformed his ways. For a cura ordering a vicario to leave, see AGN Bienes 575 exp. 15.

23. For example, the vicario of Tecolotlan in 1799 spoke of coming to this parish "por disposición del Sr. Obispo." AGN Inq. 1346 exp. 6 fol. 46. In 1796 the cura of Agua de Venado, also in the Diocese of Guadalajara, reported that it was difficult to find an assistant to staff one of his vicarías and asked the bishop to send someone. CAAG, report by Joseph Fernando Román in response to Oct. 31, 1796 circular.

24. CAAG, responses to Oct. 31, 1796 circular. The median of 33 years was quite close to the mean, reflecting the balanced number of men above and below the mean in this sample. Many of them were in their twenties but many were also 45 and older.

25. Ajofrín, 1: 69 ("Un curato en la América tiene más territorio que un obispado en España").

26. AGN RCO 82 exp. 72.

27. Ibid., exp. 99.

28. Ibid., 1768; RCO 82 exp. 88, 1764; AGN Inq. 1304 exp. 3, fols. 28–32, 1796, Zacualpan; AGN CRS 140 exp. 4, Yautepec, 1796, witness no. 8, José Miguel Rodríguez; CRS 201 exp. 1, fols. 13–19, 1780, Ixtapalapa; CRS 74 exp. 1, 1780, Molango; AGN Crim. 148 exp. 2, Almoloya, Tenango del Valle district; BEJ Papeles de Derecho, 3: fols. 500–504, 1777, implementing cedulas of Oct. 18, 1764, and June 1, 1775. The standard complaint was that the cura was too greedy to give up part of his parish revenues to an assistant. The tight-fisted cura of Zacualpan in 1796 was said to pay vicarios so little that none would stay. AGN Hist. 578A, Zacualpan report. Other examples include Hist. 578A, 1793, Teloloapan (Zacualpan report), Cacalotenango (Taxco report), Yahualica (Yahualica report).

29. The proportion of assistants to curas grew by about 4% in the archdiocese from 1767 to the early 1790's. There was no change in the Diocese of Guadalajara between 1767 and 1796, but Bishop Ruiz de Cabañas reported in January 1805 that he had added more than 100 assistants since taking office in 1796. AGI Guad. 534. If true, this would have increased the absolute number of priests in parish service by more than a quarter, but would not have raised the ratio of parishes to parish priests greatly because Cabañas had also established 31 new parishes (some of which would have had assistants as well).

30. AGI Mex. 2549, bishop's summary report on his visita, undated here, but dated March 20, 1758, in AGI Guad. 566. A similar argument was made in an Oct. 16, 1772, letter from the Audiencia of Nueva Galicia concerning the placement of tenientes required by the 1764 royal cedula. AGI Guad. 348.

31. Solórzano 4-15-54, 4-17-70; *Recop.* 1-13-20, 1-13-21, and 1-13-26. This standard was not without ambiguity. Both sources sometimes say 400 tributaries, sometimes 400 Indians. Solórzano 4-15-17 also mentions 500 Indians. The actual number of parishioners per priest varied, especially as local populations grew at different rates in the 18th century, but at least in Nueva Galicia the average was not far from the 400-tributary standard in the 1770's: there were 176 diocesan parish priests in 63 secular parishes with 314,194 parishioners, or one per 1,785 (about the equivalent of 400 tributaries if the usual 4.0–4.5 factor is used to convert total population into tributaries); AGI Guad. 341. Gerhard, "Censo,"

calculates roughly 800 parishioners per priest for the Diocese of Puebla in 1681, about half the ratio for Guadalajara a century later.

32. On Aug. 8, 1758, the archbishop of Mexico reported that he had 21 parishes to fill (only 15 of which would provide an adequate living) and more than 200 qualified competitors. "With more vacancies, there would be three hundred aspirants," he added. AGI Mex. 2549.

33. See for example, the Bishop of Puebla's justification for promoting vicarías de pie fijo. AGN Hist. 319 exp. 13, reply of March 31, 1781.

34. Solórzano 4-15-102.

35. AGN RCO 39 exp. 92. According to this source, Trent, 21st session, Reform, chs. 4, 6, grouped all assistants together. Chap. 4 provided that the bishops should "compel the rectors . . . to associate with themselves in this office as many priests as are necessary to administer the sacraments and carry on divine worship. In those, moreover, to which, by reason of distance and hardship, the parishioners cannot come without great inconvenience to receive the sacraments and hear the divine offices, they may, even against the will of the rectors, establish new parishes." Chap. 6 added that "since illiterate and incompetent rectors of parochial churches are but little suited for sacred offices, and others by the depravity of their lives corrupt rather than edify, the bishops may . . . give temporarily to such illiterate and incompetent rectors, if otherwise blameless, assistants or vicars, with a portion of the fruits sufficient for their maintenance" (translation by H. J. Schroeder, O.P.).

36. AGN Acervo 49, caja 68; AGN CRS 81 exp. 1. The first is a 1796 case involving Vicente Antonio Tello Siles of Santa Catalina Xochiatipan. The cura here received a monthly stipend of 35p. Trent, 21st session, Reform, ch. 4, gave bishops the right to determine a suitable portion of the parish emoluments to be assigned to the assistants. In a 1781 royal cedula, the crown agreed with the bishop of Oaxaca's condemnation of the practice of curas keeping most of the parish emoluments when they were replaced by a coadjutor. It ordered the bishop to be sure the coadjutors received "la renta competente para que pueda mantenerse y atender a las necesidades de los pobres, sin grabar a los demás con exacciones indevidas." AGN RCO 182 exp. 78.

There is a good summary of the position of coadjutor in *Itin.* 1-9. Its author stressed the authority of the bishop and outlined the circumstances in which a coadjutor was required. The bishop could and should assign coadjutors to any cura who was unable to serve his parish adequately. They were to be given "part of the fruits of the parish for their adequate maintenance." The position was "revocable and temporary," and the coadjutor "[had] no other jurisdiction than that which the bishop [gave] him in his title." A coadjutor was required if the cura suffered "illness of the soul or body," was incompetent in some other way, or dissipated the church's wealth, or if the population had grown too large for the cura to attend fully to the spiritual needs of his parishioners.

37. As the bishop of Yucatán noted in 1793, some of the priests who lived on capellanía proceeds were so unschooled in parish duties that they were unfit to be licensed under any circumstances. AGN Hist. 578A, Dec. 4, 1793 report.

38. The relaciones de méritos y servicios for the early 1760's concurso in the archdiocese contain a number of examples. See JCB, Juan Miguel Tinoco and Dr. Fermín Aurelio de Tagle resumés.

39. For important recent works on the secularization of parishes in the 18th century, see Mazín, "Reorganización del clero"; Mazín *Entre dos magestades*; and Belanger. Gibson, *Aztecs*, ch. 5, recognized the importance of late colonial secularizations. The extent of the secularizations varied by diocese. As Mazín, *Entre dos magestades*, p. 160, observes, where there were few secular clergy, special concessions were made to the regulars. In Oaxaca during the 18th century, the Dominicans kept 12 of their 21 doctrinas. Likewise, though

the Franciscans had been reduced to a minority position in Yucatán by 1780, they still held 21 of the 89 parishes and doctrinas there. Harrington, p. 24. In the dioceses of Guadalajara, Mexico, and Michoacán, the secularization program after 1749 was more complete.

40. Tulane VEMC 57 exp. 17 ("sobre todo los seculares están enteramente a la obediencia de VE, sin exempción alguna y promptos para egecutar sus mandatos y los míos"). To Lorenzana, secularization and reducing the size of parishes would "lead to order and the appropriate spiritual administration" (para que haia el orden y administrazión espiritual correspondiente).

41. The crown was particularly interested in identifying monasteries with fewer than eight residents. These were subject to closure, and their residents to relocation in another establishment. See, for example, BEJ Papeles de Derecho, 3: 307v–311v.

42. "Tenemos por bien, y mandamos que *por aora*, y mientras Mas no mandemos otra cosa, queden las Doctrinas y se continúen en los Religiosos . . . y que el poner y remover los Religiosos Curas todas las vezes que fuere necessario, se haga por nuestros Virreyes del Perú y Nueva España, Presidentes, y Governadores, que exercieren nuestro Real Patronazgo en nuestro nombre. . . . Y porque los Religiosos en quanto a la jurisdicción no pretendan adquirir derecho para la perpetuidad de las Doctrinas" (emphasis in the original).

43. "Si se hallasen Sacerdotes seculares iguales en número, mérito y suficiencia para las doctrinas de los Indios." Solórzano treats regular clergymen in pastoral service at length in 4-16, 4-17. Though the viceregal appointments of Franciscans as curas doctrineros routinely conformed to the preference of the provincial, it was with the proviso that the appointment was made "no en título perpetuo sino ad movile ad motum meum." Tulane Mexican Administrative Records, vol. 30, Patronato de oficio, 1725–30.

44. Condumex Library and Archive (Mexico, D.F.), Reales Cédulas collection, 1: 3–9, doc. 130. Two other points of perennial conflict between the diocesan hierarchy and Mendicants in pastoral service were the bishop's power to withhold pastoral appointments, and the formal separation of Mendicant doctrineros from the practice of ecclesiastical justice. See BN AF caja 109, exp. 1489, 1726, archbishop's refusal to appoint a particular Franciscan to the doctrina of Huichapan; and AF caja 108, exp. 1476, 1747–49, dispute between the Franciscan doctrinero of Calimaya and the cura of Tenango del Valle, who was also the juez eclesiástico for Calimaya.

45. AGI Guad. 204, March 20, 1708 relación. The secularization issue in Oaxaca is discussed in Canterla & Tovar.

46. Taylor, "Indian Pueblos," pp. 175–76; Palacio y Basave, 1: 159–75. The Mendicants in other dioceses did not improve their chances of keeping doctrinas in the 18th century by arguing for still broader powers. See BMM 135 exp. 16, for a Franciscan initiative in central Mexico in 1734. Franciscans there had been trying to beat back secularization initiatives from Spain since at least 1724. BN AF caja 127, especially 1645, fols. 13–67.

47. For examples of cooperation between Mendicants and diocesan curas, see AGN CRS 179 exp. 13, Actopan, 1763; BMM 1821, description of Apam, pp. 9–10.

48. AGN CRS 69 exp. 103 contains a copy of the 1749 cedula. This was only the first of a whole series: other cedulas followed in Feb. 1, 1753, June 23, 1757, Oct. 18, 1764, Nov. 7, 1766, July 6, 1767, Aug. 16, 1768, and March 14, 1785. See Ventura Beleña 1: doc. 262; Sierra Nava-Lasa, p. 169; and AGN RCO 130 exp. 108.

49. AGN RCO 77 exp. 77. See *Instrucciones que los vireyes*, 1: 572–79, where the viceroy, Conde de Revillagigedo (the elder) summarized these first years of secularization in a letter to his successor of October 8, 1755. The secularizations were going smoothly, he said, because of his close cooperation with the archbishop and the fact that parishioners throughout New Spain "estaban muy mal hallados con los frailes." He and the archbishop had begun cautiously, singling out for first attention the parishes that were vacant or held

"sin la formalidad debida," then turning to those in which the cura had just died. In removing sitting Mendicant curas doctrineros, he had made it a rule to defer to the advice of the bishops.

50. The old encomienda formula of escheatment on the death or resignation of the current holder, the gradual implementation of the two curatos pingües rule, and the periodic suspension of the reform are documented in Tulane VEMC 57 exp. 17.

51. The following list by colonial district is drawn from Vera, *Erecciones parroquiales*; AGI Mex. 727; and Gerhard, *Guide*: Cuernavaca 14 (Cuernavaca, Atlatlaucan [Yautepec], Jantetelco, Xiuctepec, Jonacatepec, Mazatepec, Oaxtepec, Tepoztlan, Tlaltizapan, Tlaquiltenango, Totolapa [Yautepec], Xochitepec, Yautepec, Yecapixtla); Chalco 12 (Chalco, Amecameca, Coatepec Chalco, Cuautzingo, Ecacingo, Ixtlapaluca, Xuchitepec, Mixquic, Tenango Popula, Tláhuac, Tlalmanalco, Tlayacapan); Mexico City 7 (San José, Santa Ana, Santa Cruz, Coltzingo, Santa María la Redonda, San Pablo, Santa Cruz Acatlan); Texcoco 7 (Texcoco, Acolman, Chiautla, Chimalhuacan Atenco, Coatlinchan, Huexotla, Tepetlaostoc); Xilotepec 5 (Xilotepec, Alfajayucan, Chapatongo, Huichapan, Tecozautla), Coyoacan 5 (Coyoacan, Mixcoac, San Angel, Tacubaya, Tlalpan); Tula 3 (Tula, Tepejí del Río, Tepetitlan); Cuautitlan 3 (Cuautitlan, Tepotzotlan, Tultitlan); Cuautla 3 (Jumiltepec, Ocuituco, Zacualpan de Amilpas); San Cristóbal Ecatepec 2 (Ecatepec, Tecama); Metepec 2 (Metepec, Zinacantepec); Mexicalcingo 2 (Mexicalcingo, Culhuacan); Tacuba 2 (Tacuba, Tlalnepantla); Tenango del Valle 2 (Calimaya, Capuluac); Tetela del Volcán 2 (Tetela, Hueyapan); Xochimilco 2 (Xochimilco, Milpa Alta).

52. Florescano & Gil Sánchez, *Descripciones económicas generales*, pp. 185–92.

53. In a 1753 letter to the king called "nuestra quexa" (our complaint), the Franciscans of the Santo Evangelio province in central Mexico stressed the suddenness of their dislocation and appealed for at least a more gradual secularization. BN AF caja 127 exp. 1645, fols. 70–81. Their subsequent letters to the king and the viceroy characterized the secularizations as a "violento despojo."

54. The Franciscan doctrinero of Tlaquiltenango was reprimanded in 1759 for "faltando gravemente" in his obligation to teach Christian dogma and administer extreme unction to dying parishioners. The same visitador severely admonished the doctrineros of Zacualpan and Tlayacac for their "grave carelessness and scandalous negligence." AHM L10A/8, fols. 162v–163v. At Cuautla in 1767, the visitador blamed the backsliding of parishioners on the "bad example of the pastors"—a thinly veiled criticism of the Dominican doctrinero. AHM L10A/10.

55. BN AF caja 127 exp. 1645, fols. 11–12, for 1764; caja 139 exp. 1718, fols. 22–39, for 1769; caja 89 exp. 1379, fol. 481, for 1776–77. As early as April 1761, the Franciscans of the Santo Evangelio province informed the viceroy of their "estado calamitoso." AF caja 127 exp. 1645, fols. 50ff.

56. Solórzano 4-16-35 ("aman y reverencian más a los Religiosos"). For a defense of Archbishop Lorenzana's stance on secularization that suggests Mendicant doctrineros were losing their sense of mission, see Sierra Nava-Lasa, ch. 12.

57. López Lara, p. 112.

58. Strident complaints against doctrineros for personal misconduct and abuse of office include AJANG Civil, box 5, doc. 10, 1671, Magdalena; AJANG Civil, box 49, doc. 4, 1727, Poncitlan (Jalisco); AJANG Civil, box 228, doc. 3, 1802, Cocula; Tulane VEMC 8 exp. 48, 1783, and VEMC 66 exp. 10, 1800 (abusive and outrageous conduct by Franciscan doctrineros in Puebla and Irapuato); BMM 135, various Franciscan doctrinas in the late 17th and early 18th centuries; AGN Crim. 217 exp. 4, 1703, Metepec; AGN CRS 72 exp. 3, 1730, Tetecala, Cuernavaca district; AGN DP 1 exps. 1–3, 5, 1671, Cuernavaca district, 1721 Xilotepec, 1733 Toluca, 1748 Tlaltizapan; DP 2 exps. 1–4, 6, 1668-1746, Actopan, 1675-1745 Amecameca, 1746, Temascaltepec; AGN Hist. 128 exp. 10, 1791 (against

the Franciscan doctrinero of Acaponeta); AGN Inq. 1324, fols. 1–30, 1791 (misconduct by the guardián of Toluca); BN AF caja 112 exps. 1525, 1529, 1530, 1745, Xilotepec, 1749–53, Tulancingo, 1752, Cuernavaca district (the Franciscan doctrinero blamed Indian disobedience and lack of religious fervor on their pastors, both regulars and diocesan priests); BN AF caja 110, exp. 1508, 1764, Temamatla. Many exemplary Mendicant pastors could also be mentioned, such as, in BEJ Miscelánea 458: exp. 17, the great Franciscan teacher of Sayula born in 1791; and in AGN Acervo 49 caja 116, pastoral visit, entry 28, a friar with 30 years' outstanding service in missions of the Pánuco area. The archbishop of Mexico in 1758 declared that the regulars "regularmente son más cortos en la suficiencia que los seculares." AGI Mex. 2549. An anonymous anticlerical report of abuses of office by alcaldes mayores and priests in the Diocese of Oaxaca dated Aug. 19, 1777, claimed that the curas doctrineros were hardly distinguishable from diocesan curas: "En orden a los frailes (salvo algunos que son muy pocos) biven de tal manera que las constituciones según mis cortos alcances se han buelto quimera; porque se ha metido entre ellos un género de relajamiento que ya no se distingue aquí, quien es el fraile, quien es el clérigo, ni quien es el secular porque todos a vanderas desplegadas siguen el camino de la perdición de tal manera que los frailes que siguen los haveres mundanos son los más aplaudidos." AGN RCO 126 exp. 137.

59. Texas, W. B. Stephens Coll. no 395, 1750; AGN RCO 81 exp. 30, 1761. In the Diocese of Michoacán, there was an especially prolonged and acrimonious struggle over the Augustinian doctrina and properties at Yuriria. See Mazín, *Entre dos majestades*, pp. 37–45, 59–67, 76–84, 92–96, and 154–58.

60. The appeal for the restitution of doctrinas was not altogether quixotic. The crown had been persuaded to restore (temporarily, as it turned out) the Augustinians' doctrina of Yuriria and the Franciscans' doctrina of Zitácuaro in the Diocese of Michoacán. Mazin, *Entre dos majestades*, pp. 59, 76–84.

61. BN AF caja 107 exp. 1470, fols. 20–49; caja 109 exp. 1496; Tulane VEMC 16 exp. 12, 1753 brief and investigation prepared by Juan Baptista de Bolde, guardián of Otumba.

62. See, for example, the impassioned defense of Franciscan pastoral service between 1749 and 1753 in BN AF caja 128 exp. 1651. Van Oss largely accepts the Franciscan golden-age rhetoric in his consideration of secular priests in Guatemalan parishes. See *Catholic Colonialism*, ch. 5.

63. Tulane VEMC 57 exp. 17. For additional documentation on secularizations during this period, see also in VEMC, 12 exp. 4; 21 exp. 7; 26 exp. 6; 29 exp. 9; 54 exp. 38; 55 exp. 12; 61 exp. 27; 67 exp. 47; 69 exp. 5; AGI Guad. 369; and AGI Mex. 1424, 2189, 2622–26, 2633, 2637, 2665.

64. Tulane VEMC 72.

65. *Instrucciones que los vireyes*, 1: 572–79.

66. Mazín, *Entre dos majestades*, pp. 59–67.

67. Tulane VEMC 57 exp. 17, 1768, archbishop's request for an order for auxilio, "que espero no sea necesario para contener a los pueblos." For examples of peaceful transfers in Michoacán, see AGN RCO 110 exp. 63, 1777, at Santa Ana Amatlan; and López Lara, p. 158, 1761, Zinapécuaro.

68. AGI Mex. 727, 1758, autos de visita to Colegio de Santa Cruz, informe of the Franciscan Padre Comisario General de Indios claiming that as a result of the secularizations, many friars "no tienen casas, andan vagos y prófugos sin guardar la vida monástica."

69. Tulane VEMC 8 exp. 52.

70. JCB, Lorenzo Díaz del Costero resumé.

71. Tulane VEMC 16 exp. 12.

72. BN AF caja 110 exp. 1508.

73. AGN CRS 68 exps. 4–5 ("todo el bien de nuestras almas como en tiempo de los señores frailes").

74. For another example of how good the friars looked in retrospect, see AGN CRS 75 exp. 9, 1790, Tepetitlan parish.

75. A Capuchin who visited New Spain near the peak of the secularizations, claimed there was a virtual collapse of spiritual care: "En cuanto al pasto espiritual de estos infelices, es público y manifiesto que, desde que quitaron las doctrinas o curatos a los regulares, está muy atrasado o casi perdido." Ajofrín 2: 177. Hipólito Villarroel, an ex-alcalde mayor, expressing his frustration with diocesan curas (pp. 45, 46, 49), thought their neglect of duties was leading to the collapse of the pueblos and the disintegration of Christianity. He called for the return of the friars.

76. Repercussions of secularization in the parish of Mezquitic, San Luis Potosí, are treated in considerable detail in Frye, ch. 8.

77. By late colonial times the term "español" had become a flexible category embracing people reputed to be descended from Spaniards as well as those who could definitely establish their Spanish ancestry. Among the parish priests it would have included some mestizos and other castas, and unusual individuals like don Sipriano Pérez, a vicario of Actopan in the 1790's, an orphan of unknown parentage, "reputed hereabouts as an español," who had been raised by an Indian. AGN Hist. 578A, 1793 Actopan report.

78. JCB, for the archdiocese; AHJ Manuscripts, no. G-4-719 for Guadalajara. By contrast, 50% of the members or would-be members of the cathedral chapters were either urban-born or of peninsular origin. AGI Guad. 533–35, and 540. Most were doctors and licenciados by the second half of the 18th century. The Diocese of Puebla showed the same pattern of highly educated urban priests with little or no parish service. All of the 41 leading priests described by the bishop in his April 30, 1762, report were doctors or licenciados. Only a few of the less-esteemed licenciados had served in parishes outside the city of Puebla, and then only as interim curas. AGI Mex. 2550.

79. There is no doubt of a downward trend in Guadalajara in the 19th century. By 1853–54 only 15.8% of the concursantes were from the cathedral city. CAAG unclassified. The increasing importance of priests of provincial origin should not obscure the possibility that some towns were seedbeds of seminary students in one period but not another. Teocaltiche caught my eye as the hometown of many priests in the Guadalajara concurso records for 1756–57, 1770, and 1853–54 (CAAG unclassified; AHJ Manuscripts, no. G-4-719), but few have come from this town since the Reform period, according to Father Eucario López (personal communication, 1981).

80. Castañeda, p. 278, found only one Indian admitted to the seminary in Guadalajara during the whole of the 18th century. One of the rare Indian pastors in the diocese was Br. don Antonio Canales, the son of indios caciques of Tlajomulco, who had been cura of Colotlan in the 1780's. AJANG Civil, bundle marked "1780–91 (44)," 1790, suit of José Buenaventura Canal against doña María Dolores Dábalos, sobre pesos. José Lázaro Aparicio Márquez de Alcón, a son of Indian nobles of Nochistlan, had taken only minor orders as of 1807. AGI Guad. 540.

There were seven Indian priests among the 103 who gave their family background in the resumés they submitted in a competition for vacant parishes in the archdiocese in the early 1760's. JCB. Nineteen Indian pastors and assistants are listed in the detailed but incomplete series of district reports from the early 1790's in AGN Hist. 578A.

The crown began actively promoting the idea of ordination of Indians in the 1690's. The royal cedulas to this effect appear in Konetzke, 3: doc. 41; and G. V. Vásquez, pp. 332–35. Ribadeneyra. ch. 13, para. 30, even suggested that Indians should be preferred in appointments, at least to parish benefices where Indian languages were spoken. But, as the cedula of Sept. 11, 1766, noted, existing laws encouraging ordination of Indians were not much followed. Konetzke, 3: doc. 201. See also Bayle, "España."

81. There were a few spectacular professional success stories among the late colonial Indian priests of New Spain. One became a bishop in Honduras, and several were appointed to posts in cathedral chapters. But most occupied minor parishes or remained vicarios. Typically ordained "de idioma" (qualified to minister in an Indian language), they were disdained as unworthy of promotion by members of the non-Indian clergy who were in the professional fast lane. Few Indian priests in parish service had the independent means to propel them into positions of authority or much influence within the institution, yet their nominal education and social background separated them from village tributaries.

82. *Recop.* 1-7-7. Prelates were ordered to make diligent inquiries to determine that mestizo priests met these high personal standards.

83. The 1771 provision that a third of seminary students should be Indians and mestizos appears in the records of the Fourth Provincial Council. BMM 69–70, I: ch. 16. Since the decrees of this council were not officially approved by the papacy or the crown, they did not become ecclesiastical law. Archbishop Lorenzana, who presided over the council, was one of the prelates who had little confidence in Indians and mestizos as prospective parish priests. See Moreno de los Arcos, "Dos documentos," p. 35.

84. The relaciones de méritos y servicios for priests competing for posts in the cathedral chapters are reasonably well known because they were collected by the Council of the Indies, which reviewed the files and made the final recommendations for appointments. Many of the 18th-century documents are available in the Archivo General de Indias.

Using the relaciones de méritos of the select competitors for vacant offices in the Archdiocese of Lima, Ganster, pp. 156ff, presents a picture of curas as privileged men of privileged origins. Twenty of the 40 candidates in his sample between 1730 and 1761 were from merchant families, seven were sons of high bureaucrats, seven were from Lima's aristocracy, three were from the provincial aristocracy, two were sons of physicians, and one was the son of a soldier-provincial aristocrat. Similarly, Tibesar, "Lima Pastors," found that though "the candidates for the pastorates usually were doctors from the University of San Marcos, . . . ordination was granted not only to the worthy but to those who possessed also a certain social status and enough wealth to support themselves—the *titulus patrimonii*—in a style befitting a priest." If Ganster's and Tibesar's samples are representative, the Peruvian curas were better educated and more often the children of privilege than their Mexican counterparts.

85. AGI Guad. 346. José Vicente Beltrán y Bravo was confirmed in the title by the Council of the Indies on Aug. 20, 1783. He was 25 years old at the time.

86. Examples like these come to light in Inquisition trials and criminal and civil suits rather than in official administrative reports. AGN Inq. 813 exp. 17 (Bedoya); Inq. 1308 exp. 1 (Calzada); and Inq. 1346 exp. 6 (Baldovinos).

87. AGI Guad. 544; Texas, García Coll., no. 261.

88. I have not seen a formal list of first-class parishes for Guadalajara outside the cathedral city. To judge from the number of priests in residence, the emoluments reported, and the distinctions of the curas who held them, the following 18 parishes in secular hands by the 1790's would have been the first-class parishes of this diocese (they represent about 20% of all parishes): Zacatecas, Aguascalientes, Santa María Lagos, Sierra de Pinos, Ameca, Teocaltiche, Ojocaliente, Tlaltenango, Tepatitlan, Zapotlan el Grande, Colima, San Juan de los Lagos, Xerez, Fresnillo, Zacoalco, Sayula, Zapopan, and Nochistlan. The choice doctrinas still under Franciscan control were Tlajomulco and Cocula.

89. Bachelor's degrees were awarded only to students from a recognized colegio, seminary, university, or convent school. Becerra López, pp. 295–301. Nearly all competitors for parish benefices in Mexico and Guadalajara in the late colonial period had at least a

bachelor of arts or bachelor of philosophy degree, whether they were curas, coadjutors, vicarios, or newly ordained priests. This compares with a mere 37% in the poorer Diocese of Yucatán in the years 1780–1814. Harrington, ch. 2.

90. AGI Indiferente General 245, no. 22. It would be equally important to know more about the colegios themselves. What percentage of their students were destined for the priesthood? How much did it cost to attend? What were the students' and the teachers' social backgrounds? What was the ranking of the various colegios? Some examples of classmates in close contact as pastors appear in ch. 8. A dim impression of these contacts might be charted by matching enrollment lists at school with the location of the curas and vicarios later on.

91. See, for example, Dávila Garibi, *Apuntes*, 4: 328 on five Pintados-Patróns serving as curas in the Diocese of Guadalajara at the beginning of the 19th century. In 1759, the controversial Indian cura of Yautepec (Morelos) employed two of his brothers as vicarios. AHM L10A/8, fol. 151r.

92. Most of the parish priests in the Diocese of Guadalajara in the late 18th century had studied in the Seminario San José (also known as the Seminario Tridentino or Seminario Conciliar, founded in 1699) or the Colegio de San Juan Bautista (founded by the Jesuits in 1696, closed in 1767, and reopened in 1792). In January 1805, Bishop Ruiz de Cabañas reported the Seminario Conciliar to be "in a flourishing state," with a rector, vice-rector, and 18 catedráticos. AGI Guad. 534. A few of the priests had studied at an institution in Mexico City, or at the Colegio de San Nicolás in Valladolid, the Colegio de San Francisco of San Miguel el Grande, the seminary in Durango, or the Colegio of Santo Tomás in Guadalajara. Students in the archdiocese had more schools to choose from, but most went to one of three institutions in Mexico City, the Colegio Máximo de San Pedro y San Pablo, the Colegio de San Ildefonso, or the Real y Pontificio Colegio Seminario, for their baccalaureates.

93. Castañeda, p. 279. For expectations about learning and personal conduct in the Real y Pontificio Colegio Seminario of Mexico City at the end of the colonial period, see "Exhortación del Illmo Sr Arzobispo a los individuos del Real Pontificio Seminario de México en principios del Curso Escolástico del año de 1803" (Mexico, 1803). In this lecture to the seminarians, Archbishop Lizana y Beaumont invoked San Carlos Borromeo as the patriarch of the educational system as they knew it. Carlos Borromeo's application of Tridentine reforms while he was archbishop of Milan in the 1570's and 1580's was the basic model for the training and conduct of parish priests in 18th-century Spanish America. His outline of rules for seminaries included the order of daily occupations, proper dress and personal comportment, the course of study, and an emphasis on meditation, seclusion, self-denial, the recitation of the Divine Office, and the examination of conscience. His plan for devotional practices was inspired by St. Ignatius's *Spiritual Exercises*. For an introduction to Borromeo's reforms, see Orsenigo, ch. 8; Wright, ch. 6; and especially Luria, ch. 2. On Tridentine reforms in the context of New Spain, see Poole, "Third Mexican Provincial Council"; and Poole, *Pedro Moya de Contreras*.

94. Castañeda, p. 317.

95. Ibid., pp. 306–8. The information in this section comes from Castañeda; Becerra López; and 252 relaciones de méritos y servicios of candidates for vacancies in the two dioceses during the late 18th century.

96. Becerra López, pp. 295–301. A student of law could skip the philosophy program and go directly into the five-year course of study that led to a bachelor's degree in canones y leyes.

97. Ibid., pp. 189–98.

98. Castañeda, pp. 311–14.

99. The John Carter Brown Library's collection of relaciones de méritos y servicios for the archdiocese in the early 1760's provides a sample of the academic accomplish-

ments of priests with advanced degrees—the prizes they won in school, the academies they founded, the examinations they took and how they placed, the sermons they had given, the teaching posts they held, the writings they published, etc. A well-documented example of an academic achiever was Dr. Guridi y Alcocer. See Taylor, "Conflict," pp. 285–86; and Guridi y Alcocer's own reminiscences.

100. *Constituciones que el ilustrísimo Señor Doctor Don Alonso Núñez de Haro y Peralta, del Consejo de Su Magestad y arzobispos de esta santa iglesia metropolitana de México, formó para el mejor régimen y govierno del real colegio seminario de instrucción, retiro voluntario y corrección para el clero secular de esta diócesi, fundado por S.S. Illma en el pueblo de Tepotzotlán . . .* (Mexico, 1777).

101. Everything moved up half an hour from October to March, with the wake-up call at six, and bedtime at ten.

102. Lanning, *Eighteenth-Century Enlightenment*, pp. 115ff.

103. In the neighboring diocese of Yucatán, Cartesian philosophy was introduced into the curriculum in the late 18th century but was banned in 1806. Harrington, pp. 32–35.

104. There were certainly some children of the Enlightenment (a few are discussed in Chap. 7), and there had long been parish priests with a curiosity about applied science. The regalist urge to reform ecclesiastical discipline in the late 18th century is best known in the conventual reforms, but the bishops had parish priests in mind, too. The Fourth Provincial Council in 1771 spoke of "re-establishing the exactitude of ecclesiastical discipline [and] the preachers' fervor." These men of the Fourth Council spoke of themselves as being on a mission like that of the initial conquest in the 16th century. BMM 69, 1: fols. 1ff, 276v.

105. Castañeda, p. 273, describes the many lay students in Guadalajara's colegios who pursued the carrera literaria rather than the carrera eclesiástica. Lanning's students seem to have been in the carrera literaria track. While recognizing that few, if any, high churchmen in the late colonial period were anti-Enlightenment in principle, Lanning describes a paler Enlightenment for priests in his article "Church and the Enlightenment." On the spread of "modern" works in Spanish American seminaries, see Castañeda Delgado. Seminary reforms are also discussed in Mazín, *Entre dos majestades*, pp. 35–36. For some basic information on the organization and curriculum of the conciliar seminary in Mexico City in the late colonial period, see D.P.E.P., *Noticias*.

106. *Itin.* (1771 ed.), p. 8, para. 17.

107. Trent, 23d Session, Reform, chs. 4–5. The Fourth Provincial Council elaborated on this guideline, adding that lads as young as seven were eligible for first tonsure if they were prudent boys who showed an inclination toward the office. CPM, pp. 13–23.

108. Trent, 23d Session, Reform, ch. 11.

109. CPM, pp. 13–23.

110. Trent, 23d Session, Reform, ch. 7: "The bishop shall carefully investigate and examine the parentage, person, age, education, morals, learning and faith of those who are to be ordained." Men of illegitimate birth were supposed to be excluded, although according to de la Peña Montenegro, a bishop in the Indies could grant individual dispensations, *Itin.* 3-8-1. De la Peña Montenegro noted that slaves could not be ordained, and that authorities disagreed on whether free blacks could. A detailed description of the inquiry into a candidate's personal history appears in CPM, pp. 13–23.

111. CPM, p. 17.

112. Trent, 23d Session, Reform, ch. 15, noted that ordination carried with it the power to absolve from sin but added that confession could be heard only by holders of parochial benefices and others who received special permission from the bishop. An example of a printed license to confess and administer sacraments is included in AGN Bienes 172 exp. 47 (1806).

113. Trent, 23d Session, Reform, ch. 12.

114. An example of shorter intervals is Joseph Rudesindo de Nava y Vega, who was promoted to subdeacon in June 1752, to deacon in Dec. 1752, and to presbyter in April 1753. JCB.

115. BMM 69–70, fol. 79r, March 14, 1771 debate; CPM, p. 24. *Itin.* 1-1-2, para. 18, specified 25 years of age for ordination.

116. Three of the 12 Guadalajara cases between the 1770's and 1821 appear to have been only 22 or 23 when they were ordained. Several parish priests in the archdiocese in the early 1760's mentioned receiving dispensations of seven or eight months. The number of priests ordained at 23 apparently increased in Guadalajara during the early 19th century. Of 29 priests who provided information on age at ordination in the 1853–54 concursos, 8 were ordained at 23, 6 at 24, and 1 at 22. CAAG unclassified.

117. *Instrucciones que los vireyes,* 1: 368.

118. AGI Mex. 2549, Oct. 8, 1758 report. The president of the Audiencia of Nueva Galicia in 1764 also found little to praise in the parish priests' preparation. "As soon as they finish their philosophy and moral theology, if they have studied at all, they withdraw into the *pueblos* to help the *curas,* moving continually from one parish to another." Ibid., Jan. 3, 1764, Pedro Montesinos de Lara. Castañeda, pp. 80–83, notes the poor education of priests in the Diocese of Guadalajara in the 16th and early 17th centuries, and the lack of good schooling in the city then.

119. AGN Hist. 578A, 1793, Taxco report.

120. AGI Mex. 2549, Dec. 30, 1755 informe reservado by president of the audiencia, and informes of Dec. 30, 1766, and Jan. 3, 1764: Joseph Caro Galindo, "no tiene muchas letras"; Manuel Bata and Phelipe Ramos, "de ningunas letras."

121. JCB. In the same concurso of the early 1760's, several other curas and vicarios did not mention earning a bachelor's degree, and two definitely had not completed the normal schooling. Nicolás Ximénez, cura of San Andrés Epasoyucan, studied grammar with a Franciscan in Toluca, then moral theology, but did not mention any colegio or seminary training. He had a capellanía that was too small to justify the cost of a formal education, so he went to Ixtapan to learn Nahuatl from the cura, was ordained a título de idioma in 1734, and waited more than 20 years to gain his own parish. Juan Francisco Caballero studied grammar and some philosophy and theology at the Colegio de San Ildefonso in Mexico City beginning in 1747 but left before getting his degree because of his family's poverty. He continued to study on his own in Tula and was ordained in 1757.

122. This was the way the subdelegado of Zacualpan summed up the qualifications of the vicario of Coatepec Harinas in 1793. AGN Hist. 578A, Zacualpan report. Some parish priests had so little education that they could not even handle the most basic church ritual. Joseph Manuel Sotomayor, serving in Zacualpan at the end of the 18th century, for instance, was charged not only with various personal transgressions, but also with irregularities in performing the mass. AGN Inq. 1334 exp. 3. No parish priest, however, seems to have been as profoundly ignorant as Pedro Antonio Lara, who lived on the Hacienda de Santa Cruz in the district of Huejutla in the early 1790's. If we can believe the subdelegado, Lara "doesn't know the simplest Latin; nor does it appear that he has even a nodding acquaintance with moral theology; nor does he know the ceremonies of the mass. As a result, when he celebrates mass he creates a scandal." AGN Hist. 578A, 1793, Huejutla report. The founding of the Real Colegio Seminario de Tepotzotlan in 1777 responded to this perceived need. The Fourth Provincial Council was presumably aware of this lack of formal training when it called for all candidates for the priesthood to spend at least six months in seminary.

123. AGN Inq. 1308 exp. 1. The governor of Puebla complained in 1755 that there were

too many clergymen in the Diocese of Puebla because standards for ordination were very low. AGI Mex. 2549, March 25, 1755 report.

124. *Recop.* 1-13-4 (1619). AGN CRS 67 exp. 3, Guipustla, 1768, is an example of an Indian parish trying to have its cura removed under this law. Solórzano was especially concerned that pastors know the Indian languages, 4-15-42, 44, 46. Though in 4-15-102 he mentions hiring coadjutors fluent in the local languages, he had earlier put curas in the same boat, contending that those who did not know their parishioners' language were incompetent to serve and committed a mortal sin. 2-29-47, 3-15-42–43, 3-15-48.

125. Viceroy Revillagigedo (the elder) reminded his successor in 1755 that parish priests were to know the languages of the Indians they taught and confessed. *Instrucciones que los vireyes*, 1: ch. 7. Among the priests the archbishop singled out in his report to the Council of the Indies in 1758 were various curas who understood the languages of the Indian parishioners and who, "based on their merits, seniority, and zeal," were accordingly being "promoted to other better and richer ones; . . . each of the aforementioned has enough vicarios with the same command of said languages." AGI Mex. 2549, Oct. 8, 1758 "Relación puntual que da el Señor arzobispo de México."

126. JCB. One of the priests said he was ordained "a título de administración de indios." This title does not appear in the other relaciones and probably meant a título de idioma.

127. JCB.

128. AGN Hist. 578A, Malinalco report. The subdelegado elaborated on this notion in a comment about a young vicario he regarded as poorly educated: "the lack of learning [is] common among most of those who are ordained *a título de idioma*."

129. AGN Inq. 1221 exp. 9.

130. AGN Hist. 578A, 1793, Acapulco report.

131. AGN Inq. 1348 exp. 10.

132. Lorenzana y Buitrón, *Cartas pastorales*, p. 3.

133. The full cedula is in AGN RCO 96 exp. 102; an abstract appears in Ventura Beleña, 1: 166.

134. CPM, p. 16.

135. CPM, p. 195.

136. AGI Guad. 352, "Autos formados sobre los bienes de comunidad que goza cada pueblo de yndios de los del distrito de esta Intendencia Provincia de la Nueva Galicia," 1786 and later, describes the promotion of Spanish-language schools in western Mexico at the end of the 18th century. Villarroel, p. 51, was one of many who called for denying parish benefices to priests ordained a título de idioma.

137. AGN Acervo 49, caja 116.

138. AGN Hist. 578A, 1793, Malinalco report.

139. The equating of charity with divine love is found in the *New Catholic Encyclopedia* (entry for "Charity") and in colonial writings like Palafox's pastoral letter of Nov. 12, 1640. For a brief historical presentation of the several meanings of charity, see Williams, pp. 45–46. Charity for 18th-century priests was understood to mean especially Christian love—active helpfulness springing from Christian conviction. Troeltsch, 1: 1005.

Chapter Five

EPIGRAPH: Jessopp, *Before the Pillage*, p. 116.

1. AGN Inq. 1342, fol. 125v.

2. By law the vacancies had to be filled in open, advertised competitions. See *Recop.* 1-6-24 and Solórzano 4-16-22.

3. The concursos could be more frequent if the bishop wished. Luis Piña y Mazo,

bishop of Yucatán (1780–95), convened a concurso whenever there was a vacancy—57 times in 16 years. Harrington, pp. 25–26.

4. One of the few resignations was that of Joseph Lobo, cura of Ocuilan, in 1789, in the aftermath of charges of cruelty and extortion. AGN Bienes 575 exp. 46. For resignations by more distinguished priests with delicate consciences, see Osores, entries 2, 16, 26, 33. Occasionally a cura had his licenses to confess and preach suspended and was forbidden to enter his parish for 10 years, but forced removal was rare. Under *Recop.* 1-6-38, any cura could be removed from his benefice without right of appeal simply by agreement of the prelate and the vice-patron (the audiencia was left without jurisdiction in such cases), but the law was revised in a royal cedula of August 1, 1795, which declared that no cura canonically confirmed could henceforth be removed without a show of cause and proper hearing. AGN RCO 161 exps. 196 and 254; BEJ Papeles de Derecho, 2: 248v–249v.

5. For example, AGN CRS 156 exp. 7.

6. AHJ Manuscripts, no. G-4-806 JAL/3156, "Recibos sobre provisión de curatos," 1806.

7. Hernáez, 1: 221–22; *Recop.* 1-6-24. Fallon and Harrington make extensive use of the relaciones de méritos y servicios to study the appointment process and collective biography of priests in late colonial Yucatán. Fallon's ch. 4 is devoted to the concurso process and Bishop Piña y Mazo's reform of it.

8. Hernáez, 1: 220–21 (Dec. 14, 1742).

9. Even if a priest did not place high enough to win a parish, it was important to be "aprobado"—to appear on the list of those qualified for appointment based on the examinations. Priests who had not yet gained a parish benefice would include in their relación de méritos y servicios the fact that they had been aprobados in previous concursos.

10. *Recop.* 1-1-10, and 1-6-24. Apparently the bishops did not always feel bound by the rankings of their examiners. Juan Nepomuceno Báez, cura of Nochistlan in 1795, claimed that he had received six of nine first-place votes for the Santa María de Lagos vacancy in 1790 but was not appointed. AGI Guad. 533.

11. Solórzano 4-15-83, 4-17-67. On the vice-patron's right to disregard the bishop's first choice, see *Recop.* 1-6-24 and the draft letter by the viceroy dated March 8, 1802, in Tulane VEMC 15 exp. 9.

12. Choosing the second-place candidate for the parish of Tepic in 1792 touched off a dispute. BEJ Papeles de Derecho, 1: 315.

13. *Instrucciones que los vireyes*, 1: 360. Appointments that Revillagigedo (the younger) had authorized in the Diocese of Antequera were apparently nullified because of incorrect procedures in the concurso. AGN RCO 160 exps. 141, 158, 1795.

14. Exchanges seem to have been approved routinely even though the fiscal of the audiencia occasionally recommended against them. In a Chilean judgment published for all of Spanish America, the crown ruled against a cura exchanging his parish for capellanías. AGN RCO 163 exp. 79, Feb. 14, 1796. This led to royal cedulas in Aug. 10, 1801 and Dec. 25, 1803, forbidding exchanges between curas and holders of sacristía positions. Tulane VEMC 31 exp. 26. Exchanges of this kind were not a hypothetical matter in the late colonial period, since three had been made in the Diocese of Michoacán shortly before the 1801 cedula. The principle advanced by the crown in these cedulas was that a parish benefice could not be exchanged for a beneficio simple.

15. A particularly good collection of exchange cases brought to the viceroy in the 18th century is in Tulane VEMC. They include VEMC 15 exp. 26, 1796, Ayotzingo and Cempoala (Mexico); 32 exp. 16, 1728, Villa Alta jurisdiction (Antequera); 33 exp. 6, 1796, Tzilacayoapan (Puebla); 51 exp. 29, Chalco and Jalatlaco (Mexico); 53 exp. 7, 1798–99, San Agustín Tenango and San Cristóbal Xizhuatlan (Puebla); 54 exp. 26, 1795, Cozcatlan and Coatlinchan (Mexico); 56 exp. 31, 1799, Tlalmanalco and Tacubaya (Mexico); 57 exp. 24

Amecameca and San Cristóbal Ecatepec (Mexico); and 64 exp. 27, 1797–1803, Olinalá and Zongolica (Puebla). Exchanges in the Diocese of Guadalajara are mentioned in AGN Hist. 578A, Zacatecas report (Tlaltenango and Ameca, 1787); and BEJ Papeles de Derecho, 1: 563 (Fresnillo and Lagos, 1802).

16. Tulane VEMC 15 exp. 26.

17. *Recop.* 1-1-10, 1-6-24, 1-6-29, 1-7-30; Hernáez, 1: 220.

18. For example, José Angulo y Bustamante's application to move to Temascaltepec was approved in 1789, despite (or perhaps because of?) his serious troubles in Huazalingo. AGN Bienes 575 exp. 14. Cleared of the extortion charges brought against him by his Indian parishioners there, he was soon in hot water again in his new position. Tulane VEMC 54 exp. 37.

19. *Recop.* 1-6-29 (1574); Solórzano 4-19. This seems to be contradicted by *Recop.* 1-6-34 (1620), which stipulated that the relatives of royal officials were not to be preferred. Perhaps the distinction was between men whose fathers had served the crown well in the past and those whose fathers were currently in royal service. The Fourth Provincial Council attempted to clarify this issue by stating that such candidates were to be neither favored nor discriminated against. *Recop.* 1-6-24 advised that creoles were to be preferred but pronounced peninsular-born Spaniards "equally worthy" in comparison to other candidates. In any case, family origin was supposed to be secondary to distinction in "life and example." The exception was that foreign-born candidates were not eligible unless they had a written certificate of naturalization from the crown. *Recop.* 1-6-31.

20. *Recop.* 1-6-24 and 1-6-30. In a royal cedula of April 16, 1770, the crown called for merit, not language, to be the criterion, a theme that the Fourth Provincial Council picked up the next year. Ventura Beleña, 1: 166; CPM, pp. 66–67. This was part of a growing official view that the perpetuation of Indian languages was a cause of disorder in the colonies. Merit increasingly meant learning, without much regard for the papal admonition that "the most learned is not necessarily the most suited to the examination of souls." Hernáez, 1: 220 (Dec. 14, 1742).

21. Surprisingly, some of these appeals were kept on file in the viceregal archives. For two examples from the late 18th century, see Tulane VEMC 41 exp. 3 (1788 letter from doña María Antonia Martines) and VEMC 73 exp. 29 (1795 letter from Lucas Antonio Rozados, apparently to the viceroy's wife). According to viceregal authorities in 1772 and the fiscal of the Audiencia of Guadalajara in 1778, there were strong suspicions of bribery and intercession to gain appointments for close relatives in parishes and cathedral chapters. VEMC 10 exp. 27 (referring to the cathedral chapter of Michoacán); BEJ Papeles de Derecho, 2: 185–92. For the pertinent law, which was clear on this point, see *Recop.* 1-6-34.

22. AGI Guad. 346, cartas y expedientes, no. 2, Sept. 1783.

23. CPM, p. 184.

24. Peninsular curas appear more often in the records for Mexico but were uncommon in either diocese. The most distinguished of them usually came in the company of a new bishop and were placed in the cathedral city or another first-class parish. For example, Lic. Vizente María Cassino y Cassafonda, cura of the sagrario parish in Guadalajara in 1755, was a sevillano who arrived from Campeche with Bishop Francisco de San Buenaventura Martínez de Tejada. He was judged to lead a well-ordered life and to be "of a mild and judicious temperament," acting with an "average" sense of interest in the income his parish could produce, and trying to improve his savings so he could return to Spain. AGI Mex. 2549, March 23, 1755, report.

25. Ibid., 1758 report; AGI Guad. 246, no. 13.

26. AGI Guad. 534.

27. JCB. Sometimes members of the bishop's entourage were awarded posts in the

cathedral chapter. By the 1770's, members of cathedral chapters were discouraged from interceding with the bishop on behalf of close relatives. At least in the Diocese of Michoacán, brothers and nephews of members of the cathedral chapter had secured positions in the cathedral and the seminary, presumably with family help. Joseph Quadros y Peredo, pro-secretario of the cabildo eclesiástico in Michoacán in 1772, reported that there had been 11 such cases between 1721 and 1769. Tulane VEMC 10 exp. 27.

28. Bishop Cabañas claimed in 1805 that some of his priests were taking positions outside the diocese. Some may have gone to Durango and Sonora, but there does not seem to have been a reciprocal movement of priests trained elsewhere coming into Guadalajara. AGI Guad. 534.

29. Especially in the late 18th century, many denunciations of parish priests were brought to the bishops' courts. Most were disputes over clerical fees, alleged violations of customary practices, and arbitrary demands by the priest. Charges of sexual misconduct were generally investigated by the Inquisition, and some cases for Mexico and Guadalajara in the 18th century are found in AGN Inq. But the total number of suits brought to court at the end of the colonial period would not justify for Mexico the conclusion Freeze, *Parish Clergy*, p. 31, reaches for the Russian Orthodox Church—that "perhaps the most striking feature of diocesan administration was the high frequency with which it intervened in the lives of ordinary clergy."

30. Freeze, ibid., pp. 25–26 concludes that the tendency of Russian bishops to move quite often in search of promotion weakened their ties with the parish clergy and brought on complaints of careerism.

31. In the early 1760's concurso for the archdiocese, six candidates claimed descent from conquistadores: Antonio Ramón de Cuevas, Domingo Antonio Caro, Julián Campoy y Cervantes, Antonio Flores Garcilaso de la Vega, Joseph de Prado Zúñiga y Velasco, Joseph Lucas de Santibáñez.

32. Lorenzana's position was echoed by other archbishops and bishops of New Spain to the end of the colonial period. The dean of the cathedral of Valladolid in 1785 was a particularly strong proponent of an elite class of pastors whose main distinction was their education. AGN Hist. 128 exp. 4. See also Cardozo Galué. For examples of careers of distinguished seminarians of the Colegio de San Ildefonso that included parish service, see Osores, entries 7, 9, 11, 14, 18, 23–25, 33–35, 37, and 40.

33. CAAG, Jacinto Llanos y Valdés response to Oct. 31, 1796 circular.

34. JCB. Although Bustamante said nothing else about his achievements in Tezontepec parish, he was precise about the length of his service there—eight years and five months.

35. Solórzano 4-23-6. As patron of all cathedrals and parish churches in his domain, the king was supposed to contribute to the initial construction and to supplement the resources of the parish and private donations for repairs. Ibid., 4-23-9, 4-23-10. Solórzano added that the crown's main responsibility was to contribute to construction of the first church. Royal funds for repair and reconstruction might be granted, but only selectively and by written license.

Late colonial builder-curas criticized by parishioners for overly ambitious projects were unrepentant in response. Dr. Gregorio Pérez Cancio, cura of the Santa Cruz parish in Mexico City, must have expected a sympathetic hearing from the archbishop when he wrote to him in September 1779 that "I am well aware that some will tell Your Excellency that I have sought to build a veritable basilica, and that this has hindered the construction. It is true, but the matter was aired to the satisfaction of your esteemed predecessor. I would add only that I did it for the public good and for the spiritual and temporal good of this capital city" (No ignoro que dirán a V.E. que yo he promovido una Basílica y que esto dificulta la fábrica, es verdad; pero este punto lo satisfice ante el Exmo. Predecesor digno de V.E. y ahora añado que lo ejecuté en bien del público para el bien espiritual y temporal de esta capital). Pérez Cancio, p. 176.

36. This was the position of the doctoral of the Valladolid cathedral chapter in 1779. Tulane VEMC 29 exp. 1.

37. AGI Guad. 563.

38. Parish priests in the archdiocese for the early 1760's concurso frequently mentioned among their accomplishments that they had established schools, expanded the activities of the ones they found in the parish, and secured a decent salary for the maestro. Curas in Guadalajara were more likely to mention promoting schools (and presumably doing it) in the 1770 concurso than in 1757. The 1760's was a time of particularly active promotion of Spanish in the pueblos and of Spanish-language schools by royal authorities and bishops, the increased mentions may have been a direct response to that policy shift.

39. As we will see in later chapters, cofradías were more important as financial and community organizations in the Diocese of Guadalajara. Chance & Taylor; and Taylor, "Indian Pueblos."

40. AGI Mex. 2549, March 25, 1755 report. More men who acknowledged illegitimate birth or mixed racial ancestry were apparently admitted to the priesthood in late colonial Yucatán. According to Harrington, p. 131, of the 509 priests he studied, five were Indians, three mulatos, and 78 mestizos (of whom 43 was said to be illegitimate). But the parish benefices and promotions there effectively were reserved for creoles.

41. AGN Bienes 575 exps. 14, 70. A similar case with a similar result involved Lic. Juan Antonio Xil de Andrade, cura of Cempoala (Mexico) in 1777. AGN Inq. 1113, fols. 231–54.

42. AGN CRS 136 exps. 6, 7, 1790–91; Tulane VEMC 54 exp. 37, 1793–94.

43. AGN Bienes 575 exp. 15.   44. AGN Inq. 813 exp. 17.

45. AGN Acervo 49 caja 47.   46. AGN Inq. 1191 exp. 4.

47. AGN Acervo 49 caja 49.

48. AGN Inq. 1205 exp. 28. Other examples of this pattern of harsher sentences for repeat offenders are Inq. 960 exp. 19 (the Franciscan Joseph Yriarte, of the Xalisco province, for various sexual crimes and solicitation in the confessional, 1759); Inq. 1304 exp. 3 (Joseph Manuel Sotomayor, cura of Zacualpan, for sexual crimes, suspect propositions, irreverent behavior, and lack of attention to parish duties, 1796); Inq. 1308 exp. 1 (Mariano Calzada, former vicario of Sierra de Pinos, for repeated sexual crimes and solicitation in the confessional, 1790); and Inq. 1360 exps. 1 and 2 (Athanasio Pérez Alamillo, cura of Otumba, for many irreverent propositions, 1795).

49. AGN Acervo 49 caja 156.

50. This was a long-standing pattern. As early as 1629, Ruiz de Alarcón, p. 20, remarked on "the little involvement, brief tenure, and readiness to move of the parish priests."

51. BMM 69–70, p. 63.

52. Brading, "El clero mexicano y el movimiento insurgente."

53. AGI Guad. 210. The governor of Puebla also noted that many priests "find it necessary to involve themselves in illicit commerce and other private business" because "there are so many clerics and so few positions." AGI Mex. 2549, March 25, 1755 report. In his opinion, the church was not paying enough attention to the ordination of men who would be able to support themselves in the priesthood.

54. BMM 69–70, ch. 14; CAAG, responses to the Oct. 31, 1796, circular. Apparently there was a shortage of pastors, if not of priests, after Independence. The governor's reports for the state of Mexico in 1826–27 and 1829–30 spoke of a want of men in the parishes, especially of pastors who knew Indian languages. It was attributed partly to curas being unable to afford vicarios. In the concurso of 1853–54 in Guadalajara, curas lamented the shortage of vicarios to assist them. CAAG sewn volume of relaciones de méritos.

55. Another, less useful measure of turnover is the number of vicarios competing in

the 1757 and 1770 concursos who had passed through different parishes. This measure produces Xalpan, Mecatabasco, and Zapotlanejo again, and adds two other poor parishes, Tomatlan and San Cristóbal de la Barranca. In these parishes, vicarios did serve for only very short periods, seeking better pay, more agreeable surroundings, or a parochial bene-fice as soon as they could. But this measure also produces parishes with large incomes that employed more vicarios and naturally had more of them passing through. And it leaves out the parishes that were too small or too poor to employ vicarios at all.

A rough idea of the turnover rate can be gained where the total number of vicarios on staff is known. The accompanying table for Guadalajara, based on a comparison of each

Guadalajara Parishes Served by Vicarios Competing in the Concursos of 1757 and 1770

Parish	Number of vicario concursants	Total vicarios in 1796	Vicario's income (pesos)[a]	Parish	Number of vicario concursants	Total vicarios in 1796	Vicario's income (pesos)[a]
Mecatabasco	13	1	1,092	Tequila	7	2	—
Xalostotitlan	10	1	5,656	Zapotlanejo	6	2	917
Xalpa	9	1	1,005	Tlaltenango	6	4	3,000
Zapopan	9	2	2,000	San Cristóbal	5	0	368
Ameca	9	2	1,778	Xerez	5	3	2,424
Tomatlan	8	1	703	Tepatitlan	5	4	1,200
Mascota	7	0	1,749				

[a]All data for 1774 except for Ameca (1790).

parish's vicario complement in 1796 with the number of vicarios sitting for the concur-sos of 1757 and 1770 who had served in the parish, shows the most problematical areas. Mecatabasco, Xalpa, Xalostotitlan, Tomatlan, Mascota, and San Cristóbal, in particular, stand out as poor parishes with few vicarios and many turnovers. Perhaps there had been more vicarios in these parishes in the 1750's and 1760's, or the pay was poor and the cura difficult to work with, or the vicarios there had been especially ambitious and eager to move on. More interesting is the absence of the parishes that employed the most vicarios: Zacatecas, Santa María de Lagos, and Sierra de Pinos. These three were among the most desirable parishes in the diocese.

Length of service is also suggestive of the importance of a parish. The information is incomplete, but at least for Tlaltenango and Xerez, the vicarios stayed for four or five years at a time, compared with a year or less in the poorest parishes in the table. There were important exceptions, to be sure. For example, some vicarios who had no hope of promotion returned to their hometowns for long periods of service, even though they were not located in particularly prosperous parishes.

56. CAAG, file of 55 concursants for vacant parish benefices, 1770.

57. AGI Guad. 563.

58. CAAG, with nominations for promotions in the 1770 concurso; reiterated in the Antonio Norberto Sánchez Martínez resumé, AJANG Civil, bundle labeled "1800–1809, leg. 3 (109)." Other parish benefices with small revenues that do not appear in these tables also were difficult to fill and probably had a high turnover. For example, when the parish of Tizapan el Alto was offered to Juan José de Aguirre in 1770, he declined after esti-mating its revenues at only 250p a year. CAAG, correspondence of April 12, 1770.

59. Villaseñor y Sánchez, 1: 29–31; BN AF 107 exp. 1475, fol. 53.

60. The cura of Sultepec in 1750 set out the uncertainties of holding a parish benefice in a minor silver-mining area. AGN RCO 72 exp. 29. His income could vary greatly from one year to the next, and the cycles of decline and recovery were likely to be longer than in most parishes.

61. AGI Mex. 2549–2550.

62. Zapopan and Nochistlan are the most problematical. Their incomes fluctuated and were somewhat lower than the others, and their curas appear less often in the bishops' reports. The test of length of service is a useful complement to the others, but it reveals little by itself. Some of the longest periods of service were in the choice parishes of Ameca, Nochistlan, San Juan de los Lagos, Santa María de Lagos, Teocaltiche, Xerez, Zacatecas, and Zapotlan el Grande, but individual curas also served eight or more years in Autlan, Rosario, San Cristóbal de la Barranca, Tequila, Tonalá, Valle de Salinas, and Xala.

63. The mean income reported in the mesada records for the 19 parishes that changed hands more than once is 916p. Excluding the sagrario parish of Guadalajara, it is 856p.

64. CAAG, file of 55 concursants for vacant parish benefices, 1770. Comparable figures for the 1757 concurso and for priests who applied for cathedral chapter vacancies from the 1770's to 1820's yield somewhat different results. For 1757, 7 curas waited an average of 11.7 years; for 20 in the 1770's–1820's group, the wait was 7.4 years. I would not infer change over time from these three sets of records because the 1757 sample is only half the size of the 1770 sample, and the 1770's–1820's group is not heterogeneous. It is mainly composed of privileged, well-educated curas, who would have moved more quickly than usual into parish benefices. The larger and more heterogeneous sample of 36 curas for 1853–54 gives an average wait of 7.9 years. This was somewhat lower than the 1770 figure of 8.7 years and is consistent with the expectation that fewer and less-educated priests would have competed for parish vacancies in Guadalajara in the mid-19th century.

65. The average of 6.8 years for the 1757 Guadalajara group includes the current post for curas who had not moved for at least five years. The lower 1770 figure (6.4 years) is based on a smaller group of terminated parish assignments.

66. The 1770's–1820's sample of applicants for cathedral chapter positions gives a higher average stay of 7.5 years. Again, this is not surprising, since these men held some of the best parish benefices in the diocese. Unless they gained a promotion to the cathedral chapter, there was nowhere else to go. The 1853–54 figures are substantially lower: an average of 5.1 years for curas who competed in this mid-19th-century concurso. The lower figure mainly reflects the smaller number of curas competing then. It was easier to become a cura in 1853 than in 1770 and easier to move into a better parish. Schwaller, "Implementation," p. 47, notes that the 1574 ordinance, in which parishes became benefices, encouraged long-term residence. But a benefice, by itself, did not guarantee a long tenure.

67. Dávila Garibi, *Estudio histórico*, passim.

68. Navarro de Vargas, pp. 571–77. The parish of Zinapécuaro, Michoacán, had only six curas over the period 1761–1843. Two account for fully 79 of these 82 years. López Lara. Fallon, p. 93, finds even greater horizontal mobility in late-18th-century Yucatán, where a priest could expect to serve in at least two parishes and might be assigned to as many as 17 during his career. Although there was great variation in the time spent in any one parish, the average tour of duty, he suggests, was three or four years. This average may be too low. Since Fallon notes that many priests stayed in a parish for less than a year, he apparently averaged all tours of duty he could document rather than only the figures for whole careers.

69. The data on Sotomayor, carrying his career up to 1818, comes from AGN Inq. 1304 exp. 3 and 1334 exp. 3; AGN Hist. 578A, 1793 Tixtla report; AGN Crim. 204 exp. 13; and AGN Acervo 49 caja 146.

70. In Sotomayor's 1800 deposition, he made the unusual remark that he could go home to see his parents only during vacations.

71. AGN Hist. 578A, 1793, Tixtla report.

72. Some priests ordained a título de idioma could move into the least desirable parish benefices but could not expect to advance much further. In his first 10 years beyond ordi-

nation in the early 1750's, Andrés de Salazar served short terms as a vicario in Xochitepec, Coyoacan, and Tenancingo, held the benefice of Coyuca for four years, and moved to Zacualtipan. The trials of administration there, the small income, and the unhealthy climate brought him back to the oposiciones hoping for a better appointment. JCB.

73. None of these documents says which of the Zapotlans in the Diocese of Guadalajara this was. It was probably Zapotlan de los Tecuejes (Zapotlanejo), since Zapotlan del Rey was not a parish seat and Zapotlan el Grande (Ciudad Guzmán) would have yielded a substantially larger income than the "meager rentas" Castillo spoke of.

74. AGI Indiferente General 244, 246, no. 11.

75. Cornejo Franco, pp. 232–34.

76. Ibid., p. 229, citing Agustín Rivera.

77. AGN Inq. 960 exp. 19. Yriarte was described in 1759 as "of good stature, red hair, eyes between blue and gray, almost aquiline features, and thick hair and beard."

78. In the case of Guadalajara, there was another difference between the secular parishes and the regular doctrinas: the Franciscan doctrineros tended to be younger than the secular curas and older than their vicarios. In the 1796 survey of priests for the diocese (CAAG, unclassified), 59 Franciscan doctrineros were 40.7 years old on average (median of 39), compared with 48.3 (median of 45) for the 8 curas and 35.4 (median of 33) for the 57 vicarios who reported their ages.

79. For example, Tenango del Valle (8 years), San Felipe el Grande (17), and Temascaltepec (23; AGN CRS 136 exp. 6), and Zacatecas (28; AGI Mex. 2549).

80. For example, Sultepec (13 and 22 years; AGN RCO 72 exp. 29), Milpa Alta, Tepetlaostoc (25; AGN CRS 156 exp. 5). Other long-term tenants are recorded in AGN Hist. 578A (1793): Ocuituco, Yautepec, Cuautla Amilpas district, Tejupilco, Lerma, and Tzontecomatlan in the archdiocese, and Cuquío, Zacatecas district, and Montescovedo in Guadalajara; also in JCB.

81. For example, Atitalaquia (33 years), Atenango del Río (over 11), Xaltocan (12), and Amatepec (over 9). JCB.

82. The cura of Iguala in 1771 said he had served in this district for 46 years, perhaps a record for longevity. AGN Bienes 431 exp. 17. The longtime cura of Tecozautla found the climate there especially agreeable. AGN Tierras 2179 exp. 3, fols. 34–36.

83. AGI Mex. 2549 March 23, 1755 report.

84. This was apparently the case with Diego de Cervantes, cura of the Villa de Santa María de Lagos in the 1750's. He was described as an excellent student of jurisprudence, outstanding in his zeal and dedication to the spiritual welfare of his flock, charitable, humble, and altogether indispensable. Ibid., March 23, 1755 Basarte report.

85. AGN Acervo 49 caja 116.

86. AGI Mex. 2549, Jan. 3, 1764 report.

87. AGN Hist. 578A, 1793.

88. In the 1757 Guadalajara concurso, the average stay of vicarios in one parish was 2.5 years (58 appointments for a total of 147 years). Over half of the terms (53%) were for a year or less. In the 1770 concurso, the average stay was 2.2 years (94 appointments for 207 years), with 61% of the terms being for a year or less. The figure was little changed in the 1853–54 concurso, where the average length of service by vicarios in one parish was 2.4 years (158 appointments for 384 years), and 58% of the assignments were filled for a year or less. CAAG, unclassified. The average for the archdiocese in the early 1769's was 2.2 years (158 terminated appointments for a total of 344 years), with 56% of the terms being for a year or less. JCB.

89. For example, the cura of Agua de Venado (Guadalajara) in 1796 claimed he could not find a fourth vicario willing to serve in his parish and asked the bishop to send someone. CAAG Joseph Fernando Román response to Oct. 31, 1796 circular.

90. AGN Hist. 578A, 1793. Since older vicarios rarely took part in the oposiciones, their career patterns are harder to establish than those of the curas.

91. For example, Valeriano Pulido, teniente de cura of Tenango del Valle, 1796. AGN CRS 39 exp. 1, fol. 11r.

92. AGN Inq. 1221 exp. 9.

93. AGN Inq. 1255, fols. 118–70.

94. Texas, García Coll., no. 113; JCB.

95. Poole, *Pedro Moya de Contreras*, app. 2, for a brief description of the offices. Considering the multiple screening process a man had to pass through to become a vicario, then a cura, and then a prebend, it seems likely that most members of cathedral chapters were conventional in their personal habits and privileged outlook even when they were divided by particular policies and personalities. But future case studies are apt to show more variety and conflict than general patterns can convey. Dr. Juan de Casasola, for example, was something of an outcast in the cathedral chapter of Guadalajara in 1755 because of his "excessive zeal in protecting people of low breeding, using up much of his wealth to secure the freedom of slaves." AGI Mex. 2549, March 23, 1755 report. See Cardozo Galué on the heated disputes within the cathedral chapter of Valladolid in the 1780's over certain aspects of Enlightenment thought. See also Ganster, ch. 2, on the offices and duties of the cathedral chapter of Lima.

96. BEJ Papeles de Derecho, 3: royal cedula of July 19, 1766.

97. AGI Mex. 2549; AGI Guad. 2973; Cuevas, 4: 113. Salaries of the offices of the cathedral chapter of Guadalajara apparently reached their peak in 1790, when the dean received 8,923p, the other dignitaries 7,750p, the canons 5,911p, the racioneros 4,432p, and the half-racioneros 2,243p. In 1812 the dean received 8,000p, the other dignitaries 7,000p, the canons 5,000–6,000p, the racioneros 4,000p, and the half-racioneros 2,000p. AGI Guad. 544 and AGI Indiferente General 2975.

Salaries in Puebla and Michoacán in 1755 and 1773 were higher than those in Guadalajara; both were higher than Mexico in 1755; and Michoacán's were nearly as high as Mexico's in 1773. For Puebla the respective figures for 1755 and 1773 are 6,795p and 4,456p for the dean; 5,885p and 3,862p for other dignitaries; 4,527p and 2,970p for canons; 3,169p and 2,079p for racioneros; and 1,584p and 1,039p for half-racioneros. For Michoacán, the comparable figures are 6,188p and 6,172p, dean; 5,302p and 5,349p, other dignitaries; 4,079p and 4,114p, canons; 2,885p and 2,880p, racioneros; and 1,427p and 1,440p, half-racioneros. Unlike curas, the holders of cathedral chapter posts were required to pay a *media anata* tax—one-half of the first year's salary.

98. The 1755 report on leading priests in the diocese describes Dr. Antonio Mercado, one of the canons, as a learned and respected former cura and "good ecclesiastic" who was so old and "so opaque in his mental faculties" that he could not fulfill the duties of any higher office. AGI Mex. 2549. Other members of the cathedral chapter were said to be in such poor health they had difficulty performing their duties.

99. *Recop.* 1-6-4 (1561) provided for cathedral chapter appointments by the Council of the Indies. Records of the council's deliberations over appointments to American cathedral chapters are found in the Audiencia and Indiferente General sections of AGI.

100. *Recop.* 1-6-5. This was consistent with Trent, 22d Session, Reform, ch. 2, decreeing that appointees to cathedral churches be competent to teach others and, preferably, hold an advanced university degree.

101. Solórzano 4-15-80, reiterates the preference for parish priests in appointments to the cathedral chapters.

102. AGI Guad. 207, 533, and 534; AGI Indiferente General 2975.

103. Promotion from within is clear from the bishop's report on the cathedral chapter dated Oct. 19, 1812, which gives a brief account of how each prebend reached his current

position. AGI Indiferente General 2975. Trent, 22d Session, Reform, ch. 2, included piety and good moral conduct as requisites for appointment. This usually went without saying in the appointment records.

104. AGI Mex. 2549, May 20, 1758 report.

105. Evidently 34 half-ración appointments in all were made during this period.

106. See Osores for various examples among graduates of the Colegio de San Ilde-fonso. Advanced degrees and other evidence of learning were always important, but the qualifications could change over time. The main change came during the Independence War. From 1811 to 1821, aspirants to the cathedral chapter vacancies were at pains to dem-onstrate their Spanish patriotism. Minor curas who had distinguished themselves in the fighting now competed for positions they had had no hope of winning before the Grito de Dolores. AGI Mex. 2550; AGI Guad. 535.

107. AGN CRS 47 exp. 10. Unzueta's papers were forwarded by the archbishop to secular authorities at that time. The cura of Mixcoac (Valley of Mexico), Juan de Garay y Villar, made a similar case for promotion to a cathedral chapter post in his petitions of 1783–87. Tulane VEMC 28 exp. 6.

108. The inventory of Unzueta's possessions in 1821 is in AJANG Criminal, bundle labeled "1820–21, leg. 61 (84)." His estate at that time was valued at 11,387p.

109. Despite this changing pattern of appointment, many of the applicants during the last decades of the colonial period were European Spaniards or prebends, curas, rectors, chaplains, and doctors from other American dioceses.

110. JCB; CAAG, 1770 concurso records.

111. AGN Inq. 960 exp. 19, 1759.

112. Documented, for example, in CAAG, 1770 concurso records, José Tomás Colón and Antonio Arias de Puga resumés.

113. AHJ Manuscripts, no. G-4-802, contains various petitions from parish priests to the bishop of Guadalajara in the last years of the colonial period for permission to visit the city for medical treatment or parish business. The standard two-months-per-year license is mentioned in the archbishop's pastoral letter of Feb. 2, 1762. BN LaFragua Coll., vol. 590. Bishop Joseph Gregorio Alonso de Ortigosa of Antequera specified in his pastoral visit in-structions of 1779 that curas be allowed to go to the capital for two months a year. Texas, W. B. Stephens Coll, no. 537. José Manuel de los Ríos, cura en encomienda of Atemanica, spoke proudly of "never leaving the parish for recreation or rest," as if this was unusual. CAAG, 1770 concurso records.

114. For example, the Valley of Mexico district of Tacuba in the 1790's had well-educated vicarios as well as curas. AGN Hist. 578A, 1793.

115. The cura of Otumba in 1795, Br. Athanasio Pérez Alamillo, for example, kept a house in Mexico City in which his mistress and their children lived. AGN Inq. 1360 exps. 1–2. The vicario of Zumpango de la Laguna in 1715, Domingo Soriano, tried to persuade a local Indian girl to become a servant-concubine in his house in Mexico City. Inq. 760 exp. 42. The cura of Amecameca in 1796, Dr. Ignacio Gonzales Castañeda, maintained his residence in Mexico City. AGN Templos 25 exp. 8. For the early national period, a par-ticularly interesting case is Manuel López Escudero, cura of Temamatla, Chalco district. His correspondence beginning in the late 1820's documents his comings and goings and his preoccupation with business affairs in Mexico City and on his hacienda. Texas, García Coll, no. 88. Archbishop Lizana y Beaumont pointedly warned against this kind of ab-senteeism in the cover letter to his first pastoral instruction to priests, issued on March 5, 1803. BN LaFragua Coll., vol. 893.

Chapter Six

EPIGRAPH: AGI Mex. 2549, Oct. 8, 1758, relación puntual ("como la renta de estos curatos pende generalmente de obvenciones, es mayor o menor según el número de feligreses, bautismos, casamientos, entierros, fiestas de cofradías, que suelen subsistir con algunos ganados y cortas fincas que poseen, con los sermones y otras utilidades de esta clase que no constituyen renta fixa").

1. AGN RCO 174 exp. 192. The Archdiocese of Mexico produced 1,170,746p, Michoacán 946,197p, Puebla 866,666p, Oaxaca 472,574p, and Guadalajara 447,091p. Lima (no. 2) and Havana (no. 5) were the other two dioceses that produced over 500,000p. Adding in the dioceses of Yucatán, Durango, Nuevo León, Sonora, Louisiana, and Chiapas, New Spain produced 45.2% of all Spanish American church revenues reported in 1796. The parishes of Puebla were generally regarded as the richest. AGI Mex. 2726.

2. AGN Hist. 128 exp. 4, fols. 132–38, Sept. 24, 1785, Pérez Calama informe ("Son mui escasos los premios sobresalientes de Minerva. Solamente con los curatos de dotación pingüe puede decirse que la insinuada escasez no es necesidad extrema").

3. AGI Mex. 2588, Jan. 26, 1784, report, fol. 5r.

4. "Decent" is the watchword in references to the curas' living from the time of the Council of Trent (21st Session, Reform, ch. 3) to the end of the colonial period in Spanish America.

5. Ibid., ch. 2.

6. Lorenzana y Buitrón, *Cartas pastorales*, p. 3.

7. *Itin.* 1-13-6. Papal bulls such as "Appci Ministeri" of Innocent XIII and "Pastoralis Offici" had made it clear that pastors were not to be offered a life of luxury or much comfort. The *Itinerario's* version of a decent livelihood stretches what these earlier popes had in mind.

8. Specifics about capellanías and other simple benefices held by secular priests can be found in the numerous relaciones de méritos y servicios, the occasional civil and ecclesiastical reports identifying all the priests in a diocese, the records of the bishops' pastoral visits, and the judicial records concerning individual priests. Examples of capellanía holders from the 1796 report on priests in the Diocese of Guadalajara (CAAG, unclassified) include Buenaventura González de Hermosillo (5,400p), José María Robalcaba (capellán of Hacienda Ajujúcar), Juan José Sánchez (7,000p), José Antonio Ramos (6,000p), José Ana Gómez Portugal (16,400p), Joaquín Rodríguez (6,000p), Pedro Méndez (5,000p), Antonio Balcázar (3,000p), Nicolás Cortez (4,000p), and José Norberto Mestes (4,000p). The subdelegados' 1793 reports on priests in the archdiocese (AGN Hist. 578A) provide less specific information, usually just a mention that someone supported himself mainly from a capellanía (e.g., José Espinosa in Huichapan parish) or held an hacienda chaplaincy in the district (e.g., Luis de la Urieta, Actopan parish). Two priests who submitted resumés in the 1762 competition for vacant parishes listed endowments among their qualifications: Francisco Benites de Ariza and Juan Thomas de Dios de Castro Tovio, JCB. In the same set of resumés, Juan Cassela said that because he held no capellanía, he had to study an Indian language before ordination. In litigation records, José María Alcalá y Orozco, vicario of Hueypustla in Zumpango district in 1786, offered the interest on his 8,000p capellanía as collateral. AGN CA 13 exp. 5. In 1772, the cura of Ozoloapan reportedly held 4,000p in two capellanías, one founded by Archbishop Vizarrón y Eguiarreta.

9. According to the dean at Valladolid (Michoacán), practically the only kind of endowment available to parish priests was the capellanía, and few curas or vicarios had the advantage of personal capellanías. AGN Hist. 128 exp. 4.

10. AGI Guad. 544, "Estado en donde se comprenden todas las rentas eclesiásticas de

esta diócesi de Guadalaxara de Yndias . . . 1790." Only occasionally do the pastoral visit records of the archdiocese in the late 18th century mention parish priests with capellanías, and then the holders were typically vicarios rather than curas. Among the few examples are Tlalnepantla vicario Laureano González, 1789, and San Felipe el Grande vicario Aniceto Garduño, 1792. AHM L10B/25, fol. 2r; L10B/28, fol. 128v.

11. Josef Ignacio Bustamante gives examples of young propertied priests who balked at parish assignments in his Dec. 7, 1815, letter from Zacatecas to the bishop of Guadalajara. AHJ Manuscripts, no. G-4-802. Occasionally independently wealthy priests served as interim curas, but few held parish benefices. For example, the legend on the portrait of Dr. Pedro de Villar y Santibáñez refers to him as a "modest, reliable" priest with "ricas rentas." Santibáñez served as interim cura of Real del Monte and Santa Ana, as well as two terms as rector of the University in Mexico City. Romero Flores, p. 212. Priests who owned haciendas sometimes helped out with parish duties. Brothers Francisco and José Vizente Méndez, owners of the Hacienda Totoapa el Grande, were said to be exemplary in this regard. They did not hold parish assignments but served the church at Acatlan without stipends and did the same in Tulancingo when they went there. AGN Hist. 578A, 1793, Tulancingo report.

12. AGI Guad. 210, Feb. 3, 1753, San Buenaventura y Texada report.

13. AGN Templos 95 exp. 3.

14. AGN Hist. 578A, 1793, Huichapan, Ixtlahuaca, and Pachuca reports. However, most of the landowning priests listed in the 1790's reports were not active in parish service (e.g., Bartolomé de Castro in Huichapan parish, with "unos ranchos de labor suios propios se save no tiene licencias pero se ignora el motivo, tiene muchas comodidades"; Ysidro Rubio Cisneros, Antonio Manon, José de Soto of the parish of Metepec; and Narciso Guio of Apam).

15. *Recop.* 1-18-10 (1594). Mota y Escobar, p. 31, gives the source of funding for such stipends in Nueva Galicia in the first decade of the 17th century. The crown paid the friars and secular priests who administered Indian pueblos, and encomenderos paid the parish priests in their districts, whether friars or seculars. Curas in non-Indian, non-mining towns were to be paid out of the residents' tithes; those in mining towns, where the tithe yielded little, were to be paid directly by the miners and other citizens, without any contribution from the crown. Referring to the construction of cathedral churches, Solórzano 4-23-5 (mid-17th century) indicated a three-part financial responsibility: a third from the royal treasury, a third from encomenderos of the diocese, and a third from Indians of the diocese, the last to be reduced by contributions from other wealthy Spaniards.

16. *Recop.* 1-13-21. Schwaller, in his study of the early history of royal stipends to curas (*Origins of Church Wealth*), notes that as encomiendas escheated to the crown, the number of stipended priests rose—from 119 in 1590 to 134 in 1598.

17. *Recop.* 1-13-21 provided that the stipend be paid from the tithe, and law 1-16-23 provided that four-ninths (often referred to in late colonial records as the *cuatro novenos*) of the half of the tithe not designated for the bishop and cathedral chapter (two-ninths of the total) was to go for the curas' salaries. Both *Recop.* 1-13-19 and Solórzano 4-15-73 and 2-23-21 (for Peru) stipulated that Indian tribute was to cover the stipend. Both also agreed that shortfalls in the stipends from the tithe or tribute should be covered from another branch of the royal treasury. *Recop.* 1-6-46; Solórzano 2-22-56, 4-15-74.

An unusual variant of the payment from Indian tribute is documented for the district of Tecali (Diocese of Puebla). In the 1730's the cura of Toxtepec was paid an annual stipend by the cacique of Tecali from the 20.5rr he collected from all tributaries in the district. Taylor, "Conflict," p. 275.

18. Brown Univ., Rockefeller Lib., Medina Coll., FHA 102, exp. 1, fol. 112. The crown

commonly provided money for wine and oil, along with the sínodos, in the Mendicants' doctrinas.

19. Sínodos for frontier missions of the Franciscans are documented in Velásquez, *Descentralización*. AGI Mex. 717 contains a 1704 report mentioning the payment of sínodos for the support of Dominicans in Oaxaca and the wine and oil consumed in their doctrinas. According to reports from the 1720's in AGI Guad. 113, the royal treasury owed the Franciscan doctrineros of New Spain and New Galicia some 7,950p for wine, oil, wax, maize, and the sínodos for 1719. The Marqués del Valle continued to pay an annual sum of 624p, 7rr, to the Franciscans of Toluca in the 1790's for their maintenance. AGN Hist. 578A, Nov. 26, 1793, Toluca report. He presumably used Indian tribute for this purpose, as he did in his Oaxaca districts (see AGN Diezmos 1 exp. 4, 1820, in which parish priests petitioned to have their sínodos restored now that Indian tribute had been reinstated). The frontier Indian settlements were usually staffed with regulars, but the crown also paid sínodos to secular priests if they were chosen to serve there. See, for example, AGN RCO 82 exp. 3, Jan. 12, 1762.

20. AGI Mex. 2549, Aug. 8, 1758, archbishop's report.

21. AGI Guad. 207, Dec. 22, 1708, bishop's report covering both the "four-ninths" share for curas and the "one and one-half-ninths" share for fábrica.

22. AGN RCO 86 exp. 160.

23. AGN RCO 39 exp. 32.

24. A copy of the May 28, 1724, viceregal order instructing Contadores de Cuentas del Tribunal to determine which parish priests needed stipends for their maintenance is in Tulane, Mexican Administrative Records, vol. 38. A royal cedula issued on June 1, 1765, required reports on the financing of assistants. AGN RCO 86 exp. 160. On Jan. 21, 1772, another cedula ordered the viceroys, presidents of audiencias, and governors to compile a five-year record of the income paid to parish priests, indicating how much each received from the two-ninths and how much from royal sínodos. This "plan de curatos" was also to indicate the amount of mesada tax they had paid. BEJ Papeles de Derecho, 3: 66–78. Then, in 1775, Viceroy Bucareli ordered full reports on the circumstances of parishes in the realm. Brown Univ., Rockefeller Lib., Medina Coll., FHA 43, exp. 14.

25. AGN Bienes 500 exps. 4–5; AGN RCO 85 exp. 76, Sept. 27, 1764; RCO 93 exp. 47, Aug. 25, 1768. In 1772 the Audiencia of Nueva Galicia notified bishops that there would be no more payment of sínodos. BEJ Papeles de Derecho, 3: June 12, 1772.

26. The cedula was sent to the viceroys of New Spain, Peru, and New Granada. It was published in New Spain on June 1, 1765. AGN RCO 86 exp. 160; BEJ Papeles de Derecho, 1: 389v.

27. BEJ Papeles de Derecho, 1: 522v–525v. The alcalde mayor of Tomatlan actively supported the petition at least three times between 1785 and 1794.

28. Ibid., 3: 500–504.

29. AGI Guad. 348, "Expediente formado en cumplimiento de la real cédula de 21 de enero de 1772," and "Plan exacto de los curatos," 1772; AGI Mex. 704, 1746–49 dispute over the cuatro novenos going to prebends of the Puebla cathedral chapter instead of to curas. Cedulas of 1772 and 1777, and article 223 of the 1787 Ordenanza de Intendentes, called for identifying parishes in need and distributing to them funds from the tithe. A cedula of March 13, 1777, provided that the royal treasury would contribute temporarily to curas' incomes only if the tithe and parish fees did not provide them and their assistants a decent living. Guad. 348.

30. Trent, 21st session, Reform, ch. 4; 24th Session, Reform, ch. 13 ("In parochial churches also in which the revenues are in like manner so small that they are insufficient to meet the necessary obligations, the bishop, if unable to meet the exigency by a union

of benefices, not however those of regulars, shall see to it that by the assignment of first fruits or tithes or by the contributions and collections of the parishioners, or in some other way that he shall deem more profitable, as much be collected as may decently suffice for the needs of the rector and the parish"); *Recop.* 1-15-14.

The crown did not completely withdraw its financial support for parishes and their priests. It continued to contribute funds for the construction of parish churches and sometimes for rebuilding and repair (if the damage had not been caused by misuse or neglect). In 1778, for example, the viceroy contributed 1,700p toward rebuilding the church of Ixtapaluca, Tlalmanalco district. Tulane VEMC 22 exp. 22. The crown was obliged by law to help pay for church construction from the royal tribute but was pushing for costs not paid from parish funds and local contributions to be met from the 8.3% of the tithe that originally had been designated for the construction and maintenance of church buildings. The bishops resisted this plan, stating in 1779 that this part of the tithe was too small to pay even a small part of the construction costs of parish churches and had customarily supported only the cathedral building. VEMC 29 exp. 1. Still, bishops contributed in a selective way to the construction of parish churches in poor communities, as the record of Bishop Alcalde's visita to Zapotlanejo and Real de Santa Rosa in 1776 indicates. AGI Guad. 341.

Small stipends that had been paid to missionaries of the regular orders were sometimes maintained for diocesan curas after secularization. For example, when two new vicarías de pie fijo were added to the parish of Xalpan in the Sierra Gorda after 1786 (Xalpan had been secularized from the Franciscans in 1770), the archbishop argued forcefully for a royal stipend of 1,200p. He noted that the parish was very poor and that the crown had been paying its five Franciscans 1,500p a year at the time of secularization. The royal authorities were favorably inclined, but finally authorized only 300p for the two vicarías with the expectation that the archbishop would make up the difference to meet the priests' basic needs. VEMC 7 exp. 40.

When new lieutenants were assigned in the late 18th century as permanent residents in outlying areas of parishes recently created from missions of the regular clergy, the bishops urged the crown to continue the stipends paid to the missionaries (as in the case of the two new vicarías de pie fijo of Xalpan).

31. BMM 69–70, 1: fols. 2v–3r (crown trying to abolish sínodos); AGN Bienes 500 exp. 23 (tithe salaries). Occasionally bishops set aside small sums for the support of needy curas. For example, the cura of the Santa María la Redonda parish in Mexico City was allowed 30p a month by Archbishop Rubio y Salinas in 1752, shortly after the parish was secularized. BMM 85, fols. 399–403. Paying parish priests from the tithe was a more common, if not standard, practice in 18th-century Spain. Callahan, pp. 15, 20.

32. AGI Mex. 704, 1746–49, Dr. Domingo Miguel de Aranda, cura of the sagrario parish in Puebla. Aranda also argued that curas starting out in a parish were especially needy.

33. AGI Guad. 207, Dec. 17, 1710, "El obispo de Guadalajara pone en noticia de VM lo que está executando su cabildo con el noveno de los curas."

34. AGI Mex. 2549. The 12 parish priests receiving small allotments from the tithe in 1759 were from San Pedro Analco (150p), Compostela (100p), Ameca (100p), Valle de Banderas (100p), Tala (100p), Tequila (200p), Purificación (100p), del Reyno (200p), Coahuila (50p), Huejúcar (336p), Salinas (215p), and Lampasos (100p). Figures on the distribution of the tithe in 1765 and 1769 are given in AGI Guad. 544.

35. The growth of tithe revenues is recorded in Humboldt, 1: 316; and CAAG, box of Tlajomulco parish records, June 16, 1795, certification by Francisco Cerpa Manrique, secretary of the cathedral chapter. The additions were Jolapa (200p), Xalisco (300p), Techaluta (300p), Salatitan (200p), San José de la Isla (150p), and Mesquital (200p). The royal

cedulas formally assigning 300p to Techaluta, Xalisco, and Xalostotitlan from the two-ninths on Nov. 13, 1795, and Aug. 13, 1796, are mentioned in BEJ Papeles de Derecho, 3: fols. 66–78, 502–4; and 2: fols. 299v–301r. The assignment of 200p to Salatitan was made on Feb. 1, 1791, after the cura made a persuasive case to the bishop. CAAG, box of Tlajomulco parish records. Curas from other poor Guadalajara parishes were apparently less successful in their petitions for stipends. See the 1802 petition and resumé of Joseph Diego Gómez, cura of Huaxicori, in AJANG Civil, bundle labeled "1809–19, leg. 5 (49)."

36. AGI Guad. 544, "Repartimiento de la gruesa general de diezmos," 1811. This source identifies the parishes that were added to the list after 1796.

37. BEJ Papeles de Derecho, 3: 66–78. On Dec. 21, 1777, Gálvez reported approval of the archbishop's request for stipends for curas of the poor parishes of Tempoal (300p) and Tancuichi (500p), with the stipulation that the crown would be reimbursed from the tithe. AGN RCO 112 exp. 201.

38. CAAG, box of Tlajomulco parish records, June 16, 1795, certification by Francisco Cerpa Manrique, secretary of the cathedral chapter. On Aug. 11, 1777, the bishop reported that in compliance with the cedulas of Oct. 18, 1764, and June 1, 1765, 4 new parishes, 8 ayudas de parroquia, and 10 new lieutenants had been added. He stressed that this had been accomplished without funds from the royal treasury, but it was also without cost to the cathedral, since the parish priests had underwritten the new expenses. BEJ Papeles de Derecho, 3: 66–78.

39. BEJ Papeles de Derecho, 3: 66–78, 1777. When ordered to place a teniente de cura in Juanacatlan, Bishop Alcalde skirted the issue of the two-ninths and replied on May 4, 1772, that to pay the 300p for a teniente there would leave the cura of Zapotlanejo destitute. He asked that the new teniente be paid by royal officials from the Ramo de Vacantes Mayores y Menores. The fiscal of the audiencia refused and ordered a full investigation of the parish's income and specifically of how the part of the tithe designated for parish priests was being spent. Ibid.

40. Ibid.

41. I have discussed the Diocese of Guadalajara here, but the same generalization would apparently hold for the Archdiocese of Mexico and other mainland dioceses. Archbishop Rubio y Salinas reported on June 20, 1757, for example, that his parish priests received no portion of the tithe and few had any income from interest. Cuevas, 4: 99. De la Hera, "Juicios," p. 315, notes the bishops' contention at the Fourth Provincial Council in 1771 that parish priests of New Spain did not have income from the tithe or "other fixed endowment."

42. Solórzano 4-15-50.

43. Manípulo could also mean collections for the three pascuas or high holy days of Christmas, Easter, and Pentecost. In this case it did not reduce other charges. AGN CRS 67 exp. 10, Tixtla, 1776.

44. Villarroel, p. 48.

45. Manípulos replacing other fees was far from a uniform practice in Oaxaca, though, as the published schedules of fees for that diocese show. BN Manuscripts, no. 1257 exp. 7 (1699 arancel); AGN RCO 93 exp. 103 (1703 arancel). Late colonial Oaxaca aranceles, however, included an annual contribution of 1rr from all adults (18–60 years old), and local custom often revised the arancel to include a larger manípulo called the ración ("maintenance fee"). Texas, W. B. Stephens Coll., no. 537.

46. AGN CRS 72 exp. 8. Similar deals were struck in the archdiocese in the early years of Mexico's national history. This was the case, for example, in Atitalaquia and Tulyahualco, as reported in the published informe of the governor of the State of Mexico in 1832–33, p. 55 (copy in Bancroft Library).

47. Tulane VEMC 15 exp. 5.

48. *Recop.* 1-13-7. Dominicas are described for Ytzocan in the 1760's in Pérez de Velasco, p. 79, and for Zoyatlan at the turn of the 19th century in AGN Templos 1 exp. 4. When the Sunday collection exceeded the charges for the weekly mass and the school-master's honorarium, the surplus was set aside for building repairs and new construction. The additional collections for the celebrations on special feast days are described for Zaa-chila in the Valley of Oaxaca in 1763 in AGI Mex. 727.

49. AGN CRS 130 exp. 9, fol. 395.

50. Ibid., fols. 395, 398–403. In a 1721 dispute between the cura and the officials of San Pedro Huazalingo in the parish of Yahualica, the dominica or "limosna de la misa" was 3p a week. AGN Tierras 2774 exp. 6.

51. What constituted the "minor functions" of the manuales varied somewhat. Some-times the phrase "manuales de las misas y funciones que ocurren" appears in the record of curas' incomes. CAAG, bundle labeled "curatos y cofradías, 1708–99," 1770, cura Joseph Joachin de Leiba y Carrillo's report; AGN CRS 75 exp. 6, witness no. 2, Luis de Vergara. In any case, the term "manual" appears often enough to indicate that small fees for mis-cellaneous duties were customary (as in the description of Diego Rangel, a vicario in the parish of Huichapan, who had no other income than "su salario y manuales"; AGN Hist. 578A, 1793, Huichapan report).

52. Benedictions and blessings are mentioned in *Manual breve*, fol. 70v; and AGN Inq. 1346 exp. 6, fol. 98r. On informal judicial services, fines, and certifications, see CAAG, cofradía documents (1772 petition by Indians of San Gaspar Teuchitlan to apply cofradía funds to church construction); AGN RCO 138 exp. 228, Dec. 21, 1787; RCO 149 exp. 181, June 23, 1791; AGN CRS 179 exp. 13 fol. 406r; and Tulane VEMC 7 exp. 5 (Tizayuca).

53. Tulane VEMC 43 exp. 1, Sept. 13, 1775, viceroy's letter to the bishop of Guadala-jara.

54. Examples of collecting for confession in the late colonial period: AGN CRS 74 exp. 1, fol. 4r; CRS 130 exp. 3, fol. 144; AGN Hist. 319 exp. 15; Hist. 128 exp. 7, fols. 147–54. According to *Itin.* 1-11-14, curas were entitled to collect 20% of the value of an intestate Indian's estate. I have not seen evidence that this was the practice in 18th-century New Spain, and it was specifically forbidden by *Recop.* 1-13-9 (summarizing a cedula first issued in 1609).

55. AGN CRS 75 exp. 4, fols. 274–75. But the viceroy's declaration probably did no more than ratify local practice. When the parishioners of Malacatepec (Metepec) com-plained in 1774 that the cura had violated the law in collecting two almudes of corn per Indian as first fruits, he claimed that he was simply following the local custom. CRS 75 exp. 3. In some places the first fruits were a voluntary contribution. Texas, W. B. Stephens Coll., no. 395, early 1770's, Tepeaca (Puebla). In some parishes the goods collected as tithe may have ended up in the cura's possession, sold to him by the collector at an ad-vantageous price rather than transported to the cathedral city.

56. An example of first fruits on both grain and livestock is AGN CRS 75 exp. 3; on grain alone, CRS 30 exp. 2, fols. 51ff; on livestock alone, CRS 75 exp. 6, witness no. 2, Luis de Vergara.

57. AGN CRS 30 exp. 2, fols. 51ff; CRS 75 exp. 3, fols. 96–100.

58. AGN CRS 75 exp. 6, fols. 340v–342r.

59. *Recop.* 1-16-2 (1535); Texas, W. B. Stephens Coll., no. 320, Acayucan, 1777. The first fruits on milk were supposed to be only what was recovered the first night. For an ex-ample of a complaint that the cura had violated the law on the collection of first fruits, see AGN CRS 75 exp. 3, 1774, Malacatepec.

60. Many cofradías, hermandades, and obras pías had been established in Indian pueblos of the archdiocese, but the records of pastoral visits from 1752 to 1803 reveal most to have been short of funds and property, declining, or practically inactive. In general

non-Indian cofradías and hermandades were more active and better financed in the archdiocese. AHM L10A/5–8, L10B/9–32.

61. Cofradía properties are documented in Serrera Contreras, *Guadalajara* (based on AGI Guad. 543, pastoral visit of Cabañas); Taylor, "Indian Pueblos"; and Chance & Taylor. Accounts of local cofradías and their property are well represented in CAAG, unclassified; and AJANG Civil, bundle labeled "1800–13, leg. 53 (142)." AGI Guad. 348 has a 1777 census and description of cofradías for the parish of Zapotlanejo that illustrates their importance in funding the basic masses and feasts that supported the curas. In three of the visitas, Ascatan, Tecualtitlan, and Matatan, local cofradías paid for the community's monthly mass and religious feasts. In three others, where there were no cofradías to support the religious rites, local priests were trying to establish them.

62. Two cases of curas running cofradía affairs are AGN Hist. 437 unnumbered exp. (Juan Valerio Barrientos, 1800, Mochitlan); and AHJ Manuscripts, no. G-4-802 (accounts of the cofradía of the Virgin of the Immaculate Conception, July 22, 1801, Ixtlahuacan parish). Two examples of curas compelling members to make regular contributions are AGN CRS 72 exp. 4 (1734, San Juan Huetamo, Guaymeo district); and CRS 75 exp. 7 (1789, San Andrés Timilpa, Huichapan parish). In the Huetamo case, the Indians claimed that the cura forced them to convert their livestock into spiritual property and to create cofradías, and that he whipped three Indians who would not give up their animals. Their attorney noted that under colonial law they were not obliged to found cofradías or support new feast days.

63. A rare example of a parish endowment separate from the cofradías that was to pay the cost of feast-day ceremonies is documented for Santa María la Redonda, an Indian parish in Mexico City. BMM 85, fols. 399–403, 1789.

64. AGI Guad. 543.

65. AJANG Civil, bundle labeled "1800–13, leg. 53 (142)," 1805, "Sobre patronatos laycos, menorías de misas. . . ."

66. A case in point is Tlajomulco. CAAG, Tlajomulco parish records, 1821 inventory.

67. Bishop Ortigoza of Oaxaca summarized this principle in 1779. Texas, W. B. Stephens Coll., no. 537, "Providencias de visita. . . ."

68. *Recop.* 1-13-12 (1608). Other cedulas of 1609 and 1654 against forced service for curas are in AGN CRS 51 exp. 1.

69. AGN Hist. 128 exp. 10, May 24, 1791 (complaint against the cura of Acaponeta); *Recop.* 1-15-14 (on the provision of horses); AGN CRS 136 exps. 6–7, fol. 302; Tulane VEMC 15 exp. 5 (1722, Yahualica). Apparently curas even took their beds along to the visitas as a matter of course. CRS 30 exp. 2, fols. 55ff. On official mail, see CRS 217 exp. 6, fol. 83v; and CRS 30 exp. 2.

70. AJANG Criminal, bundle labeled "1808, leg. 2 (6)," 1808, Chametla, near Real del Rosario, Nueva Galicia. According to Dr. Joseph Zelada, cura of Huizquilucan in 1762, the work the Indians did for him was customary and compensated for the meager fees he received. AGN Civil 1485 exp. 12. Unpaid labor seems to have been an especially valuable perquisite of parish benefices in Guatemala. Van Oss. *Catholic Colonialism*, p. 98, estimates its value at 2,400p a year for the average parish.

71. AGN Hist. 128 exp. 10, May 24, 1791.   72. AJANG Civil, box 223, doc. 13.

73. AGN CRS 29 exp. 2, fols. 57–58.   74. AGN CRS 51 exp. 1.

75. AGN Acervo 49 caja 97E, 1796, Indians of the four barrios of Tasquillo (Huichapan district).

76. Examples of these types of service are documented in several AGN ramos: Acervo 49 caja 97E, 1796, Huichapan; Bienes 663 exp. 25, 1818, Lolotla; Civil 1485 exp. 12, 1762, Huizquilucan; Civil 2072 exp. 19, 1788, Cempoala; CRS 29 exp. 2, 1711, Calimaya; CRS 72 exp. 17, fols. 311–12, 1797, Milpa Alta; CRS 136 exps. 6–7, fols. 302ff; Temascaltepec,

early 1790's; CRS 179 exp. 13, 1763, Actopan; CRS 217 exp. 6, 1808, Chicontepec; Crim. 232 exp. 7, 1800, Xochimilco; Hist. 128 exp. 10, 1791, Acaponeta; Templos 1 exp. 2, 1786, Guayacocotla.

77. For example, AGN CRS 72 exp. 17, 1797, Milpa Alta. The cura did not deny that he received this service but claimed that it was customary, and that the Indians of Milpa Alta paid barely half the fees they owed. The litigation in this case was initiated by an Indian, Antonio Victoriano, who complained that the town officials called him to serve too often.

78. AGN Bienes 663 exp. 25.

79. AGN Templos 1 exp. 2.

80. In principle, parishioners' holdings were among the "cosas indebidas" that curas were not supposed to request (Solórzano 4-15-50), but customary arrangements in which curas and parishioners acquiesced had the effect of law.

81. For example, AJANG Civil, box 49, doc. 6, fols. 11ff., 1724–25, Nochistlan.

82. AGN Acervo 49 caja 97E, 1796, Tasquillo; AGN CRS 179 exp. 13, fol. 404v, 1763, Actopan; AJANG Civil, box 36, exp. 7, 1726, villages near Culiacán, Guadalajara (cura was said to have told villagers that the king ordered them to sow four almudes of maize for him and to serve him without pay); CRS 67 exp. 2, 1766, villages of San Pedro y San Pablo Atlapulco and San Martín Ocoyoacac, Tenango del Valle (cura allegedly forced villages to provide him with 12 workers a month); CRS 75 exp. 6, fols. 340v–342r, 1786, Alahuistlan (a milpa large enough to sow 12 cuartillas of maize seed was set aside for cura's use); CRS 72 exp. 7., fol. 110, 1796, Hueyapan (cura complained that some local Indians had seized a piece of land his predecessors had used for their subsistence).

83. AGN Templos 25 exp. 4; AGN CRS 23 exp. 1.

84. AGN CRS 75 exp. 6, witness no. 3, Luis Mariano Moscada.

85. AJANG Civil, box 36, doc. 7, 1726, San Juan de Imala, Santiago de Navito, and San Pedro Cuilan, district of Culiacán, Guadalajara diocese (cura was charged with seizing a fishery and appropriating community lands for his own use and planting sugarcane on them with forced labor); AGN CRS 67 exp. 2, fol. 1, 1766 (cura of Ocoyoacac charged with compelling the Indians to rent him two pieces of community land for 25p a year).

86. AGN CRS 67 exp. 10.

87. AGN CRS 217 exp. 6, fol. 83v. The procurador thought this parish might be paying more to its cura than any other in the archdiocese. See also CRS 195 exp. 6, fol. 96, 1792, Zoquitlan; and AGN Tierras 2774 exp. 6, 1721, San Pedro Huazalingo, parish of Yahualica.

88. AGN CRS 39 exp. 1.

89. Clerical fees were not the main source of legal income everywhere in Spanish America. In much of southern South America no fees were collected, and pastors were paid a stipend from Indian tribute or the tithe. See Parras, p. 442; Cahill; and Hunefeldt. Parras, p. 443, and Villarroel, pp. 55–56, recommended exempting Indian pueblos from obvenciones as a way to reduce the conflicts between curas and parishioners.

90. *Recop.* 1-18-10 (based on cedulas of 1594, 1596, 1614, and 1618).

91. AGN CRS 72 exp. 8, 1785, for Archbishop Lorenzana's view that the derechos parroquiales should provide the decent living to which curas were entitled.

92. CAAG, box of Tlajomulco parish records, certification by Francisco Cerpa Manrique, June 16, 1795 ("tienen competente congrua para su honesta y decente sustentación con las obvenciones que les producen y exhigen según los aranzeles").

93. In some early-18th-century parishes, arancel-like fees for marriage and burial might be collected in a combination of cash and kind. In 1749 the fees for Indian burials in the visita of Amanalco (parish of Zinacantepec) were one hen and 9rr for adults, one chick and 4.5rr for children; for burials in the parish seat, the charge was three hens and 9rr for adults and three chicks and 4.5rr for children. Baptisms were 5rr. Marriages in the parish seat cost six hens and 2p, 5rr. BMM 135 exps. 21–24.

94. Some of the complex local arrangements for payments to curas are discussed under estimated incomes later in this section. One example of customary fees in a case in which the Indian parish chose to change to the arancel is Malacatepec, Metepec district, in 1774. The charges paid by the parish's eight pueblos, as outlined by their representatives, are shown in the accompanying table. The cura verified these contributions with two

Customary Church Fees Paid by the Eight Pueblos of Malacatepec Parish, 1774

Fee/Service	Purpose
Community	
Weekly	
12 servants	
7 rr cash	
0.5 fanega of maize	
2 rr worth of hens	Support of priests and maintenance of church property
2 rr worth of eggs	
14 cargas of firewood	
14 cargas of hay	
3.5 cargas of charcoal	
1 carga of pitch pine	
1p	Mass for patron saint
1p	Mass for souls in purgatory
Annual	
9p	Wax
0.5p	Fiscal fee
0.5p	Alcalde fee
1p	Matines de la Pascua de Resurrección
1 carga of wheat	Wine for mass
Individual	
5rr (per person)	Christmas celebrations
1 or 2rr (per year)	Home oratorio (where maintained)
5rr	Baptism
4p	Marriage
1 ox, 2 hens, and 2.5p	Funeral
2 almudes of wheat (per person)	First fruits

SOURCE: AGN CRS 75 exp. 3.

amendments: the 5rr per person was for all five principal feasts during the year, not just for Christmas, and the contributions from families with oratorios were paid to the gobernador for church ornaments, not to the priests. Other detailed examples of the variety of customary local contributions are AGN CRS 75 exp. 6, 1786, San Juan Alahuistlan, Zacualpan district; and CRS 39 exp. 1, 1796, Capuluac, Tenango del Valle.

95. For example, AGI Guad. 543, fols. 225ff, Ayó el Chico visita on Jan. 24, 1798; De la Hera, "Juicios," p. 315. An important source of income for parish priests in late-18th-century Peru was the commission they earned from the sale of indulgences (*bulas de la santa cruzada*). Cahill, p. 262. This authority was extended to the parish priests of New Spain in 1767 (at a 5% commission fee). Priestley, pp. 378–80. But the sale of indulgences was not mentioned as an important source of the curas' incomes in the documentation consulted. Decrees on the sale of indulgences in New Spain from 1750 to 1777 are found in AGN Bandos 4 exps. 18, 30; and Bandos 11 exp. 46.

96. Vera, *Colección de documentos eclesiásticos*, 1: 73–76. For the Diocese of Oaxaca, a schedule of six periodic payments or sinodales to the cura from his parishioners was established in 1617, but this was not a true arancel since it did not provide for the additional fees the cura could demand for various services. AGN CRS 178 exp. 12.

97. Revisions were made in 1683, 1748, and 1757. Vera, *Colección de documentos eclesiásticos*, 1: 77–87; BMM 135, fols. 177–80.

98. The proportion of income derived from birth, marriage, and funeral fees recorded in the 1775 reports for the Pachuca, Cempoala, and Zapotlan el Grande (Guadalajara) districts cluster in the 50–60% range: 52.6% for Atotonilco el Chico, 56.4% for Tolcayuca, 58.6% for for Tesontepec, 62.5% for Pachuca, 53% for Cempoala, 56% for Zapotlan el Grande, and 25.8% for Tuspa. Tulane VEMC 7 exp. 5; VEMC 61 exp. 18; VEMC 63 exp. 19.

99. An 1807 dispute over fees in the jurisdiction of Otumba, for example, referred to the 1767 arancel as the schedule then in force. AGN Templos 25 exp. 11.

100. Indians had hitherto been excused from having to appear before the bishop for the información matrimonial and securing a license from him. AGN RCO 62 exp. 80, Dec. 24, 1742.

101. Copies of the 1767 arancel appear in nearly all the disputes over clerical fees that followed that year. See, for example, AGN CRS 75 exp. 3.

102. *Colección de documentos históricos*, 4: 303–10, 1808. The Oaxaca arancel of 1777, by contrast, provided for a manípulo of 1rr from all persons 18 to 60 years old; 1 or 2rr and a candle for a baptism; 0.5p for a burial (2p if with misa cantada, 2.5p if with vigil and mass); and 2p for a marriage with a vigil and mass (3p if with misa cantada). For the Diocese of Puebla in 1775, the fees for Indians were 2.5p for the burial of a child, 3.5p for the burial of an adult, 7.5p for marriage outside the parish seat, 6.5p for marriage in the parish seat, and no charge for baptism. Texas, W. B. Stephens Coll., no. 537 sec. H1, pp. 299ff. Where the arancel was not followed to the exclusion of custom, the payments for community masses varied considerably, from half as much to twice as much as the arancel fees.

103. In parishes where the labor service and provisioning were not onerous and the cash contributions for the sacraments and masses were less than the arancel, the customary arrangements were usually favored by Indian parishioners as well as the cura, as indicated, for example, in AGN CRS 39 exp. 5, fols. 250–68.

104. *Colección eclesiástica mexicana* (Mexico, 1834), 3: 341ff (Bancroft Library copy). Monthly reports in CAAG suggest a seasonal pattern for the collection of obvenciones, with a peak in the spring (especially in April and May) and a trough in the summer and fall.

105. "Informe de Espinosa y Dávalos" (Mexico, 1831), p. 7 (Bancroft Library copy), based on baptism fees of 2p, 2rr, for Spaniards and 1p, 1r, for Indians; marriage charges of 7p, 3rr, for Spaniards, and 4p, 6rr, for Indians; and charges for a modest burial of 10p, 6rr, for Spaniards and 3p, 6rr, for Indians.

106. AGN CRS 217 exp. 4, fols. 61–67.

107. The area covered by the proposed parish of Achichipico yielded 788p, 7rr, from masses in 1766. AGN Bienes 431 exp. 3.

108. AGN CRS 136 exps. 6–7, answers to the cura's second interrogatory.

109. AGN CRS 204 exp. 10, para. 61.

110. CAAG, bundle labeled "curatos y cofradías, 1708–99." The rich parish of Tepeaca (Puebla) in 1775 was producing at least 800p in community masses and fiestas from its six pueblos de visita and four haciendas. Texas, W. B. Stephens Coll., no. 395, fols. 299ff.

111. The 1793 subdelegado reports on priests in the archdiocese occasionally mention curas living mainly or only on their derechos parroquiales. AGN Hist. 578A, Yahualica and Huichapan reports. However, cofradía contributions to the cura's income were important in some parishes. The five cofradías of Yahualica in 1722 contributed 38.5% of the parish income from sources other than baptism, marriage, and burial fees. Tulane VEMC 15 exp. 5. For parishes in the district of Pachuca in 1775, the proportion of the cura's income paid by cofradías ranged from 6.9% in Omitlan to 54.5% in Tizayuca, with most near the low end: Real del Monte at 8.7%, Atotonilco el Chico at 14.9%, and Pachuca at

16%. Tulane VEMC 7 exp. 5. Cofradías accounted for 12.5% of the Cempoala cura's reported income in 1775.

112. AGN Bienes 431 exp. 3. AGN CRS 13 exp. 3, fol. 44r, records additional masses for the souls of departed adults and children, the Virgin of the Assumption, and the Virgin of Candelaria in the parish of Olinalá (Guerrero) in 1781.

113. AGN Templos 25 exp. 11. This is representative of the variety of feast days celebrated in parishes of the archdiocese, but there was always some variation in the number and object of a parish's fiestas. Another good list comes from Zumpango de la Laguna in 1705. AGN Bienes 500 exp. 5.

114. AGN Bienes 500 exp. 7: Ocoyoacac 688p, San Pedro y San Pablo Atlapulco 441p, Santa María Tepeguexoyuca 286p, San Juan Coapanoaya 191p, and San Pedro Tultepec 113p.

115. AGN CA 13 exp. 9.

116. AGN Bienes 500 exp. 23.

117. AGI Guad. 352, cuad. 2, Ugarte report.

118. CAAG, 1770 Liñán and Velásquez resumés. The cura of Purificación in 1755 was said to be so poor that his obvenciones barely covered his subsistence needs. AGI Mex. 2549, March 23, 1755, Basarte report. The cura of Real de Hostotipac reported that during one four-month period in the late 1760's, he received only 2p in sacramental fees. CAAG, 1770 Ignacio García del Castillo resumé.

119. CAAG, 1778 Tala report.

120. The cura of Temascaltepec in the early 1790's claimed that his predecessor could not get the Indian parishioners to pay the fees for feast-day rites. AGN CRS 136 exp. 6, fols. 302ff. It was not always a case of the parishioners being unable or unwilling to pay. Joaquín Trujillo, cura of San Miguel Acambay, reported in 1766 that most of his parishioners lived for much of the year in distant places as farm laborers. As a result, some of their children were baptized outside the parish, and it was difficult to collect contributions from them for feast-day celebrations. CRS 156 exp. 7, fols. 229ff. AGN RCO 72 exp. 29 contains a 1750 complaint by the cura of the Sultepec mines that his parishioners wasted their money on gambling and drink to the detriment of clerical fees.

121. AGN CRS 67 exp. 3.

122. For examples of the collection of fees for funerals not presided over by priests, see AGN CRS 183 exp. 3, 1779, Tixtla; and Texas, W. B. Stephens Coll., no. 320, 1777, informe del cura de Acayucan.

123. This description of "rentas" follows BN Manuscripts, no. 1257 exp. 9. The annual income figures in the 1772 Guadalajara report were based on the "novenos, obvenciones, productos y derechos eclesiásticos"—the fees and emoluments plus any part of the tithe that the cura received as a stipend. AGI Guad. 348.

124. An unusual case in which food, fodder, and firewood were not provided in kind but paid for by an assigned peso sum is documented for Zapotlan el Grande (Guadalajara) in 1775. Tulane VEMC 61 exp. 18.

125. The 1774 figures for Guadalajara are higher, averaging 1,841p for the mesada-based figures and 2,065p per parish for the pensión conciliar–based figures. Unless some deductions and expenses have been subtracted from the 1772 figures or there was in fact a substantial increase in income from 1772 to 1774, the discrepancy suggests a margin of error of about 20% in the reported figures.

126. The offhand claim by Oaxaca curas in 1805 that it was "virtually a common thing" that "middling parishes" in the dioceses of Mexico and Puebla had emoluments and sínodos of 5,000p (AGN CRS 178 exp. 12, fols. 404ff) does not fit these figures. The 1805 figures for the archdiocese show only 15% of the 200 parishes beyond five leagues from Mexico City with rentas of 5,000p or more. Though the mean for those parishes in the

archdiocese was nearly 5,000p (4,959p), the median was 3,854p, indicating that the mean was raised substantially by a few parishes with very large incomes. No archdiocesan parish reported more than 5,000p in rentas in 1793.

127. The figure of 11,111p for Mazatepec would seem to be a misprint.

128. Monterrey and Saltillo are excluded from this list because they were separated from the Diocese of Guadalajara before the end of the colonial period.

129. AGN Hist. 128 exp. 4.

130. AGN RCO 93 exp. 103.

131. AGN Hist. 128 exp. 7, fols. 147–54.

132. This is the sense of judicial records concerning curas who lived in parishes of the archdiocese with 2,000p to 3,000p rentas in 1805. It is in the range of what Joseph Tirso Díaz, a Mexico City priest, regarded as a good income in 1770. Speaking of the income inequalities of priests, he contrasted churchmen with 2,000p to 4,000p rentas with those whose capellanía might be worth only 150p a year, if it produced anything at all. BMM 271, ch. 2.

133. AGN Hist. 578A, 1793, Zacualpan and Ixtlahuaca reports.

134. AGI Mex. 1549.

135. The proportion of modest parishes in Guadalajara was large, but nothing like the claim of Espinosa y Dávalos in 1831 that Cocula was the only parish in the diocese that provided an adequate income for the cult and cura. But both dioceses had a full share of poor parishes and small rentas. As a report on the secularization of Meztitlan de la Sierra noted, "There are towns that yield so small a profit that they do not offer a friar-cura his subsistence." AGI Mex. 727, fol. 3v of the report.

136. For example, AGI Mex. 2549, 1755, for the Diocese of Guadalajara: San Cristóbal de la Barranca, San Sebastián, San Pedro Analco, Mojarras, Techaluta, Atemanica, and Amatlan. For the Archdiocese of Mexico: JCB, 1762, Escanela, Coyuca, and Xumiltepec, Luis Román Gonzales Fuentes, Andrés Salazar, and Tiburcio de Salazar resumés; and AGN Bienes 431 exp. 7, 1771, Xacala.

137. Humboldt, 1: 85, was struck by the disparity in incomes among priests, but his statement that some curas de pueblos de indios had barely 100p to 120p a year does not square with these figures. He may have included vicarios in the very poorest parishes.

138. Even in the high income reports of 1805 for the archdiocese, 55% of the parish rentas were in the 1,000–3,000p range. Half of the Guadalajara parish rentas were in this range in 1774, but the figure fell to 27% in 1790. Van Oss and others have compared the curas' rentas with the prebends salaries to demonstrate that many curas were in an advantageous position. But direct comparison of this kind is difficult because men in both groups usually had income beyond their rentas and salaries, and the curas had substantial expenses associated with their parish duties. A comparison for Guadalajara and Mexico favors the members of the cathedral chapters. In the 1750's the canons of the archdiocese earned about 4,000p, the dean about 6,000p, the dignitaries about 5,200p, the racioneros 2,800p, and the half-racioneros 1,400p. Cuevas, 4: 113; AGI Mex. 1549. Presumably these figures would be higher for the late 18th century, when tithe income and salaries generally increased. In Guadalajara the cathedral salaries grew dramatically after 1758, when none of the offices paid even 1,000p. The dean's salary rose from 800p in 1758 to 4,437p in 1774 to 8,923p in 1790; the dignitaries' from 700p to 3,846p to 7,750p, and the canons' from 600p to 2,958p to 5,911p. The salaries of the racioneros and half-racioneros kept pace, rising from under 600p (for both) in 1758, to 2,017p and 1,035p, respectively, in 1774 and 4,432p and 2,243p in 1790. AGI Mex. 2549, "Nueva España: Año de 1758 Estado de sus iglesias . . ."; AGI Guad. 2973; Guad. 544. (A retrenchment followed, with a reduction of about 10% for all categories by 1812; AGI Indiferente General 2075.) Accordingly, only the half-racioneros and racioneros earned in the range of what the majority of the curas got in rentas, and they generally were at the high end of that range.

Relying on a short general report from the archbishop in 1767, Lopétegui & Zubillaga, p. 826, came to the misleading conclusion that most parishes of Mexico were impoverished. For a taste of what pastoral poverty in 18th-century New Spain could be, see Baegert.

Van Oss, *Catholic Colonialism*, ch. 3, suggests the average annual income (gross receipts?) of a parish in late colonial Guatemala was 2,265p (to which he would add 2,400p in unpaid labor), which is substantially more than the 1,533p and 987p averages for Mexico and Guadalajara, respectively. Whether the net income was as large as Van Oss estimates is debatable (according to him, the average parish priest had more real income than a judge on the Audiencia of Guatemala). Yucatán—like Guatemala, with fewer and larger parishes than Mexico and Guadalajara—also apparently produced higher average rentas per parish. In the older, more populous northwestern and eastern Yucatecan parishes, the average rentas were 1,646p and 1,483p in 1808. In the peripheral regions of Tabasco, Campeche, and the southeast, the average rentas were 3,000p, 2,433p, and 2,377p. Harrington, ch. 1 tables. Fallon, who also studied the financial affairs of parish priests in late colonial Yucatán, did not estimate parish incomes, but his mesada figures for 1754–59, 1760, and 1773 (p. 44), suggest substantially lower net incomes—ranging from about 150p to 3,600p annually, and clustering in the 1,000p-1,500p range. In the prosperous central diocese of Michoacán, the annual rentas approximated those of Mexico, ranging from 800p to more than 5,000p in the 1760's. About 10% of parishes there produced income of less than 1,000p. Mazín, *Entre dos majestades*, pp. 46, 113.

139. One of the better-paid assistants was Josef Antonio García de la Cadena, who received 600p a year for his services in the Hacienda Ojuelos. Since he was located 10 leagues from the parish seat of Sierra de Pinos and had ranchos under his care that were up to six leagues away, he hired another priest, Antonio Básquez, to help him. For that assistance, Básquez got 100p and board from García de la Cadena, plus 200p from the Hacienda de Gallinas for celebrating mass there each Sunday. CAAG, 1796 response of Jacinto Llanos y Valdés to request for information about priests residing in his parish. One well-educated young priest, Dr. Mariano Yriarte, declined to take up an assistant's position at a salary of 700p in the parish of San José, Zacatecas district, in 1815. He first declared that the house awaiting him was not fit to live in. When it was repaired, he pleaded that he might be killed at night responding to a call for confession. When he was promised a bodyguard, Yriarte finally declared that the income was inadequate. AHJ Manuscripts, no. G-4-802, Bustamante letter to the bishop of Guadalajara, Dec. 7, 1815.

140. In Sultepec in 1700, four assistants shared 548p from the cura's rentas. One had a capellanía that produced 400p a year; two had capellanías that produced 100p and 50p; and the fourth had no other income. AGN Bienes 500 exp. 8.

141. For examples of modest livings of assistants in the 1793 reports (AGN Hist. 578A), see José Gregorio Moreno, coadjutor of Xocotitlan, and Manuel Gonzales, vicario of Tapasco, both in the district of Ixtlahuaca; and Manuel de Chávez Nava, vicario of Tecozautla, José María Olloqui, vicario of Alfajayucan, Antonio Medina, vicario of Villa del Carbón, José Selacio Ramírez del Prado, vicario of Chiapa de Mota, José Rodríguez, vicario of San Bartolomé de las Tunas, Mariano Ruiz Miranda, vicario of Acambay, Juan José Pichardo, vicario of Aculco, Francisco Navarrete and Cristóbal Ruiz Miranda, vicarios of Xilotepec, Ignacio Basurto, vicario of Acasuchitlan, and Ignacio Sánchez, vicario of San Andrés Timilpa, all in the district of Huichapan. A particularly needy assistant was José Lázaro Aparicio Márquez de Alcon, of Nochistlan in the Guadalajara diocese, who described his circumstances in an 1807 application for vacant posts in the cathedral chapter. AGI Guad. 534.

142. Tulane VEMC 43 exp. 1, Bishop Alcalde's response to the viceroy's letter, Nov. 8, 1775.

143. For example, AGN RCO 182 exp. 78, Aug. 4, 1791, the strongly worded recom-

mendation of Bishop Ortigosa of Oaxaca. The coadjutor of Hostotipaquillo in the late 1780's apparently received all the rentas when the cura was mentally incompetent to serve. AJANG Criminal, bundle labeled "1790–99, leg. 12 (104)." Provisions for witholding stipends when the cura was absent are found in Trent, 6th Session, Reform, ch. 2; *Recop.* 1-13-18 (1583); and Solórzano 4-15-72.

144. AGN Acervo 49 caja 127; AGN CRS 39 exp. 1 (included in an expediente from 1796). Other full reports for Yahualica (Mexico) in 1722 and for two communities in the district of Chilapa in 1774 are in Tulane VEMC 15 exp. 5; and CRS 30 exp. 2. AGN Bienes 500 exp. 5 has a full list of income from sacramental fees and masses of all kinds in the Zumpango de la Laguna parish in 1705, but it does not include labor service and other contributions the cura presumably received.

Perhaps the best series of detailed reports on parish income is from 1775, prepared in response to Viceroy Bucareli's printed order of July 5, 1775. Tulane VEMC has some of the original 1775 reports prepared by alcaldes mayores or their lieutenants after inspecting the parish records in their districts. The Archdiocese of Mexico and the dioceses of Michoacán, Puebla, and Oaxaca are well represented in this collection. I examined three of these reports—for parishes in the alcaldías mayores of Pachuca and Cempoala in the archdiocese, and for parishes in the alcaldía mayor of Zapotlan el Grande in the Diocese of Guadalajara (VEMC 7 exp. 5, Pachuca; VEMC 61 exp. 18, Zapotlan; VEMC 63 exp. 19, Cempoala). The report for Cempoala shows unusually active sponsorship of celebrations in the parish seat by outlying communities, as well as of their own masses and feast days.

Zapotlan had 4,463p of income from Nov. 1774 to Oct. 1775, provided by a mix of sacramental fees, charges for Sunday and fiesta masses and processions, votive masses and novenas paid from endowments, provisions of food and supplies, and labor service. Cofradía funds covered 29.6% of the emoluments. This parish's contributions were distinctive mainly for the large number of servants at the cura's command—23 at a time throughout the year. The other two parishes in this district, Tuxpan/Tamazula and Zapotiltic, had smaller and less diverse incomes (2,203p for Tuxpan and something less than 500p for Zapotiltic), mainly derived from sacramental fees. An unusually large proportion of Tuxpan's revenues came from Indian payments in kind (28.5%).

The Pachuca district was composed of roughly half Indians and half Spaniards and castas. The curas' income there was erratic, depending on the current state of the mining economy. The Pachuca parish, including the pueblos of Pachuquilla, San Miguel Azoyatla, and San Miguel de Zerezo, produced about 2,400p a year between 1770 and 1774. Real del Monte produced about 1,630p in 1775; Tesontepec, 573p; Tisayuca, 1,093p; Tolcayuca and Acayucan, 668p; Real de Atotonilco el Chico, 1,212p; and Omitlan, 939p. Over half the income in the early 1770's came from baptism, marriage, and burial fees. Cofradía endowments provided a cushion against hard times when the mineowners did not make their usual payments for masses and maintenance of the churches, and parishioners could not pay their sacramental fees or contribute toward the cost of feast days. They supported Easter celebrations, other major feast days, and weekly masses, as well as the usual services for the cofrades and the special advocations of the brotherhood. Together, the cofradías of Pachuca, Real del Monte, Tisayuca, Atotonilco el Chico, and Omitlan provided 19% of the cura's reported income. Cofradías del Divinísimo (Blessed Sacrament) were the most common, supporting weekly misas de renovación, Holy Week and Corpus Christi celebrations in the parish, burial expenses and special masses for members, and the annual election ceremony. Primicias in this district were insignificant.

145. AGN Hist. 578A, 1793, Ixtlahuaca report.

146. AGN Hist. 318 exp. 2; *Recop.* 1-17-1 (1629). Unlike appointees to posts in the cathedral chapters, curas were exempt from the more costly media anata (half the first year's salary). Ventura Beleña, 1: 230 (Jan. 26, 1777).

147. Tobar, 2: 148.

148. BN Manuscripts, no. 1257 exp. 9 (1807). A royal order of April 12, 1802, authorized the "anualidades eclesiásticas or new contribution." BMM 153, p. 147.

149. For example, AGN CRS 204 exp. 10, para. 25.

150. BN Manuscripts, no. 1313.

151. AGN CRS 42 exp. 1, fol. 8v.

152. Tulane VEMC 7 exp. 5.

153. Ibid. 61 exp. 18; 63 exp. 19. Doctrineros from the regular clergy generally returned the fees to their orders and received maintenance and a small monthly allowance. For the two Franciscan doctrineros in Tuxpa (Jalisco) in 1775, the allowance was 5p a month. Ibid. 61 exp. 18.

154. Espinosa y Dávalos, table 2. According to one cura's notary, Ygnacio Trillo of Chiapa de Mota in 1751, notaries customarily received half the fees collected in the local ecclesiastical court. AGN Tierras 2774 exp. 10. The notary would have kept the annual census and the parish registers, and generally relieved the cura of the considerable paperwork for which he was responsible.

155. See, for example, the certification of Agustín de Acosta, cura of Monterrey, for the concurso of 1757. AHJ Manuscripts, no. G-4-719. The parish priests of Tezontepec and Tizayuca in the district of Pachuca each paid a visiting priest 100p for serving during Lent in 1775, as did the cura of Tamazula in the district of Zapotlan el Grande (Jalisco). Tulane VEMC 7 exp. 5; VEMC 61 exp. 18.

156. Tulane VEMC 7 exp. 5, estimate of alcalde mayor of Pachuca, 1775 (reported on June 4, 1776).

157. Palafox y Mendoza, *Manual*, fols. 2v, 4r, 7r.

158. Ibid., fol. 7v. See also AGN RCO 182 exp. 78 (Aug. 4, 1781).

159. *Itin.* 1-5-1. The *Itinerario* specifically excluded obvenciones from the share to be spent on charitable works.

160. For example, CAAG (unless otherwise noted), resumés of Díaz de Sandi (Mesquitic, 1806); Juan Manuel de los Ríos (Atemanica, 1770); Esparza y Gallardo (San Juan Bautista del Mezquital, 1770); Barragán (Huejuquilla, 1770); Acosta (Monterrey, 1755; AHJ Manuscripts, no. G-4719 GUA/4); Antonio Fernando Garrido (Ecacingo, 1762; JCB); and Joseph Antonio Thenorio de la Banda (Atlistaca, Puebla, 1795; Tulane VEMC 68 exp. 9): "dedicando las cortas obenciones y derechos parroquiales al culto y decencia de las mismas iglesias y socorro de las necesidades de mis feligreses." The cura of Zimatlan, Oaxaca, in 1784 said he spent all of his income on the parish. Among other charitable works, he provided food for more than 30 indigent people in his home and sponsored music training and grammar education for 18 of his charges. AGI Mex. 2588, Jan. 26, 1784, report, fol. 20r.

161. AGI Mex. 2549, informe reservado, Dec. 30, 1755.

162. In this 1755 report, the audiencia focused on the personal reputation of the curas —whether they were well educated, virtuous in their personal habits, conscientious in their parish duties, and charitable. The details are sketchy, and the court apparently had little information on many of the men. The three examples mentioned here were singled out as models of charity, but good works from the rentas are mentioned for other curas, too. Some of the parishes were described as producing so little revenue for the cura that he could not be supported from it.

163. Tulane VEMC 7 exp. 5. The cura of Zapotiltic (Jalisco) also was reported to administer the sacraments scrupulously and often without charge because of the poverty of his parishioners. The alcalde mayor's lieutenant added that this cura lost about one-third of his emoluments as a result. VEMC 61 exp. 18, 1775.

164. AGN Hist. 578A, 1793, Huichapan report.

165. Ibid., Tacuba report. "Interesado" generally was taken to mean "mixing in the temporal business activities of the laity." Ibid., Taxco report.

166. AGN Bienes 500 exp. 8, 31; AJANG Criminal, bundle labeled "1790–99, leg. 12 (104)." Commissioned by the cathedral chapter at Guadalajara in 1831 to present the diocese's case to the state legislature in its deliberations over reforming the arancel of clerical fees, Dr. Pedro Espinosa offered a longer list of usual pastoral expenses, adding in the costs of keeping the parish registers and a running census of the parish and purchasing supplies and instruments for the various masses and feast-day celebrations. He estimated the average annual expenses of a cura in this diocese to be 1,438p. *Colección eclesiástica*, 3: 320–34 (Speer Library copy: BX1428 C69).

167. This was a parish in which the beneficed cura did not reside or participate in any way. The parish income was apparently assigned wholly to the coadjutor. Under normal circumstances, a coadjutor's salary would have been an additional debit to the cura of Hostotipaquillo.

168. Palafox, *Manual*, fols. 2v–4r; *Itin.* 1-13-3. After declaring against all trade, commerce, mining, and estate ownership, the Fourth Provincial Council reiterated that "priests must only think about saving their souls and those of others, and their conversation should deal only with spiritual matters." CPM, p. 132.

169. *Recop.* 1-7-44 (1597), 1-12-2, 1-12-4, 1-12-5 (pre-1565 and 1576), 1-13-23. Solórzano 4-15-50, 4-15-60, 4-15-61, also recorded that parish priests were forbidden all trade and commerce so as to shield them from greed.

170. The Second Mexican Council (1565) forbade parish priests to trade, as did the third council. *Concilios provinciales primero, y segundo*, p. 205; *Concilio III*, pp. 338–41.

171. *Itin.* 1-13-3 (also p. 513, 1771 ed.).

172. *Colección de las ordenanzas*, pp. 73–74, 78.

173. CPM, pp. 132, 170–72.

174. CPM, p. 171. Archbishop Lizana y Beaumont's pastoral letter of March 1, 1803, pp. 29–30, is one of many exhorting priests not to dishonor their noble calling by trade and other worldly affairs: "¿Quién creyera pudiese haber Eclesiásticos, que olvidados de haber sido escogidos del Señor, y que como tales se deben apartar de los negocios seglares, especialmente de la negociación de mercadería, trafican con desmedida codicia?"

175. Pérez de Velasco, p. 99.

176. *Itin.* 1-13-5.

177. *Itin.* 1-13-6.

178. *Colección de las ordenanzas*, pp. 64–66, 78.

179. CPM, pp. 170–72.

180. Summary reports, such as AGI Mex. 2549, gobernador of Puebla's report, March 25, 1755, sometimes contain general statements about parish priests "mixing in matters of personal interest and illicit commerce, maintaining illegal liquor works," but these generalities are rarely pinned down with specific cases. Hunefeldt, p. 17, portrays parish priests in late colonial Peru as very actively involved in trade. Harrington, p. 326, finds less commercial activity among parish priests in Yucatán.

181. Examples of curas in business are AGN Hist. 578A, 1793, Taxco, Tulancingo, and Zacualpan reports (Manuel Tenorio de la Banda, vicario of Pilcayan, Manuel de Cañas, procurador of the Dieguino convent in Taxco, Josef Nicolás Martínez, cura of Atoyac, Isidro Estrada, vicario of Teloloapan); and AGI Guad. 352, Ugarte report (cura Miguel Díaz Rávago and teniente de cura Nicolás de Ochoa y Garibay of Mazamitla).

182. AGN Hist. 578A, 1793, Tixtla report (on José Miranda).

183. AGN CRS 140 exp. 4; AGN Templos 1 exp. 2.

184. Examples of repartimientos are AGN Acervo 49 caja 45 (cura of Yahualica, Hidalgo, 1806); AGN Templos 1 exp. 2 (cura of Guayacocotla, Puebla diocese, 1786).

Chinguirito was manufactured by the cura of Chimalhuacan in the archdiocese in 1802. AGN Inq. 1401 exps. 11–12. Zacualpan's cura in 1796, Joseph Manuel Sotomayor, was accused of many illegal business ventures, including operating a repartimiento, purchasing sheep for resale, and buying ore from mineworkers. Inq. 1304 exp. 3; Inq. 1334 exp. 3. He was regarded by his accusers in Zacualpan as a "slave" to cupidity and commerce.

185. Engrossment was the charge made against Ignacio de Vera Vetancur, cura of Chietla (Puebla), by the corregidor in 1777. AGN Hist. 128 exp. 3.

186. AGN Hist. 578A, 1793, Taxco report.

187. AGN Inq. 760 exp. 40. See also Inq. 1304 exp. 3, fols. 28–32, on Zacualpan's cura in 1796, Joseph Manuel Sotomayor. Isidro Acevedo, an Indian of Ixtepeji, Oaxaca, described how he worked for the parish priest there in 1808, locating mines. Acevedo said some men persuaded him to claim one of the mines as his own, then got him drunk and persuaded him to turn over his rights in the mine for 300p. He and his wife (an orphan raised by the cura) later regretted this betrayal and wanted title to the mine returned to the cura. Archivo del Estado de Oaxaca Juzgados, unclassified.

188. Some landowning priests are mentioned in the 1793 reports in AGN Hist. 578A (e.g., Felipe Zeballos Franco, a vicario in the district in Pachuca, reportedly owned a small hacienda nearby). Manuel López Escudero, the cura of Temamatla (Chalco district) from the last years of the colonial period well into the 19th century, owned an important commercial property, the Hacienda San José Axalco (valued at 83,521p in 1813). His correspondence (with complaints about being called back to the parish from business in Mexico City or on his hacienda) and accounts from the 1820's and 1830's are in Texas, García Coll., no. 88. For other priest-hacendados, see Tulane VEMC 69 exp. 4; and AGN DP 2 exp. 3. Harrington, p. 295, found a similar pattern of parish priests occasionally owning rural properties in late colonial Yucatán: 30 of 509 priests owned haciendas, and 35 more had acquired some other kind of real property while in service, such as a house or shop.

189. For example, AGN Acervo 49 caja 116, pastoral visit record, 1808–9 (complaint by Indians of Tamazunchale).

190. AGN Acervo 49 caja 68, Lucas García de Figueroa. Silverio de Nava, cura of Terrenate, Huamantla district (Puebla), rented and managed the Hacienda Tecoaque. AGN Inq. 1074, fols. 7–27.

191. AGN CRS 140 exp. 4, fol. 122r.

192. AGN Bienes 172 exp. 39 (complaint against Manuel Larrainzar, vicario of Tasquillo in 1803, who rented an hacienda in a neighboring jurisdiction).

193. AGN Tierras 2297 exp. 4. An example of a coadjutor accused of using his proceeds to buy land and livestock is AGN Acervo 49 caja 68 (Ignacio Gómez Tagle, parish of Santa Catalina Xochiatipan, 1796).

194. This was the characterization of the intendant of Durango in 1789. AGI Guad. 545. While only a few curas lived this well, he added: "It is undeniable that the worker is deserving of his pay and that he who serves the altar should be supported from it, but it is also true that he should not exceed the limits of moderation and decency appropriate to men of God."

195. An example of a cura's livestock holdings is AGN CRS 75 exp. 6, fol. 336. Harrington, p. 316, concludes that most parish priests in Yucatán (he does not distinguish curas from vicarios) owned a house, furniture, and books, but little more. The Indian cura of Colotlan, Antonio Canales, retired to his house in Guadalajara, leaving an estate in 1790 of 830p, 11 cows, 4 oxen, and 8 steers. AJANG Civil, bundle labeled "1780–91 (44)" (Canal v. Dábalos, sobre pesos).

196. CAAG, responses to Oct. 31, 1796, circular.

197. AGN Inq. 1308 exp. 1. The cura of Villa Alta (Oaxaca) in 1793 claimed that "after so many years in the benefice, I possess only three placesettings of silver, a little chafing

dish, and a few books. And with this, [a full] inventory of my possessions is made, for, as the saying goes, I don't even have a shirt [to my name]." AGN CRS 188 exp. 12, fol. 196.

198. Apparently this pattern would apply equally to the dioceses of Oaxaca and Michoacán. AGN CRS 178 exp. 12; AGN Hist. 578A, 1789 report for Valladolid.

199. AGN CRS 75 exp. 3, fols. 117v–119v.

200. Espinosa y Dávalos, p. 8. But as the many examples cited have shown, the collections were clearly often a considerable burden. As the Indian workers of the Hacienda del Salitre in the parish of San José Malacatepec explained in 1802, besides paying 0.5p for every baptism, 6p, 6rr, for marriages, 3p, 3rr, for burials, and one-half fanega each of maize, plus sheep, wool, and colts for first fruits, they had to provide a horse for the priest, 6p for mass on high holidays, wax, wine, and oil for the lamp (this alone cost 1p per week), meals for him and two companions when he came to them, and two sacristans. When they went to the parish seat to confess, they lost up to three days of work and 2rr for meals. AGN CRS 39 exp. 5.

201. BN Manuscripts, no. 1257 exp. 7, fol. 57v of the volume.

202. Despite an annual income from less secure sources of about 3,800p, the cura of Tlaquiltenango in 1803 expressed his concern about the lack of a parish treasury, cofradías, and other obras pías to pay his fees in the face of his fixed expenses for assistant pastors. It was a persistent concern of late colonial archbishops of Mexico and their pastoral visitors. AHM L10A/5–8, L10B/9–32.

203. The equation of income with respect and authority was made explicit by the dean of the cathedral chapter of Valladolid, Dr. Joseph Pérez Calama: "Los curas de renta corta en lo general no son tan respetados y obedecidos de los feligreses, como los de renta pingüe. Nada ygnora el dominio, autoridad, y respeto, que se atrae una decente dotación; y al contrario la escasez es espuesta a menosprecio." AGN Hist. 128 exp. 4, fols. 132–38, Sept. 24, 1785.

Chapter Seven

EPIGRAPH: University of Virginia, Gates Coll., item 838, ca. 1830 ("Hijos míos, el oficio que yo tengo es el de sacerdote que me lo a dado Dios y yo lo he resibido no para bien mío sino para bien de vuestras almas y por esto todo lo que pueda debo hacer que sea en bien de vuestras almas y [a]hora os ruego que por amor de Dios que cumpláis con la obligación de cristiano[s] y [*sic*] hijos de Dios que es cumplir con los Mandamientos [de] Dios y de la Yglesia también os ruego que vengáis los domingos y días de fiesta a la Sta Misa donde devemos dar gracias a Dios por lo que nos ha dado y en donde debemos pedirle todo lo [que] nesesitamos. . . . Se necesita que sean sus hijos verdaderos y teto [esto?] no puede ser sin saber la doctrina y para que aprendan voy a enseñarles un poco. Oygan").

1. "His is the solemnity of the man who believes himself a minister of the Eternal Word." Yáñez, p. 40.

2. AGN CRS 140 exp. 4, fol. 122r, 1796; or as Serna, p. 27, put it, "living under the pastors' eyes" (viviendo a los ojos de los Ministros).

3. Palafox, pastoral letter, 1653, Brown Univ., Rockefeller Lib., Medina Coll., FHA 102 exp. 1, chs. 9–16; Pérez de Velasco, p. 15. For an overview of the legal history of parishes and parish administration, see Gómez Hoyos.

4. The encompassing term "guide" appears in the decrees of the Fourth Provincial Council (1771). CPM, pp. 23–24.

5. AGN CRS 75 exp. 4, fols. 248–53.

6. AGN Tierras 2774 exp. 10, fol. 7r; Trent, 23rd Session, Reform, ch. 1. *Itin.* 1-1-1, para. 5, used the phrase "govern and reign," but as bishops made clear, curas were governors only in the sense that they acted as their agents: the cura was "an aqueduct that

carries and distributes the bishop's orders," as well as "the hands and feet of the prelate." BMM 271, ch. 89.

7. The image of sword and scripture appears in Lizana y Beaumont, pastoral letter of March 1, 1803. The struggle against the common enemy is from AGN Inq. 1346 exp. 6, fol. 102.

8. *Itin.* 1-1-2, 3-4-16. "Médico" and "médico espiritual" appear repeatedly in the literature, as in Arze, n.p.; and CPM, pp. 23–24.

9. The Council of Trent stressed the importance of the mass as a teaching tool: "that they [the pastors], either themselves or through others, explain frequently during the celebration of the mass some of the things read during the mass, and that among other things they explain some mystery of this most holy sacrifice, especially on Sundays and festival days." 22d Session, Mass, ch. 8. See also its words on teaching in 24th Session, Reform, ch. 7; and *Recop.* 1-1-10 and 1-6-46.

The manuals for parish priests and episcopal laws on the ministry also put heavy emphasis on the teaching of doctrine and preaching to Indians, and on the role of Indian assistants, as did the Fourth Provincial Council. Pérez de Velasco, p. 71; *Colección de las ordenanzas*, pp. 15, 164–67; CPM, pp. 112–16, 189. Men in the field agreed. Manuel Maruri, cura of Tepatitlan, for example, counted teaching doctrine as one of his principal parish duties. Harvard Univ., Widener Lib., 3398.38F (Maruri's 1810 resumé).

10. Trent 24th Session, Reform, ch. 4. Ricker, pp. 165–66, says that "preaching was considered the primary obligation of the pastor of souls." It was, at any rate, important enough to require the same schedule as that of teaching doctrine: every Sunday, all holy days, and daily during Advent and Lent.

11. For moral theology, Arze also recommended "Fr. Manuel Pérez" (*Farol indiano*), "Fr. Juan Baptista" (*Advertencias*, cited in *Farol indiano*, p. 7), and "the author of this small book" (Pérez de Velasco).

12. *Itinerario* was first published in Madrid. Subsequent editions: 1678, Lyons; 1698, 1726, 1737, and 1754, Antwerp; and 1771, Madrid. All, including the 1668 original, are available in the John Carter Brown Library and the Medina Collection on microfilm in the Rockefeller Library, Brown University.

13. The *Itinerario* was listed, for example, in the inventory of the possessions of Mariano Calzada, vicario of various parishes in the Diocese of Guadalajara during the 1780's. AGN Inq. 1308 exp. 1, 1790. A copy of the 1698 edition, with a few marginal notes by a parish priest in the district of Tlaltenango (Guadalajara) in the 1760's, is in the Bancroft Library. In *Farol indiano*, the cura Manuel Pérez cites the *Itinerario* often as an authoritative work and assumes that his readers owned a copy or knew the work well. Even so, he occasionally modifies some statements of "the most illustrious Montenegro" that seemed to him to be based on the author's work with Indians of Ecuador and not always appropriate to New Spain (e.g., p. 84). Paredes (1759) mentions de la Peña Montenegro among five authors who were widely known. Pérez de Velasco, pp. 35, 53, also cites the *Itinerario* as an authoritative work in pastoral theology, while using *Farol indiano* for a few adjustments to suit Mexican conditions. A treatise on Indian spiritual and temporal affairs by a Mexico City priest in 1770 cites the *Itinerario* four times and refers to "Montenegro" as "this most observant prelate." Joseph Tirso Díaz, "Papel sobre el verdadero modo de beneficiar a los yndios en lo espiritual y temporal con utilidad del estado: impugnando un proiecto acerca de lo mismo," BMM 271, chs. 66, 79, 111, 112. In a lengthy, polished report of 1784 on Indian drunkenness and the use of corporal punishment by parish priests, the cura of Zimatlan (Oaxaca), Joseph Manuel Ruiz y Cervantes, used the *Itinerario* as his principal source. AGI Mex. 2588, Jan. 26, 1784, report, fols. 2v, 3r, 11, 18r, 20r.

There are also incidental references by priests to the *Itinerario* in administrative correspondence. In 1771, the cura of Real de Jacala (Mexico) referred to it in his claim for income attached to the parochial benefice. AGN Bienes 431 exp. 7. In 1790, Manuel Morales, cura of Tlaola (Mexico), wrote to the viceroy about the poor education and bad habits of the Indians in his parish, and asked for support in promoting Spanish-language schools among them. His letter was forwarded to the archbishop, who consulted the previous cura, Cristóbal Mendoza, then the rector of the Colegio de Tepotzotlan. Apparently irritated that Morales implicitly presented his own work in a bad light, Mendoza responded that Morales was "possessed of a hypochondriac's passion" and recommended that he brush up on his de la Peña Montenegro and Pérez. The archbishop, who would not have appreciated Morales going over his head to the viceroy, agreed. In a heated reply of Jan. 1, 1791, Morales told the viceroy he did not think he needed to read these authors unless specifically ordered to do so by the archbishop because they were "full of looseness contrary to the Holy Scripture of the Gospel." Tulane VEMC 24 exp. 2. The *Itinerario* and the *Recopilación* are among the colonial books most often found today in research libraries and on the antiquarian book market.

14. *Itin.* 1-1-2, 1-1-3.

15. *Itin.* 2-10-5, 2-11-1.

16. The cura's teaching responsibilities are emphasized throughout the *Itinerario* (e.g., 2-10-5, 2-11-1).

17. Both Pérez (e.g., p. 84), and Pérez de Velasco (e.g., pp. 35ff) felt that de la Peña Montenegro's view of Indians (especially his emphasis on their "invincible ignorance" and "idolatry") and his discussions of encomienda and mine labor bore the marks of his home diocese, Quito.

18. Beginning with the second edition (1678), the title page announced a "new edition purged of many errors." By the 1771 edition, the promise was that "a great many errors" had been purged. But the errors corrected were almost all typographical and grammatical. Occasionally a reference to the *Recopilación* or other authority was added, but the 17th-century substance of the text was untouched. A first edition of the *Itinerario* expurgated for the Mexican Inquisition by Fr. Joseph de Miranda noted a few passages that were incorrect doctrine, including parts of 3-3-10 para. 2; 4-3 prologue, para. 5; and 5-4-21 para. 4. BN R278, Pen. i, handwritten marginal notes. None of these passages was deleted or changed in later editions.

19. Brown Univ., Rockefeller Lib., Medina Coll., FHA 102 exp. 1, fol. 97v.

20. The Second Provincial Council had made this point two centuries before. Noting that many curas were negligent in their teaching of the means to salvation, it ordered that all curas own a Bible, a manual for the sacraments, and several compendia on moral theology. *Concilios provinciales, primero y segundo*, ch. 2 of the council's decrees.

21. Among the 45 books in the library of Mariano Calzada, former vicario of Sierra de Pinos, Guadalajara, were a manual for parish priests, a copy of the *Itinerario*, various books of sermons, and a copy of the Council of Trent decrees in Latin. AGN Inq. 1308 exp. 1, fols. 26–27, 1790. The cura of San Bartolomé Ozolotepec, Pedro de Zúñiga y Toledo, in 1754 had an even greater library of nearly 100 volumes, valued at 259p. Most were religious books, but there were literary works by Virgil, Solís, and Gracián, Villaseñor y Sánchez's *El theatro americano*, and two booklets on mercury. AGN Tierras 2297 exp. 4, fols. 7r–35r. Too many books could be as damaging as too few. The Fourth Provincial Council gave a dark warning to its American priests in 1771 about ranging too far in their reading: "Waters from a pure source are beneficial and those that are murky, turbulent, and not cleansed of their unseen poison are noxious." CPM, 1-1-3.

22. A manual published in Mexico in 1789 and approved by Archbishop Núñez de Haro y Peralta warned readers that it superseded all others, and that priests who did not follow it exactly would be punished. *Manual de párrocos*, p. 2.

23. Another general work published in Mexico that could have served parish priests as

a moral theology text is Clemente de Ledesma, *Despertador Republicano*. I have not seen it cited in 18th-century works.

24. Manuel Pérez, pp. 8ff. Other practical guides, such as the *Manual de sacerdotes* by Puebla's Bishop Palafox (1664), were probably used only in their home diocese. The later *El ayudante de cura* (1766) is presented as the work of a wise old cura sharing his experience with beginners. Pérez de Velasco had served more than 40 years in Indian parishes, was fluent in Nahuatl, and was reputed to be a virtual apostle in his parish of Santo Domingo Ytzocan. Like Pérez, he regarded Indians as rustics and inclined to vices, but he chose to see them more as innocents than as sly children—more childlike than childish. He judged them less and focused on opportunities to reform their behavior and lead them to salvation. Not surprisingly, his manual gives special attention to the challenges of the confessional—how to lead Indians to probe their consciences and make a truthful declaration of their sins. It offers step-by-step advice to vicarios on what to do when they visit an outlying town in the parish, how to coordinate the various activities of the parish during Lent, and much more.

25. Juan Villegas, *Aplicación del Concilio de Trento*; Bayle, "Concilio de Trento."

26. Royal cedulas invoking the Council of Trent and ordering enforcement of its decrees include AGN RCO 39 exp. 92 (July 23, 1718); RCO 93 exp. 47 (Aug. 25, 1768); RCO 100 exp. 186 (June 4, 1772); and RCO 160 exp. 141 (Feb. 27, 1795). Royal officials sometimes appealed to the decrees of Trent to defend their jurisdiction against what they regarded as encroachment by curas (e.g., AGN Hist. 319 exp. 5, 1777, complaint of alcalde mayor of Cadereyta). For one of the frequent references in late colonial pastoral letters to the Council of Trent as the principal authority on the duties of parish priests, see Lizana y Beaumont, letter of March 1, 1803. Copies of the Tridentine decrees were owned by at least some parish priests, as evidenced in their citing of them to defend their performance before the audiencia. AGN CRS 75 exp. 3 (1774, Indians of San Felipe and Santiago, parish of Malacatepec, v. cura); Hist. 319 exp. 5 (1777, countercomplaint by substitute cura of Xalpan against alcalde mayor of Cadereyta); Hist. 437 unnumbered exp. (1800, "sobre que el cura del pueblo de Mochitlan Br. d. Juan Valerio Barrientos maltrata y exige derechos indebidos a sus feligreses"). The *Itinerario* cites the Trent decrees in many places, including 1-1-2, para. 14, 1-1-3, paras. 3 and 7, 1-2-1, para. 3, 1-4 prologue, para. 4, book 3 prologue, para. 11, and 4-4-8, para. 2.

27. *Concilio III*, pp. 41–43 ("deben quitarse a los indios las cosas que sirven de impedimento a la salud de sus almas").

28. Solórzano 3-26-11; *Recop.* 6-3-1 ("para que los Indios sean instruídos en la Santa Fe Católica, y Ley Evangélica, y olvidando los errores de sus antiguos ritos, y ceremonias vivan en concierto, y policía"). The Third Provincial Council declared that parish priests who did not have jurisdiction over public delinquency should report transgressions so that the guilty would be brought to justice. *Concilio III*, p. 100.

29. *Itin.* 1-5-4. The cura of Chipetlan in 1772, José María Hurtado de Mendoza, spoke of the "celo, esmero, y cuidado con que debo atender a mis pobres feligreses indios, no sólo en lo espiritual sino también en lo temporal." AGN Alcaldes Mayores 11, fols. 357-70. For a pastor's conception of the temporal aspect of his spiritual duties, see the parable set down by Antonio Pablo de Herrera y Mendoza in his resumé. JCB.

30. BN LaFragua Coll., vol. 578, undated pastoral letter of Diego Rodríguez de Rivas, bishop of Guadalajara (1763–70); 1649 pastoral letter of Juan de Palafox y Mendoza; Moxó, *Cartas mejicanas*, pp. 243–44.

31. *Itin.* 1-1-3. For the cura of Zimatlan (Oaxaca) in 1772, this meant working to curb all Indian vices, from concubinage to theft, fights, and idolatry. AGN Crim. 306 exp. 5, letter of May 6.

32. *Itin.* 3-3-13.

33. *Itin.* 1-1-2. Parish priests also assisted in the work of the episcopal court as investigators into the conduct of priests in neighboring parishes (e.g., AHJ Manuscripts, no. G-4-802, fol. 68, Dec. 28, 1814; AGN Acervo 49 caja 45, 1806, case of Mariano Joseph de Paz, cura of Huejutla).

34. Variants include Juan Joseph Ygnacio Lozano y Prieto, "cura beneficiado por su Magestad vicario y juez eclesiástico"; Nicolás Mariano Ladrón de Guevara, "cura por su Magestad y juez eclesiástico"; Juan Alexandro Piedra Palacio, "cura por Su Magestad de deste partido de Ocuituco, vicario in capite y juez eclesiástico." Tulane VEMC 15 exp. 3.

35. *Itin.* 3-4-16.

36. John Carter Brown Lib., "Práctica o fórmula de autos eclesiásticos . . . para los curas," a 1746 manuscript prepared for the cura of Huamantla (Puebla), includes forms for autos eclesiásticos in these four areas. According to *Itin.* 1-11-1 to 1-11-4, the pastor could draw up wills for Indian parishioners if there was no one licensed to do so available ("quando no se ofrece otra persona que los pueda hacer"). AGN Inq. 1113 is a complaint against the cura of Cempoala, Juan Antonio Xil de Andrade, in 1777 for controlling the formulation of a will and influencing the distribution of the estate as the executor. The cura of Xochimilco in 1792 also apparently influenced the execution of an Indian will. AGN Tierras 2670 exp. 5.

In the late colonial period, only heresy among non-Indians still came under the Inquisition (though many parish priests were involved in such cases as comisarios or local agents of the Inquisition). Indian religious deviation was supposed to be disposed of by the diocesan courts, assisted by district governors of the crown. But that curas had the authority to serve as judges of first instance in cases of "idolatry" and "superstition" among their Indian parishioners is evident in the form book prepared for the cura of Huamantla (1746), which devoted a section to "la forma de ajustar las causas de ydolatría entre yndios." ("Práctica o fórmula," cited above, fols. 30v–31v.) And that they did exercise this authority is indicated by occasional mentions of it as evidence of dedicated service in the resumés. The longtime cura of Atitalaquia (Hidalgo) reported in the early 1760's that his activities as juez eclesiástico included a 1737 prosecution of two Indian women and one man for worshipping idols representing the gods of water and cornfields. JCB, Castilla resumé. Few "idolatry" cases from the late colonial period seem to survive in the form of episcopal court trial records. Their infrequent mention in the relaciones de méritos y servicios and other evidence of priests at work in their parishes presented in this book suggest that idolatry was no longer a major issue for colonial authorities in the late 18th century.

37. Various examples of curas as jueces eclesiásticos pursuing cases of rape, incest, sodomy, and drunkenness appear in AGN Acervo 49 (e.g., caja 49). See also AGN Crim. 159, fols. 163ff (for 1797 report by Salvador Sebastián Nieto, cura of Valle de San Francisco, on drunkenness and gambling); and AGN CRS 156 exp. 7, fols. 229ff (for cura of San Miguel Acambay, Joaquín Trujillo, operating as juez verbal in cases of drunkenness and adultery, 1761).

38. AGN Tierras 2774 exp. 10. In *Incidents of Travel in Yucatán*, 1: 170, Stephens describes the cura of Ticul as "the temporal as well as spiritual physician of the village." In his *Incidents of Travel in Central America*, p. 104, he describes the cura of Esquipulas, Guatemala, as the "principal director of all the business of the town."

39. The cura of Tala also reported that he received a small fee for these services. CAAG, unclassified cofradía records (1772 petition by Indians of San Gaspar Teuchitlan and related documents).

40. AGN CRS 195 exp. 6. In the assault case, the subdelegado said that since the Indian offender did not have the money to pay the fine, his house had been sold. The subdelegado was on solid footing here, for *Recop.* 1-10-6 to 1-10-8 prohibited jueces eclesiásticos from sentencing Indians with fines or forced labor.

41. AJANG Civil, box 116, doc. 4 (Ocotlan, 1778); Civil, box 125, doc. 2.

42. AGN CRS 179 exp. 13, fol. 408r. Alvarez's predecessor in 1756 had been involved in settling a local land dispute and negotiating peace after a disturbance of public order in Actopan, AGN Civil 241 exp. 1.

43. AGN CRS 75 exp. 4, fols. 248–53 ("costumbre antiquada el que los jueses eclesiásticos [como lo es] en semejantes retiros husen de estos actos de justicia para que no se quedan impunes los delictos"; "quiere hacer el papel de juez."

44. BN LaFragua Coll., vol. 590, p. 22. Archbishop Rubio y Salinas's concern in his circular to jueces eclesiásticos and curas of Feb. 2, 1762, was how they wielded judicial authority over the Indians (priests were, for example, to "flog the vice in them, not the nation"). He did not call into question the existence of that authority.

45. Ventura Beleña, 2: 196, doc. 45 ("vagos, díscolos, ociosos, incorregibles y abandonados a la holgazanería y a la ebriedad").

46. Calderón Quijano et al., 2: 400. Earlier in the 18th century, the viceroy sometimes empowered parish priests to enforce decrees that affected alcaldes mayores, such as their unlawful collection of 0.5rr per family for fábrica (e.g., AGN Bandos 5 exps. 34–36, Cuernavaca, 1759). By the 1790's, curas were more likely to be told to implement royal decrees that restricted their own powers (e.g., BEJ Papeles de Derecho, 1: 539–40, 1791, Intendant Ugarte's order to curas to implement the new laws on the community treasuries, the use of communal lands, and restrictions on cofradía ranches).

47. Assisting the civil authorities is what the Fourth Provincial Council, ratifying the spirit of royal decrees, had in mind. CPM, p. 116.

48. Serna, p. 346.

49. Trent, 24th Session, Reform, chs. 4, 7.

50. *Recop.* 1-1-10, 1-6-46.

51. *Itin.* 1-4 prologue (obligation to teach Christian doctrine to Indians every Sunday and other holidays); 1-4-9 (duty to teach essential beliefs to children up to age 10); 2-8 prologue, 2-8-1 ("doctrina que ha de saber"); 2-8-9 (the burden of responsibility was on the cura). See also Torquemada, 3: ch. 42, p. 111, describing basic doctrine as consisting of the per signum, pater noster, ave maria, credo, salve regina, ten commandments, articles of faith, sacraments, and commandments of the church; and Omerick, BMM 113, pp. 130ff.

52. *Itin.* 1-1-2; *Concilios mexicanos primero, y segundo*, p. 125.

53. Lic. José Joaquín de la Pedreguera, cura of Jalapa, described himself as famous for his sermons. AGI Mex. 2550, 1820 resumé. In 1805 the Indians of Almoloya, Metepec district, praised their interim cura, Domingo de la Peña, for his sermons on feast days. AGN Bienes 172 exp. 37. Another effective preacher, Simón de Medina, cura of Tomatlan (Jalisco) in 1754, is described in AHJ Manuscripts, no. G-4-719 GUA/4. According to Osores, the indefatigable José Prado preached 5,667 sermons during his 42 years of service at Tlasco (Puebla) and elsewhere. Especially energetic sermonizers of unknown efficacy were Simón Thadeo de Castañeda Castro y Guzmán, who preached two or three times on Sundays against immoral conduct in various pueblos while serving as vicario of Acolman in the early 1760's, and Juan Thomás de Dios de Castro Tovio, who said in his 1762 relación de méritos that he had preached over 60 panegyrical sermons and many more moral sermons and Sunday doctrinal lectures. JCB. Very few of the published sermons of the 18th century were composed by rural parish priests. See Paredes for an example of an 18th-century sermonario.

54. Joseph Manuel Sotomayor of Zacualpan in 1796. AGN Inq. 1304 exp. 3, fols. 123ff; Inq. 1334 exp. 3, fols. 2ff. State officials in the mid-19th century expressed concern over priests stirring up their rural parishioners with Sunday sermons on religious rights; see, for example, Texas, Mariano Riva Palacio Coll., no. 6349.

55. Diocesan priests from the cathedral city were engaged by rural curas for occasional

sermons. Antonio de Osorio, vicario of Santa Ana, Zacoalco district, for example, was invited to preach in the parish church of Zacoalco three times. CAAG, resumé for 1770 concurso. In his resumé for the same concurso, Juan José Nieto Corona said he gave many sermons in and near Aguascalientes, although he no longer held a formal position. This was especially common during Lent. See, for example, in JCB, 1762 resumés of Diego de Almonacid y Salasar, reporting that he helped at Tlalnepantla during Lent, including taking the pulpit twice for six hours in all; and Joaquín Joseph Caamaño, reporting that during Lent he helped out at Tolcayuca with sermons, mass, head counts, confession, etc. Juan Thomás de Dios de Castro Tovio was the designated preacher against immoral conduct during his time as vicario of Tolantzinco in the late 1750's. JCB.

56. The first mission of this kind to Zinapécuaro (Michoacán) arrived in 1798. It consisted of nine priests, who stayed for three months. In 1803, another mission with 20 priests, came for two months. López Lara, p. 193.

57. There is no systematic study of the missionary preachers in New Spain, but the content of their sermons was probably much like that of the missionary preachers who were popular in 18th-century Spain. Preoccupied above all with what they regarded as the immorality and social and economic injustices of "modernity," they tended to emphasize Christian virtue and unity in collective as much as individual terms. See Nöel, "Missionary Preachers."

58. The guiding sentiment for the bishop of Guadalajara at this time was much the same. See the 1768 pastoral letter of Dr. Diego Rodríguez Rivas de Velasco in BN, LaFragua Coll., vol. 1005, in which he characterized the priest as the maestro and emphasized charity and the teaching of doctrina as especially great responsibilities. He wrote of the pastor's temporal as well as spiritual responsibilities, but the focus was on material growth (especially the promotion of agriculture) rather than public morals and political administration, and he closed with a reminder to obey the king.

59. Pérez de Velasco, p. 1 ("rudos indios y alguna gente de campo poco menos bozales que los indios"). Manuel Pérez's early-18th-century guide for parish priests, *Farol indiano*, pp. 15ff, 158, 163, also plays down the judicial role, emphasizing the priest's responsibilities as teacher and administrator of sacraments, but it is more in the spirit of the *Itinerario*, a work that it cites approvingly. Pérez was particularly concerned to improve the quality of confessions, which was at the heart of the pastor's judicial role, but he treated the confessor as a physician, prescribing the bad to be avoided and the good to be followed. In missions on the consolidating military frontiers of northern Mexico in the mid-18th century, administrative and judicial authority was withdrawn from the resident priests. In 1745, following the pacification of Indians on Cathuxanes mesa, the governor of Coahuila ordered the Franciscan missionaries in the region to confine their pastoral work to celebrating mass, administering the sacraments, and teaching doctrina. AGN Civil 194 exp. 4.

60. Pérez de Velasco, pp. 72, 76, 82.

61. BMM 113, pp. 106–7 ("se aprehenden las máximas fundamentales de la ley divina y natural, se deshecha la ociosidad, se procura el asseo y limpieza, se destierra la ignorancia y la idolatría, se forma un vezino Christiano útil a la sociedad, padre de familia y buen republicano").

62. Ibid., prologue ("de discreción," "aseo," and "pulidez").

63. For all the Fourth Provincial Council's emphasis on the teaching role of parish priests and on love as the means of securing spiritual salvation for their parishioners, the prelates did not ignore the responsibility of parish priests in matters of public morality. But they did not assign them the power to try or punish violators. CPM, p. 116.

64. BN LaFragua Coll., vol. 590, 1772 archbishop's circular ("Somos de nuestro oficio padres, pastores, médicos, capitanes de la Milicia Christiana, y Centinelas de la casa del Señor"). The theme of the pastor as soldier was sounded throughout the colonial period,

but it was especially common in the 16th and 17th centuries. The First Provincial Council declared in 1555 that "las armas de clérigos son las oraciones"; the second, in 1565, held that the cura "está en la milicia de Dios"; and the Council of Trent referred to "the sword of excommunication" as "the nerve of ecclesiastical discipline." *Concilios provinciales primero, y segundo*, pp. 125, 389; Trent, 25th Session, Reform, ch. 3. *Itin.* 2-3-11 picked up the theme, advising that curas should be "armado de mansedumbre"; and AGN Inq. 1346 exp. 6, fol. 102 (1799), spoke of a fight against "el común enemigo" to save souls. For late examples, see Archbishop Lizana's pastoral letter of March 1, 1803, where he calls sacred scripture the priest's "sword"; and AGN Acervo 49 caja 45, an 1815 episcopal court case in which the promotor fiscal spoke of the cura of Chalco's use of excommunication as "abuso de las terribles armas de la Yglesia."

65. AGI Mex. 2588, Jan. 26, 1784, report, fol. 9r.

66. AGN RCO 126 exp. 137 (assertion of Oaxaca's bishop in 1777: "va mui atrasada la instrucción de los yndios en la doctrina"); BN LaFragua Coll., vol. 893 (Archbishop Lizana's March 5, 1803, pastoral letter stressing the importance of teaching doctrina every Sunday before or after mass).

67. Chap. 5 presented the curas' views as evidenced in their relaciones de méritos y servicios. In the 1793 district governors' reports (AGN Hist. 578A), several curas were singled out for exemplary work in instruction: Thomás Domingo Moreno, cura of Xochimilco (Xochimilco report); and Francisco Pablo Lombardo, cura of Tasquillo, José de Roxas, cura of Chapatongo, Francisco de la Peña, cura of Villa del Carbón, and Andrés Benosa, cura of Xilotepec (all in Huichapan report). Conversely, some priests were slated for their inactivity in instruction, including Cayetano Yzquierdo, cura of Ichcateopan (Zacualpan report), Francisco Josef Vitoria, vicario of Tulancingo (Tulancingo report), generally in the district of Taxco (Taxco report), and the cura of Yahualica (Yahualica report).

68. Solórzano 4-15-1.

69. *Concilios provinciales primero, y segundo*, p. 390 ("El cura es Padre, y debe mirar por sus hijos; es Pastor, y ha de cuidar no se disipe, enferme, ó aniquile el Rebaño; es Juez, y ha de juzgar a el Penitente por las sentencias más probables; es Médico, y ha de curar con las opiniones, y medicinas más probadas; es Maestro, y ha de enseñar con las Doctrinas más sanas, y conformes á razón").

70. The subdelegado of Zacualpan, for example, wrote of the "afabilidad de verdadero padre" of José María Rincón, cura of Ixtapan, and referred to his "charidad" and "disinterés." AGN Hist. 578A, 1793, Zacualpan report.

71. CAAG, unclassified ("padre de todos por su piedad y liberalidad").

72. Summary by audiencia fiscal, AGN CRS 179 exp. 13, fol. 406r. Some parishioners also spoke of the spiritual fatherhood of the priest in the confessional. See, for example, AGN Inq. 1346 exp. 6, fol. 21v, declaration of doña Luisa de los Ríos.

73. AGN CA 13 exp. 5, 1786 (cura of Hueypustla distributed grain at cost and appealed to the crown for a 1,500p loan and relief from tribute in order to restore farm production); AGN Hist. 578A, 1793, Mexicalcingo report (cura sought lands and tools for his village parishioners); CAAG, resumé of José Antonio Barragán for 1770 concurso (the teniente de cura at Tlaltenango slaughtered his own cattle for Indians during an epidemic and famine in the 1760's); JCB, 1752, resumé of Juan Joseph de Henestrosa (as cura of Lerma he lent Indians money for tribute and sold them maize below market price in 1749–50); JCB, 1760, resumé of Manuel Joseph de Iglesias (as cura of Tarasquillo he lent money to Indians for tribute); AJANG Civil, bundle labeled "1806–07 (174)," 1809 (cura of Ixtlan, Cayetano Guerrero, served as Indian advocate in a water dispute against an hacienda); Washington State Univ., Regla Papers, folder 118, June 26, 1799 (cura represented interests of the pueblo of San Mateo in negotiations with an hacienda over rental of land); Tulane VEMC 3 exp. 9, 1787 (cura of Huejutla defended Indian interests at court over underpayment

608 ≈ *Notes to Pages 163–64*

for transporting tobacco and mail); AGN Acervo 49 caja 47, 1765 (cura of Tepecoacuilco represented a suitor whose fiancée was carried off); AGN Crim. 217 fols. 89ff, 1797 (cura of Zinacantepec, Metepec district, initiated a complaint against local Indian leaders, whom he characterized as tyrants).

74. For example, Tomás de Campo took his services to the jail of Fresnillo where, he said, he had gotten cases into court expeditiously and contributed to the liberation of many innocent people. CAAG, resumé for 1770 concurso. Lic. Joseph Antonio de Acosta, vicario of Sierra de Pinos in 1760, and Juan Ignacio de Moya Palacios, former interim cura of Zapopan in 1743, noted that they had a license to plead cases. Ibid.; AGI Indiferente General 243. Father Agüero of Yautepec put his lawyer's skills into practice in parish affairs during the 1790's, as did the cura of Teapa, Tabasco, in 1788. AGN CRS 140 exp. 4, fols. 223–36; CRS 152 exps. 6–7. In Olinalá, Juan Díaz Conti initiated a lawsuit over an Indian land rental and paid the cost himself. CRS 13 exp. 3, fols. 49ff, 1781. And the cura of Lerma lent 250p to his parishioners to press their case for land titles. JCB, 1755 resumé of Juan Joseph de Henestrosa.

75. AGN RCO 69 exp. 67.

76. *Itin.* 2-1-2, 2-1-8, 2-5-8 ("deven los juezes, por razón de su oficio, defender estos pobres," "también los curas tienen obligación a defender los Indios de sus doctrinas").

77. For more on the roles of parents and children, see Palafox's pastoral letter of 1649; and Ruiz Martínez. Pedro Pablo de Caballos, cura of Chiapa de Mota, spoke of the "consuelo paternal" he offered his Indian parishioners when they brought him small problems like arguments between spouses. AGN Tierras 2774 exp. 10. The open-ended conception of fatherhood led some parish priests informally to go far outside the bounds of their job description; see, for example, AGN CRS 140 exp. 4, fol. 95, and witnesses nos. 9, 11; and CRS 152 exps. 2–3.

78. AGN CRS 39 exp. 2, fols. 66v–67v.

79. *Itin.* 2-1-1, 2-1-2 (on amor paternal), 3-4-16 (the model of the loving father: "que para con los Indios se vista de un corazón de padre para con un hijo muy querido y necesitado").

80. *Itin.* 1-10 passim; *Colección de las ordenanzas*, pp. 36–39, 178–94. It makes a difference that in this image of the garden and the parish priest as gardener, the Indians are the plants. This is not the "horticultural metaphor" described in Clendinnen, "Franciscan Missionaries," p. 244, in which priests regarded Indians as the field, and religion as the plant that "can be rooted anywhere from seed with proper care." This alternative conception of the parish priest as gardener does appear in *Concilios provinciales primero, y segundo*, p. 387, where Lorenzana stated that "estamos nombrados Ministros de la Iglesia, y no para comodidades temporales que no nos faltarán si les sembrássemos bien la semilla espiritual."

81. CPM, p 118.

82. Pérez de Velasco, p. 46.

83. The quote in the subheading comes from the published sermon of José Julio García de Torres delivered at the Santuario de Guadalupe on Oct. 12, 1821, p. 13. I have translated "culto" as liturgy.

84. AGN Inq. 960 exp. 19, fols. 16v ff; Pérez de Velasco, p. 32. For a detailed discussion of the administration of sacraments in Indian parishes, see *Itin.* bk. 3.

85. Trent, 22d Session, Reform, ch. 4.

86. CPM, p. 156. For a good example of the fully scripted drama of the mass and other sacramental rites, with stage instructions in Spanish and the text of the drama in Latin, see *Manual breve*.

87. On the parish priest's activities before and after Sunday mass, see Pérez de Velasco, pp. 73–81. Parish priests were also called on to exercise a kind of white magic that would advance material well-being and strike a blow in the unseen struggle against Satan by

blessing a useful object or place or staging an exorcism. On the blessing of a lime kiln, see AGN Crim. 306 exp. 5, 1773, Zimatlan (Oaxaca).

88. AGN Acervo 49 caja 127, 1773, Jiquipilco. In some cases, the misas de visita were celebrated only three times a year. AGN CRS 68 exp. 3, fol. 219r. The Third Provincial Council decreed in 1585 that curas must visit every pueblo in the parish at least two times a year. *Concilio III provincial mexicano*, p. 228.

89. *Itin.* 3-1-3, 3-1-5 ("todos, hombre y mugeres, fuesen Ministros para bautizar").

90. The cura of Tlaola in 1790 complained that during his service in Tlalnepantla, one midwife performed defective baptisms on 60 dying infants. Tulane VEMC 24 exp. 2.

91. Pérez de Velasco, p. 74. Baptism was another occasion to teach. Since the godparents were expected to teach doctrina to their godchild, the priest was to be certain at the time of baptism that they at least knew the Apostles' Creed and the Lord's Prayer. Manuel Pérez, p. 13.

92. AGN RCO 62 exp. 80.

93. Seed, *To Love, Honor, and Obey*, pp. 200–215; R. Gutiérrez, pp. 315–18.

94. Pérez de Velasco, pp. 82–83, drew a close connection between confession and doctrinal instruction.

95. *Itin.* 3-4-16.

96. *Itin.* 3-4-20 ("es mejor y más acepto a Dios confesar a dos, que no a veinte de paso y mal").

97. *Itin.* 3-4-11, 3-4-14. See the detailed treatment of confession in *Itin.* 3-4 passim.

98. Pérez de Velasco, pp. 45–57.

99. *Colección de ordenanzas*, pp. 207–8. The bishop of Michoacán felt so strongly about the matter of secrecy that he threatened violators with removal from office. The Fourth Provincial Council (1771) made the same point in terms nearly as strong. CPM, pp. 194–95 (see these pages also on the prohibiting of fees). For the case of a parish priest charged with violating the secrecy of the confessional, confessing women in the sacristy with the door closed, lying down, and without clerical garb, see AGN Inq. 760 exp. 40.

100. *Itin.* 1-1-2, para. 13 ("si el Doctrinero haze oficio de juez entre sus súbditos y en el fuero Sacramental de la Penitencia los ha de juzgar, claro está que ha de tener ciencia, y conocimiento de las culpas; . . . y siendo también Médico espiritual, que ha de recetar las medicinas, según la calidad de los achaques"). See also *Itin.* 3-4-16.

101. Pérez de Velasco, p. 46.

102. AGI Guad. 563, March 15, 1816.

103. AJANG Civil, box 171, doc. 15.

104. These and other chores are summarized in *Colección de ordenanzas*, pp. 97–101. For the 16th century, see *Concilios provinciales primero, y segundo*, ch. 2, pp. 88, 90, 190, 191, 194.

105. *Recop.* 1-13-25 (1605; curas to keep books of baptism and burials and send the annual Easter population count to the viceroy); Ventura Beleña, 1: 42, June 12, 1756 (curas to report their periodic population counts and inform Indians of their exemptions from certain fees collected under the guise of tribute). Royal officials took considerable interest in the parish priests' population counts in the late 18th century. In 1773, the viceroy ordered curas to divide the population by race in order to keep better track of non-Indians in pueblos. AGN Bandos 8 exp. 28. Some parish priests were required to supervise the new royal census of 1792. For a case in which a public disturbance ensued, see AGN Crim. 243 exp. 1, Amanalco, Metepec district. Curas were also called on to report on all priests residing in their parish and those who were missing without permission.

106. AGN Alcaldes Mayores 3, fols. 172–78, 1771 (curas charged to report on their districts, to state whether an audiencia order had been enforced by the alcalde mayor, and to indicate whether, because of circumstances, a pueblo should be temporarily relieved of tribute); Alcaldes Mayores 11, fols. 353ff, 1774 (Molango cura reported abuses by the royal

lieutenant for Meztitlan de la Sierra); Alcaldes Mayores II fols. 356ff, 1772 (Chipetlan cura reported abuses by alcalde mayor of Tlapa); AGN Indios 70 exp. 69, 1795 (Tenango del Valle cura reported abuses by alcalde mayor); AGN Bandos 9 exp. 41, 1776 (viceregal orders to curas to report on population counts, economic activities, and the state of cofradías in the parish); CAAG, 1765, Tonalá (typescript of cura's report accompanying count of local population); AJANG Civil, box 67, doc. 3, 1764, Tequila (cura certified to deaths during 1763 and 1764; this was in response to an Oct. 7, 1762, order for curas and alcaldes mayores to report on cases where Indians should be relieved of tribute because of an epidemic or other extraordinary loss of population; Ventura Beleña, I: 45); AGN Crim. 203 exp. 4, 1778 (Tepoztlan cura reported on local affairs, especially Indian drinking, concubinage, and other ways in which local people did not do their Christian duties); AGN CRS 192 exp. II, 1760 (Joseph Siles appointed to investigate an idolatry case in Almoloya, Tescaliacac district); AJANG Civil, box 231, doc. I, 1804 (Poncitlan cura went to a neighboring district as investigator).

107. AGN Hist. 132 exp. 26, 1793 (witness for lieutenant of Tetecala); AJANG Civil, box 138, doc. 12, 1791 (Juchipila cura Daniel Espinosa de los Monteros reported on suitability of local men for office); AJANG Criminal, bundle labeled "1805, leg. I (24)," 1805 (San Sebastián Analco cura attested to character and habits of parishioners on trial in a domestic dispute).

108. AJANG Civil, bundle labeled "1769–60 leg. 2 (47)" (order to the cura for the declining pueblo of Totzin in 1769 to help the Indians and other settlers preserve the community).

109. AGN CRS 13 exp. 3, fols. 47–50, 1781 (Olinalá cura controlled "the papers" and caja de comunidad); CRS 156 exp. 5, 1758 (Tepetlaostoc cura kept one of the three keys to the caja de comunidad); CRS 84 exp. 5, 1799 (Fr. Mariano José de Osio, O.P., objected to the Azcapotzalco Indians' plans for "fiestas escandalosas" to celebrate a new altar; he had successfully forbidden such fiestas in the past: CRS 156 exp. 7, fols. 229ff); CRS 126 exp. 12, 1809 (Apaxtla cura supervised procession on the eve of Pentecost); CRS 188 exp. 12, 1793 (Villa Alta cura controlled licenses for dances in fiestas at Corpus Christi); AGN Inq. 1146 exp. I, fol. 63v, 1775 (Xilotepec parish ranchos needed license from cura for local bailes for the saints).

110. In 1796, the cura of Tonalisco complained to the audiencia that the subdelegado was not helping him in his efforts to get four Indians returned from Santa María del Oro. BEJ Papeles de Derecho, 2: 396–97.

111. AGN Acervo 49 caja 47, 1765 (Tepecoacuilco cura served as escribano); AHJ Manuscripts, no. G-4-808 JAL/3159 (cura signed for illiterate alcaldes in 1808–10 collection records of donations for war against France); *Itin.* I-II passim (curas could make Indian wills); AGN CRS 156 exp. 5, fols. 126–30, 1758 (Tepetlaostoc cura kept the local records for bienes de comunidad and cofradías); CRS 25 exp. 4, 1793–1803 (cura of Huiciltepec, Tecali district, Puebla, kept cofradía records); CRS 29 exp. 5, 1727 (Tlalmanalco cura received the tribute from the gobernador, then presented it to the alcalde mayor); AGN Tierras 2431 exp. 4, 1802 (Ixcatepec cura managed Indian lands that he claimed were cofradía properties).

The cura of Tlalmanalco in 1766, Dr. Pedro Ugaris, wanted to keep local Indians from renting out community lands because, he said, this practice resulted in "ociosidad" (laziness) and drunkenness. Acting as patrons, he and the alcalde mayor's lieutenant distributed community farmland among the Indians and rented out what was left over for the benefit of the caja de comunidad. He said he had "concentrated all of my efforts and desires" (dirigido toda mi industria y todos mis deseos) to persuade the Indians to work their plots for themselves and protect their lands against flood by building up the river banks. He claimed that earlier distributions of community land by the Indian cabildo had left some Indians without enough to provide for their families or pay their taxes. He regarded himself as charged with "guardar lo mandado por la Real Audiencia." Tierras 2554 exp. 11, fols. 3–4.

112. JCB, Ximénez resumé.

113. AGN Acervo 49 caja 116, 1808–9 pastoral visit.

114. Solórzano 4-23-6, 4-23-9 and 10; Palafox, *Manual de sacerdotes* ("en las Indias se suele decir, y bien, que entra por los ojos la Fe a estos pobres naturales").

115. Examples of building activity abound in the curas' resumés for late colonial concursos. The 1793 subdelegados' reports (AGN Hist. 578A) give many examples as well (all curas except as noted): Joaquín de la Plaza of Otumba and Juan Fernández Somera of Axapusco (Otumba report); Ygnacio Munive of Apango (Tixtla report); Dr. Felipe de Barcena of Taxco and Mariano Cuevas, coadjutor of Tetipac (Taxco report); Manuel Lino Guerra of Actopan (Actopan report); José Quintano of Tepexpan (Teotihuacan report); Augustín González de Castañeda of Cuzamala (Tetela del Río report); José Mariano Cuebas of Lerma (Lerma report); Dr. Tomás de Arrieta of Tacuba, Julián C. Quintana, vicario de pie fixo of San Pedro Ascapusaltongo, and José Mondragón, vicario de pie fixo of Santa Ana Xilocingo (Tacuba report); Dr. Diego Manuel de Haza of San Felipe El Grande, Miguel Flores of Atlacomulco, and Manuel Gonzales of Tapusco o Real del Oro (Ixtlahuaca report); Manuel Escoto of Tlaltenango and Pablo Ignacio Goicochea of Sierra de Pinos (Zacatecas report); Bernardino de Meza y Herrera of Chimalhuacan (Coatepec-Chalco report); and Luis Antonio de Beas of Chiapa de Mota and Luis Jose Carrillo of Aculco (Huichapan report).

Parish priests who did not engage in this kind of charity were criticized in administrative reports and judicial records for not maintaining the "debida decencia." See, for example, AGN Inq. 1304 exp. 3, fols. 123–28, 1796–99, Zacualpan; AGN Templos 25 exp. 5, 1788, Santiago Tlatlaya; Templos 25 exp. 8, 1796, Amecameca; and AGN Tierras 2774 exp. 5, 1576, Almoloya.

116. AGN Hist. 578A, 1793 reports, Zacatecas (Sierra de Pinos colegio de educandas), Otumba (Otumba side altar), Huichapan (Aculco side altar), Taxco (Taxco hospital), Tacuba (Tacuba orquesta); AGN CRS 151 exps. 4–7, 17 (various images). In his 1763 resumé, Diego de Almonacid, teniente de cura at Huitzilac, listed the pulpit, a confessional, and more. JCB.

117. JCB, Flores resumé.

118. AGN DP 3 exp. 3.

119. Torquemada, 3: 531–35. In Torquemada's telling of the pious tradition, the Indians of Otumba had no wells or streams, and their pools for collecting rainwater were polluted by European livestock. Tembleque's aqueduct carried water from springs near Cempoala.

120. AGN Hist. 578A, 1793, Tixtla report (Munive); JCB (Almonacid and Rodríguez Díaz); AHJ Manuscripts, G-4-719 GUA/4 (Castor de Aguayo).

121. López Lara, pp. 198, 202; AGN Hist. 578A, 1793, Ixtlahuaca report; Brown Univ., Rockefeller Lib., Medina Coll., FHA 162 exp. 1, 1768 pastoral letter for Guadalajara (duty to "promover en sus feligreses las grangerías, las ocupaciones y trabajos," especially to introduce new crops). Public works are covered in *Recop.* 6-1-21, 6-1-23.

122. AGN Hist. 578A, 1793, Ixtlahuaca report.

123. CAAG, resumé of Antonio Manuel Velásquez for 1770 concurso.

124. AGI Mex. 2550, 1820 resumé of José Joaquín de la Pedreguera.

125. BMM 113, p. 66. See also AGN CRS 75 exp. 5, fol. 320r.

126. AGN CRS 188 exp. 12, fols. 205v–207r; CRS 74 exp. 11 (audiencia fiscal declared that Indians should treat their cura with "debido amor y respeto"); AGN Hist. 578A, 1793, Zacualpan report (of the interim cura it was said that "lo amaban tiernamente").

127. Observation combined with obedience was a neat formula that appears often in

the colonial record; see, for example, AGN Inq. 1146 exp. 1, fol. 33v (obey the cura and fulfill the Easter duty). See also AGN CRS 156 exp. 4, 1757, Sultepec, for a cura's complaint that his Indian parishioners were not ardent in their devotion.

128. According to Pedro de Córdoba's 1544 doctrina, Indian parishioners needed to know the following in preparation for salvation: the meaning of heaven and hell; the 14 articles of faith; the Ten Commandments; the sacraments; the seven corporeal works of mercy; the seven spiritual works of mercy; and the meaning of the cross. *Itin.* 2-8 passim describes a more ambitious catechism for Indian and casta parishioners. Conspicuously absent from both works are the seven mortal sins, an omission that de la Peña Montenegro explained in *Itin.* 3-4-14. After identifying Indians as a "gente ruda," he advised that "como son estos Indios, [no] conviene enseñarles los siete pecados mortales, porque enseñarles que la gula es pecado mortal, que la pereza es pecado mortal, y la soberbia también, se sigue, que por conciencia errónea, piensan que qualquiera gula es pecado mortal, y qualquiera soberbia, y pereza y es hazer que hagan por error pecado, lo que no es."

129. Prelates saw respect and good order in society as components of spiritual well-being. Puebla's Bishop Fabián y Fuero, for example, wrote in his 1772 pastoral letter of the "necesario respeto y veneración a los párrocos, tan importante al bien espiritual de los súbditos."

130. BMM 113, p. 35.

131. For one of many references to parishioners as sheep, see AGI Mex. 2549, bishop of Guadalajara's letter of March 23, 1755.

132. For example, AGN CRS 68 exp. 2, Ozoloapan, 1769. In this record, Archbishop Lorenzana also advised the Indians not to resist their cura. For some, the fact that Indians were no longer afraid of the cura's punishment was at the root of the problem. See, for example, CRS 68 exp. 3, fols. 210v ff. Punishment and Bourbon reforms are taken up in Chap. 9.

133. AJANG Civil, box 49, doc. 4, 1727, Poncitlan, audiencia verdict.

134. AGN Hist. 319 exp. 24 ("respeten, reverencien y obedezcan a su cura and vivan christianamente y politicamente"). In AGN Templos 25 exp. 8, 1796, the audiencia ordered Indians of Amecameca to obey and respect the cura; the subdelegado ordered their "subordinación y respeto."

135. AGN CRS 75 exp. 5 ("no cumplen con la obligación de administrarles el pasto espiritual").

136. AGN CRS 68 exp. 1 ("suavidad, blandura, y amor"). A cura's sense of the reciprocal relationship was expressed by priests involved in a dispute over the celebration of mass in a sujeto of Xilotepec in 1775. The investigating cura declared that the Indians should obey the cura and fulfill their liturgical obligations in exchange for the cura's "docility, charity, and love." The cura said he was only interested in having them "fulfill their *preceptos*, which is what the *cura* is responsible for," and obey superior orders. The promotor fiscal in this case declared that the Indians were not to interfere in the spiritual government of the parish, and were to pay their fees promptly and respect and venerate the cura, and that in turn he was to teach doctrine more assiduously and keep track of who attended obligatory masses. AGN Inq. 1146 exp. 1.

137. *Concilios provinciales primero, y segundo*, pp. 387–92.

138. AGN Hist. 128 exp. 4. This late colonial claim is quite different from *Itin.* 1-1-2's warning that "ciencia" or knowledge/skill was not enough to establish the "dignidad" of a doctrinero. It also depended on age and "buena vida y costumbres." If he was a "gigante en la virtud" and prudent, that would edify more than ciencia.

139. Lizana y Beaumont's pastoral letter of March 1, 1803. See also Omerick (BMM 113) for a discussion of the wide scope of a cura's teaching responsibilities, what techniques

he should use, what he should expect to teach, what doctrina his Indians needed to know, etc.; and AGN Inq. 1146 exp. 1 (for the promotor fiscal's emphasis on the teaching role).

140. AGN CRS 192 exps. 11–12, 1760, Almoloya (promotor fiscal's order to cura).

141. AGN Acervo 49 caja 116, 1808 pastoral visit to Xochicoatlan. This is in the spirit of Pérez de Velasco, pp. 5, 15, 18–19, 45, 53, where he emphasizes the priest earning respect by his "benevolencia, afabilidad, dulzura, manso, benigno, paciencia, prudencia suma, genio apacible, benignidad, y sobre todo una gran charidad." In BMM 113, pp. 24, 79, Omerick speaks of treating parishioners with "grande amor" and "afabilidad." He does not mention punishment as a way to instill "el santo temor."

142. Pérez de Velasco, p. 102 ("La benevolencia, afabilidad y dulzura son prendas indispensables en un Ministro, cuyo empeño es el ganar a los hombres las voluntades para reducirlos a la paz con Dios. . . . no los hemos de concebir más Brutos, ni más Fieras que los Tigres, y éstos ya vemos como se mansan, se domestican, se hacen tratables: pero no a golpes, sino con alhagos. Los Ministros crueles serán temidos no ay duda de los Indios, pero los benignos serán más amados." This is in contrast to a 17th-century source like Serna, p. 360, which followed the old balance of amor and rigor.

143. For example, in 1801 the audiencia ordered a cura in the Metepec district to act with amor and suavidad. AGN CRS 74 exp. 11.

144. AGN CRS 179 exp. 13, fol. 406r, 1763. These pointed orders contrast with the general conception of the model parish priest in Solórzano 4-15-50, where the emphasis is on desinterés in the sense of a lack of greed, plus exemplary personal conduct and knowledge of Indian languages.

145. AGN RCO 92 exp. 102 ("declamaciones" and "murmuraciones").

146. "Pacífico," "suave," "humilde," "modesto," "provida," "benigno," "apacible," "timorato," "circunspección," "moderado," "paz y quietud," "muy amante de la paz," "prudente," "afabilidad de verdadero padre."

147. Places in parentheses in the list below identify the pertinent 1793 subdelegación reports in AGN Hist. 578A:

A. Benign: blando, suave, pacífico (Zacualpan); provida, modestia (Zacualpan); provida (Zacualpan); benigno, humilde (Teotihuacan); genio apacible, genio suave (Metepec); pacífico (Acapulco); afables, modestos, humildes (Ixtlahuaca); muy timorato (Zacatecas); mantiene en paz y quietud a sus feligreses (Ixtlahuaca); muy amante de la paz (Zacatecas); modestia, circunspección (Cempoala); desengañado (Tacuba); prudencia (Tixtla); afabilidad de verdadero padre (Zacualpan).

B. Selfless: desinterés (Zacualpan, Tixtla, Mexicalcingo, Metepec).

C. Zealous: indispensable celo, explicación de doctrina (Tulancingo); celo (Zacatecas); ansioso del bien de las almas (Huichapan); sólo procura el bien de las almas (Huichapan); assiduous parish service (Tetela del Río); celo, virtud (Cempoala); eficacia y exactitud en el cumplimiento (Ixtlahuaca, Zacatecas); infatigable (Taxco); puntuales en la administración (Zimapan); activo y eficaz en su ministerio (Cempoala).

D. Loving and kind: caridad, pobreza voluntaria (Zacatecas); bondad (Zacatecas); amor a los indios (Tula); lleno de caridad (Zacualpan); padre benéfico (Cuautla Amilpas); singular amor a la común (Zacatecas).

E. Exemplary personal conduct: juiciosa conducta (Zacualpan); his ejemplo (Malinalco); conducta muy arreglada (Taxco); arreglada conducta (Zacatecas); acreditado ejemplo (Zacatecas).

F. Apostolic: hombre apostólico y desengañado, celo por la salud del rebaño (Tacuba); verdadero apostol, celo desinterés, caridad, pobreza voluntaria (Zacatecas); celo verdaderamente apostólico (Zacatecas).

Less frequently mentioned was learned and talented (literatura and talento): erudición (Zacualpan, Tixtla, Metepec); distinguida letra (Zacatecas).

148. AGN Hist. 578A, 1793, Ixtlahuaca report.

149. AGN CRS 75 exp. 6, fol. 336.

150. AGN CRS 136 exp. 2, fols. 185–93. Beyond the formula, the Indians' attorneys were quick to measure the cura's conduct against the official standards of caridad. CRS 75 exp. 2.

151. AGN CRS 85 exp. 5, 1785, Huichapan district.

152. AGN CRS 156 exp. 4; CRS 136 exp. 2, fols. 185–93.

153. AJANG Criminal, box 20, doc. 2, 1806, Zapotitlan, Tuscacuesco district; AGN CRS 217 exp. 6, 1808, Tzontecomatlan.

154. AGN Bienes 172 exp. 37, 1805, Almoloya; Bienes 172 exp. 53, 1805, Huitzuco.

155. For example, AGN CRS 57 exp. 3, fols. 265f, 1796, Xichú; CRS 156 exp. 4, 1757, Sultepec.

156. CAAG, unclassified, Aug. 26, 1828, complaint by former Indians of Tuscacuesco ("proteger la iglesia como madre piadosa").

157. AGN CRS 75 exp. 5, 1785, Huichapan district; Tulane VEMC 8 exp. 21, 1803, Tlaquiltenango ("medios más suaves y prudentes"); AGN Templos 25 exp. 10 ("la mansedumbre y sufrimiento para radicar y cultivar la paz").

158. AJANG Criminal, box 20, doc. 2, 1806 ("administra sin hacérsele impresión las incomodidades de horas, tiempos ni caminos, transitando por sus barrancas aún las más fragosas con tan inalterable serenidad como si lo hiciera en llanuras de mucha comodidad").

159. AGN Inq. 1318 exp. 8 ("Era un ministro tan eficaz que a la hora que lo llamban a una confesión, a esa misma montaba a caballo sin que le sirviera de obstáculo el bueno o mal tiempo caminando por barrancas y despeñaderos . . . por páramos desiertos . . . cuando la cabalgadura no la hallaba suficiente para pasar los ríos crecidos en ella, se desnudaba y pasaba a nado los ríos"). See also JCB, 1760 resumé of Francisco Benites de Ariza; and AGN CRS 39 exp. 5, fols. 262–63, where the cura of Malacatepec in 1803 spoke of himself as "activo y diligente." Shifts in the image of the ideal cura are evident in the way priests presented themselves in their professional resumés for concursos. In the late 18th century, they were likely to emphasize their formal education and their dedication to teaching.

160. Examples of concern expressed for the moral excesses of parishioners in the archdiocese are AGN CRS 179 exp. 13, 1763, Actopan; CRS 188 exp. 7, 1790, Tlacotalpan; CRS 192 exps. 11–12, 1760, Almoloya; CRS 217 exp. 6, 1808, Tzontecomatlan; CRS 136 exp. 2, 1781, Tlaltizapan; CRS 204 exp. 3, 1726, San Juan Totolzintla; AGN Hist. 437, 1800, Mochitlan.

161. AGI Mex. 2588, Jan. 26, 1784, report.

162. De la Hera, "Derecho de los indios," presents the 1537 papal bull "Sublimis Deus" as "the Magna Carta of Indian rights." It recognized Indians as rational and human—"free by nature" from slavery, with rights to their property.

163. The characterization of Indians as people of the greatest liberty is from AJANG Civil, bundle labeled "1709–1819," 1744 Mechoacanejo case, fol. 25r (cura of Teocaltiche). The cura of Santa Fe (near Guadalajara), Pedro Miguel Quintano, pointed out even more excesses than I have listed in the text. CAAG, unclassified, 1765 dispute over cofradías. See also AGN CRS 188 exp. 7.

164. AGN CRS 188 exp. 7; CRS 136 exp. 2.

165. Parry, *Spanish Seaborne Empire*, p. 175. The ambivalence of this older meaning of liberty is evident in Sebastián de Covarrubias's *Tesoro de la lengua castellana o española* (1611). Covarrubias first defined libertad as the opposite of servitude or captivity, then warned that unlimited personal liberty could result in licentiousness and another and worse kind of servitude—the servitude of the soul. *Recop.* 6-6-14 treats Indians' natural

liberty as freedom from the servitude of slavery. By the end of the 18th century, libertad increasingly was invoked as a virtue and right in local political terms (e.g., AGN DP 3 exp. 3, fol. 47, where the attorney for the Indians of Tlaltizapan in 1797 called for the "plena libertad que deven gozar en sus elecciones").

166. For a fuller treatment and citations to the sources mentioned in the following pages, see Taylor, "'. . . de corazón pequeño.'" The sources are the standard manuals, bishops' directives, two treatises by parish priests from the 1760's and 1780's, and 41 judicial records for Mexico and Guadalajara in which parish priests commented on Indians in their letters, testimony, petitions, reports, and advice to higher authorities. For more on the Spanish rhetoric of colonialism in racial terms, see R. Gutiérrez, pp. 194–206.

167. As one Mexican cura put it in 1788, "a que sean industriosos[,] a que se civilisen para que así sean útiles al estado y a sus familias." AGN Civil 2072 exp. 19.

168. Consider, for example, Serna, p. 52: "esta miserable, y pobre gente, pequeñuelos, y pusilánimes en su naturaleza, y por esto muy expuestos a los engaños del Demonio." Fernández de Lizardi made it clear in the words of his picaresque character, Catrín de la Fachenda, that miserable did not simply mean poor: "Aunque os digo que mis padres fueron pobres, no os significo que fueron miserables." *Don Catrín de la Fachenda*, p. 5.

169. AGI Mex. 2588, Jan. 26, 1784, report. The thesis of Ruiz y Cervantes, in contrast to Hugo de Omerick (BMM 113), was that corporal punishment was a necessary instrument of the priest's responsibilities as father to unruly Indians. "To govern without punishment is a very difficult business," he claimed, citing the *Itinerario* and his own experience.

170. Ruiz y Cervantes could well be the patron of a remarkable pair of large paintings that face each other in the choir loft of the parish church at Zimatlan. One depicts the call to final judgment in which most of the risen dead are led off to hell, including one reluctant man who clutches a sheaf of papers labeled "land disputes." The other painting depicts the torments of hell that await unrepentant sinners.

171. For a still more optimistic clerical view, see Clavijero, pp. 518–23, where he praised Indian parsimony and "sobriedad," and concluded that Indians were not inferior to Europeans except in their education. Like Omerick (BMM 113) and mainstream regalist views of the time, Clavijero presented himself as an educational determinist with regard to Indians.

172. The terms used to describe Indians' human capacities assumed Spanish superiority, just as Castilian, shoes, and wheat were considered superior to Indian languages, sandals, and maize.

173. The Spaniards' hierarchical conception of colonial society made room for discriminating among Indians, especially on the basis of noble ancestry, "purity of blood," and individual virtue. Consider, as an early example, the royal cedula of March 26, 1697, on the privileges to be accorded Indians of nobility and limpieza de sangre. Konetzke, 3: 66–69.

174. Of course, this sense of class and the rhetoric of control were not peculiar to Spain and Spanish America. The epithets that Woodrow Borah identified in descriptions of Indians and the non-Indian poor for colonial Mexico—untrustworthy, gullible, drunken, lazy, and filthy—are the same as those that privileged Frenchmen used for servants and the lower classes at about the same time. Malicious, ignorant, and shameless could be added to Borah's list. In both cases, lower classes were very nearly viewed as a separate, inferior race, not fully human. See Borah, *Justice by Insurance*, ch. 4; and Fairchilds, especially p. 148.

175. On the mediating role open to parish priests, see Hicks.

176. Palafox, Nov. 12, 1640, pastoral letter.

177. Ibid. ("el camino del Señor es siempre contrario al del mundo").

Chapter Eight

EPIGRAPH: AGN CRS 156 exp. 7, fol. 229 ("No me haría fuerza esta buena harmonía de los yndios si se dirigiera a concebarlos en paz y quietud y con el debido respecto y reconocimiento a sus superiores, el párrocho que soy yo y al governador de Acambay. . . . Les manifesté el dolor que tenía en mi corazón y lo que me atormentaba ver como pastor de ellos el que haviendo puesto en los años anteriores los más eficaces medios para que cumpliesen con el anual precepto de la yglecia y no havía sacado fructo alguno").

1. Some of the variety of personalities is apparent in the sample of parish priests identified in a pastoral visit and related documents or a summary report by a prelate to the king. Just in the first few towns visited in the mountains of Hidalgo and the Huasteca in 1808, the pastoral visitor found priests of "genial flema" (Pedro José Sánchez Rosales of Zihuateutla), "afable" and "humilde" (coadjutor Fr. Ygnacio Lechuga of Zozoquiapan), "de buenas costumbres" but "tiene raras ideas, se inflama con facilidad y se produse con acrimonia" (Juan Bustamante, cura of Tianguistengo), "de buen genio, irreprensible conducta" (Dr. José Antonio Rodríguez, cura of Xochicoatlan), "sencillez inocente que forma su carácter" (Pedro Sánchez, cura of Huazalingo), and "no muy buena [conducta], inclinado a la bebida con desorden" (José Torres, vicario of Tepehuacan). An unusual secret report of March 7, 1806, about Domingo de la Peña, interim cura of Almoloya, Metepec district, described his character as "alegre, pero violento e inconstante." It went on, "su alegría no la califican de insolencia; pues aunque gustaba de música y bailes, eran domésticos de pura diversión. Y si con este motivo mismo se amistaba más con las mujeres que con los hombres de una u otra familia, no dicen huviera deshonestidad alguna; y puede atribuirse acaso al genio afeminado, o tal ves cortesano, que me conceptúo hace su carácter."

Even an occasional episcopal report to the crown would depart from the practice of describing only the leading and most virtuous curas, to fault as many as it praised. The 1755 episcopal report for the Diocese of Guadalajara identified the chantre as a man of "excesivo empeño en proteger a gente de baja esfera"; one racionero as a learned former cura incapacitated by "achaques" from his "trabajosa vida de administrar los santos sacramentos"; another racionero as lacking in "juicio para saber moderar sus operaciones y arreglarlas a una conducta exacta," a man of "tedio y repugnancia"; the cura of Aguascalientes as of "amor tierno y reverencial, muy humilde de condición"; the cura of Fresnillo as of "una virtud sólida y un genio lavorioso aunque algo violento"; the cura of Nochistlan as of "genio algo inquieto, no ha sido muy bien visto de los feligreses"; the cura of Mascota as of "rectitud de ánimo y genio manso"; the cura of Cuquío as of "buenas costumbres" but suffering from "una especial de lesión intelectual," which "lo conduze a una ligereza de ánimo nada recomendable a la gravedad de su estado"; the cura of Monterrey as an "hombre de mucho juicio"; the cura of Huauchinango as "uno de los curas que más se aplican a su ministerio sin embargo de mantenerse en un beneficio pobre y desacomodado"; and the cura of Purificación as a "buen pastor, dedicado todo al bien espiritual de sus obejas" who had not sought more desirable parishes ("el público lo estima mucho"). AGI Mex. 2549, March 23, 1755, report.

A secret audiencia report on priests in this diocese, dated Dec. 30, 1755 (also in AGI Mex. 2549), confirmed the earlier judgment of the curas of Fresnillo, Nochistlan, and Cuquío, and added a few more personalities and reputations. The cura of Zapopan was "de razonable literatura, pero mal admitido en su curato por el celo con que procura apartar a los yndios de sus embriagueses"; the cura of Colotlan was "adornado de una gran prudencia y virtud, con literatura competente"; the cura of Iscuintla was "vigilante y exacto en el ministerio de la cura, y digno de atención por su calidad"; the cura of Bolaños was "sujeto muy capaz pero de alguna nota en su origen"; and the cura of Zacatecas was "uno de los sujetos de mérito del obispado" who had the unusual habit of ceding half of his income to the church.

2. A memorable, oft-quoted source that overdraws the picture of the parish priest as greedy and lascivious is Juan & Ulloa, ch. 3.

3. Domínguez Ortiz, *Sociedad y estado*, p. 230.

4. Solórzano 4-15-50. The 1793 reports (AGN Hist. 578A) occasionally single out individuals for failings of these kinds: Ysidro Estrada, vicario of Teloloapan, "adicto a intereses," and Miguel de Estrada, vicario of Zacualpan, "demasiado apego a yntereses" (Zacualpan report); Josef Joaquín Botello, cura of Guango, "un socarrón rico afecto al dinero," and Dr. Francisco Xavier de Figueroa, cura of Valladolid sagrario, "amigo del dinero" (Valladolid report); cura of Zumpango de la Laguna, Josef Eusebio Ortega, "suma codicia." Other examples are AGN CRS 136 exp. 4, 1784, vicario José María Rodríguez of San Lorenzo Huichilapan, Lerma parish; AJANG Civil, box 36, doc. 7, 1726, Culiacán district, Sinaloa (Francisco Xabier Páez Guzmán y Sotomayor, forced labor, took over a fishery and land for sugar planting); AGN Inq. 1304 exp. 3, 1796, Zacualpan (Joseph Manuel Sotomayor, guilty of excessive derechos and "negra codicia"; he was "hijo o esclavo de este vicio," said the cura of Sultepec); Inq. 1348 exp. 14, 1795 (Joseph Díaz Conti, former cura of Xochicoatlan, Molango district, in debt—droguero); Inq. 760 exp. 40, 1715 (vicario of Temascaltepec, engaged in trade); and CRS 39 exp. 6, 1806 (Tenontepec, Oaxaca, cura took community land for his own use). At least one late colonial pastor, José Antonio López Cárdenas, cura of Temascalcingo, was fond of a market metaphor for his policy on clerical fees. He would, he said, adjust them in times of dearth, "as merchants do." AGN Templos 25 exp. 10, fol. 11r, 1805.

5. Trent, 14th Session, Reform, ch. 6.

6. CPM, p. 130.

7. Solórzano 4-15-51.

8. *Colección de las ordenanzas*, pp. 25–26. During the pastoral visit to the Toluca area in 1779, Simón Romero, vicario in the Valley of Temascaltepec, was reprimanded for having a handkerchief or hat on his head during mass. AHM L10A/21, fols. 98–103.

9. To illustrate the double disgrace of a priest gambling in clerical garb, Pérez de Velasco, p. 31, chose the following story: "A un Sugeto, para mi muy fidedigno, le oí, que entrando porque no lo pudo escusar, en una Casa de Juego, a no sé qué diligencia, advirtió que un eclesiástico, sumamente indignado, contendía sobre algún lanze, que hubo de ofrecerse en el Juego con un Mulato Baquero, según se hacía conocer por el trage, y que reconviniéndolo el eclesiástico, por haverle faltado al respecto, y veneración debida a su estado; le respondió con voz desentonada el Mulato: 'Padre mío, en arrimando la barriga a la Mesa, todos somos unos. Aquí no se juegan respectos, sino dinero: y por dinero; el suyo no es más blanco que el mío.' "

10. AHJ Manuscripts, no. G-4-802, June 7, 1819, Bustamante report.

11. AGN Inq. 1346 exp. 6, fol. 32. Brambila, p. 94, recounts an amusing popular tale of a priest in Autlan, Jalisco, who dressed and acted like a ranchero.

12. AGN Inq. 1334 exp. 3, fol. 64v. Other priests who reportedly did not dress appropriately were Rafael de Arce, vicario de pie fijo of Mexcala and Sochipalan ("algo extravagante en su vestuario y persona"), and Francisco Garrido, cura of Zinacantepec. AGN Hist. 578A, 1793, Taxco, Metepec reports.

13. Pastoral letters of Archbishop Lizana, March 1, 1803, and Sept. 24, 1807; *Colección de ordenanzas*, pp. 25–26.

14. AGN Inq. 1346 exp. 6. The same was true of a few vicarios, such as Manuel Gallo of the Guadalajara diocese, who were close to being feral priests. Inq. 1255, fols. 163ff, 1782 ("las más vezes de tránsito sin fixa residencia"). Parishioners reported an encounter with a

lapsed priest at the Hacienda de Ometuxco during a 1789 pastoral visit to Axapusco parish. A stranger in lay dress had appeared and admitted that he had been ordained. People at the hacienda tried to persuade him to give himself up to church authorities and seek forgiveness, but he said he feared confinement at Tepotzotlan and fled. AHM L10B/26, fols. 119v–120v. The former Jesuit compound at Tepotzotlan had become an ecclesiastical prison as well as a seminary. In the same visita, Manuel Bernal, a priest who had let his licenses to preach and confess lapse, was sent there for a period of solitary confinement "because of his defects." AHM L10B/26, fol. 46.

15. AGN Hist. 578A, 1793, Tixtla report.

16. AGN CRS 57 exp. 4, fols. 267ff. Other transient renegade pastors were Francisco Antonio de Urueta, who had served in rural parishes of the districts of Chalco and Cuautla (see App. C), Sotomayor (see App. C), and Josef Navarro, a widely traveled vicario in modern Hidalgo. AGN Inq. 1318 exp. 8. One of the most unpriestly priests in rural Mexico at the end of the colonial period was Pedro Antonio Lara, who resided on the Hacienda Santa Cruz in the district of Huejutla in the 1790's. According to the subdelegado of Meztitlan, he knew no Latin, was ignorant of the divine office and moral theology, did not use a breviary, and celebrated mass in an entirely irregular way. He was also a man of unbridled lust, was regularly drunk and insolent, and always carried a knife in his belt, which he was quick to use, especially when drunk. He had committed various assaults in this and neighboring districts, and the cura had secured various orders from the chancery for his removal for criminal conduct, but Lara ignored them and was still at large. AGN Hist. 578A, 1793, Huejutla report.

Priests were forbidden to bear arms without license from their prelate. According to the Fourth Provincial Council in 1771, the only occasion when firearms might be permitted was while traveling on provincial roads. CPM, p. 132. In Michoacán, priests were not allowed to bear arms at all, but their servants could do so. *Colección de ordenanzas*, p. 60. Other examples of parish priests illegally bearing arms are AGN Acervo 49 caja 43, 1625 (Ichcateopan cura carried a blunderbuss and pistol and menaced Indians of Cicapualco with them); AGN Bienes 575 exp. 46, 1789 (cura of Ocuilan carried both a blunderbuss and a club); AJANG Criminal, box 22, doc. 21, 1807 (cura of Valle de Topia, Sinaloa, customarily carried a firearm).

17. AGN Bienes 172 exp. 45.

18. AGN Inq. 1308 exp. 1, fols. 40–43, 1790, Calzada. Other problem drinkers were José María Sánchez Gallardo and Miguel Gregorio Cedeño, cura and vicario of Ajuchitlan, vicario Ignacio Alberto Ramires of Tequisquiac, Franciscan Fr. Pedro Montaño of Acaponeta, Sinaloa, and Manuel Caxica y Aguayo, cura of Huiciltepec, Puebla. AGN Hist. 578A, 1793, Tetela del Río, Zumpango de la Laguna reports; Hist. 128 exp. 10, May 24, 1791 report; Inq. 1399, exp. 12, fols. 274ff, 1800.

19. Paredes, p. 33.

20. The city of Guadalajara had a similar if weaker pull on the diocese's parish priests. In 1792 Agustín Joseph Río de la Loza was appointed to a canonry in the cathedral over the objection of the intendant, who complained that he had been away from his parish of Fresnillo for two years without license (apparently in Guadalajara). AGI Guad. 533. The urban preference of priests is evident also in the papers that crossed the bishop's desk at the end of the colonial period. They include petitions to go to Guadalajara for medical care, and reports that young priests in Zacatecas would not leave that city for rural assignments. AHJ Manuscripts, no. G-4-802.

21. AGN CRS 201 exp. 1. The cura of Tolpetlac in 1782 also lived outside the parish, presumably in Mexico City. CRS 30 exp. 3.

22. According to the subdelegado of Taxco in 1793, he had never met the cura of Pilcayan, Mariano Villegas, who resided in Mexico City. AGN Hist. 578A, Taxco report. In

an 1805 lawsuit against a neighboring hacendado, the cura of Temascalcingo mentioned in passing that he resided in Mexico City. AGN Templos 25 exp. 4. Another example is Rafael Puebla, cura of Santiago Xalpan. Hist. 578A, 1793, Cadereyta report. The 19th-century papers of Manuel López Escudero, cura of Temamatla in the district of Chalco and hacienda owner, contain a revealing letter from his agent, Martínez de Castro, who also held a parish benefice but resided in Mexico City. Martínez de Castro wrote to López Escudero with nervous humor on Aug. 10, 1831, that a meeting of bishops in the capital was rumored to be about to send the curas back to their parishes. Texas, García Coll., no. 88.

23. AGN CRS 131 exp. 1.

24. Other Mexico City residents are documented in AGN Inq. 1113, 1777, Cempoala, cura Juan Antonio Xil de Andrade; AGN CRS 140 exp. 4, 1796, Yautepec, cura Manuel de Agüero of Yautepec; CRS 136 exp. 2, 1781, Tlaltizapan, cura José Eusebio de Ortega. Among others who resided in provincial towns were Mariano Villegas, cura of Pilcayan, and Andrés López, cura of Real de Tetela. AGN Hist. 578A, 1793, Taxco, Tetela del Río reports.

25. AGN Bienes 172 exp. 44, 1805 (Tarasquillo vicario de pie fijo, Lerma district, Joseph Mariano Garfías—lax); Bienes 172 exp. 54, 1804 (coadjutor of Tenango Tepopula, Gregorio Antonio García, lax, drunk, lived in mesón, spent Fridays in Chalco where he kept a widow); Bienes 663 exp. 4, 1807 (cura of Ixmiquilpan, Joachin Negrete, 90 years old, "en una palabra, no hace nada," complained indios principales); AGN Inq. 1304 exp. 3, 1796 (Sotomayor, Real de Zacualpan, said mass in 15 minutes, did four in a row at that speed, did not pray the Divine Office, hurried through confession); Inq. 1334 exp. 3, 1793 (at Jonacatepec, Sotomayor was slow to perform last rites outside the cabecera and was careless about teaching doctrina).

26. BN LaFragua Coll., vol. 590. Customarily a cura could be away from the parish for two or three days at a time without license. *Itin.* 4-17-83, 4-17-84.

27. AGN RCO 93 exp. 47. The standard two months a year with license is mentioned in *Itin.* 1-2-1.

28. AGN RCO 182 exp. 78.

29. AGN Acervo 49 caja 116. One cura had reportedly spent seven years away from his parish when he was charged by the archbishop, but he was not relieved of office. AGN Hist. 578A, 1793, Ixmiquilpan report.

30. AGN Acervo 49 caja 116, vicario de pie fijo of Tescatepec, Sierra Gorda, 1808–9 pastoral visit; AJANG Civil, box 80, doc. 2, 1772 (cura of Sierra de Pinos, Franciso Xavier de Ocampo, resided in Villa de Aguascalientes); AGN Hist. 578A, 1793, Tulancingo report (cura Josef Nicolás Martínez of Atoyac stayed in another cabecera eight leagues away because of his "particulares negociaciones," and cura Antonio Velardo de Ontiberos of Petatam lived 30 leagues from his parish seat).

31. The cura of Ocotlan, Jalisco, from 1803 to 1819 was said to be rarely in residence, either sick or away on personal business. BEJ Miscelánea, vol. 710, exp. 8. Father Nava of Terrenate apparently lived much of the time on his farm three leagues away. AGN Inq. 1074. The vicario of Yautepec in 1799 claimed that one of the witnesses against him, the cura of Tochimilco, was often away from the parish in Puebla or on his Hacienda de Santa Catalina. Inq. 1221 exp. 9.

32. AGN Hist. 578A, 1793, Zacualpan report: Real de Tecicapan cura (of weak character, youthful "vivezas pueriles que hacen poco honor a su carácter"), Teloloapan cura (propensity for cardplaying, "aprovechando todos los intereses"). Tulancingo report: Coayutlan cura (somewhat "interesado"), Petatam cura ("emprender asumptos muy ajenos a su estado"), Petatam interim cura ("se mesclaba en tan continuados dibertimientos públicos . . . causando escándalo con su impropio exemplo," lax in teaching doctrina). Tixtla report: Chacalinitla cura ("sumergido en una pública incontinencia, hasta esta fecha

vistiéndose de militar"), vicario of Apango ("pública incontinencia"). Malinalco report: Tenancingo coadjutor ("viveza inmoderada," lax in teaching doctrina). Taxco report: Taxco vicario ("genio violento y melancólico"), Acamistla cura ("interesado"), Acamistla vicario ("de una conducta poca arreglada y mui jugador de gallos, poco aplicado al ministerio," "interesado"), Tetipac coadjutor (not very exact in his duties, off to Toluca and Mexico often for cockfights, but desinteresado), Tetipac vicario ("sea enfermedad, manía, o genio, vive tan retirado en su casa que no contesta a veces ni con los suyos," does not always respond to calls for last rites), Pilcayan cura (absent), Mexcala vicario de pie fijo ("en su conducta personal algo extravagante, así en el trato como en su vestuario y persona. Desatiende muchas veces su ministerio, por atender a la minería"). Yahualica report: cura of cabecera (lax in preaching and teaching). Cadereyta report: Real del Doctor cura (prideful, rarely preaches), Xalpan cura (habitually absent). Ixmiquilpan report: Real del Cardonal cura ("inclinado a todo género de vicios, y preocupado de amores . . . se olvida de sus obligaciones").

33. AGN Hist. 578A, 1793, Taxco report ("Ha tenido una carrera literaria mui lúcida, es de buenos talentos, bien instruído, y uno de los mejores teólogos del arzovispado. Su conducta ha ocasionado los mayores daños a muchos vecinos de este Real, donde ha residido la mayor parte del tiempo que lleva de cura de Acamistla. El tiempo que ha residido aquí, lo ha empleado en fomentar pleitos y disensiones entre los vecinos, sugiriendo y formando escritos para suscitarlos, y algunas veces produciendo escritos contra los mismos, que a un tiempo defendía. . . . Y todo el daño viene de que por lo regular patrocina negocios injustos, y aun aquéllos que tienen alguna justicia, los dirige tan mal, que parece los enrreda con estudio. . . . Ha travajado minas, y el quererse introducir injustamente en la del Poder de Dios ha ocasionado un ruidoso pleito. . . . Ocupado todo en negocios seculares agenos de su estado, tiene abandonado el cuidado de su curato y de sus feligreses"). Cayetano Yzquierdo, cura of Ichcateopan, was known for a similar mixture of traits. The subdelegado called him a man "renowned for his talent and learning," but "too active in collecting his fees. . . . He makes himself obeyed and feared by his parishioners with a majestic predominance." Hist. 578A, 1793, Ichcateopan report.

34. AGN Bienes 663 exp. 26, 1818, Lolotla district (only two masses a year); Bienes 172 exp. 36, 1803–4 (San Sebastián Querétaro interim cura negligent, rarely going out to confess); AHJ Manuscripts, no. G-4-719, 1755 (cura of Nochistlan did not go to Mesticacan for mass every 15 days); AJANG Civil, box 223, doc. 13, Santa Ana de los Negros, Zapopan district, 1803 (petition for vicario de pie fijo because many were dying without confession or proper burial); AGN CRS 75 exp. 5, 1785, Indians of San Luis de las Peras, Huichapan district (cura removed vicario de pie fijo and was not providing adequate service); Tulane VEMC 16 exp. 12 (1751–57 secularizations in the uplands of Morelos had reportedly led to the appointment of curas who were often absent or rooted in the cabecera). If the Indian petitioners of Santiago Amatepec, Villa Alta district (Oaxaca), did not exaggerate, their cura was particularly rooted in the cabecera with his "servant" and ten children. They said that when he was called to attended the dying, he sent out a message to apply a little holy water and a hot brick. Archivo del Estado de Oaxaca, Juzgados, 1807 bundle, Jan. 7, 1744, complaint against Santiago Mariano Villanueva.

35. Bishop Palafox issued the standard warning about women to seminary students: "If you wish to treat them well, don't treat with them at all. . . . What today is a thread, tomorrow is a rope, and the next day a chain." *Manual de sacerdotes*, fol. 5v. In the late colonial period, bishops still issued special pastorals on women's dress, pronouncing fashions that included bare arms and low-cut dresses the work of the devil. Women who dressed this way were temptresses and "murderers of men's [fragile] souls." See Archbishop Lizana y Beaumont's pastoral letters of Sept. 24, 1807, and Nov. 26, 1808.

36. AGN Bienes 172 exp. 53. Some parishioners of Yahualica in 1808 raised the issue of

the cura's "housemaid" (*recamarera*) not because they were outraged at his incontinence but because they regarded the woman as a tyrant and wanted her banished. AGN Acervo 49 caja 116, 1808–9 pastoral visit, report on Bartolomé Vélez Escalante.

37. AGN Hist. 578A, 1793, Zacualpan report: Miguel de Estrada (vicario of Real de Zacualpan), Ysidro Estrada (vicario of Teloloapan). Tixtla report: José Miranda (vicario of Tixtla), Mariano Munive (cura of Cachultenango), Manuel Niño de Rivera (cura, location not specified), Francisco Lazcano (vicario of Zumpango del Río). Tetela del Río report: Sebastián Patricio (vicario of Tetela). Valladolid report: Josef Joaquín Hidalgo (cura of Santa Clara del Cobre), Fr. Pablo Díaz de León (cura of Acuitzio). Acapulco report: Fr. Miguel del Castillo (capellán of hospital). Ixmiquilpan report: Manuel de Larrainzar (vicario of Ixmiquilpan), Ygnacio de la Barzena (cura of Real del Cardonal). Huejutla report: Pedro Antonio Lara (Hacienda de Santa Cruz). Zumpango de la Laguna report: Josef Eusebio de Ortega (cura of Zumpango), Ygnacio Valladolid (vicario of Zumpango), Ygnacio Alberto Ramires (vicario of Tequisquiac).

Other incidental references include AGN Civil 1603 exp. 9 (Tabasco governor's report that the clergy in his district needed reform, especially for their incontinence and rebellion); Hist. 132 exp. 27, 1794 (governor of the Marquesado del Valle's gratuitous charge that the cura of Cuernavaca was guilty of incontinence when the governor defended his lieutenant for Yautepec against charges lodged by non-Indians there); AHJ Manuscripts, no. G-4-802, 1815 (José María Romo de Vivar's petition from his post in Teocaltiche for permission to go to Guadalajara to treat his venereal infection); AGN Acervo 49 caja 116, 1808–9 pastoral visit (complaint that the cura of Santa Catarina Xochitiapan continued to have relations with a woman whom he had been forbidden to see and left the parish often to do so); and AGN Bienes 172 exp. 44, 1805 (charges of Indians of Tarasquillo, Lerma district, that, among many other wrongdoings, their vicario de pie fijo had illicit relations with a woman).

The subject came up also in a couple of Inquisition cases. In one, the alcalde mayor of Cempoala in 1777 raised this as a countercharge after he learned that the cura, Juan Antonio Xil de Andrade, had begun an inquisitorial investigation against him. The alcalde mayor claimed that Xil de Andrade was responsible for the pregnancies of three different women and had had other women living in his house. AGN Inq. 1113, fols. 231–54. In the other, a 1795 case against the cura of Otumba, Athanasio Pérez Alamillo, for heretical and seditious statements (including favoring marriage for priests), evidence was presented that for many years he had lived with Mariana de Castro and fathered children by her. Inq. 1360 exps. 1–2.

38. A royal cedula of Feb. 13, 1727, directed to the viceroy of Peru decried in general terms the scandalous conduct of priests who publicly kept whole families of women and children, and ordered prelates to reform this conduct and remove incorrigible violators from parishes and other offices. AGN RCO 46 exp. 11. The unsanctioned decrees of the Fourth Provincial Council in 1771 spoke of concubinage as an especially detestable vice among clerics and prescribed harsh punishment for repeat offenders. CPM, p. 191. The way for priests to avoid this sin, the prelates declared, was to bar "suspect persons" from their homes. A priest's servant must be over 40 years old and of blameless reputation. "The best way to overcome the temptations of the flesh is to flee them; he who courts danger will perish in it."

39. An exception was the report on Manuel de Larrainzar, assistant cura of Ixmiquilpan, whom the subdelegado regarded as ignorant, ill-mannered, and quarrelsome. He included an extended criticism of Larrainzar's apparently monogamous illicit relationship, referring specifically to the priest's carrying his mistress off to an Indian pueblo to give birth, then baptizing the infant in a filthy shack, and to his rantings in the pulpit against local vecinos who had denounced him for his unchaste behavior. AGN Hist. 578A, 1793,

Ixmiquilpan report. In this case, as in most others I have read, the incontinence was more a pretext, a wedge against a political enemy, than the primary source of complaint. Despite the occasional pastoral letter and royal cedula that called attention to incontinent priests and prescribed exemplary punishments, Phelan's claim, in *Kingdom of Quito*, pp. 245–46, "It should be pointed out that the most devastating attack an antagonist could make on a clergyman was to charge violations of celibacy," does not hold true for late colonial parish priests in New Spain.

40. AGN Bienes 172 exp. 47.

41. AGN Acervo 49 caja 49. Other cases of multiple solicitations or scandalous whippings of local women with their buttocks exposed are AGN Inq. 1297 exp. 3; Inq. 1308 exp. 1; Inq. 1324, fols. 1–30; Inq. 1348 exp. 14; and Inq. 1372 exp. 2.

42. AGN Inq. 914 exps. 14–15.

43. AGN Inq. 960 exp. 19.

44. Joseph apparently went mad in confinement at Amacueca in 1763, escaping the convent at night, pounding on people's doors, drinking heavily, and once forcing himself into the chaplain's cell and threatening his life at knifepoint. Ibid. The case of an Augustinian doctrinero with a similar history, Fr. Francisco Caietano Téllez, coadjutor of Tlaola, is reported in AGN Inq. 1205 exp. 28, 1736. As the investigation proceeded, reports of transgressions with six or seven women grew to many more. He was sentenced in 1747 to loss of his license to confess, six years' exile from the locations of his transgressions, and three years of seclusion in the convent at Chalma.

Similar cases for the diocesan clergy include Joseph Manuel Sotomayor of Zacualpan and Manuel Gallo, who had served as a vicario in various parishes in the Diocese of Guadalajara. Despite the many charges of sexual misconduct against him, Sotomayor claimed he had only been lascivious for short periods and without public scandal. His means of seduction were sometimes ambiguous enough to save him from damaging gossip and denunciation. He admitted that in approaching women committed to his charge (depositadas), he would first embrace them and if they resisted, he would disguise his intentions by saying that he embraced them out of fatherly affection, which was neither bad nor a sin. Inq. 1334 exp. 3, fol. 181, 1796. In Gallo's case, one of his young married conquests, Juana María, denounced him in 1782, four years after the event, after three confessors told her she must report Gallo to the bishop before they would grant absolution. The dam broke in 1789, when a full investigation finally documented sexual misconduct with 17 women, including two solicitations in the confessional and propositions to two of Juana María's sisters. Since Gallo "spontaneously" confessed in September 1790 before all the evidence was in, and voluntarily gave up pastoral service, he was not sentenced. In 1806, he was said to be living in blameless retirement with a middle-aged woman and saying mass daily. Inq. 1255, fols. 45ff.

A complaint was lodged in 1809 against Manuel Morales, cura of Zacualpan de Amilpas, Morelos, for incontinence. What gave weight to the complaint was the claim that he had seduced a married woman, raped two maidens, and had a child by a third, coupled with his reputation for scandalous behavior of other kinds. Tulane VEMC 42 exp. 31. Francisco Garrido, cura of Tochimilco, was investigated for concubinage under similar circumstances in 1788. VEMC 1 exp. 40; VEMC 15 exp. 3. His reputation for faithful service resulted in an exoneration by the archbishop's court.

45. Priests understood the difference. Outraged at a false charge of solicitation in the confessional, Silverio de Nava, cura of Terrenate, freely admitted that he had not been celibate, but he vehemently denied that sex had ever been connected to his duties as pastor. AGN Inq. 1074, 1768.

46. The rhetoric of misogyny and the pastor's duty to protect the family could lead to another kind of violation of the confessional that concerned the ecclesiastical courts:

breaking the seal of secrecy. In 1784, the cura of Tula, Dr. Francisco del Villar, was charged by the Inquisition with irregular conduct for forcing an unmarried pregnant woman to divulge the name of her sex partner and declaring loudly in the confessional that "he knew ahead of time that she was pregnant because she and all the women of Tula were a bunch of whores." AGN Inq. 1230 exp. 13. The vicario of Temascaltepec, Félix González Beltrán, was accused of breaking the seal of the confessional when, on more than one occasion, he pressured a man to marry a pregnant woman who had confessed to him. Inq. 760 exp. 40, 1715. Similar accusations were made against the cura of Real del Cardonal Ygnacio de la Barzena. AGN Hist. 578A, 1793, Ixmiquilpan report. In the spirit of the Council of Trent, late colonial prelates of New Spain sought to minimize the opportunities for indiscretion and to maintain "much decorum" by requiring that women not be confessed after vespers, that there be no conversation between confessor and penitent before or after confession, and that the confessional be located in an open and well-lit part of the church. CPM, pp. 194–95; *Colección de ordenanzas*, pp. 23, 206.

Ecclesiastical courts should have been concerned about parish priests violating single women who were held en depósito—confined under the priest's care, mainly in preparation for marriage or to hide the shame of pregnancy outside of wedlock. This practice is examined by Deborah E. Kanter in her doctoral dissertation, "Hijos del Pueblo."

47. Late colonial Inquisition cases of solicitation in the confessional for the two dioceses include AGN Inq. 760 exp. 40, Temascaltepec, 1715; Inq. 760 exp. 42, Zumpango de la Laguna, 1715; Inq. 814 exp. 8, Zacoalco, 1726; Inq. 1817 exp. 5, Ahualulco, 1727; Inq. 1205 exp. 28, Tlaola, 1736; Inq. 914 exps. 14–15, Lake Chapala area, 1748; Inq. 960 exp. 19, Santa María del Oro, 1759; Inq. 622 exp. 5, Ixtlahuaca, 1774; Inq. 1191 exp. 14, Mascota, 1781–82; Inq. 1255 fols. 45ff, Ameca, 1782; Inq. 1308 exp. 1, Sierra de Pinos, 1790; Inq. 1318 exp. 8, Huejutla, 1791; Inq. 1348 exp. 10, Ichcateopan, 1794; Inq. 1348 exp. 14, Xochicoatlan (Molango district), 1795; Inq. 1372 exp. 2, Sierra de Pinos, 1798; and Inq. 1221 exp. 9, Yautepec, 1799. Various other Mexican solicitation cases are mentioned in Medina, pp. 283, 290, 303–7, 340; and Lea, pp. 241–45.

An appearance before the Inquisition in 1799 was not enough to stop one particularly amorous young vicario, José Antonio Baldovinos of Colima, for whom any single creole woman between 16 and 37 was apparently fair game. Considering that some of these women confessed as often as two or three times a week, his advances were not always all that unwelcome. The oldest among the objects of his affection made him a double-edged, apparently playful confession worthy of Molière. She told him that a clergyman had caressed her in the confessional, whereupon the besotted vicario advised flight from that priest's presence. "Well, are those games and endearments so bad and sinful?," she asked, to which he replied that they were very bad and very undignified, and that she should tell him who the fellow was so he could have him expelled. But, she testified to the Inquisition, she had never had the heart to tell him that he was the author of those intimacies. Inq. 1346 exp. 6. The son of a carpenter, Baldovinos was attached to other profane pleasures as well. He especially enjoyed dances and drinking. His risky search for heterosexual gratification, which he continued in his next parish assignment at Villa de Purificación, led to a sentence in 1801 that stripped him of his license to confess. He reappeared before the Inquisition in 1806, poor and repentant, seeking the restoration of his licenses so that he could resume pastoral service.

48. AGN Inq. 1348 exp. 14.

49. In the 1790 case of Mariano Calzada, former vicario of Sierra de Pinos, one of the women he propositioned had not reported it for fear that her husband would find out. AGN Inq. 1308 exp. 1, fol. 12. In a similar case from Zumpango de la Laguna, in 1715, the two women who eventually testified against the teniente de cura (one was the wife of the maestro de escuela, the other an Indian from Tecualoyan) both said they had held back for

fear of their husband's response. Inq. 760 exp. 42. The non-Indian woman also mentioned the shame she felt and her concern that the priest might do her some harm in retaliation.

50. AGN Inq. 814 exp. 8.

51. Doña Juana María Caballero de los Olivos of Ameca, for example, delayed for four years before denouncing her former confessor, the teniente de cura of Cocula, for seduction. AGN Inq. 1255, fols. 45ff, 1782.

52. Cases of solicitation in the confessional often came to light only after other confessors denied the victims absolution until they reported the transgression to the Inquisition. Among many examples are AGN Inq. 760 exp. 11, Zoquitlan, Puebla, 1715; Inq. 760 exp. 42, Zumpango de la Laguna, 1715; Inq. 1205 exp. 28, Tlaola, 1736; Inq. 1255 fol. 45ff, Cocula, Jalisco, 1782; Inq. 1308 exp. 1, Sierra de Pinos, 1790; Inq. 1318 exp. 8, Huejutla, 1791; Inq. 1372 exp. 2, Sierra de Pinos, 1798; and Inq. 1346 exp. 6, Colima, 1799.

53. For example, Miguel Amador, vicario of Mascota in the Diocese of Guadalajara, was denounced by a criolla parishioner in 1781 for propositioning a young maiden, apparently in the confessional as well as outside. The Inquisition did not pursue the case because it was the first charge of the kind against Amador. AGN Inq. 1191 exp. 14. Charges before the archiepiscopal court against Dr. Pedro de Zúñiga, cura of Ozolotepec, for having sex with his maid were dropped in 1749 without interviewing the person who would have known best. AGN CRS 105 exp. 5.

In the case of the Franciscan doctrinero Pedro Montaño, of Acaponeta, Sinaloa, who was accused in 1791 by a vecino of having sexual intercourse with two women, the bishop declined to act on the charges not because Montaño was innocent but because the accuser and other vecinos of Acaponeta had ulterior motives. Even the vecino's accusation was less a complaint against the priest's incontinence, which was long-standing and well known, than against his habit of taking his family out on circuit, at considerable expense to parishioners. AGN Hist. 128 exp. 10.

54. AGN Inq. 1113, fols. 231–54.

55. AGN Inq. 1372 exp. 2. Early in the 18th century a married india of Xitlama charged the teniente de cura of Zoquitlan (Puebla), Joseph López, with confessing her and later having sex with her when she went to Zoquitlan on market day. He was also said to have had sex with other indias and a public affair with an unwed mestiza. Rather than denying the charges, López was contrite and escaped with a warning. Inq. 760 exp. 11, 1715.

56. Examples of sentences in cases of flagrant incontinence and solicitation in the confessional include AGN Inq. 1205 exp. 28, Tlaola, 1736; Inq. 1308 exp. 1, Sierra de Pinos, 1759; Inq. 960 exp. 19, Santa María del Oro, 1759; and Inq. 1346 exp. 6, Colima, 1799.

57. An important introduction to this virtually unstudied subject is Gruzinski, "Cenizas del deseo," which examines the investigation and trial of 123 men accused of the pecado nefando in New Spain in 1658. Though none of the 66 men whose occupation was listed was a priest, Gruzinski notes that members of the clergy were implicated by the archbishop and the alcalde del crimen of the audiencia. R. Gutiérrez, pp. 313–14, cites two late-18th-century cases of sodomy by Franciscan missionaries in New Mexico. Where 14 of the men were executed in Gruzinski's 1658 cases, sodomy was not treated as a capital offense in either of Gutiérrez's cases.

58. District officials occasionally criticized parish priests for effeminacy in their 1793 reports, but they stopped short of accusations of sodomy.

Other kinds of conduct that amounted to an abuse of office were:

A. Using the pulpit to attack enemies. At least as early as 1563, preachers were ordered not to make "scandalous remarks concerning the public and universal government" or comments that would arouse personal animosity. *Recop.* 1-12-19. Example: AGN Inq. 760 exp. 42, 1729, Domingo Soriano of Tecualoyan.

B. Spreading malicious gossip about parishioners: Rosenbach Lib., Mexican MS 462/25, pt. 4, no. 7, 1735, Fr. Manuel Maldonado of Tetela del Volcán (suit by vecinos of Hueyapan on charge of destroying a marriage by spreading unfounded rumors of adultery); AGN Hist. 578A, 1793, Acapulco report, Hippolyte chaplain of the hospital in Acapulco, Fr. Miguel del Castillo.

C. Disobeying ecclesiastical superiors: AGN Bienes 172 exp. 56, Joseph Zaragoza, vicario of Tepetlixpa (charged in the archbishop's court by his cura with insubordination, violent treatment of parishioners, and "speaking with the mouth of a drunken Indian").

D. Maltreating parishioners and the abuse of Indians: Inq. 960 exp. 19, 1759, Fr. Gregorio Yriarte, serving in Poncitlan, Jalisco (described as "con capa de pastor hacía estragos de lobo"); AGN Crim. 219 exp. 10, cura of Metepec; Crim. 231 fols. 207ff, 1787, cura of Ixtlahuaca; AGN CRS 30 exp. 3, fol. 59, 1782, cura of Tolpetlac (of whom Indian representatives said, "no ayamos amparo en el palacio de nuestro pastor"); CRS 67 exp. 3, 1768, Fermín de Tagle of Santa María Joloapan, Guipustla parish; CRS 136 exp. 4, 1784, vicario Joseph María Rodríguez, San Lorenzo Huichilapan, Lerma parish (treated Indians as enemies).

59. Only after considerable interrogation over several months and substantiation of more serious charges did the much-mentioned Sotomayor admit to being somewhat "recio" and violent with his parishioners of Zacualpan. AGN Inq. 1334 exp 3, fols. 2ff.

60. Hot-tempered priests also show up in the few bishops' reports to the crown on the clergy that contain personal evaluations. For example, AGI Mex. 2549, the archbishop's report for 1764 identified Juan Rodríguez del Castillo, cura of Teocaltiche, as "de competentes letras pero de genio violento"; Antonio Ruiz de Olachea, cura of Xerez, as of "buenas letras pero no mui buen juicio porque es iracundo"; Dr. Joseph Dávila, cura of Agua de Venado, as "de genio violento por lo que no lo quieren mucho sus parroquianos"; and Domingo Cabero y Castro, cura of Tlaltenango, as "sabe theología moral pero no muy amado de sus feligreses" because of his "genio tan áspero."

"Precipitado" usually meant a man who was quick with words that wounded. It would apply, for example, to the cura of Tejupilco, who had offended his Indian parishioners in a dispute over first fruits with his "palabras injuriosas." AGN CRS 204 exp. 10, fol. 316. Others who fit the description were the cura of Mochitlan, Juan Valerio Barrientos, for his mistreatment "de razones," his "continuo semblante de enojo o yncomodidad con ellos," and Sotomayor at Zacualpan, who habitually "injuria de palabras a sus feligreses." AGN Hist. 430, 1800; AGN Inq. 1304 exp. 3, fols. 5, 18v, 1796. The Indians of the visitas of Tamazunchale, San Luis Potosí, reportedly refused to go to their cura because he always berated them. AGN Acervo 49 caja 116, 1808 pastoral visit. One irascible priest was represented by a subdelegado in passive-aggressive terms. Francisco de Ocampo, first vicario of Taxco, was at once "violento y melancólico, lo que le hace algo retirado del comercio y sociedad." Hist. 578A, 1793, Taxco report. Another high-strung priest whose ardor apparently did him no great damage was Ygnacio de Arizávalo, coadjutor of Tenancingo, who was described by the same subdelegado as "poco sufrido, y por su viveza inmoderada suele cometer algunos errores involuntarios que desvían a los feligreses del amor que pudieran tenerle."

61. AGN CRS 75, exp. 8, fols. 420–24 ("haviéndole puesto al Br. Piña la pretención de Ordóñez, y deferido a la reconciliación y concurrencia que pretendía . . . Ordóñez se incó de rodillas, besó las manos al vicario y pretendiendo darle satisfacción le dixo: que no hallava en si huviese de motivos a los disgustos, pues cuanto a dho Padre le havían dicho, que havía hablado de él hera falso, que el indio alcalde, Antonio de Santiago hera el que handava con los chismes . . . y le suplicaba lo perdonase si en algo le había ofendido . . .

a estas razones el Br. Piña (tal vez por violencia o intrepidés de su genio) le contestó con palabras altas y de mal modo, diciéndole: que se venía santificando, que havía depuesto de su conducta, y dicho lo quitaría del pueblo; a todo satisfacía Ordóñez, diciendo que era falso; pero dicho vicario insistió en que havía proferido que lo quitaría del pueblo y administración; de que ostigado Ordóñez, viendo que no hallava razones con que satisfacer al vicario, dixo: no lo he dicho que si lo huviera dicho lo huviera cumplido: Estas palabras fueron de tanto incentibo, para fomento de cólera, en el Padre Vicario, que a grandes gritos y palmadas fuertes sobre la mesa decía, eso quiero yo que V. me quite; he de perder a V: profiriendo otras muchas razones que manifestaban ser dimanadas de la cólera que le asistía sin que fuese bastante a sosegarlo, el que por repetidas ocaciones, se estubo hincado Ordóñes de rodillas, abrasándolo y vezándole las manos; ni las medidas razones con que yo . . . procuraba sosegarlo; estando en esto observé que el Br. José María Peña salió al corredor y volvió con violencia a cojer un bastón o palo diciendo que con desacato se havían entrado hasta el corredor unos indios chupando tabaco; contube yo a dho Br. José María y al vicario, quien sobre este punto se enardeció mucho más de lo que estaba, queriendo salir en acción a apalearlos."

The receptor went on to say that the vicario seemed ready to pardon Ordóñez when the vicario's nieces entered, hysterical, saying that the Indians were making a revolt. Piña and Peña made as if to go out with saber and club to confront the Indians, but the receptor persuaded them not to do so. He told them he had gone out and found no one in the corridor or patio and no indication of an uprising, only four or five Indians, including Ordóñez's drunken brother-in-law. He returned to the cura's room to find Piña with his saber unsheathed saying that the Indians had risen up at Ordóñez's instigation and "esto quería yo, lo he de perder." Ordóñez's disclaimers and pleas for forgiveness and the receptor's assurances that there was no tumulto had no effect on the vicario, who soon fled the town with his sisters and complained to the district judge. According to the receptor, Ordóñez said "este padre me tira a perder" as they were leaving the casas curales, but nothing more provocative.

62. In a 1783 dispute over fees with Indians of San Lorenzo Huichilapan, the priest was judged to be "guiado de un zelo, aunque imprudente o que manejándose con poca discreción." AGN CRS 136 exp. 4, fol. 257r.

63. Hard-hearted was the way Indian petitioners of San Luis de las Peras described their cura in 1785. AGN CRS 75 exp. 5, fol. 327.

64. AGN Templos 1 exp. 2, 1768–88.

65. AGN CRS 68 exp. 9, 1790. Occasionally the cura was his own worst enemy when responding to charges of excessive anger and a domineering spirit. Dr. Salvador Brambila, cura of Autlan, Jalisco, in his voluminous six-year litigation against the district governor over jurisdiction in a rape case, more than made the crown's point that he was a man of great "calor" and "precipitación," and "de espíritu dominante." AJANG Civil, box 125 doc. 2. This was clearly the case with the cura of Tepetitlan. In refusing to sign the order he gave the subdelegado the high road in undermining the priest's credibility.

66. AJANG Criminal, box 33, doc. 15, 1803, coadjutor for Chametla, Sonora, Pedro García. The cura of Xaltocan was said to have started a commotion in 1747 by opposing the alcalde mayor's local execution of an audiencia order. AGN RCO 71 exp. 8, 1751. Other characterizations of pastors as obstinate and the source of local trouble: AGN Civil 865 exp. 9, fol. 23, 1772, Ocuilan; AGN Templos 25 exp. 10, 1805, Temascalcingo.

67. The prime example of an exceptionally careless pastor is Joseph Manuel Sotomayor of Zacualpan. AGN Inq. 1304 exp. 3; Inq. 1334 exp. 3, 1796–1800. Other examples include AGN Hist. 578A, 1793, Metepec report, Fr. Antonio Díaz, vicario (criticized for "desidia y poca atención"); Inq. 1113, fol. 234v, 1777, Cempoala, Lic. Juan Antonio Xil de Andrade (offered no regular misa de renovación, did not maintain an adequate supply of

communion wafers, did not fast before mass, and conducted the mass in irregular ways); and AGN Acervo 49 caja 116, 1808–9, Chiconcuautla (priest lax in keeping the font clean and replenishing the water).

68. The case of Lic. Francisco Garrido, cura of Tochimilco, who was charged with concubinage and drunkenness in 1789, is a good example. Despite telling evidence against him, he was exonerated after various curas testified to his energetic service. The promotor fiscal and archbishop reasoned that he could not be such a zealous pastor if he were guilty of public incontinence and drunkenness "porque [¿]no es conceptible que un cura enrredado en semejante desgracia pueda cumplir por si mismo con exactitud las altas obligaciones de su Ministerio; ni quien ha visto capaz de llenar esas obligaciones en el Altar, Púlpito, confesonario, administración, asseo de paramentos y arreglo de libros a un hombre sumergido en la lasiva y continuamente enagenado por la bebida como quiso pintar a este cura el Subdelegado de Tochimilco?" Tulane VEMC 15 exp. 3, fol. 4r.

69. AGN Inq. 1363 exps. 1–2, 1794–95, Otumba, cura Athanasio Pérez Alamillo; Inq. 894, fols. 264ff, 1795, Dr. Juan Antonio Montenegro, deacon from Guadalajara; Inq. 1399 exp. 12, 1800, Huiciltepec, Puebla; Inq. 1304 exp. 3 and Inq. 1334 exp. 3, 1796, Sotomayor, Zacualpan; Inq. 1205 exp. 1, 1781, Yahualica.

70. AGN Inq. 1326 exp. 2, 1795, Yecapixtla (Morelos), cura Antonio Bonavita; Inq. 894, fols. 264ff, 1795, "la religión es una pura política de que se han valido los hombres para sugetar a los pueblos," statement by a deacon with a doctorate, Juan Antonio Montenegro, Guadalajara, who claimed that he said this just for the sake of argument.

71. Many of the most outrageous perpetrators of unpriestly conduct were in fact deacons and subdeacons or diocesan priests not in parish service. Mariano Gil Caballero, a young man in minor orders from Mexico City, led such a scandalous life that his own mother denounced him to the archiespiscopal court in 1806. AGN Acervo 49 caja 45. The chancery in 1790 described Joseph Cristóbal Rivas, also in minor orders and under arrest in the ecclesiastical jail, as "enteramente abandonado, escandaloso, y de una pésima conducta." Tulane VEMC 73 exp. 41. For the Diocese of Guadalajara, a deacon reminiscent of Friar Tuck is described in AJANG Criminal, box 3, doc. 1, 1815, Pedro Barragán; and a fun-loving Mercedarian, Francisco Cádiz Oliva y Rivas, who partied and gambled his way to Guadalajara in 1799 and was killed by robbers near Tepatitlan is described in Criminal, bundle labeled "1799 leg. 1 (65)."

72. This chapter also draws on the resumés the priests prepared for the periodic competitions for vacant posts. But since only the dutiful need apply, they offer a highly selective view of parish service. Some impressive testimonial letters occasionally appear in these files. For the 1754 concurso for Guadalajara, Agustín de Acosta, cura of Monterrey, submitted a certification for candidacy from the governor of Nuevo León, in which he lavishly praised Acosta for his generosity, indefatigability, and "fervoroso cuydado de las almas." AHJ Manuscripts, no. G-4-719.

Another abundant source of documentation on the faithful conduct of parish priests is the testimony of witnesses they enlisted in their lawsuits. For example, in an 1805–6 suit brought by some Indian leaders of Zapotitlan against Ygnacio Pérez, the cura of Tuscacuesco (Jalisco), over forced labor and other mistreatment, various witnesses regarded the charges as unfair and the product of revenge. They praised Pérez for "la puntual disposición del predicho párroco en especial para las confesiones de los enfermos de los pueblos que por si administra sin hacérsele impresión las incomodidades de horas, tiempos ni caminos, transitando por sus barrancas aun las más fragosas con tan inalterable serenidad como si lo hiciera en llanuras de mucha comodidad." AJANG Criminal, box 20, doc. 2. In a dispute with Indians of Ocotlan (Jalisco), local non-Indians testified to the cura's dedication and the Indians' irreligion. One spoke of him as "este hombre parese de fierro por su constancia en el trabajo." AJANG Civil, box 231, doc. 1. This kind of evidence usually has a partisan cast and is hard to evaluate, especially if the witnesses were selected by the priest, but it should not be dismissed altogether.

73. The bishop reported on 65 parishes; 10 others were vacant at the time, and the rest were still administered by Franciscans or Augustinians. The 45 curas singled out for this praise served in Santa María de Lagos, Aguascalientes, Fresnillo, Sierra de Pinos, Xalostotitlan (2), Tepatitlan, Gutierre de Aguila, Saltillo, Cuquío, Nochistlan, Zacoalco, Tepic, Huauchinango, San Cristóbal de la Barranca, Ojocaliente, San Sebastián, Compostela, Villa de Purificación, Ameca, Senticpac, San Pedro Analco, Sayula, Pánuco, Guaynamota, Tequila, Monte Escovedo, Mesquitic, Mascota, Xala, Mojarras, Techaluta, Atemanica, Amatlan, Monterrey, Villa de Linares, Cadereyta, Valle de Guajuco, Valle de Salinas, Valle de Cerralvo, Boca de Leones, Punta de Lampasos, Ciudad de Coahuila, Valle de Santa Rosa, and one not identified by parish. AGI Mex. 2549, bishop's report, Jan. 3, 1764.

74. AGN Acervo 49 caja 116. For example, the service of the cura of Huauchinango was characterized as "conducta arreglada, prontitud exacta"; that of the cura of Guayacocotla as "costumbres arregladas, zelo en los deveres pastorales, ninguna queja contra su persona."

75. AGN Hist. 578A, 1793. They were "exact in fulfilling their duties, men of personal conduct that is very fitting to their station" (exactos en el cumplimiento, conducta muy arreglada a su estado).

76. The following quotes come from the Tulancingo, Meztitlan, Zacatecas, Cempoala, and Coyoacan reports in AGN Hist. 578A, 1793. Similar glowing descriptions appear in the reports for Zacualpan (José María Rincón, interim cura of Ixtapan), Metepec (Cayetano Sotomaior, cura of Metepec); Ixmiquilpan (José Francisco Guerrero, cura of Chilcuatla); Zacatecas (José María Díaz Ticareno, twice interim cura for Zacatecas, and Juan José de Aro, Teul); and Huichapan (Luis José Carrillo, cura of Aculco, and Andrés Benosa, European-born cura of Xilotepec).

Exemplary curas sometimes inspired exemplary conduct in their assistants, or so it was said of Gasano's primer vicario of Coyoacan, José Manuel Montes, Castro Tobio's five vicarios of Tulancingo, and the cura of Tizayuca, José María Solano, and his two assistants, José Urrueta and Cesario García (Pachuca report).

77. Alcedo, 1: 413.

78. AHJ Manuscripts, no. G-4-719.

79. AGN Hist. 578A, 1793, Tacuba, Apam, Huichapan, and Cuautitlan reports. Nearly every report in this series contains similar comments. Other kinds of surveys that yield information on some of the largely anonymous vicarios are the records of pastoral visits and late colonial censuses of priests supplied by the curas. For Guadalajara, the curas' responses to an Oct. 31, 1796, episcopal circular requesting a census of local priests (in CAAG) includes reports for Teocaltiche and Sierra de Pinos in which the curas went beyond the instructions, to praise several of their poorly educated but hard-working vicarios.

80. *Itin.* references include 22-3-1 to 22-3-5 ("limosnas que deben hacer los doctrineros de las rentas que perciben de sus Doctrinas"), 1-5-1 (the obligation to give to the poor), 1-5-4 (the obligation to give to poor Indians and not let them go without sacraments for nonpayment of fees), and 1-5-9 ("estamos obligados a dar limosna de lo superfluo a los que tienen grave necesidad . . . la razón es porque la notable necesidad del prógimo es grave mal, and as confessor to Indians, to exercise "la caridad, amor, y puntualidad"). As Bishop Palafox of Puebla had put it in 1653, "Charity is the principal virtue of the cura" (caridad es la principal virtud del Beneficiado). Brown Univ., Rockefeller Lib., Medina Coll., FHA 102 exp. 1, 1653 pastoral letter.

81. The first verse quoted by Lizana appears in Romans 12:17 in the Vulgate version of the Bible: "providentes bona non tantum coram Deo, sed etiam coram omnibus [hominibus]" (spread goodness not so much in the sight of God but especially in the sight of all

men). English versions of the verse going back to the King James omit the reference to God: "Recompense to no man evil for evil. Provide things honest in the sight of all men." For Guadalajara, one of Diego Rodríguez Rivas's pastoral letters of 1768 also concentrated on charity. BN LaFragua Coll., vol. 1005.

82. More than 40 men in these reports receive individualized attention as charitable pastors. Since the reports also remark on curas who were preoccupied with the accumulation of personal wealth, who insisted on their fees, and who practiced little charity, these attributions of charitable conduct were not without some critical judgment. See, for example, AGN Hist. 578A, 1793, Zacualpan report on Felipe Benicio Benites, cura of Apaxtla.

83. Ibid., Ixtlahuaca, Tixtla, and Zacualpan reports ("tanta caridad y desinterés que no le alcanza quanto le rinde el curato, para la mucha limosna que hace a sus feligreses y para el culto y adorno de su yglesia"; "desinterés y caridad son de tal manera singulares que nada tiene suyo quando advierte alguna neccsidad en sus feligreses"; "no se le advierte apego a yntereses y por contrario demaciado franco en repartir los que adquiere").

Other extraordinarily charitable parish priests, according to the subdelegados, were cura Martín Diego de Soto of Acapetlahuaya, Zacualpan district, coadjutor Ignacio María Castopol of Tixtla, cura Dr. Felipe de la Barcena of Taxco, cura Dr. Manuel Ramón de Escoto of Teotihuacan, cura José Gil Barragán of Real del Monte, cura Dr. José María Ramírez y Echavarri of Mexicalcingo, cura José Mariano Cueva of Lerma, cura Dr. Tomás de Arrieta of Tacuba, cura José Gutiérrez of Cacaguatepec (Acapulco district), vicarios Mariano Gutiérrez and Rafael Monroy of Ixtlahuaca, cura Francisco Ruiz de Armendáriz of Jiquipilco, vicario de pie fijo Manuel Gonzales of Tapasco (Ixtlahuaca district), cura Joseph Jacinto Llanos de Valdés of Sierra de Pinos, cura Dr. José Angel Gasano of Coyoacan, cura Luis José Carrillo of Aculco, and auxiliar Ignacio Basurto of Acasuchitlan.

The remaining notably charitable priests in these reports were coadjutor Mariano Cueva of Taxco, coadjutor Pedro de Estrada of Pilcayan (Taxco district), cura Marcelo de Arriaga of Huitzuco, cura Manuel Lino Guerra of Actopan, cura Agustín Durán of Tepecoacuilco, cura Agustín González de Castañeda of Cuzamala (Tetela del Río district), cura Francisco Miranda of Tolcayuca, cura José Mariano Cuevas of Lerma, cura Francisco Antonio Borla of Tlalnepantla, and various other curas in the district of Tacuba, cura José Francisco Guerra of Chilcuatla, cura Dr. Diego Manuel de Haza of San Felipe el Grande, vicario José Domingo Dávila of Xocotitlan, cura Antonio Anastasio Cervantes of Xerez, cura José Valerio Aldrete of Burgo de San Cosmé, cura José Luis Sánchez Urtado of Huichapan, vicario Manuel Montenegro Echarre of Huichapan, auxiliar Alexandro Ochoa of Nopala, cura Gracián de Agüero of Tecozautla, cura Francisco Pablo Lombardo of Tasquillo, the Indian auxiliar at San Bartolomé de las Tunas, and cura Andrés Benosa of Xilotepec.

84. For example, JCB, resumés of Joseph Buenaventura de Ayala, Joseph Mariano Rodríguez, Juan Manuel Tinoco, and Manuel Cassela; CAAG, unclassified, 1772, cura of Teuchitlan (in petition by Indians to apply cofradía funds to church construction); CAAG, resumés for 1770 concurso of cura José Antonio Barragán of Huejuquilla, Francisco Jacomé Robertes, cura José Ramón de Herrera of Huaynamota, cura en encomienda José Manuel de los Ríos of Atemanica, and cura Ysidro Joachín de Esparza y Gallardo of Mesquital; Cornejo Franco, resumé of Lic. Juan Manuel de el Solar, 1768, Tala; AGN Templos 25 exp. 8, 1796, Ygnacio Gonzales Castañeda. Sponsoring construction was also regarded as charity through employment.

85. CAAG, resumé of Pedro Gómez García for 1770 concurso.

86. AHJ Manuscripts, no. G-4-808, 1808, Tala cura Serafín García Cárdenas; JCB, 1760–62 resumés of curas Manuel Cassela of Atotonilco el Chico, Dr. Juan Joseph de Henestrosa of Lerma, Joseph Mariano Rodríguez of Tecoautla, Joseph Joaquín Loreto

Yturria of Tezontepec, and Dr. Manuel Joseph de Iglesias Cotillo of Tarasquillo; CAAG, resumés for 1770 concurso of cura José Ramón de Herrera of Huaynamota, cura en encomienda José Manuel de los Ríos of Atemanica, and cura Antonio Manuel Velásquez of Iscuintla and Chapala; AGI Guad. 533, 1795, resumé of cura Juan Nepomuceno Báez of Nochistlan; AGI Mex. 2550, resumé of cura Diego Narciso de Chaves of Tlanichol, 1791–1806; Tulane VEMC 68 exp. 9, cura Joseph Antonio Thenorio de la Banda of Atlistaca, Tlapa district; AGN CRS 13 exp. 3, 1780, cura Juan Días Conti of Olinalá; CRS 72 exp. 5, cura of Atlacomulco, 1737; AGN Bienes 663 exps. 5–6, 1809, cura Mariano Dionisio Alarcón of Tultitlan. Many other examples could be cited. Dr. José María Alcalá y Orozco, the idealistic young cura of Hueypustla, Tetepango district, in 1786, after exhausting his own resources and failing to get help from local hacendados in a time of devastating crop failures and famine, naively appealed to the viceroy for 1,500p to distribute among his Indian parishioners for their plantings. He even offered the future income on his 8,000p capellanía as collateral. The alcalde mayor replied that though the cura's heart was in the right place, he was new and inexperienced. He advised that pueblo property might be mortgaged or funds, if any existed, could be taken from the cajas de comunidad, but that the crown should not have to contribute. AGN CA 13 exp. 5.

87. AGI Mex. 2549, Oct. 18, 1754, Escobar report ("sin pluma alguna," "lo daba todo de limosna deducida de su congrua," "salud mui lastimada del trabajo de la administración").

88. AGI Guad. 533, 1795, resumés of Josef Jacinto de Llanos y Valdés of Sierra de Pinos and Juan Nepomuceno Báez of Nochistlan; JCB, 1762, resumé of Pascual de Roxas Mendoza Austria y Moctezuma. Also described as "el grave Pondus de aquel curato" (JCB, 1762 resumé of Juan Francisco Caballero); and "el imponderable trabajo" (AHJ Manuscripts, no. G-4-719 GUA/4, 1748, certification of Agustín de Acosta for concurso).

89. JCB, 1762, resumé of Antonio Xavier del Castillo Santa Cruz.

90. CAAG, resumé of Juan Diego de Cuevas for 1770 concurso.

91. CAAG, 1796 report.

92. Omerick, BMM 113. See also CAAG, resumé of Sisto Luna of Ixtlahuacan del Río for the 1853–54 concurso; he was on the road a lot.

93. AGN CRS 75 exp. 4, fols. 248–53, 1778, San Simón Tototepec, Zacualpan district; CAAG, 1770 concurso records (note on appointments refers to limited interest in Valle de Banderas, "por su intemperie y fragoso de sus caminos"); CAAG, resumé of José Buenaventura Gomes García for 1770 concurso (at Ixtlan since 1766, many parishioners and widely dispersed); JCB, 1762 resumés of Julián Campoy y Cervantes (six years now as cura of Lolotla, Sierra de Meztitlan, dangerous travels and remote settlements up to 20 leagues away, "caminos intratables precipicios de barrancas, ríos caudalosos, varias enfermedades"), cura Antonio Xavier del Castillo Santa Cruz of Pánuco, Joseph Buenaventura de Ayala (had spent 23 years in "ásperos y distantes curatos"), and Manuel Cassela ("hallarse sólo . . . penosísimas incomodidades por lo distante de las visitas, lo áspero de los caminos e inclemencias del tiempo").

94. JCB ("quasi imponderables . . . trabajos que ha tolerado en cuarenta y un años y meses que ha servido a la sagrada mitra" "caminando de noche con evidente peligro de la vida por lo fragoso de los caminos," "pasado las noches en el suelo sin más abrigo que su capa, y comido los más viles alimentos que muchas ocaciones ni estos se le han proporcionado").

95. AGN CRS 67 exp. 2, fol. 10r, 1766 (José Bargayanta, cura in Tenango del Valle district, often traveled four leagues round-trip to say mass).

96. JCB, 1760, resumé of Carlos Buenaventura de Arellano of Tetela del Río; Tulane VEMC 17 exp. 11.

97. CAAG, resumé of Sisto Luna for 1853–54 concurso.

98. CAAG, 1796 reports, Aguascalientes district.

99. JCB, 1762, resumé of Tiburcio de Salazar.

100. Sahagún, 3, bk. 11: 219 ("Las condiciones de las montañas son éstas: que tienen mucho heno muy verde, son airosas y ventosas, húmedas y en ellas hiela; son lugares tristes y solitarios y llorosos, son lugares cavernosos y riscosos, y pedregosos y lodosos, y [de] tierra dulce y tierra amarilla; y lugares de grandes cuestas, y de espesos, y también ralos. Hay también llanuras en las montañas, y muchos maderos y árboles secos. Hay lugares sombríos en las montañas, hay piedras llanas donde no hay hierbas ni heno; hay lugares peñascos y cóncavos como valles; son también las montañas lugares espantosos y temerosos, donde moran bestias fieras, donde no hay recreación para los hombres, sino piedras secas y riscos y cuevas, donde moran tigres y osos y gatos cervales, y donde nacen magueyes silvestres y muy espinosos, y matas de zarzas y espinos, y tunas silvestres y pinos muy recios . . . lugar donde las bestias comen a los hombres y donde matan los hombres a traición").

The drier, hotter, steep valleys going down to the coast could seem just as forbidding. Simón Thadeo de Castañeda Castro y Guzmán in 1762 described the land around Alahuistlan, one of his earlier stops, as "the most desert-like wilderness," a "dangerous land" with a "rigorous climate." JCB, 1762, resumé. Parishes toward the coasts sometimes presented a priest with the worst of mountains and tropics, or hot, dry lowlands. On the Pacific side, Joseph Antonio de Salazar, who had served for five years as the cura of Tetela del Río in the Balsas River drainage of Guerrero, wrote feelingly of "las incomodidades que ofrece la destemplanza de su País tan fragoso, quanto difícil en su administración por la distancia de sus Pueblos y abundancia de animales nossivos, ríos caudalosos y gravíssimos peligros en sus caminos de donde se hace intolerable su administración." JCB, 1762.

101. JCB, 1762 resumé of Salvador Ordóñez ("quebranto de salud . . . mojadas, serenos, nieves, trasnochadas, soles, yelos, ayres, estadas en ayunas"). Ordóñez's tale of woe is echoed in CAAG, Jocotepec response to Oct. 31, 1796, circular, reporting that Tomás Martínez de Sotomayor was in poor health because of "las gravosas administraciones que ha servido"; in AGN Hist. 578A, 1793, Ixtlahuaca report, noting that the vicario of San Felipe left because he was chronically ill "de resultas de tanto trabajo"; and in JCB, 1762, resumé of Francisco Benites de Anza, whose health was broken at Acalcingo (Ecacingo).

102. CAAG, resumé of Antonio Arias de Puga for 1770 concurso.

103. Some examples are JCB, 1760–63 resumés of cura Diego de Almonacid y Salasar of Coaxumulco, Domingo Antonio Caro of Huazalingo (had a narrow escape when his horse fell off a cliff), and Carlos Buenaventura de Arella of Tetela del Río (his vicario died in a fall into a barranca); CAAG, Jocotepec response to Oct. 31, 1796, circular, Buenaventura Villaseñor; CAAG, resumé for 1770 concurso of Francisco Jacomé Roberte, cura of Meca for seven years (mentions his falls from horses); and AGN Inq. 1308 exp. 1, 1790, Sierra de Pinos cura Mariano Calzada (injured four times in falls from horses during his six years' tenure).

104. Several examples appear in the subdelegados' 1793 reports in AGN Hist. 578A: Br. Gregorio Augustín de Villavisencio, cura of Coatepec, "enfermo habitual" (Zacualpan report), José Miguel Durán "havituales enfermedades" (Pachuca report); cura José Gutiérrez of Cacaguatepec, reportedly ill, had spent the past five months in Puebla recovering (Acapulco report); vicario José María Olloqui of Alfajayucan had let his licenses lapse because of serious illness (Huichapan report). Other examples are JCB, 1762 resumé of Simón Thadeo de Castañeda of Alahuistlan (trials of serving during an epidemic); CAAG, responses to Oct. 31, 1796, circular, reported "fiebres continuas" (José María Moreno, Teocaltiche report), and chronic illness (Antonio Ramírez, Teocaltiche report, had to leave administration for health reasons; José Domingo de Alcalá, Lagos report, relieved of administration for health reasons; Juan José Díaz, Tamazula report, relieved of administration because he was "baldado de las piernas y otras enfermedades"; Buena-

ventura Villaseñor and Tomás Martínez de Sotomayor, Jocotepec report, injured and in poor health; Joseph Matías Hernández, "de salud algo quebrantado"); AHJ Manuscripts, no. G-4-719, 1754, resumés of teniente de cura Pedro Nicolás de Arechiga of Bolaños (chronic illness) and teniente de cura Pedro Antonio Fernández de Lara of Zacoalco (served in two parishes before, substituting for sick curas); and CAAG, resumé of Antonio Domingo Rodríguez de Frías for 1770 concurso (looking for suitable climate because of poor health; he ran a fever for six months while serving as interim cura of Juchipila).

Many of the oficios, mainly petitions, to the episcopal court of Guadalajara between 1808 and 1815 had to do with the health of pastors—excusing themselves from service or seeking permission to leave the parish temporarily for health reasons. Some had been injured; others were chronically ill. AHJ Manuscripts, no. G-4-802. The permutas or exchanges of parishes between two curas were often based on health considerations, as discussed in Chap. 5.

105. CAAG, resumés of Tomás de Campo and Francisco Javier Carta submitted in 1770 concurso; JCB, 1762, resumé of Joaquín Joseph Caamaño y Colmenero; AGI Guad. 533, 1796, resumé of Joseph Antonio Fuñón; AJANG Civil, bundle labeled "1800–09, leg. 3 (109)," 1802 resumé of Antonio Norberto Sánchez Martínez; Texas, García Coll., no. 113, 1784 resumé of Valentín Mariano Ximénez.

106. AGI Mex. 2549, May 20, 1758.

107. CAAG, 1802 resumé of Joseph Diego Gómez.

108. AGI Mex. 2550, cura of Tlanichol, 1791–1806; CAAG, resumé of cura José Ramón de Herrera of Guaynamota for 1770 concurso; AGN Bienes 663 exp. 4, 1807, Ixmiquilpan district; AHJ Manuscripts, no. G-4-719 GUA/4, 1754, cura Simón de Medina y Cobarrubias of Tomatlan, certifying to the service of Juan de Palomera; CAAG, resumé of cura José Antonio Barragán of Huejuquilla for 1770 concurso, describing his service at Tlaltenango as a vicario, 1762–68; JCB, 1762 resumé of cura Antonio Flores Garcilaso de la Vega of Tantoyucan (almost murdered).

109. Doerr, pp. 18–19.

110. JCB, 1762 resumé of Joseph de Piña y Banda. Similar expressions of solitude were made by curas Manuel Ruis Coronel of Ozoloapan (Edo. de México) in 1769 ("lo solitario de este país . . . y fragosa de ella") and Pedro José Moreno of Santa María Tututepec (Hidalgo) in 1796 ("Dexo aparte los trabajos y tristezas que tiene consigo la profundíssima soledad en que los sacerdotes viven en estas tierras"). AGN CRS 68 exp. 2, fols. 55–60; CRS 130 exp. 3 fol. 74.

111. As in Francisco Benites de Ariza's expression, "se desterró a tierra caliente." JCB, 1762 resumé.

112. AGN Inq. 960 exp. 19. Joseph Diego Gómez at San Sebastián de Huaxicori expressed his loneliness in much the same way: "sin ningún consuelo humano," living among dispersed "puros indios." AJANG Civil, bundle labeled "1809–19." The cura of San Felipe del Obraje also expressed his alienation from Indian parishioners in 1771, as did Manuel Ruis Coronel of Ozoloapan in 1769. AGN CRS 68 exps. 2, 3.

113. Omerick, BMM 113, p. 93.

114. CAAG, resumé of José Manuel de los Ríos, cura en encomienda, vicario, and juez eclesiástico of Atemanica, for 1770 concurso.

115. On the pleasure of visits by seasonal confessors and missionaries, see AGN Inq. 1113, fol. 10v, witness no. 8; and Inq. 1318 exp. 8.

116. CAAG, resumé of cura José de León of Autlan for 1770 concurso.

117. One of the complaints against the cura of Huazalingo by Indian parishioners in 1789 was that he was always going to Mexico City and using pack animals and mounts belonging to the community without paying for them. AGN Bienes 575 exp. 14, fol. 24v. Various parish priests of Hidalgo and San Luis Potosí who were visited in 1808–9 were unable

to show the visitador their licenses and appointment papers, having left them in Mexico City. AGN Acervo 49 caja 116 (e.g., cura José Rafael de Otero of Tamazunchale). The frequent trips to Mexico of Francisco Marroquín, assigned to Tulancingo, are mentioned in Acervo 49 caja 49, 1780, in the criminal complaint of doña María Trinidad de Vega.

118. Few of the priests' nonofficial letters survive in public archives, but there are many complaints by parishioners that they were frequently sent out on mail deliveries and errands to Mexico City without pay. See, for example, AGN Acervo 49 caja 116, complaint against the cura of Tamazunchale, 1808. AJANG Civil, box 161, doc. 9, contains a small cache of notes that Franciscan missionaries sent to Fr. Ysidro Cadelo in New Mexico in the late 18th century.

119. For example, AGN Tierras 2554 exp. 11, Tlalmanalco, 1766. Even in Jalisco, where "Indians" constituted less than half the population of many pueblos de indios, their community leaders resisted fuller integration and occasionally called for the expulsion of non-Indians from their neighborhoods. See, for example, AJANG Civil, box 119, doc. 13, 1789-90, Atotonilco el Alto; and Civil, box 143, doc. 5, 1797, Zapotlan el Grande. An Indian coadjutor was in trouble with vecinos of Tenango Tepopula in 1804. AGN Bienes 172 exp. 54.

120. Arze, n.p. ("dan más provecho que cosijo . . . los de razón molestan mucho, murmuran no poco y sirven poquísimo").

121. CAAG, unclassified, Hurtado de Mendoza petition, April 22, 1815 ("es el que siendo dicho curato compuesto en la mayor parte de feligreses indios, que al difunto cura Cerbantes desasonaron de mil modos, informando contra su conducta ante V.Y. y el superior gobierno, temo el que igual suerte me toque, y con mayor razón conciderando que soi tenás en hacer que las gentes que están a mi cargo no falten un ápice a sus deveres y carezco de la política y tino propio para tratar a estas gentes, que exigen un gran conocimiento de su índole y constumbres"). Two examples of parish priests claiming to have been saved by non-Indians during Indian tumultos are AGN CRS 156 exp. 7, 1761, Acambay; and AGN Crim. 243 exp. 1, 1792, Amanalco.

122. The Franciscan doctrinero of Acaponeta (Sinaloa) in 1791, for example, was hated by some of the non-Indian elite, including the district governor, who brought suit against him, and was reputedly in league with others. Local Indians apparently were on the sidelines in this dispute. AGN Hist. 128, exp. 10.

123. Alienation and political impotence seem to have been at the heart of expressions of solitude by a peninsular cura in the Villa de Valles in 1791. AGN Bienes 210 exp. 26. The cura of Chimalhuacan Atenco in 1802 was the butt of disrespectful jokes. AGN Crim. 255 exp. 13. Some pastors may have been reclusive personalities as much as they were spiritual gymnasts. Where subdelegados reported voluntary solitude, they consistently attributed it to personality or self-indulgence. A "melancholy and violent temperament" was said to be the reason why Francisco de Ocampo was "somewhat withdrawn from commerce and society." AGN Hist. 578A, 1793, Taxco report. The even greater reclusiveness of Manuel José Ruiz Palencia was attributed to "illness, mania, or temperament." Ibid. The cura of Coatepec-Chalco "se bibe en su estudio divertido con sus libros mui retirado de comunicación," although he was also said to fulfill his sacramental duties; and the cura of Chimalhuacan Atenco was "aplicado a los libros y retirado de inquietudes y bicitas." Coatepec-Chalco report. A chaplain in the district of Huichapan "no administra por ser sumamente escrupuloso, sólo se vive encerrado en su casa." Huichapan report. See also JCB, 1762 resumé of cura Dr. Juan Joseph de Henestrosa of Lerma ("sólo para el cumplimiento de su obligación sale de su casa").

124. Bernanos, p. 42; *Constituciones*, passim; Tulane VEMC 53 exp. 23 (purifying the conscience through penance).

125. Berrigan, p. 70.

126. CAAG, resumé of José Antonio Barragán for 1770 concurso ("no haver algún sacer-dote inmediato para cuando necesitasse reconside[r]arme, o que en alguna enfermedad me auxiliara cuia aprehensión me ha mortificado sumamente"). Under these circumstances, arriving to bury a neighboring cura who had been his only spiritual companion must have been especially poignant. So it was for Narciso Pinto, and for Sisto Luna, who was alone after the cura died. CAAG, resumés for 1853–54 concurso.

127. Arze, n.p. ("Todo el mundo es tierra de ingratos y que el país de la gratitud es sólo el Cielo; que mi trabajo lo ve Dios, que le agradece").

128. Texas, Mariano Riva Palacio Coll., doc. 5064. This Feb. 24, 1851, letter by Manuel Cuenca, cura of Malinalco, captures the sentiments of many late colonial curas in their relaciones de méritos.

129. JCB, 1762 resumé of Juan Joseph de Monroy.

130. *Itin.* 1-1-3, para. 9.

131. Tulane, Bliss Coll., folder 5, González Calderón letter, Feb. 19, 1823. While González Calderón expressed feelings that other candidates for the priesthood may have felt, he was unlike any of the parish priests in wavering for nine years as a deacon.

132. *Recop.* 1-6-51, cited in BEJ Papeles de Derecho, 1: fols. 563–65.

133. AHJ Manuscripts, no. G-4-802.

134. AGN CRS 195 exp. 6, fol. 92v.

135. AGN CRS 75 exp. 3, fol. 179; AGN Templos 25 exp. 8.

136. AGN CRS 126 exps. 12–13, 1809, Zacualpan district. Other cases include AJANG Civil, box 49, doc. 4, 1727, Poncitlan; CRS 42 exp. 1, 1732, Tejupilco, Temascaltepec district; CRS 74 exp. 11, 1801, Amanalco; CRS 75 exp. 3, 1774, Malacatepec, Metepec district; CRS 75 exp. 4, 1775, Tototepec; CRS 75 exp. 6, 1786, Alahuistlan; CRS 75 exp. 8, 1789, San Andrés Jimilpan; CRS 130 exp. 3, 1796, Santa María Tututepec, Meztitlan district ("disturbios de motín o tumulto con riesgo de mi vida"); CRS 131 exp. 1, 1792, Cali-maya; CRS 136 exp. 2, 1781, Tlaltizapan; CRS 156 exp. 7, 1761, Acambay; CRS 156 exp. 9, 1763, Zacualpan; CRS 178 exp. 9, 1797, Yautepec; AGN Hist. 319 exp. 19, 1774, Zapo-tlan el Grande; and AGN Inq. 1304 exp. 3, 1796, Zacualpan. Whether or not the priests' lives were actually in danger, it is striking that the examples presented here and earlier in this chapter cluster in the districts of Metepec, Zacualpan, Sultepec-Temascaltepec, and modern Morelos, where disputes with parish priests were unusually frequent and heated in the late 18th century. At least some of these districts had a series of pastors of suspect conduct in the late colonial period; see Hist. 578A, 1793, Zacualpan report; and App. C.

137. AGN Hist. 578A, 1793, Taxco report; JCB, 1762 resumé of Domingo Joseph de la Mota; AGN Crim. 210, fols. 189–205. The cura of Atlistaca in the district of Tlapa re-ported in 1795 that the local Indians so hated him for his efforts to root out vice that one had tried to kill him with a machete two years before. Curiously, the cura had not re-ported the assault at the time. Tulane VEMC 68 exp. 9.

138. On parishioners poking fun at priests in 17th-century Spain as well, see Domín-guez Ortiz, "Costumbres clericales."

139. Disrespect as a justification for corporal punishment is discussed in Chap. 9. The cura of Tescaliacac, Tenango del Valle district, said he arrested five Indian parishioners in an 1801 argument over the distribution of the maize in the village granary because of their "lack of respect and disobedience." AGN CRS 84 exp. 8. The cura of Malinalco in 1798 explained that he had an Indian couple whipped because they were "tan poseídos de la embriaguez se le insolentaron en sumo grado diciéndole muchas injurias y aun la muger le entrava las manos por el rostro . . . no atendían mi respeto." AGN Tierras 2198 exp. 2. The subdelegado went out to warn the villagers against drunkenness and to respect the curas. The cura of Almoloya admitted to jailing the gobernador for disrespect. AGN Crim. 148 exp. 2. In 1796, the cura of Tetecala, Cuernavaca district, said parishioners treated him

like a "ladrón, con ningún respeto a su carácter," so he kicked the gobernador. AGN Civil 2292 exp. 3. In another case from 1796, the cura of San Bartolomé Capuluac said the charges against him stemmed from a few "resentidos de haver correxido en el pronto una notable falta de respeto con su cura." CRS 39 exps. 2–3.

Other examples include CRS 156 exp. 5, 1758, Tepetlaostoc; CRS 156 exp. 7, 1761, Acambay; CRS 130 exp. 3, 1796, Santa María Tututepec, Tulancingo district; Tierras 1554 exp. 11, 1766, Tlalmanalco; AGN Templos 25 exp. 8, 1796, Amecemeca (parishioners "faltando a mi parte al respecto . . . hasta tratarle de ladrón"); Templos 25 exp. 9, 1799, Zacualtipan, Meztitlan district (cura Joaquín de Ugalde complained to the subdelegado of Indians' "falta de subordinación y respeto"); BMM 135 exp. 17, 1752, Xiuctepec (Franciscan doctrinero thought Indians no longer showed the same respect for their parish priests); Crim. 54 exp. 1, 1791, Atitalaquia (gobernador insulted cura); AHJ Manuscripts, no. G-4-719, 1755, Valle de Mesticacan, Nochistlan district; Crim. 210, fol. 192, 1758, Pozontepec, Sultepec district (during tumulto cura was called a "perro embustero"); CRS 29 exp. 8, Xochimilco (Franciscan doctrinero complained of Indians' "palabras denigrativas o yndecorosas"); CRS 67 exp. 7, fol. 293v, 1772, Santa Cruz Atizapan, Tenango del Valle district; CRS 68 exp. 1, fol. 10, 1759, Teoloyuca, Cuautitlan district (cura complained of Indians' "gran libertad y menos respecto" in paying fees ordered by the Audiencia); CRS 75 exp. 3, 1774, Malacatepec, Metepec district (cura in arancel dispute said some people of San José failed to show him proper respect—"vertieron en su presencia todo su encono con palabras descompuestas, llegando su insolencia al extremo de intentar lanzarlo del curato"); and AJANG Civil, box 49, doc. 4, 1727, Poncitlan.

The cura of Tzontecomatlan, Guayacocotla district, responded in 1808 to the subdelegado's complaint of inadequate spiritual services by observing that he had recently suffered unusual insults, with "young Indians who I raised and now see unhappily prostituted [and who are openly] mocking in my presence." CRS 217 exp. 6, fol. 111.

140. AGN CRS 192 exps. 11–12, fols. 305–12 ("el temor que tienen generalmente estas gentes de decir algo contra algún sacerdote"). Also AGN Inq. 1360 exps. 1–2, fol. 4r.

141. AHJ Manuscripts, no. G-4-719, 1755, Valle de Mesticacan, Nochistlan district.

142. AGN CRS 75 exp. 4, fols. 248–53 ("obligado a la dirección espiritual de sus hijos," "dosilitar el ynobediente," "insolentados," "una yndómita osadía con que desobedecen, faltando a todo respecto"). Colonial chroniclers were fond of edifying tales about disrespect. The scientifically minded Alcedo recorded in his entry for the Indian pueblo of Chapultepec in the Valley of Mexico that he did not know why the community had lost four-fifths of its population, then inserted what he said was the pious local tradition that "es castigo de Dios por haber perdido el respeto a su cura y dádole mil pesares por el celo con que procuraba impedirles la idolatría, por cuya razón hoy son muy temerosos y dóciles." *Diccionario geográfico*, 1: 280.

143. *Itin.* 1-13-6. Pérez de Velasco, p. 31, warned that to command respect one must avoid compromising situations. Indignation about disrespect would be hollow if the priest had already compromised himself.

144. AGN CRS 39 exp. 1, fol. 111r, 1796. In similar words, the Augustinian doctrinero of Cuitzeo de la Laguna, Michoacán, Antonio de Fajardo, spoke of the district governor putting his standing as a priest in jeopardy, encouraging the parishioners to "quitarme la honra y crédito con que siempre he vivido." AGN Alcaldes Mayores 3, 1770. The cura of Temascaltepec, Manuel Ruis Coronel, in the 1769 dispute with Indians of Ozoloapan, wrote of their failure to show him "el devido respecto, ni a la Santa Iglesia." CRS 68 exp. 2, fol. 62. Other cases of concern with honor as well as respect are AGN Acervo 49 caja 44, exp. for San Juan del Río, 1700; AJANG Civil, box 150, doc. 7, 1791, Acaponeta, Sinaloa (cura wrote of his dignity and honor being at stake in his dispute with the subdelegado); Tulane VEMC 68 exp. 9, 1795 (cura Joseph Antonio Thenorio de la Banda of

Atlistaca was preoccupied with clearing his good name in a dispute with Indians); CRS 131 exp. 1, 1792 (cura of Calimaya fumed over "the public defamatory libel against my honor" in the course of his bitter disputes with parishioners); and AGN Templos 25 exp. 10, 1805, Temascalcingo (cura José Antonio López de Cárdenas was upset because "dicho Palacios [a local hacendado] ha injuriado gravísimamente el honor de mi parte").

145. AGN CRS 140 exp. 4, fol. 132ff. More precious than either honor or life, as Agüero's statement implicitly acknowledges, was the soul: "el alma es tesoro que no tiene precio." Pérez de Velasco, p. 32.

146. AGN CRS 136 exp. 4, 1783, Huichilapan.

147. Unity was usually expressed in organic terms, and in terms of the fear of disruption and the need for moderation. It was imbalanced, unrestrained liberty and the inclination toward indecency that worried priests, as in the cura of Teoloyuca's description of Indian resistance to paying the weekly dominica in terms of "gran libertad y menos respecto," or the complaint of Pedro José Moreno, cura of Santa María Tututepec, Tulancingo district, in 1796 of "la inobediencia y perniciosa libertad con que se conducen aquellos parrochianos." AGN CRS 68 exp. 1, fol. 10, 1759; CRS 130, exp. 3, 1796. One cura refuted political ideas of the Enlightenment to his parishioners in these terms: the equality and liberty of the French Revolution, including freedom of religion, were the cause of much evil, great bloodshed and disorder, and accursed "libertinaje." BN LaFragua Coll., vol. 792, 1808. Certeau, pp. 189–91, eloquently presents this preoccupation as universal among parish priests in their struggle with parishioners over "a governance of practices." Implicit in his formulation are over-sharp distinctions between high and low church and between high and low religion.

In situations of conflict recorded in the judicial record, priests were naturally doubtful of the virtues of personal independence and liberty. For the cura of Jamiltepec, Oaxaca, unbridled liberty was a threat to good order and honor in society: "tomándose los ruines [these "wicked people," in this case the ones protected by the subdelegado] tanta libertad que a cada paso injurian y atropellan al honrado y bien nacido de aquí." AGN CRS 188 exp. 9, 1791. The cura of Tlaltizapan in 1781 judged that liberty became libertinism among his Indian parishioners. CRS 136 exp. 2, fols. 83, 201. For a rare open mention of the boredom of service (at Tomatlan, Jalisco), see AHJ Manuscripts, no. G-4-802, 1814.

148. AGN CRS 156 exp. 5, fol. 143v. "Sujección a caveza" is also Omerick's way of talking about order in society. BMM 113, p. 89. References to the priest's paternal role—as head in a hierarchy of right order—include AGN Alcaldes Mayores 11, fols. 338–40, 1773 (Zacualpan cura expected parishioners to "sujetarse a campana"); BMM 135 exp. 16, 1734, Toluca (Fr. Martín Calderón contended that the priest must protect and discipline the Indians or they would dress and act like Spaniards and treat priests presumptuously and insolently "por quererles sugetar a la ley común de todos"); AGN Hist. 128 exp. 7, 1791 (advice to the viceroy by Pedro Fernández Ybarraran: Indians should be treated with "benignidad, [y] mansedumbre" because they are timid); and AGN Tierras 1774 exp. 9, 1749, Huatzalco, Puebla (cura claimed Indians were "unos pobres desválidos que no tienen más amparo que el mío"). One of many examples of the rhetoric of exalted station for the clergy and its commensurately high obligations is Hist. 132 exp. 2, 1772, secret report by Bishop Fabián y Fuero on the conduct of the governor of Puebla.

149. AGN CRS 136 exp. 2, May 10, 1801, letter from vicario at Tlaltizapan (humility, prudence); CRS 137 exp. 8, fols. 278–81, 1805, Alahuistlan, Zacualpan district; CRS 177 exp. 10, 1800, Mazatepec, Cuernavaca district ("genio pacifíco y buena índole"); CRS 179 exp. 13, 1763, Actopan ("suavidad, prudencia"); CRS 204 exps. 9–10, para. 78 ("amorosa paternal correspondencia"); CRS 217 exp. 6, fol. 83, 1808, Tzontecomatlan (claimed to be abjectly obedient and use "medios más suaves"—"me muestro como devo imparcial a todo . . . por estar sosegado en el curato cumpliendo con lo que está a mi cargo").

150. AGN Acervo 49 caja 146, 1772, Santiago Xalapa, Teutila district, Oaxaca.

151. AGN Alcaldes Mayores 11, fols. 448–56, 1776, Tuzamapan; Library of Congress, MMC 19 (anonymous manuscript on moral precepts, 18th-century Mexico: swift retribution promised for not maintaining churches).

152. BMM 135 exp. 16: "Dios es el rey universal por quien él de la tierra por sus leyes manda o govierna sus vasallos."

153. AGN CRS 156 exp. 5, fol. 143v ("Le han perdido el respeto. . . . Le han negado totalmente la sugesión y obediencia . . . sufriendo insolencias de los yndios a quienes para cometerlas basta tener movido pleito contra el cura, a quien creen que de esto tiene atadas las manos para corregirlos"). Frustrations of this kind could bring law-and-order sentiments to the surface. The cura of Zapotlan el Grande, Jalisco, in 1782, Bernardino Antonio de Lepe y Rivera, attributed Indian insolence there to the lack of punishment. AGN Hist. 319 exp. 18, fols. 1–4.

154. Disenchantment with the tactic of sweet persuasion was not peculiar to the late 18th century. In 1727, for example, the Franciscan doctrinero of Poncitlan lamented that his "charitativas amonestaciones" went unheeded by insolent, irreverent Indian parishioners. AJANG Civil, box 49, doc. 4.

155. AGN CRS 130 exp. 3, fol. 39.

156. AGN CRS 206 exp. 3.

157. AGN CRS 179 exp. 13 ("Estos como enfermos frenéticos se han convertido contra su pastor y médico espiritual y abusando de la protección que han tenido me han faltado al respecto, han procurado desacreditar mi conducta y bulnerar mi honra con repetidas quexas en que contra mi han prorrumpido"). The cura of Chipetlan stated his obligation in 1772 in the ample terms of parishioners' temporal as well as spiritual well-being: "mi obligación acerca del celo, esmero, y cuidado que debo atender a mis pobres feligreses yndios no sólo en lo espiritual sino también en lo temporal." AGN Alcaldes Mayores 11, fols. 357ff.

158. AGN CRS 130 exp. 3, fols. 124ff; CRS 156 exp. 7; CRS 156 exp. 5, fol. 143v; CRS 217 exp. 6, fols. 83, 95–96 ("falsos calumniadores e ynobedientes"); Tulane VEMC 49 exp. 6, 1787, Chicontepec (cura wrote of the limitless despotism of a local militia captain).

159. AGN CRS 39 exp. 1, fols. 14–16 ("no quieren entender la razón y veo que están ciegos de pasión," "ingratos," "prometen una cosa y no la hacen; la costumbre la quieren cumplir a su antojo").

160. AGN CRS 156 exp. 12 ("viven tan altivos . . . negándome la debida obediencia no quieren comparecer para lo más mínimo a este juzgado").

161. AGN Inq. 1184 exp. 21, fol. 190.

162. AGN CRS 136 exp. 6, fols. 310–18 ("las reales determinaciones le atan las manos para proseder contra los más comunes delitos").

163. AGN CRS 177 exp. 10, fols. 448–49 ("no se ven en este país, señor, más que embriagueses, concubinatos, adulterios, estupros, padres de familia ofendidos por el urto que le han hecho de sus hijas, heridas, muertes y otros males sin remedio alguno").

164. In 1752, the provisor de indios wrote: "Hallarse oy casi generalmente estos pobres indios con más ignorancia en lo necessario para su salvación que lo estuvieron a los diez años de su reducción." (The Franciscan doctrinero in this case had said that Indians no longer respected their priests as they had in the first generation.) BMM 135 exp. 17. In 1719 the priest Miguel Camacho Villavicensio wrote of two stages in the history of the church in America: the heroic age of destruction of idolatry and great conversion; and an age of defense against destruction, decay, and backsliding. Disillusioned with his 18 years of serving Indians in Mexico City, he yearned for purification and a new conquest. Ibid., exp. 18.

A fuller statement of this Counter-Reformation historical view that was especially common from the late 16th century well into the 18th was offered by the Franciscan doctrinero of Xiuctepec cited above. Pondering why there was so much variation in commitment to the faith, he concluded that, though this was a divine mystery and "we are all useless servants," laymen deserved about three-fourths of the blame, "with their natural temperaments, inclinations, and properties," and the laziness and ignorance of the clergy accounted for the rest.

165. There are many areas of silence in the written record on parish priests. Curas and vicarios in minor posts who were past striving for the attention of their superiors and who knew their own vices, as well as those of their parishioners, were less likely than younger men and newcomers to offer advice and admonitions where none were wanted. With a few exceptions, their sentiments are hard to find in archives. As Powers says of his pastor-protagonist in *Wheat That Springeth Green*, p. 111, "his eating and drinking did tend to silence the prophet in him, but so did common sense."

166. AGN Hist. 578A, 1793, Alahuistlan (Zacualpan report). In the same report, the district governor praised Cayetano Yzquierdo, cura of Ichcateopan, as a man of considerable talent and learning, and a tireless pastor, but found him "too active in collecting his fees and leaving his parishioners in fear with his dominating manner."

167. AGN Hist. 578A, 1793: coadjutor Mariano Cuevas of Tetipac, cura Agustín Durán of Tepecoacuilco, and cura Marcelo de Arriaga of Huitzuco (Taxco report); teniente de cura Josef Mariano Muñós of Apam (Apam report); cura Felipe Benicio Benites of Apaxtla and cura Joaquín María Martín de Castro of Teloloapan (Zacualpan report); and vicarios José Angel Fuente and Agustín Gutierres of Cempoala (Cempoala report). Br. Mariano Dionisio Alarcón, cura of Tultitlan in 1809, is as good an example as any of the contradictory tendencies in one priest. The picture that emerges from the testimony of witnesses he did not hand pick in a suit against him for charging excessive fees is of a cura who was charitable in the expected ways but was also preoccupied with his own income and accumulated wealth, and not inclined to dignify the cult with new ornaments or other large expenses. AGN Bienes 663 exp. 5.

168. Rigid but diligent: AGN CRS 140 exp. 4, witnesses nos. 12–20, 1796, Yautepec; CRS 197 exp. 14, fol. 178, 1802, Yautepec; CRS 201 exp. 1, 1780, Ixtapalapa; CRS 217 exp. 5, 1809, La Cañada, Querétaro; AGN Hist. 578A, 1793, vicario Ysidro Estrada of Teloloapan and cura Josef Eusebio de Ortega of Zumpango de la Laguna (Zumpango report); AGN Bienes 575 exp. 15, 1789, vicario de pie fijo Mariano Muñiz of Tepetlixpa, Chimalhuacan Atenco; AGN Inq. 1318 exp. 8, 1791, vicario Josef Navarro of Huejutla; and Tulane VEMC 15 exp. 3, 1788, cura Garrido of Tochimilco (questionable morals but dedicated to sacramental duties). For an efficient but quick-tempered pastor in the 1793 reports, see the evaluation of Dr. Jacinto Sánchez Aparicio in Hist. 578A, Tacuba report.

Some others were not very active as a rule but took a special interest in some aspect of the office. The cura of Yahualica, for example, was especially faithful in going out to administer last rites when called. Hist. 578A, 1793, Yahualica report. Some who were especially dedicated to the sacraments were said to be poorly educated and to exhibit little talent as teachers. A case in point is José Ferrara, segundo vicario of Taxco in 1793. Ibid., Taxco report.

169. AGN CRS 130 exp. 3, fol. 180.

170. As Powers put it in *Wheat That Springeth Green*, p. 63.

Chapter Nine

EPIGRAPH: AGN CRS 192 exps. 11–12, testimony of Gabriel de Santiago ("Venía el padre d. Gregorio a caballo aprisa y olló que dijo 'Ave María Santíssima,' y el gobernador respondió 'en gracia es consebida,' quitándose el sombrero").

1. Conventionally, "the yoke" referred to divine law, but it was used for colonial rule and order as well, thus combining God's law and the law of the crown in one system of

authority. It is used as a metaphor for divine law in "Apéndice a los concilios primero y segundo mexicanos," pp. 317, 324 (1539 agreements of Mexican bishops: "yugo dulce," "yugo suave"). *Itin.* 3-1-5 (referring to the gentle yoke of God's law ["es suave el yugo de su Ley"], meaning that God demands little of his faithful); BMM 135 exp. 16, 1734 (a Franciscan record speaking of "yugo o ley que profesa la cristianidad"); BN LaFragua Coll., vol. 792, p. 16 (a politico-religious treatise referring to the "iron yoke" of Spanish rule under Godoy); Aguirre Beltrán, "Delación" (the priest of Acayucan in 1787 saying the pueblos of Spanish America lived under a "yoke of flowers"); AGN Bienes 210 exp. 26, fol. 37v, 1791 (a gachupín priest preaching "the gentle yoke"); and Villarroel, p. 46 (writing of the "gentle yoke" of the king's rule in America). By the early 1820's, however, even priests were linking the yoke to oppression. Dr. José Julio García de Torres, prebend of the colegiata at the Villa de Guadalupe, for one, openly criticized "the yoke of Spanish domination" in his sermon of Oct. 12, 1821. *Sermón de acción*, p. 25.

2. Trent, 13th Session, Reform, ch. 1, instructs priests to be shepherds, not oppressors, to use exhortation more than threat, and charity more than force ("benevolence" more than "severity"). "But if on account of the gravity of the offense there is need of the rod, then is rigor to be tempered with gentleness . . . that discipline may be preserved without harshness, and that they who are chastised may be corrected." *Recop.* 1-7-27 (cited in BEJ Papeles de Derecho, 2: fols. 396–97) stated that Indians were to be corrected by ecclesiastical judges and visitadores (because of their "flaqueza" and "cortedad de ánimo") "por medios tan suaves, que ellos mismos les obliguen a su enmienda y a la perseverancia en nuestra Santa Fe Católica." Solórzano 4-16-58 affirmed the principle of moderation.

3. Local elections are discussed in Chap. 14. On curas allegedly using gossip to their own advantage or to stir up trouble for their enemies: AGN Crim. 202 exp. 1, 1789, Santa María Tixmadeje; AGN Alcaldes Mayores 11, fols. 357ff, 1772, Chipetlan; Rosenbach Lib., Mexican MS 462/25 pt. 4, no. 7, 1735, Hueyapan. On their using bribes to influence local affairs: AGN Acervo 49 caja 45, 1806 (secret letter by the provisor about cura Bartolomé Vélez Escalante, cura of Yahualica, buying influence and forming an open alliance with the subdelegados); AGN Bienes 663 exp. 6, 1809, Tultitlan (complaint of Indian officials that the cura was making bribes and promises to local people to testify on his behalf in the suit they had brought over fees and services); Acervo 49 caja 45, 1818, Ozoloapan (complaint of Indians that the deposed cura had regained the parish by means of bribes and favors).

4. *Recop.* 1-10-6 to 1-10-8. Whether these laws were routinely violated remains unclear. There are cases of late colonial priests sending or threatening to send parishioners to obrajes and sugar mills—for example, AGN Civil 1485 exp. 12 (1762, sujetos of Huizquilucan); Civil 159 exp. 13 (1785, Churubusco); and AGN Hist. 128 exp. 7 (1781, Córdoba jurisdiction)—but they appear much less often than incidents of whippings and incarceration.

5. "Apéndice a los concilios primero y segundo mexicanos," p. 317.

6. *Recop.* 6-3-16. According to *Recop.* 7-6-21, Indians might be jailed for drunkenness or other causes, but they were not liable for the costs of imprisonment.

7. AJANG Criminal, bundle labeled "1815-33 (80)," Simón Pérez accused of killing Juan de Dios, 1814, Susticacan, Xerez district ("la prisión no es pena sino custodia del reo").

8. *Colección de las ordenanzas*, pp. 164–66.

9. *Recop.* 1-13-26 (summarizing laws of 1560, 1594, 1614, and 1624) provided that parish priests could not have jails, prisons, shackles, or stocks without the formal permission of their bishop. Solórzano 4-15-57 made the same point in nearly identical words.

10. *Recop.* 7-6-1.

11. AGN RCO 37 exp. 35.

12. *Instrucciones que los vireyes*, 1: 418.

13. Ventura Beleña, 1: 60, 144.

14. CPM, p. 122.

15. Serna, p. 346 ("represión con rigor y amor").

16. AGN Acervo 49, caja 45, 1806, expediente on the conduct of Br. Bartolomé Vélez Escalante, cura of Yahualica ("violentas prisiones").

17. *Itin.* 2-6-1, 2-5-6. Indian parishioners continued to be imprisoned for "idolatry" and "witchcraft" in the 18th century, but it was usually out of the hands of the parish priest. The bishop of Oaxaca in 1787 reported that "idolaters" in his diocese were sent to the cathedral city of Antequera and detained in a house donated for that purpose by the cura of Xicayán. AGN RCO 138 exp. 229.

18. *Recop.* 1-13-6 (1594), 1-10-11 (1571), 1-10-12 (1530).

19. *Recop.* 7-8-6, cited in AGN Crim. 117 exp. 4.

20. Tulane VEMC 53 exp. 23, 1788.

21. AGN CRS 204 exp. 5.

22. AGN CRS 30, fols. 354ff, Dec. 27, 1789.

23. AGN Hist. 578A, 1793, Zumpango de la Laguna and Coyoacan reports; AGN CRS 75 exp. 4, 1775, Zacualpan jurisdiction; AGN Crim. 181, fols. 238-300, 1787, Acapetlahuaya; AGN Tierras 2670 exp. 5, 1792, Tecospa; CRS 68 exps. 4-5, 1775, Cuanacalcingo; CRS 75 exp. 11, 1790, Tetela del Río district; CRS 75 exp. 5, 1785, Huichapan district.

24. AGN CRS 179 exp. 13, fol. 406v.

25. AGN CRS 192 exps. 11-12, 1760, Almoloya, Tescaliacac district ("sin facultad").

26. The audiencia dismissed the excuses of custom and necessity in a Zacualpan case in 1775. AGN CRS 75 exp. 4.

27. AGN Tierras 1929 exp. 9.

28. AGN CRS 68 exps. 4-5, 1775-80, Cuanacalcingo (Tlaltizapan district). The cura of Tlaltizapan claimed his five requests for auxilio went unanswered. CRS 136 exp. 2, 1781.

29. I have located 49 examples of prisons and imprisonments by priests in judicial and administrative records for the period 1710-1809: 44 for the archdiocese, three for Guadalajara, and two for Puebla. The disproportionate number of cases in the archdiocese does not necessarily indicate so many more jails or complaints against them there. Most of the examples come from AGN Clero Regular y Secular, Tierras, Historia, Civil, Criminal, and Inquisición, where documentation from the archdiocese predominates.

30. 1710-19, 1; 1720-29, 2; 1730-39, 3; 1740-49, 1; 1750-59, 4; 1760-69, 5; 1770-79, 7; 1780-89, 7; 1790-99, 12; 1800-1809, 3.

31. In a 1740 case involving the cura of Tixtla, Puebla, the audiencia stated clearly that the priest "could not operate a jail without permission" ("no puede tener por sí carzel"). AGN CRS 204 exp. 5. The subdelegado of Coyoacan in 1793 noted that the cura "usa de un capítulo que tiene, equibalente a cárcel sin embargo de su prohivición." AGN Hist. 578A.

32. Cases in which the cura controlled the town jail: AGN CRS 75 exp. 11, 1790, Tetela del Río; CRS 177 exp. 10, 1800, Mazatepec, Cuernavaca district; AJANG Civil, box 116, doc. 4, 1778, Ocotlan (Jalisco). Cases in which a cura maintained his own jail (usually called a "capítulo," a term that denoted its ecclesiastical character and signified that people held there were charged with failing to fulfill duties to God and the church): CRS 156 exp. 5, fol. 146v, 1758, Tepetlaostoc; CRS 156 exp. 7, 1761, Acambay, Xilotepec district ("en un curato que llaman capítulo"); CRS 39 exp. 2, 1796, Capuluac; AGN Inq. 1146 exp. 1, 1775, Xilotepec district; AGN Hist. 578A, 1793, Zumpango de la Laguna, Coyoacan, and San Jacinto (Coyoacan report); AGN Tierras 2670, 1792, Tecospa. The capítulo sometimes was called the priest's "private jail" (cárcel privada), his "capitular jail" (cárcel capítulo), or his "jail or capítulo" (cárcel o capítulo, capítulo o cárcel privada).

33. AGN CRS 75 exp. 5. See Hernández Xolocotzi, plates 16-17, for illustrations of precolonial and 19th-century granaries that fit this description.

34. AGN Crim. 92 exp. 5, 1767, Los Reyes, Xocotitlan district, and Crim. 155, fols.

111–33, 1721, Santa Marta, Mexicalcingo district (church as jail); AGN CRS 75 exp. 4, fols. 221v–222r, 1775, San Simón Tototepec (women locked up in a chapel).

35. AGN CRS 126 exp. 12 and AGN Tierras 2179 exp. 3, fol. 44 (the "depósito" of adulterous indias); AGN Crim. 168, fols. 1–13, 1807, Apaxtla, Zacualpan district (rape victim). It was also customary for betrothed women to reside "en depósito" for a short period before they married. Arze, n.p.; Pérez de Velasco, p. 88; AGN Inq. 760 exp. 11, fols. 161–62; Inq. 1334 exp. 3, fol. 181. Some priests used their own quarters for safekeeping betrothed or pregnant young women who were not married. In a printed circular of June 10, 1756, the archbishop denounced this practice as an "intolerable abuse" that "opens wide the door to malice." Other examples of depósito include CRS 68 exp. 3, fols. 210v ff, 1771, San Felipe del Obraje; CRS 75 exp. 4, fol. 221, 1775; CRS 126, exp. 12, 1809, Apaxtla; and AGN Acervo 49 caja 68, 1796, Temascaltepec. Stories of priests demanding sex from young women in their care led to a bitter dispute in 1772 between the bishop of Puebla and the Spanish gobernador when the gobernador declared that *he* would guard the women's honor by keeping them in the municipal jail until the marriage ceremony. AGN Hist. 132 exp. 2.

36. AGN Hist. 132 exp. 7, 1791, Cadereyta and "otros distintos pueblos"; AGN CRS 179 exp. 13, 1763, Actopan; CRS 156 exp. 7, 1761, Acambay: "a room that they call the capítulo," "cárcel adentro del curato," or "dentro de las casas de su habitación."

37. AGN CRS 156 exp. 5, fols. 141, 146v. The cura of Alahuistlan, Zacualpan district, arrested "a rebel against the precept of the mass." CRS 75 exp. 6, 1786.

38. AGN Crim. 181, fols. 238–300, 1787, Acapetlahuaya ("pecados públicos, embriaguez y libertinaje"). This cura said he was arresting people mainly for drunkenness and not knowing doctrina.

39. The payments involved were usually for customary fees such as the dominica (weekly contribution) that Indians rejected in favor of the arancel (e.g., AGN CRS 68 exps. 4–5, fols. 366ff, 1775, Cuanacalcingo, Cuernavaca district), but they could also be for new fees that a cura was determined to impose (such as the attempt by the cura of Malacatepec to charge Indians of San Ildefonso for confession in 1801; AGN Crim. 152, fols. 270–312).

40. AGN Bienes 210 exp. 1, fol. 2v, Guayacocotla, 1731 (release of an Indian parishioner only after he produced a cosigner).

41. AGN Tierras 2670 exp. 5, 1792.

42. AGN CRS 75 exp. 4, fols. 221v–222r, 1775, Tototepec, Zacualpan district.

43. AGN Inq. 1074, fol. 35r, 1768, Terrenate, cura Silverio de Nava; Inq. 1205 exp. 28, 1736, Tlaola coadjutor.

44. AGN Acervo 49 caja 68.

45. Two examples are AGN CRS 130 exp. 2, 1792, Zinacantepec, Metepec district; and CRS 156 exp. 5, fols. 139–41, 1758, Tepetlaostoc.

46. AGN CRS 84 exp. 8, fol. 224r, Tescaliacac, 1801 (the gobernador and four other Indians kept in a locked room for lack of respect and obedience to the cura); CRS 156 exp. 7, 1761 (San Miguel Acambay Indian officials imprisoned for not knowing doctrina); CRS 217 exp. 6, Tzontecomatlan, 1808 (onetime gobernador arrested by the cura on suspicion of organizing secret meetings against him); AGN Crim. 148 exp. 2, fol. 22r, Almoloya, 1792 (gobernador arrested on the cura's orders for disrespect).

47. AGN CRS 136 exps. 6–7, 1790–91, San Lucas, Temascaltepec district; CRS 156 exp. 7, 1761, Acambay; CRS 75 exp. 4, fols. 221v–222r, 1775, Tototepec, Zacualpan district (for failure to submit the census).

48. AGN CRS 136 exp. 2.

49. AGN CRS 156 exp. 13, 1788, Tecualoyan.

50. AGN CRS 84 exp. 4.

51. AGN CRS 156 exp. 7, 1761, Acambay ("para exemplo y escarmiento de los demás").

52. AGN Bienes 663 exp. 25; AGN Inq. 1304 exp. 3. For an Inquisition case of a cura confining young women for not knowing doctrina and then forcing them into sex with him, see Inq. 1205 exp. 28, 1736.

53. AGN CRS 47 exp. 4; CRS 39 exps. 2, 6; CRS 47 exp. 4. Franciscan doctrineros of the Cuernavaca jurisdiction arrested Indian officials under the same circumstances in 1672. AGN Crim. 148 exp. 2.

54. AGN CRS 42 exp. 1, fols. 2r, 31–32, 1732, Tejupilco. See also Taylor, *Drinking*, ch. 4.

55. AGN CRS 188 exp. 6.

56. AGN Crim. 67 exp. 4, 1794, Hacienda Malpaís, Apam district.

57. *Recop.* 1-13-16; Solórzano 4-15-57, 4-15-59.

58. AGI Mex. 2588.

59. López Jiménez, *Algunos documentos*, pp. 39–40.

60. AGN Hist. 437, Mochitlan, 1800.

61. Real Academia de Historia, Madrid, A/III (vol. 66), fol. 221v, March 30, 1547, bishop of Oaxaca; *Colección de las ordenanzas*, p. 181 (boys and girls could be whipped over doctrina just as maestros de escuela could do to Spanish children), pp. 164–66 (paraphrase of *Recop.* law that only Indian officials could do the arresting and whipping); Serna, p. 346 (recommended prudent exemplary punishment).

62. *Itin.* laws on punishment: 1-1-2, 1-2-1, 1-4-3, 1-4-11, 1-4-12, 2-1-2, 2-1-3, 2-4-5, 2-5-6, 3-4-2, 4-2-5, 4-2-10, 5-2-5.

63. BN LaFragua Coll., vol. 590. Nevertheless, the bishop of Oaxaca still favored whippings as late as 1784, and so did Pérez de Velasco (1766) and Tirso Díaz (BMM 271, 1770). Regalists like Omerick (Tepecoacuilco, 1769) and Pedro Fernández Ybarraran (peninsular priest writing from Córdoba, Puebla, in 1791) opposed it. BMM 113 and 271. The archbishop forbade parish priests to administer whippings on March 4, 1814, following a decree from the Cortes of Cádiz to that effect of Aug. 17, 1813. BMM 153, p. 488 (manuscript copies of providencias diocesanas from the parish archive of Singuilucan).

64. For the image of the parish priest as a loving teacher and no reference to corporal punishment, see Lorenzana, pastoral letters of Oct. 5, 1766, and Oct. 12, 1767, in *Cartas pastorales*; Lorenzana, April 1, 1779, letter to a parish priest of the Archdiocese of Toledo, in *Cartas, edictos*; and CPM, pp. 116–18, 122, 129.

65. BMM 153, p. 488 (manuscript copies of providencias diocesanas from the parish archive of Singuilucan). Apparently the archbishop had been pushed into forbidding priests to order whippings by a decree of the Cortes of Cádiz of Aug. 17, 1813.

66. A priest in Tlaltenango, Zacatecas, in 1759 wrote a marginal note in his copy of the *Itinerario* expressing his concern about whether parish priests would be allowed to administer corporal punishment any longer. Bancroft Library copy, 1-4-3. The extensive use of corporal punishment in the Franciscans' California missions near the end of the 18th century is discussed in S. Cook, pp. 1–194; and Sandos.

67. AGI Mex. 2588, Jan. 16, 1784, report. The cura of San Felipe del Obraje, Metepec district, also thought his leniency had been the cause of parishioners' insolence. AGN CRS 68 exp. 3, Nov. 2, 1771, letter.

68. AGI Mex. 2588, Jan. 16, 1784, report, fols. 7v, 9r.

69. AJANG Civil, box 228, doc. 3.

70. Twenty-five of the 34 formal complaints that Indians lodged against curas for whippings in the 18th century (31 of them for the archdiocese) date from after 1770: the 1770's (7), 1780's (7), the 1790's (2), the 1800's (9).

71. AGN Inq. 1074, Terrenate, 1768, cura Silverio de Nava.

72. AGN Hist. 437.

73. For such sentences in the district of Teposcolula, Oaxaca, the early 17th century,

see CDCh, roll 3. Indians of Cicapualco, Ichcateopan district, in 1625 charged their cura, Gerónimo de Frías Quixada, with various kinds of cruel and unusual punishment. In addition to whipping and beating them without cause, he was said to have whipped an alcalde, suspended him from a pole, and attempted to castrate him, and to have whipped all the Indian officials for not repairing a road he traveled. AGN Acervo 49 caja 43.

74. I have not found examples of 18th-century curas using the more extreme forms of torture evident 200 years earlier. Apparently by now leaders of local factions and neighboring estates were more likely than priests to use or threaten unusual forms of torment. Some Indians in the parish of Guayacocotla y Chicontepec (Veracruz) in the late 1780's testified that a local estate owner and political boss named Manuel Valdés terrorized anyone who refused to contribute to his fund to pay for lawsuits against the parish priest. With the aid of some local Indians, he had them tied up and taken to the jail of his Hacienda Camaytlan, where he threatened to hang them from a tree on the hacienda and force a scalding egg into their mouths. AGN Templos 1 exp. 2. Leaders of a faction of Indians in the parish of San Felipe del Obraje supposedly threatened to "brand like beasts" local people who did not support their suit against the cura to establish a new arancel (schedule of fees) in the parish, according to Spanish and Indian witnesses for the cura. AGN CRS 68 exp. 3, fols. 309-10. The priest of Cuanacalcingo, Cuernavaca district, in 1775 had a pregnant woman whipped for missing roll call after mass. She died a month or so later, but the cura was not held accountable. CRS 68 exps. 4-5.

75. AGI Mex. 2588, Tlalixtac, Jan. 16, 1784, report. In his notion of who were the victims of physical abuse, Ferra clearly did not expect to find wives abusing husbands.

76. AJANG Civil, box 49, doc. 4, 1727; AGN CRS 68 exps. 4-5, 1775.

77. AGN Acervo 49 caja 50, 1749 ("eighteen lashes with a pause"); AGN Bienes 431 exp. 17, 1771 ("fifteen or twenty"). Called to testify in 1785 about charges that the cura of Alahuistlan whipped excessively, the creole schoolteacher, Carlos Rodríguez de Castro, said that the cura usually ordered only six to eight lashes and at most 25 "if the offense was serious, and this infrequently." AGN CRS 75 exp. 6.

78. AGN Bienes 663 exp. 22.

79. In 1819, the cacique of Ixtlahuacan (Guadalajara) complained that the cura sentenced him to 25 lashes and three months' seclusion for an argument with his wife. He fled town to avoid the punishment and appealed to the audiencia to safeguard his return and require the cura to compensate him for the corn crop he was not able to harvest. The court agreed and ordered the cura to pay him 103p. AJANG Criminal, bundle labeled "1818-19, leg. 3 (85)."

80. From Indian references to "an arroba of azotes," arroba seemed to mean "many" (see idiomatic expressions under "arroba" in *Diccionario de la lengua castellana*). For some, it may well have meant an indefinite number, so great that the person speaking had lost count. But when I began to find references to "two arrobas of lashes" and the number 25 and multiples of 25 in many sentences, it was clear that the literal meaning of "arroba" usually applied: a measure of weight equal to 25 libras.

81. One of the complaints made by Indians of San Luis de las Peras, Huichapan district, in 1785 about the cura's use of the whip was that he usually ordered no less than 50 lashes "even for a very minor offense." AGN CRS 75 exp. 5. The fiscal of the Audiencia of Mexico in 1792 blamed the cura of Amanalco for causing a disturbance in the pueblos by ordering so excessive a punishment as 50 lashes for Indians who had complained of his method of taking the census that year. AGN Crim. 243 exp. 1.

82. AGN Tierras 2198 exp. 2 ("tan fuertes . . . que asta mis carnes me partieron"). And the husband was not even the main offender, according to his testimony. He stated that in anger the cura had picked up a cáñamo de toro and given his wife the excessive number of two arrobas of lashes, then turned on him with more lashes when he complained.

Usually the claim of "crueles azotes" was made without elaboration, as in AGN Crim. 49 exp. 2, 1775, Xochimilco.

83. AGN Acervo 49 caja 49, 1739, Churubusco.

84. AJANG Civil, box 36, doc. 7, 1726, San Juan de Imala, Culiacán district (cura took over fishery).

85. AJANG Civil, bundle labeled "1709–1819 (181)," 1744, Mechoacanejo; AGN Indios 23 exp. 154, 1658, Cuehuacan, Mexicalcingo district; AGN Hist. 437, 1800, Mochitlan; AGN Bienes 663 exp. 6, 1809, Tultitlan ("maltrata por lo más leve"). In other late colonial cases, the complaint was that the priest was using minor offenses as a pretext to order many cruel whippings and other harsh punishment. AJANG Civil, box 231, doc. 1, 1804, Ocotlan.

86. AGN Templos 1 exp. 2, 1786–88, Guayacocotla; AGN Tierras 2774 exp. 9, 1749, Santo Tomás, Huatzalco district (Puebla).

87. AGN CRS 195 exp. 6, 1792, Zoquitlan (Puebla); AGN Bienes 663 exp. 6, Tultitlan, 1809 ("sólo es cura para tiranizar," said the Indian parishioners).

88. But according to AGN CRS 47 exp. 3, fols. 17–18, 1699, Tetlama, Tancítaro district, Indians used the word "contradecir" (to object) in a land dispute, which is the context in which Warman uses the phrase "Venimos a contradecir." Indians of Ayotzingo in a 1766 petition concerning the distribution of community lands referred to Vizente Roque being imprisoned for having objected to ("contradecir") the division. AGN Tierras 2554 exp. 11. As Warman implies, when it came to land, villagers thought in terms of rights more than in terms of obligations and requests.

89. AGN Bienes 210 exp. 1.

90. AGN CRS 75 exp. 5.

91. As the cura of Tlalixtac, Oaxaca, said in his report on whipping, social distinctions were customary and important. Caciques, principales, and elders who had held office were distinguished from "la pleve": "only extremely rarely are the former to be corrected with the whip." AGI Mex. 2588, Jan. 16, 1784, report.

92. AGN Acervo 49 caja 49.

93. AGN CRS 84 exp. 8, fols. 222v–224, 1801, Tescaliacac ("los más principales"); CRS 204 exp. 10, fol. 316, 1760, Tejupilco; CRS 67 exp. 3, 1768, Joloapan, Tetepango district. Similar complaints about curas not respecting status and whipping officials may be found in AGN Acervo 49 caja 43, 1625, Cicapualco, Ichcateopan district; AGN Indios 23 exp. 6, 1658, Cuehuacan, Mexicalcingo district; AGN Bienes 210 exp. 1, 1731, Guayacocotla (Veracruz); AGN CRS 72 exp. 4, 1734, San Juan Huetamo, Guaymeo district; Acervo 49 caja 49, 1739, Churubusco; AJANG Civil, bundle labeled "1709–1819 (181)," 1744, Mechoacanejo; CRS 192 exps. 11–12, 1760, Almoloya, Tenango del Valle district; CRS 23 exp. 6, 1771, Ozoloapan, Temascaltepec district; AGN Tierras 1929 exp. 9, 1772, Tlalmanalco; CRS 136 exp. 4, 1783, San Lorenzo Huichilapan, Tenango del Valle district; CRS 75 exp. 5, 1785, San Luis de las Peras, Huichapan district; CRS 156 exp. 13, 1788, San Lucas, Tecualoyan district; CRS 39 exp. 2, 1796, San Bartolomé Capuluac (Edo. de México); CRS 39 exp. 6, 1806, Amatepec, Villa Alta district (Oaxaca); Bienes 172 exp. 56, 1807, Tepetlixpa (Edo. de México); and Bienes 663 exp. 26, 1818, Lolotla, Meztitlan district.

94. For example, witnesses in a case brought against the cura of Zapotitlan in 1806 for excessive whippings testified approvingly that he had whipped only "muchachos doctrineros." AJANG Criminal, box 20, doc. 2. A royal cedula of Oct. 9, 1728, generally restricting the use of the whip on Indians, provided that children could be punished in this way as "paternal correction." Matraya y Ricci, p. 303.

95. AGN Bienes 210 exp. 1. The same priest was also charged with whipping Indian men with their pants down.

96. AGN Inq. 1297 exp. 6, 1781, Ozumba; Inq. 1324, fols. 1–30, 1791, Toluca; Inq. 1372 exp. 2, 1792, Sierra de Pinos, Zacatecas; AGN Crim. 203 exp. 4, 1778, Tepoztlan; AGN Bienes 575 exp. 14, 1789, Huazalingo.

97. AGN CRS 75 exp. 6; AGN Inq. 1074 2d num., fols. 35ff.

98. AGN CRS 204 exp. 9.

99. AGN Acervo 49 caja 50, 1749, San Miguel Tancanhuitz. Another case in which an Indian alcalde spoke of the shame of being whipped with his pants down comes from Ozoloapan in 1771. AGN CRS 23 exp. 6.

100. AJANG Civil, box 49, doc. 4, 1727, Mezcala, Jalisco; AGN Crim. 243 exp. 1, 1792, Amanalco; Crim. 284 exp. 5, 1736, Papantla.

101. Cases where Indian officials complained of an affront to their honor include AGN Bienes 210 exp. 1, 1731, Guayacocotla; AGN CRS 156 exp. 13, 1765, San Lucas, Malinalco district; CRS 67 exp. 3, 1768, Joloapan; CRS 23 exp. 6, 1771, Ozoloapan; AGN Civil 2114 exp. 8, 1780, Tolpetlac; Bienes 575 exp. 46, 1789, Ocuilan; AGN Crim. 148 exp. 2, 1792, Almoloya, Tenango del Valle district; Bienes 172 exp. 56, 1805 Tepetlixpa.

J. G. Peristiany's collection *Honour and Shame* is a helpful introduction to the meaning of honor in social terms ("Honour is the value of a person in his own eyes, but also in the eyes of society"). Unfortunately, the introduction and suggestive essay by Julian Pitt-Rivers tend to describe honor in terms of individuals and small, homogeneous groups, as if communication about honor occurred only among equals and as if "an inferior is not deemed to possess sufficient honour to resent the affront of a superior" (p. 31). This leaves out honor that was expressed in political terms, communicated across classes, and mediated by the state, as in these Mexican cases. Honor in the personal and small-group terms of the Peristiany volume can also be studied profitably for colonial Mexico. Julio Caro Baroja's chapter provides a particularly helpful historical view of honor in Spain that posits significant changes in meaning between the 16th and the 18th century.

102. AGN CRS 67 exp. 3, Joloapan, Tetepango district, Guipustla parish, 1768 ("que él no temía matar a los yndios porque sólo él era el Superior y no reconocía a otro que pudiera contenerle").

103. Attendance at mass, knowledge of doctrina, support of the schools, and fulfillment of the Easter duty are widely documented. Cases of the less common reasons of timely reporting and avoiding Christian burial are found in AGN CRS 75 exp. 6, 1786, Alahuistlan; CRS 204 exp. 9, 1760, Tejupilco towns; AGN Crim. 306 exp. 5, 1773, Zimatlan (Oaxaca).

104. Justifications for whippings on the grounds of insolence: AGN CRS 72 exp. 4, 1734, San Juan Huetamo; CRS 201 exp. 1, 1780, San Lucas Ixtapalapa (india complained about the whipping of husband); CRS 68 exps. 4–5, 1775, Cuanacalcingo (Indian came up to the cura drunk and with his hat on). When one of two Indian families of San Nicolás Coatepec, Malinalco district, disputing a lot boundary in 1798 complained to the cura, the cura had the other couple brought to him at the casas reales. In the cura's version of the encounter, they arrived drunk and insolent, laying hands on him, so he ordered them whipped. According to the husband, when he threatened to go to the district governor and show him the wounds inflicted, the cura whipped his wife again. In another case the cura claimed that when he told the gobernador to arrest a man suspected of witchcraft, the gobernador shook his staff of office in the cura's face, and a "multitud de indios" surrounded him and shouted that "no tenía que ir a buscar allí."

Other justifications: CRS 84 exp. 8, 1801, Tescaliacac (gobernador traded a carga of maize for six pounds of wax reserved for the illumination of the Host); AGN Bienes 575 exp. 14, 1798, Huazalingo (officials did not supply enough food for the cura's feast for the maestros de escuela); CRS 39 exp. 2, 1796, Capuluac (officials were pursuing litigation against cura); CRS 67 exp. 3, 1768, Guipustla parish, Joloapan (gobernador lost a letter entrusted to him; on another occasion, when an alcalde asked why the gobernador was being whipped, the cura reportedly gave him another hard one); CRS 68, exp. 3, 1771, San Felipe del Obraje (cura whipped Indians whenever they did not do just as he wished); AGN Templos 1 exp. 2, 1786–88, Guayacocotla y Chicontepec (parishioners did not perform labor service to the cura's satisfaction); AGN Tierras 2554 exp. 11, 1766, Tlalmanalco (Indian complained about the allotment he got in a distribution of community lands).

105. AGI Mex. 2588, Zimatlan, Jan. 26, 1784, report, fol. 19r.

106. AGI Mex. 2588, Tlalixtac, Jan. 16, 1784, report. The cura of pueblos in the Chilapa district in 1783 would have given an emphatic second to Ferra's preoccupation with drunkenness and the idea that it was the source of most social evils among Indians. His "equitativas correcciones" with the whip were, he said, concentrated on the evil of drunkenness, plus an occasional case of an official who allowed a parishioner to die without last rites. AGN CRS 30 exp. 2.

107. AGN Civil 2072 exp. 19, 1788, Cempoala ("detestables abominaciones"). The fear of Indians' criminal "libertad" and the view that the whip was essential to maintain order are expressed in CAAG, unclassified, 1765 cofradía dispute, Santa Fe (near Guadalajara); AGN CRS 68 exp. 3, fol. 210v, 1771, San Felipe del Obraje; AGN Civil 2114 exp. 8, 1780, Tolpetlac; and AJANG Civil, box 49, doc. 4, 1727, Poncitlan Franciscan ("sin azotes y amenazas no se puede conseguir que traigan rosario, que se muestran yndevotos").

108. AGN Tierras 2554 exp. 11, fol. 8r.

109. Tello, *Crónica miscelánea*, 4: 103–4.

110. Trent, 25th Session, Reform, ch. 3; AGN Acervo 49 caja 45, 1815, Chalco, Ygnacio Vicente Ximénez.

111. AGN CRS 75 exp. 6.

112. For example, AGN CRS 179 exp. 13, fols. 412–24, 1763–65, Actopan. In this complicated conflict among the cura, the lieutenant of the alcalde mayor, and some parishioners, the provisor of the archbishop's court called for the excommunication of the lieutenant and another man who had wounded the cura unless they came forward and repented. Both men pleaded for absolution and agreed to penance. Absolution was granted with the proviso that a public notice of the penance be posted. Some priests used excommunication purely as a political tool. On the bishops of Chiapas using it against alcaldes mayores in the early colonial period, see MacLeod, "La espada." Similar uses by parish priests in late colonial Mexico are illustrated in AGN Acervo 49 cajas 45, 48; AJANG Civil, box 59, doc. 11, box 125, doc. 2; and AJANG Criminal, box 33, doc. 15.

113. AGN Acervo 49 caja 48.

114. Omerick, BMM 113, pp. 26–27, speaks of using a musical watch to dramatize the heavenly reward. While attending to Indians in the village of Tochpan, his watch sounded the hour, "the little hammers, released, played their sonata. . . . Hearing the bell's tone and the soothing harmony of the music, they [the Indian parishioners] were amazed. They asked me the cause of that remarkable sound coming from my person and pocket. I took out the watch, and to amuse them further, I called the hour again and the watch immediately repeated its minuet, which further astonished my good Indians. I took the opportunity to apply the moment to my office and desire, explaining in a fraternal way the pleasures of fortunate eternity. And I can assure you that an oration from Father Carochi or Mijangos would not have had the same effect on their spirits even though my Nahuatl is far inferior to what [those experts] wrote and explained."

115. *Concilios provinciales primero, y segundo*, p. 125. Eighteenth-century manuals include some compelling examples of exhortations and verbal encounters intended to inspire parish priests to use spoken words to good effect. Pérez de Velasco, for example, highly recommended dramatic homilies (p. 57): "If they are excessively drunk or very lascivious, I say, 'Look at our Lord (if there is a crucifix handy). Didn't he die on a cross for your sins? Don't you confess it when you pray? And does it seem right to you that the Lord, your Father, is torn apart for your drunkenness and obscenities, and you with

the cup in your hand and bedded down with the woman while God is looking at you?' I usually wait a little while, silent as if afflicted, then add, 'What a shame! Here you are well and strong, but perhaps before the year is out you will be in Hell forever!' "

116. Trent, 13th Session, Reform, ch. 1.

117. AGN Bienes 172 exp. 37, undated petition, sewn with April 28, 1805, response of the provisor.

118. For example, Gabino Garduño of Tenango reported in 1857 that sermons of the parish priest had started rumors of an attack by the government on local religious rights and an impending nighttime arrest of the priest. Texas, Mariano Riva Palacio Coll., doc. 6349, March 27, 1857.

119. On priests and royalist propaganda, see especially three works by Hamill: "Rector to the Rescue"; "Early Psychological Warfare"; and "Royalist Counterinsurgency."

120. BN LaFragua Coll., vol. 181.

121. AGN CRS 75 exp. 9, fols. 450–65 ("Que con el arancel no han de ganar el *Cielo*"). Other examples of curas using threats to get their way: AGN DP 3 exp. 2; AGN Tierras 2198 exp. 2, 1798, Coatepec, Malinalco; and AGN Alcaldes Mayores 11, fols. 448–56, 1776, Tuzamapan. As Dening, *Bounty*, pp. 16–17, observed in another context, what made for "bad" language by a person in authority was less that it was intemperate or abusive than that it was threatening.

122. AGN Bienes 663 exp. 6.

123. AGN Inq. 1304 exp. 3. Presumably Joseph Manuel Sotomayor, cura of Zacualpan in 1796, spoke off the top of his head here as he did from the pulpit. One of his claims to fame was that he had never composed his sermons and homilies ahead of time. No one rose to defend him as an effective preacher during his lengthy trial for suspicion of blasphemy. Inq. 1304 exp. 3; Inq. 1334 exp. 3.

124. AGN CRS 67 exp. 2, fol. 76. The full text reads:

Hijo mío: vosotros con vuestras continuas borracheras, ni a Dios, ni a los superiores de el mundo queréis obedecer; pues ni a el despacho mesmo de la R^l Audiencia que vosotros propios sacasteis queréis arreglaros.

Este despacho, ya se ve que la sacasteis; porque os engañaron vuestro abogado, y apoderados; pues está todo a mi favor, como que me asiste la razón y justicia; pues siendo el pleito sobre que no queríais pagarme más que lo que expressa el arancel antiguo, manda la R^l Audiencia que me paguéis los derechos de las declaraciones no como declarados sino por ajuste que hagamos en el ínterin que sale el nuevo: en lo cual ya se demuestra que vosotros no conseguisteis lo q^e pretendías sino yo; y que assi yo gané el punto; pero después de todo para nada parecéis a verme ni a dho ajuste venís, quando cada rato se ofrece por lo que paternalmente os mando que vengáis para la Missa de la bendición que está pendiente y las de todos los domingos; porque de lo contrario ocurriré a los S^{res} Superiores y os apremiarán a que seáis obedientes y que no viváis borrachos. Dios a que en su Sta Gracia. Ocoaacac y Junio 9 de 1767.

V^{ro} el Cura q^e en Dios os ama.

125. Greene, *Power and the Glory*, pp. 167–68.

126. *Itin*. 3-4-16. An early-19th-century Chinantec confesionario taught a priest to make his authority abundantly clear at the outset. The first words he learned to say to a penitent were: "Mira hijo, que aquí vienes a confesarte como delante de Dios. Por lo mismo no ocultes ninguno de tus pecados." Univ. of Virginia, Gates Coll., doc. 837, 1838.

127. *Itin*. 3-4-16. Confession over several years to the same priest should have heightened the sense of repentance for willful disobedience.

128. The invasive, individualizing, and social control aspects of confession are empha-

sized by Tentler, *Sin and Confession*; Tentler, "Summa"; and Gruzinski, "Individualization." Gruzinski assumes more than demonstrates that, in the Salesian tradition, the confessional was the instrument of spiritual direction in New Spain, promoting a keen sense of personal guilt among Indian communicants and a guilt-induced system of control. Even the intentional meaning of Catholic doctrine and practice was not limited to individualization. Counterpoised to the emphasis on individual responsibility and salvation were the congregational aspect of the church, with its community institutions, responsibilities, and practices, and a tax system that encouraged multifamily households. AGN CRS 156 exp. 5, fol. 143v.

129. AGI Guad. 563. Politicizing the confessional in the independence period bore bitter fruit later on. Politicians in 1857 suspected that priests were using it during Easter week to persuade their parishioners not to support the new constitution. Whether they did so or not, the belief that the confessional was being used this way was widespread. Texas, Mariano Riva Palacio Coll., doc. 6435, April 18, 1857.

130. Examples of the threat of withholding absolution from unwed pregnant women who did not divulge the name of the father: AGN Inq. 760 exp. 40, 1715, Temascaltepec; Inq. 1230 exp. 13, 1784, Tula.

131. Additional examples of absolution withheld in these circumstances: AGN Inq. 622 exp. 5; Inq. 760 exp. 14; Inq. 814 exp. 8; Inq. 894, fols. 266ff; Inq. 914 exps. 14–15; Inq. 960 exp. 19; Inq. 970 exp. 6; Inq. 1191 exp. 14; Inq. 1205 exp. 28; Inq. 1221 exp. 9; Inq. 1304 exp. 3; Inq. 1308 exp. 1; Inq. 1318 exp. 8; Inq. 1346 exp. 6; Inq. 1348 exps. 10, 14; Inq. 1360 exps. 1–2; Inq. 1372 exp. 2; Inq. 1817 exp. 5; Inq. 1401 exps. 11–12.

132. Serge Gruzinski uses confessional manuals in "Individualization." Several early-19th-century manuscript confesionarios in Spanish and native languages of Oaxaca are located in the University of Virginia's Gates Collection. See especially doc. 838, a 28-page 1830's Chinantec-Spanish compendium of vocabulary and sentences the priest needed for his ministry, which provides a less formal record of how priests intended to approach penitents in the confessional: "¿Quieres confesarte?" "¿Tienes dolor de haber ofendido a Dios?" "Pues poco a poco responde a lo que te pregunto." "No tengas miedo ni vergüenza, porque si tienes miedo y vergüenza y callas los pecados te condenas." "Esperas en Dios que te perdonaría tus pecados." "¿Quieres a Dios con todo tu corazón sobre todas las cosas?" "por mandamiento de Dios y de la Yglesia." "Y creyera todo lo que la Yglesia le enseñó." "por amor de Dios y seg[u]ir su ley Santa."

Indian parishioners, in particular, were expected to confess only once a year, during Lent, and most of them did so within a week or two of Easter Sunday. *Itin.* 4-4 passim sets out the pattern for Indian confession and communion. Indians were to take communion once a year near Easter (rather than the three times recommended for non-Indians, at Christmas, Pentecost, and Easter). They could do so on any day of Lent as long as they had fasted, confessed, and been absolved. Communion by Easter was the rule, but delaying until Pentecost was acceptable since "it is not a notable delay." According to Omerick, confessions in his parish of Tepecoacuilco went on from Ash Wednesday to Corpus Christi. BMM 113.

133. JCB, n.d., resumé of Juan Miguel Tinoco.

134. Ibid., 1762 resumé of Diego de Almonacid y Salasar, describing his service in Huitzilac, Cuernavaca district.

135. Manuel Pérez, pp. 15ff, 59, 75, 84; John Carter Brown Lib., Spanish Codex Coll., no. 52, fols. 34, 36.

136. *Itin.* 3-3 to 3-4 passim.

137. *Itin.* 3-3-6, 3-3-13, 3-3-14.

138. *Itin.* 3-3-8, 3-4-14.

139. Pérez de Velasco, pp. 45–57 (like the *Itinerario*, Pérez de Velasco, p. 57, saw the

major challenge as moving Indian penitents to feel guilt); Manuel Pérez, pp. 15, 25, 59, 84, 117, 157, 165. Pérez believed that Indians failed to make proper confessions out of ignorance, fear, cunning, and forgetfulness. Since most would acknowledge only three or four minor sins, should the confessor press them about other areas of sin that they might not have committed but might then be tempted to try, or should he stop and risk leaving large areas of possible sin unexamined? Pérez doubted whether it was possible to determine how often a sin had been committed, but he felt confessors should try to find out in case one of the more sophisticated parishioners took the question to heart. As a manual of instruction, his *Farol indiano* offered little encouragement to budding confessors. Its message essentially was that what Indians said in the confessional usually could not be trusted and what they presumably left out was the most important part of an adequate confession (see especially p. 59).

140. Pérez de Velasco, p. 45. Drunkenness was one of Pérez de Velasco's practical examples of how the parishioners' way of thinking had to be taken into account to achieve an adequate confession of mortal sins: "En punto de embriaguez, aunque me digan los Indios Onitlahuan, y Onihuintic con que quieren decir: 'Me embriagué,' tampoco les pregunto luego: quantas veces, porque tengo observado, que los Indios unas veces beben por templar los bochornos, pero sólo lo que basta: otras, o porque los combidan, o porque se les antoja, y aunque se exceden en la bebida, pero no se turban: otras, beben, y tanto, que se perturban, pero no pierden el sentido; y otras, beben de modo que lo pierden, y formalmente se embriagan. Todos estos modos de beber comprehenden, y explican con la voz Onitlahuan, y dicen me embriagué. Pero como supuesta la frequencia con que los Indios beben, sería inaveriguable el número, y como en estos modos de beber, a excepción del último, aunque ay pecado venial muy notable, no ay culpa mortal, tampoco insisto mucho en averiguar las veces que han bebido, y sólo me empeño en descubrir quantas veces han bebido de modo que ayan perdido el sentido."

141. Tulane VEMC 24 exp. 2, fol. 3r, 1790.

142. Manuel Pérez, pp. 15–16, recommended that parishioners be required to demonstrate their knowledge of the rudiments of Christian doctrine before being allowed to confess.

143. Part of the case against Sotomayor in Zacualpan was that practically no Indians confessed to him because he smoked cigars when women were present, loudly mistreated the men, and failed to keep their confessions secret. AGN Inq. 1304 exp. 3, 2d foliation, fol. 1, June 22, 1796. Extensive testimony against Félix González Beltrán, vicario of Temascaltepec in 1715, suggests that he repeatedly broke the seal of the confessional and performed confessions in an undignified and provocative way that drove his parishioners away. In particular he was said to confess women in the sacristy with the door closed, lying down without wearing his habit, chewing tobacco, and making the women expose their faces. If they refused, he would not confess them. Inq. 760 exp. 40.

144. AGN Bienes 575 exp. 14. The archbishop cleared the cura of the principal charge of collecting excessive fees and did not address any of the others lodged against him. The conclusion was that the gobernador was acting out of vengeance. A related complaint by parishioners of Sierra de Pinos was that their confessor, the vicario Mariano Calzada, had driven them away by asking the young married women questions about their sexual habits. AGN Inq. 1308 exp. 1, 1790.

145. John Carter Brown Lib., Spanish Codex Coll., no. 52, fol. 245v.

146. There was a limited precedent for confession through an interpreter. According to *Itin.* 3-4-9 and 3-4-10, such confessions were permissible if the penitent was about to die, since his salvation rested in the balance.

147. Solórzano 4-15-59: "En quanto al azotar a los Indios, es opinión de sugetos muy versados en esto, que los más de los Indios son tan descuidados y de tan poca vergüenza,

que si no les azotasen no podrían atraerlos a la *doctrina* ni a Misa; y que esta ley no se debe practicar con Indios principales y otros que están ya reducidos a policía y vergüenza y como Españolizados."

148. AGN CRS 156 exp. 7.

149. Goffman discusses these issues of symbolic social acts in his classic essay "The Nature of Deference and Demeanor." Two articles that address the kinds of relationships and ambiguities of order and power in acts of deference that concern me are Shils, "Deference"; and Newby, "Deferential Dialectic."

150. The Fourth Provincial Council (1771) sought to bolster and clarify *Recop.* 1-1-26: "Por las leyes reales está mandado que quando sale el Santísimo de la Yglesia sea en procesión, o se lleva a los enfermos le acompañen todos los que le encontraren en la Calle, y haviéndose notado en las Ciudades populosas el abuso e irreverencia de que algunos que van en coche no mandan parar, y otros que paran el coche, no se apean, ni acompañan al Santísimo, manda este Concilio que todos paren de coche, se apeen, y a lo menos se pongan de rodillas hasta que pase su Magestad y pudiendo le vayan acompañando." CPM, p. 164. Communion medals that were distributed to Indian parishioners, presumably on the occasion of the first communion, or perhaps at Easter, could illustrate the connection between kneeling and the sacrament. One from Huejotzingo (Puebla) that I saw there shows a bare-chested Indian kneeling with a cross in his hand on the obverse and the cup and consecrated Host on the reverse with the words, "Praise the Most Holy Sacrament" (Alabádose Santísimo Sacramento).

151. AGN Acervo 49 caja 146, 1805, charges by Dr. Rafael José de Calera against Angel Pasqual Casabal.

152. "Apéndice a los Concilios primero y segundo," p. 315. An example of parishioners kissing the cura's hand is recorded in AJANG Civil, box 117, doc. 4. On rare occasions, the cura reversed the gesture, as the cura of Tulancingo did in 1811, when he appealed to his Indian parishioners to remain loyal to the crown. AGN Inq. 462 exp. 33.

153. AGN Hist. 578A, 1793, Zacualpan report on cura of Ichcateopan.

154. Tulane VEMC 70 exp. 45.

155. Another glimpse of pageantry confirming status and order comes from a 1710 report on clerical fees in which the Franciscans in the Diocese of Guadalajara were faulted for insisting on too much pomp in Indian pueblos. AGI Guad. 205.

156. AGI Mex. 2588, Jan. 26, 1784, report, fol. 10v. The other wing of ascent to heaven was love.

157. Making faces is mentioned by Omerick in 1769. BMM 113, pp. 73–74. According to the alcalde mayor of Autlan (Jalisco), the anger of the cura in his long and bitter dispute with royal authorities in the late 1780's over the limits of ecclesiastical jurisdiction left the community possessed by "fright, terror, and fear." AJANG Civil, box 125, doc. 2. According to a Franciscan witness, the cura of Cempoala in the vicinity of Pachuca had terrified the Indian villagers with his anger. AGN Inq. 1113, witness no. 8, fol. 10v (240v of the volume). Clearly, some curas had not caught the new spirit of the gentle pastor. The cura of Zacualtipan, Meztitlan district, in 1820 advised the subdelegado that gentle persuasions would not suffice in his dispute with local Indians over clerical fees, and he urged ominously that the magistrate apply "the most serious methods of correction." AGN Templos 25 exp. 9, fol. 22.

158. Tulane VEMC 68 exp. 9. Another case of a cura who was said to govern his parish by fear is mentioned in the secret report against Bartolomé Vélez Escalante, cura of Yahualica in 1806. AGN Acervo 49, caja 45. The report did not document the charge in detail.

159. *Itin.* 3-3-13, 3-3-14. Indians were, in one late colonial priest's words, to live "con miedo del castigo." AGN CRS 68 exp. 3, fol. 210v, 1771, San Felipe del Obraje. A wit-

ness in another case said that there was, in fact, a general fear of saying anything against a priest. AGN Inq. 1360 exps. 1–2, fol. 4r, 1795, Otumba.

160. *Itin.* 1-6-3, 2-3-4, 4-2-5.

161. AJANG Civil, box 49, doc. 4, testimony of Antonio de Lomas, comisario of Atotonilco.

162. AGN CRS 75 exp. 4. See especially the testimony of Thomas Nicolás, alguacil de la iglesia of Tototepec, who witnessed the events, fols. 257v–60v, and fol. 264.

163. In a similar case from 1775, two Indian women of the Rancho de Simapantongo, Xilotepec district, lodged a criminal complaint against the gobernador and the lay assistant (fiscal) of cura Francisco José Gutiérrez for ordering a cruel whipping of their husbands despite the women's tears and wails. The dispute centered on whether the Indians of Simapantongo were obliged to attend mass in Chapatongo, the seat of Gutiérrez's parish. The priest's response to the court in this case turned the deference argument against the women. The Indians in that settlement, he said, "swear with their chests on the ground [pecho por tierra] to obey superior orders, but they do not comply, not even with the extrajudicial agreements they had agreed to, . . . on many occasions." If the punishment was cruel—and he claimed it was not—the Indians were not entitled to a special measure of indulgence because they failed to live up to their promises sealed in genuflection to follow official orders and their own agreements. AGN Inq. 1146 exp. 1.

164. AGN CRS 47 exp. 3, fols. 17–18.

165. AGN Templos 25 exp. 11. The many appeals for viceregal protection against abusive local magistrates make the same point. See, for example, AGN Hist. 132 exp. 26, fols. 15–20, 1793, Tetecala, Cuernavaca district. Manuel Martines de Alpizar, the alcalde mayor's lieutenant of Tecozautla in the 1750's, gave a royal official's view of this practice of reciprocal duties. He claimed to have achieved a provisional settlement of a bitter dispute between villagers of San Luis de las Peras and an Indian alcalde over the alcalde's physical abuse of a local woman: "Seeing that they were Indians, I befriended them, and they seemed quite satisfied with my severe admonition to the *alcalde*, despite his objection, that he not bother this Indian woman but treat her as he does the rest." AGN Tierras 2179 exp. 3, fols. 37v–38v.

166. AGN Hist. 132 exp. 2.

167. AGN RCO 126 exp. 137.

168. "Royal piety and protection" appear in AGN RCO 93 exp. 103, a petition to the king by Indians of Chacaltianguis, Oaxaca, in 1768.

169. Headcoverings were used before European colonization, but hats were a distinctively European addition to everyday male dress, self-expression, and social intercourse. In the early colonial period, natives of central Mexico were impressed that Spanish men always seemed to have a hat. According to the 1541 *Crónica de Michoacán* (Craine & Reindorp, p. 87), one of the names that Tarascans initially used for Spaniards was "acacecha," meaning people who wear caps and hats. Some 300 years later, a visiting American was just as impressed by the ubiquitous hat and its many uses throughout Mexico: "The crowning glory of a Mexican peasant is his hat. No matter how poor he may be, he will manage to have a sombrero gorgeous with silver spangles and heavy with silver cord, or, if he prefers straw to felt, he will be equally extravagant in its decoration; and, in common with his blanket, the hat will be made to do duty for many years." Wells, pp. 26–27.

Natalie Z. Davis points to the special social importance of hats to early modern European men in her study of narratives in criminal trials from 16th-century France: "Exchanged, demanded, stolen, and especially knocked off, hats triggered trouble in remission stories." *Fiction in the Archives,* p. 38.

170. Late colonial records for these dioceses make it clear that Indians did have hats to

tip and remove. For example, Indians of Yahualica in 1739 charged their cura with trying to collect 3rr from each man to pay his lay assistants. Those who did not pay had their hats or tilmas confiscated. Tulane VEMC 15 exp. 5. Hats and pants were two of the changes in Indian dress that usually followed Spanish colonization.

When local relationships were tense, even relatives of colonial officials could be touchy about the special deference to which they felt entitled. The son of the alcalde mayor's lieutenant of Zacoalco (Jalisco) in 1753 was reportedly angered when a servant of the cura did not remove his hat as he passed the young man on the street. AJANG Civil, box 59, doc. 11.

171. Uncovering was a standard gesture of respect to one's superiors. One of the rules of the constitution of the Colegio de Tepotzotlan (1777), for example, was that students were "not to cover their heads or be seated in the presence of their elders and superiors until they are given permission." *Constituciones*, p. 12.

172. Tulane VEMC 53 exp. 23. A similar brouhaha erupted in 1774, when Mathías Gómez Marañón, the creole administrator of the Hacienda de los Quisillos in the jurisdiction of Tala, Jalisco (owned by an oidor of the Audiencia of Mexico), went to the corregidor's office to have him implement a high court order to release several Indian workers from the hacienda he had arrested. He was kept waiting a long time, but even so, when he was finally received, he addressed the corregidor with his hat in his hand. In a further slap in the face, the corregidor did not doff his own hat in return, and the two quickly fell to arguing. The corregidor ordered Marañón arrested, but he turned the tables and had the corregidor locked in his casas reales. AJANG Civil, box 121, doc. 5.

The subdelegado of Acaponeta, Sinaloa, in 1791 put himself in the same position as the cura of Cuautitlan in his description of a dispute over fireworks. On the eve of Pentecost that year, he found a Franciscan doctrinero setting off rockets in the cemetery. He approached him hat in hand and with a polite greeting, but the priest did not reply. The subdelegado told him that the day should not be marked with fireworks because houses could be set on fire, as they had been in the past. The doctrinero retorted that he would do as he pleased, and that the subdelegado was a "sángano patarrato" (a ridiculous leech). The subdelegado said he thought it best to withdraw from this dishonorable abuse. The fireworks display was repeated the next day, and the subdelegado lodged a complaint with the audiencia.

The result of this dispute was less cordial than the public reconciliation at Cuautitlan. The fiscal of the audiencia had one copy of the record sent to the Franciscan provincial, ordering him to punish the doctrinero and warn him to avoid provocations of this kind, and another copy sent to higher-ups in the audiencia with the recommendation that an arrangement be made with the provincial to remove the doctrinero. The provincial replied that the suit was the product of personal resentments harbored by the subdelegado, and that the law did not prohibit fireworks; it provided only that a license be obtained from the subdelegado. He admitted that the Franciscans at Acaponeta and the subdelegado had not maintained the "good harmony" that was expected of them, but he criticized the subdelegado for making a public issue of it. His point was that suits against public personages were especially harmful not only because dignity and honor were involved, but also because mortifying scandal against a whole corporation, not just an individual, could result ("personas públicas, constituídas en dignidad y mucho más siendo religiosos porque se interesa no sólo su personal honor también el del religioso cuerpo de que son individuos y por eso las reglas del Derecho, y los autores enceñan que se debe proceder en esta parte con mucho tiento porque no valla a ser mayor el escándalo que se cause"). His final order to the two Franciscans at Acaponeta was a "severe reprimand" and a warning to keep a harmonious relationship with the subdelegado. AJANG Civil, box 150, doc. 7.

That an official could become unworthy of the gestures of deference is an idea that the priest of the Villa de Sinaloa tried to drive home in 1800. Under orders from the bishop of Sonora, the cura had excommunicated the subdelegado and his lieutenant for Mocorito for removing a woman from the church buildings and refusing to return her to the cura. The excommunication was to mean a general shunning of the magistrates and, according to a letter written by a resident, anyone who was seen to remove his hat when passing the magistrates on the street was summoned by the cura for confession. AJANG Civil, box 171, doc. 15.

173. Tulane VEMC 8 exp. 52.

174. AGN Alcaldes Mayores 3 exp. 2 ("bastón de otate, firme, de viaje"); AGN Acervo 49 cajas 44, 1700, San Juan del Río, and 48, Temascaltepec, 1700 ("bordón").

175. That an alcalde mayor's (or his lieutenant's) authority was embodied in the staff of office is suggested by instances where the judge sent out someone else with the staff to act in his place. The lieutenant of Zacoalco in 1753 sent his son to the cura on official business carrying the staff. AJANG Civil, box 59, doc. 11. In 1776, the cura of Tuzamapan (Puebla) said he mistook a tax collector for the lieutenant's emissary because he was carrying the staff of office. AGN Alcaldes Mayores 11, fols. 448–56. Among the complaints made against the corregidor of Coyoacan in 1793 was his habit of going out without his "insignia del bastón por la cual es conocido el juez [real] en los pueblos." AGN Hist. 132 exp. 16, fol. 7r. Even an Indian alcalde's authority was embodied in the staff more than in the person, as a principal of Yanhuitlan, Oaxaca, showed when he complained of the Indian gobernador taking away his "bastón para justificar." CDCh, roll 14.

176. For example, the cura of Cuautitlan in 1788 was said not to go out without his bastón; and the cura of San Juan del Río in 1700 reportedly "siempre acostumbra traher un bordón." Tulane VEMC 53 exp. 23; AGN Acervo 49 caja 44.

177. AGN Inq. 1308 exp. 1, 1790, Mariano Calzada, former vicario of Sierra de Pinos.

178. BMM 135 exp. 16, p. 107, Fr. Martín Calderón. *Itin.* 2-3-11 used "vara de hierro" in this way. Parish priests were not to govern Indians with a vara de hierro. By implication they had to rely metaphorically on lighter, more flexible instruments. It is not clear whether Calderón got the idea of the vara de hierro from the *Itinerario* or whether there was a common source for both.

179. Fourteen cases of curas striking people with their bastón were located in the judicial records: AGN Crim. 210, fol. 190r, 1758, Aquiapa, Pozontepec; AGN CRS 204 exp. 10, fol. 316, 1760, Tejupilco; AGN Alcaldes Mayores 3 exp. 2, 1770, Cuitzeo; AGN Acervo 49, caja 48, 1771, Taxco; AGN Bienes 431 exp. 17, 1771, Iguala; CRS 75 exp. 4, 1775, Tototepec, Zacualpan district; Crim. 203 exp. 4, 1778, Tepoztlan; AJANG Civil, box 116, doc. 4, 1778, Ocotlan; Tulane VEMC 53 exp. 23, 1778, Cuautitlan; CRS 136 exp. 4, 1783, San Lorenzo Huichilapan, Tenango del Valle district; CRS 75 exp. 8, fols. 420ff, 1789, San Andrés Jimilpan; Bienes 575 exp. 14, 1789, Huazalingo; CRS 75 exp. 11, 1790, Ajuchitlan, Tetela del Río district; AJANG Criminal, bundle labeled "1823-25 (86)," 1825, Guadalajara.

180. AGN Crim. 210, fol. 190r. In another example from Tototepec, Zacualpan district, in 1775, three Indian women menaced two minor officials of the pueblo with sticks when they came to collect customary clerical fees. When the cura and his servants came up, asking why the women raised sticks against the officials, the women said they replied "for no reason, that they would soon have a court order in their favor." According to the women, the cura responded by striking one of them with his bastón, and saying that "neither the Royal Audiencia nor the Archbishop rules him." AGN CRS 75 exp. 8.

181. AGN CRS 204 exp. 10, fol. 316.

182. AGN CRS 136 exp. 4.

183. AJANG Civil, box 116, doc. 4, 1778.

184. AGN CRS 75 exp. 11. The intendant, Bernardo de Bonavía, wanted both the cura

and the subdelegado's lieutenant removed from their posts. He did remove the lieutenant, but it is not clear whether the bishop of Valladolid acted on his demand that the cura be removed, too.

185. Tulane VEMC 53 exp. 23.

186. Tulane VEMC 8 exp. 25.

187. AGN Civil 865 exp. 9, fol. 6r. See also fol. 23r ("the rest were Indians with their balcarrotas"). According to Gemelli Carreri, 1: 86, Indian men never cut their hair. For an illustration of balcarrotas in the mid-16th century, see the picture of two young nobles in Spanish dress and cropped hair accompanied by their long-haired ancestors in *Relación de las ceremonias*, plate 28.

188. AGN Hist. 319 exp. 24.

189. AGN Alcaldes Mayores 11, fols. 338–40.

190. AGN Crim. 131 exp. 24, 1796 ("Las balcarras de los yndios haun cortadas con tijera por ofensa o agrabio de los que las porten es un grabísimo delito en los que lo executan o mandan, sea quien fuere"). A similar observation by an Indian witness appears in AGN CRS 68 exp. 3, fol. 210v (also fols. 268ff): "tusa, que entre ellos es la mayor afrenta que hai."

191. If the Nahuas are representative, hair in native Mexico was traditionally thought to contain a person's power and provide protective covering for his or her soul. If it was cut, the person would sicken and die. Conversely, growing hair could cure illness. López Austin, *Human Body*, 1: 220–21.

Hair continued to have magical meaning during the colonial period, but whether cutting a man's hair was regarded as castration, as Leach, "Magical Hair," posits, is less certain. The symbolic meaning Hallpike, p. 141, suggests—that long hair is associated with being outside society and that the cutting of hair symbolizes re-entering society"—is even less relevant than the castration thesis to a case like precolumbian or colonial Mesoamerica. As Firth, pp. 297–98, points out, rather than a re-entry to social control, the cutting of hair by colonial authorities comes closer to being an "immediate transfer from one form of social control to another or emphasis on the controls of a particular type of situation."

192. John Carter Brown Lib., Spanish Codex Coll., no. 52, fol. 56.

193. Another emphatic description of Indians' long hair, the affront of having it cut off, and the rare circumstances when it could be done legally appears in Ajofrín, 2: 172–73. This Spanish Capuchin monk remarked, as he traveled through the heartland of New Spain in the mid-1760's, that "en algunas provincias no se le cortan nunca [men's hair] y acostumbran a traerlo siempre suelto, sin atarlo ni recogerlo aun para formar. . . . La mayor afrenta que se puede hacer a un indio o india, es cortarles el pelo . . . y así no se permite a las Justicias este castigo sino por gravísimos delitos y rara vez."

This was different from the English view of long-haired Indians in North America that James Axtell, pp. 174–78, describes. He finds that long hair was regarded as a sin of pride, as a symbol of the Indians' haughty independence and flouting of Englishmen and Christianity. Short hair was an "infallible guide" to an Indian's political allegiance and a requirement for his joining civilized society: "a willingness to cut his long black hair signalled his desire to kill the Indian in himself and to assume a new persona modeled upon the meek, submissive Christ of the white man's Black Book. Since this was the missionaries' primary goal, they wasted no time in persuading their native proselytes to submit to the barber's shears."

194. *Itin.* 3-1-14.

195. *Itin.* 5-2-5 ("para que quede infamado"). In the 1630's, the viceroy of New Spain declared that drunken Indians would receive the harsh sentence of 50 lashes and having their hair cut off. BN Manuscripts, no. 1358 exp. 23, fols. 363–66.

196. Arze also advised parish priests to beware of Indians cutting off their hair themselves in order to incriminate their priests before the district magistrate.

197. AGN CRS 68 exps. 4–5, fols. 416ff.

198. AGN CRS 68 exp. 3. Other 18th-century examples of curas cutting off Indians' hair as punishment are Tulane VEMC 15 exp. 5, 1739, Yahualica; and CRS 23 exp. 5, 1760, Tejupilco.

199. AJANG Civil, box 49. doc. 4. The Lienzo de Tlaxcala and the Códice Osuna, among other 16th-century pictorial manuscripts, show Spaniards grabbing Indians by the hair.

200. AGN CRS 68 exp. 2.

201. AGN CRS 75 exp. 6, fol. 366v.

202. AGN CRS 84 exp. 8. The hair-cutting priest in the notorious San Felipe del Obraje case was said to be a hair-puller as well. CRS 68 exp. 3.

203. AGN Acervo 49 caja 50.

204. AGN Acervo 49 caja 49, 1739, Churubusco; AGN Bienes 575 exp. 14, 1789, Huazalingo. As with whippings and imprisonments, a priest or magistrate needed a good reason for pulling hair, and a secure position in his district to get away with it. A hair-grabbing by the district magistrate and his minions triggered a riot in Ocoyoacac in 1708. AGN Civil 1599 exp. 9. I did not find any cases of village uprisings against priests touched off in this way.

205. AGN CRS 68 exp. 1, fol. 18v.

206. Freeze, *Parish Clergy*, p. 61.

207. According to the alcalde mayor's lieutenant, the cura of Ajuchitlan had his own 25-man police force. AGN CRS 75 exp. 11, fols. 489–92.

208. Rituals of inequality, as Sydel Silverman suggests in her paper of that title, do not only express social arrangements. They also express values, and are part of a negotiation of social arrangements. In this spirit, Bossy considers the mass in Europe from 1200 to 1700 to have been fully as symbolic of conflict and division as it was of community, peace, and order—a tension that reflected the progressive appropriation of the mass by the priesthood.

Chapter Ten

EPIGRAPH: Lumholtz, *Unknown Mexico*, 2: 475.

1. For example, the cura of Ocotlan (Jalisco) in 1804 complained of "el quaci atehismo" of his Indian parishioners. AJANG Civil, box 231, doc. 1. The cura of Tlacotalpan (Veracruz) in 1790 said he suspended marriages in the parish because the Indians who came to him did not even know the Credo. AGN CRS 188 exp. 7. Both priests made these statements in defending themselves against charges of abuse of office.

2. As early as 1546, a Nahuatl-Spanish catechism was published in Mexico for the instruction of "the boys and girls and adolescent children of the natives of this New Spain." See *Códice franciscano*, pp. 29–54.

3. CAAG, unclassified, 1774 report by cura J. Manuel Velásquez of Tala, in which he said most of his parishioners lived "in blind ignorance of the mysteries of the faith." Those of Teuchitlan, who lived dispersed on haciendas, rarely even saw a priest. The bishop of Oaxaca in 1777 asserted that many Indians there did not know enough doctrine to make a proper confession. AGN RCO 126 exp. 137.

4. *Colección de las ordenanzas*, pp. 184, 196. The classes in doctrina involved both group chants and individual recitations. These practices are occasionally documented in negative ways. José Cortés Chimalpopoca, a cacique in the district of Tacuba, petitioned in 1818 for exemption from the weekly doctrina recitations because they were led by a social inferior, the Indian fiscal de la iglesia. AGN CRS 130 exp. 10.

5. *Colección de las ordenanzas*, p. 179.

6. Manuel Pérez, p. 75.

7. Some Indians were said to regard wild game as equivalent to fish and proceeded to eat it on Fridays. John Carter Brown Lib., Spanish Codex Coll., no. 52, fols. 251–65.

8. Examples of religiously based community boycotts: AGN CRS 42 exp. 1, fol. 31, 1732, Tejupilco; CRS 39 exp. 5, fols. 262v–263v, 1803, Malacatepec.

9. AGN Hist. 437, unnumbered 16-fol. expediente, "Sobre que el cura del pueblo de Mochitlan Br. d. Juan Valerio Barrientos, maltrata y exige derechos indebidos a sus feligreses." This kind of passive resistance stopped short of the habit of flight discussed in Chap. 14.

10. CPM, p. 172; *Manual breve*, fols. 143v–144r. The significance of the mass both as an isolated ceremony and as an integral part of the church year is summarized in Hardison, pp. 82–83.

11. BMM 271, ch. 7.

12. The 1775 pastoral visit record ordered an end to this "inaudita, abominable, y bárbara costumbre [of failing to take communion before marriage that] se observa por los naturales de este partido." AHM L10B/13, fol. 207v.

13. *Colección de las ordenanzas*, pp. 5–8.

14. Ibid., pp. 23, 206–8.

15. General compliance is documented in the 1793 reports for central Mexico (AGN Hist. 578A) and pastoral visit records from 1752 to 1803 (AHM L10A/5–8, L10B/9–32). Curas were just as likely to note failures as successes in their resumés or administrative reports in the knowledge that failures would probably be uncovered by a pastoral visitor or a district governor.

16. AGN Acervo 49 caja 116. On Sept. 11, 1809, the gobernador de la mitra expanded on the report for the Huehuetlan mission and noted: "viven todas muy distantes y derramadas por los montes y jamás oyen misa, ni se confiesan, originándose estos defectos de no tener sugeción alguna al padre ministro o misionero." AGN CRS 126 exps. 12–13, fols. 296–301.

17. AGN Crim. 120 exp. 25. Reportedly no men and only a few women in the visitas attended mass.

18. It is hard to tell from the record how serious the open religious opposition in 1769 was, since the visitas' Indians were then engaged in a bitter dispute over clerical fees. But if Zelada is to be believed, it was not a temporary protest. According to him, the district had a long history of "idolatry" in the mountains (partly because many of the men made their living as charcoal burners) and violent resistance to priests who interfered. One of his predecessors, a Dr. Negrete, had to call for a detachment of soldiers to put down one of their tumultos. Tulane VEMC 39 exp. 15. The cura of San Gabriel Chilac in the district of Tehuacan (Puebla) made a similar appraisal of his parish in 1801. He regarded his parishioners as perhaps "the most superstitious in all America." He complained especially of their extreme drunkenness, poor attendance at mass, animal sacrifices, desecration of holy garments with sacrificial blood, witchcraft, and other improper ceremonies. The subdelegado agreed that the whole district was prone to disobedience but said that the Indians were not so bad as the cura claimed. He considered the priest a major part of the problem. AGN Hist. 413, fols. 236–39.

19. AGN CRS 201 exp. 5.

20. AGN CRS 177 exp. 10.

21. AGN Acervo 49 caja 146, Oct. 6, 1816. According to the cura of Pilcayan parish, over half the 216 people who had not taken communion in 1802 were hacienda residents. Acervo 49 caja 45.

22. AGN CRS 131 exp. 1. Other cases of mass refusal to confess in resistance to the

cura or church policy include CRS 204 exp. 5, 1740, Tixtla (cura accused parishioners of noncompliance during a suit over cofradías and clerical fees); CRS 156 exp. 7, 1761, San Miguel Acambay (Indians stopped doing the Easter duty in protest over the division of the parish); AGN Crim. 203 exp. 4, 1778, Tepoztlan (less than half the parishioners were even attending mass, and a campaign to have the cura removed was under way); AGN Templos 1 exp. 2, 1786–88 (few of Guayacocotla y Chicontepec cura Ladrón de Guevara's Indian parishioners had confessed or taken communion during Lent in 1786; they had lodged a complaint against him for forced labor and mistreatment early in the year and, according to an Indian witness from the Rancho de Huixtlzapoli, he and his son had been discouraged from confessing by the leaders in the suit against the priest when they were on their way to the cabecera to do so); CRS 136 exps. 6–7, 1790–91, San Francisco Temascaltepec (cura accused parishioners of noncompliance during a suit over cofradías and clerical fees); CRS 57 exp. 4, 1796–99, Xichú (countercharges against the cura for mistreatment after he had entered a suit against the parishioners for failure to meet their obligations; the parish was divided over him, and he alleged that his accusers were mulatos who did not belong in the community); and AGN Acervo 49 caja 146, Aug. 26, 1816, Jonacatepec (cura Joseph Manuel de Sotomayor reported that a third of his parishioners had not fulfilled the Easter duty despite a mission of Fernandines and his other efforts; he blamed the wantonness of the military unit stationed there and the fact that none of the soldiers had confessed).

23. The bishop of Oaxaca in 1777 commented that many Indians were not allowed to confess or take communion because of their ignorance of Catholic doctrine. AGN RCO 126 exp. 137. I have not found similar statements for Mexico or Guadalajara, or much evidence that parishioners were turned away from the confessional by priests for lacking sufficient knowledge of the faith. Other circumstances that contributed to the evasion of confession were priests charging fees for the service and fear of harsh punishment from especially stern priests. An example of a priest being too exacting is AGN Hist. 578A, 1793, Huichapan report, Ygnacio Sánchez.

24. AJANG Civil, box 36, doc. 7.

25. In the words of one district governor, "An Indian would rather die . . . than confess through an interpreter." AGN Hist. 578A, 1793, Ixmiquilpan report.

26. AGN CRS 39 exp. 6, 1806, Santiago Amatepec, Tezontepec parish, Villa Alta district (Oaxaca).

27. AGN Crim. 148 exp. 2. Perhaps the people of Almoloya were not as ignorant of Spanish as they seemed. Their nonparticipation might be explained by the fact that they were in the midst of a bitter dispute with the cura over fees and his use of force.

28. BMM 271, ch. 7.

29. AGN Hist. 128 exp. 7.

30. Tulane VEMC 24 exp. 2. This case exposes the difficulty of interpreting the generalizations of a parish priest or his parishioners in administrative and judicial records. Morales had direct experience of religious practices in an Indian parish, and his observations have some of the bite and specificity that reflect that experience. But his predecessor, Cristóbal Mendoza, then the rector of the Colegio at Tepotzotlan, responded that Morales was a victim of self-deception rooted in excessive zeal (not to mention the attention this alarmist report might draw to an ambitious young priest from a reforming, regalist archbishop). The lay people of this parish were not such devious, shallow Christians as the cura held, in Mendoza's judgment. True, the Indians of Tlaola were afraid to confess, but they attended mass, said their prayers, and took communion. Mendoza's commentary is sensible, but he was hardly a disinterested party in the matter. Without more information about that place and time, the differences between the Morales and Mendoza versions of the religious practices of the Indians of Tlaola cannot be reconciled.

31. John Carter Brown Lib., Spanish Codex Coll., no. 52, fol. 226v.

32. The cura of Sultepec in 1757 probably spoke for most of his fellow pastors when he said that his Indian parishioners were not ardent Catholics, that he was disappointed by their attendance at mass and their failure to confess regularly. AGN CRS 156 exp. 4. In places where mass was not paid for from mandatory derramas, the administrative and judicial record for village practices regarding attendance at mass reads much like this description of confessions. Cases in which mass was not allowed by the parishioners usually occurred during larger disputes with the cura. CRS 42 exp. 1, fol. 31, 1732, Tejupilco; AGN Templos 25 exp. 4, fol. 308, 1769, Tlayacapan. Some did not comply because of fear or hatred of the parish priests. AGN Tierras 2774 exp. 9, fol. 3r, 1749, Huazalingo; AGN Crim. 202 exp. 1, fol. 171r, 1789, Tixmadeje, Huichapan district. Others were discouraged from attending by a district lieutenant or a local leader or hacendado. Crim. 25 exp. 23, 1773, Xilotepec (lieutenant); Manuel Pérez, p. 49 (compadres and patrones); Templos 1 exp. 4, fol. 249r, 1806–8 Xalpatlahuaca, Tlapa district (gobernador); Crim. 111 exp. 3, 1777, Tultitlan, Tacuba district; AJANG Civil, box 90, doc. 16, 1776, Tuxpan.

In parishes where collections were made for mass, the usual excuse for boycotts and refusals to pay was poverty. CRS 68 exp. 1, 1759, Teoloyucan, Cuautitlan district; CRS 67 exp. 3, 1768, Joloapan, Tetepango district; Tulane VEMC 66 exp. 5, 1775, Zumpango (cura reportedly overcharged); CRS 84 exp. 3, 1780, Tlacochahuaya, Cuernavaca district; AGN RCO 190 exp. 133, 1803, Villa de Medellín (Puebla).

There could be other reasons not to attend mass, as when district governors patrolled the church grounds waiting to arrest parishioners who had not paid the tribute or other taxes (BMM 135, exp. 16, 1734, Toluca; Crim. 304, fol. 150, 1767, Papantla) or because parishioners were too drunk to attend (AGI Mex. 877, 1726 report on the parish of Jalatlaco, Oaxaca; AHJ Manuscripts, no. G-4-802, Dec. 7, 1815, Zacatecas, letter from Josef Ignacio Bustamante to bishop of Guadalajara; Tierras 2179 exp. 3, 1756, Xilotepec, Tula district (case against Indian alcalde for beating a woman; in his defense, the alcalde said the charge was brought in revenge for his vigilance against Indian vices, especially the gatherings of people in taverns during mass and lack of church attendance). Sunday markets could both encourage and discourage attendance at mass. In the parish of San Juan Yagila in the Villa Alta district of Oaxaca, people from visitas would come to mass in the cabecera only if there was a Sunday market. Tierras 2771 exp. 5, 1780. For Atotonilco el Alto in 1789, people went to market elsewhere, leaving few behind to attend mass. AJANG Civil, box 117, doc. 4.

33. Tulane VEMC 66 exp. 5, 1775, Zumpango; AGN CRS 188 exp. 7, 1790, Tlacotalpan (Veracruz). There were growing gender differences in participation in rural, mainly Indian parishes. Men much more than women tended to reject the formal ideology of Catholicism (especially original sin, and ideas about pollution and purification) by the late colonial period, and to skip mass. At Huauchinango (northern Veracruz) in 1790, the pastoral visitor noticed "el intolerable y abominable abuso de ponerse varios hombres de todas calidades y estados en el cementerio y arcos a notar murmurar y sindicar a las pobres mugeres que van a misa los días festivos sobre si van bien o mal vestidas y sobre otros puntos que no es justo individualizar de que nace que algunas no se atreven a ir a misa y otras se enfadan y tal vez con el mal exemplo de los hombres padecen ruina espiritual." AHM L10B/26, fol. 96.

Even in less-acculturated parishes, men usually had the lead in public—holding the offices, serving at the altar, and the like—and were thus the ones priests were likely to identify as allies or enemies, although in the late 18th century, a parish priest would sometimes speak of relying on a particular woman as an invaluable ally in promoting the liturgy and combating drunkenness. The parish priest of Tzontecomatlan singled out María Josefa in this way in 1792, but their collaboration led to rumors of illicit sexual relations between them. AHM L10B/27, fol. 198v. As midwives, women were in the best position to administer conditional baptism; they usually dressed the images in church, were more attached than men to female saints other than the Virgin Mary, may have taken more responsibility for worship at home, and were more likely to confess during the year; and wives in troubled marriages more often than husbands turned to priests for protection and remedy (if the petitions to pastoral visitors are a reliable indication). In most respects, however, the differences were still outweighed by the common and complementary practices. Parish priests and lay witnesses drew few distinctions between men and women in the matter of devotion, where one might have expected them to do so.

34. Tulane VEMC 24 exp. 2, 1790, Tlaola (midwife baptisms); AGN CRS 156 exp. 9, fols. 366ff, 1763–64, Zacualpan, Cuautla Amilpas district (fiesta without mass). Burying the dead was not necessarily an act of rebellion. When the cura of Olinalá in 1781 complained that his parishioners of Anathechan owed him fees for burial, their representatives replied that in principle fees were owed, but that since the cura had not come to their pueblo to perform the ceremony, they had buried the dead themselves. CRS 13 exp. 3. But it often clearly was, as when, according to the cura of Actopan in 1763, the gobernador urged people not to take cadavers to the church for burial but to throw them down the barrancas or hang them from trees. CRS 179 exp. 13. Parishioners of Ozoloapan and Huizquilucan also reportedly buried their own. AHM L10B/21, fols. 35v–40v, 92r–97v, 1779.

35. The most frequent complaint of late colonial parish priests in pueblos de indios was that lay people were tardy in paying for their fiestas, masses, and other services or declined to pay them for specious reasons. It was common for Indian parishioners to ask for marriages and burial on credit, then to pay the debt little by little. BMM 271 (1770), ch. 8; AGN CRS 75 exp. 3, 1774, Malacatepec parish, Metepec district. The bishop of Oaxaca summed up the clerical viewpoint on this kind of indebtedness in his Aug. 21, 1778, reply to an anonymous complaint against the alcaldes mayores and parish priests of the province: "the pastor's fees are paid late, badly, or never." AGN RCO 126 exp. 137. Many parish priests would have supported this judgment, like Antonio Arpide, Franciscan doctrinero of Xiuctepec in 1752, who lamented that Indians rushed off to remove faithful pastors who displeased them, and paid their fees badly or not at all. BMM 135 exp. 17, fols. 111–27. Cura Luis Antonio de Veas prefaced his summary of the income of Jiquipilco parish in 1773 with a bitter marginal comment about clerical fees: "Para no perder los derechos parroquiales se ha de saber que a excepción de mui pocos, todos son drogueros y que a fin de hacer drogas hacen los mayores esfuerzos, aunque sea difamando al cura, por lo que si posible es, pillarse los derechos antes que la fiesta se haga, que el novio se case, etc." AGN Acervo 49, caja 127, "Directorio de la parroquia Jiquipilco." For a Nueva Galicia example, see AJANG Civil, box 143, doc. 20, 1793, San Juan Alaya.

Though priests were under pressure to forgive debts, especially debts for spiritual services, out of charity, some found the conventional plea of poverty less than persuasive and were likely to attribute delays to the "malicia" of their Indian parishioners instead. AGN CRS 42 exp. 1, 1732, San Pedro Tejupilco, Temascaltepec district; CRS 204 exp. 3, fols. 146–53, 1726, Totolzintla, Tixtla district.

36. In 1796, the priest in Santa María Tututepec, Tulancingo district (where a millenarian movement had developed in 1769 and the Indians were still regarded as "disobedient and practicing a pernicious freedom"; Taylor, *Drinking*, p. 124), fearful for his life, spoke of one his predecessors being attacked with a "cloud of rocks" when he tried to calm a group of angry parishioners with the consecrated Host in his hands. AGN CRS 130 exp. 3, fols. 124ff.

37. By 1799, there was reportedly a santocal or home altar in every Indian house. Texas, García Coll., no. 273, "Apunte del genio, condición, y trabaxos de los yndios," fol. 1r. An example is the oratorio kept by an alcalde of San Gregorio in the jurisdiction of Xochi-

milco in 1736. AGN Crim. 49 exp. 30. Serna, p. 69, mentions Indians keeping images of saints in their houses, a point that Stephanie Wood takes up in detail in "Adopted Saints." Wood also develops the idea of late colonial Indians as sincere Christians in "Cosmic Conquest." Cline documents the early stages of Christianization from native wills and census records for Culhuacan and six Morelos communities in *Colonial Culhuacan* and "Spiritual Conquest." Bishops encouraged prayers and other devotions at home. In the Diocese of Michoacán, lay people were allowed to have holy water in their homes so they could cross themselves and sprinkle their children when they arose in the morning and again at bedtime to ward off the Devil. *Colección de las ordenanzas*, p. 154.

38. Pérez de Velasco, p. 53. Freeze, *Parish Clergy*, p. xxiv, quotes an early-19th-century Russian Orthodox priest to the same effect: "They work six days a week for the serf-owner, on the seventh for themselves, and they visit the Church only on main holidays. . . . As a result, they are without the slightest grasp of the faith, the Ten Commandments, or morality." Most parish priests in these two dioceses would not have said that their parishioners did not attend church on Sunday or could not recite the rudiments of the faith.

All Souls' Day—the Day of the Dead—also acquired a special importance in the practice of local religion, especially in the archdiocese, where it appears in the parish accounts as a special feast day sponsored by the pueblo with masses and other solemnities that made it more costly than most fiestas. As in modern practice, it was also a time for elaborate feasting by families in honor of their ancestors. See expenditures in the accounts for Jiquipilco for 1773 and the districts of Cempoala and Pachuca for 1775. AGN Acervo 49 caja 127 (1733); Tulane VEMC 7 exp. 5 and 63 exp. 19 (1775).

39. Even in the course of disputes with priests over sacramental fees, Indian parishioners expressed their wish for baptism and extreme unction (e.g., AGN Crim. 148 exp. 2, 1792, Almoloya, Tenango del Valle district). Occasionally, Indians would not present their children for baptism (e.g., AGN Inq. 1230 exp. 13, 1784, Tula—with good reason in this case). But with infant mortality a realistic prospect, and the belief that those who died without baptism would go to limbo instead of heaven, infant baptism was a particularly compelling sacrament.

40. AGN Inq. 1334 exp. 3, fol. 107r, 1796, Zacualpan (the Indians' only practice of religion supposedly was attendance at mass).

41. AGN CRS 156 exp. 1, 1756, San Gaspar, Metepec district; AGN RCO 93 exp. 103, 1768, Chacaltianguis, Cosamaloapan district; CRS 67 exp. 3 fols. 1–9, 1768, Joloapan, Tetepango district; CRS 178 exp. 9 fol. 294r, 1797, Yautepec.

42. AGN Templos 1 exp. 2, 1786, testimony of vecino Manuel Arispe of Rancho de Achichipique about the conduct of cura Nicolás Mariano Ladrón de Guevara.

43. AGN CRS 156 exp. 1, 1756, San Gaspar, Metepec district. In this dispute over clerical fees, the Indian representatives claimed that many couples did not marry because of the high fees and the failure of curas to follow the formal agreement (*convenio*) made with the Franciscan doctrinero in 1749. (This community in fact refused to request any of the sacraments during the course of this lawsuit.) Other examples of villagers avoiding marriage because of high fees are AGN CRS 204 exp. 3, 1726, Totolzintla, Tixtla district; AGN RCO 93 exp. 103, 1768, Chacaltianguis, Cosamaloapan district; CRS 30 exp. 2, 1774, Xocutla, Chilapa district (the marriage fee in this case was 16p); CRS 204 exp. 3, 1726, Totolzintla, Tixtla district; and CRS 178 exp. 9, 1797, Yautepec. Another reason for more baptisms and last rites than marriages may have been that before marriage, the couple was expected to demonstrate an adequate understanding of church doctrine. Infant baptism and last rites did not call for such an examination, but I have not found many priests saying that they denied marriages because the couple was not adequately prepared in doctrina.

44. AGN CRS 203 exp. 4. The question then arises how children of common-law unions could receive baptism. The answer may be that only the godparents would bring

the infant to the ceremony. In 1784, a fellow priest accused cura Francisco del Villar of Tula of detaining the godparents in such cases until they divulged the names of the parents. The rumor was that this was his way of forcing the couple to marry and pay him the fee. AGN Inq. 1230 exp. 13.

45. Torres, p. 97; Mota y Escobar, p. 33.

46. Navarro de Vargas, p. 570 ("que eran Matronas Benerables, las quales le ayudaron varonilmente").

47. AGN CRS 130 exp. 9, fol. 400. Gregorio Alonso would have been a good candidate for Fr. José Díaz de la Vega's gallery of Christian Indian heroes. BMM 240, "Memorias piadosas de la nación yndiana recogidas de varios autores . . . 1782." Díaz de la Vega concentrated on the most brilliantly successful, especially those who became church dignitaries or prelates, but he occasionally included an exemplary villager, like Salvadora de los Santos (ch. 12), an Otomí noblewoman from Querétaro who was known for her pious works, especially in the epidemic of 1772, and for her powers of predicting the future.

48. AGN CRS 156 exp. 5.

49. AGN RCO 126 exp. 137.

50. Summary information about these additional expenses in the districts of Cempoala and Pachuca in 1775 is available in Tulane VEMC 7 exp. 5 and 63 exp. 19.

51. AGN Hist. 319 exp. 15.

52. AGN Templos 25 exp. 2, fol. 38r. Yet another instance is the complaint of the native leaders of Zacualtipan, Meztitlan district, in 1799 of the cura's "unrestrained avarice [and] caprice," and the free rein he gave to his whims. Templos 25 exp. 9, fols. 8ff.

53. AGN CRS 75 exp. 3.

54. AGN Bienes 575 exp. 46.

55. Serna, p. 16; pastoral letter of Archbishop Lizana, March 1, 1803, p. 11; Lombide, "Instrucción al defensor," in AJANG Criminal, bundle labeled "1800, leg. 1" (undated 19-folio expediente). Lombide's retort to the wolf metaphor was to turn it on its head: "Rather, I merited the name of unfortunate pastor who had to shepherd wolves rather than sheep." In accusing the Franciscan doctrinero of Poncitlan of solicitation in the confessional, Dr. Thomas Cuber y Linián charged that "in the guise of a shepherd, he committed the depredations of a wolf." AGN Inq. 914 exp. 15, fols. 143–56, 1758. Zeph. 3:3 and Jer. 5:6 are two of several verses in the Old Testament that identify wolves as enemies of the flocks and a symbol of the punishment to be visited on the Jews for their sins.

56. AGN CRS 75 exp. 5. An earlier case in point from Tlajomulco in the Diocese of Guadalajara is discussed in Calvo, pp. 173–82.

57. AGN CRS 75 exp. 5, 1785–88. This case took up an issue that had been pending since 1785. At that time, the archbishop's court ordered the cura to provide all the services required, and the Indians to fulfill their obligations, but it had not reinstated the vicario de pie fijo on the grounds the pueblo had waited four years before complaining about the termination of the post.

58. AGN Bienes 663 exp. 4.

59. AGN Crim. 71 exp. 6, fol. 172v. The cura was somewhat out of touch as well as out of sympathy with this tradition. He referred to the famous Franciscan as "Luis de Valencia."

60. AGN DP 2 exp. 4, fol. 313r. Another example of parishioners declaring that the church was theirs is DP 1 exp. 1, fol. 90 and passim, 1671, Xochitepec and Alpoyecan, Cuernavaca district. The Indians of these pueblos hid the church ornaments and stopped attending services over a fee dispute with the Franciscan pastors. The tension over who the church buildings belonged to helps to explain the great interest of late colonial parish priests in rebuilding and adding to the existing structures—so that the building would become at least partly theirs. A logical extension of the disputes against curas in these terms

of Christian doctrine and feelings of superiority as Christians was to press for the ordination of local men. I have not seen petitions to this effect for Mexico or Guadalajara, but one for Chacaltianguis (Oaxaca) in 1768 appears in AGN RCO 93 exp. 103.

61. AGN Crim. 79 exp. 1, fol. 6r.

62. AGN Templos 25 exp. 11 ("Todos estamos tristes, confusos y consternados a el concidurar sólo que se nos hallan de prohivir tan sagrados auxilios y mucho más sube de punto nuestra consternación si concideramos no encontrar amparo que nos protexa").

63. AGN CRS 217 exp. 6. As usual, the matter was not as simple as the Indian leaders and the lieutenant made out. The lieutenant was locked in a bitter rivalry with the cura, and the parishioners had been at odds with the cura over mistreatment, fees, and the annual elections. This triangle of contention is discussed in detail in Part Four. Another example of parishioners seeking more adequate spiritual services is CAAG, cofradía records for Santa Fe, 1764 (request that the bishop order the cura to go to Santa Fe once a month to celebrate mass sponsored by a local cofradía at 18p a year). Rancheros in the Diocese of Guadalajara were famous for their religious zeal after independence. An example of the same zeal in the 18th century is the eloquent appeal for a cura by vecinos of the Valle de Mesticacan, Nochistlan district, in 1755, so that they would live and die as Christians. AHJ Manuscripts, no. G-4719 GUA/4.

64. AGN Crim. 166, fols. 185–272.

65. AGI Mex. 2588, Jan. 26, 1784, report, fol. 9r.

66. AGN CRS 126 exp. 12, 1809, Tanicpatlan, Ichcateopan district (example of when the cura was unable to stem violence with a saintly symbol).

67. For an example of village leaders in search of a father to guide them ("We lack a lord who will guide us, and so we go along like orphaned and lost youths"—no tenemos Sor quien nos dirija pues andamos como unos jóvenes huérfanos y perdidos), see AJANG Civil, box 223, doc. 10, 1801, Tlajomulco.

68. Tulane, Mexican Administrative Records, vol. 38, patronato de oficio records, March 18, 1728.

69. AGN CRS 192 exp. 3.

70. AGN Bienes 172 exp. 37, 1805. The court acknowledged the priest's blameless pastoral work but was less impressed by his personal qualities. In a secret report by José Antonio de la Vega, he was judged "cheerful but violent and erratic" (alegre pero violento e inconstante) and of an "effeminate temperament." Other late colonial examples are AGN Hist. 578A, 1793, Tezontepec, Pachuca report ("muchas exprecciones de sus feligreses que sentirían su ceparación o transporte a otro curato"); CAAG, unclassified, undated petition (ca. 1800) by Indians of La Barca for their much-loved cura to remain; and AGN CRS 192 exp. 3, n.d. (ca. 1802), Miacatlan, Mazatepec parish, Cuernavaca district.

71. AJANG Criminal, bundle labeled "1824, leg. 2 (38)."

72. There was a factional split over the cura of Miacatlan in 1803, to cite one example. AGN CRS 192 exp. 3.

73. AGN CRS 74 exp. 11. The people of Amanalco had a history of strained relations with their parish priests, including a tumulto in 1792 that led the cura to flee the district. AHM L10B/14, fol. 104v.

74. Arze, n.p. The 16th-century bishop Vasco de Quiroga is a more famous example of a cleric who was warmly remembered centuries after his death. Moxó, p. 229, wrote this late colonial appreciation (1805) of him: "Y ¿qué diré de los indios del vecino reyno de Michoacán? ¿Cuán grande, cuán extraordinario es el reconocimiento que profesan a su primer obispo el venerable Señor Don Vasco de Quiroga, que murió el en año de 1556? ¿No es cosa que causa asombro ver que después de dos siglos y medio no se ha entibiado todavía en los corazones de aquellos naturales el antiguo afecto acia su grande amigo y protector? ¿Que hablan de Quiroga, como si le estuviesen aun mirando? ¿Que cuentan la

historia de los increíbles favores que le debieron sus antepasados, como si ellos mismos hubiesen sido testigos de estos remotísimos sucesos?"

75. AGN Tierras 2670 exp. 5. The court responded quickly, ordering that Alcántara's wife, whom the priest had arrested in the dispute, be released, and that the district judge report on the larger issue within six days.

76. AGN CRS 75 exp. 4.

77. AJANG Criminal, bundle labeled "1824, leg. 2 (38)," "Desavenencia entre habitantes por la venida del cura Miguel Márquez."

78. AJANG Civil, box 143, doc. 20. When a cura berated the Indian gobernador of Cuaunacuacacingo (Cuanacalcingo/Pueblo Nuevo), Cuernavaca district, in 1775 for persisting in a lawsuit against him over fees, the gobernador responded (according to the cura) that "the *cura* would eventually leave, while he would still be there to pursue the litigation." AGN CRS 68 exps. 4–5, fols. 366ff.

79. AGN CRS 72 exp. 7, fol. 123. In reply to the complaint by parishioners of San Pedro Tejupilco in 1732 that he was charging excessive fees, the cura said that the pueblo of San Lucas owed him 170p in back fees, and he wanted them paid. The Indians were malicious more than poor, he claimed. They delayed and delayed "so that with the passage of time [the debts] would be forgotten." CRS 42 exp. 1.

80. Moxó, pp. 205–6, remarked that Mexican Indians had a particular passion for *romerías*. He was thinking especially of the long-distance travels to famous shrines, but the statement would hold even better for the shorter journeys to shrines in the district and the processions of saints and lay people in and near their pueblos.

81. It was the church hierarchy's intention that parish priests keep close watch over religious festivals in America, as their counterparts in Spain were expected to do. This meant above all Indian fiestas. The Second Provincial Council in 1565 specifically directed that Indians not have processions unless their parish priest was present. *Concilios provinciales primero, y segundo,* p. 194. Similar concerns were repeated throughout the colonial period, For Michoacán in the late 17th century, see *Colección de ordenanzas,* pp. 234–35. A characteristic cura's complaint about local processions acquiring a life of their own separate from his authority is in CAAG, 1802 records of the Cofradía de la Purísima Concepción of Ixtlahuacan (Jalisco), where the cura reported that the Indians of Ixtlahuacan went out "in processions by themselves without the accompaniment of a priest. They go into the fields and the streets of the pueblos 'on visits' or to fulfill a vow, the women carrying the images with notable indecency." The cura did not say whether the indecency resulted from the manner in which the images were carried or the fact that women carried them, but it was presumably the latter. Parish priests were sometimes blamed for failing to control these activities, as if they, alone, could do so. A peninsular friar at Churubusco in 1810 blamed the parish priests for allowing unruly processions and fiestas. Tulane VEMC 70 exp. 64. In 1793, the subdelegado of Ixmiquilpan blamed an assistant pastor for not eliminating night processions that created problems for law enforcement. AGN Hist. 578A, 1793, Ixmiquilpan report. (But as we will see later in this chapter, it could be dangerous to interfere with local traditions of procession.)

My focus on rural parishes, especially pueblos de indios, is not meant to suggest that urban fiestas and processions were less important. Mexico City, in particular, was famous for its pageantry and public commotions on the great religious feast days. See Rockefeller Lib., Brown Univ., Medina Coll., FHA 15 exp. 2, corregidor's circular of Feb. 10, 1789; and Sutro Library, Felipe Zúñiga y Ontiveros, "Efemérides," 1763–74, entry for June 1767 (estimate that 5,000 people took part in the Corpus Christi procession in 1767).

82. *Concilios provinciales, primero y segundo,* 1555, pp. 65–69.

83. The obligatory feast days for non-Indians according to the Fourth Provincial Council in 1771 were Sundays; the moveable feasts of Resurrection Sunday, Christ's Ascension,

Pentecost Sunday and the two days thereafter, and Corpus Christi; and the fixed feasts in honor of the Circumcision of Christ and Epiphany (January), the Purification of Mary (February), Saint Joseph and the Annunciation (March), the birth of Saint John the Baptist and Saint Peter and Saint Paul (June), San Hipólito (Mexico City only) and the Assumption of the Virgin (August), the birth of Mary (September), All Saints' Day (November), and the Immaculate Conception, the Day of the Virgin of Guadalupe, Christmas, and Saint Stephen (December). Indians were not obliged to celebrate seven of these days: Saint Joseph, the birth of Saint John the Baptist, San Hipólito, All Saints, the Immaculate Conception, the Virgin of Guadalupe, and Saint Stephen. CPM, pp. 146–57.

84. Tulane VEMC 15 exp. 5. AGN Templos 25 exp. 11 lists the fiestas from which the parish priest derived income for his services in San Nicolás Oztoticpac during 1807: fiesta titular (yielding 25p); Palm Sunday high mass, procession, and blessing of the fronds (5p); Feast of the Purification of the Virgin (4p); Holy Saturday (5p); Ash Wednesday (4p); high masses during Lent (6p); high mass on the Day of Saint Joseph (3p); low masses on the Monday, Tuesday, Wednesday, and Friday of Easter week (2p each); sermon on Good Friday (5p); Easter Sunday (6p); the Feast of the Holy Spirit (6p); the Day of the Assumption of Christ (2p); the Day of the Holy Trinity (3p); the Day of Saint Peter and Saint Paul (2p); the Day of the birth of Mary (3p; on this day the feast of Our Lady of Guadalupe was also celebrated at a cost of 15p); All Souls' Day (5p 2rr); the Day of San Nicolás Obispo (3p); Christmas (10p). He also received fees on the patron saints' days of the visitas.

85. The 300–1,000 peso range for annual fiesta expenses is based on figures for priest's revenues from fiestas in rural parishes of Pachuca district in 1776, and assumes that the priest's revenue was roughly a quarter of total expenditures. Tulane VEMC 7 exp. 5.

86. BEJ Papeles de Derecho, 1: 573v–580.

87. AGI Guad. 352, cuad. 1, "Autos formados sobre los bienes de comunidad . . . de la Nueva Galicia" (after 1786), fol. 86v.

88. AGN Civil 1485 exp. 13, 1782, Azcapotzalco. Another example of a república feast is AGN CRS 192 exps. 11–12, 1760, Almoloya, Tenango del Valle district.

89. Arze, n.p. The Dominican doctrinero of Azcapotzalco in 1799 said local Indians had to take advances from haciendas to pay the fiesta expenses, which obligated them to long terms of debt servitude. AGN CRS 84 exp. 5. The subdelegado of Atotonilco el Alto reported in 1791 that the local Indians spent virtually all of their ready cash on fiestas. AJANG Civil, bundle labeled "1791–98, leg. 20 (175)" (suit brought against Indians of Atotonilco el Alto in 1791 "por no haber sacado en la cuaresma el paso de Santa Rosa").

90. AGN CRS 156 exps. 2–3. In 1760, Indians of Tejupilco complained that their cura was trying to institutionalize the feast of the Virgin of Guadalupe and add charges to other festivities. CRS 156 exp. 5. In a sweeping statement, the intendant for Michoacán criticized the clergy in his territory for introducing many new fiestas in order to increase their incomes. AGN Hist. 578A, 1793, Michoacán report. In 1794, an anonymous letter complained on behalf of the pueblos of San Angel, Xochimilco, Tacuba, Tlalnepantla, and Azcapotzalco that the local priests forced them to supply companies of mock soldiers to serve during Holy Week. Hist. 437, "Quexa anónima a nombre de los pobres . . ."

91. AGN Civil 2095 exp. 4, 1790, San Miguel Almoloya, Tenango del Valle district.

92. AGN CRS 130 exp. 3, fol. 71v.

93. Ibid., exp. 5. In another case, the cura of Hueyapan in the late 1760's reported that his Indian parishioners resisted celebrating even the feast of the patron saint and had stopped paying fees for the fiestas they did celebrate. AGN CRS 72 exp. 7.

94. Lorenzana, *Cartas pastorales*, edict 12; CPM, pp. 116, 118.

95. AGN Bandos 15 exp. 30, Nov. 17, 1789, (May 2, 1789 cedula); Rockefeller Lib., Brown Univ., Medina Coll., FHA 55 exps. 8, 50 (March 23, 1790, April 16, 1791, cedulas). In 1790, the fiscal of the Audiencia of Mexico called for reducing the number of fiestas; the

intendant of Guadalajara and various subdelegados followed suit in 1791. Tulane VEMC 73 exp. 41; AGI Guad. 352. The intendant of Guadalajara renewed his campaign in 1796, instructing subdelegados to allow only the fiestas of Corpus Christi and the patron saint to be celebrated with funds from the community treasury. He asserted that expensive fiestas were the "primary cause of the [local treasuries'] destruction" and called on parish priests, as well as district governors, to "eradicate these entrenched abuses of the Indians." AHJ AMAJ, packet 8, copy of circular to subdelegados in 1816 libro de demandas de tierras.

96. In the early 16th century, what worried the clergy even more than the goings-on outside the church were the ecstatic mass flagellations and, to their eyes, profane communion that could take place inside. Clendinnen, "Ways to the Sacred," sheds new light on the likely meaning of these and other Indian religious practices of the period.

97. "Apéndice a los concilios primero y segundo," pp. 314–15.

98. BEJ Papeles de Derecho, 4: 165–76.

99. Bullfighting in pueblos de indios of Morelos is considered further in App. C. See AGN Indios 15 cuad. 2 exp. 45, 1649 (Indians of San Juan Parangaricúytiro and Santiago Tragavandela, Michoacán, given permission to celebrate their fiestas as usual, dressing up as soldiers with blunderbusses and other weapons, wearing masks, and putting on bullfights—juegan toros—and "various dances with guitars and other musical instruments"); and AJANG Criminal, box 8, doc. 6, 1805, Tlaltenango (Indians said to like to "correr sus toros").

100. Priests were especially concerned about the implications for social disorder when Indian leaders, like the alcalde de San Gregorio, Xochimilco district in 1736, and the gobernor of Tultitlan, Tacuba, in 1777, drank heavily or sold liquor. AGN Crim. 49 exp. 30, 1736; Crim. 111 exp. 3, 1777. The cura of Huizquilucan in the 1760's associated his parishioners' general disobedience with liquor. He claimed that distilled drinks were sold just outside the church doors on Sundays, and that most of the men got drunk instead of attending mass. Crim. 120 exp. 25. For a fuller discussion of official views on Indian abuse of alcohol, see Taylor, *Drinking*, ch. 2.

101. Pérez de Velasco, pp. 49ff. His point to confessors was that the term in Nahuatl for "I became drunk"—Onitlahuan—could mean moderate drinking to cool off from the heat, social drinking without drunkenness, heavy drinking with slurred speech and diminished motor control, or drinking to the point of passing out. Querying Nahuatl-speaking Indians in their language about drinking, he warned, was likely to result in a misleading catalogue of drinking occasions.

102. Malinchis: AJANG Criminal, bundle labeled "1811, leg. 1 (39)," 1808, Teocaltiche (report of homicide of José María Hernández). Tlaxilacalis: CAAG, typescript copy of Domingo Aldaz Hernández's June 1689 report on the parish of Tapalpa. Huehuentris o Tlaxcaltecos: AGN Crim. 25 exp. 23, 1773, Xilotepec. Live passion of Christ, Nescuitiles, Palo del Volador: Lorenzana, *Cartas, edictos*, Feb. 11, 1769, pastoral letter. Tastuanes: AJANG Civil, bundle labeled "1800–19 (109)," 1815, San Andrés, Tlaquepaque district. Danza de los Negros: AJANG Criminal, bundle labeled "1800–01," 1801, Sayula (masked dancers murdered a spectator). Santiaguitos, Moros y Cristianos: Warman, *Danza*, passim; AGN CRS 156 exp. 9, 1763, Zacualpa, Cuautla Amilpas district; Crim. 120 exp. 25, 1769, Tescaluca, Huizquilucan. Matachines: AJANG Civil, box 231, doc. 1, 1804, Ocotlan.

103. Matachines has become a common term for fiesta dancers in Mexican pueblos. Toor, p. 336, writes of a society of matachín dancers who called themselves the "Soldiers of the Virgin," again reflecting the martial character of most dances. Games were another kind of fiesta "performance." At Nochistlan (Jalisco), Indian witnesses in a 1788 investigation of local drinking and the effects of obrajes recently established there said that they played a game called jugar a la conta, in which a flaming ball was moved from place to place with sticks. AJANG Criminal, bundle labeled "1700–93, leg. 84 (16)."

104. Masks are mentioned with some concern but no indication of the precolonial tradition in AGN Indios 15 cuad. 2, exp. 45, San Juan Parangaricúytiro, 1649; AGN Hist. 319 exp. 18, 1782, Zapotlan el Grande; AJANG Criminal, bundle labeled "1800–01," 1804, Sayula; AJANG Civil, bundle labeled "1800–10, leg. 3 (109)," Aug. 21, 1815, petition by the officials of San Andrés, Tlaquepaque district, and the subdelegado's report.

105. Taylor, *Drinking*, ch. 2. Examples of heavy drinking in public and private fiestas: Texas, W. B. Stephens Coll., no. 537, p. 99, 1771, Xaltocan; Tulane VEMC 62 exp. 1, 1796, Capuluac; AGN Crim. 29 exp. 6, 1796, Xochitepec, Xochimilco district; AJANG Criminal, bundle labeled "1811, leg. 1 (39)," 1801, Sayula (murder case against José Asencio Aldan); AGN Crim. 71 exp. 6, 1806, Amecameca. Responding to official concern about drunken disorders and generally unseemly conduct during Holy Week, the Fourth Provincial Council called for "greater order" and renewed emphasis on spiritual rather than mundane high spirits by not allowing liquor or food to be sold in the cemeteries during the procession of Christ's crucified body. CPM, pp. 161.

106. In 1762, for example, the Indians of San Andrés, Tenango del Valle district, chased the district governor's lieutenant and his two alguaciles out of town when they came searching for tepache on the day of the fiesta titular. At one house, the lieutenant reported finding many Indian men and women getting drunk around a big pot of tepache. AGN Crim. 123 exp. 21.

107. Texas, W. B. Stephens Coll., no. 537, pp. 75–117. Replacing a soldier's outfit with a candle (a symbol of penitence and purity) was an effort to focus the participant's attention on the spiritual significance of the Easter season. The Fourth Provincial Council intended to control fiesta excesses—whether mundane excesses like drinking and extravagant dress or excesses of mortification with the lash that seemed to the prelates more barbaric than devout—in much the same way by having participants in processions carry symbols of mortification and purification. CPM, p. 161.

108. Tulane VEMC 62 exp. 1. This complaint led to an order from the archbishop that all parish churches close at 10:00 P.M. on Thursday and Friday of Holy Week.

109. AGN CRS 206 exp. 3. The cura placed particular emphasis on the practice of maintaining lighted candles for the saints. Even in cathedrals, he observed, the lamp of the sacrament was kept lit.

110. AGN CRS 84 exp. 5.

111. AJANG Criminal, bundle labeled "1820–21, leg. 60 (84)." At the inquest it could not be established who struck the fatal blow.

112. Taylor, *Drinking*, chs. 2–3.

113. AJANG Criminal, bundle labeled "1810, leg. 3 (15)."

114. Ibid., bundle labeled "1819 (52)."

115. In 1794, cura Martín de Verdugo of Cuernavaca listed the fireworks used in the major religious feasts at Yautepec as "cohetes, boladores, y buscapiés, cámaras, bombas, arboleras, ruedas." The first three were flying, fiery missiles, which he regarded as especially dangerous and wanted banned. AGN Hist. 132 exp. 27, Jan. 19, 1794, report. Ysidro Gómez Tortolero, pastor at San Pedro Lagunillas, Compostela district, in 1808 complained that his parishioners squandered their church funds on fireworks, drink, and fandangos instead of the spiritual necessities; and the accounts of the Immaculate Conception cofradía for Ixtlahuacan (Jalisco) for expenses in the Corpus Christi and patron saint festivities in 1801 note expenses for "whistles, drums, and fireworks." AHJ Manuscripts, no. G-4-802, Sept. 19, 1808, July 22, 1801. The creole estate owner elected to the post of captain of the armed forces for the Easter week festivities in 1773 complained about the heavy burden of expenses, which included three to four pounds of gunpowder. Texas, W. B. Stephens Coll., doc. 537, pp. 75–118, Zumpango.

116. Brandes, "Fireworks," pp. 186–87.

117. Clendinnen, "Ways to the Sacred," pp. 105–30.

118. AGN Bandos 11 exp. 63.

119. BEJ Papeles de Derecho, 4: 165–76, "El comandante Governador de Guadalajara representa a VM los males que ocasiona no tener los jueces con qué subsistir y propone medios."

120. AGN CRS 206 exp. 3, fol. 202r.

121. AGN Crim. 71 exp. 6.

122. AJANG Criminal, box 45, doc. 6. Gallos seem to have been mostly urban and non-Indian, as suggested, for example, by AJANG Criminal, bundle labeled "1798 (125)," concerning the homicide of José Guillermo Velásquez of the barrio San José Analco in Guadalajara on Sept. 15, 1793, during "a gallo that was wandering through that barrio."

123. AJANG Civil, box 140, doc. 5, 1791.

124. In 1808, the cura of San Pedro Lagunillas, Compostela district, complained of "the continuous disorders from fandangos, card games, and drunkenness." AHJ Manuscripts, no. G-4-802, Sept. 9, 1808. Though the descriptions in the following pages come from the Diocese of Guadalajara, fandangos were popular in parts of the archdiocese as well. Fandangos are mentioned in late colonial records for districts of the modern state of Morelos, and in 1773, the cura of Xilotepec complained that the lieutenant allowed fandangos day and night in the town, and gallos in the streets. AGN Crim. 25 exp. 23. Farther north, the cura of Valle de San Francisco (San Luis Potosí) in 1797 was concerned about the fandangos sponsored by the subdelegado with lower-class dancers and singers. Crim. 159, fols. 163–80.

125. AJANG Criminal, bundle labeled "1813, leg. 1 (23)."

126. Ibid., bundle labeled "1809, leg 1 (126)."

127. Ibid., bundle labeled "1819–20 (61)." Cruz was released from jail in Oct. 1820 with a formal pardon.

128. Ibid. Fandangos at houses of prostitution produced a share of belligerent drunks ready to pick a fight with anyone they came across. On Dec. 3, 1808, José María Meza Guerra, a mulato tributary of Sayula, had a night on the town, first visiting the house of "La Muerta," Josefa Macías Lugo, and ending up at the mezcal store, thoroughly drunk, shouting, brandishing his saber, and inviting a fight. José Agramontes, the alcalde de la cárcel, appeared and ordered Meza to stop in the name of the king. Full of his authority, Agramontes found Meza "disrespectful, rash, and daring" when he tried to arrest him. Agramontes drew his sword "in defense of the Royal Jurisdiction" and, in the confusion, ran Meza through, killing him outright. AJANG Criminal, bundle labeled "1808, leg. 48 (91)."

129. Menéndez Valdés, pp. 56–57, 77–79. Menéndez Valdés reported a population of 21,091 for the district.

130. For marriages, they went to the homes of the parents of both the bride and the groom.

131. AGN Hist. 319 exp. 18, 1782. Although Lepe criticized Alcalde Mayor Vicente de Leis y Oca's weak responses to Indian insolence and was, in turn, criticized by him for excessive zeal that made matters worse, the alcalde mayor's version of the fiesta behavior of Zapotlan's Indians is similar to Lepe's. When ordered by the audiencia to comment on Lepe's report, Leis y Oca naturally was more concerned about his own troubles with Indians not paying their tribute and appearing in threatening crowds at his door, but he agreed with the cura's account of their fiesta behavior. He added that the Indians were disobedient to both officials in other ways. At that moment, he said, an Indian alcalde and the town scribe were under arrest for falsifying the cura's signature on an official document. Leis y Oca said he had been warned about Indian insolence in this district when he accepted the post, but it had been worse than he imagined. Though he thought the cura had aggravated the situation with rash actions, he agreed with him on the need for some

severe punishments to control the "pride and malice of these Indians." The fiscal of the audiencia recommended a less hasty course of action: warnings to all, and further investigations by the alcalde mayor that might firmly identify the leaders and serve as the basis for their trial and punishment.

132. AJANG Civil, box 143, doc. 5.

133. AJANG Criminal, box 45, doc. 6, 1793. Cura Joseph Buenavista de Estrada y Monteros of Jilotepec described gallos in 1773 as "desordenados fandangos que arman no sólo de día sino a desoras de la noche, corriendo ese alboroto que llaman vulgarmente gallo, por las calles públicas." AGN Crim. 25 exp. 23.

134. AGN Inq. 1318 exp. 5. The Inquisition declined to pursue the charges because most of them involved Indians, over whom it did not have jurisdiction, and the others were not clearly demonstrated.

135. AGN Hist. 132 exp. 22. Leis y Oca had been alcalde mayor since early 1781. The signatures of petitioners were all in one hand, perhaps that of the cura's notario receptor, José Antonio Alamán, who wrote a vehement denunciation of Leis y Oca later in the year.

136. AGN Inq. 1297 exp. 9.

137. AGN Hist. 578A, 1789 report by Intendant Juan Antonio de Riaño, and 1793 report by the subdelegado of Ixmiquilpan. In 1791, the subdelegado observed that Indians in and around Atotonilco el Alto were required to contribute to too many religious events. He sought support for his intention to enforce the recent royal laws on the number of fiestas to which they had to contribute. AJANG Civil, bundle labeled "1791–98, leg. 20 (175)." In 1769, the cura of Santa María Tututepec, Tulancingo district, complained to the audiencia that the teniente de justicia was influencing his Indian parishioners to stop supporting many of the customary fiestas. AGN CRS 130 exp. 3, fols. 69v–71v.

138. AGN Hist. 578A, 1793, Xochimilco report; AJANG Civil, box 80, doc. 2 (a particularly bitter dispute between an alcalde mayor and a cura over funeral processions in Sierra de Pinos, Zacatecas, in 1772); Civil, box 140, exp. 5, 1791, Juchipila.

Chapter Eleven

EPIGRAPH: Pérez de Velasco, pp. 76–77 (Veerá Vmd a un Indio, o India, hincado de rodillas en la grada de algun Altar, donde cita colocado un Crucifixo y advertirá, que enclavijadas las manos, suspirando, y bañado en lágrimas, le repite sus deprecaciones. Después se pone en pie, sube al altar, se acerca a la Imagen, le quiere llegar la mano, y retirándola en ademán de medroso, la besa, se signa con ella y se aparta. Y yo digo: Si este Indio después de tantas genuflexiones, tantas y tan expresivas demonstraciones de Devoción, le llega con tanto miedo a la Imagen, y no se atreve a llegar la mano, porque le parece osadía el tocar la Imagen de Jesu-Christo: Y vee que el Sacerdote, sin especial reverencia sin tiento, con much aceleración eleva, y baja la Hostia consagrada; que sin concierto, ni orden la bendice, y que después, al signar el Cáliz con ella, en varios descompasados reboloteos parece que la baila: Teniendo por su Maestro y Director al Ministro este Indio, ¿aprenderá en esta Misa el respecto, la reverencia que debe tener a Christo Señor Nuestro Sacramentado?)

1. The distinction between supplication and contrition was important to colonial priests. In the words of a Mexico City cura in 1779, "No es culto de Dios el dolor y sentimiento del pobre; no se hizo para la casa del Señor el que se labre con los sudores ajenos y miserables de los más desválidos de la tierra. Solo son para los altares los gemidos de un corazón arrepentido, no las lástimas y quejas de quien se mira despojado." Pérez Cancio, p. 151. It was one of the priests' standard criticisms of the religious practices of Indians during the colonial period.

2. See Nolan & Nolan.

3. On church edifices in medieval Europe as images or models of heaven, see von

Simson, especially pp. 8–9. In the 1743 reports of the archdiocese's parish priests, the more religious art approached "perfection," the more it became a passageway to the sacred. This was in the spirit of the Council of Trent decrees. Solano, 1: 251–52, 256, 262, 263.

4. As a mid-18th-century bishop of Michoacán put it, "Dios quiere hacer ostentación de su gran poder." Mazín, *Entre dos majestades*, p. 107.

5. Cook.

6. Tello, 3: 22.

7. Alcedo, 1: 49.

8. Although the relationship between saints and believers was intimate as well as reverential, the appeal for intercession was made with a pomp and solemnity that increased the distance between supplicant and saint, subject and authority. Believers probably approached them with even greater reverence, but the images that moved had given signs of divine presence, of readiness to hear.

9. Thanks to Nolan & Nolan, one can begin to speak more confidently of the cult of saints and images in Spain and Spanish America in comparison to each other and to practices in other parts of Western Europe. Shrines to miraculous found images of saints or Christ were especially common in Spain (pp. 257, 260). They were also common in Spanish America, although the short history of Christianity in America meant that few of the objects discovered in the colonial period had been known and lost, as they often were in Spain and Portugal. Iberian shrines associated with apparitions and found objects mostly were located on hilltops or hillsides with caves (p. 311). This was the usual pattern in Mesoamerica as well. These similarities are not necessarily American imitations of Spanish antecedents, but the similarities at least made the American manifestations familiar to Spanish authorities, and perhaps more acceptable to them. But whereas found-object shrines in Spain usually were built around an image of Mary, the crucifix was the more common cult found-object in central Mexico. Since Christ was presented to colonial Indians at the altars of their churches as an almost inaccessible figure, perhaps rural parishioners in some parts of Mesoamerica were especially open to signs of the Son of God's direct communication and patronage in the open air.

10. Sardo (Chalma); Kiracofe (Amecameca's Sacromonte). Mexico City was the home of a number of miraculous images of the crucified Christ, including the Santo Cristo de los Desagravios, which reputedly had sweated blood, the Señor de la Misericordia, and the self-restoring Santo Cristo de Santa Teresa, brought from Ixmiquilpan. Sedano, 1: 207; 2: 42–43, 174–75. Among the archdiocese's less famous shrines were the Sanctuary of the Crucified Christ of Cuezala in the Ichcateopan district; the miraculous Christ of Totolapa (northern Morelos); and the Santuario de Nuestra Señora de Tonatico in the parish of Ixtapan (Edo. de México). AGN Tierras 2431 exp. 6, 1790; AHM L10B/21, fols. 118r, 275v–276r. As the names of these sanctuaries suggest, the two great sources of miracles were crucifixes (or other images of Christ) and images of Mary. Solano, vols. 1–2, passim.

11. AHM L10B/28, fol. 107. For other images moved to a parish seat or urban location in the archdiocese at the behest of church officials, see Solano, 1: 46, 71, 127, 252; and 2: 478.

12. Escobar, pp. 463–69.

13. Other miracle-working crosses west of Lake Chapala at Sayula and Autlan were reported by Mota Padilla (1742), pp. 390–92. Bishop Alcalde referred to a Señor del Mesquite at Zacoalco, which he wanted moved to the parish church. AGI Guad. 341, record of visita pastoral, 1776. Farther south, in the district of Zapotlan el Grande, various crude images of Christ were much esteemed and put on display in Holy Week processions in the 1790's. AGN Inq. 1318 exp. 5, 1793. Lockhart, *Nahuas After the Conquest*, p. 245, also mentions the association of crosses with miracles.

14. CAAG, unclassified, 1721 exp., "Autos pertenecientes a la cofradía del Santo Cristo de la Expiración del pueblo de Jocotepec."

15. Everett Gee Jackson (p. 75), who saw the Santo Cristo de la Expiración image while traveling in the Chapala area in the 1920's, says of this "interesting piece of primitive sculpture": "Obviously some Indian had noticed that the form of a tree root with two branches above and one below had something in common with the form of a man's body. He had imagined just how to carve it here and there to bring about a closer resemblance, and then he had painted it black, and attached it to a crude cross." *Burros and Paintbrushes*, p. 75.

16. For his part in the forgery, Bernabé Rodríguez, the town scribe of Jocotepec and native of Tonalá, was exiled under penalty of 200 lashes if he returned.

17. AGN Tierras 1048 exp. 8.

18. Wood, "Adopted Saints," especially 278–91; Lockhart, *Nahuas After the Conquest*, pp. 235–51.

19. Christian, *Apparitions*, p. 14.

20. In many parishes, one person was made responsible for collections to support a saint. For example, in the San Diego barrio of Tlayacapan (Morelos), a woman was selected to be the "Madre Magna" of Our Lady of the Nativity. Her main responsibility was to collect napkins made by the unmarried girls of her neighborhood and the parcialidad of Tecpan, and present them to the cura to support the cult. This practice reached the ecclesiastical courts in 1769 because an Indian widow serving as the Madre Magna that year had not turned in the napkins, claiming that the parents refused to allow it on the grounds that they were paying many other church fees. AGN Templos 25 exp. 4. A tension between the parish priest and local cults of saints cannot be assumed, since he was sometimes the one who introduced parishioners to an unfamiliar saint or encouraged the devotion of one he especially favored in their existing stock of images. A saint might be pitted against the parish priest, but that may not have been common.

21. AGN Tierras 2621 exp. 6.

22. JCB.

23. *Concilios provinciales primero, y segundo*, p. 67. Saint Joseph's feast day was not obligatory for Indians (CPM, pp. 146–47), and by the late colonial period, he was a patron mainly of gente de razón. In the district of Pachuca (Hidalgo) in 1775, only gente de razón paid for the novena and feast for him. Tulane VEMC 7 exp. 5.

24. Motolinía, p. 173: "In this land the devotion of both Spaniards and natives to Saint Francis is so great, and God has in his name performed so many miracles and marvels, and so openly, that it may truly be said that God had reserved for him the conversion of those Indians."

25. AGN Inq. 1146 exp. 1, fol. 59. With more local parish histories on the order of López Lara's study of Zinapécuaro, Michoacán, a satisfying synthesis of this pivotal subject might be possible.

26. According to local tradition, Santiago had come to Spain to preach the gospel, and his martyred remains had later arrived from Jerusalem and been buried there. A great pilgrimage cult began in the 9th century at Compostela, with the discovery of the purported relics and subsequent stories of the apostle's personal appearance in a decisive victory over the Moors near Logroño. For an engaging introduction to the "creed" of Saint James in Spanish history and his position as the patron saint of Christian Spaniards, see Kendrick.

27. Weckmann, I: 149–51, lists 11 instances in which Santiago was invoked in battles against Indians in Mexico during the 16th century. An early tradition of Santiago appearing at a decisive moment for the Spanish in Mexico is recorded in the account of Cortés's secretary. According to López de Gómara (who never visited America), I: 92–93, a mysterious man on horseback appeared and vanished three times during a fierce Indian attack on Spaniards at Tabasco, to turn the native armies back until Cortés and reinforcements could come to the rescue. Some of the men believed that the unknown cavalryman was

"the apostle Santiago, patron saint of Spain." Cortés preferred to think it was Saint Peter, his special guardian. Either way, says López de Gómara, it was judged a miracle. At p. 85 of the preceding chapter, López de Gómara says Cortés invoked Santiago, as well as God and Saint Peter, in another engagement with coastal natives. Lasso de la Vega commemorated the apparition at Tabasco in his epic poem *Mexicana* (1588), p. 94. Bernal Díaz, who took part in the battle, wrote that if Santiago had appeared there, he had not been privileged to witness the saint's presence. Díaz del Castillo, pp. 63–64.

Another tradition along the same lines comes from the city of Querétaro. Its parish church was dedicated to Santiago in honor of his intervention in the decisive battle against Otomí and Chichimec Indians in 1531. Alcedo, 3: 265.

Valle, *Santiago en América*, the most extensive study of the saint, written from an ardently Catholic and hispanophile viewpoint, identifies 14 reports of apparitions by Santiago in Spanish America from 1518 to 1892. New Spain cases (seven, including the Tabasco and Querétaro cases) date from the 16th century, a phenomenon that he interprets in much the same way as Trexler, *Church and Community*, p. 15, does, as a result of Indians seeing Santiago as "the new telluric force, invincible [and] irresistible . . . with his message of terror" (p. 15).

28. Ajofrín, 1: 221. The Spaniards awoke "esforzados y animosos," the Indians "confusos y asustados; y luego, sin venir a las armas, se entregaron humildes y rendidos."

29. Warman, *Danza*, pp. 20, 60.

30. Trexler, "We Think," pp. 208, 216. What I would question, though, is the extent to which these mock battles succeeded in carrying out the Spaniards' intent. From several sources that document mainly Spanish intentions, Trexler infers a more throughgoing and unchanging Spanish control in Indian communities than I think is justified. In contrast to Trexler, Baumann sees Tlaxcalan nobles as scripting the early post-Conquest moros y cristianos events to impress the viceroy and heighten their prestige in the colonial world as loyal, courageous Christian subjects.

31. Lumholtz, 2: 329, records a similar belief about Santiago at Zapotlan el Grande (Jalisco) in the late 19th century: Santiago "is a good deal of a liar and has made himself rich at the expense of the Indians. Though the people do not like him he always has his way because he frightens them." Choy Ma, pp. 421–37, develops the theme of the Spanish encouraging Indians to see Santiago as a symbol of defeat and submission. But he concentrates mainly on the Spanish side, and though he holds out the possibility of an Indian reworking that would see Santiago as a liberating force, he offers little evidence from the Indian perspective, and for that matter, little evidence at all for Mexico after the 16th century. One of the few pieces of evidence Choy Ma musters for the Indians in Mexico accepting the Spanish version of Santiago is an illustration in Diego Durán's *Historia de las Indias de Nueva España* (probably drawn in the 1560's or 1570's). But the picture he refers to (plate 62) does not show a mounted Santiago trampling an Aztec warrior, as Choy, p. 431, would have it. According to Durán's surrounding text (2: 573–74), it shows a Spanish rider who invoked the saint's name before engaging the enemy. What made the episode remarkable to Durán and worthy of an illustration was that the rider was a woman who had led a bold assault on Indian forces in a seemingly impregnable location outside Tetlan (Tetela del Volcán, Morelos?) when Cortés was on the point of turning away.

Choy Ma believes that the idea of Santiago as "Indian-slayer" rather than "Moor-slayer" is also supported by a change in colonial images of the saint, in which prostrate Indians replaced turbaned Moors under the horse's feet (p. 432). An inventory of images of Santiago, with their makers, dates, and owners, would be needed to test this hypothesis fully. For Mexico, the colonial images I know from published sources, visits to parish churches in Jalisco, Michoacán, and the Estado de México, and the Franz Mayer Collection in Mexico City show exotic Moors rather than Indians as Santiago's victims. One

Santiago "mata-indios" from Santa María Chiconautla (Edo. de México) is mentioned in the exhibition catalogue *Mexico: Splendors of Thirty Centuries* (Washington, D.C., 1983), p. 346, and described briefly in the abstract of Asunción García Samper's paper for the conference on "Manifestaciones religiosas en el mundo colonial americano," Tlaxcala, Mexico, April 1-6, 1991 ("El Santiago Mata-indios, una manifestación religiosa en Santa María Chiconauhtlan").

Santiago in either guise seems to have been a more captivating character in Indian parishes of Peru during the colonial period. And he was more often "mata-indios" in Peruvian representations. Of the 21 colonial Santiagos illustrated in Pablo Macera's *Pintores populares*, two appear to be "mata-indios," and seven others show llamas or alpacas (wholly native animals) near the horse's raised front legs. Macera, p. xlii, posits a change in representations of Santiago at Cuzco during the colonial period, from mainly "mata-indios" at the beginning to a mounting preference for "matamoros" in the 17th and 18th centuries. For a brief discussion of Santiago in colonial Peru, with two more illustrations of "mata-indios," see Gisbert, pp. 195-98 and the illustrations at pp. 198, 211; and for a more recent important essay on the subject, see Silverblatt.

32. Torres, p. 47 ("monstrándose verdadero hijo del trueno en vencer y amedrentar a los indios . . . también se ostentó rayo para alumbrarlos; y así, luego que llegó el venerable Padre Segovia, le refirieron el caso muy admirados, y valiéndose de él, el varón apostólico les comenzó a predicar la fidelidad de Dios Nuestro Señor para con los cristianos"). According to an 18th-century account, Padre Segovia also promoted the cult at Tetlan, an Indian pueblo between Guadalajara and Tonalá, after learning from local Indians that Santiago had protected the forces of Nuño de Guzmán during a battle there. Valle, ch. 2. Felipe Guaman Poma de Ayala, the early-17th-century Peruvian Indian author, also asociated Santiago's power with thunder and lightning. *El primer nueva corónica y buen gobierno*, ed. John V. Murra and Rolena Adorno (Mexico City, 1980), 2: 376-77. Santiago is widely known in central Mexican villages today as the "son of thunder." Warman, *Danza*, pp. 113-35. Did Indians in different places spontaneously make the association on their own, learn it from other Indians, or learn it mainly from Spaniards?

33. In "We Think," p. 194, Trexler presents the messages of the "military theatre of the conquest" as Indian obedience and the honor of being a Spaniard. He describes no particular ambiguity, only Indian submission and Spanish destiny to rule. I am suggesting that the cult of Santiago conveyed the honor of being a Christian, as well as the honor of being a Spaniard. As Christians, colonial Indians might also enlist the saint's support.

34. Valle, pp. 10-12. That Santiago was a common Christian name and surname for Indian nobles in the 16th century also suggests his patronage and power. See, for example, the names of Indian officials meeting at Amecameca on Nov. 7, 1599, in Lemoine Villicaña, pp. 36-37.

35. Valle, p. 51. According to Carrillo y Gariel, *Imaginería popular*, pp. 13-24, among 2,156 ciudades, villas, pueblos, and barrios in 1950, Santiago was second only to Mary in popularity, with 207 namings (9.6%).

36. The representation of Santiago on a white mount with sword upraised was also standard in Spanish accounts before the colonization of America began. Kendrick, p. 42 and plates 2a and 10a. The white horse recalls Rev. 6:2 in the New Testament: "And I saw, and behold, a white horse, and its rider . . . and he went out conquering and to conquer." Valle, p. 83, lists some images of Santiago he located in Mexico. Weismann, p. 58, suggests that most of the Mexican Santiagos were made in the 17th century. A spiritual geography is needed for Santiago in New Spain. My examples come from rural communities of central and western Mexico, where he continues to be venerated. Warman, *Danza*, pp. 113-35, finds the current veneration to be centered in the states of Veracruz, Puebla, Morelos, Jalisco, Zacatecas, Mexico, and the Distrito Federal.

37. Clendinnen discusses questions of communication across cultures, syncretism, and the practice of religion in 16th-century Mexico in "Franciscan Missionaries"; "Ways to the Sacred"; and " 'Fierce and Unnatural Cruelty.' "

38. Clendinnen, " 'Fierce and Unnatural Cruelty.' "

39. *Relación de las ceremonias y ritos y población y gobierno de los indios de la provincia de Michoacán (1541)*. Facsimile of Ms. c.IV.5 of El Escorial (Morelia, 1977), pp. 238, 241, 264–65, 266.

40. Horses appear prominently in the 16th-century Indian pictorials of the Conquest. In book 12 of the Florentine Codex they are depicted as restless, always in motion, with legs raised, kicking up dust. Sometimes they are massed for a charge, mouths open and teeth bared. Anderson & Dibble, pp. 29, 30, 65, 69, 80. In the Códice de Tlatelolco (ca. 1564) and the Lienzo de Cuauhquechollan (Puebla), horses appear in battle rearing up on their hind legs, with mouths and large eyes wide open and ears laid back. Glass, plates 41, 45. In the Lienzo de Tlaxcala, they appear in nearly all the fighting scenes as solid, outsized, branded creatures, often rearing up (like Santiago's mount) or with big teeth, tongue, and virile member showing. Sometimes the neck of the charging horse is stretched well forward, as if the animal were about to attack with its mouth. The artist of the Lienzo de Tlaxcala (as well as the creators of other 16th-century pictorials like the Códice Osuna) was particularly impressed by horses' capacity for food and frequently showed them eating (e.g., Glass, plate 49).

41. Cited in Bustamante, *Memoria*, probably based on a translation of Chimalpahin's "Compendio de la historia mexicana, 1064–1521" in Bustamante's possession (per *Handbook of Middle American Indians*, 15 [1975]: 331). In nearly the same words, Torquemada, 1: 496, wrote that Santiago's horse, "with his mouth, forelegs, and hindlegs, did as much damage as the horseman with his sword" during the Spaniards' battle with the Aztecs in Tenochtitlan shortly before the Noche Triste. Purporting to paraphrase Indian testimony about this apparition of Santiago along with the Blessed Virgin, Torquemada says that the Spaniards would have been annihilated had not "la imagen de Nª Sª les hechaba Tierra en los ojos, y que un Caballero mui grande, vestido de bla[n]co, en un caballo blanco, con Espada en la mano, peleaba sin ser herido, y su caballo con la boca, Pies, y Manos, hacía tanto mal, como el Caballero con su Espada. Respondíanles los Castellanos: Ai veréis, que vuestros Diosos son falsos, esa Imagen es de la Virgen Madre de Dios, que no pudiestes quitar del Altar, y ese Caballero es el Apostol de Jesu-Christo Santiago, a quien los Castellanos llaman en las Batallas, y le hallan siempre favorable." Unless Bustamante borrowed without attribution from Torquemada rather than Chimalpahin, these two early-17th-century accounts of the warrior horse may have come from a common oral tradition in and near the Valley of Mexico.

42. Poinsett, p. 87.

43. Aguirre Beltrán, *Medicina y magia*, pp. 98–112; Musgrave-Portilla.

44. John Carter Brown Lib., Spanish Codex Coll., no. 52, fols. 251–65. In prehispanic terms, the personal association between an animal and an individual apparently took two distinct forms, the nahualli and the tonalli. López Austin, *Cuerpo humano*, 1: 427–30, regards both as spiritual entities that could separate from the human body. The tonalli resided in the head and was associated with an animal counterpart (known in Spanish as the tona) that was identified shortly after birth. The tonalli could escape the body during dreams, drunkenness, or coitus. If it was lost, or if the animal counterpart died, the person would also die soon. In the colonial period the identification of animals as counterparts or embodiments of people was apparently not limited to the first days of life. Ribadeneyra records the belief that adults turned into animals when they died: "After an adult Indian dies, they watch out on the day of his burial for the first animal to come to the door of the church. Believing that the deceased is to become that animal, they buy it and take it

home." Another common belief, he said (fols. 251–65), was that deceased relatives became oxen, and he himself had heard Indians speak of this or that ox being like their father or mother.

The nahualli, according to López Austin, resided in the liver. Only wizards (known in Spanish as naguales because of their association with this spiritual entity) could release this spirit into a powerful animal that would act out the wizard's will. Everyone had a tona or animal counterpart, but not everyone was a nagual. The prehispanic wizards were elite men associated with the fiercest animals.

If López Austin is correct about the sharp distinction between nahualli and tonalli, that distinction declined sometime during the early colonial period. By the 17th century, naguales were said to transform themselves (not just release their liver-spirit) into animals, often domesticated animals such as dogs and goats, perhaps indicating that these colonial wizards were commoners who could not claim the most powerful animal associates. (See Aguirre Beltrán, *Medicina y magia*, pp. 98–112, and Musgrave-Portilla, pp. 45, 57, on the idea of transformation, the increasing importance of dogs, and a decline in the distinction between tona and nagual.) Also during the colonial period, a dualistic conception of supernatural powers both nurturing and destroying may have given way to the more Christian notion of black magic, in which the wizard was essentially malevolent and often took the form of a small black dog.

45. The idea of a culture of conquest and its "other face"—Indian reworkings—is explored in Warman, *Danza*; and Baumann.

46. The literal meaning of "chichimec" is not certain but the various dictionary definitions suggest unwelcome intruder. Siméon says it means "those who suck milk from the breast" (from *chichi*, suckle); that is, those who prey on others. Robelo says it derives from *chichiman*, "unknown region." And Santamaría says it means "dog on a leash" (from *chicho* for dog and *mecatl* for rope); or, alternatively, in English "dog with a rope" (i.e. dog who punishes). A more historical reflection on the meaning of "Chichimec," and a slightly different derivation of the word, comes from Diego Muñoz Camargo, the Tlaxcalan mestizo who served several times as the gobernador of his province near the end of the 16th century, and saw groups of his compatriots sent north with Spanish expeditions to settle in the Chichimec zone. In addition to writing that "Chichimec" comes from "men who eat raw meat and drink and suck the blood of their prey," Muñoz Camargo observed a growing—and increasingly pejorative—use of the word to mean "savage": "Chichimecas puramente quiere decir 'hombres salvajes' como atrás dejamos referido aunque la derivación de este nombre procede de 'hombres que comían las carnes crudas,' y se bebían y chupaban la sangre de los animales que mataban . . . . Y ha quedado este nombre de chichimecas el día de hoy ya arraigado tanto que aquellos que viven como salvajes, y se sustentan de caza y monterías y hacen crueles asaltos, y matanzas en las gentes de paz, y aquéllos que andaban alzados con arcos y flechas como alarbes son tenidos por chichimecas, especialmente en los tiempos de ahora, son más crueles y espantosos que jamás lo fueron, porque en otros tiempos, que ha menos de cuarenta años, no mataban sino cazas y animales fieras y silvestres, y ahora matan hombres y saltean caminos. . . . Por manera que el nombre de chichimeca, que solía ser la cosa más noble entre los naturales, ha venido a ser y a parar que los que llaman el día de hoy chichimecas se ha de entender por hombres salteadores y robadores de caminos, y todos aquellos indomésticos que habitan las tierras de la Florida y la demás tierra que está por ganar y conquistar" (quoted in Román Gutiérrez, p. 323).

47. Warman, *Danza*, p. 81; Weckmann, 1: 151–52.

48. Warman, *Danza*, pp. 97–98.

49. Nathan Wachtel's daring interpretation of four "dances of the Conquest" from Peru and Mexico follows a more conquest/resistance approach. Upstreaming from modern descriptions to colonial practices in ch. 2, he emphasizes a pervasive "violent shock,"

"destructuration," and "permanent trauma" of the Conquest, with some Indian resistance by rebellion and reworking of these ritual performances. His approach does not attend to complications of time and place. Two other relatively recent studies of dances of the Conquest are Díaz Roig; and Bricker, "Historical Dramas."

50. Warman, *Danza*, p. 100.

51. AGN Inq. 303, fols. 69–71 (the Augustinian guardian's short report on Indian "idolatry" in the vicinity of Ixmiquilpan, 1624). The description of María's dream is not full enough to be certain that she regarded intercourse with the Spaniard as submission rather than a more neutral or reciprocal communication. In either case, his power supposedly was transferred to her without mediation or supplication. Similar 17th-century cases of young non-Indian men appearing to Indian curanderas and diviners in their dreams or in a drug-induced state and giving them secret powers and incantations were recorded by Ponce (cura of Zumpahuacan), p. 379; and Ruiz de Alarcón (cura of Atenango), p. 52. In Ruiz de Alarcón's description, an Indian woman named Mariana consulted ololiuhqui (psychedelic morning glory seeds) for advice about a wound that had not healed. A young man, whom she judged to be an angel, appeared to her and told her not to worry, that God saw her poverty and would favor her. That night, the young man crucified her and taught her his powers of curing. Ponce mentions that diviners using ololiuhqui claimed that young black men or Christ or angels appeared and told them what they wanted to know.

52. Serna, p. 38 ("Santiago el mozo, ayudadme, varón fuerte vencedor y hombre valeroso, valedme y ayudadme, que [no] se perderán las obras y hechuras de Dios todo poderoso"). Other 17th-century accounts by parish priests of local religious practices in central Mexico pueblos also mention conjurers of the clouds and the belief that the clouds and winds were angels and gods. Ponce, p. 379; Ruiz de Alarcón, pp. 23–24. In Ponce's description, presumably for Zumpahuacan, conjurers called teciuhpeuhque made many hand signals and blew the clouds and winds.

53. John Carter Brown Lib., Spanish Codex Coll., no. 52, fols. 251–65, para. 54, "abusos que frecuentemente se advierten en los yndios."

54. AGN Crim. 120 exp. 25, fol. 286v. Huizquilucan was notorious for its militant independence from parish priests. Late colonial pastoral visits warned the Indian parishioners about burying their dead, slaughtering cofradía cattle without permission, wasting money on fireworks, failing to attend mass, and keeping an indecent image of Nuestra Señora de los Remedios. The 1779–80 visita record advised the parish priest to be patient and promote schools. The one for 1792–93 noted in passing that local Indians had lodged various judicial complaints against their parish priests. AHM L10B/21, fols. 92–97; AHM L10B/28, fols. 196–203. Horses and riders were admired by all classes in colonial Mexico. Mota y Escobar, p. 34, writing about Nueva Galicia at the turn of the 17th century, spoke of the Indians' particular love of horses (and trees). The many horse thefts recorded in 18th-century Indian districts suggest both the presence of horses in Indian pueblos and how much they were coveted.

55. I am not certain when the Danza de Santiaguito was forbidden by the crown. The cura of Zacualpan de las Amilpas complained in 1763 that the pueblo of Temoac—which he regarded as a lawless, idolatrous place—resisted his attempts to end the dance, even though other pueblos in the district had complied with the prohibition. AGN CRS 156 exp. 9, fols. 366ff. On Feb. 11, 1769, Archbishop Lorenzana and his provisor published a pastoral letter calling for an end to that dance, as well as to the Nescuitiles, the Palo del Volador, and live representations of the passion of Christ. Because of Santiago's association with the Reconquista, the Danza de Santiaguito could have been a variation on the old moros y cristianos pageants. But there was probably no one standard dance. At least, celebrations on his day or in which his image appeared varied (several variations are described in the text). At Tecali (Puebla), where Santiago was the patron saint, Indians

danced the Hahuixtle, or "Dance from before the Conquest," on his feast day, with some dancers arrayed around a teponastle (the hollowed log drum) and others, "dressed as Chichimecs," pursuing captive deer in a mock hunt. AGI Mex. 839–41, 1735. Various modern versions of the Santiago dances are mentioned in Warman, *Danza*, pp. 113–35; and Mata Torres. Toor, p. 350 (see also plate 68) describes what was probably a relatively standard form from Cuetzalan (Puebla) in which a dancer representing Santiago el Caballero wore a miniature horse on a painted belt and fought soldiers to the accompaniment of flute and drum music. Only Santiago did not wear a mask, perhaps suggesting that the saint was now an Indian or to draw attention to the horse as his "mask." Whoever played that role was responsible for "feeding" the "horse" throughout his tenure. According to Toor, "The newly elected Santiago receives the horse from the outgoing one, and has to take care of him until the next fiesta the following year. He keeps him either on the household altar or in a small box-like stable, made especially for the purpose. Santiago obligates himself to feed the horse a bowl of corn and another of water every day. If he does not do this faithfully, the horse may run away to another village."

56. BMM 69–70, diario of the Fourth Provincial Council, 1771, fols. 200v–201r. The "Dance of the Santiaguitos" came up in the Council's discussion of Indian "idolatry." José Miguel Guridi y Alcocer, the scholarly priest of Acaxete (Puebla), also regarded the dance as evidence of Indians' pagan spirit. Sutro Lib., "Discurso sobre los daños del juego," 1799, fol. 81v. In one of his rare references to Mexico in this treatise, Guridi spoke of the old pagan spirit only being encountered in small, unimportant Indian pueblos, in such dances as the torito (little bull) and Santiagos, "which is the main one" (sólo se encuentra en los pueblitos de poca consideración que han fundado los yndios como danza torito y santiagos que es el principal).

57. BMM 69–70, fols. 200v–201r ("El provincial de San Francisco dexó haver oído algunos Ynteligentes ser un llanto de su Conquista. El cura de Otumba añadió que sólo les ha podido percivir una voz, que no entendió, y de que preguntados los yndios, respondieron significar lo mismo que arrogante, o sobervio, lo que aplicaban al Santo Apostol").

58. AJANG Civil, bundle labeled "1800–19, leg. 3 (109)," Aug. 21, 1815, petition by the officials of San Andrés and subdelegado's report. The relevant passage in the subdelegado's report reads: "tiene el nombre de Tastuanes y se contrahe a vestirse varios indios muy ridiculamente con máscara y que montado uno de ellos a caballo y con espada en mano que es el que llaman Santiago comienza a darles a los demás de sintarazos que resisten con un palo que trae cada uno en la mano, pero ya despues que se embriagan los que eran antes sintarazos se buelven cuchilladas de suerte que cada año resultan de su danza uno, dos o más heridos aunque de esto ni dimana queja alguna pues los pacientes sufren aquello por decir que viene de Santiago. No es lo más lo que llevo espuesto a Vuestra Excelencia sino es que así en castellano como en mexicano son muchas las obsenidades que hablan y también las acciones indecentes que hacen al tiempo que manifiestan estarle quitando la piel al que hace de Santiago."

Drawing on Santoscoy, Warman, *Danza*, pp. 108–10, describes the dance of the tastuanes in this same town of San Andrés, plus three others near Guadalajara (Huentitlan, Mezquitan, and Tonalá), in 1889. (See also Valle, pp. 57–59). The 1815 and 1889 descriptions are not exactly parallel or equally detailed, but the same basic structure is recognizable in both: a mounted Santiago engaged horseless masked men (apparently infidel Moors in 1815, minions of the Devil in 1889) in combat. He escaped many times but eventually was captured, taken off his horse, and humiliated. The apparent differences in the 1889 version are that the saint was killed; the tastuanes' struggle against him was sanctioned by the judgment of kings; the dance was held on the day of Santiago rather than (or in addition to?) the day of San Pedro; and the tastuanes were not represented only as Moors (some of the names of tastuanes indicate that they were infernal characters—Barrabas and Satan).

The differences between the descriptions, if they are real differences between the performances, suggest changes in degree rather than kind. The inversion of the saint's power is common to both. (Warman suggests that the traditional message of good triumphing over evil had been inverted in 1889. But given that the tastuanes were the king's subjects and measured the community's lands and executed the saint on royal orders, the performance seems to confirm the integrity and legitimacy of the community more than it signified the victory of evil over good. Following Musgrave-Portilla's interpretation of the Devil and nagualism after the Conquest, perhaps evil is not exactly the way the Barrabas figure and his compatriots were understood. Warman's description does not indicate that the king was, himself, the Devil.)

Warman treats this dance in 1889 as an example of radical change within the moros y cristianos tradition after Mexico's national independence, and as evidence of a more independent popular culture and diminishing influence of the priesthood that emerged during the anarchy of Mexican political life in the years before the Reform period. Judging by the 1815 description, the "radical" change in this case occurred before national independence. The subdelegado in 1815 did not say how old the version of the dance of the tastuanes he described was, but he gave no indication that it was a new practice.

For additional information about past and present dances of the tastuanes in pueblos of the Zapopan and Tonalá districts adjacent to Guadalajara, see Mata Torres.

59. The Toxcatl festival is described and richly interpreted in Carrasco, *To Change Place*, pp. 31–57; and Clendinnen, *Aztecs*, pp. 104–10, 147–48.

60. Valle, pp. 30–33, citing Tello's *Crónica miscelánea*, recounts the pious tradition of 1541 and Tello's comment that "Indians in the pueblos of Galicia reenact this miracle each year."

61. McKinley describes this conception of Santiago's violence in a modern Dance of the Santiagos at Xalacapan in the district of Zacapoaxtla (Puebla).

62. Valle, p. 53, recounts an oral tradition from Janitzio, an island pueblo on Lake Pátzcuaro, about Santiago as village protector during the Independence War. When royalists tried to take the pueblo, Santiago came down from the hill, whereupon the local patriots multiplied and scattered the enemy. Valle sees the pueblo's modern moros y cristianos dance as a representation of reciprocity and community responsibility.

63. One of the best-known village Santiagos, from Tupátaro, Michoacán, seems tame and approachable, like the friendly little images of Mary described in Weismann, especially p. 173. Edward Weston wrote a memorable description of this Santiago when he went to see it in the 1920's: "Here in Tupátaro the villagers were more than hospitable, and excited as children when I asked permission to photograph their Santiago. Santiago was a childlike expression. They must feel more than mere reverence for a saint, he must be like them—one of them. So Santiago was. He could have been displayed in any American department store amongst the toys,—a super toy. All details had received careful, tender attention. He was booted and spurred, over his neck hung a little sarape, around the waist a real faja, and his spirited hobby horse had been branded! Because of a recent fiesta the horse was still wreathed with roses." *Daybooks*, 1: 176. Weston's photograph of the image is reproduced in Gruening, p. 250; and Brenner, p. 69.

64. As Díaz del Castillo, p. 99, put it: "Since they now have no more idols in their high temples, he [Cortés] would leave them a great lady who was the Mother of our Lord Jesus Christ, whom we believe in and venerate, and . . . they should treat her as their lady and intercessor."

65. The special importance of images of the Immaculate Conception in the Mexico and Guadalajara dioceses built on the prominent place of Franciscans in the introduction of Christianity there. They were enthusiastic promoters of this tenet of the faith. By contrast, the Dominicans, whose evangelizing efforts centered farther south in Oaxaca and Chiapas, were longtime opponents of a feast for Mary Immaculate. See Reumann.

66. Mary is depicted in this image with dark skin, but the features are not obviously Indian. According to Nolan & Nolan, p. 202, nearly all of the 172 dark-skinned images they found in European shrines were of the Virgin Mary.

67. An important, still unresolved matter in the debate is the dating of the "Nican Mopohua," an account of the apparition written in Nahuatl and attributed to Antonio Valeriano, an early student of the Colegio de Santa Cruz de Tlatelolco. The original manuscript has apparently not been seen since the late 17th century. Among the modern scholars who question the antiquity of the Guadalupe apparition tradition are Francisco de la Maza; Jacques Lafaye; and Mauro Rodríguez. Torre Villar & Navarro de Anda contains the principal historical texts on the Guadalupan tradition. A more recent, especially extensive interpretation is O'Gorman, *Destierro de sombras*.

68. Lafaye, p. 299. Lafaye has made a valuable contribution to an understanding of the Guadalupe tradition as "the central theme of the history of creole consciousness," but as in other writings that refer to the cult's history, his book treats it from the standpoint of protest and assumes rather than demonstrates a widespread early devotion by the "Indians," rooted in oppression and a cosmogony that bred eschatalogical hopes. See Lafaye, pp. 22, 29, 242–43, 277, and 288.

69. Nicholson, *Art*, pp. 67–79. Perhaps the gods were not as threatening and remote as they are presently understood to have been, or at least that the memory of them by native chroniclers long after the Conquest had been tinged with Christian beliefs and an idealizing nostalgia. Chimalpahin, pp. 234–35, writing after 1620 about people of Chalco who sought the advice of their gods at the arrival of the Spaniards, said, "so they brought out the gods, which were like our mothers and our fathers." For an introduction to the multiple meanings of Tonantzin, see Sylvest.

70. For a more fully documented discussion of the Virgin Mary in colonial Mexico, see Taylor, "The Virgin of Guadalupe." The cult of the Virgin of Guadalupe before independence has long been conventionally held to be a message of national destiny rooted in the Indian past, whether the authors are foreign novelists and world travelers like Graham Greene ("This Virgin claimed a church where she might love her Indians and guard them from the Spanish conqueror. The legend gave the Indian self-respect; it gave him a hold over his conqueror; it was a liberating, not an enslaving legend." *Lawless Roads*, p. 103); Mexican literary figures like Octavio Paz ("Tonantzin/ Guadalupe was the imagination's answer to the situation of orphanhood in which the Conquest left the Indians. . . . The Indians took refuge in the skirts of Tonantzin/Guadalupe." *El ogro filantrópico*, p. 49); Mexican scholars like Wigberto Jiménez Moreno (The Virgin of Guadalupe in the 16th century "immediately became the Virgin of the Indians and before long, the Virgin of those born in Mexico, the Mexicans." Jiménez Moreno et al., p. 285); or foreign scholars like Ena Campbell ("The Indian population accepted her as the miraculous incarnation of the Aztec earth and fertility goddess Tonantsi"; "Guadalupe's image began to appear everywhere." Campbell, pp. 7, 9).

71. Díaz del Castillo, p. 6. Drawing from Torquemada's *Monarquía indiana*, Padden, *Hummingbird*, p. 144, mentions the incident of Mary casting dust into the Indians' eyes. Some material in this section is drawn from my article "The Virgin of Guadalupe in New Spain." It is used by permission of the American Anthropological Association from *American Ethnologist* 14: 1, February 1987. Not for further reproduction.

72. Padden, *Hummingbird*, chs. 8–9.

73. Christian, *Apparitions* and *Local Religion*.

74. Christian, *Local Religion*, pp. 4, 13–14, 213–15.

75. Ibid., pp. 207–8.

76. Ibid., p. 98. Cabrera y Quintero documents an exception to Christian's suggestion that Mary was not appealed to in epidemics: the great epidemic of 1737 in Mexico City.

77. Padden, *Hummingbird*, p. 99.

78. Only one other saint's day was included in the list, the Day of Saint Peter and Saint Paul. *Concilios provinciales primero, y segundo*, pp. 68–69. *Recop.* 1-1-24 summarizes a royal cedula of 1645 declaring the Virgin Mary "Patroness and Protectress, as in our kingdoms [of Spain]."

79. Hernáez, 2: 586 (Oct. 10, 1760).

80. Palafox, 1649 pastoral letter, pp. 35–36.

81. Juan de Palafox y Mendoza, *Carta pastoral y dictámenes de curas* (Madrid, 1653), fol. 139v.

82. Palafox, *Manual de sacerdotes*, fol. 10v.

83. CPM, pp. 166–67; John Carter Brown Lib., Spanish Codex Coll., no. 52, fol. 213v.

84. Rockefeller Lib., Brown Univ., Medina Coll., FHA 54 exp. 19.

85. Tulane VEMC 68 exp. 9, 1797 petition, attached to Aug. 8, 1797, doc. See also the volume of petitions in AGN Acordada 15.

86. AGN Inq. 1213 exp. 18, 1785, Molango, is one of many examples of a priest attempting to soothe a crowd by holding up an image of the Virgin.

87. Josefina Muriel, *Hospitales de la Nueva España* (Mexico, 1956); López Lara, ch. 5.

88. Taylor, "Indian Pueblos," pp. 172–73.

89. For example, the cura of Jocotepec parish in 1794 reported a sharp decline in cofradía property and income after the epidemic of 1786, but mayordomos were still elected annually to care for the hospital buildings and images, lead the customary devotions, and provide for an occasional beggar. CAAG, Martínez Mataraña report, Sept. 2, 1794.

90. Venegas Ramírez, p. 104. The CAAG records indicate that Indian pueblos of Jalisco almost always kept the hospital chapels in good repair.

91. CAAG, unclassified, 1772 petition of the cabildo of San Gaspar Teuchitlan, Tala district, to apply cofradía funds to church construction.

92. AGI Guad. 341, 1776, Zacoalco, Bishop Alcalde visita (shortly after secularization of the parish).

93. AJANG Civil, box 231, doc. 1. Bishop Alcalde, in his pastoral visit to Zacoalco in 1776, denied a petition by local Indians for mass in a chapel dedicated to Our Lady of Guadalupe. He ordered its image of Mary and another called the Señor del Mesquite transferred to the parish church in order to encourage devotion there and discourage rivalries between that chapel and the cura's seat. AGI Guad. 341.

94. Alcedo, 1: 259. The Guadalajara parish churches of Santa Anita Tisac, Senticpac, San Pedro Tlaquepaque, Amatitan, Ixtlan, Amacueca, Zacoalco, Magdalena, Ahualulco, and Talpa all boasted miraculous images of the Virgin Mary. Mota Padilla, *Historia de la conquista*, pp. 390–92.

95. Jiménez Moreno, "Indians," 428.

96. For brief accounts of the various pilgrimage shrines to Mary in Mexico, see Vargas Ugarte.

97. A bitter dispute in 1679 between the Indian cofradía to Guadalupe at Tepeyac and Spanish devotees of the Virgin of Guadalupe in Mexico City over the collection of alms indicates both their rivalry and the appeal of Guadalupe in the capital. The Indian cofradía had long been allowed to collect alms, but licenses had also been granted to the Spaniards to collect "outside and within this city." The provisor of the ecclesiastical court in that year clarified the situation to the advantage of the Spaniards of the capital, allowing the Indian cofrades to solicit in the city only from Indian homes. AGN Acervo 49, caja 174.

The brief account of the development of devotion to Our Lady of Guadalupe in the text is not meant to suggest an unbroken line of growth from the 1520's on. Various administrators and rent collectors for the sanctuary in the second quarter of the 17th century spoke of it as "very poor" and "in great need." Acervo 49, caja 140, July 11, 1633, and

Dec. 25, 1649. Still, the image of the Virgin of Guadalupe had already become good business by then. Joseph Ferrer claimed to have sold "medidas de Nuestra Señora de Guadalupe" at the sanctuary and in Mexico City since the 1620's, paying the vicar 100p a year and 50p worth of medidas for the privilege, and commissioning a large painting of the apparition that was displayed in the sanctuary. AGN Acervo 49, caja 149, folder 3. The "medidas," of his own invention, appear to have been ribbons cut to the height of the painting of the Virgin and stamped in gold or silver with her image and name.

98. AGN Acervo 49 caja 140, folder 23, Pérez petition. This was not the first time that officials of the sanctuary had attempted to enlarge their territorial base for the collection of alms. In 1633, the cobrador de rentas sought a license for Dr. Antonio de Esquibel Castañeda to collect for the sanctuary in Querétaro "and other parts." Ibid., folder 24, Ruiz González petition.

99. For a study of Marian devotion at Tepeyac in 1556, it is important but not essential to know whether the image to which Bustamante referred was modeled after the Spanish Guadalupe, the sculpted figure for which the shrine was presumably named, as Lafaye thinks, or the famous picture of the Virgin on Juan Diego's cloak, the Mexican Guadalupe. See Taylor, "Virgin of Guadalupe," p. 26, n. 6.

100. According to Hermosillo, fol. 109r, Archbishop Juan Pérez de la Serna (1613–25) had enlarged the sanctuary's fábrica (funds for construction, repairs to buildings, and maintenance of the cult) "with his singular devotion and infinite care." Hermosillo referred to this image as "inspiring great devotion" (devotísima). A survey of art objects in Mexico City in the 17th century probably would yield many representations of Guadalupe. Vera, *Erecciones parroquiales*, p. 19, records a copy of the Guadalupe painting in the church of Santa Catarina in 1634. Various private palaces and religious buildings from the 17th and 18th centuries in downtown Mexico City display stone images of the Virgin of Guadalupe in exterior niches. Late-17th-century records in AGN suggest that much of the financial support for the sanctuary was coming from well-placed families in Mexico City, and that by then the sanctuary held substantial property and liens on property in the city. The two principal donors for construction of the new church at Tepeyac were prominent men of Mexico City, Lic. Bentura de Medina Picazo and Capt. Pedro Ruiz de Castañeda, who donated 80,000p between them and proposed to collect donations during the period of construction. Acervo 49 caja 140, folder 7, July 7, 1694, license granting the two the right to collect donations.

101. Hakluyt, 6: 314–15. In a 1575 letter to the king, Viceroy Martín Enríquez (1568–80) spoke of a shrine to Our Lady of Guadalupe that had become popular among "the people" (la gente) 20 years before when a cattleman (ganadero) spread the word that he had regained his health by going there. *Cartas de Indias*, pp. 39–40.

102. López Sarrelangue, *Una villa mexicana*, p. 132.

103. Ibid., p. 305; Hanke & Rodríguez, 1: 315 (1592), 2: 192 (1644). The Shrine of Guadalupe at Tepeyac and the cathedral continued to be closely associated in the 17th century. Vicars of the sanctuary were sometimes cathedral dignitaries (in 1644, for example, the vicar was the maestrescuela of the cathedral; AGN Acervo 49, caja 174), and archbishops continued to speak of themselves as patrons of the cult (ibid., caja 140, May 11, 1657). The Villa de Guadalupe continued to be the place where distinguished emissaries from Spain were met until the end of the colonial period (witness the viceregal decree of June 4, 1779, that the new viceroy, Martín de Mayorga, be received there; AGN Bandos 11 exp. 13), and it was apparently the place of investiture for viceroys in the late colonial period. Tulane VEMC 22 exp. 15, royal order of April 20, 1789.

104. The tradition recorded by Ajofrín, 1: 77, in the 1760's was that the Tepeyac image was taken by canoe to the city, and the flood waters immediately began to recede: "the city was left as dry as before, and the sainted image was returned by the causeway with-

out difficulty." Ajofrín believed that floods had been stopped at the very edges of the city in 1763, 1764, and 1765, after nine days of public worship (novenarios) were offered to the Virgin of Guadalupe in her sanctuary.

105. Cabrera y Quintero, p. 23; *Gacetas de México*, 3: 78. In 1737, the Inquisition ordered three nights of festival lights on the façade of its palace and the house of the inquisitors in Mexico City in honor of the new patroness of the city. AGN Inq. 862, fols. 260–63.

106. *Gacetas de México*, 3: 78.

107. Quoted in Lafaye, p. 284. The flowering of the devotion in Mexico City in the 18th century is documented in many ways, including the many sculpted images of the Virgin of Guadalupe that still grace exterior niches of late colonial buildings in the heart of the city; the broad public appeals to her in times of need (e.g., the "oraciones" printed in Mexico City at the time of the earthquakes of 1776; AGN Inq. 1103 exp. 17, fols. 187–90); the active interest of the secular clergy; the celebrations organized in the city's monasteries and convents (e.g., the 1723 festivities in the Convento de San José de Carmelitas Descalzas mentioned in AGN Templos 157 exp. 20, fols. 128–32); Archbishop Lorenzana's promotion of the cult as providentially centered in Mexico City in the late 1760's (she appeared "para que los cortesanos y vecinos de México vengan a suplicar en sus necesidades; aquí para defender la Capital de entrada, o invasión de enemigos; aquí donde tributar las primicias de su veneración los Exmos Virreyes, e Illmos Prelados . . ."); Lorenzana, *Historia de Nueva España*, p. 211; Archbishop Núñez de Haro's 1776 order for an annual *repique a vuelo* of all the church bells in the city on December 11 and 12 in honor of the city's patroness and the "patroness of this entire kingdom" (AGN Bandos 9, fol. 262); the "indecent" processions in the city in which her image was carried in front as a standard (Inq. 1099 exp. 11, 1776); and the consecration of the main bell of the cathedral in her name on March 8, 1792 (Sedano, 1: "Campana" entry).

By the time Mota Padilla wrote, at least two bishops of Guadalajara, Galindo (1701–2) and Mimbela (1714–21), had been fervent devotees of the Virgin of Guadalupe, and presumably promoted public devotion to the image there; and the merchants of Guadalajara would soon join the wave of urban interest in her by making her their patroness in 1749. Bishops Martínez de Tejada (1752–56) and Alcalde (1771–92) continued to promote the veneration of the image in the diocese. Dávila Garibi, *Apuntes*, 3: 110, 280–83, 640–42, 655–57, 717–19, 806–7, 935–50.

108. Fernández de Lizardi, *Obras*, 1: 157. Fernández de Lizardi went on to say that "everyone knows about this; many of those who ran to Tepeyac are still living."

109. AGN RCO 52 exp. 134, Dec. 28, 1733; RCO 68 exp. 32, Aug. 21, 1748; RCO 69 exp. 16, July 22, 1749; RCO 71 exp. 42, Dec. 14, 1751; Ventura Beleña, 1: 2d enumeration, pp. 126–28; Cuevas, 4: 41; Pompa y Pompa. The crown added its support for elevating the Virgin of Guadalupe to patroness of all New Spain in a Dec. 7, 1756, real servicio that declared her image and sanctuary to be "a pious and indispensable legacy" (legado pío y manda forzosa) in the districts of Mexico, Guadalajara, and Guatemala. RCO 77 exp. 17. On Sept. 7, 1756, the new colegiata obtained an order from the Council of the Indies requiring people in New Spain to provide for "the sanctuary and representation of that holy image" in their wills. AGI Mex. 2531. Even if compliance was far from complete, the sanctuary's wealth and recognition must have been enhanced by a royal cedula that year to the same effect. Tulane VEMC 50 exp. 11.

Further institutional evidence of the cult consolidating and growing in the late 18th century includes a 1792 order to honor the apparition of Our Lady of Guadalupe on the twelfth day of each month. BN LaFragua Coll., vol. 1573.

110. Paredes, p. lxxiii. Jesuits had been particular advocates of the Virgin of Guadalupe since the 17th century. See Frost. In 1759, the crown authorized the establishment of a school for Indian girls in Mexico City dedicated to Our Lady of Guadalupe, the Co-

legio Real de Indias Educandas de Nuestra Señora de Guadalupe. Olaechea, pp. 360–62. Judging by a 1791 reference, the few students in the school were from the Mexico City Indian neighborhoods of San Juan and Santiago. AGI Mex. 2546, "Sobre un testimonio del expediente instruído a instancia del Marqués de Castañiza . . .," Feb. 7, 1811.

111. Lorenzana, *Cartas pastorales*, pp. 195–216. Following Lorenzana's lead, Omerick, BMM 113, p. 113, recommended that curas use the Virgin Mary, especially the Virgin of Guadalupe, to promote religious teaching among Indians because they "live proud and happy . . . when they are told that that most fortunate Indian Juan Diego was worthy of Our Lady's apparitions." Omerick went on to become a canon in the colegiata at the Villa de Guadalupe.

112. AGN Bandos 9 exp. 36; carta pastoral, March 25, 1803, p. 12. Archbishop Lizana reiterated the connection between the sanctuary of Guadalupe and Mexico City in his order to the college of canons at the Villa de Guadalupe on Dec. 22, 1807, to celebrate the news of victory against the English at Buenos Aires by giving the same service as the one to be given in the cathedral the following day.

113. AGN CRS 204 exps. 9–10; JCB, 1762, resumés of Casell, Ximénez, and Loretoyturría. An acclaimed chapel in Cuernavaca to Our Lady of Guadalupe, completed shortly before 1789, owed its existence to the personal sponsorship of Dr. Manuel de la Borda. AHM L10B/26, fol. 2r.

114. JCB. Parish priests sometimes made reference to their published and unpublished writings about Our Lady of Guadalupe in their resumés. Luis de Mendizábal y Zubialdea, an ordained priest of the Diocese of Puebla, listed a poetic work called "Idilio guadalupano" among his achievements. AGI Mex. 2550, 1819.

115. JCB, Xuárez de Escovedo resumé, 1762.

116. AGN CRS 156 exps. 2–3.

117. AGN CRS 136 exp. 8. The cura of Meztitlan de la Sierra (Hidalgo) in 1780 was charged by his Indian parishioners with keeping half of the wax left over from the annual celebration of the Virgin of Guadalupe for himself. CRS 74 exp. 1, fol. 4r. The cura of Atitalaquia said he was responsible for an altar to the Virgin of Guadalupe in his parish church. JCB (he did not specify when it was built; he served this parish from 1736 to 1758).

References to growing Guadalupan devotion in judicial records are hard to assess. Usually, it is shown more as a product of the priest's initiative than as a spontaneous popular movement, but that is partly in the nature of the evidence. Judging by the witnesses who came to the defense of cura Mariano Dionisio Alarcón of Tultitlan against charges of being unbending in his collection of sacramental fees, he was exceptionally devoted to the Guadalupan cult. The picture they painted was of a priest who filled the calendar with free services and charity in the Virgin's name that apparently won adherents: he said a mass in her honor every Saturday and afterwards distributed four or five pesos' worth of medio reales to the poor (5p of medio reales would serve 80 people). AGN Bienes 663 exp. 5, 1809. A different aspect of a priest's devotion was displayed by cura Ygnacio Gonsales Castañeda of Amecameca in 1796. He urged a quick resolution to his arancel dispute with the parish so he could return in time to celebrate the feast of Guadalupe on Dec. 12. AGN Templos 25 exp. 8.

Late colonial priests in the north actively supported devotion to the Virgin of Guadalupe as well, sometimes too actively from the official point of view. In 1805, Br. Ignacio Theodoro de Therán y Zamora, chaplain in Chihuahua, wrote an apology to the viceroy for his unauthorized effort to build a new sanctuary (hermita) to her. Tulane VEMC 73 exp. 36, March 8, 1805.

118. Ajofrín, 1: 117–20.

119. Ibid., 2: 174.

120. AGN Acervo 49 caja 127. The 1743 relaciones geográficas for the Archdiocese of Mexico, which contain some information on miraculous images and popular devotion, rarely mention Our Lady of Guadalupe. The great exception is the image and church dedicated to her in the city of Querétaro. Solano, 1: 253. But the cult seems to have made considerable headway thereafter. AHM files for 1775 (L10B/13) and 1792–93 (L10B/28) reveal two haciendas in the districts of Ixtlahuaca and Sultepec carrying the name; a chapel to Guadalupe on the outskirts of Temascalcingo; and Guadalupe as patroness of Atlacomulco. Santa María Jalatlaco, in the Tenango del Valle district, which had also taken her as patroness, had an especially active cofradía dedicated to her in 1775; yet the hermandad in her honor in nearby Tescaliacac was about to be terminated for neglect (L10B/13, fols. 38v ff, 51v ff). Late-18th-century pastoral visits tell a similar tale, recording "an exquisite chapel of Our Lady of Guadalupe" in Xiuctepec, donated by Dr. Manuel de la Borda (L10B/26, second visita to Cuernavaca, 1789, fols. 2–5); and the special dedication of the towns of Atlacomulco and San Juan del Río to this image of Mary (L10B/28, 1792, fols. 142, 144).

121. AGN Acervo 49 caja 116. The seven pueblos with obras pías for the Virgin of Guadalupe were Tianguistengo (out of 6 obras pías there), Molango (out of 13), Lolotla (out of 12), Misión Villa de Valles (out of 2), Misión de Tampico (out of 4), Misión de Ozuluama (out of 4), and Xochiatipan (out of 3). Similarly, five of the 10 communities named for Guadalupe (beyond the Villa de Guadalupe at Tepeyac) listed in Alcedo, 2: 136 (1786–89), were missions.

122. AHM L10B/26, fols. 58v, 64v ff, 79v.

123. Cuevas, 4: 129, says the chapel of Our Lady of Guadalupe outside the city of San Luis Potosí was informally established by a "pious gentleman," Francisco Castro y Mampaso, among others. A principal document for the idea of a widespread devotion to the image of the American Guadalupe by the mid-17th century is a letter to the Pope written by Bishop Fray Tomás de Monterroso of Oaxaca, dated May 10, 1667, and published in translation by Cuevas, 4: 35. Written in support of the petition by the archdiocese's cathedral chapter for papal recognition of the apparition, Monterroso's statement was a short but enthusiastic general endorsement. It claimed that "all of New Spain" believed in the apparition to "a poor Indian," that "I saw the multitudes of people from Mexico City and other pueblos of New Spain who come to visit the sanctuary," and that "there is an image of Our Lady of Guadalupe in almost all the pueblos of New Spain." Monterroso specified only the devotion of capitalinos, and he did not say he had seen for himself copies of the image in the pueblos. Perhaps he was inferring a general circulation of the image from copies he would have seen in provincial towns and cities such as Antequera.

124. Nine of the 10 communities named for the Virgin of Guadalupe listed in Alcedo, 2: 136, were located in the north.

125. Andrés Cavo, *Historia de los tres siglos de México durante el gobierno español* (Jalapa, 1836), 2: 170–71.

126. AGN Intendencias 51 exp. 5, fol. 54, 1805, informe of Luis María de Luna López Portillo, Hacienda de la Parada de Luna, Armadillo. Expansion of the cult in the 17th century is also suggested by the efforts of sanctuary administrators to extend the collection of offerings. In 1633 the rent collector, Juan Ruiz González, sought a license from the ecclesiastical court of the archdiocese to allow Dr. Antonio de Esquibel Castañeda, "who is going to Querétaro and other places," to collect alms for the Virgin of Guadalupe. AGN Acervo 49, caja 140, folder 24. In 1649, the mayordomo of the sanctuary urged a more ambitious program of collection: "it is necessary to ask for [offerings] throughout the archdiocese," he said, having already made a temporary agreement with Diego de Venavides to do so. Acervo 49, caja 140, folder 18.

127. Vera, *Informaciones*. A Dominican testified in this 1666 investigation to an Indian

having recovered from a mortal arrow wound after appealing to the Virgin of Guadalupe at her shrine. But it was not until 1789 that the cura and Indians of Tulpetlac in the Valley of Mexico were granted permission to erect a chapel on the spot where Our Lady of Guadalupe was said to have appeared to Juan Bernardino, uncle of Juan Diego. AGN Bienes 575, exp. 11. According to Sahagún, 3: 299, Indians were coming to worship at Tepeyac in the second half of the 16th century "from very distant places, from over twenty leagues away, from all these settlements in the district of [the city of] Mexico," as they had done before the Conquest, even though there were other churches to the Virgin closer by. He said they called her Tonantzin, as well as Our Lady of Guadalupe, and was concerned about a confusion of the precolonial goddess with Mary, but he says little about who the pilgrims were, where they came from, or what they believed. Perhaps the Indian devotion to Guadalupe in the early colonial period corresponded roughly to the territory of pilgrimage and worship of Tonantzin at Tepeyac (whatever that territory may have been), but too little is known about the worship of that goddess to tell.

Other, later indications of popular and Indian devotion to the image and shrine of the American Guadalupe include a petition of the administrator of the sanctuary in 1649 that speaks of the Virgin of Guadalupe as "an image of such devotion and so worthy of note because of the apparition" (AGN Acervo 49, caja 140, folder 23); the archbishop's mention in a record of May 11, 1657, of natives and other people going there for the sacraments (ibid.); and an archiepiscopal order dated Jan. 16, 1677, that the glass case covering the image should no longer be opened for devotees to kiss the image or touch it with their hands or with religious images and rosaries (ibid., folder 8).

128. The fiestas in 1756 that I can document now are for Mexico City and other principal towns (AGN Inq. 986 exp. 10, fols. 167–72), but additional evidence may well show that the papal confirmation of Guadalupe's patronage that year was what triggered priests to promote annual celebrations in the countryside. AGN CRS 204 exps. 9–10, 1760, Tejupilco; CRS 156 exp. 5, fol. 146, 1758, Tepetlaostoc (Edo. de México).

The public devotion to the Virgin Mary, especially to the image of the Virgin of Guadalupe, of parish priests in the Archdiocese of Mexico at the end of the colonial period is richly documented. Cura José Mariano Cuebas of Lerma (Edo. de México) was reported to have finished a chapel to the Virgin of Guadalupe largely at his own expense and to have personally led his parishioners in carting rocks for the construction. AGN Hist. 578A, 1793, Lerma report. And in 1811, the cura of Tepehuacan complained of his Indians' paganism and insolence, despite his many gifts to them, including a sanctuary to María Santísima de Guadalupe. García & Pereyra, 5: 186–87. Vicario Luis Venegas of Tetelpa in the parish of Tlaquiltenango (Morelos) gave a provocative sermon in praise of the Virgin to his parishioners in 1804, in which he proposed that she be made the "captain" of armies and public celebrations such as dances, bullfights, and plays. AGN Bienes 172, exp. 51. In 1809, the cura of Tultitlan (Valley of Mexico) was said to celebrate a mass every Saturday for Our Lady of Guadalupe. Bienes 663 exp. 5.

129. Paul Wheatley, "City as Symbol," Inaugural Lecture delivered at the University College, London, Nov. 20, 1967.

130. A couple of other ways to explore the expansion of the cult in the 17th and 18th centuries suggest themselves. One might learn much from looking at parish inventories and wills for evidence of paintings, prints, altars, medals, and other representations of the image. Unfortunately, some of the best physical evidence, like medals worn or kept at home, escapes the formal record. Occasionally, such medals are recovered in excavations. A bronze medal with the Guadalupe image, the providential inscription, "No other nation has been so favored" (non fecit taliter omni nationi), and the date 1805 was discovered at Amilpa in the district of Autlan (Jalisco). Brambila, p. 102. But whether this medal was actually struck in 1805 is open to question. Robertson, *Visit to America*, 1: 54, bought

a brand new medal dated 1805 at the Basílica de Guadalupe in 1851. It might be profitable also to look specifically at the missionaries who founded houses of charity (*hospicios*) in Guadalupe's name. Perhaps her most energetic missionary devotee was the Spanish Franciscan Antonio Margil de Jesús, who died in 1726 after four decades of service from Nicaragua to Texas. He was famous as the founder of the Colegio de la Santísima Cruz of Querétaro in 1683 and the Apostólico Colegio de Nuestra Señora de Guadalupe of Zacatecas in 1706. For more on his life and work, see Guerra; and Ríos. The friars of the Zacatecas colegio were sent out on short visits to established doctrinas of western and north-central New Spain in preparation for long-term missionary service, mainly in the north. Cura Juan Nepomuceno Báez of Nochistlan (Jalisco) reported in 1788 that he had twice called in the Zacatecan friars of Guadalupe to help stamp out drinking and other vices. AJANG Criminal, bundle labeled "1700–93, leg. 84 (16)."

131. For example, the cofradía of Nuestra Señora de Guadalupe in Tamazunchale—the one cofradía named for Guadalupe in a survey for the district of San Luis Potosí in 1798—was founded in 1749. AGN CRS 72 exp. 20, fol. 451. The cofradía of Nuestra Señora de Guadalupe in the Villa de Orizaba was founded in 1781. AGN RCO 120, exp. 134. Non-Indian brotherhoods dedicated to the Virgin of Guadalupe sometimes appear in ecclesiastical court records; for example, CRS 151 exp. 14 contains the 1796 petition of Felipe Francisco Tenorio, merchant of the Villa de Tlapa (Guerrero) and guardian of the Hermandad de Nuestra Señora de Guadalupe, for permission to collect alms for a mass on the twelfth of each month.

132. For tables and other information about these naming patterns, see Taylor, "Virgin of Guadalupe." For patterns of Marian naming for the sagrario parish of Mexico City similar to those described below, see Boyd-Bowman.

133. It is not clear from the baptismal registers who chose the names. Undoubtedly, the parish priest influenced many of them, since he performed the ceremony of baptism and may have been the only participant who kept close track of the saints' days. The standard entry in the registers contains the phrase "a quien le puse por nombre" (to whom I put the name), which may or may not indicate that the priest chose the name. The early guides for parish priests and manuals for the administration of sacraments suggest that the priest should not allow certain names, but that within those limits, parents and godparents could choose whatever they wanted. *Manual breve*, fol. 2, instructed, "No consienta el Sacerdote que le pongan algún nombre del testamento viejo, ni de gentiles, o judíos, ni alguno ridículo, sino de los que se acostumbran poner en la Sancta Iglesia, o de algún Santo, o Santa del nuevo testamento"; and *Itin.* 3-1-18 stated, "Reparen mucho los Doctrineros en que a los Indios que bautizan, no se les pongan los nombres que usaban ponerlos los padres en la Gentilidad." The Fourth Provincial Council endorsed this view in 1771: "Los Párrocos no pondrán a los Bautizados nombres de Indios Gentiles, ni tampoco los tomaran del Testamento viejo; porque para no confundirlos con los Judíos, y no equivocar la verdad de la Ley de Gracia con su sombra, que lo fue la Antigua, o escrita, está mandado que solo so pongan nombres de Santos de la Ley Evangélica." CPM, pp. 162–63. The archbishop of Guadalajara echoed these traditional parameters in his visit to Jocotepec in 1874. He urged the cura not to allow either unusual names, even if they came from Roman martyrs, or the names of saints from the Old Testament. Names should be drawn from the New Testament, and preferably those of saints well known to Christians for their virtues. CAAG, record of the archbishop's visita.

Two pieces of evidence work against the idea that it was simply the priest who chose the names: changes in naming did not usually coincide with changes in curas; and the pattern of naming varied within parishes even though one priest baptized all the infants. For example, in the parish of Tlajomulco, the frequency of Marías and Guadalupes was substantially different in the town of Tlajomulco and the rest of the parish, with many more

Indian Marías in the town than in the outlying villages and estates, and more non-Indian Guadalupes in the outliers than in the town.

134. Eliade, *Patterns*, pp. 240, 259, 262, 332.

135. Weismann, p. 173.

136. Marina Warner, *Alone of All Her Sex: The Myth and Cult of the Virgin Mary* (New York, 1976), p. 285. The deep belief by colonial priests in the Virgin Mary as spiritual advocate and intercessor is illustrated by the 1692 will of cura Francisco de Fuentes of Yahualica (Hidalgo), in which he invoked "por mi abogada a la puríssima Virgen María Señora Nuestra concebida sin la culpa original desde el primer ynstante de su ser, para que interceda con su santíssimo hijo." AGN Templos 95, exp. 3.

137. Greenberg, *Santiago's Sword*, pp. 46–47; Taussig, *Devil*, p. 210.

138. The concept of communitas is succinctly stated in Turner & Turner, pp. 250–51, and used in connection with the colonial Guadalupe in their ch. 2.

139. Lafaye, p. 288.

140. Taylor, "Conflict."

141. AGN Inq. 1213 exp. 6 ("Vea Ud. la temporal y Eterna"). In Zacoalco, the protection of Mary in earthly affairs may well have been associated with the image of Guadalupe in the late colonial period. In his visita of 1776, Bishop Alcalde denied a petition of Indians from Zacoalco for mass to be celebrated in a chapel dedicated to Guadalupe for fear of drunkenness and disorderly conduct, and ordered that her image be moved to the parish church. AGI Guad. 341.

142. AGN RCO 93 exp. 103 ("protección de la Virgen María para libertarse de tantas opresiones").

143. AGN Inq. 1360 exps. 1–2.

144. AGN Inq. 1145 exp. 8, fols. 98–105.

145. BMM 113, pp. 115ff. In the view of de la Peña Montenegro, the misconception of the Trinity as three people was common among Indians. *Itin.* 2-8-4.

146. AGN Crim. 308. Much of the evidence for Guadalupe as an emblem of revolt and liberation in the last years of Spanish rule comes, again, from Mexico City and non-Indians: the Revolt of the Machetes in Mexico City in 1799, and the disturbances between creoles and peninsulares in Valladolid around Dec. 12, 1809. García, I: 335.

147. For example, in 1811, cura José Antonio Zúñiga of Temascaltepec was reported to have proclaimed "Viva Nuestra Señora de Guadalupe y mueran los Gachupines y sus sequases amigos." AGN Inq. 462 exp. 34.

148. AJANG Civil, bundle labeled "1809–19, leg. 5 (49)," Dec. 19, 1810, "Decreto sobre impedir a los naturales de Juchipila y Aposol que bejen la casa y haciendas de D. Julián Muñana." In central Mexico, cries of "Viva Nuestra Señora de Guadalupe" were heard during the overrunning of Atlacomulco and San Juan de los Jarros, and the killing of peninsular Spaniards there on Nov. 1–3, 1810. AGN Crim. 229, fols. 263–303.

149. AGN Hist. 428 exp. 3 ("el día de Nuestra Señora de Guadalupe habían de alumbrar en su santuario cirios compuestos de mixtos para que a cierta señal ardiese el templo y en la confusión volar el palacio del Exmo Señor Virrey que debía estar ya minado"). An earlier rumored plan to destroy the sanctuary and also the image of the Virgin of Guadalupe was investigated by the Inquisition in 1771. Joseph Guerrero, a 26-year-old creole living in Mexico City, claimed that various local notables were plotting to burn the sanctuary and turn the kingdom over to the English. The plan was to destroy the image in the belief that if it ever deteriorated by itself, the world would be destroyed. The Inquisition judged Guerrero's disclosure to be the rantings of an inveterate liar and sacrilegious criminal. AGN Inq. 1097 exp. 18.

150. Turner, *Dramas*, pp. 98–155.

151. Eric Wolf, "Virgin of Guadalupe," pp. 37–38.

152. Clearly Indians, especially in central Mexico, were being drawn to the Virgin of Guadalupe in the late colonial period, but the evidence at present is fragmentary or very general. Most of it has been cited already. Some is shaky at best. For example, in 1779, the Council of the Indies provided for six posts in the colegiata to be filled by experts in Indian languages: four in Nahuatl, one in Mazahua, and one in Otomí. This may indicate that many devotees came to the shrine from places where these languages were spoken. But it could also indicate where the colegiata planned to promote the cult. AGI Mex. 2531, June 10, 1779. My four examples of Indians in central Mexico invoking the Virgin of Guadalupe in their petitions to authorities in Mexico City date from the last decades of the colonial period. One was an individual petition, and three were in the name of communities: AGN Crim. 48, exp. 12, fol. 331r, petition of Manuel José, indio esclavo of Rodrigo del Valle, Trapiche de San Diego (near Yautepec, Morelos), 1775 ("y así pido y suplico a la grandessa de vuessa exxelencia que por N^{ra} Señora de Guadalupe mande el que se me dé papel para buscar amo"); AGN CRS 68 exp. 3, fol. 296, petition of Indians of San Agustín, Ixtlahuaca district (Edo. de México), April 9, 1772 ("que por amor de Dios y N^a S^a de Guadalupe suplican al presente S^r juez el arancel"); Crim. 222, exp. 51r, petition of Nicolás Juárez and "todos de mi pueblo . . . San José Cocotichan" and operarios de la Hacienda de Atoyac, Chalco district, Dec. 12, 1785 ("Pido y suplico q^e p^r la corona del Rey N° S^r y p^r N S^a de Guadalupe nos aga Vxa Justicia"); and AGN Bienes 172 exp. 45, petition of the gobernador of San Juan Bautista Tescatepec (Tlaxcala), 1805 ("Suplicamos por María Santísima de Guadalupe").

A collection of 1799 petitions for clemency by people detained by the Acordada (AGN Acordada 15) yields five appeals in her name; they seem to be more closely associated with urban residence than anything else. Two of the three Indian petitioners (fols. 94, 163, 285) resided in Mexico City, and the other lived in the city of Guanajuato. Of the two non-Indians, one was from the city of Querétaro and the other was not identified by place. Most of the petitions make no reference to the image of the Virgin of Guadalupe.

Other examples of Indian veneration of the Virgin of Guadalupe: Crim. 49 exp. 30, 1736, San Gregorio, Xochimilco district (oratory in Indian's home with a large picture of her); Colín, no. 562, 1762, Calimaya, Metepec district (at the time of the elections, some voters were off visiting the sanctuary); CRS 74 exp. 1, fol. 4r, 1780, Molango, Hidalgo (Indians celebrated Guadalupe's apparition with an annual village fiesta); CRS 206 exp. 3, 1798, Sultepec (customarily named mayordomos for various saints on the day of the Virgin of Guadalupe); Crim. 108 exp. 14, 1801, Tulancingo (Indian couple attended a recitation of the rosary for Nuestra Señora de Guadalupe); Crim. 3 exp. 10, 1805, Teocalzingo, Zacualpan district (some Indians celebrated the Virgin's birth by placing candles and flowers before an image of the Mexican Guadalupe). Moxó, pp. 205–6, speaks in his letters of 1805 of large numbers of Indian pilgrims visiting Tepeyac. No doubt many more examples will be found in the late colonial records, especially in the inventories of church ornaments, books of pastoral visits, and the directorios.

153. Sardo, pp. 61–66. Sardo's text closely follows a 17th-century account by the Jesuit devotee of the Virgin of Guadalupe, Francisco de Florencia.

154. Fernández de Lizardi, *Obras*, 1: 99.

155. AGN Templos 24. Although permission was not granted in 1813, by 1818 a grand church to Guadalupe was under construction in Zacapoaxtla, guided by cura Miguel Pérez Trabanca. José Rebollar Chávez, "El templo guadalupano en Zacapoaxtla," *La Voz Guadalupana*, 13, no. 7 (1946): 20–22. Some curas appealed to the Virgin of Guadalupe for aid against the early insurgency. For example, cura Jacinto Sánchez de Aparicio of Actopan reported on Aug. 21, 1811, that he and the priests of his district were celebrating a novenario of solemn masses for her intercession with God and the Christ of the Armies. García & Pereyra, 5: 246ff (doc. 49).

156. Meier, pp. 479–80. A good short summary of Morelos's devotion to the image of Guadalupe and the mystery of the Immaculate Conception is in Villoro, *Proceso*, pp. 103–4.

157. López Sarrelangue, *Una villa mexicana*, p. 258.

158. Humboldt, 1: 126. This view was not original to Humboldt, although he probably was its most influential proponent outside of Mexico. Clavigero and other late colonial creoles who idealized the ancient Indian past had expressed it decades before Humboldt visited New Spain. An enthusiastic 19th-century admirer of Humboldt expanded on his vision of Indians in these terms: "The cross was planted here in a congenial soil, and as in the Pagan East the statues of the divinities frequently did no more than change their names from those of heathen Gods to those of Christian saints, . . . so here the poor Indian still bows before visible representations of saints and virgins, as he did in former days before the monstrous shapes representing the unseen powers of the air, the earth, and the water; but he, it is to be feared, lifts his thoughts no higher than the rude image which a rude hand has carved." Calderón de la Barca, letter 38.

159. Warren explores the idea of Indians creating a philosophy to make sense of subordination after European colonization. In doing so, she questions the emphasis of much scholarship in Mesoamerican anthropology on the survival of precolonial traditions.

160. Curas and bishops calling for revered images to be placed in the parish church is a pattern suggested by examples cited earlier in the chapter. Even a household saint might be appropriated in this way. Victoria Juárez of Atitalaquia (Hidalgo) appealed to the pastoral visitor in 1789 for the return of her image of Christ of the Column, which the cura had taken to the parish church. The cura had done the right thing, the visitor concluded, "porque en la Parroquia tiene esta Santa Ymagen mejor culto." AHM L10B/25, fol. 150.

161. Sariola, p. 152.

Chapter Twelve

EPIGRAPH: AGN Tierras 2670 exp. 5 ("A más de esto el cura ha metido su hoz en mies agena").

1. Guadalajara's last colonial bishop, Juan Ruiz de Cabañas, described cofradías as "una junta, hermandad o sociedad cristiana de algunas personas que, no viviendo en comunidad ni obligándose por algunos votos o juramentos, se unen de común consentimiento para emplearse en algunas obras de piedad y practicar ciertos ejercicios espirituales con la aprobación de los legítimos superiores." Quoted in Serrera Contreras, *Guadalajara*, pp. 351–52.

2. *Concilio III*, 3-8-2, 3-14-3. Examples of curas exercising control over cofradía affairs in the Diocese of Guadalajara in the 17th century are CAAG, unclassified, "Sobre vender el ganado de la cofradía," 1669, Axixic (licensed the sale of cofradía livestock or other property for any purpose); and CAAG, unclassified, 1683, Ameca (lent money from the cofradía treasury to his compadres and sold livestock without consulting cofrades).

3. Solórzano 4-15-101.

4. *Recop.* 1-4-1, 2-31-8, 2-31-9. The cura of Cuquío (Jalisco) in 1829 claimed that other laws in the *Recopilación* (1-4-2, 1-4-4, 1-22-22, and 2-31-9) provided that bienes de cofradías de indios were the property of the church and subject only to ecclesiastical jurisdiction, and that Indians could not dispose of them. The laws he cited have no direct bearing on cofradías, nor do they provide any obvious basis for the cura's sweeping claim of ecclesiatical jurisdiction. CAAG, unclassified, document beginning "[el cura] da cuenta de los procederes de aquellos yndígenas en el repartimiento . . . de la cofradía de la Purísima."

5. CAAG, unclassified, 1721, Jocotepec, "autos pertenecientes a la cofradía del Santo Cristo de la Espiración"; AGN CRS 75 exp. 2, 1724 (Indians of Tecomatlan, Malinalco district, said the cura handled the accounts); CRS 72 exp. 4, 1734, San Juan Huetamo, Guaymeo district (suit against cura, "sobre que no les compela a fundar cofradías"); AGN

Tierras 2774 exp. 10 fol. 7r, 1751, Chiapa de Mota (cura keeping the cofradía records); AHJ Manuscripts, no. G-4-719, "Entrega del curato de Theocuitatlan," 1755, and certification for concurso of Agustín de Acosta, n.d. (after 1748); AGI Guad. 352, 1786 and later, report on bienes de comunidad compiled and submitted by Intendant Ugarte y Loyola, especially the reports on Huauchinango, Mascota, and Tequila; CRS 75 exp. 6, 1786, Alahuistlan (cura controlled a cofradía rancho); CRS 75 exp. 7, 1789, Timilpa, Huichapan district (cura presided over cofradía affairs); AJANG Civil, box 139, doc. 8, 1791, Moyahua, Juchipila district (cura said to manipulate cofradía property for his own use); Guad. 352, 1798, Ullate report, Santa María del Oro (cura held the financial records and would not show them to subdelegado); AGN Hist. 437, 1800, document titled "Sobre que el cura del pueblo de Mochitlan . . . maltrata y exige derechos indebidos," fols. 2–4, 9–14; AJANG Civil, bundle labeled "1803 (147)," 1803, Mecatabasco, Juchipila district; Guad. 534, Jan. 17, 1805, Bishop Cabañas, "Reflexiones . . . para la pública felicidad y mejora de costumbres de los pueblos" (wanted curas to control and report to him); CAAG, box of mainly 17th-century cofradía records, Tomatlan, 1805 and 1813; CAAG, unclassified, Jan. 20, 1817, letter of cura José Antonio Hurtado de Mendoza, San José de Gracia; CAAG, unclassified, Aug. 26, 1828 (complaint by former Indians of Tuscacuesco against cura); CAAG, unclassified, 1830, "Los indígenas de San Marcos, curato de Etzatlan, sobre despojo de cofradías" (cura took the property for himself).

6. By official count, there were at least 121 formally constituted cofradías in the Diocese of Guadalajara in 1805, compared with 117 in the archdiocese. Serrera, *Guadalajara*, p. 358. But Bishop Cabañas mentioned 403 cofradías in his pastoral visits (ibid., p. 371), and the pastoral visit records of the archdiocese identify many more than 117 cofradías and hermandades. In his report of April 9, 1791, Intendant Jacobo Ugarte of Guadalajara remarked on the special importance of cofradía properties there. They were, he said, the mainstay of parish finances in his province because clerical fees produced little income for the curas and vicarios, parishes received no part of the tithe, and few of them had substantial endowments for anniversary masses. AGI Guad. 352, cuad. 2. Ugarte's observation is supported by many individual cases in CAAG and BEJ Papeles de Derecho. The pastoral visit records for the archdiocese reveal a different story, despite the intention of making sodalities the centerpiece of parish finances.

7. "Prioste" was used interchangeably with "mayordomo" in Jalisco. CAAG, unclassified, 1765, Santa Fe (near Guadalajara), cacique Francisco Juan report; AGI Guad. 352, Ugarte report, cuad. 2, April 9, 1791.

8. AGN CRS 136 exps. 6–7.

9. Tulane VEMC 7 exp. 5, June 4, 1776, Pachuca report. Singling out the Divinísimo as the "super" cofradía is the pattern in late colonial pastoral visit records for the archdiocese (AHM L10A/5–8, L10B/9–32); and it was the stated policy of the visitador on his stops at Malinaltenango (Edo. de México) and Mexcala (Guerrero) in the late 1770's. AHM L10B/13, 1775, fol. 275; AHM L10B/21, 1779–80, fol. 266r.

10. CAAG, unclassified, 1776, "Sobre que las cofradías de Tlaxomulco se unan en la del Santíssimo sacramento." For more on this umbrella group, see AGN CRS 75 exp. 7, 1789, San Andrés Timilpa, Huichapan district (everyone was an hermano); CRS 25 exp. 4, fol. 206, 1793, Tecali district (Puebla); and AJANG Civil, bundle labeled "1809–19 (49)," 1802 resumé of Joseph Diego Gómez (established the first cofradía at Huaxicori, which was dedicated to Nuestro Amo).

11. Tulane VEMC 7 exp. 5, Pachuca, June 4, 1776, report; VEMC 3 exp. 5, Tepoztlan, 1791; CAAG, unclassified, July 3, 1829, "antes llamados indios" of Atotonilco el Alto.

12. Tulane VEMC 7 exp. 5, June 4, 1776, Pachuca report.

13. AGN CRS 25 exp. 4, fol. 206. Except for the hospital cofradías, colonial Mexi-

can sodalities attended less to poor relief than their urban counterparts in early modern Spain. See Flynn.

14. See, for example, the community cofradías in the districts of Pachuca and Yahualica. Tulane VEMC 7 exp. 5 and VEMC 15 exp. 5, 1775–76.

15. On Franciscan hospitals and their association with Mary Immaculate, see Taylor, "Indian Pueblos."

16. CAAG, unclassified, 1721, Jocotepec, "autos pertenecientes a la cofradía del Santo Cristo de la Espiración."

17. AGN CRS 206 exp. 3. In this case, the community, not the mayordomo, reportedly paid for the mass on the saint's day. Gruzinski, "Indian Confraternities," adds an important dimension to the study of sodalities in his discussion of these less formal religious associations.

18. Vetancurt, 1: 173.

19. Even in cabeceras of the archdiocese, the number of cofradías ranged from many to none. Amanalco (Edo. de México) had none in 1779, whereas Teloloapan (Guerrero) had seven that were "not in bad condition." AHM L10B/21, fols. 98–103, 273–74. On the "deplorable state" of cofradías in parts of the archdiocese, see AHM L10B/10, 1767–69, fols. 16–19 (Cuernavaca district); L10B/21, 1779–80, fols. 98–103 (Valle de Temascaltepec Cofradía de las Animas); and L10B/28, 1792–93 (various communities in the Valley of Toluca). During late colonial visitas in the archdiocese, cofradías were sometimes "extinguished" because of lax government and parlous financial condition. This meant that the prestigious standing and semi-independent government of cofradía status were withdrawn by the bishop, not necessarily that the cult disappeared. In this way, cofradías officially became hermandades. Xilotepec (Hidalgo) and Real de Temascaltepec (Edo. de México) are examples of communities where non-Indian cofradías were comparatively numerous and rich. L10B/13, fol. 237, L10B/28, fols. 164–65. Pescador, "Devoción," offers an especially close study of the late colonial history of a non-Indian cofradía in Mexico City. Another important contribution to the history of late colonial urban cofradías is Belanger, ch. 3.

20. AHM L10B/10, 1767–69, entries 6–10, and fols. 57r, 79v, and L10B/27, 1791–92, fols. 97v–100r, show Meztitlan's cofradías in decline. There were fewer and generally less-well-supported cofradías in the Valley of Toluca and Morelos, but great differences from one parish to the next even there.

21. Pérez-Rocha, "Mayordomías," p. 12. Apparently the earliest cofradías had many members and originally supported their activities from general contributions. By 1579, Chalco's cofradía of the Virgen del Rosario, founded about 1563, had received land donations from various principales and other natives of the pueblo and was on the way to a self-sustaining endowment. *Papeles de Nueva España*, 4: 64. Cases of Indians donating lands to cofradías: AGN Tierras 2776 exps. 23–24, 1764, Ecatepec; AGN Inq. 1146 exp. 1, 1775, Xilotepec; AGN Templos 1 exp. 2, pre-1786, Camotipan, Guayacocotla district (Veracruz); AGN Crim. 147, fols. 146–84, 1794, Tenango del Valle. It is not always clear whether lands were donated to cofradías or whether cofradías were allowed to used community lands— lands held "por razón de pueblo." Examples of cofradías using community lands: CAAG, unclassified, 1769 Tlajomulco report on Cofradía de Nuestra Señora de la Limpia Concepción; AGN CRS 136 exps. 6–7, 1790–91, Temascaltepec; Tierras 2670 exp. 3, 1792, Milpa Alta (supported fiestas from rental of community monte); CRS 25 exp. 4, 1793 Huiciltepec, Puebla.

22. For example, at Lerma (Edo. de México) in 1792, the Cofradía de las Animas was supported by a 1,400p lien at 5% annual interest, some magueyes, and "jornalillos" of the members. AHM L10B/28, fol. 2r.

23. Some 16th- and 17th-century examples of fiesta expenses being covered by *derramas*: AGN Civil 822, fols. 220–23, 1576, Tlacolula, Oaxaca; AGN Crim. 230 exp. 17, 1641,

Ixtlahuaca (gobernador forced Indians to pay 4rr per adult for the fiestas de las tres pascuas); Crim. 54 exp. 14, fol. 308r, 1690, Tlapanaloya (fiestas supported from general collections by the gobernador).

24. CAAG, cofradía records, box 2, Tala, 1759–62.

25. The 150–500 range of livestock held by hospital cofradías in Jalisco is based on the records contained in four labeled boxes of colonial cofradía records in CAAG. Serrera Contreras, *Guadalajara*, p. 372, concludes that cofradía property was even more substantial because the recorded inventories in late colonial inspections were incomplete.

26. CAAG, unclassified cofradía records, Tecolotlan, Aug. 16, 1817, cofradía inventory; CAAG, unclassified cofradía records, Ameca, 1812, "cuentas de cofradía."

27. AGI Guad. 543, Cabañas visita, cuad. 3, 1798, fols. 109–21.

28. AGI Guad. 543, cuad. 4, 1798.

29. For example, AGI Guad. 543, Cabañas visita, cuad. 3, 1798, fols. 80–87 (Juanacatlan and Tecuaititlan), fol. 222 (Teocuitatlan).

30. AHM L10B/21, fols. 35–40.

31. AGN CRS 25 exp. 4, fols. 270, 308 (cofradía created 1755). Other examples of curas creating cofradías: AHJ Manuscripts, no. G-4-719, 1755, Nochistlan, "Autos formados sobre pedir ministro independiente del cura reverendo, los vesinos españoles del Valle de Mesticacan," and Zapotlan (cura Pedro Ignacio del Castillo y Pesquera claimed to have established the Cofradía del Santísimo); CAAG, resumés for 1770 concurso of Antonio Manuel Velásquez (founded a cofradía at Chapala) and José Manuel de los Ríos (revived the Cofradía del Santísimo at Atemanica); AGN Hist. 578A, 1793, Tacuba report (cura Dr. Tomás de Arrieta created a new hermandad and added ornamentos); Hist. 437, fols. 9–14, 1800, Tixtla-Mochitlan; AJANG Civil, bundle labeled "1809-19 (49)," 1802, resumé of Joseph Diego Gómez (founded the Cofradía de Nuestro Amo at Huaxicori). The income-generating possibilities were less obvious and less closely supervised by priests in the specialized sodalities, but even there the cura usually received fees for an annual mass and some support for the care of a side altar or image in the church.

Van Oss, *Catholic Colonialism*, pp. 175–76, notes that in many places in colonial Guatemala, cofradías were the curas' "largest single source of revenue." Harrington, pp. 25–27, 339, found this to be considerably less true in neighboring Yucatán. There, in contrast to other Mesoamerican dioceses, much of the land still attached to cofradías was sold off by the bishop between 1780 and 1795.

32. AGN CRS 72 exp. 8. Other examples of curas making Indians create new cofradías include CRS 72 exp. 4, 1734, San Juan Huetamo, Guaymeo district; JCB, 1762, Joseph Buenaventura de Ayala and Nicolás Ximénez resumés; AGN Civil 2095 exp. 4, 1790, San Miguel Almoloya, Tenango del Valle district (making Indians contribute for "fiestas no señaladas"); and AGN Hist. 578A, 1793, Zacualpan report, vicario of Acapetlahuaya.

33. AJANG Civil, bundle labeled "1809-19 (49)," 1802, Joseph Diego Gómez resumé.

34. AGN CRS 137 exp. 5, fol. 198.

35. AHJ AMAJ, packet 1, 1828–29, "Juicio seguido por varios indígenas de Tizapanito contra el ayuntamiento sobre entrega de 200 cabezas de ganado pertenecientes a cofradías" (describing an 18th-century founding). Examples from the archdiocese include AGN Templos 1 exp. 2, pre-1786, Camotipan, Guayacocotla district, Veracruz (an Indian donated a little land to the Cofradía del Santísimo); AGN Crim. 147, fols. 146–84, 1794, Tenango del Valle (milpa for support of the fiesta of San Cayetano); BEJ Papeles de Derecho, 1: fols. 226v–229v, 1795, Tamazula (community again asked to establish a cofradía; first application made in 1793); and AGN Tierras 2621 exp. 6, 1818, Tenayuca, Valley of Mexico (pueblo members customarily left their share of community lands to a saint).

36. CAAG, cofradía records, box 2, 1746, document concerning cofradía founded 10 years before in Zacoalco by Antonio de Espinosa, with encouragement of the cura.

37. AGN CRS 72 exp. 4. See also AGN Tierras 2431 exp. 4, 1802, Ixcatepec (cofradías began with voluntary contributions of cattle by parishioners).

38. BEJ Papeles de Derecho, 1: fols. 226v–229v, 334v (1791, Cuquío; 1795, Tamasula).

39. On administrative costs, see Tulane VEMC 63 exp. 19, 1775, Cempoala; and AGN CRS 72 exp. 11, 1794, Mexico City. The Indians of Tapantla, Autlan district (Jalisco), complained in 1791 of the following excessive charges by their cura for the visita de cofradía: 5p for the colegio seminario, 8p for himself, 4p for the notary, and one cow apiece for him and the notary. CAAG, bundle labeled "Cofradías de los años de 1765–96."

40. CAAG, bundle labeled "Cofradías de los años 1765–96," Sept. 1, 1787, report of cura Fr. Ignacio Yslas of Atoyac. Similar examples for the archdiocese include Tulane VEMC 15 exp. 5, 1739, Yahualica (five cofradías supported weekly masses, fiesta titular, and more); VEMC 7 exp. 5, 1775, Pachuca (archicofradía, 100p for 50 misas de renovación, 48p for Easter week fees, 45p for Corpus Christi, 13p for San Pedro función, 9p for misa cantada de los cofrades, 6.5p for cabildo de elección; Animas cofradía of San Salvador Tizayuca, Monday masses, fiestas titular, and the anniversary mass; Santo Cristo cofradía of Orizaba, masses on the last Friday of the month, on the first Friday of Lent, on Good Friday, on the day of the Holy Cross, on the Sunday of Corpus Cristi week and the following Sunday, on the Day of the Transfiguration of Christ, and on Christmas, as well as the anniversary mass); VEMC 63 exp. 19, 1775, Cempoala (four cofradías de españoles paid 102p each for weekly or monthly masses, fiestas to the patron saints, anniversary masses, elections of mayordomos, and inspection of accounts; two cofradías paid 29p each for the same services); AGN CRS 25 exp. 4, 1783–93, Huiciltepec (Puebla); and CRS 136 exps. 6–7, 1790, San Francisco Temascaltepec (Santísimo Sacramento cofradía, 12p for Corpus, 12p for Jueves Santo, 1p a month for mass, 4p for Todos Santos).

41. AGN CRS 137 exp. 8, fols. 278–79. In deploring the excessive expenses of cofradías, late colonial curas were taking a cue from their bishops and royal decrees.

42. CAAG, unclassified, March 3, 1765, letter of cura Pedro Miguel Quintano. Arguing that Indians should not administer cofradía properties, the cura wrote "es ocasión de muchos y graves pecados porque la cofradía les costea la panocha de que fabrican bebidas para la continua embriaguez . . . [which leads to] luxuria, adulterio, incestos, estupros, fornicaciones, etc., irrespectos a sus superiores, tranquilidad, litigios y como tienen tan a su disposición la carne, usan abundantemente de ella, aun en tiempos prohibidos (por la iglesia). De la cofradía sacan los tributos . . . etc., y con esta confianza se dan tanto al ocio y floxedad."

43. AJANG Civil, bundle labeled "1795, leg. 35 (1)."

44. For litigation against the cura: AGN CRS 25 exp. 4, 1793–1803, Huiciltepec; CRS 137 exp. 8, 1804–5, Alahuistlan, Zacualpan district. For land measurements and titles (all from CAAG, unclassified): 1690, Tizapan (Indians misusing cofradía property, selling livestock); 1769, Tizapanito (ten bulls sold for the community's two cofradías to pay for land measurement); 1800, Tizapan (petition to use 200p from two cofradías for land measurement); 1803, Tonila measurement record; 1806, Tizapan (petition to use 50p from cofradía funds for a composición de tierras). For tribute: CAAG, unclassified, March 3, 1765, letter of cura Pedro Miguel Quintano of Santa Fe (near Guadalajara). For emergency relief from famine and epidemic: CRS 25 exp. 4, fol. 206, 1793–1803, Huiciltepec; CAAG, unclassified, Nov. 25, 1822, "Sobre arreglo y aprobación del reglamento de las cofradías de la parroquia de Tala."

Bishop Cabañas appreciated the charitable uses of cofradía treasuries as welfare funds in his diocese when he wrote in 1788: "Estos fondos, bajo la apariencia de cofradías, son unos montes de piedad, con que no sólo se consulta por los ordinario a la conservación del pasto espiritual de todo el obispado, al culto debido a Dios y a sus templos, privados hasta el día de los ordinarios auxilios, sino aun en el socorro de las necesidades de los pobres de todas clases en los casos de enfermedad, inopia o esterilidad, como se verificó en la rigurosa peste y general hambre que poco ha experimentamos." Cited in Serrera Contreras, *Guadalajara*, p. 352.

45. AGN CRS 156 exp. 11.

46. CAAG, resumés of cura José Antonio Barragán of Huejuquilla and Felipe de Liñán of Tepic for 1770 concurso.

47. AGI Guad. 352, cuad. 2, fol. 87, Oct. 12, 1786 Ugarte report.

48. Examples of cofradía expenditures in Guadalajara: CAAG, cofradía records, box 4, 1669, Ajijic, "sobre vender el ganado de la cofradía," and 1688, Atotonilco el Bajo (request to use 200p of cofradía funds for hospital chapel construction); CAAG, unclassified, 1772, San Gaspar Teuchitlan, Tala district (petition to apply cofradía funds to church construction); AGI Guad. 341, 1776, pastoral visit, Tapalpa. See also in CAAG, unclassified, various requests by parish priests for cofradías to purchase ornamentos for the church (e.g., 1726, Tecolotlan, Autlan district). For Mexico: AGN CRS 72 exp. 4, before 1734, Huetamo, witness no. 1, Juan de Suaso y Pardo; CRS 130 exp. 9, 1802, San Felipe, Metepec district; Tulane VEMC 36 exp. 17, 1802–3, Alahuistlan.

49. AGN CRS 130 exp. 9, 1802, San Felipe, Metepec district.

50. During his pastoral visit to Zapotlan del Rey, Juanacatlan district, in 1776, Bishop Alcalde of Guadalajara intervened to order that cofradía funds be used to repair the church. AGI Guad. 341. He also contributed 1,000 pesos of his own funds to the cause.

51. Papeles de Derecho and AFRANG 293 in BEJ and AGI Guad. 250 and 352 (Ugarte report) document the strength and wealth of cofradías compared with the cajas de comunidad at this time.

52. AGN Tierras 2431 exp. 4 ("Que desde el origen de nuestro vecindario concurrieron sus individuos voluntariamente a poblar seis ranchos. . . . Estos intereses se establecieron con el objeto de asegurarle al pueblo una subsistencia que rindiese lo suficiente a desempeñar las expensas que antes salían de los sudores del común para acudir a los menesteres de la yglesia, a el costo de los paramentos sagrados, a las limosnas de missas . . . a diferentes advocaciones, y también para soccorrer varias indigencias públicas").

53. Cofradía livestock frequently grazed on lands within the pueblo patrimony. According to cura Felipe de Liñán of Tepic, he had built up the cofradías at Tuspa and Acaxala in the early 1760's; and over the objection of Indian parishioners, he had separated out 80 cattle from a herd in which they had mixed cofradía and community animals. CAAG, resumé for 1770 concurso.

54. AGN Tierras 261 exp. 6, 1818, Tenayuca, is one example of a pueblo in which people by custom donated their share of the community lands to the support of a saint or special advocation. For further comparisons of community and cofradía lands, data on property, and information on Oaxaca cofradías, see Serrera Contreras, *Guadalajara*, especially pp. 341–72; Taylor, "Indian Pueblos"; and Chance & Taylor.

55. AGN CRS 137 exp. 5. A similar informality can be seen in the pious funds of Alahuistlan, Zacualpan district, in 1805. CRS 137 exp. 8.

56. AGN CRS 72 exp. 4. Indians of San Gerónimo, Cholula district (Puebla), in 1729 claimed the vicario meddled in affairs of the community treasury. They obtained a decree from the audiencia ordering him to desist. He replied that the pueblo had gained the decree by misrepresenting the facts, that the properties in question were "destinados a la iglesia" and therefore should not be considered bienes de comunidad. CRS 47 exp. 4.

57. AGN CRS 42 exp. 1.

58. For other laws, see Brooks, ch. 4.

59. AGN Bandos 4 exp. 16.

60. AGN Bandos 9 exp. 41.

61. Enlarging community treasuries at the expense of pious funds was the intent of the March 26, 1783, "Reglamento para el pueblo de Apasco" (Tetepango district, Hidalgo). It called for reducing or eliminating payments from the bienes de comunidad for religious

fiestas, wax, ornaments, church repairs, and schoolmasters, and oversight of the caja de comunidad finances by the alcalde mayor. Vásquez, pp. 336–42. Serrera Contreras, *Guadalajara*, pp. 339–55, discusses the struggle over the two funds in the Diocese of Guadalajara after 1783.

62. Ventura Beleña, 2: pp. viii–xi (following p. 427). In looking at Indian pueblos as revenue-generating enterprises for the state ("medios para la captación de moneda"), Lira, "Cajas de comunidad," highlights the Ordenanza de Intendentes as establishing the rules for the cajas and stresses the fiscal motives for reform. Nava Oteo, in her study of cajas de comunidad in the Valley of Teotihuacan, also sees the Ordenanza de Intendentes as an important event.

63. AGI Guad. 352, Ugarte report. An example for the archdiocese of an Indian community appealing to the Ordenanza de Intendentes to make its case for the priest to be removed from cofradía administration is AGN CRS 75 exp. 7, 1789, Timilpa, Huichapan district.

64. BEJ Papeles de Derecho, 1: 334v.

65. AGN CRS 136 exps. 6–7.

66. BEJ Papeles de Derecho, 1: 573v–580v, 1796, Sayula; AGN CRS 25 exp. 4, 1783–93, Huiciltepec (dissolution issue).

67. AGN CRS 25 exp. 4.

68. AGN CRS 72 exp. 12, Aculco, Xilotepec district.

69. AGN RCO 167 exps. 288, 291, Aug. 26, 1797.

70. BEJ Papeles de Derecho, 2: 354–55; Papeles de Derecho, 3: 79–83.

71. AGN Bandos 16 exp. 27. The bando quoted a royal cedula of March 8, 1791, to this effect.

72. Tulane VEMC 53 exp. 22.

73. AGN CRS 72 exp. 12.

74. AGN CRS 137 exp. 8, fols. 275v, 287–89. In support of his position, the fiscal protector cited cedulas of Sept. 6, 1788, Nov. 16, 1789, and Nov. 25, 1802.

75. The audiencia fiscal de lo civil for Guadalajara, in an opinion in a dispute over the Cofradía del Santísimo Sacramento on March 27, 1798, noted that though cofradía matters pertained to the church, the lands of cofradías were still royal property, even though they had passed "into other hands." No matter what their use the properties of the cofradía were temporal and mundane ("bienes temporales y profanos"). BEJ Papeles de Derecho, 2: 354r–355v. Records in the cathedral archive of Guadalajara show that disputes over the nature of cofradía properties continued there in the early 19th century. A case reached the courts in 1809–10 disputing the ownership of a rancho attached to the hospital at Tlajomulco. The audiencia fiscal and the legal representative of the Royal Treasury asserted that it was hospital property and, therefore, within the crown's jurisdiction. The bishop argued strongly for ecclesiastical control, even though the hospital was not then in service, noting that the Cofradía of the Immaculate Conception had been despoiled of these lands in 1799 but recovered them in 1801. CAAG, unclassified, "Liquidación de reales pertenecientes a los arriendos del sitio de Cacaluta." The old conflicts between parish priests and parishioners over cofradía properties continued during the 1820's, but secular officials were then well on the way to taking over the administration of cofradía finances and, in Acatlan de Juárez, priests were resigned to the dissolution of sodality properties. See especially the 1823–28 records for Tizapanito in CAAG and AHJ AMAJ, packet no. 1; and the July 3, 1829, petition of the "antes llamados indios" of Atotonilco el Alto in CAAG.

76. AGN CRS 137 exp. 5, fol. 194r, 1802, San Simón Tototepec, Zacualpan district (Indians were ordered to keep the accounts, and the cura was ordered not to interfere); CRS 137 exp. 8, fols. 187–89, Alahuistlan, Zacualpan district, Aug. 22, 1805 (audiencia ordered that cofradía funds not be squandered on "fiestas, comidas, embriagueses, y gastos

superfluos y generalmente toda especie de disipación sino que se inviertan precisamente en los destinos [y] objetos piadosos").

77. For example, in an 1817 dispute in Acatlan, Tulancingo district, in which the cura was accused of adding new fiestas to those that local cofradías already sponsored, the audiencia ordered the cofradías to support only the celebrations and duties set down in their constitutions. AGN CRS 136 exp. 8.

78. The selection of cofradía leaders by gobernadores was reported at Alahuistlan in 1786. AGN CRS 75 exp. 6. In 1763, the town officials of Tlajomulco complained bitterly when the cura tried to influence the election, refused to convene until he desisted, and petitioned the audiencia to remove his candidate. CAAG, cofradía records, installation of Juan Antonio de Aguila as mayordomo of the Immaculate Conception cofradía.

79. On cofrades' demand to name their own officers: AGN CRS 75 exp. 11, fol. 496, 1791, Ajuchitlan, Tetela del Río district (cura said the Indians now demanded the right to name the mayordomos); CRS 75 exp. 7, 1788, San Andrés Timilpa, Huichapan district. In the second case, the Indians complained that the cura was trying to force the reelection of his favorite. They wanted the justicia (the alcalde mayor or his lieutenant) to preside. The fiscal de la Real Hacienda and the audiencia agreed, citing articles 13 and 14 of the 1786 Ordenanza de Intendentes for New Spain.

Even so, some curas continued in their old ways. The lieutenant of Aculco in 1796 complained that the cofradías there were governed by mayordomos who were "elected" by the cura—that "the individual favored by the parish priest is always elected." CRS 72 exp. 12. At Moyahua, Zacatecas (Guadalajara) in 1791, Indian parishioners asked that the cura no longer be allowed to choose the mayordomos, but they agreed that he could continue to certify the outcome and veto the cofrades' choice "for good reason." AJANG Civil, box 139, doc. 8.

80. CAAG, cofradía records, box 4, 1669, Ajijic ("Sobre vender el ganado de la cofradía").

81. Cofradía property and general observations from the Cabañas visita of 1797–1804 are discussed in Serrera Contreras, *Guadalajara*, pp. 339–75. This pattern of decline is presented in more detail in Taylor, "Indian Pueblos," p. 174.

82. AGI Guad. 543, Cabañas visita, cuad. 3, fols. 243v–250r; yet Teuchitlan, Tala district, increased its herd from 200 cattle in 1772 to 371 cattle and 83 horses in 1802.

83. See Taylor, "Indian Pueblos," pp. 174–75. A decline was evident but not so dramatic in the five Indian pueblos of the Zapotlanejo district, where the cofradía herds declined by 20% between 1770 and 1801, from 1,870 to 1,497. A similar pattern of declining herds is evident for the archdiocese in the pastoral visit records. AHM L10A/5–8, L10B/9–32.

84. AGI Guad. 543, cuad. 3, fols. 80–87, 122–29, Cabañas visita to Zapotlanejo and Tlajomulco; Guad. 352, cuad. 2, Ugarte report of April 9, 1791, and 1791 observation by cura of Chapala that Indians were trying to sell cofradía livestock to pay tribute; CAAG, unclassified, Feb. 12, 1792, Mecatabasco (cura complained of Indians distributing cofradía cattle among themselves); CAAG, unclassified, 1803 (payment of 400p out of cofradía funds for a land measurement); CAAG, unclassified, 1804, Jamay, "Sobre que se tome providencia para que los yndios del pueblo de Jamain no disipen los biene. de su cofradía" (cura sought the bishop's intervention to prevent the Indian alcalde and others from selling livestock); CAAG, unclassified, 1803 (payment of 400p out of cofradía funds for a land measurement); AJANG Civil, bundle labeled "1805, leg. 45," 1805, "Sobre venta de bienes de obras pías y capellanías."

85. The cedulas on the sale of obras pías and capellanías dated Jan. 23, 1805, June 3, 1806, and May 27, 1807, are included in an expediente entitled "1805, Sobre venta de bienes de obras pías y capellanías," in AJANG Civil, bundle labeled "1805, leg. 45 (134)."

86. CAAG, cofradía records, 1815, "Sobre enagenación de los fondos de la parroquia de la villa de Purificación." This was the cura of Purificación's plan for the 8.75 sitios and 12 caballerías of "church" lands on which rent was no longer being paid. The war contributed to more confusion in the cofradías and the opportunity for mayordomos to appropriate livestock for their own use. See, for example, AJANG Criminal, bundle labeled "1818 (89)," 1818, where the lieutenant finally arrested the mayordomo of Xalpa. In some cases, the confusion and loss of property provided curas with the opportunity to reclaim their management as an emergency measure to protect what remained. The cura of San José de Gracia (Guadalajara) in 1817, for instance, justified his management of cofradía finances and failure to hold elections for mayordomos in recent years as an unavoidable war measure. CAAG, unclassified, Jan. 20, 1817, Hurtado de Mendoza letter.

87. CAAG, cofradía records. The pattern of declining numbers of livestock, inattentive management, and malfeasance was evident in some parishes before the 1780's. In 1765, the cacique of Santa Fe (near Guadalajara) spoke of the "total ruin" of the Immaculate Conception cofradía's possessions because of the corrupt management of an aged principal, Manuel Salvador, who had served as prioste for two years. The cura, Pedro Miguel Quintano, corroborated this part of the cacique's claims in a letter to the bishop of March 3, 1765, adding that the cofrades "disponen tan a su arbitrio y antojo de todo — venden, arriendan, matan, regalan, y destruyen los bienes sin poderse averiguar sino es quando unos pelean con otros, que entonces rencorosos, y por venganza se descubren sus maldades." CAAG, cofradía records, box 2.

88. AGI Guad. 352, cuad. 2, Ugarte report.

89. A sample of late colonial disputes between priests and parishioners over the administration and property of cofradías: AGN CRS 47 exp. 4, 1729, San Gerónimo, Cholula district ("sobre extorciones que les infiere el vicario de su partido"; example of curas intervening to protect church property before the late 18th century); CRS 42 exp. 1, 1732, Tejupilco; CRS 72 exp. 4, 1734, Huetamo; CAAG, unclassified, 1772, San Gaspar Teuchitlan, Tala district (Indian parishioners' petition to use cofradía funds to build church); CRS 72 exp. 8, 1785, Tlaxpa, Tepejí del Río district; CRS 75 exp. 6, 1786, Alahuistlan; CRS 75 exp. 7, 1788–89, San Andrés Timilpa, Huichapan district; CRS 136 exps. 6–7, 1790–91, Temascaltepec (cura arranged for rent of sitios to non-Indians in order, he claimed, to generate cofradía income); AJANG Civil, box 139, doc. 8, 1791, Moyahua; AGN Templos 159 exp. 50, 1793, San Miguel Quaxusco, Malinalco district; CRS 25 exp. 4, 1793–1803, Huiciltepec, Puebla; AGN Crim. 147, fols. 146–84, 1794, Tenango del Valle; Templos 25 exp. 7, 1795, Tequisquiac; CRS 140 exp. 4, 1796, Yautepec; CRS 206 exp. 3, 1798, San Miguel Totomaloyan, Alahuistlan district; CRS 84 exp. 7, 1800, Yautepec; CRS 130 exp. 9, 1802, San Felipe, Metepec district; AGN Tierras 2431 exp. 4, 1802, Ixcatepec; CAAG, unclassified, 1802, Acatic, Tepatitlan district ("sobre despojo del manejo de los bienes de las cofradías de dich pueblo"); Tulane VEMC 36 exp. 17, 1802–3, Alahuistlan; CRS 137 exp. 5, 1803, San Simón Tototepec, Zacualpan district; VEMC 36 exp. 17, 1803, Alahuistlan; CRS 137 exp. 8, 1805, Alahuistlan; Crim. 178 fols. 239–47, 1807, Zimapantongo; AJANG Civil, bundle labeled "1800–1809 (109)," 1819, Xalpan; CAAG, unclassified, Nov. 25, 1822, Tala, Ahuisculco, Teuchitlan ("sobre arreglo y aprobación del reglamento de las cofradías de la parroquia de Tala"; cura wanted to rent out cofradía lands and Indians resisted violently, saying the properties belonged to them).

Not all parish priests lost control of cofradía properties. Their literacy, management experience, and interest in controlling the finances made them indispensable in some cases; but confronting both subdelegados and pueblos over the matter without a firm legal right presented them with a formidable problem.

90. AGN CRS 72 exp. 12. Other cases similar to Aculco include CRS 75 exp. 11, 1789–91, Ajuchitlan, Tetela del Río district; CRS 195 exp. 12, 1794, Chilpancingo; CRS 72

exp. 18, 1798, Ixtlahuaca; AGN Hist. 437, 1800, Mochitlan; CRS 195 exp. 16, 1800, Xalat-zingo; and CRS 137 exp. 8, 1804, Alahuistlan. For an earlier struggle between a cura and an alcalde mayor over control of cofradía lands, see AGN Tierras 1776 exps. 23–24, 1764, Ecatepec. Most earlier conflicts between curas and district governors over cofradías found the governor accusing the priest of stealing from them, not disputing original jurisdiction (e.g., AGN Inq. 1113, fols. 231–54, 1777, cura Juan Antonio Xil de Andrade of Cempoala).

91. AGN Hist. 132 exp. 30.

92. Examples of curas with a strong, if contested role in cofradía affairs in the last years of the colonial period: AGN CRS 75 exp. 7, 1788, San Andrés Timilpa, district of Huicha-pan; CRS 136 exps. 6–7, 1790, San Francisco Temascaltepec; CRS 25 exp. 4, 1793, Tecali; Tulane VEMC 53 exp. 22, 1794, Real de Huautla; CRS 140 exp. 4 and CRS 84 exp. 7, 1796, Yautepec; AGN Hist. 437, 1800, Mochitlan; AGN Tierras 2431 exp. 4, 1802, Ixca-tepec; CRS 137 exp. 5, 1803, San Simón Tototepec; AGN Crim. 178, fols. 239–47, 1807, Zimapantongo. Example of a cura "electing" a non-Indian mayordomo: CRS 72 exp. 12, 1791, Aculco. Some curas, even when they acceded to the new policy influenced cofradía finances by ordering whippings of mayordomos who did not pay for the required masses, as in Crim. 147, fols. 146–84, 1794, Tenango del Valle.

93. AGN Hist. 437.

94. On curas of Guadalajara dismantling cofradía properties: CAAG, unclassified, Aug. 26, 1828, Tuscacuesco (cura charged with selling the bienes de cofradía and keep-ing the proceeds); CAAG, unclassified, 1829–33, Zapotlan el Grande, Tamazula (petitions from curas to sell lands of cofradías); CAAG, unclassified, 1830, Chapala (complaint by cofrades of the María Santísima cofradía in Chapala that the cura seized their properties for his own use: "Sólo bemos despilfarros").

95. CAAG, cofradía records, 1829, "El cura de Cuquío da cuenta . . ." ("Los indígenas han repartido todos los fondos entre ellos mismos en tanto grado que no sólo los agos-taderos en que pacea el ganado de la cofradía llamada de la purísima, sino también los corrales y plaza de rodeo. En cuya virtud me veo en la necesidad de rentar otro agosta-dero o de vender el poco mueble que queda; tanto por lo que se entrañara mudándolo, como por los ladroncillos que poco a poco acabarán con ella; siéndome más doloroso la altanería con que dichos indígenas se portan, ceducidos estos de unos quantos calaveras que no importa nombrarlos, llegando a tanto grado que han vendido un hospital"). "Cala-veras" (skulls) in the cura's usage means "persons of poor judgment and little prudence," according to the early editions of the *Diccionario de la lengua castellana*.

96. AHJ AMAJ, uncatalogued 19th-century records.

97. AGN Templos 25 exp. 7; also AGN CRS 42 exp. 1, fols. 6r, 8, 1732, Tejupilco. Jocotepec, in the Diocese of Guadalajara, was said to have always managed its own cofra-días (CAAG, unclassifed, Sept. 2, 1794, report by the cura José Antonio Martínez Mar-taraña), as had Acatic, Tepatitlan district (CAAG, unclassified, 1802, "Sobre despojo del manejo de los bienes de las cofradías de dicho pueblo"). Intendant Ugarte reported on a rich cofradía of Mascota in which the cura was not involved. AGI Guad. 352, cuad. 2.

98. AGN CRS 137 exp. 5.

99. AJANG Civil, box 90, doc. 16.

100. AGN Tierras 2431 exp. 4.

101. CAAG, unclassified, Feb. 12, 1792, complaint by Mecatabasco cura González de Hermosillo.

102. Gibson, *Aztecs*, p. 129.

103. Examples of informal, individual sponsorship include the mayordomías for the saints at Totomaloyan in 1786 described above, mayordomo sponsorship of a feast for the community of San Miguel Almoloya, Tenango del Valle district, Edo. de México on the Day of the Holy Cross (May 3) in 1760 (AGN CRS 192 exps. 11–12, 1760–86), and the

custom of mayordomos of Malinaltenango sponsoring celebrations during Holy Week, mentioned in 1784 (AGN Templos 25 exp. 4, 1769–84). For the theses that individual sponsorship became the norm in the 19th century and that the civil-religious hierarchy grew then as the presence of parish priests declined, see Chance & Taylor.

104. AGN CRS 136 exps. 6–7, fols. 320–22. Other examples of the selection of mayordomos for their "wealth" are AGN Hist. 132 exp. 27, 1794, Yautepec; and AJANG Criminal, bundle labeled "1811–20, leg. 2 (20)," 1816, Totatiche, Tlaltenango district.

105. AJANG Civil, bundle labeled "1791–98, leg. 20."

106. In his campaign to promote cofradías, Archbishop Lorenzana was inclined to encourage new mayordomos to finance them. AHM L10B/10, 1767–69, fol. 143v.

107. AGN Inq. 1334 exp. 3, fols. 181–82, 1796–1800.

108. AGN Civil 2095 exp. 4. In the context of the larger history of cofradías, these examples of curas actively promoting private sponsorship do not support the idea that priests' repressive power is sufficient to explain individual sponsorship. On the other hand, they also raise doubts about functionalist interpretations that leave parish priests out of the history of cofradía affairs (discussed further in Chance & Taylor).

109. Chance & Taylor.

110. See, for example, CAAG, box of Tlajomulco cofradía records, 1840, Cajititlan.

111. "Descripción de Alahuiztlán" ("Familias de españoles, cuya casta no se sabe de cierto . . . por ser foráneos y traspuestos a esta jurisdicción").

112. AGN CRS 75 exp. 6, fol. 371, July 1787.

113. The parishes of Apaxtla and Coatepec de los Costales, and the area called Ceutla in the parish of Tetela del Río, just south of the district of Tixtla, were identified as trouble spots by the pastoral visitor, whereas in 1780 Alahuistlan was a parish of "peaceful and orderly" Indians, where "so many boys and girls go to school and pray the catechism that in the afternoon more than 300 girls assemble, and at night the same number of boys." AHM L10B/21, 1779–80, fols. 269r, 271v, 273, 274r. People of Ceutla were particularly famous for living outside the law, and beyond the priests' influence. In the words of the pastoral visitor in 1780, "en los confines de este curato y en los de Chilpancingo, Acapulco y Coyuca hay un sitio llamado Ceutla, mui grande, fértil fecundado con varios ríos de los que el mayor es él del Papagayo, y compuesto de varias rancherías de gente foragida que viven de las siembras de tabaco de que hacen contrabandos; aora seis años de orden del Superior Govierno y Gefes de este Ramo, se pasó por un comisionado acompañado de treinta hombres al destrozo y ruina de dichas siembras, lo que executaron, y me aseguraron que valdría como catorce mil pesos lo que se quemó. Todas aquellas gentes viven como regularmente se dice, sin Dios, ley, ni Rey, no reconocen jurisdicción alguna y viven como bestias, porque ni aun ocurren a dichos curatos a bautizar los que nacen. Y me aseguraron algunos de los que fueron al destrozo del tabaco que después que lo verificaron y prendieron como quince personas entre hombres, mujeres y niños, por haberse huido los demás, se han vuelto a reunir, viven en la misma forma; y hasta apóstatas de algunas Religiones aseguran que hay en dicho Ceutla. Este es un mal difícil de remediar porque el referido sitio, que pertenece a la Castellanía de Acapulco, dista treinta leguas a lo menos del más inmediato de dichos curatos."

114. The events of 1786–88 are documented in AGN CRS 75 exp. 6.

115. Castro was 27 years old at the time of his deposition. During his four years in Alahuistlan, there had been two curas.

116. AGN Hist. 578A, 1793, Sultepec report; Osores, 1: 68.

117. AGN CRS 206 exp. 3.

118. Tulane VEMC 36 exp. 17.

119. AGN CRS 137 exp. 8, fol. 275v.

120. A marginal note in ibid., fol. 279, ordered the subdelegado to forward the document of Sept. 8, 1804, without delay.

121. Ibid., fol. 283 ("Por ahora lo que puedo informar a VE es que dhos bienes son radicados por los mismos naturales con el nombre de cofradías, pero no son de Yglecia, ni bienes espirituales, como dho cura representa, pues es público y notorio que son puramente profanos sin que ninguno de los demás curas tenga tales pretenciones pues todos están bien impuestos de su verdadero fundamento").

122. See Chance & Taylor for more on structural differences between the 19th- and 20th-century cofradías. We posit that whereas cofradía sponsorship of the official cult was an artifact of colonial rule, the same cannot be so clearly said of individual sponsorship and an elaborate ladder of offices.

123. This is the emphasis of Brooks; and Gruzinski, "Indian Confraternities."

124. Farriss, *Maya Society*, especially ch. 11, describes priests as exercising little influence over Indian cofradías in Yucatán, a conclusion supported by AGI Mex. 2546, Nov. 4, 1818, "En cumplimiento de la real orden con que se les dirigió una carta documentada del Reverendo Obispo de Yucatán," a Council of the Indies decree referring to a letter of the bishop of Yucatán, who wanted to sell cofradía haciendas dedicated to various images in the jurisdiction of Kinctul because they yielded no income to the church. The Indian gobernadores objected, gaining the support of the audiencia and, here, the Council of the Indies.

125. One exception is the mestizo mining community of Huautla (Morelos), where, in 1794, no one was willing to serve as mayordomo of the Divinísimo cofradía because of the large debt it owed to the cura and the fear that the mayordomo would be made personally responsible for it. But even here the cofrades sought to solicit contributions and renew their commitment to the cult. Tulane VEMC 53 exp. 2.

Chapter Thirteen

EPIGRAPH: AGN Bienes 575 exp. 14, fol. 24r ("Luego dise el Sr. cura que nosotros somos judíos no queremos que ayga Escuelas no creemos la Ley de Dios por eso no los queremos los maestros. No es verdad están enoxados todos los pobres naturales porque no les enseñan sus hijos bien porque el cura les ha dicho a los maestros que no los enseñan las cartas ni escrivir ni la lengua castellana solo las oraciones porque si lo han de saber bien entonses sabran defenderse cada uno solo").

1. Pérez de Velasco, pp. 18, 71. As one dissatisfied cura wrote to a fiscal who had failed to collect a burial fee, "Tienes obligación no sólo de celar y velar el pueblo mas también la tienes de cobrar los derechos de la iglesia." AGN CRS 75 exp. 5, fol. 324, 1785, San Luis de las Peras, Huichapan district. Fiscales and other lay officials are described for the Cuernavaca district in Haskett, *Indigenous Rulers*, pp. 114–23. The fiscal post there appears to have been a prestigious one filled by members of "the highest levels of local indigenous society."

2. Pérez de Velasco, p. 18.

3. AGN CRS 179 exp. 13, fol. 408.

4. José Cortés Chimalpopoca, an Indian noble from the jurisdiction of Tacuba, claimed in 1818 that his hereditary privileges exempted him from appointment to minor offices such as fiscal, escribano, topil, alguacil, and regidor. AGN CRS 130 exp. 10. The first generations of fiscales enjoyed more prestige and probably more political and spiritual power than their successors. In the 16th century, the fiscal was called an alcalde or alguacil, or by the Nahuatl terms for calpulli officers (calpixqui, tepixqui, and tequitlato), and was regarded as a member of the Indian cabildo. Guarda, p. 61. Lockhart, "Some Nahua Concepts in Postconquest Guise," also draws upon 16th-century evidence to describe the

fiscales as major figures in local politics. Since late colonial fiscales were supposed to be over 50 years of age, it would be surprising if many of them had not held other community offices even where the office of fiscal generally had become less important.

5. *Recop.* 6-3-7 called for a fiscal in every Indian community, and two in communities with more than 100 Indians. This law was invoked in AGN CRS 136 exp. 2, fols. 185–93, 1781, Huispaleca and Pueblo Nuevo, Cuernavaca district; and CRS 179 exp. 13, fol. 409, 1763, Actopan.

6. Examples of fiscales subordinate to a fiscal mayor: AGN Tierras 2179 exp. 3, fols. 50–53, 1756, Xilotepec (rancherías within the parish); AGN CRS 179 exp. 13, fol. 409, 1763, Actopan; CRS 75 exp. 9, fol. 451, 1790, Tepetitlan, near Tula (visitas of the parish). Examples of two fiscales in a pueblo: AGN Acervo 49 caja 50, 1749, Tampamolon; AGN Crim. 141, fols. 376–90, 1776, Ozumba; CRS 136 exp. 2, fols. 185–93, 1781, Tlaltizapan; CRS 75 exp. 6, 1786, Alahuistlan; AGN Hist. 437 unnumbered exp., fols. 9–14, 1800, "Sobre que el cura del pueblo de Mochitlan Br. d. Juan Valerio Barrientos maltrata y exige derechos indebidos a sus feligreses"; AGN Bienes 663 exp. 19, 1817, Lerma.

How fiscales from different communities were interconnected is not yet clear. Many fiscales in the visitas would have had a localized view of their responsibilities, but it was natural for the cura and the fiscal of the parish seat to try to coordinate their activities. Indians of Santa María Atengo and San Francisco Zayula in the parish of Tepetitlan complained in 1790 that their fiscales were "*fiscales* in name only," that they were effectively named from the parish seat and controlled by the fiscal there. CRS 75 exp. 9. Like the fiscales menores, fiscales in the visitas were sometimes called alguaciles de la iglesia or alguaciles de la doctrina, suggesting their ideally subordinate position in the parish hierarchy. Tierras 2179 exp. 3, 1757, testimony of Andrés Osorio, Xilotepec; Hist. 578A, 1793, Zumpango de la Laguna report. From the cura's point of view, they were there to assist him when he visited the outlying villages of the parish—taking the annual census, collecting fees, making arrests at his orders, and overseeing the rotational labor of local parishioners in the head town. CRS 75 exp. 4, fols. 257v–260v, 1775, Tototepec, Zacualpan district; Crim. 141, fols. 359–75, 1817, Tlayacapan.

7. AGN Crim. 283 exp. 3, fol. 279v, 1719, Santa Lucía (Oaxaca); AGN Tierras 2179 exp. 3, 1756, Xilotepec, testimony of Vicente Flores.

8. AGN CRS 75 exp. 6, fol. 366v, 1786 (as messenger); AGI Guad. 385, diario for audiencia, Jan. 4, 1803, entry, "Reo Santiago el campanero indio, uno de los cómplices en la sublevación intentada en el pueblo de San Juanito."

9. *Recop.* 6-3-7 (1618). The days of the child fiscal, which seems to have been the friars' preference in the first generation of Spanish colonization, were long past in the 18th century. See Trexler's study, "From the Mouths of Babes," in *Church and Community*, for a discussion of the use of Indian youths in the evangelization of the early 16th century. Another of his studies in the same collection, "Aztec Priests," highlights the Spanish authorities' consistent preference for the Indian elite as religious and civil officers as a way to reinforce their own social order founded on rank.

10. AGN Bandos 7 exp. 91; Pérez de Velasco, p. 71.

11. All six of the fiscales of pueblos in the parish of Xilotepec who gave their ages when they testified in a 1721 suit were over 40 years old. Two of them said they were caciques y principales. AGN DP 1 exp. 2. See also AGN Tierras 2179 exp. 3, 1756, Xilotepec, testimony of Matheo Osorio (fiscal, age 65); AGN CRS 192 exps. 11–12, 1760, Almoloya, testimony of Pasqual Gabriel (current fiscal and former gobernador and alcalde, 51); and CRS 179 exp. 13, fol. 409, 1763, Actopan (fiscal, 51); CRS 75 exp. 8, fol. 429v, 1789, San Andrés Jimilpan (fiscal, 56). In the minor pueblos, the financial burden of the office would have driven away some of an already small pool of distinguished candidates. In one parish the fiscal had to pay part of the cost of replenishing the stock of wax, oil, incense, and flour for

the sacramental bread. CRS 39 exp. 2, 1796, San Bartolomé Capuluac. In many parishes, he was held responsible for the difference between the clerical fees he could collect and what was owed. CRS 130 exp. 2, 1792, Metepec district.

12. AGN CRS 29 exp. 8, 1738, Xochimilco district; JCB, Joseph Lucas de Santibáñez resumé, San Lucas Mazatepec.

13. Pérez de Velasco, p. 71 (the fiscal was to "observar las embriagueses, incontinencias, y demás excesos para avisarlos a VM"). For fiscales reporting to curas: AGN CRS 156 exp. 7, 1761, Acambay (failure to practice the religion); CRS 179 exp. 13, 1763, Actopan (public concubinage); CRS 75 exp. 6, fols. 351–52, 1786, Alahuistlan (escape of a prisoner); AGN Acervo 49 caja 45, 1810, Chimalhuacan Atenco, ("Ynformación sobre repentina muerte de Domingo Guerrero . . .").

14. AGN CRS 136 exp. 4, fol. 269r, 1783, San Lorenzo Huichilapan.

15. Making arrests: AGN Acervo 49 caja 50, 1749, Tancanhuitz, Tampomolon parish; AGN CRS 179 exp. 13, fol. 406v, 1763, Actopan; CRS 75 exp. 4, 1775, Zacualpan district; AGN Inq. 1146 exp. 1, 1775, Xilotepec; AJANG Civil, box 116, doc. 4, 1778, Ocotlan. Placing fiancées en depósito: CRS 179 exp. 13, fol. 409, 1763, Actopan. Accompanying the priest to stop a party: CRS 192 exps. 11–12, 1760, Almoloya. Serving as truant officer: BN LaFragua Coll., vol. 590, Feb. 2, 1762, pastoral letter of Archbishop Rubio y Salinas; AGN Hist. 437 unnumbered exp., fols. 9–14, 1800, Tixtla. Carrying orders: CRS 156 exp. 7, fols. 229ff, 1761, Acambay. Taking roll: CRS 201 exp. 1, 1780, San Lucas Ixtapalapa. Transporting prisoners: Tulane VEMC 53 exp. 23, 1788, Cuautitlan. Accompanying the priest-as-judge: CRS 192 exps. 11–12, 1760, Tescaliacac district. Taking charge of ecclesiastical jail: CRS 42 exp. 1, fol. 31, 1732, Tejupilco.

16. *Concilio III*, p. 225. In 1759 a Franciscan doctrinero at Amacueca (Jalisco) tried to excuse his habit of whipping women in his cell for penance by saying that the fiscal sometimes wielded the whip. AGN Inq. 960 exp. 19.

17. AGN Crim. 221, fols. 210–25.

18. AGN Inq. 1146 exp. 1. Other cases of alleged brutality by fiscales include AGN Crim. 234, fols. 79ff, 1638, Actopan (Indian complaint against the fiscal for agravios, derramas, confiscating possessions, etc.); Crim. 230 exp. 17, 1641, Ixtlahuaca; Crim. 123 exp. 25, 1735, Tenango del Valle; AGN Acervo 49 caja 49, 1739 suit against Francisco de Vergara of Churubusco (fiscal carrying out indiscriminate whippings ordered by vicario, grabbing the hair of a woman and dragging her a block, threatening spouses whose partners were not attending mass); CDCh, roll 14, exp. 207, 1742, Chilapa; Crim. 141, fols. 376–90, 1776, Ozumba; AGI Mex. 2588, 1784, Ruiz y Cervantes report, fols. 16v–17r; and AGN Hist. 578A, 1793, Ixmiquilpan (Indians feared the fiscal of Real del Cardonal).

19. Collecting dominicas: AGN CRS 156 exp. 5, 1758, Tepetlaostoc; CRS 130 exp. 2, 1792, Metepec district; CRS 130 exp. 9, 1809, Papalotla, Texcoco district. Supervising community labor for the church: CRS 75 exp. 6, 1786, Alahuistlan. Collecting other parish fees: CRS 188 exp. 9, 1791, Jamiltepec; AGN Hist. 578A, 1793, Zumpango de la Laguna report.

20. AGN CRS 156 exp. 12, 1765, Tlapanaloya, Tetepango district.

21. Collecting excessive fees: AGN CRS 75 exp. 9, 1790, visita near Tula.

22. Responsibility for fees: AGN CRS 130 exp. 2, 1792, Metepec district.

23. *Recop.* 6-3-7.

24. AGN CRS 179 exp. 13, 1763, Actopan; AGN Tierras 2431 exp. 6, late 1780's, Zacualpan district.

25. Pérez de Velasco, p. 71; BMM 271, ch. 86.

26. Allowing fiscales to have any part in confessions was considered a great scandal. AGN Hist. 578A, 1793, Minas de San Antonio, Cadereyta report; Real del Cardonal, Ixmiquilpan report.

27. AGN CRS 39 exp. 2, 1796, Capuluac; AGN Templos I exp. 2, 1798, Guayacocotla y Chicontepec. Usually the fiscal read the banns in marriage ceremonies and received 4rr for his services. AGN DP 2 exp. 6, fol. 492v, 1763, Tlachichico, Actopan; CRS 179 exp. 13, fol. 408r, 1763, Actopan ("leen las amonestaciones de los indios en su lengua").

28. AGN CRS 179 exp. 13, fol. 408r, 1763, Actopan ("dicen las orasiones del oficio de sepultura [en muchos casos inexcusables]"); CRS 68 exp. 2, 1768, Ozoloapan; CRS 75 exp. 5, fols. 327–28, 1784, San Luis de las Peras, Huichapan district.

29. AGN CRS 156 exp. 5, fols. 126–30, 1758, Tepetlaostoc.

30. Tulane VEMC 15 exp. 5, 1739, Yahualica; AGN CRS 68 exp. 1, fol. 10, 1759, Teoloyucan; CRS 192 exps. 11–12, 1760, Almoloya, testimony of Pasqual Gabriel; CRS 156 exp. 7, fols. 229ff, 1761, Acambay; CRS 67 exp. 3, fol. 119, 1768, Joloapan, Tetepango district.

31. *Recop.* 1-13-6; Solórzano 4-15-57.

32. The royal cedula of Sept. 19, 1763, is summarized in AGN Bandos 8 exp. 43.

33. For example, the flustered or distracted cura of Actopan in 1763 argued for his continuing right to appoint fiscales by citing several irrelevant laws of the *Recopilación*, as if an appeal to older law would save the day. AGN CRS 179 exp. 13, fol. 408r. The provisor of the archdiocese tried to salvage some ecclesiastical control over the selection of fiscales by instructing villages to forward three names to the bishop, from which one would be chosen. The Indian leaders of Zacualpan de las Amilpas replied by insisting that the cura confirm the man they elected. CRS 156 exp. 9, fols. 366ff. Five years later, the cura of Tetepango was charged under the 1763 cedula by both the alcalde mayor and the Indians with failing to obey the law against priests naming the fiscales. Rather than claim that he had the right to name them in the future, he argued for popular elections instead of election by vocales. CRS 67 exp. 3, fol. 119.

34. AGN RCO 101 exp. 20.

35. AGN Bandos 8 exp. 43; Ventura Beleña, 1: 166.

36. AGN RCO 149 exp. 181. The cedula read: "me dignase declarar por punto general que las elecciones de Fiscales en los pueblos de Yndios, tocan a sus Repúblicas." Whether or not this viceregal cedula can be taken as expressing a royal preference for the election of fiscales at the time as well (a preference that was not articulated until 1794, in a plan for new missions in Nayarit; López Jiménez, *Algunos documentos*, p. 30), there was apparently no further attempt to change established practices in this regard after 1774.

37. AGN CRS 217 exp. 5. See also CRS 75 exp. 6, 1786, Zacualpan district; AGN Crim. 200 exp. 4, 1800, Dangú; and AGN Bienes 663 exp. 25, fols. 8ff, 1815, Tianguistengo. In Acolman, the custom was apparently to elect the fiscal at the time of the annual elections to community office, but the cura claimed the power to appoint an interim fiscal when a vacancy occured between elections. Crim. 145 fols. 235ff, 1774.

38. Where village electors sent three names to the bishop to choose from, the parish priest's ranking was probably decisive. For this reason, Indians of Zacualpan de las Amilpas refused to submit three names and demanded that the cura confirm the man they elected. AGN CRS 156 exp. 9, fols. 366ff, 1763.

39. Tulane VEMC 24 exp. 4, archbishop's instruction on schools (probably from 1754).

40. Three cases of non-Indians appointed as fiscales in Indian pueblos stand out: a recently arrived lobo-cum-creole who served as fiscal of Barrio San Andrés Totoltepec, San Agustín de las Cuevas parish, in 1765; a mulato who served as interim fiscal of Acolman in 1774; and a mestizo who served as fiscal of Tulpetlac, Ecatepec district, in 1780. AGN Crim. 49 exp. 10; Crim. 145, fols. 145ff; AGN Civil 2114 exp. 8. In all three cases, parishioners protested the violent excesses of these cura appointees.

41. AGN RCO 126 exp. 137 ("un fiscal que desde los principios de la justa adquisición de las Yndias, acostumbran dar los pueblos a los párrocos").

42. AGN Bienes 575 exp. 63, Malinalco, 1789 ("mis fiscales representan mi propia persona").

43. Indian leaders of Asunción Ixtapa, Zacualpa district, said through their attorney on Sept. 20, 1769, that the cura regarded the fiscales as his servants. AGN CRS 75 exp. 2. The priest of Acaponeta in 1791 had the fiscales of his parish perform a variety of petty tasks for him on a rotating basis. According to José Antonio Cresencio, who testified in a suit against that cura, the priest had ordered the fiscal to go find him a pair of scissors so that he could trim the mane of a horse that an Indian had brought to drink at the convent's trough without permission. AJANG Civil, box 150, doc. 7. The injunction against using fiscales beyond their oficio was published in *Recop.* 6-3-7, but that law concerned convening catechism classes. Without clear stipulations about what was not included in a position with such broad responsibilities, the law had little bite and was rarely invoked by fiscales against their priests.

44. AGN CRS 67 exp. 3, 1768, Tetepango district; CRS 39 exp. 2, 1796, Capuluac; AGN Bienes 575 exp. 14, 1789, Huazalingo; AGN Hist. 437 unnumbered exp., 1800, Mochitlan ("Sobre que el cura del pueblo de Mochitlan . . ."). In the last case, a lieutenant fiscal was whipped for not attending mass one *día de precepto*. The list goes on: in 1625, the cura of Ichcateopan was reported to have run after the fiscal with a knife (AGN Acervo 49, caja 43, suit brought by Indians of Cicapualco); in 1672, Franciscan doctrineros were accused of whipping six fiscales for not making parishioners pay full fees according to the arancel (BMM 135, fol. 198); in 1771, the cura of Ozoloapan gave the fiscal a humiliating whipping with his pants down (CRS 23 exp. 6); in 1775, the cura arrested the fiscal of Cuanacalcingo (Tlaltizapan district, Morelos) in retaliation for the pueblo preferring charges against him for excessive fees (CRS 68 exps. 4–5); and in 1783, the cura of Quechultenango, Chilapa district, admitted to whipping the fiscal for letting a woman die without confession (CRS 30 exp. 2, fols. 51ff).

45. For example, the cura of San Lucas Tecualoyan in 1788 was said to have beaten the fiscal on his own as the instigator of community strife and rebellion. AGN CRS 156 exp. 13.

46. AGN Bienes 663 exps. 5–6, 1809, Tultitlan; AGN DP 1 exp. 2, 1721–24, Jilotepec parish.

47. AGN Inq. 1074, 2d numeration, fols. 1r, 35r, Huamantla; AGN CRS 30 exp. 2, fols. 41ff, Chilapa.

48. AGN Crim. 306 exp. 5.

49. AGN Templos 25 exp. 4, 1784, Coatepec, Zacualpan district.

50. AGN CRS 68 exp. 3, fol. 210v.

51. AGN Crim. 120 exp. 25. In 1817, the vicario of Lerma charged the fiscal, the fiscalito, and 16 others with "idolatry." AGN Bienes 663 exp. 19. See also AGN Inq. 510 exp. 112 on fiscales and "superstitions." Ruiz de Alarcón, pp. 32–33, 68, cites instances of an Indian fiscal and a sacristán participating in "idolatry" in central Mexico.

52. As Lockhart, "Some Nahua Concepts," p. 472, suggests, a fiscal who was elected by the community could be one of the most important figures on the pueblo council. Appointment by the cura did not guarantee a fiscal's unswerving loyalty. The cura of Teoloyuca observed in 1759 that, although he had named the fiscal, the man turned out to be insolent toward him and closely connected to his local enemies. AGN CRS 68 exp. 1, fol. 10.

53. AGN CRS 192 exps. 11–12, 1760, Almoloya (according to the fiscal, local Indians angrily regarded him as a soplón); CRS 23 exp. 6, 1771, Ozoloapan (pueblo officials charged that the fiscal continually went to the cura with "gossip in order to make trouble for the Indians": "chismes para molestar a los indios").

54. AGN CRS 75 exp. 4, fols. 257v–260v.

55. AGN Bienes 663 exps. 5–6. In this case two other fiscales also testified against the cura.

56. Pérez de Velasco, p. 18, warned against such fiscales: "En los pueblos, especialmente siendo cortos, tienen los curas y vicarios muchos fiscales que les cuenten los pasos y observen los movimientos, y que ay algunos de tal malevolencia que con qualquiera aunque levísimo motivo de sospecha, los acusan de delinquentes."

57. AGN CRS 156 exp. 7, fols. 229ff, 264–75.

58. Examples of exceptionally close fiscal-cura relationships: AGN Tierras 2179 exp. 3, 1756, Xilotepec; AGN CRS 192 exps. 11–12, 1760, Almoloya; Tierras 2554 exp. 11, 1766, Tlalmanalco; AGN Crim. 79 exp. 1, 1777, Tlamatlan; AGN Bienes 575 exp. 14, 1789, Huazalingo; AJANG Criminal, bundle labeled "1818 (89)," 1816–18, Tonalá. When fiscales turned in local people for "idolatry" and secret ceremonies, they challenged alternative spiritual leaders—a daring move. One of the examples of a fiscal reporting the discovery of "idols" appears in Navarro de Vargas, p. 580.

59. AGN Templos 1 exp. 2, witness no. 3. The fiscal of Ozoloapan in 1768 found a menacing crowd gathered against him when he tried to collect fees owed to the cura. AGN CRS 68 exp. 2. A similar situation was faced by the fiscal and the gobernador of Malacatepec, Metepec district, when they carried an unpopular order from the cura. CRS 75 exp. 3. The fiscal of Almoloya was nearly killed in a similar tumulto in 1760. CRS 192 exps. 11–12. In 1732, at Tejupilco, some Indians wanting to free the alcalde from the ecclesiastical jail tried to kill the fiscal who was serving as guard. CRS 42 exp. 1.

60. Guarda, pp. 65–66; Chance, pp. 164–65.

61. AGN CRS 68 exp. 3, fols. 300–301. 62. AGN CRS 57 exp. 3.

63. Navarro de Vargas, pp. 577–78. 64. *Recop.* 6-3-6.

65. Cura Joseph Sotomayor, facing an array of charges for his activities in Zacualpan and other parishes, defended himself at one point by claiming that a local Spaniard had waged a personal campaign against him out of malice, and that the sacristán had been his enemy's accomplice. AGN Inq. 1334 exp. 3, fol. 180r, 1801. Whether this was true or not, the charges against Sotomayor were so numerous and well-founded that the Inquisition did not pursue this facet of his defense.

66. *Recop.* 6-3-6 called for the sacristán to "guardar los oranmentos y barrer la iglesia." In 1771, the Fourth Provincial Council added that he was responsible for "the decoration of the temples and their altars, [and] the good order and cleanliness of the ornaments and valuables." CPM, p. 128.

67. In a 1795 dispute over the sacristán in La Cañada, Querétaro, the cura complained that the man elected by the pueblo was drunk and dishonest and had not posted a bond or provided guarantors. The audiencia fiscal judged that the pueblo could elect whoever it pleased, but that the man chosen had to put up a bond at court "in accordance with the law." Tulane VEMC 8 exp. 25.

68. CPM, p. 128.

69. AGN CRS 204 exp. 9, fols. 312–18, 1760, Tejupilco.

70. AGN CRS 204 exp. 9, 1760, Tejupilco; CRS 140 exp. 4, 1796, Yautepec; CRS 136 exp. 2, fol. 201, 1781, Tlaltizapan.

71. The cura of Tejupilco used the Spanish analogy in 1760 to press for his creole sacristán to be the schoolmaster. AGN CRS 204 exp. 9, para. 70. Father Cirilo de Castilla objected to what he said was a law that sacristanes in the cabeceras were to teach Spanish. Cited in AGN RCO 74 exp. 54, June 28, 1754.

72. The ruling in the La Cañada case (see n. 67 above) suggests that the courts would have favored the election of sacristanes, but no cedula seems to have been issued to that effect, and I do not know of other evidence that villages in the Mexico and Guadalajara dioceses knew of, or were moving to test, that possibility after 1795.

73. AGN CRS 204 exp. 9.

74. AGN CRS 67 exp. 3, 1768, Tetepango (four "sacristanes" served two-week shifts without pay); AGN Crim. 232 exp. 7, 1800, Xochimilco (six-man rotations every three weeks); CRS 39 exp. 5, 1803, San José Malacatepec (two "sacristanes" served weekly shifts for 1p a week).

75. AGN CRS 68 exp. 2, fols. 55–60, 1769, Ozoloapan; CRS 39 exp. 6, 1806, Tenontepec, Villa Alta (Oaxaca).

76. AGN Acervo 49 caja 49. Parishioners said that it was the cruelty of both the cura and the fiscal toward the current sacristán that kept anyone else from agreeing to serve.

77. AGN Tierras 2776 exps. 23–24.

78. AGN CRS 30 exp. 2, fols. 51ff, 1774, Chilapa district (buried someone without telling the cura); Tulane VEMC 8 exp. 25, Cañada, 1795 (sold oil for the lamp and was drunk and dishonest).

79. AGI Mex. 2588, 1784, Ruiz y Cervantes report, fols. 16v–17r (sacristán administered cruel floggings); Tulane VEMC 53 exp. 23, fol. 25r, 1788, Cuautitlan (took prisoners to the alcalde mayor).

80. AGN CRS 67 exp. 3, 1768, Tetepango. As an outgrowth of the disputes over the arancel of 1767, the trend increasingly was toward paid service for assistants, as at San José Malacatepec in 1803. CRS 39 exp. 5.

81. AGN Civil 2072 exp. 19, 1788, Zacualpan.

82. The usual description of the cantor's job was that he would "oficiar las misas." AGN CRS 136 exp. 2, fol. 83v, 1781, Tlaltizapan; AJANG Civil, box 180, doc. 24, 1793, Tonalá.

83. For example, the cura of Tonalá in 1793 approached the audiencia about removing the chief cantor, who had held office for 40 years, for chronic drunkenness and incompetence. In reply, the fiscal saw no obstacle to that, affirming that the position was for one year at a time, and a cantor thus had to be formally reappointed. AJANG Civil, box 180, doc. 24.

84. Early on, in 1539, the bishops of Mexico instructed their parish priests to choose a few of the most able Indians as acolytes, exorcists, ostiarios, and cantores. "Apéndice a los concilios primero y segundo," p. 324.

85. Texas, W. B. Stephens Coll., no. 320, 1777, Acayucan (Oaxaca); AGN CRS 130 exp. 3, fol. 23r, 1796, Tututepec, Tulancingo district; AGN DP 1 exp. 2, 1721–24, Xilotepec (mentions the fees cantores received for assisting at mass). The Franciscan doctrineros at Cuernavaca apparently objected strenuously to cantores in the pueblos burying the dead. DP 1 exp. 1, 1671. Technically, a valid baptism, unlike extreme unction, could be administered in emergencies by any communicant who knew the procedure. *Itin.* 3-4-16. Though midwives often baptized infants who died in childbirth or in the first hours of life, if time permitted, the church preferred to have one of the priest's lay assistants perform the baptism so that it was done properly.

86. For example, Martín Vásquez, the cantor of Tlaxiaco (Oaxaca), was reported to be the leader of a faction there in 1601. CDCh, roll 2, leg. 1.

87. AJANG Criminal, bundle labeled "1815, leg. 2 (138)," "Sobre la prisión del indio escribano de Taltenango, Tomás Miramontes" ("concerbación de nros dros paz y tranquilidad sin que se nos incomode veje o perturbe contra las soberanas intenciones . . . con facultad de poder sostituto quanto le combenga y especialmente para que inste la solicitud pendiente de las fatigas de nro personal trabajo").

88. AGN Indios 23 exp. 154, 1658, Culhuacan (cura accused of making the cantores work his chinampas after singing, and of confiscating and selling their property); AJANG Criminal, bundle labeled "1824 (38)," 1824, Techaluta.

89. Weber, p. 361.

90. AGN Acervo 49, caja 44, 1700, San Juan del Río, testimony of Ysidro de Torreblanca in dispute between cura Nicolás Flores and Lt. Francisco Básquez.

91. It was the parish priest who had been charged with establishing schools by the Third Provincial Council of 1585 (*Concilio III*, p. 35), and late colonial records often refer to him as the "cura maestro de doctrina" (for example, AGN DP 1 exp. 2, 1721, Xilotepec).

92. BMM 271, ch. 79; Kanter, "Indian Education," pp. 23–27. The campaign for Spanish schools gained momentum after 1750, but there were earlier efforts. A cedula of May 25, 1720, suggests that the viceregal decree of Sept. 30, 1716, calling for Spanish schools in Indian pueblos had borne some fruit. It refers to a letter from Archbishop Lanciego recounting how he established many escuelas de la lengua castellana during his pastoral visits. AGN RCO 41 exp. 23. Royal cedulas to that effect had been issued since the late 17th century. The principal royal cedulas on establishing Spanish-language schools in Indian pueblos appear in Konetzke, vol. 3: doc. 1, May 30, 1691; doc. 20, Dec. 20, 1693; doc. 21, April 2, 1694; doc. 23, Aug. 7, 1694; doc. 52, June 16, 1700; doc. 101, July 11, 1718; doc. 105, May 25, 1720; doc. 166, Sept. 11, 1766; doc. 214, May 10, 1770; doc. 245, Feb. 22, 1778; and doc. 265, Nov. 5, 1782.

The clearest articulation of the crown's intent to make civil authorities responsible for Spanish-language instruction in the late 18th century was the royal cedula of Feb. 22, 1778. Corregidores and alcaldes mayores were charged with maintaining Spanish, literacy, and catechism schools in the pueblos, though they had to appoint maestros agreeable to the curas. The effects of this decree are not clear from my research. A consulta from the Council of the Indies of 1778 or 1779 called for the residencias of corregidores to include an inquiry into whether they had promoted such schools. AGI Guad. 343. The residencia of the alcalde mayor of La Barca in 1781 did, in fact, include a question about Spanish-language instruction in its interrogatory. AJANG Civil, box 104, doc. 7. The 1778 cedula was reissued in New Spain on Jan. 24, 1782. Ventura Beleña, 1: 210. A later cedula (Nov. 5, 1782) repeated the call for Spanish-language schools in the pueblos de indios, and urged the priests to persuade their parishioners of the need to speak Spanish. RCO 123 exp. 164.

The radical position taken by several bishops at the Fourth Provincial Council, that Indian languages should be extinguished as soon as possible, was countered by the moderate, prevailing view expressed by the oidor Antonio de Ribadeneyra. It favored establishing Spanish-language schools in the pueblos but without expecting to extinguish native languages. John Carter Brown Lib., Spanish Codex no. 52. The support for Spanish-language schools by Archbishops Rubio y Salinas, Lorenzana, and Núñez de Haro y Peralta is well documented in their pastoral visits. AHM L10A/7–8; L10B/9 (1759–60); L10B/10 (1767–69); L10B/11–28 (1775–92).

93. Bishop Palafox of Puebla wrote of the ideal of two schools divided by sex, with a man to teach the boys and a woman to teach the girls. Rockefeller Lib., Brown Univ., Medina Coll., FHA 102 exp. 1, 1653, pastoral letter. A 1716 viceregal law specified knowledge of Spanish by the maestro, and separate schools for boys and girls. John Carter Brown Lib., call no. bBB M6113. In a 1762 circular, Archbishop Rubio y Salinas called for women of good character to teach girls. BN LaFragua Coll., vol. 590. The Fourth Provincial Council (1771) and a cedula of Feb. 22, 1778, specified that the maestros be competent, of good customs, and examined in doctrina. The council added that Indians who could teach only in their own tongue were to be avoided. CPM, p. 4. The bishop of Oaxaca, during his pastoral visit of 1779, specified that teachers should be fluent in Castilian. Texas, W. B. Stephens Coll., no. 537. The cura of Villa Alta (Oaxaca) in 1793 complained of the subdelegado's choices for maestros and said that all should be Spaniards of good character. AGN CRS 188 exp. 12, fols. 210–11.

I have found only one case of a male teacher and a female teacher in an Indian pueblo: in Xuchicoatlan near Huazalingo in 1789. Both were described as castizos. AGN Bienes

575 exp. 14, fol. 22r. Where there was only one maestro, the boys were to be taught in the morning, and the girls in the late afternoon. *Colección de las ordenanzas*, p. 181. An example of the practice appears in AJANG Criminal, bundle labeled "1806, leg. 2 (11)," testimony of Juan María Flores in a suit brought by Indians of Zapotitlan against the cura over injurias in 1806.

Indian girls were to attend school from the age of seven to ten. *Colección de las ordenanzas*, p. 181; John Carter Brown Lib., call no. bBB M6113. Though no reference is made to the age range for boys, since the Third Provincial Council (1585) provided that all children under twelve were to attend catechism class, the school age for boys was probably seven to ten or eleven. *Concilio III*, 1-1-2. In a memorandum to the archbishop of June 22, 1790, the viceroy fixed adulthood at the age of sixteen, but I have not seen evidence that Indians from twelve to fifteen continued to attend school. Tulane VEMC 73 exp. 41.

No distinction seems to have been made between boys and girls in the basic curriculum of rudimentary literacy, Spanish language, and doctrina. In any case, the aim was to impart received knowledge, not to stimulate independent thought. The emphasis was on memorizing the rudiments of the Spanish language and the religion that would, if acted on, presumably be sufficient for salvation. Every day the children were called on to recite certain parts of the catechism aloud and listen to an explanation of them by the maestro. CPM, p. 4. Simón Thadeo de Castañeda Castro y Guzmán, vicario of Alahuistlan in 1762, described the commencement of school each day as a procession of about 60 children chanting the doctrina. JCB.

94. AGN Tierras 2621 exp. 7, 1818.

95. Villarroel, pp. 50–51.

96. John Carter Brown Lib., call no. bBB M6113. The Franciscan guardian for the province of Xalisco in the mid-17th century instructed the friar-pastors to find a Spanish-speaking Indian to teach doctrina to the boys and girls of the parish. Tello, 4: 84. *Colección de ordenanzas*, p. 18, called for curas to appoint an able Indian man to teach doctrina to boys on Sundays and a comparable Indian woman to teach the girls. The cura of Villa Alta (Oaxaca) in 1739 not only strongly opposed the appointment of Indian maestros in principle, but was particularly upset that the subdelegado was appointing Indian youths 16 to 18 years old. AGN CRS 188 exp. 12, fols. 210–11.

97. According to AGI Guad. 352, 1791, Ugarte report. If the maestro was a local Indian, the state favored sacristanes. The escribano of Tepechitlan (Nueva Galicia) in 1815 was also serving the parish as a cantor. AJANG Criminal, bundle labeled "1815, leg. 2 (138)," "Sobre la prisión del indio escribano de Taltenango, Tomás Miramontes."

98. Some single and casta maestros: AGN Inq. 760 exp. 40, 1715, Temascaltepec (35-year-old mulato bachelor); JCB, 1750's, Bizente Joseph Ramires resumé, Misquiahuala (Indian in training for the priesthood); AGN CRS 68 exp. 4, fol. 409, 1775, Tlaltizapan (mulato); Inq. 1119 exp. 2, 1777, Ocotlan, Jalisco (27-year-old español bachelor in 1775); AGN Bienes 575 exp. 14, fol. 22r, 1789, Xuchicoatlan (castizos). The Indian cura of Atenango del Río in 1762 mentioned that he had hired a maestro de razón. JCB, Br. Pasqual de Roxas Mendoza Austria y Moctezuma's resumé.

Some maestros designated by don: CRS 75 exp. 4, 1775, Zacualpan district (40-year-old married teacher in Ixcatepec and 35-year-old teacher in Tototepec); AGN Tierras 2621 exp. 6, 1818, Tenayuca, Valley of Mexico ("hombre de bien, de conducta irreprehensible"); CRS 75 exp. 6, 1786, Alahuistlan (married 27-year-old). Ocotlan had an español teacher in 1775. Inq. 1119 exp. 2. And the maestro of Ayó el Chico (Jalisco) in the early 1790's was described as a "vecino de conocidas costumbres"—perhaps another español. AGI Guad. 352, Ugarte report. In general, however, creole maestros in Indian pueblos must have been unusual.

99. One case of village initiative is San Martín Texiutlan, near Guadalajara. In a 1773

petition for pueblo status separate from Jocotepec, the village leaders proudly said that they had established a school and hired a maestro. AGN Tierras 1048 exp. 8.

100. AGN Inq. 1119 exp. 2.

101. John Carter Brown Lib., call no. bBB M6113, 1716; Tulane VEMC 24 exp. 4, 1754(?); Heath, pp. 50–51; AGN RCO 123 exp. 164, 1782; AHM L10B/25, 1788, fol. 21r.

102. Ability to pay was mentioned in the 1782 cedula. AGN RCO 123 exp. 164. One real per month for every child in school may have been regarded as the standard for an appropriate salary, AHM Mexico L10B/21, 1779–80, fol. 7r.

103. The examples are Xilotepec, 1756, 52p a year and one cuartilla of maize a week (AGN Tierras 2179 exp. 3); Tuzamapan, 1776, 104p a year (AGN Alcaldes Mayores 11, fols. 448–56); Zitácuaro, 1778, 20rr a week, or 120p for a 48-week year (Tulane VEMC 25 exp. 15); Santa María la Redonda, Mexico City, 1789, 48p a year and maintenance (BMM 85, fols. 399–403); La Barca, ca. 1790, 120p a year (AGI Guad. 352, Ugarte report); Villa Alta, 1793, 6rr a week or 39p a year (AGN CRS 188 exp. 12, fols. 198–99); and Santa María Ajoloapa, Ecatepec district, 1794, 2p a week or 96–104p a year (AGN Templos 159 exp. 55). In the missions of Nayarit in the 1790's, the maestro was to receive 48p a year and maintenance. "Plan para las misiones, 1794," in López Jiménez, *Algunos documentos*, p. 36.

104. AGI Guad. 352, early 1790's, Ayó el Chico (sacristy); AGN Crim. 166, fol. 354bis (estanquillo de cigarros); AGN Templos 24, fol. 54r (interpreter).

105. See Ugarte's report on schools in AGI Guad. 352. Colonial decrees continued to call for payment from the arcas. Ventura Beleña, 1: 209–10, Jan. 14, Nov. 5, 1782. But royal officials did press pueblos to pay from the local treasury when they could. (On May 23, 1792, the fiscal de lo civil of the audiencia ruled that the Indians of Tlacotalpan should pay the maestro from their fondos de comunidad "as the royal cedulas prescribe." AGN CRS 188 exp. 7.) Some examples of pueblos paying from the community treasury: Tulane VEMC 66 exp. 5, 1778, Zumpango; Guad. 352, ca. 1790, La Barca; VEMC 28 exp. 4, 1792, Santa María Acamuchitlan, Temascaltepec.

106. John Carter Brown Lib., call no. bBB M6113, 1716; Tulane VEMC 24 exp. 4, arch-bishop's instruction, 1754, AGN RCO 123 exp. 164, 1782 cedula, which put the produce of a plot of tierra de pan llevar cultivated by the community first, and the arcas second. In 1778, the cura of Zitácuaro reported that he had arranged for each pueblo to plant a pedazo de tierra de comunidad for the maestro's salary, which would be supplemented by indi-vidual contributions. VEMC 25 exp. 15. At Tlaltenango in the early 1790's, the maestro was paid with one day's labor in the harvest by each Indian. AGI Guad. 352, Ugarte report.

107. AGI Guad. 352, Ugarte report.

108. AGN RCO 123 exp. 164, 1782. The maestro of Tonalá (Nueva Galicia) in the early 1790's was paid solely from contributions. AGI Guad. 352.

109. Supporting schools with user fees was Viceroy Bucareli's solution in 1772, and also the viceroy's plan for the missions of Nayarit in 1794. Heath, pp. 50–51; López Jiménez, *Algunos documentos*, p. 36. The method was used in the parish of Tuzamapan in 1776. AGN Alcaldes Mayores 11, fols. 448–56. The archbishop's instruction of 1754(?) emphati-cally opposed payment by the parents alone: lacking sufficient funds from the treasury or a communal plot, the maestro was to be paid by the común "y nunca por los padres de niños." Tulane VEMC 24 exp. 4.

110. Tulane VEMC 25 exp. 15.

111. AGN CRS 156 exp. 5, 1758, Tepetlaostoc; AGN Templos 1 exp. 4, Zoyatlan, 1806–8.

112. AGN CRS 188 exp. 12, fols. 198–99, 1793.

113. Curas paying maestros: BMM 85, fols. 339–403 (Santa María la Redonda, 1789); AGN Hist. 578A, 1793, Coyoacan report; AGN DP 3 exp. 3, fol. 34v (Tlaltizapan, 1797).

114. *Recop.* 1-13-5 (1634, 1636); Tulane VEMC 24 exp. 4, archbishop's instruction, 1754(?).

115. AGN CRS 156 exp. 5, 1758, Tepetlaostoc.

116. AGN Alcaldes Mayores 11, fols. 448–56, 1776, Tuzamapan.

117. Archbishop Rubio y Salinas's 1762 circular, BN LaFragua Coll., vol. 590; AHM L10B/26, fols. 154v–155r, 1790. The *Colección de ordenanzas*, p. 178, called for the curas to do weekly examinations of the maestros on what they were to teach and the pupils on what they had learned.

118. JCB. Other examples from this concurso include Pasqual de Roxas Mendoza Austria y Moctezuma, Simón Thadeo de Castañeda Castro y Guzmán, Bizente Joseph Ramires, Francisco de Rivera Butrón, and Joachin Joseph Truxillo. See also the resumé for Valentín Mariano Ximenes for schools established in Totolapa parish, 1778, in Texas, García Coll., no. 113.

119. The 1754 resumés are in AHJ Manuscripts, no. G-4-719, GUA/4. The 1770 resumés and others scattered through the final years of colonial rule, including 1806, were in unmarked cardboard boxes in the cathedral archive of Guadalajara when I examined them in 1980. By the 1790's, leading candidates for half-ración posts in the cathedral chapter also emphasized their accomplishments in education. In 1795, Dr. Josef Antonino González Martínez's main accomplishment as cura of Tonalá seems to have been the founding of escuelas de primeras letras. In the same concurso cura Miguel Martínez of Aguascalientes mentioned establishing an escuela de primeras letras when he was interim cura of Cuquío in 1779. AGI Guad. 533. The successful applicant for a media ración in 1821, Gabriel Sánchez de Llenero, listed the founding of schools in three pueblos of the parish of Salatitan among his accomplishments. Guad. 540. District governors occasionally praised curas for establishing schools, as in AGN Hist. 578A, 1793, Teotihuacan and Sierra de Pinos reports.

120. AGN Crim. 210, fols. 189–205.

121. AGN Civil 865 exp. 9.

122. AGN CRS 75 exp. 4, fol. 263.

123. AGN Bienes 575 exp. 14.

124. AGN CRS 188 exp. 7. The audiencia fiscal de lo civil commented on May 23, 1792, that there were "various [schools] operated by individuals for public instruction and education" in Tlacotalpan but not a separate school for Indians.

125. AGN RCO 126 exp. 137.

126. The appointment of maestros was a particularly contentious matter in the Villa Alta district. In 1790, the subdelegado complained of a vicario removing the maestros of Roayaga and Yazona. AGN Hist. 132 exp. 14. In 1793, the cura of Villa Alta objected to the subdelegado appointing maestros without consulting him. AGN CRS 188 exp. 12, fols. 210–11. Villa Alta was one of the most lucrative subdelegaciones in New Spain because of the cochineal trade, and royal governors there were especially eager to consolidate their power and reduce the influence of the parish clergy.

127. AGN CRS 68 exps. 4–5, 1775–81.

128. AGN Acervo 49 caja 44.

129. Villarroel, p. 51, implied that there was a good deal more conflict between curas and maestros in his time (1780's) because curas ordained a título de idioma opposed the teaching of Spanish. As a onetime alcalde mayor, he may well have known parish priests who opposed Spanish schools (AGN Bienes 575 exp. 5, Huazalingo, 1789, seems to provide an example), but his opinions here (and elsewhere) must be judged in the light of his antagonism toward parish priests generally, and his failure to acknowledge the place of alcaldes mayores like himself in what would have been at least a three-way conflict. The many cases of priests promoting and paying for Spanish schools, and of beneficed curas who were not fluent in Indian languages, also call Villarroel's view into question as a generalization for the late colonial period.

130. Kanter, "Indian Education," p. 41.

131. AGN CRS 156 exp. 5, 1758, Tepetlaostoc; AGN Bienes 431 exp. 17, 1771, Iguala; AGN Crim. 203 exp. 4, 1778, Tepoztlan; Bienes 575 exp. 14, 1789, Huazalingo; Bienes 210 exp. 26, 1791, Cozcatlan.

132. Allowing schools to shut down was a complaint of the curas of Tepetlaostoc in 1758 and Tuzamapan, Xonotla parish (Real de Tetela district), in 1776. AGN CRS 156 exp. 5; AGN Alcaldes Mayores 11, fols. 448–56. Intendant Ugarte observed in the early 1790's that many schools had closed in Nueva Galicia. AGI Guad. 352.

133. AGN DP 3 exp. 4 ("No hay forma de pagar el maestro ya una congrua suficiente para su sustento o ya aquello por lo que con ellos se han pactado[,] ya haciéndoles drogas el salario o ya demorándoselos por tanto tiempo que no teniendo con que mantenerse se ven precisados a desertar"). Additional examples of Indians not paying maestros: AHM L10B/21, fol. 7r, 1779, Amanalco; AGN Bienes 575 exp. 14, 1789, Huazalingo; AGN CRS 188 exp. 12, 1793, Villa Alta, Oaxaca; AGI Guad. 352, early 1790's, Ugarte report; AGN Acervo 49 caja 116, 1808, pastoral visit to the highland parishes of Hidalgo.

134. Tulane VEMC 66 exp. 5. A lack of wherewithal was the claim of the Zumpango parish in 1775. The cura countered that the villagers had the money to pay for a maestro.

135. For example, Zitácuaro in 1778 resisted paying the maestro's salary on the grounds that it was a new charge. Tulane VEMC 25 exp. 15. The lieutenant also mentioned the opposition to a new contribution but thought there was a second reason for it: Indians were averse to additional Christian discipline.

136. AGN Acervo 49 caja 116, especially the entries for Chiconcuautla, Tlaola, Santa Ana Tianguistengo, Tlacolula, and Tepehuacan. Zozoquiapan was reported to have schools in operation.

137. AGN Bienes 431 exp. 17 (Iguala); Tulane VEMC 24 exp. 2 (Tlaola); Bienes 210 exp. 26 (Cozcatlan).

138. JCB, 1762, Simón Thadeo de Castañeda resumé (parents in Tláhuac hid their children from the schoolmaster to keep them at home for domestic chores); AGN Acervo 49 caja 116, 1808, Chiconcuautla.

139. AGI Guad. 352, 1791.

140. AGN Templos 1 exp. 2 (Guayacocotla and Chicontepec); AGN Bienes 663 exp. 6 (Tultitlan); Bienes 575 exp. 14 (Huazalingo).

141. AJANG Civil, bundle labeled "1709–1819 (181)," record from April 1744.

142. Tulane VEMC 24 exp. 2.

143. AGN RCO 74 exp. 54. Father Cirilo de Castilla proposed the founding of a new colegio, where Indian priests would teach Indian children, who in turn would teach Indians in their pueblos, a plan reminiscent of the royal cedula on Indian education of July 12, 1691. Kanter, "Indian Education," pp. 8–9.

144. Tulane VEMC 24 exp. 2, 1790, Tlaola.

145. AGN Crim. 306 exp. 5, 1773, Zimatlan. The cura of Ixtapan in 1773 reported that Indians there also resisted the placement of maestros de escuela for instruction in Spanish as well as doctrina. AGN Alcaldes Mayores 11, fols. 338–40.

146. BMM 113, pp. 32–33 ("no hay otra cossa en el pueblo que el Indio fulanillo por que todos le admiran como un milagro de su nación y efectivamente lo es; pero luego que sale de la edad pupilar todos conspiran contra su havilidad y aplicación. Unos dicen que es ladino y Bachiller, toman este honrroso sobre escrito, por lo mismo que parlante, truan o loquas, y que presto será bellaco. Otros notan que le estaría mejor cuidar el rebaño, la pastería de los bueyes, espantar los tordos en la milpa, hazer oficio de topile y otros inferiores de la república. Los menos temerarios se lastiman dando voces de que aquel individuo hará falta en los repartimientos de minas, obras públicas y peonajes de haciendas a que se deben aplicar. Otros le profetissan que vendrá a parar en una horca porque tomando

conocimiento de los manjares y modo de vestir de los españoles, no pudiendo arribar a este luxo por medios lícitos, se verá en presisión de hacerse ladrón de los caminos públicos. Otros se duelen porque dicen que aspirara a tomar mujer blanca o española echando a su familia este borrón y dándole a la propia un nuevo lucimiento").

147. The cacique's Spanish sojourn is documented in AGI Guad. 377; and AGN RCO 174 exp. 123.

148. For instance, there were Spanish-language schools in all the pueblos of Ozoloapan parish in 1780 and Tultitlan parish in 1788; and in Atlapulco and Tolpetlac, sujetos of Ocoyoacac, and various sujetos in the district of Temascaltepec in 1792. AHM L10B/21, fol. 100v, L10B/25, fol. 21r, L10B/28, fols. 16v, 73r ff.

149. AHM L10B/21, fol. 274r ("Hay escuelas de lengua castellana y los jóvenes especialmente están bastantemente instruidos en este ydioma").

150. On the Tzeltal revolt, see Bricker, *Indian Christ*; Klein; Gosner; and Wasserstrom. See also Farriss, *Maya Society*, p. 318.

151. Farriss, *Maya Society*, pp. 335–36, 341–43; Collins.

Chapter Fourteen

EPIGRAPHS: AGN CRS 68 exp. 3, fols. 210v ff ("Antes les recreaba la voz de sus pastores, y seguían como corderos mansos sus silvos, aora huyen de sus caricias como pudieran de las ferocidades del lobo"); AGN Inq. 1399 exp. 12 ("Después de concluída su confesión y de haverle absuelto, me preguntó que si era pecado embriagarse y fornicar y hurtar . . . porque a su cura el Br. d. Manuel Caxica y Aguayo le havía oído predicar en el púlpito que no era pecado fornicar, hurtar, ni embriagarse, y que sólo es pecado tener pleito").

1. Burridge's "triangle" of authority, in *Mambu*, led me to this way of presenting local and district politics in New Spain. In broad outline, it can describe face-to-face authority in various early modern European states and colonies with an official church.

2. AJANG Criminal, bundle labeled "1806–7 (74)." The noun mandón—commander —also appears in the following documents, sometimes referring to the gobernador, more often to the body of principales: AGN Crim. 92 exp. 5, fol. 72r, 1767, Los Reyes, Ixtlahuaca district (mandón); AGN DP 1 exp. 2, fol. 160v, 1721–24, Huichapan (gobernador y mandones); DP 1 exp. 7, 1774, Temoaya, Ixtlahuaca district (elders called mandones). As with the use of "república," the distinction between the current officeholders and the body of principales is not always clear. An especially informative work on elections and elected officials in the district of Cuernavaca is Haskett, *Indigenous Rulers*, chs. 2–5. Also on elected offices and requirements for officeholding, see Alanís Boyso, *Elecciones*, pp. 12–13, 18–21.

3. Governance by younger men was usually pointed out as exceptional and inappropriate. For example, the cura of Temascaltepec in 1809 remarked that the alcaldes of Pipioltepec and Acatitlan were barely old enough to serve as topiles. BMM 251.

4. How the power of local officeholders changed in these regions during the three centuries of colonial rule is beyond the scope of this book. Gobernadores probably enjoyed greater influence and legitimacy during the 16th century, when more of them inherited their prominent place in the community and held office continuously for many years (d. Diego de Guzmán, "indio cacique y principal" of Tlajomulco, Jalisco, for example, was gobernador from 1567 to 1588). By the 18th century, gobernadores and alcaldes usually held office for only one year at a time, as the *Recopilación* provided; were more susceptible to removal from office for misconduct; and were hemmed in in other ways. (For examples of removal by high court decree, see AGN Indios 66 exp. 75, 1777, Nochistlan, Oaxaca; and AJANG Criminal, bundle labeled "1818 leg. 3 (89)," 1818, Tonalá [alcalde]). But cases of gobernadores serving five or more consecutive terms can be found in the late colonial

period, too: Rosenbach Lib., Mexican MS 462/25, pt. 7, no. 2, 1727, Huichapan; AJANG Civil, bundle labeled "1709–1819 (181)," 1744, Mechoacanejo; AGN DP 2 exp. 4, 1746, Tetitlan and Actopan (gobernador was said to be an ally of the Augustinian doctrineros, who had let him be reelected eight times); AGN Crim. III exp. 3, 1777, Tultitlan, Tacuba district; AGN Indios 66 exp. 75, 1777, Nochistlan, Oaxaca; AJANG Civil, box 205, doc. 2, 1790, Mechoacanejo. There was great variation even in the 16th century. Guzmán's successor in Tlajomulco was removed from office by judicial decree when, three years after he arrived, local Indians complained of his misconduct. Tello, *Crónica miscelánea*, 4: 23.

5. *Badianus Manuscript*, plates 70–71.

6. Eighteenth-century English usage recorded in the *Oxford English Dictionary* recognized this meaning of "republic" as the body politic, which was not necessarily coterminous with the community ("any community of persons, animals, etc. in which there is a certain equality among the members"). Villarroel uses "comunidad política" in his preface. "República" was also used to mean the current officeholders as a group. AGN CRS 39 exp. I, fol. III. There seems to have been a general shift in electors during the late colonial period from a hereditary aristocracy to "los ancianos y demás que han tenido oficios de república." Chávez Orozco, "Instituciones democráticas," pp. 162–64, finds this pattern prevalent in the vicinity of Toluca by the 1760's. On election procedures, see Alanís Boyso, "Corregimiento," pp. 467–70. Haskett, *Indigenous Rulers*, pp. 29–32, notes a pattern of territorial representation among electors and officeholders that gradually came to exclude some outlying settlements, but did not much alter the traditional elite composition of officeholders.

7. AGN Crim. 139 exp. 15. See also Chávez Orozco, "Instituciones democráticas."

8. AJANG Civil, box 172, doc. 22; Civil, box 267, doc. 17; Civil, box 172, doc. 22 ("aunque viejos carecen de los servicios, instrucción y méritos que los constituien padres de república").

9. AGN CRS 75 exp. 6, fols. 340v–342r, 1786, Alahuistlan, Zacualpan district. Vaqueros de cofradía were the caretakers mentioned in this document.

10. Francisco Antonio Lorenzana y Buitrón, "Reglas para que los naturales de estos reynos sean felices en lo espiritual, y temporal," June 20, 1768 (4 pp.), Brown Univ., Rockefeller Lib., Medina Coll., FHA 40, exp. 2.

11. AJANG Civil, box 22, doc. 8 ("para la administración de la Real Justicia, cobro de los reales tributos y reparo de las urgencias de dicho nuestro pueblo").

12. AGN Acervo 49 caja 50, 1749, Tancanhuitz (primicias); AGN Crim. 203 exp. I, 1769, Tepoztlan (collection for an organ); Tulane VEMC 3 exp. 5, 1791, Tepoztlan (clerical fees); AGN Civil 171 exp. 14, 1791, San Martín, Tonalá district (collection for Candlemas).

13. AGN CRS 67 exp. 2, 1766, Atlapulco, Ocoyoacac.

14. CDCh, roll 14, exp. 231, 1743, Yanhuitlan.

15. AGN Crim. 123 exp. 4.

16. AJANG Civil, box 205, doc. 2.

17. Archivo del Estado de Oaxaca, bundle labeled "1767–70," 1762, alcalde of Santa María Asunción Ocotlan; AGN Crim. 149, fols. 497ff, 1774, Tlacotepec, Metepec district (gobernador claimed the right to hit an Indian because he was drunk). As the *Recopilación* laws would predict, drunkenness was the most common justification: AGN Crim. 72 exp. 6, San Francisco Yicapujalco, Zacualpan district (officials claimed they did their best to obey the law and prevent drunkenness); Crim. 123 exp. 4, 1753, Tenango del Valle; Crim. 280, fols. 135ff, 1783, Gilozingo. For an example of disrespect, see Crim. 92 exp. 5, 1767, Los Reyes, Ixtlahuaca district. The cura of Santa María Apaxtla, Zacualpan district, claimed that the Indian gobernador Marcos Juan had applied a death sentence on his own. Crim. 166, fols. 185–272.

18. AGN Crim. 139 exp. 15. Another example of a pueblo-run jail is AGN Acervo 49 caja 47, 1765, Tepecoacuilco. Topiles mayores were in charge of it.

19. A sample of the charges of financial abuses: AGN Crim. 148, fols. 263ff, 1634, Ocoyoacac (Indians complained that gobernadores collected for fiestas and kept over half for themselves); Crim. 219, fols. 25ff, 1638, San Mateo Atengo, Metepec district (gobernador complained that other local officials extracted money on the pretext of tribute and litigation but kept it for themselves); Crim. 580 exp. 6, 1692, Temascalcingo (gobernador charged three principales with hiding tribute money); BMM 135 exp. 18, 1703, Mexico City (gobernador was said to have falsified death books for tribute purposes); AGN CRS 42 exp. 1, fol. 11, 1732, San Pedro Tejupilco, Temascaltepec district (Indian witness claimed that officials there had long hidden tributaries and collected the full amount, keeping the difference for themselves); AJANG Civil, bundle labeled "1709–1819 (181)," 1744, Mechoacanejo (cura accused leaders of overcollecting tribute and keeping the excess); AJANG Civil, box 171, doc. 14, 1791, San Martín, Tonalá district (alcalde accused two former alcaldes of not turning over the money they collected for tribute); CRS 136 exps. 6–7, fol. 304, 1790–91, Temascaltepec (cura said that república members forced macehuales to cultivate a cofradía milpa, then kept the proceeds for themselves); AGN Crim. 162, fols. 1–16, 1791–92, Otumba (complaint that a former gobernador was skimming tribute).

20. AGN Crim. 148, fols. 59ff, 1634, Ocoyoacac (two Indians charged the gobernador with taking their corn); AGN Indios 11 exp. 170, 1639, Amecameca (Indian charged that officials took away his maguey fields); Crim. 230 exp. 17, 1641, Ixtlahuaca (gobernador accused of forcing macehuales to serve without pay on nearby haciendas, till his fields, tend his livestock, and provide three corn grinders and two loads of pulque blanco every week); Rosenbach Lib., Mexican MS 462/25 pt. 7, no. 2, 1727, Huichapan (Indians complained of gobernador's extortions); Crim. 242 exp. 6, 1728, Santiago Jocotitlan (involuntary service for the gobernador); AGN Tierras 2554 exp. 11, 1766, Tlalmanlalco; CAAG unclassified, 1772, petition from San Gaspar Teuchitlan, Tala district; Tierras 2621 exp. 16, 1777, Indians of San Andrés v. gobernador of Tlalnepantla, district of Tacuba; AJANG Civil, box 171, doc. 14, 1789, San Martín, Tonalá district (alcaldes accused of taking solares from their enemies); AJANG Criminal, bundle labeled "1815 leg. 2 (138)," 1815, Tlaltenango. The possibility always existed for officials to be bribed with favors. For example, in 1774, two Indians of Acolman complained the gobernador had been bribed with "pulque, aguardiente, pan y otras cosas." Crim. 145, fols. 235ff.

21. AGN Crim. 580, 1644, San Miguel Hinacatepec, 1678, Metepec, 1749, Metepec district (suits against gobernadores for "excesos y malos tratos"); Crim. 730, 1703, Tultitlan (gobernador charged with excesos); Crim. 203 exp. 2, 1769, Tepoztlan (gobernador accused by townspeople of using excessive force, imprisoning and whipping them to extract contributions to purchase an organ for the church); Crim. 149, fol. 497, 1774 Tlacotepec, Metepec district (gobernador charged with adultery and mistreating Indians); AJANG Civil, box 149, doc. 4, 1794, Mecatabasco, Juchipila district (alcaldes accused of cruel whippings and forced labor); Crim. 15 exp. 2, 1797, Tenancingo, Malinalco district (Indians complained of the gobernador's abuses); Crim. 154, fols. 536–52, 1798, San Angel, Xochimilco district (official used excessive force in arresting a drunken Indian); Crim. 233 exp. 24, 1803, Belem, Xochimilco district (gobernador charged with beating an Indian couple severely in an argument over the quality of cloves); Crim. 171, fols. 220–27, 1808, Chiconcuac, Texcoco district (a topil charged the gobernador with cursing and attacking him); AJANG Criminal, bundle labeled "1817–1822 leg. 1 (159)," post-1817, San Sebastianito, Tonalá district (alcalde charged with whipping a widow when she told him to stop beating her son; he said he whipped her for being disrespectful).

22. AGN Crim. 179, fol. 13, 1759, San Luis de las Peras (Indians complained of malos tratos by a drunken alcalde); Crim. 177 exp. 12, 1763, San Francisco Chilpa, Tultitlan district (alcalde drunk and abusive, charged with beating townspeople); Crim. 17 exp. 19, 1766, Almoloya, Tianguistengo district (cura accused the gobernador of chronic drunkenness, of bursting into church to beat a tequitlato, and of making Indians work on feast days); Crim. 111 exp. 10, 1786, Azcapotzalco (Indian complained that the drunken alcalde and other officials beat him while he was asleep); Crim. 67 exp. 6, 1809, San Francisco Tonalapa (two Indians claimed the gobernador came into their home drunk, hit them, and jailed their mother); Crim. 120 exp. 17, San Pedro Xalostoc (an Indian accused the alcalde of tormenting the community with "fines and aggravations," especially of jailing people so that he could buy more alcohol for himself).

23. AGN Crim. 560, 1748 Tetela; AJANG Civil, box 205, doc. 2, 1790, Mechoacanejo, Jalisco (alcalde accused of drunkenness, of selling community property for his own benefit, of whipping and imprisoning people arbitrarily, of extorting money, and of taking land from two local Indians for his father-in-law).

24. AGN Crim. 228 exp. 1, 1766, San Miguel, Tlayacapan district (village woman raped on the road by the alcalde and his companions). The alcalde of San Nicolás Tlachaloya had an adulterous relationship with the wife of Antonio Domingo during his terms in 1815 and 1816 and arrested Antonio when he became angry. The outraged macehual subsequently killed his wife. Crim. 170, fols. 134–201.

25. AGN Civil 1485 exp. 13.

26. AGN CRS 39 exp. 3 ("no tiene lugar de trabajar para tener dinero").

27. Bernardo Antonio, mayordomo cobrador de tributos by appointment of the gobernador for Barrio San Pablo, Xochimilco, found his wife arrested in 1806 when he fell short 10p (by his estimate) or 30p (by the subdelegado's) in the tribute payment. AGN Civil 2072 exp. 17. In 1784, the ex-gobernador of Chichicastla, Meztitlan district (Hidalgo), petitioned for the embargo put on his property to be lifted because he had covered the remaining tribute. He thought that freezing his assets was unjust because the tributaries in arrears were not members of his pueblo, but hacienda residents. AGN Tierras 2772 exp. 23. AGN CRS 72 exp. 17, 1797, Milpa Alta, describes the gobernador's financial responsibilities, including covering the tribute of others from his own purse if they did not pay.

28. BEJ Papeles de Derecho, 3: 103–5, Feb. 11, 1791 ("deben sufrir por sus oficios").

29. AGN Crim. 129 exp. 8.

30. AJANG Criminal, bundle labeled "1806–1807 (74)" ("que alcalde ni que nada, yo soy el que manda y assí metan al alcalde en el zepo").

31. AJANG Criminal, bundle labeled "1809 (127)." A regidor of San Sebastián Analco was wounded under the same circumstances in 1813. Ibid., bundle labeled "1813–14, leg. 1 (116)."

32. Ibid., bundle labeled "1816 leg. 1 (32)" ("que ningún carajo tiene que meterse con él, que aquélla era su muger y haría con ella lo que quisiera").

33. AGN CRS 156 exp. 5.

34. AGN CRS 136 exp. 2.

35. AGN CRS 29 exp. 8, 1738, San Antonio Tecomic, Xochimilco district; AHJ Manuscripts, no. G-9-752 ZAS/3155, 1752, Guanusco, Juchipila district; AJANG Criminal, bundle labeled "1815 leg. 1 (78)," 1815, San Pedro Tlaquepaque, Guadalajara district; Criminal, bundle labeled "1818 leg. 2 (89)," 1818, Tonalá.

36. In the 1750's, curas could also declare men who did not know the Spanish language ineligible for office. Tulane VEMC 24 exp. 4.

37. AGN Crim. 111 exp. 3, 1777, Tultitlan; AGN Tierras 2431 exp. 6, 1790, Acapetlahuaya, Zacualpan district; AGN Crim. 179, fols. 50ff, 1797, Tuxtepec (alcalde came to the

cura's offices drunk); AGN Civil 2292 exps. 7–8, 1818, Malinalco (cura claimed the gobernador promoted drunkenness).

38. AJANG Criminal, bundle labeled "1815 leg. 1 (78)" ("hasta el grado de increparme a cada paso mirándome con desprecio y total olvido en toda clase de funciones del pueblo"; "Tu cuando fuiste alcalde en tu año castigaste a todos los Principales, y por eso te castigamos a ti"; ". . . y porque más se inclina a las máximas de las gente de razón que a las del Pueblo"). The case ended with an audiencia order for the two alcaldes to be replaced for the remainder of the year by the regidores más antiguos.

Once having passed the cura's scrutiny, some were reelected. Alanís Boyso found this to be the case for gobernadores and alcaldes in the election patterns for 26 pueblos of the corregimiento of Toluca from 1729 to 1811. "Corregimiento," pp. 471–77. Haskett, *Indigenous Rulers*, p. 126, also found reelections among the gobernadores of the Cuernavaca district: about one term in five was filled by someone who had held the office before.

39. AGN Crim. 202 exp. 1. Other cases of pueblo officials who found themselves the objects of disrespect, lawsuits, and violence by community members include the alcaldes of Navito and Imala (Sinaloa) in 1726, the alcalde of Xilotepec (Hidalgo) in 1756, and the gobernador of Acolman (northeast of the Valley of Mexico) in 1774. AJANG Civil, box 36, doc. 7; AGN Tierras 2179 exp. 3; AGN Crim. 145, fols. 238ff.

40. AGN CRS 130 exp. 10.

41. AGN CRS 39 exp. 3, fols. 84v–86r, Capuluac (collecting manípulos); CRS 140 exp. 4, fols. 160, 166, 1796, Zamatitlan and Oacalco, Yautepec district, Morelos (representing pueblo to audiencia); AGN Templos 25 exp. 11, 1807, Otumba and Cuautlancingo (signing for gobernadores); AHJ Manuscripts, no. G-4-808, 1808–10 (assisting with donation records); AJANG Civil, bundle labeled "1806–7 (174)," 1809, Jamay (counting votes); AJANG Criminal, bundle labeled "1809, leg. 2 (127)," 1809–10, Guisculco, and bundle labeled "1818 (63)," 1817, Tonalá (framing official communications for illiterate alcaldes and gobernadores); Criminal, bundle labeled "1815 (138)," 1815, Tlaltenango (assisting in elections).

42. AGI Guad. 352, 1790's reports on bienes de comunidad sometimes identify escribanos as the maestros.

43. The escribano of San Martín, Tonalá district, Jalisco, had served for 16 years before his removal by the subdelegado in 1791. AJANG Civil, box 172, doc. 22. On the reelection of escribanos, see Alanís Boyso, "Corregimiento," p. 469. As with other offices, the election procedures could vary, depending on the influence of the principales and local pressures for more popular selection. At Tlaltenango in 1815, the escribano was selected by the cabildo. AJANG Criminal, bundle labeled "1815 (138)." At Timilpa, Huichapan district, in 1789, there were two candidates for each office, including escribano—one nominated by the república and one by the común. AGN CRS 75 exps. 7–8. The escribanos of San Martín, Tonalá district, in 1791, and Tututepec, Tulancingo district, in 1796 were sons of an alcalde and gobernador, respectively. AJANG Civil, box 171, doc. 14; AGN CRS 130 exp. 3.

44. CAAG, unclassified, Autos pertenecientes a la cofradía del Santo Cristo, 1721, Jocotepec (an outsider from Tonalá became escribano); AJANG Criminal, bundle labeled "1811 legs. 2, 3," 1806–7, San Martín de la Cal, Cocula district (escribano was a recently arrived mulato accused of promoting much litigation).

45. AJANG Criminal, bundle labeled "1815, leg. 2 (138)" ("conserbación de nuestros derechos, paz, y tranquilidad sin que se nos incomode, veje, o perturbe contra las soberanas intenciones . . . con facultad de poder sostituto quanto le combenga y especialmente para que inste la solicitud pendiente de las fatigas de nuestro personal trabajo").

46. AJANG Civil, box 178, doc. 6, 1798, Huentitan (Jalisco).

47. AJANG Civil, box 160, doc. 6.

48. AGN Crim. 207 exp. 10 ("tiene a su disposición 500 yndios para que peleen contra los españoles; que no ha de ser esta Conquista como la de Hernán Cortés").

49. AJANG Civil, bundle labeled "1709–1819 (181)."

50. AGN CRS 30 exp. 2.

51. CAAG unclassified, 1721, Jocotepec, cofradía del Santo Cristo litigation (in 1720 escribano falsified episocopal decrees granting indulgences for visiting the found image of the crucifixion of Christ); AGN Hist. 319 exp. 18, fols. 11–12, 1782, Zapotlan el Grande (alcalde and escribano arrested for forging the cura's signature); Hist. 319 exp. 24, 1782, Santo Domingo Hueyapan (escribano de república accepted bribes of 2–3p from community officials to draw up false wills months after death of testator); AJANG Civil, box 172, doc. 22, 1792, San Martín, Tonalá district (escribano accused of tampering with testaments and land papers to benefit himself and others); AJANG Criminal, bundle labeled "1818 leg. 2 (89)," 1818, Tonalá (escribano admitted falsifying subdelegado's signature at the request of alcalde); Criminal, bundle labeled "1819–1820 leg. 6 (58)," 1819, Asguetlan, Colotlan district (escribano allegedly sent note to the subdelegado on behalf of community officials without their review and approval).

52. Distribution of cases of open resistance to priests by decade: 1720–29, two cases (2.4%); 1730–39, one case (1.2%); 1740–49, six cases (7.3%); 1750–59, five cases (6.0%); 1760–69, 18 cases (21.9%); 1770–79, 17 cases (20.7%); 1780–89, 14 cases (17.1%); 1790–99, nine cases (10.9%); and 1800–1809, 10 cases (12.1%).

53. In an 1804 petition for elevation to cabecera status, the pueblo of Huixtaca in the district of Taxco presented itself as a model of docility and humility, "obedient to whatever decrees and orders are sent, . . . whether royal or ecclesiastical." Rosenbach Lib., Mexican MS 461/25 pt. 28, no. 8. Huixtaca's absence from the conspicuous lawsuits and violent disputes of the late 18th century would appear to support the claim. On the other hand, pueblos appealing for favor from the superior courts could be expected to lay claim to a record of obedience and respect, whether or not it was fully deserved, as, for example, in AGN CRS 47 exp. 3, 1699, Santa Ana Tetlama, Tancítaro district, Michoacán ("postrados y arrodillados a tos pies, venimos a pedir. . . . Besamos los pies de VE"); AGN Tierras 2179 exp. 3, fols. 37v–38v, 1756, San Luis de las Peras, Xilotepec district (submissive to justicia); CRS 68 exp. 1, fol. 18v, 1759, Coyotepec, Cuautitlan district (Indians always respected and feared the cura); and AGN Templos 25 exp. 11, 1807, Otumba district ("siempre hemos estado engreídos en el patrosinio de nuestro soberano"). Some did clearly demonstrate great loyalty to the cura: AJANG Civil, box 59, doc. 9, 1756, Zacoalco (asked for cura's pardon); CRS 74 exp. 11, 1801, Amanalco, Metepec district. For the Franciscan doctrinero Miguel Camacho Villavicensio in 1719, the best predictor of Indians who were "encoxidos y humillados" was whether they dressed in tilmas. BMM 135 exp. 18.

54. AHM L10B/28, fol. 104v ("a fin de evitar el mal concepto que tienen en otras partes").

55. Delumeau, p. 155: "Protest against the loose morals of the lower clergy topped the list of complaints put forward by the inhabitants of La Lonpierre."

56. Fully half of the 39 complaints to pastoral visitors between 1765 and 1792 centered directly on priests' fees and labor demands, as against only two complaints about a priest's personal conduct. AHM L10B/28, fol. 168, L10B/13, fol. 257v. A similar pattern of conflict with curas of Peru over fees and labor, plus land, is described in O'Phelan Godoy, "El norte." Economic matters were also the main grievances against parish priests in Ireland in the early 19th century. Connolly, pp. 237–48. Frye, ch. 8, provides a case study of economic and political conflicts between priests and parishioners in San Luis Potosí during the late 18th century.

57. *Recop.* 6-3-2, 6-3-15, 4-9-13, 4-9-1.

58. AJANG Civil, bundle labeled "1709–1819 (181)."

59. AJANG Civil, box 119, doc. 12 ("a los hijos toca proponer, al cura elegir, y a los señores alcaldes mayores nombrar"). He would choose one of three they proposed, and the alcalde mayor would install him, the cura said.

60. AJANG Civil, box 17, doc. 2 (La Barca); Civil, box 22, doc. 8 (Atotonilco el Alto); Civil, bundle labeled "1769–60, leg. 2 (47)" (Tetapan, province of Amula).

61. AGN CRS 72 exp. 7, fols. 101–10.

62. AGN Bandos 8 exp. 43; Bandos 7 exp. 91; Bandos 8 exp. 28; Bandos 10 exp. 1.

63. Brown Univ., Rockefeller Lib., Medina Coll., FHA 54 exp. 16, August 25, 1789 ("no ha de ser para obligar a los electores a que nombren los judiciales que los párrocos quieran").

64. BEJ Papeles de Derecho, 1: 292 ("aunque contribuirá mucho con sus asistencia para el esplendor y seriedad del acto, no tiene jurisdicción alguna en él"). Amended, these instructions became audiencia regulations on March 9, 1791. They provided for (1) elected officials to be "of Indian caste and from the pueblo," as certified by the subdelegado and cura; (2) a subdelegado's deputy to have the commission in writing; (3) the judge or his deputy to "presidir las elecciones and combocar para ellas y no sólo authorizar con su presencia sino también con su firma entera"; and (4) "no han de omitir recomendar el mérito de los más inclinados, aplicados, y aptos para la agricultura y persuadir a los yndios y especialmente a los justiciales a ella y su obligación de influir a su aumento." AJANG Criminal, box 38, doc. 32.

65. In cases before the Audiencia of Mexico, it was the Ordenanza de Intendentes more than an audiencia instruction that was invoked (e.g., AGN CRS 75 exp. 7, 1789, San Andrés Timilpa, Huichapan district; CRS 195 exp. 6, 1792, Zoquitlan, Tehuacan district).

66. AGN CRS 39 exps. 2–3.   67. AGN RCO 149 exp. 181.

68. Tulane VEMC 8 exp. 25.   69. AGN CRS 75 exp. 11; CRS 137 exp. 5.

70. AJANG Civil, box 138, doc. 12; and Civil, box 140, doc. 5.

71. AJANG Civil, box 139, doc. 8.

72. AGN CRS 195 exp. 6 ("¿ . . . por razón de evitar disenciones en los pueblos quando se elijan sugetos de castas infectas que perturban miserablemente la paz?").

73. That curas were not ousted from power everywhere is illustrated by Texas, Mariano Riva Palacio Coll., no. 6491, where the párroco of Amanalco in the district of Villa de Valles was reported to control local elections as late as 1837. But by 1789, it was becoming rare to find parish priests "naming the *gobernador* and seeing to his election," as the Indians of Tixmadeje claimed theirs did that year. AGN Crim. 202 exp. 1.

74. AJANG Criminal, box 20 doc. 2, 1806, Zapotitlan, testimony of Reyes de los Angeles.

75. AJANG Civil, box 172, doc. 22; Civil, box 171, doc. 14; Civil, box 206, doc. 1.

76. Ibid., box 149, doc. 4.

77. AJANG Criminal, box 8, doc. 6.

78. A case of vote fraud is AJANG Civil, bundle labeled "1806–7 (174)," 1807–9, Jamay, in which Pedro Felipe was excluded from office for having tampered with election results as far back as 1792.

79. The move toward broader suffrage seems to have been especially true of pueblos in Jalisco. Another case of all "hijos" voting that is not mentioned in the text is Xomulco, Ahuacatlan district. AJANG Civil, box 119, doc. 1285, 1749.

80. AJANG Civil, box 22, doc. 8. For more on Atotonilco el Alto, see Taylor, "Indian Pueblos," especially pp. 167–68.

81. AJANG Civil, box 267, doc. 17. On the practical matter of whether a more restricted electorate would yield better government in Tlajomulco, the subdelegado advised the audiencia that it would make little difference. The principales who wanted the old sys-

tem of restricted voting were, he said, just as bad as the group that had levered itself into office by the expanded suffrage. Tlajomulco was well known for disputed elections in the late colonial period. Disputes over the election of mayordomos went back at least to 1763, with the cura claiming the power to approve the nominees in the annual election. CAAG unclassified, 1763, record of the removal of a mayordomo of the Purísima Concepción cofradía. The tension over elections was apparently not simply a product of internal divisions, because the subdelegado complained in 1815 that the cura was still confirming elections in one of the outlying sujetos, Santa Cruz, without the knowledge of civil authorities.

82. AGN CRS 67 exp. 33. The cura's move in this case was done with the cooperation of the alcalde mayor.

83. In 1729, Indian officials of San Gerónimo, Cholula (Puebla), complained that the vicario was taking money from the arca to cover his clerical fees and masses. Similarly, in 1778, the pueblo of Anathecan, Olinalá parish, and the district lieutenant complained that the cura was managing the caja de comunidad and using the funds for church construction in a pueblo of less than 30 tributaries. AGN CRS 13 exp. 3. The 16th-century legislation is compiled in *Recop.*, book 6, titles 4 and 10. Solórzano 4-16-66 summarized it in the mid-17th century.

84. AGN Bandos 9 exp. 41, Aug. 29, 1776. An example of the audiencia requesting an inspection by the contador when expenditures from the cajas in the district of Zitácuaro became an issue in 1778 is documented in Tulane VEMC 25 exp. 15.

85. *Recop.* 6-4-31.

86. Reports and instructions on establishing and operating the arcas and bienes de comunidad for Nueva Galicia in the 1780's and 1790's are located in AGI Guad. 250, 352; AFRANG 293; and BEJ Papeles de Derecho, 1: 573v–80, 539–41, 2: 25v–26, 89v–91r, 351–53, 4: 409–14 and 494–507. See also Nava Oteo; and Lira, "Cajas de comunidad." District judges were expected to promote the cajas, as the 1786 residencia of the alcalde mayor of Sayula shows. AJANG Civil, box 106, doc. 1. Apparently they were active in doing so until independence. Civil, box 261, doc. 11, 1808–16; Civil, bundle labeled "1806–1828 (92)," 1817, Tlajomulco (pueblo officials objected to the subdelegado's attempts to increase the caja's cash reserves by renting out community lands).

87. Lira, "Cajas de comunidad" (cajas of Indian pueblos as source of capital for Banco Nacional de San Carlos after 1782); AFRANG 293, 1794, Autlan (contributions to Real Caja de Filipinas); AJANG Civil, bundle labeled "1800–1813," 1806 consolidación record in which funds from the bienes de comunidad of Indian pueblos had entered the treasury of the Ramo de Consolidación "en calidad de préstamo patriótico" (pueblos from seven districts of Nueva Galicia contributed 5,769p).

88. The question of putting caja funds to religious use was not new to the courts. What changed was the intensity with which the issue was pursued and the new determination to scrutinize public expenditures minutely. For an earlier case in which a corregidor would not approve the use of funds from the arca to pay for religious construction, see AGN Tierras 2771 exp. 7, 1764, Xilotepec. In this case, the audiencia decided that the arca funds could be spent to finish a side altar but warned the pueblo officials that in the future they should expect to follow the corregidor's judgment.

89. AGN Tierras 2771 exp. 12.

90. Tulane VEMC 28 exp. 4, 1794, Santa María Acamuchitlan, Temascaltepec district (request to sell community livestock to purchase decent implements for the mass; the case was left pending by the audiencia fiscal, who wanted more information on the expenses involved and the funds in the caja); AGN CRS 137 exp. 7, 1803, Axapusco, Tacuba district (request for a license to use caja funds for church ornaments and other needs of the parish; an investigation was ordered and the decision left pending, but the audiencia fiscal expressed his opinion that the amount requested should be reduced because so much

had been spent on church construction and ornaments there in the past); AGN Templos 25 exp. 11, 1808, Ostotipac and San Salvador Quautlancingo, Otumba district (audiencia's approval of pueblos' request to pay for parish celebrations from the caja, as the crown had allowed them to do in the past, "if they cannot do so by other means").

91. AGN CRS 179 exp. 10; Tulane VEMC 8 exp. 51.

92. AGN Templos 25 exp. 5.

93. The caja of Otumba got 546p, 4rr, from land rents in 1793. Nearly all of that sum (533p) was expended, the greater part of it on derechos parroquiales (361p) and the schoolmaster's salary. In Oztoticpac that year, nearly 350p of the 434p of income from rents and sales was expended, 204p of which went for derechos parroquiales. Chávez Orozco, *Cajas de comunidades.* AGN Templos 159 exps. 50 and 56 contain accounts for San Miguel Quaxusco, Malinalco district, in 1793 (where the income was used up on fiestas and masses); Ajoloapa, Ecatepec district, in 1794 (where 20p of the 96p expended went for lime and construction materials to repair the church, 14p for the fiesta titular, and 4p to complete the tithe); and Santos Reyes Acosac in 1794 and 1795 (where over half the funds expended went for candle wax, fireworks, fees to the cura, and oil for the lamp). Most of the expenses of Yautepec (Morelos) in 1796 were also for mass and other religious events. AGN Crim. 203 exp. 3.

94. Hidalgo suits over labor service: AGN Tierras 2774 exp. 6, 1721, Huazalingo, Yahualica district; Tulane VEMC 15 exp. 5, 1739, Yahualica; Tierras 2774 exp. 9, 1749, Huazalingo; AGN Templos 25 exp. 2, 1753–54, Chapula (Meztitlan report); AGN CRS 153 exp. 6, 1755, Santo Tomás, San Mateo, and San Gabriel Cempoala; Tierras 2179 exp. 3, 1756, Peras, Xilotepec district; CRS 156 exp. 10, 1763, Santa María Amealco, Huichapan district; CRS 67 exp. 3, 1768, Joloapan, Tetepango district; AGN Crim. 79 exp. 1, 1777, Tlamatlan, Meztitlan district; AGN Civil 2072 exp. 19, 1788, Cempoala; AGN Bienes 575 exp. 14, 1789, Huazalingo; AGN Hist. 578A, 1793, Tepehuacan (Meztitlan report); AGN Acervo 49 caja 97E, 1796, Tasquillo, Huichapan district; CRS 130 exp. 3, 1796, Santa María Tututepec; Templos 25 exp. 9, 1799, Santa María Zacualtipan, Meztitlan district; Civil 2282 exp. 3, 1805, Huejutla; CRS 136 exp. 8, 1817, Acatlan, Tulancingo district; Bienes 663 exp. 25, 1818, Tlatepingo, Lolotla parish. There was also a concentration of service disputes involving curas in the district of Tixtla (Guerrero): CRS 67 exp. 10, 1776, San Juan Tetelzingo; CRS 183 exp. 3, 1779, San Juan Tetelzingo; Hist. 578A, 1793, Apango (Tixtla report); Hist. 437, 1800, Mochitlan.

95. *Recop.* 1-14-81, 1594 ("sino fuere en casos y cosas muy necesarios, y entonces pagándoles lo que merecieren, y el Gobierno hubiere tasado por sus jornales . . . pues solamente toca a los Religiosos la doctrina y alivio de los naturales").

96. *Recop.* 1-13-11, 6-12-3, 6-12-48.

97. *Recop.* 6-12-43 ("A los curas de Pueblos se reparten Indios, varones, y hembras, que les guisen de comer, hagan pan de maíz, y pesquen las Vigilias, y Quaresmas; y porque es muy dañoso, y perjudicial: Ordenamos que no se permita tal repartimiento para estos efectos, ni otro alguno, y guárdese lo dispuesto en los servicios personales"). For the Audiencia of Mexico, another clear statement against personal service to parish priests was made on May 4, 1656. Ventura Beleña, 1: 58.

98. Within three years, the 1793 circular prohibiting priests from requiring free personal service was invoked and quoted in two suits. AGN CRS 130 exp. 3, Santa María Tututepec, Meztitlan district; CRS 130 exp. 5, Zinacantepec, Metepec district.

99. See *Pintura del gobernador,* fol. 501v, for an example of a claim of excessive, unpaid service in the 16th century. The resistance to labor service was not always by litigation. In 1725, the Franciscans at Tlaxcala collected the tilmas of all Indians as they came to work during the day because otherwise most would flee: "los más se huyen y hacen burla e irrisión de los Padres." BMM 135 exp. 8.

100. AGN Tierras 2774 exp. 6. Huazalingo was back in court over a similar issue of personal services in 1789. AGN Bienes 575 exp. 14.

101. AGN CRS 68 exps. 4–5. Other 18th-century disputes over servicios involuntarios and pay beyond the Hidalgo cases set out in n. 94 above include CRS 29 exp. 2, 1711, Calimaya; CRS 153 exp. 7, 1755, Malacatepec, Metepec district; CRS 204 exps. 9–10 and CRS 23 exp. 5, 1760, Tejupilco and sujetos, Temascaltepec district; AGN Civil 1485 exp. 12 and Tulane VEMC 39 exp. 15, 1762, two sujetos of Huizquilucan; CRS 156 exp. 13, 1765, San Lucas and San Mateo, Tecualoyan parish, Malinalco district; CRS 156 exp. 11, 1765, Zumpahuacan, Malinalco district; AGN Templos 25 exp. 3, 1768, San Lucas, Temascaltepec district; CRS 136 exp. 2, 1781, two sujetos of Tlaltizapan (Morelos); CRS 75 exp. 6, 1786, Alahuistlan, Zacualpan district; and AJANG Civil, box 143, doc. 20, 1793, San Juan de Alaya.

102. AGN CRS 153 exp. 6.

103. Tulane VEMC 15 exp. 5. Huazalingo, in this parish of Yahualica, complained in 1721 that it alone supplied one topil, one sacristán, one zacatero, one molendera, and one tortillera. AGN Tierras 2774 exp. 6.

104. AGN Acervo 49 caja 97E; AGN CRS 30 exp. 2.

105. AGN CRS 153 exp. 7. Labor service was also extensive in Michoacán. In 1770, shortly after the secularization of the parish of San Gerónimo Purenchícuaro, the Indians of San Nicolás Acuitzio complained that the cura was demanding two indios panaderos, two refitoleras, two cavallerizos, two barrenderos, one potrero, one zacatero, one aguador, three carreteros, one pastor, and two carpinteros, plus four men to chase crows away from the cornfields, and that he demanded the same number from Tiripitío. AGN CRS 51 exp. 1.

106. AGN CRS 67 exp. 3. Other labor disputes turning on the 1767 arancel are CRS 67 exp. 6, 1770, San Gaspar Amatepec and Santiago Atlaya, Zacualpan district; CRS 75 exp. 6, 1786, Alahuistlan, Zacualpan district; AGN Bienes 575 exp. 14, 1789, Huazalingo; AGN Acervo 49 caja 97E, 1796, Tasquillo, Huichapan district; and Bienes 663 exp. 6, 1809, Tultitlan. For an earlier example, AGN CRS 153 exp. 7, 1755, Malacatepec, Metepec district.

107. AGN CRS 75 exp. 3.

108. AGN CRS 30 exp. 2.

109. AGN CRS 72 exp. 17. In 1766, Atlapulco and Ocoyoacac, Tenango del Valle district, complained that 12 servants a week were too many in a time of scarcity. AGN CRS 67 exp. 2.

110. AGN CRS 72 exps. 14 and 17, 1795–97, Milpa Alta. The cura of Jonacatepec reported in 1796 that parishioners had stopped serving the church, claiming that the arancel exempted them from doing so. AGN Civil 2121 exp. 10. On providing transportation for confession, see AHJ G-4-719 GUA/4, 1755, "Autos formados sobre pedir ministro independiente," Mesticacan, Nochistlan district; López Jiménez, *Algunos documentos*, p. 31, 1794, Nayarit; and CAAG, resumé of cura José Antonio Barragán of Huejuquilla for 1770 concurso.

111. AGN CRS 136 exp. 2, as had been agreed on on Oct. 26, 1775.

112. *Itin.* 1-7-4, 2-2-6.

113. AGN Tierras 2179 exp. 3.

114. AGN Templos 25 exp. 3.

115. AGN CRS 183 exp. 3.

116. AGN Hist. 578A, 1793, Zumpango de la Laguna report; Hist. 437, 1800, Mochitlan, Tixtla district.

117. AGN Civil 2072 exp. 10.

118. AGN CRS 72 exp. 10 ("según la costumbre de la tierra y el jornal que ganen en otras ocupaciones"). Contrast this to the 1711 dispute at Calimaya, where the viceroy ordered the visitas of Nativitas Tarimoro, San Andrés, Concepción, San Miguel Chapul-

tepec, and San Mateo Mexicalcingo to provide weekly servants to tend the priests' live-stock, and "traerles leña, agua y zacate y carbón como lo demás, que es estilo." AGN CRS 29 exp. 2.

119. The demand for a "justo precio" was raised, for example, in AGN 136 exp. 8, 1817, Acatlan, Tulancingo district.

120. AGN CRS 136 exps. 6–7.

121. For example, the cura of Tejupilco testified that he paid "los salarios de la molen-dera y demás yndios de servicio doméstico de mi parte y sus vicarios" at the going rate in the district, when Indians of the cabecera and San Miguel Ixtapa and San Juan Acati-tlan brought suit for involuntary labor in 1760. AGN CRS 204 exps. 9–10. See also AGN Civil 1485 exp. 12, 1762, San Juan and San Francisco, Huizquilucan parish; and AGN Hist. 128 exp. 7, 1791, letter of Sept. 15, 1791. Indians of Tamazunchale told the pastoral visitor making his rounds in 1808–9 that the priest made them work without pay in his sugar-cane fields, building fences, and making deliveries to Mexico City. Later, they admitted he paid them 1.5r a day for the work, but they claimed that it was still inappropriate be-cause the fields were a day's walk away. AGN Acervo 490 caja 116.

122. A quotable example of a sweeping complaint of this kind made on behalf of Indian plaintiffs is in AGN CRS 136 exp. 4, fols. 264ff, Oct. 11, 1783, letter of Bartolomé Díaz Borrego, solicitador for the Indians of San Lorenzo Huichilapan, Tenango del Valle district: "Sería esto lo menos, aunque con semejantes contribuciones casi destruien estos infelises indios toda su sustancia sin que les quede para hacer las demás, a que los estrecha o igual o maior obligación como son los de los reales tributos, i subvenir a sus necesidades cotidianas i las de sus familias. Lo más es, la tiranía con que se les exije i el rigor que guía al Padre Vicario en todas sus operaciones."

123. *Diccionario de la lengua castellana* ("la mutación de las cosas que por lo común tienen estado fijo o se creía que le debían tener").

124. AGN CRS 75 exp. 9, 1790, Indians of Atengo and San Francisco Zayula v. cura of Tepetitlan (complaint of "novedades" by parish priests since secularization, "que cada cura ha introducido a su antojo"); CRS 178 exp. 13, 1805, San Juan Bautista Jiquipilco, Ixtlan district (objection to the cura "innovating," raising fees "a su antojo"); AJANG Civil, bundle labeled "1795 leg. 35," 1795, San Sebastián Achichipico ("inobación en la limosna de las misas de dichas cofradías").

125. But some curas were convinced their Indian parishioners were wholly animated by blind custom. In 1792, the cura of Calimaya complained of visita Indians "viviendo en su antigua libertad," resisting a trip to the cabecera for confession "por sólo el pretexto de no haver sido essa la costumbre." AGN CRS 131 exp. 1, fol. 82. Another spoke of his parishioners wanting to return to custom after trying an innovation permitted by royal policy. CRS 204 exp. 5, 1740, Tixtla.

126. AGN CRS 136 exp. 2, fol. 138 ("en todo aquello que les es faborable la constum-bre la abrasan con suma tenacidad y siguen el arancel en lo que les es útil"). See also fols. 196–209. Appealing to custom could obviously serve personal interests, as well as principle. The Indian gobernador of Papalotla, Texcoco district, in 1809 was not simply a high-minded defender of custom when he invoked it against the cura for preventing him from taking charge of the Sunday collection. AGN CRS 130 exp. 9.

127. Did not know idioma: AGN RCO 69 exp. 5, 1749; RCO 96 exp. 102, 1770. Re-spect and dignity of officials at stake: BMM 135, fols. 197–224, 1672; AGN CRS 192 exps. 11–12, 1760 (gobernador traveled to Mexico City to show his wounds and complain of ex-cessive behavior); CRS 136 exp. 4, 1783 (cura jailed and shamed the gobernador as "plei-tista y perturbador del público"); AGN Tierras 2431 exp. 6, 1790 (revenge over pleito or humiliation); AGN Civil 49 exp. 4 (alcalde's desire for revenge over humiliation).

128. AGN CRS 75 exp. 6, 1786, Alahuistlan.

129. Litigation (at least that involving Indians) seems to have followed a different trajectory in Castile in the early modern period from New Spain's. Kagan, in his study of lawsuits in Spain during the 16th and 17th centuries, traces a "legal revolution" in which "the formal adjudication of disputes [by all kinds of people] was sharply and dramatically on the rise." But by the second quarter of the 17th century (and on through the 18th), litigation in the royal courts became much less common as disputes increasingly came to be played out in other ways. In New Spain, by contrast, litigation seems to have been a growth industry through much of the colonial period, perhaps declining some in the late 17th and early 18th centuries, but increasing dramatically during the reigns of Fernando VI, Charles III, and Charles IV.

Litigation in Castile, as Kagan studied it, seems different in two ways from litigation in New Spain, and these differences may help to explain the contrasting long-term pattern (if, in fact, litigation did not pick up again in Spain during the late 18th century). Most suits in Castile were pursued by individuals, and mainly by aristocrats and urban residents, whereas the bulk in New Spain were pursued in the name of the corporate interests of a predominantly rural population. Kagan's premise that litigiousness "was a function of a world view that placed greater emphasis on individual rights than on individual responsibilities" does not hold so well for the colonial situation, since it was the failure of royal officials to fulfill individual responsibilities that provoked much of the Indian litigation. Despite the many signs of diminished royal power in New Spain during the 17th century, the judicial state and the habit of litigation apparently remained greater there than in the mother country.

130. The Indians of Tecospa, Xochimilco district, confidently reminded the court in 1792 of the shrinking definition of a parish priest's duties when they declared that "la materia es muy agena de su ministerio." AGN Tierras 2670 exp. 5.

131. AGN CRS 42 exp. 1. Van Young, "Conflict and Solidarity," regards litigation in the name of the community as an expression of collective solidarity that counterbalanced the forces of internal division. The cases presented in this study suggest that the impetus for and the meaning of such litigation were more ambiguous.

132. AGN CRS 25 exp. 4, fol. 193v ("Sin consumir lo que con tanto afán y trabajo adquerían y devían emplear en mantenerlas en pleitos como al presente, desatendiendo sus campos y bagando"). The lieutenant of Zacoalco (Jalisco) in 1798 was accused of a miscarriage of justice when he jailed a local man who had written to the audiencia in Guadalajara and made two trips there to complain of the lieutenant's conduct. AJANG Criminal, box 32, doc. 2.

133. AGN Inq. 1304 exp. 3 ("Los gastos han acobardado a los querellantes").

134. One of many examples of such exaggeration is Rosenbach Lib., Mexican MS 462/25 pt. 4, no. 7, 1735, Hueyapan, Morelos.

135. The Nava case is documented in AGN Inq. 1074; Inq. 1145 exp. 24; and Inq. 1209 exp. 13. Another case of false charges, made against the cura of Cosamaloapan (Veracruz) in the 1780's, is traced in Tulane VEMC 61 exp. 9; VEMC 66 exps. 10, 11, and 22; VEMC 67 exp. 5; and VEMC 74 exp. 42. Arze took care in 1766 to warn young would-be parish priests that Indians were capable of maliciously wounding themselves in order to bring charges of cruelty against their priests. For another case of local notables using litigation to take revenge on a parish priest, see AJANG Criminal, box 20, doc. 2, 1806, Zapotitlan, in which a man who had been declared ineligible for office by the cura initiated a suit against him for abusos.

136. BMM 271, ch. 12 ("la verdad es que los yndios por más que los suponen amantes de su suelo, y pegado a él, mui bien saben salir de allí, por mui largas temporadas, quando interviene su propio interez. No, no son tan sencillos como los creen muchos").

137. Mota y Escobar, pp. 34–35.

138. BMM 1722, vols. 2, doc. 21 (referring to the abandonment of the congregación at Yasauila, Oaxaca, in 1611), and 4, doc. 53 (describing migration of Indians out of Tlaxcala in the 1620's).

139. Miguel Camacho Villavicensio, Franciscan doctrinero of an Indian parish in Mexico City, complained in 1719 of many rural Indians coming into his parish and wanted the royal law on Indians maintaining their original residence enforced. BMM 135 exp. 18. From the other end, some rural priests reported that many of their parishioners had left for parts unknown. AGN Civil 2166 exp. 5, 1766, Alfajayucan, Huichapan district; AGN CRS 25 exp. 4, 1799, Huiciltepec (Puebla). See also on Indian vagrancy, M. Pérez, p. 2.

Village Indians residing on estates: AGN CRS 72 exp. 4, witness no. 4, 1734, Huetamo, Michoacán ("Se hallan muchos hijos de este pueblo desamparados en otras jurisdicciones sirviendo de baqueros en estancias de ganado"); CRS 156 exp. 7, fols. 229ff, 1761, Acambay, Xilotepec district, Hidalgo ("He observado que los yndios de todo el partido la mayor parte del año se viven en la tierra adentro trabajando en las siembras, . . . cosechas, y trasquilas"); BEJ Papeles de Derecho, 1: 41–43, 1794, Cocula (many Indians were medieros, operarios on ranchos and haciendas in the district); AGN Tierras 1772 exp. 17, 1802, Cuahuayutla, Guerrero (pueblo had declined during cura's three years there, with many parishioners leaving to hide or work in ranchos of the district; he wanted an order for their repatriation). Returns on weekends: AGN CRS 75 exp. 6, 1786, Alahuistlan, Guerrero (salt pits). Traders: AGN Policía 23 exp. 2, 1782(?), Ecatepec district.

140. New York Public Library, "Yndize comprehensibo de todos los goviernos . . . del virreynato de Mexico," 177?, fol. 29r, reported that in some places (here the example was Metepec) it was difficult to collect the tribute because "sus tributarios suelen trasponerse."

141. AJANG Civil, bundle labeled "1809–1819 leg. 5 (49)," relación de méritos of Joseph Diego Gómez ("su fácil inclinación a dejar sus naturalezas y huir a los montes"); AGI Guad. 352 report by Luis de Ullate, fol. 10r.

142. Various of the witnesses against Manuel Gallo, charged with soliciting women in several parishes of central Jalisco between 1782 and 1795, had left their pueblos during the famine and epidemic of 1785–86 and could not be located. AGN Inq. 1255. In 1782, the alcalde mayor of Ecatepec reported that a number of Indians had left Tolpetlac during the last smallpox epidemic. AGN CRS 30 exp. 3.

143. AJANG Civil, box 18, doc. 5 ("Estamos en ánimo todos los de los pueblos que si dicho Chaide prosigue con la vara de justicia a sacar nuestras familias y despoblar los pueblos y benimos a vesindar a la galisia para tener quietud y sosiego").

144. AGN Bienes 575 exp. 46.

145. The pueblos of Jalisco, in particular, tended to be relatively outside-oriented, and migration from them was largely by individual choice. See Taylor, "Indian Pueblos."

146. Indians fleeing cura's cruelty: AJANG Civil, bundle labeled "1769–60 (47)," 1767, Mazatan and Tetapan, province of Amula.; AJANG Criminal, bundle labeled "1806 leg. 22 (11)," 1805, Zapotitlan, Tuscacuesco district. See also citations in n. 150 below.

147. AJANG Civil, box 231, doc. 1, 1804, Ocotlan (either 14 or 26 families were said to have left because of mistreatment by the cura and their inability to pay tribute and other taxes any longer).

148. AGN CRS 39 exp. 5. The abandonment of pueblos in fees disputes is also reported in AGN CRS 68 exp. 3, 1771, for San Felipe del Obraje, San Lucas, and San Juan Bautista.

149. AGN CRS 68 exp. 2, fols. 113f, 1769, Ozoloapan.

150. AGN Acervo 49 caja 43, 1625, Cicapualco, Ichcateopan district (Indians fled to escape cura's impositions); AGN DP 1 exp. 1, 1671, Cuernavaca district (14 pueblos, including Mazatepec and Tetlama, reported that many Indians were moving away as a result

of excessive charges by the Franciscan doctrineros); AGN CRS 47 exp. 4, 1729 (Indians of San Gerónimo, Cholula district, Puebla, said to have fled to avoid the cura's wrath and what they feared would be sentences to obraje service); AGN Bienes 210 exp. 1, 1731, Guayacocotla (gobernador, past gobernador, two alcaldes, and other officials claimed the interim cura's cruelty had caused many Indians to flee, "dejando desiertos los pueblos"); CRS 42 exp. 1, 1732, Tejupilco (Indians of San Lucas, in arrears in fees to cura, left because of the bad harvest and pressure from the cura to pay); AGN Crim. 284 exp. 5, 1736, Papantla (tumulto against the teniente de cura and alcalde mayor); Tulane VEMC 15 exp. 5, 1739, Yahualica (some Indians had fled to the monte in order to avoid the cura's jail, whippings, and fees); AGN Acervo 49 caja 49, 1739, Churubusco (84 indios ausentes, many of whom reportedly had fled the gratuitous abuse of the cura); AGN Tierras 2779 exp. 9, 1749, Huazalingo, Yahualica district (an Indian priest from a noble family of the pueblo was said by cura to be the cause of much migration to "otras tierras por la grandíssima opresión"); CAAG, resumé of cura José Antonio Barragán of Tlaltenango for 1770 concurso; AGN Alcaldes Mayores 3, fols. 172–78, 1771, San Juan Bautista Amecac, Atlixco district (Indian witnesses said various pueblos were being abandoned because of fear of the cura and his abuses); Aguirre Beltrán, "Delación," 1787, Acayucan; AGN Templos 25 exp. 9, 1799, Zacualtipan, Meztitlan district (Indians took flight to the monte to avoid cura's abuse); VEMC 8 exp. 21, 1803, Tlaquiltenango (roughly half of the Indian families had reportedly moved away as a result of conflicts with the lieutenant); VEMC 54 exp. 22, 1805, Meztitlan district (Indians of Nonoalco refused to be governed by the gobernador Zocsoquipan and took flight when a detachment of soldiers was sent in; here only the men fled—the women took refuge in the church); Bienes 663 exp. 25, 1818, Tlaltepingo, Lolotla parish (pueblo abandoned to avoid cura's abuse); Texas, Mariano Riva Palacio Coll., no. 4550, 1850, Zacualpan (official complained that local people were hiding for two or three days at a time to avoid the 1rr/month mandatory contribution).

151. Large numbers of people from some Valley of Mexico communities were used to living in Mexico City all or part of the year. See the appeal of the cura of Cuautitlan for his parishioners' repatriation in 1798. AGN Civil 2224. Smaller numbers of Indians from farther away also moved there for long stretches, usually for compelling reasons. For example, Nicolás de Castilla, cura of Atitalaquia in the mid-1730's, had tracked down an adulterous widow and widower who had fled to Mexico City. By then, they had married in Mexico City, but Castilla had the marriage invalidated so that he, as their parish priest, could sanction it. JCB, 1760 resumé.

152. AGN CRS 136 exp. 2, fols. 185–93.

153. AGN CRS 29 exp. 2, witness no. 4, Mathías Moreno, 1711, Calimaya; CRS 192 exps. 11–12, 1760, Almoloya, Tescaliacac district; AGN Bienes 575 exp. 14, 1789, Huazalingo; CRS 136 exps. 6–7, 1790–91, Temascaltepec. The pattern in Nueva Galicia was similar for pueblos within a few days travel from Guadalajara (e.g., AGN Hist. 319 exp. 18, 1782, Zapotlan el Grande).

154. AGN Tierras 2173 exp. 9, 1756, Peras; AGN CRS 75 exp. 6, 1789, Timilpan.

155. Sultepec, for example, engaged a local attorney for a complaint in 1756. AGN CRS 156 exps. 2–3.

156. Viceregal circular of Oct. 19, 1799, quoted in Taylor, *Landlord and Peasant*, p. 83: "The following is a well-known public abuse: Indians in growing number are traveling to the viceregal and provincial capitals, remaining there for many days on the pretext of engaging in lawsuits or entering petitions on behalf of their towns. Serious problems have resulted. There is a shortage of agricultural labor; residents of the countryside are growing accustomed to the laziness and vices of the cities; small towns are burdened with supporting their representatives; and there is a growing shortage of supplies in the capitals. I have found it advisable to order that no Indian town can send more than one or two represen-

tatives to engage in litigation or for any other purpose. Subdelegados, alcaldes ordinarios, and judicial officials are to take care that no more than two Indians from any town in their jurisdiction leave as representatives to a capital or city. Magistrates in the capitals are to recognize only two such representatives and should order others to leave."

A less oblique but still nonviolent type of resistance to the parish priest, one that often accompanied litigation, was refusal to attend mass, learn doctrina, pay clerical fees, serve the parish, or send children to school. See Ch. 17.

157. Instances of each have been cited throughout the study. Here I list only a few of many examples. Rejecting rites of baptism and burial: AGN Crim. 120 exp. 25, 1769, Huizquilucan (Indians were said to hide their sick and infants from the cura); Crim. 203 exp. 4, 1778, Tepoztlan. Locking church doors: AGN CRS 42 exp. 1, fol. 11, 1732, San Pedro Tejupilco. Mass: CRS 204 exp. 5, 1740, Tixtla; Crim. 305 exp. 5, 1768, Xichú; Crim. 120 exp. 25, 1769, Huizquilucan (the men especially); Crim. 203 exp. 4, 1778, Tepoztlan. Not attending doctrina classes: AGN Alcaldes Mayores 11, fols. 448–56, 1776–80, Tuzamapan, Puebla; AGN Acervo 49 caja 116, 1808–9, Chiconcuautla. Refusing mass and confession: CRS 204 exps. 9–10, 1760, Tejupilco, Temascaltepec district; CRS 156 exp. 7, 1761, Acambay, Xilotepec district; AGN Inq. 1146 exp. 1, 1775, Simapantongo, Xilotepec district; Acervo 49 caja 116, 1808–9, Tepehuacan district (few confess). Not confessing serious sins: AGN Bienes 575 exp. 14, 1789, Huazalingo.

158. AGN Crim. 120 exp. 25, 1769, Huizquilucan; Taylor, *Drinking*, p. 124, 1769, Meztitlan; Crim. 79 exp. 1, 1777, Coamelco and Cholula, Meztitlan district (Indians stopped fulfilling the precepto anual and attending mass over a change in parish boundaries); AGN CRS 131 exp. 1, 1792, Calimaya (cura estimated that 5,000 people had not confessed and taken communion).

159. AGN Crim. 79 exp. 1, 1777, Coamelco, Meztitlan district; Crim. 145, fols. 235ff, 1774, Acolman; AGN Civil 2114 exp. 8, 1780, Tolpetlac; AGN CRS 159 exp. 3, 1785, Churubusco. Lay officials refusing to do their duty was especially common in the enforcement of periodic labor service.

160. AGN CRS 217 exp. 4. As the cura of Acapetlahuaya said of a former gobernador who brought suit against him in 1790, "simula una profunda humildad bajo de una fina hypocrecía." AGN Tierras 2431 exp. 6, fols. 5–11.

161. AGN Templos 25 exp. 8, 1796, Amecameca; AGN Crim. 255 exp. 13, 1802, Chimalhuacan. Other cases are cited in connection with the discussion of disrespect in Ch. 9.

162. AGN Hist. 437 ("Se quedan como mudos, y no se la responden, ni aun los muchachos").

163. AGN CRS 30 exp. 2, 1774 ("Me miran cados y no me hablan; proceden en fin, como si les hubiese inferido los mas acerbos insultos").

164. AGN CRS 146 exps. 12–13. Interfering with objects of the local church was a sure way to stir up general anger and violence, as the cura of Xaltocan learned when he tried to remove images and ornaments from the old parish seat to his new residence at Santa Ana Nestralpa in 1747. AGN RCO 71 exp. 8; AGI Mex. 704; AGI Indiferente General 244. Another example is AGN Crim. 157, a 1799 tumulto at Atlautla, Chalco district, over the cura selling an old side altar to Ozumba. Indian witnesses testified that they feared he would also sell their image of the Virgin of Sorrows. The protesters repented after the priest preached to them in their language. In the Xaltocan case, Indian witnesses said it was not just the objects themselves that were at issue, but their fear that the loss of them would mean no more masses in the local church. The cura was moved to Zumpahuacan shortly after the incident.

165. At Acambay, Jilotepec district, in 1761, villagers rose up against the cura when he imprisoned the indio capitán after they would not be reconciled to a division of the parish, refused to confess, and had lodged a complaint against him. AGN CRS 156 exp. 7.

In popular disturbances not directed against the cura, he could sometimes pacify the crowd; but not always, as the cura of Ixmiquilpan found in 1746, when he was pushed aside after threatening to bring out the monstrance and a revered image of the Virgin in order to let God punish a throng of Indians protesting a land measurement, and as the cura of Papantla found in 1767, when he stepped in during a violent commotion against the alcalde mayor. AGN Crim. 57 exp. 1; Crim. 304.

166. Other cases of tumultos against curas include JCB, 1743, Tepecoacuilco, and 1747, Zacualpan, against Domingo de la Mota; AGN Crim. 210, fols. 189–205, 1758, Pozontepec, Sultepec district; AGN CRS 192 exps. 11–12, 1760, San Miguel Almoloya, Texcaliacac district; Crim. 306 exp. 6, 1769, San Sebastián Agua de Venado (Jalisco); AGN Civil 865 exps. 8–9, 1772, Ocuilan, Malinalco district (by Indians of San Juan Azingo); Crim. 90, 1773, Tlalmanalco; CRS 75 exp. 4, 1775, San Simón Tototepec, Zacualpan district; Crim. 203 exp. 4, 1778, Tepoztlan; AGN Hist. 319 exp. 18, 1782, Zapotlan el Grande (Jalisco); CRS 159 exp. 3, 1785, Churubusco; CRS 75 exps. 7–8, 1789, Timilpa, Huichapan district; AGI Guad. 352, Ugarte report on bienes de comunidad, 1787–, Mazamitla, ca. 1790; Hist. 578A, 1793, Taxco report (cura of Cacalotenango while at Apaxtla); AGN Inq. 1379 exp. 7, 1796, Toluca (justicia feared tumulto because of Franciscan guardian's provocative acts); and AGN Templos 25 exp. 8, 1796, Amecameca.

167. AGN Crim. 57 exp. 1, 1746, Ixmiquilpan; Crim. 305 exp. 5, 1768, Xichú; AGN CRS 130 exp. 3, 1796, Tututepec. Priests sometimes said their lives were in danger, but cases of direct attack were rare.

168. AGN Bienes 431 exp. 17, letter of vicario of Acamistla, May 31, 1771 ("si quemaban [al cura] con casa y todo si les resultaría a ellos algún daño").

169. AGN Civil 865 exp. 9.

170. JCB, Domingo de la Mota resumé; AGN Crim. 210, fols. 189–205.

171. AGN CRS 130 exp. 3 ("Toda esta raza ha sido siempre mui inquieta y enemiga de los curas"). My research into conflict between priests and parishioners in the dioceses of Mexico and Guadalajara reveals little of the nativist millenarianism that Florescano sees as a response to the modernizing project of the later Bourbons. *Memoria mexicana*, chs. 4, 5. Barabas, *Utopías indias*, ch. 5, posits a utopian millenarianism as the basis of Indian "socio-religious movements" in Mexican history. But her book is short on 18th-century evidence outside of Chiapas and Yucatán. Bricker, *Indian Christ*, sees a prophetic tradition but little of a "longing for ancient times" in the revitalization movements of Yucatán and Chiapas during the 18th century.

172. AGN CRS 156 exp. 5, fols. 117r, 123, 139–41 ("han estudiado modos con que restituirse a su antigua vida"; "como conserben siempre el govierno en ellos, hamás sabrán el cura y alcalde mayor lo que allí pasa, sino es que siempre se quedarán entre ellos los negocios que se ofrescan"; "unos gentiles o brutos sin el menor pusesión ni reconocimiento a superior alguno eclesiástico o secular"; "cuyo carácter ha sido siempre la audacia, la protervidad y orguyo y una continua indocilidad no sólo respecto de su cura, sino en respecto de las justicias seculares, que con más livertad y rigor pueden castigándolos reprimirlos, [that they only] reconocían por superiores . . . [a sus] tlatoques").

Other observations in a similar vein include AJANG Civil, bundle labeled "1769–1760 leg. 2 (47)," 1760, Santiago, Autlan district ("quieren vivir sin ley y sin rey"); JCB, 1762 resumé of cura Juan Faustino Xuarez Escovedo of Ocotepec, Cuernavaca district ("los que en estos altos vivían con toda libertad. Los halló muy colmados de abusos, arreglados a las costumbres supersticiosas de sus antepasados"); AGN CRS 156 exp. 9, 1763, Zacualpan de las Amilpas, Morelos ("no tienen mas costumbre que su voluntad"); CRS 156 exp. 12, 1765, Tlapanaloya, Tetepango district ("viven tan altivos y sobre si que negándome la debida obediencia no quieren comparecer para lo mas mínimo a este juzgado"); AGN Bienes 431 exp. 18, 1771, Xochitepec (Tetelpa and two subordinate pueblos "viven con una plena libertad sumergidos en visios sin justicia real ni eclesiástico que los reprenda"); AGN Alcaldes Mayores II, fols. 338–40, 1773, Ixtapan, Zacualpan district (Indians accustomed to "vivir barbaramente en los montes y sin sujetarse a campana"); CRS 131 exp. 1, fol. 82, 1792, Calimaya (disobedient and resolved to "seguir viviendo en su antigua libertad, tenaz resistencia"); CRS 130 exp. 3, 1796, Tututepec, Meztitlan district (cura claimed that malcontents "desenfrenan por todas partes en hablillas contra su cura, muestran ningún temor a Dios ni a los superiores que se burlan de sus determinaciones"); CRS 177 exp. 10, fols. 448–49, 1800, Mazatepec, Morelos ("no se ven en este país, señor, más que embriagueses, concubinatos, adulterios, estupros, padres de familia ofendidos por el urto que le han hecho de sus hijas, heridas, muertes, y otros males sin remedio alguno aun el sueño no se puede tomar por la mucha algaravía nocturna"); CRS 137 exp. 8, 1805, Alahuistlan, Zacualpan district ("proceden tan absolutos que ni dan las quentas ni abisan"); CRS 130 exp. 9, fol. 401v, 1809, Papalotla (too great an "espíritu de independencia"); CRS 126 exps. 12–13, fols. 302–4, 1809, Apaxtla, Ichcateopan, and Zacualpan districts (cura wrote of the "altanería" of Indians of Tlaicpatlan, quoting the cabecillas as spreading the word "que no hay más rey que ellos . . . que no obedecen a ningún juez, sino sólo viven a su livertad").

173. AGN CRS 68 exp. 3 ("y con ella el indio, como instrumento auténtico de su libertad, tenía la de governarse por si con independencia de todo superior").

174. AGN CRS 75 exp. 6.

175. To decry the independence and disorder of subjects is in the nature of a ruler's natural concern for authority and power. The Duque de Linares, viceroy of New Spain, expressed himself in language similar to that of these priests in his instructions to his successor in 1716: "La naturaleza del pueblo o vulgo que compone *al todo* del lugar (*la Nueva España*) no sé si mi rudeza podrá definirla, por que no distingo grandes cualidades en los afectos, desde el indio mas ínfimo hasta el caballero más elevado, pues sus fines son vivir en una absoluta libertad, creyendo que con decir que conocen al Rey por su Soberano, han cumplido con su obligación de vasallos." Quoted in Rivera, 3: 249–50.

176. *In and near Zacualpan*: AGN Crim. 210, fol. 196, 1758, Pozontepec, Sultepec district; AGN Alcaldes Mayores II, fols. 338–40, 1773, Ixtapan parish; AGN CRS 75 exp. 6, 1786, Alahuistlan; CRS 137 exp. 8, 1805, Alahuistlan; CRS 126 exps. 11–12, 1809, Tanicpatlan, Apaxtla parish; CRS 217 exp. 4, 1809, Pilcayan. *Morelos*: JCB, Ocotepec, Cuernavaca district, 1759–62, resumé of cura Juan Faustino Xuarez de Escovedo; CRS 156 exp. 9, 1763, Zacualpan de las Amilpas; AGN Bienes 431 exp. 18, 1771, Xochitepec; CRS 136 exp. 2, 1781, Huispaleca and Pueblo Nuevo, Tlaltizapan parish; AGN Hist. 132 exp. 26, 1793, San Francisco Tetecala, Cuernavaca district; AGN DP 3 exp. 3, 1797, Tlaltizapan; CRS 177 exp. 10, 1800, Mazatepec. *Vicinity of Metepec, Valley of Toluca*: Crim. 123 exp. 21, 1762, San Andrés, Tenango del Valle district; CRS 68 exp. 3, 1771, San Felipe del Obraje, San Lucas, and San Juan Bautista, Ixtlahuaca district; CRS 131 exp. 1, 1792, Calimaya (in 1625, the provisor observed that the jurisdiction of Toluca was particularly rife with cases of incest, adultery, and sacrilegious conduct); AGN Acervo 49 caja 43 exp. 5). *Hidalgo*: CRS 156 exp. 12, 1765, Tlapanaloya, Tetepango district; AGN Inq. 1146 exp. 1, 1775, Simapantongo and Chapatongo, Xilotepec district; Crim. 79 exp. 6, 1777, Meztitlan district; CRS 130 exp. 3, 1796, Tututepec.

177. AGN Tierras 2198 exp. 2, April 19, 1798, report of subdelegado's lieutenant ("Viven con libertad empleados en los vicios principalmente en los de la embriaguez y latrocinio"). The pastoral visitor to the Malinalco district in 1775 encountered the same kind of resistance. The people of Ocuilan had driven their cura out three years before with lawsuits and threats on his life. Now the visitador attempted a reconciliation, but the Indians absolutely refused. They agreed to establish the cofradías required of them only after the archbishop promised to appoint a new cura. During the same visita, Zumpahuacan Indians petitioned for the removal of their cura, too; then, in the 1779–80 visita,

they leveled apparently false charges against his successor for excessive fees, earning the visitador's characterization of them as "indios bastantemente inquietos y díscolos." AHM LioB/13, fols. 79r, 113v; LioB/21, fol. 276. See also AGN Templos 25 exp. 4, 1784, royal provisión to alcalde mayor of Zacualpan; and Tierras 2554 exp. 11, 1766, Ayotzingo (Tlalmanalco lieutenant reported the Indians' "mucha floxedad y ninguna obediencia a las superiores órdenes"). Another instance, for Nueva Galicia, is Zapotlan el Grande in the 1780's. AGN Hist. 319 exp. 18.

178. AGN Crim. 79 exp. 6.

179. AGN Crim. 210, fols. 189–205.

180. AGI Guad. 352, 1787– , Ugarte report on Indian bienes. He added that curas sometimes encouraged Indians in their preference for their own tongues so as to keep creoles and Europeans at a convenient distance. Pueblos in Nueva Galicia are occasionally mentioned in the same way. The Franciscan doctrinero of Poncitlan in 1727 spoke of the Indian parishioners' "mucha libertad y ningún temor a la justicia." At Mezcala, the Indians had put the lieutenant in stocks for bothering them. The doctrinero appealed for a lieutenant at Poncitlan and placement of some non-Indians in the town. AJANG Civil, box 49, doc. 4.

181. "Libertad" appears frequently in the sections of the *Recopilación* that treat Indian rights and duties. See especially 6-2, entitled "De la libertad de los Indios"; and 6-1-1, 6-1-2, 6-1-19, 6-1-21 to 23, 6-1-32. Their legal libertad was qualified by many restrictions and obligations (see especially 6-3). There were always mixed signals. Even as the crown opened pueblos to forasteros and non-Indian residents and promoted greater political freedom in the late 18th century, it held Indians to a variety of restrictions. The fiscal of the Audiencia of Guadalajara was careful in 1796 to remind Indian pueblos that Indians did not have the liberty to move wherever they wanted. BEJ Papeles de Derecho, 2: 396–97. Liberty was not identified with equality in official and semiofficial Spanish sources (e.g., BN LaFragua Coll., no. 792, 1808). Attorneys for Indian litigants invoked the principle of limited freedom, too, when it served them, as when the cura of Ecatepec was charged with increasing fees in 1765 "de su libre y espontánea voluntad." Tulane VEMC 68 exp. 20.

182. AGI Mex. 842, last "legajo" on Santiago Tecali, fol. 80v.

183. Tetchiness: AGN Crim. 232 exp. 7, 1800, San Luis Telazaltemalco, Xochimilco district.

184. AGN CRS 136 exp. 2, fols. 83v, 192r ("Están viviendo con una total independencia y sumo libertinaje sin poder allar medio de que valerme para reducirlos . . . continuos esclavos sin ración ni sueldo del cura"). Villagers of Huautla in the Huejutla district likewise complained that the cura treated them "as if we were his slaves, not his parishioners." AGN DP 3 exp. 8, 1812.

185. AGN DP 3 exp. 3, 1797 ("plena libertad que deven gozar en sus elecciones").

Chapter Fifteen

EPIGRAPHS: Humboldt, *Political Essay*, 1: 127; AGN CRS 68 exp. 3, fol. 210v. Manuel Abad y Queipo, a leading peninsular priest of Michoacán in the last years of colonial rule, made a comment much like Humboldt's: "The Indians govern themselves, and all the [local] magistrates are of the copper-colored race. In each village there are eight or ten old Indians who live at the expense of the rest in absolute idleness, basing their authority either upon their claim to an illustrious birth, or upon political trickery which has become hereditary. These chiefs have a great interest in keeping their fellow citizens in the most profound ignorance, and thus they contribute more than anyone to the perpetuation of the prejudices, ignorance, and barbarism of ancient habits." Quoted in Simpson, p. 95.

1. Lockhart, *Nahuas After the Conquest*, is the landmark study. The expression of shared values that was so prominent a feature of Indian colonial life is evident even in the homicides and drinking that occurred in local communities. See Taylor, *Drinking*, chs. 2–3.

2. The opening petitions in lawsuits usually indicate who was claiming to represent the community. Occasionally, almost the whole community would appear with the petition, as in AJANG Civil, bundle labeled "1769–60 (48)," Indians of Mazatan and Tetapan v. Lt. Antonio Gómez, 1767. More often the principales sent a delegation or appeared before the judge themselves, as in AGN Bienes 210 exp. 1, 1731, Guayacocotla (gobernador, ex-gobernador, two alcaldes, escribano, two regidores, and two other principales); AGN Acervo 49 caja 46, 1739, Churubusco ("gobernador, alcaldes, común y naturales"); AGN Hist. 319 exp. 15, 1782, Cacaguatepec, Acapulco district (the principal official). But in many cases the petitions were entered by two or three individuals in the name of the pueblo. Sooner or later, their right to represent the community was challenged, even when, as in the following examples, they were high officeholders: AGN CRS 30 exp. 3, 1782, Tolpetlac, Ecatepec district; CRS 75 exp. 6, 1786, Alahuistlan, Zacualpan district; AGN Templos 1 exp. 2, 1786–88, Guayacocotla (Veracruz); AJANG Civil, box 142, doc. 11, 1795, Tlaltenango; CRS 126 exps. 12–13, 1809, Tepehuacan, Sierra Gorda.

3. Gibson, *Aztecs*, p. 190.

4. Oaxaca had the most political divisions of this kind. Taylor, *Drinking*, p. 23. Petitions for cabecera status began earlier there than in the dioceses of Mexico and Guadalajara, in the second half of the 17th century. See, among others, CDCh, roll 21, leg. 2, 1674; AGN Indios 26 cuad. 2 exp. 177, 1682; Indios 31 exp. 45, 1692; Indios 36 exp. 145, 1704; Indios 39 exp. 17, 1714; AGN Civil 167 exp. 8, 1721; Indios 54 exp. 210, 1737; Indios 55 exp. 181, 1743; Indios 55 exp. 241, 1744; Indios 60 exp. 114, 1765; Indios 60 exp. 150, 1766; Indios 61 exp. 172, 1767; Indios 64 exp. 111, 1773; AGN Crim. 306 exp. 5, 1773; Indios 70 exp. 187, 1800.

5. A larger sample of cabecera-sujeto disputes could be developed from AGN Indios and General de Parte.

6. Van Young, "Conflict and Solidarity"; Taylor, "Indian Pueblos."

7. Cabecera-sujeto friction and attempts to split off were not simply rooted in demographic changes in which sujetos became larger than cabeceras (a common pattern in central Mexico). There were more petitions for political autonomy in Oaxaca than anywhere else, perhaps a reflection of more localized political identities that run deep in that region's past. The highlands of Puebla seem to have been in between the Oaxaca and central Mexico patterns; see Taylor, "Conflict."

8. Temascaltepec had 54 cabeceras in all in 1801. Gerhard, *Guide*, p. 270.

9. The standard complaints of the curas and gobernadores in the six Meztitlan and Guayacocotla cases were that the Indians of the sujetos lived dispersed in inaccessible hamlets in the montes without pastoral care and sometimes without paying tribute or serving in the cabecera. Some were slow to build and maintain a local church; others were under the influence of unscrupulous estate owners in the district or subject only to their own authority. In any case, they resisted labor service and had altogether little to do with the parish priests. AGN Templos 1 exp. 2, 1786, Guayacocotla; AGN Hist. 578A, 1793, Yahualica report; AGN CRS 130 exp. 3, 1793–96, Santa María Tututepec; Tulane VEMC 54 exp. 22, 1805, Nonoalco, Zocsoquipan district; CRS 217 exp. 6, 1808, Tzontecomatlan; AGN Bienes 663 exp. 26, 1818 Lolotla.

10. AGN CRS 156 exp. 7, 1761, Acambay; AGN Inq. 1146 exp. 1, 1775–79, Simapantongo; CRS 75 exp. 5, 1785, San Luis de las Peras; CRS 75 exp. 9, 1790, Santa María Atengo and San Francisco Zayula. The fifth case, a dispute over the management of cofradía finances, had in the background an appeal by San Andrés Timilpa (Huichapa district) for a division of the parish that would make this pueblo a parish seat. CRS 75 exp. 7, 1789.

11. AGN CRS 204 exp. 10. The cabecera gobernador is sometimes represented (and perhaps deserves to be represented) as a tyrant in these situations of cabecera-sujeto tensions. For example, in 1767, residents of Los Reyes, already deeply resentful of the gober-

nador of Xocotitlan, Ixtlahuaca district, for doing the cura's bidding and allying himself with the "mulatos de razón" in the vicinity, were infuriated when he arrested the headman (mandón) and his wife for lack of respect. They snatched him and were taking him off to Mexico City when the alcalde mayor arrived to free him. AGN Crim. 92 exp. 5.

12. AGN Cofradías 13 exp. 9. Tototepec documented its claim of coequal standing with the pastoral visit record of 1721, which called both it and Acapetlahuaya cabeceras, and a 1609 order for the parish-wide fiestas to alternate between the churches of these two pueblos. The pastoral visitor in 1779 denied an earlier petition of Tototepec, Ixcatepec, and Almoloya to form a separate parish, but he did recommend that Tototepec be made the seat of a vicario de pie fijo. AHM L10B/21, fol. 272r. In resisting the call for a labor draft to help rebuild the rectory of Temascaltepec in 1768, the Indians of San Lucas drew on a local tradition of contesting such claims, having obtained an order from the audiencia in 1744 against involuntary labor in the cabecera. The elders ultimately agreed to help with the rebuilding as long as the workers were paid and all settlements in the parish participated. AGN Templos 25 exp 3. San Miguel Tecomatlan, Malinalco district, had pursued the arancel as a means of avoiding service in the cabecera in 1724. Its residents also complained of having to travel to the cabecera to hear mass. AGN CRS 72 exp. 2. In 1809, Pipioltepec, Temascaltepec parish, resisted unification with Acatitlan, a plan promoted by the cura to bring residents closer to his cabecera and simplify parish administration. BMM 251.

Within these patterned tendencies, the actions of particular pueblos can surprise. They were not neatly predictable, even within one parish in a district. Acting independently could mean defending the cura. Indians of Capula brought suit against the gobernador of the parish seat, Pozontepec, in 1757 when he arrested their alcalde because they would not contribute to his complaint against the cura on behalf of the parish. They acted as firm supporters of the cura, testifying against the gobernador's charges of forced labor. AGN CRS 156 exp. 4. In 1769, visitas in the parish of Ozoloapan had grievances against the cura and his attachment to the cabecera, and saw the possibilities of the new arancel as a way to increase their independence, but each seemed to act on its own. CRS 68 exp. 2.

13. AGN CRS 29 exp. 2, 1711, Calimaya (visitas of San Mateo Mexicaltzingo, San Miguel Chapultepec, San Andrés, and La Concepción); CRS 29 exp. 11, 1754, Malacatepec (San José split off as new parish); AGN Tierras 2771 exp. 9, 1804, Mexicalcingo (Santa María Nativitas, a sujeto of Tenango del Valle, sought license to elect its own gobernador on the grounds that it had more than 600 families, a church, and a school). The other two Toluca Valley examples of sujeto-cabecera tension both involved collective actions (alborotos), one in the pueblo of San Lucas, Amanalco parish (Metepec district), against a census by three "comisionados de baja esfera" in 1792, and another, Xocotitlan district in 1767, against the gobernador for arresting their alcalde. AGN Crim. 243 exp. 1; Crim. 92 exp. 5. Denied permission to have its own church in 1784, San José del Tunal, a barrio of Atlacomulco, got its wish in 1793, after the pastoral visitor assured himself that the residents had resolved their internal conflicts. AHM L10B/28, fol. 143v.

14. AGN Crim. 162, fols. 94–104, 1749, Oztoticpac (Indians of Belém launched a tumulto against the gobernador for his arrest of their alcalde); AGN CRS 156 exp. 5, 1758, Santo Tomás Apipilhuasco (bitterly resisted the cura and gobernador of Texcoco over the payment of fees); CRS 30 exp. 3, 1782, Tolpetlac, near Ecatepec (then constructing a large church, the pueblo complained of the cura overcharging for his services as they were preparing to request a vicario de pie fijo); Crim. 232 exp. 7, 1800, San Luis Telazaltemalco, Xochimilco district (complained of the new cura at San Gregorio interfering with their "liberty" by obliging them to serve him in the cabecera and allowing the manager of his estate to whip them harshly).

15. AGI Mex. 704; AGN RCO 71 exp. 8. The two cases from the Tixtla district oc-

curred in 1740 and 1779. In the first case, Indians complained that the cura did not celebrate mass in the barrios and visitas; in the second, Indians of San Juan Tetelzingo "and others of the district of Tixtla" resisted labor service in the cabecera on the grounds that they were arancelados. AGN CRS 204 exp. 5; CRS 183 exp. 3. The three Morelos cases turned on the curas' efforts to standardize the collection of first fruits, to move a periodic market from a sujeto to the cabecera, and to secure labor service from visitas for the cabecera. CRS 156 exp. 9, Temoac, Zacualpan de las Amilpas parish, 1763; CRS 136 exp. 2, Huispaleca and Cuanacalcingo (Pueblo Nuevo), Tlaltizapan district, 1781; CRS 72 exp. 10, Tlaquiltenango, 1789.

16. See Taylor, "Indian Pueblos."

17. The *Oxford English Dictionary* definition of faction presented in the text corresponds to the definition of "facción" in the *Diccionario de la lengua castellana*, which goes on to give "parcialidad" and "bando" as synonyms ("la parcialidad de gente amotinada o rebelada; bando, pandilla, parcialidad, o partido en las comunidades o cuerpos"). However, the entry for "parcialidad" gives a pejorative twist to the meaning, stressing the idea of separation from within and applying the term directly to Indians: "la unión de algunos, confederándose para algún fin, separándose del común y formando cuerpo aparte; el conjunto de muchos que componen una familia o facción, lo que es común entre los indios." The intendant of Mexico used "parcialidad" in its negative meaning in a June 22, 1791, letter asking for the removal of the interim cura (actually the coadjutor) of Asuchitlan (Guerrero): "El qual podrá tal vez ser buen vicario o desempeñar otro destino subordinado; pero ciertamente no lo considero a propósito para que tenga la primera facultad eclesiástica en Axuchitlan, donde se perturbó la paz por desavenencias suscitadas entre sus cabezas, vecinos, y naturales, haviendo costado sumo trabajo tranquilizarlos luego que me encargué de la Yntendencia; pero es temible se renueven las *parcialidades* [emphasis added] con la animosidad que reina entre los primeros." AGN CRS 75 exp. 11, fols. 479–80.

18. Champagne, "Change, Continuity, and Variation." Haskett, *Indigenous Rulers*, pp. 38–41, describes sharp divisions and conflict without separation in the Cuernavaca district. The concentration of homicides within the nuclear family in central Mexico as well as Oaxaca during the late 18th century also suggests more controlled political conflict than factionalism in this sense. Taylor, *Drinking*, ch. 3.

19. AJANG Civil, box 17, doc. 2. In addition to cases mentioned in the following text, I found two others for the Diocese of Guadalajara. One, in 1713, had to do with a district judge in Xerez, Zacatecas, who accentuated divisions in neighboring pueblos by promoting gobernadores and alcaldes he knew would oppose their missionary priests. The other involved a heated jurisdictional dispute between the cura and the alcalde mayor over the years 1784–90 that divided the community of Autlan ("dividido en opiniones y vandos"). Civil, box 18, doc. 5; Civil, box 125, doc. 2.

20. AGN CRS 130 exps. 3, 7. This complicated dispute continued in 1798 without a clear resolution.

21. AJANG Civil, box 172, doc. 22 ("juzgándose con autoridad para crear nuebos principales, han acompañádose en sus cabildos o juntas de otros indios, que aunque viejos carecen de los servicios, instrucción y méritos que los constituien padres de república").

22. Ibid., box 119, doc. 12.

23. Ibid., bundle labeled "1806–1828." An extensive list of election disputes for central Mexico in the 18th century is appended to Chávez Orozco, "Instituciones democráticas," 3(4): 378–82. In a 1791 case from Puebla, two groups of principales launched criminal suits against each other in an effort to get their favorites elected. AGN Crim. 54 exp. 2, San Pedro Tlasquapa, Acatlan and Piaxtla district.

Principales also divided bitterly enough among themselves to go to court when current officials favored their associates with a disproportionate share of the best community lands: AGN Tierras 2621 exp. 15, 1731, Tultitlan; Tierras 2554 exp. 4, 1764, San Juan Tlapisaqua; Tierras 2554 exp. 1, 1800, Chalco.

24. AGN CRS 75 exp. 4.

25. AGN CRS 39 exps. 1–2 ("Observo que andan divididos unos por la costumbre, y otros por el arancel cuio inconveniente necesita toda la autoridad de V.E. para remediarse").

26. AGN DP 2 exp. 4. The audiencia fiscal thought that the clamor would stop once the parishioners grew used to the arancel. He recommended that it be reconfirmed, and the high court agreed in its order of July 5, 1748.

27. AJANG Civil, box 142, doc. 11; AJANG Criminal, box 8, doc. 6.

28. AJANG Criminal, bundle labeled "1790–1799 (35)," 1797, Xalpa barrio de abajo, Juchipila district (against the cofradía mayordomo, "sobre pesos"); Criminal, bundle labeled "1818 leg. 2 (89)," 1818, Xalpa (barrio de abajo complained against cura's trying to transfer its cofradía to the pueblo); Criminal, caja 5 leg. 1 exp. 6, June 6, 1810, Teocaltiche (barrio de abajo blamed for tumulto against teniente). See also Criminal, bundle labeled "1820 leg. 5 (27)," which mentions that the victim of a murder in 1819, Sipriano Martín de Avila, was from the barrio de arriba of Tlajomulco. In 1756, the principales of San Lucas, Cajititlan district, near Guadalajara, were divided over where the ruined parish church should be rebuilt, which suggests residential loyalties. One group went to court over the alcalde's choice. AJANG Civil, box 62, doc. 6.

29. Lockhart, *Nahuas After the Conquest*, chs. 1–3.

30. AGN Tierras 2621 exp. 9. Tampamolon (near Villa de Valles, San Luis Potosí) had a Huasteca parcialidad. AGN Acervo 49 caja 50, 1749.

31. AGN Civil 2072 exp. 19; Gerhard, *Guide*, p. 69.

32. Chávez Orozco, "Instituciones democráticas," 3(2): 162–63. For the earlier cases, AGN Crim. 55 fols. 122–35, 1642, Ixmiquilpan; Crim. 230, fols. 379–87, 1641–42, Ixtlahuaca; Crim. 216, fols. 184ff, 1685, Atlacomulco.

33. AGN Crim. 226, fols. 401ff.

34. AGN Hist. 319 exp. 24.

35. AGN CRS 130 exp. 5. See also for cases that spread at the initiative of one person or a small group, AGN DP 1 exp. 2, 1722, arancel dispute involving the cabeceras of Huichapan and Xilotepec and the sujetos of Tecaxic, San Agustín, San Juanico, Santiago, San Sebastián, Amealco, San Bartolomé, Tlahuac, and San Andrés (cura blamed a local mestizo and two Indian officials and their few "parciales" for intimidating members of the pueblo into pressing for the arancel; again, various Indian witnesses for the cura said they did not favor the arancel); CRS 156 exp. 5, 1758, Tepetlaostoc (cura blamed three Indians for putting the pueblo of Apipilhuasco in an uproar by promising that as long as they were elected to office the cura and alcalde mayor would know nothing of local affairs); DP 3 exp. 3, 1797, Tlaltizapan (cura charged that the complaint against him over fees was promoted by a principal he had struck from the list of candidates for gobernador); and AGN Bienes 172 exp. 41, 1806, Tejupilco (two bandos and two lawsuits, which the cura blamed on one man who seduced Indians into complaints to the audiencia, possibly with the encouragement of a former cura interino).

36. AGN CRS 75 exp. 11. This record provides only the lieutenant's and intendant's versions of the conflict.

37. CPM, p. 183 (5-2-4) ("La experiencia enseña que muchas veces los Indios presentan memoriales con acusaciones contra clérigos encabezándolos en nombre de los Gobernadores, Alcaldes, Justicia y Común de Naturales, y frecuentemente ninguno firma; y aún se averigua haverlos formado una sola persona mal intencionada, y de otras castas; y para cortar estos recursos, manda este Concilio, que los obispos averiguen secretamente si son

ciertas las quexas de los Naturales; si son inducidos; si proceden de malicia; si han inter-
venido los Governadores, y Justicias, y que se reconozcan las firmas").

38. *Recop.* 1-7-29, 6-10-8.

39. In the 1560's d. Domingo, cacique and gobernador of Tlacolula (Oaxaca), reportedly collected by derrama for the high holy days and other fiestas of the pueblo, doling
the money out as he wished. AGN Civil 822, fols. 220–23. Similarly, in 1634, officials of
Ocoyoacac (Edo. de México) were accused by macehuales of collecting for each of the
pueblo's eight fiestas but spending much of the money and food on banquets for themselves. AGN Crim. 148, fols. 263ff. Juan de Palafox y Mendoza of Puebla, in his 1653
pastoral letter (fol. 154v), instructed his parish priests not to allow gobernadores to "echar
derramas desproporcionadas."

40. AGN CRS 42 exp. 1.

41. AGN Acervo 49 caja 68, 1796, cura Vicente Antonio Tello Siles of Santa Catalina
Xochiatipan v. Ygnacio Gomez Tagle, his coadjutor ("sobre no ministrarle alimentos").

42. AGN CRS 23 exp. 6, 1767, Ozoloapan (manípulos of 1rr per person for four annual
celebrations); CRS 30 exp. 2, 1774, Xocultla and Nazintlan, Chilapa district (manípulos of
1rr per casado and one-half real per viudo); CRS 13 exp. 3, Anathechan, parish of Olinalá
(1.5rr per month per family for mass); CRS 39 exp. 1, 1796, Capuluac, Tenango del Valle
district (cura reported custom of each family paying 1r a year for the rectory's upkeep).

43. AGN CRS 72 exp. 8, 1785, Otlazpa, Tlaxpa; CRS 75 exp. 7, 1789, Timilpa, Huichapan district (Hidalgo).

44. BMM 113.

45. BMM 135 exp. 17 ("no pueden sacar el dinero suficiente para pelear porque el
modo de sacarlo es echar derramas de a peso o cuatro reales cada cabeza para empezar,
proseguir y acabar el pleito, no que no cessan de pedir los cabezillas ni los demás dexan
de darlo con mucho gusto quantas veces se lo piden aunque el pleito se dilate mucho
tiempo"). Examples of willing subscription to derramas for litigation could be added at
length.

46. AJANG Civil, bundle labeled "1806–7 (174)," 1808 ("casi todos los indios están
prontos a contribuir derrama").

47. AGN CRS 65 exps. 4–5, 1775; Tulane VEMC 3 exp. 5, 1794.

48. AGN Crim. 54 exp. 14.

49. AGN Crim. 217, fols. 89ff. Priests sometimes sought the arrest of local Indians
who, in the words of the cura of San Felipe del Obraje, "exigen derramas en perjuicio de
ambas Magestades." AGN CRS 68 exp. 3, 1771.

50. AGN CRS 39 exps. 2–3.

51. Though Gregorio Velásquez of San Mateo is named as Santa María's ally in litigation, the record has little more to say about him.

52. AGN CRS 29 exp. 2. Other early examples of legal entrepreneurship are AGN
Crim. 54 exp. 14, 1690, Tlapanaloya, Atitalaquia district (Hidalgo); AJANG Civil, box 17,
doc. 2, 1708, La Barca (Jalisco); Crim. 630 exp. 4, 1720, Teposcolula district (Oaxaca); and
AGN DP 1 exp. 2, 1721–24, Huichapan and Xilotepec (Hidalgo). Examples can probably
be found for the 16th century as well.

53. A study of land litigation in similar terms is one way to enlarge on this discussion.
Stephanie Wood's doctoral dissertation and unpublished essays on the Techialoyan manuscripts contribute to this subject.

54. Two examples of ignorant or ineffectual elected officials in such suits. The gobernador of Milpa Alta (fringe of Valley of Mexico) in 1790 could not sign his name, much less
communicate effectively in Spanish. He proved unable to defend his office and the interests of the community against a local strongman. AGN Crim. 131 exp. 21. In 1801, a tribu-

tary of Tlajomulco (Jalisco) went to the audiencia to plead for some discretion in future elections—that the current alcaldes "no ser sujetos hábiles que sepan desempeñar." What was needed, he said, were "peritos . . . pastores que nos encaminen por una senda que nos conduzga a una vida arreglada." AJANG Civil, box 223, doc. 10.

55. AHJ Manuscripts, no. G-9-752 ZAS/3155. Bentura spent three months in jail in Guadalajara. He was released by the audiencia on Dec. 12, 1752, and removed from office.

56. One of the many cases of gobernadores as front-runners is AGN Templos 25 exp. 4, 1769, Tlayacapan, in which the "gobernador y demás viejos" diverted money collected each year for Easter week celebrations to litigation against the cura and ordered Indians not to pay the clerical fees or attend the Easter events.

57. Indians could no longer argue so effectively at court against non-Indian residents, but the cofradía issue was viable, since the crown's policy was to take the management of local resources out of the cura's hands.

58. AGN CRS 136 exps. 6–7. The cura justified his rentals to non-Indians on the ground of the local settlement patterns. He said that the cabecera's 150 Indian families "viven separados en los pedazos de tierra que el común les ha signado y a las orillas del pueblo tienen otro pedazo de tierra cada familia para sus sementeras que muchos no cultivan por su descidia por lo que el pueblo está sin formación." But only 130 of the more than 700 non-Indian families in the district lived "a orillas del pueblo." The rest lived leagues away in the mountains without schools or pastoral care. Because these Spaniards and castas had tried for 30 years to get the Indians to rent them plots to build their houses in the cabecera without success, he said, he had agreed to intercede (fols. 304–5).

59. AGN CRS 204 exps. 9–10, 1760 ("pobre indio reducido a su cotón y demás miserias regulares entre ellos, y oi viste muy decente, carga armas, es criador de ganados y dueño de rancho y de trapiche").

60. The alcalde mayor of Zacatlan de las Manzanas (Puebla) in 1786 complained that rebellions and litigation in his district were being carried out by non-Indians who were "apoderados de los empleos de república." They were also convenient scapegoats for the alcalde mayor's wish to represent himself as an innocent victim. See Taylor, "Conflict."

61. AGN Crim. 166, fols. 354bis ff.

62. AGN CRS 25 exp. 4.

63. AJANG Civil, box 17, doc. 2.

64. AGN CRS 137 exp. 5 ("el seductor de los yndios de su pueblo que los trae alborotados y mobió para este presente asunto"). Juan Diego, the shaman behind the false charges against Father Nava of Terrenate in 1768, was also the escribano del pueblo. AGN Inq. 1074, fols. 68ff (Nava's deposition), and fol. 1r of second numeration; Inq. 1145 exp. 24; Inq. 1209 exp. 13.

65. AGN CRS 72 exp. 7, 1767, Santo Domingo Hueyapan; CRS 68 exps. 4–5, 1775, Cuanacalcingo.

66. AGN CRS 130 exp. 5.

67. AGN CRS 68 exps. 4–5. According to the cura, Barrera resented having been removed as schoolmaster by the previous parish priest and was playing on the opposition of many from Cuanacalcingo to labor service for the church.

68. AGN Bienes 210 exp. 26.

69. BMM 113, 1769.

70. Friedrich, *Agrarian Revolt.*

71. AGN CRS 156 exp. 12. A secret episcopal investigation into charges against the cura of Yahualica in 1806 concluded that two families of nanahuacos and bajoneros "who are known to tribunales superiores" were responsible. AGN Acervo 49 caja 45, exp. on conduct of Bartolomé Vélez Escalante.

72. AGN CRS 130 exp. 3, fols. 65v ff, 78v ff, 164.

73. AGN Bienes 431 exp. 17.

74. AGN DP 3 exp. 3.

75. AGN CRS 217 exp. 6.

76. *Diccionario de la lengua castellana.*

77. Alan Knight, 1: 112–13; Díaz Díaz, especially p. 5.

78. Luisa Paré, p. 338 ("Un ejercicio informal y personal del poder a nivel local o regional en áreas rurales, caracterizado por sus actividades de mediación entre el pueblo y el aparato gubernamental, actividades posibles gracias al control y a la manipulación de los canales de comunicación, especialmente del sistem de autoridad").

79. Other helpful sources on caciquismo are Friedrich, *Agrarian Revolt* and *Princes of Naranja*; the essays in Kern, *Caciques*; Dennis, "Oaxacan Village President"; and Islas García, *Apuntes para el estudio del caciquismo*. Islas treats caciquismo as the exercise of power over a community from without, hence locating its origins in the Spanish encomienda and overseer system of the 16th century. For the 18th century, he regards the isolation of settlements and the predilection for military offices, but not the "spiritual and economic climate," as conducive to caciquismo (p. 23). In his opinion, respect for the law and the civil authority lessened the need for armed force and impeded the development of caciquismo at the time. Eighteenth-century caciquismo was not, I think, as closely associated with a monopoly of the best village lands, as Knight, 1: 112–13, finds for Mexico in the second half of the 19th century. Knight's emphasis on a close connection between caciquismo and the control of land and labor leads him to find the main origins of caciquismo after independence. Díaz Díaz emphasizes roots in the Independence War (p. 5). The militarization of both Spain and much of Spanish America in the early 19th century helps to explain caciquismo in both as more than a vague cultural affinity.

80. A well-known example of caciquismo in the 1920's that drew on the legal skills of the leader is Primo Tapia of Naranja, Michoacán. See Paul Friedrich's various writings on Tapia, especially *Agrarian Revolt* and *Princes of Naranja*.

81. Roniger, p. 72.

82. See, for example, AGI Guad. 383, 1795–1803, for rising militarization in Nueva Galicia. See also MacLachlan, *Criminal Justice*; and Taylor, "Sacarse de pobre." In the mid-18th century, officers of the Acordada enjoyed extraordinary freedom from supervision by the audiencia in pursuing bandits, which would have contributed to the arbitrary use of force. AGI Guad. 120, 1753, "Sobre que por la Audiencia de Guadalaxara no se impida el libre uso de la comisión de la Acordada."

83. As early as Jan. 8, 1743, royal authorities gave citizens on the costa del mar del sur permission to arm for defense against possible English invasion, and requested a report on how many arms were available. AGI Guad. 306.

84. Tulane VEMC 54 exp. 22.

85. AJANG Criminal, bundle labeled "1809 leg. 2 (127)," 1809–10.

86. AGN Acervo 49 caja 146, Sotomayor report, Aug. 26, 1816 ("despotismo" quote); AJANG Civil, bundle labeled "1800–1809 (109)," 1815, Tlajomulco (cura claimed the subcomandante had taken over the community like a tyrant); AJANG Criminal, bundle labeled "1815 leg. 2 (138)," 1815, Tacámbaro (cura claimed that the visitador mariscal de campo was acting like a caudillo and claiming to have the authority to decapitate offenders). On the scorched earth policy of José de la Cruz around Lake Chapala in the early years of the Independence War, see Taylor, "Banditry and Insurrection."

87. AJANG Civil, bundle labeled "1806–7 (174)," 1807–9, Jamay.

88. AGN Tierras 2621 exp. 15, 1731, Tultitlan (gobernador gave lands allotted to certain principales to one of his political allies); Tierras 2550 exp. 10, 1736, Tepetitla, Chalco district (some naturales complained of an alcalde who obliged them to labor on community lands he had appropriated for himself); AGN Crim. 560, 1748, Santa María Tetela (gobernador stole tribute payments from the caja de comunidad, sold ranchos de cofradía, and sent minor offenders to obraje owners); Crim. 177 exp. 12, 1763, San Francisco Chilpa,

Tultitlan district (alcalde, charged with repeated assaults against people while drunk, claimed this was a pretext to remove him from office); Crim. 149, fols. 497ff, 1774, Tlacotepec, Metepec district (cacique Rufino Calixto, charged with adultery and mistreating Indians, replied that the moderate beatings he administered were his duty as gobernador).

89. AGN Tierras 2179 exp. 3. The alcalde was found guilty, deprived of "voz y voto," ordered to pay 20p each to two injured parties, and warned of more severe punishment in the future.

90. AGN Tierras 1431 exp. 6 ("en donde y en su casa publicamente los de su república lo cuidaban y asistían, como a personaje grande y oráculo de ellos").

91. AGN Tierras 2774 exp. 9. An example of an Indian reporting abuses by a gobernador's relatives is documented in AGN Crim. 181, fols. 484–97, 1785, at San Antonio in the parish of Tecozautla, where the Cruz brothers, caciques of Tecozautla were accused of loitering on the roads half drunk, beating up passersby, and drinking in pulquerías and refusing to pay. The accuser said they were able to get away with such misconduct because their cousin was the gobernador and would not act against them.

92. Rosenbach Lib., Mexican MS 462/25 pt. 7, no. 2.

93. AGN CRS 67 exp. 3 ("Ai unas familias, los Hernández que [no siendo tributarios ni útiles para cosa alguna] pretenden con crecido empeño ser governadores para por este medio tener avasallados a los pobres naturales y servirse de ellos por cuyo motivo se halla frecuentemente aquel miserable pueblo dividido en dos vandos"). With the aid of the alcalde mayor, the cura successfully promoted the candidacy of a non-Hernández for gobernador. He later soured on this man, too, but the alcalde mayor continued to support the new gobernador as the least of the evils.

94. AGN Bandos 8 exp. 28, June 9, 1773 ("ha perdido el respeto a Oficiales y a todos, aporreándolos, como si fueran sus criados; ha quitado tierras al Pueblo, enagenándolas a otros; y lo que es más, por su propia mano con general escándalo ha azotado hasta a las Viudas; si les coxe algo a los hijos, los encarcela, y les arranca multa; obligándolos, en precaución de todos estos perjuicios, a que muchos hayan desertado el Pueblo, por no tener arbitrio de ocurrir al Alcalde Mayor").

95. AJANG Civil, box 142, doc. 11. For more on colonial Tlaltenango, see Jiménez Pelayo.

96. AJANG Criminal, box 8, doc. 6.

97. BMM 113, 1769. The law could be a negative source of personal political power when it did not seem to reach a budding leader. At Xichú, San Luis de la Paz district (Guanajuato), in 1768, an Indian tumulto in the parish church at Easter time in which the priest was assaulted was blamed by neighboring Spaniards on an "untrustworthy" (caviloso) Indian named Felipe Gonzales. Gonzales's claim to be a prophet was shored up, witnesses said, because though civil and religious officials tried to arrest him many times, he was still at liberty. AGN Crim. 305 exp. 5.

98. AGN Crim. 131 exp. 21 ("hacerles escriptos a los yndios para este juzgado [y] haciéndose asimismo apoderado de ellos y ocurriendo a su nombre a ajitar sus solicitudes.... Tiene el pueblo sublevado").

99. *Hidalgo*: AGN Crim. 43 last exp., 1615, Actopan; AGN DP 1 exp. 2, 1722, Huichapan district pueblos; Rosenbach Lib., Mexican MS 462/25 pt. 7, no. 2, 1727, Chiapa de Mota and sujetos, Huichapan district; AGN Tierras 2774 exp. 9, 1749, Huazalingo, Yahualica district; Tierras 2179 exp. 3, 1756, San Luis de las Peras, Huichapan district; AGN CRS 156 exp. 7, 1761, Acambay, Xilotepec district; DP 2 exp. 6, 1763, sujetos of Actopan; CRS 67 exp. 3, 1768 Joloapan, Tetepango district; AGN Inq. 1146 exp. 1, 1775, Simapantongo, Xilotepec district; Crim. 181, fols. 484–97, 1785, Tecozautla, Xilotepec district; CRS 130 exp. 3, 1796, Tututepec, Tulancingo district; AGN Bienes 172 exp. 39, 1803, Tasquillo, Alfajayucan district; Tulane VEMC 54 exp. 22, 1805, Meztitlan.

Morelos: Crim. 560, 1748, Tetela; BMM 135 exp. 17, 1752, Tejalpa; CRS 156 exp. 6, 1761, Tejalpa; CRS 72 exp. 7, 1767, Hueyapan; AGN Templos 25 exp. 4, 1769, Tlayacapan; CRS 68 exps. 4–5, 1775, Cuanacalcingo; Crim. 203 exp. 4, 1778, Tepoztlan; AGN Hist. 319 exp. 24, 1782, Hueyapan; DP 3 exp. 3, 1797, Tlaltizapan; CRS 178 exp. 9, 1797, Yautepec.

Nueva Galicia: AJANG Civil, box 49, doc. 4, 1727– , Poncitlan district; Civil, box 90, doc. 16, 1776, Tuspa; Hist. 128 exp. 10, 1791, Acaponeta; Civil, box 171, doc. 14, 1791, San Martín, Tonalá district; Civil, box 142, doc. 11, 1795, Tlaltenango; Civil, box 178, doc. 6, 1795, Cuquío district; AJANG Criminal, box 8, doc. 6, 1805; Tlaltenango; Civil, bundle labeled "1806–1807 (174)," 1807–9, Jamay; Criminal, bundle labeled "1809 leg. 2 (127)," 1809, San Andrés Guisculco, near Mesticacan; Civil, bundle labeled "1800–1809 (109)," 1815, Tlajomulco; Criminal, bundle labeled "1818 leg. 2 (89)," 1818, Tonalá.

Temascaltepec-Zacualpan: Crim. 210, fols. 189–205, 1758, Pozontepec, Sultepec district; CRS 23 exp. 6, 1767, Atexcapan; CRS 75 exp. 4, 1775, Tototepec, Zacualpan district; Tierras 2431 exp. 6, 1790, Zacualpan district; CRS 126 exps. 12–13, 1809, Tanicpatlan, Apaxtla parish, Zacualpan district.

Valley of Mexico area: Tierras 2621 exp. 15, 1731, Tultitlan; Tierras 2550 exp. 10, 1736, Tepetitla, Chalco district; CRS 68 exp. 1, 1759, Teoloyucan, Cuautitlan district; AGN Crim. 177 exp. 12, 1763, Chilpa, Tultitlan district; Tierras 2554 exp. 11, 1766, Tlalmanalco; AGN Bandos 8 exp. 28, 1773, Coatepec; Crim. 111 exp. 3, 1777, Tultitlan.

Metepec: DP 1 exp. 7, 1749–78, Temoaya; Crim. 92 exp. 5, 1767, Xocotitlan, Ixtlahuaca district; CRS 68 exp. 3, 1771, San Felipe del Obraje; Crim. 149, fols. 497ff, 1774, Tlacotepec; CRS 39 exp. 3, 1793, Capuluac; CRS 130 exp. 5, 1796, Zinacantepec; Crim. 217, fols. 89ff, 1797, Zinacantepec.

Malinalco: AGN Civil 1674 exp. 16, 1787, Tenancingo. *Guerrero*: Bienes 431 exp. 17, 1771, Iguala; VEMC 68 exp. 9, 1795–97, Atlistaca, Tlapa district; Templos 1 exp. 4, 1806–8, Xalpatlahuaca, Tlapa district. *Veracruz*: VEMC 49 exp. 6, 1787, Camotipan, Chicontepec district; CRS 217 exp. 1, 1808, Tzontecomatlan, Guayacocotla district. *Guanajuato*: Crim. 305 exp. 5, 1768, Xichú, San Luis de la Paz district. *Puebla*: Bienes 210 exp. 26, 1791, Cozcatlan; CRS 25 exp. 4, 1793–1803, Huiciltepec. *Michoacán*: AJANG Criminal, bundle labeled "1815 leg. 2 (138)," 1815, Tacámbaro.

100. AGN CRS 130 exp. 3 ("famosos . . . por pleitistas, . . . los más perversos de todos quantos havitan estas cierras"; "es el principal caveza y Padre del pueblo y el que está siempre atento a defenderlos, de donde resulta que quanto un Gobernador quiere se hace y esto aunque muchos lo repugnen, callan y obedecen"). The investigator found the Indians of Tututepec different from their neighbors in ways that made them more like mestizos: "Estos se distinguen de los demás yndios de esta cierra no sólo en sus costumbres sino hasta en sus trages, siendo en estos mui iguales a la gente de razón y casi todos sin balcarras como la usan los demás yndios; se distinguen también en sus tratos y comercios; porque quando los demás de esta cierra se entretienen y ocupan en el cultivo de sus tierras y beneficio de sus frutos, éstos otros al modo de la gente de razón tienen lleno toda la cierra de sus comercios no sólo con géneros de la tierra, como son sus sombreros, machetes, paños chicos y grandes, sesotes, fresadas, y hasta jabón, sino mercería y otros géneros de España."

101. AJANG Civil, box 49, doc. 4.   102. AGN CRS 72 exp. 7.

103. AGN Crim. 111 exp. 3.   104. AGN Civil 1674 exp. 16.

105. AJANG Criminal, bundle labeled "1818 leg. 2 (89)," Sept. 1818 (contra el indio alcalde Toribio Covarrubias, por sedición).

106. AGN CRS 126 exp. 12, fol. 287v ("La dominación de éste ha llegado a tal extremo que siempre que iba a la casa de comunidad mandaba a sus alguaciles como regidor que era, le repicasen las campanas, en cuia casa hacía juntar a todos los del pueblo y desde que salía hasta que bolvía a su casa le repicaban. . . . El dicho con su campanero el otro regidor llamado Domingo, anduvieron de casa en casa mobiendo y convocando a todos los yndios

que se levantaran contra mi citado vicario d. Bernardo Martínez y Sandoval a causa de que éste havía puesto en depósito a una yndia por pedimento de la madre, que se hallaba amancevada dos años ha con un yndio casado").

107. A similar complexity reduced to a supposed one-man tyranny is reflected in another cura's account of friction with a sujeto. This case comes from Pozontepec (Edo. de México) in 1758, when the cura of Sultepec attempted to place a resident vicario there. The pueblo erupted in violence following prolonged litigation against the placement. The cura recognized that 12 men from two barrios made decisions for the pueblo, but he was convinced that an indio ladino from Sultepec, Sebastián Miguel de Celis, as "apoderado de todos [de] este curato y principal caveza," was behind it and had told the Indians to oppose their cura. The cura was particularly distressed that the people of Pozontepec greeted Celis's arrival with a great peal of bells and lavish banquets, and that at his behest, the tributaries had thrice contributed one real apiece for the lawsuit against him. AGN Crim. 210, fols. 189–205.

Special respect was also shown to Joseph Zárate, a "coyote" who represented the Indians of Texalpa (Tlayacapan district, Morelos) in their 1761 dispute with the parish priest over clerical fees. When the people of Texalpa went off to the cabecera of Atlatlaucan to receive the audiencia's judgment, they traveled on foot alongside the mounted Zárate. AGN CRS 156 exp. 6. To cite just one other of the cases of curas speaking of a few local men exercising the power of caudillos, the cura of Teoloyuca, Cuautitlan district, wrote that he was afraid to go to Coyotepec now because the fiscal, the alcalde, and the fiscal's brother and father, "acting like *caudillos*, have the plebe in an uproar" (como caudillos tienen inquieta la pleve).

108. AGN Templos 1 exp. 4.

109. Tulane VEMC 49 exp. 6 ("Caudillo . . . en estos payses por su caudal, empleos, valimientos, and su refinada astucia. . . . influye desisivamente en todos los suzesos de consideración en estos territorios, teniendo dominado enteramente al justicia. . . . Exerce un despotismo sin límites no sólo con sus dependientes y soldados sino con toda clase de gentes . . . tiemblan los que podían atestiguar sobre estos y otros particulares").

110. My organization of cases into themes also sacrifices some of the complexity that can be recovered from the richest of the judicial case records.

111. AGN Tierras 2554 exp. 11 ("a quien todo deferían y obedecían sin otro motivo para los yndios que la utilidad que se imaginaban tenían en el adelantamiento de las pensiones en que nunca los de razón se manifestaban más liberal quando avía algún litis en punto de tierras porque entonces eran los yndios a cuyo nombre y costo se seguía el pleyto; porque los gastos se cargaban a las tierras y la utilidad y provecho era para el arrendatario cuya parcialidad vencía. Razón porque en treinta años no faltaron pleytos sobre tierras en este pueblo"). "Adalid" meant "caudillo de gente de guerra," according to the 1822 edition of the *Diccionario de la lengua castellana*. The cura did not suggest that the estate owners had coerced the Indians into renting their repartimiento lands. The implication was that personal bonds, including compadrazgo, were built into the rental arrangements. For a clearer but less detailed case of Indians relying on a creole Spanish patron for financial support, see AGN CRS 42 exp. 1, 1732, in which the Indians of Tejupilco offered a creole as their fiador (cosigner).

112. For an earlier case of political divisions in Tlalmanalco, see AGN Crim. 227 exp. 9, 1693. The cura's unusually long and detailed account of actions and interests in this case give it credibility in spite of his obvious self-interest.

113. Paz, "In Search of the Present," p. 34.

Chapter Sixteen

EPIGRAPHS: *Recop.* 6-1-1 (1580) ("Que los Indios sean favorecidos, y amparados por las Justicias Eclesiásticas, y Seculares. . . . Es nuestra voluntad encargar a los Vireyes, Presidentes, y Audiencias el cuidado de mirar por ellos, y dar las órdenes convenientes, para que sean amparados, favorecidos, y sobrellevados. . . . Y rogamos y encargamos a los Prelados Eclesiásticos, que por su parte lo procuren como verdaderos Padres espirituales de esta nueva Christiandad, y todos los conserven en sus privilegios, y prerogativas, y tengan en su protección"); AGN CRS 195 exp. 6 ("Aunque la Autoridad Real es tan poderosa y respetable, no por eso son despreciables los sacerdotes").

1. Although the titles are analogous, most district governors outside of provincial cities were called alcaldes mayores, rather than corregidores. "Alcalde mayor" was intended to designate the royal governor of a less important district, one that was smaller in territory and population. *Recop.* 5-2-31. Convenient as the triangle of authority concept is, it is a simplification that does not give adequate attention to other potential power players whose activities intertwined with those of the priests, district governors, and members of pueblos. In particular localities, their influence in local politics was decisive, but they do not appear to have been at the center of political conflict in many predominantly Indian parishes in the late 18th century. Hacendados and rancheros, for instance, were influential figures in many places. Some were clearly rivals to curas and justicias for power, especially for the control of village resources. See, for example, AGN Tierras 2554 exp. 11, 1766, Tlalmanalco; AGN CRS 23 exp. 6, 1767, Ozoloapan, Temascaltepec district; AGN Inq. 1074, 1768, Terrenate, Tlaxcala; AGN Templos 1 exp. 2, 1786, Hacienda Camaytlan, Guayacocotla and Chicontepec district, Veracruz; CRS 197 exp. 14, 1802, Mazatepec, Morelos (anticlerical hacendado accused of intimidating vicarios). A few here and there were regional bosses who manipulated lieutenants against parish priests or controlled both in order to gain control over Indian lands and labor. AGN Civil 1599 exp. 9, 1708, Ocoyoacac, Metepec district; AGN Hist. 437, 1800, Mochitlan, Tixtla district (Guerrero). But for the most part, their conflicts with curas were confined to estate issues, such as clerical fees owed by hacienda residents, curas supporting land suits by pueblos against the estate, or hacendados working their peones on Sundays and preventing them from attending mass. Such conflicts are documented in CRS 29 exp. 7, 1737, Tulancingo (over fees); BMM 135, 1749, Zinacantepec, district of Metepec (over the arancel for clerical fees); AGN Acervo 49 caja 68, 1762, Tepeapulco, Otumba district (over funeral charges); BMM 502, 1777, Xochitepec, Puebla (over gañanes forced to work on Sundays); CRS 39 exp. 5, 1803, Hacienda del Salitre, Malacatepec, district of Metepec (rancor over fees); AGN Templos 25 exp. 10, 1805, Temascalcingo, Ixtlahuaca district (over fees). They seem much like those between curas and residents of visitas described in earlier chapters.

The relationship between curas and district governors was sometimes complicated by one or both of them owning local estates. For cases of district governors as hacendados and rancheros, see AGN Tierras 2084 exp. 1, 1728, near Xalostoc, Ecatepec district; AGN Alcaldes Mayores 3, fols. 172–78, 1771, Amecac, district of Atlixco, Puebla; Tulane VEMC 53 exp. 23, 1788, Cuautitlan, Valley of Mexico; and Aguirre Beltrán, "Delación," 1807, Acayucan, Veracruz. But hacendados could also be allies, friends, and even kinsmen of the parish priest. See, for example, AGN Cofradías 13 exp. 5, 1786, Hueypustla, Edo. de México (two brothers of the cura owned haciendas in the district); AGN Hist. 578A, 1793, Taxco report (vicario of Acamistla lived on his brother's hacienda in the district); CRS 57 exp. 3, 1796–99, Xichú (several hacendados gave glowing accounts of the cura's service); AJANG Civil, box 231, doc. 1, 1804, Ocotlan, Jalisco (Indians complained that the cura punished them to please an hacendado); BMM 251, 1809, Pipioltepec, Temascaltepec district (cura supported an hacendado's plan for a new congregation of Indians);

VEMC 54 exp. 37, 1793, Temascaltepec (cura interfered with the subdelegado's effort to arrest an hacienda administrator for failing to pay just wages); and CRS 75 exp. 3, 1774, Macatepec, Metepec district (cura, hacendado, and royal officials cooperated to control local unrest). The need for productive land and the labor of village Indians gave hacendados a vital interest in the political affairs of pueblos. Further research in AGN Tierras and local land records should clarify the complex relationships between private estate owners or managers and political power beyond the estate boundaries.

In addition, every alcaldía mayor of central and western Mexico had at least a small nucleus of traders, artisans, schoolmasters, muleteers, and tax collectors. Local peninsular and creole (and sometimes casta and Indian) merchants could be especially important in local politics and trade. Some served as lieutenants; others allied themselves with the lieutenant or alcalde mayor to promote their mutual interests; others were themselves lieutenants. See, for example, AJANG Civil, box 86, doc. 1, 1768, Cocula (merchant lieutenant); Civil, box 82, doc. 7, 1769, Zacoalco (merchant lieutenant); BMM 271, 1770 (Tirso Díaz wrote of local merchants depending on the lieutenant's goodwill to prosper); CRS 188 exp. 6, 1789, Choapan, Villa Alta district, Oaxaca (peninsular merchant promoted Indian opposition to the cura); and Hist. 132 exp. 34, 1793, Sayula, Jalisco (lieutenant and merchants controlled local trade). This influence might be played out in other ways as well. See, for example, CRS 42 exp. 1, 1732, Tejupilco, Temascaltepec district (Spanish vecino acted as the Indians' cosigner); Crim. 284 exp. 5, 1736, Papantla, Veracruz (a creole "compadre" of various Indians was accused of instigating a tumulto); AGN Acervo 49 caja 46, 1763, Xochitepec, Morelos (a local peninsular defied the cura); and AJANG Civil, box 228, doc. 7, 1802, Zapotlanejo, Jalisco (local notables including the owner of the mesón worked against the lieutenant).

At a distance, lawyers in the audiencia capitals of Mexico City and Guadalajara also could be important players in local politics. See, for example, CRS 74 exp. 11, 1801, Amanalco, Metepec district (audiencia warned a Mexico City attorney not to interfere in minor business such as the cura's absence from the parish); and Templos 25 exp. 9, 1801, Zacualtipan, Meztitlan district, Hidalgo (legal representative in Mexico City was arrested as a mischief maker). See also BMM 1745, ledger of Vicente Garviso, a Mexico City lawyer who represented Indian pueblos from 1814 to 1834.

2. *Recop.* 5-2-1 and 5-2-10 speak of three-year terms, and the alcalde mayor of Xerez in 1713 had received a three-year appointment. There was some variation in the 18th century, but most sources refer to a standard "quinquenio" or document a five-year term (e.g., BMM 271, ch. 101, 1770). Villarroel, pp. 332, 337, objected to fixed five-year terms for alcaldes mayores who had performed well. The terms of alcaldes mayores are discussed briefly by Alanís Boyso, *Introducción*, pp. 19–25. He concludes that though three to five years was standard, an appointment could be extended at the king's pleasure. In any case, the outgoing alcalde mayor was expected to serve until his replacement arrived.

3. *Recop.* 5-2-11 called on alcaldes mayores and lieutenants to "carry a *vara de justicia* and listen to everyone benignly"; *Recop.* 5-2-19 and 5-2-29 also emphasized their judicial authority. If absent or ill, an alcalde mayor or subdelegado could delegate his authority to hear Indian cases to a lieutenant or some other reliable man who was an officer of the cabildo de españoles. Ventura Beleña, 1: 211, July 7, 1781.

4. Corruption and the barely diluted power of the alcaldes mayores are highlighted in a recent collection of essays on provincial government before the Ordenanza de Intendentes: Borah, *El gobierno provincial*.

5. Anonymous complaints against district governors or lieutenants: AGN RCO 126 exp. 3, 1777, Oaxaca; AGN Hist. 132 exp. 4, 1782, Querétaro; Hist. 132 exp. 6, 1786, Cholula (Puebla); Hist. 132 exp. 22, 1786, Zapotlan el Grande (Jalisco); Hist. 132 exp. 10, 1790, Querétaro; Hist. 132 exp. 18, 1792, Villa de Valles (San Luis Potosí); Hist. 132 exp. 30,

1792, Aculco (Hidalgo); Hist. 132 exp. 16, 1793, Coyoacan (Valley of Mexico); Hist. 132 exp. 26, 1793, Cuernavaca (Morelos); Hist. 132 exp. 27, 1794, Yautepec (Morelos); Hist. 132 exp. 28, 1794, Huajuapan (Oaxaca); Hist. 132 exp. 29, 1794, Maravatío (Michoacán).

6. AGN Civil 1485 exp. 10. An example of a lieutenant avenging himself on an Indian who wrote a complaint against him to the audiencia is AJANG Criminal, box 32, doc. 2, 1798, Zacoalco (Jalisco).

7. In 1793, for example, Indians of Tlaquiltenango pleaded with the viceroy for special protection because their alcalde mayor enjoyed the unqualified backing of the gobernador of the Marquesado del Valle. AGN Hist. 132 exp. 26, fols. 15–20.

8. The later Bourbons encouraged the appointment of military officers as district governors, but the practice was not new, and in some districts, it was more common in the 17th century than in the 18th. According to Alanís Boyso, *Corregidores*, pp. 32–38, whereas military men were especially prominent among the corregidores in Toluca during the late 17th century, their representation fell off soon after; only one corregidor between 1700 and 1810 had been a military officer.

9. Examples of governors charging priests with sexual misconduct: AGN Inq. 760 exp. 11, 1715, Zoquitlan (Puebla); AGN Hist. 128 exp. 3, 1777, Chietla (Puebla); Hist. 578A, 1793, Tixtla and Ixmiquilpan reports.

10. Villarroel, pp. 469–70, complained of this kind of priestly complaint.

11. Lynch, *Bourbon Spain*, p. 372.

12. *Hidalgo-Querétaro-San Luis Potosí*: Xilotepec district, AGN Tierras 2179 exp. 3, 1756; Tierras 2771 exp. 7, 1764; AGN Crim. 25 exp. 23, 1773; AGN Inq. 1146 exp. 1, 1775; AGN CRS 72 exp. 2, 1796. Meztitlan district, AGN Templos 25 exp. 2, 1753; AGN Alcaldes Mayores 11, fols. 353ff, 1774; CRS 136 exp. 5, 1785; Inq. 1213 exp. 18. Huichapan district, CRS 75 exp. 7, 1789; CRS 75 exp. 5, 1785. Tetepango district, CRS 67 exp. 3, 1768; CRS 195 exp. 8, 1793. Tulancingo district, CRS 130 exps. 3, 7, 1796–97. Ixmiquilpan district, Inq. 1209 exp. 12, 1783. Yahualica district, AGN Bienes 575 exp. 14, 1789. Pachuca–Real del Monte district, Tulane VEMC 43 exp. 2, 1775; VEMC 66 exp. 13, 1808. Querétaro, AGN Acervo 49 caja 44, 1700; Hist. 319 exp. 5, 1777; Acervo 49 caja 48, 1777; CRS 217 exp. 5 1809. San Luis Potosí, Crim. 159, fols. 163–80, 1797.

Guerrero-Morelos: Tlapa district, Alcaldes Mayores 11, fols. 357ff, 1772; Templos 1 exp. 4, 1806. Chilpancingo district, Inq. 862, fols. 393–407, 1737; CRS 195 exp. 12, 1794. Tetela del Río district, CRS 75 exp. 11, 1790. Tixtla district, CRS 204 exp. 5, 1740. Ichcateopan district, Acervo 49 caja 47, 1765. Taxco district, Acervo 49 caja 48, 1761. Olinalá district, CRS 13 exp. 3, 1781. Cuernavaca district, CRS 140 exps. 4–5, 1796; CRS 177 exp. 10 and CRS 197 exp. 14, 1800–1802. Tlayacapan district, CRS 156 exp. 6, 1761; AGN RCO 84 exp. 77, 1764. Tlaltizapan district, CRS 136 exp. 2, 1781. Tlaquiltenango district, VEMC 8 exp. 21, 1803.

Valley of Mexico area: Cempoala district, Inq. 1113, fols. 231–54, 1777; VEMC 9 exp. 1, 1789. San Cristóbal Ecatepec district, Tierras 2776 exps. 23–24, 1764; VEMC 68 exp. 20, 1765. Tlalmanalco district, Tierras 1929 exp. 9, 1772; Bienes 663 exp. 24, 1817. Ixtapalapa district, CRS 201 exp. 1, 1780. Churubusco district, CRS 159 exp. 3, 1785. Xochimilco district, AGN Civil 2095 exp. 3, 1787. Otumba district, VEMC 51 exp. 6, 1811. Cuautitlan district, VEMC 53 exp. 23, 1788. Coyoacan district, Hist. 132 exp. 16, 1793.

Zacualpan-Temascaltepec-Malinalco-Metepec-Tenango del Valle: Zacualpan district, Alcaldes Mayores 11, fols. 338ff, 1773; CRS 75 exp. 4, 1775; Inq. 1326 exp. 2, 1795; CRS 137 exp. 8, 1805. Temascaltepec district, Acervo 49 caja 48, 1700; CRS 204 exps. 9–10, 1760; Acervo 49 caja 146, 1805. Metepec district, CRS 164 exp. 4, 1747; CRS 130 exp. 5, 1796. Malinalco district, Bienes 575 exp. 63, 1789. Ixtlahuaca district, CRS 72 exp. 2, 1796. Toluca district, BMM 135 exp. 16, 1734. Tenango del Valle district, CRS 84 exp. 8, 1801.

Nueva Galicia: Acaponeta district, AJANG Criminal, bundle labeled "1815 leg. 5 (101),"

1737; AGN Hist. 128 exp. 10, 1791; AJANG Civil, box 150, doc. 7, 1791; AJANG Criminal, box 12, doc. 27, 1808. Ahuacatlan district, AJANG Civil, box 119, doc. 12. Autlan district, AJANG Civil, box 125, doc. 2, 1784. Colima district, VEMC 26 exp. 3, 1760. Cosalá district, AJANG Civil, caja 4 leg. 2, exp. 14, 1807; AJANG Criminal, bundle labeled "1806–7 (74)." 1806–10. Cuquío district, AJANG Civil, box 120, doc. 5, 1786. Chametla district, AJANG Criminal, bundle labeled "1808 leg. 2 (6)," 1808. Huejuquilla district, CAAG, 1770 concurso records. Juchipila district, AJANG Civil, box 140, doc. 5, 1791. Ocotlan district, AJANG Civil, box 116, doc. 4, 1778; AJANG Civil, box 89, doc. 6, 1778; AJANG Civil, box 103, doc. 10, 1783. Santa María del Oro district, BEJ Papeles de Derecho, 2: 396–97, 1796. Sayula district, AJANG Civil, box 119, doc. 3, 1776. Sierra de Pinos district, AJANG Civil, box 80, doc. 2, 1772. Sinaloa district, AJANG Civil, box 171, doc. 15, 1800. Tequila district, AJANG Criminal, bundle labeled "1719–1800 leg. 1," 1796. Tlajomulco district, AJANG Civil, bundle labeled "1800–1809 leg. 3 (109)," 1815. Valle de Topia district, AJANG Criminal, box 22, doc. 21, 1807. Zacoalco district, AJANG Civil, box 59, doc. 11, 1753. Zapotlan el Grande district, Hist. 319 exp. 18, 1782; Hist. 132 exp. 22, 1786; Inq. 1318 exp. 5, 1793; BEJ Papeles de Derecho, 1: 458–59. Zapotlanejo district, AJANG Civil, box 228, doc, 7, 1802.

Oaxaca: Villa Alta, CRS 188 exp. 6, 1789; Hist. 132 exp. 14, 1790; CRS 188 exp. 12, 1793. Xicayán, CRS 188 exp. 9, 1791. Teposcolula, CRS 84 exp. 1, 1775. Atlatlauca, Archivo del Estado de Oaxaca, Juzgados bundle for 1806. Acayuca, Aguirre Beltrán, "Delación," 1807. Teutila, Acervo 49 caja 146, 1772.

Puebla: Chiautla de la Sal, Tierras 2771 exp. 12, 1786. Quimixtlan, AGI Indiferente General 3027, 1799. Tehuacan, CRS 195 exp. 6, 1792. Tetela de Xonotla, Alcaldes Mayores 11, fols. 448ff, 1776. Tochimilco, Inq. 821 exp. 24, 1728.

Tabasco district: CRS 152 exps. 6–7, 1788; AGN Civil 1603 exp. 9, 1813. *Tlaxcala district*: Huamantla, Inq. 1074, 1768. *Veracruz district*: Jalapa, RCO 33 exp. 165, 1708. Guayacocotla, Templos 1 exp. 2, 1786. *Michoacán*: Cuitzeo district, Alcaldes Mayores 3 exp. 1, 1770. Pátzcuaro district, Hist. 437, 1792. Zacatula district, RCO 182 exp. 95, 1801. Taximaroa district, CRS 30, fols. 354ff, 1789. San Miguel el Grande district, AGN Civil 59, 1761.

13. *Recop.* 5-2-7. For a similar 1611 instruction to alcaldes mayores, see Ventura Beleña, 1: 38.

14. AGN RCO 69 exp. 67, July 12, 1739, is an example of justicias being especially charged with the good treatment of Indians.

15. *Recop.* 5-2, 6-1, 6-10.

16. *Recop.* 6-1-27 and BEJ Papeles de Derecho, 4: 409–14 (granting permission for the sale of private Indian holdings); AGN Crim. 630 exp. 4, 1720, Yolomecal (overseeing regional markets); AGN Tierras 1048 exp. 8, 1773, Jocotepec district, Jalisco, and Tierras 2554 exp. 6, 1801, Tlalmanalco (supervising boundaries and performing other duties as land judge); Crim. 730, unnumbered exp. for June 9, 1781, Escapusaltongo, Tacuba district (approving Indian land rentals; here a district judge denied a principal's request to rent out land); Tierras 1772 exp. 23, 1784, Chichicastla, Meztitlan district, and Crim. 52 exp. 10, 1796, Tejupilco (embargoing Indian property; the last case also includes taking depositions and serving as judge of first instance in a murder case); BEJ Papeles de Derecho, 1: 573–80, 1796 (approving Indians' repartimientos de tierras).

17. AJANG Civil, box 200, doc. 13. Many minor disputes that did not require review or judgment by the audiencia were settled informally, by juicio verbal, without a written record of the proceedings.

18. AJANG Civil "caja 12," 1728, "Sobre azotes que mandó dar d. Francisco Arze."

19. The royal cedula of Aug. 13, 1799, ordering military officers on active duty not to serve as subdelegados suggests that even this practice was not unknown in New Spain. AGN RCO 173 exp. 254.

20. Calderón Quijano et al., *Virreyes de Nueva España . . . Carlos III*, 1: 364–69. The alcalde mayor of Sayula in 1780, Manuel Baamonde, continued to be a military officer—a capitán de ejército. Extolling "la ilustre carrera de armas," he proposed the formation of a battalion of infantrymen from militia companies in his district to defend the ports of San Blas and Navidad. AGI Guad. 347.

21. AGI Guad. 345, relación de méritos of Francisco Javier de Arriola; AGN Hist. 132 exp. 5.

22. AGN Crim. 120 exp. 2, 1774, San Cristóbal Ecatepec (two pueblos sought the removal of their military lieutenant for mistreatment); AJANG Civil, bundle labeled "1803, leg. 1 (147)," 1806, Tlajomulco (Indians of Santa Anita said that the subdelegado, who held a military commission, mistreated them in various ways and had sent in 50 armed men in response to the erroneous rumor of an alboroto). Such complaints escalated during the Independence War when even more district governors were military men. An example is AJANG Criminal, bundle labeled "1813–1812 (42)," 1813, Tepatitlan. Some, like the military subdelegado of Temascaltepec in 1805, hired a "director" to advise them in legal matters. AGN Acervo 49 caja 146.

23. See, for example, the town council of Mexico City's 1771 representation to the king, advertised in Philadelphia Rare Books and Manuscripts Catalogue 5 (1989), now in the Bancroft Library. For a milder expression of these antipeninsular sentiments, see Eguiara y Eguren.

24. By law, the power of alcaldes mayores to select and remove their lieutenants was limited. Under *Recop.* 5-2-42, appointments of lieutenants required a license from the viceroy, and under 5-2-36 the viceroy and audiencia could remove lieutenants when harm ("daño") was being done. In practice, alcaldes mayores had a freer hand with appointments than removals. Removals initiated by the alcalde mayor occasionally did occur, but usually because of friction with parish priests and at the priests' request (e.g., AGN CRS 195 exp. 6, 1792, Tehuacan, Puebla). After 1789, removal required the approval of the intendant. On lieutenants, see Borah, *El gobierno provincial*, ch. 4.

25. BEJ Papeles de Derecho, 1: 295–305. In law, they could not administer justice unless their superior was out of the district and had appointed them to do so. Despite a nepotism rule forbidding corregidores to appoint relatives to offices in their districts (*Recop.* 5-2-45), some alcaldes mayores and subdelegados had brothers and cousins as lieutenants, and peninsular subdelegados in the late colonial period were inclined to appoint peninsulares as lieutenants when they could, whether they were members of their retinue or established local residents. Relatives: AGN Hist. 132 exp. 7, 1791, Cadereyta. Peninsular lieutenants: AJANG Civil, box 86, doc. 1, 1768, Cocula (long-time resident); Civil, box 82, doc. 7, 1769, Zacoalco; Civil, box 205, doc. 2572, 1789, Teocaltiche (regarded as "much worse" than his predecessors); AJANG Criminal, bundle labeled "1780–89 leg. 14 (121)," 1795, Zacoalco; AFRANG 570, 1800, Zacoalco.

26. Insubordination was the complaint of the subdelegado of Tlaltenango in 1815 and the alcalde mayor of Atlixco in 1771. The offender in the first case, the lieutenant of Tepechitlan, had served for 15 years. The man in the other, the lieutenant of Amecac, had served for 14. AJANG Civil, bundle labeled "1809–19 leg. 5 (49)"; AGN Alcaldes Mayores 3, fols. 172–78. The lieutenant of Tepechitlan in 1815 was a retired captain. Landowning lieutenants include the lieutenant of San Cristóbal de la Barranca (Jalisco), with an haciendita de caña y trapiche in 1787, and the lieutenant of Ocotlan (Jalisco), with a rancho in 1778. Merchants include the lieutenant of Zacoalco (Jalisco) in 1769 and the lieutenant of Cocula in 1768. AJANG Civil, box 111, doc. 5; Civil, box 89, doc. 6; Civil, box 82, doc. 7; Civil, box 86, doc. 1. Borah, *El gobierno provincial* p. 48 and ch. 4, posits that many lieutenants purchased the office despite legal prohibitions, and that others were appointed by the merchants who cosigned the alcaldes mayores' bonds of office.

27. AGN CRS 197 exp. 14.

28. AJANG Civil, box 111, doc. 5, contains reports for Tepatitlan, La Barca, Lagos, Teocaltiche, Xalostotitlan, San Juan, Villa Encarnación, Aguascalientes, Sierra de Pinos, Real de Charcas, Ahualulco, Cuquío, Charcas, Hostotipaquillo, Ahuacatlan, Santa María del Oro, Tepic, Senticpac, Acaponeta, Fresnillo, Villa de Llerena, Real de Nieves, Mazapil, and Tequila.

29. Calderón Quijano et al., *Virreyes de Nueva España . . . Carlos III*, 1: 364–69.

30. AGN RCO 99 exp. 27; AGN Alcaldes Mayores 3, fols. 263–65. Salaries for a few alcaldías mayores of New Spain in the late 17th century are listed in *Recop.* 5-2-1. For a 1765 list of alcaldías mayores of New Spain by class, see BN AF caja 139 exp. 1717.

31. Calderón Quijano et al., *Virreyes de Nueva España . . . Carlos III* 1: 364–69.

32. *Recop.* 5-2-9.

33. AGN RCO 147 exp. 200, Dec. 14, 1790; *Instrucciones que los vireyes*, 2: 322–23 (1794; according to Viceroy Revillagigedo, 5% of the tribute yielded only about 300p a year on average, with great variation); BEJ Papeles de Derecho, 4: 165–76 (1798). For an early-18th-century arancel for fees of the alcaldes mayores, see Brown Univ., Rockefeller Lib., Medina Coll., FHA 15 exp. 17, 1723.

34. BMM 271. That few of the sources of income described below were unique to the 18th century is indicated by complaints made against the alcalde mayor of Colima in 1603. "Relación de agravios de los naturales de la provincia de los Motines de Colima contra su Alcalde Mayor y Juez Congregador," *Boletín del Archivo General de la Nación* (Mexico), n.s., 1.2 (April-June 1960): 201–13.

35. AGN Tierras 2084 exp. 1, 1728, Ecatepec (accused along with his scribe of arbitrary arrests and fines, and of being a papelista); AGN Acervo 49 caja 47, 1765, Tepecoacuilco "Criminales contra Antonio de Estrada" (used multas for personal gain); AGN Crim. 131 exp. 32, 1794, Xochimilco (district governor refused to release a women without payment of 4p "costs"); AJANG Criminal, bundle labeled "1813-12 leg 3 (42)," 1813, Tonalá (fined old indio 4p and imprisoned him for a week for not attending the commemoration of the new constitution). See also AGN Crim. 176, fols. 523–31, 1787, Escapulsantongo (complaint by india Luis María, "sobre que el teniente de Tlanepantla la puso presa por haver tenido una riña con un vecino suyo").

36. AGN Crim. 710, 1742, Cuautitlan; AGN RCO 86 exp. 140, 1765, Yautepec; AGN Alcaldes Mayores 11, fols. 338–40, 1773, Ixtapan.

37. Underreporting tributaries: AJANG Criminal, bundle labeled "1799, leg. 1," Felipe Montes de Oca (as alcalde mayor of Tomatlan, Jalisco, in 1765). Leveling excessive fees: AGN Hist. 132 exp. 26, 1793, Cuernavaca district, Morelos (for land measurements); AJANG Civil, box 172, doc. 17, 1793, Sayula, Jalisco (on estates). The second case involved the estate of a man who died intestate. His widow protested the subdelegado's taking inventory at all, claiming that her husband owed nothing to anyone. According to her complaint, the subdelegado had broken into her house, seized it, and surrounded it with guards. Collecting unauthorized taxes: AGN CRS 72 exp. 11 (for attending cofradía meetings); CAAG, cura José Antonio Barragán of Huejuquilla resumé for 1770 concurso (said alcalde mayor collected 3p-12p from all vecinos during periodic visitas and jailed any who refused to pay). In 1767, a landowning widow complained that the alcalde mayor of La Barca imposed several unjust fees: 10p alcabala, even though she did not sell anything locally (she said she paid the alcabala to the alcalde in Guadalajara when she sold a cow or two there), 10p para la carcel y casas reales, and 6p for fiestas reales. AJANG Civil, box 172, doc. 7.

Charging for visitas was forbidden by *Recop.* 5-2-16. In 1713, the alcalde mayor of Xerez was ordered to repay fees he collected on visita or face a 500p fine. AJANG Civil, box 18, doc. 5. Fees for certifying elections were regulated. AGN RCO 71 exp. 31, Sept. 28, 1751.

38. AJANG Criminal, bundle labeled "1818 (63)," 1817 (alcalde de segundo voto Manuel Andrés v. d. Juan Rada, sobre injurias).

39. According to cura José Antonio Barragán of Huejuquilla, the alcalde mayor collected one fanega de maíz from all Indian tributaries annually. CAAG, resumé for 1770 concurso.

40. AJANG Civil, box 11, doc. 5, 1658, Magdalena, Itzatlan district.

41. *Recop.* 5-2-26 (1552, 1563).

42. AJANG Civil, box 11, doc. 5, 1658, Magdalena, Itzatlan district (alcalde mayor sent tributaries to the mines as punishment); Civil, box 243, doc. 7, 1808, Zapopan (subdelegado took prisoners from jail and used them as his domestic servants).

43. AGN Crim. 54 exp. 14, 1690, Tlapanaloya; Crim. 193, fols. 377ff, 1726, San Marcos Guaquilpa (lieutenant of Calpulalpan made the Indians work his fields); Aguirre Beltrán, "Delación," p. 70, 1807, Acayucan (subdelegado said to control Indian labor and to be the biggest planter, hiding his ownership behind the names of stand-ins).

44. AGN RCO 86 exp. 140.

45. AGN Alcaldes Mayores 11, fols. 338ff ("Listo el dinero, los gigantes se convierten en pigmeos, lo que se comprueba con preguntar ¿qué alcalde mayor ha salido mal de su residencia?"). Tirso Díaz thought that in residencias, "everything was arranged for about 500 pesos." BMM 271, ch. 102.

46. AGI Guad. 346, carta reservada concerning charges against Eusebio Sánchez Pareja, Sept. 1783. For superficial residencia inquiries in Nueva Galicia during the late 18th century, see AJANG Civil, box 162, doc. 2, 1772, La Barca and Poncitlan; Civil, box 104, doc. 7, 1781, La Barca; Civil, box 120, doc. 9, 1783–86, Tuscacuesco; Civil, box 120, doc. 11, 1786–87, Hostotipaquillo; Civil, box 106, doc. 1, 1786, Sayula; Civil, box 111, doc. 3, 1789, Tequila; Civil, box 141, doc. 9, 1790–91, Etzatlan; and Civil, box 149, doc. 14, 1794, Amula. Some serious charges against the subdelegado of Tonalá were investigated in a residencia of 1809–11. AJANG Civil, box 3, doc. 2, 1811; Civil, bundle labeled "1809 leg. 2 (127)." Adrián de Ceráin, former corregidor of Toluca, was particularly indignant that a priest was spreading the word in 1792 that Ceráin would lose in his residencia. AHM L10B/28, fol. 10v.

47. AGN RCO 40 exp. 162. According to the cura of Santiago Tecali (Puebla) in the 1730's, there was also a 1723 law against repartimientos. AGI Mex. 840.

48. See Rodolfo Pastor's paper in Borah, *El gobierno provincial* (ch. 12). The important commercial role of alcaldes mayores in cochineal and mining regions during the first half of the 17th century is well documented in Hoberman, *Mexico's Merchant Elite*, chs. 2–4. Hoberman also provides examples of merchants posting the bonds of office for alcaldes mayores.

49. AGN RCO 71 exp. 147.

50. Calderón Quijano et al., *Virreyes de Nueva España . . . Carlos III*, 1: 169. In 1792, the corregidor of Villa de Valles (San Luis Potosí) was accused of continuing the repartimiento and forcing Indians to sell him maize. AGN Hist. 132 exp. 18.

51. *Instrucciones que los vireyes*, 2: 45.

52. B. Hamnett, *Politics and Trade*.

53. New York Public Library, "Yndize comprehensibo de todos los Goviernos, corregiminetos, y alcaldías mayores que contiene la Governación del virreynato de México . . . [177?]." For example, the Colima entry offers the following brief summary of the alcalde mayor's commercial activity: "El comercio le tiene el Alcalde Mayor en la sal llamada de Colima que es mui especial[,] en las crías de ganado mayor, siembras de maízes, cortes de madera y carbón, hortalizas, arros, azúcares, mieles y algunos repartimientos que hace de efectos de la Puebla." For further documentation on alcaldes mayores' repartimientos and commerce, see AGN Alcaldes Mayores 11, fols. 357ff, 1772, Chipetlan, district of

Tlapa (control of cotton distribution and forced production of cotton cloth); AGN CRS 75 exp. 6, 1786, Alahuistlan (the forced sale of salt for silver processing); AGN Civil 1485 exp. 10, 1787, Tacuba (repartimiento de mulas); AJANG Civil, box 141, doc. 9, 1790–91, Etzatlan (local merchant, brother of alcalde mayor, assumed the office when he died); AGN Hist. 132 exp. 26, 1793, Cuernavaca (reparto de toros, mulas, and horses); CRS 188 exp. 12, 1793, Villa Alta (schoolteachers forced to sell cloth, hats, and brandy for subdelegado at exorbitant prices and had their salaries witheld until the goods were paid off); Hist. 132 exp. 28, 1794, Huajuapan, Oaxaca (the forced sale of mantas, chapanecos, and sombreros at high prices in exchange for the choicest Indian livestock); AGN Crim. 220, Metepec (repartimiento abuses and manipulation of maize sales).

54. AGN RCO 130 exp. 82, Feb. 20, 1785. This was in keeping with *Recop.* 5-2-34, which provided that "no se ausenten de los pueblos principales sin licencia." The message of this cedula was apparently lost on the alcalde mayor of Malinalco. In 1789, he resided in San Angel and left the administration of his district to a lieutenant. AGN Bienes 575 exp. 63. The 1785 cedula described the alcaldes mayores' commercial activities: "Some are financial backers [habilitadores of merchants]; others trade by their own hand; and many have intimate connections of other kinds [with merchants]." A subdelegado acting as a small-scale habilitador is documented for Tonalá (Jalisco) in 1795. A local Indian complained that the subdelegado had lent him money for his pottery trade; then, when the Indian was unable to repay the loan on time, the subdelegado claimed his mules, which were worth more than the debt. AJANG Civil, bundle labeled "1797–1794 (129)."

55. AGN Alcaldes Mayores 3, fols. 172–78. No salary was apparently typical.

56. Calderón Quijano et al., *Virreyes de Nueva España . . . Carlos III,* 1: 251–53, mentions audiencia decrees against the sale of tenientazgos in 1784. The text of the principal decree is in Brown Univ., Rockefeller Lib., Medina Coll., FHA 48 exp. 9. The Fourth Provincial Council (1771) objected to lieutenants "renting" their positions. De la Hera, "Juicios," p. 313. The practice did not disappear with the 1784 decrees. The alcalde mayor of Cadereyta was accused in 1791 of accepting bribes in exchange for teniente appointments. AGN Hist. 132 exp. 7.

57. De la Hera, "Juicios," p. 313. The lieutenant of Zacoalco (Jalisco) in 1769 reportedly paid 500p for the post. AJANG Civil, box 82, doc. 7. According to AJANG Civil caja 4 leg. 2 exp. 10, as late as 1806 lieutenants in Nueva Galicia were still paying 400p and more a year for their offices.

58. AJANG Civil, box 162, doc. 2, fol. 80r, 1772, La Barca (lieutenant traded in chiles, cheese, and beef, "gritándoles y regañándoles"); AGN Hist. 132 exp. 26, 1793, Tetecala, Cuernavaca district (reparto of mules by lieutenant); Civil, box 149, doc. 14, 1794, Tuscacuesco (lieutenants "engaged in a little commerce"); Civil, box 149, doc. 14. According to Tirso Díaz, lieutenants who had purchased their position were likely to be permitted to engage in commerce on their own or to be given a share of the collections owed to their superiors. Some seem to have been paid a salary. BMM 271, chs. 93–97.

59. AGN Crim. 730, 1703, Tultitlan (extortion); AJANG Civil, box 18, doc. 5, 1713, Xerez; Crim. 193, fols. 377ff, 1726, San Marcos Guaquilpa; AGN Alcaldes Mayores 3, fols. 172–78, 1771, Amecac, Atlixco district (accepted bribes); AGN CRS 75 exp. 11, 1790, Ajuchitlan, Tetela del Río district (lieutenant admitted that he had accepted a "gratificación" of 20p from the governor, but "tuvo a bien devolvérselos para que en ningún tiempo se le pueda calumniar de este crimen"); Crim. 159, fols. 163–80, 1797, Valle de San Francisco, San Luis Potosí (demanded 20p or a horse from those he found drunk); Tulane VEMC 8 exp. 21, 1803, Tlaquiltenango (bribes and arbitrary fines);VEMC 8 exp. 21, 1803 Tlaquiltenango; AJANG Criminal, box 12, doc. 27, 1808, Chametla (received "estipendios" for not interfering with illegal gambling); AGN Crim. 131 exp. 26 (arrested 14 men and

women he found in the same sweat bath and charged 5p each for their release); Crim. 156, fols. 1–17, n.d., Ozumba.

60. AGN Alcaldes Mayores, 11 fols. 353–56 ("todo lo compone con dinero").

61. AGN Crim. 137 exp. 2 ("No tienen más juez que el gobernador"). For cases illustrating the tumulto situations mentioned in the text: Crim. 232 exp. 2, 1720, Milpa Alta; Crim. 155 fols. 111ff, 1721, Santa Marta, Mexicalcingo district; Crim. 204 exp. 12, 1734, Huaxintlan; Crim. 117 exp. 4, 1751, Actopan; Crim. 123 exp. 4, 1753, Tenango del Valle; Crim. 123 exp. 21, 1762, San Andrés, Tenango del Valle district; Crim. 178 exp. 1, 1766, Alfajayucan; Crim. 104 and 107 exp. 1, 1772, Meztitlan and Zacualtipan; Crim. 15 exp. 3, 1797, Tenancingo; Crim. 154, fols. 536–52, 1798, San Angel; AGN Hist. 334 exp. 5, 1798, Tetela de Xonotla; Crim. 226, fols. 401ff, 1799, Amecameca; Crim. 181, fols. 201ff, 1800, Ixtapan; Crim. 76 exp. 1, 1803, Tacubaya; Crim. 184 exp. 5, Papantla.

62. AJANG Civil, box 111, doc. 5, fol. 37 ("tomando conocimiento en todo género de causas de los indios assí civiles como criminales, haciendo testamentos, oyendo demandas y sentenciándolas").

63. AJANG Civil, box 59, doc. 9. There is an extensively documented case of an alcalde mayor of Colima, his lieutenant, two schoolmasters, and three militia officers besieged and driven out of town by members of the cabildo of the Villa de Colima and Indians of Coaquimatlan in 1762. The cura of Colima did not participate in the "tumulto" against the alcalde mayor, but the two had been locked in a bitter jurisdictional dispute for several years, and he was deeply critical of the alcalde mayor during the investigation that followed. The main complaint of the local creoles was the alcalde mayor's arbitrary, sweeping infringement of their traditional prerogatives—confiscating their firearms, imposing a branding fee and new salt tax on everyone, demanding the alcabala on exempted goods, and interfering with the illegal liquor trade. The cura recognized that the alcalde mayor was carrying out viceregal orders in most of these initiatives but pointed to his inflexible application of them, which had resulted in hunger, the collapse of local commerce, and the needless killing of Indians of Coaquimatlan by militia troops. AGN Crim. 288–89.

64. AJANG Criminal, bundle labeled "1805 leg. 1 (25)," charges against Diego Vallejo and others; Criminal, bundle labeled "1807 leg. 1 (76)," 1807, charges against d. José Perfecto Martín.

65. AJANG Criminal, box 33, doc. 3. Similar cases of dangerous disrespect in the Guadalajara audiencia district include AJANG Civil, box 59, doc. 9, 1756, Zacoalco; Civil, box 121, doc. 5, 1764, Tala (riña between an hacendado and the corregidor); Criminal, box 45, doc. 6, 1793, Zapotlan el Grande; Criminal, bundle labeled "1806 leg. 1 (120)," 1804, Tequila; Criminal, box 8, doc. 6, 1805, Tlaltenango; Criminal, bundle labeled "1807 leg. 1 (76)," 1805, Las Cañadas; Criminal, bundle labeled "1811 legs. 2–3," 1806, Tepatitlan; Criminal, bundle labeled "1807 leg. 1 (76)," 1807, Tequila (contra José Demetrio Guzmán); Criminal, bundle labeled "1809 leg. 1 (126)," 1809, Sayula; Criminal, caja 5 leg. 1 exp. 1, 1810, Teocaltiche; Criminal, bundle labeled "1811–20 leg. 2 (20)," 1811, San Martín de la Cal; Criminal, bundle labeled "1815–1833 (80)," 1817, Tonalá (woman insulted subdelegado); Criminal, bundle labeled "1818 leg. 2 (89)," 1818, Tonalá; Criminal, bundle labeled "1818–19," 1819, Ixtlahuacan; Criminal, bundle labeled "1821 leg. 2 (54)," 1821, San Pedro Tlaquepaque.

66. Guardar armonía, paz y quietud are mentioned, for example, in AJANG Civil, box 119, doc. 3, 1726, Sayula; AGN Inq. 1146 exp. 1, 1775, Xilotepec; AJANG Civil, box 116, doc. 4, 1778, Ocotlan; Tulane VEMC 53 exp. 23, 1788, Cuautitlan; AJANG Civil, box 150, doc. 7, 1791, Acaponeta; and VEMC 51 exp. 6, 1811, Otumba. *Recop.* 3-1-4 (1555) called for "toda paz y conformidad" between ecclesiastical and secular authorities.

67. The fiscal of the Audiencia of Nueva Galicia in 1804, for example, expressed con-

cern that the cura and lieutenant of Ocotlan (Jalisco) were too friendly, opening the door to mistreatment of Indians. AJANG Civil, box 231, doc. 1. Solórzano 3-26-16, citing a cedula of 1597 (summarized in *Recop*. 1-6-33), noted that doctrineros should not be relatives of encomenderos because kinship could result in hidden abuses.

68. Phelan develops this theme of institutionalized mutual suspicion in "Authority and Flexibility," pp. 53–54 ("Motivated by an abiding distrust of its agents overseas, the Crown gradually fashioned during the course of the 16th century a complex bureaucratic pyramid with multiple, partly independent and partly interdependent hierarchies. Under this system the conflicts between the various bureaucracies were continuous and acrimonious, since their jurisdictions often overlapped"), and at greater length in *Kingdom of Quito*.

For a brief introduction to the counterpoint of conflict and cooperation in the association of parish priests and district governors, see Rosa Camelo's paper in Borah, *El gobierno provincial* (ch. 9). See also Cahill, pp. 275–76, who emphasizes struggles between curas and district governors in southern Peru, with curas having the upper hand.

69. AGN CRS 72 exp. 12, 1772, Aculco, Xilotepec district (cura's claim); CRS 188 exp. 9, 1791, Jamiltepec, Oaxaca (cura's claim); AGN Hist. 578A, 1793, Ixmiquilpan report (subdelegado's claim); Tulane VEMC 51 exp. 6, Otumba, 1811 (cura's claim).

70. CPM, p. 163. Audiencia warnings: AJANG Civil, box 119, doc. 3, 1776, Sayula; Civil, box 116, doc. 4, 1778, Ocotlan; Tulane VEMC 53 exp. 23, 1788, Cuautitlan; VEMC 66 exp. 13, 1808–9, Pachuca. Ecclesiastical court warnings: AGN Inq. 1209 exp. 12, 1783, Ixmiquilpan; VEMC 53 exp. 23, Cuautitlan 1788; AJANG Civil, box 150, doc. 7, 1791, Acaponeta.

71. AGN Bienes 663 exp. 24, 1817, Tlalmanalco. Attempts at such reconciliation were a common feature of late colonial pastoral visits.

72. For example, in speaking of mutual responsibilities of the church and civil authorities for the good treatment of Indians, *Recop*. 6-10-6 (1582) first mentions the royal justicias, then adds that prelates have the same obligation because of "their responsibilities for the spiritual and temporal welfare of those natives." *Recop*. 6-1-21 (1552) charges "nuestras justicias" with seeing that the Indians work and act properly, giving the parish priest an important but secondary mission: "encargamos a los doctrineros que persuadan a los Indios a lo referido en esta nuestra ley." The responsibility for Indian tribute clearly fell to the district governors, but the Audiencia of Mexico in 1762 called for the curas, as well as alcaldes mayores, to advise on cases where Indian communities hit by epidemics should be relieved of tribute. Ventura Beleña, 1: 45. *Itin*. 2-2-2 offered the potentially controversial opinion that confessors should see that Indians paid only a just tribute, one that was in proportion to their means. As the repeated warnings to ecclesiastical judges not to infringe on the royal jurisdiction suggest (*Recop*. 1-7-31, 1-10-1, 1-10-2, 3-1-5), there were two judicial spheres, even though the boundaries between them were not sharply drawn.

73. *Recop*. 1-1-6, 1-1-7, 1-1-9; Ventura Beleña, 1: 209 (Oct. 10, 1769, circular instructing royal officials to "help" religious authorities promote the Spanish language). *Itin*. 2-7-5 and 2-7-8 specified that the cura and the district governor shared responsibility for eliminating Indian drunkenness "because drunkenness is against both spiritual and corporal well-being."

74. *Recop*. 1-10-11, 5-2-23; AGN Bandos 8 exp. 33, Aug. 18, 1773; Bandos 16 exp. 43, Dec. 22, 1791.

75. See also Ventura Beleña, 1: 60, May 4, 1656, forbidding doctrineros to jail Indians, make them burden bearers, or bother them in other ways, and instructing justicias to see that the priests acted benignly and to ensure that the Indians were well treated.

76. *Recop*. 5-10-7 (1530); Brown Univ., Rockefeller Lib., Medina Coll., FHA 14 exp. 7, 1723, royal provisión.

77. *Recop.* 6-10-8, 1-12-8.

78. For example, Richard Morse's comment in Bakewell et al., eds., *Readings in Latin American History* (Durham, N.C., 1985), 1: 417: "Corregidors of Indian towns regularly exploited their wards for personal gain, often in conspiracy with priests and Indian caciques."

79. AGN CRS 30, fols. 354ff. See also CRS 156 exp. 7, 1761, Acambay; Brown Univ., Rockefeller Lib., Medina Coll., FHA 55 exp. 63, 1773; CRS 75 exp. 8, 1789, Jimilpan; and AGN Templos 25 exp. 8, 1796, Amecameca (cura went to court to get the subdelegado's cooperation in collecting clerical fees).

80. The lieutenant of Ajuchitlan, Tetela del Río district, in 1790 complained that the cura's way to seek royal auxilio was to ask for the keys to the jail. AGN CRS 75 exp. 11. Other examples of justicias accusing priests of ignoring the requirement of royal auxilio are AGN Tierras 1929 exp. 9, 1772, Tlalmanalco; CRS 75 exp. 4, 1775, Tototepec, Zacualpan district; CRS 75 exp. 5, 1785, San Luis de las Peras, Huichapan district; CRS 84 exp. 8, 1801, Tescaliacac, Tenango del Valle district. An example of a district governor accusing the priest of frivolous demands for royal auxilio is Tulane VEMC 53 exp. 23, 1788, Cuautitlan, after the cura struck the lieutenant with his bastón when he refused to arrest Indians who had not taken part in an Easter procession.

81. AGN CRS 204 exp. 5, 1740, Tixtla (Guerrero); CRS 68 exp. 2, 1769, Ozoloapan (Edo. de México); AGN Alcaldes Mayores 11, fols. 338–40, Ixtapan, Zacualpan district, 1773–74; CRS 68 exps. 4–5, 1775, Cuanacalcingo (Morelos); AJANG Civil, box 119, doc. 3, 1776, Sayula (Jalisco); Alcaldes Mayores 11, fols. 448–56, 1776–80, Tuzamapan (Puebla); AJANG Civil, box 116, doc. 4, 1778, Ocotlan (Jalisco); CRS 136 exp. 2, 1781, Tlaltizapan (Morelos); AGN Hist. 132 exp. 22, 1786, Zapotlan el Grande (Jalisco); CRS 195 exp. 8, 1793, Misquiahuala, Tetepango district (Hidalgo); CRS 177 exp. 10 and 197 exp. 14, 1800–1802, Mazatepec (Morelos); AJANG Criminal, box 12, doc. 7, 1805, Chametla (Sinaloa); AGN Crim. 71 exp. 6, 1806, Amecameca; AGN Acervo 49 caja 116, 1808–9 (record of pastoral visit), Tepehuacan (Hidalgo).

82. AGN CRS 195 exp. 8 (Misquiahuala); CRS 177 exp. 10, CRS 197 exp. 14 (Mazatepec).

83. John Carter Brown Lib., "Práctica o Fórmula de autos eclesiásticos, para los curas, Notarios y Ministros en su Govierno eclesiástico, en el Pue. de Huamantla, este año de mill setecientos Quarenta y Seis." The section entitled "Forma de ajustar las causas de ydolatría entre yndios" specified that the juez eclesiástico (usually the cura) was to make the preliminary investigation, take depositions, and remit the case to the provisor of the episcopal court for instructions. If ordered to proceed, the juez eclesiástico was to see that a defense counsel was appointed within three days; notify the accused of the formal charges; receive confessions and complete the interrogations in the presence of the defense counsel, giving him the opportunity to raise objections; provide the defense counsel with a copy of the prosecution record for his certification; record the defense; ratify the record and remit it to the provisor for judgment; and notify the accused and the defense counsel of the judgment and sentence. In this description of the proceedings, the alcalde mayor or his lieutenant was limited to imparting royal auxilio by arresting the accused on the juez eclesiástico's order, inspecting the site of the alleged idolatry in the company of the juez eclesiástico, and taking custody of the accused's property when the juez eclesiástico asked him to do so. The secular magistrate would also have executed the sentence. See AGN Civil 59 for a 1761–62 dispute over jurisdiction in a case of "superstition" (the common view by now), Villa de San Felipe, San Miguel el Grande district (Valladolid).

84. AGI Mex. 2582, "El fiscal Posada da cuenta del expediente formado a petición de los indios de los pueblos de Corzocon en que exponen las medidas que se han tomado contra ciertos abusos que perjudicaban a los indios"; AGN RCO 138 exp. 229; reiterated for Nueva Galicia in BEJ Papeles de Derecho, 2: 178–79. The practical effect of this

redefinition of mixed jurisdiction probably was not great, since comparatively few "idolatry" cases were adjudicated in the late 18th century.

85. AGN Bandos 15 exp. 27. An earlier escalation of official criticism of priests occurred in the aftermath of the expulsion of the Jesuits and the violent protests of the late 1760s. AGN Crim. 304, 1767, Papantla; AJANG Civil, bundle labeled "1769–1760," 1767, Zapotitlan (Jalisco); Crim. 307 exp. 2, 1768, Chalchicomula (Puebla); Crim. 306 exp. 6, 1769, Agua de Venado. See also AGN RCO 92 exp. 102, March 17, 1768, ordering all ecclesiastics to stay out of government affairs and say nothing against the king: "se guarde al Trono el respeto que la Religión Cathólica inspira, y ninguna persona dedicada a Dios por su profesión se atreva a turbar por tales medios los ánimos y orden público, ingiriéndose en los negocios de Govierno, tan distantes de su conocimiento, como improprios de sus ministerios espirituales."

86. AGN DP 3 exp. 1 ("desafueros y tropelías contra la Real Justicia").

87. AGN CRS 75 exp. 6, 1786, Alahuistlan (cura pressed for a resident lieutenant). For parish priests' complaints that parishioners were more inclined to obey the justicia: CRS 156 exp. 9, 1763, Zacualpan de las Amilpas; AJANG Civil, box 119, doc. 13, 1790, Atotonilco el Alto; CRS 188 exp. 12, 1793, Villa Alta (cura claimed that the Indians "reconocen más superioridad en dicho subdelegado que en otro alguno por tenerlos engañados con su decantada authoridad y favor que logra de Vuestra Excelencia"); CRS 195 exp. 12, 1794, Chilpancingo.

88. BMM 271, ch. 102 ("El cura y demás ministros eclesiásticos ya se guardarán de hablar he intervenir en el remedio de tales escándalos, porque en brebes días dará por sí o por otros una quexa tan bien tramada y pertrechada de testigos que le haga caminar a una reclución, perder el mérito adquirido en su empleo, la reputación y fama para con el Prelado y por consiguiente para todos").

89. An idea of their networks of local supporters sometimes can be traced through the witnesses they summoned in litigations. For example, the following character witnesses appeared on behalf of Miguel José Losada, cura of Xichú (Guanajuato) in 1796, when he was charged with mistreatment of parishioners: three Spanish farmers, a Spanish hacienda administrator, a Spanish saltpeter refiner, a Spanish militia corporal, an Indian cacique, and three principales. All of them were dones. His Indian adversaries retorted that this was hardly an unbiased assembly of notables. They claimed that five were present or former fiscales, one was the cura's servant, another was an hacendado who opposed Indian interests, another was involved in a rental dispute with the pueblo, and two more had acted against the pueblo before. AGN CRS 57 exp. 4.

90. AGN Hist. 578A, 1793, especially the cura of Chicuautla, Ixmiquilpan report; the curas of Ixtlahuaca and Temascalcingo, Ixtlahuaca report; and the cura of Xochimilco, Xochimilco report. Administrative reports of this kind were superficial snapshots that could be misleading. Some glossed over conflicts that were not acute at the moment. For example, the subdelegado of Cuautitlan praised the cura and lieutenant of Teoloyucan for maintaining very good relations. In fact, there had been litigation between Teoloyucan and the curas of Cuautitlan for years. AGN CRS 68 exp. 1, 1759; Tulane VEMC 53 exp. 23, 1788.

91. AJANG Civil, box 104, doc. 7, 1781, La Barca; Civil, box 103, doc. 10, 1783, Ocotlan (lieutenant and cura were compadres); Civil, box 171, doc. 14, late 1780's, Tonalá; AGN CRS 130 exp. 5, 1796, Zinacantepec, Metepec district (lieutenant and cura cooperated); AJANG Criminal, bundle labeled "1811–1820 leg. 2 (20)," Aug. 15, 1811 (lieutenant took refuge in cura's house when three drunken men started a disturbance against him).

The subdelegado testified for the cura of Capuluac in 1796 against charges by local Indians over excessive fees and other abuse: "ha tratado y comunicado con frecuencia a dicho cura y puede asegurar que no habrá muchos que le excedan en conducta, celo, actibidad en el cumplimiento de su ministerio tratando a los naturales sus feligreses con el amor y equidad que le exigen sus christianos honrrados y arreglados procedimientos." He went on to speak of "algunos espíritus inquietos como son los que hablan en el precedente escrito concebido en la parte sustancial de falseada[,] resentidos de las correcciones con que dicho cura solicita cortarles el arraigado bicio de la embriaguez de que están poseídos." AGN CRS 39 exp. 3, fols. 98–101.

92. Probably a variant of temachtiqui, or teacher.

93. AGN Tierras 2198 exp. 2 ("Mui Señor mío: el día de ayer en la mañana se me precentó Santiago pidiéndome llamase a Pedro Juan y su muger que no sé qué sitio estaban acarriando una poca de piedra y que le hiciera que se la devolviesen y yo por ser tan enemigo de chismes de los yndios les persuadí que fueran ante VM para ese chisme y en esta persuasión llegó su muger de Juan ya mui borracha luego inmediatamente llegó Juan y otros en forma de tumulto en contra de Santiago; diciéndome tantas insolencias como quiera que todos estaban borrachos no atendían mi respecto y tal fue el atrebemiento de la muger de Juan como el meterme las manos a la cara y con tanta insolencia, les dí unos quartazos y así Vd se serbirá de llamarlos y corregirlos su borrachera y atrebimientos. Pues en tiempo de confesiones no sesan los tepaches no solo ellos sino otros se me han presentado tan ebrios y aunque estos como el escribano y Salvador el Temachti an estado borrachos pero estos no se me an insolentado pero será mui bueno Vmd les ponga una amenaza quisá assí se contendrán porque digo a Vmd que no es para tolerar estos y más en este tiempo de la Santa Quaresma. Dios guarde a Vmd muchos años, su afectísimo capellán que sus manos besa, Cornelio López").

94. However, priest-governor cooperation could mean personal loyalty. For example, the lieutenant and cura of Ocotlan (Jalisco) in 1783 were said to be compadres. AJANG Civil, box 103, doc. 10.

95. AGN CRS 67 exp. 3, fols. 147v ff.

96. Again, this tendency was far from universal. For some cases of curas at odds with local non-Indians, see AGN Acervo 49 caja 50, 1746, Ixmiquilpan; Acervo 49 caja 49, 1760, Actopan; AGN Bienes 172 exp. 54, 1803–4, Tenango Tepopula (vecinos brought charges against the Indian coadjutor); Acervo 49 caja 45, 1810, Chimalhuacan Atenco (cura in dispute with vecinos of San Vicente Chicoloapa said he had little success with the non-Indians in his parish); Acervo 49 caja 116, 1808–9, pastoral visit to Santo Tomás Tlacolula, Meztitlan district (the 30 gente de razón families of the Ranchería Yllatipan reportedly refused to attend mass).

97. AGN CRS 136 exp. 2, fol. 206v.

98. In the early 1790's, for example, two Indians charged the cura of Temascaltepec with illegally renting out pueblo lands and intending "to destroy the *pueblo* and make it into a Spanish town." AGN CRS 136 exps. 6–7, 1790–91. In 1727, the cura of Poncitlan wanted "algunos vecinos" to be allowed to settle in town and rent some Indian land, but the Indians would not agree to it. AJANG Civil, box 49, doc. 4.

99. AGN Civil 1599 exp. 9. Similar statements appear in AJANG Civil, box 119, doc. 13, 1776, Sayula; box 117, doc. 4, 1789, Atotonilco el Alto; and box 143, doc. 5, 1797, Zapotlan el Grande. The gente de razón of Amanalco, Metepec district, came to the cura's aid in a 1792 tumulto, as did those of Acambay in 1761. AGN Crim. 243 exp. 1; AGN CRS 156 exp. 7. In a 1768 arancel dispute of Joloapan against the cura of Guipustla, all the cura's witnesses were Spaniards. CRS 67 exp. 3. In a 1771 arancel dispute at San Felipe del Obraje, the cura called six Spaniards and four Indian principales as witnesses. CRS 68 exp. 3.

100. AGN CRS 156 exp. 5, 1758, Tepetlaostoc (cura said Indians of Apipilhuasco disobeyed both him and the justicia); AGN Templos 25 exp. 4, 1784, Zacualpan (alcalde mayor supported the cura of Malinaltepec in his litigation over fees and disrespect by

the Indians of Coatepec, who were equally insolent and disobedient, the cura said, to the alcalde mayor); AJANG Criminal, bundle labeled "1700–1793 (16)," 1788, Nochistlan (Indians were reported to be disrespectful to the justicia, and the cura was powerless to control them); Templos 25 exp. 9, 1799, Zacualtipan, Meztitlan district (the cura and justicia were agreed on the Indians' "falta de subordinación"); AJANG Criminal, bundle labeled "1815 leg. 2 (138)," 1815, Tlaltenango (cura and justicia cooperated against the troublesome Indian escribano).

Tumultos against both: AGN Civil 2292 exps. 10–11, 1733, Atlacomulco; AGN Crim. 304, 1767, Papantla; Crim. 307 exp. 2, 1768, Chalchicomula; Crim. 306 exp. 6, 1769, Agua de Venado; CAAG, cura Ysidro Joachin de Esparza y Gallardo of Mesquital, resumé for 1770 concurso.

101. AJANG Civil, box 49, doc. 4, 1727, Poncitlan; Civil, bundle labeled "1769–60," 1767, Mazatan and Tetapan, Zapotitlan district (Franciscan doctrinero spoke up for the lieutenant in a suit against him by local Indians, saying he had saved the life of the previous parish priest, and that the Indians did not respect their priests); Tulane VEMC 25 exp. 15, 1778, Zitácuaro (cura and justicia cooperated on the schools initiative and shared a judgment of Indians as people of "mucha desidia, floxedad, [y] poca aplicación").

102. AGN Inq. 1399 exp. 12, fol. 274 ("la poca veracidad de estas gentes, de la hypocrecía con que cubren su malicia, principalmente quando conservan en su corazón algún resentimiento, como sin duda respiran estos lo tienen contra su cura por el litigio que siguen desde ahora seis años sobre aranceles, obenciones, cofradías y tierras"). See also AGN CRS 75 exp. 2, 1769, Zacualpan (in which the Indians' attorney complained that both the lieutenant and the cura were "disgustados" with the Indians).

103. AGN CRS 47 exp. 3, 1699, Tetlama, Tancítaro district; AGN Crim. 730, 1713, Cuautitlan district; AJANG Criminal, bundle labeled "1818 leg. 2 (89)," Xalpan, Tlaltenango district (Indians complained that the lieutenant had not processed their suit against the cura).

104. AGN Hist. 319 exp. 15 ("Si estas [quexas] las exponemos a ellos [the priests] a más de no ser atendidos[,] después de maltratarnos lo hazen peor; si nos quexamos a los juezes seculares nos sucede lo mismo, por contemporisarse éstos con aquellos; de modo que precisamente por estos respectos, nos reduse nuestra mala suerte a una esclabitud perpetua"). Other examples of Indians and others charging parish priests and district governors with collusion: AGN RCO 93 exp. 103, 1768, Chacaltianguis, Cosamaloapan district (Oaxaca); AGN Crim. 203 exp. 2, 1769, Tepoztlan; RCO 126 exp. 137, 1777, Oaxaca; AGN Templos 25 exp. 9, 1799, Zacualtipan, Meztitlan district; AJANG Civil, box 231, doc. 1, 1804, Ocotlan (Jalisco).

105. AJANG Civil, box 117, doc. 4.

106. Ibid., box 59, doc. 11 ("Vuestra Real Jurisdicción se halla perdida y despreciada en este pueblo").

107. AGN CRS 67 exp. 3; AGN RCO 182 exp. 95, 1801 ("los excesos en que incurrían frecuentemente los curas párrocos y otros eclesiásticos para imponer la pena condigna a los culpados"). The intervention of district governors in fiestas, elections, cofradías, testaments drawn up by curas for other priests, and idolatry cases, are examples of this expanding authority. The issue of parish priests making testaments for other priests and inventorying their estates after death was raised in 1767. Tulane VEMC 26 exp. 3, 1767, Colima.

108. Ventura Beleña, 1: 144, Dec. 8, 1786. In jurisdictional disputes, the jueces eclesiásticos were advised by the audiencia to use "regulado y prudente método."

109. AJANG Civil, box 125, doc. 2. Brambila was the cura of Purificación in 1799. AGN Inq. 1346 exp. 6, fol. 32. Other jurisdictional disputes in which excommunication was employed: AGN Inq. 862, fols. 393–407, 1737, Chilpancingo (Guerrero); AGN Civil 59, 1761–62, Valladolid; AGN RCO 84 exp. 77, 1764, Tochimilco; AGN Acervo 49 caja 47,

1765, Tepecoacuilco; AGN Tierras 1929 exp. 9, 1772, Tlalmanalco; AJANG Civil, box 171, doc. 15, 1800, Villa de Sinaloa.

110. Some of the important cases of clashes between priests and district governors in the archdiocese are AGN CRS 68 exp. 3, 1771, 1774, San Felipe del Obraje, Ixtlahuaca district (in which the lieutenant took the cura's rage over the notification that he must post the arancel as an "ultraje a la jurisdicción real"); CRS 95 exp. 4, 1775, Tototepec, district of Zacualpan (where the cura was accused of imprisoning and punishing without royal auxilio: "pretende abusar de su autoridad para atropellar las determinaciones de esta Real Audiencia"); AGN Hist. 128 exp. 3, 1777, Chietla (Puebla); AGN Inq. 1113, fols. 231–54, 1777, Cempoala (in which the cura's charges against the alcalde mayor for sodomy and other gross misconduct turned into an investigation of the cura's sex life, gambling, and weaknesses as a pastor; the Inquisition eventually suspended the case because of the alcalde mayor's ardor in pursuing it); CRS 201 exp. 1, 1780, Ixtapalapa (in which the cura was unrepentant and uncooperative when the audiencia charged him with illegal whippings); Tulane VEMC 51 exp. 6, 1811, Otumba (in a dispute over amancebados, which was traditionally an ecclesiastical matter; the subdelegado claimed the cura acted as if he were "the absolute authority in this pueblo"); and AGN Bienes 663 exp. 24, 1817, Tlalmanalco. See also Hist. 578A, 1793, Taxco, Tetela del Río, and Yahualica reports for apparent examples described in some detail by district governors.

Two examples of impertinent public statements by parish priests in central Mexico that parallel the anticlerical ones by district governors are Inq. 1304 exp. 3, 1796; and Inq. 1360, exps. 1–2. In the first, the subdelegado of Zacualpan said he sat in the back of the church on Sunday to avoid the cura's gaze and sharp tongue, only to be singled out during the sermon with a salvo to the congregation that they "flee from that man who distances himself from the church and attends mass where he cannot (and doesn't have to) hear it." In the second, the cura of Otumba reportedly declared "que los Reyes estaban puestos por castigo de los hombres, como Dios havía puesto a Saúl."

Several of the cases of sharp and sweeping conflict in the Diocese of Guadalajara that are discussed in the following pages involved longtime curas and recently appointed district governors. One that is not mentioned elsewhere comes from the district of Tehuacan in the neighboring diocese of Puebla in 1792. The cura of Zoquitlan presumed that he was still entitled to certify local elections and order whippings when Indian parishioners did not fulfill their sacramental obligations, as he had done for 20 years. The subdelegado, whose French surname, Quilty Valois, was itself provocative, declared that the cura had no aptitude for his duties, that he acted as if he were the juez real in his parish, and that his lack of civility was intolerable. The rancor over election certifications, corporal punishment, and highhandedness between officials in this case was rooted in a deeper conflict over the cura's interference in local commerce. From the pulpit, the cura reportedly advised his Indian parishioners to drink homemade tepache rather than aguardiente de caña in order to break their ties with Spanish cochineal merchants. CRS 195 exp. 6.

111. AJANG Criminal, bundle labeled "1719–1787–1800, leg. 1," 1796, Tequila, subdelegado v. teniente párroco of Real de San Pedro Analco.

112. AJANG Civil, box 228, exp. 7.

113. AJANG Criminal, box 22, doc. 21.

114. Ibid., bundle labeled "1810 leg. 3 (15)," June 22, 1810, causa contra el presbítero d. Salvador Parra. See also ibid., caja 9 leg. 3 exp. 68.

115. Tulane VEMC 8 exp. 21. The case was filed without a verdict on Dec. 14, 1805, because the cura did celebrate the mass in question.

116. AGN Bienes 663 exp. 24. The tabernacle at issue was the special monumento that housed the consecrated Host during Holy Week: "Aparato que el jueves santo se forma en las iglesias, colocando en él en una arquita a modo de sepulcro la segunda hostia que

se consagra en la misa de aquel día, para reservarla hasta los oficios del viernes santo, en que se consume." *Diccionario de la lengua castellana*, p. 546.

A heated rivalry between the interim cura and subdelegado of Real de Cosalá (Guadalajara) between 1806 and 1810, in which the cura meddled in local litigation, and the subdelegado was of the view that the cura's pastoral duties should occupy all of his time, also came to a head during Easter week in 1807. The subdelegado forbade the traditional night processions as unruly, and the cura retaliated by withholding the key to the monumento on Maundy Thursday. As the cura said, the key was not supposed to be held by laymen, but that had clearly been the custom here and elsewhere. AJANG Civil caja 4 leg. 2 exp. 14, 1807; AJANG Criminal, bundle labeled "1806–1807 (74)," 1806–10. For another dispute over precedence and ceremony, see AGN Inq. 821 exp. 24, 1728, Tochimilco (Puebla), in which the alcalde mayor complained about the seating at mass on Palm Sunday in 1726.

117. AGN CRS 75 exp. 13. Two years later, the subdelegado of Tetela del Río, Joseph Antonio Velasco (who had been the subdelegado since 1789), criticized a vicario of the new coadjutor of Asuchitlan in much the same terms: "es caprichudo y temoso: varias vezes ha intendado mezclarse en los asuntos de la Real Jurisdicción, tratándola con desprecio, pero yo he procedido a su defensa en la parte posible." AGN Hist. 578A, 1793, Tetela del Río report.

118. AGN Acervo 49 caja 48.

119. AJANG Criminal, box 12, doc. 27. For a much earlier example of an alcalde mayor telling his Indian subjects not to obey the cura, see "Relación de agravios de los naturales de . . . Motines de Colima," 201–13. The archdiocese's visitador to the Huasteca in 1808 expressed suspicion of the lieutenant of Tampomolon, who "spoke ill of all ecclesiastics." AGN Acervo 49 caja 116.

120. AGN CRS 188 exp. 12, 1793, Villa Alta, Oaxaca; AGN Acervo 49 caja 146, 1805, Temascaltepec; AJANG Criminal, bundle labeled "1808 leg. 2 (6)," 1808, Chametla. For a similar, earlier complaint, see AGN Acervo 49 caja 48, 1700, Temascaltepec. See also Arze y Miranda's warning in his instructions to prospective tenientes de cura of 1766 that the alcaldes mayores and their lieutenants were often the parish priest's enemies.

121. AGN CRS 136 exp. 5. Angry over the corregidor's judgment against him in a property dispute, the cura of La Cañada, Querétaro district, made a similar sweeping complaint of anticlericalism in 1809. AGN CRS 217 exp. 5. Another case that a priest blamed on the subdelegado's enmity toward him and priests in general came to court in 1808. According to the cura of Pachuca, the subdelegado spread a rumor among the residents that he had chipped the parish church's piece of the Santo Lignum (Christ's cross) and patched it with wax. When a group of vecinos demanded to see the relic and the subdelegado ordered the cura to show it, he refused on the grounds that "el era cura de aquel lugar y que las notificaciones se le debían hacer de ruego y encargo." When the subdelegado repeated his order because a restless crowd had gathered, the cura responded that it was late—after nine in the evening—but that he would take the relic to the Franciscan guardian for his inspection. The cura declined to display the relic on September 14, as was the custom, and the matter went to the Audiencia of Mexico. The fiscal determined that part of the relic was, indeed, missing and had been replaced with wax. He wanted to know the condition of the wood when it first came to Pachuca but, in any case, he blamed the cura for the uproar, judging that "ha faltado a la buena armonía." Tulane VEMC 66 exp. 13.

122. AJANG Civil, box 120, doc. 5, 1786, Cuquío; BEJ Papeles de Derecho, 1: 458–59, 1795, Zapotiltic; AGN CRS 130 exp. 3, fols. 78ff, 1796, Tututepec. Irreverence was also implied by the curas of Xilotepec (Hidalgo) in 1773 and Valle de San Francisco (San Luis Potosí) in 1797. AGN Crim. 25 exp. 23; Crim. 159, fols. 163–80. The justicia of Ixtlahuaca (Edo. de México) failed to contribute to his cofradía, according to the cura in 1798. AGN CRS 72 exp. 18. Again, this kind of behavior was not new. For an early-18th-century

example of a choleric, irreligious alcalde mayor, see AGN Inq. 565 exp. 4, 1705, Autlan (Jalisco).

123. AJANG Civil, bundle labeled "1800–1809 leg. 3 (109)," subdelegado José Espinosa.

124. AGN Hist. 132 exp. 2 ("No hay quien no le note la falta de reverencia con que se le ve las vezes que va, indecentemente abierto, perdone V. Exa, de piernas, mirando sin compostura a todas partes i como pudiera estar en la calle, sin arrodillarse quando lo hazen todos los fieles por la veneración a el templo o por pedir esta circunstancia de rendimiento algunos de los misterios que entonces se representan").

125. AJANG Criminal, bundle labeled "1797–1800 leg. 1," document labeled exp. 34, contra George Márquez, 1792; AGN Alcaldes Mayores 3 exp. 1, 1770; AGN Inq. 1213 exp. 18.

126. AGN Inq. 546 exp. 5.

127. AGN Hist. 132 exp. 16, fol. 6v. For cases in which curas accused district governors of encouraging immoral behavior, see AGN CRS 204 exps. 9–10, 1760, Tejupilco, Temascaltepec district (Edo. de México); CRS 188 exp. 6, 1789, Choapan, Villa Alta (Oaxaca); CRS 188 exp. 12, 1793, Villa Alta (Oaxaca); CRS 130 exp. 3, 1796, Tututepec (Hidalgo); and CRS 39 exp. 5, 1803, Malacatepec (Edo. de México).

128. AJANG Civil box 116 doc. 4 ("dueño absoluto de la jurisdicción real que administro"). The lieutenant of Olinalá in 1781 claimed he wanted nothing more than to "cumplir la real provisión," and berated the cura for infringing on his jurisdiction over cofradías and encouraging Indians to litigate against their land rentals and go to ecclesiastical court without the lieutenant's permission. AGN CRS 13 exp. 3. Other examples of district governors and priests occupied with their own dignity: AGN Inq. 821 exp. 24, 1728, Tochimilco; AJANG Civil, box 59, doc. 11, 1753, Zacoalco; CRS 156 exp. 6, 1761, Atlatlaucan; CRS 68 exp. 3, 1771, San Felipe del Obraje; Inq. 1146 exp. 1, 1775, Xilotepec; AGN Hist. 132 exp. 14, 1790–91, Villa Alta; AGN Bienes 663 exp. 24, 1817, Tlalmanalco. For an earlier example, see AGN Acervo 49 caja 44, 1700, San Juan del Río.

129. AJANG Criminal, box 12, doc. 27 ("En fin a lo más pronto estaré en ese pueblo por mi o por un comisionado a purificar el asunto pues para administrar justicia no hay cosa que me impida [salvo las atenciones del servicio del soverano] ni jamás he oído ni oidré con enfado, . . . porque mi empleo es para en Gral oír y administrar justicia y por último VM save que en esto y en quanto guste puede con satisfacción orden lo que le agrade").

130. On charges of incontinencia, see AGN CRS 84 exp. 1, 1775, Yolotepec (Oaxaca); AGN Inq. 1113, fols. 231–54, 1777, Cempoala; and AGN Hist. 578A, 1793 Tixtla report. The intendant of Durango in 1789 was deeply critical of wealthy curas who lived without the appropriate "moderación y decencia." AGI Guad. 545.

131. AGN Hist. 132 exp. 14. The subdelegado of Huejutla (Hidalgo) in 1793 wrote at some length about Padre Pedro Antonio Lara, resident of the Hacienda de Santa Cruz, as a law unto himself. AGN Hist. 578A, Huejutla report.

132. The chronological information on Villarroel comes from Borah, "Alguna luz sobre el autor de las *Enfermedades políticas*." Villarroel probably filled out his term at Cuautla, since he was still listed as the alcalde mayor there in 1765. BN AF caja 139 exp. 1717.

133. AGN RCO 86 exp. 140 quotes the archbishop's report of April 19, 1762, in which he mentioned inadequate spiritual care by the parish clergy, but mainly blamed the "idolatry" and collective action at Yautepec in 1761 on justicias who fomented drunkenness, condoned illicit sex, resisted using corporal punishment, and levied various charges on Indian pueblos in order to enrich themselves.

134. AGN Alcaldes Mayores 11, exp. beginning at fol. 357 ("Si las quejas han sido contra mi antesesor desde luego serán infundadas, supuesto a que en los dos meses que exerzo el oficio no he tenido el más mínimo reclamo acerca de su conducta ni he enten-

dido aya causado extorsión alguna. Me persuado a que todo sea impostura y que se llevaría la quexa a este Superior Govierno por influxo de algún cura, que es la fuente de donde regularmente brotan las discordias, como la experiencia nos lo manifiesta en este desgraciado reino. No ai cura que directa o yndirectamente no influia contra el alcalde mayor para forticarse con la ruina de su adversario; para con esta mal aventurada política, ussar a su arvitrio de la autoridad, que jusga tener para ingerirse en todos los casos y cosas ajenas de su ministerio. El estilo y dogmas que regularmente enseñan algunos de dichos curas a los yndios es: que con qualquier orden o providencia que les dé el alcalde mayor ocurran ante si y siguen el semblante que les pone, da pauta a los yndios para que obedezcan o no lo que les manda el alcalde mayor si el alcalde mayor se opone [como es justo] a esta coruptela, inmediatamente se sigue el cisme, el reclamo y la quexa al superior govierno de donde dimana el trastorno del alcalde mayor, la buena armonía, la desolación del territorio, la falta de respeto en los yndios a la justicia y el engreimiento de los curas autorizados para perder a otro y todos los que sigan en el oficio").

135. Villarroel, pp. 416, 320.

136. Ibid., pp. 332, 89, 458.

137. Ibid., pp. 335, 469. Villarroel wanted the alcalde mayor to be the primary judge for virtually everything but Indian land cases (p. 85).

138. AGN Hist. 319 exp. 5 ("buscó modo de mortificarme porque le iba legalmente a la mano, a beneficio de aquellos vezindarios").

139. Ibid. ("pues todo quanto determiné y emprendí lo hize creyendo servía en ello a Dios, a la Religión, a Nuestro Cathólico Soberano, a la sagrada mitra, y a la República").

140. Judging by anonymous charges against the subdelegado of Cadereyta in 1791, the license of district governors and parish priests in this district continued, but with a distant collusion between them, more than conflict. The subdelegado was accused of selling tenientazgos to unsuitable mulatos and allowing curas to operate jails. AGN Hist. 132 exp. 7. Two years later, the subdelegado of Cadereyta mildly criticized the cura of San José del Pinal, 25 leagues from the cabecera, for exceeding his authority: "suele salir a rondar de noche, quitándole las vezes a la jurisdicción Real pero esto tal vez lo habrá echo movido de su piadoso zelo, sobre cuyo asumpto le tengo recombenido vervalmente." AGN Hist. 578A, Cadereyta report.

141. An earlier (1737) bitter dispute between the alcalde mayor and the Franciscan doctrinero at Acaponeta over jurisdiction and their personal animosity is recorded. AJANG Criminal, bundle labeled "1815 leg. 5 (101)."

142. *Recop.* 1-14-73 limited the audiencias and other secular courts to making inquiries against regular priests only in cases of public scandal. In such cases they could "require" the provincial or prelate to administer punishment commensurate with the offense. If such punishment was not applied, the case was to be presented to the Council of the Indies for disposition. *Recop.* 1-6-38 provided that priests could be removed from benefices by mutual agreement of the prelate and the vice-patron.

143. The 1791 case is documented in AJANG Civil, box 150, exp. 7; and AGN Hist. 128 exp. 10.

144. AJANG Civil, box 89, doc. 6, 1778; Civil, box 103, doc. 10, 1783–85. A lieutenant of Xilotepec seemed to be at fault for the abuses and lack of cooperation in 1773; two years later, it was the cura. AGN Crim. 25 exp. 23; AGN Inq. 1146 exp. 1.

145. AJANG Civil, box 80, doc. 2. The lengthy debate between the fiscal of the audiencia and the promotor fiscal of the diocese is recorded on fols. 18–43. According to the promotor fiscal, the posas amounted to "un responso que se canta puesto el cuerpo sobre una mesa con sus belas correspondientes."

146. Other cases in which the audiencia favored the district governor include AGN Inq. 1146 exp. 1, 1775, Xilotepec; AGN CRS 195 exp. 6, 1792, Zoquitlan, Puebla; and

AJANG Criminal, box 22, doc. 21, Valle de Topia, 1807- . Although the suit between the cura of Yolotepec (Oaxaca) and the alcalde mayor of Teposcolula in 1775 ended without a verdict because the cura died, his detailed complaint about the alcalde mayor's abuses of Indians and reparto de efectos turned into an investigation of his own alleged sexual misconduct. AGN CRS 84 exp. 1. Curas' complaints against district governors seem to have received less serious attention than the governors' complaints against curas in the late 18th century. Sometimes they were simply disregarded or dismissed as vague. See AGN Alcaldes Mayores 11, fols. 338–40, for a 1773 example from Ixtapan, Zacualpan district.

Though judicial opinion and royal decrees tipped against many customary rights of parish priests at this time, some decrees were intended to mark legal limits to these changes. A royal cedula of Dec. 21, 1787, confirmed the ecclesiastical courts' jurisdiction over concubinato cases but noted that the ecclesiastical judges were not to levy fines in such cases and were to execute the crown's general pardons. In February 1796, the viceroy circulated a royal cedula that protected curas from removal without due process (i.e., agreement between the prelate and the vice-patron that a cura should be removed was not regarded as sufficient cause). Tulane VEMC 23 exp. 5.

147. Brown Univ., Rockefeller Lib., Medina Coll., FHA 162 exp. 1 (1768 pastoral letter); FHA 163 exp. 1 (1769 pastoral letter). Two years later at the provincial council, Lorenzana and three bishops sounded a warning against the danger to the faith and the political order caused by irreligious foreign soldiers in the emerging colonial army—"capaz de pervertir este Reino, inficcionar la Religión y costumbres, sembrar malas semillas que insensiblemente van minotando la fidelidad al Soberano legítimo, el respeto a lo sagrado [y] un libertinaje pésimo e infernal . . . y todo lo pone en una confusión" (Oct. 24, 1771). Bravo Ugarte, *Historia de México*, 3: 23.

148. AGN RCO 182 exp. 84 ("¡Ha, Señor! Y como siente el clero americano ver tan lejos a su Rey y Protector, a su Monarca el Sol de España, cuyas luzes gozan los dichosos europeos"). The royal cedula in question was issued on Feb. 10, 1795. The biographies in Osores indicate that many clerics with law degrees were licensed to plead Audiencia of Mexico cases in the 18th century.

149. The question of ecclesiastical immunity in the late colonial period is probed in Farriss, *Crown and Clergy*.

150. AGN Civil 1603 exp. 5, fols. 26ff.

151. BN Manuscripts, no. 1314, Dec. 12, 1799 ("si los siglos de ignorancia produxeron desórdenes y abusos en el exercicio de la jurisdicción e inmunidades eclesiásticas, el siglo pretendido de las luzes disputando hasta lo más sagrado y arroyando como un torrente precipitado, la verdad con el herror, la piedad con el fanatismo y la autoridad con la superstición, ha destruido en el todo estos sagrados derechos o los ha reducido a una sombra de lo que deben ser").

152. AJANG Civil, box 80, doc. 2, fol. 23v (words of the promotor fiscal of Guadalajara in a 1772 case of licensing public processions).

153. AGN CRS 126 exps. 12–13, within fols. 296–301 ("en varios pueblos del curato de Tepehuacan hay indios que no oyen misa, no cumplen con los preceptos de Nuestra Santa Madre Yglesia, no llaman a confesión para enfermos, no quieren tener escuelas, y han perdido enteramente la subordinación a los eclesiásticos que es el principio elemental para llegar a no tener alguna a las potestades seculares. Como las historias acreditan, que la Religión Católica ha sido siempre el apoyo más sólido de los tronos"). For a similar view nearly 50 years before, but without imagining the collapse of colonial rule, see AGN CRS 179 exp. 13, fol. 406v, 1763, Actopan.

154. BMM 271. Peninsular curas serving outside the first-class parishes could probably not be counted on to take a blandly regalist position on parish reforms either. The district governor of Iguala (Guerrero) described the peninsular cura interino there in 1793 as

"genio fuerte y violento y algo inquieto. . . . Se ha querido introducir en las funciones de la Jurisdicción Real, sin embargo de las recombenciones amistosas que le han sido echas por mi." AGN Hist. 578A.

155. AGN Hist. 128 exp. 7 ("Es innegable que muchos señores governadores subalternas han abusado de su autoridad por condescender con sus pasiones [their subjects'], con injuria de la religión, en detrimento de la justicia y abatimiento del estado y los pueblos").

156. BMM 113, pp. 37–39; AGN Acervo 49 caja 47.

157. BMM 135 exp. 17, 1752–53, Fr. Arpide, Xiuctepec (Morelos); AGN CRS 23 exp. 6, 1767, Ozoloapan; AGN Templos 25 exp. 4, fol. 5v, 1769, Tlayacapan; AGI Mex. 2588, Jan. 26, 1784, report of cura Joseph Manuel Ruiz y Cervantes, Zimatlan (Oaxaca). Occasionally, a cura blamed the district governor for Indian disobedience or suggested that his anticlericalism was the cause of a local dispute. See AGN Crim. 25 exp. 23, 1773, Xilotepec; and Crim. 159, fols. 163–180, 1797, Valle de San Francisco (San Luis Potosí). In these two cases, the curas charged district governors with failing to provide auxilio, failing to punish Indian crimes, and encouraging drinking and gambling. The result, they claimed, was new insolence by the Indians and poor attendance at mass. "From judges to tyrants" comes from the cura of Acayucan (Veracruz) in 1787, quoted in Aguirre Beltrán, "Delación," p. 70. Such claims rarely received a sympathetic hearing in the audiencia. See, for example, CRS 156 exp. 5, 1758, Tepetlaostoc; and CRS 188 exp. 12, 1793, Villa Alta (Oaxaca). In 1809, the cura of La Cañada, Querétaro district, implied that Corregidor Domínguez (Father Hidalgo's ally in the plot against the viceregal government in 1810) had seized his bath house and mineral spring without due process because he was anticlerical. CRS 217 exp. 5.

158. AGN CRS 177 exp. 10, fols. 448–49.

159. In 1820, for example, the cura of Otumba referred to the "funesta y temible anarquía eclesiástica entre mis feligreses." AGN CRS 37 exp. 5.

160. AGN CRS 188 exp. 12, fol. 213 ("influyendo y persuadiendo a los naturales a que no nos obedescan, respeten, ni reverencien, protegiendo todos quantos negocios quieren promover contra nosotros, y dándoles a entender que estamos sujetos a su jurisdicción ordinaria sin excepción alguna y essa tan perversa doctrina ha logrado el fruto que su mal corazón desea en él de estos neóphitos, pues ya para ellos sus párrochos y demás ministros eclesiásticos somos unos yndividuos despreciables y no nos prestan obediencia, ni respeto alguno, y aun se entiende a más lo que con el más profundo dolor estamos advirtiendo, y es, el que ya se ba resfriando entre dichos naturales la devoción y fervor que iban adquiriendo en las cosas sagradas"). As early as 1766 Arze y Miranda, himself a former cura in the Diocese of Puebla, warned vicarios to be especially careful about administering whippings because district governors now encouraged Indians to be disrespectful toward their parish priests and encouraged them to litigate such matters.

161. AGN CRS 156 exp. 5, fol. 146v; CRS 136 exps. 6–7, fol. 306v. The promotor fiscal of the Diocese of Guadalajara used the same expression in the 1772 Sierra de Pinos case. AJANG Civil, box 80, doc. 2.

162. BMM 113, pp. 102–3. Examples of curas' appeals against reform: AGN CRS 137 exp. 8, 1805, Alahuistlan (cura urged the audiencia in 1805 "not to innovate" in the administration of community ranchos); CRS 178 exp. 12, 1805 Oaxaca (curas asked that "we may not suffer reform" in the arancel).

In an earlier statement of the cura's sense of predicament over eroding judicial authority, Martín Calderón—a Franciscan serving in Toluca in 1734—appealed for a return to the wide judicial powers of the 16th-century "evangelists." To his mind, Indians were bound for perdition unless parish priests had the power to "subject them to the yoke of the law for their spiritual well-being" because they were naturally inclined to irrational behavior. BMM 135 exp. 16, Jan. 4, 1734. Perhaps only a Franciscan would see the decline of judicial authority so emphatically in terms of a 16th-century high-watermark and Indian incapacity, but the more common combination in the late 18th century of a sense of decline and greater optimism about Indian capacity for reform had more unsettling political possibilities.

163. AGN CRS 217 exp. 6 ("burlándose a mi presencia aun los yndios jóvenes que he criado y veo infelismente prostituidos").

164. AGN CRS 179 exp. 13, fol. 406r. Additional evidence of this bitter dispute in Actopan, dating back to 1761, is in AGN Civil 2208 exps. 4–9. The cura issued an order of excommunication for the alcalde mayor and his chief lieutenant, while the alcalde mayor was quick to claim that his actions were "in defense of the Royal Jurisdiction."

165. AJANG Civil, box 197, doc. 10 ("para que como padre me haga saber el giro por donde pueda caminar").

166. Ibid., box 119, doc. 3 ("que después de Dios no tengo a quien apelar a más de a V. md porque es nuestro padre"). Other examples are AGN Crim. 77 exp. 9, 1771, Molango, Hidalgo (Indian widow appealed to the justicia "como a padre"); and AJANG Civil, box 89, doc. 6, 1778, Ocotlan, Jalisco (Indian officials testified that the lieutenant treated them like his sons).

167. AGN CRS 39 exp. 2, fols. 67–68, 1796, Capuluac. CRS 67 exp. 2, fol. 76, contains an intimidating 1767 letter from the cura of Ocoyoacac to the Indian gobernador of Atlapulco that addresses him repeatedly as "hijo." Or, as the cura of Olinalá wrote to the lieutenant on May 17, 1778, "Suplico a Ud se contenga de estar molestando a los dichos hijos." CRS 13 exp. 3.

168. AGN CRS 75 exp. 4, fols. 248–53 ("verdaderos hijos, como se berifica en el castigo que más es como de padres a hijos que como de jueces a [?]eos [reos?]"). Indian principales, especially the leading officeholders, were political fathers, too. The gobernador of Zacoalco (Jalisco) in 1769, for example, brushed aside a complaint by three principales against the new lieutenant because he, as "padre de Nuestra República y tributario de Su Magestad," spoke for the community. Indians of Tlajomulco (Jalisco) in 1808 complained that their alcalde had acted, "not as a benevolent father, but as a devouring lion." And the subdelegado of Tonalá in 1791 criticized the Indian alcalde of San Martín for designating new principales who, "even though they are elderly, lack the service, training, and merits that would make them *padres de república*" (aunque viejos carecen de los servicios, instrucción y méritos que los constituien padres de república). AJANG Civil, box 172, doc. 22; Civil, box 267, doc. 17; Civil, box 172, doc. 22. But rural Indians of all categories were inevitably treated as "hijos del pueblo" in their dealings with the colonial state.

Chapter Seventeen

EPIGRAPHS: AGN CRS 75 exp. 3, within fols. 117v–119v, San Felipe and Santiago, parish of Malacatepec, district of Metepec ("Este [arancel] se erigió con el santo fin de que los yndios sintieran la maior comodidad y no con el de engrosar a los curas el bolsillo"); CRS 75 exp. 5, fol. 326 ("Diles a los hijos de ese pueblo que los derechos parroquiales están mandados por derecho natural, por derecho divino, por derecho eclesiástico, y por derecho real, que no es limosna voluntaria como a ustedes les parese pues así como yo estoy obligado a darles a ustedes el pasto espiritual, así lo están ustedes a darme el pasto corporal como lo dice San Pablo").

1. AGN Acervo 49 caja 127, 1773, Jiquipilco, directorio.

2. AGN CRS 67 exp. 2, fol. 69v, dispute involving Ocoyoacac and Atlapulco, Tenango del Valle district ("Esta es una controversia frecuentísima entre los curas y naturales sus feligreses, y lo ha sido de muchos días a esta parte").

3. Only a handful of curas in the subdelegados' 1793 reports were singled out as having

escaped such a dispute. One was Pedro Berrio del Rincón, interim cura of Atotonilco el Chico, whom the subdelegado of Pachuca described as "de un manejo distinguido, pues no ha crusado en sus derechos parroquiales sentimiento de queja a sus feligreses." AGN Hist. 578A.

4. AGN Acervo 49 caja 116 ("no hay indio que en el día no quiera relebarse de lo que antes ha pagado a sus curas").

5. AJANG Civil, box 49, doc. 4, 1727, Poncitlan; Civil, bundle labeled "1795 leg. 35 (1)," 1795, Achichipico; AJANG Criminal, bundle labeled "1806 leg. 2 (11)," 1805, Zapotitlan.

6. *Metepec-Toluca-Lerma*: AGN DP 1 exp. 3, 1733, Toluca; AGN Civil 2292 exps. 10–11, 1733, Atlacomulco; AGN CRS 72 exp. 5, 1737, Atlacomulco; BMM 135 exps. 21–24, 1749, Zinacantepec; DP 1 exp. 7, and Tulane VEMC 69 exp. 1, 1749–69, Metepec district; CRS 153 exp. 3, 1751, Atotonilco; CRS 153 exp. 7, 1755, Malacatepec; CRS 178 exp. 13, 1756, Jiquipilco; JCB, Lucas García de Figueroa resumé, 1762, Lerma; Civil 2292 exp. 5, 1767, Otompan (Toluca); AGN CRS 68 exp. 3, 1771, San Felipe del Obraje; AGN Acervo 49 caja 127, 1773, Jiquipilco; CRS 75 exp. 3, 1774, Malacatepec; VEMC 28 exp. 12, 1775, Almoloya; CRS 136 exp. 4, 1783, Huichilapan; AGN Crim. 243 exp. 1, 1792, Amanalco; CRS 131 exp. 1, 1792, Calimaya; CRS 130 exp. 2, 1792, Zinacantepec; Crim. 148 exp. 2, 1792, Almoloya; Crim. 146, fols. 316–25, 1795, Almoloya; CRS 130 exp. 5, 1796, Zinacantepec; CRS 39 exp. 5, 1803, Malacatepec; CRS 84 exp. 10, 1804, Zinacantepec; CRS 178 exp. 13, 1805 Jiquipilco; AGN Templos 25 exp. 10, 1805, Temascalcingo.

Tenango del Valle: Civil 1599 exp. 9, 1708, Ocoyoacac; CRS 153 exp. 2, 1746, Ocoyoacac; Civil 2292 exp. 13, 1757, Chapultepec; CRS 67 exp. 2, 1766, Ocoyoacac; CRS 67 exp. 9, 1775, Ocoyoacac; AGN Hist. 578A, 1793, Tenango district; CRS 39 exps. 1–3, 1795–96, Capuluac.

Malinalco: CRS 72 exp. 2, 1724, Tecomatlan; CRS 156 exp. 11, 1765, Zumpahuacan; CRS 156 exp. 13, 1765, Tecualoya; AGN Bienes 575 exp. 46, 1789, Ocuilan; Hist. 578A, 1793, Tenancingo; CRS 84 exp. 6, 1800, Cuapasco; CRS 84 exp. 13, 1807, Ocuilan; Civil 2292 exps. 7–8, 1818, Malinalco.

Temascaltepec-Sultepec: CRS 42 exp. 1, 1732, Tejupilco; DP 2 exp. 3, 1746, Temascaltepec district; AGN RCO 72 exp. 29, 1752, Sultepec; CRS 156 exps. 2–3, 1756, Pozontepec; CRS 156 exp. 4, 1757, Capula; Crim. 210, fols. 189–205, 1758, Pozontepec; CRS 23 exp. 5 and 204 exps. 9–10, 1760, Tejupilco; CRS 23 exp. 6, 1767, Ozoloapan; Civil 2282 exp. 2, 1768, Guajulco; Templos 25 exp. 3, 1768, San Lucas; CRS 68 exp. 2, 1769, Ozoloapan; CRS 75 exp. 10, 1790, Valle de San Francisco; CRS 136 exps. 6–7, 1790–91, Temascaltepec; DP 3 exp. 4, 1799, Temascaltepec district.

Zacualpan: CRS 75 exp. 2, 1769, Ixtapan; CRS 67 exp. 6, 1770, Zacualpan district; CRS 75 exp. 4, 1775, Tototepec; CRS 75 exp. 6, 1786, Alahuistlan; Inq. 1334 exp. 3, 1796, Zacualpan; Crim. 166, fols. 185–272, Apaxtla.

Hidalgo: DP 1 exp. 2, 1721, Jilotepec; AGN Tierras 2774 exp. 6, 1721, Huazalingo (Yahualica); CRS 153 exp. 1, 1721, Tlaquilpa (Cempoala); DP 2 exps. 1, 3, 1727, Actopan; VEMC 15 exp. 5, 1739, Yahualica; DP 2 exps. 1, 3, 4, 1746, Actopan; Templos 25 exp. 2, 1753, Tianguistengo; CRS 153 exp. 6, 1755, San Gabriel (Cempoala); JCB, Nicolás Jiménez resumé, 1750's, Epasoyucan (Cempoala); CRS 156 exp. 7, 1761, Acambay (Jilotepec); DP 2 exp. 6, 1763–64, Actopan; CRS 156 exp. 12, 1765, Tlapanaloya (Tetepango); CRS 156 exp. 14, 1768, Acambay; CRS 75 exp. 1 and CRS 156 exp. 14, 1768–90, Acambay; Crim. 308, 1769, Sierra de Tututepec (Tulancingo); Inq. 1146 exp. 1, 1775, Simapantongo (Jilotepec); Crim. 79 exp. 1, 1777, Coamelco, Cholula (parish of Tlamatlan, Meztitlan district); CRS 74 exp. 1, 1780, Molango (Meztitlan); AGN Diezmos 8 exp. 1, 1778, Tepejí del Río; CRS 72 exp. 8, 1785, Tlaxpa (Tepejí del Río); CRS 75 exp. 5, 1785, San Luis de las

Peras (Huichapan); CRS 136 exp. 5, 1785, Molango (Meztitlan); Crim. 202 exp. 1, 1789, Tixmadeje (Huichapan); CRS 75 exp. 9, 1790, Atengo (Tepetitlan); Hist. 578A, 1793, Atotonilco el Chico (Pachuca report); Hist. 578A, 1794, Yahualica (Yahualica report); Acervo 49 caja 97E, 1796, Tasquillo (Huichapan); CRS 130 exp. 3, 1796, Tututepec (Tulancingo); CRS 130 exp. 8, 1799, Tulancingo district; Templos 25 exp. 9, 1799, Zacualtipan (Meztitlan); DP 3 exps. 5-6, 1806, Jilotepec; DP 3 exp. 8, 1812, Huautla (Huejutla); CRS 136 exp. 8, 1817, Acatlan (Tulancingo).

Querétaro-Guanajuato-San Luis Potosí: Acervo 49 caja 50, 1749, Villa de Valles; Crim. 305 exp. 4, 1768, Xichú; Bienes 210 exp. 26, 1791- , Cozcatlan (Villa de Valles); CRS 57 exp. 3, 1796-99, Xichú; Bienes 172 exp. 36, 1803, San Sebastián Querétaro; Acervo 49 caja 116, 1808-9, pastoral visit to Tamazunchale, Tampomolon, Tancanhuitz, and Yahualica.

Guayacocotla y Chincontepec: Bienes 210 exp. 1, 1731; Templos 1 exp. 2, 1786-88; CRS 217 exp. 6, 1808, Tzontecomatlan.

Morelos: DP 1 exp. 1, 1671, Cuernavaca district; BMM 135, 1672, Cuernavaca district; CRS 72 exp. 3, 1730, Tetecala; Civil 2121 exp. 10, 1736, Jonacatepec; Crim. 174, fols. 157-239, 1740, Guecaguasca (Jamiltepec parish, Cuautla district); CRS 204 exp. 6, 1743, Ocuituco (Cuautla); DP 1 exp. 5, 1748, Tlaltizapan; BMM 135, 1752, Tetecala; DP 2 exp. 5, 1760-61, Hueyapan (Cuautla); CRS 156 exp. 8, 1761, Ocuituco; CRS 156 exp. 9, 1763, Zacualpan de las Amilpas; CRS 68 exps. 4-5, 1775, Cuanacalcingo; CRS 72 exp. 7, 1777, Hueyapan; Crim. 203 exp. 4, 1778, Tepoztlan; CRS 136 exp. 1, 1780, Cuanacalcingo; CRS 84 exp. 3, 1780, Tlacochahuaya; CRS 136 exp. 2, 1781, Tlaltizapan; DP 3 exp. 1, 1786, Tlaquiltenango; AGN CRS 72 exp. 10, 1789, Tlaquiltenango; VEMC 53 exp. 6, 1791- , Tepoztlan; VEMC 3 exp. 5, 1794, Tepoztlan; CRS 140 exps. 4-5, CRS 178 exp. 9, 1797, Yautepec; Civil 2292 exp. 3, 1796, Tetecala; DP 3 exp. 3, 1797, Tlaltizapan; CRS 177 exp. 10, 1800, Mazatepec.

Chalco district, in or near Morelos: DP 2 exp. 2, 1677, 1745, Amecameca; CRS 156 exp. 6, 1761, Tlayacapan; Templos 25 exp. 4, 1769, Tlayacapan; Diezmos 8 exp. 1, 1778, Ozumba; VEMC 62 exp. 37, 1793, Tenango Tepopula; Templos 25 exp. 8, 1796, Amecameca; CRS 130 exp. 9, 1816, San Miguel Atlautla.

Guerrero: CRS 204 exp. 3, 1726, Tixtla district; CRS 204 exp. 5, 1740, Tixtla district; Bienes 431 exp. 17, 1771, Iguala; CRS 30 exp. 2, 1774, Xoxutla (Chilapa); CRS 67 exp. 10, 1776, Tetelcingo (Tixtla); CRS 183 exp. 3, 1779, Tixtla district; Hist. 319 exp. 15, 1782, Cacaguatepec (Acapulco); Crim. 181, fols. 238-300, 1787, Acapetlahuaya (Ichcateopan): CRS 75 exp. 11, 1790, Ajuchitlan (Tetela del Río); Hist. 578A, 1793, Zumpango del Río (Tixtla report); CRS 195 exp. 12, 1794, Chilpancingo (Tixtla).

Valley of Mexico area (see also Cempoala under Hidalgo and Chalco above): Cuautitlan district, DP 2 exp. 7, 1748-59, Teoloyucan; CRS 68 exp. 1, 1759, Teoloyucan; DP 3 exp. 2, 1797, Cuautitlan; VEMC 3 exp. 4, 1820, Coyotepec. Huizquilucan, Tacuba districts, VEMC 39 exp. 15, 1762, Huizquilucan; Civil 1485 exp. 12, 1762, Huizquilucan; Crim. 120 exp. 25, 1769, Huizquilucan; CRS 130 exp. 10, 1818, Tacuba. San Cristóbal Ecatepec district, VEMC 68 exp. 20, 1765, Acosac; Civil 2114 exp. 8, 1780, Tolpetlac; CRS 30 exp. 3, 1782, Tolpetlac. Xochimilco district, CRS 29 exp. 8, 1738, Tecomic; Crim. 232 exp. 7, 1800, Xochimilco district.

Other: Acervo 49 caja 46, 1739, Churubusco; CRS 156 exp. 5, 1758, Tepetlaostoc district; CRS 67 exp. 5, 1768, Tlalnepantla; Acervo 49 caja 44, 1778, Tacubaya; Templos 25 exp. 11, 1807, Oztoticpac (Otumba).

7. JCB, 1762, Simón Thadeo de Castañeda Castro y Guzmán resumé. Mazín *Entre dos majestades*, p. 107, notes the same problem of collecting fees in Michoacán.

8. New fees, higher charges: Tulane VEMC 16 exp. 12, 1757, Ozumba; AGN CRS 204 exp. 9, 1760, Tejupilco; CRS 156 exp. 12, 1765, Tlapanaloya, Tetepango district; CRS 75

exp. 9, 1790, Santa María Atengo, Tepetitlan parish; CRS 75 exp. 10, 1790, San Lucas del Valle de San Francisco, Temascaltepec district; AGN Crim. 152, fols. 270–312, 1801, San Ildefonso, Metepec district.

Fiestas: CRS 72 exp. 4 fol. 63, 1734, Huetamo; CRS 156 exps. 2–3, 1756, Sultepec pueblos; CRS 156 exp. 5, fol. 146v, 1758, Tepetlaostoc; CRS 204 exp. 9, fols. 312–18 and 338–62, 1760, Tejupilco; AGN Inq. 1146 exp. 1, 1775, Xilotepec ranchería.

Complaints of breaking custom were legion, particularly on fees. For example, AGN DP 2 exp. 5, 1760, Hueyapan; CRS 156 exp. 8, 1761, Ocuituco, Cuauhtla Amilpas district; CRS 156 exp. 12, 1765, Tlapanaloya, Tetepango district; Crim. 79 exp. 1, fol. 19v, 1777, Tlamatlan, Meztitlan district; CRS 84 exp. 3, 1780, Tlacochahuaya, Cuernavaca district; VEMC 62 exp. 37, 1793, Tenango Tepopula, Tlalmanalco district; Inq. 1146 exp. 1, 1775, Xilotepec (a rancho claimed the new cura was breaking custom by not coming to administer baptism and last rites; the Indians decried his "antiguas novedades," trying to make them have mass every Sunday); CRS 136 exps. 6–7, 1790–91, San Francisco Temascaltepec (cofradía lands); CRS 137 exp. 5, 1803, San Simón Tototepec, Zacualpan district (obra pía ranchos).

But the diocesan priests did have to depend on obvenciones more than the regulars: CRS 75 exp. 5, 1785, San Luis de las Peras, Huichapan district (cura would not say a votive mass in a visita during the week without a 4p fee); CRS 30 exp. 2, 1774, Xocutla and Nazintlan, Chilapa district (to Indians' complaints in these recently secularized pueblos of "unjust services and contributions," cura replied that there was no custom here despite the Indians' claim that there was, and that in any case the agreements with the Mendicant doctrineros "no han sido adaptables a los clérigos").

9. AGN CRS 156 exp. 9. Other examples of diocesan curas in a quandary about the appropriate fees to charge include CRS 156 exp. 8, 1761, Ocuituco, Cuautla district (cura of this formerly Augustinian doctrina sought clarification about fees because he did not know what they should be); and CRS 68 exp. 1, 1759, Teoloyucan, Cuautitlan district (cura was uncertain what to charge because Indians were not paying the arancel but could or would not document the customary arrangement). Other examples of Indian parishioners taking the comings and goings of the new secular curas as occasions to alter the terms of their sponsorship of the parish priest: CRS 156 exp. 12, 1765, Tlapanaloya, Tetepango district; CRS 204 exp. 5, following fol. 198, 1740, Tixtla (petition by gobernador and others).

10. AGN CRS 156 exp. 7.

11. Trent, 24th Session, Reform, ch. 13: "In parochial churches also in which the revenues are in like manner so small that they are insufficient to meet the necessary obligations, the bishop, if unable to meet the exigency by a union of benefices, not however those of regulars, shall see to it that by the assignment of first fruits or tithes or by the contributions and collections of the parishioners, or in some other way that he shall deem more profitable, as much be collected as may decently suffice for the needs of the rector and the parish."

12. Summarized in *Recop.* 1-8-9. The first and second provincial councils for the viceroyalty (1555, 1565) did not move directly toward aranceles. Parish priests could receive contributions but were subject to stiff penalties if they charged for the sacraments. *Concilios provinciales primero, y segundo*, pp. 188–89.

13. These laws, some of which invoked the Council of Trent or provincial councils, were summarized in *Recop.* 1-7-43 (1642), 1-8-9 (1538), 1-13-6 (1560, 1594, 1614, 1624), 1-13-13 (1643), and 1-18-10 (1594), and cited repeatedly in 18th-century fee disputes. Solórzano 4-15-58 stated that curas were to follow aranceles.

14. One of the third council's decrees called on curas not to demand "cantidad alguna que excede a la señalada en el arancel público"; that is, "lo que justamente les esté regu-

lado." The decree added that "cuando lo percibiesen o cobrasen asienten lo que sea en un libro, en que expresen el día, mes y año, firmando la nota correspondiente en unión de los procuradores del lugar o del pueblo, para que siempre haya memoria del hecho, y se cierre la puerta a las calumnias y falsos testimonios." *Concilio III*, p. 223.

15. In Antequera, for example, the two important aranceles were issued in 1617 (with minor modifications in 1699 and 1703) and 1805. AGN CRS 178 exp. 12; CRS 39 exp. 6; BN, Manuscripts, no. 1257 exp. 7.

16. For earlier instructions to parish priests to abide by the terms of the arancel, see the 1638 schedule for the archdiocese in *Colección de documentos eclesiásticos*, 1: 75; and AGN RCO 39 exp. 32, 1718.

17. On the variation of customary derechos within a parish, see BMM 135, exps. 21–24, 1749, Zinacantepec parish (parish fees took the form of a local schedule that combined chickens, cash, and candles); CRS 68 exp. 3, 1771, San Felipe del Obraje, Metepec district; CRS 75 exp. 3, 1774, Malacatepec, Metepec district; and CRS 72 exp. 10, 1789, Tlaquiltenango.

18. AGN CRS 204 exps. 9–10. See CRS 75 exp. 2 for 1769 records of lingering dispute in Ixtapan.

19. AGN CRS 204 exps. 9–10, fol. 316 ("Los trata con palabras injuriosas ya sea al gobernador ya a los alcaldes ya a los regidores y a otros viejos que han obtenido semejantes cargos de república, y aun muchas vezes por causas sumamente ligeras los manda azotar publicamente en la puerta de la yglesia los días domingos a vista y en presencia de todos los hombres y mujeres, que en semejantes días ocurren a la misa; llegando a tanto extremo su mal trato que le tiene dado orden a sus vicarios para que sin reserva alguna executen lo proprio como ansí lo hazen, hasta llegar ellos con sus proprias manos a quitarles las balcarrotas, y a darles con el bastón: de suerte que según se me informa, por haverse doceado, que el cura intenta azotar al gobernador interino a los alcaldes assí de aquella cavezera como del pueblo de San Simón y tres viejos, temorosos de que ponga en execución semejantes amenazas; se han retirado de tal modo que ni aun asisten a la misa").

20. I did not find a verdict in this record. By the 1770's, it would likely have been a brief order for all parties to obey the arancel, and for the Indians to pay first fruits.

21. *Colección de documentos eclesiásticos*, 1: 73–75.

22. A 1670 addendum is mentioned in AGN CRS 67 exp. 2, fols. 11ff. The 1683 revision appears in *Colección de documentos eclesiásticos*, 1: 76–80; the one of Dec. 2, 1691, is mentioned in AGN CRS 72 exp. 2, 1724, Malinalco; and CRS 68 exp. 2, 1769, Ozoloapan. These amendments added a few services not listed in 1638 but did not change the terms of that arancel. For the 1720 arancel of Archbishop Lanciego, see AGN RCO 59 exp. 47. According to a note in AGI Mex. 2531, the Mexico City government submitted a memorial in 1739 "sobre haberse dejado de observar de algún tiempo a esta parte el arancel de derechos parroquiales que formó su Arzobispo d. Fr. José Lanciego." Archbishop Rubio y Salinas noted in his 1752 pastoral visit that he was finalizing an arancel to "servir para todas las parrochias de nuestra Diócesis." AHM L10A/5, unnumbered folio near the beginning. His Nov. 11, 1757, arancel appears in *Colección de documentos eclesiásticos*, 1: 80–87; and BN LaFragua Coll., no. 564. Apparently it applied only to Mexico City. Rubio y Salinas wrote that the earlier arancel (of 1720?) was not in effect when he assumed office, and that when he had tried to implement it in 1750, doubts were raised at court and by the priests of the sagrario parish. Van Oss, *Catholic Colonialism*, p. 178, describes a similar chronology of aranceles for Guatemala: the first arancel, published in 1660, served until 1787; its replacement was in effect until 1822.

23. Some cases in which the 1637 arancel was invoked: AGN Tierras 2774 exp. 6, 1721, Huazalingo; AGN CRS 23 exp. 5, 1733, 1760, Tejupilco; Tulane VEMC 15 exp. 5, 1739, Yahualica; CRS 153 exp. 2, 1746, Ocoyoacac; AGN DP 2 exp. 5, 1760, Cuautla; VEMC 68

exp. 20, 1765, San Cristóbal Ecatepec; CRS 156 exp. 11, 1765, Malinalco; CRS 67 exp. 2, 1766, Ocoyoacac. Lorenzana's arancel of 1767 referred to the current one as being more than a century old.

24. On calidad, see McCaa.

25. AGN CRS 68 exp. 3, fol. 210v, 1771 fiscal; CRS 130 exp. 3 fol. 44, 1796 (the audiencia wanted uniformity).

26. AGN CRS 68 exp. 3 fol. 210v, 1771, San Felipe del Obraje ("seminario de quexas, disturbios, y pleitos").

27. AGN CRS 72 exp. 8, 1785, Tlaxpa ("Cortar las raíces de los pleitos"). See also AGN Acervo 49 caja 127, 1773, Jiquipilco (directorio carried out "para que sesen discordias").

28. Lorenzana's point about the early aranceles is supported not only in the amendments to the 1637–38 arancel and the variety of interpretations of it in individual cases, but in a 1775 report by the bishop of Durango noting that an arancel originally issued in 1648 had been amended to apply special local fee schedules in the districts of Alamos (1725), Real del Rosario (1725), Culiacán (1729), Papasquiaro (1739), Parras (1761), and Albuquerque and Villa Nueva in New Mexico. BEJ Papeles de Derecho, 2: 373–76.

29. See *Colección de documentos históricos*, 4: 1, 301–12. Sentiment in the Fourth Provincial Council in 1771 was strongly in favor of the arancel. CPM, p. 116.

30. BN LaFragua Coll., no. 564 ("poner fin a la dilatada controversia"), quoting a royal cedula of Dec. 24, 1746.

31. BEJ Papeles de Derecho, 2: 373–76.

32. Ventura Beleña, 2: 196, doc. 45 ("perdonarlos a los pobres y miserable gente").

33. Some of the standard verdicts: AGN CRS 75 exp. 3, 1774, Malacatepec; CRS 68 exps. 4–5, 1775, Cuanacalcingo, Cuernavaca district; CRS 75 exp. 4, 1775, Zacualpa; CRS 136 exp. 4, 1783, Huichilapan, Tenango del Valle district; CRS 130 exp. 3, 1796, Tututepec, Tulancingo district; AGN Templos 25 exp. 9, 1799, Zacualtipan, Meztitlan district; CRS 39 exp. 5, 1803, Malacatepec; Templos 25 exp. 10, 1805, Temascalcingo.

34. The cura of Temascalcingo in 1805 noticed this pattern in audiencia judgments during the last third of the 18th century. AGN Templos 25 exp. 10. Although royal laws and audiencia verdicts apparently did not speak of it, the arancel was sometimes presented to the courts by attorneys for the pueblos as a kind of liberation for Indians and, by implication, a method for the crown to recover political power from the clergy. See, for example, the argument in AGN CRS 68 exp. 3, fols. 268–91, Sept. 2, 1771, San Felipe del Obraje, that custom, as opposed to the arancel, had made the Indians "feudatarios de los curas ministros."

35. AGN CRS 75 exp. 2.

36. Ibid. exp. 3, fols. 117v–119v, 143, 1774, Malacatepec, Metepec district ("aborrece el arancel"); AGN Hist. 319 exp. 15, 1782 ("no observando ni teniendo más aranzel que el que le influye su codicia").

37. AGN CRS 153 exp. 7, 1755, Malacatepec (claim that cura was imposing old custom); CRS 75 exp. 6, 1786, Alahuistlan, Zacualpan district (pueblo did not want cura's custom); AGN DP 3 exp. 1, 1786, Tlaquiltenango (claim that cura would not follow either custom or the arancel); AGN Bienes 575 exp. 46, 1789, Ocuilan, Malinalco district (claim that cura was not following the arancel); CRS 136 exp. 8, 1817, Acatlan, district of Tulancingo, Hidalgo (Indians wanted custom abolished).

38. AGN CRS 72 exp. 2.

39. AJANG Civil, box 49, doc. 4 ("para negarle el servicio").

40. AGN CRS 42 exp. 1 (title page: "sobre que se arregle al arancel y no los obligue a servicios involuntarios").

41. AGN Civil 1485 exp. 12 ("mandaron se libre a estas partes testimonio que sirba de

Real Provición como lo piden con la pena de 200 pesos"). In a similar early 1760's case, San Gaspar Amatepec and Santiago Atlaya in the district of Zacualpan complained of personal service. The cura responded that they were not arancelados and therefore could be compelled to perform traditional service. They countered by requesting the arancel, "so that they will know what they have to pay." The audiencia granted their request on April 29, 1763, and ordered the alcalde mayor to enforce the arancel's provisions. AGN CRS 67 exp. 6.

42. AGN Templos 25 exp. 3, 1768, San Lucas, Tejupilco parish; AGN CRS 75 exp. 3, 1774, San Felipe and Santiago, Malacatepec parish, Metepec district; CRS 183 exp. 3, 1779, Tetelcingo, Tixtla parish; CRS 136 exp. 1, 1780, Cuanacalcingo and Huispaleca, Tlaltizapan parish; AGN Acervo 49 caja 97E, 1796, four barrios of Tasquillo, Huichapan district; AGN Crim. 232 exp. 7, 1800, Telazaltemalco, San Gregorio parish, Xochimilco district.

43. AGN CRS 75 exp. 3.

44. AGN Templos 15 exp. 9. Another 1790's Hidalgo petition for the arancel in order to stop personal services appears in AGN CRS 130 exp. 3, Tututepec, Tulancingo district.

45. AGN CRS 75 exp. 3, last document, Jan. 8, 1777, petition. In June 1779, the Indians of San José Malacatepec finally agreed to pay "punctually" the fees prescribed in the arancel, but the parishioners of Asunción Malacatepec still balked at following either the terms of the arancel or their customary arrangement. AHM L10B/21, fols. 98r–103r.

46. The visitas of Cuanacalcingo and Huispaleca in the parish of Tlaltizapan (Morelos), for example, were advised in 1780 that their court order forbidding personal service did not mean they could withhold the semaneros who performed services essential to the spiritual mission of the parish—in this case, a fiscal, sacristanes, acolytes, a bellringer, and a general assistant (topil). AGN CRS 136 exps. 1–2. For another example, see CRS 75 exp. 6, 1786, Alahuistlan, Zacualpan district.

47. As late as 1800, a court case revealed that the small pueblo of Telazaltemalco, San Gregorio parish, Xochimilco district, was being forced to provide six men and one boy to serve for three-week periods in the cabecera. AGN Crim. 232 exp. 7.

48. AGN CRS 183 exp. 3. A similar case from 1768 is documented for San Lucas, Temascaltepec district. AGN Templos 25 exp. 3. Solórzano 4-17-84 and 4-17-85 regarded the construction of the pastor's residence as an obligation of Indian parishioners. By extension, they were also presumably responsible for repairing it.

49. A sample of 27 cases of arancel suits against new curas were concentrated in the years after 1750: 1720's (1 case); 1730's (1); 1740's (2); 1750's (6); 1760's (5); 1770's (1); 1780's (1); 1790's (6); 1800's (4). Those late colonial cases include AGN CRS 153 exp. 7, 1755, Malacatepec, Metepec district; CRS 156 exp. 1, 1756, San Gaspar, Metepec district; AGN Crim. 210, fols. 189–205, 1758, Pozontepec, Sultepec district; CRS 156 exp. 5, 1758, Tepetlaostoc; CRS 23 exp. 5 and CRS 204 exps. 9–10, 1760, Tejupilco, Ixtapan, and Acatitlan, Temascaltepec district; CRS 156 exp. 6, 1761, Atlatlaucan, Tlayacapan district; CRS 156 exp. 8, 1761, Ocuituco, Cuautla district; JCB, 1762, Epasoyucan; CRS 23 exp. 6, CRS 68 exp. 2, 1766–69, Ozoloapan; CRS 183 exp. 3, 1779, Tixtla; CRS 136 exp. 2, 1781, Tlaltizapan; CRS 188 exp. 7, 1790, Tlacotalpan; CRS 136 exps. 6–7, 1790–91, Temascaltepec; CRS 131 exp. 3, 1792, Calimaya; CRS 39 exp. 3, 1795, Capuluac; AGN Templos 25 exp. 8, 1796, Amecameca; CRS 130 exp. 5, 1796, Zinacantepec, Metepec district; Crim. 232 exp. 7, 1800, Telazaltemalco, Xochimilco district; AJANG Civil, box 231, doc. 1, 1804, Ocotlan (Jalisco); AGN Templos 25 exp. 10, 1805, Temascalcingo, Ixtlahuaca district; Templos 25 exp. 11, 1807, Oztoticpac, Otumba district; CRS 217 exp. 6, 1808, Tzontecomatlan.

50. Complaints of curas' "innovations" in collecting fees: AGN CRS 75 exp. 4, 1775, Tototepec, Zacualpan district; CRS 74 exp. 1, 1780, Molango, Meztitlan district; AGN

Bienes 575 exp. 46, 1789, Ocuilan, Malinalco district; CRS 72 exp. 10, 1789, Tlaquil-tenango, Cuernavaca district; CRS 75 exp. 9, 1789, Tepetitlan, Tula district; CRS 75 exp. 10, 1790, Valle de San Francisco (San Luis Potosí); CRS 57 exp. 4, fol. 267, 1796–99, Xichú, San Luis de la Paz district; AGN DP 3 exp. 4, 1799, Temascaltepec; AGN CRS 130 exp. 8, 1799, Tulancingo; AGN Templos 25 exp. 9, 1799, Meztitlan; AGN Crim. 232 exp. 7, 1800, Xochimilco; AGN CRS 178 exp. 13, 1805, Jiquipilco, Ixtlahuaca district; Templos 25 exp. 10, 1805, Temascalcingo, Ixtlahuaca district; Tulane VEMC 3 exp. 4, 1820, Coyotepec, Cuautitlan district.

51. AGN CRS 75 exp. 9, fol. 451.

52. Indian parishioners who "won" the arancel: AGN CRS 153 exp. 1, 1721, San Pablo Tlaquilpa, Cempoala district; CRS 153 exp. 3. 1751, Atotonilco, Metepec district; CRS 156 exp. 4, 1754, Sultepec; CRS 156 exp. 10, 1763, Amealco, Huichapan district; CRS 156 exp. 13, 1765, San Lucas, San Mateo, and Santiago de Tecualoyan, Malinalco district; CRS 204 exps. 9–10, 1760, Tejupilco; CRS 68 exp. 2, 1769, Ozoloapan, Temascaltepec district. The cura of Zinacantepec, Metepec district, in 1796 thought the suit against him over the arancel had been lodged because some local leaders believed they had driven his predecessor out of the parish with a similar complaint. CRS 130 exp. 5.

53. AGN CRS 204 exps. 9–10, fols. 338–62, ch. 78 ("que como por costumbre lo [the arancel] sacan siempre que les ba nuevo cura, lo avían también sacado para mi parte desde su ingreso al curato, antes que tomassen conocimiento de su porte").

54. AGN CRS 39 exp. 3, fols. 98–101, July 21, 1796 ("Ha tratado y comunicado con frecuencia a dicho cura y puede asegurar que no habrá muchos que le exedan en con-ducta, celo, y actibidad en el cumplimiento de su ministerio tratando a los naturales sus feligreses con el amor y equidad que le exigen sus christianos honrrados y areglados pro-cedimientos. . . . algunos espíritus inquietos como son los que hablan en el precedente escrito concebido en la parte sustancial de falseada resentidos de las correcciones con que dicho cura solicita cortarles el arraigado bicio de la embriaguez de que están poseídos. Todo el ruidoso aparato de su representación según me hallo informado es sobre haberles fixado el cura el arancel para que se areglen a éste para la contribución de derechos parro-quiales por no querer cumplir con los asignados por constumbre").

55. See, for example, provisor's ruling in AGN Hist. 319 exp. 5, 1777, Xalpan, Cade-reyta district.

56. AGN Civil 2114 exp. 8, 1780, Tolpetlac, Ecatepec district (cura complained of Indians' "revoluciones y sediciones" and "la criminal libertad que desean").

57. Quest for despachos: AGN CRS 47 exp. 4, fols. 39ff, 1729, San Gerónimo, Cho-lula district (Puebla); CRS 67 exp. 2, fol. 76, 1766, Atlapulco and Ocoyoacac, Tenango del Valle district; CRS 68 exp. 2, fol. 66, 1769, Ozoloapan, Temascaltepec district; CRS 75 exp. 9, fols. 451, 458v, 1790, Atengo and Sayula, Tepetitlan parish, near Tula, Hidalgo.

58. AGN Alcaldes Mayores 11, fol. 338 ("sino es por letra [de] los mandatos de los superiores").

59. In 1785, the cura of the Villa de la Peña de Francia, Huichapan district (Hidalgo), accused the Indians of San Luis de las Peras of treating clerical fees as voluntary offerings now that they had the arancel. AGN CRS 75 exp. 5. Late colonial pastoral visitors in the archdiocese encountered this attitude, too, especially in the 1770's. AHM L10B/13, fols. 34r, 225v–226v; L10B/21, fols. 84, 98r–103r. Other cases of Indian parishioners requesting the arancel and then following it and the usual spiritual obligations only selectively include CRS 23 exp. 6, 1767, Ozoloapan, Temascaltepec district; CRS 68 exp. 3, fol. 210v, 1771, San Felipe del Obraje, Ixtlahuaca district; CRS 68 exps. 4–5, 1775, Cuanacalcingo; CRS 136 exp. 2, fols. 196–209, 1781, Huispaleca and Cuanacalcingo (Pueblo Nuevo), Tlaltiza-pan parish, Cuernavaca district (cura's defense); Tulane VEMC 3 exp. 5, 1791, Tepoztlan;

CRS 130 exp. 8, 1799, Huitlalpa, Tulancingo district; and CRS 217 exp. 4, 1809, Pilcayan, near Taxco.

60. AGN CRS 68 exp. 3 ("el arancel manda que no se lleven derechos y así qualquiera cosa que se les exija les parece fuera de arancel . . . imaginan que el cura no puede obligar a los indios aranzelados al cumplimiento de la ley de Dios, por cuya idea ni en sus pueblos tienen doctrina; ni vienen a esta cabecera los niños los sábados en comunidad"; "aseverándoles que el arancel se dirige a dexarlos a su arbitrio"; "instrumento auténtico de su libertad . . . para su resguardo").

Other cases in which visitas or whole parishes used the arancel as license to suspend other payments of duties include AGN Bienes 431 exp. 17, 1771, Iguala (cura claimed the Indians were "insolentados o bien engreídos con el despacho que obtuvieron de aranceles"); CRS 75 exp. 4, fols. 221v–222r, 1775, San Simón Tototepec, Zacualpan district (cura reported "con el motivo de estar en el arancel se han revestido de una total ynobediencia y se han querido exhimir aun de las precisas obligaciones de christianos, pues assí para la escuela, como para el presepto de la misa se experimenta en ellos la maior reveldía"); and Tulane VEMC 3 exp. 5, 1794, Tepoztlan (cura accused Indians of spreading the rumor that with his having to obey the arancel, all the misas and fiestas would stop).

61. Tulane VEMC 15 exp. 5; AGN CRS 136 exps. 6–7. Since there was almost always more involved than a disagreement over fees, the citations would be nearly as long as the list of arancel cases. One example from Nueva Galicia is AJANG Criminal, bundle labeled "1806 leg. 2 (11)," April 22, 1805, Zapotitlan (Indians v. cura). Calling for the arancel also allowed Indian parishioners to avoid compromises and deals, or so they expected. CRS 72 exp. 8, fols. 139–63, 1785, Tlaxpa v. cura of Tepejí del Río (this was the opinion of the lieutenant, Juan Josef de Bringas).

Indians treating the arancel as license to do as they wished: AGN CRS 23 exp. 5, 1760, Tejupilco, Temascaltepec district; CRS 23 exp. 6, 1767, Ozoloapan, Temascaltepec district; CRS 75 exp. 3, 1777, San Felipe and Santiago, parish of Malacatepec (cura said "ellos ni quieren vivir arreglados ni vivirán por el arancel, ni quieren pagar, ni quieren ser castigados"); AGN Templos 15 exp. 4 and Templos 25 exp. 8, 1796, Amecameca.

The arancel disputes also invited opportunities for personal enrichment and power building, as the discussion of legal entrepreneurs in Ch. 15 suggests.

62. For an example of customary payments that differed from one visita to another and from the cabecera, see AGN CRS 72 exp. 10, 1789, Tlaquiltenango parish, Cuernavaca district.

63. Though judicial respect for custom was more common before the mid-18th century (e.g., AJANG Civil, box 17, doc. 2, 1708, La Barca, where the Audiencia of Nueva Galicia supported traditional election procedures), it was still a consideration near the end of the century. In recommending action on a cura of Totomaloyan's appeal that an annual celebration on December 12 for the selection of new mayordomos be forbidden because it always became a drunken orgy, the fiscal of the Audiencia of Mexico warned that "como en material de costumbres en los pueblos, no deve procederse para removerlas, sin perfecto conocimiento de la causa." Yet he supported the cura's appeal. AGN CRS 206 exp. 3, fol. 202r, 1798.

64. Tulane VEMC 39 exp. 15, 1762, Huizquilucan. A richly documented case of vacillation in a visita comes from the parish of Teoloyuca in the Valley of Mexico. In 1759, the cura charged that Indians of the visita of Coyotepec were not paying their fees on the pretext that they wanted to follow customary practices. He wanted them to pay the arancel, just as the parishioners of the cabecera did. Through their attorney, the leaders of Coyotepec replied that since the cura would not accept the arancel they had followed from the time of Archbishop Aguiar y Seixas, they had struck an agreement with him some

while ago in order to avoid lawsuits. But now that Teoloyuca had agreed to the arancel of another archbishop (presumably the Lanciego arancel of 1720), the cura wanted to impose it on them. They complained that it was unfair for the cura to enrich himself at their expense, since theirs was a small pueblo with poor lands, and they were always being called to do unpaid repair work on the Huehuetoca drainage project. As the case grew with more claims and counterclaims, the fiscal summarized his frustration with the people of Coyotepec in a Feb. 27, 1760, recommendation to the audiencia. He observed that they had wanted their customary practice, and the audiencia had approved. Then they wanted the arancel, and that was ordered. Now they wanted only part of the arancel and offered "weak reasons" for this latest preference. He advised a stern order for the Indians to obey the arancel, and for the gobernador and indio fiscal to be incarcerated for a few days as a warning to the rest. The audiencia agreed, but allowed a few modifications to the arancel. Still the leaders of Coyotepec were not satisfied. They responded that the cura was not following the arancel fee for marriages (to which the cura replied that what appeared to be excess charges were his legitimate fees as the juez eclesiástico). Finally, on April 6, 1761, the audiencia ordered the Indians of Coyotepec "to keep perpetual silence in their disorderly complaints" about the arancel, and to obey it "without interpretation." AGN CRS 68 exp. 1.

Other cases of parishioners changing their minds about the arancel or failing to follow it are AJANG Civil, box 49, doc. 4, 1727, Poncitlan; CRS 204 exp. 5, 1740, Tixtla; CRS 153 exp. 2, 1746, Cuapanoaya, Ocoyoacac parish, Metepec district; CRS 68 exp. 1, fols. 19v-21, 1759, Teoloyucan, Cuauhtitlan district; CRS 156 exp. 7, fol. 264, 1761, Acambay, Xilotepec district; CRS 156 exp. 9, fols. 376-80, 1763-64, Zacualpan, Cuautla Amilpas district; CRS 156 exp. 12, fols. 442-51, 1765, Tlapanaloya, Tetepango district; CRS 68 exp. 3, 1771, San Felipe del Obraje, Ixtlahuaca district; AGN Inq. 1146 exp. 1, fol. 51, 1775, Xilotepec; CRS 74 exp. 1, 1780, Molango, Meztitlan district; CRS 136 exp. 2, fol. 201, 1781, Huispaleca, Cuernavaca district; CRS 136 exp. 4, fols. 264-70, 1783, Huichilapan, Tenango del Valle district; CRS 72 exp. 8, 1785, Tlaxpa v. cura of Tepejí del Río; and CRS 39 exp. 2, 1796, Capuluac.

65. Among others, Joseph de Rojas, subdelegado for Tenango del Valle, could report that "cada uno [of the parish priests in his district] procura cobrar sus derechos conforme al Real Aranzel que les está puesto." AGN Hist. 578A, Nov. 23, 1793, report.

66. AGN Hist. 578A, report of Jan. 29, 1794. In his words: "Todos giran vajo un mismo pie en punto de obenciones, siendo ciertas contribuciones que hacen los yndios a sus párrocos, o mensal o anualmente, y assí no ay tropiezo en los matrimonios, entierros, bautismos, fiestas, etc. por saverse el tanto de limosna que a cada cosa corresponde; ni de consiguiente, lugar a exceso en los derechos; y aunque puede haverlo en el modo de exigirlos, o bien pretendiendo cobrarlos de los verdaderamente pobres, o no concediendo una justa espera a los que pronto no pueden satisfacerlos, no ha llegado hasta el día a mi noticia queja alguna de esta naturaleza." See also AGN Acervo 49 caja 127, 1773, Jiquipilco directorio (done "para que sesen discordias"); AGN CRS 72 exp. 8, 1785 royal provisión, paraphrasing the 1767 arancel, Tlaxpa v. cura of Tepejí del Río ("deseando corten las raíces de los pleitos"); and Tulane VEMC 28 exp. 12, 1775, Almoloya ("ruidoso pleito" since 1773).

67. See, for example, on arancel disputes as a way to avoid even customary payments, at least until the litigation was over: AGN CRS 23 exp. 5, 1760, Tejupilco, Temascaltepec district; CRS 183 exp. 3, 1779, Tetelcingo, Tixtla district; CRS 178 exp. 13, 1805, Xiquipilco, Ixtlahuaca district; AGN Templos 25 exp. 10, 1805, Temascalcingo, Ixtlahuaca district; Templos 25 exp. 11, 1807, Oztoticpac and Cuautlancingo, Otumba district.

68. AGN Acervo 49 caja 116, 1808-9, pastoral visit, Tamazunchale, Tampamolon, Huehuetlan, Santa Catarina Xochiatipan. Curas' conflicts with district governors had long been evident, but before, the tension was mainly over the alcalde mayor as the bearer of bad news and the administrator of royal orders. AGN DP 1 exp. 1, 1671, Cuernavaca dis-

trict; BMM 135, fols. 197–224, 1672, Cuernavaca district; AGN CRS 75 exp. 6, 1786, Alahuistlan, Zacualpan district; CRS 39 exp. 5, 1803, Malacatepec, Metepec district; CRS 75 exp. 4, fols. 210–12, 248–53, 1775, Tototepec, Zacualpan district; AGN Hist. 319 exp. 15, 1782, Acapulco district. For an example of a late colonial audiencia promoting such conflict, see CRS 183 exp. 3, 1779, Tixtla. Before 1789, there were more cases of alcaldes mayores supporting curas on the arancel issue, as in AGN Civil 2292 exps. 10–11, 1733; and BMM 135, exps. 21–24, 1749, Metepec district.

69. Cited by the attorney for the pueblo of Tututepec (Hidalgo) in 1796. AGN CRS 130 exp. 3. In the post-1789 adjudications over fees, the audiencias were less than ever inclined to take the curas' side. This Tututepec case is one of the few in which Indian parishioners were blamed for the litigation (fols. 110ff).

70. Ventura Beleña, 1: 166, doc. 258 ("No lleven excesivos derechos parroquiales a los indios; que se formen Aranceles equitativos y proporcionados a su pobreza").

71. Nevertheless, some curas and district magistrates still cooperated in fees disputes. Examples are AGN CRS 136 exps. 6–7, 1790–91, Temascaltepec; CRS 39 exp. 2, 1796, Capuluac; AGN Templos 25 exp. 9 fols. 22ff, 1799, Zacualtipan, Meztitlan district; and CRS 130 exp. 8, 1799, Huitlalpa, Tulancingo district.

72. AGN Hist. 578A, Malinalco report.

73. AGN DP 3 exp. 1 ("enfurecido dicho párroco empezó a prorrumpir palabras mui descompuestas e indignas de su carácter y ministerio"; "sus desafueros y tropelías contra la Real Justicia").

74. AGN Hist. 578A, 1793, Tixtla report ("su inmoderada pasión de interés y desde el ingreso a este pueblo dejó de hacer huso del arancel, cobrando los derechos parroquiales por la quota arvitraria que les impone").

75. AGN CRS 195 exp. 12.

76. AGN CRS 75 exp. 11, fols. 403–4 ("Luego que lo saludé me dixo como le va al Señor Cura[,] estará muy enojado por el arancel de los naturales del Pueblo de San Miguel[,] pero me hace Ud. favor de decirle al Señor Cura, que ni yo, ni mi Theniente nos hemos mesclado en nada; pues d. José de Navas les hizo el borrador del escrito que presentaron en la Real Audiencia, dichos naturales de donde dimanó dicho arancel, a lo que le respondí a dicho Señor Mayor, el Señor Cura no se enojó por dicho aranzel sino el en modo con que fue su Teniente de Ud. a hazérselo saber, pues estaba dicho Señor Cura bañándose y no dejó que acabara, sino que entró a la sala diciéndole a los que llevava consigo, entren Uds. Señores, esto y otros pasages").

77. AGN CRS 130 exp. 3.

78. For the *Itinerario*'s respect for custom, see 1-3-4 (approval of late mass on Sunday where "la costumbre es general" and Indians had to travel a long distance); 1-6-1 ("la costumbre para hacer ley, ha de ser voluntaria y libre"); and 4-5-5 (excusing Indians from fasting under certain circumstances even without a bull, empowered not by derecho but by "costumbre recibida y aprobada").

79. Curas for the arancel: AGN CRS 30 exp. 2, 1773, Chilapa; CRS 30 exp. 3, 1782, Tolpetlac; AGN Templos 25 exp. 11, 1807 Otumba. (Some curas wanted the arancel, even if it meant temporary confusion and a small reduction in income, because it produced cash rather than a welter of goods, cash, and services, and was easier for them to administer.) For an example of a cura still pleading custom as late as 1803, see CRS 39 exp. 5, fol. 268v, Malacatepec, Metepec district.

80. AGN CRS 178 exp. 12.

81. BN Manuscripts, no. 1257 exp. 7.

82. For example, AGN Bienes 431 exp. 17, 1771, Iguala; AGN Civil 2114 exp. 8, 1780, Tolpetlac ("la criminal libertad que desean"); AGN Crim. 148 exp. 2, 1792, Almoloya.

83. AGN CRS 67 exp. 10, 1776, San Juan Tetelcingo, Tixtla district (cura did not

make the arancel available); CRS 74 exp. 1, 1780, Molango, Meztitlan district (cura forced custom); CRS 136 exp. 5, 1785, Molango, and CRS 140 exp. 4, 1796, Yautepec (cura blatantly disregarded arancel); AGN Bienes 172 exp. 36, 1803, San Sebastián Querétaro (cura did not obey the arancel).

84. AGN CRS 75 exp. 9 fol. 451, 1790 ("no han de ganar el cielo"). The cura of Acambay in 1761 had reportedly used a similar tack with the parishioners who resisted being brought into his parish, advising them that they would be going to hell for disobeying him. CRS 156 exp. 7.

85. AGN Bienes 210 exp. 1, 1731, Huayacocotla; AGN CRS 140 exp. 4, 1796, Yautepec (witness no. 9 said Father Agüero of Yautepec was a "tirano en los derechos de casamientos y entierros"); AGN Templos 25 exp. 10, 1805, Temascalcingo (royal provisión of Jan. 15 characterized cura as rigid and arbitrary).

86. AGN Bienes 172 exp. 37.

87. AGN CRS 72 exp. 5. The cura obtained an audiencia order for Indian families to pay the funeral fees by selling some of the property of the deceased. The teniente de cura for Capuluac in 1796 claimed that after he once forgave a man's fee "de pura gracia," all the parishioners expected it. AGN CRS 39 exp. 1. In an earlier case, the cura of Atlacomulco, district of Metepec, buried without charge many poor parishioners who died in the epidemic of 1737, only to find that more prosperous families then demanded the same consideration, leaving him, he said, without sufficient revenue to pay his vicarios and meet his own needs. CRS 72 exp. 5.

88. Parras, 2: 442. The Morelos case is discussed in App. C.

89. Solano, 2: 312–14. The example of Ozoloapan first appeared in a different context in my article "Santiago's Horse," in *Violence, Resistance, and Survival in the Americas* (Washington, D.C.: Smithsonian Institution Press), pp. 153–89, copyright 1994 Smithsonian Institution. I thank the Smithsonian Institution Press for permission to use it here.

90. AHM L10B/28, fols. 91–96; BN AF caja 107 exp. 1475, fol. 53; von Mentz, *Sultepec*, pp. 32–33.

91. AGN CRS 23 exp. 6. This claim to protection under an existing arancel indicates that the parish had been through an earlier and well-remembered fees dispute. Ruis Coronel did not look into the earlier dispute, but it was well known to the cura of Tejupilco in 1760. He blamed the gobernador of Tejupilco for the recent disputes between the people of the districts of Amatepec and Ozoloapan against their curas. AGN CRS 204 exps. 9–10 (para. 79 of the cura's defense against charges by representatives of Tejupilco, San Miguel Ixtapan, and San Juan Acatitlan, Temascaltepec district).

92. AGN CRS 23 exp. 6, fols. 225–28 ("porque para gobernar el pueblo él sólo basta por razón de su empleo de alcalde que es empleo muy grande y bolviendo a mirar al fiscal dixo que los fiscales vienen con chismes al cura para incomodar y molestar a los yndios y por eso ya tenía mandado al fiscal de su pueblo que se abstubiera de ellos, porque si no, lo haría abstener, y llamándolo posteriormente varias ocaciones para que se dispusiera poner en su pueblo una escuela de ninguna manera contestó desobedeciendo en todo mis órdenes, lo que he sufrido y tolerado manejándome con la mayor prudencia").

93. The hacendados and their mayordomos of Ozoloapan had financial reasons to push for the arancel for their indios gañanes: its charges for sacramental fees were lower than the customary practice in this parish. AGN CRS 39 exp. 5, 1803. A decade earlier, hacienda Indians in this parish also appealed to the pastoral visitor to order the cura to perform marriages gratis or at a reduced charge. AHM L10B/28, fols. 72r–v and 103r (1792).

94. AHM L10B/21, fols. 35v–40v; L10B/28, fol. 96 ("porque los yndios querían ser dueños de la Yglesia y Campanas y disponer de todo a su arbitrio").

95. AGN CRS 156 exp. 5 ("Dirigir a aquella vida christiana y arreglamiento entre todos los yndios, que tengan escuela, asistan a la misa, quenta y doctrina, evitarles los continuos amancebamientos, embriagueses y otros culpas"). The Santo Tomás Indians,

he said, were living like "unos gentiles o brutos sin el menor susesión ni reconocimiento a superior alguno eclesiástico o secular, sin administración de sacramentos sin oyr missa sin doctrina sin escuela sin cuenta ni arreglamiento alguno político ni christiano."

96. Archbishop Rubio y Salinas (1749–65) proudly reported the founding of 228 schools in 1754 alone. Tulane VEMC 24 exp. 4.

97. The visita of Santo Tomás consisted of several small settlements that had been consolidated in the early 17th century. Gerhard, *Guide*, p. 314.

98. AGN CRS 156 exp. 5 ("Mui estimadíssimo compadre y mui señor mío—los indios de este pueblo se han insolentado de manera que ya la cuenta es irrición pues no ay forma de que assistan; y los pocos que asisten no ay forma de contribuir con el medio cada quinze días, y en apurándoles dan la vuelta y se van riendo, y ahora con la prisión del governador [que algún respecto cauzaba] se han acabado de insolentar y esto es no sólo en la cabecera sino también en los barrios . . . pues lo que se junta no alcanza ni para pagar la missa, por lo que dize a la escuela es lo mismo pues no basta para que imbíen a sus hijos el que a tarde y mañana los soliciten el fiscal y sus topiles; por lo que se halla en la actualidad quasi desierta la escuela").

99. Tulane VEMC 69 exp. 1.

100. AGN Crim. 304, fol. 150, 1768, Papantla, following 1767 revolt.

101. AGN CRS 137 exp. 8, fols. 178–79, 1805, Alahuistlan, Zacualpan district.

102. AGN CRS 75 exp. 3, fol. 103, 1774, Malacatepec, Metepec district (attorney for San Felipe and Santiago called the customary labor service to the cura "una especie de esclavitud"); AGN Acervo 49 caja 97E, 1796, Tasquillo, Huichapan district (attorney charged that the cura and his dependents regarded the Indians "como esclavos comunes, cargándoles a su antojo").

Parish priests of the Diocese of Antequera came close to openly denying the supremacy of royal law in their 1805 complaint against a new arancel. They labeled it a "novedad" and declared that they should not have to "suffer reform." AGN CRS 178 exp. 12.

103. So far as the cura of Alahuistlan in 1805 was concerned, "nada se puede inovar." AGN CRS 137 exp. 8.

Conclusion

EPIGRAPH: AGN Hist. 319 exp. 5, within fols. 7–8 ("Hago sombra y abrigo, como Dios me manda").

1. Manuel Abad y Queipo's lengthy defense of ecclesiastical immunity in 1799 is particularly well known. Hernández y Dávalos, 2: 823–52. Bustamante emphasized the immunity issue in *Cuadro histórico*, 1: 444 and 2: 378–79. For a modern treatment of church-state relations in the late colonial period that emphasizes the immunity issue and relies on the administrative record in the Archivo General de Indias (which features bishops and royal policy makers), see Farriss, *Crown and Clergy*.

2. AGN DP 3 exp. 1 ("indisputable autoridad . . . para hacerle observar todo lo justo").

3. Viceregal concern about the loyalty of priests was expressed in an 1813 call for district reports on their politics and the quality of their pastoral service (10 of these reports—8 of them for the archdiocese—are located in AGN OG 5). No such reports on subdelegados and their lieutenants were apparently commissioned.

Though these 1813 reports provide a valuable survey of the political choices and apparent sympathies of 272 parish priests between 1810 and early 1814, they must be used with caution. There are four areas of concern. (1) Curas are identified and evaluated quite systematically, but for the most part vicarios and other priests living in these districts are not. (2) The instructions did not prescribe a method for classifying the politics of the priests. The result is various classifications by different reporters, making comparisons between districts difficult and weakening the reliability of summary figures (on the other hand, the open-ended instructions allowed reporters to express their opinions about individual priests more freely). (3) As specific as the characterizations often are, reducing a priest's politics to a few words inevitably oversimplifies and sometimes misleads. This weakness is highlighted by the fact that 14 of the 20 instances in which a parish priest was evaluated by more than one reporter offer rather different judgments about his politics (Vicente and Juan José Zeñil of Zimapan, Miguel Vásquez and Nicolás Galindo of Meztitlan, Juan María Bustamante of Tianguistengo, Pedro Ugalde of Lolotlan, José Francisco Sánchez of Molango, Rafael Sánchez Espinosa of Tlanichol, José Ignacio Díaz of Huazalingo, Rafael Barrientos of Calnali, Joaquín Negrete of Ixmiquilpan, Lic. Ignacio López Aguado of Tepehuacan, Dionisio de Zúñiga of Tenango del Valle, and José María Velasco of Tescaliacac). And (4), in the polarized political climate of the time, some reporters were inclined to classify people as either insurgents or royalists when evidence of their conduct was ambiguous or changing. For Toluca—the fullest of these reports—the reporter included an index in which he reduced many of the priests to a one-word evaluation as insurgent or faithful to "la buena causa." Where the long description of someone in the Toluca report does not correspond to his "insurgent" classification in the index, I have placed him in a category that more closely fits the long description.

4. Trabulse touches on these social tenets of Enlightenment thought through the writings of Clavigero. "Clavigero, historiador." How priests, especially parish priests, participated in the intellectual, political, and cultural changes of the 18th century is not entirely clear. Wigberto Jiménez Moreno, in one of his seminal essays, projected Mexico's "entry into modernity" and "modern thought" through three generations of clerical intellectuals. Led by Jesuit humanists, the first generation, born between 1718 and 1731, began a revolution in ideas by adopting Cartesian philosophy. The second, born between 1732 and 1745, was more directly under the influence of French Enlightenment thought. The third, born between 1746 and 1759 and exemplified by Miguel Hidalgo, pursued the political implications of the second generation's thinking and was influenced by the ideas of Montesquieu and Rousseau, British America's independence war, and the French Revolution. Jiménez Moreno saw a dramatic increase in the impact of these ideas—"al principio dejaron sentir su influjo en círculos pequeños, pero que al final conquistaron a un público numeroso." His metaphor for this change is ramparts of older thinking being breached and modernity bursting in. "Antecedentes históricos." Other interpretations in this vein include Góngora, *Studies*, ch. 5; Córdova-Bello, *Reformas del despotismo*; Navarro B., *Cultura mexicana*; and the three works by Lanning in the Bibliography.

Other scholars are less certain about the influence of the Enlightenment on the clergy. For Spain, Nöel describes a Catholic Enlightenment, in which the clergy favored the practical measures for physical improvement through education and applied science and shared the growing optimism about the human potential for change, but was united in its opposition to the *philosophes'* fundamental ideas of individual rights, intellectual and religious freedom, and political equality. "Clerical Confrontation"; "Missionary Preachers"; "Opposition." Priests were less united about regalism, with its implicit assault on clerical authority, and about the virtues of unrestrained rationality. As men who influenced others with their words, Nöel considers traditionalist missionary preachers to have been far more important in 18th-century Spain than Enlightenment thinkers—stirring "crowds of tens of thousands," as opposed to a minority of the educated. These preachers stressed social obligations and charity in the face of commercial, industrial, and financial changes, which they viewed as a threat to Christian virtue—the source of greed, social and economic injustice, and immorality. In their sermons against the proud and powerful, they set themselves against the monarchy and merchants, posing "a challenge to the economic aims and political stability of the ruling order." "Missionary Preachers," p. 892. But Spanish preachers rose to defend the king and muted their criticism of the modernizing state once the French Revolution began. In the New Spain of 1810 insurgent parish priests also defended the king (at least half-heartedly) against godless French invaders, but they did not mute their criticism of the Bourbons' "afrancesado" path to modernity.

The studies of 18th-century clerical ideology in New Spain of Brian Connaughton, Oscar Mazín, Francisco Morales, and Javier Malagón-Barceló parallel Nöel's representation of the upper clergy in Spain as standing for traditional values in innovative ways. In particular, Connaughton's *Ideología y sociedad en Guadalajara (1788–1853)* indicates an engagement with the issues and intellectual currents of the day and rather flexible responses that did not simply oppose Enlightenment thought. Church leaders were trying to claim a prominent place in a changing society, often accepting national aspirations and some new forms without abandoning their moral theology, the idea of an organic, hierarchical society, or the political guarantees of a state church.

The Diocese of Michoacán became something of a cradle of Enlightenment thought—with conspicuous adherents in Juan Benito Díaz de Gamarra (resident from 1745 to 1783), José Pérez Calama (1740–92), Antonio de San Miguel (bishop from 1785 to 1804), and Manuel Abad y Queipo (resident from 1784 to 1815, member of the cathedral chapter, then bishop-elect in 1810); some prominent priests taking part in an early independence conspiracy in the episcopal capital (1808); and Miguel Hidalgo, the Father of Independence—but their inclination toward ameliorating legal and social inequalities and toward reason and experimentation arose in traditional sources such as Aquinas, Luis Vives, Melchor Cano, and Francisco Suárez as well. Their thought has the appearance of a modernized scholasticism more than a breaching of old ramparts. For a convenient short treatment of Díaz de Gamarra and Pérez Calama, San Miguel's 1804 prescription for social reforms, and Abad y Queipo's May 30, 1810, thoughts on social and economic reforms that might ward off a general insurrection, see Joseph Pérez, "Tradition et innovation"; "Un notable escrito"; and Hernández y Dávalos, *Colección,* 2: 891–96, respectively.

In "Hidalgo: La justificación de la insurgencia," Herrejón proposes that even Hidalgo's political outlook was built more on recessive features of traditional Catholic theology than 18th-century French thought. But whether he was more the philosophe or the traditionalist, Hidalgo with his doctorate, wide reading, optimism about change, and years of privilege near the top of the episcopal hierarchy was hardly representative of parish priests. Though also atypical in the sense that he had an urban parish, the well-educated builder-cura Dr. Gregorio Pérez Cancio better captures the feelings of many of his fellows in the archdiocese in the late 18th century. His lengthy record of the rebuilding of the parish church of Santa Cruz (Mexico City) offers few hints of Enlightenment thought, but it is ripe with indignation against uncharitable peninsular Spaniards who contributed little and demanded much from the impoverished Indian parishioners. See his *La Santa Cruz,* p. 154, for example. A more measured treatment for late-eighteenth-century Mexico that includes the famous case of Anastasio Perez de Alamillo is Greenleaf, "The Mexican Inquisition and the Enlightenment."

5. A suggestive treatise on the social significance of the Ten Commandments called *Conveniencia de la Religión, y el Estado* was published in Mexico City in 1805 under license from the vicar general and the viceroy. The author was Juan Francisco Domínguez, the then-80-year-old senior pastor of the sagrario parish and bishop-elect of Cebú in the Philippines. Love, good order, and other positive virtues are Domínguez's main message: "Love ties with golden chains the subjects to the prince, the servants to the masters, and the children to the parents. . . . By this love . . . the Republic lives, the happiness of the State is perpetuated" (pp. 23, 27). For the second and fifth commandments, he turns negative injunctions into positive virtues: "This [second] Commandment is conceived in negative terms but in reality it is affirmative: to love the sacred name of God." "Thou shalt not kill," he added, "is more a matter of loving than [not] hating, of doing good than of not doing bad" (p. 130). At a time when the public role of parish priests had been curtailed,

Father Domínguez's treatise was a reminder, perhaps a veiled warning, to royal authorities that the church and religion were vital parts of the social and political order of New Spain.

6. Ward, 1: 239; Alamán, 3: 213. Major studies of the Independence War with challenging new perspectives and appraisals by Christon Archer and Eric Van Young are nearing completion. Published articles and review essays by both authors suggest rather different views of the role of parish priests in insurgent movements between 1810 and 1821—different both from each other and from the interpretation advanced here. See notes 7, 14, 64, and 67 below, and the following articles: "Bite of the Hydra," "Cutting Edge," "Insurrection," "Viva Nuestra Señora de Guadalupe!," "Where Did All the Royalists Go?," and "What Goes Around" by Archer; and "Conclusion: The State as Vampire," "Cuautla Lazarus," "Islands," "Mad Messiah," "Quetzalcoatl," and "To See Someone Not Seeing" by Van Young.

7. Pablo Richard, p. 82. Other writers subscribe to Richard's view, if not to his exact figure. Elías Martínez, for example, contends that most Franciscans were active partisans and overwhelmingly pro-insurgent between 1810 and 1819; and Ward, 1: 238–40, notes that besides Hidalgo, Morelos, and Matamoros, there were "numberless others." Archer evidently agrees with Ward's vision of the mass defection of the "omnipotent" clergy. "Bite of the Hydra," pp. 73, 75, 78–80, 91.

8. Bravo Ugarte, "Clero y la Independencia: Ensayo estadístico," pt. 2, tabulates just 26 insurgents among 1,072 curas in New Spain (2.4%). Simpson, p. 172, follows the same line of interpretation, characterizing diocesan priests as "the very backbone of conservatism." Other authors have suggested that local elites representing the royal government involved in appropriating surplus production for themselves and the crown in fees and taxes would form the core of royalist partisans. If so, most parish priests should have leaned toward the royalists.

9. Hernández y Dávalos, 4: 452.

10. Alamán, 2: 330, 3: 213.

11. According to Bustamante, *Cuadro histórico*, 1: 455–56, the bishop of Puebla claimed on Nov. 14, 1811, that the curas of Ayutla, Tesmalaca, and Tlapa were kidnapped by insurgents under Morelos.

12. App. B adds 25 names to Bravo Ugarte's total of ten vicarios, almost three times fewer than the number of curas. Percentages of insurgent vicarios cannot be calculated without better information on the total number of vicarios and other assistants to the curas in all of the dioceses. There were certainly more vicarios than curas, perhaps by a factor of 1.4 : 1. Using that factor and increasing by half the number of vicarios known to have participated in the insurgency still suggests that their involvement was minimal, compared with curas. Assuming that about a quarter of the vicarios were replaced with recently ordained priests during the war, as few as one in 50 may have joined the insurgency. (Though the figure of one-quarter for replacements is only a guess, it does not seem too high despite the disruptions of the war and dangers of going to a rural parish. Bishop Cabañas reported in 1816 that both of his seminaries in Guadalajara were in operation and training priests for parish service. AGI Guad. 563. He did not suggest that the number of seminarians was smaller than usual.)

Still, the ratio of three curas to one vicario in App. B may be too high. As several of the entries indicate, the term "cura" could be used rather loosely to mean parish priests of all kinds, including vicarios de pie fijo. The 1813 district reports in AGN OG 5 may also skew the figures to the curas' side. Since the curas' politics were the main concern, the vicarios may be underrepresented. As a rule, vicarios would have been less likely than their superiors—the curas—to occupy conspicuous leadership positions in the struggle.

It is clear from those reports that vicarios did not necessarily follow their cura's politics. For example, the cura of Huichapan was judged "pésimo" and his vicario "sobresaliente";

the cura of Tepejí del Río, "pésimo" and his vicario "bueno"; the cura of Xilotepec "sobre-saliente," and his vicarios "indiferentes"; the cura of Guitepec a reliable royalist and his vicario "perverso como patriota"; the cura of Mazatepec "good in all ways" and his vicario "de opinión sospechosa"; the cura of Xochitepec "indiferente" and his vicario "muy bueno en todos sentidos"; the cura of Calimaya an active royalist and his vicarios "indiferentes"; and the cura of Lerma an insurgent sympathizer and his vicario a royalist. The vicarios of a parish were sometimes divided, too. For example, one of the vicarios of Xochimilco, Mariano Durán, was "indiferente"; the other, Rafael Truxillo, was an ardent royalist.

13. The text here is based on Farriss's figure of 401 in the appendix to *Crown and Clergy*. As the listings in Bravo Ugarte and Farriss indicate, most of the priests involved in the insurgency were not pastors: 55 of 91 (60.4%) in Bravo Ugarte, 164 of the 244 diocesan priests (67.2%) in Farriss. (Farriss does not always indicate which of the 157 regulars who were implicated in the insurgency were serving as doctrineros.) By Farriss's figures, about one in ten diocesan and regular priests supported the insurgency in various ways at some time between September 1810 and late 1819 (401 of 4,229). In fact, there would have been more than 4,229 priests living in mainland New Spain between 1810 and 1819.

14. According to Archer, "Dineros," pp. 51–52, the Bajío remained a focal point of insurgency throughout the years 1810–21. My study of priests and parishioners in Mexico and Guadalajara cannot directly explain why that area (located largely in the Diocese of Michoacán) would be the main center of the early Independence movement, and why parish priests there would be especially prominent insurgent leaders. Brian Hamnett's study of regions in the Independence War suggests that the underlying reasons for an explosive alliance of "lower classes" and "the professional bourgeoisie" against peninsulares in the Bajío were economic: a "lower class consciousness of a deterioriating or threatened position," born of material deprivation; and creole professionals finding opportunities for advancement and prosperity closed off by royal favoritism to peninsulares. *Roots of Insurgency*, pp. 3–12. But that does not fully explain why the insurrection was sustained and widespread there. Hamnett lays it in part to the presence of a large, more or less proletarianized rural population of estate laborers and tenants who lived precariously, were often recent migrants or deracinated Indians, and maintained wide contacts, but he also sees religion as the great mobilizing force, providing clerical leadership and moral justification. His emphasis is on ideology—that "religion" and "profound Marian associations" could provide "a unifying ideology capable of attracting the large numbers of people drawn from disparate groups in society" (pp. 13–19). But then the question becomes, why were priests not as widely accepted as political leaders in other places where religious fervor and Marian devotion were strong?

The late colonial history of local religion in various parts of central and western Mexico offers three clues: (1) Catholic religiosity that looked to priests for more than the sacraments and was expressed in regional as well as local practices was exceptionally strong in the Bajío; (2) parish priests were accepted as community leaders there more than in many parts of the archdiocese during the decades before 1810; and (3) the area was known more for its aggravated disputes between district governors and parish priests than for conflicts between priests and parishioners. All three points are suggested by the experience of the Diocese of Guadalajara, which adjoins and to some extent overlaps the Bajío, and has a similar history of commercial agriculture, trade, and mining. The first point is suggested also by Giffords' study of ex-voto paintings. The Bajío was a principal center of the production and consumption of votive paintings on tin in the early 19th century, reflecting a burgeoning mass culture of popular devotion expressed in a conventionalized, orthodox way. The second and third points are encapsulated in the strongly worded 1793 report of Juan Antonio de Riaño on priests residing in his intendancy of Guanajuato. Riaño wrote of the "incredible" influence of the clergy there, which he characterized as "noxious and prejudicial." He identified several priests who were especially provocative in their dealings with him. AGN Hist. 578A, Sept. 16, 1793, report.

15. The main differences between the distribution by modern state and region for insurgent and royalist parish priests in the sample were that the proportion of insurgents was greater in the tierra caliente (28.7% to 15.4%), and the proportion of royalists was greater in the central highlands (49.2% to 20.4%). A principal source of information about royalist parish priests is García & Pereyra, vol. 5, in which the authors attempt to demonstrate that nearly all parish priests were royalists. But that finding is problematical for three reasons. For one thing, they presume that any priest who was not making trouble for the crown or pointedly suspected of insurgent sympathies was a royalist. For another, some ardent royalists, including a number of priests on my list, could as well be counted as insurgents since they shifted from one camp to another. More important, most of the 20 royalist examples in García & Pereyra come from modern Hidalgo and Querétaro. My own sample of royalists in App. B indicates that Hidalgo became a royalist stronghold. A breakdown by diocese of the 65 men who could be identified by place (excluding the AGN OG 5 reports, which show a particular concentration of royalists in Hidalgo) shows that 37 came from Mexico, compared with 9 for Guadalajara, 9 for Michoacán, 6 for Puebla, and 5 for Antequera. The importance of royalist priests and their parishioners in the modern state of Hidalgo did not escape the notice of Alamán. The pueblos of Meztitlan district were especially pro-royalist after September 1811, it seemed to him, contributing "people, captained by the *curas*, on the frequent expeditions that the royal troops made throughout the territory." Alamán, 2: 412.

16. *Proceso instruído*, p. 20; Bustamante, *Cuadro histórico*, 1: 350.

17. Pardoned pastors (*indultados*) who had returned to parish service as of 1813 include cura José Francisco Sánchez of Molango (Hidalgo); cura José Rafael Sánchez of Tlanichol (Hidalgo); vicario José Mariano Lesama of Tulancingo (Hidalgo); coadjutor José Rafael Campuzano of Tejupilco (Edo. de México); cura José Antonio López Cárdenas of Acamistla (Guerrero); and vicario Felipe Gómez of Huehuetoca (Edo. de México). Many curas suspected of having supported insurgents were not formally charged or pardoned. AGN OG 5.

18. Ironically, both Couto and Pedreguera subsequently applied for vacancies in the cathedral chapter of Puebla. In his 1820 resumé, Couto, who narrowly escaped execution in 1817 after five years of insurgent activity, presented himself as a respectable senior priest who, as he delicately put it, had "taken refuge among dissidents in the war." Resumés for both men are in AGI Mexico 2550. Few members of cathedral chapters or the Colegiata of Nuestra Señora de Guadalupe joined the insurgency, but, superficially, there was little to separate Francisco Antonio de Velasco, the canon of the Colegiata who did join, from José Mariano Beristáin de Souza, a member of the cathedral chapter of Mexico, who did not. Both were creoles educated in Spain with Spanish doctorates; and Beristáin, perhaps more than Velasco, took pride in the intellectual accomplishments of Americans (see his *Bibliotheca Hispano-Americano*). But Beristáin's gratitude to Spain for his education and advancement turned pride in creole accomplishments that had revolutionary possibilities into even higher praise for and attachment to Spanish mentors. Alamán, 2: 554, claimed that Velasco was an opportunist who turned insurgent in order to avoid arrest by the Inquisition for his personal misconduct.

19. But clearly not all. For a cura who, despite a bitter dispute with the subdelegado in 1805, preached against Hidalgo's independence movement from the beginning, see the case of Dr. Rafael José de Calera. AGN Acervo 49 caja 146; and García & Pereyra, 5: 23.

20. Juan José Crisanto Sánchez, who had been the chaplain of the Hacienda del Astillero (Diocese of Guadalajara) since at least 1796, admitted in March 1811 that he had published Hidalgo's proclamations. CAAG, report for Cuquío in response to Oct. 31, 1796,

circular requesting information on priests in all parishes of the diocese; AJANG Criminal, caja 9 leg. 3 exp. 18. In 1813, Pablo Victoria, a clergyman residing on the Hacienda de la Pala in the district of Sahuayo (Diocese of Michoacán), was arrested and charged with publishing insurgent proclamations. He provided 33 witnesses to prove his innocence, but in Nov. 1814 he was still under arrest and ordered held until the war was over. Criminal, caja 11 leg. 2, exp. 19. As cura of Temascaltepec, José Antonio de Zúñiga had been closely associated with a local hacendado in the 1809–10 litigation over the resettling of several Indian rancherías. BMM 251.

21. Examples of clashes with royal authorities in the late 1780's: AGN Cofradías 13 exp. 5, 1786, Tetepango (cura was turned down in his plea for a loan of 1,500p from the viceroy to aid his starving parishioners, even though he offered to put up the interest on his 8,000p of capellanías as collateral); Tulane VEMC 3 exp. 9, 1787 (a cura concerned about just wages for Indian labor); AGN CRS 152 exps. 6–7, 1788, Teapa, Tabasco (dispute with the district governor in which the cura protested the miserable working conditions and poor pay of cacao hacienda peones). The royal government could have trouble even with "a very diligent cura" in the late colonial period. CRS 177 exp. 10, fols. 447–49, 1800, Mazatepec.

22. Callahan, *Church*, pp. 80–81, detects a vague sense of impending doom among Spanish priests during the second half of the 18th century that, by the 1790's, was turning into vengeful calls for moral regeneration. The cura of Apaxtla, Ichcateopan district (Guerrero), expressed his despair over the "deplorable state" of Tanicpatlan's spirituality with this kind of vehemence when he wrote to the archbishop's court in 1809: "con lágrimas de sangre se debe llorar la perdición de aquellas almas, pues han abandonado absolutamente la religión, aunque yo desde el principio del pleito siempre he procurado con amor suave cediendo todos los derechos que corresponde a un párroco y humillándome a todo quanto ellos han querido menos a lo que disuena contra nuestra Santa Religión." AGN CRS 126 exps. 11–12.

23. Alamán, 2: 11. Alamán mentioned a few virtuous insurgent curas as exceptions that, for him, proved the rule — notably José María Mercado, with his "great reputation for virtue," and Salto, the vicario of Teremendo, a man of "exemplary virtue" in his pastoral service who was pardoned in July 1811 but went back to the insurgency and was executed in 1812. 2:11; 3: 210. A safer inference from Alamán is that few of the insurgent priests were among the leading lights or most promising younger clergymen at the time. For example, none of the insurgent curas identified in App. B appears in Félix Osores's compendium of distinguished alumni of the Colegio de San Ildefonso in Mexico City, which is especially strong on his contemporaries from the late 18th and early 19th centuries.

24. Alamán, 3: 213. "El Padre Chocolate" — Father Muñoz of Valladolid — is also mentioned in AGN OG 5, fol. 220.

25. Tulane VEMC 1 exp. 40, 1788, Tochimilco; VEMC 15 exp. 3, 1789–90, Tochimilco; AGN Hist. 578A, 1793, Metepec report; AGN CRS 130 exp. 5, fols. 241ff, 1794, Zinacantepec; García & Pereyra, 5: 229–31, Aug. 12, 1811; AGN OG 5, 1813.

26. AGN Acervo 49 caja 116, pastoral visit report for Tepehuacan; García & Pereyra, 5: 34. Anselmo Vicente Ambrosio Aguila, an Indian priest in San Juan Acazingo (Diocese of Puebla) in 1809, was a similar case. Tulane VEMC 62 exp. 30.

27. AGN Inq. 1304 exp. 3, 1796–1800; Inq. 1334 exp. 3, 1796–1812; AGN Acervo 49 caja 146, 1816.

28. Alamán, 2: 228. Alamán also singled out José Antonio Torres, vicario of Cuitzeo, calling him "el azote del Bajío" (the scourge of the Bajío). He alleged that Torres was so ignorant he could barely understand the divine office that priests prayed every day. 3: 688–89.

29. Ibid., 4: 722.

30. Bustamante, *Cuadro histórico*, 1: 434.

31. Ibid., 2: 16.

32. Ibid., 2: 232–34.

33. Two parish priests from the dioceses of Mexico and Guadalajara who approach Alamán's vision of the insurgent priest are Joseph Díaz Conti and Salvador Parra. Díaz Conti, who held a law degree, created a scandal in the mid-1790's as a vicario in Molango and Atotonilco el Grande for various solicitations in the confessional and keeping several concubines. In January 1811, he was denounced by one of his female confessees for praising Miguel Hidalgo and expressing anti-peninsular sentiments. AGN Inq. 462 exp. 5; Inq. 1348 exp. 14. Parra was notorious in the Diocese of Guadalajara in the 1790's and 1800's for disobeying, demeaning, and assaulting district judges, consorting with outlaws, and sexual misconduct. He was reported to the Audiencia of Guadalajara in June 1810 (while cura of Valle de Topia) on suspicion of treason for uttering untoward remarks about peninsulares and praising the creole insurgents of Caracas, Venezuela. As of January 1813, he was still in prison, without having been formally charged. See the scattered records on his political troubles in AJANG Civil, box 228, doc. 7 (1802); AJANG Criminal, box 22, doc. 21 (1807); Criminal, bundles labeled "1719-1787-1800 leg. 1" (1796) and "1810 leg. 3" (1810, 1813); and Criminal, caja 9 leg. 3 exp. 68 (1810).

Alamán and Bustamante differed in their general view of priests in the insurgency. Alamán saw a body of especially disreputable priests in an increasingly corrupt priesthood to be the evil geniuses of the insurgency; Bustamante deplored the fact that not enough priests were committed to the insurgency to ensure its early success. But both historians include most of the same priests in their detailed narratives and characterize them similarly. Though Bustamante, as a moderate liberal and former insurgent, is inclined to emphasize royalist atrocities, both authors represent individual priests in much the same way, whether they were men of virtue or posturing egotists and irresponsible in their use of power. In two cases that Bustamante would have known best (and where Alamán apparently relied on the *Cuadro histórico* for his information about them), the pro-insurgent sentiments of priests are muffled by Alamán: Antonio Labarrieta who, according to his former student Bustamante, gave pro-independence sermons when his old seminary colleague Hidalgo took the city in 1810; and José Antonio Martínez de Segura, the octagenarian cura of Tetela de Xonotla, who sheltered Bustamante in 1815 and reportedly gave financial and moral support to the insurgents. Bustamante, *Cuadro histórico*, 1: 95, 2: 196; Alamán, 2: 67-68, 4: 255.

34. AGN Hist. 578A.

35. AGN Templos 25 exp. 11.

36. Tulane VEMC 51 exp. 6. In a secret investigation, all five witnesses declared the charge of insurrection to be unfounded.

37. AGN CRS 75 exp. 6. See Ch. 12 for his prominent part in the Alahuistlan disputes.

38. AGN Hist. 578A.

39. BMM 251.

40. AGN Inq. 462 exp. 34 ("Muchachos, ya tenemos cañones para matar a todos los gachupines que tanto tpo nos han tenido usurpada nuestra América. Ya se acabó España no tendremos aguardiente, bretaña, puntabiés y otras cosas pero tendremos nro charape, manta y otros lienzos que fabricamos. ¡Viva Nuestra Señora de Guadalupe y mueran los gachupines y sus sequaces amigos!").

41. Juan Bustamante, cura of Tianguistengo, is a more clear-cut example of a priest who switched from insurgent to royalist. He had been characterized in the 1808 pastoral visit as an upstanding priest, but a man of "raras ideas," "se inflama con facilidad y se produse con acrimonia." AGN Acervo 49 caja 116. Early in the Hidalgo insurrection, he was denounced by another priest for persuading his parishioners to turn against the king and

for serving as pastor to 6,000 insurgents. García & Pereyra, 5: 206–7. Although all three military commanders who reported on his conduct in Dec. 1813 found him to be quietly at work in his parish and a royalist supporter, they did not agree on his earlier role in the insurgency or whether he could be trusted now. AGN OG 5, reports for Zimapán, Tulancingo, and Pachuca. In 1815, he was still the cura of Tianguistengo, writing a commissioned report for the archbishop. AGN Bienes 663 exp. 25.

Others who evidently changed their minds include the former vicario of Tulancingo (Hidalgo), José Mariano Ledesma; cura José del Castillo of Tututepec (Hidalgo); cura José Francisco Sánchez of Molango (Hidalgo); cura José Antonio López Cárdenas of Acamistla (Guerrero); vicario Felipe Gómez of Almoloya (Edo. de México); vicario José María Pereda of Tianguistengo (Hidalgo); vicario Ignacio Terrón of Tenango del Valle (Edo. de México); cura José Ignacio Muñoz of Xocotitlan (Edo. de México); cura Rafael Caballero of Coatinchán (Edo. de México); and Rafael Sánchez Espinosa, cura of Tlanichol (Hidalgo). Some curas reportedly made a point of treating both sides cordially: Miguel Quiros, vicario de pie fijo of Real del Oro, Xocotitlan district, and Juan and José Salinas, vicarios of Temascaltepec. AGN OG 5.

42. This kind of neutrality was apparently all that José María Morelos asked for, at least in the early years of the insurgency. Or so the short letter he sent to the cura of Tiosintla from his headquarters at Chilapa in late 1811 suggests: "Muy Sr. mio. Para evitarle todo sobresalto le pongo a V. esta diciendo que puede V. estar sin cuidado exerciendo su ministerio, pues no benimos metiendonos en puntos de Religion, sino puramente quitando el Gobierno politico y militar a los Europeos que tanto tiempo hace nos tienen usurpado: bajo este supuesto no hay que temer nada, sino cuidar de sus feligreses. Dios gue. a V. Ms. as. que le desea su Servidor, Jose Maria Morelos, General del Sur." Texas, García Coll., folder 130, file 1, typescript of a copy of the letter in AGI, dated Jan. 22, 1812.

The following were reported by royalist military commanders in late 1813 to be dedicated pastors but indifferent patriots: interim cura Cándido Ybarrola of Tempoal, cura José Simbrón of Singuilucan, the vicarios Matías Alvarado of Cuernavaca, Pedro Gomez of Guitepec, and Sebastián Ocampo of Mazatepec, cura Joseph Asareo Ximénez of Xochitepec, vicario Joseph Arrellano of Xochitepec, vicarios Mariano Camacho, Domingo Ximénez, Cristóbal Arámbulo, and José María Ramos of Metepec, cura José Antonio Vega of Almoloya, and vicarios José Gregorio Moreno and Mariano Bega of Almoloya.

43. García & Pereyra, 5: 248ff.

44. Alamán, 4: 63–64, 2: 569; Bustamante, *Cuadro histórico*, 1: 315. Other examples appear in Alamán, 3: 248, 4: 355, and Hernández y Dávalos, 5: 208–9.

45. Bustamante, *Cuadro histórico*, 3: 48; Alamán, 4: 286.

46. Alamán, 4: 475.

47. J. López, *Insurgencia*, 2: doc. 260. Cabañas's pastoral letter of April 4, 1812, criticized "many of our priests" for not actively supporting the royalists, as if "giving frequent and punctual information" about local unrest and "denouncing, discovering, and persecuting the infamous revolutionary and factious insurgents . . . were opposed to the meekness and leniency of their character." Toral blamed the curas in particular: "Contemplo responsables a los Curas porque con la resistencia que hicieron para la Misión, creo que han dado margen a que los Eclesiásticos de buenos sentimientos se retraigan a trabajar a favor de nuestra justa Causa, como lo prueba inequivocadamente lo que me pasa con el Cura Interino de San Sevastián Dr. d. José María Cabrales. Este Eclesiástico es un sujeto de las mejores prendas, del más realzado Patriotismo, y de la más sana conducta. Desde que se presentó aquí la misión extraordinaria nos manifestó los deseos que tenía de coadyubar a nuestros fines, y se subscribió gustoso en la lista de los Misioneros, pero no ha hecho función de tal, temeroso de la Censura de sus Compañeros." Hernández y Dávalos, 5: 353. Members of the cathedral chapter of Mexico in their March 28, 1811, exhortation

to their parish clergy to combat the insurgency, claimed that no cura "from this fortunate Archdiocese" had turned insurgent, but they noted that "some have not been heroes." Hernández y Dávalos, 2: 906–8.

Calleja's complaint followed the receipt of a series of reports he had commissioned at the end of 1813 on the politics of priests. Eight of these reports by district military commanders from the following headquarters in the Archdiocese of Mexico appear in AGN OG 5: Zimapan, Huichapan, Cuernavaca, Texcoco, Pachuca, Xochimilco, Tlalmanalco, and Pánuco. After eliminating the curas and vicarios for whom two or more inconsistent evaluations appear in the reports, 272 parish priests in these eight military districts remain. I divided them into six groups: (1) outstanding royalists (20 cases), (2) royalists (99 cases), (3) largely untested or passably loyal to the king and the Spanish colonial government (23 cases), (4) indifferent to the royalist cause, or sympathies unknown (70 cases, many of them pastors who did not provide intelligence on insurgent movements in their vicinity), (5) suspected of insurgent sympathies (40 cases, including individuals characterized as "pésimo"—"awful," "terrible"), (6) insurgents, or active supporters of insurgents (20 cases). Groups 2–5 contain a variety of descriptions of individual priests (15 different descriptions within group 2; 11 within group 3; 12 within group 4; and 18 within group 5).

Of these 272 parish priests, 7% were clearly insurgents at the time (group 6: 20 cases, included in App. B), 44% were regarded as royalists (groups 1 and 2: 119 cases, included in App. B), and 49% were in the middle—suspect, indifferent, untested, or undetermined (groups 3, 4, and 5: 133 cases). Despite the reporters' (and Calleja's) doubts about the loyalty of many of the pastors in the middle, all were still at work in their parishes.

48. Fleeing at the approach of insurgents: Alamán, 3: 154, 1810–11, Sultepec; AGN Templos 25 exp. 9, 1811, Zacualtipan (Joaquín de Ugalde, longtime cura, whose only professional blemish was a fees dispute in 1808, left in early 1811 "por temor a los insurgentes").

Declining reassignment: AGN Acervo 49 caja 116, 1815, Sierra de Pinos (José Antonio Hurtado de Mendoza, lieutenant cura, declined to go to the Indians of pueblo nuevo); García & Pereyra, 5: 22; CAAG, box of Tlajomulco records.

Cooperating with the local group in power: AJANG Criminal, caja 9 leg. 3 exp. 18, 1811, Hacienda del Astillero (chaplain Juan José Crisanto Sánchez admitted on March 9, 1811, that he had posted Hidalgo's proclamations, but said he did so under duress from "the rabble"; he was pardoned); García & Pereyra, 5: 34 (José María Torres, cura in Tepeapulco district, Hidalgo, said he had buried two insurgent leaders as they demanded, but wrote to the bishop to reaffirm his loyalty).

Ringing church bells and offering holy water: García & Pereyra, 5: 194ff (Joaquín Zavala, cura interino of Matehuala, reported to his royalist superiors that this did not pacify the indios rebeldes under Huacal who entered the town in June 1811).

Supporting both sides: AHJ Manuscripts, no. G-4-802 (Juan Nepomuceno Romero in 1814); Bustamante, *Cuadro histórico*, 1: 259 (cura Garza of Aguayo, a self-proclaimed royalist pursued for insurgent sympathies). Bustamante was almost as harsh as Calleja in his judgment of these kinds of "survivors," regarding them as two-faced temporizers. *Cuadro histórico*, 1: 590.

49. One peninsular cura complained of the local stereotype of "gachupines" as "recios de genio, altivos y sobervios." He preferred to call himself an "ultramarino." AGN Bienes 210 exp. 26, fols. 37–39. The anti-gachupín feelings of laymen and American-born parish priests in the late colonial period are abundantly documented. Perhaps the most vivid and extended example is the memorial sent to the king by the ayuntamiento of Mexico City in 1771 complaining of the appointment of peninsulares to many offices, and their prejudices against Americans. Manuscript copy advertised in Philadelphia Rare Books and Manuscripts Catalogue Five, now in Bancroft Library. The cura or vicario of Tlal-

tenango (Zacatecas) who annotated his copy of the *Itinerario* during the 1770's lamented that peninsular priests were being appointed to parish benefices without knowing the local Indian language, even though royal law preferred the appointment of natives of the province. Bancroft Library copy, p. 25. In 1801, a group of five young men of Guadalajara, one of them associated with the cathedral ("había sido de aquella iglesia catedral"), were caught plotting against colonial rule, swearing to "derramar la última gota de sangre en defensa de la patria y bengarse de las incomparables infamias del Govierno y de todos los Europeos por el sobradísimo abatimiento e infeliz estado a que se hallaban reducidos por ellos." AGI Guad. 383, March 1803, sentencing of Josef Simón Méndez Monacillo. See also AGN Hist. 132 exps. 26–27, 1793, Tetecala, Cuernavaca district (people would swear allegiance to the king and the viceroy, but not to the peninsular lieutenant governor of the Marquesado del Valle); AGN CRS 197 exp. 14, 1802, Mazatepec; AJANG Criminal, box 6, doc. 1, 1807, Zacoalco; and AGN Inq. 462 exp. 5, 1811, Mexico City.

The outrage of parish priests and their rural parishioners at "gachupines" was especially directed against peninsular lieutenants of the district governors who were also merchants: AJANG Civil, box 86, doc. 1, 1768, Cocula (Jalisco); Civil, box 82, doc. 7, 1769, Zacoalco (Jalisco); AGN CRS 188 exp. 6, 1789, Choapan (Oaxaca); Civil, box 205, doc. 5, 1789, Teocaltiche (Jalisco); AGN Hist. 132 exp. 26, 1793, San Francisco Tetecala (Morelos); AJANG Criminal, bundle labeled "1780–1789 leg. 14," 1795, Zacoalco (Jalisco); CRS 197 exp. 14, 1802, San Francisco Tetecala (Morelos).

50. AGN OG 5.

51. Brading, "Tridentine Catholicism," p. 22.

52. Nöel, "Clerical Confrontation," p. 109. An exception was Hugo de Omerick, writing during the high tide of Lorenzana's regalist initiatives in 1769. BMM 113.

53. AGI Mexico 2588, 1784, Zimatlan (Oaxaca), Joseph Manuel Ruiz y Cervantes treatise.

54. AGN Alcaldes Mayores 11, fols. 357–70.

55. Sermon delivered by Dr. José Julio García de Torres in the presence of Iturbide at the Colegiata de Guadalupe on Oct. 12, 1821. Luis Villoro, in his celebrated *El proceso ideológico de la revolución de independencia*—as challenging a book today as it was when first published in 1953—transcends a dichotomized view of self-rule in Mexico after 1808 that would have it either a traditionalist reaction against liberal innovations from Spain or a democratic/bourgeois revolution. He posits a struggle of various movements informed by both the traditionalist and the liberal stream, but plays down the importance of preconceived ideas in the early years. Rather, it was the war itself—"the intoxication of liberty"—that galvanized ideas for "the popular revolutionary consciousness" and its leaders (especially parish priests). Villoro proposes a two-step process that saw the "instantaneísmo" of the popular movement overtaken by middle-class leadership, and the transition of those leaders from an appeal to Spanish legal tradition (and against French innovators) for the exercise of sovereignty in the absence of the king to modern democratic ideas. Villoro's chief concern is the popular revolution and its diversion into a bourgeois vision of constitutionalism and representative government. The traditionalist stream interests him less, and then mainly in terms of middle-class leaders in 1808. Parish priests in the early movements are represented as men of praxis, embodying the spontaneous, popular revolutionary consciousness and seemingly unattached to the moral theology that defined their public roles before the war. See especially Villoro, *Proceso*, pp. 78–102.

56. Quoted in Elías Martínez, p. 156 ("mantener nuestra religión, nuestra ley, la patria y pureza de costumbre").

57. Esparza, pp. 157–58 ("Sí, Oaxaqueños, sois objetos muy preciosos a los ojos del Eterno"; ". . . al mismo tiempo que pesa sobre la desgraciada México afligida por la tiranía . . . vosotros véis la protección y vigilancia del cielo"; ". . . no hacemos más que

abandonar la recámara de esta bella casa, para situarnos en las puertas, y entradas de ella";
". . . sois sin contradicción, libres, felices e independientes").

58. Hernández y Dávalos, 2: 78 ("se mira que en algunos está la cristiandad falleciendo es estar los ultramarinos; pues bien se mira que no tenéis otro objeto que la abaricia y así ésta es la causa de este movimiento . . . pues defendemos la Patria y Religión").

59. García & Pereyra, 5: 82.

60. Ibid., pp. 109ff (Huitzuco), 121ff (Tepatitlan, district of Tula), 128ff (Real del Cardonal), 130ff (Atitalaquia), 144ff (Tepehuacan), 153ff (Zacualtipan), 161ff (Amealco), 201ff (Oapan). There were also Indian royalists in the Hidalgo area during the early years of the independence period. Indians of Huautla, Huejutla district, for example, declared their unconditional faith in the Spanish monarchy, referring to their pueblo in the political relationship as "the weak sex." AGN DP 3 exp. 8.

61. Van Young, "Comentario," p. 62; Van Young, "Islands in the Storm," p. 140, n. 23.

62. Alamán, 4: 406–7.

63. AGN Inq. 1213 exp. 6, fols. 77–80 ("Ningún Christiano se puede condenar").

64. AGN CRS 68 exp. 3, fol. 219, 1771, San Felipe del Obraje, Ixtlahuaca district (Edo. de México). According to the cura in this fee dispute, one of the leaders of the litigation, Bernardo González, told the Indians that "dicho arancel les exima de toda obediencia y pensiones y que havía venido del cielo embiado del eterno padre. Con este razonamiento quedaban los indios alucinados y gustosíssimos abrazaban el aranzel: y para su resguardo les daba el dicho Bernardo una cedulilla que decía *Aranzelado*, por la que les llevaba dos o quatro reales, y con ella el indio, como instrumento authéntico de su libertad, tenía la de governarse por sí con independencia de todo superior."

There are promising new treatments of millenarianism as the key to popular insurrection during the independence period, but the issue of how religious convictions translated into rebellion at that time is far from resolved. Millenarianism is the main theme of Enrique Florescano's interpretation of popular mentality in Mexico during the colonial and early national periods, *Memoria mexicana*. Its roots, he suggests, are largely indigenous: a reworking in Christian terms of precolonial prophetic traditions and the idea of a new golden age on the return of a culture hero. His narrative in chs. 4 and 5 connecting the colonial and independence periods is more suggestive than conclusive. The 18th-century cases he identifies are few and situated outside the areas where popular insurrections occurred after the Grito de Dolores, and the evidence for the independence period is sketchy. Rodolfo Pastor, in his study "La Virgen y la revolución," also starts from the position that the Indian rebellions of this time were "always fundamentally messianic," but he emphasizes a Christian framework, especially a prevailing apocalyptic symbolism of Mary Immaculate. Eric Van Young, too, regards millenarianism as the mobilizing principle of rural insurrections during the independence period. He notes that "messianic belief . . . functioned to focus popular—largely Indian and peasant—energies on the struggle for a political break with Spain," and that "much of the Mexican countryside was awash with [an] amalgam of rumor, hope, and messianic expectation." "Raw and the Cooked," p. 76; "Islands in the Storm," pp. 130, 155. But Van Young is less concerned than Florescano and Pastor with specifically indigenous or Christian antecedents because he finds that two secular figures, the Spanish king Ferdinand VII and the creole military officer Ignacio Allende, were the main objects of rural messianic hopes. See especially "Quetzalcoatl."

The emphasis on millenarianism has tended to draw a sharp line between high and low religion and to see Indian/peasant religious beliefs and practices as a self-made, self-contained system. But late colonial evidence of local religious and political practices, such as the Santiago performances and the Ozoloapan disputes discussed in Chs. 11 and 17, suggest that Indian villagers did not often regard themselves as agents of a precolonial revival or enemies of the colonial state and its religion. True, where Indians who believed that they were chosen Christians went on to make invidious comparisons to their social betters and to distinguish between Christianity and the church, dreams of a new order had millennial possibilities. But such dreams were rarely acted on in central and western Mexico—rarely, at least, beyond the local level where they had helped to define a colonial identity.

65. AGN CRS 75 exp. 6, fol. 371, 1786, Alahuistlan (Guerrero); AGN Hist. 132 exp. 26, 1793, Tetecala (Morelos).

66. AJANG Criminal caja 3 leg. 1 exp. 6 ("No hay fuerza alguna que pueda oponerse a las tropas del Rey pues aquellos naturales más bien han querido dar su dinero y caballos a los rebeldes que sus personas"). Díaz was a former associate of Miguel Hidalgo at the seminary in Valladolid, and succeeded him as vice-rector. He served as José Antonio Torres's chaplain in lowland Jalisco and Colima, joined Hidalgo in Guadalajara (but reportedly took no part in the killing of peninsulares there), and eventually became associated with the constitutionalists at Apatzingán. His captors sent him to Manila in February 1815.

If political tradition has much to do with Mexico's national disunity in the 19th century, these examples of faith and resistance in the behavior of rural villagers in central and western Mexico (where the majority of future Mexicans resided at the end of the colonial period) suggest an interpretation that differs from that of Louis Hartz, ed., *The Founding of New Societies: Studies in the History of the United States, Latin America, South Africa, Canada, and Australia* (New York, 1964), chs. 1–3. Borrowing (not always faithfully) from his contributor Richard Morse's paper, "The Heritage of Latin America," Hartz looks at colonial society from the top and treats Spaniards as the shapers of colonial history. He portrays Spanish America as a feudal, authoritarian society, whose servile masses had no experience in self-government. Theirs was a society that rested on the iron grip of the encomienda, landless Indians, a tradition of "Indian absolutism," "popular submissiveness," and "the incapacity of the people to assume Enlightenment responsibilities." Once the legitimacy of the imperial government was challenged after 1808, the social and political order inevitably collapsed into anarchy.

The Indian resistance and accommodations I have documented in this study (especially in Part Three) suggest that the weakness of Mexican national governments in the 19th century had less to do with popular submissiveness, Indian absolutism, and a lack of political mobilization than with the long-standing political strength and experience of localities and regions that connected rural settlements to provincial towns and imperial officials. Political participation was considerably greater than one would expect from Hartz's summary. The curas of Ozoloapan certainly felt the sting of a local political initiative that was not simply the product of a petty tyrant's machinations. In arguing that a "native spirit of independence" was the principal source of Mexico's disunity, the late-19th-century North American commentator David Wells comes closer to the militant myopia of districts and pueblos like Ozoloapan, Atexcapan, and Alahuistlan. *Study of Mexico*, pp. 84–85.

This political strength of localities and, to a lesser extent, regions should not be regarded just as a prehispanic legacy or a function of spatial separation, as Brand, p. 40, suggests. It was also promoted by the position of Indians in colonial society as laboring, producing, tribute-paying subjects of the crown. As members of corporate pueblos de indios, they fitted into the Hapsburgs' idea of a mediated, patrimonial state. For the future national state, a major problem was the weakness of a middle ground of territorial and institutional loyalties between local communities and the crown's audiencias and viceroy. With the decline of the court system and the accustomed legitimacy of the highest political leaders in the decades following independence, comparatively few rural constituencies thought their interests were well served by state and national governments.

67. Van Young, "Raw and the Cooked," pp. 76–77, makes this important distinction between the likely outlook of creole leaders and Indian followers. His approach to politi-

cal culture and popular ideology in the independence period draws a sharp distinction between elites and masses ("a kind of binary opposition"), leaves little room for leaders and mediators who were not of the local community, and minimizes the impact of the state on local society (on the last, for example, he writes on p. 94: "What seems to have mattered to most people was not state but community. In the case of early-19th-century Mexico, therefore, I favor this paraphrase of a sociological motto that has recently gained some currency: Taking the state back out"). I have learned much from Van Young's well-researched, often ingenious studies, but his approach seems to rule out of order the colonialism as a shared culture that this history of priests and parishioners suggests is a key to Mexico's 18th-century history. We agree on many particulars, including doubts about the still-popular idea that priests were dominant village notables who could call out "the masses" when they wished, but we part ways on the place he would give to parish priests, effectively reducing them to objects of independent colonial villagers' scorn, to be resisted, and otherwise almost irrevelant to the social, political, and religious history of rural Mexico. Florescano offers a similar view of conflict with curas in *Memoria mexicana*, pp. 182ff, 245, except that he regards the priests as more powerful adversaries who promoted modernizing ideas against which Indian peasants reacted.

68. Anaya's letter, filled with the language of a holy war, appears in Montiel & Huesca, pp. 91–101.

69. Bustamante, *Cuadro histórico*, 1: 443–44. On Feb. 22, 1811, the viceroy ordered captured insurgents, including priests, executed on the spot. Hernández y Dávalos, 2: 408. A fuller justification for the execution of insurgent priests without recourse to ecclesiastical courts was made by viceregal bando on June 25, 1812. See Hernández y Dávalos, 4: 305–16, for the text of the bando, along with legal commentary; a July 6, 1812, protest against it to the cathedral chapter of Mexico by unnamed priests as a violation of ecclesiastical immunity; and the promotor fiscal's response.

Morales, p. 81, describes the insurgents under Hidalgo and Morelos as more conciliatory toward royalist clergy than vice versa. More of the insurgent priests in App. B were executed by royalists than the other way around. But the implications for anticlericalism can be overstated. Even more of the insurgents were pardoned. Occasionally, they became active royalists, but most were politically inconspicuous thereafter.

70. Alamán, 2: 100–101 (cura of San Sebastián, San Luis Potosí, was arrested and mistreated by insurgent sympathizers as he fled for refuge in Querétaro in Dec. 1810); 2: 355 (Indians of Jocotitlan, Ixtlahuaca district, Edo. de México, reportedly stoned the cura when he tried to pacify them with the Blessed Sacrament in April 1811); García & Pereyra, 5: 34, 36 (the reported killing of priests by insurgents in Ixmiquilpan in 1813). José María Ortiz Navarro, the vicario de pie fijo of Acatitlan in the parish of Tejupilco, explained his part in the insurgent band of "Vargas" in 1817–18 as unavoidable given the leader's view of priests. Vargas had threatened his life and exclaimed, "los sacerdotes son cabalmente los mayores enemigos de su Patria y creo que decapitando a uno se exemplaresen los demás, y si esto no bastare seguiré la seqüela hasta concluir con los del carácter de V." AGN Acervo 49 caja 45, exp. on the conduct of the interim cura of Usuluapan (Ozoloapan).

71. García & Pereyra, 5: 135–38: "les dije que era el cura; entonces quitándose el sombrero me dijeron: 'Padrecito, perdone Su Merced, con quien no queremos nada, es con esos malditos gachupines, que hasta las criaturas ensartan las lanzas.' " Described 18 years before as a dedicated pastor but impetuous and not particularly charitable (AGN Hist. 578A, 1793, Zacualpan report [Apaxtla parish]), Benítez represented himself to the cathedral chapter as anti-insurgent, and asked for guidance in case the insurgents returned.

72. Villoro, *Proceso*, regards anticlericalism as part of pro-independence sentiment, too, but he sees it coming late in the war. His two examples are Fr. Servando Teresa de Mier and José Joaquín Fernández de Lizardi. Fernández de Lizardi's pointedly pro-Masonic

and seemingly anticlerical tracts of 1822 and 1823 went beyond corruption in the clergy and the cruelty of royalist curas in the war to sharp words about fanaticism and superstition in Catholic practices. BEJ Miscelánea, vol. 10 exps. 1–3. But his "Last Will and Farewell" in *Don Catrín de la Fachenda y fragmentos de otras obras*, pp. 243–58, emphasizes that he was a faithful Catholic and not against the clergy as such: "nunca he aborrecido al clero sino sus abusos."

An example of overt anticlericalism by a royalist from the beginning of the war appears in AJANG Criminal, bundle labeled "1815 leg. 2 (138)," a record of the 1815 trial of Ignacio Ximenes de Guante, a priest living in Tacámbaro (Michoacán), who was charged with insulting the "Visitador Económico, Político, [y] Eclesiástico" Manuel Díaz some years before. In his deposition, Díaz made his own intentions clear: "Yo estoy persuadido que para reprimir la audacia de los clérigos de esta clase se hace preciso que el Govierno se rebista de todo su poder y les haga sentir el peso terrible del brazo de la justicia."

Whether or not there was more anticlericalism among royalists during the war, the reputation would have followed naturally from the cutting comments, poor church attendance, and other anticlerical moves made by some district governors in the late colonial period (sometimes cued to regalist initiatives by higher authorities in Guadalajara, Mexico City, and Madrid).

73. Bustamante, *Cuadro histórico*, 2: 498.

74. Alamán, 3: 536 (Huatusco); Bustamante, *Cuadro histórico*, 1: 278 (Calpulalpan).

75. Bustamante, *Cuadro histórico*, 2: 498.

76. AGN Crim. 229, fols. 263ff, Atlacomulco (insurgent cries of "Viva Nuestra Señora de Guadalupe"); Alamán, 2: 101 (shouts of "Viva Nuestra Señora de Guadalupe" while mistreating a cura, late 1810, at Pueblo of Tierra Nueva, between San Luis Potosí and Querétaro); 2: 413 (people in the Bajío and adjacent areas continued to rally to the call of Our Lady of Guadalupe and "Mueran los gachupines"); 2: 411, Tecpan (Oct. 13, 1811, town renamed in honor of Nuestra Señora de Guadalupe); 2: 554 (Dr. Francisco Antonio de Velasco, former canon of the Colegiata at the Basílica of Guadalupe, took a store of Guadalupe medals with him into the insurgency).

77. Bustamante, *Cuadro histórico*, 1: 617–19.

78. Calderón de la Barca, p. 564. See especially Alamán, 2: 426 and 3: 248, for his general commentary inspired by particular examples. His conclusion centers on Morelos's severity: "Entre las calidades que distinguían a Morelos, no se contaba por desgracia la humanidad y generosidad para con los vencidos" and "poco dispuesto estaba éste a la clemencia, por lo que castigó con severidad a algunos de los vecinos." He wrote also of Morelos's "energía feroz."

79. An example of this kind of tension and anguish for a Spanish clergyman of the time is developed in Martin Murphy, *Blanco White: Self-Banished Spaniard* (New Haven, Conn., 1989).

80. Herrejón, *Morelos*, p. 257.

81. Dromundo, pp. 15–17. Dromundo says Morelos was not a muleteer (as some contend), but lived on the Hacienda de Tehuejo in the district of Apatzingán from age 14 to 25.

82. Herrejón, *Morelos*, pp. 35–36, 129.

83. Orozco Farías, p. 208, Feb. 1, 1798.

84. Texas, García Coll., folder 130, typescript of Morelos's Nov. 22, 1799, reply to complaints against him.

85. Herrejón, *Procesos*, p. 124.

86. Herrejón, *Morelos*, p. 214.

87. Timmons, pp. 40–41.

88. The slogan Hidalgo emblazoned on his banner was publicized by Abad y Queipo in his decree of excommunication, Sept. 24, 1810, which Morelos had read before his meet-

ing with Hidalgo in October. Orozco Farías, pp. 180–84. In Hidalgo's decree of Jan. 11, 1811, he insisted on the religious basis of his insurrection, much as Morelos would in the following years. Hidalgo promised to "defend it [the Catholic faith] in its pure form" from foreigners "who disfigure it" and to respect the high clergy. If "Religion, King, and country" were to be defended, European Spaniards had to be removed from government in America. But in art. 1 of this decree, he added that the arrest of Europeans would be limited to laymen, "and in no way should include Señores Eclesiásticos except in cases of high treason." J. López, *Insurgencia*, 1: doc. 120.

Morelos used a version of Hidalgo's slogan as an oath of allegiance for new adherents in 1812, elaborating only on the meaning of "bad government" (in terms of gachupín selfishness): "Viva Nuestra Señora de Guadalupe; Viva Nuestra Santa Religión; Viva la América y muera el mal govierno que corrompía destruyendo con sus maleficiosas constumbres e imposiciones probechosas para ellos, en sus repartimientos y combeniencias y adversas por sus desdichas a todo Americano." AGN OG 919, fols. 33–34, Tlaxiaco (Oaxaca).

89. Orozco Farías, pp. 186, 189, 210–11.

90. Alamán, 2: 317–20. How Morelos's forces grew so rapidly as he traversed the tierra caliente is not entirely clear from the secondary literature. Morelos's own contacts through trade and travel may have been important. Many of his supporters would have come from settlements along his line of march in the tierra caliente (as Mercado's did in northwestern Jalisco at the end of 1810; J. López, *Insurgencia*, 1: doc. 94). Kinship and the support of local strongmen attracted by Morelos's early military successes seem to have been especially important to his expanding base. His small band of followers from Carácuaro would have had relatives and former neighbors up and down the region who might be enlisted. In a 1734 dispute over cofradías in San Juan Huetamo, just southeast of Carácuaro, a mestizo witness from Huetamo, Diego Joseph Yáñez, testified that "many sons of this *pueblo* are living in other jurisdictions, serving as cowboys on cattle ranches." AGN CRS 72 exp. 4. The cura of Cuaguayutla (Guerrero) in 1802 decried the effective collapse of this pueblo because many of the Indians were hiding or living on ranchos in the vicinity. AGN Tierras 2772 exp. 17. In a way, the tierra caliente was a poor version of the Bajío—with its ranching, cotton and textile production, rural migrations, respect for priests, and comparatively large casta population. Brian Hamnett, *Roots of Insurgency*, pp. 142–48, suggests that early military successes in the tierra caliente attracted the indispensable support of independent coastal and upland caciques farther south, especially the Galeanas and Bravos, who brought with them bands of personal followers. He posits that their interest in Morelos's anti-gachupín insurrection resulted from "disputes and hostilities concerning the expansion and abuse of mercantile power." By working through the "existing structure of relationships in the locality," rather than subverting them, "Morelos strove to prevent the degeneration of the movement into race and class war."

91. Alamán, 2: 423, 4: 334, 338.

92. Lemoine, *Morelos y la revolución*; Churruca, "Fuentes del pensamiento de Morelos"; Churruca, *Pensamiento*. Chávez Orozco, "Pensamiento social y político," treats Morelos as a democratic agrarianist, "a century ahead of his time." Among other sources, Carlos Herrejón's commentaries on the records of Morelos's career as a parish priest and his interrogations by the Inquisition in 1815 (*Morelos; Procesos*) are especially important to the interpretation I am advancing. Brading, *First America*, pp. 578–81, offers a similar interpretation of Morelos's political ideas.

For Villoro, *Proceso*, p. 99, Morelos was a thinker born of the revolution—"the most authentic representative of the distinctly popular revolutionary conscience"—without important intellectual antecedents in moral theology or the European Enlightenment. To the extent that European political philosophies influenced Morelos toward the end, they were, in Villoro's view, a product of his seduction by middle-class leaders. Churruca, in contrast to Lemoine and Villoro, recognizes that religion must have influenced Morelos's political thought, but he describes that influence mainly in formal terms—in terms of Morelos's possible justification of revolution by theological jurisprudence, of his vision of divine intervention in the insurgency, and of the similarity between biblical passages and several texts by Morelos. "Fuentes del pensamiento de Morelos," pp. 140–45.

93. Villoro, *Proceso*, p. 98, notices this shift. A parish priest who made this positive connection between liberty and equality 15 years before the Mexican War of Independence began, and expressed it in terms of the French Revolution, is documented in AGN Inq. 1360 exps. 1–2 (Athanasio Pérez Alamillo, cura of Otumba).

94. Timmons, p. 51; *Morelos: Documentos inéditos*, 1: 128–38. Morelos's short decrees during the years of his insurgency were frequently peppered with anti-gachupin remarks. See Hernández y Dávalos, 4: 865–66, 5: 163–66, 213–14, and 6: 221. For what Morelos may have understood by "Machiavellian schemes," see Fernández de Lizardi's "Machiavellian Decalogue," in *Don Catrín de la Fachenda y fragmentos de otras obras*, pp. 69–70. Here Machiavelli represents the opposite of the principles of the Ten Commandments: look out for yourself and beware of love and friendship (the first commandment is "On the surface, treat everyone in a pleasant manner, but love no one"); and resort to lies, deception, and flattery whenever necessary. José María Mercado, another parish priest-insurgent under Hidalgo (from Ahualulco, Guadalajara Diocese), was equally vehement about his crusade against European Spaniards. His letters to his father and to Hidalgo in Dec. 1810 speak of "el gusto que me a causado la vengansa que Dios me a consedido de mis Enemigos" and promise to "perseguir a nuestros traidores Enemigos hasta el cavo del Mundo." J. López, *Insurgencia*, 1: docs. 82, 94.

95. Alamán, 2: 426, 3: 248, 4: 722.

96. Morelos's conciliatory words to the commander of Fort San Diego at Acapulco in April 1813—to the effect that he did not routinely kill European Spaniards and made war only against "the declared enemies of our nation"—cloaked the strong anti-gachupín sentiments he often expressed in other circumstances. Lemoine, *Morelos: Su vida revolucionaria*, p. 287. Still, he did repeatedly emphasize that his forces did not kill innocent children, only "*gachupines* of outrageous malice" (no matamos criaturas inocentes, sino gachupines de inaudita malicia). *Morelos: Documentos inéditos*, 1: 139, undated. And in his response to the eleventh charge brought against him by the Inquisition after his capture in 1812 (that he falsely claimed the king would not return or would return only as the agent of Napoleon), Morelos replied that he had only criticized those European Spaniards who had acted badly ("sólo se ha hablado mal de aquellos que son malos en su modo de obrar"). *Morelos y la Iglesia*, pp. 105–6.

97. Timmons, p. 49. For a particularly harsh order by Morelos, calling for the execution of any of his soldiers who robbed and sacked, see Hernández y Dávalos, 4: 487 (Sept. 30, 1812). This followed a caustic order on Sept. 12, 1812, for the arrest of a fellow priest and officer in his forces, José María Ramos, who had left Chilapa without a pass and made trouble in Tepecoacuilco. Hernández y Dávalos, 4: 416–17.

98. See his 1812 message to the people of Tehuantepec called "Desengaño de la América y traición descubierta de los europeos," and his message to the people of Oaxaca of Jan. 29, 1813. *Morelos: Documentos inéditos* 1: 128–37, 155–58.

99. In his communiqué to Calleja of April 12, 1812, for example, Morelos addressed the general as someone who would die for Napoleon while the insurgents died for "la verdadera Religión y su Patria." Ibid., p. 326. Similarly, during the siege of Cuautla in early 1812, he appealed to creoles on the royalist side to join him "in defense of our holy religion and our Patria in order to restore the rights that the *gachupines* have taken from us for 300 years." Chávez Orozco, *Sitio*, p. 94. Morelos spoke of his concern to prevent "the adulteration of our Holy Religion" and of his habit of thinking of dioceses when he thought

of electoral units. Hernández y Dávalos, 4: 662–63 (Nov. 7, 1812). The first two articles of the oath of allegiance sworn by the town fathers of Tlaxiaco, Oaxaca, when Morelos passed through in December 1812 were "Long Live Our Lady of Guadalupe" and "Long Live Our Holy Religion." AGN OG 919, fols. 33–34. The king was also part of Morelos's formula from 1810 to 1812, but he was mentioned after "religion," as in "Religión, Rey, y Patria." *Morelos: Documentos inéditos*, 1: 137 (1812).

100. Texas, García Coll., folder 130, "Documentos relativos a José María Morelos, 1795 a 1815," file 2 ("No quiero dejarlos empeñados, ni menos sacrificarlos: Soy cristiano tengo alma que salvar y he jurado sacrificarme antes por mi Patria y mi Religión, que desmentir un punto de mi Juramento").

101. *Morelos: Documentos inéditos*, 1: 137, 158, 326 (March 23, 1813). In a longer note to Calleja during the siege of Cuautla in 1812, Morelos wrote: "He who dies for the true religion and for his country, does not die unhappily but gloriously. . . . You are not the one who determines the final moment of this army, but rather it is God, who has decided the punishment of the Europeans." Quoted in Timmons, p. 70. According to Bustamante, Morelos's followers revered him as a kind of messenger from heaven ("genio superior"). Other writers note that some followers regarded his young son, Juan N. Almonte, as endowed with supernatural powers of prediction and healing. Díaz Díaz, p. 31; *Morelos y la Iglesia*, p. 105; Alamán, 2: 530.

102. Bustamante, *Cuadro histórico*, 1: 62; *Morelos y la Iglesia*, pp. 103–4. Given Morelos's explanation of his own motives, his request on Oct. 21, 1810, for a leave of absence at partial pay (one-third of the clerical fees collected) was not as "incredible" as Lemoine finds it in *Morelos y la revolución*, p. 243.

103. *Morelos y la Iglesia*, p. 104.

104. Herrejón, *Procesos*, p. 115. While Morelos sought to avoid direct confrontation with his superiors in the church, bishops were quick to condemn the continuing insurgency. Bishop Cabañas's first pastoral letter after his return to Guadalajara in 1812 condemned the insurgents as "a mob of thieves and assassins," and sought to reclaim the principles of union and Christian charity for the royalists. J. López, *Insurgencia*, 2: doc. 260.

105. Herrejón, *Procesos*, pp. 104–6, 110, 137–38. Morelos did not say why he considered parts of the Apatzingán constitution impracticable or ill-conceived, but there are clues in his earlier writings, experience as insurgent leader, and training as a priest. Above all, he would have doubted the wide powers granted to congress and the weak, divided executive branch of government. (Macías, pp. 106–17, considers this constitution, with its weak executive, a reaction *against* Morelos and Rayón as discredited military dictators.) In addition, the constitution did not devote much attention to the matters for which he showed such deep concern in his "Sentimientos de la nación": a partnership between the new national state and the Catholic church, the principle of hierarchy, and social justice and charity. Why did he sign the document? His humility, desire for unity in the insurgency, and belief in its principles of independence and managed liberty may be the best answer. In framing official pronouncements, he was prepared to subordinate his own views to the wisdom of more learned congressmen; witness his comment in his letter of June 15, 1814, to the Junta Insurreccional about a manifesto prepared the same day in the name of the congress that called for unity of the people against the royalists under Calleja: "Nada tengo que añadir al manifiesto que vuestra majestad ha dado al pueblo sobre puntos de anarquía mal supuesta. Lo primero porque vuestra majestad lo ha dicho todo, y lo segundo, que cuando el señor habla, el siervo debe callar. Así me lo enseñaron mis padres y maestros." Torre Villar, *Constitución de Apatzingán*, p. 379. (See also pp. 410–13, commentary by Pedro de Alva and Nicolás Rangel in 1924 on Morelos's concern for unity and discipline among the insurgents.)

Most scholars consider the Apatzingán constitution to be largely Morelos's work (Villoro, Macías, and Herrejón are notable exceptions). The effect has been to highlight Enlightenment origins to his political thought after 1812, leaving a curious contradiction between his religion and politics. See, for example, Churruca Peláez, "Fuentes del pensamiento de Morelos," pp. 145–47; and in Herrejón, *Repaso*, the papers of Juan Hernández Luna, pp. 151–60, Jorge Mario García Laguardia, pp. 161–66, Manuel Rodríguez Lapuente, pp. 167–70, and Daniel Moreno, pp. 181–84. If, as Herrejón suggests, Morelos took little or no part in framing the constitution and read little in contemporary European and North American political philosophy, the contradiction and seeming compartmentalization of his thought is less apparent, and a moral theology foundation for his eclectic political outlook—in the words of Edmundo O'Gorman, "at once monarchical and republican"—comes to the fore. *Supervivencia política*, p. 12.

106. Morelos specifically recalled reading works by three other authors: Grosin, Echarri, and Benjumea. Herrejón, *Morelos*, pp. 56–62, identifies and briefly discusses these works. All had to do with moral theology and the obligations of pastors. "Grosin" was Francisco Santos y Grosin's 1790 revision of Francisco Lárraga's *Promptuario de la theología moral*, first published in 1704. "Echarri" could be either or both of two works by Francisco Echarri, *Directorio moral* and *Instrucción y examen de ordenandos*. "Benjumea" probably consisted of some of the theological tracts of Blas de Benjumea dealing with canon law and moral theology.

107. Dussel, *Historia general*, 1: 569–70.

108. On Morelos's fear of anarchy and concern for good order, status, and discipline, see Hernández y Dávalos, 3: 401–2 (Oct. 13, 1811), 3: 450 (Dec. 13, 1811), 4: 865–66 (Feb. 20, 1813), and 5: 163–66 (Sept. 18, 1813).

109. *Itin.* 1-1-7, 1-4-10, 1-5-1 to 1-5-4.

110. *Itin.* 1-5-4. Or 1-13-6: "por obligación de caridad estamos obligados a dar limosna de lo superfluo a los que tienen grave necesidad . . . la razón es porque la notable necesidad del prógimo es grave mal: luego gravemente ofende las leyes de caridad, quien pudiendo sin dificultad socorrer al prógimo, y librarle de aquel mal, no lo hace." Charity was prime evidence of the practice of virtue, which Morelos regarded as the highest purpose of the insurgency, and which appears prominently in the *Itinerario*: as in 3-3-13, "Estos temores sirven de espuelas para la virtud."

The *Promptuario de la theología moral* ("Grosin"), another of the works Morelos recalled reading (see n. 106 above), also gave special attention to Christian charity, as well as a loving God and the Ten Commandments more than the Seven Mortal Sins. Treatise 21, one of the longest, is devoted to charity in terms of the Ten Commandments. Invoking the bien común (the common good), it emphasizes the fundamental obligation to help those in extreme need. It also provides for a hierarchy of charity: it is owed to the father, before the mother, children, and others, because "por los Padres debemos el ser." Treatise 34 emphasizes restitution for sins such as seizing the property of others, and Treatise 36 treats usury, both of which also resonate with Morelos's political program.

111. *Itin.* 3-4-3, 3-4-16.

112. Herrejón, *Procesos*, pp. 121–22 (from Mark 10:44).

113. For an earlier example of the use of the term Siervo, see González Dávila, 1: 77 (1648).

114. Hernández y Davalos, 3: 677–85 (April 26, 1810, circular to priests in the archdiocese by the gobernador de la mitra calling them to defend "religión y patria").

115. *Itin.* (1771 ed.), p. 210 ("que como Christo dió la vida por nosotros; así también debemos aventurar las nuestras por la salud del prógimo, que está en extrema necesidad").

116. Villoro, *Proceso*, p. 103.

117. Morelos renamed the town of Tecpan (Guerrero) in the Virgin of Guadalupe's honor in late 1811 (Alamán, 2: 422); her name became the countersign of his troops; and

he set aside pressing military affairs to observe her feast day, preaching at Izúcar de Mata-moros (Puebla) on Dec. 12, 1811, and making a detour to Carácuaro for the observance in 1813. It was apparently on Dec. 12, 1815, preoccupied with "making peace with his God," that Morelos unburdened himself of strategic information about insurgent activity. Tim-mons, p. 163.

118. *Morelos: Documentos inéditos*, 1: 155–58, March 23, 1813, bando (tithes and derechos parroquiales); "Sentimientos de la nación," Sept. 1813 (tithes and first fruits).

119. Herrejón, *Morelos*, p. 214 (letter of Dec. 30, 1808). Obviously, not all parish priests who opposed and were hurt by the reform of cofradías and cajas de comunidad became insurgents, any more than all of those who wholeheartedly practiced the ethic of charity in their parish service joined the early insurgency. Manuel Urizar, vicario of Huitzuco, near Taxco, an unchaste but especially charitable priest in the years before the Indepen-dence War, for example, does not appear in the insurgent rolls after 1810. AGN Bienes 172 exp. 53.

120. Lemoine, *Morelos: Su vida revolucionaria*, p. 287.

121. The *Itinerario* repeatedly refers to the priest's obligation to protect the humble, as do 16th- and 17th-century royal laws and legal commentaries (e.g., Solórzano 4-7-34: "como recibe la Iglesia a su abrigo a todos los que se hallan faltos de propia defensa"). Priests knew they should practice exemplary charity whether they did so or not. For ex-ample, the priest of Villa Alta (Oaxaca) wrote in 1793 of his voluntary poverty: "pues después de tantos años de beneficio sólo tengo tres cubiertos de plata, un braserito y unos pocos libros y con esto ya está hecho el inventario de mis bienes, pues como suele de-cirse ni camisa tengo . . . y en esta cituación he vivido siempre mui contento, porque no amo los ynterezes; y sólo quisiera tener muchas riquezas para mis amados los pobres, y el fomento de ésta mi yglesia." AGN CRS 188 exp. 12, fols. 205v–207r. As Gilly, p. viii, ob-serves, Morelos was on the road to "la otra razón, la libertadora; la otra comunidad, la de las libres individualidades solidarias; y la otra modernidad, la de todos."

122. On Morelos's respect for private wealth, see his decree of Oct. 13, 1811, in Her-nández y Dávalos, 3: 401–2 ("It is not our intention to proceed against the rich as such. [This is against] Divine Law, which prohibits robbing and taking the property of someone else without the owner's agreement, and prohibits even the thought of coveting things that belong to others"). On the absence of Christian virtue in the conduct of Spaniards in America, see *Morelos: Documentos inéditos*, 1: 136–37 (1812). Morelos's declaration that such gachupines were "enemies of God, of his Church, and of all mankind" suggests that he did regard them as heretics.

123. *Itin.* 3-4-14.

124. Lemoine, *Morelos: Su vida revolucionaria*, pp. 370–73.

125. Nöel, "Missionary Preachers," pp. 885, 890.

126. Lemoine, *Morelos: Su vida revolucionaria*, p. 28; AGN CRS 178 exp. 9, fols. 295–302, 1797 ("revolution" as a dirty word). In his bando to the inhabitants of Oaxaca on Jan. 29, 1813, Morelos wrote that the only social distinctions were to be based on "virtue placed at the service of the Church and the State." *Morelos: Documentos inéditos*, p. 156 ("que solo la Virtud han de distinguir al hombre y lo han de hacer útil a la Yglecia y al Estado"). This phrase was italicized.

127. Mariano Beristáin de Souza, *Discurso político-moral*. González y González, pp. 165, 168–69, 190, treats Beristáin as a creole Mexican nationalist, a representative of the dis-covery of patria and desire for independence. Judging by this sermon, Beristáin is better understood as a pan-Hispanic nationalist, for he here argues against Mexican indepen-dence and for a vision of Mexican literary achievements in Spanish context.

128. Dromundo, pp. 81–89.

129. Villoro, *Proceso*, pp. 98-105, is among those who view the "Sentimientos" as a liberal document. But the term "liberal" appears in Morelos's art. 11 as the opposite of tyrannical, suggesting that he still thought of liberal and liberty more in terms of the absence of tyranny and oppression than in terms of unqualified individual rights.

130. For an example of "sentimientos" as a prominent word in the vocabulary of late colonial priests, see Lizana y Beaumont, *Sentimientos religiosos*. In embracing "sentiments" as his watchword, Morelos drew away from the kind of unabashed faith in reason of much Enlightenment thought. " 'Have courage to use your own reason!'—that is the motto of Enlightenment," Immanuel Kant wrote in his essay "What Is Enlightenment?" (1784). *Critique of Practical Reason*, p. 286.

131. Parry, *Spanish Theory of Empire*, pp. 174-75.

132. The terms of this meeting of apparent opposites in the 18th century are illuminated by Hirschman, *Passions and Interests*. His thoughts on how new ideologies arose from the old in the 18th century rather than being "independently conceived, insurgent ideologies" are especially helpful in understanding the conservative, even reactionary side of Morelos. Hirschman's prime example is Montesquieu, who also emphasized the traditional balancing of qualities (like political powers or honor and profit) and the moderation of passions with interests. But Montesquieu went much beyond Morelos in his belief in the salutary political consequences of economic expansion and in wedging interest between the old opposites of reason and passion. Montesquieu would have objected less than Morelos to the instrumentalism of the Bourbon reforms in 18th-century Spanish America.

133. Ortner, *High Religion*, p. 195, provides a definition of praxis against which Morelos's actions are measured here: "sustained engagement in activity built on an alternative logic, different from the routines of everyday life, and different from intentional action, which, though nonroutine, shares the logic of everyday life."

134. Weinstein, pp. 3, 12-15. Torquemada put this sentiment in more familiar terms (3: within pp. 531-35): "It is a greater thing to love than to be loved by all" (es más amar que ser amado de todos).

135. Morelos and other insurgent priests would not have been altogether satisfactory symbols for modern liberation theology in Enrique Dussel's terms: standing for the church of the poor, but against the church that served the colonial state. *Historia general*, 1: 271. Morelos was not a relativist in matters of doctrine and authority. He would not have warmed to the "every path to God is a legitimate path" relativism espoused by Bishop Samuel Ruiz of San Cristóbal de las Casas, Chiapas, in 1985 (quoted by Ronald Wright, p. 268) or to the notion of priests as followers or mainly associates in spiritual matters. And he did not see social justice so clearly in class terms. His view of charity and social order was more hierarchical, paternalistic, and respectful of established authority and existing inequalities of wealth.

136. O'Gorman elaborates on this mentality in *México: El trauma de su historia*, pp. 11-15. He finds creoles' nationalism to be rooted in (1) a sense of spiritual and moral superiority (which included a vision of themselves as superior Iberians), and (2) traditional Catholic values that were hostile to what was modern, rationalist, innovative, and liberal. As he says in his earlier *Supervivencia política*, p. 12, "Los que secundaron la obra de Hidalgo fueron monárquicos y republicanos a la vez, que estos dos corrientes se encontraron dentro del pensamiento de Morelos." To speak of the importance of tradition and moral theology in the role of parish priests during the struggle for independence is not to suggest that they were fixed or uncomplicated, tightly bound ideas. This is not Américo Castro's timeless Iberian determinism in which "There is no need . . . to look around among ideas gestated outside Spain for motives and incitements for the independence of Hispano-American colonies. The principal reason lay in the very process of Spanish his-

tory, within which Las Casas's strange form of Christianity turned eventually into rational criticism." *Spaniards*, pp. 590–91.

137. Kolakowski, p. 226.

Appendix C

1. Womack, p. 29.

2. An example of the artisans in Morelos pueblos is AGN Crim. 159, fols. 44–57, where the principals and witnesses in a murder case from Tlayacapan in 1810 all spoke of themselves as tailors, chandlers, muleteers, and other nonagriculturalists. On vagrancy and migration at the turn of the century, see AGN CRS 177 exp. 10.

3. The Morelos ratio is based on census reports for Jonacatepec, Yautepec, Jantetelco, Cuautla, Tlaltizapan, Tlaquiltenango, Xaltengo, and Zacualpan in 1759–60. AHM L10A/8. The Toluca figure is based on detailed reports for the parishes of Capuluac, Tescaliacac, Jalatlaco, Tianguistengo, Malinalco, Tenancingo, Tecualoya, Tenango del Valle, Calimaya, Metepec, Zinacantepec, Almoloya, Ozolotepec, Temoaya, Jiquipilco, Ixtlahuaca, Xocotitlan, San Felipe el Grande, Atlacomulco, Temascalcingo, Amealco, Acambay, and Xilotepec in 1775. AHM L10B/12. The gente de razón of Morelos cabeceras were more likely than those of the Toluca region to be classified as mulatos.

4. Judging by the reports of curas' annual income, the parishes administered by these four towns were among the 19 richest in the archdiocese. See App. A.

5. For a discussion of "centrifugal" pueblos de indios near Guadalajara, see Taylor, "Indian Pueblos."

6. Alcedo, 1: 258.

7. For the Taxco labor drafts and their results in Tepoztlan, see Haskett, "Our Suffering with the Taxco Tribute."

8. Warman, *We Come to Object* (originally published in Mexico City as *Y venimos a contradecir: Los campesinos de Morelos y el estado nacional*); de la Peña, *Herederos de promesas*.

9. de la Peña, *Herederos*, p. 51.

10. Ibid.

11. Tutino, *From Insurrection to Revolution*, pp. 188–91.

12. Martin, *Rural Society*; von Wobeser, *Hacienda azucarera*; von Mentz, *Pueblos de indios*.

13. Martin, *Rural Society*, p. 178.

14. Ibid., p. 194.

15. Haskett, *Indigenous Rulers*, p. 196. Haskett also considers precolonial concepts, the Indians' vigorous defense of their landholdings, and the written Nahuatl tradition in pueblos of the Cuernavaca district in "Indian Town Government"; and "Indian Community Land and Municipal Income in Colonial Cuernavaca: An Investigation Through Nahuatl Documents," paper presented to the annual meeting of the American Historical Association, Dec. 1987.

16. Ibid., p. 14. The following quote is from p. 85.

17. Archbishop Rubio y Salinas's pointed attempt to purify local religious practices and moral conduct is the main example. During his pastoral visit of 1759–60, Rubio y Salinas went beyond exhorting parishioners to give up the superstitious practices, drunkenness, and scandalous dances he heard about. He suspended the license for mass at Apitzaco (a barrio of Yautepec) because of the indecency of its chapel; threatened to close the churches of all the visitas of Tlaltizapan unless they were put in good order right away; ordered the removal of a "ridiculously dressed" Christ from the parish church of Tlaquiltenango unless it was made decent; and threatened to suspend all the pueblos' outdoor processions and ceremonies in the hills unless they received formal permission from the

cura. AHM L10A/8, fols. 42, 47, 49, 152v, 158v, 163r. Subsequent events in Yautepec and some upland parishes are discussed later in this appendix.

18. Among the area parishes secularized between 1750 and 1777 were Atlatlaucan, Jantetelco, Xiuctepec, Jonacatepec, Mazatepec, Oaxtepec, Tepoztlan, Tlaltizapan, Tlaquiltenango, Totolapa, Xochitepec, Yautepec, and Yecapixtla (all in Cuernavaca); and Jumiltepec, Hueyapan, and Ocuituco (Cuautla). The 12 Chalco parishes were Amecameca, Coatepec Chalco, Cuautzingo, Ecacingo, Ixtapaluca, Xuchitepec, Mixquic, Temamatla, Tenango Popula, Tláhuac, Tlalmanalco, and Tlayacapan. The figure of 70 for the archdiocese's secularized parishes in this period (based on Vera, *Erecciones parroquiales*; Gerhard, *Guide*; and scattered archival evidence) will undoubtedly grow with additional research.

19. Tulane VEMC 16 exp. 12. In the early 1750's, the new secular curas of Atlatlaucan, Tetela, and Ocuituco reportedly did not know Nahuatl well and used translators in the confessional. They did not employ vicarios at the time. The cura of Atlatlaucan reportedly used Franciscans for parish work that required the native language.

20. The Indians of Tlaquiltenango district, for example, were said to be fluent in Spanish. AGN CRS 72 exp. 10, 1789. I have not gathered enough evidence to construct a geography of Spanish and Nahuatl for this area in the late colonial period. Apparently, most Indians in the southwestern district of Mazatepec were fluent only in Nahuatl; and the same was true in nearby Tetelpa and Xoxocotla (vicario Luis Venegas, who spoke Nahuatl, said that the people of his pueblos were "indios cerrados" and required a priest who spoke their language). CRS 197 exp. 14, 1802; AGN Bienes 172 exp. 51, 1805. Indians of Jonacatepec, Huautla, and Oapan, and of the upland parishes of Tlalnepantla and Yecapixtla were reported by the pastoral visitor in 1779 to know little Spanish, but Indian leaders of Totolapa who testified in a 1742 dispute were identified as very well versed in Spanish (the past alcalde and the fiscal were both described as "ladino en la lengua castellana que habla y entiende con toda perfección," and the current alcalde ordinario of San Guillermo and the sacristán mayor of Totolapa were called "sumamente ladino"). AHM L10B/21, fols. 105v, 256–77; Texas, Borden-Clarke Coll., no. 17. The pastoral visit records from 1779 on mention Mexicano and Spanish being spoken in the lowland parishes. According to Haskett, *Indigenous Rulers*, p. 144, "a majority of the jurisdiction [of Cuernavaca]'s ruling group was unable to speak Spanish even in the later eighteenth century." His 18th-century evidence covers 1700 to 1769.

21. Bolde relied especially on a detailed complaint by the Indian gobernador and 12 Indian witnesses of Atlatlaucan. BN AF 107 exp. 1470, fols. 20–49; Tulane VEMC 16 exp. 12. The impassioned brief against secularization made by the ayuntamiento of Mexico City in 1753 also uses this particular area for its specific examples. BN AF 128 exp. 1651. Even in this area there were complaints by parishioners against the doctrineros shortly before secularization. For charges against the Augustinian doctrinero of Totolapa by Indian officials of Nepopoalco in 1742–43, see Texas, Borden-Clarke Coll., no. 17. Perhaps this doctrinero could not have prevented the charges of physical abuse and unwarranted fees in any case. The root of these charges and the doctrinero's countercharges seems to have been a bitter rivalry between the cabecera of Totolapa and its dependency, Nepopoalco.

22. AGN CRS 68 exps. 4–5. The petitioners apparently felt the lightening of their pockets more than the insecurity of their souls. Their specific complaint when they asked for the return of the regulars was that they did not have to pay for mass and confession when the friars were in charge. Br. Francisco Benites de Ariza claimed in his 1760 resumé that the parishioners of Ecacingo made life so trying for their parish priests that his 21 months' service there was a record, friars included. JCB.

23. AGN CRS 84 exp. 3. Some licenciados and doctores in parish service in Morelos

plainly had their eyes on a cathedral chapter appointment from the beginning. José Joaquín de Unzueta, who had served 16 years as cura of Atenango del Río, Xuchitepec, and Jonacatepec, made his ambitions clear in a dossier prepared for the archbishop in 1793. He dwelled on the books he had bought and the reading he had done more than his work as a pastor. CRS 140 exp. 4. Unzueta did in fact gain a media ración, but in Guadalajara rather than Mexico. AGI Guad. 533; AJANG Criminal, bundle labeled "1820–21 leg. 61" (inventory of Unzueta's estate at the time of his death in 1821).

24. Militia forces had to be sent to Ameca, for example, in the secularization of the parish in 1799. Brambila, p. 112.

25. BMM 135, fols. 197–224. The investigator recommended that the friar be sent to another monastery. For complaints against regulars in Tepoztlan, see Haskett, *Indigenous Rulers*, pp. 43–44.

26. AGN DP 1 exp. 1. The 13 towns were San Felipe Agueguetzingo y Santiago Xoxotlan, San Juan Evangelista Xochitepec, San Sebastián Cuentepec, San Francisco Agueguetzingo, Santa María Concepción Alpoyecan, San Andrés Ascatlicpac, San Agustín Tetlama, San Lucas Mazatepec, San Francisco Tetecala, San Gaspar Cohuatlan, San Miguel Huixitlan (Huajintlan), San Juan Cuahuatetelco, and Santo Tomás Miacatlan.

27. AGN CRS 72 exp. 3.

28. AGN Civil 2121 exp. 10, 1736. For a similar case involving the Augustinians of Xumiltepec with the pueblo of Huecahuasco (near Ocuituco) in 1740, see AGN Crim. 174, fols. 157–239. The various pre- and post-secularization arancel disputes for Morelos are cited in the notes to Ch. 17.

29. AGN DP 1 exp. 5 ("Mueran, mueran, porque la Audiencia nos engañó con los aranceles que antes nos llevaban menos los frailes aora por el aransel nos lleban más").

30. BMM 135 exp. 17; BN AF caja 112 exp. 1530. In another kind of pre-secularization dispute, a group of mulato and creole rancheros living near Santo Domingo Hueyapan complained in 1735 that the Dominican doctrinero there was a tyrant, forcing the daughter of one parishioner to have sex with him, interfering in the private affairs of others, and spreading malicious gossip. The cura replied that the plaintiffs were his enemies. They harbored others who disobeyed him and neglected their Christian duty to attend mass. In secret testimony, several Indian leaders and creoles of Hueyapan said they had no complaint against the cura, that he fulfilled his duties, and that the dispute was between him and a group of non-Indians led by Miguel de Arisa. The complaint had been lodged, the investigator noted, after the cura issued a preliminary excommunication against the group for not attending mass. Rosenbach 462/25, pt. 4, citizens of Hueyapan vs. Fray Manuel Maldonado. For more on Hueyapan's struggles with parish priests, see AGN CRS 72 exp. 7, 1777; and AGN Hist. 319 exp. 24, 1782.

31. AGN CRS 84 exp. 3. Cheryl Martin connects secularization and fees disputes in her paper "Secularization, Clerical Finance and Parish Life in Late Colonial Mexico: The Case of Morelos." In another example, the cura of Zacualpan (Cuautla district), Juan de Ayuso Peña, reported to the archbishop in 1763 that his Augustinian predecessors had left him no instructions about the normal fees for clerical services. As a result of the confusion, his Indian parishioners were not paying even what the old arancel prescribed and had renewed an old fee dispute that long antedated secularization. Having exhausted the extrajudicial remedies, he now entered a formal complaint with the ecclesiastical court. CRS 156 exp. 9. A similar problem faced Thadeo Antonio de Acosta in the former Augustinian doctrina of Ocuituco in 1761. The audiencia's laconic order on Feb. 27, 1760, for Indians to follow the current arancel and respect the cura had had little effect. For the former Dominican doctrina of Santo Domingo Hueyapan, the new cura in 1760, Br. Juan López de Arteaga, sought the arancel because his Indian parishioners now refused to pay him what they had paid to the friars. CRS 156 exp. 8; AGN DP 2 exp. 5. See also CRS

156 exp. 6 for Atlatlaucan, where the cura was able to persuade village leaders that the arancel was also in their interest. They requested it in 1761, which apparently resolved the dispute to the satisfaction of all concerned.

32. For examples of cases turning specifically on labor demands, see AGN CRS 136 exp. 2, 1776–81, Tlaltizapan; and Tulane VEMC 53 exp. 6, 1791, Tepoztlan.

33. AGN CRS 72 exp. 10; AGN DP 3 exp. 1.

34. AGN DP 3 exp. 3. But apparently some of the parishioners of Tlaltizapan had chosen the arancel before Vásquez del Campo arrived. In 1778, their leaders appealed to the pastoral visitor for a reduction of fees. He denied the appeal and ordered them to pay the full charges listed in the arancel, not to bury their dead, and not to have processions without the cura's permission. AHM L10B/20, fols. 212–13, Cuanacalcingo. Conflict between Cuanacalcingo and its parish priests in the late colonial period is abundantly documented elsewhere in the book.

35. A shining exception, if his account is credible, was Diego de Almonacid y Salasar, interim cura of Xumiltepec in 1751 and vicario of Huitzilac from 1756 until at least 1760, when he composed his relación de méritos for the concursos of 1762–63. In Huitzilac he had organized and helped pay for a badly needed public well, a pulpit, a confessional, and the completion of a side altar to San Bartolomé. In spite of breaking his right arm horribly in a fall from his horse while returning from the visita of Coaxumulco, he celebrated mass the same day in the head town. By his account, when he turned the parish of Xumiltepec over to its propietario in 1752, the parishioners "wept inconsolably over his departure." JCB.

36. AGN CRS 156 exp. 9, fols. 366ff ("no tienen más costumbre que su voluntad"). This cura's view of his parishioners was shared by his counterpart in the district of Mazatepec and Xochitepec in 1760. He termed the Indians of San Miguel Huajintlan "very rebellious and contrary." JCB, Joseph Lucas de Santibáñez resumé. It was a defiance that this community showed both earlier and later. In the 1730's the alcalde mayor had brought suit against the Indians of Huajintlan for disrespect to the judge and insubordination over fishing rights in the Río Amacusac, and in 1780, the pastoral visitor found them still on bad terms with their cura, neglecting to follow the arancel or maintain a primary school. AGN Crim. 204 exp. 12, 1734; AHM L10B/21, fol. 84.

37. The cura asked for the arrest of four men whom he regarded as the leaders of the collective actions. He also petitioned that the market held at Temoac every five days be moved to the head town of Zacualpan. The audiencia's verdict, on Sept. 27, 1764, called for the publication of the arancel then in force and legal proceedings against the accused leaders.

A fondness in Morelos villages for bullfights that favored the bull and expressed the same contentious localism seen in the late colonial evidence was reported in the late 1930's by Nathaniel Wolff in a newspaper story about apprentice matadors of Mexico City. Word came from "the tiny village of Vista Hermosa, Morelos" that there would be bulls to fight during the community fiesta on March 21:

> They had about twenty bulls to fight, most of which had appeared previously at these fiestas. They are privately owned and not allowed to be killed. That means that they are "educated" and are able to distinguish between the man and the cape, or *muleta*. They always go for the man. The chief of the bulls was a monster seven years old. He was bigger than any bull you ever saw in the *Toreo*. He was the village pride because he had already killed more than a dozen people. His name was Ojos Negros—"Black Eyes." The boys had no choice.
>
> When Ojos Negros broke into the ring the first thing he did was to tear off the cheek of a woman who was holding her face too close to the interstices of the rail

fence. Then Mario stepped on the place. He slipped. He was thrown out of the ring by the bull and his right thigh gashed open to the white of the bone. A *ranchero*, who wished to show how much better he was than the city *toreros*, jumped before the bull. The *ranchero* got it in the belly, dying almost immediately.

At this point one of Mario's friends grabbed a sword and stabbed Ojos Negros fatally. That annoyed the public. They wanted to put the "murderers" of the village pride in prison, to prevent their getting away. They refused them a horse to take the wounded boy to the highway. (Quoted in Kirk, pp. 25–26).

38. BEJ Papeles de Derecho, 4: 165–76, Oct. 16, 1778, report by the comandante gobernador of Guadalajara: "éstos [gente de razón] gustan de juegos y toros y aquéllos [Indians] de danzas y bebidas."

39. Rangel, p. 142.

40. AGN CRS 156 exp. 9.

41. AGN CRS 136 exp. 2, fols. 78–79. Cuanacalcingo had been involved in fees disputes since 1775. CRS 68 exps. 4–5; AHM L10B/20, fols. 212–13. Parishioners in the vicinity of modern Morelos near the end of the colonial period were notorious for making fun of the priest, if not of the liturgy. In 1802, three Indians of La Magdalena called upon the cura of Chimalhuacan Atenco, asking him to come confess a sick member of the community. The cura noticed that one of the three was covering his face, as if to stifle a laugh. The cura's assistant arrived in La Magdalena to find that the man was not gravely ill, only drunk. When asked what ailed him, he replied that his heart hurt because no mass had been celebrated in the pueblo. The cura's reaction was to write the archbishop and lament that "the disorders in the parish increase each day . . . only dissension and insolence reign." He said he feared a general uprising and blamed the pernicious influence of mulatos and lobos. AGN Crim. 255, fols. 287–88.

42. AGN DP 3 exp. 3, fol. 47.

43. AGN Indios 13 exp. 224, 1641, Ozumba; Indios 13 exp. 325, 1641, Tlalmanalco; Indios 21 exp. 162, 1657, Tlahuac; Indios 24 exp. 352, 1670, Chalco district (gobernadores of the principal communities agreed to pay 600p per year to the asentista for the privilege of selling pulque).

44. Two years after the Mexico City riots, the alcalde mayor of Cuernavaca was ordered to enforce the pulque laws and keep the Indian women of Santa María from selling it. AGN Indios 32 exp. 184, 1694. The preliminary investigation in this case dwelled on the bad effects of the drink, that it caused laziness, violence, litigiousness, and other outrages. There had long been a concern to control adulterated pulque and drunkenness, but this was a turn away from the pro-pulque attitude of earlier royal decrees. In the early 18th century, representatives of pueblos in this area said they produced only for their own use ("para beber entre sí") and complained of the pulque asentista trying to collect the old fees as if they were still selling the drink. AGN Crim. 1 exp. 29, 1705, Chalco; AGN Civil 2229 exp. 7, 1722, Xumiltepec; Civil 1508 exp. 8, 1738, San Sebastián Achichipico. For the same reason, pueblos in the Cuautla district resisted paying pulque taxes in the 1780's. AGN Pulques 2, fol. 252.

45. AGN Pulques 2, fol. 133.

46. Ibid. According to this report, only Huitzilac continued to actively market pulque. Commercial production also continued in the upland parishes of Tepoztlan, Tlalnepantla, and Atlatlaucan. AHM L10B/21, fols. 110r, 119, 1779–80; Haskett, *Indigenous Rulers*, p. 182.

47. The 18th-century laws on alcoholic beverages for New Spain are assembled in BN Manuscripts, nos. 1358–61; and AGN Aguardiente de Caña. Mezcal was selectively licensed, especially in the first decade in the Bajío, where it did not compete with pulque. AGN General de Parte 24 exps. 122, 179. But not in Puebla, where the pulque asentista

reported that his revenues were declining because of competition from the illegal production of local distilled drinks. General de Parte 23 exp. 9, 1714. Chinguirito was permitted in Guatemala from at least 1753 to 1766. But royal decrees before 1767 generally forbade native brandies as noxious beverages and undesirable competition for imported liquor. For details, see Hernández Palomo, chs. 2–5.

48. AGN Crim. 29 exp. 6, fol. 76r, 1796, Xochitepec (defense attorney said of the Indians of this area, "siempre que toman pulque acaban de embriagarse con aguardiente"); Crim. 203, fols. 404–87, 1816, Huitzilac (Indian who admitted to killing his wife on Candlemas said he had spent the entire day getting drunk on pulque and aguardiente); Crim. 39 exp. 18, 1818, Cuernavaca (Indian murderer said he received aguardiente after working all day on an irrigation project).

49. BN Manuscripts, nos. 1358–61. Nine years before, in 1758, the protomedicato had declared chinguirito to be more healthful than grape brandy. The same experts who favored local aguardientes in 1767 regarded pulque as unsanitary, "una de la bebidas más nocivas que la malicia humana ha discurrido contra su propia salud." Ibid., no. 1358, exp. 11. At a time when Indians were expected to assimilate more fully into colonial society and adopt the civilized habits of their superiors, pulque was regarded as an "Indian drink" that reduced other classes of people who drank it to the level of Indians ("se hacen indios"). Pulquerías were treated in these reports as the cause of Indian deaths and irreligion.

50. AGN Civil 1798 exp. 5, Marqués de Branciforce, Jan. 30, 1797, authorizing the pardon and release of those who had violated the old prohibition laws.

51. According to the 1797 plan to enforce the new liquor tax laws in the Cuernavaca district, pulque came from the pueblos, fields, and ranchos of the Indians, and aguardiente from the barrancas and the small and large sugar mills far from the district capital. AGN Aguardiente de Caña 13, fol. 23. In fact, the sugar plantations may not have produced the bulk of the liquor. The treasury authorities were worried that plantation owners in the Izúcar area were selling their syrup at high prices rather than upping the production of aguardiente, thereby avoiding taxation. Ibid., last expediente, Feb. 12, 1797.

52. Local observers like Manuel Morales, cura of Mazatepec in 1802, were impressed by the excessive and disorderly drinking: "No se ven en este país, señor, más que embriagueses, concubinatos, adulterios, estupros, padres de familia ofendidos por el urto que le han hecho de sus hijas, heridas, muertes, y otros males sin remedio alguno aun el sueño no se puede tomar por la mucha algarabía nocturna." AGN CRS 177 exp. 10, fols. 448–49. Pueblos of Morelos received special mention from pastoral visitors in the late colonial period for their drunkenness. AHM L10A/8, fol. 158r; L10B/10, fol. 49 (at Yecapixtla the visitador wrote of "los vicios de embriaguez y luxuria que tanto dominan en estos pueblos"); L10B/21, fol. 51r. Examples of drunken binges that ended in personal affronts or lethal violence: AGN Indios 21 exp. 160, 1657, Cuernavaca; AGN Crim. 159, fols. 44–57, 1810, Tlayacapan; Crim. 203, fols. 404–87, 1816, Huitzilac; Crim. 103 exp. 12, 1818, Jonacapa.

53. AGN Crim. 507 exp. 17.

54. AGN CRS 68 exp. 4, fol. 438v.

55. Minos, pp. 17–28.

56. AHM L10A/8, fol. 163r, 1759–60; L10B/21, fol. 110r, 1779–80; Dussel, *Historia general*, 5: 146 (unauthorized tour of the Christ of Tlayacapan, 1751). A cacique-schoolmaster of Tlaltizapan was discovered in 1760 with 18 works of "diabolical rites" written in Nahuatl. Gruzinski, *Man-Gods*, p. 169. Priests who tampered with local images and other instruments of the faith were in for trouble. At Atlautla in the parish of Chimalhuacan, the cura raised a tumulto in 1799 when he tried to sell an old side altar and use the proceeds for a new one. AGN Crim. 157 fols. 93–132.

57. Minos, pp. 44–45, 64–66, has a 1771 appeal to the cura of Xichiltepec by the fiscal

of San Gerónimo Metl for his support in tribute assessments and against a neighboring Spanish landlord, and an 1864 account of the pueblo of Tehuistla relocating on the other side of the Río del Estudiante in the 18th century after a vicario drowned trying to cross the river to reach it.

58. AGN CRS 136 exp. 2, Jan. 29, 1782, Cuanacalcingo; AGN Inq. 1304 exp. 3 and 1334 exp. 3, fol. 107r, 1796, Zacualpan (see also AGN Acervo 49 caja 147, Aug. 26, 1816, letter of Joseph Manuel Sotomayor, now at Jonacatepec); CRS 140 exp. 4, 1796, Yautepec (testimony of d. Andrés de San Julián and confession of the cura); CRS 177 exp. 10, fols. 442–46, 488–89, 1800, Mazatepec (cura claimed that 716 individuals—roughly equal numbers of men and women—plus some families and nearly the entire pueblo of Coatetelco had not fulfilled the precepto anual); AGN Crim. 255 exp. 13, 1802, Chimalhuacan. The bitter late-18th-century disputes with curas in the districts of modern Morelos over sacramental fees, first fruits, and labor service expose similar resistance to the priest's leadership. These disputes and sentiments were not unique to Morelos, but their undercurrent of vehemence seems unusual. Notable examples are CRS 72 exp. 7, 1767, Hueyapan; CRS 68 exps. 4–5, and CRS 136 exp. 2, 1775–82, Tlaltizapan; AGN Civil 2292 exp. 3, 1796, Santa María de la Asunción Tetecala; and CRS 72 exp. 10, 1804, Tlaquiltenango. Late colonial curas in this area also claimed to be struggling against "superstitions," especially in the 1750's and 1760's. The former cura of San Salvador Ocotepec said of his service, "con crecido trabajo ha reducido a estos pobres a la Ley de Dios los que en estos altos vivían con toda libertad . . . los halló muy colmados de abusos, arreglados a las costumbres supersticiosas de sus antepasados"; and Francisco Herrera Cervantes y Pozo said he exposed idolatry among the Indians of Chalco in 1760 and arranged for the penitents to be treated mercifully. JCB, Xuárez de Escobedo and Cervantes y Pozo resumés. The pastoral visitor to the area in 1759–60 was concerned about superstitions and rites in the hills in the parish of Tlaquiltenango, and the visitor in 1767 gave a special 30-minute lecture against superstition at Yecapixtla. AHM L10A/8, fol. 163r; L10B/10, entry 49. Indian and casta seers and their practices that were thought to be evidence of witchcraft were brought to the Inquisition's attention in the 17th century: for example, AGN Inq. 303, fols. 78–80, 1624, Tlaquiltenango (an old woman diviner and Indians took ololiuhqui—morning glory seeds—to have visions); and AGN Inq. 435, fols. 12–13, 1656, Achichipico (mestiza principal of Achichipico charged with practicing witchcraft with ololiuhqui).

59. AGN CRS 68 exps. 4–5.

60. AGN CRS 136 exp. 2, fols. 166r–167r, July 16, 1781.

61. AGN CRS 68 exps. 4–5, fol. 409.

62. Indian women were as conspicuous as men in some other public protests against colonial authority in late-18th-century Morelos. At Zacualpan de las Amilpas, where townspeople resisted the cura's demands and the audiencia's order to pay the customary clerical fees in 1763, Spanish witnesses spoke of Indian women as well as men howling and screaming in protest. D. Rafael Francisco Rodríguez testified that in the loud defiance of the alguacil mayor's visit to enforce the audiencia decree, "the Indian women are worse than the men." AGN CRS 156 exp. 9, fols. 357v ff.

63. AGN Crim. 203 exp. 4. Ten years later, Gamboa's successor complained that the leader, José Tenepantla, still made trouble for the parish priests and was protected by the alcalde mayor (fols. 180ff). The long bill of particulars that parishioners of Tepoztlan agreed to abide by in 1779 provides a fuller account of their "abuses and disobedience": they were to pay their clerical fees promptly, according to the customary arrangement; to pay the cura punctually the tithe and first fruits; to hear mass on the prescribed days and submit to roll call; to call the cura promptly to confess the sick and bury the dead; to reestablish primary schools in the head town and sujetos, and send their children to them and to catechism classes; to attend and participate in reciting the catechism on Sundays;

and to refrain from selling or taking out loans on their children and making young men serve in the homes of their future in-laws. Men and women were not to bathe together in the sweat baths; the gobernador was to assist the cura whenever asked; and the gobernador and other officials of the community were to leave the property of the local churches and all spiritual and ecclesiastical matters strictly to the priests. All were to "live quietly and peacefully, to obey and respect their cura as their spiritual Father, to live and act from now on as Christians who seek salvation, and to work to prevent drunkenness and other public sins." AHM L10B/21, fols. 50v–51r.

As elsewhere, Morelos Indians also expressed their opposition to colonial authorities by passive resistance and flight. The pastoral visitor's exhortation to parishioners of Tlaltizapan in 1778 that they provide for the weekly renovation mass and supply of Hosts met with sullen silence. AHM L10B/20, fol. 192r. In the Cuanacalcingo labor dispute, the Indians refused to comply with the audiencia's order on the grounds that only their elected officials could authorize compliance. The officials were conveniently absent whenever the court's emissary appeared. Temporary or permanent migration was a threat and an established practice in some of these disputes. AGN Hist. 132 exp. 29, fols. 9–11, 1794, Cuernavaca; AGN CRS 68 exp. 4, cura Ortega's letter of Dec. 15, 1780. New migration was a particular worry to colonial authorities in late colonial Morelos because of what they regarded as already widespread vagrancy. In Lt. Matute's elliptical observation during a dispute with the cura of Mazatepec in 1800, "Residence in many *haciendas*, *ranchos* and settlements is seasonal, and the residence of many inhabitants moveable because of their vice of vagrancy." CRS 177 exp. 10, fols. 394–95.

64. For example, the cura of Tlaltizapan, in his dispute with Indian parishioners over labor service, urged the audiencia to verify his side of the dispute by calling the hacienda administrators and other "vecinos de razón" in the parish to testify. AGN CRS 136 exp. 2, fol. 206v.

65. AGN Acervo 49 caja 146, Aug. 26, 1816, Joseph Manuel Sotomayor letter.

66. AGN CRS 177 exp. 10, fols. 448–49. The heat generated by rivalries between district governors and parish priests in late colonial Morelos is documented on the alcalde mayor's side by Hipólito Villarroel, whose withering blasts against lazy, corrupt, venal, and obstructionist parish priests have already been discussed in some detail. Villarroel's sweeping conclusions were undoubtedly informed by his experience in the field (on which, see Borah, "Alguna luz"). But Villarroel's partisan account, composed in the mid-1780's, may well reveal more about the thinking of an angry ex–district governor than about the conditions and classes of people described. In any case, as I have said, its claims require independent corroboration at nearly every point. Manuel de Agüero at Yautepec, Miguel José Losada at Tlaquiltenango, and Manuel Morales at Mazatepec had serious conflicts with the district governor in the last two decades of the colonial period. AGN CRS 140 exp. 4, 1796; CRS 178 exp. 9, 1797; CRS 177 exp. 10, 1800; CRS 197 exp. 14, 1802; CRS 192 exp. 3, 1802; AGN Bienes 172 exp. 51, 1804. When anonymous charges were brought against the district governor of Yautepec in 1794, his superior—the governor of the Marquesado del Valle at Cuernavaca—rose to his defense, declaring that the suit was a trumped-up attack by "my capital enemy, the *cura* of the *cabecera* of Cuernavaca." AGN Hist. 132 exp. 27, fol. 5r.

67. AGN CRS 192 exp. 3, Oct. 27 and Oct. 31, 1802, letters to Father Morales from one of his brothers. The cura's lawyer successfully discredited the case against his client, noting especially the suspicious uniformity of the testimony against him and an unblemished record in his previous appointments. Still, the courts were not overly sympathetic. In March 1803, the ecclesiastical court and the audiencia simply dismissed his latest counter-charges against the lieutenant.

68. When Morales initiated the struggle at court in 1800, the lieutenant and his allies

criticized the cura in return for not hiring as many vicarios as the parish required for adequate spiritual care. AGN CRS 177 exp. 10. This was also their most substantial complaint in 1802 when they brought their own formal charges against Morales. CRS 197 exp. 14. While sharply critical of Morales for launching the complaint against his "most humble and compliant" lieutenant, the alcalde mayor of Cuernavaca in 1800 certified to the cura's diligence and the good order of his parish records. CRS 177 exp. 10, fol. 447. In 1809, however, Morales (now cura of Zacualpan de las Amilpas) was accused of various illicit relations with Indian women. Tulane VEMC 42 exp. 31.

69. AGN Inq. 1304 exp. 3 and 1334 exp. 3, Zacualpan, 1796 (Sotomayor); AGN CRS 140 exp. 4, 1796, Yautepec (confession of Manuel de Agüero); Martin, *Rural Society*, p. 190. Lieutenants were also the targets of heated complaints to the high courts for personal misconduct and the abuse of office. AGN Crim. 205, 1764, Cuernavaca; AGN Hist. 132 exp. 26, 1793, Tetecala, Tlaquiltenango, and Jonacatepec.

70. Nine years later, the audiencia fiscal reviewed the file and noted that the matter of how the cult of the Eucharist would be funded had been left pending in 1794. Since there had been no subsequent complaints, he recommended that the case be closed, and that the subdelegado take care that cofradía meetings be held only if a representative of the crown presided. The priest could be present, but only in the passive role of "rector de la casa." Tulane VEMC 53 exp. 22, 1794–1803. Another case of a parish priest accused of consuming the Host is in AGN CRS 136 exps. 6–7, 1790, San Francisco Temascaltepec.

71. AGN CRS 192 exp. 3. Morales considered himself to be in a struggle for the souls of his parishioners against heretical healers and diviners. AGN Inq. 1397, fols. 205–16, 1800 (case against Juan el cojo, mulato).

72. AGN CRS 68 exps. 4–5.

73. AGN CRS 72 exp. 3, 1671; BMM 135, exp. 16, arts. 4–5, 1734.

74. JCB, resumé no. 137.

75. AGN Hist. 132 exp. 26.

76. AGN CRS 177 exp. 10, fols. 394–95.

77. Even Manuel Morales, the popular cura of Mazatepec during the last years of the colonial period, was understood by the Inquisition to have acted "scandalously" in church. He was said to have been careless with the liturgy and let his temper get the best of him. While distributing the consecrated wafers at communion he had once shouted, "So you want to bite me, do you?" which stirred laughter in the church. On another occasion he had interrupted the mass and gone into the congregation to berate a parishioner. AGN Inq. 1397 last fol., June 15, 1808.

This is not to say that the districts of Cuernavaca and Cuautla did not have many largely inconspicuous curas and vicarios, active in their pastoral duties. The subdelegados who reported on the priests in their districts in 1793 did not dwell on misconduct, although Antonio de la Landa y Garcés was so recently appointed to Cuernavaca that he was unable to individualize their personal qualities. Juan Felipe Velásquez of Cuautla found nothing particularly negative to report; some of the curas were new, and he knew nothing about them, but he singled out the Dominican doctrinero of Cuautla, Pedro Alva, and the cura of Ocuituco, Juan Alexandro Piedra Palacio, for praise as discreet, judicious, and learned pastors. AGN Hist. 578A. At least a faction in most parishes supported the local priest. For example, when Manuel Urizar, vicario of Huitzuco, was charged in 1805 with sexual misconduct, the Indian gobernador and others rose to his defense, praising his "most honorable conduct and great many acts of charity. . . . We have never before seen such a devoted minister, as is well known throughout the tierra caliente." AGN Bienes 172 exp. 53.

78. AGN Inq. 1221 exp. 9; Inq. 1401 exps. 11–12. In separate Inquisition cases, the curas of Yecapixtla and Otumba were accused in 1795 of various provocative political and moral

declarations about the French Revolution and the priesthood. AGN Inq. 1326 exp. 2; Inq. 1360 exps. 1–2.

79. For the final picaresque twists to Sotomayor's public career, see his prim Aug. 26, 1816, letter in AGN Acervo 49 caja 146 and the dispute with his parishioners in 1818 in AGN Crim. 204 exp. 13. Haskett describes this final episode: "a nervous curate of Jonacatepec became alarmed when members of the municipal council were discovered plotting in the home of the town's governor. Convinced they intended to revolt, he denounced them to the military authorities, only to find that they had been working out the details of a criminal suit against the unpopular curate himself." *Indigenous Rulers*, p. 196.

80. AGN Bienes 172 exp. 51.

81. Tulane VEMC 8 exp. 21 ("un antípoda a todo lo que toca a la jurisdicción real"; "mi carácter y religión me nesesitan a la mansedumbre y sufrimiento para radicar y cultivar la paz"; "un hombre sobervio, temerario, favuloso, arrojado, audas").

82. In the same spirit, but without working out the historical possibilities in detail, is Ingham, *Mary, Michael, and Lucifer*. In his interpretation of local religion and religious change in Tlayacapan, Ingham emphasizes "the Catholicity of traditional culture" and sees within the religious ritual and symbolism counterpoints between conflict and solidarity that express social relationships. For the colonial period, he is inclined to follow Foster and Ricard into an emphasis on Europeanization, missing the continuities in habits of conception that Clendinnen, Lockhart, and others see. Perhaps this is more appropriate for Tlayacapan than it would be for many other communities of central Mexico in the 18th century.

83. Martin's illuminating discussion of the Yautepec disputes in the 1790's and 1800's in *Rural Society*, ch. 8, brings together the principal evidence from AGN.

84. BMM 113, pp. 102–3.

85. JCB, de la Mota resumé.

86. AGN RCO 82 exp. 140, which says that people from other pueblos followed the flight to Popocatepetl. According to Sedano, 1: 34, the guilty Indians were paraded in an auto de fe in Mexico City "around 1760." Gruzinski, *Man-Gods*, ch. 5, provides a fuller description of the 1761 events from records sent to the Council of the Indies. The related case against Luisa Carrillo, between 1761 and 1768, appears in AGN Inq. 1073, fols. 13–119 and 225–53. Witnesses in this case also referred to Pérez's "idol" as an image of the Virgin. Carrillo's daughter, María Gertrudis Anastasia, mentioned the use by Pérez and Pascual de Santa María of a statue of a child with a dog's head and the devil's tail.

87. Gruzinski, *Man-Gods*, pp. 162–63.

88. Judging by testimony in the case against Luisa Carrillo, Pérez's appeal was less Indian v. non-Indian than this quote suggests. Carrillo herself was said to be a mestiza or mulata. See AGN Inq. 1073 exp. 2, especially the testimony of María de la Cruz (loba) and Carrillo's daughter and husband (mulatos) in fols. 29–43. The vicario of San Pedro Ecacingo claimed to have apprehended "fifty-six idolaters from various jurisdictions," who had gathered in a cave in his district to "worship the idol that Antonio the shepherd (the main criminal in this matter) possessed," and sent them to the judge at Yautepec. JCB, 1760, Benites de Ariza resumé.

89. BN AF caja 107 exp. 1470, part of case assembled for the Franciscan guardian at Ozumba. This nostalgia for former Augustinian pastors of Totolapa in 1753 seems out of phase with the heated complaints of Nepozualco's gobernador and república against the Augustinian cura ministro of Totolapa in 1742–43 for neglect of his duties and for whipping the sacristanes of visitas. Pastor Joseph de Sevilla replied that these Indians did not support the church enthusiastically and what few church ornaments they had were poorly cared for. This particular dispute apparently stemmed from Nepozoalco's campaign for a

resident priest and an end to all service in Totolapa. Texas, Borden-Clarke Coll., no. 17. Other doctrinas in this area had been subdivided this way in recent years and may also have been in some turmoil. Father Sevilla claimed that recent subdivisions of Chimalhuacan Chalco, Tepetlixpa, Atlautla, Tlalnepantla, and Atlatlaucan had caused great hardships for the friars.

90. Tulane VEMC 16 exp. 12. On a bitter fee dispute in the parish of Atlatlaucan in 1761–62 led by a "coyote," Joseph Zárate, see AGN CRS 156 exp. 6.

91. AHM L10A/8, fols. 152v, 158, 163r, and unfoliated entries 49 and 50.

92. AGN RCO 84 exp. 140.

93. AGN RCO 82 exp. 72, 1762; RCO 86 exp. 160, 1765.

94. Agüero paid 125p in mesada tax at the time he took over the Yautepec parish in 1772. AGI Mex. 2726 (summary of the mesadas paid that year). He left the parish for good in 1807 to become a prebend in the cathedral chapter of the archdiocese. Martin, *Rural Society*, p. 187.

95. AGN Civil 1341 exp. 4.

96. Ibid., exp. 1.

97. AGN Civil 1889.

98. AGN Civil 1520 exp. 4, fol. 42 ("Hombre, es Ud. muy fatal").

99. Evidently del Cerro was behind another long-running suit brought against Agüero in 1796 for debts and libelous insults, initiated by d. Manuel de Ortuna. AGN Civil 1520 exp. 4. While both del Cerro and Agüero used their privileged positions to enrich their estates, the conflict between them does not seem to have been rooted in a rivalry of office, at least not on Agüero's part. In Jan. 1794, Father Agüero was called to testify in the case of unsigned accusations against del Cerro's successor as lieutenant of Yautepec. The anonymous accuser, claiming to speak for Yautepec's vecinos, dueños de tiendas, trapiches and haciendas de azúcar, charged the lieutenant with forced contributions for the feast of the Immaculate Conception and abuses in the sale of livestock. Agüero testified on the lieutenant's behalf that there had been no forced contributions from any hacienda. AGN Hist. 132 exp. 27.

100. AGN CRS 140 exps. 4–5, 1796–97. How important the cofradía property issue was to the dispute is not clear from this record. Agüero claimed that he had founded the cofradías in question, not usurped control of institutions and estates that had been under the direction of laymen (fol. 276v).

101. AGN CRS 140 exp. 4, fol. 267 ("Ni sol, ni agua, ni malos caminos ni cosa alguna le a impedido el asistir, llamado aún en las oras más incómodas de la noche a qualesquiera feligrés suyo").

102. An account of Agüero's successors and the political problems of Lt. Manuel de Porras is given in Martin, *Rural Society*, pp. 187–92.

103. A trace of this kind of network is the letter sent by the gobernador of Cuanacalcingo to the gobernador and officials of Ticuman on March 10, 1781, asking them to attend a meeting the following day to organize against the parish priest. AGN CRS 68 exps. 4–5, fol. 448. Haskett briefly considers Indian contacts across communities in *Indigenous Rulers*, p. 17.

104. Brian Hamnett, *Roots of Insurgency*, pp. 71–72, 154, 174, juxtaposes Indian villagers and hacendados of Morelos in this way.

105. The figures on Morelos's forces vary. Tutino, *From Insurrection*, p. 188, says 5,500, Timmons, p. 69, 4,000–4,500. The Morelos area had been penetrated by Hidalgo's forces in Oct. 1810. But according to Alamán, 2: 327–29, after occupying Cuernavaca and 21 haciendas, they were expelled the following month with the aid of 57 hacienda dependents, most of them from the estates of Gabriel Yermo. In Nov. 1811, Xochitepec was sacked by insurgents. See Van Young, "Comentario," p. 58; and AGN Crim. 204 exps. 10–11.

106. In June, the remaining insurgent forces at the Hacienda de Temilpa under Francisco Ayala were defeated by Capt. José Gabriel de Armijo. Alamán, 3: 164–66.

107. According to Alamán, 2: 490–91, except for "la poca gente allegadiza de las inmediaciones de Cuautla, los demás eran todos negros y mulatos de la costa."

108. For example, cofradías and images of Our Lady of Guadalupe at Tlayacapan and Atlatlauca are listed in a 1705 summary of emoluments for the district of Cuernavaca. AGN Bienes 500 exps. 4–5.

109. The three known parish priests who joined Morelos are Mariano Matamoros and his vicario, Matías Zavala; and José Antonio Valdivieso, cura of Ocuituco. The two priests who are not certainly parish priests are Joaquín Díaz and Eduardo Zavala. Both were from Tlayacapan. *Morelos: Documentos inéditos*, 1: 219–20; María y Campos, pp. 32–33; Alamán, 4: 63. A possible addition is a vicario of Santo Domingo, who provided helpful intelligence to Matamoros at Izúcar. *Proceso instruído*, p. 69. My total on the parish priests is based on an incomplete list of parishes and pastors for the districts of Cuernavaca and Cuautla in 1805 in Florescano & Gil, pp. 185–92.

110. María y Campos, p. 22.

111. *Proceso instruído*, pp. 14–21, 62, 69, 81–82, 93–94; María y Campos, pp. 13–14, 22, 32–33. According to Salido Beltrán, p. 62, 200 troops were enlisted at Jantetelco.

112. The district of Sultepec, adjoining the modern border of Morelos to the northwest, was the one exception that occurred to Matamoros. He was not certain whether insurgents operated successfully there because local pueblos freely supported the insurgency or whether they did so under duress. *Proceso instruído*, pp. 81–82. The local support there could well have been freely given. In 1811, the cura of Sultepec, Francisco Garrido, reported that priests and residents of the cabecera were supporting Father Hidalgo's insurrection because a number of them were his relatives. García & Pereyra, 5: 32. See also Alamán, 2: 345, 537–38; 3: 149–51, 154; 4: 719. Though Garrido's checkered career of misconduct and inattention to his pastoral duties in the 1790's (AGN Hist. 578A, Metepec report) might have made him a candidate for political protest after 1810, he apparently did not join the movement. Morelos continued recruiting fighters from pueblos and ranchos of the Cuautla area after the siege. See Hernández y Dávalos, 5: 274 (commission to Capt. José María Larios of Jan. 25, 1814). On insurgent activity in Morelos after the siege, see Alamán, 4: 420–21.

113. For instance, two rival factions combining Indian, mestizo, and mulato villagers, creole hacendados, and peninsular merchants that had struggled over control of land, water, and political power at the district level might well cancel each other out in a wider struggle, or both might remain on the sidelines.

114. AGN Civil 1674 exp. 25, José María Niña report. In the same expediente, the subdelegado of San Miguel el Grande briefly described an hacienda that had been settled by many tenants, and the need for a teniente de campo there.

115. BN AF caja 112 exp. 1530.

116. H. McLeod, p. 60.

Bibliographical Material

Bibliographical Note

Several long runs of judicial and administrative records that encompass the Archdiocese of Mexico and the Diocese of Guadalajara housed in archives and libraries in Mexico, Spain, and the United States proved especially useful in building a history of parish life in the eighteenth century, notably the proceedings of civil and criminal court cases in the Archivo General de la Nación (AGN, Mexico City), the Archivo Judicial de la Audiencia de la Nueva Galicia (AJANG, Guadalajara), and the Viceregal and Ecclesiastical Mexican Collection of Tulane University (New Orleans); the sets of episcopal court records in AGN and the Guadalajara cathedral archive; the Inquisition's administrative and judicial papers; pastoral visit books in the Archivo Histórico de la Mitra (Mexico City) and the Guadalajara cathedral archive; the professional resumés and manuscripts of priests that are scattered from the Archivo General de Indias (AGI) in Seville, to university libraries on both U.S. coasts, to the Biblioteca Nacional de México, to the cathedral archives; royal cedulas and audiencia findings in AGN and AJANG; parish registers filmed for the Church of Jesus Christ of Latter-day Saints in Salt Lake City; and the financial records that seem to turn up everywhere.

The rich case records, detailed administrative reports for a particular year on priests, schools, ecclesiastical property, or parish income (for which AGI is the premier source), digests of law and legal opinion, the records of the Fourth Provincial Council, pastoral letters and other published works that parish priests knew well, and broken runs of sodality reports and sermons not only added depth to the serial information, but suggested answers to some of their own mysteries in the patterns over time.

The Notes contain citations to the following archives:

Alderman Library, University of Virginia, Charlottesville, VA: William Gates Collection
Archivo del Estado de Oaxaca, Oaxaca City, Juzgados section
Archivo Fiscal de la Real Audiencia de Nueva Galicia, Biblioteca del Estado de Jalisco, Guadalajara

Archivo General de Indias, Sevilla. Sections:
    Audiencia de Guadalajara
    Audiencia de México
    Indiferente General
Archivo General de la Nación, Mexico. Ramos:

Acervo 49 (provisorato records)	Historia
Acordada	Hospital de Jesús
Aguardiente de Caña	Impresos Oficiales
Alcaldes Mayores	Indios
Bandos	Inquisición
Bienes Nacionales	Intendencias
Civil	Operaciones de Guerra
Clero Regular y Secular	Policía
Cofradías y Archicofradías	Pulques
Criminal	Reales Cédulas Originales
Derechos Parroquiales	Templos y Conventos
Diezmos	Tierras
Epidemias	
General de Parte	

Archivo Histórico de Jalisco, Guadalajara:
    Archivo Municipal de Acatlán de Juárez
    Mexican Manuscripts (general classification)
Archivo Histórico de la Mitra, Mexico City
Bancroft Library, University of California, Berkeley: Mexican Manuscripts
Benson Library, University of Texas, Austin. Latin American Collection:
    Borden-Clarke Collection
    García Collection
    Mariano Riva Palacio Collection
    Muse Purchase
    Wallace B. Stephens Collection
Biblioteca del Estado de Jalisco, Guadalajara:
    Archivo Fiscal de la Real Audiencia de Nueva Galicia
    Archivo Judicial de la Real Audiencia de Nueva Galicia. Civil and Criminal sections.
    Colección Miscelánea
    Papeles de Derecho (MS 300)
Biblioteca Nacional, Mexico City:
    Archivo Franciscano
    Colección LaFragua
    Manuscripts (general classification)
Cathedral Archive of the Arzobispado de Guadalajara
Firestone Library, Princeton University, Princeton, N.J.: Western Americana Collection
Hispanic Society of America, New York City
Instituto Nacional de Antropología e Historia library, Museo de Antropología, Mexico City: Colección de Documentación del Castillo de Chapultepec, Sección Oaxaca
John Carter Brown Library, Providence, R.I.: Spanish Codex Collection
Latin American Library, Tulane University, New Orleans:
    Bliss Collection, Collection II
    Mexican Administrative Records
    Viceregal and Ecclesiastical Mexican Collection
Library of Congress, Washington, D.C.: Mexican Manuscripts Collection

New York Public Library, New York City
Real Academia de Historia, Madrid
Rockefeller Library, Brown University, Providence, R.I.: Medina Collection (microfilm)
Rosenbach Library, Philadelphia: Mexican Manuscripts section
Speer Library, Princeton University, Princeton, N.J.
Sutro Library, California State Historical Society, San Francisco
Washington State University, Pullman: Regla Papers
Wilson Library, University of North Carolina, Chapel Hill

Bibliography

With some exceptions (pastoral letters, *relaciones de méritos y servicios*, *aranceles*, *cédulas*, *bandos* or other laws, short circulars, proclamations, and sermons that were published individually), all printed works not cited in full in the Notes are listed here. I have included certain uncited works from the fields of religious studies, anthropology, political science, sociology, and history that contributed to my thinking about power, religion, culture, and change in colonial Latin America. Unless otherwise indicated, all Spanish-language books are published in México, D.F.

Acosta Gómez, Ricardo. *Los templos de Sierra de Pinos, Zac. y sus ministros.* San Luis Potosí, 1984.
Adams, Richard N. *Energy and Structure: A Theory of Social Power.* Austin, Tex., 1975.
Aguirre, Ignacio. *Noticias varias de la Nueva Galicia: Intendencia de Guadalajara.* Guadalajara, 1878.
Aguirre, Manuel J. *Ensayo histórico de Teocaltiche.* 1971.
Aguirre Beltrán, Gonzalo. "Delación del cura de Acayucan, D. Joaquín de Urquijo," *México Agrario*, 4, no. 1 (1972): 63–73.
———. *Formas de gobierno indígena.* 1953.
———. *Medicina y magia: El proceso de aculturación enla estructura colonial.* 1963.
———. *Regiones de refugio.* 1957.
———. *El señorío de Cuauhtochco: Luchas agrarias en México durante el virreinato.* 1940.
Ajofrín, Fr. Francisco de. *Diario del viaje que pororden de la Sagrada Congregación de Propaganda Fide hizo a la América septentrional en el siglo XVIII* [1763]. 2 vols. Madrid, 1958.
Alamán, Lucas. *Historia de México: Desde los primeros movimientos que prepararon su independencia en el año de 1808 hasta la época presente.* 5 vols. 1985.
Alanís Boyso, José Luis. *Corregidores de Toluca: Apuntes para su estudio, 1590–1810.* 1976.
———. "Corregimiento de Toluca: Pueblo y elecciones de república en el siglo XVIII," *Historia Mexicana*, 25 (1976): 455–77.

———. *Elecciones de república para los pueblos del corregimiento de Toluca, 1729-1811.* 1978.

———. *Introducción al estudio de los corregidores y alcaldes mayores del Marquesado de Valle (títulos de 1590 a 1810).* 1977.

Alcedo, Antonio de. *Diccionario geográfico histórico de las Indias occidentales o América* [1786-89]. 4 vols. Madrid, 1967.

Aldridge, A. Owen, ed. *The Ibero-American Enlightenment.* Urbana, Ill., 1971.

Alvarez Mejía, Juan. "La cuestión del clero indígena en la época colonial," *Revista Javeriana,* 2 parts, 45 (1956): 57-67, 209-19.

Amira de Narte, Sejo. *Clamores de la América y recurso a la protección de María Santíssima de Guadalupe en las presentes calamidades.* 1811.

Anderson, Arthur J. O. "Sahagún's 'Doctrinal Encyclopaedia,'" *Estudios de Cultura Nahuatl,* 16 (1983): 109-22.

Anderson, Arthur J. O., and Charles E. Dibble, eds. *The War of Conquest: How It was Waged Here in Mexico.* Salt Lake City, 1978.

Anderson, Perry. *Lineages of the Absolutist State.* London, 1974.

Andrews, George Reid. "Spanish American Independence: A Structural Analysis," *Latin American Perspectives,* 12 (1985): 105-32.

"Apéndice a los concilios primero y segundo mexicanos," in Nicolás León, ed., *Bibliografía mexicana del siglo XVIII* (1907), pt. 4: 308-30.

Archer, Christon I. *The Army in Bourbon Mexico, 1760-1810.* Albuquerque, N.Mex., 1977.

———. "Bite of the Hydra: The Rebellion of Cura Miguel Hidalgo, 1810-1811," in Jaime E. Rodríguez, ed., *Patterns of Contention in Mexican History* (Wilmington, Del., 1992): 69-93.

———. " 'La Causa Buena': The Counterinsurgency Army of New Spain and the Ten Years' War," in Jaime E. Rodríguez, ed., *The Independence of Mexico and the Creation of the New Nation* (Los Angeles, 1989): 85-108.

———. "The Cutting Edge: The Historical Relationship Between Insurgency, Counterinsurgency, and Terrorism During Mexican Independence, 1810-1821," in Lawrence Howard, ed., *Terrorism: Roots, Impact, Responses* (New York, 1992): 29-45.

———. "Los dineros de la insurgencia, 1810-1821," in Carlos Herrejón, ed., *Repaso de la Independencia* (Zamora, Michoacán, 1985): 39-55.

———. "Insurrection-Reaction-Revolution-Fragmentation: Reconstructing the Choreography of Meltdown in New Spain During the Independence Era," *Mexican Studies/Estudios Mexicanos,* 10, no. 1 (winter 1994): 63-98.

———. " 'Viva Nuestra Señora de Guadalupe!': Recent Interpretations of Mexico's Independence Period," *Mexican Studies/Estudios Mexicanos,* 7, no. 1 (winter 1991): 143-65.

———. "What Goes Around Comes Around: Political Change and Continuity in Mexico, 1750-1850," in Jaime E. Rodríguez, ed., *Mexico in the Age of Democratic Revolutions, 1750-1850* (Boulder, Colo., 1994): 261-80.

Arcila Farías, Eduardo. *Reformas económicas del siglo XVIII en Nueva España.* 2d ed. 2 vols. 1974.

Ariès, Philippe. *The Hour of Our Death.* New York, 1981.

Arregui, Domingo Lázaro de. *Descripción de la Nueva Galicia.* Seville, 1946.

Arze y Miranda, Andrés de. Introduction to Andrés Miguel Pérez de Velasco, *El ayudante de cura instruído en el porte a que le obliga su dignidad en los deberes a que le estrecha su empleo y en la fructuosa práctica de su ministerio.* Puebla, 1766. The Arze piece is unpaginated.

Asad, Talal. "Anthropological Conceptions of Religion: Reflections on Geertz," *Man,* 18 (1983): 237-59.

Ave María Puríssima: Breve instrucción a los christianos casados; y útiles advertencias a los que pretenden serlo . . . 1791.

Avila Martel, Alamiro de. "Actividades del cabildo secular de Santiago en el campo eclesiástico durante el siglo XVI," in Avila Martel, *Estructuras, gobierno y agentes de la administración en la América española (siglos XVI, XVII y XVIII)* (Valladolid, Spain, 1984): 9-42.

Axtell, James. *The Invasion Within: The Contest of Cultures in Colonial North America.* New York, 1985.

Babcock, Barbara, ed. *Reversible World: Symbolic Inversion in Art and Society.* Ithaca, N.Y., 1978.

The Badianus Manuscript, an Aztec Herbal of 1552. Translated, with an Introduction and notes, by Emily Walcott Emmart. Baltimore, 1940.

Badone, Ellen, ed. *Religious Orthodoxy and Popular Faith in European Society.* Princeton, N.J., 1990.

Baegert, Johann Jakob. *Observations in Lower California.* Berkeley, Calif., 1952.

Balandier, Georges. *Political Anthropology.* New York, 1970.

Bancroft, Hubert H. *The Works of Hubert Howe Bancroft.* 39 vols. San Francisco, 1882-90.

Barabas, Alicia. *Utopías indias: Movimientos sociorreligiosos en México.* 1989.

Barbier, Jacques. "Toward a New Chronology of Bourbon Colonialism," *Ibero-Amerikanisches Archiv,* 6 (1980): 335-53.

———. "Tradition and Reform in Bourbon Chile: Ambrosio O'Higgins and Public Finances," *The Americas,* 34 (1978): 381-99.

Basurto, J. Trinidad. *El arzobispado de México: Obra biográfica, geográfica y estadística.* 1901.

Bauer, Arnold J. "The Church and Spanish American Agrarian Structure, 1765-1865," *The Americas,* 28 (1971): 78-98.

———. "The Church in the Economy of Spanish America: *Censos* and *Depósitos* in the Eighteenth and Nineteenth Centuries," *Hispanic American Historical Review,* 63 (1983): 707-33.

———, ed. *La iglesia en la economía de América latina, siglos XVI a XVIII.* 1986.

Baumann, Roland. "Tlaxcalan Expression of Autonomy and Religious Drama in the Sixteenth Century," *Journal of Latin American Lore,* 13 (1987): 139-53.

Bayle, Constantino. "Cabildos de indios en la América Española," *Missionalia Hispánica,* 8 (1951): 5-35.

———. "Los clérigos y la extirpación de la idolatría entre los neófitos americanos," *Missionalia Hispánica,* 3 (1946): 53-98.

———. *El clero secular y la evangelización de América.* Madrid, 1950.

———. "La comunión entre los indios americanos," *Revista de Indias,* 4 (1943): 197-254.

———. "El Concilio de Trento en las Indias españolas," *Razón y Fe,* 45 (1945): 257-84.

———. "España y el clero indígena en América," *Razón y Fe,* 2 parts, 31 (1931): 213-25, 521-35.

———. "Los niños indígenas en la cristianización de América: Una página conmovedora de historia," *Razón y Fe,* 44 (1944): 267-83.

Bazant, Jan. *A Concise History of Mexico from Hidalgo to Cárdenas, 1805-1940.* New York, 1977.

Becerra López, José Luis. *La organización de los estudios de la Nueva España.* 1963.

Beemer, Margaret Anne. "Godly Interchange: The Appropriation of Nonchristian Symbols in the Development of Christianity in Spain and the Valley of Mexico." Ph.D. diss., University of California, Los Angeles, 1988.

Behar, Ruth. "The Struggle for the Church: Popular Religion and Anticlericalism in Post-Franco Spain," in Ellen Badone, ed., *Religious Orthodoxy and Popular Faith in European Society* (Princeton, N.J., 1990): 76-112.

Belanger, Brian C. "Secularization and the Laity in Colonial Mexico: Querétaro, 1598-1821." Ph.D. diss., Tulane University, 1990.

Bellah, Robert. *Beyond Belief: Essays on Religion in a Post-Traditional World.* New York, 1970.

Benítez, Fernando. *Los demonios en el convento: Sexo y religión en la Nueva España.* 1985.

Beristáin de Souza, José Mariano. *Biblioteca hispano-americana septentrional*. 3d ed. 5 vols. 1947.

———. *Discurso político-moral y cristiano que en los solemnes cultos que rinde al santísimo sacramento en los días del carnaval* . . . 1809.

Bernal Díaz, *see* Díaz del Castillo

Bernanos, Georges. *The Diary of a Country Priest*. New York, 1954.

Berrigan, Daniel. *The Mission: A Journal*. New York, 1986.

Berryman, Philip. *Liberation Theology: Essential Facts About the Revolutionary Movement in Latin America and Beyond*. Philadelphia, 1987.

Beutler, Gisela. *La historia de Fernando y Alamar: Contribución al estudio de las danzas de moros y cristianos en Puebla (México)*. Stuttgart, 1984.

Bierhorst, John. *The Mythology of Mexico and Central America*. New York, 1990.

Bitterli, Urs. *Los "salvajes" y los "civilizados": El encuentro de Europa y ultramar*. 1981.

Black, Donald, ed. *Toward a General Theory of Social Control*. 2 vols. New York, 1984.

Blau, Peter. *Exchange and Power in Social Life*. New York, 1964.

Bobb, Bernard. *The Viceregency of Antonio María Bucareli in New Spain, 1771-1779*. Austin, Tex., 1962.

Bonomi, Patricia. *Under the Cope of Heaven: Religion, Society, and Politics in Colonial America*. New York, 1986.

Borah, Woodrow. "Alguna luz sobre el autor de las *Enfermedades políticas*," *Estudios de Historia Novohispana*, 8 (1985): 51-79.

———. "The Collection of Tithes in the Bishopric of Oaxaca During the Sixteenth Century," *Hispanic American Historical Review*, 21 (1941): 386-409.

———. "Discontinuity and Continuity in Mexican History," *Pacific Historical Review*, 48 (1979): 1-25.

———. *Justice by Insurance: The General Indian Court of Colonial Mexico and the Legal Aides of the Half-Real*. Berkeley, Calif., 1983.

———. "Notes on Civil Archives in the City of Oaxaca," *Hispanic American Historical Review*, 31 (1951): 723-49.

———. "Tithe Collection in the Bishopric of Oaxaca, 1601-1867," *Hispanic American Historical Review*, 29 (1949): 498-517.

———, ed. *El gobierno provincial en la Nueva España, 1570-1787*. 1985.

Borges Morán, Pedro. *El envío de misioneros a América durante la época española*. Salamanca, Spain, 1977.

Bossy, John. *Christianity in the West, 1400-1700*. Oxford, Eng., 1985.

———. "The Counter-Reformation and the People of Catholic Europe," *Past & Present*, 1970, no. 47: 51-70.

———. "Holiness and Society," *Past & Present*, 1977, no. 75: 119-37.

———. "The Mass as a Social Institution, 1200-1700," *Past & Present*, 1983, no. 100: 29-61.

Bourdieu, Pierre. *Outline of a Theory of Practice*. Cambridge, Eng., 1977.

Bouwsma, William J. "Christian Adulthood," in Erik H. Erikson, ed., *Adulthood* (New York, 1978): 81-93.

Bowser, Frederick P. "The Church in Colonial Middle America: Non Fecit Taliter Omni Nationi," *Latin American Research Review*, 25 (1990): 137-56.

Boxer, C. R. *The Church Militant and Iberian Expansion, 1440-1770*. Baltimore, 1978.

Boyd-Bowman, Peter. "Los nombres de pila en México desde 1540 hasta 1950," *Nueva Revista de Filología Hispánica*, 19 (1970): 12-48.

Boyer, Richard. "Absolutism Versus Corporatism in New Spain: The Administration of the Marquis of Gelves, 1621-1624," *The International History Review*, 4 (1982): 475-503.

Boys, Mary C. *Educating in Faith: Maps and Visions*. New York, 1989.

Brading, D. A. "El clero mexicano y el movimiento insurgente de 1810," *Relaciones: Estudios de Historia y Sociedad*, 1981, no. 5: 5-26.

———. "Facts and Figments in Bourbon Mexico," *Bulletin of Latin American Research*, 4 (1985): 61–64.

———. *The First America: The Spanish Monarchy, Creole Patriots, and the Liberal State, 1492–1867*. Cambridge, Eng., 1991.

———. "Government and Elite in Late Colonial Mexico," *Hispanic American Historical Review*, 53 (1973): 389–414.

———. *Haciendas and Ranchos in the Mexican Bajío: León, 1700–1860*. Cambridge, Eng., 1978.

———. "Images and Prophets: Indian Religion and the Spanish Conquest," in Arij Ouweneel and Simon Miller, eds., *The Indian Community of Colonial Mexico* (Amsterdam, 1990): 184–204.

———. *The Origins of Mexican Nationalism*. 3d ed. Cambridge, Eng., 1985.

———. *Prophesy and Myth in Mexican History*. Cambridge, Eng., 1985.

———. "Tridentine Catholicism and Enlightened Despotism in Bourbon Mexico," *Journal of Latin American Studies*, 15 (1983): 1–23.

Brambila, Crescenciano. *El nuevo obispado de Autlán*. Colima, 1962.

Brand, Donald. *Mexico: Land of Sunshine and Shadow*. Princeton, N.J., 1966.

Brandes, Stanley H. "Fireworks and Fiestas: The Case of Tzintzuntzan," *Journal of Latin American Lore*, 7 (1981): 171–90.

———. *Power and Persuasion: Fiestas and Social Control in Rural Mexico*. Philadelphia, 1988.

Bravo Ugarte, José. "El clero y la Independencia: Ensayo estadístico," *Abside*, 2 parts, 5 (1941): 612–30; 7 (1943): 406–9.

———. "El clero y la Independencia: Factores económicos e ideológicos," *Abside*, 15 (1951): 199–218.

———. *Diócesis y obispos de la iglesia mexicana, 1519–1965*. 2d ed. 1965.

———. *Historia de México*. 3 vols. 1941–59.

Brenner, Anita. *Idols Behind Altars*. New York, 1929.

Bricker, Victoria R. "Historical Dramas in Chiapas, Mexico," *Journal of Latin American Lore*, 3 (1977): 227–48.

———. *The Indian Christ, the Indian King: The Historical Substrate of Maya Myth and Ritual*. Austin, Tex., 1981.

Bringas, Diego Miguel. *Friar Bringas Reports to the King: Methods of Indoctrination on the Frontier of New Spain, 1796–1797*. Ed. Daniel S. Matson and Bernard L. Fontana. Tucson, Ariz., 1977.

Brooks, Francis. "Parish and Cofradía in Eighteenth-Century Mexico." Ph.D. diss., Princeton University, 1976.

Brown, Kendall W. *Bourbons and Brandy: Imperial Reform in Eighteenth-Century Arequipa*. Albuquerque, N.Mex., 1986.

Brown, Peter R. L. *The Cult of Saints: Its Rise and Function in Latin Christianity*. Chicago, 1981.

———. *Society and the Holy in Late Antiquity*. Berkeley, Calif., 1982.

Burke, Kenneth. *The Rhetoric of Religion*. Boston, 1961.

Burke, Peter. "A Question of Acculturation?," in *Scienze, credenze occulte livelli di cultura* (Florence, Italy, 1982): 198–204.

Burkhart, Louise M. *The Slippery Earth: Nahua-Christian Moral Dialogue in Sixteenth-Century Mexico*. Tucson, Ariz., 1989.

Burridge, Kenelm. *Mambú: A Melanesian Millennium*. London, 1960.

———. "Revival and Renewal," in Eliade, ed., listed below, 12: 368–74.

Bustamante, Carlos María. *Cuadro histórico de la revolución mexicana, iniciada el 15 de septiembre de 1810 por el c. Miguel Hidalgo y Costilla . . .* 3 vols. 1961.

———. *El indio mexicano o avisos al rey Fernando Séptimo para la pacificación de la América septentrional . . .* [1817–18]. Ed. Manuel Arellano Zavaleta. 1981.

———. *Memoria principal de la piedad y lealtad del pueblo de México, en los solemnes cultos de nuestra Señora de los Remedios . . .* 1810 (Sept. 4).

———. *Tres estudios sobre don José María Morelos y Pavón (1822, 1825).* Facsimile ed. 1963.

Cabrera y Quintero, Cayetano. *Escudo de armas de México.* 1746.

Cacho, Xavier. "Francisco Xavier Clavigero, S.J., 1731-1787," in Alfonso Martínez Rosales, ed., *Francisco Xavier Clavigero en la Ilustración mexicana, 1731-1787* (1988): 31-40.

Cahill, David. "*Curas* and Social Conflict in the *Doctrinas* of Cuzco, 1780-1814," *Journal of Latin American Studies,* 16 (1984): 241-76.

Caillois, Roger. *Man and the Sacred.* Glencoe, Ill., 1959.

Calderón de la Barca, Frances. *Life in Mexico: The Letters of Fanny Calderón de la Barca, with New Material from the Author's Journals.* Garden City, N.Y., 1966.

Calderón Quijano, José Antonio. "El Banco de San Carlos y las comunidades de indios de Nueva España," *Anuario de Estudios Americanos,* 19 (1962): 1-144.

Calderón Quijano, José Antonio et al. *Los virreyes de Nueva España en el reinado de Carlos III.* 2 vols. Seville, 1968.

———. *Los virreyes de Nueva España en el reinado de Carlos IV.* 2 vols. Seville, 1972.

Callahan, William J. *Church, Politics, and Society in Spain, 1750-1874.* Cambridge, Mass., 1984.

———. "Two Spains and Two Churches, 1760-1835," *Historical Reflections,* 2 (1975): 158-81.

Callaway, Carol H. "The Church of Nuestra Señora de la Soledad in Oaxaca, Mexico." Ph.D. diss., University of Maryland, 1989.

Callcott, Wilfrid H. *Church and State in Mexico, 1822-1857.* Durham, N.C., 1926.

Calvo, Tomás. *La Nueva Galicia en los siglos XVI y XVII.* Guadalajara, 1989.

Cameron, J. M. *Images of Authority: A Consideration of the Concepts of Regnum and Sacerdotium.* New Haven, Conn., 1966.

Campbell, Ena. "The Virgin of Guadalupe and the Female Self Image: A Mexican Case History," in James J. Preston, ed., *Mother Worship: Theme and Variation* (Chapel Hill, N.C., 1982): 5-24.

Campbell, Leon G. "Church and State in Colonial Peru: The Bishop of Cuzco and the Túpac Amaru Rebellion of 1780," *Journal of Church and State,* 22 (1980): 251-70.

———. "Recent Research on Bourbon Enlightened Despotism," *New Scholar,* 1-2 (1981): 29-50.

Canons and Decrees of the Council of Trent. Tr. H. J. Schroeder. Rockford, Ill., 1978.

Canterla, Francisco, and Martín de Tovar. *La iglesia de Oaxaca en el siglo XVIII.* Seville, 1982.

Cardozo Galue, Germán. *Michoacán en el siglo de las luces.* 1973.

Carlsen, Robert S., and Martin Prechtel. "The Flowering of the Dead: An Interpretation of Highland Maya Culture," *Man,* 26 (1991): 23-42.

Carmagnani, Marcello. *El regreso de los dioses: El proceso de reconstitución de la identidad étnica en Oaxaca, siglos XVII y XVIII.* 1988.

Carrasco, David. *Quetzalcoatl and the Irony of Empire: Myths and Prophecies in the Aztec Tradition.* Chicago, 1982.

———. *Religions of Mesoamerica.* New York, 1990.

———, ed. *To Change Place: Aztec Ceremonial Landscapes.* Boulder, Colo., 1991.

Carrasco, Pedro. "La transformación de la cultura indígena durante la colonia," *Historia Mexicana,* 25 (1975): 175-203.

Carrillo y Gariel, Abelardo. *El Cristo de Mexicaltzingo: Técnica de las esculturas en caña.* 1949.

———. *Imaginería popular novoespañola.* 1950.

———. *El traje en la Nueva España.* 1959.

Carroll, Michael P. *The Cult of the Virgin Mary: Psychological Origins.* Princeton, N.J., 1986.

Carroll, Warren H. *Our Lady of Guadalupe and the Conquest of Darkness.* Front Royal, Va., 1983.

Cartas de Indias. Madrid, 1877.

Casanueva, Fernando. "Politique, evangelisation et revoltes indiennes à la fin du XVIIIe siècle: Le cas du sud chilien," in *L'Amérique espagnole à l'époque des lumières: Tradition-Innovation-Représentations* (Paris, 1987): 203–19.

Castañeda, Carmen. *La educación en Guadalajara durante la colonia, 1552–1821.* Guadalajara, 1984.

Castañeda Delgado, Paulino. "La condición miserable del indio y sus privilegios," *Anuario de Estudios Americanos,* 28 (1971): 245–335.

———. "La Hierarchie ecclésiastique dans l'Amérique des lumières," in *L'Amérique espagnole à l'époque des lumières: Tradition-Innovation-Représentations* (Paris, 1987): 79–100.

Castro, Américo. *The Spaniards: An Introduction to Their History.* Tr. William F. King and Selma Margaretten. Berkeley, Calif., 1971.

Catecismo para el uso de los párrocos hecho por el IV Concilio provincial mexicano, celebrado el año de MDCCLXXI. 1772.

Certeau, Michel de. *The Writing of History.* Tr. Tom Conley. New York, 1988.

Cervantes, Fernando. "Christianity and the Indians in Early Modern Mexico: The Native Response to the Devil," *Historical Research,* 66 (1993): 177–96.

Champagne, Duane. "Change, Continuity, and Variation in Native American Societies as a Response to Conquest," in William B. Taylor and Franklin Pease G. Y., eds., *Violence and Resistance in the Americas: Native Americans and the Legacy of Conquest* (Washington, D.C., 1993): 208–25.

Chance, John K. *Conquest of the Sierra: Spaniards and Indians in Colonial Oaxaca.* Norman, Okla., 1989.

Chance, John K., and William B. Taylor. "Cofradías and Cargos: An Historical Perspective on the Mesoamerican Civil-Religious Hierarchy," *American Ethnologist,* 12 (1985): 1–26.

Chase, Stuart. *Mexico: A Study of Two Americas.* New York, 1931.

Chávez Orozco, Luis. *Las cajas de comunidades indígenas de la Nueva España.* Vol. 5 of *Documentos para la historia económica de México.* 1934.

———. "Las instituciones democráticas de los indígenas Mexicanos en la época colonial," *América Indígena,* 4 parts, 3 (1943): 73–82, 161–71, 265–76, 365–82.

———. "El pensamiento social y político de Morelos," in Carlos J. Sierra, ed., *Inmortalidad de Morelos* (1965): 145–48.

———. *El sitio de Cuautla.* 2d ed. 1962.

Chevalier, François. "Les Municipalités indiennes en Nouvelle Espagne, 1520–1620," *Anuario de Historia del Derecho Español,* 15 (1944): 352–86.

Chimalpahin C., Francisco de San Antón Muñón. *Relaciones originales de Chalco Amaquemecan* [1620's]. 1965.

Choy Ma, Emilio. "De Santiago Matamoros a Santiago Mata-indios," in Choy Ma, *Antropología e Historia* (Lima, 1979): 333–437.

Christian, William A., Jr. *Apparitions in Late Medieval and Renaissance Spain.* Princeton, N.J., 1981.

———. "Folk Religion: An Overview," in Eliade, ed., listed below, 5: 370–74.

———. *Local Religion in Sixteenth-Century Spain.* Princeton, N.J., 1981.

Churruca Peláez, Agustín. "Fuentes del pensamiento de Morelos," in Carlos Herrejón, ed., *Repaso de la Independencia: Memoria del Congreso Sobre la Independencia Mexicana, Octubre 22 y 23 de 1984.* (Zamora, Michoacán, 1985): 127–59.

———. *El pensamiento insurgente de Morelos.* 1983.

Cintrón Tiryakian, *see* Tiryakian

Clavigero, Francisco Javier. *Historia antigua de México.* 3d ed. 1964.

Clendinnen, Inga. *Ambivalent Conquests: Maya and Spaniard in Yucatán, 1517–1570.* Cambridge, Eng., 1987.

———. *Aztecs: An Interpretation.* Cambridge, Eng., 1991.

———. "The Cost of Courage in Aztec Society," *Past & Present,* 1985, no. 107: 44–89.

———. "Disciplining the Indians: Franciscan Ideology and Missionary Violence in Sixteenth-Century Yucatán," *Past & Present,* 1982, no. 94: 27–48.

———. " 'Fierce and Unnatural Cruelty': Cortés and the Conquest of Mexico," *Representations,* 1991, no. 33: 65–100.

———. "Franciscan Missionaries in Sixteenth-Century Mexico," in Jim Obelkevich, Lyndal Roper, and Raphael Samuel, eds., *Disciplines of Faith: Studies in Religion, Politics, and Patriarchy* (London, 1987): 229–45.

———. "Landscape and World View: The Survival of Yucatec Maya Culture Under Spanish Conquest," *Comparative Studies in Society and History,* 22 (1980): 374–83.

———. "Ways to the Sacred: Reconstructing 'Religion' in Sixteenth-Century Mexico," *History and Anthropology,* 5 (1990): 105–41.

Cline, S. L. *Colonial Culhuacan, 1580–1600: A Social History of an Aztec Town.* Albuquerque, N.Mex., 1986.

———. "The Spiritual Conquest Re-examined: Baptism and Church Marriage in Early Sixteenth-Century Mexico," *Hispanic American Historical Review,* 73 (1993): 453–80.

Coatsworth, John H. "Economic History and History of Prices in Colonial Latin America," in Lyman L. Johnson and Enrique Tandeter, eds., *Essays on the Price History of Eighteenth-Century Latin America* (Albuquerque, N.Mex., 1990): 21–34.

———. "La historiografía económica de México," *Revista de Historia Económica,* 6 (1988): 277–91.

———. "Limits of Colonial Absolutism," in Karen Spalding, ed., *Essays in the Political, Economic and Social History of Colonial Latin America* (Newark, Del., 1982): 25–51.

———. "The Mexican Mining Industry in the Eighteenth Century," in Nils Jacobsen and Hans-Jürgen Puhle, eds., *The Economies of Mexico and Peru During the Late Colonial Period, 1760–1810* (Berlin, 1986): 26–45.

Códice Franciscano: Siglo XVI. 1941.

Códice Sierra. 1906.

Cohen, Abner. *Two-Dimensional Man: An Essay on the Anthropology of Power and Symbolism in Complex Society.* London, 1974.

Cohn, Bernard. *An Anthropologist Among the Historians and Other Essays.* New Delhi, 1987.

Colección de documentos eclesiásticos de México o sea antigua y moderna legislación de la iglesia mexicana. Ed. Fortino H. Vera. 3 vols. Amecameca, 1887.

Colección de documentos históricos inéditos o muy raros referentes al Arzobispado de Guadalajara. Ed. Francisco Orozco y Jiménez. 6 vols. Guadalajara, 1922–26.

Colección eclesiástica mexicana. 3 vols. 1834 (Bancroft Lib.).

Colección de las ordenanzas, que para el gobierno de el obispado de Michoacán hicieron y promulgaron con real aprobación . . . 1776.

Colección de los aranceles de obvenciones y derechos parroquiales que han estado vigentes en los obispados de la República Mexicana . . . 1857.

Colín, Mario. *Indice de documentos relativos a los pueblos del Estado de México: Ramo de Indios.* 1968.

Collier, George A., Renato I. Rosaldo, and John D. Wirth, eds., *The Inca and Aztec States, 1400–1800: Anthropology and History.* New York, 1982.

Collins, Anne C., "The *Maestros Cantores* in Yucatán," in Grant D. Jones, ed., *Anthropology and History in Yucatan* (Austin, Tex., 1977): 233–47.

Colpe, Carsten. "Syncretism," in Eliade, ed., listed below, 14: 218–27.

Concilio III provincial mexicano, celebrado en México el año 1585. 2d ed. Barcelona, 1870.

Concilio provincial mexicano IV celebrado en la Ciudad de México el año de 1771. Queré-taro, 1898.

Concilios provinciales primero, y segundo, celebrados en la muy noble, y muy leal ciudad de México . . . 1769.

The Confessions of St. Augustine. Tr. Edward B. Pusey. New York, 1957.

Connaughton, Brian F. *Ideología y sociedad en Guadalajara (1788–1853).* 1992.

Connolly, S. J. *Priests and People in Pre-Famine Ireland, 1780–1845.* New York, 1982.

La conquista de México: Lienzo de Tlaxcala. Artes de México series, unnumbered, [1965?].

Constable, Giles. "Resistance to Tithes in the Middle Ages," *Journal of Ecclesiastical History,* 13 (1962): 172–85.

Constituciones que el ilustrísimo Señor Doctor Don Alonso Núñez de Haro y Peralta . . . formó para el mejor régimen y govierno del real colegio seminario de instrucción, retiro voluntario y corrección para el clero secular de esta diócesi, fundado por S.S. Illma. en el pueblo de Tepotzotlán . . . 1777.

Cook, John W. "Iconography: Christian Iconography," in Eliade ed., listed below, 7: 57–64.

Cook, Sherburne F. *The Conflict Between the California Indian and White Civilization.* Berkeley, Calif., 1976.

Cook, Sherburne F., and Woodrow Borah. *Essays in Population History: Mexico and the Caribbean.* Vol. 1. Berkeley, Calif., 1971.

Córdoba, Pedro de. *Christian Doctrine for the Instruction and Information of the Indians.* Tr. Sterling A. Stoudemire. Coral Gables, Fla., 1970.

Córdova-Bello, Eleazar. *Las reformas del despotismo ilustrado en América (siglo XVIII hispanoamericano).* Caracas, 1975.

Cornejo Franco, José. "Relaciones de méritos y servicios," *Anuario de la Comisión Diocesana de Historia del Arzobispado de Guadalajara,* 1968: 221–49.

Corona Núñez, José. "Religiones indígenas y cristianismo," *Historia Mexicana,* 10 (1961): 557–70.

Costeloe, Michael P., "The Administration, Collection, and Distribution of Tithes in the Archbishopric of Mexico, 1800–1860," *The Americas,* 23 (1966): 3–27.

———. *Church and State in Independent Mexico: A Study of the Patronage Debate, 1821–1857.* London, 1978.

———. *Church Wealth in Mexico: A Study of the Juzgado de Capellanías in the Archbishopric of Mexico, 1800–1856.* Cambridge, Eng., 1967.

———. *Mexico State Papers, 1744–1843: A Descriptive Catalogue of the G.R.G. Conway Collection in the Institute of Historical Research.* London, 1976.

Council of Trent, see *Canons and Decrees*

Covarrubias Horozco, Sebastián de. *Tesoro de la lengua castellana o española según la impresión de 1611, con las adiciones de Benito Remigio Noydens publicadas en la de 1674.* Barcelona, 1943.

Crahan, Margaret. "Civil-Ecclesiastical Relations in Hapsburg Peru," *Journal of Church and State,* 20 (1978): 93–111.

———. "Clerical Immunity in the Viceroyalty of Peru, 1684–1692: A Study of Civil-Ecclesiastical Relations." Ph.D. diss., Columbia University, 1967.

———. "Spanish and American Counterpoint: Problems and Possibilities in Spanish Colonial Administrative History," in Richard Graham and Peter H. Smith, eds., *New Approaches to Latin American History* (Austin, Tex., 1974): 36–70.

Craine, Eugene R., and Reginald C. Reindorp. *The Chronicles of Michoacán.* Norman, Okla., 1970.

Cuevas, Mariano. *Historia de la iglesia en México.* 5 vols. Tlálpam, D.F., 1921–24. (Republished El Paso, Tex., 1928.)

D.P.E.P. *Noticias de la Nueva España: Estado de la Universidad (1799).* 1945.

Dávila Garibi, José Ignacio. *Apuntes para la historia de la Iglesia en Guadalajara*. 7 vols. 1956–77.

———. *Biografía de un gran prelado: El Exmo. e Ilmo. Sr. Doctor D. Juan Cruz Ruiz de Cabañas y Crespo*. Guadalajara, 1925.

———. *Estudio histórico sobre la parroquia de Ocotlán*. 2d ed. Guadalajara, 1918.

Davis, Natalie Z. *Fiction in the Archives: Pardon Tales and Their Tellers in Sixteenth-Century France*. Stanford, Calif., 1987.

———. "The Sacred and the Body Social in Sixteenth-Century Lyons," *Past & Present*, 1981, no. 90: 40–70.

———. "Some Tasks and Themes in the Study of Popular Religion," in C. Trinkhaus and H. Oberman, eds., *The Pursuit of Holiness in Late Medieval and Renaissance Religion* (Leiden, 1974): 307–36.

De la Hera, *see* Hera

Dehouve, Danièle. *El tequio de los santos y la competencia entre los mercaderes*. 1976.

Delumeau, Jean. *Catholicism Between Luther and Voltaire: A New View of the Counter-Reformation*. London, 1977.

Dening, Greg. *The Bounty: An Ethnographic History*. Melbourne, 1988.

———. *History's Anthropology: The Death of William Gooch*. Lanham, Md., 1988.

———. *Islands and Beaches: Discourse on a Silent Land. Marquesas, 1774–1880*. Honolulu, 1980.

———. *Xavier: A Centenary Portrait*. Armadale, Australia, 1978.

Dennis, Philip A. "The Oaxacan Village President as Political Middleman," *Ethnology*, 12 (1973): 419–27.

"La descripción de Alahuiztlán, 1789," *Tlalocan* 2, no. 2 (1946): 106–9.

Díaz del Castillo, Bernal. *Historia verdadera de la conquista de la Nueva España*. Madrid, 1982.

Díaz Díaz, Fernando. *Caudillos y caciques: Antonio López de Santa Anna y Juan Alvarez*. 1972.

Díaz Roig, Mercedes. "La danza de la Conquista," *Nueva Revista de Filología Hispánica*, 32 (1983): 176–95.

Diccionario de autoridades. Facsimile of 1726 original. 3 vols. Madrid, 1969.

Diccionario de la lengua castellana. 6th ed. Madrid, 1822.

Diehl, Carl Gustav. "Replacement or Substitution in the Meeting of Religions," in Sven S. Hartman, ed., *Syncretism* (Stockholm, 1969): 137–61.

Documentos históricos mexicanos. Ed. Genaro García. 1910.

Doerr, Harriet. *Consider This, Señora*. New York, 1993.

Domínguez, Juan Francisco. *Conveniencia de la Religión, y el Estado: En diez discursos sobre los mandamientos de Dios*. 1805.

Domínguez Ortiz, Antonio. "Costumbres clericales en la España barroca," *Historia 16*, 8 (1983): 27–30.

———. "La crisis española del siglo XVIII," *Arbor*, 118 (1984): 41–56.

———. *Sociedad y estado en el siglo XVIII español*. Barcelona, 1976.

Dow, James. *The Shaman's Touch: Otomí Indian Symbolic Healing*. Salt Lake City, 1986.

Dromundo, Baltasar. *José María Morelos*. 1970.

Dumont, Louis. "A Modified View of Our Origins: The Christian Beginnings of Modern Individualism," in Michael Carrithers, Steven Collins, and Steven Lukes, eds., *The Category of the Person: Anthropology, Philosophy, History* (Cambridge, Eng., 1985): 93–122.

Durkheim, Emile. *The Elementary Forms of Religious Life*. Tr. Joseph W. Swain. New York, 1965.

Dussel, Enrique D. *Caminos de liberación latinoamericana (Interpretación histórico-teológica de nuestro continente latinoamericano)*. Buenos Aires, 1972.

———. *Historia de la iglesia en América Latina*. 2d ed. Barcelona, 1972.

————, ed. (and author of vol. 1). *Historia general de la iglesia en América Latina.* 9 vols to date. Salamanca, Spain, 1981–.

Eck, Diana L. *Darsan: Seeing the Divine Image in India.* Chambersburg, Pa., 1981.

Eckhoff, T. "The Mediator, the Judge, and the Administrator in Conflict Resolution," *Acta Sociologica,* 10 (1967): 148–72.

Egaña, Antonio de. *Historia de la iglesia en la América Española, desde el descubrimiento hasta comienzos del siglo XIX: Hemisferio sur.* Madrid, 1966.

Eguiara y Eguren, Juan José de. *Prólogos a la Biblioteca Mexicana* [1775]. Tr. and ed. Agustín Millares Carlo. 1944.

Eisenstadt, S. N. "Religious Diversity," in Eliade, ed., listed below, 12: 312–18.

Eliade, Mircea. *Patterns in Comparative Religion.* New York, 1958.

————. *The Sacred and the Profane.* New York, 1961.

————. *Shamanism: Archaic Techniques of Ecstasy.* Princeton, N.J., 1970.

————, ed. *The Encyclopedia of Religion.* 16 vols. New York, 1987.

Elliott, J. H. "Self-Perceptions and Decline in Early Seventeenth-Century Spain," *Past & Present,* 1977, no. 74: 41–61.

Elton, G. R. *Political History: Principles and Practice.* New York, 1970.

Engstrand, Iris. "The Enlightenment in Spain: Influences Upon New World Policy," *The Americas,* 41 (1985): 436–45.

Ensayo de una memoria estadística del distrito de Tulancingo. 1825.

Escobar, Matías. *América thebaida: Vitas patrum de los religiosos hermitaños de N. P. San Agustín de la provincia de San Nicolás Tolentino de Mechoacán* [1729]. Morelia, Michoacán, 1970.

Esparza, Manuel, ed. *Morelos en Oaxaca: Documentos para la historia de la independencia.* Oaxaca, 1986.

Espinosa, Fr. Isidro Félix de. *Crónica de los Colegios de Propaganda Fide de la Nueva España* [1746]. Washington, D.C., 1964.

Estructuras, gobierno, y agentes de administración en la América española (siglos XVI, XVII, XVIII). Valladolid, Spain, 1984.

Evans, E. J. "Some Reasons for the General Growth of English Rural Anticlericalism, c. 1750–c. 1830," *Past & Present,* 1975, no. 66: 84–109.

Fabian, Johannes. "The Anthropology of Religious Movements: From Explanation to Interpretation," *Social Research,* 46 (1979): 4–35.

Fairchilds, Cissie. *Domestic Enemies: Servants and Their Masters in Old Regime France.* Baltimore, 1986.

Falassi, Alessandro, ed. *Time Out of Time: Essays on the Festival.* Albuquerque, N.Mex., 1987.

Fallon, Michael J. "The Secular Clergy in the Diocese of Yucatán, 1750–1800." Ph.D. diss., Catholic University of America, 1979.

Farriss, Nancy M. *Crown and Clergy in Colonial Mexico, 1759–1821.* London, 1968.

————. *Maya Society Under Colonial Rule: The Collective Enterprise of Survival.* Princeton, N.J., 1984.

Fernández de Lizardi, José Joaquín. *Don Catrín de la Fachenda y fragmentos de otras obras.* Ed. Jefferson Rea Spell. 1944.

————. *The Itching Parrot, El periquillo sarniento.* Tr. Katherine Anne Porter. Garden City, N.Y., 1942.

————. *Obras.* 3 vols. 1963–68.

————. *El periquillo sarniento.* Barcelona, 1933.

Fernández de Recas, Guillermo. *Aspirantes americanos a cargos del Santo Oficio.* 1956.

Fernández Munilla, Juan. *Informe sobre el clero regular y secular del corregimiento de Querétaro. Año de 1793.* Querétaro, 1946.

Figuera, Guillermo. *La formación del clero indígena en la historia eclesiástica de América, 1500–1810.* Caracas, 1965.

Firth, Raymond. *Symbols Public and Private*. London, 1973.

Fisher, J. R. *Government and Society in Colonial Peru: The Intendant System, 1784-1814*. London, 1970.

Florencia, Francisco de. *Las novenas del santuario de Nuestra Señora de Guadalupe de México* . . . Madrid, 1785.

———. *Origen de los dos célebres santuarios de la Nueva Galicia obispado de Guadalaxara* . . . [1694]. 1757.

———. *Zodiaco mariano . . . los cultos de SS. Madre por medio de las más célebres y milagrosas imágenes de la misma Señora, que se veneran en esta América Septentrional y Reinos de la Nueva España*. 1755.

Flores Caballero, Romeo. *Counterrevolution: The Role of the Spaniards in the Independence of Mexico, 1804-1838*. Tr. Jaime E. Rodríguez. Lincoln, Neb., 1974.

Flores Galindo, Alberto. *Buscando un Inca: Identidad y utopía en los Andes*. Lima, 1987.

———, ed. *Independencia y revolución (1780-1840)*. 2 vols. Lima, 1987.

Florescano, Enrique. "El indígena en la historia de México," *Historia y Sociedad*, 15 (1977): 70-89.

———. *Memoria mexicana*. 1987.

———. "El poder y la lucha por el poder en la historiografía mexicana," *Nova Americana*, 3 (1980): 199-238.

———. *Precios del maíz y crisis agrícolas en México, 1708-1810*. 1968.

Florescano, Enrique, and Isabel Gil Sánchez. "La época de las reformas borbónicas y el crecimiento económico, 1750-1808," in *Historia general de México* (1976) 2: 183-301.

———, eds. *Descripciones económicas generales de Nueva España, 1784-1817*. 1973.

———. *Descripciones económicas regionales de Nueva España: Provincias del centro, sudeste, y sur, 1766-1827*. 1976.

———. *Descripciones económicas regionales de Nueva España: Provincias del norte, 1790-1814*. 1976.

Florescano, Enrique, and Victoria San Vicente, eds. *Fuentes para la historia de la crisis agrícola (1809-1811)*. 1985.

Floris Margadant S., Guillermo. *Carlos III y la iglesia novohispana*. 1983.

Flynn, Maureen. *Sacred Charity: Confraternities and Social Welfare in Spain, 1400-1700*. Ithaca, N.Y., 1989.

Fogelson, Raymond, and Richard N. Adams, eds. *The Anthropology of Power: Ethnographic Studies from Asia, Oceania, and the New World*. New York, 1977.

Foster, George. *Culture and Conquest: America's Spanish Heritage*. New York, 1960.

"Franciscan Report on the Indians of Nayarit, 1673" (tr. Dan S. Matson), *Ethnohistory*, 22 (1975): 193-221.

Fraser, Valerie. *The Architecture of Conquest: Building in the Viceroyalty of Peru, 1535-1635*. Cambridge, Eng., 1990.

Freeze, Gregory L. *The Parish Clergy in Nineteenth-Century Russia: Crisis, Reform, Counter-Reform*. Princeton, N.J., 1983.

———. *The Russian Levites: Parish Clergy in the Eighteenth Century*. Cambridge, Mass., 1977.

Friedrich, Paul. *Agrarian Revolt in a Mexican Village*. Englewood Cliffs, N.J., 1970.

———. *The Princes of Naranja: An Essay in Anthrohistorical Method*. Austin, Tex., 1986.

Frost, Elsa Cecilia. "El guadalupanismo," *Estudios: Filosofía, Historia, Letras*, 7 (1986): 49-66.

Frye, David L. "Local Memory, Local History, and the Construction of Identity in a Rural Mexican Town." Ph.D. diss., Princeton University, 1989.

Fulbrook, Mary. "Legitimation Crises and the Early Modern State: The Politics of Religious Toleration," in Kaspar von Greyerz, ed., *Religion and Society in Early Modern Europe, 1500-1800* (London, 1984): 146-56.

————. *Piety and Politics: Religion and the Rise of Absolutism in England, Würtemberg and Prussia.* Cambridge, Eng., 1983.

Las gacetas de México: Reproducción de las de Castorena y Ursúa (año 1722), Sahagún de Arévalo (año 1728 y 1742). 3 vols. 1950.

Gadow, Hans. *Through Southern Mexico: Being An Account of the Travels of a Naturalist.* London, 1908.

Galarza, Joaquín. *Lienzos de Chiepetlan: Manuscrits pictographiques et manuscrits en caractères latins de San Miguel Chiepetlan, Guerrero, Mexique.* 1972.

Ganster, Paul. "A Social History of the Secular Clergy of Lima During the Middle Decades of the Eighteenth Century." Ph.D. diss., University of California, Los Angeles, 1974.

García, Genaro, ed., *Documentos historícos mexicanos.* 7 vols. 1910.

García, Genaro, and Carlos Pereyra, eds. *Documentos inéditos o muy raros para la historia de México.* 36 vols. 1905–11.

García de Torres, José Julio. *Sermón de acción de gracias a María Santísima de Guadalupe, por el venturoso suceso de la independencia de la América septentrional.* Oct. 12, 1821.

García Gutiérrez, Jesús. *Apuntes para la historia del origen y desenvolvimiento del regio patronato indiano hasta 1857.* 1941.

————, ed. *Bulario de la iglesia mexicana: Documentos relativos a erecciones, desmembraciones, etc. de diócesis mejicanas.* 1951.

García Icazbalceta, Joaquín, ed., *Cartas de religiosos de Nueva España, 1539–1594.* 1941.

García Martínez, Bernardo. *Los pueblos de la sierra: El poder y el espacio entre los indios del norte de Puebla hasta 1700.* 1987.

García Ugarte, Marta Eugenia. "Andares políticos de don Félix Osores Sotomayor: Cura párroco de la provincia queretana," *Eslabones,* 1991, no. 1: 57–67.

Garner, Richard L. "Exportaciones de circulante en el siglo XVIII (1750–1810)," *Historia Mexicana,* 30 (1982): 544–98.

————. "Price Trends in Eighteenth-Century Mexico," *Hispanic American Historical Review,* 65 (1985): 279–325.

————. "Prices and Wages in Eighteenth-Century Mexico," in Lyman L. Johnson and Enrique Tandeter, eds., *Essays on the Price History of Eighteenth-Century Latin America* (Albuquerque, N.Mex., 1990): 73–108.

————. "Silver Production and Entrepreneurial Structure in Eighteenth-Century Mexico," *Jahrbuch für Geschichte von Staat, Wirtschaft und Gesellschaft Lateinamerikas,* 17 (1980): 157–85.

Garrard, John. "Social History, Political History and Political Science: The Study of Power," *Journal of Social History,* 16 (1983): 105–22.

Gawthrop, Richard, and Gerald Strauss. "Protestantism and Literacy in Early Modern Germany," *Past & Present,* 1984, no. 104: 31–55.

Geertz, Clifford. "History and Anthropology," *New Literary History,* 31 (1990): 321–36.

————. *The Interpretation of Cultures: Selected Essays.* New York, 1973.

Gemelli Carreri, Juan F. *Viaje a la Nueva España: México a fines del siglo XVII.* 2 vols. 1955.

Genovese, Eugene D. *Roll, Jordan, Roll: The World the Slaves Made.* New York, 1974.

Gerhard, Peter. "Un censo de la Diócesi de Puebla en 1681," *Historia Mexicana,* 30 (1981): 530–60.

————. *A Guide to the Historical Geography of New Spain.* Cambridge, Eng., 1972.

————. *The North Frontier of New Spain.* Princeton, N.J., 1982.

Gibson, Charles. *The Aztecs Under Spanish Rule: A History of the Indians of the Valley of Mexico, 1519–1810.* Stanford, Calif., 1964.

————. *Spain in America.* New York, 1966.

Giffords, Gloria Kay. *Mexican Folk Retablos: Masterpieces on Tin.* Tucson, Ariz., 1974.

Gilly, Adolfo. *Nuestra caída en la modernidad.* 1988.

Gilmore, David. "Andalusian Anti-clericalism: An Eroticized Rural Protest," *Anthropology,* 8 (1984): 31–44.

Giménez, Gilberto. *Cultura popular y religión en el Anáhuac.* 1978.

Giménez Fernández, Manuel. *El concilio IV provincial mexicano.* Seville, 1939.

Ginzburg, Carlo. *The Cheese and the Worms: The Cosmos of a Sixteenth-Century Miller.* Baltimore, 1980.

Gisbert, Teresa. *Iconografía y mitos indígenas en el arte.* La Paz, 1980.

Glass, John B. *Catálogo de la colección de códices.* 1964.

Goffman, Erving. "The Nature of Deference and Demeanor," *American Anthropologist,* 58 (1956): 473–502.

Gómez Canedo, Lino. *La educación de los marginados durante la época colonial: Escuelas y colegios para indios y mestizos en la Nueva España.* 1982.

Gómez Hoyos, Rafael. *La iglesia de América en las leyes de Indias.* Madrid, 1961.

Góngora, Mario, "Estudios sobre el galicanismo y la 'Ilustración católica' en América española," *Revista Chilena de Historia y Geografía,* 125 (1957): 96–152.

———. "The Enlightenment, Enlightened Despotism, and the Ideological Crisis in the Colonies," in his *Studies in the Colonial History of Spanish America.* Tr. Richard Southern (Cambridge, Eng., 1975): 159–205.

Gonzalbo Aizpuru, Pilar. "Del tercer al cuarto concilio provincial mexicano," *Historia Mexicana,* 35 (1985): 5–31.

González Dávila, Gil. *Teatro eclesiástico de la primitiva iglesia de la Nueva España en las indias occidentales* [1648]. 2d ed. 2 vols. Madrid, 1959.

González Navarro, Moisés. *Repartimientos de indios en Nueva Galicia.* 2 vols. 1953.

González Sánchez, Isabel, ed. *El obispado de Michoacán en 1765.* Morelia, Michoacán, 1985.

González y González, Luis. "El optimismo nacionalista como factor de la independencia de México," in *Estudios de historiografía americana* (1948): 153–215.

Gosner, Kevin. "Soldiers of the Virgin: An Ethnohistorical Analysis of the Tzeltal Revolt of 1712 in Highland Chiapas." Ph.D. diss., University of Pennsylvania, 1983.

Graff, Gary W. "Spanish Parishes in Colonial New Granada: Their Role in Town Building on the Spanish-American Frontier," *The Americas,* 33 (1976): 336–51.

Gramsci, Antonio. *Letters from Prison.* Tr. Lynne Lawner. New York, 1973.

———. *Selections from the Prison Notebooks of Antonio Gramsci.* Tr. and ed. Quintin Hoare and Geoffrey Nowell Smith. New York, 1971.

Granados y Gálvez, Fr. Joseph Joaquín. *Tardes americanas . . . breve y particular noticia de toda la historia indiana . . . trabajadas por un indio y un español.* 1778.

Greenberg, James B. *Blood Ties: Life and Violence in Rural Mexico.* Tucson, Ariz., 1989.

———. *Santiago's Sword: Latino Peasant Religion and Economics.* Berkeley, Calif., 1981.

Greenblatt, Stephen. *Marvelous Possessions: The Wonder of the New World.* Chicago, 1991.

Greene, Graham. *The Lawless Roads.* London, 1950.

———. *The Power and the Glory.* Harmondsworth, Eng., 1984.

Greenleaf, Richard E. "The Inquisition and the Indians of New Spain: A Study in Jurisdictional Confusion," *The Americas,* 22 (1965): 138–66.

———. "The Inquisition in Eighteenth-Century Mexico," *New Mexico Historical Review,* 60 (1985): 29–60.

———. "The Mexican Inquisition and the Enlightenment," *New Mexico Historical Review,* 41 (1966): 181–91.

———. *The Mexican Inquisition of the Sixteenth Century.* Albuquerque, N.Mex., 1969.

———, ed. *The Roman Catholic Church in Colonial Latin America.* New York, 1971.

Grigsby, Thomas L. "In the Stone Warehouse: The Survival of a Cave Cult in Central Mexico," *Journal of Latin American Lore,* 12 (1986): 161–79.

Groethuysen, Bernard. *The Bourgeois: Catholicism v. Capitalism in Eighteenth-Century France.* New York, 1968.

Gruening, Ernest. *Mexico and Its Heritage.* New York, 1928.

Gruzinski, Serge. "Las cenizas del deseo: Homosexuales novohispanos a mediados del siglo XVII," in Sergio Ortega, ed., *De la santidad a la perversión, o, de porqué no se cumplía la ley de Dios en la sociedad novohispana* (1986): 255–82.

———. *La Colonisation de l'imaginaire: Sociétés indigènes et occidentalisation dans le Mexique espagnol, XVIe–XVIIIe siècle.* Paris, 1988.

———. "From Baroque to the Neo-Baroque: The Colonial Sources of the Postmodern Era," in Olivier Debroise, Elisabeth Sussman, and Matthew Teitelbaum, eds., *El corazón sangrante/The Bleeding Heart* (Seattle, 1991): 62–89.

———. "La guerra de las imágenes," *Nexos*, 148 (1990): 5–9.

———. "Indian Confraternities, Brotherhoods and *Mayordomías* in Central New Spain," in Arij Ouweneel and Simon Miller, eds., *The Indian Community of Colonial Mexico* (Amsterdam, 1990): 203–21.

———. "Individualization and Acculturation: Confession Among the Nahuas of Mexico from the Sixteenth Century to the Eighteenth Century," in Asunción Lavrin, ed., *Sexuality and Marriage in Colonial Latin America* (Lincoln, Neb., 1989): 96–115.

———. *Man-Gods in the Mexican Highlands: Indian Power and Colonial Society, 1520–1800.* Stanford, Calif., 1989.

———. "Normas cristianas y respuestas indígenas: Apuntes para el estudio del proceso de occidentalización entre los indios de Nueva España," *Historias*, 15 (1986): 31–41.

———. "La red agujerada: Identidades étnicas y occidentalización en el México colonial (siglos XVI–XIX)," *América Indígena*, 46 (1986): 411–33.

———. "La 'segunda aculturación': El estado ilustrado y la religiosidad indígena en Nueva España (1775–1800)," *Estudios de Historia Novohispana*, 8 (1985): 175–201.

Guaman Poma de Ayala, Felipe. *El primer nueva corónica y buen gobierno.* Ed. John V. Murra and Rolena Adorno. 2 vols. 1980.

Guarda, Gabriel. *Los laicos en la cristianización de América.* Santiago, Chile, 1973.

Guerra, José. *Fecunda nube del cielo Guadalupano . . . Relación breve de la vida exemplar del V.P.F. Antonio Margil de Jesús.* 1726.

Guía de forasteros en Jalisco para el año de 1828. Guadalajara, 1828.

Gulliver, P. H. "On Mediators," in Ian Hamnett, ed., *Social Anthropology and Law* (New York, 1977): 15–53.

Guridi y Alcocer, José Miguel. *Apuntes de la vida de d. José Miguel Guridi y Alcocer, formados por él mismo en fines de 1801 y principios del siguiente de 1802.* 1906.

Gutiérrez, Ramón A. *When Jesus Came, the Corn Mothers Went Away: Marriage, Sexuality, and Power in New Mexico, 1500–1846.* Stanford, Calif., 1991.

Gutiérrez Casillas, José. *Historia de la iglesia en México.* 1974.

Gutiérrez de Arroyo, Isabel. "El nuevo régimen institucional bajo la Real Ordenanza de Intendentes de la Nueva España (1786), *Historia Mexicana*, 39 (1989): 89–122.

Gutiérrez y Ulloa, Antonio. *Ensayo histórico político del Rno. de la Nueva Galicia con notas políticas y estadísticas de la Provincia de Guadalaxara* [1816]. Ed. Juan López. Guadalajara, 1983.

Hakluyt, Richard, ed. *The Principal Navigations, Voyages, Traffiques, and Discoveries of the English Nation.* 8 vols. New York, 1906.

Hall, David D. *The Faithful Shepherd: A History of the New England Ministry in the Seventeenth Century.* Chapel Hill, N.C., 1972.

———. *Worlds of Wonder, Days of Judgment: Popular Belief in Early New England.* New York, 1989.

Hallpike, C. R. "Social Hair," in Ted Polhemus, ed., *The Body Reader: Social Aspects of the Human Body* (New York, 1978): 134–46.

Halperín Donghi, Tulio. *Reforma y disolución de los imperios ibéricos, 1750–1850.* Madrid, 1985.

Hamill, Hugh M. "Caudillismo and Independence: A Symbiosis?," in Jaime E. Rodríguez, ed., *The Independence of Mexico and the Creation of the New Nation* (Los Angeles, 1989): 163–74.

———. "Early Psychological Warfare in the Hidalgo Revolt," *Hispanic American Historical Review,* 41 (1961): 206–35.

———. *The Hidalgo Revolt: Prelude to Mexican Independence.* Gainesville, Fla., 1966.

———. "The Rector to the Rescue: Royalist Pamphleteers in the Defense of Mexico, 1808–1821," in Roderic I. Camp, Charles A. Hale, and Josefina Zoraida Vásquez, eds., *Intellectuals and Power in Mexico* (Los Angeles, 1991): 49–61.

———. "Royalist Counterinsurgency in the Mexican War for Independence: The Lessons of 1811," *Hispanic American Historical Review,* 53 (1973): 470–89.

Hamnett, Brian R. "The Appropriation of Mexican Church Wealth by the Spanish Bourbon Government: The 'Consolidación de Vales Reales,' 1805–1809," *Journal of Latin American Studies,* 1 (1969): 85–113.

———. *Politics and Trade in Southern Mexico, 1760–1821.* Cambridge, Eng., 1971.

———. *Roots of Insurgency: Mexican Regions, 1750–1824.* Cambridge, Eng., 1986.

Hamnett, Ian, ed. *Social Anthropology and Law.* New York, 1977.

Hanke, Lewis, and Celso Rodríguez, eds. *Los virreyes españoles en América durante el gobierno de la Casa de Austria: Mexico.* 5 vols. Madrid, 1976–78.

Hardison, O. B., Jr. *Christian Rite and Christian Drama in the Middle Ages: Essays in the Origin and Early History of Modern Drama.* Baltimore, 1965.

Harrington, Raymond P. "The Secular Clergy in the Diocese of Mérida de Yucatán, 1780–1850: Their Origins, Careers, Wealth and Activities." Ph.D. diss., Catholic University of America, 1983.

Harris, Max. "Indigenismo y Catolicidad: Folk Dramatizations of Evangelism and Conquest in Central Mexico," *Journal of the American Academy of Religion,* 58 (1990): 55–68.

Hartman, Sven S., ed. *Syncretism.* Stockholm, 1969.

Haskell, Thomas L. "Capitalism and the Origins of the Humanitarian Sensibility," *American Historical Review,* 2 parts, 90 (1985): 339–61, 547–66.

Haskett, Robert. "Indian Town Government in Colonial Cuernavaca: Persistence, Adaptation, and Change," *Hispanic American Historical Review,* 67 (1987): 203–31.

———. *Indigenous Rulers: An Ethnohistory of Town Government in Colonial Cuernavaca.* Albuquerque, N.Mex., 1991.

———. " 'Our Suffering with the Taxco Tribute': Involuntary Mine Labor and Indigenous Society in Central New Spain," *Hispanic American Historical Review,* 71 (1991): 447–75.

Heath, Dwight B. "New Patrons for Old: Changing Patron-Client Relationships in the Bolivian Yungas," in Arnold Strickon and Sidney M. Greenfield, eds., *Structure in Latin America: Patronage, Clientage and Power Systems* (Albuquerque, N. Mex., 1972): 101–38.

Heath, Shirley B. *Telling Tongues: Language Policy in Mexico, Colony to Province.* New York, 1972.

de la Hera, Alberto. "Los comienzos del derecho misional indiano," in *Estructuras, gobierno, y agentes de la administración en la América española (siglos XVI, XVII, y XVIII)* (Valladolid, Spain, 1984): 43–59.

———. "El derecho de los indios a la libertad y a la fe: La bula 'Sublimis Deus' y los problemas indianos que la motivaron," *Anuario de Historia del Derecho Español,* 26 (1956): 89–181.

———. "Notas para el estudio del regalismo en el siglo XVIII," *Anuario de Estudios Americanos*, 31 (1974): 409–40.

———. "Reforma de la inmunidad personal del clero en Indias bajo Carlos IV," *Anuario de Historia del Derecho Español*, 30 (1960): 553–59.

———. *El regalismo borbónico en su proyección indiana*. Madrid, 1963.

———, ed. "Juicios de los obispos asistentes al IV Concilio mexicano sobre el estado del virreinato de Nueva España," *Anuario de Historia del Derecho Español*, 31 (1961): 307–26.

Hermosillo, Fr. Gonzalo de. *Sitio, naturaleza y propiedad de la ciudad de México . . .* 1618.

Hernáez, Francisco Javier, ed. *Colección de bulas, breves y otros documentos relativos a la iglesia de América y Filipinas*. 2 vols. Brussels, 1879.

Hernández Palomo, José Jesús. *El aguardiente de caña en México (1724–1810)*. Seville, 1974.

Hernández Xolocotzi, Efraím. "Maize Granaries in Mexico," *Botanical Museum Leaflets* (Harvard University), 13 (1949): 153–92.

Hernández y Dávalos, Juan E. *Colección de documentos para la historia de la guerra de independencia de México de 1808 a 1821* [1877–82]. 2d ed. 6 vols. Liechtenstein, 1968.

Herr, Richard. *The Eighteenth-Century Revolution in Spain*. Princeton, N.J., 1958.

Herrejón, Carlos. "Hidalgo: La justificación de la insurgencia," *Relaciones*, 1983, no. 13: 35–40.

———. *Morelos: Vida preinsurgente y lecturas*. Zamora, Michoacán, 1984.

———. *Los procesos de Morelos*. Zamora, Michoacán, 1985.

———. *Repaso de la Independencia*. Zamora, Michoacán, 1985.

———. *Textos políticos en la Nueva España*. 1984.

———, ed. *Humanismo y ciencia en la formación de México*. Zamora, Michoacán, 1984.

Herrero, Javier. *Los orígenes del pensamiento reaccionario español*. Madrid, 1971.

Hexter, J. H. *Reappraisals in History: New Views on History and Society in Early Modern Europe*. New York, 1961.

Heyden, Doris. "Caves," in Eliade, ed., listed above, 3: 127–33.

———. "Flores, creencias y el control social," in *Actes du XLIIe Congrès International des Américanistes* (Paris, 1976), 6: 85–94.

Hicks, Frederick. "Politics, Power, and the Role of the Village Priest in Paraguay," in Dwight B. Heath, ed., *Contemporary Cultures and Societies of Latin America: A Reader in the Social Anthropology of Middle and South America*. 2d ed. (New York, 1973): 387–95.

Hirschman, Albert O. *The Passions and the Interests: Political Arguments for Capitalism Before Its Triumph*. Princeton, N.J., 1977.

Hoberman, Louisa. "Hispanic American Political Theory as a Distinct Tradition," *Journal of the History of Ideas*, 41 (1980): 199–218.

———. *Mexico's Merchant Elite, 1590–1660: Silver, State, and Society*. Durham, N.C., 1991.

Hobsbawm, Eric. "Religion and the Rise of Socialism," *Marxist Perspectives*, 1978, no. 1: 14–33.

Huber, Brad R. "The Reinterpretation and Elaboration of Fiestas in the Sierra Norte de Puebla, Mexico," *Ethnology*, 26 (1987): 281–96.

Huerta, María T., and Patricia Palacios, eds. *Rebeliones indígenas en la época colonial*. 1976.

Hufton, Olwen H. "Attitudes Towards Authority in Eighteenth-Century Languedoc," *Social History*, 3 (1978): 281–302.

Humboldt, Alexander von. *Political Essay on the Kingdom of New Spain*. Tr. John Black. 2 vols. New York, 1811.

Hunefeldt, Christine. "Comunidad, curas y comuneros hacia fines del período colonial: Ovejas y pastores indomados en el Perú," *HISLA: Revista Latinoamericana de Historia Económica y Social*, 2 (1983): 3–31.

Ibarra, Ana Carolina. " 'Los poderes creadores de un instante': La historia de José de San Martín en la independencia," *Eslabones*, 1991, no. 1: 5–15.

Ingham, John M. *Mary, Michael, and Lucifer: Folk Catholicism in Central Mexico.* Austin, Tex., 1986.

"Inscripciones colocadas durante el gobierno del Exmo. Sr. Virrey Conde de Revilla Gigedo en esta Nueva España," *Anales del Museo Nacional de Arqueología, Historia y Etnología,* 5 (1914): 279–87.

Instrucción reservada que el Obispo-Virrey Juan de Ortega Montañés dió a su sucesor en el mando el Conde de Moctezuma. Ed. Norman F. Martin. 1965.

Instrucciones que los vireyes de Nueva España dejaron a sus sucesores. 2 vols. 1873.

Isérn, Juan. *La formación del clero secular de Buenos Aires y la Compañía de Jesús.* Buenos Aires, 1936.

Islas García, Luis. *Apuntes para el estudio del caciquismo en México.* 1962.

Jackson, Everett Gee. *Burros and Paintbrushes: A Mexican Adventure.* College Station, Tex., 1985.

Jacobsen, Nils, and Hans-Jürgen Puhle, eds. *The Economies of Mexico and Peru During the Late Colonial Period, 1760–1810.* Berlin, 1986.

James, Mervyn. *Society, Politics, and Culture: Studies in Early Modern England.* Cambridge, Eng., 1986.

Jessopp, Augustus. *Before the Great Pillage, with Other Miscellanies.* London, 1901.

Jiménez Moreno, Wigberto. "Antecedentes históricos del cambio social y económico en el México contemporáneo," *Anales del Instituto Nacional de Antropología e Historia,* 43 (1962): 139–45.

———. "The Indians of America and Christianity," *The Americas,* 14 (1958): 411–31.

Jiménez Moreno, Wigberto, José Miranda, and María Teresa Fernández. *Historia de México.* 1963.

Jiménez Pelayo, Agueda. *Haciendas y comunidades indígenas en el sur de Zacatecas.* 1989.

Johnson, H. B. "Portrait of a Portuguese Parish: Santa María de Alvarenga in 1719," *Estudos de Historia de Portugal,* 2 (1983): 181–201.

Johnson, Lyman L., and Enrique Tandeter, eds. *Essays on the Price History of Eighteenth-Century Latin America.* Albuquerque, N.Mex., 1990.

Jones, Peter M. "Parish Seigneurie and the Community of Inhabitants in Southern Central France during the Eighteenth and Nineteenth Centuries," *Past & Present,* 1981, no. 91: 74–108.

Juan, Jorge, and Antonio de Ulloa. *Discourse and Political Reflections on the Kingdoms of Peru . . . 1749.* Ed. John J. TePaske; tr. TePaske and Besse A. Clement. Norman, Okla., 1978.

Juárez Nieto, Carlos. *El clero en Morelia durante el siglo XVII.* Morelia, Michoacán, 1988.

Kagan, Richard. *Lawsuits and Litigants in Early Modern Spain.* Chapel Hill, N.C., 1981.

Kant, Immanuel. *Critique of Practical Reason and Other Writings in Moral Philosophy.* Ed. and tr. Lewis White Beck. Chicago, 1949.

Kanter, Deborah E. "Hijos de Pueblo: Family, Community, and Gender in Rural Mexico, the Toluca Region, 1730–1830." Ph.D. diss., University of Virginia, 1993.

———. "Indian Education in Late Colonial Mexico: Policy and Practice." M.A. thesis, University of Virginia, 1987.

Kantorowicz, Ernst H. *The King's Two Bodies: A Study of Mediaeval Political Theology.* Princeton, N.J., 1957.

Kaplan, Steven L., ed. *Understanding Popular Culture: Europe from the Middle Ages to the Nineteenth Century.* Berlin, 1984.

Kendrick, T. D. *St. James in Spain.* London, 1960.

Kern, Robert, ed. *The Caciques: Oligarchical Politics and the System of Caciquismo in the Luso-Hispanic World.* Albuquerque, N.Mex., 1973.

Kidd, Barbara Anne. "From Priest to Shaman. A Study of Colonial Nahuatl Nativism." Ph.D. diss., Tulane University, 1982.

Kiracofe, James B. "Constructing a Matrix for the Miraculous: A Study of Christianization and the Transformation of the Sacramental Imagination in Sixteenth-Century Mexico." M.A. thesis, University of Virginia, 1990.

Kirk, Betty. *Covering the Mexican Front*. Norman, Okla., 1942.

Klein, Herbert S. "Peasant Communities in Revolt: The Tzeltal Republic of 1712," *Pacific Historical Review*, 35 (1966): 247–64.

Klor de Alva, J. Jorge. "Colonizing Souls: The Failure of the Indian Inquisition and the Rise of Penitential Discipline," in Mary Elizabeth Perry and Anne J. Cruz, eds., *Cultural Encounters: The Impact of the Inquisition in Spain and the New World* (Berkeley, Calif., 1991): 3–22.

———. "Spiritual Conflict and Accommodation in New Spain: Toward a Typology of Aztec Responses to Christianity," in George A. Collier, Renato I. Rosaldo, and John D. Wirth, eds., *The Inca and Aztec States, 1400–1800: Anthropology and History* (New York, 1982): 345–66.

Knight, Alan. *Mexican Revolution*. 2 vols. Cambridge, Eng., 1986.

Kolakowski, Leszek. *Religion*. New York, 1982.

Konetzke, Richard, ed. *Colección de documentos para la historia de la formación social de Hispanoamérica*. 5 vols. Madrid, 1953–62.

Korn, Peggy K. "Topics in Mexican Historiography, 1750–1810: The Bourbon Reforms, the Enlightenment, and the Background of Revolution," in *Investigaciones contemporáneas sobre historia de México* (1971): 159–95.

Koster, Adrianus. "The Kappillani: The Changing Position of the Parish Priest in Malta," in Eric R. Wolf, ed., *Religion, Power, and Protest in Local Communities: The Northern Shore of the Mediterranean* (Berlin, 1984): 185–212.

Kubler, George. *Mexican Architecture of the Sixteenth Century*. 2 vols. New Haven, Conn., 1948.

———. "On the Colonial Extinction of the Motifs of Pre-Columbian Art," in Samuel K. Lothrop et al., eds., *Essays in Pre-Columbian Art and Archaeology* (Cambridge, Mass., 1961): 14–34.

Kuethe, Allan J. "La desregulación comercial y la reforma imperial en la época de Carlos III: Los casos de Nueva España y Cuba," *Historia Mexicana*, 41 (1985): 265–92.

Kuethe, Allan J., and G. Douglas Inglis. "Absolutism and Enlightened Reform: Charles III, the Establishment of the *Alcabala*, and Commercial Reorganization in Cuba," *Past & Present*, 1985, no. 109: 118–43.

Ladd, Doris M. *The Mexican Nobility at Independence, 1780–1826*. Austin, Tex., 1976.

Lafaye, Jacques. *Quetzalcóatl and Guadalupe: The Formation of Mexican National Consciousness, 1531–1813*. Tr. Benjamin Keen. Chicago, 1976.

Lamb, Ursula. "Religious Conflicts in the Conquest of Mexico," *Journal of the History of Ideas*, 17 (1956): 526–39.

Lanning, John T. "The Church and the Enlightenment in the Universities," *The Americas*, 15 (1959): 331–50.

———. *The Eighteenth-Century Enlightenment in the University of San Carlos de Guatemala*. Ithaca, N.Y., 1956.

———. "The Enlightenment in Relation to the Church," *The Americas*, 14 (1958): 489–96.

Lárraga, Francisco. *Promptuario de la theología moral . . .* [1704]. 4th ed., revised by Francisco Santos y Grosin. Madrid, 1790.

Larson, Brooke. "Caciques, Class Structure and the Colonial State in Bolivia," *Nova Americana*, 2 (1979): 197–235.

Lasso de la Vega, *see* Lobo Lasso de la Vega

Lavrin, Asunción. "The Church as an Economic Institution," in Richard E. Greenleaf, ed., *The Roman Catholic Church in Colonial Latin America* (New York, 1971): 182–94.

———. "The Execution of the Law of *Consolidación* in New Spain: Economic Aims and Results," *Hispanic American Historical Review*, 53 (1973): 27–49.

———. "Misión de la historia e historiografía de la iglesia en el período colonial americano," *Anuario de Estudios Americanos*, 46 (1989): 11–44.

———. "Mundos en contraste: Cofradías rurales y urbanas en México a fines del siglo XVIII," in Arnold J. Bauer, ed., *La iglesia en la economía de América latina, siglos XVI a XVIII* (1986): 235–76.

———. "Rural Confraternities in the Local Economies of New Spain: The Bishopric of Oaxaca in the Context of Colonial Mexico," in Arij Ouweneel and Simon Miller, eds., *The Indian Community of Colonial Mexico* (Amsterdam, 1990): 224–49.

———, ed. *Sexuality and Marriage in Colonial Latin America*. Lincoln, Neb., 1989.

Lea, Henry C. *The Inquisition in the Spanish Dependencies*. New York, 1908.

Leach, Edmund. "Concluding Remarks," in Antony Hooper and Judith Huntsman, eds., *Transformations of Polynesian Culture* (Auckland, 1985): 219–23.

———. "Magical Hair," in John Middleton, ed., *Myth and Cosmos: Readings in Mythology and Symbolism* (Garden City, N.Y., 1967): 77–108.

Lears, T. J. Jackson. "The Concept of Cultural Hegemony: Problems and Possibilities," *American Historical Review*, 90 (1985): 567–93.

Ledesma, Clemente de. *Despertador republicano que por las letras del ABC compendia el segundo tomo de noticias theológicas morales*. 1699–1700.

Lemoine Villicaña, Ernesto. *Morelos: Su vida revolucionaria a través de sus escritos y de otros testimonios de la época*. 1965.

———. *Morelos y la revolución de 1810*. 2d ed. Morelia, Michocán, 1984.

———. "Un notable escrito póstumo del obispo de Michoacán, fray Antonio de San Miguel, sobre la situación social, económica y eclesiástica de la Nueva España, en 1804," *Boletín del Archivo General de la Nación*, 2d series, 5 (1964): 5–65.

———. "Relación de agravios de los naturales de la provincia de los Motines de Colima contra su alcalde mayor y juez congregador," *Boletín del Archivo General de la Nación*, 2d series, 1 (1960): 201–12.

———. "Visita, congregación y mapa de Amecameca de 1599," *Boletín del Archivo General de la Nación*, 2d series, 2 (1961): 5–46.

Linati, Claudio. *Trajes civiles, militares y religiosos de México (1828)*. Ed. and tr. Justino Fernández. 1956.

Lira, Andrés. "Las cajas de comunidad," *Diálogos*, 1982, no. 108: 11–14.

———. "Los indígenas y el nacionalismo mexicano," *Relaciones*, 1984, no. 20: 75–94.

Lira, Andrés, and Luis Muro. "El siglo de la integración," in *Historia general de México* (1976) 2: 83–181.

Liss, Peggy K. *Atlantic Empires: The Network of Trade and Revolution, 1713–1826*. Baltimore, 1983.

Litle, Marcella M. "Sales Taxes and Internal Commerce in Bourbon Mexico, 1754–1821." Ph.D. diss., Duke University, 1985.

Lizana y Beaumont, Francisco Javier de. *Sentimientos religiosos, con los que ... desea instruir a sus amados diocesanos: En la Semana Santa, visitas y estaciones que en ella se practican en las iglesias*. 1808.

Llaguno, José A. *La personalidad jurídica del indio y el III Concilio Provincial Mexicano (1585)*. 1963.

Lobo Lasso de la Vega, Gabriel. *Mexicana* [1594]. Madrid, 1970.

Lockhart, James. *The Nahuas After the Conquest*. Stanford, Calif., 1992.

———. "Some Nahua Concepts in Postconquest Guise," *History of European Ideas*, 6 (1985): 465–82.

———. "Views of Corporate Self and History in Some Valley of Mexico Towns: Late

Seventeenth and Eighteenth Centuries," in George A. Collier, Renato I. Rosaldo, and John D. Wirth, eds., *The Inca and Aztec States, 1400–1800: Anthropology and History* (New York, 1982): 367–94.

Lockhart, James, and Stuart B. Schwartz. *Early Latin America: A History of Spanish America and Brazil.* Cambridge, Eng., 1983.

Lohmann Villena, Guillermo. "Religion and Culture in Spanish America," *The Americas,* 14 (1958): 383–98.

Lomnitz-Adler, Claudio. *Evolución de una sociedad rural: Historia del poder en Tepoztlán.* 1982.

Lopétegui, León, and Félix Zubillaga. *Historia de la iglesia en la América española desde el descubrimiento hasta comienzos del siglo XIX: México, América central, Antillas.* Madrid, 1965.

López, Juan, ed. *Insurgencia de la Nueva Galicia en algunos documentos.* 2 vols. Guadalajara, 1984.

López Austin, Alfredo. *Cuerpo humano e ideología: Las concepciones de los antiguos nahuas.* 2 vols. 1980.

———. *The Human Body and Ideology Concepts of the Ancient Nahuas.* Tr. Thelma Ortiz de Montellano and Bernard Ortiz de Montellano. 2 vols. Salt Lake City, 1988.

López de Gómara, Francisco. *Historia de la conquista de México.* 2 vols. 1943.

López Jiménez, Eucario, ed. *Algunos documentos de Nayarit.* Guadalajara, 1978.

———. *Cedulario de la Nueva Galicia.* Guadalajara, 1971.

———. *Centenario de la Arquidiócesis de Guadalajara.* Guadalajara, 1964.

———. *Descripción del partido y jurisdicción de Tlaltenango hecha en 1650 por D. Francisco Manuel de Salcedo y Herrera.* 1958.

López Lara, Ramón. *Zinapécuaro: Tres épocas de una parroquia.* 3d ed. Morelia, Michoacán, 1984.

López Sarrelangue, Delfina. "Mestizaje y catolicismo en la Nueva España," *Historia Mexicana,* 23 (1973): 1–42.

———. *Una villa mexicana en el siglo XVIII.* 1957.

Lorenzana y Buitrón, Francisco Antonio. *Cartas, edictos y otras obras sueltas del Excelentísimo Señor D. Francisco Antonio Lorenzana, Arzobispo de Toledo, Primado de las Españas.* Toledo, Spain, 1786.

———. *Cartas pastorales y edictos del Illmo Señor Don Francisco Antonio Lorenzana y Buitrón, Arzobispo de México.* 1770.

———. *Historia de Nueva España escrita por su esclarecido conquistador Hernán Cortés aumentada con otros documentos y notas por el Ilustríssimo . . . Arzobispo de México.* 1770.

Lumholtz, Carl. *Unknown Mexico.* 2 vols. New York, 1902.

Luria, Keith P. *Territories of Grace: Cultural Change in the Seventeenth-Century Diocese of Grenoble.* Berkeley, Calif., 1991.

Lynch, John. *Bourbon Spain, 1700–1808.* Oxford, Eng., 1989.

———. "La segunda conquista de América: 1765–1808," *Historia 16,* 1977, no. 1: 60–70.

MacAndrew, John. *The Open-Air Churches in Sixteenth-Century Mexico.* Cambridge, Mass., 1965.

MacCormack, Sabine. "From the Sun of the Incas to the Virgin of Copacabana," *Representations,* 1984, no. 8: 30–60.

———. " 'The Heart Has Its Reasons': Predicaments of Missionary Christianity in Early Colonial Peru," *Hispanic American Historical Review,* 65 (1985): 443–66.

———. "Pachacuti: Miracles, Punishments, and Last Judgment; Visionary Past and Prophetic Future in Early Colonial Peru," *American Historical Review,* 93 (1988): 960–1006.

———. *Religion in the Andes: Vision and Imagination in Early Colonial Peru.* Princeton, N.J., 1991.

Macera, Pablo. *Pintores populares andinos*. Lima, 1979.

———. *Trabajos de historia*. 2 vols. Lima, 1977.

Macías, Anna. *Génesis del gobierno constitucional en México: 1808–1820*. 1973.

MacLachlan, Colin M. *Criminal Justice in Eighteenth-Century Mexico: A Study of the Tribunal of the Acordada*. Berkeley, Calif., 1974.

———. *Spain's Empire in the New World: The Role of Ideas in Institutional and Social Change*. Berkeley, Calif., 1988.

MacLeod, Murdo J. "La espada de la Iglesia: Excomunión y la evolución de la lucha por el control político y económico en Chiapas colonial, 1545–1700," *Mesoamérica*, 1990, no. 20: 199–214.

———. "Papel social y económico de las cofradías indígenas de la colonia en Chiapas," *Mesoamérica*, 1983, no. 4: 64–86.

McCaa, Robert. "*Calidad, Clase,* and Marriage in Colonial Mexico: The Case of Parral, 1788–1790," *Hispanic American Historical Review*, 64 (1984): 477–502.

McKinley, Arch. "The Account of a Punitive Sentence," *Tlalocan*, 2, no. 4 (1948): 368–73.

McLeod, Hugh. *Religion and the People of Western Europe, 1789–1970*. New York, 1981.

McManners, John. *French Ecclesiastical Society Under the Ancien Regime: A Study of Angers in the Eighteenth Century*. Manchester, Eng., 1960.

McNeill, William H. *Population and Politics Since 1750*. Charlottesville, Va., 1990.

Madsen, William. *Christo-Paganism: A Study of Mexican Religious Syncretism*, in Middle American Research Institute Publications (New Orleans), 19 (1957): 105–80.

———. "Religious Syncretism," *Handbook of Middle American Indians*, 8 (1967): 369–91.

Malagón Barceló, Javier. "Los escritos del cardenal Lorenzana," *Boletín del Instituto de Investigaciones Bibliográficas*, 4 (1970): 223–63.

———. "La obra escrita de Lorenzana como Arzobispo de México," *Historia Mexicana*, 23 (1974): 437–65.

Mann, Michael. *The Sources of Social Power*. Vol. 1: *A History of Power from the Beginning to A.D. 1760*. Cambridge, Eng., 1986.

Manual breve y forma de administrar . . . 1638. (John Carter Brown Lib. ed., BA 638.)

Manual de párrocos para la administración del sacramento de matrimonio y de las exequias, enteramente conforme al ritual romano . . . [1789]. 1803.

María y Campos, Armando de. *Matamoros, teniente general insurgente*. 1964.

Marichal, Carlos. "La Iglesia y la crisis financiera del virreinato, 1780–1808: Apuntes sobre un tema viejo y nuevo," *Relaciones*, 1989, no. 40: 103–29.

Markman, Peter T., and Roberta H. Markman. *Masks of the Spirit: Image and Metaphor in Mesoamerica*. Berkeley, Calif., 1989.

Martin, Cheryl E. "Popular Speech and Social Order in Northern Mexico, 1650–1830," *Comparative Studies in Society and History*, 32 (1990): 305–24.

———. *Rural Society in Colonial Morelos*. Albuquerque, N.Mex., 1985.

———. "Secularization, Clerical Finance and Parish Life in Late Colonial Mexico: The Case of Morelos." Paper delivered at the Southern Historical Association convention, Memphis, Tenn., 1982.

Martín Rivera, José de. "La vida cotidiana de la cristiandad americana," in Enrique Dussel, ed., *Historia general de la Iglesia en América latina* (5 vols. to date; Salamanca, Spain, 1981–), 5: 95–164.

Martínez, Elías. "Los franciscanos y la Independencia de México," *Abside*, 24 (1960): 129–62.

Martínez Albiach, Alfredo. *Religiosidad hispana y sociedad borbónica*. Burgos, Spain, 1969.

Martínez Reyes, Gabriel. *Finanzas de las 44 diócesis de Indias, 1515–1816*. Bogota, 1980.

Mata Torres, Ramón. *Los tastuanes de Nextipac*. Guadalajara, 1987.

Matraya y Ricci, Juan Joseph. *Catálogo cronológico de las pragmáticas, cédulas, decretos, órdenes y resoluciones reales generales emanados después de la Recopilación de leyes de Indias* [1819]. Buenos Aires, 1978.

Matson, Daniel S., and Bernard L. Fontana, eds. *Friar Bringas Reports to the King: Methods of Indoctrination on the Frontier of New Spain, 1796-1797*. Tucson, Ariz., 1977.

Maunier, René. *The Sociology of Colonies: An Introduction to the Study of Race Contact*. 2 vols. London, 1949.

Mayer, Brantz. *Mexico As It Was and As It Is*. New York, 1844.

Maza, Francisco de la. *El guadalupanismo mexicano*. 1953.

Mazín Gómez, Oscar. *Entre dos majestades: El obispo y la iglesia del Gran Michoacán ante las reformas borbónicas, 1758-1772*. Zamora, Michoacán, 1987.

———. "Reorganización del clero secular novohispano en la segunda mitad del siglo XVIII," *Relaciones*, 1989, no. 39: 69-86.

Medina, José Toribio. *Historia del Tribunal del Santo Oficio de la Inquisición en México*. 2d ed. 1952.

Meier, Matt S. "María insurgente," *Historia Mexicana* 23 (1974): 466-82.

Mello e Souza, Laura de. *O diablo e a terra de Santa Cruz*. Sao Paulo, 1987.

Melville, Elinor G. K. *A Plague of Sheep: Environmental Consequences of the Conquest of Mexico*. New York, 1994.

Memmi, Albert. *The Colonizer and the Colonized*. Boston, 1967.

Memorias y descripciones de la Nueva Galicia, año del Señor de 1579. Guadalajara, 1976.

Menéndez Valdez, José. *Descripción y censo general de la Intendencia de Guadalajara, 1789-1793*. Ed. Ramón María Serrera Contreras. Guadalajara, 1980.

Merrill, William L. "Conversion and Colonialism in Northern Mexico: The Tarahumara Response to the Jesuit Mission Program, 1601-1767," in Robert W. Hefner, ed., *Conversion to Christianity: Historical and Anthropological Perspectives on a Great Transformation* (Berkeley, Calif., 1993): 129-63.

Meyers, Albert, and Diane Hopkins, eds., *Manipulating the Saints: Religious Brotherhoods and Social Integration in Postconquest Latin America*. Hamburg, 1988.

Miller, Arthur G. "Transformations of Time and Space: Oaxaca, Mexico, circa 1500-1700," in Susanna Küchler and Walter Melion, eds., *Images of Memory: On Remembering and Representation* (Washington, D.C., 1991): 141-75.

Miller, Arthur G., and Nancy M. Farriss. "Religious Syncretism in Colonial Yucatán: The Archaeological and Ethnohistorical Evidence from Tancah, Quintana Roo," in Norman Hammond and Gordon R. Willey, eds., *Maya Archaeology and Ethnohistory* (Austin, Tex., 1979): 223-40.

Minos, Agapito Mateo. *Apuntaciones históricas de Xoxutla a Tlaquiltenango (Estado de Morelos)*. 1923.

Mintz, Sidney W., and Richard Price. *An Anthropological Approach to the Afro-American Past: A Caribbean Perspective*. Philadelphia, 1976.

Miquel i Vergés, José María. *Diccionario de insurgentes*. 1969.

Miranda, José. *Vida colonial y albores de la independencia*. 1972.

Montiel, Rosalba, and Irene Huesca, eds. *Documentos de la guerra de independencia en Oaxaca*. Oaxaca, 1986.

Moore, Sally F. *Law as Process: An Anthropological Approach*. London, 1980.

Moore, Sally F., and Barbara G. Myerhoff, eds. *Symbol and Politics in Communal Ideology: Cases and Questions*. Ithaca, N.Y., 1975.

Mora Mérida, José Luis. "Comportamiento político del clero secular de Cartagena de Indias en la preindependencia," *Anuario de Estudios Americanos*, 35 (1978): 211-31.

———. *Iglesia y sociedad en Paraguay en el siglo XVIII*. Seville, 1976.

Morales, Francisco. *Clero y política en México (1767-1834): Algunas ideas sobre la autoridad, la independencia y la reforma eclesiástica*. 1975.

Morazzani de Pérez Enciso, G. *La intendencia en España y en América*. Caracas, 1966.

Morelos: Documentos inéditos y poco conocidos. 3 vols. 1927.

Morelos y la Iglesia Católica. 1948.

Moreno de los Arcos, Roberto. "Dos documentos sobre el arzobispo Lorenzana y los indios de Nueva España," *Históricas*, 1982, no. 10: 27–38.

———. "Humanismo y ciencias en el siglo XVIII," in Carlos Herrejón, ed., *Humanismo y ciencia en la formación de México* (Zamora, Michoacán, 1984): 325–37.

———. "Visión de la Nueva España," in Jaime E. Rodríguez, ed., *Latin America in the Eighties: Proceedings of the PCCLAS*, 10 (1982–83): 1–9.

Moreno García, Heriberto. "El humanismo ilustrado y el agro novohispano," in Carlos Herrejón, ed., *Humanismo y ciencia en la formación de México* (Zamora, Michoacán, 1984): 237–67.

———, ed. *En favor del campo: Gaspar de Jovellanos, Manuel Abad y Queipo, Antonio de San Miguel, y otros*. 1986.

Mörner, Magnus. *La corona española y los foráneos en los pueblos de indios de América*. Stockholm, 1970.

Morse, Richard. "Claims of Political Tradition," in Peter Bakewell, John J. Johnson, and Meredith D. Dodge, eds., *Readings in Latin American History* (Durham, N.C., 1985), 1: 414–28.

———. "The Heritage of Latin America," in Louis Hartz, ed., *The Founding of New Societies: Studies in the History of the United States, Latin America, South Africa, Canada, and Australia* (New York, 1964): 123–77.

Mota Padilla, Matías de la. *Historia de la conquista de la provincia de la Nueva Galicia* [1742]. 1870.

———. *Historia del Reino de Nueva Galicia en la América septentrional*. Guadalajara, 1973.

Mota y Escobar, Alonso de la. *Descripción geográfica de los reinos de Nueva Galicia, Nueva Vizcaya, y Nuevo León* [1603]. 2d ed. 1940.

Motolinía [Toribio de Benavente]. *History of the Indians of New Spain* [1541]. Washington, D.C., 1951.

Moxó, Benito María de. *Cartas mejicanas escritas en 1805*. Genoa, 1838.

Muldoon, James. *Popes, Lawyers, and Infidels*. Philadelphia, 1979.

Muller, Gene A. "The Church in Poverty: Bishops, Bourbons, and Tithes in Spanish Honduras, 1700–1821." Ph.D. diss., University of Kansas, 1982.

Muro Romero, Fernando. "Instituciones de gobierno y sociedad en Indias (1700–1760)," in *Estructuras, gobierno, y agentes de la administración en la América española (siglos XVI, XVII, y XVIII)* (Valladolid, Spain, 1984): 163–231.

Musgrave-Portilla, L. Marie. "The Nahualli or Transforming Wizard in Pre- and Postconquest Mesoamerica," *Journal of Latin American Lore*, 8 (1982): 3–62.

Nandy, Ashis. *The Intimate Enemy: Loss and Recovery of Self Under Colonialism*. New Delhi, 1983.

———. "The Politics of Secularism and the Recovery of Religious Tolerance," in Veena Das, ed., *Communities, Riots and Survivors in South Asia* (New Delhi, 1990): 69–93.

———. *The Tao of Cricket: On Games of Destiny and the Destiny of Games*. New Delhi, 1989.

Nash, June. "The Aztecs and the Ideology of Male Dominance," *Signs: Journal of Women in Culture and Society*, 4 (1978): 349–62.

Nava Oteo, Guadalupe. "Cajas de bienes de comunidades indígenas," *Anales del Instituto Nacional de Antropología e Historia*, época 7, no. 2 (1969): 349–59.

Navarro B., Bernabé. *Cultura mexicana en el siglo XVIII*. 2d ed. 1982.

Navarro de Vargas, Joseph. "Padrón del pueblo de San Mateo Huitzilopochco, inventario de su iglesia y directorio de sus obvenciones parroquiales [1734]," *Anales del Museo Nacional de Arqueología, Historia, y Etnología*, época 3, no. 1 (1909): 553–99.

Navarro y Noriega, Fernando. *Catálogo de los curatos y misiones de la Nueva España seguido de la memoria sobre la población del reino de Nueva España* [1813, 1820]. 1943.

Newby, Howard. "The Deferential Dialectic," *Comparative Studies in Society and History*, 17 (1975): 139–64.

Nicholson, Henry B. *Art of Aztec Mexico: Treasures of Tenochtitlan*. Washington, D.C., 1983.

———. "Religion in Pre-Hispanic Central Mexico," *Handbook of Middle American Indians*, 10 (1971): 395–446.

Nöel, C. C. "The Clerical Confrontation with the Enlightenment in Spain," *European Studies Review*, 5 (1975): 103–22.

———. "Missionary Preachers in Spain: Teaching Social Virtue in the Eighteenth Century," *American Historical Review*, 90 (1985): 866–92.

———. "Opposition to Enlightened Reform in Spain: Campomanes and the Clergy, 1765–1775," *Societas*, 3 (1973): 21–43.

Nolan, Mary Lee. "The Mexican Pilgrimage Tradition," *Pioneer America*, 5 (1973): 13–27.

Nolan, Mary Lee, and Sidney Nolan. *Christian Pilgrimage in Modern Western Europe*. Chapel Hill, N.C., 1989.

Noticias varias de Nueva Galicia, Intendencia de Guadalajara. Guadalajara, 1878.

Núñez de la Vega, Francisco. *Constituciones diocesanas del obispado de Chiapa*. 1988.

Nutini, Hugo. "Pre-Hispanic Component of the Syncretic Cult of the Dead in Mesoamerica," *Ethnology*, 27 (1988): 57–78.

———. "Syncretism and Acculturation: The Historical Development of the Cult of the Patron Saint in Tlaxcala, Mexico (1519–1670)," *Ethnology*, 15 (1976): 301–21.

———. *Todos Santos in Rural Tlaxcala: A Syncretic, Expressive, and Symbolic Analysis of the Cult of the Dead*. Princeton, N.J., 1988.

Oakley, Francis. *The Western Church in the Later Middle Ages*. Ithaca, N.Y., 1979.

O'Crouley, Pedro Alonso. *A Description of the Kingdom of New Spain*. Ed. and tr. Seán Galvin. San Francisco, Calif., 1972.

O'Day, Rosemary. *The English Clergy: The Emergence and Consolidation of a Profession, 1558–1642*. Leicester, Eng., 1979.

O'Day, Rosemary, and Felicity Heal, eds. *Princes and Paupers in the English Church, 1500–1800*. Leicester, Eng., 1981.

O'Dea, Thomas F. *The Sociology of Religion*. Englewood Cliffs, N.J., 1966.

O'Gorman, Edmundo. *Destierro de sombras: Luz en el origen de la imagen y culto de Nuestra Señora de Guadalupe del Tepeyac*. 1986.

———. *Historia de las divisiones territoriales de México*. 4th ed. 1968.

———. *México: El trauma de su historia*. 1977.

———. *La supervivencia política novo-hispana: Reflexiones sobre el monarquismo mexicano*. 1969.

Olaechea, Juan B. "Doncellas indias en religión," *Missionalia Hispánica*, 27 (1970): 360–62.

O'Neil, Mary R. "*Sacerdote ovvero strione*: Ecclesiastical and Superstitious Remedies in Sixteenth-Century Italy," in Steven L. Kaplan, ed., *Understanding Popular Culture: Europe from the Middle Ages to the Nineteenth Century* (Berlin, 1984): 53–83.

———. "Superstition," in Eliade, ed., listed above, 14: 163–66.

O'Phelan Godoy, Scarlett. "El mito de la 'independencia concedida': Los programas políticos del siglo XVIII y del temprano XIX en el Perú y Alto Perú (1730–1814)," in Inge Buisson et al., eds., *Estudios sobre la formación del estado y de la nación en Hispanoamérica* (Bonn, 1984): 55–92.

———. "El norte y las revueltas anticlericales del siglo XVIII," *Historia y Cultura*, 12 (1979): 1–17.

———. "Por el rey, religión y la patria: Las juntas de gobierno de 1809 en La Paz y Quito," *Boletín del Instituto Francés de Estudios Andinos*, 17 (1988): 61–80.

———. "Las reformas fiscales borbónicas y su impacto en la sociedad colonial del Bajo y el Alto Perú," *Historia y Cultura*, 16 (1983): 113–28.

———. *Un siglo de rebeliones anticoloniales: Perú y Bolivia, 1700–1783*. Cuzco, 1988.

Ornelas Mendoza y Valdivia, Nicolás Antonio de. *Crónica de la Provincia de Santiago de Xalisco, 1719–1722*. Guadalajara, 1962.

Orozco Farías, Rogelio, ed. *Fuentes históricas de la Independencia, 1808–1821*. 1967.

Orsenigo, C. *Life of St. Charles Borromeo*. Tr. Rudolf Kraus. St. Louis, Mo., 1947.

Ortega, Sergio, ed. *De la santidad a la perversión, o por qué no se cumplía la ley de Dios en la sociedad novohispana*. 1985.

Ortega y Medina, Juan. *Estudios de tema mexicana*. 1973.

Ortiz Vidales, Salvador. *La arriería en México: Estudio folklórico, costumbrista e histórico*. 1929.

Ortner, Sherry B. *High Religion: A Cultural and Political History of Sherpa Buddhism*. Princeton, N.J., 1989.

———. "Theory in Anthropology Since the Sixties," *Comparative Studies in Society and History*, 26 (1984): 126–66.

Osores, Félix. *Noticias bio-bibliográficas de alumnos distinguidos del Colegio de San Pedro, San Pablo y San Ildefonso*. 2 vols. 1908.

Oswald, Felix. *Summerland Sketches, or Rambles in the Backwoods of Mexico and Central America*. Philadelphia, 1908.

Ouweneel, Arij. "Growth, Stagnation, and Migration: An Explorative Analysis of the Tributario Series of Anáhuac (1720–1800)," *Hispanic American Historical Review*, 71 (1991): 531–77.

———. "Raíces del 'chiaroscuro' en México: Algunas consideraciones acerca de esta compilación," in Arij Ouweneel and Cristina Torales Pacheco, eds., *Empresarios, indios, y estado: Perfil de la economía mexicana (siglo XVIII)* (Amsterdam, 1988): 1–15.

Padden, Robert C. *The Hummingbird and the Hawk: Conquest and Sovereignty in the Valley of Mexico, 1503–1541*. Columbus, Ohio, 1967.

———. "The Ordenanza del Patronazgo, 1574: An Interpretative Essay," *The Americas*, 12 (1956): 333–54.

Pagden, A. R. *The Fall of Natural Man: The American Indian and the Origins of Comparative Ethnology*. Cambridge, Eng., 1982.

———. *Spanish Imperialism and the Political Imagination*. New Haven, Conn., 1990.

Palacio y Basave, Fr. Luis del Refugio de. *Recopilación de noticias y datos que se relacionan con la milagrosa imagen de Nuestra Señora de Zapopan y con su colegio y santuario*. 2 vols. Guadalajara, 1942.

Palafox y Mendoza, Juan de. *Manual de sacerdotes*. 1664.

———. *Tratados mejicanos* [1647–]. 2 vols. Madrid, 1968.

Palmer, Gabrielle. *Sculpture in the Kingdom of Quito*. Albuquerque, N.Mex., 1987.

Papeles de Nueva España. Ed. Francisco del Paso y Troncoso. 9 vols. 1905–48.

Paré, Louise. "Diseño teórico para el estudio del caciquismo actual en México," *Revista Mexicana de Sociología*, 34 (1972): 335–54.

Paredes, Ignacio de. *Promptuario manual mexicano, que a la verdad podrá ser utilíssimo a los Parrochos para la enseñanza; a los necessitados Indios para su instrucción; y a los que aprenden la lengua para la expedición. . . . Añádese por fin un Sermón de Nuestra Santíssima Guadalupana Señora . . .* 1759.

Parker, David. "The Tridentine Order and Governance in Late Colonial Brazil, 1792–1821." Ph.D. diss., University of Washington, 1982.

Parnell, Philip C. *Escalating Disputes: Social Participation and Change in the Oaxacan Highlands*. Tucson, Ariz., 1988.

Parras, Fr. Pedro Joseph. *Gobierno de los regulares de la América*. Madrid, 1783.

Parry, J. H. *The Spanish Seaborne Empire*. New York, 1966.

———. *The Spanish Theory of Empire in the Sixteenth Century.* Cambridge, Mass., 1940.

Pasos O., Tzahacil. *La iglesia como aparato ideológico y de estado en la Nueva España (1800–1815).* 1982.

Pastor, Rodolfo. *Campesinos y reformas: La Mixteca, 1700–1856.* 1987.

———. "La comunidad agraria y el estado en México: Una historia cíclica," *Diálogos,* 1982, no. 108: 16–26.

———. "Los religiosos, los indios y el estado en la Mixteca, 1524–1810: Sobre el trasfondo y función social de la ideología." Paper presented to the Sixth Conference of Mexican and U.S. Historians, Chicago, 1981.

———. "La Virgen y la revolución: Sistema religioso y comportamiento político en Mesoamérica," *Estudios: Filosofía, Historia, Letras,* 7 (1986): 29–47.

Patiño, José Alejandro. "Topografía del curato de Tlaxomulco," in *Noticias varias de Nueva Galicia* (Guadalajara, 1878): 183–224.

Payne, Harry C. "Elite Versus Popular Mentality in the Eighteenth Century," *Studies in Eighteenth-Century Culture,* 8 (1979): 3–32.

Paz, Octavio. "In Search of the Present," *New Republic,* Jan. 7–14, 1991: 33–38.

———. *El ogro filantrópico: Historia y política, 1971–1978.* 1979.

———. *One Earth, Four or Five Worlds: Reflections on Contemporary History.* San Diego, Calif., 1985.

Pazos, Manuel R. "Los misioneros franciscanos de Méjico y la enseñanza técnica que dieron a los indios," *Archivo Ibero-Americano,* 33 (1973): 149–90.

Peel, J. D. Y. "Syncretism and Religious Change," *Comparative Studies in Society and History,* 10 (1968): 121–41.

Pelikan, Jaroslav. *The Riddle of Roman Catholicism.* New York, 1959.

———. *The Vindication of Tradition.* New Haven, Conn., 1984.

Peña, Guillermo de la. "Evolución agrícola y poder regional en el sur de Jalisco," *Revista Jalisco,* 1980, no. 1: 38–55.

———. *Herederos de promesas: Agricultura, política y ritual en los Altos de Morelos.* 1980.

Peña Montenegro, Alonso de la. *Itinerario para parochos de indios, en que se tratan las materias más particulares tocantes a ellos, para su buena administración.* Madrid, 1668. (Other editions: Madrid, 1771; Lyons, 1678; Antwerp, 1698, 1726, 1737, 1754.)

Pérez, Joseph. *Los movimientos precursores de la emancipación en Hispanoamérica.* Madrid, 1977.

———. "Tradition et innovation dans l'Amérique des Bourbons," in *L'Amérique espagnole à l'époque des lumières: Tradition-Innovation-Répresentations* (Paris, 1987): 237–46.

Pérez, Manuel. *Farol indiano y guía de curas de indios: Summa de los cinco sacramentos que administra los ministros evangélicos en esta América, con los casos morales que suceden entre los indios.* 1713.

Pérez Cancio, Gregorio. *La Santa Cruz y Soledad de Nuestra Señora: Libro de fábrica del templo parroquial* [1784]. 1970.

Pérez de Velasco, Andrés Miguel. *El ayudante de cura instruído en el porte a que le obliga su dignidad en los deberes a que le estrecha su empleo y en la fructuosa práctica de su ministerio.* Puebla, 1766.

Pérez Herrero, Pedro. "Los beneficiarios del reformismo borbónico: Metrópoli versus élites novohispanas," *Historia Mexicana,* 41 (1991): 207–64.

———. *Plata y libranzas: La articulación comercial del México borbónico.* 1988.

Pérez Lugo, J. *La cuestión religiosa en México: Recopilación de leyes, disposiciones legales y documentos para el estudio de este problema político.* 1926.

Pérez Memem, Fernando. *El episcopado y la independencia de México (1810–1836).* 1977.

Pérez-Rocha, Emma. "Mayordomías y cofradías del pueblo de Tacuba en el siglo XVIII," *Estudios de Historia Novohispana,* 6 (1978): 12.

————, ed. *Colección de documentos en torno a la iglesia de San Gabriel Tlacopan.* 1988.

Pérez Verdía, Luis. *Apuntes históricos sobre la guerra de independencia en Jalisco.* 2d ed. Guadalajara, 1953.

————. *Historia particular del Estado de Jalisco desde sus primeros tiempos de que hay noticia hasta nuestros días.* 3 vols. Guadalajara, 1910–11.

Peristiany, J. G., ed. *Honour and Shame: The Values of Mediterranean Society.* Chicago, 1963.

Pescador Cantón, Juan Javier. *De bautizados a fieles difuntos: Familia y mentalidades en una parroquia urbana: Santa Catarina de México, 1568–1820.* 1992.

————. "Devoción y crisis demográfica: La cofradía de San Ygnacio de Loyola, 1761–1821," *Historia Mexicana*, 49 (1990): 767–801.

————. "La piedad popular y el más allá: Entierros y cofradías en una parroquia de la ciudad de México, 1600–1800." Unpublished manuscript, 1991.

Phelan, John L. "Authority and Flexibility in the Spanish Imperial Bureaucracy," *Administrative Science Quarterly*, 5 (1960): 47–65.

————. *The Kingdom of Quito in the Seventeenth Century: Bureaucratic Politics in the Spanish Empire.* Madison, Wis., 1967.

————. *The People and the King: The Comunero Revolution in Colombia, 1781.* Madison, Wis., 1978.

Pietschmann, Horst. "Consideraciones en torno al protoliberalismo, reformas borbónicas y revolución: La Nueva España en el último tercio del siglo XVIII," *Historia Mexicana*, 41 (1991): 167–205.

Piho, Virve. *La secularización de las parroquias en la Nueva España y su repercusión en San Andrés Calpan.* 1981.

Pintura del gobernador, alcaldes y regidores de México . . . (Códice Osuna). Madrid, 1878.

Platt, Tristan. "The Andean Soldiers of Christ: Confraternity Organization, the Mass of the Sun and Regenerative Warfare in Rural Potosí (18th–20th Centuries)," *Journal de la Société des Américanistes*, 73 (1987): 139–92.

Poinsett, Joel R. *Notes on Mexico, Made in the Autumn of 1822 . . .* Philadelphia, 1824.

Pompa y Pompa, Antonio. "Cómo fue celebrada la confirmación del patronato guadalupano en 1756," *La Voz Guadalupana*, 8, no. 2 (1941): 13, 14, 20.

Ponce, Pedro. "Breve relación de los dioses y ritos de la gentilidad," in *Tratado de las idolatrías, supersticiones, dioses, ritos, hechicerías y otras costumbres gentílicas de las razas aborígenes de México* (1953) 1: 369–80.

Poole, Stafford. "Church Law on the Ordination of Indians and *Castas* in New Spain," *Hispanic American Historical Review*, 61 (1981): 637–50.

————. *Pedro Moya de Contreras: Catholic Reform and Royal Power in New Spain, 1571–1591.* Berkeley, Calif., 1987.

————. "The Third Mexican Provincial Council of 1585 and the Reform of the Diocesan Clergy," in Jeffrey A. Cole, ed., *The Church and Society in Latin America* (New Orleans, 1984): 21–37.

Porras Muñoz, Guillermo. *El clero secular y la evangelización de la Nueva España.* 1987.

————. *Iglesia y estado en Nueva Vizcaya (1562–1821).* Pamplona, Spain, 1966.

Powers, J. F. *Morte d'Urban.* Garden City, N.Y., 1962.

————. *Wheat That Springeth Green.* New York, 1988.

Powers, William K. *Beyond the Vision: Essays on American Indian Culture.* Norman, Okla., 1987.

Price, S. R. F. *Rituals and Power: The Roman Imperial Cult in Asia Minor.* Cambridge, Eng., 1984.

Priestley, Herbert I. *José de Gálvez, Visitor-General of New Spain (1765–1771).* Berkeley, Calif., 1916.

Prieto, Guillermo. "El cura del pueblo," *El Album Mexicano*, 2 (1849): 271–73.

————. *Memorias de mis tiempos (1828–1853)*. 2 vols. 1906.

Proceso instruído en contra de D. Mariano Matamoros. Morelia, Michoacán, 1964.

Quirarte, Martín. *El problema religioso en México*. 1967.

Raeff, Marc. "The Well-Ordered Police State and the Development of Modernity in 17th- and 18th-Century Europe," *American Historical Review*, 80 (1975): 1221–43.

Rafael, Vicente. "Confession, Conversion, and Reciprocity in Early Tagalog Colonial Society," *Comparative Studies in Society and History*, 29 (1987): 320–39.

Ramírez, José R. "La parroquia de Arandas," in *Anuario de la Comisión Diocesana de Historia del Arzobispado de Guadalajara* (1968): 281–311.

Rangel, Nicolás. *Historia del toreo en México, época colonial, 1529–1821*. 1924.

Rausch, Jane. *A Tropical Plains Frontier: The Llanos of Colombia, 1531–1831*. Albuquerque, N.Mex., 1984.

Rebollar Chávez, José. "El templo guadalupano en Zacapoaxtla," *La Voz Guadalupana*, 13, no. 7 (1946): 20–22.

Recopilación de leyes de los reynos de las Indias. 4 vols. Facsimile of 1681 original. Madrid, 1973.

Rees Jones, Ricardo. *El despotismo ilustrado y los intendentes de la Nueva España*. 1979.

Reher, David S., "¿Malthus de nuevo?: Población y economía en México durante el siglo XVIII," *Historia Mexicana*, 41 (1992): 615–64.

Relación de las ceremonias y ritos y población y gobierno de los indios de la provincia de Michoacán (1541): Reproducción facsímil del Ms. C.IV.5 de El Escorial. Morelia, Michoacán, 1977.

Reumann, John. "Mary," in Eliade, ed., listed above, 9: 251.

Reyes Garza, Juan Carlos. "El presbítero José Antonio Díaz ¿Protoprócer de la independencia en Colima?" *Eslabones*, 1991, no. 1: 16–20.

Ribadeneyra y Barrientos, Antonio Joachin. *Manual compendio de el regio patronato indiano para su más fácil uso en las materias conducentes a la práctica . . .* Madrid, 1755.

Ricard, Robert. *The Spiritual Conquest of Mexico*. Berkeley, Calif., 1966.

Richard, Pablo. *Death of Christendoms, Birth of the Church: Historical Analysis and Theological Interpretation of the Church in Latin America*. New York, 1987.

Ricker, Dennis P. "The Lower Secular Clergy of Central Mexico, 1821–1857." Ph.D. diss., University of Texas, 1982.

Ríos, Eduardo Enrique. *Life of Fray Antonio Margil, O.F.M.*. Ed. and tr. Benedict Leutenegger. Washington, D.C., 1959.

Rivera, Agustín. *Principios críticos sobre el vireinato de la Nueva España i sobre la revolución de independencia*. 3 vols. Lagos de Moreno, Jalisco, 1887–89.

Robelo, Cecilio. *Diccionario de aztequismos*. 1940.

Robertson, William. *The History of America*. 3d ed. 3 vols. London, 1780.

Robertson, William P. *A Visit to Mexico by the West India Islands, Yucatán and United States*. 2 vols. London, 1853.

Rodríguez, Mauro. *Guadalupe: ¿Historia o símbolo?* 1980.

Román Gutiérrez, José Francisco. *Sociedad y evangelización en Nueva Galicia durante el siglo XVI*. 1993.

Romero Flores, Jesús. *Iconografía colonial*. 1940.

Roniger, Luis. "Caciquismo and Coronelismo: Contextual Dimensions of Patron Brokerage in Mexico and Brazil," *Latin American Research Review*, 22 (1987): 71–100.

Rosaldo, Renato. "The Rhetoric of Control: Ilongots Viewed as Natural Bandits and Wild Indians," in Barbara A. Babcock, ed., *The Reversible World: Symbolic Inversion in Art and Society* (Ithaca, N.Y., 1978): 240–57.

Roseberry, William. "Hegemony and the Language of Contention," in Gilbert M. Joseph and Daniel Nugent, eds., *Everyday Forms of State Formation: Revolution and the Negotiation of Rule in Modern Mexico* (Durham, N.C., 1994): 355–66.

Ruiz de Alarcón, Hernando. "Tratado de las supersticiones y costumbres gentílicas que oy viven entre los indios naturales desta Nueva España [1629]," in *Tratado de las idolatrías, supersticiones, dioses, ritos, hechicerías y otras costumbres gentílicas de las razas aborígenes de México* (1953), 2: 17–180.

Ruiz Martínez, Cristina. "La moderación como prototipo de santidad: Una imagen de la niñez," in Sergio Ortega, ed., *De la santidad a la perversión, o de por qué no se cumplía la ley de Dios en la sociedad novohispana* (1985): 49–66.

Russell, Anthony. *The Clerical Profession.* London, 1980.

Sabean, David. *Power in the Blood: Popular Culture and Village Discourse in Early Modern Germany.* Cambridge, Eng., 1984.

Sahagún, Bernardino de. *Historia general de las cosas de Nueva España.* 5 vols. 1938.

Salido Beltrán, Roberto. *Campaña de Morelos en 1812.* Guadalajara, 1964.

Salomon, Frank. "Nightmare Victory: The Meanings of Conversion Among Peruvian Indians (Huarochirí, 1608?)." *1992 Lecture Series, University of Maryland,* Working Paper no. 7. College Park, Md., 1990.

Salvucci, Linda K. "Costumbres viejas, 'hombres nuevos': José de Gálvez y la burocracia fiscal novohispana (1754-1800)," *Historia Mexicana,* 33 (1983): 224–64.

Salvucci, Richard, and Linda K. Salvucci. "Crecimiento económico y cambio en la productividad de México, 1750–1895," *HISLA: Revista Latinoamericana de Historia Económica y Social,* 10 (1987): 67–89.

Sánchez, Pedro J. *Historia del seminario conciliar de México.* 1931.

Sánchez Flores, Ramón. *Zacapoaxtla, república de indios y villa de españoles.* Puebla, 1984.

Sandos, James A. "Junípero Serra's Canonization and the Historical Record," *American Historical Review,* 93 (1988): 1253–69.

Santamaría, Francisco J. *Diccionario general de americanismos.* 1941.

Santoscoy, Alberto. *La fiesta de los tastoanes, estudio etnológico-histórico.* Guadalajara, 1889.

Sardo, Joseph Joaquín. *Relación histórica y moral de la portentosa imagen de Nuestro Señor Jesuchristo Crucificado aparecida en una de las cuevas de San Miguel de Chalma.* 1810.

Sariola, Sakari. *Power and Resistance: The Colonial Heritage in Latin America.* Ithaca, N.Y., 1972.

Sarrailh, Jean. *La España ilustrada de la segunda mitad del siglo XVIII.* 1957.

Schmidt, Leigh Eric. *Holy Fairs: Scottish Communions and American Revivals in the Early Modern Period.* Princeton, N.J., 1989.

Schmitt, Karl M. "The Clergy and the Independence of New Spain," *Hispanic American Historical Review,* 34 (1954): 289–312.

Schwaller, John Frederick. *The Church and Clergy in Sixteenth-Century Mexico.* Albuquerque, N.Mex., 1987.

———. "The Implementation of the Ordenanza del Patronazgo in New Spain," in Jeffrey A. Cole, ed., *The Church and Society in Latin America* (New Orleans, 1984): 39–49.

———. "The Ordenanza del Patronazgo in New Spain, 1574–1600," *The Americas,* 42 (1986): 253–74.

———. *Origins of Church Wealth in Mexico: Ecclesiastical Revenues and Church Finances, 1523–1600.* Albuquerque, N.Mex., 1985.

Schwartz, Marc J., ed. *Local-Level Politics: Social and Cultural Perspectives.* Chicago, 1968.

Scott, James C. *Domination and the Arts of Resistance: Hidden Transcripts.* New Haven, Conn., 1990.

———. "Hegemony and the Peasantry," *Politics & Society,* 7 (1977): 267–96.

———. *Weapons of the Weak: Everyday Forms of Peasant Resistance.* New Haven, Conn., 1985.

Sedano, Francisco. *Noticias de México.* 2 vols. 1880.

Seed, Patricia. "The Colonial Church as an Ideological State Apparatus," in Roderic A. Camp, Charles A. Hale, and Josefina Zoraida Vásquez, eds., *Intellectuals and Power in Mexico* (Los Angeles, 1991): 397-415.

———. *To Love, Honor, and Obey in Colonial Mexico: Conflicts over Marriage Choice, 1574–1821*. Stanford, Calif., 1988.

Segre, Enzo. *Las máscaras de lo sagrado: Ensayos italo-mexicanos sobre el sincretismo nahuat-católico de la Sierra Norte de Puebla*. 1987.

Seneri, Pablo. *El penitente instruído para confesarsse bien*. 1695.

Sennett, Richard. *Authority*. New York, 1980.

Serna, Jacinto de la. "Manual de ministros de indios para el conocimiento de sus idolatrías, y extirpación de ellas," in *Colección de documentos inéditos para la historia de España* (Madrid, 1892), 104: 1–267.

Serra, Fr. Angel. *Manual de administrar los santos sacramentos a los españoles y naturales de esta Provincia de los Gloriosos Apóstoles San Pedro y San Pablo de Michuacán . . . 1731*.

Serrera Contreras, Ramón. "Estado económico de la intendencia de Guadalajara a principios del siglo XIX: La "relación" de José Fernando de Abascal y Sousa de 1803," *Jahrbuch für Geschichte von Staat, Wirthschaft und Gesellschaft Lateinamerikas*, 11 (1974): 121–48.

———. *Guadalajara ganadera: Estudio regional novohispano, 1760–1805*. Seville, 1977.

Shennan, J. H. *Liberty and Order in Early Modern Europe: The Subject and the State, 1650–1800*. New York, 1986.

Shiels, W. Eugene. *King and Church: The Rise and Fall of the Patronato Real*. Chicago, 1961.

Shils, Edward. *Center and Periphery: Essays in Macrosociology*. Chicago: 1975

———. "Deference," in Edward O. Laumann, Paul M. Siegel, and Robert W. Hodge, eds., *The Logic of Social Hierarchies* (Chicago, 1970): 420–48.

Sierra Nava-Lasa, Luis. *El cardenal Lorenzana y la Ilustración*. Madrid, 1975.

Silva Riquer, Jorge. "La consolidación de vales en el obispado de Michoacán, 1804-1809," in Virginia Guedea and Jaime E. Rodríguez, eds., *Five Centuries of Mexican History/Cinco siglos de historia de México* (Mexico, D.F., 1992), 2: 65–80.

Silverblatt, Irene. "Political Memories and Colonizing Symbols: Santiago and the Peruvian Mountain Gods of Colonial Peru," in Jonathan D. Hill, ed., *Rethinking History and Myth: Indigenous South American Perspectives on the Past* (Urbana, Ill., 1988): 174–94.

Silverman, Sydel. "The Peasant Concept in Anthropology," *Journal of Peasant Studies*, 7 (1979): 49–69.

———. "Rituals of Inequality: Stratification and Symbol in Central Italy," in Gerald D. Berreman, ed., *Social Inequality: Comparative and Developmental Approaches* (New York, 1981): 163–81.

Siméon, Rémi. *Diccionario de la lengua nahuatl o mexicana*. 1st Spanish ed. 1977.

Simpson, Lesley B. *Many Mexicos* [1941]. 4th ed., Berkeley, Calif., 1967.

Smith, Carol A. "Local History in Global Context: Social and Economic Transitions in Western Guatemala," *Comparative Studies in Society and History*, 26 (1984): 193–228.

———, ed. *Regional Analysis*. 2 vols. New York, 1976.

Smith, Hilary D. *Preaching in the Spanish Golden Age: A Study of Some Preachers of the Reign of Philip III*. Oxford, Eng., 1978.

Smith, Jonathan Z. *Map Is Not Territory: Studies in the History of Religions*. Leiden, 1978.

Sodi de Pallares, María Elena. *Historia del traje religioso en México*. 1950.

Solano, Francisco de, ed. *Relaciones geográficas del Arzobispado de México, 1743*. 2 vols. Madrid, 1988.

Solórzano Pereira, Juan de. *Política indiana*. Facsimile of 1647 original. 5 vols. Madrid, 1930.

Sparks, Rosa Consuelo. "The Role of the Clergy During the Struggle for Independence in Peru." Ph.D. diss., University of Pittsburgh, 1972.

Sperber, Jonathan. *Popular Catholicism in Nineteenth-Century Germany*. Princeton, N.J., 1984.

Spufford, Margaret. *Contrasting Communities*. Cambridge, Eng., 1974.

Starr, Frederick. *Catalogue of a Collection of Objects Illustrating the Folklore of Mexico*. London, 1899.

————. *In Indian Mexico*. Chicago, 1908.

Stein, Stanley, "Prelude to Upheaval in Spain and New Spain, 1800–1808: Trust Funds, Spanish Finance and Colonial Silver," in Richard L. Garner and William B. Taylor, eds., *Iberian Colonies, New World Societies* (State College, Pa., 1985): 185–202.

Stein, Stanley, and Barbara Stein. *The Colonial Heritage of Latin America; Essays on Economic Dependence in Perspective*. New York, 1970.

Stephens, John Lloyd. *Incidents of Travel in Central America, Chiapas, and Yucatan*. London, 1854.

————. *Incidents of Travel in Yucatan* [1843]. 2 vols. Norman, Okla., 1962.

Stern, Steve J. *Peru's Indian Peoples and the Challenge of Spanish Conquest: Huamanga to 1640*. Madison, Wis., 1982.

Stewart, Omer T. *Peyote Religion*. Norman, Okla., 1987.

Stoetzer, O. Carlos. *El pensamiento político en la América española durante el período de la emancipación*. 2 vols. Madrid, 1966.

Strickon, Arnold, and Sidney M. Greenfield, eds. *Structure and Process in Latin America: Patronage, Clientage and Power Systems*. Albuquerque, N.Mex., 1972.

Sugawara, Masae. "Reformas borbónicas y luchas de clases, 1763–1810," in Enrique Semo, ed., *México: Un pueblo en la historia* (1981), 1: 315–42.

————, ed. *La deuda pública de España y la economía novohispana, 1804–1809*. 1976.

Sullivan, Lawrence E. *Icanchu's Drum: An Orientation to Meaning in South American Religions*. New York, 1988.

————. "Sound and Senses: Toward a Hermeneutics of Performance," *History of Religions*, 26 (1986): 1–33.

Sylvest, Edwin E. *Nuestra Señora de Guadalupe: Mother of God, Mother of the Americas*. Dallas, 1992.

Szewczyk, David M. *The Viceroyalty of New Spain and Early Independent Mexico: A Guide to Original Manuscripts in the Collections of the Rosenbach Museum and Library*. Philadelphia, 1980.

Szuchman, Mark D., ed. *The Middle Period in Latin America*. Boulder, Colo., 1989.

Tackett, Timothy. "The Citizen Priest: Politics and Ideology Among the Parish Clergy of Eighteenth-Century Dauphiné," *Studies in Eighteenth-Century Culture*, 7 (1978): 307–28.

————. *Priest and Parish in Eighteenth-Century France*. Princeton, N.J., 1977.

————. *Religion, Revolution and Regional Culture in Eighteenth-Century France: The Ecclesiastical Oath of 1791*. Princeton, N.J., 1986.

Tackett, Timothy, and C. Langlois. "Ecclesiastical Structures and Clerical Geography on the Eve of the French Revolution," *French Historical Studies*, 11 (1980): 352–70.

Taggart, James M. *Nahuat Myth and Social Structure*. Austin, Tex., 1983.

Talavera S., Francisco. "Cuaderno de la danza de la conquista," *Revista Jalisco*, 1980, no. 2: 46–62.

Taussig, Michael T. "Culture of Terror, Space of Death: Roger Casement's Putumayo Report and the Explanation of Torture," *Comparative Studies in Society and History*, 26 (1984): 467–97.

————. *The Devil and Commodity Fetishism in South America*. Chapel Hill, N.C., 1980.

————. *Shamanism, Colonialism, and the Wild Man: A Study in Terror and Healing*. Chicago, 1986.

Taylor, William B. "Banditry and Insurrection: Rural Unrest in Central Jalisco, 1790–1816," in Friedrich Katz, ed., *Riot, Rebellion, and Revolution in Mexican History* (Princeton, N.J., 1988): 205–46.

————. "Between Global Process and Local Knowledge: An Inquiry into Early Latin American Social History, 1500–1900," in Olivier Zunz, ed., *Reliving the Past: The Worlds of Social History* (Chapel Hill, N.C., 1985): 115–90.

———. "Conflict and Balance in District Politics: Tecali and the Sierra Norte de Puebla in the Eighteenth Century," in Arij Ouweneel and Simon Miller, eds., *The Indian Community of Colonial Mexico* (Amsterdam, 1990): 267–91.

———. "'. . . de corazón pequeño y ánimo apocado': Conceptos de los curas párrocos sobre los indios en la Nueva España del siglo XVIII," *Relaciones*, 1989, no. 39: 5–67.

———. *Drinking, Homicide, and Rebellion in Colonial Mexican Villages.* Stanford, Calif., 1979.

———. "Indian Pueblos of Central Jalisco on the Eve of Independence," in Richard L. Garner and William B. Taylor, eds., *Iberian Colonies, New World Societies: Essays in Memory of Charles Gibson* (State College, Pa., 1985): 161–83.

———. *Landlord and Peasant in Colonial Oaxaca.* Stanford, Calif., 1972.

———. "Sacarse de pobre: El bandolerismo en la Nueva Galicia, 1774–1821," *Revista Jalisco*, 1981, no. 2: 34–45.

———. "The Virgin of Guadalupe in New Spain: An Inquiry into the Social History of Marian Devotion," *American Ethnologist*, 14 (1987): 9–33.

Tedlock, Barbara. "A Phenomenological Approach to Religious Change in Highland Guatemala," in Carl Kendall et al., eds., *Heritage of Conquest: Thirty Years Later* (Albuquerque, N.Mex., 1983): 235–46.

Tello, Francisco Antonio. *Crónica miscelánea de la sancta provincia de Xalisco.* 4 vols. Guadalajara, 1945–68.

Tentler, Thomas N. *Sin and Confession on the Eve of the Reformation.* Princeton, N.J., 1977.

———. "The Summa for Confessors as an Instrument of Social Control" and "Response and *Retractatio*," in Charles Trinkhaus and Heiko A. Oberman, eds., *The Pursuit of Holiness in Late Medieval and Renaissance Religion* (Leiden, 1974): 103–25, 131–40.

TePaske, John. "The Atlantic Empire in the Eighteenth Century: Spanish America," *International History Review*, 6 (1984): 511–18.

———. "The Financial Disintegration of the Royal Government of Mexico During the Epoch of Independence," in Jaime E. Rodríguez, ed., *The Independence of Mexico and the Creation of the New Nation* (Los Angeles, 1989): 63–83.

———. "General Tendencies and Secular Trends in the Economies of Mexico and Peru, 1750–1800: The View from the *Cajas* of Mexico and Lima," in Nils Jacobsen and Hans-Jürgen Puhle, eds., *The Economies of Mexico and Peru During the Late Colonial Period, 1760–1810* (Berlin, 1986): 316–39.

Thomas, Keith. *Religion and the Decline of Magic.* London, 1971.

Thompson, E. P. *The Making of the English Working Class.* London, 1963.

———. "Patrician Society, Plebeian Culture," *Journal of Social History*, 7 (1974): 382–405.

Tibesar, Antonine. "The Lima Pastors, 1750–1820: Their Origins and Studies as Taken from Their Autobiographies," *The Americas*, 28 (1971): 39–56.

———. "The Shortage of Priests in Latin America: A Historical Evaluation of Werner Promper's *Priesternot in Lateinamerika*," *The Americas*, 22 (1966): 413–20.

Timmons, Wilbert H. *Morelos: Priest, Soldier, Statesman of Mexico.* El Paso, Tex., 1963.

Tiryakian, Josefina Cintrón. "Campillo's Pragmatic New System: A Mercantile and Utilitarian Approach to Indian Reform in Spanish Colonies of the Eighteenth Century," *History of Political Economy*, 10 (1978): 233–57.

Tobar, Balthasar de. *Compendio bulario indico.* 2 vols. Seville, 1954–66.

Toor, Frances. *A Treasury of Mexican Folkways.* New York, 1947.

Torquemada, Juan de. *Monarquía indiana* [1615]. Facsimile of 1723 ed. 3 vols. 1943–44.

Torre Villar, Ernesto de la. "Algunos aspectos acerca de las cofradías y la propiedad territorial en Michoacán," *Jahrbuch für Geschichte von Staat, Wirtschaft und Gesellschaft Lateinamerikas*, 4 (1967): 410–39.

———. "Aspectos sociales de los instrumentos de pastoral cristiana en Nueva España," *Historia Mexicana*, 38 (1989): 609–22.

———. "La iglesia en México, de la guerra de independencia a la Reforma: Notas para su estudio," *Estudios de Historia Moderna y Contemporánea*, 1 (1965): 9–34.

———. ed. *La constitución de Apatzingán y los creadores del estado mexicano*. 1964.

Torre Villar, Ernesto de la, and Ramiro Navarro de Anda, eds. *Testimonios históricos guadalupanos*. 1982.

Torres, Fr. Francisco Mariano de. *Crónica de la Sancta Provincia de Xalisco*. 1960.

Tovar Pinzón, Hermes. "El estado colonial frente al poder local y regional," *Nova Americana*, 1982, no. 5: 39–77.

Trabulse, Elías. "Clavigero, historiador de la Ilustración mexicana," in Alfonso Martínez Rosales, ed., *Francisco Xavier Clavigero en la Ilustración mexicana, 1731–1787* (1988): 41–57.

Tracy, Patricia J. *Jonathan Edwards, Pastor: Religion and Society in Eighteenth-Century Northampton*. New York, 1980.

Trexler, Richard C. *Church and Community, 1200–1600: Studies in the History of Florence and New Spain*. Rome, 1987.

———. "We Think, They Act: Clerical Readings of Missionary Theatre in Sixteenth-Century New Spain," in Stephen Kaplan, ed., *Understanding Popular Culture: Europe from the Middle Ages to the Nineteenth Century* (Berlin, 1984): 189–227.

Troeltsch, Ernst. *The Social Teachings of the Christian Churches*. Tr. Olive Wyon. 2 vols. Chicago, 1981.

Turner, Victor. "The Center Out There: Pilgrim's Goal," *History of Religions*, 12 (1973): 191–230.

———. *Dramas, Fields, and Metaphors: Symbolic Action in Human Society*. Ithaca, N.Y., 1974.

———, ed. *Celebrations: Studies in Festivities and Ritual*. Washington, D.C., 1982.

Turner, Victor, and Edith Turner. *Image and Pilgrimage in Christian Culture*. New York, 1978.

Tutino, John. "Creole Mexico: Spanish Elites, Haciendas, and Indian Towns, 1750–1810." Ph.D. diss., University of Texas, 1976.

———. "From Colonial Reconstruction to Symbiotic Exploitation: Agrarian Structure in the Valley of Mexico, 1600–1800," in *Historia General del Estado de México*, vol. 3, forthcoming.

———. *From Insurrection to Revolution in Mexico: Social Bases of Agrarian Violence, 1750–1940*. Princeton, N.J., 1986.

———. "Patterns of Culture in Mexican History: From Colonial Hegemony to National Conflict." Paper presented to the Eighth Conference of Mexican and U.S. Historians, San Diego, Calif., 1990.

Tylor, Edward B. *Anahuac: Or Mexico and the Mexicans, Ancient and Modern*. London, 1861.

Usigli, Rodolfo. *Corona de luz: Pieza antihistórica en tres actos*. New York, 1967.

Valle, Rafael Heliodoro. *Santiago en América*. 1946.

Van Oss, Adriaan C. *Catholic Colonialism: A Parish History of Guatemala, 1524–1821*. Cambridge, Eng., 1986.

———. "Comparing Colonial Bishoprics in Spanish America," *Boletín de Estudios Latinoamericanos y del Caribe*, 1978, no. 24: 27–66.

———. "Pueblos y parroquias en Suchitepéquez colonial," *Mesoamérica*, 1984, no. 7: 161–79.

Van Young, Eric. "The Age of Paradox: Mexican Agriculture at the End of the Colonial Period," in Nils Jacobsen and Hans-Jürgen Puhle, eds., *The Economies of Mexico and Peru During the Late Colonial Period, 1760–1810* (Berlin, 1986): 64–90.

———. "Comentario," in Carlos Herrejón, ed., *Repaso de la Independencia* (Zamora, Michoacán, 1985): 56–65.

———. "Conclusion: The State as Vampire—Hegemonic Projects, Public Ritual, and

Popular Culture in Mexico, 1600–1990," in William H. Beezley, Cheryl English Martin, and William E. French, eds., *Rituals of Rule, Rituals of Resistance: Public Celebrations and Popular Culture in Mexico* (Wilmington, Del., 1994): 343–74.

———. "Conclusions," in Susan E. Ramírez, ed., *Indian-Religious Relations in Colonial Spanish America* (Syracuse, N.Y., 1989): 87–102.

———. "Conflict and Solidarity in Indian Village Life: The Guadalajara Region in the Late Colonial Period," *Hispanic American Historical Review*, 64 (1984): 55–79.

———. "The Cuautla Lazarus: Double Subjectivities in Reading Texts on Popular Collective Action," *Colonial Latin America Review*, 2 (1993): 3–26.

———. *Hacienda and Market in Eighteenth-Century Mexico: The Rural Economy of the Guadalajara Region, 1675–1820.* Berkeley, Calif., 1981.

———. "Islands in the Storm: Quiet Cities and Violent Countrysides in the Mexican Independence," *Past & Present*, 1988, no. 118: 130–55.

———. "The Mad Messiah of Durango and Popular Rebellion in Mexico, 1800–1815," *Comparative Studies in Society and History*, 21 (1986): 386–413.

———. "Quetzalcóatl, King Ferdinand, and Ignacio Allende Go to the Seashore; or Messianism and Mystical Kingship in Mexico, 1800–1821," in Jaime E. Rodríguez, ed., *The Independence of Mexico and the Creation of the New Nation* (Los Angeles, 1989): 109–27.

———. "The Raw and the Cooked: Elite and Popular Ideology in Mexico, 1800–1821," in Mark D. Szuchman, ed., *The Middle Period in Latin America: Values and Attitudes in the 17th–19th Centuries* (Boulder, Colo., 1989): 75–102.

———. "To See Someone Not Seeing: Historical Studies of Peasants and Politics in Mexico," *Mexican Studies/Estudios Mexicanos*, 6 (1990): 133–59.

Vargas Ugarte, Rubén. *Historia del culto de María en Ibero-América y de sus imágenes y santuarios más celebrados.* Madrid, 1956.

Vásquez, Genaro V. *Doctrinas y realidades en la legislación para los indios.* 1940.

Vásquez de Espinosa, Fr. Antonio. *Descripción de la Nueva España en el siglo XVII.* 1944.

Velásquez, María del Carmen. *La descentralización administrativa y el pago de los sínodos a las misiones norteñas del siglo XVIII.* Guadalajara, 1974.

———. *El estado de guerra en Nueva España, 1760–1808.* 1950.

Venegas Ramírez, Carmen. *Régimen hospitalario para indios en la Nueva España.* 1973.

Ventura Beleña, Eusebio. *Recopilación sumaria de todos los autos acordados de la Real Audiencia y Sala del Crimen de esta Nueva España.* Facsimile of 1787 original. 2 vols. 1981.

Vera, Fortino. *Apuntamientos históricos de los concilios provinciales mexicanos y privilegios de América.* 1893.

———. *Erecciones parroquiales de México y Puebla.* Amecameca, Edo. de México, 1889.

———, ed. *Informaciones sobre la milagrosa aparición de la Santísima Virgen de Guadalupe recibidas en 1666 y 1723.* Amecameca, Edo. de México, 1889.

Vetancurt, Agustín de. *Teatro mexicano. Descripción breve de los sucesos exemplares, históricos, políticos, militares y religiosos del nuevo mundo occidental de las Indias* [1697]. 3 vols. 1961.

Villarroel, Hipólito. *Enfermedades políticas que padece la capital de esta Nueva España en casi todos los cuerpos de que se compone y remedios que se la deben aplicar para su curación si se quiere que sean útil al rey al al público* [ca. 1785]. 1979.

Villaseñor y Sánchez, José Antonio de. *Suplemento al Theatro americano (la ciudad de México en 1755).* Ed. Ramón Serrera Contreras. 1980.

———. *Theatro americano, descripción general de los reynos y provincias de la Nueva España, y sus jurisdicciones* [1746–48]. 2 vols. 1952.

Villegas, Juan. *Aplicación del Concilio de Trento en Hispanoamérica, 1564–1600: Provincia eclesiástica del Perú.* Montevideo, 1975.

Villegas G., Jesús Gerardo. *Cosas de Tlajomulco: Sucedidos que parecen cuentos.* Guadalajara, 1965.

Villoro, Luis. *El proceso ideológico de la revolución de independencia.* 4th ed. 1984.

———. "La revolución de independencia," in *Historia general de México* (1976) 2: 303–56.

von Mentz, Brígida. *Pueblos de indios, mulatos y mestizos, 1770–1870: Los campesinos y las transformaciones protoindustriales en el poniente de Morelos.* 1988.

———, ed. *Sultepec en el siglo XIX: Apuntes históricos sobre la sociedad de un distrito minero.* 1989.

von Simson, Otto. *The Gothic Cathedral: Origins of Gothic Architecture and the Medieval Concept of Order.* Princeton, N.J., 1962.

von Tempsky, G. F. *Mitla. A Narrative of Incidents and Personal Adventures on a Journey in Mexico, Guatemala, and Salvador in the Years 1853 to 1855.* London, 1858.

von Wobeser, Gisela. *La hacienda azucarera en la época colonial.* 1988.

Vovelle, Michel. *Piété baroque et déchristianisation en Provence au XVIIIe siècle.* Paris, 1973.

Wachtel, Nathan. *The Vision of the Vanquished: The Spanish Conquest of Peru Through Indian Eyes, 1530–1570.* New York, 1977.

Ward, Henry G. *Mexico.* 2d ed. 2 vols. London, 1829.

Warman, Arturo. *La danza de los moros y cristianos.* 2d ed. 1985.

———. *"We Come to Object": The Peasants of Morelos and the National State.* Tr. Stephen K. Ault. Baltimore, 1980.

Warren, Kay B. *The Symbolism of Subordination: Indian Identity in a Guatemalan Town.* Austin, Tex., 1978.

Washburn, Douglas A. "The Bourbon Reforms: A Social and Economic History of the Audiencia of Quito, 1760–1810." Ph.D. diss., University of Texas, 1984.

Wasserstrom, Robert. *Ethnic Relations in Central Chiapas, 1528–1975.* Berkeley, Calif., 1983.

Watanabe, John M. "From Saints to Shibboleths: Image, Structure, and Identity in Maya Religious Syncretism," *American Ethnologist,* 17 (1990): 131–50.

Weber, Eugen. *Peasants into Frenchmen: The Modernization of Rural France, 1870–1917.* Stanford, Calif., 1976.

Weber, Max. *The Sociology of Religion.* Tr. Ephraim Fischoff. Boston, 1963.

Weckman, Luis. *La herencia medieval de México.* 2 vols. 1984.

Weinstein, Michael A. *The Polarity of Mexican Thought: Instrumentalism and Finalism.* University Park, Pa., 1976.

Weismann, Elizabeth W. *Mexico in Sculpture, 1521–1821.* Cambridge, Mass., 1950.

Weismann, Elizabeth W., and Judith Hancock Sandoval. *Art and Time in Mexico from the Conquest to the Revolution.* New York, 1985.

Wells, David A. *A Study of Mexico.* New York, 1887.

Weston, Edward. *Daybooks.* 2 vols. New York, 1961.

Williams, Raymond. *Keywords: A Vocabulary of Culture and Society.* New York: 1976.

Wilson, Bryan R. *Magic and the Millennium: A Sociological Study of Religious Movements of Protest Among Tribal and Third-World Peoples.* London, 1973.

Wolf, Eric R. *Europe and the People Without History.* Berkeley, Calif., 1982.

———. "Introduction," in Wolf, ed., *Religion, Power, and Protest in Local Communities: The Northern Shore of the Mediterranean* (Berlin, 1984): 1–14.

———. "The Virgin of Guadalupe: A Mexican National Symbol," *Journal of American Folklore,* 71 (1958): 34–39.

Wolf, Eric R., and Edward C. Hansen. "Caudillo Politics: A Structural Analysis," *Comparative Studies in Society and History,* 9 (1967): 168–79.

Womack, John. *Zapata and the Mexican Revolution.* New York, 1969.

Wood, Stephanie. "Adopted Saints: Christian Images in Nahua Testaments of Late Colonial Toluca," *The Americas,* 47 (1991): 259–93.

———. "Corporate Adjustments in Colonial Mexican Indian Towns: Toluca Region, 1550–1810." Ph.D. diss., University of California, Los Angeles, 1984.

———. "The Cosmic Conquest: Late Colonial Views of the Sword and Cross in Central Mexican *Títulos*," *Ethnohistory*, 38 (1991): 176–95.

Wright, A. D. *The Counter-Reformation: Catholic Europe and the Non-Christian World*. New York, 1982.

Wright, Ronald. *Time Among the Maya: Travels in Belize, Guatemala, and Mexico*. New York, 1989.

Wrightson, Keith, and David Levine. *Poverty and Piety in an English Village: Terling, 1525–1700*. New York, 1979.

Wrong, Dennis. *Power: Its Forms, Bases, and Uses*. New York, 1980.

Yáñez, Agustín. *Edge of the Storm*. Tr. Ethel Brinton. Austin, Tex., 1963.

Sources of Figures and Maps

FIGURES

1 Data from Ricardo Acosta Gomez, *Los templos de Sierra de Pinos, Zac. y sus ministros* (San Luis Potosí, 1984). Photographs courtesy of Bernardo del Hoyo.

2 Claudio Linati, *Trajes civiles, militares y religioso de México*. Mexico, D.F., 1978. Print courtesy of DeGolyer Library, Southern Methodist University.

3 Alonso de la Peña Montenegro, *Itinerario para parochos de indios* . . . [1668], pp. 255 (a), 38 (b). Courtesy, The Bancroft Library, University of California, Berkeley.

4 Photograph courtesy of Bernardo del Hoyo.

5 Efraím Hernández Xolocotzi, "Maize Granaries in Mexico," *Botanical Museum Leaflets* 13 (Harvard University, Jan. 17, 1949)

6 AGN Ilustración no. 4933. Courtesy of the Archivo General de la Nacion, Mexico.

7 R. W. Hardy, *Travels in the Interior of Mexico, in 1825–26, 1827, and 1828* (London, 1829).

8 H. G. Ward, *Mexico*, 2d ed. (London, 1829), 2: 260. Print courtesy of DeGolyer Library, Southern Methodist University.

9 Alfonso Alberto de Velasco, *Exaltacion . . . de la soberana imagen de Christo Señor Nuestro Crucificado* [1699] (Mexico, 1790)

10 Cayetano Cabrera y Qintero, *Escudo de armas de México* (Mexico, 1746). Courtesy of the John Carter Brown Library at Brown University.

MAPS

1 Adapted from *The North Frontier of New Spain*, Revised Edition, by Peter Gerhard, p. 19, "Diocesan Boundaries." Copyright © 1982 by Princeton University Press, trans-

ferred 1991 to the University of Oklahoma Press. Revised edition copyright © 1993 by the University of Oklahoma Press.

2, 5 Adapted from *A Guide to the Historical Geography of New Spain*, Revised Edition, by Peter Gerhard, p. 16, "Political Divisions in 1786." Copyright © 1972 by Cambridge University Press, transferred 1991 to the University of Oklahoma Press. Revised edition copyright © 1993 by the University of Oklahoma Press.

3, 4 Adapted from *The North Frontier of New Spain*, Revised Edition, by Peter Gerhard, p. 41, "Nueva Galicia in 1786." Copyright © 1982 by Princeton University Press, transferred 1991 to the University of Oklahoma Press. Revised edition copyright © 1993 by the University of Oklahoma Press.

Index

Index

In this index an "f" after a number indicates a separate reference on the next page, and an "ff" indicates separate references on the next two pages. A continuous discussion over two or more pages is indicated by a span of page numbers, e.g., "57-59." *Passim* is used for a cluster of references in close but not consecutive sequence.

Library of Congress Cataloging-in-Publication Data

Taylor, William B.
   Magistrates of the sacred : priests and parishioners in
eighteenth-century Mexico / William B. Taylor.
      p.   cm.
   Includes bibliographical references and index.
   ISBN 8-8047-2456-3 (cloth) : ISBN 0-8047-3659-6 (pbk.)
   1. Catholic Church—Mexico—History—18th century.
2. Church and state—Mexico—History—18th century.
3. Mexico—Church history—18th century.   I. Title.
BX1428.2.T38   1996
282'.72'09033—dc20   95-22982
                                                              CIP
   ⊗ This book is printed on acid-free, recycled paper.

Original printing 1996

Last figure below indicates year of this printing:

05   04   03   02   01   00   99   98